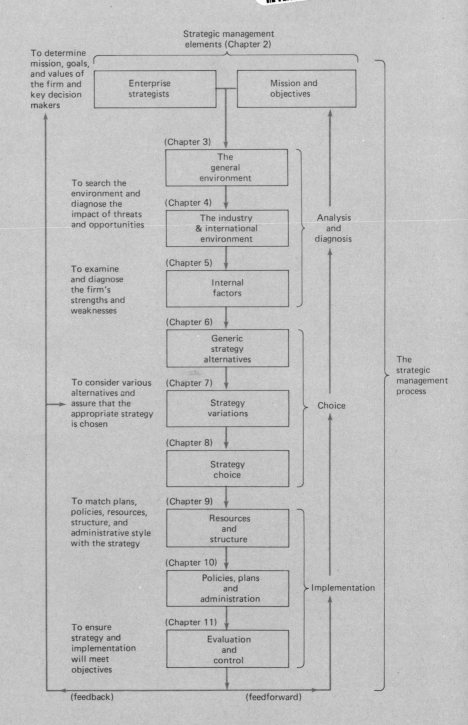

Strategic management
elements (Chapter 2)

To determine
mission, goals,
and values of
the firm and
key decision
makers

| Enterprise strategists | | Mission and objectives |

(Chapter 3)

To search the
environment and
diagnose the
impact of threats
and opportunities

The
general
environment

(Chapter 4)

The industry
& international
environment

Analysis
and
diagnosis

To examine
and diagnose
the firm's
strengths and
weaknesses

(Chapter 5)

Internal
factors

(Chapter 6)

Generic
strategy
alternatives

To consider various
alternatives and
assure that the
appropriate strategy
is chosen

(Chapter 7)

Strategy
variations

Choice

(Chapter 8)

Strategy
choice

The
strategic
management
process

To match plans,
policies, resources,
structure, and
administrative style
with the strategy

(Chapter 9)

Resources
and
structure

(Chapter 10)

Policies, plans
and
administration

Implementation

To ensure
strategy and
implementation
will meet
objectives

(Chapter 11)

Evaluation
and
control

(feedback)   (feedforward)

BUSINESS POLICY AND STRATEGIC MANAGEMENT

McGraw-Hill Series in Management

Fred Luthans and Keith Davis, *Consulting Editors*

BUSINESS POLICY AND STRATEGIC MANAGEMENT

FIFTH EDITION

Lawrence R. Jauch
Northeast Louisiana University

William F. Glueck
Late of the University of Georgia

McGRAW-HILL BOOK COMPANY

New York   St. Louis   San Francisco   Auckland   Bogotá
Hamburg   London   Madrid   Mexico   Milan   Montreal   New Delhi
Panama   Paris   Saõ Paulo   Singapore   Sydney   Tokyo   Toronto

This book was set in Times Roman by the College Composition Unit in cooperation with Waldman Graphics, Inc. The editor was Kathleen L. Loy; the cover was designed by Caliber Design Planning, Inc.; the production supervisor was Leroy A. Young.
New drawings were done by Fine Line Illustrations, Inc.
Project supervision was done by The Total Book.
R. R. Donnelley & Sons Company was printer and binder.

BUSINESS POLICY AND STRATEGIC MANAGEMENT

1 2 3 4 5 6 7 8 9 0 DOCDOC 8 9 2 1 0 9 8 7

ISBN 0-07-032347-X

Library of Congress Cataloging-in-Publication Data

Jauch, Lawrence R.
  Business policy and strategic management.

  (McGraw-Hill series in management)
  Glueck's name appears first on the earlier edition.
  Includes bibliographies and index.
  1. Corporate planning.   I. Glueck, William F.
II. Title.   III. Series
HD30.28.J375   1988   658.4'012   87-16859
ISBN 0-07-032347-X

ABOUT THE AUTHORS

LAWRENCE R. JAUCH is the Biedenharn Professor in Management at Northeast Louisiana University. He has taught at Kansas State University and Southern Illinois University at Carbondale. He completed his dissertation with Dr. Glueck while they were both at the University of Missouri. Professor Jauch is the coauthor of 14 texts and supplements, and has published over 50 papers, monographs, and cases. He has consulted with planning executives in several countries. Dr. Jauch is currently on the editorial review boards of *The Academy of Management Review* and *The Journal of Management Case Studies*. He chaired the Business Policy and Planning Division of the Academy of Management in 1983–84.

WILLIAM F. GLUECK was Distinguished Professor of Management at the University of Georgia at the time of his death in 1980. He was a Fellow and President of the Academy of Management. Professor Glueck authored over 20 books (including *Strategic Management and Business Policy* and *Readings in Business Policy from Business Week*, both published by McGraw-Hill) and over 150 articles, monographs, and cases. He was a Fulbright scholar and spent many years as a food industry executive. He served on the editorial review boards of *Long Range Planning, Journal of Business Strategy,* and *Academy of Management Journal*.

To Bill

CONTENTS

TABLE OF CASES

PREFACE

The fifth edition of this book, like its predecessors, is designed to meet the needs of students of business policy and strategic management. It contains two parts: text and cases.

The following additions and changes have been made in the text of the fifth edition.

1 The text has been rewritten and updated, especially to reflect the major structural changes in the U.S. and world economies which impact strategic thinking.

2 The discussion and the model have been altered to stress a greater integration of topic areas.

3 Chapter 2 has been expanded to include a discussion of the roles of the general manager.

4 The discussion of the environment has been expanded to two chapters. Discussions of the industry environment and the international environment have been included.

5 International strategy material has been incorporated in other chapters as well, especially 7, 8, and 10.

6 The chapter on strategy alternatives has been expanded to two chapters (6 and 7). This helps students better grasp the concept of types of strategies and their variations.

7 The majority of exhibit vignettes describing applied concepts have been updated to provide meaningful illustrations of key points and topics as they are applied by various organizations.

8 Much of the elaboration of research studies and theories which were in supplementary modules in the previous edition have been deleted. Thus the readability of the basic text has been improved, but the integrity of previous editions has been maintained as explained below.

A key strength of previous editions of this book was the attempt to summarize the state of the art of business policy and strategic management. This included a blending of both prescriptive and descriptive ideas of theorists, practitioners, and researchers in the field. The body of work on the process and content of strategic management has been expanding rapidly. If an attempt had been made to incorporate all this material in the basic text of this latest edition, the result would have been confusion for the reader. The basic material still rests on a firm foundation of up-to-date research, theory, and practice. Extensive references are also available to the reader. But many of the details of some research and various additional techniques, theories, and viewpoints formerly part of the supplementary modules have been condensed or eliminated. The key conclusions and findings from this supplementary material are highlighted and summarized in the chapter itself. Those interested in exploring particular subtopics in greater depth might refer to the instructor's manual where extensive references are provided beyond those cited in the book. These were reduced to provide room for new text and case materials.

The case section of the book is changed and improved also.

1 First, there are more cases. This edition includes 32 cases, but several have multiple parts.

2 Most of the cases are completely new or rewritten for this book. This makes the course more interesting and helps the instructor deal with the "solutions are in the fraternity files" problem.

3 The vast majority of case are dated in the 1980s.

4 The section on the case method has been improved (Chapter 12), and a detailed sample case is elaborated in the Instructor's Manual to illustrate application of text material.

5 The mix of cases reflects the interests of users. For example, there are nearly equal numbers of enterprises in service-oriented business as there are in manufacturing. Five of the 32 cases deal with entrepreneurial or small businesses, and five specifically address international issues. Three deal with businesses based on technological developments, two are not-for-profit organizations, and two deal directly with social responsibility issues as they impact strategy and implementation. Hence, industries covered range from "high tech" to "smokestack." The cases cover settings all over the United States and several in Canada. The cases also include firms basing operations in Brazil, England, India and Israel. The case mix as a whole, then, also reflects structural changes in U.S. and world economies and industries.

For the instructor, a new feature in the instructor's manual—Demonstrating Strategy—allows flexible use of one of the cases in either an integrative fashion or a chapter by chapter format. This facilitates the ability of students to apply text material to the difficult task of case analysis.

As we prepare to face the challenges of the 1990s, it is increasingly evident that managers are planning the strategies of their enterprises for their own survival and that of our civilizations. We hope that this book will contribute something to that mission.

This book is the product of many people. First and foremost is the foundation laid down in the first three editions by the coauthor, William F. Glueck. His untimely death in 1980 was a blow to many of us. His inspiration and guidance are sorely missed. I continue to dedicate this edition to his memory and have made every attempt to continue the tradition of excellence he exhibited in all his endeavors.

I am also most grateful to all the contributing case authors for their useful material. Several of the cases in this edition were written by former students of Bill Glueck's; they are now scattered around the United States.

I would also like to thank those who reviewed the book at various stages in its development. They include Helen Deresky, State University of New York at Plattsburgh; Bahman Ebrahimi, North Texas State University; Duane Ireland, Baylor University; Aaron Kelly, University of Louisville; Mary Frances Lewis, Illinois State University; Michael Pitts, Virginia Commonwealth University; Michael Shaner, St. Louis University; and Gerald Speth, University of Indianapolis.

I should also mention the influence of many colleagues in the Academy of Management. I have been fortunate to have had the opportunity to receive and review the work of a large number of scholars active in advancing the field of strategic management. They are too numerous to mention here, but the references attest to their significant influence on my thinking and the development of this edition.

My appreciation also goes to Audrey Preston, Donna Reynolds, and Tammy Nack, who assisted in the preparation and typing of the manuscript, and to the Management Department at Southern Illinois University at Carbondale and Northeast Louisiana University for providing work environments conducive to productive efforts. My editor, Kathleen L. Loy, provided additional motivation to complete the task in a timely fashion, for which I am grateful. Last but not least, my family has had to bear my petulance for far too long; I trust their indulgence and tolerance have not been stretched beyond the limits.

As is customary, I will accept blame for errors of commission and omission. I hope that any errors that are discovered will be brought to my attention so that they may be corrected in future editions.

Lawrence R. Jauch

CHAPTER OUTLINE

CHAPTER 1

AN INVITATION TO STRATEGIC MANAGEMENT

OBJECTIVES

- To learn what the strategic management process is
- To understand why strategic management takes place
- To learn how strategic management takes place in modern businesses
- To learn about strategic decision-making processes
- To understand how strategic management is practiced in the not-for-profit and public sectors

INTRODUCTION

This book is about decision making and actions which determine whether an enterprise excels, survives, or dies.[1] This process is called "strategic management." The job of strategic managers is to make the best use of a firm's resources in a changing environment.

If you looked at a list of the largest and most successful firms in 1908, 1938, or 1968 and compared it with a list of those in 1988, you'd be amazed! Few of the leaders then are leaders now despite their economic power then. That's what happens when strategic management is inadequately done.

Let's look at this situation in a different way. Most of us have a work life of about 42 years. Put yourself in the shoes of a person who retired in 1985. Exhibit 1.1 gives

---

[1]We use the terms "enterprise," "organization," "company," and "firm" interchangeably. Some are profit-seeking, others not-for-profit; but all can utilize a strategic management process. Similarly, terms such as "manager," "strategist," or "executive" are substitutes for variety.

EXHIBIT 1.1 TEN COMPANIES' EXPERIENCES DURING ONE BUSINESS EXECUTIVE'S WORK LIFE

Company	1943	1985
American Can	Manufacturer of tin cans, packages and containers	Financial, specialty retailing and packaging company with almost half its operating income deriving from financial services
Coleman	Small manufacturer of lamps, stoves, heaters, and accessory items	Leading manufacturer of outdoor recreational equipment including camping gear, trailers, sailboats, and target guns
Genentech	Did not exist	Genetic research corporation in an emerging industry
W.T. Grant	One of the larger variety-store retailers	Out of business
Honeywell	Leading manufacturer of various types of temperature-controlling and heat-regulating devices	Major producer of information processing and control systems for environmental, industrial, and aerospace applications
IBM	Engaged mainly in manufacturing, selling, and leasing various kinds of tabulating, accounting, and payroll machines, typewriters, and related supplies	World's largest manufacturer of computers and information-processing equipment and systems, ranging from microcomputers to large-scale mainframes
Parker Pen	Major producer of fountain pens and patented pencils with network of approximately 40,000 retailers	Leading manufacturer of pens and other writing instruments but derived more than 80 percent of its revenues from temporary help services
Pitney Bowes	Small manufacturer of postage meter machines and related equipment	World's largest manufacturer of postage meters and mailing equipment, and manufacturer of dictation systems, copiers, facsimile machines and retail labeling equipment
Raytheon	Small producer of cathoderay tubes and other electronic equipment	Leading factor in air defense missile systems and other government electronics products
Wheeling Steel	Large profitable steel producer and principal manufacturer of finished steel and fabricated steel products	Now known as Wheeling-Pittsburgh Steel; the nation's seventh largest integrated steel producer filed for protection under Chapter 11 of the Federal Bankruptcy Code

a brief summary of what 10 firms were like when the retiree began work and what they were like at that person's retirement.

A close examination will show examples of success and failure and stability and complete change, as well as many stages in between. Some of these changes occurred because of pressures from the outside—from government, competitors, and consumers. Others developed because the employees and management made decisions to change the nature of the business. The exhibit also tells of firms that haven't changed their businesses—they just approached them differently.

Just as this executive experienced these changes in a lifetime, so will you. You may experience even more changes than these in your career.

Because this book focuses on top-level decisions, you may have a problem with the relevance of the subject matter for your short-term career interests. But several reasons can be given for why the knowledge you can gain in the study of strategic management is practical and useful for your early career stages:

1 You are likely to perform better in your function, regardless of your level in the organization, if you know the direction in which the organization is going. As the manager of a subunit, you would like to know how what you do fits into the broader picture. If you know how your function contributes, you should be able to do a better job of helping the organization reach its objectives. If your unit is successful and higher-level managers realize how you contributed to this success, this will reflect positively on you. Furthermore, lower-level units often interpret strategies and policies set at higher levels. If you understand why those were established, you can implement them more effectively. Finally, if you understand how your job relates to others in the organization, you will be in a better position to effectively work with peers when cooperation is called for and compete for resources when the time comes.

2 In your study of the strategic management process you will begin to identify factors which may lead to significant changes in the organization. Some of these strategic changes could be positive or negative to you personally. For instance, a major divestiture could eliminate your unit! Or a new market thrust or product development could make your unit more critical for organizational performance. If you understand what factors may be pushing the organization in certain directions and how your job fits in, you might decide to change or keep your job. Foresight about critical organization changes can be a real asset to your career.

3 If you are aware of the strategies, values, and objectives of higher-level managers, you are in a better position to assess the likelihood of acceptance of proposals you might make. For instance, you might be in a position to suggest better ways to meet competition, improve the production or R&D effort, increase personnel skills, and so on. Or if you are auditing the financial statements, you might discover a way to improve the treatment of accounts. As you consider offering your suggestions, tying the reasons to your assessment of the interests of higher-level managers is likely to enhance their acceptance and your visibility.

Thus we believe that an understanding of how and why strategic decisions are made can be helpful to you in terms of securing resources beneficial to your subunit, improving your job performance, and enhancing your career development. This book's purpose is to help you make sense of the strategic management process while you are a first-line manager and a middle manager. It is also designed to help prepare you to become a successful top manager. Its goal is to show you that if you understand the business policy and strategic management process before you get to the top, you'll be a more effective manager. And you are more likely to reach the top once you understand this process [1].[2]

The book also is designed to fulfill a teaching function in schools of business, management, and administration. The material is designed to help you integrate the functional tools you have learned. These include the analytical tools of production-operations management, marketing management, financial management, accounting, physical distribution and logistics, and personnel and labor relations. All these provide help in analyzing business problems. This book and the materials in it provide you with an opportunity to learn *when* to use which tools and how to deal with trade-offs when you cannot maximize the results or preferences of all the functional areas simultaneously.

This book contains two types of material. The first is the *textual* material, which reviews what we know about business policy and strategic management. Second, there are *cases,* which are descriptions of businesses and of other organizations that provide the reader with an opportunity to analyze the strategic management of real organizations and prescribe improvements for them. They look at all aspects of the company that seem important for understanding the business as a whole. More will be said about case analysis in Chapter 12. The task of understanding a company's strategy and judging its effectiveness is not an easy one. It requires that you look at how the company has come to grips with the challenges and opportunities facing it. It requires that you make judgments about whether the business or other organization is well run and how to improve its operations and results. This is a challenging job, the job of top managers of divisions or companies. It will provide you with a new understanding of how companies succeed or fail.

WHAT IS STRATEGIC MANAGEMENT AND BUSINESS POLICY? [2]

''Strategic management'' is the term currently used to describe the process on which the book focuses. It will be defined shortly. But first let's review previously used terms for this process so that they will not be unfamiliar to you if you come across them. ''Business policy'' is a term traditionally associated with the course in business schools devoted to integrating the educational program of these schools and understanding what today is called strategic management. In most businesses in earlier times (and in many smaller firms today), the focus of the manager's job was on today's decisions for today's world in today's business. That may have been satisfac-

---

[2]Reference footnotes are not used in this text. Instead, end-of-chapter references are grouped into numbered sections. These sections are referred to in the text by bracketed numbers, and labels in the references indicate general topical areas. The references provided are those which we specifically cite or make direct use of in the text. Your instructor may wish to provide additional research references on selected topics which provide more depth on given subjects and which provide the basis for many of our statements and summaries of research.

tory then. However, the changes illustrated in Exhibit 1.1 and similar ones taking place all around led to a different approach to management.

Instead of focusing all their time on today, managers began to see the value of trying to anticipate the future and to prepare for it. They did this in several ways.

• They prepared systems and procedures manuals for decisions that must be made repeatedly. This allowed time for more important decisions and ensured more or less consistent decisions.

• They prepared budgets. They tried to anticipate future sales and flows of funds. In sum, they created a planning and control system.

Budgeting and control systems helped, but they tended to be based on the status quo—the present business and conditions—and did not by themselves deal well with change. These systems did provide better financial controls and are still in use. Later variations included capital budgeting and management-by-objectives systems.

Because of the lack of emphasis on the future in budgeting, long-range planning appeared. This movement focused on forecasting the future by using economic and technological tools. Long-range planning tended to be performed primarily by corporate staff groups, whose reports were forwarded to top management. Sometimes their reports and advice were heeded (when they were understood and were credible); otherwise, they were ignored. Since the corporate planners were not the decision makers, long-range planning had some impact, but not as much as would be expected if top management were involved. Then, too, they were producing first-generation plans.

''First-generation planning'' means that the firm chooses the most probable appraisal and diagnosis of the future environment and of its own strengths and weaknesses. From this, it evolves the best strategy for a match of the environment and the firm—a single plan for the most likely future.

Today's approach is called ''strategic planning'' or, more frequently, ''strategic management.'' As will be seen in Chapter 2, the board of directors and corporate planners have parts to play in strategic management. But the starring roles are for the general managers of the corporation and its major operating divisions. Strategic management focuses on ''second-generation planning,'' that is, analysis of the business and the preparation of several scenarios for the future. Contingency strategies are then prepared for each of these likely future scenarios. We return to this topic at the end of the chapter.

But these are our distinctions, and the terms ''long-range planning,'' ''strategic planning,'' and ''strategic management'' have as many definitions as there are experts. The terms ''strategic management,'' ''strategy,'' and ''policy'' will be used often in this book. So let's define our terms.

Strategic management is a stream of decisions and actions which leads to the development of an effective strategy or strategies to help achieve corporate objectives. The strategic management process is the way in which strategists determine objectives and make strategic decisions.

Strategic decisions are means to achieve ends. These decisions encompass the definition of the business, products and markets to be served, functions to be performed, and major policies needed for the organization to execute these decisions to achieve objectives.

Plans and policies are guides to action. They indicate how resources are to be allocated and how tasks assigned to the organization might be accomplished so that functional-level managers execute the strategy properly.

A strategic business unit (SBU) is an operating division of a firm which serves a distinct product-market segment or a well-defined set of customers or a geographic area. The SBU is given the authority to make its own strategic decisions within corporate guidelines as long as it meets corporate objectives.

The strategic management process for a business which has organized itself with only a single SBU is given in Exhibit 1.2. Each of the strategic management elements and decisions in the strategic management process is explained in more detail in Chapters 2 through 11, as indicated in Exhibit 1.2. This model is used throughout the book to relate the material to that covered previously and that which will come later. The phases of the model in Exhibit 1.2 are as follows:

• *Strategic management elements:* The general managers who are involved in the process of determining strategy to accomplish objectives are first described in Chapter 2. Then we discuss the mission, business definition, and objectives of the enterprise. We also describe a gap analysis in some detail here.

• *Analysis and diagnosis:* Determining environmental problems and opportunities and internal strengths and weaknesses. This involves recognizing problems and/or opportunities and assessing information needs to solve the problems and heuristics for evaluating the information.

Chapter 3 presents factors in the general environment, such as economic, technological, and government conditions, which create threats and opportunities for the firm. Chapter 4 discusses analysis of the industry and international environments and presents a tool to help summarize the diagnosis of the environment: ETOP. Chapter 5 covers the analysis of internal conditions which provide strengths the strategist can use and weaknesses that prevent strategies or need correcting. This chapter also suggests a tool to focus the diagnosis of internal factors: SAP.

• *Choice:* Generating alternative solutions to the problem, assessing them, and choosing the best ones.

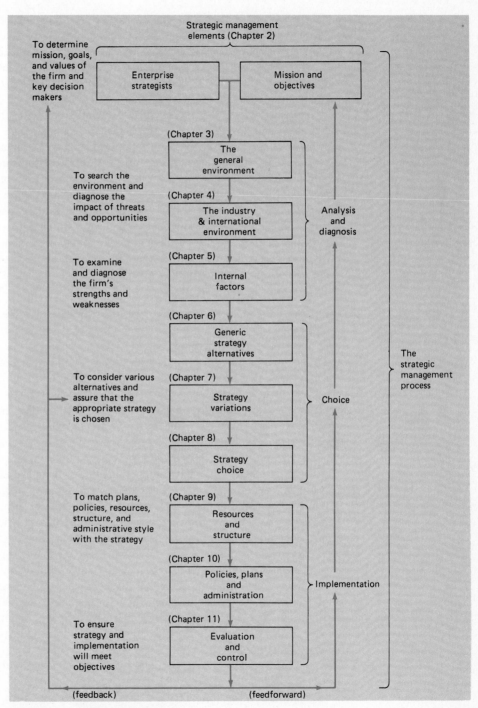

EXHIBIT 1.2   A model of strategic management.

Chapter 6 maps out generic strategy alternatives of expansion, stability or retrench-ment, and combinations. Chapter 7 extends this discussion to describe different ways in which such generic strategies can be carried out. Chapter 8 describes the factors that affect how managers might choose from among the strategy alternatives. It ex-plains the use of the ETOP and SAP as applied to closing gaps in objectives, while recognizing the impact of the strategists.

* *Implementation:* Making the strategy work by building the structure to support the strategy and developing appropriate plans and policies.

Chapter 9 describes resource allocation, organization structure, and planning proc-esses. Chapter 10 explores policies to be developed for functional areas and the leadership aspects of implementation. These administrative processes must be inte-grated with the strategy to close gaps in order to attain desired objectives.

* *Evaluation:* Through review of results and future possibilities, determining whether the strategy is working and taking steps to make it work.

Chapter 11 is a part of implementation in that the evaluation, feedback, and control of the strategy under way is important. But evaluation also includes feed forward to serve as an input to determine whether the strategy and plans as decided will work before proceeding with the choice.

As the diagram suggests, these phases are integrated. While it is convenient to discuss them as if they were a sequential step-by-step series of activities, in reality each phase affects all the other phases. Thus as strategists are performing analyses, the implementation of past strategies and choices will be considered. The choice phase for new strategic directions requires a consideration of the ability to implement. For the most part, however, we will discuss each phase of the strategic management process separately, because it is extremely difficult to discuss all the parts simulta-neously. In fact, strategic management is a *continuous* process. To say that it is a process rather than a series of steps is not just a shift of words. The parts of the process are interacting. Analytically we can separate them; in reality we can't. As cases and businesses are analyzed, the integrated whole requires comprehensive ex-plorations. This process, then, is a guide to improving strategic thinking.

Note, too, that Exhibit 1.2 is also drawn up for the firm which is using first-generation planning, the most frequent approach at present. More advanced firms are using second-generation or contingency planning. In this system, the choice and im-plementation decisions appear as in Exhibit 1.3. Note that in this case the firm chooses several scenarios of the future environment (analysis and diagnosis) and strengths and weaknesses given different futures. It then prepares several strategies and plans and short- and medium-range implementations of the strategies. When the future arrives, the firm puts into effect that strategy which it is capable of implementing and which comes closest to meeting the environmental conditions outlined in each scenario and strategy. For simplicity's sake, Exhibit 1.2 will be used throughout the book. But you should keep in mind that if contingency planning is used, the modification of the model in Exhibit 1.3 applies.

Exhibit 1.2 is also drawn for a single-business-unit firm. For a firm that is a multiple-strategy business unit, the model must be modified.

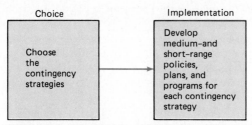

Choice   Implementation

EXHIBIT 1.3   **Strategic management model for second-generation planning (modifies Exhibit 1.2).**

STRATEGIC MANAGEMENT IN MULTIPLE-SBU BUSINESSES [3]

In small businesses or in businesses which focus on one product or service line, the "corporate-level" strategy serves the whole business. This strategy is implemented at the next lower level by functional plans and policies. This implementation process will be discussed in Chapters 9 and 10. This relationship is illustrated in Exhibit 1.4.

In conglomerates and multiple-industry firms, the business often inserts a level of management between the corporate and functional levels. In some firms, these units are called "operating divisions" or, more commonly, strategic business units (SBUs). In these firms, the strategies of these units are guided by the corporate strategies, but they may differ from one another. This situation operates as shown in Exhibit 1.5.

Each SBU sets its own business strategies to make the best use of its resources (its strategic advantages) given the environment it faces. The overall corporate strategy sets the long-term objectives of the firm and the broad constraints and resources within which the SBU operates. The corporate level will help the SBU define its scope of operations. It also limits or enhances the SBU's operations by means of the resources it assigns to the SBU. Thus at the corporate level in multiple-SBU firms, the strategy focuses on the "portfolio" of SBUs the firm wishes to put together to accomplish its objectives.

For example, Mobil Corporation hired a new chief executive with the charge of revitalizing Montgomery Ward, one of its poor-performing SBUs. The SBU is being pared down and turned into a specialty retailer since it has not been able to compete well as a general merchandiser. Corporate-level management set goals and has its own strategy (that of divesting Ward if it doesn't perform); but the SBU has determined its own strategy for how to redefine its business and compete effectively.

EXHIBIT 1.4   **Relationship of corporate strategy and functional plans and policies at single-SBU firms.**

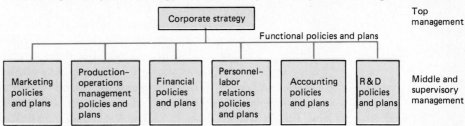

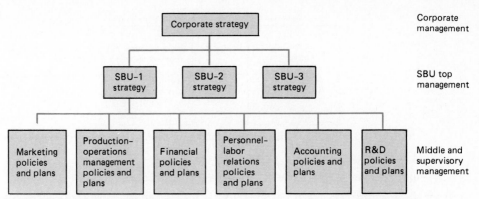

EXHIBIT 1.5   **Relationship among strategies and policies and plans in firms with multiple SBUs.**

Some writers make distinctions between corporate strategy, business strategy, and functional-level strategy, maintaining that corporate strategy focuses on the mission of the firm, the businesses that it enters or exits, and the mix of SBUs and resource allocations. Business strategy, then, focuses on how to compete in an industry or strategic subgroup, and how to achieve competitive advantage. At the functional level, plans and policies to be carried out (by marketing, manufacturing, personnel, and so on) are designed to implement corporate and business strategy to make the firm competitive. We discuss all these issues at various places in the book. Mission and business definition are discussed in Chapter 2; Chapters 6 to 8 describe entry, exit, and SBU mix; and Chapter 9 describes resource allocation. Chapter 4 describes the international and industry competition; and Chapters 4, 10, and 11 discuss how to compete and use and develop competitive advantages. But we agree with Boswell that the distinction between business and corporate strategy is partly artificial. They are interrelated. And, as Roger Smith, chairman of GM, has stated, "Unless we want to play a perpetual game of catch-up, we . . . have to do more than just meet our competition on a day-to-day basis. We have to beat them in long-term strategy." Choices about *how to compete* should be considered in the decision about *whether* to exit or enter a business, as our earlier example about Montgomery Ward illustrated. And the implementation of a strategy will determine how effectively the choice will be carried out. Hence, we believe that the process described here can assist in the reader's thinking about business *and* competitive strategy.

As mentioned before, the model in Exhibit 1.2 is for a single-SBU firm. For a multiple-SBU firm the model is adjusted so that the process is conducted at corporate *and* SBU levels. The results of these processes feed into one another. However, at both levels, the process involves appraisal, choice, implementation, and evaluation.

Strategic decision making in multiple-SBU firms involves interrelationships between corporate-level and business-level planning. As can be seen in Exhibit 1.6 the corporate-level executives first determine the overall corporate strategy. They do this after examining the level of achievement of objectives relative to their SBUs and other businesses they could enter. Next they assess how the SBUs are doing relative to each

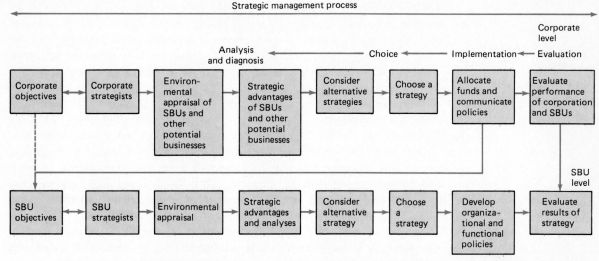

EXHIBIT 1.6   A model of the strategic management process for a firm with multiple SBUs using first-generation planning.

other and potential SBUs. Then they allocate funds to the SBUs and establish policies and objectives with them.

At this point the SBUs analyze, within the guidelines set by the corporate level, how they can create the most effective strategy to achieve their objectives.

This model is, of course, a simplified representation. Depending on various organization designs, the interrelationships among units and planning processes can be quite complex in a series of iterative interactions across levels and subunits. Moreover, conflicts between the corporate level and the SBU level can create problems for both. SBU managers usually seek greater resource allocations in an attempt to expand their units. Corporate level, however, may wish to stabilize a unit or use cash flows from one unit to support another SBU. For example, while the head of the tobacco unit at Philip Morris in the early 1980s wanted growth in cigarette volume and new-product development, funds were being used to promote sales of the Miller Brewing acquisition. Discussions between SBUs and corporate level must consider overall goals and resource needs.

WHAT IS A STRATEGY? [4]

> *A strategy is a unified, comprehensive, and integrated plan that relates the strategic advantages of the firm to the challenges of the environment. It is designed to ensure that the basic objectives of the enterprise are achieved through proper execution by the organization.*

A strategy is the means used to achieve the ends (objectives). A strategy is not just any plan, however. A strategy is a plan that is *unified:* it ties all the parts of the enterprise together. A strategy is *comprehensive:* it covers all major aspects of the enterprise. A strategy is *integrated:* all the parts of the plan are compatible with each other and fit together well. These are prescriptions; we will return to some descriptions of strategy after clarifying some terms.

A strategy begins with a concept of how to use the resources of the firm most effectively in a changing environment. It is similar to the concept in sports of a game plan. Before a team goes onto the field, effective coaches examine a competitor's past plans and strengths and weaknesses. Then they look at their own team's strengths and weaknesses. The objective is to win the game with a minimum of injuries. Coaches may also not wish to humiliate an opponent with a 100-0 score. They may wish not to use all their best plays but to save some for future opponents. So coaches devise a plan to win the game.

A game plan is not exactly a strategy, however. A game plan is oriented toward only one game. A strategy for a firm is a long-run plan. A game plan is oriented against one competitor only, and is only for one game, not a whole season. A firm deals with a number of competitors simultaneously and with the government, suppliers, owners, labor unions, and others. A strategy is oriented toward basic issues such as these: What is our business? What should it be? What are our products, functions, and markets?[3] What can our firm do to accomplish objectives? The Dallas Cowboys' coach doesn't ask questions such as these. Still, it may help you understand the concept of strategy as a plan which is the result of analyzing strengths and weaknesses and determining what the environment has to offer so that the firm can achieve its objectives.

Exhibit 1.7 suggests the original strategy of Federal Express and various alternative strategies the firm considered to expand the business. Note that the firm could expand products, markets, or functions, or all three. These are only one set of strategies that firms consider based on their configuration of goals, external conditions, and internal factors. Chapter 6 describes strategies in more detail.

Strategies, as suggested, must also be implemented effectively. Players can drop the ball or miss their blocking assignments. The coach may have an excellent game plan, but the game is played on the field. For successful performance, then, the unified, comprehensive, integrated plan includes operational concerns. Most of you are probably more familiar with operational management and plans. Exhibit 1.8 highlights some of the differences.

The strategic plan, then, must be integrated with operational concerns. This will be discussed later in the book. But recognize here the importance of both. Exhibit 1.9 points out one example of how strategy and implementation must be combined for success. In other words, the probability of success is enhanced with the combination of good strategic planning *and* good strategic implementation. Good strategy with poor implementation or poor strategy with good implementation is likely to lead to problems.

---

[3]Note: When we refer to products, mentally add the word ''service'' if appropriate for the kind of organization you are analyzing.

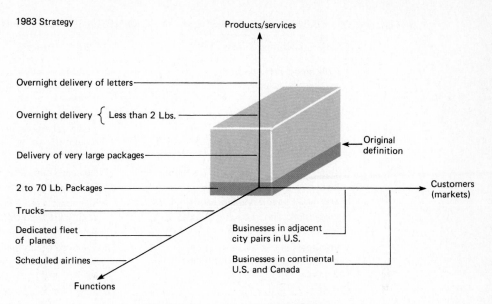

1983 Strategy

Products/services

Overnight delivery of letters

Overnight delivery { Less than 2 Lbs.

Original
definition

Delivery of very large packages

2 to 70 Lb. Packages

Customers
(markets)

Trucks

Dedicated fleet
of planes

Businesses in adjacent
city pairs in U.S.

Scheduled airlines

Businesses in continental
U.S. and Canada

Functions

(A) Original strategy with initial expansion

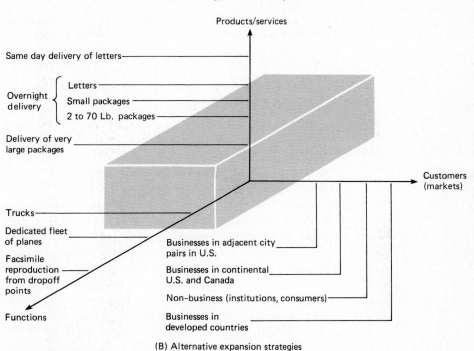

Products/services

Same day delivery of letters

Letters

Overnight
delivery { Small packages

2 to 70 Lb. packages

Delivery of very
large packages

Customers
(markets)

Trucks

Dedicated fleet
of planes

Businesses in adjacent city
pairs in U.S.

Facsimile
reproduction
from dropoff
points

Businesses in continental
U.S. and Canada

Non-business (institutions, consumers)

Functions

Businesses in
developed countries

(B) Alternative expansion strategies

EXHIBIT 1.7 **Strategy alternatives to expand Federal Express.**
Adapted from George S. Day, Strategic Market Planning *(St. Paul, Minn.: West, 1984.)*

EXHIBIT 1.8 DIFFERENCES BETWEEN OPERATIONAL MANAGEMENT AND STRATEGIC PLANNING

Operational management	Strategic planning
1 Concerned with goals derived from established objectives.	1 Concerned with the identification and evaluation of new objectives and strategies.
2 Goals usually have been validated through extensive past experience.	2 New objectives and strategies can be highly debatable; experience within the organization or in other companies may be minimal.
3 Goals are reduced to specific subgoals for functional units.	3 Objectives usually are evaluated primarily for corporate significance.
4 Managers tend to identify with functions or professions and to be preoccupied with means.	4 Managers need a corporate point of view oriented to the environment.
5 Managers obtain evidence of their performance against goals relatively promptly.	5 Evidence of the merit of new objectives or strategies is often available only after several years.
6 Incentives, formal and social, are tied to operating goals.	6 Incentives are at best only loosely associated with planning.
7 The "rules of the game" become well understood. Experienced individuals feel competent and secure.	7 New fields of endeavor may be considered. Past experience may not provide competence in a "new game."
8 The issues are immediate, concrete, and familiar.	8 Issues are abstract and deferrable (to some extent) and may be unfamiliar.

Source: Robert Mainer, "The Impact of Strategic Planning on Executive Behavior," a special commentary (Boston: Boston Consulting Group, 1968), pp. 4–5.

IS STRATEGIC MANAGEMENT USED? [5]

You might be wondering if the concepts in this book are applied in practice. Do organizations really go to all this trouble? A number of studies support the idea that *strategic management is now widely practiced in industry*. For years, strategic management was advocated but received little attention. Now it seems to be practiced by most large- and medium-sized firms and by the more sophisticated smaller firms. And in 1977, *Business Week* initiated a weekly section called "Corporate Strategies" describing strategic management in various enterprises. Each week this section is one of the longest in the magazine, and it is a source for many of the exhibits in this book. We think that those who practice strategic management have a higher probability of success, which we will discuss shortly. Before we do so, you might be interested in some sketches of firms which have tried strategic management approaches (Exhibit 1.10).

Note that the exhibit contains both successes and failures. Just because a firm practices strategic management doesn't guarantee success. Their plans can be good as well as bad. Several of the plans that didn't work may have been based on faulty assumptions or unforeseen changes in the environment, or may have been the result of diversification away from areas that managers knew something about. Moreover,

EXHIBIT 1.9   STRATEGY MINUS IMPLEMENTATION = PROBLEMS

When F. Ross Johnson moved in to head Standard Brands in 1976, he faced a firm with a 10-year history of emphasis on short-term earnings, low marketing budgets, and increased prices, all of which had resulted in one of the food processing industry's slowest-growing companies. The firm had failed to develop new products and had become more dependent on the cyclical corn syrup refining business. Johnson mapped out a bold new strategy and recruited a new planning staff to map out the details. Unfortunately, over the next 4 years Johnson learned a bitter lesson: "A good strategy—unaccompanied by equally good execution—is not the answer to any company's problems."

The firm's efforts in the next 2 years resulted in "some of the most celebrated failures in the food industry." The first new product developed internally was a marketing disaster when it failed the consumer taste test. A line of snack foods going head-on against industry leader Frito-Lay also failed. Of course, unexpected price increases didn't help either. But the major problems resulted from poor implementation.

For one thing, the new planning team failed to make needed changes in an antiquated marketing structure. Second, the corporate planners were making centralized operating decisions which they were ill-prepared to handle. Third, too many outsiders unfamiliar with the business were placed in leadership positions. Finally, the legacy of previous resource allocations made a turnaround more difficult.

In 1978, Johnson changed his approach, concluding that "proper implementation requires the experience of operating specialists—not the heavy-handed rule of the half-dozen corporate planners who were hired to develop the strategy." A commitment was made to allocate greater resources for promotion and new-product development; sales and distribution functions were reorganized; the reins of control were passed to operations specialists, many of whom were already within the company's executive ranks; and a program was started that began to promote and transfer operating executives within the company so that they could develop broader experience. As can be seen, implementation and strategy must go hand in hand for a firm to be successful.

Source: Adapted from "When a New Product Strategy Wasn't Enough," *Business Week,* Feb. 18, 1980, pp. 142–146.

many firms may have relegated planning to a formal planning staff and not involved the line managers who were charged with implementing plans. Moreover, even good plans might not be successful because of poor implementation.

Our next section will discuss the reasons why strategic management should be practiced; and Chapter 2 will discuss the role of the planning staff and the line in this process. The entire book deals with ways in which strategic management can be executed more successfully to improve the probability of success.

Many firms in the United States apparently use these approaches. What about firms in other countries? This book has been written from the perspective of authors who have lived most of their lives in the United States. We have consulted or traveled in Canada, Latin America, Europe, Asia, Africa, and Australia. But our knowledge of these areas is based mostly on reading, so most of this book is based on practices in North America. However, the ideas in this text are used to varying degrees by firms in other countries. And as Chapter 4 will explain, the international environment must be carefully examined as a basic source of opportunity and threat. Be assured that international firms are thinking strategy. These ideas are also applied by many non-profit enterprises and the public sector. The Appendix indicates the extent to which those concepts have been applied in these organizations and different areas of the world.

EXHIBIT 1.10   A SAMPLING OF STRATEGIC PLANNING'S TRACK RECORD

Plans That Didn't Work . . .			. . . and Plans That Did		
Company	Strategy	BW assessment	Company	Strategy	BW assessment
Adolph Coors	Regain lost market share and become a national force in the beer industry	Largely unsuccessful because of weak marketing clout	Abbott Laboratories	Become less vulnerable to cost-containment pressures in traditional hospital products	Won a leading share of the diagnostic-products market through acquisitions and internal development and built a highly profitable dietary supplements business
American Natural Resources	Offset sagging natural gas sales by diversifying into trucking, coal mining, oil/gas exploration, and coal gasification	Ran into trouble because anticipated gas shortages and higher prices failed to materialize	Bausch & Lomb	Regain dominance in soft contact lenses through intensive marketing and aggressive pricing; become a major force in lens solutions	Boosted share of daily-wear lens market to 60 percent
Exxon	Diversify into electrical equipment and office automation, offset shrinking U.S. oil reserves by investing in shale oil and synfuels	Failed because of poor acquisitions, management problems in office automation, and falling oil prices	Bekins	Return to profitability by selling real estate, building market share in basic moving business, and remedying poor diversification moves	Increased moving's market share through improved marketing; divested bad businesses
General Motors	Gain market share by outspending U.S. competitors in the race to offer more fuel-efficient, downsized cars	Failed as import market share grew; modified strategy to pursue diversification	Borg-Warner	Offset the cyclicality of manufacturing-related businesses	Expanded into financial and protective services through acquisitions and internal development; services now account for a third of earnings
International Multifoods	Diversify away from flour milling by developing niche products in consumer foods and expanding restaurant business	Largely unsuccessful because of management timidity, problems overseas, and the recession	Dayton Hudson	Maintain impressive sales and earnings growth by diversifying retail operations	Jumped to number 5 in retailing by dramatically expanding Target, Mervyn's promotional apparel, and B. Dalton Booksellers chains

EXHIBIT 1.10   (*Continued*)

Plans That Didn't Work . . .			. . . and Plans That Did		
Company	Strategy	BW assessment	Company	Strategy	BW assessment
Napco Industries	Become the dominant distributor of nonfood items to grocery stores	Ran into trouble through bad acquisitions, logistical and management problems, and the recession	Gould	Move from an industrial and electrical manufacturer into an electronics company via divestitures and acquisitions	Built electronics to 100 percent of earnings by buying nine high-tech companies and divesting old-line operations
Oak Industries	Diversify into subscription TV and cable TV equipment	Failed because cable TV competition was underestimated; also did not keep abreast of TV equipment technology	National Intergroup	Improve efficiency of and reduce dependence on steel operations	Became an efficient steelmaker by modernizing; diversified into financial services, sold a steel plant to workers, and sold a 50 percent share of steel operations to Nippon Kokan
Shaklee	Streamline product lines and become the leading nutritional products company	Ran into trouble because of the recession and sales-force turnover	New England Electric System	Reduce dependence on oil by switching to coal, developing other fuel sources, and promoting conservation	Switch to coal saved over $200 million, cut oil consumption 58 percent
Toro	Capitalize on brand recognition and reputation for quality in mowers and snowblowers by expanding into other home-care products	Failed because of snowless winters and distribution mistakes; new management changed strategies	Ralston Purina	Refocus on basic grocery products and feed business	Shed mushroom and European pet food divisions, revitalized core business through product development and improved marketing
Trailways	Survive in the bus business by striking alliances with independent carriers and persuading regulators to hold Greyhound to 67 percent of intercity bus traffic	Failed because of deregulation and Greyhound's market-share war	Uniroyal	Revive ailing tire business and abandon lackluster businesses	Shut two U.S. tire plants, shed many foreign and U.S. operations, and is expanding in specialty chemicals

Source: Companies were selected from those whose strategies were described by *Business Week* in 1979 and 1980 and reassessed by *Business Week*, September 17, 1984, pp. 62–68.

WHY STRATEGIC MANAGEMENT? [6]

Up to this point in the chapter, you have been introduced to the concepts of strategic management, strategies, SBUs, and similar ideas. You've probably been saying, "That's interesting. And some firms use strategic management. But why should I be interested?" After all we just told you that many of these plans don't work. In the introduction to this chapter we gave you three personal reasons why you should be interested in these topics. This section will give you some other reasons for learning more about strategic management.

A number of reasons are given by authors and executives as to why firms (and other institutions) *should* engage in strategic management. Exhibit 1.11 lists some of the major points and some common reactions from those who question the value of this process.

Our position is as follows:

1 Some of the irony about change is that it makes planning more difficult. However, firms need not just react to change; they can proact or even make changes happen. Much will be said in this book about changes businesses face and how these changes have increased dramatically in the past half century. Strategic management allows a firm's top executives to anticipate change and provides direction and control for the enterprise. It will also allow the firm to innovate in time to take advantage of new opportunities in the environment and reduce the risk because the future was anticipated. In addition, it helps ensure full exploitation of opportunities. While the manager of a utility may not know the price of oil, the demand for electricity, regulations regarding nuclear power, or technological changes to allow the use of solar energy, decisions about investment in a new plant to come on stream 20 years from now cannot wait. Long-term planning is absolutely necessary, with assumptions about these factors in the future. Assumptions may not be right; but decision makers are paralyzed if they wait for complete certainty (which never comes).

In sum, strategic management allows an enterprise to base its decisions on long-

EXHIBIT 1.11   REASONS FOR AND REACTIONS TO THE VALUE OF STRATEGIC MANAGEMENT

Pros	Cons
1 Strategic management allows firms to anticipate changing conditions.	Conditions change so fast, managers can't do any planning, especially long-term planning.
2 Strategic management provides clear objectives and direction for employees.	Objectives must often be vague and general.
3 Research in strategic management is advancing so that the process can help managers.	Managers pay little attention to research, and studies are not well done.
4 Businesses which perform strategic management are more effective.	There are many reasons for success, and many firms are effective without *formal* planning.

range forecasts, not spur-of-the-moment reactions. It allows the firm to take action at an early stage of a new trend and consider the lead time for effective management. "Chance," said Louis Pasteur, "favors the prepared man." The strategic management process stimulates thinking about the future. Plans resulting from the process should be flexible enough to allow for unanticipated change.

2 As we will note in Chapter 2, there are proponents of vague objectives with some interesting reasons for their position. Nonetheless, most people perform better (in terms of quality and quantity) if they know what is expected of them and where the enterprise is going. This can also help reduce conflict. Effective strategic management points the way for the employees to follow. Strategic management provides a strong incentive for employees and management to achieve company objectives. It serves as the basis for management control and evaluation. Strategic management also ensures that the top executives have a unified opinion on strategic issues and actions.

3 While there are methodological problems in research in this area, many good studies are now being done. Just 20 years ago much of what was known about strategic management was based on single case studies or anecdotal evidence. The last few years have seen an explosion of research. We cite some of this evidence in support of the positions taken in the book. The references [7] for this section cite some of the recent summaries of research. In 1977, the Business Policy and Planning Division of the Academy of Management held a conference summarizing the research in the area, and special conferences devoted to research in strategic management are held every year in the United States and Europe. And two new journals devoted entirely to strategic management were launched in 1980 and 1981.

In general, we know more about effective strategic management than we did, and this makes its study more worthwhile. As for whether managers pay attention to this research, all we can suggest is that our earlier section noted that strategic management is now widely practiced. Indeed, much of the research efforts focus on what those practices are.

4 There is no such thing as a definitive study which *proves* that strategic management *causes* better performance. In fact, some studies suggest better performance leads to strategic planning. There are some studies and theorists suggesting that strategic planning makes no difference for performance. But the majority of studies suggest that there is a relationship between better performance and *formal* planning [8]. Our summary statement is that *businesses which perform formal strategic planning have a higher probability of success than those which do not.*

There are many reasons for this proposition. Some of them are as follows:

• Strategic management is one way to systematize the most important of business decisions. Business involves great risk taking, and strategic management attempts to provide data so that reasonable and informed gambles can be made when necessary.

• Strategic management helps educate managers to become better decision makers. It helps managers examine the basic problems of a company.

• Strategic management helps improve corporate communication, the coordination of individual projects, the allocation of resources, and short-range planning such as budgeting.

Because of the studies of strategic management, many businesses make sure it is a part of their management development programs. The American Assembly of Collegiate Schools of Business strongly suggests that accredited schools of business should teach strategic management, believing that persons exposed to strategic management will develop a broad understanding of the general manager. Strategic management focuses on business problems, not just functional problems such as those of a marketing or financial nature. Strategic management helps build a knowledge of management and develops the attitudes necessary for being a successful business generalist and practitioner. It should also help individuals learn how to assess a business so that they can determine whether they wish to be employed by it or purchase its stock.

Successful companies are successful for many reasons: adequate resources, good people, luck, good products and services, and so on. This is *not* to say that strategic management is all you need to make a success of your business career, but it looks as if it is worth learning about.

STRATEGIC DECISION-MAKING PROCESSES

We began this chapter by stating that this book is about a particular set of decisions. So far we have outlined the strategic planning process, defined strategy, and indicated where it's used and why it's important. In this section we will examine decision-making approaches. Since the remainder of the book will come back to these ideas again and again, it's useful to understand the framework underlying the approach we will follow.

Before outlining the framework, we should point out that in any applied field which combines art and science, you are likely to find two approaches—prescriptive (or normative) and descriptive. Prescriptive approaches tell you how things *ought to be done*. Descriptive approaches tell you how things *are done*. A common theme running through this book is that a blending of these two approaches is likely to be more fruitful. Keeping this in mind, let's look at some prescriptive and descriptive explanations of strategic decision making.

How Does a Decision Maker Make a Decision?

Various theories have been suggested about how decisions are made. Let us examine these first. Most writers focus on three approaches: rational-analytical, intuitive-emotional, and behavioral-political.

Rational-Analytical Decision Maker [9]

In this model, the decision maker is a unique actor whose behavior is intelligent and rational. The decision is the choice this actor makes, in full awareness of all available feasible alternatives, to maximize advantages. The decision maker therefore considers all the alternatives as well as the consequences of all the possible choices, orders these consequences in the light of a fixed scale of preferences, and chooses the alternative that procures the maximum gain.

This is the oldest decision theory. It prescribes a rational, conscious, systematic, and analytical approach. It has been criticized because

1 The decision maker is often not a unique actor but part of a multiparty decision situation.

2 Decision makers are not rational enough or informed enough to consider all alternatives or know all the consequences. And information is costly.

3 Decision makers make decisions with more than a maximization of objectives in mind. They tend to "satisfice," that is, make a decision expected to yield a satisfactory, as opposed to an "optimal," outcome. Besides, the objectives may change.

So descriptions of actual decision making question the validity of "rational" processes.

Intuitive-Emotional Decision Maker [10]

The opposite of the rational decision maker is the intuitive decision maker. This decision maker prefers habit or experience, gut feeling, reflective thinking, and instinct, using the unconscious mental processes. Intuitive decision makers consider a number of alternatives and options, simultaneously jumping from one step in analysis or search to another and back again.

Some who prescribe intuition or judgment as the preferred approach point out that in many cases, judgment may lead to "better" decisions than "optimizing" techniques. For example, consider sensitivity analysis on a tool such as the economic order quantity (EOQ). EOQ models suggest that there is an optimal order quantity considering trade-offs of ordering and holding costs. Yet you can stray far from optimal in most cases without a very significant impact on total cost differentials. Here, then, judgment concerning other factors in the decision situation could lead to a better *overall* decision about order quantities, rather than holding fast to deciding what the rational model prescribes. In fact, the timing of when to implement a decision based on the analysis may require an intuitive feel for what the data are telling you. In many cases, judgment such as this might be preferable to relying on the analysis. Recognize, then, that analytical models are tools to *help* the decision maker refine judgment.

Those opposed to this approach argue that

1 It does not effectively use all the tools available to modern decision makers.

2 The rational approach ensures that adequate attention is given to consequences of decisions before big mistakes are made.

Political-Behavioral Decision Making [11]

A third point of view suggests that real decision makers must consider a variety of pressures from other people affected by their decisions. An organization interacts with a variety of stakeholders in a series of interdependent exchange relationships. Unions exchange labor for decent wages and job security. Customers exchange money for products and services. Owners exchange capital for expected returns on investment. Suppliers exchange inputs for money and continued business. Government exchanges protection and economic security for taxes. Even competitors exchange information with one another through trade associations or other contacts. The list of agents and expectations goes on. *A stakeholder is any group or individual who can affect or is affected by the achievement of an organization's purpose.*

Each stakeholder gives the organization something and expects something in return. To the extent an organization has a favorable exchange relationship (gets a bit more than given) compared with other organizations and stakeholders, it has more power. More powerful stakeholders have more influence over decisions because the organization is more dependent on these stakeholders. A majority stockholder can have a greater influence on decisions about reinvestment versus dividend payout than if stock is widely held by many small owners. If the firm is labor-intensive, more attention may be paid to union leaders' demands for better wages than to the desires of stockholders for more profit, because the union might shut the firm down.

Given these realities, decision makers do a juggling act to meet the demands of the various stakeholders. Through political compromise, they attempt to merge competing demands so that a coalition of interests emerges that will support the decision.

This mode of decision making is a descriptive theory suggesting that the organization in which the decision maker works limits the choices available. Decisions are made when the several people involved in the process agree that they have found a solution. They do this by mutual adjustment and negotiation following the rules of the game—the way decisions have been made in the organization in the past. The decision maker must consider whether the decision outcome can be implemented politically.

A Synthesis on Decision Making

The human being is a mix of the rational and the emotional. We also know that the environment is a mixture of the analyzable and of chaotic change and pressures. Strategic management decisions therefore are made in a typically human way: using the rational, conscious analysis and intuitive, unconscious "gut," in light of political realities.

As stated earlier, some prescribe that one component or another *should* be larger. However, because of individual differences and differences in the stability of the environment, the amount of the rational versus the intuitive versus the political varies by the decision maker and the decision situation. In some cases the analytical component is very large; in others, the emotional set may dominate. For example, Bill Ziff, the magnate behind the billion dollar Ziff-Davis Publishing Company, sold off much of his empire because he became "more and more bored." He put TV stations up for sale because, he says, "they were not a turn on." But as Exhibit 1.12 suggests, the interaction of the three approaches (shaded area) defines where we think much decision making probably occurs. We would prefer that the analytical component be larger than the others. In fact, we prescribe an analytical-rational approach, tempered by realities in the situation. Thus when you set about to make decisions, you should apply the tools you learn. But truly rational analysis will also incorporate analysis of

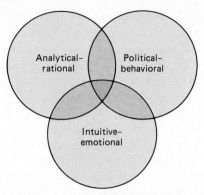

EXHIBIT 1.12   Components of strategic decision processes.

the political-behavioral and intuitive dimensions in the decision situation. Indeed various techniques such as dialectic inquiry, devil's advocacy, hierarchical analysis, and influence diagrams have evolved to help managers with these complex and messy problems. These systems allow managers to recognize and rationally structure the judgmental and political factors which will undoubtedly influence them [12].

Thus we suggest that a blending of these prescriptive and descriptive approaches helps you better understand how decision makers operate. And as you assess cases or business problems, attempt to diagnose the political or emotional realities of the situation in addition to using the analytical tools at your disposal. The recommendations you make are likely to be much more meaningful if you do this. Now, let's explain the significance of these ideas for the strategic management model used in this book.

Strategic Management and Strategic Decisions [13]

As you look again at Exhibit 1.2, note that the phases in the model are interrelated. As we examine strategic management elements, we will outline who the decision makers are, what organizational objectives are sought, and how those objectives are arrived at. You will find that the processes involved in making decisions about objectives involve political pressures and value orientations of individuals involved with the organization. As we discuss the analysis and diagnosis of external and internal factors, you will find that there are analytical approaches and that there are also descriptions of how perceptions and political influences affect the assessments made. Our discussion of choosing among alternatives will suggest some analytical techniques to aid in the identification of strategies and prescriptions about why some might be better than others under certain circumstances. But often there are only a few proposals recommended to strategists that will be considered at any given time. In addition to rational analysis, political factors and intuition play a role in the selection of a proposal. For implementation, behavioral-political factors become particularly critical. And as evaluation is done, a rational analysis of criteria is possible; but the interpretation and explanation of results may involve other elements.

Related to this is the issue of whether strategic change is evolutionary or revolutionary. A major line of work in this area is based on the assumption that incremental processes are, and should be, the prime mode used for strategy setting. Such a philosophy is best represented by the work of Quinn and Mintzberg. Quinn describes how 10 large companies actually arrived at their most important strategic changes. He suggests that *formal rational planning* often becomes a substitute for control instead of a process for stimulating innovation and entrepreneurship. He recommends that incremental processes be consciously used to integrate the psychological, political, and informational needs of organizations in setting strategy.

Earlier we provided a prescriptive definition of strategy as a unified, comprehensive, and integrated plan. Mintzberg describes strategy as a pattern in a stream of decisions. The pattern may not be comprehensive, unified, or integrated. This descriptive definition implies that decisions are often made piecemeal, and outcomes may be unintended. In essence, the strategy may be changed in an evolutionary manner without executives even realizing it.

However, there may be hidden costs in incremental changes. In particular, piecemeal approaches to strategy and structure may result in internal disharmonies. Making decisions about individual projects on their own merits, without considering broader strategic implications, can result in an "emerging" strategy which is de facto different from the intended strategy. Thus delays in these changes might better be made until such time that a "quantum," or revolutionary, change is justified by reconfiguring the entire system—its strategy, structure, policies, resource allocations, and so on.

Perhaps the dispute can be explained by noting that prescription and description do not converge. Descriptively, a number of researchers observe incremental evolutionary adjustments to strategy being the norm in practice; prescriptively, in order to achieve internal and external consistency, strategy change is often viewed as necessarily revolutionary. This book attempts to blend these perspectives.

Another way to look at this is to ask, What might encourage a decision maker to begin to think about the need to make a strategic change? We think that a gap analysis is a useful way to explain this. Exhibit 1.13 shows a scheme we will be referring to from time to time. It suggests several important considerations for strategic decision makers to ponder.

As a result of decisions made in the past, the organization has evolved in a particular way with a particular strategy to accomplish a set of desired outcomes. At any given time (t_1), a formal evaluation might be made of how the strategy is working. Perhaps more commonly, a proposal for some new activity or change in the strategy will be

EXHIBIT 1.13   Strategic gap analysis.

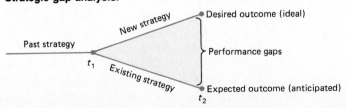

offered for consideration. In the process of contemplating the need for change, the proposal is likely to be considered in relation to the gap between the *expected outcomes* of continuing with the existing strategy and the *desired outcomes* from making a change for the future (t_2) with the proposed new strategy.

As we go through the book, we will discuss a number of conditions which could lead to this gap. For instance, Chapter 2 discusses objectives and decision makers. If these change, then desired outcomes could be altered, leading to a perceived need for change. As external conditions are assessed (Chapters 3 and 4), the expected outcomes could be altered if significant changes are expected (i.e., continuing with the past strategy might not allow the firm to take advantage of an opportunity to reach a more desirable outcome, or its continuation could lead to outcomes which are unsatisfactory). A diagnosis of internal factors (Chapter 5) might reveal that certain areas of the firm are declining in performance and that the expected results of continuing as is will lead to a gap. Similarly, as implementation is considered (Chapters 9 to 11), continuing past policies or procedures may suggest that they will no longer lead to expected outcomes, or better ways might be found to accomplish desired outcomes. Hence, an ''incremental'' project proposal might trigger a more comprehensive process of strategic thinking which may lead to revolutionary change.

At the choice stage (Chapter 8), several conditions must exist in the nature of this gap before decisions will be made to make a change or accept a proposal.

1 *The gap must be perceived to be significant.* Some theories refer to this as a minimum threshold of perception. The idea is that if you expect to be close to where you want to be, no change is required. If you want a 10 percent market share and expect to get 9½, you may not change anything.

2 *The decision maker must be motivated to reduce the gap.* Given multiple outcomes, the gap, even if significant, must pertain to an important objective. The trade-off required to reduce a gap in one objective at the expense of a larger gap in a more important objective may reduce the motivation to make any alterations.

3 *The decision maker must believe that the gap can be reduced.* If the organization is seen as incapable of reducing the gap, the gap may be ignored. If the gap is a sales decline in corn and the decline is expected to be due to inadequate rainfall, the choice may be to continue to try to grow corn.

If any of the three conditions is *not* present, it is likely that no change will be made or that the desired outcomes will be changed to be consistent with expected outcomes.

If a change is made and the overall process is effective, the desired outcomes will be reached; then the process will start all over with new and probably higher desired outcomes. As a change is implemented, if the desired outcomes prove to be unrealistically high, or if unforeseen changes in the environment occur, or if the implementation is ineffective, the desired outcomes might have to be lowered incrementally, or a contingency plan might have to be put into effect to deal with the new circumstances (Chapter 11). In all these instances, note that the various phases shown in Exhibit 1.2 are linked together. In effect, this gap analysis can occur at any stage in the overall process. For example, an internal analysis might reveal that the firm is not currently capable of reaching the desired outcomes with its current resources. It could try to build additional resources to reduce the gap if management believes it can reduce the gap this way; if not, this resource constraint could be a reason for resolving the gap differential by altering desired outcomes. Thus strategic choice and evaluation are ongoing in all parts of the model outlined in Exhibit 1.2 and can lead to strategic change, goal alterations, or changes in implementation.

If you look carefully at the three conditions which must prevail before the gap will trigger action, you will note that perception, motivation, and belief are involved. As we explained before, intuitive, rational, and political decision factors will converge to influence the managers' thinking regarding the nature of a gap (Exhibit 1.12). Exhibit 1.14 shows how these factors have influenced the assessment of strategic gaps of a large advertising agency.

Before discussing our last topic, we should point out that our primary emphasis in this book is on the strategic management *process* more than the *content* of strategy. That is, we emphasize planning processes for strategic management, decision-making approaches for formulating objectives and strategies, and processes for implementing strategy. Thus we focus on the factors influencing strategy selection and implementation. This does involve examining various types of strategies and ways to implement them. But we do not attempt to prescribe *the strategy* a firm should follow or *the policies and plans* to implement a *particular* strategy in a *particular environment*. There are two major reasons for this:

• While some patterns are evident, firms are unique, and content must often be situation-specific.

EXHIBIT 1.14   THE GAPS AT LEO BURNETT

Leo Burnett is one of the top 10 ad agencies in the United States in total billings. Yet it has the smallest number of clients among that group, with only one new account added in the last year. Its strategy is to land "blue-chip" accounts—"companies that need advertising, increase their ad spending over the years, and pay their bills on time."

Its approach has been to stick with a campaign for a client year after year, such as the "Friendly Skies" slogan of United, the "Good Hands" pitch of Allstate, Star-Kist's Charlie the Tuna, and Kellogg's Tony the Tiger. Many clients are strong backers of what they see as winning campaigns. But some smaller clients—such as Litton Industries, with an account estimated at $5 million—have left for other agencies. And many on Madison Avenue suggest that the agency's creative work has become un-even, pointing to the uninspired introduction of RCA's videodisc.

Such a potential gap is not perceived to be significant to Burnett officials. They are content with their traditional way of doing business, and they have eschewed trying to grow by gaining more clients or diversifying into other service areas as many of their competitors have done. CEO John Kensella states, "We plan to stay an advertising agency. We're willing to plan for the long term and wait for the pieces of business we want. We want to do the best work possible for our clients, make sure our people are well-paid, and see that our stockholders make money. None of that has anything to do with size."

Clearly, the gap (perceived by Burnett executives) between the desired outcomes and expected future outcomes is insufficient to lead them to alter their strategy.

Source: Adapted from "A Blue-Chip Strategy Pays Off," *Business Week*, Nov. 16, 1981. pp. 188ff.

- There is little generalizable research available which supports the generic content statement that "firm A will reach objective B with strategy C in environment D by implementing plan E."

In the analysis of cases, you will have an opportunity to apply the process to arrive at prescriptions for the content of a strategy plan for a given firm. And you will find common approaches and factors which must be considered in the analysis. But it is unlikely that there is *one best way* to successful strategic management.

TIMING AND STRATEGIC MANAGEMENT [14]

Before we summarize, the topic of timing deserves mention, since it will also crop up again. In the gap analysis, we did not specify a time period, yet that could also influence the analysis. If your desired outcome is to double the market share in a 2-year time period, your assessment about gaps between expected and desired outcomes will be different than if that desired outcome were to extend over a 10-year period. Very different interpretations will be given to a diagnosis of internal and external conditions, depending on whether your plan is long-term or short-term.

Descriptively, the terms short-range and long-range have no precise meaning but rather express relative periods of time. In the oil industry, or in the case of electric utilities, it is often necessary to extend plans 20 to 30 years into the future. Forest products companies such as Georgia-Pacific have reforestation plans that extend well into the latter half of the next century. The average lapse of time from the sowing of a fir seedling to its harvest at maturity is 99 years. At the other extreme, long-range plans for the manufacturers of children's toys may extend no more than 6 months to a year. In such industries it is virtually impossible to safely predict how quickly popular fads will come and go. Under such circumstances, examples of short-range plans might include a weekly production meeting and a quarterly budget.

Though no set answer can be given to the question, How long should a long-range plan be?, certain prescriptive criteria can be suggested as guidelines.

1 How far into the future do the firm's *fixed commitments* extend? Such commitments would include long-term indebtedness and contracts. If a firm is obligated to make mortgage or lease payments over 30 years, for instance, it would seem wise to have a financial plan for that period of time.

2 How much *uncertainty* is associated with the future? Without exception, predictive efficiency drops off over time. In some instances, the future may even be unpredictable after only a few years. In such cases it makes little sense to develop complex plans covering extended time horizons. While plans could be based on pure intuition or guesswork, their true value would be limited. On the other hand, the absence of uncertainty can lead to long-term plans which *shouldn't* be made, because they become overly rigid. For years, firms in regulated industries could develop long-term plans without concern that conditions would change radically. These firms, such as Western Union, often became bloated, slow-moving, and poorly positioned to deal with change. When deregulation occurred, they were ill-prepared to deal with the need to plan strategically, or they were locked into long-term fixed commitments which did not allow them to maneuver readily. Many failed, while others, such as some trucking firms, began to apply strategic thinking. That is, managers began to anticipate the future and devise flexible plans to proactively move their firms in desired directions.

3 What is the *lead time* required to ready a product or service for sale? For example, it typically takes 3 to 5 years for a new series of computers to reach the market following its development. So planning periods are strongly influenced by product development considerations. While the lead time for a new line of women's dresses may be only 6 months, many firms are forced to plan well into the future if their products are ever going to be developed at all.

Given these considerations, it is not uncommon to find that planning is often done on a "rolling" basis. Under this system an organization may develop a 5-year plan of future operations and update it on an annual basis. Thus as the current year of a 5-year plan closes, the plan is extended, or rolled forward, to include a "new" fifth year. Such a procedure allows an organization to revise its plans on the basis of new information and to maintain a degree of flexibility in its commitments. It is at this time that a comprehensive gap analysis of the entire business is desirable. Thus both long-range, or strategic, plans and short-term or operational, plans to implement strategy can be integrated with one another.

Unfortunately, many U.S. executives seem to have abandoned long-term strategic management to concentrate on short-term profitability. There are a number of reasons for this, including pressure from Wall Street, and rewards for short-term results rather than long-term performance.

For example, managers often buy back stock, or pursue other strategies to protect their own position of control or improve the stock price. Short-term investor interest (often large institutional holders who buy and sell large blocks of stocks or bonds) will often force the hand of management. And as we pointed out earlier, some failures in plans are due to faulty strategic planning. Again, there could be other reasons for lack of success. But strategic plans do often rest on premises or assumptions about the future which may be uncertain or unreliable. Instead of abandoning strategic thinking in favor of short-term performance, however, we believe the concept should be expanded to the next generation—contingency management. Here, the firm uses *anticipatory flexibility* by establishing a long-term plan which anticipates a probable future, but incorporates flexibility to maneuver and alter the plan if the assumptions on which it is based are found to be inaccurate. This is slightly different from the notion of "surprise" management. That is, managers can try to anticipate surprises (such as an environmental disaster, death of a president, or a new-product introduction by a competitor) and plan a contingency response which would be ready in such an eventuality. However, the idea behind anticipatory flexibility is not necessarily to provide a specific plan for a surprise. Rather, it is to achieve the ability to alter a strategy in several directions—usually requiring slack in the system. In other words, the plan to begin with recognizes that diversions or variations are likely as time goes on. This does not negate the usefulness of surprise management. Rather, flexibility complements a contingency plan. Our concept of strategic management is also grounded in this concept, which will be referred to again.

Consistent with this is the idea that strategic management requires some risk taking. Exhibit 1.15 serves to tie together our thoughts in this regard. Note that Pepsi incor-

EXHIBIT 1.15   TAKING THE PEPSI CHALLENGE

From within the ranks of the consumer product marketing giants, PepsiCo, Inc., has emerged as this generation's innovator and new product leader. Pepsi has accumulated a wide variety of consumer product successes despite recent slips and tumbles experienced by other industry powerhouses including Phillip Morris, Procter & Gamble, and Coca-Cola. Besides having the nation's best-selling soft drink, Pepsi has helped Taco Bell and Pizza Hut become two of the fastest-growing restaurant chains in the country. Pepsi was hoping to flex its marketing magic once again by purchasing Seven-Up to reverse the falling market shares and profits of the lemon-lime soft drink. But that deal fell through.

The backbone of this confidence is a "fast-moving, risk-oriented management with an exquisite sense of timing." While Pepsi employs analytical research and test-marketing tools similar to those of its rivals, it also realizes the importance of instincts or intuition as decision-making assets. Because the demands of regional, national, and even international markets can change so rapidly, a degree of intuition is essential to flexibility in keeping a step ahead of the competition. Executives at Pepsi value their instincts so much that they have risked millions by being the first out with a 100 percent NutraSweet formula, even before a test market could be performed for fear that Coca-Cola would be tipped off. Pepsi's top management allows its managers to operate with a great deal of autonomy and encourages quick actions in return for expected performance. When opportunities arise, usually the difference between success and failure is not that of failing to recognize the opportunity but instead that of not correctly and quickly acting upon the opportunity before the competition does.

However, does a point exist where even the best intuition or good hunch won't be enough to go on when determining investment allocations? This point does exist in some organizations, while not being present in others, depending upon the risk or comfort level of each individual management team. As in every case, though, for each company not willing to take a chance on a hunch, there is another one ready to take the risk in search of larger market shares and profits. And at this time Pepsi has accepted the challenge!

Source: Adapted from A., Dunkin, "Pepsi's Marketing Magic: Why Nobody Does It Better," *Business Week,* Feb. 10, 1986. pp. 52–57

porates intuitive and rational decision making along with a concern about anticipating the future and taking risks as they make incremental moves toward their long-range strategy and goals.

SUMMARY

This chapter has introduced you to the world of strategy and strategic management. It has shown you how budgeting evolved into long-range planning, which in turn has evolved into strategic planning and strategic management.

The chapter has also defined some key terms.

• Strategic management is a stream of decisions and actions which leads to the development of an effective strategy or strategies to help achieve corporate objectives.

• Strategic decisions are means to achieve ends. These decisions encompass the definition of the business, products to be handled, markets to be served, functions to be performed, and major policies needed for the organization to execute these decisions to achieve objectives.

• A strategic business unit (SBU) is an operating division of a firm which serves a distinct product-market segment or a well-defined set of customers or a geographic area.

• A strategy is a unified, comprehensive, and integrated plan that relates the strategic advantages of the firm to the challenges of the environment. It is designed to ensure that the basic objectives of the enterprise are achieved through proper execution by the organization.

• Policies are guides to action. They indicate how resources are to be allocated and how tasks assigned to the organization might be accomplished so that functional-level managers execute the strategy properly.

The strategic management process was set up and differences in the process between single-SBU and multiple-SBU firms were clarified. Then it was emphasized that for ease of presentation the parts of the strategic management process would be discussed one at a time. But in reality the phases of the strategic management process are interactive; the process is continuous, with several parts occurring simultaneously. Strategies and policies must be formulated and implemented with each other in mind.

Several examples of the use of strategic management were provided, suggesting that this approach is widely used in larger organizations, even though there are successes and failures. The Appendix also indicates that the concepts are used in different parts of the world and in nonprofit enterprises and the public sector.

Why strategic management is instituted was discussed next. The main reasons are as follows:

• Strategic management helps firms anticipate future problems and opportunities.

• Strategic management provides clear objectives and directions for the future of the enterprise.

• Research in strategic management can be helpful to practicing managers, and it seems to suggest that formal planning contributes to success.

This last reason is important enough to summarize in propositional form. This method will be used in the summaries of the chapters throughout the book.

Proposition 1.1

Businesses which develop formal strategic management systems have a higher probability of success than those which do not.

This chapter also introduced you to some basic concepts running through the book. We noted that this text tries to integrate both *descriptive* and *prescriptive* approaches to strategic management. And we indicated that the focus of the book is on the *process* of strategic management. The most basic process discussed is decision making; we outlined three basic modes: rational-analytical, intuitive-emotional, and behavioral-political. Our synthesis suggests that all three modes are used in strategic decision making, and we showed how these ideas relate to our model of the strategic management process.

We also discussed how these concepts relate to gap analysis. Before a decision is made,

- A gap must exist between desired outcomes and the expected outcomes.
- The gap must be perceived to be significant, thus deserving attention.
- The decision maker must be motivated to reduce the gap.
- The decision maker must believe that something can be done about the gap.

Proposition 1.2

Decision making is a multiphase process. Effective decision makers combine rational and intuitive approaches to making complex, unstructured decisions. They also consider the political feasibility of the decisions.

Finally, the chapter pointed out the importance of timing for strategic decisions and strategic planning. We noted that long-term strategic plans versus short-term operational plans are situation-specific. The time frame for strategic planning is probably based on the nature of the time associated with fixed commitments, the degree of uncertainty in the future, and the lead time needed for start-up. In any case, *anticipatory flexibility* is seen as a superior way to account for the need for long-term strategy while allowing for short-term changes as assumptions are proved right or wrong.

The appendix for this chapter describes strategic management in nonbusiness settings and in different parts of the world. In the chapters that follow, we examine in more detail the strategic management process and important issues about strategic management. Chapter 2 discusses the key elements of strategic management: the strategic decision makers and the decision outcomes (objectives). Then the strategic management process is described, beginning with Chapter 3.

We hope that you will find the journey that lies ahead of you both interesting and rewarding. We hope that you will take advantage of the opportunities available to you.

Appendix: Users of Strategic Management [15]

The primary focus of Chapter 1, and of the book in general, is on strategic management in the private sector in North America. But perhaps more than a third of you will spend all or parts of your careers in not-for-profit or public sectors. Further, as our world gets "smaller," you need to be aware of what's going on in other countries. This appendix will introduce you to our ideas about how the concepts of strategic management are applied in these different settings. Chapter 4 elaborates on the international setting.

The public sector includes federal, state, and local government bodies and federal corporations such as Amtrak, Conrail, the U.S. Postal Service, Canadian National Railways, Renault,

British Air, and Rolls-Royce. (With changes in governments, some of these organizations are being moved to the private sector.) Collectively, these are huge employers of managers and specialists. The not-for-profit sector includes nongovernment, nonprivate groups. Examples of these include most community general hospitals, private colleges and universities, independent research institutes such as the Midwest Research Institute, trade unions, political parties, churches and synagogues, charities such as the Red Cross, interest groups like the NAACP or Common Cause, consumer cooperatives, and arts organizations such as symphonies, ballet companies, museums, and repertory theaters. We will classify countries following our description of public and not-for-profit sectors.

Is strategic management useful in the public and not-for-profit sectors? It appears that it is. Many of the enterprises in these sectors are managed like small- and medium-sized businesses, since they have many of the same characteristics.

There are similarities and differences between the private and other sectors. Many enterprises in the nonprivate sector are more complicated to manage because the manager has to face many more constraints (such as active and diverse stockholders) than in the private firm. It appears reasonable to conclude that these institutions will receive benefits similar to what businesses receive if their management groups practice effective strategic management.

Cases that focus on the operations of several nonbusiness sectors have been included in this book. These allow you to apply the tools of strategic management across different sectors.

We are learning more about the strategic management of public and not-for-profit enterprises. Several authors have described the strategic management of these two sectors in general. Others focus on part of the strategic management process for all these enterprises, such as environment forecasting. But most of the information is written about strategic management of specific institutions. Let us review briefly some of the better studies of these institutions.

Strategic Management of Hospitals [16]

In the United States, community hospitals are in the not-for-profit sector, except for the 850 or so proprietary (for profit) hospitals. There are about 3500 not-for-profit hospitals. In other countries, including Canada, all hospitals are in the public sector. The mental hospitals and Veterans Administration and municipal hospitals in the United States are in the public sector and number about 2700. The focus of this section is on the not-for-profit hospitals.

In our opinion, these institutions are the most difficult enterprises to manage. The hospital administrator must deal first with many objectives, and many of these are hard to quantify. The objectives include quality patient care, research, professional training, cost efficiency, growth in size, and community prestige. The administrator is responsible to a board of trustees, which is usually composed of community leaders and physicians. Although the members of the medical staff can use the hospital facilities, usually they are not the hospital employees. The hospital's funds come from patients, donors, and third-party groups such as Blue Cross, Medicare, and insurance companies. The employees vary from highly trained professionals to semiskilled workers.

One study found that even though the law requires hospitals to be involved in strategic management, most hospitals practice it informally (if at all) on a regular basis. Webber and Dula, using concepts similar to those in this book, have outlined how hospitals could improve their strategic management.

Strategic Management of Colleges and Universities [17]

In the United States there are over 3000 colleges and universities, many of which are in the public sector. Typical of these are the state universities such as the University of California and the University of Wisconsin, municipal universities, and local or state-supported colleges such as Dade County Community College. The third-sector (private or independent) colleges and universities vary from wealthy, well-known institutions such as Harvard and Stanford to hundreds of colleges known mostly to their alumni and local communities.

The university presidents and chancellors are faced with a multitude of objectives, many of which are hard to measure. These include effective teaching, the creation and dissemination of research, and service to society, not to mention the unofficial goals such as developing winning sports teams. The president's strategic management also involves a board of regents (often prominent citizens or alumni), faculty with tenure, the professional staff (sometimes unionized), and sometimes a militant student body. Funds come from tuition, research grants, donations, legislatures, and ancillary operations such as dormitories, the food service, the bookstore, bowl games, and television stations.

Universities are faced with serious strategic challenges from time to time. California universities in the public sector faced the challenge of Proposition 13. All universities face the reality of a significant decline in the number of students in the 1980s because of a lower birthrate.

Strategic management offers some sources of help for universities. Several writers have described effective strategic management for colleges and universities not too differently from the approach of this chapter. And there is one case study which indicates that success and failure do result from the strategies chosen. For example, the past successes of Swarthmore, Antioch, and Reed Colleges have been attributed to the strategic management of these institutions. New York University is financially and educationally sounder because of President Sawhill's turnaround strategy in the late 1970s. And Beloit College has survived because of its turnaround strategy. It is possible to identify specific strategies of colleges. For example, the New School for Social Research has flourished because of its approach to adult education.

Outside the United States, most universities, schools, and hospitals are owned and financed by the government. In these cases there is little direct fund raising or "market"-support activity. But strategic decisions are required there too. Since long-term financial support decisions are based on factors such as population and on performance criteria such as student-staff and patient-staff ratios, strategic plans are also important for their success. And in western Europe, some mergers have taken place among these institutions.

Strategic Management of Churches and Synagogues [18]

Like their less "holy" peers, churches and synagogues face environmental challenges and internal problems. There are approximately 300 national church and synagogue bodies and hundreds of thousands of local churches and synagogues.

Priests, ministers, or rabbis are sometimes subject to a hierarchy of bishops or central headquarters. Sometimes they face a church or synagogue board. Their income comes from gifts and endowments. Membership fluctuates as member values, the local community, and the internal organization change. For example, *Fortune* reported on the financial problems of Roman Catholic religious orders. Their membership has declined rapidly, and remaining members tend to be older, while the orders' fixed costs such as those for buildings or pensions are increasing.

Various experts have shown how strategic management can help improve church and synagogue performance. Adair has reported on how the Church of England (Anglican church) has tried strategic management to stem its decline in participation and membership. Hussey has helped outline and implement a strategic management system for a small Methodist church; and Reimnetz, a Lutheran pastor, has shown how a strategic management system helped church educational services.

Strategic Management of Arts Organizations [19]

Most of the arts organizations in the United States are small "businesses," with relatively few employees. Symphonies, opera companies, ballet troupes and other dance companies, theater groups, and museums are the most typical. Many of these enterprises hire people for part-time rather than full-time work.

The managers of these institutions have a difficult time generating financial support from ticket sales, gifts, and grants. Ancillary businesses, such as stores, have been used to supplement revenues. The managers' titles vary from curator to impressario. Most of these institutions survive because of the talent and dedication of their leaders. Success also comes from a dedicated and competent group of volunteers who substitute for paid employees and help raise money.

Relatively little has been written about strategic management of the arts. But a couple of writers have shown how strategic management can help make the arts organization more effective too.

Strategic Management in the Public Sector [20]

The public sector includes all enterprises whose major direct source of funds is a government body. Most often, these enterprises are owned by the government. Sometimes they are quasi-independent corporations such as the U.S. Postal Service, Air Canada, and Conrail.

Public enterprises sometimes pursue objectives different from those of private- and third-sector enterprises. Public managers must be able to deal with more complex internal and external environments than private- and third-sector managers. The hierarchy to which public managers are responsible is usually divided among executive (mayor or city manager, governor, prime minister, president) and legislative (Parliament, Congress, legislature, city council) branches. And out-of-office politicians and the press seek to expose the public managers. (They are called "inefficient bureaucrats" by these two groups.)

Politicians can interfere with the public manager's job. Often, they want the merit system to be bent according to their will. This is a remnant of the spoils system. Voters organize into pressure groups to influence the executive and legislative bodies and thus the public managers. These characteristics of the public manager's job and environment should lead you to conclude that strategic management is much more complex and difficult in the public sector, which is indeed the case.

Despite the difficulty, some analyses provide clues for effective strategic management in the public sector. At the federal level, the Tennessee Valley Authority prospered because of good strategy. And James Webb was an excellent strategist for NASA. Strategic management could be used by the Congress, and it could be improved at the federal level, according to several authors.

Strategic management can be practiced at the state and provincial levels. George Romney used strategic management while he was the governor of Michigan. Michael Howlett, a professional politician, and Muskin, an academic, provide some useful information for initiating and implementing strategic management at this level. Finally, at the local level, strategic management makes sense too. It works in city government, according to some writers.

A special case of strategic management in the public sector involves the military. Probably the first major institutions engaged in strategic management were the military organizations. Earlier works on business strategy used many terms developed by such military theorists as von Clausewitz; these terms have been used recently to describe marketing tactics. It is generally recognized that much of the success of the great generals of history was due to their strategic planning. You would probably not know about generals such as Rommell and MacArthur without the strategic planning done by themselves and their staffs. Of course, the implementation of strategy also affects success in the military setting.

Strategic Management in Other Settings [21]

Little is known about the strategic management of unions, political parties, independent research institutes, charities, and interest groups. Other institutions rise or fall partly because of the effectiveness or weakness of their strategies. There are no more Whig or Federalist political parties. Some unions such as the Knights of Labor and the IWW did not succeed. The literature is just beginning on the strategic management of these groups but is developing well for the strategic management of libraries. Much more work must be done in these settings. However, it appears fruitful to encourage this work to make these enterprises more effective and responsive to societal needs.

This appendix should lead you to conclude that strategic management can contribute to the meeting of objectives in the not-for-profit and public sectors. Those interested in these sectors should gain from this book too.

Strategic Management Around the World [22]

It appears that the factors affecting strategic management in countries other than the United States and Canada include educational, behavioral, legal and political, and economic factors. After reading, traveling, and thinking about this issue, we find it useful to think about effective strategic management by dividing the world into three categories. Chapter 4 will present another scheme to categorize countries according to types of resources they have, since this takes on strategic significance as the international environment is analyzed.

Fully Developed Countries

The fully developed nations' economic, educational, behavioral, and legal and political conditions are most like those in the United States and Canada. Basically these countries include Australia and New Zealand, Israel, South Africa, Japan, and most European countries (United Kingdom, West Germany, France, Austria, U.S.S.R., Belgium, Luxembourg, the Netherla, Switzerland, Italy, Sweden, Norway, Denmark, and Finland).

A quick glance at this list indicates that there are significant political differences (U.S.S.R. versus West Germany), cultural differences (Israel versus Japan), and other differences among this group.

References for this section indicate that the *processes* used by managers in these developed countries are more similar to than different from the processes used in the United States and Canada. However, the content or outcome of strategic choices varies due to the factors just mentioned. Thus more U.S. managers are trying to learn why the Japanese have become more successful in world markets.

Developing Countries

Very little has been written about strategic management practices in developing countries such as Brazil, Mexico, Argentina, Venezuela, Chile, Spain, Portugal, Nigeria, Saudi Arabia, Iran, Libya, Taiwan, India, Greece, Singapore, Korea, China, and most of eastern Europe (especially Yugoslavia, East Germany, Rumania, Czechoslovakia, and Poland). In some of these countries, however, with planned economies, we would expect that long-range planning concepts are in use.

Third-World Countries

We know almost nothing about strategic management in the 90 or so third-world countries such as Egypt, Upper Volta, Bolivia, Burma, Pakistan, and the Philippines. It is suspected that relatively little strategic management goes on in these countries and little in the developing countries. But there are sophisticated firms in countries such as Brazil, Mexico, Venezuela, Saudi Arabia, and Iran.

It appears that the material in this book is directly relevant to developed countries and the more sophisticated firms in the developing and third-world countries. As we move to a more global economy, our expectation is that more firms will begin to use the concepts outlined in this book, tailored to the unique circumstances faced by each. That's why we have added an extended discussion on the international environment in Chapter 4.

REFERENCES

[1] Basic References about Strategic Thinking

Ansoff, H. I.: *Implementing Strategic Management* (Englewood Cliffs, N.J.: Prentice-Hall, 1985).

Abell, D. F.: *Defining the Business: The Starting Point of Strategic Planning* (Englewood Cliffs, N.J.: Prentice-Hall, 1980).

Hofer, C., and D. Schendel: *Strategy Formulation: Analytical Concepts* (St. Paul, Minn.: West, 1978).

[2] The Evolution and Definition of Strategic Management

Ansoff, H. I.: "Strategy Formulation as a Learning Process: An Applied Managerial Theory of Strategic Behavior," *International Studies of Management & Organization,* vol. 7 (Summer 1977), pp. 58–77.

Ginter, P. M., and D. D. White: "A Social Learning Approach to Strategic Management: Toward a Theoretical Foundation," *Academy of Management Review,* vol. 7 (1982), pp. 253–261.

Hall, W. K.: "SBUs: Hot, New Topic in the Management of Diversification," *Business Horizons,* vol. 21 (February 1978), pp. 17–25.

Kudla, R. J.: "Elements of Effective Corporate Planning," *Long Range Planning,* vol. 9, no. 4 (August 1976), pp. 82–93.

[3] Strategic Management for Multiple SBU Firms

Ellis, J. E.: "Ward's Makes a Desperate Move Uptown," *Business Week,* Aug. 26, 1985, pp. 34–35.

Lorange, P.: *Corporate Planning: An Executive Viewpoint* (Englewood Cliffs, N.J.: Prentice-Hall, 1980).

Vancil, R. F.: "Strategy Formulation in Complex Organizations," *Sloan Management Review,* vol. 17 (Winter 1976), pp. 1–18.

[4] Defining Strategy

Boswell, J. S.: *Business Policies in the Making* (London: George, Allen & Unwin, 1983).

Chaffee, E. E.: "Three Models of Strategy," *Academy of Management Review,* vol. 10 (1985), pp. 89–98.

Hobbs, J. M., and D. R. Heany: "Coupling Strategy to Operating Plans," *Harvard Business Review,* vol. 55 (May–June 1977), pp. 119–126.

Porter, M. E.: *Competitive Strategy* (New York: Free Press, 1985).

Shirley, R. C., "Limiting the Scope of Strategy: A Decision Based Approach," *Academy of Management Review,* vol. 7 (1982), pp. 262–268.

Smith, R. B.: "The 21st Century Corporation," speech to the Economics Club of Detroit, Sept. 9, 1985.

[5] The Use of Strategic Management

Barnes, J. H.: "Cognitive Biases and Their Impact on Strategic Planning," *Strategic Management Journal,* vol. 5 (1984), pp. 129–137.

Boulton, W. R., S. G. Franklin, W. M. Lindsay, and L. W. Rue: "How Are Companies Planning Now?—A Survey," *Long Range Planning,* vol. 15 (1982), pp. 82–86.

Capon, N., J. V. Farley, and J. Hulbert: "International Diffusion of Corporate and Strategic Planning Practices," *Columbia Journal of World Business,* vol. 15 (Fall 1980), pp. 5–13.

Curtis, D. A. (ed.): *Strategic Planning for Smaller Business* (Boston: Heath, 1983).

Henry, H. W.: "Then and Now: A Look at Strategic Planning Systems," *Journal of Business Strategy,* vol. 1 (Winter 1981), pp. 64–69.

"Publisher's Memo," *Business Week* (January 9, 1978).

[6] The Value of Strategic Management

Bresser, R. K., and R. C. Bishop: "Dysfunctional Effects of Formal Planning," *Academy of Management Review,* vol. 8 (1984), pp. 588–599.

Camillus, J. A.: "Strategic Planning Systems in the Eighties," paper presented at the Strategic Management Society Conference, 1984.

Miller, D.: "Common Syndromes of Business Failure," *Business Horizons,* vol. 20 (November 1977), pp. 43–53.

Saunders, C. B. and F. D. Tuggle: as answered by David Hussey, "Who Says Planners Don't?" *Long Range Planning* (October 1977), pp. 83–85.

[7] Some Summaries of Strategic Management Research

Anderson, C., and F. Paine: "PIMS: A Reexamination," *Academy of Management Review* (July 1978), pp. 602–612.

Hofer, C.: "Research on Strategic Planning," *Journal of Economics and Business,* vol. 28 (Spring–Summer 1976), pp. 261–286.

Lamb, R. B. (ed.): *Advances in Strategic Management,* vol. 1–3 (Eastchester, N.Y.: JAI Press, 1983, 1985).

Schendel, D. E. and C. W. Hofer: *Strategic Management: A New View of Business Policy and Planning* (Boston: Little, Brown, 1979).

[8] Formal Planning and Organization Success

Armstrong, J. S.: "The Value of Formal Planning for Strategic Decisions," *Strategic Management Journal,* vol. 3 (1982), pp. 197–212.

Baird, I. S.: "Assessing the Effectiveness of Planning Systems," paper presented at the Academy of Management Meetings, 1984.

Donham, W.: "Essential Groundwork for a Broad Executive Theory," *Harvard Business Review,* vol. 1 (October 1922), pp. 1–10.

Frederickson, J. W.: "The Comprehensiveness of Strategic Decision Processes," *Academy of Management Journal,* vol. 27 (1984), pp. 445–466.

Kudla, R. J.: "The Effects of Strategic Planning on Common Stock Returns," *Academy of Management Journal,* vol. 23 (1980), pp. 5–20.

Robinson, R. B., and J. A. Pearce: "The Impact of Formalized Strategic Planning on Financial Performance in Small Organizations," *Strategic Management Journal,* vol. 4 (1983), pp. 197–207.

[9] Rational Decision Models

Beach, L. R., and T. R. Mitchell: "A Contingency Model for the Selection of Decision Strategies," *Academy of Management Review,* vol. 3 (July 1978), pp. 439–449.

Eilon, S.: "More Against Optimization," *Omega,* vol. 5 (1977), pp. 627–633.

Lenz, R. T., and M. A. Lyles: "Paralysis by Analysis: Is Your Planning System Becoming Too Rational?" *Long Range Planning,* vol. 18 (August 1985), pp. 64–72.

———— and ————: "Crippling Effects of 'Hyper-Rational' Planning," working paper 956, College of Commerce, University of Illinois, 1983.

Murray, M.: *Decisions: A Comparative Critique* (Marshfield, Mass.: Pitman, 1986).

Simon, H. A.: *Administrative Behavior* (New York: Free Press, 1957).

[10] Intuitive Decision Making

Isaack, T.: "Intuition: An Ignored Dimension of Management," *Academy of Management Review,* vol. 3 (October 1978), pp. 917–922.

Mintzberg, H.: "Planning on the Left Side and Managing on the Right," *Harvard Business Review,* vol. 54 (July–August 1976), pp. 49–58.

Rowan, R.: "Managerial Hunches and Intuition," *Fortune,* Apr. 23, 1979, pp. 111 + .

————.: *The Intuitive Manager* (Boston: Little, Brown, 1986).

[11] Political Decision Theory

Dill, W. R.: "Strategic Planning in a Kibitzer's World," in Ansoff, Declerk, Hays (eds.). *From Strategic Planning to Strategic Management* (New York: Wiley, 1976), pp. 125–136.

Freeman, R. E.: *Strategic Management: A Stakeholder Approach* (Boston: Pitman, 1984).

Gray, B., and S. S. Ariss: "Politics and Strategic Changes Across Organizational Life Cycles," *Academy of Management Review,* vol. 10 (1985), pp. 707–723.

MacMillan, I. C.: *Strategy Formulation: Political Concepts* (St. Paul, Minn.: West, 1978).

Mitroff, I. I.: *Stakeholders of the Organizational Mind* (San Francisco: Jossey-Bass, 1984).

Narayanan, V. K., and L. Fahey: "The Micro-Politics of Strategy Formulation," *Academy of Management Review,* vol. 7 (1982), pp. 25–34.

Pfeffer, J.: *Power in Organizations* (Marchfield, Mass.: Pitman, 1981).

[12] Techniques to Integrate Decision Modes

Hart, S., M. Boroush, G. Enk, and W. Hornick: "Managing Complexity Through Consensus Mapping," *Academy of Management Review,* vol. 10 (1985) pp. 587–600.

Ramaprasad, A. and E. Poon: "A Computerized Interactive Technique for Mapping Influence Diagrams," *Strategic Management Journal,* vol. 6 (1985), pp. 377–392.

Schweiger, D. M., and P. A. Finger: "The Comparative Effectiveness of Dialectical Inquiry and Devil's Advocacy," *Strategic Management Journal,* vol. 5 (1984), pp. 335–350.

————, W. R. Sandberg, and J. W. Ragan: "Group Approaches for Improving Strategic Decision Making," *Academy of Management Journal,* vol. 29 (1986), pp. 51–71.

Schwenk, C. R.: "Effects of Planning Aids and Presentation Media on Performance and Affective Responses in Strategic Decision Making," *Management Science,* vol. 3 (1984), pp. 263–272.

Welles, C.: "What's Next for the Unpredictable Bill Ziff?" *Business Week,* Apr. 14, 1986, pp. 102–106.

[13] Integrative Decision Making

Burgelman, R. A.: "On the Interplay of Process and Content in Internal Corporate Ventures," *Academy of Management Proceedings* (1984), pp. 2–6.

Carter, E. E.: "Project Evaluations and Firm Decisions," *The Journal of Management Studies* (1971), pp. 253–279.

Cosier, R. A.: "Dialectical Inquiry in Strategic Planning: A Case of Premature Acceptance?" *Academy of Management Review,* vol. 6 (October 1981), pp. 643–648.

Donaldson, G., and J. W. Lorsch: *Decision Making at the Top* (New York: Basic Books, 1983).

Hambrick, D. C., and S. Finkelstein: "Managerial Discretion," in B. Staw and L. L. Cummings (eds.). *Research in Organizational Behavior,* vol. 9 (Eastchester, N.Y.: JAI Press, 1987).

Lindblom, C. E.: *The Policy Making Process* (Englewood Cliffs, N.J.: Prentice-Hall, 1980).

Mason, R. O., and I. I. Mitroff: *Challenging Strategic Planning Assumptions* (New York: Wiley, 1981).

Miller, D. H., and P. H. Friesen: *Organizations: A Quantum View* (Englewood Cliffs, N.J.: Prentice-Hall, 1984).

Mintzberg, H., and J. A. Waters: "Of Strategies, Deliberate and Emergent," *Strategic Management Journal,* vol. 6 (1985), pp. 257–272.

Murray, E. A.: "Strategic Choice as a Negotiated Outcome," *Management Science,* vol. 24 (May 1978), pp. 960–972.

Murray, M.: *Decisions: A Comparative Critique* (Cambridge, Mass.: Ballinger, 1986).

Quinn, J. B.: *Strategies for Change: Logical Incrementalism* (Homewood, Ill.: Irwin, 1980).

[14] Timing in Strategic Management

Ansoff, H. I.: "Managing Strategic Surprise by Response to Weak Signals," *California Management Review,* vol. 18 (Winter 1975), pp. 21–33.

Bedeian, A. G., and W. F. Glueck: *Management* (Elmhurst, Ill.: Dryden, 1983).

Camillus, J. C.: "Reconciling Logical Incrementalism and Synoptic Formalism—An Integrated Approach to Designing Strategic Planning Processes," *Strategic Management Journal,* vol. 3 (1982), pp. 277–283.

Graham, R.: "The Timing of Radical Organizational Change: The Revitalization Process at AT&T," working paper, Wharton School, University of Pennsylvania, 1981.

Leff, N. H.: "What You Don't Know Can Hurt You," *Business Week,* Mar. 14, 1983, p. 12.

Maremont, M.: "How Western Union Went from Bad to Worse," *Business Week,* Jan. 28, 1985, pp. 110–116.

Priest, A. L.: "Why Corporate Stock Buybacks Don't Really Pay Off," *Business Week,* June 25, 1984, pp. 33.

Tushman, M. L., W. H. Newman, and E. Romanelli: "Convergence and Upheaval," working paper S.C. #49, Graduate School of Business, Columbia University, 1985.

"What Deregulation Has Done to the Truckers," *Business Week,* Nov. 9, 1981, pp. 70+.

[15] Users of Strategic Management

Hatten, M. L., "Strategic Management in Not-for-Profit Organizations," *Strategic Management Journal,* vol. 3 (1982), pp. 89–104.

Hay, R. D.: *Strategic Management for Non-Profit Organizations* (Santa Barbara, Calif.: Kinko's, 1986).

Lachman, R.: "Public and Private Sector Differences," *Academy of Management Journal,* vol. 28 (1985), pp. 671–680.

Nutt, P. C.: "A Strategic Planning Network for Nonprofit Organizations," *Strategic Management Journal,* vol. 5 (1984), pp. 57–75.

Ring, P. S. and J. L. Perry: "Strategic Management in Public and Private Organizations," *Academy of Management Review,* vol. 10 (1985), pp. 276–286.

Unterman, I., and R. H. Davis: "The Strategy Gap in Not-for-Profit," *Harvard Business Review,* (May–June, 1982), pp. 30–40.

[16] Hospitals Use Strategic Management

Carper, W. B., and R. J. Litschert: "A Comparative Analysis of Strategic Power Hierarchies in For Profit and Not-For-Profit Hospitals," paper presented at the Academy of Management meeting, 1982.
——— and ———: "Strategic Power Relationships in Contemporary Profit and Nonprofit Hospitals," *Academy of Management Journal,* vol. 26 (1983), pp. 311–320.
Webber, J., and M. Dula: "Effective Planning Committees in Hospitals," *Harvard Business Review* (May–June 1974), pp. 133–142.

[17] Universities Apply Strategic Management

Clark, B., and M. Trow: "The Organizational Context," in T. Newcomb and E. Wilson (eds.), *College Peer Groups* (Chicago: Aldine, 1966).
Doyle, P., and J. Lynch: "Long Range Planning for Universities," *Long Range Planning,* vol. 9 (December 1976), pp. 30–46.
Huff, A. S., and J. M. Ranney: "Assessing the Environment for an Educational Institution," *Long Range Planning,* vol. 14 (1981), pp. 107–115.
Thomas, R.: "Corporate Strategic Planning in a University," *Long Range Planning,* vol. 13 (1980), pp. 70–78.

[18] Religious Groups Use Strategic Management

Adair, J.: "Formulating Strategy for the Church of England," *Journal of Business Policy,* vol. 3 (1973), pp. 3–12.
Hussey, D.: "Corporate Planning for a Church," *Long Range Planning,* vol. 7 (April 1974), pp. 61–64.
Reimnetz, C.: "Testing a Planning and Control Model in Non Profit Organizations," *Academy of Management Journal* (March 1972).
Wasdell, D.: "Long Range Planning and the Church," *Long Range Planning,* vol. 13 (June 1980), pp. 99–108.

[19] Arts Organizations Apply Strategic Management

Margolis, S., and J. Traub: "Business Comes to the Arts," *The MBA* (March 1978), pp. 11–25.
Raymond, T., and S. Greyser: "The Business of Managing the Arts," *Harvard Business Review* (July–August 1978), pp. 123–132.

[20] Strategic Management in the Public Sector

Cartwright, J.: "Corporate Planning in Local Government," *Long Range Planning* (April 1975), pp. 46–50.
East, R. J.: "Comparison of Strategic Planning in Large Corporations and Government," *Long Range Planning,* vol. 5 (1972).
Howlett, M.: "Strategic Planning in State Government," *Managerial Planning* (November–December 1975), pp. 10–16; 24ff.
Muskin, S.: "Policy Analysis in State and Community," *Public Administration Review,* vol. 37 (May–June 1977), pp. 245–253.

[21] Strategic Management in Other Organizations

Keating, B. P., and M. O. Keating: "Goal Setting and Efficiency in Social Service Agencies,"
Long Range Planning, vol. 14 (1981), pp. 40–48.

Kennington, D.: "Long Range Planning for Public Libraries—A Delphi Study," *Long Range
Planning,* vol. 10 (April 1977), pp. 73–78.

McGrath, W.: *Development of a Long Range Strategic Plan for a University Library* (Ithaca,
N.Y.: Cornell University Libraries, 1976).

[22] Strategic Management in Other Countries

Bazzaz, S. J., and P. H. Grinyer: "Corporate Planning in the U.K.: The State of the Art in
the 70s," *Strategic Management Journal,* vol. 2 (April–June, 1981), pp. 155–168.

Gotcher, J. W.: "Strategic Planning in European Multinationals," *Long Range Planning* (October 1977), pp. 7–13.

Hayashi, K.: "Corporate Planning Practices in Japanese Multinationals," *Academy of Management Journal,* vol. 21 (1978), pp. 211–226.

"Progress in Planning: An International Review," Special Issue of *Long Range Planning,* vol.
15 (1982).

"The Stalled Soviet Economy: Bogged Down by Planning," *Business Week,* Oct. 19, 1981,
pp. 72–83.

STRATEGIC MANAGEMENT ELEMENTS

CHAPTER OUTLINE

STRATEGIC MANAGEMENT ELEMENTS

OBJECTIVES

* To understand the roles of the general manager
* To learn who the strategists of an enterprise are, how these groups relate to each other, and how the strategists affect the strategic management process
* To understand what mission and objectives are, how they are formed and change, and how they relate to the strategic management process

INTRODUCTION

Our discussion of strategic management begins with an analysis of the strategic management elements: the strategists who are involved in the process and the mission and objectives of the enterprise. We also apply some of the decision-making concepts discussed in Chapter 1 as they relate to the formation of objectives. Exhibit 2.1 presents the model of strategic management, highlighting the chapter's focus. We will elaborate on these elements and integrate them into their place in the strategic management process. We begin by defining the actors in the process of strategic management—those involved with strategic decisions and actions. Then we move to the starting point of the process—mission and objectives.

THE GENERAL MANAGER—MORE THAN JUST A STRATEGIST [1]

General managers are key players in the strategic management process. Before discussing the particular strategic roles they play, we find it useful to determine who the

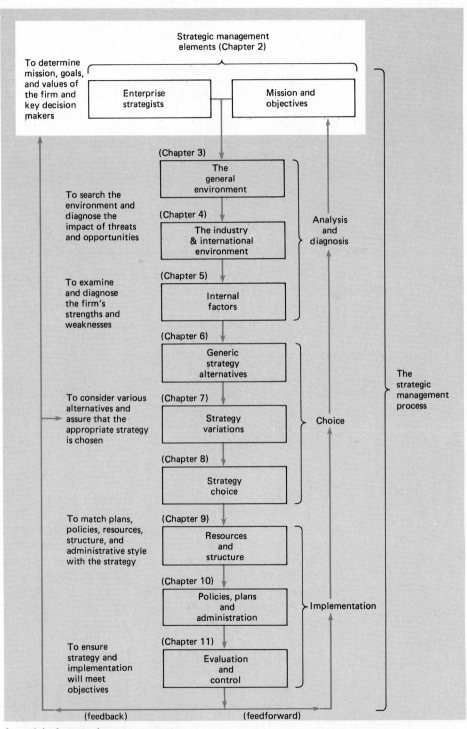

EXHIBIT 2.1   A model of strategic management.

general managers are and what they do in organizations, for they are more than just strategists.

The general managers of a firm are executives at the pinnacle of the enterprise or SBUs who are responsible for the survival and success of the corporation. They have titles such as chairman of the board, president, senior vice president, executive vice president, and vice president. If the business is divided into strategic business units or operating divisions, then the persons at the top of these units are also general managers.

But who are these people called general managers (GM), and what do they do? A 1976 study of general managers in the top 500 U.S. corporations revealed the following profile based on the most frequently found characteristics. The typical GM was a male who made over $200,000 a year. He was about 60 years old and probably graduated from college but did not take advanced work. He probably came from a working-class family and worked his way through the marketing part of the organization.

Yet such a profile tells us little. Other backgrounds and ways to the top may depend on economic conditions and strategies of the organization. For instance, in the late 1970s many corporations became more interested in profit margins than in building up their market share or entering new businesses; this led to an increase in the number of GMs promoted from the controllers' ranks.

While a 1982 study found little differences from those of the 1976 study, other conditions are changing the face of corporate elites. A record number of acquisitions, mergers, and proxy battles have squeezed out "redundant" managers. Foreign competition and slower-growing domestic markets have also forced out some managers. Accelerated technological change requires general managers with different skills. And deregulation has created major change for formerly protected companies. Hence, old-line traditional industrial leaders are being displaced by high-tech entrepreneurs (Steven Jobs, formerly of Apple, An Wang of Wang Laboratories), service gurus (Donald Burr of People Express, William McGowan of MCI), corporate rejuvenators (Lee Iacocca of Chrysler, John Welch of General Electric), and asset shufflers (T. Boone Pickens of Mesa Limited Partners). These individuals, and others like them, are having an impact on corporate direction, and are serving as new role models for other chief executives and general managers. They have often founded their own firms, are on the frontiers of deregulated industries, are saving smokestack industries by borrowing skills and values from entrepreneurs, or are shifting assets and consolidating the old economic base. With an economy in transition, new people such as these are emerging as general managers.

Still, the general manager needs a variety of skills and has many roles to play, just as they have always had. Top-level jobs are assumed to require more emphasis on conceptual skills with less need for human relations or administrative skills and low requirements for technical abilities. The jobs of lower-level managers are seen as emphasizing technical requirements without much need for conceptual ability. So the skill mix changes with the demands of the job. Top managers are urged to be generalists rather than specialists. While this approach has some value in helping us understand managers and their jobs, we still must ask, What does the GM do?

WHAT DO GMs DO?

The traditional impression is that the GM is a reflective thinker who maps out strategy, designs an organization to implement the plan, and guides troops through the necessary maneuvers to accomplish objectives using vast experience and insight. The GM is the entrepreneur (sets goals), strategist (plans), organization builder (organizes), leader (directs), and chief implementer (controls). The task is to lead the firm or SBU through uncharted territory in less-than-certain circumstances.

These tasks may not be so neatly compartmentalized as you might suspect. Human, technical, economic, and political circumstances are only partly subject to rational analysis. The general manager must integrate pieces of a puzzle, some of which may be missing, distorted, or not even yet made, and most of which are continuously changing. According to the Harvard Business School, general-management leadership "requires judgment, courage, empathy, the ability to articulate and persuade."

Exhibit 2.2 contrasts what general managers actually do with what theorists say they should do. The studies indicate that the general manager must simultaneously handle several different activities on a schedule which provides little time for contemplation. In the process, intuition and judgment become the preferred decision-making models. Mintzberg's list of roles provides an example of the different types of activities a GM may be asked to perform. Let's use his categories of interpersonal, informational, and decisional roles to guide the discussion.

Interpersonal Roles   As the symbolic *figurehead* of the organization, the GM performs numerous routine ceremonial duties of a legal or social nature. This is often important in legitimizing the firm to outsiders. As a *leader,* the GM has responsibility for staffing the organization and training and motivating subordinates. In the *liaison*

EXHIBIT 2.2   A CONTRAST OF THEORY AND RESEARCH ON THE GENERAL MANAGER (GM)

Areas	The research says that general managers	The theorists say that general managers should
1 Time allocations	Avoid spending great amounts of time on one issue	Spend concentrated time to get results
2 Time horizons	Seek activities that are current, preferring "hot" information	Formulate effective strategies that require consideration of major current and future trends
3 Information sources	Prefer verbal sources and avoid documented information	Formulate effective strategies that require thorough environmental and organizational analysis
4 Planning processes	Discuss strategy in meetings, but such work is fragmented and lacks focus	Formulate effective strategies that require commitment, focus, and concentrated effort
5 Basic purposes	Have work that is fragmented with no concentration of effort or pattern of activities	Have as a basic purpose that of establishing organizational goals and developing the strategies needed to achieve them

Source: Adapted from C. W. Hofer, and C. N. Toftoy, "How CEOs Set Strategic Direction for Their Organizations," paper presented at the Academy of Management Meeting, 1984.

role the manager maintains a network of outside contacts to obtain favors and information. Note that the GM can accomplish liaison tasks while engaged in activities related to the figurehead role.

Informational Roles In the role of *monitor,* managers read periodicals and reports, make plant tours, or observe meetings to seek information about the organization and its environment. As a *disseminator,* the GM transmits much of the information received to outsiders and insiders. Information about the organization is also transmitted to outsiders through the mail, phone calls, or board meetings as the manager acts as a *spokesperson* for the organization. Once again, note how the liaison, leader, or figurehead role can do double duty for the collection and distribution of information.

Decision Roles As an *entrepreneur,* the GM performs strategic functions of initiating projects to take advantage of opportunities. Strategy and review meetings are conducted to do this and to correct problems or solve crises when the role shifts to that of *disturbance handler.* As *resource allocators,* managers authorize budgets and approve requests for the allocation of human, monetary, and material resources. Finally, the top manager is responsible for representing the organization as a *negotiator* for contracts with labor unions, major suppliers, or major customers.

In effect, the GM must spend substantial amounts of time in being the organizational leader and personal leader and in communicating with stakeholders outside and inside the organization. This would seem to leave little room for involvement with strategic planning or for service as the "architect of organization purpose." Yet this role seems to encompass all the others.

The formulation of strategy, goals, and plans for implementation is often considered the exclusive realm of the general manager. Yet many different individuals may be involved in the strategic management process. *Boards of directors,* who review the results of the strategies and *chief executive officers,* are the main corporate-level strategists. *Corporate planning staffs* help top managers in planning and implementing the strategies, and *consultants* may be hired to help corporate planners or do the corporate planning work if there is no corporate planning staff. *General managers* of strategic business units and *lower-level participants* are also involved with goal setting and strategy formation and implementation. So our next sections focus on the strategic management role of these participants in the process.

CORPORATE-LEVEL STRATEGISTS

The board of directors and chief executive officers (CEOs) are the primary groups involved with corporate-level strategy making. In the special case of start-ups or family-owned businesses, the entrepreneur is both the general manager and chief strategist. This section describes the role of these groups in the strategic management process.

The Board of Directors and Strategic Management [2]

The ultimate legal authority in businesses is that of the board of directors. In other institutions, equivalent boards (e.g., trustees) have similar authority. Boards are held responsible to the stockholders for the following duties: ensuring the continuity of management (replacing or retiring ineffective managers); protecting the use of stock-holders' resources; ensuring that managers take prudent action regarding corporate objectives; approving major financial and operational decisions of the managers; representing the company with other organizations and bodies in society; maintaining, revising, and enforcing the corporate charter and bylaws.

The board is legally mandated to control the organization and be centrally concerned with maintaining operations and effectiveness. It is often seen as the representative of the owners, so knowledge of the organization's operations, business acumen, and industry perspective are key prerequisites for membership.

Until the 1960s, many boards consisted mainly or exclusively of top-level managers. Obviously, these "inside" boards would simply ratify their own decisions. But more boards have accepted "outside" members, and some boards have a majority of outsiders. Some boards are even taking on leaders of labor unions with which they deal.

Are outside boards any different from inside boards? Maybe. Some outsiders are selected simply because they are friends of top managers or because they represent a minority group. If one assumes that executives don't wish to provide information detrimental to their own policies or proposals, a passive outsider may act much the same as an insider. According to one official of the Securities and Exchange Commission (SEC), "We saw directors treated like mushrooms—something you keep in the dark and heap manure on."

In the past, most boards were not actively involved in the strategic management of firms except in times of crisis, when their major act was to replace the chief executive. Now, outside boards are becoming more active for several reasons. First, shareholder suits have increasingly charged directors with failure to fulfill their responsibilities. (The Penn Central bankruptcy is credited with precipitating these actions.) Second, the New York Stock Exchange has required its members to form audit committees composed of *outside directors,* and most of the largest U.S. corporations now have these committees. Third, the SEC has increased investigations of the negligence and misconduct of directors. Fourth, the 1977 Foreign Corrupt Practices Act requires directors to be alert to political payoffs by corporations.

Membership on boards is increasingly being used as a means to more closely link the corporation to other organizations. For instance, to obtain a large loan the company may "elect" a banker to the board. Even competitors may be on the board, although this is prohibited by the Clayton Act of 1914. And those representing powerful political interests may be seated on the board.

The increase in outsiders has paralleled changes in the structure of many boards. Many boards have created nominating committees for recruiting and selecting new *outside* directors. There has been an increase in audit committees even though management still controls the source of the data. Outside directors are being paid more, and nonbusiness groups are more active in demanding representation. Overall, there has been a subtle but important shift in board membership and management control. Activists are replacing mushrooms.

Nonetheless, the percentage of outside directors on boards of the largest 1000 industrial companies dropped in 1986 to 57 percent from 63 percent in 1985. The cost or unavailability of liability insurance and the increasing time burdens due to a wave of takeovers and divestitures have made the director's job less appealing to many.

Can the Board Actively Pursue Strategy Formulation? [3]

With more active outsiders, more boards are involved with linking strategy with subsequent corporate action. They are beginning to support new strategies, attract resources, and protect the organization from outside threats. For instance, the outside directors at Mead Corporation helped management fight off a takeover attempt. As the board is used to link the company with powerful outsiders, even more outsiders may be selected.

Boards are likely to become more active in evaluating corporate strategy and performance. With more active outside members with managerial experience, boards may become more than rubber stamps in evaluating major strategic changes. And they are likely to evaluate corporate performance on both financial and nonfinancial grounds. The board rarely runs the company. Yet the power of the board in strategic formulation is often apparent when "strategic decision points" are reached. That is, the board is important with respect to issues of mission and identity (e.g., approving mergers) or the selection of a new chief executive officer. Indeed, the greatest power most boards (and stockholders) have to influence strategy rests in their ability to remove a CEO and appoint a new one.

To the extent that outside directors continue their recent decline in number and directors act with an eye toward preventing personal liability, active questioning and scrutiny of executives' strategic recommendations may suffer. And efforts to make boards effective guardians of shareholder interests may fail.

Effective strategists discuss their strategies with the board to find out how the board feels about their stewardship. But the primary active role in strategic management remains with the top manager of the firm, and many top managers are members of the board.

The CEO as Strategist [4]

Crucial to the success of strategic management is the role of the corporate-level general manager: the chief executive officer (CEO). The CEO is responsible for defining what business the firm is in and matching the best product-market opportunities with the best use of the enterprise's resources. This person must conceptualize the strategy and then initiate and maintain the strategic management process.

It has been argued that the large number of work interruptions and variety of demands from the roles of the general manager described earlier do not allow the CEO time for reflective thinking or planning on the job. Managers have a great deal to do. Planning is only one of several activities competing for a manager's attention. Planning often involves thinking, paperwork, and time alone. Most managers do not like or have precious little time for these activities. Managers tend to prefer to be doers, not thinkers. Further, managers prefer to act on immediate problems because they generate immediate feedback. If a customer makes a rush order and the manager helps out, the customer's thanks are given *now*. Planning deals with future events, and the rewards (if any) are deferred into the future. Most of us prefer to take our rewards now rather than later. Moreover, the number of roles expected of the manager as supergeneralist may become so difficult that it is beyond the capability of any one person. The formal experience and training of today's CEOs may not have prepared them to cope with their environment. Thus some go so far as to suggest that CEOs spend more time *managing the process* of strategic planning than they do making strategic decisions. Yet we believe that the roles played by the CEO set the tone for strategic formation.

Even though different styles will exist among organizations and CEOs, when managers devote time to specific kinds of activities, the roles overlap. In a negotiating session information may be collected and disseminated to insiders or outsiders, and decisions may be made concerning resource allocation which in effect result in strategic decisions. Thus while Mintzberg found that only 13 percent of the manager's time was devoted to strategy per se, strategic planning is intertwined with other functions. Further, he found that the CEO alone was making major key decisions about programs to solve particular problems or exploit particular opportunities. Thus the CEO is a pivotal figure in strategic formation. Moreover, managerial values (discussed later in this chapter) influence how the CEO may perform these roles (see Exhibit 2.8). Some fear that managers' values have shifted from entrepreneurial risk taking to a greater concern for the short-term bottom line. This may lead to a lack of innovation and new-product development. But the changes noted earlier may be a response to these conditions. Hence, CEO roles and values play a significant part in strategic management.

As various roles are performed, more or less emphasis on particular roles and values will influence the type of planning in the organization. In very large organizations, the emphasis may rest with resource allocation and internal negotiation to ratify decisions made at divisional levels. More time will be devoted by the CEO to figurehead or liaison functions with external groups and boards of directors. In smaller firms the entrepreneur role is likely to be of more critical importance. Let's look a little more closely at this special case.

Entrepreneurs as Strategists [5]

Entrepreneurs are individuals who start a business from scratch. Several hundred entrepreneurs do that each hour in the United States, and the pace seems to be accelerating. Financial incentives and the lure of an opportunity to make a new-product contribution seem to motivate more individuals to strike out on their own. About 95 percent of U.S. businesses are entrepreneurships or family businesses. Family businesses are of two types. *The family-operated firm* is a business whose major ownership influence is a family, and *all* or most of the key executives are family members. *A family-influenced firm* is a business whose major ownership influence is a family, and some of the key executives are family members.

The entrepreneur is the main (and in most cases the only) strategist in the entrepreneurial firm. The strategic management of a family business falls between that of entrepreneurial firms and that of corporate firms. The chief strategist of the family firm must consider the preferences of the family members who are active in the management of the firm and/or lead family members of the ownership group. These family members are part of the coalition which runs a family firm. In this way, the strategists of the family firm are somewhat like the corporate strategists. In some family firms, the chief strategist has the full support of the family, which does not interefere except in a crisis. In such cases, the family business strategist can operate much like an entrepreneur in developing a strategy.

It has been found that there are a few differences between owner-managed and publicly held companies with regard to objectives, strategies, and strategic decision factors. One significant objective that you can find in a family or entrepreneur's business is the desire to remain independent and provide an outlet for family investment and careers for the family. When the chief strategist leaves this position, a difficult transfer-of-power situation arises. Owner-managers also seem to stress sales

EXHIBIT 2.3 A FEW FAMILY BUSINESSES AS OF 1985

• Lester Crown is taking over for his ailing 89-year-old father Henry. The family has controlling interest in General Dynamics, own big blocks of stock in (and hold sway over) another half-dozen public corporations, and operate a vast portfolio of real estate holdings. Net worth is estimated at around $1.5 billion.

• Samuel C. Johnson is the chairman and chief executive of S. C. Johnson & Son, the $2 billion consumer products giant his great-grandfather founded in 1886.

• Forest Mars, Sr., still controls the candy company which makes Snickers, M&Ms, 3 Musketeers, Milky Way, and other candies.

• Sanford "Sandy" McDonnell is the CEO of McDonnell Douglas in St. Louis. James "Mr. Mac" McDonnell (Sandy's uncle) is chairman of the board.

• M. G. "Jerry" O'Neill was chairman of General Tire & Rubber Co. until an outsider was brought in. His family has run the company since 1915.

• Frederick Stratton, Jr., is the chief operating officer of Briggs & Stratton Corp., producer of lawn-mower engines and other products.

• Sam M. Walton built over 817 Wal-Mart Stores, Inc., from a single five-and dime in Newport, Arkansas. The family's 39 percent stake in Wal-Mart shares is worth about $4.2 billion.

A few other family-influenced firms you may have heard of include:

• Du Pont family: 17.5 percent of E. I. Du Pont worth $3.3 billion

• John Dorrance and family: 57.5 percent of Campbell Soup worth $2.1 billion

• David Packard: 17.2 percent of Hewlett-Packard worth $1.9 billion

• Bancroft family: 54.7 percent of Dow Jones & Co., Inc., worth $1.9 billion

• Bronfman family: 38.5 percent of Seagram Company worth $1.9 billion

• Ford family: 7.7 percent of Ford Motor Company worth $1.1 billion

• August Busch: 13 percent of Anheuser-Busch worth $85.7 million

• Joan Kroc: 8.6 percent of McDonalds worth $710 million

Source: Adapted from "The Crown Family Empire," *Business Week,* March 31, 1986, pp. 50–54; "Sam Walton of Wal-Mart," *Business Week,* Oct. 14, 1985, pp. 142–147; "Trying to Bring Out the Old Shine at Johnson Wax," *Business Week,* Aug. 13, 1984; "General Tire," *Business Week,* Feb. 13, 1984, pp. 76–80; "Where Management Style Sets Strategy," *Business Week,* Oct. 23, 1978; "Briggs and Stratton 39 Year Old Chief Begins to Alter Stodgy Image of Firm," *Wall Street Journal,* Oct. 10, 1978; "Mars," *Business Week,* Aug. 14, 1978; "Super Rich Owners of American Business," *U.S. News and World Report,* July 21, 1986, pp. 36–44.

growth, have greater use of labor than capital, and adopt a policy of charging lower prices than publicly held firms.

There are thousands of examples of entrepreneurial and family strategies and strategists. Two of the more publicized entrepreneurs you might be familiar with are Ted Turner (sports teams and cable broadcasting) and John DeLorean (bankrupt auto manufacturer). Exhibit 2.3 furnishes examples of a few more who are less notable, perhaps. And the number of these types of business leaders appears to be increasing. The business world has rediscovered some satisfaction in creating and building a company. The more humanistic values usually involved in a family business have regained their appeal along with concerns of becoming just another number in the large corporate organization. Plus, more top posts at family businesses are opening up as founders approach retirement age and their baby-boom children are ready to take over.

The control of a family business firm often evolves from the control of the previous family business executive. And the strategic management process often does involve members of the family other than the current chief strategist. While most entrepreneurs are men, increasing numbers of women are starting their own businesses. And while they are not yet a large force, more women are also emerging as venture capitalists (those who are willing to risk investing in chancy enterprises).

When an entrepreneur's organization has been successful and evolves into a large firm, the individual is often faced with a problem. The motivations and skills of starting a firm and building it are often no longer appropriate to the demands of operating the larger firm. Its challenges may call for competent managers who can see beyond the brilliance of the founder's original vision. The entrepreneurs often find that these challenges are not what interest them. At that point (which is difficult to pinpoint) it is time for new strategists to take over.

Strategists and Failure [6]

So far we have examined strategists and entrepreneurs in corporate or family firms which seem to be successful. But not all strategists are successful. What kinds of problems might cause failure?

Several analyses have found how the corporate-level strategist fails by pursuing the following defective strategies:

• *The firm fails when power-hoarding strategists create overambitious, incautious strategies which ignore environmental signals.* These strategists have not developed adequate strategic management systems.

• *The firm fails when power-hoarding strategists refuse to change the past strategy.* This again is true because these strategists do not accept advice from subordinates and don't search the environment themselves.

• *The firm fails when the chief strategists do not create a strategy.* These strategists expect the firm to run itself without a strategy.

• *The firm fails because the strategists create an overambitious strategy given the weakened resource base of the firm.* In this case, the strategists have not adequately analyzed their strategic advantages and disadvantages.

Other analyses found similar problems and suggested that managers were preoccupied with current structural problems or improving personnel skills needed in the future. When this occurs, we usually find that management succession results, or the family business is sold. A later Exhibit (2.9) provides an example of executive succession after the founder of Control Data Corp. experienced difficulties. However, many executives are reluctant to let go. The thrill of having power and the feeling that no one else can do the job quite as well keep some strong-willed corporate leaders (Harry Gray of United Technologies, David Lewis of General Dynamics, Armand Hammer of Occidental Petroleum) at the helm well into their seventies or eighties in a few cases.

BUSINESS-LEVEL STRATEGISTS

We have now discussed how the top manager, sometimes in conjunction with board members, plays the major role in setting corporate-level strategy. Four other groups of individuals are potentially involved in crucial roles in strategic management. These include SBU managers, corporate planners, consultants, and lower-level managers. Let's examine their roles in strategic management.

SBU Executives as Strategists

If a firm is organized into SBUs, the head of the SBU plays the general-manager role at the business level. If corporate strategists encourage it, SBU managers set the strategies for their units or businesses. Essentially, the SBU strategists perform roles similar to those of top managers for their businesses and attempt to get the best results in their business segment given their resources and the corporate objectives. In first-generation planning, they create multiple strategies on a contingency basis.

Earlier we indicated that entrepreneurs are involved with starting their own businesses. But the corporate world has recognized some value in establishing an entrepreneurial climate within some of their SBUs. The word often heard to describe this is "intrapreneurship." In essence, the SBU manager is encouraged to develop new ventures, or the SBU itself may be a new venture established within the existing corporation. For example, the MacIntosh computer was developed by a separate newly created unit within the Apple organization. Apple did not want to stifle the creativity or enthusiasm of this new-product development by housing it within the mainstream. However, creation of internal ventures are ultimately expected to be consolidated into the ongoing organization. As ventures grow and require new levels of investment, corporate involvement increases. Corporate procedures and objectives may conflict with the independent start-up environment of new ventures—more structure and control is introduced. Hence, the SBU manager under these circumstances plays the role of entrepreneur and strategist. As with independent entrepreneurs, SBU managers may have to be replaced when the entrepreneurial functions are completed as the venture becomes more important to corporate level.

Planners and Strategic Management [7]

Some firms, mostly large and complex ones, have provided their chief executives and SBU managers with planning staffs. These planners are staff specialists who are trained in strategic management techniques and who provide staff-support services and recommendations on strategic management decisions. A planning staff can participate in many aspects of the strategic management process, such as identifying new business opportunity, maintaining environmental scanning, reviewing strategic performance, providing analyses of strategy alternatives, and so on.

There is some debate about whether a planning staff should *do* planning or *facilitate* planning done by the line. There is an argument that specialists can take time to closely examine proposals and projects without having the burdens of running existing operations.

Critics of this approach point out the usual problems of acceptance by line managers of staff activities and recommendations. Using a staff to do planning increases the probability that planning will be done but decreases the probability that the plans developed will be used. One writer characterizes this as a "paralysis of analysis." Planners may be seen as having their heads stuck in the clouds, while from the staff point of view the line managers have their feet stuck in the mud. This can lead to the isolation of a separate planning staff. Indeed this appears to have occurred in the late 1970s when strategic planners were allowed to become dominant figures in their companies. As their power grew and the influence of operating managers declined, hostility escalated. The result: few of the strategies were implemented.

This problem occurred at Standard Brands (see Exhibit 1.9). Just as some suggest that the CEO should manage the process of planning, others urge that the planning staff should contribute not by doing but by "selling" a planning "culture" to the line. Thus the task of the planning staff would be to develop a plan for implementing planning throughout the organization. These authors also argue that a planning staff can play an evaluative role and a consulting role.

Practitioners in the 1980s appear to be doing just that. Some of the leading proponents of strategic management have cut the size of their planning staffs at corporate, group, and divisional levels. General managers, having participated in the process of putting together strategic plans are now more aware of the usefulness of strategic planning. The new generation of CEOs believe that they and their key general managers should be the strategic thinkers.

Thus in practice the role of a planning staff varies with the organization and the power of other participants in strategic planning. The staff members may not play a significant role unless they are represented in the power structure and can influence decisions regarding the implementation of plans. *But most of the evidence indicates that a planning staff rarely, if ever, seriously participates in the strategic choice process.* This is the crucial job of the general manager, and the staff serves as the executive's research and follow-through team.

Throughout the book, the roles which can be performed by corporate planners will be discussed. This is especially true with respect to the chapters on analysis and diagnosis (Chapters 3 and 5), alternative choice preparation (Chapter 6), and implementation (Chapters 9 and 10) and evaluation (Chapter 11). Chapter 9 will describe in more detail the operations of corporate planning staffs.

Strategic Management Consultants [8]

Another influence on the strategist can be a consultant in strategic management. Many consultants offer advice in the area of strategic management. Much of this advice comes in the form of designing and helping to implement a formal strategic management system for an enterprise. Others conduct studies as part of the strategic management process. In this respect, they are serving the role of corporate planning departments when no department exists or when management prefers an outsider's view. Some of these consultants become chief strategists of firms after their interaction with them. Further, some CEOs have also developed advisory boards to give advice on technical matters or to evaluate special projects or trends affecting the business.

Like corporate planning departments and their executives, the consultant serves primarily as an adviser to the chief strategist and performs such strategic management duties as the strategist requests. In the case of small businesses, firms using consultants in this fashion perform better.

Lower-Level Participants [9]

Suffice it to say that when you find yourself in middle-management positions, you will not be intimately involved with strategic choice. But you may be providing data or ideas which can affect future choices at higher levels. And lower levels implement strategy (or prevent its implementation). To the extent that you understand who has power and what their roles and values are, you are in a better position to offer ideas and suggestions which have a higher probability of acceptance and recognition. And you can implement plans and policies consistent with strategic intent. This is one way to increase the visibility and power of your own subunit. Thus we encourage you to consider the roles and values of strategists carefully.

Next we turn to the starting point of the strategic process which these actors influence—mission and objectives.

MISSION AND OBJECTIVES

The two most basic questions faced by corporate-level strategists are, (1) What business are we in? and (2) Why are we in business?

An answer to the first question requires a consideration of the mission definition, or the scope of the business activities the firm pursues. The second question involves establishing objectives to be accomplished. Both questions help define the nature of the business and provide a framework for analysis, choice, implementation, and evaluation processes.

The Mission and Business Definition [10]

For long-term survival (often viewed as the ultimate objective), most organizations must legitimize themselves. This is normally done by performing some function which is valued by society. Of course, some functions are valued more highly than others, and priorities can change over time. In the United States, professional sports teams are valued for their entertainment function, and they have become big business.

Organizations which make a net contribution to society are likely to be called "legitimate." These organizations are likely to be allowed to survive over the long term. Challenges to legitimacy are not frequent, but once made they can damage survival potential or limit the scope of action and increase the cost of doing business. For example, over a dozen of the largest U.S. defense contractors were under investigation in 1985 for cost and labor mischarges, bribery and kickbacks, defective pricing, and so on (e.g., the infamous $400 toilet seats). Congress acted to stop payments on some contracts and made it harder to acquire the more lucrative contracts because the legitimacy of the action of these firms was called into question.

Many organizations define the basic reason for their existence in terms of a mission statement. Such a definition can provide the basic philosophy of what the firm is all about. It usually emanates from the entrepreneur who founded the firm or from major strategists in the firm's development over time. The mission can be seen as a link between performing some social function and more specific targets or objectives of the organization. Thus the mission can be used to legitimize the organization.

When the mission of a business is carefully defined, it provides a statement to insiders and outsiders of what the company stands for—its purpose, image, and character. Exhibit 2.4 indicates how Hallmark defines its mission. When Hallmark considers strategic proposals, it can refer back to its definition with a basic question: Does the proposal fit our mission?

Mission definitions can be so broad as to be meaningless, or they can merely be public pronouncements of ideals which few could ever reach. As you will see later,

EXHIBIT 2.4   THE MISSION OF HALLMARK

"When you care enough to send the very best" is one of America's most recognized corporate slogans. What does it stand for? What business is Hallmark in? What is its mission?

Hallmark's strategy has been one of diversification far beyond cards. Its customers are also buying books, candles, party supplies, pewter and crystal items, bath products, fine pens and pencils, and jewelry. How do these all fit? What's the grand vision?

Several key elements are involved. The company has creative talents, processing talents, and marketing skills all focused around an image of quality. And it has to provide its 6000 independent dealers with a number of relatively high priced items to create volume and revenue beyond that created solely by cards. Thus items in its product mix are design-oriented and sold primarily to women. Hallmark's self-defined mission: bring quality to social expression.

When it acquired a costume jewelry manufacturer, industry sources saw it as "a shrewd move . . . to expand . . . the lines sold through its traditional outlets. Women don't know if jewelry is good quality or bad. If you can't trust Hallmark, who can you trust?" With jewelry and related items dealers can round out their inventories with numerous products in Hallmark's mix. The acquisition fit neatly into Hallmark's creative, quality, design-oriented, social-expression philosophy.

Hallmark has consciously and carefully created a clearly defined mission and strategies to implement it. Its mission is an ideological position statement of its image and character and what the company stands for and is trying to achieve. It provides a basis upon which to determine the scope of products, markets, and technologies in its domain.

Sources: Adapted from "Hallmark Now Stands for a Lot More than Cards," *Business Week,* May 29, 1978, pp. 57–58; "Hallmark Tries Out the Jewelry Trade," *Business Week,* Nov. 3, 1975, p. 29.

the specificity and breadth of goal or mission statements are important considerations for strategists. But a good mission statement focuses around customer needs and utilities. For example, AT&T is in communications, not telephones; Tenneco is in energy, not just oil and gas; MGM provides entertainment, not just movies. The customer needs for communication, energy, or entertainment are not product-specific—nor are mission statements. Avon defines itself as being in the beauty business. The mission of most public universities is to provide teaching, research, and public service—but many also provide entertainment (sports teams).

The mission must be clear enough so that it leads to action. Organizations must at some point establish specific targets to shoot for which will be used as guides for evaluating progress. NASA's mission in the 1960s was to begin space exploration and land a man on the moon. Without establishing specific goals to get to along the way, we might be still waiting for that first "small step." So firms also must express their mission and philosophy by establishing statements about the grand design, quality orientation, atmosphere of the enterprise, and the firm's role in society.

After Roger Smith took over as chairman of General Motors, he moved quickly to solve some problems at GM and altered its strategy. As part of the process, he distributed "culture cards" to be carried in the pockets of executives to remind them of their new mission. The card reads

> The fundamental purpose of General Motors is to provide products and services of such quality that our customers will receive superior value, our employees and business partners will share in our success, and our stockholders will receive a sustained, superior return on their investment.

Other firms consciously (or subconsciously) develop "core principles," or norms, which guide decision making or behavior. These principles serve as mechanisms for self-control to guide managers at all levels of the organization. Hence, if quick decisions are needed at lower levels of an organization, such core principles serve as guides to making decisions or taking action consistent with the overriding mission and strategy of the business. These are different from policies in that they are frequently part of the culture, or ways of doing things, that emerge in the informal organization.

In practical, everyday decision making, most organizations are not immediately concerned with questions of continued existence. Survival for most is relatively assured within the time frame of thinking of those in charge. And the mission tends to become an ideological position statement which is only occasionally referred to in support of legitimization. So what tends to occupy the minds of the molders of organization purpose are various objectives to improve performance. However, prescriptively, a mission statement and core principles ought to serve as guidelines for strategic decisions rather than as a set of platitudes. Otherwise, short-term thinking can get in the way of the long-term best interests of the organization in society.

Business Definition

Part of the mission statement is the definition of the business itself. By this we mean a description of the products, activities, or functions and markets that the firm presently pursues. Products (or services) are the outputs of value created by the system to be sold to customers. Markets can refer to classes or types of customers or geographic regions where the product and/or service is sold. When we refer to functions, we mean the technologies or processes used to create and add value. For example, in agriculture one might plant and grow seeds, harvest crops, mill grain, process the grain into various food products, and distribute or retail the finished product. Each stage adds value and represents a separate function. Some firms do all the functions while others do a limited number or only one. Consider a full-service airline versus a no-frills carrier. One operates full-service ticket counters in airports and downtown locations; the other may ticket on the plane, offer no interline ticketing, offer few fare options, and so on. The no-frills airline may use first-come–first-serve seating versus ticketing at gates. On board, the no-frills carrier may not serve food or drink or charge extra for the service. The full-line carrier may provide free baggage checking while the no-frill firm charges or provides no interline baggage connection. Each of these options represents a service or function configuration. Functions of ticketing, gate operations, on-board service, and baggage handling can provide options for adding value to services provided.

A good business definition will include a statement of products, markets, and functions. For example, a business definition for Apple might state the following: *We design, develop, produce, market, and service microprocessor-based personal computers in United States and foreign countries*. In contrast, Tandy might be defined as *a U.S. manufacturer and retailer of consumer electronic equipment*. Note that Tandy performs fewer functions than Apple and is a bit more restricted geographically, but it has a wider product definition. *Westinghouse manufactures, sells, and services equipment and components which generate, transmit, distribute, utilize, and control electricity*. Note that this definition includes a very broad line: it specifies a focus around which the products are related but ignores market issues (except for the notion that its markets involve electricity). In its 1985 Annual Report, Schulumberger asks, What are our businesses? The answer:

> First, we are an oilfield services company, bringing technology to the oil industry anywhere, anytime. [We are] also an electronics company. We are ready to expand in the international markets through leadership in electricity, . . . electronic payments, . . . instruments, bringing technology to the utilities, to the aerospace industry, to the banking community . . .

A good statement of the business definition of the firm should meet certain criteria: it should be as precise as possible and indicate major components of strategy (products, markets, and functions). Some go a bit further than this by also indicating how the mission is to be accomplished. Note that Hewlett-Packard (Exhibit 2.5) meets the criteria of defining the mission and business definition and takes the next step of indicating the kind of management desired and policies necessary to attain the mission. Each of these aspects is described in more detail throughout the book.

Defining the mission and business definition is the starting point of strategy analysis. It answers the question, What business are we in? When performing the initial gap analysis described in Chapter 1, we find that such a statement indicates where the firm's current strategy has been going up to this point in time, and what results

EXHIBIT 2.5   THE MISSION AND BUSINESS DEFINITION OF HEWLETT-PACKARD

Hewlett-Packard's business is concentrated on developing high-quality products which make unique technological contributions and are so innovative that customers are willing to pay premium prices. Products are limited to the areas of electronic testing and measurement and to technologically related fields. Customer service, both before and after the sale, is given primary emphasis. The financial policy is to use internally generated funds to finance growth and avoid long-term debt and to resort to short-term debt only when sales growth exceeds the return on net worth. H-P seeks to attract high-caliber and creative employees with the opportunity to share in the success of the company through high wages, profit sharing, and stock-purchase plans. Job security is increased by keeping fluctuations in production schedules to a minimum by avoiding consumer-type products and by not making any products exclusively for the government. The managerial policy is to practice "management by objective" rather than management by directive; corporate objectives provide unity of purpose, and H-P gives employees the freedom to work toward these goals in ways that they determine are best for their own area of responsibility. The company exercises its social responsibility by building plants and offices that are attractive and in harmony with the community, by helping to solve community problems, and by contributing both money and time to community projects.

Source: Adapted from D. Crites and R. Atherton, "Hewlett-Packard (A)," in W. F. Glueck, *Business Policy and Strategic Management* (New York: McGraw-Hill, 1980), pp. 384–385.

might be expected if it continues. From there, once objectives have been specified and other analyses have been performed, determinations can be made about whether such a definition can continue successfully, or must be altered to close gaps. In other words, the strategic management process starts with the current business definition but proceeds with other questions: What business should we be in? Who are our customers? How do we serve them? That is, some conditions might call for a strategic change in products, markets, or functions, or changes in the way in which that business definition is going to be accomplished (competitive strategy and policies). For example, long after cars, interstate highways, and airplanes sent many railroad companies into bankruptcy court, some railroad companies are reemerging with new corporate identities. The Reading Company, a major regional railroad established in 1833, now owns only 16 miles of track. Like many former railroad firms, Reading is now a major real estate operator (even though the Monopoly game board earns it immortality as a railroad).

A problem many firms find themselves with is that through acquiring a series of businesses unrelated to their mission or business definition, they become conglomerates, with little to tie them together other than financial objectives. Many firms have found a need to return to basic business definitions because they cannot effectively manage the diversity. It took General Mills longer than most, but after 17 years of trying they finally sold off their toy division and nonfood lines to "get back to the kitchen," which they knew best about.

Changing the business definition is one of the basic strategy alternatives to be described in Chapter 6. But before strategy determination is made, the other major aspect of strategic gap analysis is a determination of whether desired objectives will be attained. Analysts must determine if continuation with the mission and adherence to the business definition will lead to expected outcomes close to those desired. Our next section, then, begins the examination of objectives themselves to answer the question, Why are we in business?

What Objectives Are Pursued? [11]

Objectives are the ends which the organization seeks to achieve through its existence and operations.[1] A variety of different objectives are pursued by business organizations. Some examples include continuity of profits; efficiency (for example, lowest costs); employee satisfaction and development; quality products or services for customers or clients; good corporate citizenship and social responsibility; market leadership (for example, to be first to market with innovations); maximization of dividends or share prices for stockholders; control over assets; adaptability and flexibility; service to society.

It is important that several points be made about objectives so that you understand their nature fully. These are as follows:

• The list just given contains 10 objectives, which is not to suggest that most organizations pursue 10 objectives or these exact 10. But research clearly demonstrates that firms have many objectives. *All but the simplest organizations pursue multiple objectives*.

• Many organizations pursue some objectives in the short run and others in the long run. For example, with respect to the list of 10 objectives, many firms would view efficiency and employee satisfaction as short-run objectives. They would probably view profit continuity, service to society, and good corporate citizenship as long-run objectives. Some other objectives such as adaptability or asset control may be medium-range objectives. *In sum, the objectives pursued are given a time weighting by strategists*.

One of the major dilemmas of corporate-level strategists is the short-term–long-term trade-off decision. With the logic of net present value and the importance of return on investment, combined with pressures from Wall Street and corporate raiders for good quick profits and cash flows, modern managers have been pressured toward short-term thinking. This kind of thinking also filters down to the business level, where a desire for quick returns may influence SBU managers. There appears to be less patience to invest in the future in the United States than there is in other countries (such as Japan). This lack of patience can have a severe impact on strategic decision making; and the timing of goal accomplishment needs careful analysis in this regard.

• Since there are multiple objectives in the short run at any one time, normally some of the objectives are weighted more highly than others. The strategists are responsible for establishing the priorities of the objectives. Priorities are crucial when resources and time are limited. At such times, trade-offs between profitability and

---

[1]We use the terms ''objective'' and ''goal'' synonomously.

market share, etc., must be known so that the major objective of the particular time is achieved. Thus *strategists should establish priorities for each objective among all the objectives at corporate and SBU levels.*

• There are many ways to measure and define the achievement of each objective. For example, some objectives can be measured through the use of an efficiency criterion; others may be measured in terms of effectiveness. Efficiency is the ratio of inputs to outputs. Effectiveness refers to the degree of achievement of a goal in relation to some ideal. At times, trade-offs between efficiency and effectiveness are required. For example, installing pollution-control equipment may be effective in achieving clean-air goals, but these goals may be achieved at the expense of a goal of efficient plant operation. At other times, trade-offs of efficiency goals within units of an organization are required. This is a basic factor in *suboptimization.* As each subsystem seeks efficiency, the entire system may lose effectiveness. For example, a credit manager is charged with establishing a policy to minimize credit losses; a sales manager is asked to maximize sales. If they both maximize in their own way, conflict is likely. Sales to some classes of customers will increase credit risk. Trade-offs in the goals of each unit may be called for. Here, goal priorities of the whole organization need to take precedence. In each part of the organization such goal conflicts are likely and require resolution. The guidance should come from mission definitions. *The implementation phase of strategic management involves clarifying the measurement of achievement of objectives.*

• There is a difference between official objectives and operative objectives. Operative objectives are ends *actually* sought by the organization. They can be determined by analyzing the behavior of the executives in allocating resources. Official objectives are ends which firms *say they seek* on official occasions such as public statements to general audiences. The objectives that *count* are those the strategists put their money and time behind. For instance, executives' official goals may focus on providing employees with a quality work environment; whether operative goals are the same depends on how much money is spent to improve actual working conditions.

An official goal may be to contribute to social responsibility; yet a firm may fail to spend money on pollution-control equipment or even fight regulations designed to prevent acid rain because of the costs involved. Or a firm may state that it wishes to integrate activities of SBUs to achieve synergy while its organization structure grants decentralized autonomy to divisions which prevent this from happening. Anderson, Clayton & Co. has searched for an acquisition in the food business for a decade; but analysts suggest its refusal to take on a debt to clinch a big acquisition really suggests that its operative goal is to not discourage potential buyers of the firm itself. According to one former officer, "they are managing the company to be sold."

• *There may be limits to the attainment of some goals.* Some firms may try to maximize shareholder wealth but find that they are constrained by the need for funds to achieve lower-cost operations to meet competition. Excessive increases in market share might come at the cost of unpleasant antitrust consequences, which, in effect, could be counterproductive from a survival perspective. Again, there are trade-offs among goals which managers must make.

• Finally, *objectives are not strategies*. Strategies are means to an end. Note that expansion was not among the objectives listed. Expansion is one type of strategy but not an end in itself. In itself, expansion of sales or assets may not improve performance. But cutting back (retrenchment) in certain areas of the operation could also be a way to increase efficiency and improve performance. So expansion and retrenchment are ways in which goals can be achieved, and both can lead to performance increases (e.g., growth in returns). Not all managers agree with this distinction, but we believe it is an important one. (This is a problem with strategic management terminology in general.)

One other issue regarding objectives which has become important to strategists is the priority attached to objectives relating to social responsibility [12]. Social responsibility is an ill-defined term, but the basic idea is that the economic functions provided by business *ought to be* performed in such a way that other social functions are, at worst, unharmed and, at best, promoted. Thus businesses are urged to be as concerned with human rights, environmental protection, equality of opportunity, and the like, as they are with providing outcomes such as economic efficiency.

Several dilemmas arise. A major problem is how to define socially responsible behavior. Value systems are so diverse that achieving consensus on this issue is difficult. Equally problematic is the fact that economic organizations automatically take resources from organizations in other sectors and often detract from performing other societal functions. Businesses weren't designed to promote public health, safety, and welfare (though some use charitable giving as a marketing ploy). A common example is detrimental health effects from pollution created by the production of goods. Do we stop producing goods? Do we increase costs to the extent that other societal goals are adversely affected? For instance, a completely safe automobile might be so expensive that possible cost increases to protect human safety become detrimental to economic well-being. Cost-benefit trade-offs are extremely difficult to make.

In some cases, external threats can be so severe as to call into question the legitimacy of the mission of the organization, as in the case of utilities which generate power with nuclear plants. Policies to deal with these concerns include ignoring the issue, using public relations campaigns to try to mitigate unfavorable publicity, and altering goal priorities and changing strategies. Some creative strategists try to turn these kinds of threats into opportunities. For instance, some coal companies have increased the value of land originally used for strip-mining by converting the strip mines into recreation complexes. But these options are not always available. In any case, decision makers are being urged to increase the priority given to these concerns by some.

On the other hand, businesses are also criticized if they stray too far from their economic function. For instance, business firms are chastised for creating political action committees as a means to influence their environment.

While research evidence is mixed, the predominant view is that social responsibility bears little (positive or negative) relationship to financial performance objectives. Clearly, then, establishing goal priorities and resource allocation requires a consideration of issues beyond simple economic efficiencies.

Why Objectives [13]

Why do firms have objectives, and why are they important to strategic management? There are four reasons.

1 *Objectives help define the organization in its environment.* Most organizations need to justify their existence, to legitimize themselves in the eyes of the government, customers, and society at large. And by stating objectives, they also attract people who identify with the objectives to work for them. Thus objectives define the enterprise.

2 *Objectives help in coordinating decisions and decision makers.* Stated objectives direct the attention of employees to desirable standards of behavior. It may reduce conflict in decision making if all employees know what the objectives are. Objectives become constraints on decisions.

3 *Objectives provide standards for assessing organizational performance.* Objectives provide the ultimate standard by which the organization judges itself. Without objectives, the organization has no clear basis for evaluating its success.

4 *Objectives are more tangible targets than mission statements.* The products of an organization or the services it performs (outputs) are probably the most familiar terms in which people tend to think of objectives or goals. (It's easier to see Hallmark as a producer of cards and gifts than to imagine the company as being in "the social-expression business.") Output goals may also be thought of in terms of quality, variety, and the types of customers or clients who are the intended target. Nonetheless, it may be deceptively easy to link output goals with mission definitions. For instance, Henry Ford's original mission of "providing transportation for the common man" was easily seen through the production of the Model A. But the private hospital offering a large range of services with the best doctors and equipment may be available to only a few rich clients; it may be profitable with these services and judged effective by some, but others will argue that it fails to satisfy a larger mission of equal health care treatment (note the social responsibility element here).

Mission and objectives ought to be considered at each stage of the strategic management process. In the assessment of environmental conditions, expected changes may force rethinking about goal priorities (e.g., changing government tax regulations may suggest a different treatment of dividend payout or retained earnings). In an analysis of internal conditions, a goal of employee welfare might alter perceptions about unionization. In choosing alternative strategies, a change in business definition could lead to decisions to get out of some businesses in favor of others. If a goal of flexibility is desired, the implementation of a strategy could lead to a new form of organization structure. So at each stage of the process, mission, business definition, and objectives should guide decision making.

To carry this a bit further and illustrate how objectives relate to the process as a whole, we consider the gap analysis as outlined in Exhibit 2.6. Point A is the current level of attainment an enterprise has reached at this time (t_1). Point B is the ideal point at which management would like to see itself at some point in the future (t_2). If, as a result of following the strategic management process, the firm sees itself

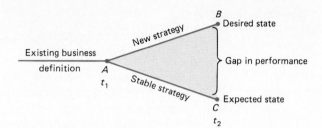

EXHIBIT 2.6 **Gap analysis for objectives.**

pursuing the *same strategy* with a given set of assumptions about its environment, management may believe it will arrive at point C at t_2. The gap of interest which could trigger either *strategic change or goal change* is that between B and C. Note that the gap between the existing state and the desired state is not as important as the gap between the *expected state* and the *desired state*.

As we discussed in Chapter 1, the perception of this gap is important in terms of significance, importance, and reducibility. With these conditions in mind, note that several basic choices are available. If the gap is significant, important, and reducible, an attempt could be made to alter strategy so that the expected state (point C) will come closer to the desired state (B). If the gap is significant and important but not reducible, point B might be altered (e.g., expectations might be lowered). If the gap is significant and reducible but not important, once again point B can be altered. The goal that is sought becomes less critical when compared with other goals. If the gap is *neither* significant, important, nor reducible, no change will occur—a stability strategy (continuing past approaches in similar ways) is likely to be followed.

This is a prescriptive way to examine the analysis of objectives as a component of the strategic management process. But other factors influence the nature of the perceptions of these gaps as objectives are formulated. These are discussed next.

How Are Mission and Objectives Formulated? [14]

We believe that missions and objectives are formulated by the corporate-level strategists. But these executives do not make choices in a vacuum. Their choices are affected by several factors: the realities of the external environment and external power relationships, the realities of the enterprise's resources and internal power relationships, the value systems and goals of the top executives, and past strategy and development of the enterprise. Let us discuss each of these influencing factors and then summarize.

The first factor affecting the formulation of mission and objectives is *forces in the environment*. As discussed in Chapter 1, the stakeholders with whom the organization has an exchange relationship will present demands or claims (expectations). These can be thought of as constraints on objectives. The stakeholders may vary, the nature of their constraints (expectations or claims) can change, and their power vis-à-vis the organization and one another may change. Taken together, they represent one set of forces within which managerial objectives must be established. The claims of the most powerful stakeholders will be met, so long as the entire set of objectives falls within the constraints imposed by the set of stakeholders.

Suppose that managers want to choose maximization of sales as an objective. They may have to modify this objective because of governmental regulations regarding excess profits, antitrust legislation, consumer labeling, and so on. Trade unions may require higher-than-market wage rates or fringe benefits which lead to higher costs (possibly reducing sales). Competitors may sell other products or services at unrealistically low prices and spend excessive amounts on advertising. Suppliers may become monopolized and charge outrageous prices. If the organization is more dependent on suppliers than on any other stakeholders, the operative objective may very well be limited by the availability and cost of supplies. As discussed in Chapter 1, then, the political-behavioral realities of the situation influence the choice of objectives.

So the prudent strategist will ask a variety of questions when establishing mission, objectives, and strategy: Who are the critical stakeholders? What are our critical assumptions about each stakeholder? How do stakeholders affect each division, business, or function at various points in time. And what changes can be expected among the stakeholder groups in the future?

The second factor affecting the formulation of mission and objectives is the *realities of the enterprise's resources and internal power relationships*. Larger and more profitable firms have more resources with which to respond to forces in the environment than do smaller or poorer firms.

In addition to this, the internal political relationships affect mission and objectives. First, how much support does management have relative to others in the organization? Does the management have the full support of the stockholders? For example, Paul Smucker has the support of the Smucker family stockholders to emphasize quality as an objective for his jam and preserves firm. If the management has developed the support of employees and key employee groups like the professional employees' lower and middle management, then it can set higher objectives that employees will help achieve.

Mission and objectives are also influenced by the power relationships among the strategists either as individuals or as representatives of units within the organization. Thus if there is a difference of opinion on which objectives to seek or the trade-offs among them, power relationships may help settle the difference.

A final internal factor is the potential power of lower-level participants to withhold information and ideas. To the extent that this occurs, the evaluation of past goal attainment and expectations about the future can be affected. For instance, consider the sales manager who tries to hide the fact that a competitor's new product is starting to hurt sales. This might be an attempt to protect the unit, but it could mislead top managers regarding future goals and strategies. Or lower-level managers might decide whether or not to forward a proposal which could lead to goal changes on the basis of what they *think* top management is (or is not) ready to accept. Thus the exercise of this type of informal power can play a role in the selection of objectives.

Mintzberg has advanced a theory about formulation of objectives that combines the stakeholder forces described earlier with the internal power relationships. He believes that power plays result from interactions of internal and external coalitions.

EXHIBIT 2.7 SIX PURE POWER CONFIGURATIONS AFFECTING OBJECTIVES FORMULATION

External coalition	Internal coalition	Power configuration
Dominated	Bureaucratic	The Instrument
Passive	Bureaucratic	The Closed System
Passive	Personalized	The Autocracy
Passive	Ideologic	The Missionary
Passive	Professional	The Meritocracy
Divided	Politicized	The Political Arena

Source: Henry Mintzberg, *Power In and Around Organizations* (Englewood Cliffs, N. J.: Prentice-Hall, 1983), p. 307.

• The external coalition includes owners, suppliers, unions, and the public. These groups influence the firm through social norms, specific constraints, pressure campaigns, direct controls, and membership on the board of directors. Mintzberg specifies three types of external coalitions, noted in Exhibit 2.7.

• The internal coalition includes top management, middle-line managers, operators, analysts, and support staff. These groups influence the firm through the personnel control system, the bureaucratic control system, the political system, and the system of ideology. Mintzberg specifies 5 types of internal coalitions, shown in Exhibit 2.7.

Mintzberg says that there are six basic power configurations, as shown in Exhibit 2.7. In the instrument power configuration, one external influence with clear objectives, typically the owner, is able to strongly influence objectives through the top manager. In a closed-system power configuration, power to set objectives rests with the top manager, who sets the objectives. This is also true in the autocracy power configuration. In the missionary power configuration, objectives are strongly influenced by past ideology and a charismatic leader. Ideology tends to dictate the objectives. In the meritocracy power configuration, the objectives are set by a consensus of the members, most of whom are professionals.

Thus the formulation of mission and objectives can be a simple process: the top manager sets them subject to the environment. Or, more frequently, they are set by a complex interplay of past and present, internal and external role players.

The third factor affecting the formulation of mission and objectives is the *value system of the top executives*. Enterprises with strong value systems or ideologies will attract and retain managers whose values are similar. These values are essentially a set of attitudes about what is good or bad, desirable or undesirable. These in turn will influence the perception of the advantages and disadvantages of strategic action and the choice of objectives. Exhibit 2.8 lists the extremes of six selected values. Let's look at each of these to see how they might affect objectives.

EXHIBIT 2.8 VALUES TOWARD VARIOUS GROUPS IN THE
STRATEGIC SITUATION

1 Very combative	Very passive
2 Very innovative	Noninnovative
3 Risk-oriented	Risk-aversive
4 Quality	Quantity
5 Autocratic	Participative
6 Personal goals	Shareholder goals

The following list corresponds to the continuum in Exhibit 2.8. Each dimension is explained below:

1 Some executives believe that to be successful a firm must attack in the marketplace. Others believe that you ''go along to get along.''

2 Some executives believe that to succeed a firm must innovate. Others prefer to ''let others make the mistakes first.''

3 Some executives know that to ''win big, you must take big risks.'' Others comment, ''Risk runs both ways.''

4 Some executives believe that one becomes successful by producing quality. Others go for volume.

5 Some executives believe that one should treat employees in a manner that makes them know who the boss is. Others believe that cooperation comes from a participative style.

6 Some executives believe that they should be primary beneficiaries of corporate success while others think the business is operated for the benefit of stockholders.

You can see that one set of executives with the set of values on the left would be inclined to emphasize a different set or different level of objectives than those who accept the set of values on the right in Exhibit 2.8. For instance, risk-oriented innovators might see significantly larger gaps between where they want to be and where they expect to be than risk averters. Managers on the left on number 6 will avoid hostile takeovers to protect their jobs, even if it comes at the expense of shareholder loss. Corporate raiders often recognize this, and receive ''greenmail'' for their effort.

Prescriptively, from a ''maximizing'' decision perspective, these and other kinds of values *ought not* be considered when goals are being established. Yet some believe that it is better to recognize the inevitability of their influence on decision makers. That is, even if they are not explicitly stated, value assumptions will be implicit in decision premises and the types and forms of data collected. Consequently, stating these values in the form of assumptions is one technique recommended to force these values explicitly into the open. If they are included, the bases upon which decisions are made can be considered ''more rational'' than if decision makers pretended that these factors don't exist. Exhibit 2.9 suggests that value shifts do affect the mission and goals of a business.

EXHIBIT 2.9 EXECUTIVE SUCCESSION SHIFTS VALUES, GOALS, AND STRATEGY

Control Data Corp. is in trouble. The company lost approximately $400 million in 1985 and analysts expect it to do no better than break even in 1986. Also, the company owes nearly $400 million in loans. In 1985 Control Data went into technical default on $217 million of those loans. It is up to Robert Price, the president and now chairman and CEO of the company, to lead it out of trouble. Price recently succeeded William Norris, the founder of Control Data. Norris's retirement indicates a change in direction for the company.

The idealistic Norris vowed to use computers to serve "society's unmet needs." The operation of Control Data reflected Norris's position. For example, the company had to write off $9.7 million on a business of building energy-saving earth-sheltered homes. The pragmatic Price has a different philosophy. He sees Control Data's mission as "using computer technology to solve problems." Price is currently selling off Norris's altruistic but unprofitable ventures. Also, he is trying to revitalize the company's longtime revenue sources.

Norris, as founder, probably had enough power to lead the company in the direction he wanted, even if the board did not agree with him. Does Price have that power? It could be argued that Price is a reflection of the board of directors' values, since he now becomes the vehicle by which the board hopes to lead the company toward a more profitable direction.

Note that a shift in values after succession led to a change in mission and goals for this organization and has resulted in a retrenchment strategy.

Source: Adapted from "Can a Gentleman Farmer Get Control Data Out of Its Ditch?" *Business Week,* Jan. 27, 1986, pp. 44–45.

The fourth factor affecting the formulation of mission and objectives is the *awareness by management of the past development of the firm.* Management does not begin from scratch each year. It begins with the most recent mission and objectives. These may have been set by strong leaders in the past. The leaders consider incremental changes from the present, given the current environment and current demands of the conflicting groups. The managers have developed aspiration levels of what the objectives ought to be in a future period. But by muddling through, they set the current set of objectives to satisfy as many of the demands and their wishes as they can. The momentum of the large organization and its strategies and policies are all currently designed to accomplish the existing mission and objectives. Just as it takes time to turn a large ship around, it usually takes time to make major corporate changes.

Let's summarize what has been said so far on how mission and objectives are established. The factors are shown in Exhibit 2.10. Mission and objectives are not the result of managerial power alone. These result from the managers' trying to satisfy the needs of all groups involved with the enterprise. These coalitions of interests (stockholders, employees, suppliers, customers, and others) sometimes have conflicting interests. As the strongest coalition group, managers try to reconcile the conflicts. Management cannot settle them once and for all. Management "bargains" with the various groups and tries to produce a set of objectives and a mission which can satisfy the groups at that time. The goals of these groups are considered in relation to past goals. This is a very complicated, largely consensus-building process with no precise beginning or end. And at any given time, only a few specific goals can be grasped and comprehended by any single executive. Thus there appears to be a need for some grander vision as expressed by a mission definition.

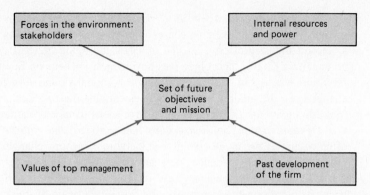

Note: Each of these factors represents a set of constraints on the establishment of the priorities among future objectives. The set of mission and objectives considered at any one time is also limited.

EXHIBIT 2.10   Factors influencing the formulation of objectives and mission.

Mission and objectives will become a meaningful part of the strategic management process only if corporate strategists formulate them well and communicate them and reinforce them throughout the enterprise. *The strategic management process will be successful to the extent that general managers participate in formulating the mission and objectives and to the extent that these reflect the values of management and the realities of the organization's situation.* These factors also play a role in strategic choice, as we explain in Chapter 8.

Why Do Mission and Objectives Change?

Although organizations tend toward stability, mission and objectives change over time. As discussed before, objectives could change on the basis of a rational analysis of a gap between expected and desired states. That is a normative approach. But what might lead to the determination of the states themselves? Are there some factors which would lead to different perceptions regarding the gaps between goals and how the future goal states might be arrived at?

On the basis of the foregoing discussion of how mission and objectives are formulated, we can present some descriptive reasons why mission or objectives might change.

• The aspiration levels of managers could alter goal orientations. They may begin to extrapolate past achievements and say that the enterprise can do more. Or they may look at what relevant competitors or other enterprises have achieved and decide to match or exceed these levels. The arrival of a new CEO from outside the organization is the most prevalent condition under which mission and goals are reconsidered. New managers from the outside who are not tied or committed to past strategy and ideology are more likely to alter the mission, objectives, and strategies of an organization than are new CEOs from the inside.

• *The mission can change in a crisis.* When a firm's market disappears, for example, or its reason for being ceases, a crisis exists. Some firms supplying equipment to the oil industry discovered this in 1974 and again in 1982 and 1986. Faced with an uncertain future, their objectives have begun to focus on flexibility. When the cure for polio was found, the mission of the National Foundation for Infantile Paralysis changed. So the attainment of objectives can also lead to a crisis. Or, new opportunities can create an identity crisis if a firm seeks to take advantage of them.

• *Demands from coalition groups that make up the enterprise can change.* This often occurs as the membership or leadership of groups changes or as internal power groups change. For instance, new government or labor leaders or new competitors can alter the way a business sets its goal-priorities. Similarly, if the comptroller becomes more powerful internally, the firm might begin to stress shorter-term financial goals.

• *Normal life-cycle changes may occur which alter goal orientations.* Exhibit 2.11 suggests a stage of development approach. Though the analogy with humans can be taken too far, there may be changes in objectives or strategies which "naturally" occur in the aging process. Of course, organizations may have more control over the sequencing and timing of these stages than humans. Yet it is often difficult for an organization to know what stage it is in. And we're not sure what might precipitate organizational aging or movement. We do know that commitment to the past may hinder change, and new agents in coalition groups are likely to hasten it.

These four classes of factors—aspirations, crisis, demands, and development—can be used to predict the likelihood that mission and objectives will remain similar to those of the past or be subject to redefinition. Thus in considering how mission and

EXHIBIT 2.11   ORGANIZATIONAL DEVELOPMENT AS ANALOGOUS TO HUMAN DEVELOPMENT

Human stage	Prime life thrust	Organizational objectives	Strategic focus for an organization
Birth	Trauma and survival	Survival—create new entity	Identify an entrepreneurial idea and find resources
Infancy	Adaptation and self-interest	Define mission and search environment	Define products, markets, and functions to offer
Youth	Rapid, uneven growth spurts	Quantitative growth	Increase market share; claim more territory
Young adult	Procreation and search	Achieve uniqueness and establish niche	Redefine products, markets, and functions
Adult	Establishment of self	Qualitative growth—gain reputation	Reap rewards; mine markets for benefits
Maturity	Status quo	Stabilize and contribute to society	Maintain position with stability
Old age	Survival	Survival	Procreate and retrench parts that are no longer healthy

objectives are formulated, we must examine various pressures for stability or change before a gap analysis can be effectively done.

The Specificity of Mission and Objectives [15]

Our final area of concern with these basic elements of strategic management deals with how broadly or narrowly mission and objectives should be, or are, defined. Let's separately examine mission definition and then look at objectives.

Mission

As strategists define their mission, they are usually urged to seek a *common thread* to which activities can be related. The common thread is often stated in terms of the *scope* of products, but markets or technologies in the domain of the enterprise are also used. The problem is that the firm might define the scope so broadly that strategic decisions or objectives tied to the mission become meaningless. On the other hand, an overly narrow mission definition can lead to the oversight of factors that are potentially important to the success of the enterprise. Exhibit 2.12 shows part of the dilemma.

EXHIBIT 2.12   ASPECTS OF THE PRESENT AND FUTURE DOMAIN OF TWA

Trans World Airlines is in the business of moving people from one destination to another. About half its customers (business executives) want face-to-face interaction with people at another location. They want to get there quickly and conveniently and at a relatively low cost. What are their alternatives? What business is TWA really in? What is its domain?

Most analysts see TWA as being in the commercial airline industry. Some see it as part of the transportation industry. A few suggest that its domain includes communications. Each has different implications.

If the domain is the airline industry, then some relevant key competitors are PanAm, Eastern, and United. Claims over similar territories and clients are made. But this tends to ignore the potential threats of customers using alternative modes of transportation—cars, buses, trains, private aircraft. When regularly scheduled air traffic has some advantages over these other modes, ignoring them and the factors which might lead to customers using them could result in a loss of business. This becomes clearer as you consider the communications domain.

The Wall Street Journal reports that face-to-face communication with clients and colleagues is now possible with satellite-linked TV screens. At one trial of such an approach, "participants said video conferences could substitute for a majority of face-to-face business meetings, for quicker decision-making and reduced travel time and expense." IBM and AT&T are heavily involved in these developments. Do you remember Ma Bell's response when the 1974 energy crisis hit? A series of ads promoted the use of the telephone by salespeople, encouraging salespeople to contact clients from the office instead of using the company car. Will executives soon "travel by long distance and stay awhile"? *Business Week* reports that videoconferencing is indeed an increasingly popular approach to reduce travel time and cost without loss of executive effectiveness. Exhibit 3.5 shows how this technology is gaining acceptance.

Sources: Adapted from "Dogfight in Space: The Competition Heats Up in Domestic Satellites," *The Wall Street Journal*, Sept. 8, 1978, p. 1; *Business Week*, July 7, 1980, p. 81; "Videoconferencing: No Longer Just a Sideshow," *Business Week*, Nov. 12, 1984, pp. 116–120.

If the domain of TWA is defined too narrowly, executives may miss important technological or competitive activities occurring outside the more limited domain of ''other air carriers.'' As a result, the firm may risk the potential loss of a large part of its customer base.

Thus the domain must be sufficiently broad so that decision makers will be sensitive to important issues it may face in the future. Of course, overgeneralization, the opposite of myopia, may lead to a lack of focus on relevant issues as well. Should an airline view itself as being in the vacation business, it could lose sight of its basic mission. Paper Mate now views itself as in ''office products'' with the acquisition of Liquid Paper. A radio is a product, but manufacturers of radios are in the business of providing a means of delivering audio information and/or entertainment. The Boston Consulting Group statement on this issue is instructive:

> Unfortunately, there is a prevalent notion that if one merely defines one's business in increasingly general terms—such as transportation rather than railroading—the road to successful competitive strategy will be clear. Actually, that is hardly ever the case. More often, the opposite is true. For example, in the case of the railroads, passengers and freight represent very different problems, and short haul vs. longer haul are completely different strategic issues. Indeed, as the unit train demonstrates, just coal handling is a meaningful strategic issue.

Thus perhaps one of the best ways to determine a common thread is to seek out synergies which could be obtained between old and new activities. ''Synergy'' refers to the idea that the whole is greater than the sum of its parts ($2 + 2 = 5$). Here, if a firm can find new activities which utilize the strengths or benefits of old activities, it is likely to create more value for all activities. As noted in Exhibit 2.4 Hallmark found synergy in its markets, products, *and* technologies. Another suggestion is to give careful attention to the *utilities* provided for customers (e.g., cost, time, location, convenience) by the functions performed by the enterprise. Careful attention to categories of goods and services (rather than ''products'') and synergies can lead to more useful definitions of the organization's mission and domain. For instance, Sears began its move into providing financial services to complement its existing insurance business by using its broad base of retail outlets and large number of charge customers as a point of departure.[2] In essence, mission and business definition can change. It must be periodically evaluated as part of the strategic management process.

A final point before turning to the specificity of objectives is the idea that these issues of domain definition are stated in different terms at different levels of the organization, but similar questions emerge. For instance, the scope question at the corporate level implies issues concerning the overall degree of diversification in the portfolio of business operations. At the SBU levels, the breadth of the product-market scope or degree of vertical integration (technology scope) is the more common issue. At functional levels, the issues often are debated in terms of product-market segmentation or positioning.

---

[2]Sears has been one of the few which has succeeded with unrelated diversifications because of their ability to manage some synergies well.

Objectives

The differences among levels also occur in that objectives are successively narrower as one moves down into an organization. But in more general terms, firms tend to evolve through stages of more precisely defining their objectives. These are as follows:

1 *Formulation of general objectives, usually not in written form.* Once administrators are aware of the desirability of objectives, they begin to formulate them. If you ask top management what its objectives are, you might be given them in general terms. You will not find them in writing anywhere.

2 *Formulation of general, written objectives.* The next step is to get the objectives in writing, perhaps in annual reports. By the time this stage is reached, the firm is fairly large and formalized.

3 *Formulation of specific objectives.* The hurdle that appears at step 4 is to get the executives to specify the objectives. For example, an objective may be changed *from* "increase the return on investment" *to* "increase the return on investment to 6 percent in the next year." (Note the greater specificity and timing involved.)

4 *Formulation and ranking of specific objectives.* The final and most difficult step is to ask management to compute the trade-offs between objectives. This requires management to say, for example, that the return on investments (ROI) is more important than the market share and having the market share is more important than having satisfied employees. This step is found only in the most sophisticated of firms.

There are various techniques for moving the firm through these steps. One of the most popular is the management-by-objectives (MBO) technique. MBO is used to develop a company philosophy requiring top management to proceed through step 4 in formulating objectives. Then middle and lower management are expected to translate these objectives into specific targets at their level to better ensure the achievement of the objectives, as shown in Exhibit 2.13.

Finally, most management theorists suggest that objectives should not only be formal, specific, measurable, prioritized, and time-based, they should also be challenging and obtainable. There should be a reasonable opportunity for achieving goals to avoid frustration; but if they are too easily obtainable, then little satisfaction or achievement is likely. For example, in 1980 IBM declared it would match or beat the information processing industry's growth in all segments (ranging from up to 12 percent per year for mainframe computers to 40 percent for personal computers). In 1985, the company planned to double revenues by 1990, and double them again by 1994. These are lofty goals, but the company has achieved many of them; and the pace of investment has been accelerated even though economic problems and industry slowdowns created challenges to the objective.

Many firms, however, prefer to rely on more general definitions instead of publicly stated specific goals or targets. For example, one automobile industry analyst suggested that "Ford still doesn't know where it's going." But the chairman of the board, Donald Peterson, insists that Ford knows where it is headed, but he is vague on the specifics. The only goal he admits to is that of making Ford "a customer-driven company." Why do managers do this? Quinn argues that broad goal statements are preferable because specific and rigid goal pronouncements can rigidify positions,

EXHIBIT 2.13 TRANSLATION OF STRATEGIC OBJECTIVES INTO SPECIFIC TARGETS

Corporate-level strategic objectives	Corporate and/or SBU specific targets
1 Improve return on assets	1 Increase return on net assets (after taxes) from 12 to 19 percent in 3 years
2 Increase overall profit	2 Increase overall profit margin from 4 to 6 percent in 3 years
3 Increase sales by (a) Improving market penetration in existing markets	3 (a) Product A: Increase market penetration from 15 to 20 percent next year Product B: Increase market penetration from 20 to 25 percent in 2 years
(b) Opening up new markets	(b) Move product from development fo production (planned market penetration, 5 percent) in next year
4 Increase manufacturing productivity	4 Purchase new equipment: $3 million next year Establish a methods engineering department; improve rework rate by 5 percent over next year
5 Improve management-union relations	5 Establish new industrial relations department and examine management's approach to labor problems immediately; reduce turnover rate 3 percent next year

eliminate creative options, cause resistance, centralize the organization, and alert the opposition to a target for counterattack, particularly as competitors lure away top talent who have inside knowledge about specific plans. He argues for more generality so executives can keep their options open and generate identity, cohesion, and commitment around an idealized mission. Others argue that the effective manager sets general objectives to give a sense of direction but is never committed *publicly* to a specific set of objectives. In other words the manager should have objectives but should not state them publicly. Public statements of specific objectives might be avoided because it is impossible to set down specific objectives which will be relevant for any reasonable period of time since things change too fast; objectives may not be clear enough so that everyone in the organization will understand what they mean; details complicate the task of reaching objectives. If it is felt that employees will not accept the strategist's objectives, then it is useful to be vague and avoid this problem. Finally, some executives prefer to state vague and general goals because their performance evaluation is tied to accomplishment. After-the-fact explanations of goal attainment are much easier if the goals are not specific, time-based, measurable, and publicly known. Justifying that a firm has achieved ''industry leadership'' is easier on several grounds than having to show that ''we will lead our industry by attaining the highest ROI by 1990.'' Chapter 11 will refer to this again as we consider the evaluation of the performance of a firm.

SUMMARY

Chapter 2 has focused on the two strategic management elements: the mission and objectives and the strategists.

The first strategic element is that of the actors in the process. We described the general manager as an executive at the pinnacle of an enterprise or SBU. While new types of general managers are coming on the scene, these individuals have a complex task. They are organization leaders, personal leaders, and designers of mission and strategy. They play informational, interpersonal, and decision-making roles. Enormous amounts of time are spent in communicating with internal and external stakeholders while they play these roles.

Since our focus is on the strategic management role, we next described the corporate-level and business-level strategists.

• *The board.* The board of directors has the ultimate legal authority, but it primarily reviews strategies and CEOs, and it influences strategy through CEO selection and replacement.

• *Top managers.* They may be professional managers or entrepreneurs, and they are the primary decision makers.

The failure of an organization to achieve its objectives can often be traced to a breakdown at the level of the board or top management group.

Other actors influencing the development of strategy and its implementation include SBU managers, who perform roles similar to those of top managers; corporate planners, who can facilitate and do planning; consultants, who can provide advice on specific problems; and lower-level managers, who interpret policy and offer proposals up the line.

Consultants are more objective advisors

Proposition 2.1   *The Authors*

With respect to the strategists, we propose that strategic management is most effectively performed by general managers. In larger firms, the executives may receive assistance from corporate planning staffs. In firms of various sizes, the top executives may receive assistance from consultants and guidance from the board of directors.

In all cases, we suggest that effective implementation will more likely occur if general managers and operating managers are directly involved in the strategic management process.

The second element is the starting point of the strategic management process—mission and objectives.

A mission statement defines the basic reason for the existence of an organization and helps legitimize its function in society. The business definition clarifies the nature of existing products, markets, and functions the firm presently provides.

Objectives are those ends which the organization seeks to achieve through its existence and operations. Objectives are an integral part of the strategic management process. They are the ends the firm seeks and the criteria used to determine its effectiveness.

Objectives are an integral part of the strategic management process. They are the ends the firm seeks and the criteria used to determine its effectiveness.

The chapter emphasized the following points about objectives:

- All but the simplest organizations pursue more than one objective.
- Two types of objectives can be distinguished: operational objectives are the objectives that are actually pursued; official objectives are the objectives that managers say they are seeking.
- Strategists should establish the current priorities of each objective among all the objectives, but they often don't.
- There may be limits to the attainment of some goals.
- Objectives are ends, not means.
- Social responsibility is becoming a more important consideration among the multiple objectives sought by business.

Organizations have objectives for a number of reasons: objectives help define the organization in its environment: objectives help in coordinating decisions and decision makers; objectives provide standards for assessing organizational performance; objectives are more tangible targets than mission statements.

The formulation of mission and objectives is a complex process which involves

- An analysis of the gaps between desired and expected goal attainments
- The realities of the external environment and external power relationships
- The realities of the enterprise's resources and internal power relationships
- The value systems and goals of top executives
- The past strategy and development of the enterprise

Proposition 2.2

Mission and objectives are formed for an organization when its top managers react to a complex interplay of the demands of groups in the environment and inside the firm. The managers incrementally adjust the mission and objectives, considering these demands, their own values and aspirations, and past strategy.

Changes in mission and objectives depend on several factors: the aspiration levels of managers can change; an organizational crisis may be at hand; demands from coalitions can change; normal life-cycle development may occur.

Managers are urged to define their objectives in formal, specific, time-based, prioritized, measurable terms which are challenging and attainable. But they tend to resist being specific about objectives because specificity tends to reduce flexibility. Consequently, many managers rely on more general mission statements.

If an enterprise is not achieving its objectives, it has several choices:

- Claim that the objectives being achieved will ultimately lead to long-term mission attainment.
- Change the objectives so that those being met are the objectives.
- Change the strategy in order to achieve the objectives.

- Change the strategists and keep the objectives and strategy, assuming that new strategists can achieve the objectives.

To conclude, recognize that organizations pursue multiple purposes, which are time-based. Some purposes are means to ends, while others conflict with one another and require trade-offs. An organization is usually called efficient *and* effective only if short-term and intermediate goals are attained as it moves toward its long-term mission. But even the mission and goals change over time. Finally, a complex set of factors and pressures from internal and external forces must be considered by the strategists.

As an aspiring manager you must be aware of the nature of goals and general managers and the types of conditions likely to lead to change. Middle managers interpret policy and can be held responsible for problems. To interpret wisely, you must understand the pressures faced at the top and why certain strategies or policies are being formed and pursued. More than one career has been stifled simply because the manager was on the wrong side of a power struggle. This chapter has provided some ideas about the basic dynamics involved in these processes. Finally, as you prepare ideas and proposals for consideration by your supervisors, you will find it useful to know "where they are coming from" and what roles they play. Your proposals will have a better chance for acceptance if you understand how they fit on "the agenda" of the organization.

Now that we know a little more about the strategic elements—the decision makers and their decisions about mission and objectives—we can move on to Chapter 3, which continues the discussion of the strategic management process with the analysis of the firm's environmental opportunities and threats.

REFERENCES

[1] The General Manager

Bourgeois, L. J.: "Strategic Management and Determinism," *Academy of Management Review,* vol. 9 (1984), pp. 586–596.

Burck, C. G.: "A Group Profile of the Fortune 500 Chief Executive," *Fortune,* May 1976, pp. 173–174+.

Chandy, P. R. and T. Klammer: "The Big Firm CEO," *Collegiate News and Views,* vol. 37 (1984), pp. 1–5.

Christensen, C. R., K. R. Andrews, J. L. Bower, R. G. Hammermesh, and M. E. Porter: *Business Policy: Text and Cases* (Homewood, Ill.: Irwin, 1982).

Hambrick, D. C., and P. A. Mason: "Upper Echelons: The Organization as a Reflection of Its Top Managers," *Academy of Management Review,* vol. 9 (1984), pp. 193–206.

Kotter, J. P.: *The General Managers* (New York: Free Press, 1986).

Levinson, H., and S. Rosenthal: *CEO: Corporate Leadership in Action* (New York: Basic Books, 1983).

Mintzberg, H.: *The Nature of Managerial Work* (New York: Harper & Row, 1973).

Nussbaum, B., J. W. Wilson, D. B. Moskowitz, and A. Beam: "The New Corporate Elite," *Business Week,* Jan. 21, 1985, pp. 62–81.

Sigband, N. B.: "The Changing Role of the CEO," research monograph, University of Southern California, 1984.

"Turnover at the Top," *Business Week,* Dec. 19, 1983, pp. 104–110.

[2] The Board of Directors

Baum, L., and J. A. Byrne: "The Job Nobody Wants," *Business Week,* Sept. 8, 1986, pp. 56–61.

Cochran, P. L., R. A. Wood, and T. B. Jones: "The Composition of Boards of Directors and Incidence of Golden Parachutes," *Academy of Management Journal,* vol. 28 (1985), pp. 664–671.

Jones, T. M., and L. D. Goldberg: "Governing the Large Corporation: More Arguments for Public Directors," *Academy of Management Review,* vol. 7 (1982), pp. 603–611.

"Labor's Voice on Corporate Boards: Good or Bad?" *Business Week,* May 7, 1984, pp. 151–153.

Mizruchi, M. S.: "Who Controls Whom? An Examination of the Relation Between Management and Boards of Directors in Large American Corporations," *Academy of Management Review,* vol. 8 (1983), pp. 426–423.

Zahra, S. A.: "The Composition of Board of Directors and Company Strategic Behavior and Performance," working paper 85-03, Old Dominion University, Norfolk, VA, 1985.

[3] The Board as Strategists

Boulton, W.: "The Evolving Board: A Look at the Board's Changing Roles & Information Needs," *Academy of Management Review,* vol. 3 (October 1978), pp. 827–836.

"End of the Directors' Rubber Stamp," *Business Week,* Sept. 10, 1979, pp. 72–77.

Wommack, W. W.: "The Board's Most Important Function," *Harvard Business Review,* vol. 57 (September–October 1979), pp. 48–52 +.

[4] Top Managers as Strategists

Donaldson, G., and J. W. Lorsch: *Decision Making at the Top* (New York: Basic Books, 1983).

Hambrick, D. C.: "Strategic Awareness within Top Management Teams," *Strategic Management Journal,* vol. 2 (July–September 1981), pp. 263–280.

Hickson, D. J., R. J. Butler, D. Cray, G. R. Mallory, and D. C. Wilson: *Top Decision* (San Francisco: Jossey Bass, 1986).

Hofer, C. W., and C. N. Toftog: "How CEOs Set Strategic Directions for their Organizations," paper presented at the Strategic Management Society Conference, 1984.

Mintzberg, H.: "The Manager's Job: Folklore and Fact," *Harvard Business Review* (July–August, 1975), pp. 49–61.

Shrivastava, S.: *The Executive Mind* (San Francisco: Jossey Bass, 1983).

————: *Executive Power* (San Francisco: Jossey-Bass, 1986).

Sturdivant, F. D., J. L. Ginter, and A. G. Sawyer: "Managers' Conservatism and Corporate Performance," *Strategic Management Journal,* vol. 6 (1985), pp. 17–38.

[5] Entrepreneurs

Ehrlich, E.: "America Expects Too Much from its Entrepreneurial Heroes," *Business Week,* July 28, 1986, p. 33.

"Following the Corporate Legend," *Business Week,* Feb. 11, 1980, pp. 62–66 +.

"The New Entrepreneurs," *Business Week,* Apr. 18, 1983, pp. 78–89.

Pave, I.: "A Lot of Enterprise is Staying in the Family These Days," *Business Week,* July 1, 1985, pp. 62–63.

Sykes, H. B.: "Lessons from a New Ventures Program," *Harvard Business Review* (May–June, 1986), pp. 69–74.

Van de Ven, A. H., R. Hudson, and D. M. Schroeder: "Designing New Business Startups," *Journal of Management,* vol. 10 (1984), pp. 87–107.

[6] The CEO and Failure

Bibeault, D. B.: *Corporate Turnaround* (New York: McGraw-Hill, 1982).

"Chief Executives Who Won't Let Go," *Business Week,* Oct. 8, 1984, p. 39.

Dalton, D. R., and I. F. Kesner: "Organizational Performance as an Antecedent of Inside/ Outside Chief Executive Succession," *Academy of Management Journal,* vol. 28 (1985), pp. 749–762.

Jauch, L. R., T. N. Martin, and R. N. Osborn: "Top Management Under Fire," *The Journal of Business Strategy,* vol. 1 (Spring 1981), pp. 33–41.

Pfeffer, J., and A. Davis-Blake: "Administrative Succession and Organizational Performance," *Academy of Management Journal,* vol. 29 (1986), pp. 72–83.

[7] The Corporate Planning Staff

Hunsicker, J. Q.: "The Paralysis of Analysis," *Management Review* (March 1980), pp. 9–14.

Javidan, M.: "What Does Top Management Expect from Its Corporate Planning Department?" ASAC 1982 Conference, University of Ottawa.

Lorange, P.: "Divisional Planning: Setting Effective Direction," *Sloan Management Review* (Fall 1975), pp. 77–91.

———: "Formal Planning Systems," in C. Hofer and D. Schendel, *Strategic Management: A New View of Business Policy and Planning* (Boston: Little, Brown, 1979).

"The New Breed of Strategic Planner," *Business Week,* Sept. 17, 1984, pp. 62–68.

[8] Strategic Management Consultants

"An Advisory Council to Back Up the Board," *Business Week,* Nov. 12, 1979, pp. 131 + .

"Consultants Move to the Executive Suite," *Business Week,* Nov. 7, 1977.

Robinson, R. B., Jr.: "The Importance of 'Outsiders' in Small Firm Strategic Planning," *Academy of Management Journal,* vol. 25 (1982), pp. 80–93.

[9] Lower-Level Managers' Impact on Management

Jauch, L. R., and H. K. Wilson: "A Strategic Perspective for Make or Buy Decisions," *Long Range Planning,* vol. 12 (December 1979), pp. 56–61.

Mechanic, D.: "Sources of Power of Lower Participants in Complex Organizations," in W. W. Cooper, J. J. Leavitt, and M. W. Shelly (eds.), *New Perspectives in Organizational Research* (New York: Wiley, 1964).

Wheelwright, S. C., and R. L. Banks: "Involving Operating Managers in Planning Process Evolution," *Sloan Management Review* (Summer 1979), pp. 43–59.

[10] Mission and Business Definition

Abell, D. F.: *Defining the Business: The Starting Point of Strategic Planning* (Englewood Cliffs, N.J.: Prentice Hall, 1980).

Beam, A., and J. H. Dobrzynski: "General Mills: Toys Just Aren't Us," *Business Week,* Sept. 16, 1985, pp. 105–109.

Payne, S.: "Stepping Up the Attack on Contract Abuse," *Business Week,* July 1, 1985, p. 24.

Schlumberger Annual Report, 1985.

"Some Old Railroads Never Die—They Just Stop Running Trains," *Business Week,* Nov. 19, 1984, pp. 88–89.

Whiteside, D. E.: "Roger Smith's Campaign to Change the GM Culture," *Business Week,* Apr. 7, 1986, pp. 84–85.

[11] The Objectives of Businesses

"Anderson Clayton: Shopping Around for a Food Company or Grooming to Be a Takeover Target?" *Business Week,* Jan. 23, 1984, pp. 62–67.

Richards, M.: *Setting Strategic Goals and Objectives* (St. Paul, Minn.: West, 1986).

"Will Money Managers Wreck the Economy? Their Short-Term View Derails Companies' Long Term Plans," *Business Week,* Aug. 13, 1984, pp. 86–93.

[12] Social Responsibility Objectives

"Amex Shows the Way to Benefit from Giving," *Business Week,* Oct. 18, 1982, pp. 44–45.

Aupperle, K. E., A. B. Carroll, and J. D. Hatfield: "An Empirical Examination of the Relationship Between Corporate Social Responsibility and Profitability," *Academy of Management Journal,* vol. 28 (1985), pp. 446–463.

Cochran, P. L., and R. A. Wood: "Corporate Social Responsibility and Financial Performance," *Academy of Management Journal,* vol. 27 (1984), pp. 42–56.

Preston, L. E. (ed).: *Research in Corporate Social Performance and Policy* (Greenwich, Conn.: JAI Press, 1982).

Wartick, S. L., and P. L. Cochran: "The Evolution of the Corporate Social Performance Model," *Academy of Management Review,* vol. 10 (1985), pp. 758–769.

[13] The Purpose of Objectives

Pearson, G. J.: "Setting Corporate Objectives as a Basis for Action," *Long Range Planning,* vol. 12 (August 1979), pp. 13–19.

Simon, H.: "On the Concept of Organizational Goal," *Administrative Science Quarterly,* vol. 9 (June 1964), pp. 1–22.

[14] Formulating the Mission and Objectives

Cyert, R., and J. March: *A Behavioral Theory of the Firm* (Englewood Cliffs, N.J.: Prentice-Hall, 1963).

Freeman, R. E.: *Strategic Management: A Stakeholder Approach* (Boston: Pitman, 1984).

Guth, W. D.: "Formulating Organizational Objectives and Strategy: A Systematic Approach," *Journal of Business Policy,* vol. 2 (Autumn 1971), pp. 24–31.

Mintzberg, H.: *Power In and Around Organizations* (Englewood Cliffs, N.J.: Prentice-Hall, 1983).

Samuelson, R. J.: "A Misuse of Management Power," *Newsweek,* June 25, 1984, pp. 56–57.

Zeleny, M.: *MCDM Past Decade and Future Trends: A Source Book of Multiple Criteria Decision Making* (Eastchester, N.Y.: JAI Press, 1984).

[15] Narrow vs. Broad Mission and Objectives

Edid, M., W. J. Hampton and R. A. Melcher: "Now That It's Cruising, Can Ford Keep Its Foot on the Gas?" *Business Week,* Feb. 11, 1985, pp. 48–52.

Harris, M. A.: "IBM Sets Its Sights High," *Business Week,* Feb. 18, 1985, pp. 85–98.

Ohmae, K: *The Mind of the Strategist* (New York: McGraw-Hill, 1982).

Perspectives on Corporate Strategy (Boston: Boston Consulting Group, 1970), p. 42.

CHAPTER OUTLINE

THE GENERAL ENVIRONMENT

OBJECTIVES

- To introduce the sectors in the general environment which are crucial to the survival of a firm
- To examine the ways the environment may be analyzed
- To explore the factors affecting a diagnosis of the environment
- To indicate how the environmental analysis and diagnosis phase can be used in the strategic management process

INTRODUCTION [1]

With Chapter 3, we begin the discussion of the environment's impact on the strategic management process. The environment includes factors outside the firm which can lead to opportunities for or threats to the firm. Chapter 3 examines socioeconomic, technological, and governmental factors. Chapter 3 also introduces ways in which the factors can be *analyzed* and *diagnosed*. Chapter 4 examines the industry factors: customers, suppliers, and competition. We also explore the international environment in Chapter 4.

> *Environmental analysis is the process by which strategists monitor the environmental sectors to determine opportunities for and threats to their firms.*

Analysis is the tracing of an opportunity or threat to a source. It also involves breaking a whole into its parts to find its nature, function, and relationship. Strategic management requires searching for opportunities and threats and determining where they come from and which ones are coming.

> *Environmental diagnosis consists of managerial decisions made by assessing the significance of the data (opportunities and threats) of the environmental analysis.*

These decisions lead to other decisions on whether to react to, ignore, try to influence, or anticipate the opportunities or threats discovered. Thus managers' *perception* of the environment may be different from its objective condition.

In effect, diagnosis is an *opinion* resulting from an analysis of the facts to determine the nature of a problem with a view to acting to take advantage of an opportunity or to effectively manage a threat.

In Chapters 1 and 2 we discussed the use of gap analysis as an aid to strategists. As we begin the analysis stage, the analyst is trying to determine whether assumptions about the environment affecting the firm in the future will permit the current strategy to be continued so that the firm can reach desired outcomes. In some cases, if the environment presents more opportunities, the strategy might be changed so that new higher objectives can be reached. If threats appear, objectives may be changed or the strategy might be adjusted so that performance gaps will not grow too large.

Specifically, Exhibit 3.1 outlines the environmental analysis and diagnosis process. As you can see, first the strategists consciously examine the relationship between the firm's strategy and their perceptions of the environment. This is necessary as a basis for comparing current strategy with potential future strategy. Then the strategists

EXHIBIT 3.1   THE ENVIRONMENTAL ANALYSIS AND DIAGNOSIS PROCESS

Environment of the firm	Strategists analyze and diagnose gaps

General (Chapter 3)
  Socioeconomic
  Technological
  Governmental
Industry (Chapter 4)
  Customers
  Suppliers
  Competition
International (Chapter 4)
	Analysis
	1 Identify the current strategy the firm uses to relate to the environment. What are the assumptions or predictions about the environment on which current strategy is based?
	2 Predict the future environmental conditions. Are the assumptions or predictions the same as in step 1? Is there a gap?
	Diagnosis
	3 Assess the significance of the gap between the current and future environments for the firm. Are changes in objectives needed? Do changes in strategy appear useful to consider? Will they reduce the gap?

attempt to assess the future environment. These are the analysis steps. If there are no gaps, then the current strategy can be fruitfully pursued. If there are gaps, then the strategists determine whether these will have a significant effect on the current strategy or objectives.

This brings us back to our model of the strategic management process. Exhibit 3.2 highlights the analysis and diagnosis phase of the strategic management process, focusing especially on the external environment. It is a concern for the achievement of objectives in the future which motivates the analysis and diagnosis phase of strategic management. Hence, an analysis of gaps could lead to the adjustment of objectives (Chapter 2) or to a consideration of the need for a new strategy. If the decision is to adjust the strategy, alternative strategies must then be generated (Chapters 6 and 7) and a new strategy chosen (Chapter 8) and implemented (Chapters 9 to 11).

WHY ENVIRONMENTAL ANALYSIS AND DIAGNOSIS? [2]

Although some of the reasons why effective strategists analyze and diagnose the environment have already been hinted at, let's summarize a number of them briefly for purposes of clarity.

Managers must systematically analyze and diagnose the environment, since environmental factors are prime influencers of strategy change. Consider a few examples of environmental changes with negative consequences. (Others will be given in the chapters.)

1 Aramco was a large firm in Saudi Arabia that produced crude oil. It was owned primarily by American firms. The Saudi government nationalized the firm.

2 Large increases in the sales of soft drinks and other beverages were influenced by the popularity of nonreturnable containers. Some governmental bodies are passing laws against these containers.

3 In 1948, some of the largest firms in the United States were Paramount, Warner Brothers, and MGM. Enter the television networks: CBS, NBC, ABC.

4 Many persons made a good living running diaper-service companies. Suddenly Procter & Gamble brought out Pampers (disposable diapers), and others joined the parade.

5 Not so long ago, copies were made by typing stencils. These were put on duplicating machines made by firms such as A. B. Dick and Company. Xerox, IBM, and others came along with a new product which captured the market from the stencils.

Environmental analysis and diagnosis gives strategists time to anticipate opportunities and to plan to take optional responses to these opportunities. It also helps strategists develop an early warning system to prevent threats or develop strategies which can turn a threat to the firm's advantage.

In the 70 years between 1918 and 1988, almost half of the 100 largest American firms went out of business or became significantly less important to our society. Often a company becomes convinced that it is almost invincible and need not examine what is happening in the marketplace. When the company ceases to adjust the environment to its strategy or does not react to the demands of the environment by changing its

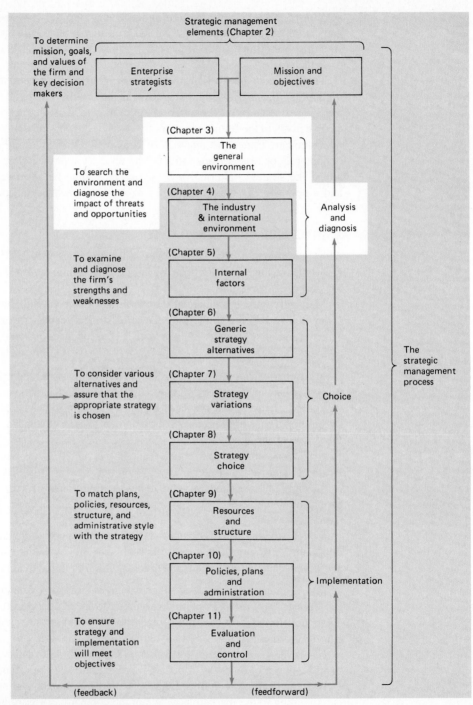

EXHIBIT 3.2   **A model of strategic management.**

strategy, the result is lessened achievement of corporate objectives. One extreme example was provided by W. T. Grant. That firm went bankrupt when it failed to meet competitive changes and the needs of its markets.

Managers need to search the environment to (1) determine what factors in the environment present threats to the company's present strategy and objectives accomplishment and (2) determine what factors in the environment present opportunities for a greater accomplishment of objectives through an adjustment in the company's strategy. Just as important, the analysis needs to recognize the inherent risks involved in trying to take advantage of opportunities. As has been observed, "opportunism without competence is a path to fairyland." And there are usually threats inherent in any opportunity.

Without systematic environmental search and diagnosis, the time pressures of the managerial job can lead to inadequately thought-out responses to environmental changes. It is clear that because of the difficulty of assessing the future, not all future events can be anticipated. But some can and are. To the extent that some or most are anticipated by this analysis and diagnosis process, managerial decisions are likely to be better. And the process reduces the time pressures on the few which are not anticipated. Thus the managers can concentrate on these few instead of having to deal with all the environmental opportunities and threats in a pressure-cooker environment.

Firms which systematically analyze and diagnose the environment are more effective than are those which don't. Successful firms do more and better environmental analysis and diagnosis than do failing firms. The amount and sophistication of the analysis and diagnosis meet the demands of the environment.

The primary responsibility for environmental analysis and diagnosis rests with top management in a single-SBU firm. In multiple-SBU firms, this responsibility is shared by the SBU top executives and corporate top managements. They may use corporate planners and consultants to help them with this task. How these strategists perform the analysis and diagnosis will be discussed at the end of the chapter.

Before that, this chapter will describe the sectors in the general environment that are to be analyzed and diagnosed; the techniques used for analysis; and who is likely to do environmental analysis. The next chapter examines the industry and international environments in more detail. And we provide an overall tool, the environmental threat and opportunity profile (ETOP), to help you combine the analyses in the strategic management process.

THE GENERAL ENVIRONMENT [3]

There are a large number of factors which affect the firm in each sector of the environment. And these factors interact with one another. Exhibit 3.3 shows these relationships for a typical integrated oil company.

There are many ways to organize the sectors for analysis and diagnosis. The categories used in this chapter are socioeconomic, technological, and governmental. (Note that Exhibit 3.3 includes these and other sectors to be covered in Chapter 4.) Let's examine each sector to determine the kinds of factors that need analysis and diagnosis.

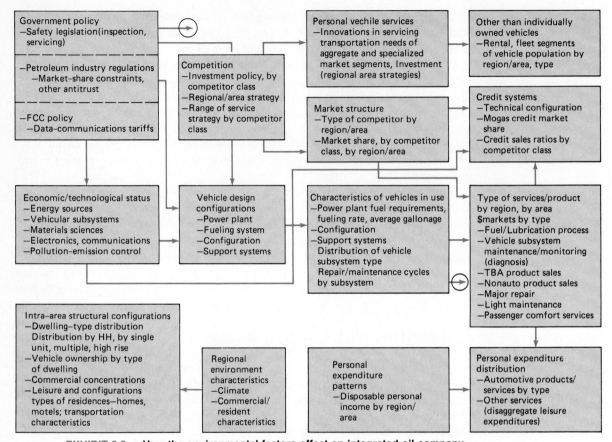

EXHIBIT 3.3 **How the environmental factors affect an integrated oil company.**
(H. Klein, "Incorporating Environmental Examination into the Corporate Strategic Planning Process,"
unpublished doctoral dissertation, Columbia University, New York, 1973.)

Socioeconomic Sector

There are a variety of factors which affect the demand for products and services and the costs of providing them. This section explores the economic, climatic, and social factors which help or hinder a firm in the attainment of objectives.

The Economy [4]

The state of the economy at present and in the future can affect the fortunes and strategy of the firm. The specific economic factors that many firms analyze and diagnose include:

• The stage of the business cycle. The economy can be classified as being in a depression, recession, recovery, or prosperity stage.

• The inflationary or deflationary trend in the prices of goods and services. If inflation is very severe, wage and price controls may be imposed.

• Monetary policies, interest rates, and devaluation or revaluation of the currency in relation to other currencies.
• Fiscal policies: tax rates for firms and individuals.
• Balance of payments, surpluses, or deficits in relation to foreign trade.

Each of these facets of the economy can help or hinder the achievement of a firm's objectives and lead to success or failure for the strategy. For example, recessions often lead to unemployment, which can lead to lower sales if the firm produces discretionary goods. If monetary policy is tightened, funds for needed plant additions may be too costly or unavailable. But other policies lead to interest-rate changes. As the interest rates rose in the late 1970s and early 1980s, less money was available for investment. As the cost of money declined in the mid-1980s, firms scrambled to refinance old debt, and more money then became available for new investment. Tax policies can reduce the attractiveness of investment in an industry or reduce the after-tax incomes of consumers, who then lower their spending levels. Changes in the balance of payments may either discourage trading partners from continuing to purchase goods from one another or encourage them to continue trading. In the early 1980s a large number of governments throughout the world were linking imports to exports, bartering goods, and protecting jobs.

Each of these facets can be an opportunity or a threat. For example, most people see inflation as a threat to corporate objectives. But for some industries, such as catalog merchandising, it has been an opportunity for better business. And disinflation is seen as a mixed blessing. High-inflation rates in the 1970s and early 1980s created the appearance that profits were good. With rates of inflation at only 3 or 4 percent in the mid-1980s, while costs were lower, firms couldn't raise prices as fast either. Hence, corporate profits, after subtracting for inflation, have been relatively flat. This has led to cost cutting, quality control, product diversification, and better debt management.

Business Week maintains that there are five separate economies in the United States.

1 *Old-line industry*. The basic manufacturing industry faces serious international competition and is in the throes of restructuring.

2 *Energy*. The United States has natural resources and good technology but can squeeze financing available to other industries.

3 *High technology*. This area can function independently of the rest of the U.S. economic scene and shows tremendous growth potential.

4 *Agriculture*. The United States has a temperate climate, and demand can grow with population, but the pace of productivity may slacken, leading to accelerating farm inflation.

5 *Services*. Employment should grow fast, and internationalization is likely; this sector should begin to show productivity gains.

Demand patterns, the availability of capital, inflation, the balance of payments, and the like affect these industries differently. So a change in economic conditions may be good for one firm but bad for another. Strategists must determine what economic factors are most important to their business and attempt to predict the changes which are likely in those conditions. That is, of course, easier said than done given the numerous explanations of why the economy operates as it does. But the best possible estimates of important economic conditions must be made as inputs for strategic decision making.

Climatic Factors [5]

Effective strategists often have climate and ecological concerns. Threats from unforeseen weather changes can be seen by firms whose products are seasonal. Ski resorts and manufacturers of snowmobiles and snowblowers were forced to change their evaluations and marketing methods when a low-snow winter occurred one year in the United States. One firm diversified into lawn mowers as a result. Large food distributors can be paralyzed by an abnormal storm that keeps their trucks off the road. Food processors may be caught with inadequate supplies because of an extended drought. However, several businesses derive opportunity by providing climate-forecasting services. One example is Oceanroutes, which employs 65 full-time meteorologists. They plot weather and sea conditions leading to the best routes for steamship lines so that time and fuel costs are minimized. Sears employs two weather forecasters for preseason and in-season decision making about inventories of merchandise such as air conditioners and snow tires. Finally, ecological issues such as the protection of endangered wildlife and the acid-rain controversy affecting the United States and Canada can affect plant location decisions and other strategic decisions. Vlasic decided to locate a pickle plant near the ocean so that the brine effluent would not foul fresh water.

Social Factors [6]

The last set of socioeconomic factors focuses on the values and attitudes of people—customers and employees—which can affect strategy. These values translate into lifestyle changes which affect the demand for products and services or the way firms relate to employees. Some examples may help you see how these factors can create threats and opportunity.

• In 1986, a government commission issued a report suggesting that pornography was creating social ills. Even though *Playboy* and some other magazines were deemed ''not obscene,'' some retailers under consumer pressure (such as Southland's 7-11 units) no longer carry this merchandise.

• At one time, it was thought that the normal thing for a family unit to do was to have two to four children. Today not all individuals accept this, and change of attitude has had a big impact on P&G (Pampers), Gerber (baby food), builders (houses versus condominiums), Mattel (toys), and others.

• It used to be common for retired people, single people, widows, and widowers to live with relatives. Now there is a trend toward living alone, and this has had a big impact on builders, appliance manufacturers, food packers, magazine publishers, and others.

• For years most married women stayed home. Now, most work. This has caused problems for firms that sold door to door (Avon and Fuller Brush) and has increased business for a variety of firms, such as those offering nursery school service, prepared foods, restaurants (two-employee families eat out more frequently), and home security systems, to name a few.

• At one time, people lived in one place. Now there are thousands of people who are nomads—almost like the bedouins of Jordan. They live in campers and motor homes and move from place to place as jobs open up or as the spirit moves them. This provides opportunities for and threats to firms.

• Increased education has led to new attitudes on the part of employees about how many hours they wish to work, the quality of life they expect at work, and the kind of supervisory style they expect can affect how strategies are developed and implemented. New benefits programs are also needed for new lifestyles.

• Ignoring different cultural values can mean the failure of new marketing programs. Campbell Soup withdrew from markets in Brazil because housewives believed they were not fulfilling homemaker roles if they served canned soups. And many ad campaigns lose their meaning or take on negative connotations when translated into another language.

• After the Three Mile Island nuclear plant incident, more people started to question the safety of nuclear power. New-plant construction and uranium mining in Canada, the United States, and Australia have been cut drastically, while coal operators are seeing new opportunities.

So strategists must keep up with changes in educational levels and social values in order to assess the potential impact on their strategies. Typical responses of firms to these social factors, however, vary from changes in their strategy or policies to attempts to change social values and attitudes through public-relations efforts. For example, Exhibit 3.4 shows one firm that changed strategy in response to social change.

EXHIBIT 3.4   DRINKING DRIVES SEAGRAM'S

SADD and MADD (Students or Mothers Against Drunk Driving) aren't the only societal groups affecting alcoholic consumption these days. Today's health-conscious young professional orders a salad and diet soda more often than bourbon and beef for lunch. Older executives too are skipping lunch in favor of a jog or a squash match. "The change is drastic, nationwide, and here to stay." In the words of one liquor executive, the shift is nothing less than "the sobering of America."

With public sentiment against drunk driving and "happy hours" growing, Congress pushing for a national drinking age of 21, and higher excise taxes taking effect in 1985, further declines in liquor sales seem inevitable.

Joseph E. Seagram & Sons has been driven to alter its strategy since its traditional strength in "brown liquors"

has witnessed a revenue drop of 4% in just two years. Not only is America drinking less alcohol, but vodka, gin, rum, and specialty liquors attract more buyers—areas where Seagram is weakest. Only Royal Crown Canadian experienced a jump in sales while 7 Crown and V.O. lost 6 to 7% in sales over a 4-year period in the mid 1980s.

Seagram is seeking product diversification (purchased Wine Spectrum from Coca-Cola), is stressing product development into sweeter and weaker drinks, is looking toward foreign markets where alcohol consumption is still growing, and is likely to make future beverage acquisitions. Clearly, Seagram's strategy is a response to sweeping social changes in its environment. Note that this "threat" is an opportunity for other firms, such as soft drink producers.

Source: Adapted from "How Seagram is Scrambling to Survive 'The Sobering of America,' " *Business Week* (Sept. 3, 1984), pp. 94–96.

Technological Sector [7]

Besides examining socioeconomic factors for their possible impact on products, markets, or ways of doing business, effective strategists search the environment for changing technology that might affect the firm's raw materials, operations, and products and services. Changing technology can offer major opportunities for improving goal achievement or threaten the existence of the firm. Examples of product and service breakthroughs include transistors, lasers, efficient batteries for electric cars, genetic farming, computers, miniature integrated circuits, xerography, and synthetic fibers. The change in production methods in the printing industry made possible by the use of computerized typesetting is an example of how changing technology affects operating procedures. Numerical control of machines and the use of industrial robots has revolutionized the structure of some industries. An example of changes in distribution is the use of computer-controlled "sails" on cargo ships. Raw materials change too. Some possible changes we see involving raw materials are the use of lignite by Phillips Petroleum, shale oil for petroleum, log houses, and garbage to generate electric power.

Technical change, of course, affects the product or service life cycle. The demand for a product or service seems to pass through a life cycle. At first, the product experiences remarkable sales growth. Then it matures, and finally it declines. Sometimes the cycle can lead to growth after decline has set in. It appears, for example, that the dairy business is declining, as is gasoline retailing. The hard-liquor business appears to be mature, as do theme parks and chain food stores. The U.S. fishing industry and home canning are examples of industries and activities which have experienced growth after decline. Firms spend a great deal of energy trying to determine where they are in the cycle so that they can decide how to invest their efforts. In some cases it is necessary to invest in research and development to improve products so that their life cycle can be extended or replace products near the end of their life cycle. In other cases, environmental scanning is needed to determine what technological change will mean to existing products in terms of production processes. Technological change can also affect distribution methods, raw materials, or the skills needed by the work force.

Whether technological change comes fast or slow is a function of the creativity of people, receptiveness on the part of industry, and the availability of venture capital. For instance, 16 U.S. electronics companies want to start a joint venture to do R&D to counter the erosion in competitive ability versus the competitive ability of the Japanese. While such a venture would provide more funds than any one firm could muster, there is a concern about antitrust implications. So government incentives through tax policies, funding, and regulations also play a role in technological change. In the mid-1980s, America's scientific establishment sounded alarms because of declining and tight government budgets. Both universities and industry have become dependent on governments for almost half their funding. The concern is that further declines in R&D expenditures could erode long-term competitive advantage for U.S.-based businesses.

A willingness to innovate and take risks also seems to be a critical component. Furthermore, technological change requires a receptive socioeconomic climate, as suggested in Exhibit 3.5. Even so, investments in technology involve other risks. For

EXHIBIT 3.5   HAVE TV, WILL TRAVEL

Videoconferencing technology has been available for some time as a substitute for travel-weary corporate managers. The Picturephone was displayed at the 1964 World's Fair by AT&T. The convenience of conducting business meetings over long distances via the TV screen, however, has been offset by high prices, poor picture quality, and human aversion to substitutes for face-to-face meetings.

Now the first two problems are being tackled. Recent advances in special computers which code signals into digital computer bits have allowed costs to decline and quality of transmission to improve. Sears installed a network to link 26 cities for full-motion videoconferencing in 1985. And Exxon, Xerox, 3M, IBM, and others are expanding networks or jumping in, prompting speculation that smaller firms will follow. More conference rooms were wired in 1984 than were set up in the 3 previous years combined.

However, some firms still have trouble getting people to use the technology. Rockwell International requires workers to indicate in writing why videoconferencing cannot substitute for their proposed travel. Yet their system linking Dallas and Los Angeles is only used 30 hours a month, mainly for general business-review sessions. "It intimidates some people, and others just like to travel."

While travel savings are important, some companies believe this technology can offer a competitive edge. For example, Boeing completed a new aircraft development project ahead of schedule by linking executives, technicians, and pilots to make instant design decisions.

Still, the potential threat to the airlines will not make significant inroads until humans can be convinced that such technology satisfies their needs and can be used to accomplish their objectives.

Source: Adapted from "Videoconferencing: No Longer Just a Sideshow," *Business Week,* Nov. 12, 1984, pp. 116–120.

example, competing technologies (such as video discs vs. cassettes, or digital audio discs vs. digital tape) may require large investments without assurance that the technology will be accepted. Hence, threat and opportunity from technology also involves other factors.

Not all sectors of the economy are likely to be equally affected by technological change. Some sectors are more volatile than others. There are few good measures of likely volatility. One is the amount spent on research and development. One would expect that the more an industry spends, the more likely it is that changes will come. If this is true, the industries producing aircraft and missiles, communication equipment and electrical components, and drugs and medicine are much more volatile than the industries producing lumber, wood products, furniture, textiles, and primary ferrous metals. Strategists in industries affected by volatile technological change must be much more alert to changes than those in more stable industries. However, advanced indicators about the nature of change in technology are available; there is usually adequate time for strategists to prepare for the impact of change.

Government Sector [8]

Federal, state or provincial, and local governments increasingly affect how businesses operate. They legislate on such matters as wage and price controls, equal employment opportunity, safety and health at work, the way that consumer credit is administered, the place that the plant can be located, the chemicals that the plant can emit into the air, the amount of noise that the product can make, the way in which the firm can run advertising, and the kinds of ads that can be run. The laws and regulations change how businesses operate on a day-to-day basis.

Government philosophies about its relationships with business can change over time. This is an important aspect for strategists to examine. For instance, Exhibit 3.6 indicates some major milestones in the deregulation of three major U.S. industries. As these shifts took place, new threats and opportunities faced the firms in these industries and those connected to them. For instance, transportation costs, financial plans, and communications options have all been affected, to say nothing of the changing nature of competition in the industries directly affected.

Action by governments also affect the strategic choices of businesses. They can increase a business's opportunities or threats or sometimes both. Some examples of *opportunities* include the following:

• *Governments are large purchasers of goods and services.* It is estimated that about one-fifth of purchases are made by governments. In some industries, such as the aircraft and aerospace industries, they are the major purchasers. The U.S. General Services Administration spends over $5 billion a year on paint, pens, paper clips, desks, chairs, etc., to keep the bureaucracy going. Government policy decisions also create new industries or additional businesses. Examples include General Signal's business increase in mass transit equipment and in cleaning up water, banks' increase in business from collecting student education loans, the space shuttle program, and the manufacture of pipelines for transporting coal.

• *Governments subsidize firms and industries and thus help them survive and prosper.* For example, state and provincial governments subsidize by reducing property taxes and paying the entire cost or part of the cost of training new employees. Federal

EXHIBIT 3.6　MAJOR STEPS IN THE DEREGULATION OF FINANCE, TELECOMMUNICATIONS AND TRANSPORTATION

Finance		Telecommunications		Transportation	
1970	Federal Reserve frees interest rates on selected bank deposits	1968	Supreme Court decision permits non-AT&T equipment to be connected to AT&T's system	1978	Congress starts the process of airline deregulation
1975	SEC orders bankers to cease fixing commissions on stock sales	1969	FCC gives MCI the right to hook its long-distance system into local phone systems	1980	Congress deregulates trucking and railroads
1977	Merrill Lynch offers the Cook Management account in order to compete with banks	1974	Justice Department files antitrust suit against AT&T	1982	Congress deregulates intercity bus service
1980	Federal Reserve allows banks to pay interest on checking accounts	1979	FCC allows AT&T to sell nonregulated services	1986	Civil Aeronautics Board out of business
1981	Sears Roebuck becomes a one-stop financial supermarket	1984	AT&T divests its local phone companies		

Source: Adapted from: "Deregulating America," *Business Week*, Nov. 28, 1983, pp. 80–89.

governments subsidize directly by means of ownership or partial ownership in projects like Comsat, Amtrak, Via Rail Canada, British Leyland, and Air Canada. France and Japan seek to support industries where the government believes strength and opportunity best match. The federal government helped the U.S. shoe industry with a $56 million subsidy because of foreign competition, funneled $2.2 billion of its business to minority-owned firms, gives tax breaks to AT&T, bailed out Chrysler, subsidizes new experiments in energy with ERDA money, and provides firms with patents and royalty protections.

• *Governments protect home producers against "unfair" foreign competition.* Governments do this by imposing import restrictions, tariffs, and antidumping provisions. The steel and shoe industries are benefiting further at present. Governments also help exporters by participating in trade treaties.

• *Government policy changes can lead to increases in opportunities and new business for firms.* If firms are willing to search the government environment and respond to changes, business can increase. Banks can now pay interest on checking accounts, which can mean more business and profits for them—and more competition for the thrift institutions. The FCC has increased the number of TV stations, which means that there are more business opportunities for those wanting to start new stations and more competition for the present stations. NASA has created opportunity for numerous technological advancements, many of which have become consumer products.

Besides encouraging and helping, the government creates *threats* when it affects survival and profits negatively. Many laws and regulations can limit the strategic options of many firms. Some of these laws and regulations include the following:

• *U.S. and state antitrust laws which limit mergers.* Some mergers have been prevented by antitrust policies and lawsuits.

• *Government regulations that significantly affect the strategic options of whole industries.* States and provinces limit the ability of utilities to increase profits; thus the utilities have limited amounts for capital spending and the construction of new power plants. Indeed, Detroit Edison provides an example of the plight of several companies that started nuclear power plants in the late 1960s and early 1970s. Plans were announced in July 1968 for a new plant estimated to cost $230 million with targeted start-up in February, 1974. Because of licensing bottlenecks, new environmental rules, redesigns for new safety rules and nuclear waste storage, and the intervening inflation and interest costs due to delays, costs had risen to $3.1 billion with a start-up in 1985. The "nuclear" option doesn't even seem available to power companies at this point in time.

• *Governmental policies that change economic conditions, tax laws, etc., can create threats to individual businesses.* Exhibit 3.7 provides one example.

Aside from laws and regulations, government policy changes can lead to increases in threats to firms. As indicated above, policy changes can lead to opportunities for some firms and threats to others. But some produce mostly threats to industries. The EPA threatens the auto business. State laws controlling the weights of trucks limit where certain trucking businesses can compete. Antiredlining regulations limit where

EXHIBIT 3.7   TAXES CHANGE THE BUSINESS DEFINITION OF INTEGRATED RESOURCES

Integrated Resources faces a major business definition change as a result of shifts in governmental tax regulations.

Even though Integrated has acquired over $7 billion in real estate and has expertise in property investing, it is not a real estate company. And while it has about $6 billion of life insurance policies in force, it is not a life insurance company either. Integrated services over 125,000 clients who invested in about 500 tax-sheltered limited partnerships. Enter Congress and the IRS.

Congress has intensified its efforts to close tax loopholes and shut down tax-shelter sales companies. The Internal Revenue Service has challenged more and more tax-shelter deals, and uncertainty over future tax-code tightening further dims sales prospects.

According to one of the cofounders of Integrated, the best thing that could happen to Integrated would be for Congress to "leave the tax system alone for three to five years." But this doesn't seem to be in the cards.

Hence, Integrated is diversifying out of tax shelters, and some of its real estate programs have become less tax-oriented. The investment program dabbles in equipment leasing, energy, and cable TV. But two of the fastest growing segments of business are leveraged buy-outs of operating businesses and restaurant franchising. The company is thinking about marketing everything from variable annuities to mutual funds and money market accounts. Says one cofounder, "I would like to become a household word in managing finances."

It seems that governmental tax policy changes have moved this firm to rethink its basic mission definition.

Source: Adapted from "A Tax-Shelter Specialist That Wants to Change Its Spots," *Business Week*, Oct. 8, 1984, pp. 149–151.

a thrift institution can lend its money. And California almost passed a law that would have severely hurt the tobacco industry. Several states banned the sale of Tylenol when poison was found in one bottle.

A special case of a threat from the government is government competition with the private sector. From their beginnings, the U.S. and Canadian governments have performed certain services and produced certain products which put them in competition with firms. For example, Safeway Stores has to compete with U.S. military commissaries. A firm competing in the food industry or in some other industry likely to be involved with government competition must consider what government "firms," with no profit requirement and no tax payments, could do in the industry and must monitor the environment to see if the government is making moves toward entering the industry.

As in other sectors, threats to one firm may offer opportunities to another as a result of government actions. For instance, strict air-pollution regulation could threaten coal-burning utilities but provide opportunity for those who install smokestack scrubbers.

As you can see, government can be quite pervasive. In fact, it can influence every other environmental sector. Government strongly influences socioeconomic conditions through fiscal policy, zoning, and other regulations. It can thwart or promote innovation and technology directly or indirectly. It can affect supplies of labor and materials and especially supplies of capital. Government itself can be a direct competitor, or it can influence competition, for example through the enforcement of antitrust laws. An interesting example of how a typical firm can be affected is given in Exhibit 3.8.

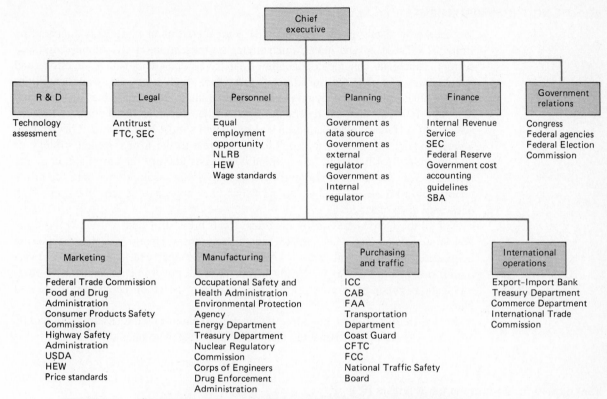

EXHIBIT 3.8   **Typical industrial corporation and federal government relations.**
(M. Weidenbaum, "Public Policy: No Longer a Spectator Sport for Business." Reprinted by permission from the Journal of Business Strategy, *vol. 1, no. 1 (Summer 1980). Copyright © 1980, Warren, Gorham and Lamont, Inc. 210 South St., Boston, Mass. All rights reserved.)*

It shows how a "shadow" organization of public officials matches the organization chart.

Corporations have finally come to the point where proactive postures are increasingly witnessed in efforts to influence government. Of course, there have always been attempts to influence legislators and regulators or public officials. But firms now are more willing to push for favorable rulings and even take regulators to court instead of negotiating. What perhaps bothers strategists most about government is uncertainty. Constant change or new interpretations or efforts make planning difficult. So political action committees and a variety of approaches are used to try to influence government actions and reduce uncertainty.

In sum, firms must search the environment, try to influence government policy, and try to seize the opportunities and mitigate the threats that government policy presents.

ANALYZING THE ENVIRONMENT

We have now discussed the sectors in the general environment typically analyzed by strategists. These are the items which strategists must monitor. By monitoring these sectors, strategists can identify conditions to determine their nature, function, and relationships. For example, social trends and values, such as concerns about smoking, may eventually find their way into government regulations. (Some states ban smoking in public facilities and the federal government has considered banning all tobacco advertising.) Hence, interrelationships among sectors must be analyzed. This leads to a determination of whether the condition is a threat to the firm's current strategy or an opportunity for the future. In addition, strategists identify the current strategy the firm uses to relate to the environment and reanalyze the assumptions about the firm's relationship to the environment, noting which ones appear to be still true and which ones may have changed.

Not all the factors are equally important to all firms. In Chapter 4 we will outline how strategists pay more attention to some than to others. Here, recall that the mission helps determine which aspects or sectors should be analyzed. For instance, TWA might look at the FCC as well as at the CAB in its governmental analysis if communication is seen as relevant to the mission of transportating people from place to place.

Before we move on to diagnosis, we want to explain how the environment can be analyzed, describe environmental analysis, and discuss who does the analysis.

Techniques for Environmental Analysis [9]

Earlier in the chapter, it was noted that the strategist assesses the future before making a diagnosis. This is done by forecasting. At this point, we will review *how* the strategist analyzes the environment. This analysis is done by means of a search of verbal and written information, spying, forecasting and formal studies, and information systems.

First of all, there is the gathering of verbal information, that is, information that we hear. This information can be gathered informally or formally (for example, at meetings and conferences).

Sources of verbal information include

- Such media as radio and television
- The firm's employees, such as peers, subordinates, and supervisors
- Others outside the firm, including (1) customers of the enterprise, (2) persons in the industry channels (for example, wholesalers and brokers), (3) suppliers doing business with the firm, (4) competitors and their employees, (5) financial executives such as bankers, stockholders, and stock analysts, (6) consultants, and (7) government and university employees.

Written or documentary information is what we learn by reading from information prepared by others for various purposes. Managers read newspapers, trade journals, industry newsletters, and general publications. In some firms top managers subscribe to clipping services, which search periodicals and papers and summarize the information for them. A number of experts point out that much can be learned from reading the annual reports and 10K's of significant competitors. The 10K is a very detailed annual report. The federal government requires that all firms listed on the stock exchange must submit a 10K to the Securities and Exchange Commission.

There are a number of sources which can tell you where to locate information on a business if you are searching the environment as a manager or analyzing a case as a student. A summary of a variety of information sources is appended to Chapter 4. The Freedom of Information Act in the United States allows competitors to acquire information about firms which do business with the government or which are in a regulated industry. However, attempts are being made to reduce the easy access to government information about competitors.

Another solution is to design a management information system (MIS) to bring the information to the strategists [10]. This approach formalizes the line and staff gathering of the information desired by the strategists on a regular basis. Many experts advocate this approach, although some feel that a formal MIS fails to work properly, since information is often limited, untimely, or unreliable. Another version of an MIS is a strategic information system (SIS), which some firms have developed. Strategic databases can be developed by relying on inputs from customers, suppliers, competitors, internal managers, the sales force, R&D units, and so on. These are often organized on the basis of answering questions which must be addressed in the strategic management process: What opportunities are available? What environmental conditions will affect us? What competitive actions will affect us? What strengths do we have? What weaknesses do we have? Strategic databases can be built from various information sources (see appendix to Chapter 4) such that the strategic management process is facilitated. Problems similar to the MIS are to get managers to accept and use the SIS adequately.

A third technique for environmental analysis, one normally used to gather information about potential or actual competitors, is spying. The top executive (or, more likely, a middle-level executive encouraged, however surreptitiously, by a top executive) employs an individual or individuals to determine trade secrets. The spy can be an employee of the competitor, one of the competitor's suppliers or customers, or a "professional" spy. Although it varies by industry and functional areas, industrial espionage appears to be increasing. This observation is based on survey data and expenditures on systems to protect trade secrets and industrial processes.

A fourth approach to analyzing the environment is formal forecasting [11]. Normally it is performed by corporate planners or other staff personnel or consultants at the request of top management. There is a group of consultants specializing in this called "futurists," and there are a number of journals dealing with this subject, such as *Technological Forecasting and Social Change, Journal of Environment and Planning, Early Warning Weekly, Futures,* and *Journal of Forecasting.*

The advent of personal computers and software to do economic forecasting has made it cheaper and easier to test many different policies or strategies with what-if scenarios. While there are problems with all models, most are a good tool to organize thinking.

All the factors in the environment have been subjected to forecasting, some more successfully than others. And a number of forecasting techniques are available. Another technique is polling. Many firms pay thousands of dollars yearly to receive reports of social attitudes about the economy, government, their products, and so on. Of course, market research departments can provide important pieces of environmental information as well.

Descriptions of Environmental Analysis [12]

In the previous section, we outlined the *prescription* for performing an analysis on all sectors of the environment. Here, we want to summarize the *descriptive* conclusions about these approaches.

First, strategists generally seem to be more concerned with the economy than with any other factors, although competition is also seen as important. Other factors become more important depending on the general state of the economy. Second, strategists do seem to spend a significant amount of time (up to 2 hours daily) analyzing the environment in some fashion, though this varies by industry. Third, the primary method is making verbal contacts inside and outside the firm, although this varies by level in the organization, with lower levels using more written sources. Fourth, formal prediction techniques such as forecasting, modeling, and using an MIS are viewed skeptically by many strategists, but the use of these techniques may be increasing. Finally, even though they are concerned, some executives may be psychologically unprepared to cope with change.

To summarize, there are several prescriptive implications of the realities of environmental analysis:

1 It is critical for strategists to develop an effective network of human sources to provide inputs for environmental analysis. These should be well-informed, knowledgeable sources inside the organization (in various functions and in all geographic areas) and outside the organization.

2 Those who favor MIS or SIS approaches must learn how to get their findings more quickly and more easily to this informal network if they are to have any impact at all. A strategic information system could help here.

This brings us to the role of managers in diagnosing the meanings of the findings of environmental analysis. They do not just react automatically to what they find—*they* must impute meaning to it and make decisions accordingly.

The Role of Strategists in Analysis and Diagnosis [13]

As discussed in Chapter 2, there are several groups of strategists involved in strategic management. How does each group relate to the environmental analysis and diagnosis phase of strategic management? Exhibit 3.9 summarizes this relationship.

As can be seen, the top managers of corporations or SBUs are involved in verbal search behavior and supplement their work with help from corporate planners and occasionally the board. Again, these people engage in verbal search and occasionally

EXHIBIT 3.9   THE ROLE OF STRATEGISTS IN THE ANALYSIS AND DIAGNOSIS OF THE ENVIRONMENT

	Analysis				
Strategists	Verbal search	Documentary search	Formal forecasts and studies	MIS/ SIS	Diagnosis and decision making
Top managers	Regularly	Rarely	Rarely	Rarely	Performs
Corporate planners	Regularly	Occasionally	Occasionally	Rarely	Advises as requested
Board of directors	Occasionally	Rarely	Rarely	Rarely	Occasionally advises
Consultants	Rarely	Occasionally	Rarely	NA	Occasionally hired to advise

use other methods of search. Then the top managers diagnose the significance of the findings. Let's examine that issue now.

DIAGNOSIS OF THE ENVIRONMENT

After analysis is complete, the strategists must diagnose the results. They assess the significance of the opportunities and threats discovered by the analysis of environmental conditions.

In Chapter 1, we discussed the conditions under which decisions would be made. The first condition was that the strategists perceive a gap between expected accomplishment and desired accomplishment. This is the decision-recognition phase. The environmental analysis may indicate a gap due to threats or opportunities. Once this is recognized, the strategists focus on the threats and opportunities if they are motivated to improve the future and feel that the company can do something to close a gap which may exist due to environmental factors.

The diagnosis requires the strategists to decide which sets of information to believe and which data to ignore, and to evaluate some information as important and other information as less important. This is the heart of diagnosis.

In Chapter 2, we discussed the strategists and their jobs and values. Since they are doing the diagnosis, it is useful to recall that value systems, internal power, etc., are important to the strategic management process. Here, similar factors emerge to affect a diagnosis of the environment: factors about the strategists, factors about the strategist's job, factors about the group of strategists, factors in the strategist's environment.

Diagnosis and Strategists' Characteristics [14]

A large number of characteristics of the strategist determine how well and whether the strategist diagnoses opportunities in and threats from the environment. Only a few can be discussed here.

The more *relevant experience* the strategist has, the greater the tendency to do a more accurate and higher-quality diagnosis. Older executives take longer to diagnose but usually do a better job of it. Cognitive capabilities can also be developed through training and education to improve diagnostic ability (one of the reasons for this book).

The *higher the aspiration* level of the strategist—in other words, the more motivated the executive is—the better the diagnosis (assuming data are available and used). Motivation is affected by the strategist's needs (for example, the need for achievement, the need for affiliation, and the need for power) and the rewards received for performance. Diagnosis may not be effectively performed if the rewards are based on short-run actions and results. This leads to behavior which may not be conducive to good diagnosis. A junior-level marketing executive is rewarded for today's and this week's sales, not for sales forecasting. A junior-level operations executive is rewarded for getting today's work out, not for planning a plant addition for 5 years from now. The junior accountant is rewarded for getting statements out on time. If the whole career learning is based on speedy feedback and rewards for short-run results, the executives carry these behavior patterns into senior management positions.

Individuals' perceptions of the environment are based upon their predispositions for dealing with the uncertainty of information. The *perceptual mode* influences the kind of diagnosis made. Persons who are *risk-aversive* will perform environmental analysis conservatively, analyzing and diagnosing one attribute at a time. Those who are willing to take risks will focus on gambling, varying more than one attribute at a time. Risk seekers vs. risk averters also react differently to environmental conditions. Some see the glass half empty, others see it half full. Some are *reflective,* while others are *impulsive.* Some strategists take a small amount of information and seek a speedy "gestalt closure." They impulsively diagnose and quickly act. Executives who are *dogmatic,* whose "minds are made up," make rapid diagnoses on the basis of inadequate information. Some strategists are so dogmatic that they tend to ignore the environment, or they believe it to be more stable than it really is. (For example, Singer executives believed that their sewing machine business was in great shape in 1979.) Many organizations have found it useful to include in their executive group an individual who disagrees with the basic belief systems of the other executives to make sure that contrary possibilities are brought up and discussed. This is the maverick executive, or the devil's advocate. People with *abstract conceptual structures* process many dimensions of information and use a complex approach to integration. The ability to deal with abstract aspects is valuable for the diagnosis of changes in the environment.

The *psychological mood* at the time of diagnosis (or any decision) can make an executive feel optimistic or pessimistic. Problems in their private lives can make them devote less time to diagnosis or give them a pessimistic attitude toward diagnosis and analysis.

Other than the mood at the time, the psychological ability to accept change is important to environmental diagnosis (and the entire strategic management process). It is widely observed that people resist change. This is not just perversity. We spend our time and use our ego building present procedures and ways of doing things. To change these is to experience in a small way death and predeath, retirement. If the old ways must change, the "old" executives can be threatened.

All these factors and more in the strategist determine whether diagnosis takes place, how well diagnosis is performed, and some of the outcomes of the diagnosis. For instance, if the strategist is risk-oriented and optimistic, a greater search for change is likely. Opportunities are more likely to be perceived than threats from the same data. Moreover, a *proactive* rather than *reactive* posture is likely to result. That is, strategies to force change can result. This is most easily seen in the technology sector. Proactive innovators create change; others react. While changes in some sectors of the environment are beyond *control,* they are not beyond the *influence* of strategists.

Diagnosis and the Strategist's Job [15]

The second set of factors influencing diagnosis concerns the nature of the executive's job. Several factors seem important.

Time pressures and stress seem to reduce the emphasis placed on environmental analysis and diagnosis. Executives can have many things to do; for example, they meet customers, promote people, and handle ordinary tasks. And ordinary short-run tasks have a way of filling up the day. Simon called this phenomenon "Gresham's law of planning": present pressing duties drive out long-run consideration. It should be pointed out that top managers can create the conditions for more or less stress by means of effective delegation and similar management techniques.

The *significance of the decision* will influence how much time executives devote to diagnosis. More time is given if the relative impact of a "correct" diagnosis is great.

If the firm has substantial *resources,* it can take the time and use extensive resources to analyze and diagnose the environment. If the resource base is weak, this may prevent effective diagnosis.

If managers believe that they have *discretion* to make decisions, they will engage in search activities more so than if they feel they are unable to make a decision. This applies more to the activities of SBU executives than to the activities of top corporate managers.

Diagnosis and the Group of Strategists [16]

In many cases, diagnosis is performed by several strategists—the top management team. The kind and amount of diagnosis which takes place will be affected by the presence or absence of *team spirit,* the extent to which the strategists are a *cohesive group* (without serious conflict), and by the *power plays* which may be taking place within this group. If there is significant conflict, diagnosis may become a battle: if one executive diagnoses the situation one way, a rival will take the opposite position. If there is good team spirit, all can bring their talents to the diagnosis and probably improve the process. However, Janis cautions that if the group is overly cohesive, it may make an inaccurate diagnosis or ignore important information. As before, a devil's advocate may be a useful addition to a top management group.

Descriptively, you should be aware that planning groups may believe that top management is not prepared to deal with change. As a result, senior managers may be shielded from bad news or threats in the environment.

THE ENVIRONMENT-STRATEGY INTERFACE [17]

The preceding sections indicate that the process of diagnosis is affected by a number of factors. But how do firms use the diagnosis?

Managers view the impact of their environment in different ways. Some see ambiguity (uncertainty) as threatening and some see it as opportunistic. Some perceive changes as threats or opportunities which merely require adaptation of the organization or its strategy. In other words, many executives respond reactively to change. Others view their environment proactively. They seek to make choices about which parts of the environment can be manipulated and then seek to set up a strategy to start manipulating. For example, in the governmental sector, firms set up political action committees or use public relations offices to influence governmental policy and decision makers in ways favorable to them. In the technological sector, some firms scan the research and then move their labs in the direction the technology appears to be moving. Other firms seek to strike out on their own to gain acceptance for the technological direction in which they have chosen to proceed.

A very interesting descriptive study of how firms deal with technological changes in the environment serves to point out that a variety of strategic choices are actually made by firms. Cooper et al. studied how diesels replaced steam locomotives, transistors affected vacuum tubes, ball-point pens affected fountain pens, nuclear plants affected fossil-fuel boilers, and electric razors challenged safety razors. Some of the key findings follow:

- Sales of the old technology continued to expand, in some cases 40 years after the new technology was introduced.
- When sales did decline, it took from 2 to 11 years for sales of the new technology to exceed sales of the old one.
- New technologies often created new markets and invaded old markets by capturing a series of submarkets sequentially.
- The commercial introduction of new technology often was made by a firm outside the traditional industry.
- All but one of 15 firms made an effort to participate in the new technology, three by acquisition.
- An early and rapid commitment to new technology was often unsuccessful.
- The old technology reached its highest stage of development after new technology was introduced, and all companies continued to invest heavily in the old technology.

A number of implications can be drawn from this study. But a major conclusion is that strategic responses to environmental threats can vary significantly. Moreover, there is ample time to respond to environmental change, and attempts to influence the nature of the change and its impact can be made. Furthermore, environmental assessment seems to require a broader definition of the scope of the firm's mission so that the firm can detect changes occurring outside the traditional view of its industry. Finally, it may be relatively difficult to change past strategy, even in view of significant competitive threats.

Thus while environmental assessment is a critical process, you should also be aware

EXHIBIT 3.10   A LONG-TERM ECONOMIC ASSUMPTION GUIDES THIS STRATEGY

Andre Horn, chairman of Joy Manufacturing, is a believer in economic theory. In the fall of 1981, Joy used the controversial "long-wave" theory of Russian economist Nikolai Kondratieff to foresee the worst recession in decades. Months ahead of competitors, Joy dropped uncompetitive businesses and cut its work force in half. Despite a 37 percent drop in sales, Joy stayed in the black in 1983 while most rivals suffered losses.

Horn believes that the world economy is in a 10-year transition period between two 45- and 60-year growth cycles. During the transition, which Horn believes began in 1979, the United States is shedding excess capacity. A sustained growth period should begin in 1990 according to this theory. In step with these cycles, Joy has laid out a strategy to survive early in the transition and then to reposition itself for the next upturn by increasing its presence in capital goods.

Horn is once again warning that capital goods producers will face another wrenching downturn during the 1980s. This time, instead of slimming down, Joy is embarking on an acquisition plan to double its size by 1990.

In this case, long-term economic assumptions have led to a sequential strategy of retrenchment to be followed by expansion. Note that perceptions of threat and opportunity, and strategic choices, varied based on economic assumptions.

Source: Adapted from "Joy Mfg.: Out to Double Its Size as It Predicts a 1990s Boom in Capital Goods," *Business Week,* Apr. 9, 1984, pp. 61–62.

that internal conditions may vary and consequently constrain the very usefulness of this process.

Exhibit 3.10 indicates how one firm has made some long-term economic assumptions and pursues a strategy to fit these expectations. Again, there appear to be a variety of ways that firms can choose to look at the general environment. And strategic choices about how to deal with the environment allow for substantial managerial discretion.

SUMMARY

It is the crucial job of top management to create the conditions for effective analysis and diagnosis of the environment. This means that the management must determine what factors in the environment are most crucial, which in turn influences what information will be gathered and where in the enterprise it will be analyzed and diagnosed.

The general environment includes factors in several sectors outside the firm which can lead to opportunities or threats. These include the socioeconomic, technological, and governmental sectors.

Strategists try to cope with the environment through analysis and diagnosis. Environmental analysis is the process by which strategists monitor the environmental settings. Analysis is the process of identifying observed conditions (socioeconomic, technological, etc.) in order to determine whether they present a threat for existing strategy or an opportunity for a new strategy. Environmental diagnosis consists of decisions made as a result of the environmental analysis. These decisions are an assessment of the significance of the opportunities and threats discovered by the analysis. In effect, diagnosis is an opinion resulting from an analysis of the facts to determine the nature of a problem with a view toward acting to take advantage of an opportunity or to effectively manage a threat. Exhibit 3.1 outlined the analysis and diagnosis process to examine the important gaps associated with the environment.

Propositions 3.1 and 3.2 summarize why environmental analysis and diagnosis is performed.

Proposition 3.1

A firm whose strategy fits the needs of its environment will be more effective.

Proposition 3.2

The major causes of growth, decline, and other large-scale changes in firms are factors in the environment, not internal developments.

The chapter discussed in some detail the three sectors in the general environment which strategists analyze and diagnose.

- The socioeconomic sector includes economic, climatic, and social factors.
- The technological sector affects raw materials, operations, and the product or service life cycle.
- The government sector seems to be increasingly important, since its roles include tax collector, regulator, competitor, customer, researcher, and supplier. It has an impact on every other environmental sector.

Then the methods of analyzing the environment were discussed. The methods used include the gathering of verbal and written information, the use of clipping services, the use of management information systems (MIS), formal forecasting, and spying. The conclusions of this section can be summarized in Propositions 3.3. to 3.5.

Proposition 3.3

Most top managers gather information about the environment verbally. Written information, forecasting, and MIS are not significant sources of information for analyses by top managers, but their use may be increasing.

Proposition 3.4

The more information contacts the strategist seeks, the better is the environmental analysis. In larger organizations, the contacts are primarily internal. In smaller organizations, the contacts are normally external.

Proposition 3.5

The more sectors and the more factors that are analyzed, the more effective is the environmental analysis.

Next we examined the role of the strategists in environmental analysis and diagnosis. Again, the top managers are the crucial analysts and diagnosticians. They may be helped by a corporate planning staff and consultants in larger organizations.

Then we discussed the diagnosis of the data generated in analysis. How the data are diagnosed depends on

- Factors concerning the strategist, such as experience, motivation, perception, and psychological mood
- Factors related to the strategist's job, such as time pressures and stress, resource availability, and discretion
- Factors in the strategist's group, such as team spirit, cohesiveness, and power plays

Environmental analysis and diagnosis is a crucial part of the strategic management process. If the environment is ignored (or partially ignored) by strategic decision makers, the process cannot be effective. Effective strategists try to anticipate what is coming, or attempt to influence the environment in favorable directions. Usually the lead time for change is long, not overnight. This requires a long-term strategic vision and commitment to strategic management. As Cooper points out, diesel locomotives were first built in 1924 and received great publicity. But it was not until 1934 that General Motors produced its first diesel, and the Baldwin and Lima Companies remained in the steam locomotive field even after 20 years of declining sales (and increasing diesel sales).

If a firm focuses its analysis primarily internally, in all but the most stable environments its strategic management process will also be less effective. You should recognize that environmental analysis interrelates with the formation of objectives, the generation of alternative strategies, and the other aspects of strategic management.

Chapter 4 examines in more detail some other sectors of the environment managers focus on as well. Many of the approaches and factors discussed here for the general environment also apply to diagnosis of the industry and international environments. We won't repeat those ideas. But we will introduce other tools for diagnosis to help summarize conclusions from the analysis of the general, industry, and international environments. The sectors of the general environment described here must be added to those from the industry and international environments for a comprehensive picture of threats and opportunities for the firm and its strategy.

REFERENCES

[1] The Role of the Environment in Strategic Management

Aguilar, F.: *Scanning the Business Environment* (New York: Macmillan, 1967).

[2] The Importance of Environmental Analysis

Bourgeois, L. J.: "The Environmental Perceptions of Strategy Makers and Their Economic Correlates," working paper, University of Pittsburgh, 1978.

Grinyer, P. H., and D. Norburn: "Planning for Existing Markets: Perceptions of Executives and Financial Performance," *Journal of Royal Statistical Society,* vol. 138 (1975), part I, pp. 70–97.

[3] Categorizing the Environment

Lenz, R. T. and J. L. Engledow: "Alternative Models for Analyzing Organizational Environments," working paper, Graduate School of Business, Columbia University, 1983.

[4] Economic Factors

"America's Restructured Economy," *Business Week,* June 1, 1981, pp. 55–100.

Farrell, C., T. Mason, and R. Mitchell: "The Rush is On to Cut the Cost of Debt," *Business Week,* Mar. 24, 1986, pp. 33–34.

Menosh, E., K. Pennar, S. Weiss, and D. Cook: "Living with Disinflation," *Business Week,* July 15, 1985, pp. 54–60.

Pennar, K., N. Jonas, S. Bartlett, H. Gleckman, and B. Riemer: "Hooray for Cheap Money," *Business Week,* Mar. 24, 1986, pp. 30–33.

Toffler, A.: *The Third Wave* (New York: Morrow, 1980).

[5] Climatic Factors

"Perverse Weather," *Business Week,* Feb. 27, 1978, pp. 60ff.

"Struggling to Cope without Snow," *Business Week,* Feb. 18, 1980, p. 66.

[6] Social Factors

Burck, C.: "Changing Habits in American Drinking," *Fortune,* Oct. 1976, pp. 156–161, 164 ff.

"Bidding for an Elusive Market," *Business Week,* Nov. 7, 1977, p. 72.

"Campbell Soup Fails to Make It to the Table," *Business Week,* Oct. 12, 1981, p. 66.

Higgins, J. C., and D. Romano: "Social Forecasting: An Integral Part of Corporate Planning?" *Long Range Planning* (April 1980), pp. 82–86.

"New Benefits for New Lifestyles," *Business Week,* Feb. 11, 1980, pp. 111–112.

Sease, D.: "The Nomads," *The Wall Street Journal,* Aug. 21, 1978.

[7] Technological Factors

Chase, M.: "U.S. Electronics Firms Consider Joining in Research Venture to Counter Japanese," *The Wall Street Journal,* Mar. 1, 1982, p. 7.

Clark, E., and A. Hall: "America's R&D Establishment Is Not Just Crying Wolf," *Business Week,* Mar. 24, 1986, p. 38.

"The Dark Side of the Business Tax Cuts," *Business Week,* June 11, 1984, pp. 135–138.

Sahal, D.: *Patterns of Technological Innovation* (Reading, Mass.: Addison-Wesley, 1981).

"Thinner Cream for the Dairy Business," *Business Week,* July 31, 1978.

Ulman, N.: "Bon Voyage: After Years of Decline, U.S. Fishing Industry Is Beginning to Boom," *The Wall Street Journal,* July 25, 1977.

"Vanishing Innovation," *Business Week,* July 3, 1978.

Wasson, C.: *Dynamic Competitive Strategy and Product Life Cycle* (St. Charles, Ill: Challenge Books, 1974).

[8] Governmental Factors

"Behind AT&T's Change at the Top," *Business Week,* Nov. 6, 1978.

"Breaking a Bottleneck in Long Haul Trucking," *Business Week,* Mar. 6, 1978.

"Business Comes Out Swinging at Regulators," *Business Week,* Apr. 7, 1980, p. 112.

"Deregulating America," *Business Week,* Nov. 28, 1983, pp. 80–89.

"General Signal Cashes In on Federal Dollars," *Business Week,* Mar. 21, 1977.

Shipper, F. and M. M. Jennings: *Business Strategy for the Political Arena* (Westport, Conn.: Greenwood Press, 1984).

"Too Many Cereals for the FTC," *Business Week,* Mar. 20, 1978.

"Where Utilities and Antinuclear Activists Agree," *Business Week* Apr. 16, 1984, pp. 185–187.

[9] Techniques for Environmental Analysis

Bowman, E.: "Strategy, Annual Reports, and Alchemy," *California Management Review,* vol. 20 (Spring 1978), pp. 64–71.

Fahey, L., and V. K. Narayanan: *Macro Environmental Analysis for Strategic Management* (St. Paul, Minn.: West, 1986).

Montgomery, D. et al.: "The Freedom of Information Act: Strategic Opportunities and Threats," *Sloan Management Review* (Winter 1978), pp. 1–13.

Thietart, R. A., and R. Vivas: "Strategic Intelligence Activity: The Management of the Sales Force as a Source of Strategic Information," *Strategic Management Journal,* vol. 2 (1981), pp. 15–25.

[10] The MIS System for Analysis

Hershey, R.: "Competitive Intelligence for the Smaller Company," *Management Review,* vol. 66 (January 1977), pp. 18–22.

King, W. R. and D. Cleland: "The Strategic Information Subsystem," *Strategic Planning and Policy* (New York: Van Nostrand Reinhold, 1978).

Mintzberg, H.: *Impediments to the Use of Management Information* (New York: National Association of Accountants, 1975).

Radford, K. J.: "Some Initial Specifications for a Strategic Information System," *Omega,* vol. 6 (1978), pp. 139–144.

[11] Forecasting

Armstrong, J. S.: *Long Range Forecasting* (New York: Wiley, 1985).

————: "How Expert are the Experts?" *INC* (December 1981), pp. 15–16.

Holloway, C.: "Does Futures Research Have a Corporate Role?" *Long Range Planning* (October 1978), pp. 17–24.

"How Personal Computers Are Changing the Forecaster's Job," *Business Week,* Oct. 11, 1984, pp. 123–124.

LeBell, D., and O. J. Krasner: "Selecting Environmental Forecasting Techniques from Business Planning Requirements," *Academy of Management Review* (July 1977), pp. 373–383.

Rippe, R.: "The Integration of Corporate Forecasting and Planning," *Columbia Journal of World Business,* vol. 11 (Winter 1976), pp. 54–61.

Wheelwright, S., and S. Makridakis: *Forecasting Methods for Management* (New York: Wiley, 1977).

[12] What Executives Analyze

Glueck, W. F.: *Business Policy and Strategic Management,* 3d ed. (New York: McGraw-Hill, 1980).

"Japan's Business Intelligence Beehive," *Business Week,* Dec. 14, 1981, p. 52.

Lewis, M. F.: "Assessment of Environmental Issues—A Three-Industry Comparison," paper presented at the Academy of Management meeting, New York, 1982.

[13] Who Does Environmental Analysis

Engledow, J. L., and R. T. Lenz: "Whatever Happened to Environmental Analysis?" *Long Range Planning,* vol. 18 (April 1985), pp. 93–106.

——— and ———: "The Evolution of Environmental Analysis Units in Ten Leading Edge Firms," working paper #S.C. 39, Graduate School of Business, Columbia University, 1984.

Preble, J. F.: "The Selection of Delphi Panels for Strategic Planning Purposes," *Strategic Management Journal,* vol. 5 (1984), pp. 157–170.

[14] Strategists' Characteristics Affecting Diagnosis

Duncan, R. B.: "Characteristics of Organizational Environments and Perceived Environmental Uncertainty," *Administrative Science Quarterly,* vol. 17 (1972), pp. 313–327.

Miller, D., M. F. R. deVries, and J. Toulouse: "Top Executive Locus of Control and the Relationship to Strategy Making, Structure, and Environment," working paper, McGill University, Montreal, December 1980.

O'Hanlon, T.: "Behind the Snafu at Singer," *Fortune,* Nov. 5, 1979, pp. 76–80.

Taylor, R.: "Psychological Determinants of Bounded Rationality," *Decision Sciences,* vol. 6 (July 1975), pp. 409–429.

———: "Age and Experience as Determinants of Managerial Information Processing and Decision Making Performance," *Academy of Management Journal,* vol. 18 (1975).

[15] Job Characteristics Affecting Diagnosis

Anderson, C. et al.: "Managerial Response to Environmentally Induced Stress," *Academy of Management Journal,* vol. 20 (1977), pp. 260–272.

Dickson, J.: "The Relation of Individual Search Activity to Subjective Job Characteristics," *Human Relations,* vol. 29 (1976), pp. 911–928.

ElSawy, O. A.: "Understanding the Process by Which Chief Executives Identify Strategic Threats and Opportunities," *Academy of Management Proceedings,* 1984, pp. 37–40.

Simon, H.: *Administrative Behavior: A Study of Administrative Processes in Administrative Organization,* 3d ed. (New York: Free Press, 1976).

[16] Group Factors Affecting Diagnosis

Janis, I. L.: *Victims of Groupthink* (Boston: Houghton Mifflin, 1972).

[17] The Environment-Strategy Interface

Aplin, J. C., and W. H. Hegarty: "Political Influence: Strategies Employed by Organizations to Impact Legislation in Business and Economic Matters," *Academy of Management Journal,* vol. 23 (1980), pp. 438–450.

Boulton, W. R., W. M. Lindsay, S. G. Franklin, and L. W. Rue: "Strategic Planning: Determining the Impact of Environmental Characteristics and Uncertainty," *Academy of Management Journal,* vol. 25 (1982), pp. 500–509.

Cooper, A. et al.: "Strategic Responses to Technological Threats," *Proceedings of the Academy of Management* (1973).

Jauch, L. R. and K. L. Kraft: "Strategic Management of Uncertainty," *Academy of Management Review,* vol. 11 (1986), pp. 777–790.

Lenz, R. T.: "Environment, Strategy, Organization Structure and Performance: Patterns in One Industry," *Strategic Management Journal,* vol. 1 (July–September 1980), pp. 209–226.

Smircich, L., and C. Stubbart: "Strategic Management in An Enacted World," *Academy of Management Review,* vol. 10 (1985), pp. 724–736.

CHAPTER OUTLINE

CHAPTER 4

THE INDUSTRY AND INTERNATIONAL ENVIRONMENT

OBJECTIVES

* To introduce the sectors in the industry environment which should be analyzed and diagnosed
* To introduce the international environment
* To examine ways the industry environment can be analyzed
* To introduce the environmental threat and opportunity profile (ETOP) for summarizing the results of analysis and diagnosis of the environment
* To indicate how the ETOP can be used in the strategic management process

INTRODUCTION

This is the second chapter that focuses on the analysis and diagnosis of environmental factors that present threats and opportunities to the firm. Exhibit 3.1 listed the general, the industry, and the international environments as areas strategists must examine for factors which could lead to strategic gaps. The last chapter introduced the general environment and described various aspects of performing analysis and diagnosis. As Exhibit 4.1 indicates, this chapter describes the industry and international environments. It also provides additional techniques for analyzing these sectors of the environment, as well as an overall tool—the environment threat and opportunity profile—which can be used to summarize all the environmental conditions to help focus the diagnosis on the most significant factors affecting the strategy of the firm. The appendix provides some sources of information that you can use to find information on all the sectors of the environment.

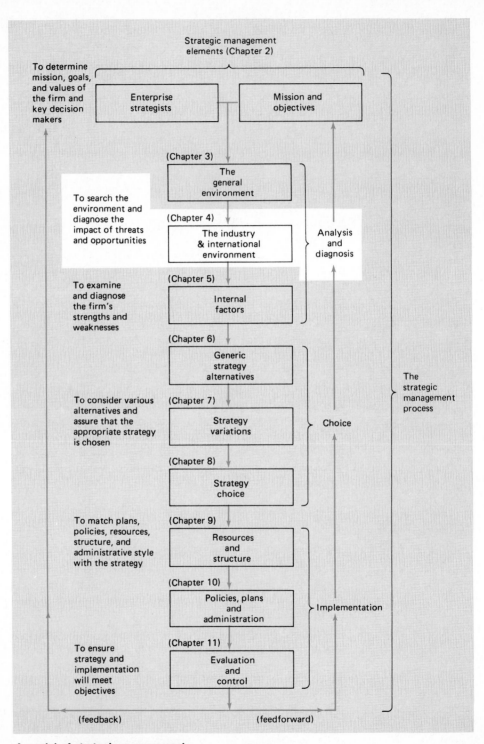

EXHIBIT 4.1   **A model of strategic management.**

THE INDUSTRY ENVIRONMENT [1]

The strategies and objectives of a firm (or its SBUS) will be affected by the attractiveness of the industry in which it chooses to do business and its relative competitive position within that industry. An industry can be conceived of as a set of firms which are in competition with one another for customers of their goods and services and which rely upon others that supply critical inputs (supplies). This section of the chapter describes these three sectors of the industry environment—customers, suppliers, and competitors.

Customer Sector

Effective strategists are concerned with who their customers are and their customers' needs and desires. They are also interested in who and where potential customers might be and trends in the future which may lead to changes in customer buying patterns. In effect, opportunities come through identifying and providing for customer utilities, and threats come from failures to meet changing customer requirements. This sector explores three factors that strategists include as part of their industry analysis of the customer sector—buyer identification, demographic factors which create changes in certain customer classes, and geographic locations of markets.

Buyer Identification [2]

Different customers have various reasons for interest in a product or service. They have needs, desires, or requirements to be satisfied by the purchase. Marketers generally indicate three distinct classes of customers. Each of these groups have somewhat different factors that affect their decisions to purchase, as illustrated in Exhibit 4.2.

EXHIBIT 4.2   FACTORS INFLUENCING DIFFERENT BUYERS

Consumers		
Availability	Price	Variety
Convenience	Quality	Warranty
Credit	Reputation	

Retailers and/or Wholesalers	
Competitive product	Product turnover
Consumer recognition	Profit potential
Product availability	Promotional and merchandising support
Product line breadth	Supply dependability

Industrial and/or Institutional Buyers		
Cost vs. profitability	Price	Product performance
Financing	Product information	Source availability
Legal conformity	Product line	Technical assistance

These factors vary in importance depending on the type of product as well. For instance, industrial purchasers of durable goods may be less concerned with price and more concerned with setup or maintenance costs of equipment as a factor in their own profitability. These same purchasers may be very price-sensitive to commodities (such as pens or paper). Exhibit 4.3 indicates how consumer products firms are adapting their strategies as consumer needs have shifted and as demographic changes (discussed below) have come into play.

Strategists identify the nature of these customers and their utilities in order to avoid threats of loss of customers and to find or create opportunities for themselves to find new customers or sell more to existing ones. Again, these customers and their needs may not be static. Our next section indicates a critical factor in the consumer segment to which environmental analysts should pay close attention.

Demographic Factors [3]

There are several important conditions associated with the general population that affect the market for goods and services for different industries. Economists and marketing experts often refer to these as "primary demand factors." The most important of these are as follows:

• *Changes in population.* As the total population changes, the demand for products or services changes. If there are fewer people to buy a good or service, this affects the primary demand for products and services. The population growth rate for the United States, Canada, and the rest of the developed world is declining. The Third

---

EXHIBIT 4.3   THE NEW CONSUMER MAKEUP

The blush is off the cosmetics markets due to changes in the consumers of makeup and their needs and desires. The last big surge was fueled by baby-boom girls who started wearing makeup as teenagers and continued to be heavy users as they moved into the work force in record numbers. But recently, revenues have been flat, and long-term trends look ominous. Avon, Max Factor, and Revlon have suffered large profit declines and loss of market share.

While the number of working women is expected to continue rising, the population of teenagers is declining. With more women working, fewer are left at home to answer the door when a sales representative calls, and fewer are available to become members of the sales force. Moreover, working women have less time and are apt to buy makeup where they do the rest of their shopping—the food stores and discount outlets. Another factor is the shifting reasons believed to motivate the purchaser. Notes a vice president at Revlon, who sells both mass-market and prestige brands, "Cosmetics companies used to sell fantasies and dreams. Women now buy reality and value."

To keep pace with changing consumer lifestyles, values, and demographics, cosmetics firm are using several strategies. Shifts in distribution approaches are being made. For example, Avon now sells at the office. New customers—men—are being targeted by Estee Lauder's skin-care products. And many firms are expanding product lines, revising old products, and changing advertising practices. Clearly, changing patterns of purchase behavior by consumers have provided both threats and opportunities for the strategists of cosmetic firms.

Source: Adapted from A. Dunkin and C. Dugas, "How Cosmetics Makers Are Touching Up Their Strategies," *Business Week,* Sept. 23, 1985, pp. 66–73

World's is not. This can affect a firm's location strategy. If you are operating in a region of a country where the population is declining, you may move your business to a fast-growing area. Or if the population of a city is growing or shifting to the suburbs, this can affect where you concentrate your effort. Population movement to the sunbelt, for example, hurt some firms and helped others.

• *Age shifts in the population.* As the total population changes, the age distribution changes. If the birthrate declines and health care improves, more older people and fewer babies populate an area. Primary demand declines or increases. Because there are fewer babies, strategy changes are taking place in the bubblegum, toy, and soft-drink industries. Even enrollment patterns at colleges and universities are affected by age changes.

• *Income distribution of the population.* In some areas of the world a majority of the income is in a few hands, and most of the people have little money. Sometimes this is true of races. In other areas, there are fewer differentials between upper-, middle-, and lower-income persons and between races. If the middle-income group is smaller than it was 10 years ago, this will affect the primary demand for goods and services with regard to some autos, but not Rolls-Royces.

These kinds of changes create threats and opportunities, and affect strategies of different types of firms and different industries. For instance, in the early 1980s, demographers defined a group known as the Yuppies—young urban professionals—who were the subject of intense efforts by marketers. In the mid- to late 1980s, marketers discovered the "graying of America." The *parents* of the Yuppies in general had greater disposable income and were more inclined to purchase certain classes of products and services. Lodging chains, retailers, airlines, travel agencies, hospitals, and even the Yellow Pages have discovered new opportunities to attract senior citizens. With a growing diversity in market segments and consumer lifestyles, mass marketing is giving way to segmentation.

Geographic Factors

The effective strategist also scans the geographic environment to look for opportunities and threats as part of analyzing the customer sector. Essentially the strategist is trying to determine if conditions are better elsewhere for achieving corporate or SBU objectives. The strategist seeks new locations to add to current locations. Or the strategist can search the environment for areas in which to relocate (either in the same region or in a new region). Sometimes a change involves moving corporate headquarters to a new region. It could also mean moving the plant or operations location from the city to a suburb or from one city to another. A change can come about because of shifts in the general population, because the firm wants a population of customers with the required income for purchasing goods and services or because costs are lower or the quality of life is better in the new location. So while this factor is primarily concerned with the location of markets for customers, other factors such as operating costs could be involved too.

In the customer sector of the industry environment, then, the firm's strategy must take into account who its customers are, what they want, how they are changing, and where they are located.

Supplier Sector [4]

Suppliers provide capital, labor, materials, and so on to a firm. Effective strategists are concerned about supplier changes in the environment. The strategist is concerned with the cost and availability of all the factors of production used in the business. The cost and availability of raw materials, subassemblies, money, energy, and, to a lesser extent, employees are affected by the power relationships between the firm and the supplier, as described by Porter, who has summarized the relative power of suppliers as follows:

1 The power the supplier has to raise prices and lower buyer profits is dependent on how far the supplier is from the free-competition model. The farther away the supplier is, the greater its power.

2 The power the supplier has to raise prices and lower buyer profits is lessened if the buying firm is a monopolist or oligopolist.

3 The power the supplier has to raise prices and lower profits is greatest when the buyer is not an important customer. The supplier has the least power when there are substitute materials available at a reasonable cost and the most power when there are no acceptable substitutes.

4 The power of the supplier is greatest when the supplier can integrate forward, that is, purchase or control the channel in front of it. For example, a shoe factory could buy the shoe store that sells its shoes.

5 The supplier threat in item 4 can be offset if the buyer can integrate backward and is in a very profitable industry or if it can purchase or control the supplier. For example, the shoe factory could purchase the leather company.

The power of the buyer also affects the cost of supplies. The buyer's power is at a maximum when the buyer's industry is concentrated, when the buyer represents a significant portion of the supplier's business, and if the buyer can virtually integrate backward. The buyer's power is at a minimum when the buyer's industry is competitive, when the cost of switching to a substitute is high, when the supplier's product is an especially important part of the production process, and when the supplier can virtually integrate forward.

Availability and Cost of Raw Materials and Subassemblies

In addition to bargaining with suppliers of raw materials over cost and availability, strategists must search the environment to examine long-run trends in the availability and cost of materials. Some materials are increasing in cost. For example, water used to be a cheap resource. In some areas (for example, Arizona) water is becoming more expensive and its availability is uncertain. Oil refiners (and others) have had to cope with dramatic changes in the supply and cost of crude oil as a basic raw material ever since OPEC became a force in 1974. Shortages and excesses have occurred, as have rapid price increases and decreases over the past 15 years. As will be discussed in Chapter 7, many firms are more and more buying subassemblies and entire products from outside sources—a distinct change in function strategy due to lower costs.

Availability and Cost of Energy

The petroleum situation is one in which key suppliers may be able to cut off the supply, and the long-run costs of petroleum are likely to rise. Strategists must decide what to do—use substitutes, withdraw from a business that relies on energy, or expect rising costs. Similar conditions exist as natural gas, nuclear power, and hydropower become more costly, thus limiting some substitution potential. While coal is a substitute, pollution control costs become a limiting factor. New technologies may help, but energy may be an important strategic factor for firms dependent on this input.

Availability and Cost of Money

Actions by central banks like the Federal Reserve and the Bank of Canada and international currency fluctuations affect the availability of money and the cost to suppliers of money: banks, thrift institutions, and other lenders. Strategists must be aware of conditions in the money market and how they will affect strategy. The cost or availability of capital can limit a firm's strategic options, as we discussed in Chapter 3.

Availability and Cost of Labor

Strategists cannot develop a strategy without determining whether skilled employees are available and at what cost. Coal companies wanted to expand faster than the availability of well-trained miners would permit in the late 1970s. Sports businesses are being affected by the explosion in player costs. And competition is fierce for engineers, technicians, and skilled labor in high technology areas.

Many firms have turned to locating facilities in foreign countries to take advantage of lower-cost labor; some have stopped domestic production entirely and get products from suppliers who have a competitive edge due to low labor costs.

Finally, in addition to availability and cost, lead time must be recognized as a potentially limiting factor for strategies. If the supply of factors of production is not available *when* needed, the strategy may not be effective, or it may be limited in terms of its timing. Exhibit 4.4 provides an example of several issues that strategists can consider in their analysis of supply factors.

Competitor Sector [5]

Besides looking at primary demand and supply factors, strategists examine the state of competition the firm must face, because this also determines whether a firm will remain in its current business and what strategies it will follow in pursuing its business. Four factors must be examined regarding competition: entry and exit of major competitors, substitutes and complements for current products and services, and major strategic changes by current competitors, as shown in Exhibit 4.5.

Entry and Exit of Major Competitors

One of the first questions a strategist asks about the competitive environment is, How has the competition changed? Are there new competitors entering our business?

EXHIBIT 4.4   THE POWER OF SUPPLY

In late 1982, IBM announced plans for a "passive investment" of $250 million for a 12 percent stake of Intel, a semiconductor maker. Intel was IBM's only outside source of supply for computer chips at the time. Observers speculated this was the opening salvo in a change in strategy for many high-tech U.S. companies who may be abandoning a strategy of backward vertical integration (self-control of raw-material inputs).

The prevalent opinion was that IBM was trying to block the Japanese before they do to computers what they did to the U.S. television industry. Japanese TV makers used low bidding to undermine the component suppliers that supported the industry. The same thing began happening with integrated circuits—the vital components of all computers. The independent semiconductor firms began facing financial problems as the Japanese offset new innovations with lower-priced competitive chips. United States chipmakers couldn't get their innovation investment back.

IBM was quite concerned about depending on foreign suppliers of chips. So the move to invest in Intel was seen as a way to make sure its supplier was adequately financed to remain a key supplier. And IBM was establishing unusually close relationships with other outside suppliers. Other computer, communications, and semiconductor firms were similarly increasing cooperation with one another through strategies of joint ventures, technology exchanges, and other ownership agreements.

In effect, supply factors of availability of money and raw materials are involved here. But the relative power of suppliers and buyers is also being altered to offset a threat of greater power by the foreign competitors and suppliers.

Source: Adapted from "IBM and Intel Link Up to Fend Off Japan," *Business Week,* Jan. 10, 1983, pp. 96–98; "Reshaping the Computer Industry," *Business Week,* July 16, 1984, pp. 84–98; and "Chip Wars: The Japanese Threat," *Business Week,* May 23, 1983, pp. 80–96.

Old rivals leaving it? If competitors leave, many times the probability of achieving corporate objectives increases. When RCA and GE left the computer business, this increased IBM's, Burrough's, and Control Data's chances of success. Indeed, Burroughs later acquired Sperry to reduce competition even more. Most of the time this is the case. But when GAF left the amateur photography business, Kodak wasn't completely happy. For this left the industry consisting of Kodak, Berkey, Inc., 3M, and Japanese firms making film and print paper. The exit of GAF left Kodak in a vulnerable position regarding charges by Berkey of assuming a monopoly position.

The opposite case involves the entry of new competitors. New competition often makes it tougher to achieve objectives unless together the current and new companies can increase the primary demand. Surely watch companies such as Bulova weren't pleased when Texas Instruments entered their business. American and Canadian businesses are often concerned when competitors from abroad enter the North American market. Examples include Japan's Sharp Corporation entering the U.S. computer business and Alumax, a joint venture of Mitsui and Amax, challenging the big three in aluminum.

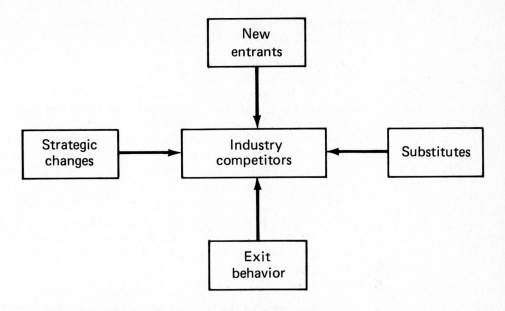

EXHIBIT 4.5   Factors to be analyzed in the competitor section.

Whether entry or exit takes place depends on the barriers to entry or exit. Porter contends that the following factors must be assessed with respect to their impact on *barriers to entry* in an industry:

• *Product differentiation.* There is strong customer loyalty to existing brands. Often the cost of getting customers to switch brands is high.

• *Economies of scale.* The costs of production, distribution, selling, advertising services, R&D, and financing decline as more units are sold. If economies of scale exist, then a firm that wishes to enter must do so at a unit-cost disadvantage, or the firm must enter the industry at the scale of the existing competitors.

• *Absolute cost advantages.* These are cost advantages deriving from patents, control of proprietary technology or especially skilled labor, control of superior raw-material sources, experience which leads to lower costs, capital at low cost, and depreciated assets which are useful, or experience or learning-curve advantages.

• *Access to marketing channels.* If the present firms own or have strong influence over the major channels, it can be very costly to enter a business.

• *Likely reaction of current firms.* If current firms will "live and let live," a proposed entry may be viable. If they "fight us on the beaches," it may be too costly.

Porter also explains *barriers to exit* from an industry. He contends that many firms do not leave an industry even though their objectives are not being met because

• *Managerial values prevent it.* Managers may be so tied to the industry psychologically that the firm doesn't exit.

• *Other products or services are related to exit candidates.* If other profitable products share marketing channels, production facilities, and other forms of joint activity, the firm may stay in the industry.

• *Costs are sunk in assets.* The costs of doing business in many industries include having large sums of money invested in assets that are useful only to the industry. Thus when the chemical business is bad, few leave it who have huge investments in plant, R&D, and other assets.

• *Direct exit costs are high.* Firms will not leave an industry whose direct exit costs (severance pay, relocation costs, etc.) are high.

• *Indirect costs may reduce exit behavior.* Some managers believe that social responsibility to the community and their employees prevent them from leaving a business or a particular location.

In effect, the combination of these barriers may serve to create new competitive conditions, and strategists should assess the impact of these barriers when they consider the likelihood of new firms entering their markets, or when considering strategies of entering or exiting themselves.

Availability of Substitutes

How profitably and successfully a firm operates depends in part on the availability of quality and less costly substitutes for the firm's products or services; and how competitive the substitute is will determine how viable the substitute is. Successful strategists also scan the environment for the loss or potential loss of business to substitutes. Thus sugar companies must be concerned about fructose and corn syrup. Marathon Oil must be concerned about the potential of solar energy as well as Peabody Coal. Can companies must pay attention to alternative packaging materials. Some substitutes may have cost advantages or other characteristics valued by buyers.

Major Strategic Changes of Current Competitors

While strategists are concerned with the previous two factors, they probably watch more carefully when major competitors change their strategies in significant ways. Xerox has had to react to much more aggressive competition from copier competitors such as IBM, Savin, SCM, and Kodak. When Pepsi offered to buy Seven-Up, Coca-Cola countered with an offer for Dr Pepper, even though both deals were later abandoned.

The amount of concern about the competition varies with the economic structure of the industry. An industry can be a monopoly (as nickel used to be) or an oligopoly (like the auto and aluminum industries), or it can be engaged in monopolistic competition (like parts of the computer industry) or competition (like the wheat production industry). Greater rivalry among firms in an industry leads to much more competition on the basis of price, quality, service, and other factors which can affect whether objectives are reached or not. Exhibit 4.6 provides an example of an industry in the throes of such change.

In essence, strategic groups tend to evolve in an industry. These groups tend to segment and compete more directly with one another. For instance, the beer business has a group of national competitors (such as Anheuser-Busch and Miller), local and regional brewers, and some who are attempting to become national. Firms can enter or exit segments. Coors is seeking to join the national brewer segment, while Falstaff became a regional brewer after it found it could not compete on a national basis. Heileman is a "national" brewery based on its strategy of acquiring and operating a series of regional breweries and brands and evolving a national brand name. Barriers

---

EXHIBIT 4.6   ON ENTRIES, EXITS, AND COMPETITIVE BEHAVIOR

In the summer of 1978, personal computers were high-tech toys selling slowly. But a few farsighted software developers saw great potential for these 30-pound paperweights. A graduate student at Harvard made a decision to go into business for himself selling an imaginative electronic spreadsheet he dreamed up at school. A year later, his program was commercially introduced as VisiCalc, and an industry was born.

Within 8 years since 1978, the personal computer software business has become a $5 billion industry with 14,000 companies and 27,000 different products. But the entry stage appears to be over. In 1985, 57 software firms were bought out, up from 23 in 1984. Many others died quietly. Changing competitive behavior can be explained by shifts in another industry environment factor—buyer behavior.

Until recently, software producers sold to individuals who used computers mostly on the job—and had discretion to buy programs they wanted. Now corporations want to tie computers into information networks. Data-processing managers have taken over the buying function, and they are a hard sell. "The package has to be from someone reputable; it's got to be bug free; the manual's got to be good; it's got to be teachable; and it's got to have some reason to displace what we already have."

These changes in buyer patterns have forced competitive behavior changes. Software makers have had to develop better quality control, special corporate sales and support forces, and high-volume pricing policies. And new-product development is important. One-product companies who can't keep the creative juices flowing to think up and produce follow-up products will not grow big enough to gain corporate acceptance and will likely exit the industry.

This is leading to speculation that three tiers (or strategic groups) will emerge in the industry structure. Several major competitors will sell all the basic software needed for word processing, spreadsheets, graphics, communications, and database management. A second tier of smaller firms will write programs for specific jobs in niche markets too small or narrow to concern larger firms. The third tier will be software makers that can't reach corporations. They will be able to survive by selling through retailers to individuals who now make up about half the market. But they also face increasing rivalry and buyer problems. Retailers are skeptical of small firms whose simple product line may generate little traffic. It is more profitable for the retailer to push fewer and fewer products, especially if service and support are necessary for the user.

It appears that in a very short time, this industry has gone from introduction to rapid growth to a shakeout stage. Consolidation in the industry and further exits are likely among those unable to switch from the entrepreneurial seat-of-the-pants management to more professional operating procedures.

Source: Adapted from A. R. Field, C. L. Harris, B. Buell, R. Brandt, and S. Ticer,: "Software: The Growing Gets Rough," *Business Week,* Mar. 24, 1986, pp. 128–139.

to entry to or exit from strategic group segments on an *intraindustry* basis (mobility) are the same as those for *interindustry* movement described earlier.

As the competition is analyzed, strategic moves are carefully watched, especially by those in one's strategic group. For example, are competitors developing cost advantages? Are they taking market share? How are they doing it (e.g., price, promotion, etc.)? Are they encroaching on market niches or developing new products? In other words, executives are examining relative competitive position and behavior, both to see what threats competitors are creating and to look for opportunities for improving their own position.

Thus competitor action can provide a significant opportunity or threat. The analyst must assess these characteristics of the competitor sector to determine their impact. On the basis of these and other factors, Porter summarizes the intensity and direction of competitive rivalry in a set of propositions.

• Rivalry increases and industry profits fall as the number of competitors in the industry increases and they become more similar in relative size and bargaining power.
• Rivalry increases as overall industry growth slows.
• Rivalry increases where fixed costs are high, efficient increments to capacity are large, or external factors lead to recurring or chronic excess capacity.
• Rivalry increases as products in the industry become less differentiated (more standardized as commodities) from the buyer's viewpoint.
• Rivalry becomes more volatile as firms in the industry become more diverse in personality, strategic approaches, and historic origins.

Industry Analysis and Diagnosis [6]

The appendix provides a variety of sources of information which can be used to gather data about customers, demographics, suppliers, and competitors along with other aspects of the general environment. Exhibit 4.7 is an intriguing commentary on how several techniques for competitor analysis have been utilized by business firms. As Chapter 3 indicated, there are a number of ways to proceed with analysis of environmental factors.

Yet it is particularly useful to get a sense of the favorability of the industry environment for the future strategy of the firm. Each factor can be subjected to an examination of threats or opportunities (e.g., do demographic trends provide opportunity or threat to our products?). But such a piecemeal approach may not result in an overall assessment useful for strategy generation. If the strategist is concerned with major strategic issues such as expansion into or retrenchment out of an industry, an overall assessment of the industry is necessary. Here, several of the factors we discussed earlier along with other criteria can be integrated, as shown in Exhibit 4.8, to begin to diagnose this segment of the environment.

By exploring these factors, strategists can determine profit potentials and begin to draw conclusions about the favorability of their current industry or new ones they may choose to consider as part of the business definition. Of course, these diagnoses

EXHIBIT 4.7   ARE THEY REALLY SPYING?

A 1982 issue of *Business Week* reported that microelectronics has supported a boom in the practice of "bugging" corporate offices. Counterbugging services are fast-growing businesses, even though it is illegal to make, sell, or possess eavesdropping devices in the United States. But this type of spying is only one of a number of techniques for competitive intelligence gathering, others of which are less "questionable" from a legal standpoint.

"The most serious and closed-mouth practitioners of competitive intelligence are often found among industry leaders." IBM has a "Commercial Analysis Department," Texas Instruments keeps "fairly formal files," and Citicorp has a manager whose title is "Manager of Competitive Intelligence." While clandestine activities are not usually disclosed, a picture of techniques for analysis does emerge. Examples include analyzing government contracts to discern technological strengths; back engineering—taking apart a competitor's product; preparing call reports—urging sales personnel to report on competitors from what they hear from customers; filing patent

mistakes to throw off competitors who review patent files; reviewing trade publications, 10K reports, annual reports, and securities analyses; debriefing engineers and scientists after professional meetings; hiring competitors' key employees; holding quarterly meetings to review competitor products with experts from marketing, manufacturing, engineering, and finance; monitoring the test marketing done by competitors; and feeling out firms involved with direct mail and catalogs, for they have lead times for publishing new offerings.

The key to the analysis is putting together bits of information in a puzzle to get an overall picture of future developments. In most companies, the process is informal. But those using formal approaches claim that they can "come up with amazingly clear pictures." As one executive put it, "The most important information to us is, 'What is his basic strategy?' " Clearly, an analysis of the competitive environment is important for strategists, and a variety of techniques are useful for obtaining "pieces of the puzzle."

Sources: Adapted from "Business Sharpens Its Spying Techniques." *Business Week,* Aug. 4, 1978, pp. 60–62; "New 'Bugs' Make Spying Easier," *Business Week,* July 12, 1982, pp. 74–75.

are not done in a vacuum. Relative firm power must be considered, which is the subject of Chapter 5.

Note that one of the factors noted in Exhibit 4.8 in two places is foreign opportunity and threat. This is the final sector of the environment that we explore.

EXHIBIT 4.8   ANALYSIS AND DIAGNOSIS OF THE INDUSTRY ENVIRONMENT

Markets and customers
  1 Size (present and potential)
  2 Growth and cyclicality (product life cycle)
  3 Customer segments and utilities
  4 Foreign opportunities
Suppliers
  1 Availability of needed inputs
  2 Costs of inputs
  3 Exits and entry of suppliers
  4 Power of suppliers

Competitors
  1 Concentration ratio (number of firms and market-share control)
  2 Capacity utilization
  3 Exits and entry barriers, especially foreign threats of entry
  4 Competitive behavior
  5 Strategic groups and mobility across strategic groups
  6 Availability and costs of substitutes from other industries

THE INTERNATIONAL ENVIRONMENT [7]

Many strategic managers now operate in what has been termed the "global village." United States business managers must consider threats and opportunities in the international business community. Nor can non-U.S. managers ignore what is going on in America or the rest of the world. Governments, economies, and business firms are increasingly intertwined in foreign trade and competition. Since World War II, the volume of goods traded between nations climbed from less than $100 billion to more than $1 trillion. In 1983, the 100 largest U.S.-based multinational companies earned an average of 37 percent of operating profits abroad. And direct foreign investment in the United States exceeds $70 billion, largely from Japanese, West German, and French firms.

With a focus on international competition, we have witnessed encroachment of international rivals into one another's market territories. International status and domestic prosperity has been linked to trade expansionism. Domestic economies of scale have financed pricing penetration into overseas markets by both U.S. and foreign firms. New competitors have forced innovations, price cutting, and quality improvements, but at a cost of competitive instability. This has further led to economic and strategic linkages among trading partners, such that mergers, joint ventures, cross licensing, and other strategies have become endemic.

Within this context, the international environment is a "special case" of the general and industry environments deserving special attention by strategists. That is, all the other factors—socioeconomic, government customer, competitor, and so on—discussed before apply here, as well as being shown in Exhibit 4.9. But the nature of the threats and opportunities take on a different focus. Compared to firms operating in a single country, the international environment is more competitive, heterogeneous,

---

EXHIBIT 4.9 EUROPE'S ENVIRONMENT

Strategists in multinational corporations are diagnosing threats to their business from broad changes occurring in Europe. A number of forces seem to be operating:

• *Socioeconomic:* Monetary exchange rates are increasingly uncertain; the European monetary system is expected to falter; economic growth is slowing.

• *Supply:* Labor unions seem to be increasingly hostile as unemployment increases; the availability of capital is decreasing as more capital is being used to pay for oil.

• *Technology:* Nationalistic policies are leading to government support of "home-grown" industrial development.

• *Competition:* Outmoded industries are not competitive in world markets.

• *Government:* There are increasing regulations on business and restrictions on operations; governments are seen as less stable; Europe has lost hope for unity, and this has led to greater nationalism.

While few U.S. companies are abandoning Europe, U.S. firms are reorienting their investment strategies by investing in services and improving plants rather than building new capacity. Some see joint ventures as a means for maintaining a presence with less risk. And European multinationals are investing more in the United States and in third-world countries. Note that elements of hostility, volatility, and the degree of development are involved in the assessments and strategic choices being made.

Source: Adapted from "Europe's Economic Malaise," *Business Week,* Dec. 7, 1981, pp. 74–79.

and complex because of different societies and cultures; educational practices; legal, political, and economic structures; and ideologies about appropriate business practices. Relative values of currencies vary rapidly and can quickly turn profits into losses. And government-to-government as well as firm-to-government relationships can have a bearing on attaining objectives. This is amply illustrated by comparing the differences between U.S. and multinational operations that affect strategic management noted in Exhibit 4.10.

The following sections discuss some of the threats and opportunities firms face in the international environment. The perspective is usually that of the U.S.-based multinational or international firm. That is, the multinational is a firm which operates in a number of countries, with offices or production facilities located outside the U.S. borders. However, the threats or opportunities could be reversed if the perspective were of a firm looking at U.S. companies entering their markets or seeking to enter U.S. territories. In each case, you should be aware that the sectors of the general or industry environments are interconnected with the discussion.

Opportunities for International Activities [8]

First, we should recognize that the economic world is not composed only of haves and have-nots. There are *resource-rich* countries such as in the OPEC bloc and many parts of Africa. There are *labor-rich,* rapidly developing countries, such as Hong Kong, Singapore, Korea, Mexico, Brazil, and Taiwan. These are countries which have done better than some others that have as much labor but have not grown. There are also *market-rich* countries, such as Europe, Brazil, Mexico, Phillipines, and many South American countries. These countries have some purchasing power in contrast to other countries such as India or China that although they possess large populations, they suffer from lack of purchasing power. Of course, there is business that can be done in the U.S.S.R. and Warsaw pact countries, but there are attendant difficulties because of extra legal hurdles.

In each instance, then, different opportunities prevail. For example, Northern Electric added the United States to its Canadian markets, while Dr Pepper entered European and Asian markets. The opportunities for market expansion were great in these market-rich areas. In western Europe and Japan, gross domestic product expansion (similar to GNP) was on the rise in 1986 because of lower oil prices, thus creating significant opportunity for business expansion. On the other hand, many U.S. firms have set up "off-shore" manufacturing operations to use lower-cost advantages available in the labor-rich areas. Raw material or energy resource requirements might be satisfied by foreign activities, such as INCO engaging in worldwide exploration, mining, and production of nickel where rich ore deposits are more readily available. The strategy sometimes involves internal investment and development. Often, as a result of governmental or political restrictions, joint ventures are set up with firms in the "host" countries involved. For example, United Technologies established six separate joint ventures in Britain, Belgium, China, Taiwan, Japan, and France between 1984 and

EXHIBIT 4.10   COMPARING U.S. AND INTERNATIONAL OPERATIONS

Factor	U.S. operations	International operations
Language	English used almost universally	Local language must be used in many situations
Culture	Relatively homogeneous	Quite diverse, both between countries and within a country
Politics	Stable and relatively unimportant	Often volatile and of decisive importance
Economy	Relatively uniform	Wide variations among countries and between regions within countries
Government interference	Minimal and reasonably predictable	Extensive and subject to rapid change
Labor	Skilled labor available	Skilled labor often scarce, requiring training or redesign of production methods
Financing	Well-developed financial markets	Poorly developed financial markets; capital flows subject to government control
Market research	Data easy to collect	Data difficult and expensive to collect
Advertising	Many media available; few restrictions	Media limited; many restrictions; low literacy rates rule out print media in some countries
Money	U.S. dollar used universally	Must change from one currency to another; changing exchange rates and government restrictions are problems
Transportation/ communication	Among the best in the world	Often inadequate
Control	Always a problem; centralized control will work	A worse problem; centralized control won't work; must walk a tightrope between overcentralizing and losing control through too much decentralizing
Contracts	Once signed, are binding on both parties, even if one party makes a bad deal	Can be voided and renegotiated if one party becomes dissatisfied
Labor relations	Collective bargaining; can lay off workers easily	Often cannot lay off workers; may have mandatory worker participation in management; workers may seek change through political process rather than collective bargaining
Trade barriers	Nonexistent	Extensive and very important

Source: R. G. Murdick, R. C. Moor, R. H. Eckhouse, and T. W. Zimmerer, *Business Policy: A Framework for Analysis,* 4th ed. (Columbus, Ohio: Grid, 1984).

1986, along with two independent start-ups in Spain, a merger in Italy, and co-production in Australia of aircraft, air conditioning, elevators, and other products.

Other opportunities may involve economic considerations such as more favorable tax advantages from operating in "duty-free" zones. Even with the communists taking over Hong Kong in the late 1990s, opportunities for businesses there are expected to be good for some firms.

Other sources of opportunity include the chance to secure sources of funding from international investors who believe conditions are good for investing in the United States. In some cases, a joint venture is set up in the United States where the domestic firm markets the foreign firms' outputs. Or, several domestic and foreign producers may set up joint operations for manufacturing and marketing, as has happened in the auto industry. Conversely, the U.S. firm may seek a foreign partner to license or market its goods. This route is taken by increasing numbers of smaller U.S. manufacturers.

Hence, opportunity exists for some firms to produce in one country, assemble in another, and market in yet others, as the "global economy" and the firm evolves. For example, firms may first get their feet wet by limited exporting or licensing. Then the firm might use foreign sales offices and/or joint venturing. If successful, international divisions for marketing and/or production might be established. Eventually, the firm may be engaged in multinational activities.

Companies go multinational when it appears that they can achieve objectives of high-level sales, higher profits, lower costs, and employee satisfaction. However, going multinational is a complex decision. For example, tax structures, product and service preferences, and employee skill levels can be different. Chapter 10 describes this in more detail. The firm may face expropriation of its properties. Sometimes going multinational means getting involved in local politics, as ITT found out in Chile and United Brands found out in Central America. A multinational strategy can complicate a firm's structure and top executive relationships, consideration of which brings us to the discussion of threats from the international environment.

Threats from International Activities [9]

A major threat to many U.S. firms appears to come from international competitors. Those possessing advantages of natural resources and labor have begun using them. Exhibit 4.11 indicates a list of two dozen U.S. industries which have experienced significant market-share losses in the last decade or so. And now the U.S. semiconductor industry appears threatened.

In industry after industry, manufacturers are closing up shop and becoming marketing organizations for other producers, mostly foreign. Autos, steel, machine tools, industrial robots, fiber optics, and semiconductor chips are some of the markets where the United States is losing (or has lost) dominance. This forces the U.S. economy to become more service-oriented. It is harder to achieve parity in productivity growth and personal income in service sectors compared to manufacturing, leading some to suggest that the U.S. economy is headed for serious trouble. Moreover, the advantages in service may be no less vulnerable to competition than are those in autos or steel.

EXHIBIT 4.11   THE IMPACT OF FOREIGN COMPETITION ON SOME U.S. INDUSTRIES
(Data by year reflect imports as a percent of the total U.S. market)

Industry	1972	1984	Industry	1972	1984
Blowers and fans	3.6	29.2	Precious jewelry	4.9	24.9
Converted paper	10.4	20.1	Printing machinery	8.5	22.9
Costume jewelry	10.4	28.6	Radios and TV	34.9	57.5
Dolls	21.8	54.7	Semiconductors	12.3	30.5
Electronic computers	0.0	14.2	Shoes	17.1	50.4
Lighting fixtures	4.2	17.4	Sporting goods	13.0	23.2
Luggage	20.7	52.4	Telephone equipment	2.1	12.1
Men's and boy's outerwear	8.7	26.8	Tires	7.2	15.1
Men's and boy's shirts	17.8	46.1	Women's blouses	14.9	33.0
Musical instruments	14.9	25.2	Women's suits and coats	7.3	24.5
Fertilizers	4.3	19.4	Wool yarn	6.1	17.4
Power handtools	7.5	23.2	Zinc	28.4	51.5

Source: *Business Week*, Oct. 7, 1985, pp. 94–95.

Some of the reasons for these inroads reflect not only competitive strength of foreign competitors but internal weaknesses on the part of U.S. firms. For instance, U.S. products are often not competitive because of poorer quality, and many firms lack technological superiority because of past failure to invest in R&D. While U.S. firms invented robots, the Japanese put them to more effective use earlier than U.S. firms. However, U.S. firms are not entirely to blame. Government assistance (reflecting U.S. ideology) is usually not competitive with foreign governments who often work closely with their own corporations to secure major contracts, obtain insurance, or provide other financial subsidies. And business behavior is sometimes not competitive with foreign firms because of U.S. restrictions such as tax laws, antibribery rules, or environmental regulations. The U.S. government can also create threats to importers if protectionism sentiments lead to further restrictions on world trade (though this could be an opportunity for selected domestic producers in protected industries). And of course, monetary policy affecting the value of the dollar helped imports in the early 1980s at the expense of U.S. manufacturers. Similarly, freight costs as well as labor rates (U.S. workers often earn two to five times foreign counterparts) put U.S. firms at a cost disadvantage.

The Japanese seem to have commanded the most attention of U.S. managers as key competitors in industry after industry. When the Japanese began showing up at U.S. trade shows and scientific meetings in the 1960s, they were an amusing sight to many Americans as they listened intently to interpreters and took hundreds of photographs. But they became less entertaining when Japanese products from automobiles to televisions flooded the market. Now the Americans are starting to look over the Japanese shoulders to find out what they are up to. With increased investment opportunity as a result of a higher rate of savings, lower cost of labor, a culture of cooperation, and unstinting efforts to improve quality and productivity to solve problems of insufficient labor availability, Japan has been able to overcome a total absence of natural resources to become a world economic powerhouse. And they are starting to lead the world in many new technological breakthroughs in selected areas where they have focused research efforts.

To dispel the rumor that the Japanese are infallible, let us hasten to add that they are experiencing their own foreign-competition problems. Strengthening of the Japanese yen has shifted price advantages to the "four tigers"—South Korea, Singapore, Taiwan, and Hong Kong. Korea competes directly with Japan in autos, steel, and videocassette recorders both in Japanese and U.S. markets. It might be noted that several of these firms, notably in Singapore, are subsidiaries of U.S. companies. Hence, the multinational U.S. firm which faces some threats from "foreign" competition can turn this into opportunity by shifting production to locations which possess certain competitive advantages (in this case labor cost).

Aside from competition, U.S. firms seeking to operate in foreign countries face a variety of threats because of restrictions placed on them by host countries such as

* Ownership. Typically, the host country or firm from the host country must own a major or controlling interest.
* Employment. Almost always, host countries demand that certain positions in management and technological areas be held by host-country nationals.
* Profits and fees. Typically, profits and fees are set at some maximum level.
* Internal debt capital. Internal debt capital is often set according to a preestablished formula.
* Training and development. Insistence on training and development for host-country nationals is common.
* Host-country markets. Most host countries demand development of their exports.
* Technological bases. Most host countries seek technologically based industry rather than extractive industry.

These factors can make the decision to operate in the host country particularly problematic. The threats may offset the opportunities or advantages originally thought available.

Finally, threats may come from a variety of sources of potential risk when operating in a foreign country. Examples of these include

1 Political risks: war, occupation by foreign powers, disorders caused by territorial claims, ideological differences, conflict of economic interests, regionalism
2 Social risks: civil wars, riots, unequal income distribution, union militancy, religious divisions, antagonism between social classes
3 Economic risks: continuous slow GNP growth, strikes, rapid rise in production costs, fall in import earnings, sudden increase in food or energy imports
4 Financial risks: fluctuating currency exchange rates, repatriation of profits and capital, changing tax policies

These risks can even exist in "friendly" countries, as an anti-U.S. backlash was seen in Britain in 1986 after several U.S. firms made attempts to buy British-government-owned businesses. In some instances, governments may expropriate your business, or you may lose substantial amounts of money as exchange rates move up or down.

Firms must decide whether the environment they are examining is subject to these risks before deciding to set up operations. Once there, policies may be needed to guide managers in maneuvering in the host country in ways different from domestic operations. Or the firm may have to decide, as some are now in South Africa, whether the risks of staying are worth the costs of abandoning a location.

While it may be noted that U.S. firms have been losing competitive ability in the world arena, stronger efforts have been made to improve productivity and quality and restore competitive strength. But many firms have done this by exploring international strategies to take advantage of the opportunities of collaboration and avoid some of the threats we have noted.

The final point we wish to make in this section is that in the special case of a multinational business, the complexity and scope of the business suggest that environmental analysis must be far-reaching indeed. A greater emphasis on the socioeconomic, government, and competitor sectors seems to be called for. While common sense suggests that overseas risk is greater in less-developed countries, greater volatility in developed countries may be more significant. Sudden changes in currency exchange rates, so-called nontariff trade restrictions, licensing laws, political embargos, etc., can be as damaging as coups, revolts, or seizures. And since the stakes may be higher in developed markets, the ultimate losses may be greater. In fact, Garreau suggests that within North America itself there are nine distinct regions with their own sociopolitical and economic configurations which create quite different markets and strategic situations.

Now that we have examined all the sectors of the environment, it should be quite clear that strategists cannot do in-depth analysis and diagnosis of all the various factors. Our next section provides suggestions for limiting this task.

FOCUSING THE DIAGNOSIS [10]

The strategist usually has a limited amount of time and limited cognitive skills for diagnosing the information gathered in the analysis phase. If they let themselves, managers can be bombarded with information from the environment. They are faced with choices on what information to continue to examine and whether they should act upon that information. They must avoid a breakdown in effective diagnosis because of information overload. To avoid this cognitive strain, the strategist has several options.

One is to delegate some diagnosis and focus on the most significant diagnosis duties. Instead of the top manager doing all the diagnosis, the management team can be involved in the diagnosis. The team in turn can delegate some of the less crucial diagnoses to the subordinates. The initial diagnosis of each factor could be delegated to the functions most affected (e.g., technology to R&D, economic to finance, customer to marketing, supplier to production). These diagnoses can be pooled and integrated by the top management team or strategists. The key is systematic linking of the diagnoses together.

A second approach is to try to train the strategists in more effective diagnosis. One technique which a few firms have experimented with is the use of scenarios. The approach that GE uses is shown in Exhibit 4.12. Royal Dutch Shell in London has adapted this technique to training. Its goal is to open the executives' minds to possible futures which they don't want to come. Shell creates two scenarios—far enough away from the present condition yet not the most visionary possibilities. Then the top managers of Shell make operating and strategic change decisions based on these two *possible* futures. It is not important whether the scenarios become the future. They are a training vehicle which stretches executives' minds so that they can deal more effectively with the future environment—whatever it is.

A third approach is called issues analysis. This is related to scenario building and

EXHIBIT 4.12   How scenarios are constructed at General Electric Company.
(General Electric Company.)

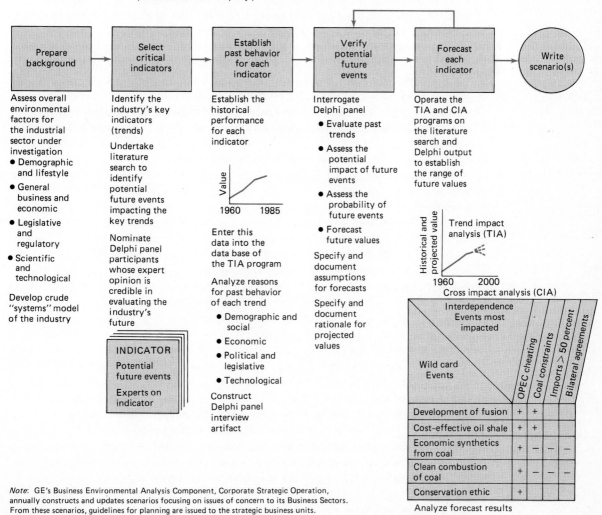

Note: GE's Business Environmental Analysis Component, Corporate Strategic Operation, annually constructs and updates scenarios focusing on issues of concern to its Business Sectors. From these scenarios, guidelines for planning are issued to the strategic business units.

contingency planning. An "issue" is a factor (internal or external such as emerging political, social, or economic trends or controversies) which if it develops, could have a significant effect on the firm in the future. Issues are identified, a probability is assessed with respect to its possible occurrence, and a weight is given to its expected effect. These issues are brought to the attention of management so proactive behavior may be taken to deal with the issue. For example, the issues staff at Atlantic Richfield was tracking 140 issues in 1985 that might be brought to the attention of top executives, planners, and government or public relations staff. However, not all issues can be diagnosed ahead of time. Surprises, or unanticipated events, are bound to arise. Nonetheless, management can prepare contingency plans to be put into effect if such events arise. For example, if a supplier suddenly becomes a competitor, the firm could be prepared ahead of time to respond appropriately. The key is to diagnose possible surprises (errors in the computing system, terrorist action in a foreign plant, takeover bids, etc.) and sketch out a plan to be put into effect. For more-probable and important surprises, a detailed plan is desirable.

The last approach for reducing information overload is satisficing instead of maximizing when maximization is beyond the capabilities of the strategist or will cause serious cognitive strain. That is, the manager doesn't try to get an optimal focus or diagnosis but settles for doing an acceptable job given the time pressures and other demands.

Certain characteristics of the environment may operate in ways which demand more or less attention by the strategist. We think that several general characteristics are important in explaining what factors can be diagnosed. [11]

Diagnosis of the environmental analysis data is influenced by how *dependent* the firm is on the environment. The more powerful the stockholders or key owners, the more their perception of the environment might influence the diagnosis. As discussed earlier, if the power of government is great vis-à-vis the organization, the firm is more dependent on the government and its actions. As discussed in Chapters 1 and 2, exchange relationships with a number of agents in the environment can lead to dependence, thus influencing strategists. Dependence can be a threat or an opportunity. For instance, firms develop interdependent relationships with competitors (through trade associations, for example) which can lead to an opportunity to improve performance. Of course, threats can occur if the organization is overly dependent (as in the case of some firms with few customers).

The degree of *development and complexity* in the environmental sector can be important to the diagnosis. A highly developed economy creates more sources of data and a greater infrastructure to support diagnosis. In less-developed countries, analysis and diagnosis may be hindered by the absence of accurate or timely information. If complexity is greater, diagnosis becomes more difficult and more important.

A *hostile* environment is one where the factors being diagnosed tend to be unfavorable for the organization. For instance, economic conditions might be recessionary, or social values may be negative toward some operations (e.g., electric power companies). Firms in more competitive industries usually perceive greater hostility in this sector. The more hostile the competitive environment, the more vital the diagnosis of that sector is, and the more quickly the firm responds to challenges. While this seems to stress the threats, you should be aware that the opposite of hostility—favorableness—can provide opportunities and also will command managerial attention. Estimates of favorable customer demand and favorable changes in governmental policies (such as deregulation) are examples of environmental changes which could create opportunities and should lead to greater attention and diagnosis. Note that *developed* environments tend to be viewed more favorably also.

Volatile environments are those in which substantial change occurs but is infrequent, irregular, and thus less predictable. (Some call this uncertainty.) Recall that earlier we noted how technological factors are particularly subject to volatility. Comprehensive and timely diagnosis is more necessary in *volatile, dynamic* environments than in stable environments. Firms which face dynamic, uncertain, and *complex* environments develop more complete diagnoses (and strategies). Those not doing so are more likely to fail.

Once again, both opportunities and threats can result from volatility, although many executives tend to perceive change negatively. Indeed, *The Wall Street Journal* reported that many executives are frustrated and spend significantly more time examining volatile currency exchanges. In fact, some multinationals buy several services which forecast exchange rates, because predictions vary widely.

Closely related to volatility is the question of how *time* affects diagnosis. If time pressures are great, diagnosis may have to be speedily done. Thus near-term or long-term environmental change is important to assess. Some suggest that a useful approach is monitoring sectors for signs which are weak or strong. For instance, weak signs of changes in the composition of the work force with regard to women began appearing in the early 1970s. The signs became stronger over time that significant changes were occurring. As a sign becomes stronger, a more extensive diagnosis of the sector is necessary. These changes over time can create "double-edged swords" of threat and opportunity. Consider the impact of the women's movement on Avon, noted in Exhibit 4.3. Exhibit 4.13 suggests another aspect of changes in an environmental factor over time. Thus possible gains from every opportunity can also present a threat of "downside" risk to a firm.

The cost of the search and luck are the final factors affecting diagnosis. If the cost of the search is excessive for the firm, this may cause the executives to do less diagnosing than they might prefer. And as with most decisions in life, luck is a factor. Sometimes a diagnosis is done on the right factor at the right time by chance or luck. This can help or hurt the diagnosis.

ENVIRONMENTAL THREAT AND OPPORTUNITY PROFILE: ETOP [12]

In Chapter 3, diagnosis was defined as an assessment of the significance of information developed in analysis. Specifically, how significant is the difference between the future environment and the present environment with regard to our strategy to achieve the objectives? Diagnosis seeks a statement of the problems and opportunities the environment is offering us.

If first-generation planning is used, this diagnosis is based on the most probable future. If second-generation planning is used, several scenarios of the future are

EXHIBIT 4.13   FROM OPPORTUNITY TO THREAT AT ENVIROTECH

The major line of business for Envirotech until 1980 was construction projects to help companies and municipalities meet pollution control regulations. From 1970 to 1980, total sales grew from $60 million to $580 million; half this total was accounted for by an agglomeration of 30 companies involved in controlling air and water pollution which Envirotech had acquired, thereby becoming the largest pollution control business in the United States.

The company's first strategic plan was put together in 1976. It noted that the pollution control business would slow down by 1983 or 1984. Thus weak signs of a slow-down were evident. In fact, the waste-water treatment market began to deteriorate in 1978. Management assumptions and perceptions concerning market growth and changes in regulations and government funding were inaccurate.

There were, of course, internal management difficulties, such as signing long-term, fixed-price construction contracts in areas where Envirotech had little expertise. But the major problem was a volatile environment.

Envirotech made a proactive effort to influence change. In late 1979, the CEO met with government policymakers to try to convince the Environmental Protection Agency to change its regulations. This had no impact, and Envirotech has sold or shrunk most of its acquisitions and reduced employment from 8900 to 5600.

In 1981, the company made plans to abandon air quality control after the completion of some 130 projects. Water pollution control equipment still represents 15 percent of Envirotech's business, but the company plans to emphasize mining and mineral processing machinery.

Clearly, what was once an opportunity became a threat for Envirotech. It anticipated this, but not soon enough. It made efforts to proact, but in the end it was forced to react by changing its strategy. Reports indicated that Envirotech was up for sale in late 1981.

Sources: Adapted from "Envirotech: Controlling the Red Ink That's Polluting Its Balance Sheet," *Business Week,* Oct. 19, 1981, pp. 140–141; "Envirotech Offer by Baker International," *The Wall Street Journal,* Nov. 18, 1981, p. 14.

drafted, with best-case, most-probable, and worst-case assumptions. Then several diagnoses are made.

To do this effectively, managers should use a systematic technique. Several available approaches are listed in the references. The one we suggest is the preparation of an environmental threat and opportunity profile (ETOP), which allows you to conveniently summarize the diagnoses of all the various sectors of the environment which you have deemed most important to the strategic gaps facing the firm.

An example of an ETOP is given in Exhibit 4.14. Note that the environmental sectors in the analysis are listed in summary fashion for simplicity's sake. In a more extensive diagnosis, the subfactors would be examined first and then the summary ETOP would be prepared, as shown in this exhibit. For example, instead of showing only the "socioeconomic" sector, a more extensive profile would list the subfactors: economic, climatic, and social. As you analyze cases and businesses, this approach should be used for each factor. For each one, a time-based prediction of the most likely events must be prepared (for first-generation plans).

The firm shown in this ETOP is Alza Corp., a small company which markets a unique type of intrauterine device called Progestasert. While the ETOP appears generally negative, Alza has been given what seems to be the possibility of increasing annual sales from the current $1 million up to $100 million. That prospect, however, is very risky and many factors will influence management's strategy, just as various factors influenced the opportunity. Unfortunately, Alza's product was introduced in 1976, just after A. H. Robins Company withdrew its IUD, the Dalkon shield, from

EXHIBIT 4.14   ENVIRONMENTAL THREAT AND OPPORTUNITY PROFILE (ETOP)
FOR ALZA CORPORATION

Environmental sectors	Impact of each sector
Socioeconomic	− Perception of public about IUDs − Influence on public of Searle's and A. H. Robins' withdrawal from the market − Possibility of increased legal problems + Planned Parenthood and doctors support IUD products + Huge market demand for pregnancy prevention
Technological	+ Product is unique; not just an IUD + Does not use estrogen with its side effects 0 Must be replaced yearly
Government	+ FDA approval continues − More legal problems may change government support
Customer	− Best used in monogamous relationships; U.S. divorce rate = 50% + Loyalty of present IUD users
Supplier	− Liability insurance agreement may change; rates may become too high to afford

Competitor	+ Searle's and A. H. Robins' withdrawal from the market
	− Allegations posed against IUD makers
	− Birth-control pills becoming safer
	− Condom alternative also prevents STDs; has reached a 40
	   percent female market
	− Makers of alternative forms of birth control will step up
	   marketing efforts

International	+ Chinese government policies promote single-child families

Note: + indicates opportunity; − indicates threat; 0 indicates neutral impact.

the market, because of allegations that it caused injury and even death.[1] As of January, 1986, G. D. Searle & Co. had decided to remove its last remaining IUDs from the market. This decision was also caused by a rapidly increasing number of lawsuits. (The FDA, doctors, and Planned Parenthood all endorse Alza's product, but the risk of legal tangles is high—although they have never lost a case—and the company may not be able to afford the liability insurance necessary.) Although Alza could inherit the abandoned IUD market, there are good and bad attributes to their product, and producers of alternative birth control methods are stepping up market penetration based on their own strengths.

The environment basically created this opportunity for the company. Pressure from the public has caused competitors to abandon the market to Alza. The public's perception that Progestasert is as dangerous as the other IUDs is Alza's biggest threat. (There is the probability that the company will get hit by more lawsuits itself, even though it has support from doctors, Planned Parenthood, and the U.S. government

[1]Robins then went into Chapter XI bankruptcy.

through the FDA.) However, IUDs are recommended mostly for women in stable, exclusive relationships—a market that could be diminishing with the ever-increasing U.S. divorce rate. Also, increased legal problems could cause the government to withdraw its approval. Technologically, the product is unique; it is made of plastic and does not have the side effects of estrogen associated with contraceptive pills. The fact that Progestasert must be replaced every year is described as a threat, but in reality, many women in the U.S. normally go to a gynecologist once a year for other reasons, so this may not be a drawback after all.

The exit of competition by IUD manufacturers has created the opportunity for Alza to take over this niche but also signals their unwillingness to continue defending the product. Other potential competitive entrants with their eye on this market are the birth-control-pill manufacturers who have lowered estrogen levels and stepped up marketing (as has VLI Corp., makers of contraceptive sponges, and condom makers). The latter can also promote the fact that condoms prevent sexually transmitted diseases (STDs). Alza's supply of liability coverage is not assured in the future, so financial and/or legal risk is a large problem.

The future strategies Alza's management is considering all attempt to find a solution to the legalrisk problem considered as the most significant threat:

1 Sell Progestasert to another company to produce and market
2 Find a marketing partner to share risk with the company
3 Create a separate division and thus insulate the rest of the company

Alza has already diversified into alternative drug-delivery systems that are more lucrative. The threats posed by the current environment affecting the birth-control industry may cause Alza's management to withdraw or to simply minimize exposure and risk to the company. However, the opportunities to increase involvement exist and could be seized by Alza.

The summary ETOP can be prepared so that top management can identify the most critical sectors of the environment and focus intensively on their potential impact on the strategy of the firm as a whole and key aspects of its operations. That is, top managers could focus on some areas and delegate others. We suggest that top management should focus on the areas which are perceived to be more developed, more volatile, and more hostile (or favorable) and where greater organizational dependence exists. Prescriptively, long-term signals should be diagnosed; descriptively, near-term factors are likely to command more attention. This focus should then lead to detailed predictions about the sector in question.

A more detailed ETOP should be developed to focus the diagnosis more precisely. It should provide data and estimates for revenue and cost implications of these factors as well as estimates on the likelihood that certain events will occur and their timing. The key, then, is to identify the relevant trends expected and assess their likely impact. This diagnostic tool, ETOP, will be matched with the strategic advantage profile (SAP), described in Chapter 5. Together, these diagnostic tools provide the input for generating strategic change alternatives and determining whether gaps might exist between expected and desired outcomes and why.

SUMMARY [13]

This chapter completes our look at the environmental factors which create threats and opportunities. We continued our description of the sectors in the environment which strategists analyze and diagnose beyond the general environment discussed in Chapter 3.

First we described the industry environment as consisting of customers, suppliers, and competitors. Effective strategists must analyze who their customers are, where potential customers might be located, and what changes in customer buying patterns might occur. This involves identifying buyers and their utilities, assessing basic demographic factors which create primary demand for products or services, and scanning the geographic environment for potential markets and customers.

Strategists also must determine the availability and costs of supply conditions including raw materials, energy, money, and labor. We noted that the power of suppliers (and buyers) can influence a firm and its strategy.

Then we discussed the competition. The exit and entry of competitors, the possibility of substitute products or services, and major strategic changes by competitors are the important factors to be analyzed and diagnosed in this sector of the industry environment.

We concluded our look at the industry environment by indicating how to put together a diagnosis of these various sectors to draw conclusions about the favorability of an industry. This is an important component of the overall environmental analysis as an input to the strategic management process.

Next we pointed out that the international environment is an increasingly important source of opportunity and threat to business firms. The global village includes all other aspects of the environment but is a special case deserving special attention by strategists. Effective strategists examine opportunities and threats from areas of the nation and the world other than the ones they are presently doing business in. But we pointed out how because of heterogeneity and complexity, analysis here is more difficult but must be far-reaching.

Next we discussed how managers focus the diagnosis to limit cognitive strain and to make the process more effective. This can be done by delegating some of the diagnoses to vice presidents or by scenario building. Top managers must still narrow their focus and more closely monitor the areas which presently are likely to offer the most significant opportunities and threats. Propositions 4.1 to 4.6 provide some clues on how to focus the top manager's analysis and diagnosis.

In effect the focal zone of the strategist is narrowed by the conditions of each factor. Exhibit 4.15 illustrates this point. In this case, the competitor sector may be seen as volatile and uncertain, with new competitors entering and strategies changing. Thus there is a greater focus on this sector than on any other. Few changes may be occurring with suppliers, but technologies may be changing. Due to competitive conditions, the government in this example is viewed as relatively unimportant. There may be problems in the economy or social changes which are requiring more managerial attention. Few geographic factors are of importance, but the international environment is increasing in significance.

Proposition 4.1

The more dependent the enterprise is on a sector, the more it will focus its environmental analysis on that sector of the environment.

Proposition 4.2

The more developed the sector, the more a firm will focus on that sector of the environment.

Proposition 4.3

The more hostile the sector, the more vital the diagnosis of that sector.

Proposition 4.4

The more volatile and uncertain the sector, the more the diagnosis will focus on that sector.

Proposition 4.5

The greater the time pressure and cost of search, the less likely it is that in-depth diagnosis will result.

Proposition 4.6

The greater the complexity of the environment, the more sectors managers must focus on.

So the executive does not seriously analyze and diagnose the shaded area of Exhibit 4.15 but closely analyzes and diagnoses the white area (focal zone), where most of the current opportunities and threats are coming from. The effective executive systematically diagnoses these areas, using a mechanism like the ETOP to make sure that effective analysis and diagnosis takes place.

EXHIBIT 4.15   How the focal zone is narrowed.

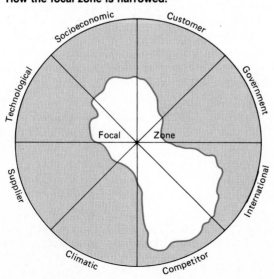

The ETOP can be used to systematically summarize all aspects of the environment. This tool when combined with the strategic advantage profile (SAP) to be described in the next chapter provides a basic input to the generation of strategic alternatives and choice of strategy in the overall strategic management process.

Appendix: Business Facts: Where to Find Them*

This appendix provides business executives, government officials, academicians, and students with a concise reference list of sources for locating published material which can be used in analyzing business operations. The list contains references to both primary data sources and bibliographical publications.

Sources of primary data and statistical information:

1 Government publications
2 Trade publication statistical issues
3 Business guides and services

General reference sources of business information and ideas:

4 Indexes
5 Periodicals and periodical directories
6 Bibliographies and special guides
7 Trade associations
8 Other basic sources
9 Specialized Sources: On-line data bases

Sources of Primary Data and Statistical Information

1 Government Publications

Probably no one collects more business information than the U.S. government does through its various agencies. The Department of Commerce maintains excellent reference libraries in field offices in many major cities, for example, and the Small Business Administration assists with business problems and maintains field offices in over 85 cities.

A Indexes *The Federal Register* (National Archives). Published daily. Contains all regulatory matter issued by all governmental bodies.

Monthly Catalog of United States Government Publications (GPO), issued monthly. A comprehensive list by agencies of federal publications issued during each month.

Monthly Checklist of State Publications (GPO), issued monthly. A record of state documents and publications received by the Library of Congress.

B Selected Basic Sources The following list of selected sources is representative of the types of information available through the government.

---

*This appendix was adapted by the authors from an article of the same title by C. R. Goeldner and L. M. Dirks originally published in *MSU Business Topics* in 1976. That article was based on an article by S. M. Britt and I. A. Shapiro, "Where to Find Marketing Facts," *Harvard Business Review,* September–October 1962. Updates are adapted from J. S. Mulitonovich, "Business Facts for Decision Makers" *Business Horizons,* March–April 1985, pp. 63–80.

Business Conditions Digest (U.S. Department of Commerce, Bureau of Economic Analysis), published monthly. Provides many economic time series statistics used by forecasters and planners.

Commerce Business Daily (U.S. Department of Commerce: Office of Field Operations), published daily. Lists U.S. government procurement invitations, contract awards, sales of surplus property, and foreign business opportunities.

County Business Patterns (U.S. Department of Commerce, Bureau of the Census), issued annually. A volume showing county, state, and U.S. summary statistics on employment, the number and employment size of reporting business units, and taxable payrolls for approximately 15 broad industry categories. The statistics are particularly suited to analyzing market potential, establishing sales quotas, and locating facilities.

Economic Indicators, issued monthly. A digest of current information on economic conditions of prices, wages, production, business activity, purchasing power, credit, money, and federal finance presented in charts and tables.

Employment and Training Report of the President (U.S. Manpower Administration), published annually. Reports employment, earnings, size, and demographic characteristics of the labor force. Historical data and projections included.

Federal Reserve Bulletin (Board of Governors of the Federal Reserve System), issued monthly. A source of statistics on banking, deposits, loans and investments, money market rates, securities prices, industrial production, flows of funds, and various other areas of finance.

Foreign Economic Trends and Their Implications for the United States (U.S. Bureau of International Commerce), pamphlets issued semiannually or annually for each country. Prepared by embassies; contains analysis of economic trends and possible implications in various countries.

Index of Patents Issued from the U.S. Patent Office (U.S. Patent Office), published annually. Volume 1 indexes patents by name of patentee. Volume 2 lists patents by subject of invention.

Monthly Labor Review (U.S. Department of Labor, Bureau of Labor Statistics), issued monthly. A compilation of trends and information on various current labor statistics.

Small Business Bibliographies (U.S. Small Business Administration), published irregularly. Briefly describes particular business activities.

Statistical Abstract of the United States (U.S. Department of Commerce, Bureau of the Census), issued annually. A standard summary of statistics on the social, political, and economic organization of the United States.

Statistical Yearbook (New York: United Nations), issued annually. A body of international statistics on population, agriculture, mining, manufacturing, finance, trade, education, and so forth.

Survey of Current Business (U.S. Department of Commerce, Bureau of Economic Analysis), issued monthly. The official source for gross national product, national income, and international balance of payments. A survey that brings about 2600 different statistical series up to date in each issue under these headings: General Business Indicators; Commodity Prices; Construction and Real Estate; Domestic Trade; Labor Force, Employment and Earnings; Finance; Foreign Trade of the United States; Transportation and Communications; and several headings on specific raw material industries.

C Census Data   By far the most extensive source of information on the United States and its people and businesses is census data. The list provided gives a sampling of the information available through the census surveys. Because the census surveys are conducted at regular intervals, trends can be noted and comparisons made by using similar data from several census years. The following are all from the U.S. Department of Commerce, Bureau of the Census.

Bureau of the Census Catalog of Publications, issued quarterly with monthly supplements and accumulated into an annual volume. An index of all available Census Bureau data.

Census of Agriculture. Reports data for all farms and for farms with sales of $2500 or more by county and by state.

Census of Housing, issued every 10 years. Reports data on structure, household characteristics, ownership, etc., in several volumes.

Census of Manufacturers, issued every 5 years. A presentation of geographic and industrial data on manufacturers. *Final Industry Reports* includes a series of separate reports on the value of shipments, capital expenditures, value added by manufacturing, the cost of materials, and employment for approximately 450 manufacturing industries. The data are classified by geographic region and state, employment size, class of establishment, and degree of primary products specialization.

Census of Population, issued every 10 years. There are several series, two of which are the following: *Series B: General Population Characteristics.* A description and cross-classification of the number of inhabitants of the United States, with characteristics about age, sex, race, marital status, and relationship to head of household for states, counties, Standard Metropolitan Statistical Areas, etc. *Series C: General Social and Economic Characteristics.* Describes and cross-classifies the number of inhabitants. Data include nativity and parentage, state of birth, mother tongue, school enrollment by level and type, years of school completed, families and their composition, occupation groups, and class for states, counties, Standard Metropolitan Statistical Areas, etc.

Census of Retail Trade. A compilation of data for states, Standard Metropolitan Statistical Areas, etc., by kind of business. Data include number of establishments, sales, payroll, and personnel.

Census of Selected Services. Includes data on hotels, motels, beauty parlors, barbershops, and other retail service organizations. The survey also includes information on the number of establishments, receipts, and payrolls for states, Standard Metropolitan Statistical Areas, counties, and cities.

Census of Wholesale Trade. Presents statistics for states, Standard Metropolitan Statistical Areas, and counties on the number of establishments, sales, payrolls, and personnel by kind of business.

2   Trade Publications

Publications serving specific industries often compile data annually in special articles, factbooks, or issues. Some of those available are the following:

Appliance (Elmhurst, Ill.: Data Chase Publications), monthly.

Broadcasting (Washington, D.C.: Broadcasting Publications), weekly.

Chain Store Age—Super Markets (New York: Lebhar-Friedman Publications), published monthly with an extra issue in July.

Computerworld (Newton, Mass.: Computerworld), published 51 times a year.

Drug and Cosmetic Industry (New York: Drug Markets, Inc.), monthly.

Editor & Publisher (New York: The Editor & Publisher Company), weekly.

Forest Industries (San Francisco: Miller Freeman), monthly.

Implement & Tractor (Kansas City, Mo.: Intertec Publishing Corporation), published 24 times a year.

Men's Wear (New York: Fairchild), twice a month.

Merchandising Week (Cincinnati, Ohio: Billboard Publications), weekly.

Modern Brewery Age (Stamford, Conn.: Business Journals), tabloid published weekly; magazine issued every other month.

National Petroleum News (New York: McGraw-Hill), magazine issued monthly and twice in May.

Quick Frozen Foods (New York: Harcourt Brace Jovanovich), monthly.

Sales Management (New York: Bill Communications), magazine published twice a month, but once in December.

Survey of Buying Power, published in July. A prime nongovernment authority for buying income, buying power index, cash income, households, merchandise line sales, population, and retail sales for the United States. The data are divided into national and regional summaries and market rankings, metro-market data by states and county-city data by states. Some data on Canada are now included.

VENDing Times (New York: VENDing Times), journal published monthly with one extra issue in February and in June.

3 Business Guides and Services

Directory of Corporate Affiliations (Skokie, Ill.: National Register Publishing Company), published annually; includes quarterly updates. Directory lists approximately 3000 parent companies with their 16,000 divisions, subsidiaries, and affiliates; an index of "who owns whom."

Moody's Industrial Manual (New York: Moody's Investors Service), published annually. A brief background, a description of the business and products, a history, a mergers and acquisition record, and a principal plants and properties list are given for each company. Principal officers and directors are given as well as 7 years' worth of financial statements and a 7-year statistical record for each company.

Standard & Poor's Corporation Services (New York: Standard & Poor's). Some of these services include *Industry Surveys,* an annual publication with three to four current surveys of each industry and a monthly section called "Trends and Projections"; *The Outlook,* a weekly stock market letter; *Stock Guide,* a monthly summary of investment data on common and preferred stocks; and *Trade and Securities,* a monthly listing of statistics on business and finance, stocks and bonds, employment, foreign trade, production, and so forth.

Standard & Poor's Register of Corporations, Directors and Executives (New York: Standard & Poor's), issued annually; three volumes. Volume 1 includes an alphabetical list of nationally known corporations with the titles of their important executives, the names of directors and principals, and annual sales. Volume 2 provides an alphabetical list of directors and executives in the United States and Canada. Volume 3 indexes corporations by Standard Industrial Classification, geographic area, new individuals, obituaries of individuals, and new companies.

Standard Directory of Advertisers (Skokie, Ill.: National Register Publishing Company), published annually in two editions, classified and geographical; plus *Directory of Advertising Agencies* and an updating service. A concise record of more than 17,000 companies and their agencies doing national and regional advertising. Each entry includes the company name, address, and telephone number; the names of top executives, including financial, marketing and advertising, and purchasing managers; the approximate sales; and the agency. Most listings also include advertising budget information and the method of product distribution.

Standard Rate & Data Service Publications (Skokie, Ill.: Standard Rate & Data Services). These publications provide information required by advertisers and agencies for preparing advertising and placing it in various media. In addition, a good deal of consumer market data are provided in *Newspaper Rates and Data, Spot Radio Rates and Data,* and *Spot Television Rates and Data.*

Thomas Register of American Manufacturers and Thomas Register Catalog File (New York: Thomas Publishing), issued annually; 11 volumes. A directory that classifies manufacturers by products and services and also includes an alphabetical list of 60,000 brand or trade names. This work is a source of information on companies incorporated for less than $1 million.

General Reference Sources of Business Information and Ideas

4 Indexes

Accountants' Index (New York: American Institute of Certified Public Accountants). A detailed list by author, subject, and title of publication covering the fields of accounting, auditing, data processing, financial management and investments, financial reporting, management, and taxation.

Advertising Age Editorial Index (Chicago: Crain Communications). An index which cross-references the 52 issues of *Advertising Age* articles by key words, subject category, company name, and author. Some abstracts.

Applied Science & Technology Index (New York: H. W. Wilson). A cumulative subject index to periodicals in the fields of aeronautics and space science, automation, chemistry, construction, earth sciences, electricity and electronics, engineering, industrial and mechanical arts, materials, mathematics, metallurgy, physics, telecommunications, transportation, and related subjects.

Business Periodicals Index (New York: H. W. Wilson). A cumulative subject index covering periodicals in accounting, advertising, the automotive field, banking, communications, finance, insurance, labor, management, marketing, and taxation and periodicals of specific businesses, industries, and trades.

F & S Index of Corporations and Industries (Cleveland, Ohio: Predicasts). An index which covers company, industry, and product information from more than 750 business-oriented newspapers, financial publications, special reports, and trade magazines. Information is arranged by SIC number, by company name alphabetically, and by company according to SIC groups.

Public Affairs Information Service Bulletin (New York: Public Affairs Information Service). A selective list by subject of the latest publications relating to economics and public affairs.

The Wall Street Journal Index (Princeton, N.J.: Dow Jones). An index of all articles that have appeared in *The Wall Street Journal*.

5 Periodicals and Periodical Directories

Business periodicals feature articles of use and of interest to the business manager. Frequently research studies or new developments are reported in these specialized journals. The following list illustrates some of the periodicals available: *Academy of Management Journal, Accounting Review, Business Week, Dun's, Fortune, Harvard Business Review, Industrial Marketing, Journal of Advertising Research, Journal of Business, Journal of Finance, Journal of Marketing, Journal of Marketing Research, Journal of Retailing, Management Accounting, Management Science, Nation's Business, Personnel, Personnel Management, Sales Management.* In addition to general business periodicals, there are hundreds of trade publications covering almost every field. The following directories can help you find these periodicals.

Ayer Directory of Publications (Philadelphia: Ayer Press, 1975), issued annually. A comprehensive listing of newspapers and magazines and trade publications of the United States (by state), Canada, Bermuda, the Republic of Panama, the Republic of the Philippines, and the Bahamas.

Business Publications Rates and Data (Skokie, Ill.: Standard Rate & Data Services), issued monthly. A listing of more than 3000 U.S. business, trade, and technical publications arranged according to 175 market-served classifications.

Management Contents (Skokie, Ill.: Management Contents Inc.), published biweekly. Lists the tables of contents of hundreds of periodicals in accounting, finance, management, marketing, and related disciplines.

Ulrich's International Periodicals Directory, 15th edition (New York: Bowker), two volumes. Issued every 2 years. An index of subject entries for more than 55,000 in-print periodicals published throughout the world.

6 Bibliographies and Special Guides

Bibliographies and other guides can quickly lead you to original sources of information on selected topics. Examples of bibliographies and special guides are provided in the following selections.

Bibliography of Publications of University Bureaus of Business and Economic Research (Boulder, Col.: Business Research Division, University of Colorado), issued annually. A bibliography of publications by bureaus of business and economic research and by members of the American Association of Collegiate Schools of Business.

Encyclopedia of Business Information Sources, 2d edition (Detroit: Gale Research Company), two volumes. Edited by Paul Wasserman et al. A listing of primary subjects of interest to managerial personnel, with sources of information on each topic.

Management Information Guides (Detroit: Gale Research Company). A group of bibliographical references to information sources for various business subjects. Each volume includes books, dictionaries, encyclopedias, filmstrips, government and institutional reports, periodical articles, and recordings on the featured subject.

The Marketing Information Guide (Garden City, N.Y.: Hoke Communications), cumulative indexes issued quarterly. An annotated bibliography that shows both the source and the availability for each item listed.

National Planning Association Publications (Washington, D.C.: Planning Association), published annually. An annotated bibliography for the publications of the National Planning Association.

7 Trade Associations

Don't overlook trade sources. Many trade associations maintain research departments and collect basic data on sales expenses, shipments, stock turnover rates, bad-debt losses, collection ratios, returns and allowances, and net operating profits. One of the following directories will help you locate a particular trade association.

Encyclopedia of Associations (Detroit: Gale Research Company).

National Trade and Professional Associations of the United States and Labor Unions (Washington, D.C.: Columbia Books), issued annually.

8 Other Basic Sources

In addition to the specific references listed, the following are general sources of valuable information for the researcher.

Commercial Atlas & Marketing Guide (New York: Rand McNally), published annually. A volume containing statistics and maps. It provides data on population estimates, principal cities, business centers and trading areas, county business, and sales and manufacturing units; also zip code marketing information and transportation data for the United States. General reference maps of Canada and foreign countries are included.

The Conference Board Record (New York: The Conference Board), monthly. A report to management on business affairs which provides an analysis and interpretation of current statistical tabulations.

Exporter's Encyclopedia (New York: Dun and Bradstreet), published annually. Detailed facts on shipments to every country in the world. Covers regulations, types of communication and transportation available, foreign trade organizations, general export information, and listings of ports.

National Economic Projection Series (Washington, D.C.: National Planning Association), published annually. A report providing forecasts of the gross national product and its principal components, including historical and projected 5-, 10-, and 15-year forecasts for capital investment, consumption and savings, government revenues and expenditures, output and productivity, and population and employment.

P. Wasserman, C. Georgi, and J. Woy, *Encyclopedia of Business Information Sources* (Detroit: Gale Research Co., 1983). Quick survey of basic information sources covering 1215 subjects.

9 Specialized Sources: On-Line Databases

Computer technology has revolutionized the search for business facts. By using a database, decision makers benefit from the accessibility and adaptability of massive resources now available. This tool is expensive but can be cost-effective when measured by time savings.

The actual process of a computer search is a simple one. A questionnaire is completed, specifically describing the problem and indicating important authors, journals, or key facts useful in retrieving references. Citations are printed immediately or mailed.

Three major vendors offer on-line interactive search access to hundreds of databases. Bibliographic Retrieval Services (Scotia, N.Y.) and DIALOG/Lockheed Informations Services (Palo Alto, Cal.) store general bibliographic data. SDC Search Service (System Development Corporation, Santa Monica, Cal.) emphasizes technical and statistical information.

Listing of computer based services can be found in the following directory.

Directory of Computer Based Services (Washington, D.C.: Telenet Communications Corp.), published annually. Lists data banks, commercial service bureaus, educational institutions, and companies that offer interactive computer-based services to the public through the nationwide Telenet network.

The business databases are divided into three areas: bibliographies, statistics, and directories.

Bibliographies On-line interactive search access to various bibliographic databases.

Management Contents (Skokie, Ill.: Management Contents, Inc.), monthly. Current information on a variety of business and management-related topics for use in decision making and forecasting. Articles for 200 U.S. and foreign journals, proceedings, and transactions are fully indexed and abstracted to provide information in areas of accounting, design sciences, marketing, operations research, organizational behavior, and public administration.

Monthly Catalog of U.S. Government Publications (Washington, D.C.: U.S. Government Printing Office). Published monthly with annual cumulations. Reports, studies, fact sheets, maps, handbooks, and conferences.

Predicasts Terminal System (Cleveland: Predicasts, Inc.). Bibliographic and statistical database providing instant access to many business journals and other special reports for searches of current articles, statistics, geographic location of companies.

Statistics In-depth statistics easily adapted for a wide variety of manipulations.
Economic Time Series
Business International/Data Time Series (Business International Corp.). PTS/U.S. Time Series (Predicasts, Inc.).
Marketing Statistics
BLS Consumer Price Index (Department of Labor, Bureau of Labor Statistics).
BLS Producer Price Index (Department of Labor, Bureau of Labor Statistics).
Financial Statistics
Disclosure II (Washington, D.C.: Disclosure, Inc.), 1977 to present; updated weekly. Extracts of reports filed with the U.S. Securities and Exchange Commission by publicly owned companies. 11,000 company reports provide a reliable and detailed source of public financial and administrative data. Source of information for marketing intelligence, corporate planning and development, portfolio analysis, legal and accounting research.

Directories
CATFAX
Directory of Mail Order Catalogs.
EIS Industrial Plants (Economic Information Systems, Inc.).
Foreign Traders Index (Department of Commerce).
Trade Opportunities (Department of Commerce).

REFERENCES

[1] Industry Attractiveness

Hax, A. C., and N. S. Majluf: *Strategic Management* (Englewood Cliffs, N.J.: Prentice-Hall, 1984).

[2] Identifying Buyers and Their Utilities

Boulton, W. R.: *Business Policy* (New York: MacMillan, 1984).
Kiechel, W., III: "The Food Giants Struggle to Stay in Step with Consumers," *Fortune,* Sept. 11, 1978, pp. 50–56.
"Listening to the Voice of the Marketplace," *Business Week,* Feb. 21, 1983, pp. 90–91.

[3] Demographic Factors

"Americans Change," *Business Week,* Feb. 20, 1978, pp. 64–69.
Brown, P.: "Last Year It Was Yuppies—This Year It's Their Parents," *Business Week,* Mar. 10, 1986, pp. 68–74.

[4] Supplier Factors

"A Capital Crunch That Could Change an Industry," *Business Week,* Mar. 23, 1981, pp. 82–84.
Menzies, H.: "Why Sun Is Educating Itself Out of Oil," *Fortune,* Feb. 27, 1978, pp. 42–44.
Norris, W. C.: "A Risk Avoiding, Selfish Society," *Business Week,* Jan. 28, 1980, p. 20.
Porter, M. E.: *Competitive Strategy: Techniques for Analyzing Industries and Competitors* (New York: Free Press, 1980).

"Venture Capitalists Raid Silicon Valley," *Business Week,* Aug. 24, 1981, p. 112.

"The Wave of the Future: Shipping by Sail," *Business Week,* Aug. 24, 1981, p. 112.

"Why the Next Oil Crisis Could Be a Disaster," *Business Week,* Nov. 23, 1981, pp. 132–133.

[5] Competitor Factors

Abernathy, W. J., K. B. Clark, and A. M. Kantrow: "The New Industrial Competition," *Harvard Business Review* (September–October 1981), pp. 68–81.

Grossman, R.: "Why IBM Reversed Itself on Computer Pricing," *Business Week,* Jan. 28, 1980, p. 84.

Levy, R.: "The Big Battle in Copiers," *Dun's Review* (May 1977), pp. 97–99.

Porter, M. E.: *Competitive Advantage* (New York: The Free Press, 1985).

Sammon, W. L., Kurland, M. A., and R. Spitalnic: *Business Competitor Intelligence* (New York: Wiley, 1984).

[6] Industry Analysis and Diagnosis

Galbraith, C. S., and C. H. Stiles: "Firm Profitability and Relative Firm Power," *Strategic Management Journal,* vol. 4 (1983), pp. 237–249.

Hatten, K.: "Heterogeneity within an Industry: Firm Conduct in the U.S. Brewing Industry, 1952–1971," *Journal of Industrial Economics,* vol. 26 (December 1977), pp. 97–113.

[7] The Global Village

"Drastic New Strategies to Keep U.S. Multinationals Competitive," *Business Week,* Oct. 8, 1984, pp. 168–172.

Garland, J., and R. N. Farmer: *International Dimensions of Business Policy and Strategy* (Boston: Kent, 1986).

"Global Trade Skirmish Looms as Restrictions on Services Multiply," *The Wall Street Journal,* Oct. 5, 1981, p. 1.

Lorange, P.: "A Framework for Strategic Planning in Multinational Corporations," *Long Range Planning* (June 1976), pp. 30–37.

Pearce, J. A., and R. B. Robinson: *Strategic Management* (Homewood, Ill.: Irwin, 1985).

Porter, M. E.: *Competition in Global Industries* (New York: Free Press, 1986).

[8] International Opportunities

Comes, F. J., and J. Rossant: "France Gets Set for a Capitalist Comeback," *Business Week,* Mar. 31, 1986, pp. 42–44.

"The Future of Hong Kong," *Business Week,* Mar. 5, 1984, pp. 50–64.

Glasgall, W., F. J. Comes, R. A. Melcher, S. Miller, R. Lewald, and L. Armstrong: "In Western Europe and Japan, The Party is Just Beginning," *Business Week,* Feb. 10, 1986, p. 80.

King, R. W., A. Borrus, and J. Heard: "UTC adds Westland to Its Growing Foreign Arsenal," *Business Week,* Feb. 24, 1986, pp. 88–89.

Yang, D. J., and D. Griffeths: "China: A Dream Market for Western Arms Makers," *Business Week,* Feb. 24, 1986, p. 48.

[9] International Threats

"America Starts Looking Over Japan's Shoulder," *Business Week,* Feb. 13, 1984, pp. 136–140.

Cetron, M.: *The Future of American Business* (New York: McGraw-Hill, 1985).

"The Four Tigers Are Pouncing on Japan's Markets," *Business Week,* Mar. 24, 1986, p. 48.

Haner, F. T.: "Rating Investment Risks Abroad," *Business Horizons,* vol. 22 (April 1979), pp. 18–23.

"The Import Invasion: No Industry Has Been Left Untouched," *Business Week,* Oct. 8, 1984, pp. 172–174.

Jones, N.: "The Hollow Corporation," *Business Week,* Mar. 3, 1986, pp. 57–59.

Melcher, R. A.: "Yanks, Go Home," *Business Week,* Mar. 24, 1986, p. 50.

"Why Carmakers Will Mourn if Export Quotas Die," *Business Week,* Feb. 18, 1985, pp. 46–47.

Wilson, J. W., M. Berger, P. Hann, and O. Port,: "Is It Too Late to Save the U.S. Semiconductor Industry?" *Business Week,* Aug. 18, 1986, pp. 62–67.

[10] Focusing the Diagnosis

Amara, R. C. and A. J. Lipinski: *Business Planning for An Uncertain Future: Scenarios and Strategies* (New York: Pergamon, 1982).

Gottschalk, E. C., Jr.: "Firms Hiring New Type of Manager to Study Issues, Emerging Troubles," *The Wall Street Journal,* June 10, 1982, p. 21.

Hofer, C. W.: *Instructor's Manual to Accompany Strategic Management* (St. Paul, Minn.: West, 1981).

Kalaska, P.: "Multiple Scenario Approach and Strategic Behavior in European Companies," *Strategic Management Journal,* vol. 6 (1985), pp. 339–356.

Wack, P.: "The Use of Scenarios at Shell," International Research Seminar in Strategy, Saint-Maximin, France, June 1979.

[11] Diagnosis and the Strategist's Environment

Ansoff, H. I.: "Managing Strategic Surprise by Response to Weak Signals," *California Management Review,* vol. 18 (Winter 1975), pp. 21–33.

Bourgeois, L. J.: "Strategic Goals, Perceived Uncertainty, and Economic Performance in Volatile Environments," *Academy of Management Journal,* vol. 28 (1985), pp. 548–573.

Engwall, L.: "Response Time of Organizations," *Journal of Management Studies,* vol. 13 (February 1976), pp. 1–15.

"Exchange Rates: Pick a Forecast," *Business Week,* Apr. 26, 1982, p. 108.

Osborn, R. N., J. G. Hunt, and L. R. Jauch: *Organization Theory* (New York: Wiley, 1980).

Pine, A.: "Wide Swings in Imported Currencies Vex Businessmen, Bankers, Government Aides," *The Wall Street Journal,* Dec. 29, 1981, p. 30.

Regan, D.: "Uncertainty Is Breeding Fear," *Fortune,* Oct. 19, 1981, pp. 62–67.

Smart, C., and I. Vertinsky: "Strategy and the Environment: A Study of Corporate Responses to Crises," *Strategic Management Journal,* vol. 5 (1984), pp. 199–213.

[12] Systematic Ways to Diagnose the Environment

DeSouza, G. R.: *System Methods for Socioeconomic and Environment Impact Analysis* (New York: Arthur D. Little, 1979).

"Searle's Troubles Give Alza Its Big Break," *Business Week,* Feb. 24, 1986, pp. 123–125.

[13] Summary

Paine, F., and C. Anderson: "Contingencies Affecting Strategy Formulation and Effectiveness: An Empirical Study," *Journal of Management Studies,* vol. 14 (1977), pp. 147–158.

INTERNAL ANALYSIS AND DIAGNOSIS

CHAPTER OUTLINE

INTERNAL ANALYSIS AND DIAGNOSIS

OBJECTIVES

- To describe the process of internal analysis and diagnosis
- To introduce internal strategic factors and to illustrate how they affect a firm's objectives
- To examine some techniques which have been developed and used for internal analysis
- To consider factors that affect the diagnosis of internal strengths and weaknesses

INTRODUCTION [1]

This chapter completes the three-chapter unit on analysis and diagnosis. Chapters 3 and 4 focused on analysis and diagnosis of the environment to determine which opportunities and threats could be significant to the firm in the future. Chapter 5 describes the parallel process which involves determining the strengths and weaknesses the firm has at present or might develop. These are diagnosed in order to develop competitive advantages, and to minimize weaknesses, or consider how they will limit strategy or can be corrected.

Every firm has strengths and weaknesses. The largest firms have financial strengths, in comparison with smaller firms, but they tend to move more slowly and be less able to serve small market segments effectively. No firm is equally strong in all its functions. Proctor & Gamble was known for its superb marketing, Maytag is known for its outstanding production and product design. American Telephone and Telegraph is known for its outstanding service and personnel policies. Yet each of these firms is

> *Internal analysis is the process by which the strategists examine the firm's marketing and distribution, research and development, production and operations, corporate resources and personnel, and finance and accounting factors to determine where the firm has significant strengths and weaknesses. Internal diagnosis is the process by which strategists determine how to exploit the opportunities and meet the threats the environment is presenting by using strengths and repairing weaknesses in order to build sustainable competitive advantages.*

not strong "across the board." Within a company, each division has varying strengths and weaknesses. General Electric was strong in jet engines and weak in computers a few years ago. So a firm must determine what its distinctive competencies are—what makes it unique to the competitive arena—so that it can make decisions about how to use these abilities now and in the future. And it must determine whether weaknesses will limit strategic options or identify weaknesses which can be overcome.

Exhibit 5.1 indicates how strengths and weaknesses at ITT may influence that company's strategy.

EXHIBIT 5.1   THE STRENGTHS AND WEAKNESSES AT ITT

ITT spent $105 million in 1985 to introduce to the United States its System 12, a sophisticated telephone switch which has been routing calls and data abroad since 1981. System 12 is ITT's most crucial vehicle for cracking the telecommunications market dominated by AT&T and Northern Telecom Ltd. While analysts and customers agree that the System 12 is very innovative and "quite a step forward," its complexity is producing time delays resulting in an increasing flow of lost customers. ITT spent more than $1 billion developing System 12, eliciting from some analysts the opinion that it should be dropped in the United States, a move that could add 25 cents a share to earnings. On the other hand, System 12 seems crucial to Chairman Rand Araskog's strategy. Its failure could jeopardize his own future.

ITT perceived a technological opportunity—cracking the telecommunications market with an innovative telephone switching system. In its effort to exploit this opportunity, ITT utilized its financial and marketing (distribution, promotion, sales) strengths. Yet these strengths have not successfully evolved into a strategic advantage, as less than 10 percent of the 129 million lines ordered since 1978 have been delivered; and after 3 years, only one quarter of the 10,000 lines installed in Salamanca, Spain, are working. The successful conversion of strengths into advantages was thwarted by a prevailing weakness, not in the finance or marketing areas but in the product development and organization and management areas. Three teams were set up in the United States and Europe to develop System 12. According to M. Peter Thomas (former president of ITT's Network Systems Division), "The product is so complex and the organization is so complex that without focused management it was hard to design a major system." This fault in the strategic planning stage resulted in the numerous delivery delays leading to decreased customer confidence. In addition, ITT may have expended too much of its resources in pursuit of this perceived opportunity, allowing other advantages to atrophy to the point where ITT's future could be dependent upon the success or failure of this single project.

In a stunning reversal of strategy, Araskog announced an attempt in mid-1986 to sell most of the telecommunications business to the French. If the deal is rejected, he may not find a buyer at a reasonable price, leading to more problems for ITT's troubled balance sheet.

Source: Adapted from "The Project ITT Can't Seem to Bring Home," *Business Week,* Feb. 17, 1986, pp. 52–55; "Behind the ITT Deal: Will Araskog's Radical Surgery Work?" *Business Week,* July 14, 1986, pp. 62–65.

Unless the executives are fully aware of their competitive advantages, they may not choose the one opportunity of the many available at the time that is likely to lead to the greatest success. Unless they regularly analyze their weaknesses, they will be unable to face the environmental threats effectively. In effect, these assessments must be combined with environmental analysis so that decisions can be made about how to use or add strengths and minimize weaknesses.

This chapter focuses on how to analyze the internal factors realistically and diagnose their significance. It is at this point that executives can develop a strategic advantage profile (SAP) and match it with an environmental threat and opportunity profile (ETOP) to create optimal conditions for adjusting or changing strategies or policies.

Exhibit 5.2 reminds us of how this process fits into the total strategic management process. And as before, we are interested in how the internal factors relate to the gap analysis. That is, management performs internal analysis and diagnosis to identify clearly the current strengths and weaknesses of the firm. Management also examines the most probable *future* strengths and weaknesses. On the basis of these assessments, expectations are developed about goal attainment given the internal and external conditions. If gaps exist between desired and expected objectives, new strengths must be developed or weaknesses preventing goal attainment must be overcome.

Since this chapter parallels Chapters 3 and 4, much of what was said there applies here and will not be duplicated. The similarities include the definitions of analysis and diagnosis, the purposes of analysis and diagnosis, and factors affecting diagnostic decisions.

This chapter also provides parallel information on the internal factors. This includes

- Strategic factors to be analyzed and diagnosed
- Techniques and problems of internal analysis
- The role of strategists in internal analysis and diagnosis
- Diagnosis and preparation of a summary assessment (SAP)

INTERNAL FACTORS TO BE ANALYZED

In the discussion of internal factors, it is not possible to consider in depth the material presented in courses such as marketing management and personnel and labor relations. Some of the leading books on the subject are listed in the references for each section. All that will be attempted here is a listing of the most crucial internal factors and a presentation of brief illustrations of the competitive advantages (and weaknesses) that are possible. The order of discussion does not indicate importance—it is just a convenient ordering of line and staff factors and follows a fairly typical budgeting format. But you should remember that each area interacts with the others.

Marketing and Distribution Factors [2]

Marketing and distribution means moving goods or services from the producer to the customer. It starts with finding out what customers want or need and whether the product and/or service can be sold at a profit. This requires doing market research,

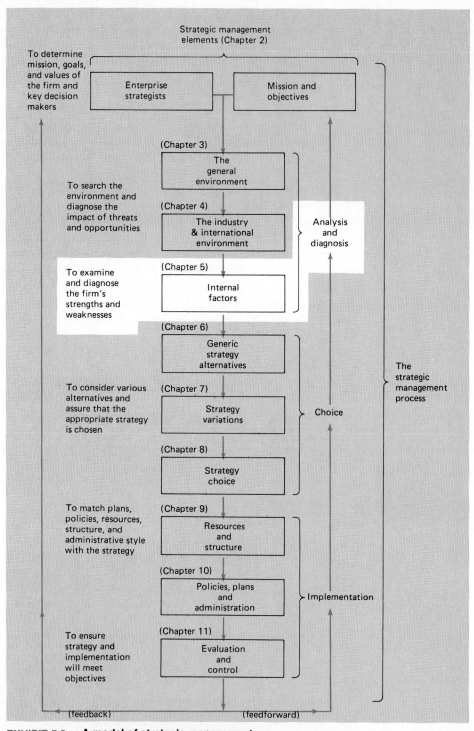

EXHIBIT 5.2   **A model of strategic management.**

EXHIBIT 5.3   INTERNAL FACTORS: MARKETING AND DISTRIBUTION

1 Competitive structure and market share: To what extent has the firm established a strong market share in the total market or its key submarkets?

2 Efficient and effective market research system.

3 The product-service mix: quality of products and services.

4 Product-service line: completeness of product-service line and product-service mix; phase of life cycle the main products and services are in.

5 Strong new-product and new-service leadership.

6 Patent protection (or equivalent legal protection for services).

7 Positive feelings about the firm and its products and services by the ultimate consumer.

8 Efficient and effective packaging of products (or the equivalent for services).

9 Effective pricing strategy for products and services.

10 Efficient and effective sales force: close ties with key customers. How vulnerable are we in terms of concentrating on sales to a few customers?

11 Effective advertising: Has it established the company's product or brand image to develop loyal customers?

12 Efficient and effective marketing promotion activities other than advertising.

13 Efficient and effective service after purchase.

14 Efficient and effective channels of distribution and geographic coverage, including internal efforts.

identifying the market, developing product, testing customer reaction, working out production and costs, determining distribution and service requirements, and deciding on advertising and promotion approaches.

As simple as this sounds, many corporations all but forgot such basics in the 1970s when inflation kept revenue high. But vast economic and social changes have made marketing strengths more important for most firms. The recession in the early 1980s and demographic and life-style shifts created problems for those who pursued mass marketing and brand loyalty as the keys to marketing success. Likewise, intense international competition, rapid technological change, and deregulation have created new weaknesses in typical marketing approaches. The changing nature of competition, then, requires a close look at marketing strengths and weaknesses in order to build competitive advantage in increasingly fragmented markets. Exhibit 5.3 is a list of the marketing and distribution factors. The strategist is looking to see if the firm is substantially stronger in marketing and distribution than its competitors.

As you look at the factors, you will see that strength can come from a variety of approaches. The operational marketing questions of segmentation, positioning, and mix (product, price, promotion, distribution) are quite important to the firm's ability to compete effectively. Of course, firms compete on any and all of these factors. Some firms prefer approaches involving low prices, lower quality, more promotion, and wide distribution; others prefer orientations toward higher prices, higher quality, and custom design.

An assessment of the weaknesses in relation to market potential also suggests areas where improvements can be made. For instance, if there appears to be a gap in the product line, new-product development or acquisition is called for to fill out the existing line or create new ones. A gap in distribution might lead to efforts to build intensity, exposure, or coverage. If usage gaps exist, price or promotion can lead to increased frequency of purchase, or new uses or users (customers) can be found for products.

Just as important as these questions are other areas which focus on how the marketing organization functions. For instance, the organization may have the ability to accumulate better knowledge about its markets than the competition has. If properly used, this can become a major advantage with respect to assessing the need for changes and determining their timing. Similarly, if the marketing organization maintains good relationships with production or new-product engineering, the translation of marketplace needs into the timely creation of goods or services can lead to a competitive edge.

Finally, the importance of marketing to the overall success of the company needs evaluation. In some firms, such as those which supply to a few customers who specify their precise needs (e.g., defense contractors), the marketing function need not be particularly strong. In other industries, the greatest share of internal resource allocation may go to marketing units (e.g., consumer products producers). As competitive needs are assessed, the relative strength of marketing and the way it is managed in relation to major competitors may lead to indications of strength or weakness. Exhibit 5.4 provides an example of how marketing has become a weakness at Proctor & Gamble due to the way it is managed in a changing environment.

EXHIBIT 5.4   MARKETING BY THE NUMBERS

Like all packaged-goods marketers, Proctor & Gamble operates in a tougher world than the past, when it had the midas touch. The firm has stumbled lately. It no longer has commanding leads on branded products such as Crest and Pampers. And its competitors are smarter.

P&G's traditional strengths—a massive commitment to product research and exhaustive test marketing—have not been as potent as in the past. Its markets are mature, and "the old mass audience delivered by mass media for the mass markets isn't working anymore," says one P&G alumnus.

P&G's earlier successes often came from a strategy of acquiring brand names (e.g., Charmin, Duncan Hines, Folger's); and using marketing expertise, it put those names on one product after another to dominate its field. But the firm has yet to turn recent acquisitions into big profit producers. Proctor has done little more than reformulate some new products while competitors have captured substantial new business by segmenting markets and products. Insiders suggest that the problems at P&G reflect a corporate culture which is stifling. Decisions are "made by the numbers." In an age when creative thinkers often get freedom to try ideas without interference from the top, P&G remains bureaucratic and centrally controlled. The president wants to "know what the facts are." He is a no-nonsense analyst who gets involved in nitty-gritty matters, with a fetish for memoranda and a burdensome system of communication. This slow-moving perfectionist style worked to P&G's advantage during less-competitive times. But now this approach is hurting some key markets.

Recently, President Smale has been showing greater flexibility. P&G is working more closely with retailers; it has cut down on its memos and livened up its ads. Forgoing its usual thoroughness, P&G rolled out half a dozen products since 1984 with no test marketing. However, unless its weaknesses resulting from insularity and adherence to centralization are reduced, Proctor's past marketing glories may not provide the strengths to accomplish its goal of doubling unit volume each decade.

As Exhibit 5.8 points out, P&G still faces problems from competitors who are beating them to the punch, but this "defensive" posture fits the style of its current management practices.

Source: Adapted from Z. Schiller and A. Dunkin: "P&G's Rusty Marketing Machine," *Business Week*, Oct. 21, 1985, pp. 111–112.

EXHIBIT 5.5   INTERNAL FACTORS: R&D AND ENGINEERING

1 Basic research capabilities within the firm	8 Well-equipped laboratories and testing facilities
2 Development capability for product engineering	9 Trained and experienced technicians and scientists
3 Excellence in product design	10 Work environment suited to creativity and innovation
4 Excellence in process design and improvements	11 Managers who can explain goals to researchers and research results to higher managers
5 Superior packaging developments being created	12 Ability of unit to perform effective technological fore-casting
6 Improvements in the use of old or new materials	
7 Ability to meet design goals and customer requirements	

R&D and Engineering Factors[3]

The research and development (R&D) and engineering function can be a competitive advantage for two prime reasons: (1) It can lead to new or improved products for marketing, and (2) it can lead to the development of improved manufacturing or materials processes to gain cost advantages through efficiency (which could help to improve pricing policies or margins). Exhibit 5.5 presents the list of factors which might be analyzed in the R&D and engineering area.

In Chapter 3 we noted that major technological changes often occurred outside the immediate industry. Even so, research and development can provide significant strength for the ongoing business.

The R&D process is commonly viewed as proceeding through the stages of basic research, applied research, developmental research, and commercialization. Exhibit 5.6 graphically represents the time savings in producing a new product, process, or service with accelerated developmental research. One axis shows the time lapse from a basic research breakthrough to commercialization and the other shows the R&D states. The actual improvement in time will vary, but under unaccelerated conditions, the normal gap between a research breakthrough and commercialization is about 25 years. The figure was developed by looking back from commercialization to basic research. Accurate forecasts of the commercial applications of basic or developmental research are rare and difficult to produce. But for the individual firm assessing its own R&D capabilities, the key is to examine the ability to produce product or process improvements and the timing and effectiveness of its future efforts.

A firm can choose to pursue an offensive approach to R&D or pursue defensive "fast second" or "imitator" approaches. Exhibit 5.7 describes the kinds of differences you would expect in these approaches to R&D. The offensive approach would accelerate the applied and developmental research efforts (B_1 in Exhibit 5.6). The "fast second" approach would emphasize accelerated developmental research (B_2 in Exhibit 5.6). The "imitator" would wait for commercial developments and follow up with minor changes or improvements (B_3 in Exhibit 5.6). Exhibit 5.8 suggests when these various approaches might be more suitable to use.

Some firms do both offensive and defensive R&D work. For example, TDK corporation (Japan) characterizes its work as positive technology, negative technology,

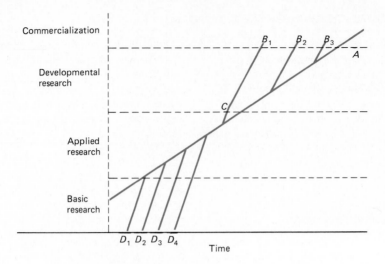

A   TYPICAL R&D PROCESS
B_{1-3} ACCELERATED DEVELOPMENTAL RESEARCH
C   ACCELERATED APPLIED RESEARCH
D_{1-4} BASIC RESEARCH FINDINGS

EXHIBIT 5.6   **Looking back from successful commercialization: transforming basic research into viable products.**
(Based on B. Gold, "Technological Diffusion in Industry: Research Needs and Shortcomings." The Journal of Industrial Economics, vol. 39 [March 1981], pp. 247–269.)

or nonexistent technology. Positive technology involves research for the purpose of upgrading existing technologies and improving products. Research on negative technology is done on processes, materials, or technology which could present a threat to existing technology. While this entails time, cost, and risk, it enhances the possibility of accumulation of new technology and keeps a firm abreast of potential substitutions. Nonexistent technology research focuses on new developments which could provide threat or opportunity in the future. Without this, delays in research of negative technology would be inevitable, and new products would cease to be developed.

As with marketing, the importance of R&D to success in business is much higher

EXHIBIT 5.7   A COMPARISON OF OFFENSIVE AND DEFENSIVE R&D APPROACHES

	Offensive	Defensive
Products or processes	Dramatically new ones	Improvement of existing ones
Production design	Flexible and responsive	Rigid, with efficiency goals
Volume	Less emphasis on cost per unit	High-volume emphasis
Implementation	New divisions or new firms	Existing structures
Timing	Longer term	Immediate impact
Environment	Proact—Use R&D to achieve change suited to your research	React—Adjust R&D to needs forecasted

EXHIBIT 5.8 AN INNOVATOR TURNED IMITATOR

In 1986, Procter & Gamble unveiled its newest product innovation, Ultra Pampers, a diaper endorsed by the National Pediatrics Nurses Association for helping to maintain healthy skin. The recent introduction signals a comeback in a market that P&G virtually created but lost ground in when it failed to realize that consumers would pay more for better-quality diapers. Last spring, Kimberly's Huggies took the number one market-share position with its contoured fitting diapers. P&G's comeback resulted from a $500 million revamp of diaper-making equipment. Kimberly is presently changing its equipment to make an equivalent product.

According to P&G, it is using a proven strategy of demonstrating consumer benefit, however slight, to take over market share. Other examples of P&G's product-differentiation strategy include the addition of tartar control to Crest and the introduction of Liquid Tide, a laundry detergent with superior cleaning power. However, competitors continue to innovate (e.g., the pump dispenser for toothpaste), leaving P&G to follow in their footsteps. Note how this relates to the management style discussed in Exhibit 5.4.

The strategy pursued by P&G adds light to our discussion of R&D with regard to offensive and defensive approaches. Although the biggest firms are thought to be fast seconds, this seems to vary with the level of technology. Reportedly, P&G lost ground to "nimbler competitors" in the market in the recent past, by lacking in offense—or innovative leads. It has assumed the imitator position in both diapers and the pump toothpaste, eventually making up lost market share. Where technologies are relatively simple, the imitator position may be quite suitable. Changes are slower but more lasting and much less modifiable, making the imitator spot more attractive. In other areas, where technology is more complex, the innovator or fast-second position is usually more desirable. Innovators, however, are usually smaller firms and often come from outside the industry.

Source: Adapted from "Procter and Gamble Banks On a New Baby: Ultra Pampers," *Business Week,* Feb. 24, 1986, pp. 36–37.

for some than for others. For instance, computer or pharmaceutical firms generally have much larger R&D budgets (5 or 6 percent of sales) than do many other industries (which are in the 1 percent range). Yet even there, some firms choose to innovate with new products, while others develop new applications or minor improvements. Of equal importance, R&D is seen as a way to improve productivity in manufacturing. Increased R&D has led to increasing factory automation after two decades of neglect in the United States. Even the service industries are recognizing the need to boost productivity. In the United States, capital investment in technology per worker averaged less than $450 per worker in the 1960s through mid-1970s. By the mid-1980s, this figure jumped to over $1000 per worker (in constant dollars).

It might be noted that while many U.S. firms have been lagging in long-term commitment to investment in risky R&D with unknown time and payoff lags, Japanese companies have surged ahead. Now many of the imitators are becoming the inventors. But even here, different firms pursue different approaches. Sony is an innovator; Matsushita is a copycat in the consumer electronics arena.

Production and Operations Management Factors [4]

Exhibit 5.9 lists the factors for analyzing production and operations management.

If we were to identify one functional area where North American firms have become less competitive in relation to overseas competitors, it would be operations. The United

EXHIBIT 5.9 INTERNAL FACTORS: PRODUCTION AND OPERATIONS MANAGEMENT

1 Lower total cost of operations compared with competitors' total costs	7 Efficient and effective offices
2 Capacity to meet market demands	8 Strategic location of facilities and offices
3 Efficient and effective facilities	9 Efficient and effective inventory-control systems
4 Raw materials and subassemblies costs	10 Efficient and effective procedures: design, scheduling, quality control
5 Adequate availability of raw materials and subassemblies	11 Efficient and effective maintenance policies
6 Efficient and effective equipment and machinery	12 Effective vertical integration or supplier relations
	13 Flexibility in operations

States used to be cited as the leader in this area. Now it seems that Japanese, Taiwanese, Korean, or European firms are the leaders. In particular, the Japanese have pushed hard on factors 1, 6, and 10 through the use of robots (five times more in use than in the United States, even though they were invented by Americans) and quality-control circles in a national effort to improve productivity. If we are to be able to compete, we cannot continue to yield whole businesses such as television and radio manufacturing and clothing to overseas competition. Steel may be the next major loss. Efforts are being made now in U.S. industry to improve quality. "Doing it right the first time" may provide more benefit to the bottom line than any realistic boost in sales volume—and frequently for an investment that is returned in less than a year.

Consider the U.S. steel firms. Their facilities are out of date and they haven't been able to raise funds to modernize. They are at a serious disadvantage against the Japanese on factors 1 and 2, though they are showing signs of making a turnaround.

With regard to factors 1 and 6, Eastern Airlines used to compete with Delta. Delta's equipment was newer and less costly to operate. Delta had a cost advantage. With the newer equipment there are fewer breakdowns, too, and so Delta had an advantage on factor 11.

With regard to factor 3, consider some of the major food chains. Safeway and Kroger have larger and newer stores than A&P. A&P has had to spend large sums to try to catch up. A&P also has factor-8 problems. Many of its stores were located in older neighborhoods with no parking. And A&P is inadequately represented in the faster-growing areas.

Consider factors 4 and 5. Ashland Oil does not own its own crude oil. In the 1973–1974 oil crisis, only government policy allowed it to continue in the gasoline business. Exxon did not have these problems.

Your exposure to production and operations management provided you with tools to help you decide how a firm can improve with regard to factors 9 to 12. The development of careful production planning and control systems, productivity improvements, supplier relations, and plant capacity and location decisions can lead to important competitive advantages for a firm. If a firm can produce at a lower cost, has the capacity to handle business when others can't, or can get raw materials at favorable prices, it has a competitive advantage.

Finally, factor 13 suggests that operations flexibility could become a competitive advantage. Since the beginning of this century, efficiency through economies of scale

EXHIBIT 5.10   THE INCREDIBLE SHRINKING PLANT

The reduction of plant size to more manageable scales is well under way at Westinghouse. A new office furniture plant at Grand Rapids employs 600 people. Its general manager, Russell Nagel, used to run a 5000-worker appliance factory before Westinghouse got out of that business. Nagel sees an enormous difference between managing big and small plants.

In the large-appliance plant, Westinghouse was trying to develop and manufacture an energy-efficient low-cost refrigerator. Nagel recalls, "For six or eight months we couldn't get the key guys from marketing and manufacturing into the same room to talk about what we were trying to do." At any given time, many were out of town or working on other projects. Westinghouse introduced the product a year late.

It is easier to keep tabs on what is happening at the new furniture factory. When Nagel took over, he realized almost immediately that it was throwing away at least $100,000 a year of wood scrap. Within a few weeks, he set up a task force of managers and union workers to deal with the problem. Within a few months they reduced the scrap to $7000 a year. "The bottom-line effect of being able to identify goals and communicate them quickly in a smaller environment is dramatic," says Nagel. "Ten years ago, if you asked me whether by going to smaller plants, you gave up a lot of efficiencies, I would have said 'yes.' Now, I can't think of any."

Source: Adapted from "Small Is Beautiful Now in Manufacturing," *Business Week,* Oct. 22, 1984, pp. 152–156.

has dominated the thinking of production executives. Longer and bigger runs can cut per-unit costs. But as we noted before, technological and economic international competitive conditions are changing the ground rules. Because of nonunion and foreign competition, it is increasingly difficult to run large plants at capacity. And as technological change shortens product life cycles (e.g. consumer electronics), plants become obsolete sooner than expected. Combined with computer-aided design and manufacturing, productivity can be raised but large plant capacities become uncompetitive.

Manufacturing people are now discussing diseconomies of scale. Huge manufacturing complexes are being replaced with newer, smaller plants which are becoming more automated, as suggested in Exhibit 5.10. While some firms still use economies of scale to gain advantage, others are finding that they have more flexibility to shift production requirements in smaller plants, achieve greater productivity, and eliminate some bureaucracy, which often leads to smoother labor relations. In an era where mass marketing gives way to a focus on needs of fragmented population groups which seem to change rapidly, flexibility in operations can very well become a competitive strength. Firms can increase process flexibility and product design flexibility, as well as add flexibility to the production infrastructure (personnel, training, inventory, quality control, and planning and scheduling). This creates aggregate manufacturing flexibility.

Corporate Resources and Personnel Factors [5]

Exhibit 5.11 lists a set of corporate resources and personnel factors which can provide competitive advantages for a firm. Each of the factors can add to the ability of a firm to achieve its objectives. Some firms are well known for these factors. General Electric, for example, has advantages with regard to most of them.

EXHIBIT 5.11   INTERNAL FACTORS: CORPORATE RESOURCES AND PERSONNEL

1 Corporate image and prestige.

2 Effective organization structure, climate, and culture.

3 Company size in relation to the industry (barrier to entry).

4 Strategic management system.

5 Enterprise's record for reaching objectives: How consistent has it been? How well does it do compared with similar enterprises?

6 Influence with regulatory and governmental bodies.

7 Effective corporate-staff support systems.

8 High-quality employees.

9 Balanced functional experience and track record of top management: Are replacements trained and ready to take over? Do the top managers work well together as a team?

10 Effective relations with trade unions.

11 Efficient and effective personnel relations policies: staffing, appraisal and promotion, training and development, and compensation and benefits.

12 Lower costs of labor (as measured by compensation, turnover, and absenteeism).

13 Effective management information and computer systems.

Some firms have attracted and held high-quality, highly productive, and loyal employees and managers. IBM, Texas Instruments, and other firms are known for this. Since these people make the decisions for all functions, this can be a crucial advantage. Many firms have purchased other firms just to get their top-quality managerial, professional, and other employees. By the same token, an organization's structure, climate, and culture can be a key advantage. Disney is well known for an overriding emphasis on a few core principles which guide decisions, employee behavior, and the operations of its business.

Being unionized can be a competitive disadvantage because of the loss of flexibility or because of the higher direct costs of labor. Some firms are unionized but have had good relations with efficient and effective unions, leading to potential advantage.

Many of these factors become particularly important when managers try to determine whether a strategy can be implemented. Weaknesses in these areas could lead to a decision of not attempting a given strategy because of the inability to carry it out effectively. For example, an acquisition candidate whose organization structure is incompatible with the structure of your firm could be a poor choice. Or a strategy to close a plant could be affected by union contracts.

Thus, factors 8 to 12 deal with the so-called people issues. And managers (whether labeled personnel, industrial relations, or human resources managers) who deal with these issues are recognized at some leading companies as a source of competitive strength. More of these managers are reporting to the CEO and are involved in making strategic decisions. If companies are constantly acquiring, merging, spinning off new divisions, entering new businesses, or getting out of old ones, management must consider the human resource questions involved—matching skills with jobs, keeping key personnel after a merger, solving human problems that arise with new technology or the closing of a plant, and so on. According to one of the new breed of human resource managers, ''Chief executives have finally come to realize that people are what give you a competitive edge, and we're telling them how to get the right people.''

Finally, with the advent of management information systems development, and usage, many firms are finding that they can turn data and information power into a potent strategic weapon. Exhibit 5.12 suggests a number of ways that firms can

EXHIBIT 5.12   TEN WAYS TO USE INFORMATION TECHNOLOGY

1 **Better financial management.** By setting up computer links between the treasurer's office and your banks, you can obtain financial information faster—and that means better cash management.

2 **Customer service.** By letting customers tap into your database to track their orders and shipments, you build loyalty and smooth relations.

3 **Locking in customers.** By creating exclusive computer communications with customers for order entry and exchange of product and service data, you can help thwart competitors.

4 **Market intelligence.** By assembling and manipulating data on demographics and competitors, you can spot untapped niches, develop new products, and avoid inventory crunches.

5 **New businesses.** Information technologies make whole new operations possible. Federal Express, for one, could not work without computer-equipped trucks and facilities.

6 **Product development.** By providing a toll-free number for consumer questions and complaints, you get ideas for product improvements and new products. In-house electronic publishing can help turn out product manuals faster for speedier introductions.

7 **Sales.** Giving salespeople portable computers so that they can get messages faster and enter orders directly adds up to quicker deliveries, better cash flow, and less paperwork.

8 **Selling extra processing power.** By using off-peak processing power to develop completely new services for outsiders, you can transfer some of the high costs of building your information network.

9 **Telemarketing.** Testing cold leads by telephone first—using computer runs to ferret out the best prospects—helps slash sales-force expenses and boost productivity.

10 **Training.** Training or retraining workers using videodisks lets them learn at their own speed—and lets you cut training costs.

Source: Adapted from J. Hamilton and C. L. Harris, "Information Power," *Business Week,* Oct. 14, 1985, pp. 108–116.

develop strengths by using information technology to gain a competitive edge. Quick access to up-to-date data on which to base decisions and make plans is now available to strategists from all over the corporation. In fact, many firms have installed a chief information officer (CIO) in their organizations. These new managers often have several functions and characteristics:

- Oversee the company's technology, including data processing, office systems, and telecommunications
- Report directly to the chairman or CEO
- Concentrate on long-term strategic use of information, leaving day-to-day operations of the computer room to subordinates.

Finance and Accounting Factors [6]

Exhibit 5.13 lists some of the major factors in finance and accounting. The appendix to this chapter provides a summary of financial analyses which can be done to help you assess this area.

One objective of the analysis is to determine if the focal firm is stronger financially than its competitors (Exhibit 5.13, factor 1). Can it hold out longer or compete more effectively because it has the financial strength to do so?

Analysis of the comparative financial condition of the firms is primarily done to determine whether the firm is capable of undertaking a particular strategy, or if it is advisable to do so. For example, many entrepreneurs fail to account for their financial

EXHIBIT 5.13   INTERNAL FACTORS: FINANCE AND ACCOUNTING

1 Total financial resources and strength—liquidity, leverage, profitability, activity, cash flows	5 Advantageous tax conditions and insurance to minimize risk exposure
2 Low cost of capital in relation to the industry and competitors because of stock price and dividend policy	6 Efficient and effective financial planning, working capital, and capital budgeting procedures
3 Effective capital structure, allowing flexibility in raising additional capital as needed; financial leverage	7 Efficient and effective accounting systems for cost, budget and profit planning, and auditing procedures
4 Amicable relations with owners and stockholders	8 Inventory valuation policies

weakness in their start-up phase. Their firms go ''belly-up'' because of the cash-flow weakness if they have not planned for it. And many firms have planned costly plant expansions only to find that they are financially incapable of paying for them.

Another purpose of financial analysis is to help pinpoint strengths or weaknesses in other functional areas, from operational and strategic perspectives. The other factors listed add efficiency (factors 2, 5, and 6) or a strategic value (factors 3 and 4) to a firm. The accounting staff function (factor 7) is a necessary one for legal and management information purposes. Accounting policies for inventory valuation (factor 8) can have strategic value when changed in response to inflation and other external changes.

This last point suggests two other important ideas to keep in mind as the financial position of the firm is analyzed. First, the financial value of a firm must be carefully considered in terms of the basis upon which the valuation is made. Stock market prices may reflect *short-term* judgments of analysts. And these judgments may be based on changes in the accounting treatment of assets for tax purposes, which may make returns appear better than they are. The book value may be ridiculously out of date based on long-term historical costs or the method of depreciation used.[1] In either case, if a firm or subunit is being valued for acquisition (or for divestiture or liquidation), the financial valuation process itself must be assessed in addition to other factors affecting such decisions. So the assessment of strength or weakness depends on the analytical approach and the interpretation of ''hard'' numbers.

A second major issue is the working capital needs for strategic versus ongoing operations. Because of past strategic choices, firms may have tied up so much cash that future options are limited. This happened to Ford and Seagrams. On the other hand, cash-rich firms must determine how long existing strengths will provide a continuous flow of funds and decide how to invest this wisely. Thus timing questions are important to financial analysis.

The final issue we wish to raise concerns the process of financial management. Earlier we suggested that the way valuations are made influences the content of the financial analysis. Also, other corporate resources factors were seen to be important, including the quality of management. Factors 4, 6, and 7 in Exhibit 5.13 hint at the

---

[1]Some analysts now suggest the computation of a Q ratio to aid investment decisions. This is the ratio of the market value of physical assets to the cost of replacing those assets.

important role of the policies and procedures established for performing financial analysis. Thus the role of the financial executive in providing support for planning can lead to a strategic advantage for the firm. Too often, the chief financial manager is seen as important only at budget preparation stages or for providing "number crunching" as input for decisions. These roles are important. But frequently the financial executives are excluded from real involvement in strategic planning because it is believed that they have short-term orientations, focus on selective components rather than on comprehensive pictures, and value precision over less tangible issues. (These remarks often apply to executives in other functional areas as well.) As a result, decision processes can suffer from what has been called a "paralysis of analysis." It is suggested that the chief financial officer's tasks of forecasting capital structure, determining resource allocation and cash flows, and raising external funds are critical functions in determining the competitive advantage of the firm.

Thus a firm at a particular time can be strong (or weak) financially, and this condition allows it to make (or prevents it from making) strategic changes. Financial ratio and accounting analyses help measure this strategic advantage. But an analysis should also be made of the process of financial management, since it too can provide advantages for the firm. Of course, as suggested in the section on corporate resources, the quality of management in any of the functional areas can provide advantages for the firm.

In sum, firms can have competitive advantages on a number of the factors just discussed. Strengths usually lead to greater "slack"—a cushion of resources which allows an organization to be flexible and adapt internally or externally. Slack enhances the ability of a firm to choose from a greater number of alternative strategies. Weaknesses or disadvantages limit the strategic options of a firm. The list of resources and factors also serves as a checklist of items to analyze about a firm (or a case) with a view to improving its operations and identifying its distinctive competencies. It is not an exhaustive list. But it does provide a useful beginning.

ANALYSIS OF STRENGTHS AND WEAKNESSES

There are a variety of ways each area of potential competitive advantage (or disadvantage) might be analyzed. First we will provide some prescriptions for how analysis should be done. Then we will summarize some evidence about whether it is done that way and what is analyzed.

Techniques of Internal Analysis [7]

As suggested earlier, a number of basic references for each area of internal analysis have been provided. It is beyond the scope of this book to summarize the techniques of analysis for the areas most business school curriculums cover in detail. For instance, a partial but far from comprehensive list of tools is identified in Exhibit 5.14.

Data for analysis and diagnosis of the factors come from several sources. One source is the data gathered in the environmental analysis and diagnosis stage of strategic management. The other source is the internal data generated in doing business

EXHIBIT 5.14   A FEW TOOLS FOR INTERNAL ANALYSIS

Finance and accounting: Capital asset pricing model; pay-back; accounting return; present value; internal rate of return; financial ratios (see appendix); fixed and variable budgets

   Human resources: Turnover analysis; morale surveys; training budgets; analysis of personnel needs and capabilities

   Marketing: Sales forecasts; market-share analysis; price-volume relationships; sales-force analysis; product and market-lines analysis

   Operations: Inventory analysis; aggregate and shop-floor simulations; break-even analysis; labor, material, and overhead-cost analysis; materials requirement planning (MRP); operations-research techniques

   R&D: Patents generated; project analysis; value analysis

and available from the management information system and the functional departments (such as marketing). One writer has suggested that the annual report, with all its faults, is another valuable source of information. So as before, verbal sources, documents, formal studies, or a management information system can provide data inputs for analysis.

In addition to these sources, there are two other analytical aids you might use to guide the internal analysis. The first is the functional-area profile. This type of profile is shown in Exhibit 5.16 (pages 172–173). The idea is to present a matrix of functional areas with characteristics common to each.

Then the strategist prepares the functional-area resource-deployment matrix (Exhibit 5.15). The firm records where it is spending its dollars and currently exerting its efforts. This information should be recorded each year so that the firm can determine the relative importance of each functional area (compared with competitors' functional areas) over time. This approach allows the firm to analyze the strategic deployment of funds and its strengths and weaknesses over time as compared with those of competitors.

We also wish to make some suggestions about how you can apply some of these techniques for strategic analysis. First, each area must be considered with respect to what its policies and approaches were, are, and will be. That is, how do current conditions *relate to* the past attainment of objectives, future expectations, or internal requirements? This question is critical to the overall gap analysis, and the answer will help you determine which areas are most important for the future. As we noted before, what is viewed as a strength now may become a weakness later. Looking at each area over time allows you to see if advantages are being developed or are deteriorating. For instance, a decline in the number of patents being generated may be a sign of potential problems in R&D or new-product development. Increasing grievances may suggest labor problems. An increase in the cost of goods sold could indicate production difficulties. Increases in the rework rate may indicate quality-control problems. A host of indicators in each area can be examined over time. In finance, the ratios noted in the appendix can be examined over several years, and pro formas can be prepared for the future. Each indicator also must be analyzed in relation to goals or requirements.

For instance, are sales quotas being met? Does the trend in debt to equity suggest

EXHIBIT 5.15 A FUNCTIONAL-AREA RESOURCE-DEPLOYMENT MATRIX

Functional areas	Resource-deployment emphasis	5 years ago	4 years ago	3 years ago	2 years ago	1 year ago	This year	Next year
R&D + engineering	% of strategic development dollars							
	Focus of efforts							
Manufacturing	% of strategic development dollars							
	Focus of efforts							
Marketing	% of strategic development dollars							
	Focus of efforts							
Finance	% of strategic development dollars							
	Focus of efforts							
Management	% of strategic development dollars							
	Focus of efforts							

problems in meeting any conditions of loan agreements with bankers? Are our hiring procedures meeting the requirements of the Equal Opportunity Employment Commission so that we can continue to secure government contracts? Any of these areas could be sources of weaknesses or strengths. For example, your firm may be a favored employer if its hiring practices are ''better'' than those of competitors.

Second, the analysis can be done on a piecemeal basis, with each area viewed independently of the others. However, the strengths and weaknesses must be compared *in relation to* one another. Trade-offs will inevitably result, but it is better to consider the needs and desires of each area together rather than let each suboptimize. Consider Exhibit 5.17 as a case in point. Manufacturing may see strength through a policy of long, steady mass production runs of a limited product line. Finance may set policies which value a low finished-goods inventory and high turnover for cash-flow improvement. It may suggest capital budgeting and investment policies which minimize the number of factories and warehouses, freight costs, etc. So far so good; these policies

EXHIBIT 5.16   TYPICAL FUNCTIONAL-AREA PROFILE

	R&D engineering (conceive/design/develop)	Manufacturing (produce)

Focus of financial deployments	$ for basic research
	$ for new product development
	$ for product improvements
	$ for process improvements
		$ for plant
		$ for equipment
		$ for inventory
		$ for labor

Physical resources	Size, age, and location of R&D facilities Size, age, and location of development facilities	No., location, size, and age of plants Degree of automation Degree of integration Type of equipment
Human resources	Nos., types, and ages of key scientists and engineers Turnover of key personnel	Nos., types, and ages of key staff personnel and foremen Turnover of key personnel
Organizational systems	System to monitor technological developments System to control conceptual/design/development process	Nature and sophistication of purchasing system; production scheduling and control system; quality control system
Technological capabilities	No. of patents No. of new products % of sales from new products Relative product quality	Raw materials availability Trends in total constant $ per-unit costs for raw materials and purchased parts; direct labor and equipment Productivity Capacity utilization Unionization

could be seen as ways to improve efficiency and gain a competitive advantage. But suppose marketing and sales efforts are directed toward the exclusive distribution of high-quality, high-priced, custom-designed outputs. The company has developed promotion policies to tap a market opportunity in this area. Its goal is better customer service through well-stocked warehouses and a wider product line. Suddenly, the assessment of production and finance strengths takes on a different meaning. And the

Marketing (distribute/sell/service)	Finance (finance)	Management (plan/organize/control)

$ for sales and promotion
$ for distribution
$ for service
$ for market research
	$ for short-term cash management
	$ for raising long-term funds
	$ for allocating long-term funds
	$ for management development
		$ for planning system
		$ for control system
		$ for management development

No. and location of sales offices No. and location of warehouses No. and location of service facilities	No. of lock boxes No. of major lenders Dispersion of stock ownership No. and types of computers	Location of corporate headquarters
Nos., types, and ages of key salespeople Marketing staff Turnover of key personnel	Nos., types, and ages of key financial and accounting personnel Turnover of key personnel	Nos., types, and ages of key managers and corporate staff Turnover of key personnel
Nature and sophistication of distribution system; service system; pricing and credit staff; market research staff	Type and sophistication of cash management system; financial markets forecasting system; corporate financial models; accounting system	Nature of organizational culture and values Sophistication of planning and control systems Delegation of authority Measurement of reward systems
Trends in total constant $ per-unit costs for sales and promotion; distribution and service % retail outlet coverage Key account advantages Price competitiveness Breadth of product line Brand loyalty Service effectiveness	Credit rating Credit availability Leverage Price-earnings ratio Stock price Cash flow Dividend payout	Corporate image prestige Influence of regulatory and governmental agencies Quality of corporate staff Organizational synergies

types and numbers of personnel to manufacture custom-designed products, staff warehouses, process and ship orders, etc., become quite different. Clearly this is an extreme example. But the point should be clear that what may be a strength in each area can result in overall weakness if the company is "pushing the cogs" in opposite directions.

In a similar view, weaknesses must be compared with strengths. Weaknesses may prevent us from taking advantage of an opportunity. They can prevent us from readily shifting strategies. But too many executives put on unneeded "blinders" by emphasizing weaknesses instead of strengths. Instead of taking a pessimistic view ("if anything can go wrong, it will"), successful strategists often take an optimistic view ("we didn't know it couldn't be done, so we did it"). Thus instead of allowing weaknesses to dominate, it is often more fruitful to take advantage of an opportunity by capitalizing on strengths. However, this must be done within the legitimate, *real* constraints which may exist because of the firm's weaknesses.

In addition to being compared over time in relation to goals and to one another, strengths and weaknesses are compared in relation to environmental conditions. The comparison is usually based on competitors, but it could include the firm's position relative to technological changes, suppliers, or the product life cycle.

Most strategists are concerned with how their firms are placed strategically relative to competitors in similar businesses. It is vital that the proper comparisons be made. For example, as the PIMS data have shown, companies with a high degree of investment intensity are often less profitable than those with lower investment-sales ratios. Similar differences exist if the firm being compared is substantially different on characteristics other than investment intensity. Thus a statement about the mission of the business as discussed in Chapter 2 becomes important as a basis for determining the relevant comparison groups. Furthermore, aside from the group itself, the company within the group that you compare your firm with makes a difference with regard to the interpretation of strengths and weaknesses. Consider ratio analysis, for example. Besides studying changes of your organization over time, should you compare these with industry *averages* or with the changes experienced by leaders? If low performers on ROI in the industry have high liquidity, for example, is the high liquidity of your firm a strength or a weakness? That may depend on other factors unique to your firm's own situation. In other words, many industries are composed of different strategic groups. Comparing ratios of Anheuser-Busch to Heilemann or LoneStar or with beer-industry averages may not make much sense. Hence, comparisons with leaders of strategic groups (or to upper- and lower-quartile performers) is more likely to reveal valid and meaningful conclusions than using "industry averages" as the basis for comparing financial ratios or other data such as marketing outlays, plant size, R&D expenditures, labor costs, and so on. Indeed, TWA was criticized when its former CEO urged executives to measure their company against industry averages than to shoot for the top. So caution in the interpretation of data is required.

It is also important to compare firms which are in the same or similar phases of the product-service life cycle. If our firm's main products or services are in the maturity stage of the life cycle, improper comparisons would be made with a firm whose main products are in the growth phase of the cycle. One representation of the life cycle is given in Exhibit 5.18.

Finally, it is important to compare strengths and weaknesses relative to their overall significance to the strategy of the firm. Crisis managers can get bogged down in analyzing fine details and "lose sight of the forest for the trees." Daily operational fluctuations and problems may drive attention away from areas of strength or weakness that are far more important to overall success. Of course, clinical judgment is required

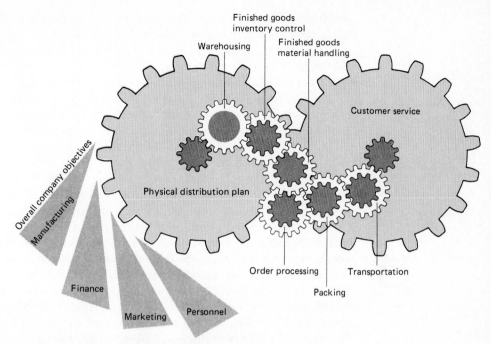

EXHIBIT 5.17   **"Cogwheels" in a physical distribution system.**
(R. Ball, "Physical Distribution: A Suitable Case for Treatment," Long Range Planning [February 1980], p. 3.)

EXHIBIT 5.18   **A common product-service life cycle.**

Phase I (Development)	Phase II (Growth)	Phase III (Maturity)	Phase IV (Shakeout)	Phase V (Decline)
Development of the product and/or service and/or process and/or market characterized by: inception; missionary work; lack of customer knowledge; much personal selling and service; continued product and/or service development; little or no competition	Growth of product and/or service and/or process and/or market characterized by: demand exceeding supply; increase in production capacity; order taking; little promotion; low sales effort; competitors enter market	Maturity of product and/or service and/or process and/or market effort; low margin mass selling; over-capacity in production; much competition	Industry consolidation; many firms exit; some focus on specific niches; others merge or take over market share from those leaving; beginning of slow decline in demand and capacity	Decline of product and/or service and/or process and/or market characterized by high substitution, decreased demand, and competitors leaving the market

for determining which areas and indicators these are. (We have more to say about this in the section on diagnosis.) The key is to identify areas and indicators which top management should focus on. Four key questions can be asked as you examine the five areas: What does this firm do particularly well? Do these competencies count, and if so, when? What does the firm do poorly? Does it matter? As companies and cases are analyzed, our advice is to not worry about head colds—if pneumonia seems to be indicated, that requires more serious analysis. (Nonetheless, if it appears that the head cold can become pneumonia, it may require treatment.)

Descriptions of Internal Analysis [8]

The discussion of analysis so far has been prescriptive. There is little descriptive research on whether and how strategists actually perform strategic advantage analysis. On the basis of a few studies two things are clear. One is that the process of internal analysis is subject to internal bias by level and type of executive. There is often disagreement among executives about the distinctive competence of their firm. Second, it does not appear that clear patterns of strengths or weaknesses emerge. Each firm seems to be unique in how it develops and uses its advantages.

But this isn't very helpful. The question is, How do you identify and use competitive advantages? You identify them on the basis of the diagnosis and analysis of strengths and weaknesses discussed earlier in the chapter. For example, distinctive competence could result from a superior delivered low-cost position or a differentiated product offering. Competitive advantages could consist of superior quality, superior service or technical assistance, a strong brand name, a unique or innovative product or service, or the status of being a full-line producer with wide distribution. Such advantages result from the strength of superior skills or resources, lower costs of manufacturing or distribution, lower cost of capital, design expertise, good trade relationships, fast and flexible response capabilities, and so on. Identification of these involves careful analysis of the various factors identified earlier.

One of the factors discussed in the operations and corporate resources sectors was whether size was a strength or weakness. The "advantage" of size deserves special treatment since we think that too many believe "bigger is better." A larger size in relation to the competition is normally viewed positively. It can give strength by allowing greater economies of scale or providing barriers to entry. However, there are some potential weaknesses associated with a larger size. Diseconomies of scale can result from rapid increases in size as we discussed earlier. The organization becomes more difficult to manage. This is typical of young, overly aggressive companies. Furthermore, large firms often become the targets of regulators, legislators, consumer activists, and competitors; many equate size with the potential for misuse of power. Moreover, small firms or SBUs are often thought to have an advantage of flexibility that allows them to change and maneuver, while larger firms or units find it more difficult to do this.

Another dilemma associated with size is its relationship to goals. A number of studies suggest that size is not necessarily directly correlated with better performance.

For instance, expansion may entail internal diseconomies of scale. And there may be limits to continued growth in a particular business. Under certain circumstances, the size of the market share itself is related to returns in a U-shaped fashion where large *and* small shares may be related to higher ROI than medium market shares.

For example, the do-it-yourself retail business has long been dominated by small mom-and-pop hardware stores and lumberyards. Several large firms (K Mart, Home Centers of America, etc.) believed they could jump in, build mammoth stores, offer discount prices, and attract customers with advertising. Instead of killing off the little guys, the big chains are fighting each other for market share and sites needed to break even on large warehouse stores. Massive advertising, cost cutting, and loss leaders to build traffic have cut gross margins tremendously. And the little guys fought back by forming alliances for buying and advertising clout and by offering personal service to the naive new do-it-yourselfers.

These and other examples suggest that expansion strategies carry with them seeds of potential competitive disadvantage where sheer size creates new management problems. Hence each firm must determine whether it is better to be a big fish in a little pond or a little fish in the sea. There are advantages in both situations, and strength or weakness can go along with a large size. Careful thought must go into the diagnosis of whether conditions being analyzed are strengths or weaknesses.

There are also some descriptions about how businesses can strengthen their competitive position and develop distinctive competence. Ohmae suggests that managers should use their analysis of strengths and weaknesses in ways which lead to competitive advantage.

1 The first approach is to readjust resource allocation to strengthen certain areas of the business. If management allocates resources exactly the same way competitors do, there will be no change in competitive position. So this approach suggests that resources should be concentrated in areas where there are key success factors (KSF) so the firm can gain a strategic advantage. Even though a firm may have no more total resources than competitors, it can achieve distinction if it focuses those resources on one crucial point.

One typical example here is the use of market segmentation. A Japanese shipbuilder segmented customer groups into seven markets and ship types into 12 product categories. After identifying key product market groups, it focused its resources and attention on these sectors to gain competitive advantage.

2 It may be that the KSF struggle is being waged, but a firm may exploit differences between itself and a competitor. Here the strategist either (*a*) makes use of the technology, sales network, and so on, of those of its products which are not directly competing with the products of competitors or (*b*) makes use of other differences in the composition of assets. Thus relative superiority is used to avoid head-on competition.

Ohmae provides an example of a Japanese film producer who could not compete with Fuji on the basis of an image problem associated with its name. Advertising could not overcome the negative connotations. However, it had a relative advantage in its costs of production; hence, it lowered prices and started to do battle on economic issues where it possessed superiority.

3 A competitor in a well-established stagnant industry may be hard to dislodge. Here an unconventional approach may be needed to upset the key factors for success that the competitor has used to build an advantage. The starting point is to challenge accepted assumptions about the way business is done, or the nature of products or processes, and gain a novel advantage by creating new success factors.

For example, a camera manufacturer wondered why photographs have to go through the negative stage before being printed, or why a camera couldn't have a built-in flash to spare users the trouble of finding and fixing an attachment. Federal Express wondered why packages were delivered point to point instead of funneled through a centralized facility. Challenging basic assumptions with questions can lead to novel ideas.

4 Finally, a competitive advantage may be obtained by means of innovations which open new markets or lead to new products. Innovation often involves finding new ways of satisfying the customer's utility function.

Suppose that you manufacture coffee and determine that the utility function of target customers is superior taste. What determines coffee taste? Kind and quality of beans, type of roast, fineness of grind, time between grinding and brewing, water hardness and temperature, style of brewing, and so on. Some of these are beyond the manufacturer's control. But others involve degrees of freedom: Water hardness could probably be overcome by incorporating a regenerable filter in the machine. The approach here is to think creatively for innovations which expand degrees of freedom to accomplish goals and develop new strengths.

In each of these approaches the principal point is to avoid doing the same thing as the competition on the same battleground. So the analyst must decide which of these approaches might be pursued to develop a sustainable distinctive competence.

The Role of Strategists in Analysis and Diagnosis

Exhibit 5.19 shows how each of the groups of strategists is involved in internal analysis and diagnosis.

If you compare this exhibit with Exhibit 3.9 you'll note that the role performances are similar, except that from what the research tells us, firms perform internal analysis less frequently and less formally, which is why there are differences between the exhibits. Given some findings that internal analysis is time-consuming and distorted, we might understand why managers are reluctant to perform internal analysis themselves. Outside consultants are not necessarily a panacea, however. An investment firm's report, for instance, may inject a bias for emphasizing financial specifics. Prescriptively, several approaches are probably useful with top management discussion on points of disagreement.

Of course, in a single-SBU firm, advantages are analyzed and diagnosed at the corporate level. In multiple-SBU firms, they are analyzed at the SBU level and then reevaluated at the corporate level and compared across SBUs.

EXHIBIT 5.19   THE ROLE OF STRATEGISTS IN INTERNAL ANALYSIS AND DIAGNOSIS

	Analysis				
Strategists	Verbal search and interviews	Docu- mentary search	Formal studies	MIS	Diagnosis and decision making
Top managers	Occasionally	Rarely	Rarely	Rarely	Performs
Corporate planners	Occasionally	Rarely	Occasionally	Rarely	Advises as requested
Board of directors	Occasionally	Rarely	Rarely	Rarely	Occasionally advises
Consultant	Rarely	Rarely	Rarely	NA	Occasionally hired to advise

DIAGNOSIS OF STRENGTHS AND WEAKNESSES [9]

As indicated earlier, the diagnostic process for internal factors parallels that process for environmental factors. Similar factors such as the strategist's characteristics, the strategist's job, and the strategist's environment affect the decision. Focusing on diagnosis of internal factors is similar to focusing on the environmental diagnosis as described in Chapter 4. However, we will add some other factors, since we are discussing the importance of subunits to the organization and its strategy.

Organization theorists suggest that the most critical units are those in the "technical core." Essentially, these are the units which perform the basic transformation of inputs into outputs called for by the mission definition. Note that this need *not* necessarily include mass production (though it could), because other types of missions do not call for this kind of transformation. Hence banks, wholesalers, retailers, and real estate and travel agents have a technical core that is somewhat different from the technical core of cigarette manufacturers. The core units for the organization in question are the primary areas for the initial diagnosis of strengths and weaknesses.

However, other units not in the technical core attempt to build their power and become important to the organization so that they may increase their share of resource allocation. Identifying these units is also important for narrowing the diagnosis of strengths and weaknesses. These units can be identified by determining how many other units they are interconnected with, whether they have a direct impact on the technical core units, and whether they are specialized in such a way that they can help reduce uncertainty. Let's consider an example. Suppose that a data processing unit builds a management information system which provides useful data for estimates of sales and production scheduling as well as for tracking the performance of warehouse operations. It has positioned itself to deal with important uncertainties, and its work flow is important input for decisions by several core units. We can expect that its potential power in the organization may lead it to become an important unit for the diagnosis of strengths and weaknesses. To the extent that other subunits are dependent on a given unit, it is more powerful and requires analysis by top management.

Of course, this discussion relates essentially to functions within SBUs. At the corporate level of analysis in a multiple-SBU firm, similar suggestions are made. But here one is analyzing the importance of entire strategic business units to overall corporate performance and strategy. That is, how dependent is the corporation on a given SBU? At this level, more global assessments of SBU strengths and weaknesses are often made and are based on relative competitive position and environmental opportunity. Chapter 7 examines how these factors can be combined to assist in strategic decision making.

Once the key areas for diagnosis have been analyzed, it is useful to prepare a strategic advantage profile (SAP) for the firm being analyzed. Similar to the ETOP, this is a tool for providing a picture of the more critical areas, which can have a relationship to the strategic posture of the firm in the future.

Exhibit 5.20 presents an example of an SAP for a hypothetical firm. Note that this firm has weaknesses in channels of distribution, facilities, and R&D and is experiencing union difficulties. This may preclude certain strategies, such as market expansion in the southwest. On the other hand, it may suggest to managers that a conscious choice to correct this weakness is important. The final conclusions depend on environmental factors, objectives, and the pattern of other strengths and weaknesses identified. For example, the financial strengths could lead to a decision to invest in updated facilities or build a sales force in the southwest if the environment shows opportunity there. Chapter 8 describes in more detail how the SAP is combined with other factors to lead to strategic decision making.

If first-generation planning is used, this diagnosis is based on the most probable future. If second-generation planning is used, several scenarios of the future are drafted—with best-case, most-probable, and worst-case assumptions. Then several diagnoses are made.

As in the preparation of an ETOP, several stages may be required before the final SAP is displayed. That is, each of the subfactors identified in Exhibits 5.3, 5.5, 5.9, 5.11, and 5.13 should be subjected to the comparative analysis discussed in our section

EXHIBIT 5.20   STRATEGIC ADVANTAGE PROFILE

Internal area	Competitive strength or weakness
Marketing	+ Product line is extensive, and service is excellent. − Channels of distribution are weak in the southwest.
R&D	− No R&D performed.
Operations	+ Excellent sourcing for raw materials. − Facilities are old and becoming outdated.
Corporate resources	0 Company size is about average for the industry. 0 Profits have been consistent but average. − Union employees complain frequently.
Finance	+ Balance sheet shows ability to obtain needed capital; low debt-equity ratio, high working capital position, and favorable stock price.

Note: + indicates strength; 0 indicates neutral; − indicates weakness.

on techniques for analysis. For example, a set of financial ratios (see the appendix) can be exhibited as a supplement to the SAP. Then a *diagnosis* of the most important ones for the organization is summarized in the final SAP.

This latter stage is probably the most crucial and most difficult. In effect, the comparative analyses require you to consider the environmental factors and time simultaneously. Let's clarify this statement.

Suppose that your analysis shows a high quick ratio for the firm compared with the ratio of your major competitor. One assessment could be that there is a potential cash management weakness. But suppose you also identified in the ETOP a threat of insufficient capital available to the industry for needed investment. Now your perception of the cash position of this firm may turn out to indicate strengths. Similarly, a high inventory position which might otherwise be viewed as a weakness could be considered a strength if demand conditions appear to be growing or if a strike appears likely.

By the same token, assessments of environmental opportunities and threats can be altered depending on your diagnosis of the internal factors. Let's say that your environmental analysis indicated a threat of the exit of sources of supplies of raw materials for your industry. Your internal analysis, however, shows that your purchasing agent has developed close contacts with the remaining suppliers; your firm is assured of a steady stream of needed inputs. Now the perception of the supplier threat is one of an opportunity to gain a competitive advantage due to your firm's particular strength in this area.

In these examples note that diagnosis involves the perception of threats and opportunities and strengths or weaknesses *in relation to one another*. The analysis of data and information can be done independently. But diagnosis requires that you consider integrating the relative information to draw conclusions. One further step is needed, however.

We have discussed this as a static process. You should recognize that events can change. Thus diagnosis also involves estimating scenarios of likely future conditions to reflect dynamic realities.

Consider the example where your firm's strength of supply contacts offsets a threat of the exit of suppliers. How long will that strength exist? Will the suppliers remain loyal or bend to pressure to supply your firm's competitors? Will the competitors alter their strategy? For instance, some may leave the business. Some may integrate backward to make their own raw materials. Others may try new methods or materials to reduce their dependence on the remaining suppliers. Each of these alternatives might be considered by your competitors. They, too, are looking to build a competitive advantage.

Another issue related to time is the question of how long a strength will remain if it is relied on extensively or overused. For instance, the KSF approach prescribes building a unique strength by concentrating resources in a single area or in a few areas. For instance, a football team may rely on a single superstar to carry the ball. Several conditions may result over time. First, competitors may start to "key on" the factor—they may try to attack it, steal, or copy your firm's strength. If the strength happens to be technological, it can become obsolete. If the strength lies in personnel, key people may resign, retire, or die. Finally, if one area receives the bulk of the resources, other areas where new competitive advantages might be generated will not develop their potential. Suppose, for example, that you have analyzed your firm's work force and found that it is made up of highly skilled and trained personnel. This could be a competitive advantage, but you observe that the facilities, machines, tools, and materials that they need to do their work effectively are out of date or lead to inefficiencies. Thus your firm cannot *use* its strength as a potential competitive advantage unless resources are allocated to correct the weakness. Some of the other approaches suggested earlier may be necessary.

Of course, the obverse problem should be recognized. If resources are spread too thinly across many areas, there is a danger that the firm will not develop a distinctive competence. Firms (and individuals) have been known to seize an opportunity without commensurate ability. As Christensen et al. suggest, "Opportunism without competence is a path to fairyland." This is particularly a danger when managers believe that they have superior ability and can succeed at almost anything on the basis of past success. And as we mentioned before, if the strengths of interdependent units are actually working against one another (Exhibit 5.17), the resulting suboptimization may lead to a competitive disadvantage.

The weaknesses of an organization may inhibit or preclude certain strategies from being considered as capable of implementation. For example, a firm with an abnormally high debt-equity ratio may find it is unable to pursue a merger because it has reached its debt "limits." Nonetheless, the role of perception creeps in here in terms of the diagnosis of this weakness. That is, the debt weakness might be corrected with an issuance of equity, assuming other financial factors are reasonable and the equity markets (environmental factor) are favorable. So it is with other weaknesses. More than one entrepreneur has been heard to remark that "We didn't know it couldn't be done, so we went ahead and did it."

In effect, a firm should develop a strategy over time which revolves around an area of distinctive competence. With this approach the firm can develop slack resources that can evolve into new areas of strength when old ones falter (and they inevitably do). At the same time, the weaknesses which are identified as potentially important to the future should receive management attention. This may require a strategy to acquire personnel or other strengths which are currently lacking, if the firm is incapable of developing them because of internal resource weaknesses.

Many U.S. companies are trying to be more competitive these days with the kind of strategic thinking we have identified here. Many firms are planning to invest in more efficient plants and equipment, invest in more research and development, improve quality of service to customers, adopt more aggressive marketing tactics, and try to reduce labor costs in an effort to develop sustainable competitive advantage. Exhibit 5.21 shows a firm in this process.

As you may have noticed, the discussion has begun to address the pros and cons of alternative strategies. The Boston Consulting Group suggests that the number of competitive advantages and the size of the advantages lead to different kinds of strategies. Exhibit 5.22 explains this. For example, if there are many ways to create advantages such as in the fast food business but the size of those advantages is small, then the firm should probably seek to stabilize.

EXHIBIT 5.21   DEVELOPING A STRATEGIC ADVANTAGE

Compared with AT&T, GTE, and IBM, Continental Telephone would hardly be viewed by most as a firm with the kinds of strengths needed to compete in the booming market for transmitting data communications. In the amalgam of 1800 rural telephone exchanges spread over 37 states, 30 percent of the subscribers still share party lines. The holding company has little research and development and no manufacturing capability of its own. Compared with the assets of AT&T, its $3 billion in assets is minuscule, and its 1980 revenue of $1.1 billion was just over 2 percent of the revenue of its giant competitor. The price-earnings ratio is about standard for regulated utilities but far lower than the ratios of the computer companies expected to play a major role in the market.

However, a key strength is an aggressive management team atypical of the management of regulated telephone companies. At age 70, the founder and chairman believes that the best defense is a good offense. A carefully planned series of acquisitions and joint ventures has been designed so that the company can develop the strengths it needs to become a major supplier of data and voice communication services.

A joint venture with Fairchild (Am Sat) gives Continental strength in satellite transmission. A satellite receiving station can be set up for 10 percent of the cost of what AT&T needs to lay out comparable ground lines. The purchase of Executone, a PBX marketing firm, provided a base from which to build a business in intelligent terminals and digital telephone switches, which will become the hub of the automated office. The joint-venture approach, in particular, provides Continental with a way to use its limited resources to enter areas that it could not enter on its own.

Of course, some observers are skeptical. A GTE executive sees little synergy in the recent acquisitions (but Continental executives see them as complementary). And the task of integrating the pieces into a single network is difficult to accomplish. Further, AT&T, GTE, IBM, and Xerox are not standing still. If it's a game for giants, Continental does not yet qualify.

The perception at Continental, though, is that it has a head start, and it can keep the customers it gets before its regulated competitors are allowed to enter the fray. Furthermore, Continental sees its size as an advantage. Even if it captures only 5 percent of the market, that will represent a revenue increase of almost 700 percent. It can turn its business around faster and has already started putting the pieces together.

The weaknesses it believes require long-term development are the need for aggressive marketing and the need for skilled personnel who can manage and integrate high technology. Additional acquisitions and joint ventures are planned to correct these weaknesses.

You might note that several of the points discussed in this chapter are brought together here. Perceptions of relative strength and weakness, relevant comparison groups, long-term development of resources, and the relationship between competitive advantage and environmental threats and opportunities have all helped determine the way in which this firm has chosen to orient itself strategically.

Source: Adapted from "Continental Telephone: Taking On the Giants in Telecommunications," *Business Week,* Feb. 9, 1981, pp. 50–56.

However, we think that this ignores some of the environmental factors described in our earlier chapters. And it is hoped that you can find ways to increase either the size or number of advantages to increase your options. Thus, diagnosis of combining the ETOP and the SAP should lead to examining a wider variety of strategy alternatives than is suggested here, which is the subject of Chapters 6 and 7.

SUMMARY

The chapter described the internal analysis and diagnosis process paralleling the environmental analysis process covered in Chapters 3 and 4. Internal analysis and diagnosis is the process by which the strategists examine the firm's internal factors to

Size of the competitive advantage which can be achieved

	Small	Large
Many	**Key competitive feature:** Many ways to gain an edge, but the size of the edge counts for little in the marketplace. Strategy prescriptions: ● Carve out a position and hold it. ● Emphasize profits now. ● Minimize investment. ● Be cautious about expansion.	**Key competitive feature:** A specialized approach to the many market segments is essential and so is creating and protecting the advantage in serving these segments. Strategy prescriptions: ● Seek a niche. ● Get in position to serve selected segments. Spend heavily to build and fortify the chosen advantage. ● Stay ahead of rivals who aspire to gain the same advantage. ● Watch out for change.
Few	**Key competitive feature:** Almost a pure cost–price game; on other factors, all firms are in about equal position. In the absence of price–cost differences, there is a virtual competitive stalemate. Strategy prescriptions: ● Use aggressive cost reduction strategies. ● Emphasize ways to improve efficiency. ● Manage to increase cash flow. ● Look for diversification opportunities.	**Key competitive feature:** Only those who get and keep one of the large competitive advantages will survive; usually low cost is the primary advantage that is available. Often, the name of the game is volume. Strategy prescriptions: ● Pursue economies of scale. ● Ride the experience curve downward by getting volume up. ● Go after the customers of weak firms. ● If weak, get out or look for new ways to compete.

Different ways a competitive advantage can be created

EXHIBIT 5.22 **Strategies based on competitive advantages.**
(Adapted from an approach suggested by Alan Zakon, Boston Consulting Group, in an address to the Academy of Management, 1982.)

determine where the firm has significant strengths and weaknesses. This is needed so the firm can exploit opportunities, meet threats, and correct weaknesses inhibiting a desired strategy or putting the firm at a competitive disadvantage.

The areas covered in the chapter include internal factors to be analyzed and diagnosed, techniques of internal analysis, the reality of internal analysis, the role of strategists in this process, and the diagnosis of the internal factors.

The internal factors that management analyzes and diagnoses are marketing and distribution, R&D and engineering, production and operations management, corporate resources and personnel, and finance and accounting. Each of these factors was broken down and each subcategory was illustrated to help you digest the internal analysis and diagnosis process. It was suggested that strengths are needed to build slack to give firms greater strategic options, and weaknesses must be overcome where possible.

Techniques of internal analysis were described. Data and indicators of various subfactors should be gathered so that *relative comparisons* can be made. Comparisons are necessary in the following areas to get a clearer picture of strengths and weaknesses: past, present, and future conditions; internal goals and external requirements; the way that each functional area relates to other functional areas; and environmental factors: competitors, technology, suppliers, and the product life cycle. Two analytical tools were suggested as useful guides for the analysis, and four key questions were suggested to help identify distinctive competencies—What does the firm do well? Do these competencies count? What does the firm do poorly? Does it matter?

Research on internal analysis indicates that this process is not scientific. But very little research has been done on this subject. The studies which exist indicate that executives perceive strengths and weaknesses differently and that firms seem to be unique in their particular pattern of competitive advantages. That uniqueness can be developed into competitive advantages in a variety of ways.

A brief section on the role of strategists in the internal analysis and diagnosis process suggests the need to formalize the process of internal analysis for better strategic management.

The chapter concludes with our suggestions for performing internal diagnosis. Focusing the diagnosis is affected by factors outlined in Chapter 4. But in addition, the analyst should determine the areas of greatest importance to strategic performance: technical core units and units which are pervasive and can reduce uncertainty. Once the diagnosis is focused, the strategic advantage profile (SAP) is defined and its development is outlined.

The strategic advantage profile is a tool for making a systematic evaluation of the enterprise's internal factors which are significant for the company in its environment.

What this profile does is give a visual representation of what the company is as a result of developing from past strategic decisions and interaction with its environment. Suggestions are offered for interpreting an internal analysis.

In sum, the chapter focused on how to analyze the internal factors realistically and how to diagnose their significance. Then the executive can develop an SAP and match it with the ETOP to create conditions for adjusting or changing strategies or policies.

The process is summarized in proposition form as follows:

Proposition 5.1

A firm whose strategy fits its environment, considering its competitive advantages, will be more effective than one whose strategy does not.

Proposition 5.2

A firm which develops slack resources through distinctive competence will be more effective than one which does not.

This chapter completes the analysis and diagnosis discussion. Chapter 6 begins the three-chapter discussion of the choice phase of the strategic management process. We have now examined conditions (internal and external) which might create a gap between the ideal and expected positions of the firm in the future. Next we will examine ways in which the gap may be reduced, by examining strategy alternatives and the choice of a strategy.

Appendix: Using Financial Analysis*

One of the most important tools for assessing the strength of an organization within its industry is financial analysis. Managers, investors, and creditors all employ some form of this analysis as the beginning point for their financial decision making. Investors use financial analyses in making decisions about whether to buy or sell stock, and creditors use them in deciding whether or not to lend. They provide managers with a measurement of how the company is doing in comparison with its performance in past years and with the performance of competitors in the industry.

Although financial analysis is useful for decision making, there are some weaknesses that should be noted. Any picture that it provides of the company is based on past data. Although trends may be noteworthy, this picture should not automatically be assumed to be applicable to the future. In addition, the analysis is only as good as the accounting procedures that have provided the information. When making comparisons between companies, one should keep in mind the variability of accounting procedures from firm to firm.

There are four basic groups of financial ratios: liquidity, leverage, activity, and profitability.

Depicted in Exhibit 5.23 are the specific ratios calculated for each of the basic groups. Liquidity and leverage ratios represent an assessment of the risk of the firm. Activity and profitability ratios are measures of the return generated by the assets of the firm. The interaction between certain groups of ratios is indicated by arrows.

Typically two common financial statements are used in financial analyses: the balance sheet and the income statement. Exhibit 5.24 is a balance sheet and Exhibit 5.25 an income statement for the ABC Company. These statements will be used to illustrate the financial analyses.

Liquidity Ratios

Liquidity ratios are used as indicators of a firm's ability to meet its short-term obligations. These obligations include any current liabilities, including currently maturing long-term debt. Current assets move through a normal cash cycle of inventories—sales—accounts receivable—cash. The firm then uses cash to pay off or reduce its current liabilities. The best-known liquidity ratio is the current ratio: current assets divided by current liabilities. For the ABC Company the current ratio is calculated as follows:

$$\frac{\text{Current assets}}{\text{Current liabilities}} = \frac{\$4,125,000}{\$2,512,500} = 1.64 \ (1988)$$

$$= \frac{\$3,618,000}{\$2,242,250} = 1.61 \ (1987)$$

*Prepared by Elizabeth Gatewood, University of Georgia.

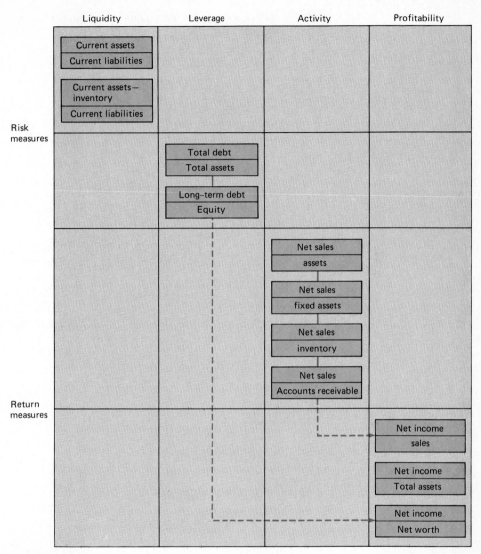

EXHIBIT 5.23   Financial ratios.

Most analysts suggest a current ratio of 2 to 3. A large current ratio is not necessarily a good sign; it may mean that an organization is not making the most efficient use of assets. The optimum current ratio will vary from industry to industry, with the more volatile industries requiring higher ratios.

Since slow-moving or obsolescent inventories could overstate a firm's ability to meet short-term demands, the quick ratio is sometimes preferred to assess a firm's liquidity. The quick ratio is current assets minus inventories, divided by current liabilities. The quick ratio for the ABC Company is calculated as follows:

$$\frac{\text{Current assets } - \text{ inventories}}{\text{Current liabilities}} = \frac{\$1,950,000}{\$2,512,500} = 0.78 \text{ (1988)}$$

$$= \frac{\$1,618,000}{\$2,242,250} = 0.72 \text{ (1987)}$$

A quick ratio of approximately 1 would be typical for American industries. Although there is less variability in the quick ratio than in the current ratio, stable industries would be able to safely operate with a lower ratio.

EXHIBIT 5.24   ABC COMPANY BALANCE SHEET AS OF DECEMBER 31

		1988		1987
Assets				
Current assets:				
Cash		$ 140,000		$ 115,000
Accounts receivable		1,760,000		1,440,000
Inventory		2,175,000		2,000,000
Prepaid expenses		50,000		63,000
Total current assets		$4,125,000		$3,618,000
Fixed assets:				
Long-term receivables		$1,255,000		$1,090,000
Property and plant	$2,037,000		$2,015,000	
Less: Accumulated depreciation	862,000		860,000	
Net property and plant		1,175,000		1,155,000
Other fixed assets		550,000		530,000
Total fixed assets		$2,980,000		$2,775,000
Total assets		$7,105,000		$6,393,000
Liabilities and Stockholders' Equity				
Current liabilities:				
Accounts payable		$1,325,000		$1,225,000
Bank loans payable		475,000		550,000
Accrued federal taxes		675,000		425,000
Current maturities (long-term debt)		17,500		26,000
Dividends payable		20,000		16,250
Total current liabilities		$2,512,500		$2,242,250
Long-term liabilities		1,350,000		1,425,000
Total liabilities		$3,862,500		$3,667,250
Stockholders' equity:				
Common stock (104,046 shares outstanding in 1983; 101,204 shares outstanding in 1982)		$ 44,500		$ 43,300
Additional paid-in capital		568,000		372,450
Retained earnings		2,630,000		2,310,000
Total stockholders' equity		$3,242,500		$2,725,750
Total liabilities and stockholders' equity		$7,105,000		$6,393,000

EXHIBIT 5.25   ABC COMPANY INCOME STATEMENT FOR THE YEARS ENDING DECEMBER 31

		1988		1987
Net sales		$8,250,000		$8,000,000
Less: Cost of goods sold	$5,100,000		$5,000,000	
Administrative expenses	1,750,000		1,680,000	
Other expenses	420,000		390,000	
Total		7,270,000		7,070,000
Earnings before interest and taxes		$ 980,000		$ 930,000
Less: Interest expense		210,000		210,000
Earnings before taxes		$ 770,000		$ 720,000
Less: Federal income taxes		360,000		325,000
Earnings after taxes (net income)		$ 410,000		$ 395,000
Common-stock cash dividends		$ 90,000		$ 84,000
Addition to retained earnings		$ 320,000		$ 311,000
Earnings per common share		$ 3.940		$ 3.90
Dividends per common share		$ 0.865		$ 0.83

Leverage Ratios

Leverage ratios identify the source of a firm's capital—owners or outside creditors. The term "leverage" refers to the fact that using capital with a fixed interest charge will "amplify" either profits or losses in relation to the equity of holders of common stock. The most commonly used ratio is total debt divided by total assets. Total debt includes current liabilities and long-term liabilities. This ratio is a measure of the percentage of total funds provided by debt. A total debt–total assets ratio higher than 0.5 is usually considered safe only for firms in stable industries.

$$\frac{\text{Total debt}}{\text{Total assets}} = \frac{\$3,862,500}{\$7,105,000} = 0.54 \ (1988)$$

$$= \frac{\$3,667,250}{\$6,393,000} = 0.57 \ (1987)$$

The ratio of long-term debt to equity is a measure of the extent to which sources of long-term financing are provided by creditors. It is computed by dividing long-term debt by the stockholders' equity.

$$\frac{\text{Long-term debt}}{\text{Equity}} = \frac{\$1,350,000}{\$3,242,500} = 0.42 \ (1988)$$

$$= \frac{\$1,425,000}{\$2,725,750} = 0.52 \ (1987)$$

Activity Ratios

Activity ratios indicate how effectively a firm is using its resources. By comparing revenues with the resources used to generate them, it is possible to establish an efficiency of operation. The asset turnover ratio indicates how efficiently management is employing total assets. Asset turnover is calculated by dividing sales by total assets. For the ABC Company, asset turnover is calculated as follows:

$$\text{Asset turnover} = \frac{\text{Sales}}{\text{Total assets}} = \frac{\$8,250,000}{\$7,105,000} = 1.16 \text{ (1988)}$$

$$= \frac{\$8,000,000}{\$6,393,000} = 1.25 \text{ (1987)}$$

The ratio of sales to fixed assets is a measure of the turnover on plant and equipment. It is calculated by dividing sales by net fixed assets.

$$\text{Fixed asset turnover} = \frac{\text{Sales}}{\text{Net fixed assets}} = \frac{\$8,250,000}{\$2,980,000} = 2.77 \text{ (1988)}$$

$$= \frac{\$8,000,000}{\$2,775,000} = 2.88 \text{ (1987)}$$

Industry figures for asset turnover will vary with capital-intensive industries, and those requiring large inventories will have much smaller ratios.

Another activity ratio is inventory turnover, estimated by dividing sales by average inventory. The norm for American industries is 9, but whether the ratio for a particular firm is higher or lower normally depends upon the product sold. Small, inexpensive items usually turn over at a much higher rate than larger, expensive ones. Since inventories are normally carried at cost, it would be more accurate to use the cost of goods sold in place of sales in the numerator of this ratio. Established compilers of industry ratios such as Dun and Bradstreet, however, use the ratio of sales to inventory.

$$\text{Inventory turnover} = \frac{\text{Sales}}{\text{Inventory}} = \frac{\$8,250,000}{\$2,175,000} = 3.79 \text{ (1988)}$$

$$= \frac{\$8,000,000}{\$2,000,000} = 4 \text{ (1987)}$$

The accounts receivable turnover is a measure of the average collection period on sales. If the average number of days varies widely from the industry norm, it may be an indication of poor management. A too low ratio could indicate the loss of sales because of a too restrictive credit policy. If the ratio is too high, too much capital is being tied up in accounts receivable, and management may be increasing the chance of bad debts. Because of varying industry credit policies, a comparison for the firm over time or within an industry is the only useful analysis. Because information on credit sales for other firms is generally unavailable, total sales must be used. Since not all firms have the same percentage of credit sales, there is only approximate comparability among firms.

$$\text{Accounts receivable turnover} = \frac{\text{Sales}}{\text{Accounts receivable}} = \frac{\$8,250,000}{\$1,760,000} = 4.69 \ (1988)$$

$$= \frac{\$8,000,000}{\$1,440,000} = 5.56 \ (1987)$$

$$\text{Average collection period} = \frac{360}{\text{Accounts receivable turnover}}$$

$$= \frac{360}{4.69} = 77 \ \text{days} \ (1988)$$

$$= \frac{360}{5.56} = 65 \ \text{days} \ (1987)$$

Profitability Ratios

Profitability is the net result of a large number of policies and decisions chosen by an organization's management. Profitability ratios indicate how effectively the total firm is being managed. The profit margin for a firm is calculated by dividing net earnings by sales. There is wide variation among industries, but the average for American firms is approximately 5 percent.

$$\frac{\text{Net earnings}}{\text{Sales}} = \frac{\$410,000}{\$8,250,000} = 0.0497 \ (1988)$$

$$= \frac{\$395,000}{\$8,000,000} = 0.0494 \ (1987)$$

A second useful ratio for evaluating profitability is the return on investment—or ROI, as it is frequently called—found by dividing net earnings by total assets. The ABC Company's ROI is calculated as follows:

$$\frac{\text{Net earnings}}{\text{Total assets}} = \frac{\$410,000}{\$7,105,000} = 0.0577 \ (1988)$$

$$= \frac{\$395,000}{\$6,393,000} = 0.0618 \ (1987)$$

The ratio of net earnings to net worth is a measure of the rate of return or profitability of the stockholders' investment. It is calculated by dividing net earnings by net worth, the common-stock equity and retained-earnings account. ABC Company's return on net worth, also called ROE, is calculated as follows:

$$\frac{\text{Net earnings}}{\text{Net worth}} = \frac{\$410,000}{\$3,242,500} = 0.1264 \ (1988)$$

$$= \frac{\$395,000}{\$2,725,750} = 0.1449 \ (1987)$$

It is often difficult to determine causes for lack of profitability. The Du Pont system of financial analysis provides management with clues to the lack of success of a firm. This financial tool brings together activity, profitability, and leverage measures and shows how these ratios interact to determine the overall profitability of the firm. A depiction of the system is set forth in Exhibit 5.26.

The right side of the figure develops the turnover ratio. This section breaks down total assets into current assets (cash, marketable securities, accounts receivable, and inventories) and fixed assets. Sales divided by these total assets gives the turnover on assets.

The left side of the figure develops the profit margin on sales. The individual expense items plus income taxes are subtracted from sales to produce net profits after taxes. Net profits divided by sales gives the profit margin on sales. When the asset turnover ratio on the right side of Exhibit 5.26 is multiplied by the profit margin on sales developed on the left side of the figure, the product is the return on assets (ROI) for the firm. This can be shown by the following formula:

$$\frac{\text{Sales}}{\text{Total assets}} \times \frac{\text{Net earnings}}{\text{Sales}} = \frac{\text{Net earnings}}{\text{Total assets}} = \text{ROI}$$

EXHIBIT 5.26   Du Pont's financial analysis.

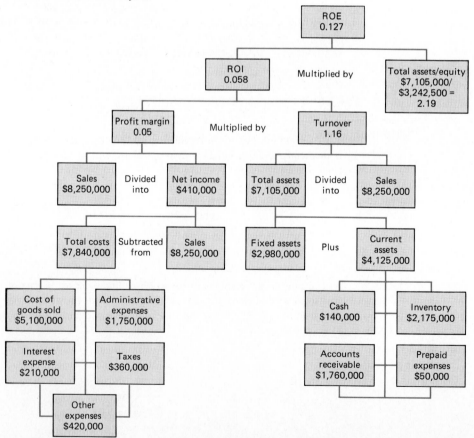

The last step in the Du Pont analysis is to multiply the rate of return on assets (ROI) by the equity multiplier, which is the ratio of assets to common equity, to obtain the rate of return on equity (ROE). This percentage rate of return could, of course, be calculated directly by dividing net income by common equity. However, the Du Pont analysis demonstrates how the return on assets and the use of debt interact to determine the return on equity.

The Du Pont system can be used to analyze and improve the performance of a firm. On the left, or profit, side of the figure, attempts to increase profits and sales could be investigated. The possibilities of raising prices to improve profits (or lowering prices to improve volume) or seeking new products or markets, for example, could be studied. Cost accountants and production engineers could investigate ways to reduce costs. On the right, or turnover, side, financial officers could analyze the effect of reducing investment in various assets as well as the effect of alternative financial structures.

There are two basic approaches to using financial ratios. One approach is to evaluate the corporation's performance over several years. Financial ratios are computed for different years, and then an assessment is made about whether there has been an improvement or deterioration over time. Financial ratios can also be computed for projected, or pro forma, statements and compared with present and past ratios.

The other approach is to evaluate a firm's financial condition and compare it with the financial conditions of similar firms or with industry data in the same period. Such a comparison gives insight into the firm's relative financial condition and performance. Financial ratios for industries are provided by Robert Morris Associates, Dun and Bradstreet, and various trade association publications. (Associations and their addresses are listed in the *Encyclopedia of Associations* or the *Directory of National Trade Associations*.) Information about individual firms is available through *Moody's Manual,* Standard and Poor's manuals and surveys, annual reports to stockholders, and the major brokerage houses.

To the extent possible, accounting data from different companies must be standardized so that companies can be compared or so that a specific company can be compared with industry data. It is important to read any footnotes of financial statements, since various accounting or management practices can have an effect on the financial picture of the company. For example, firms using sale-leaseback methods may have leverage pictures that are quite different from what is shown as debts or assets on the balance sheet.

Analysis of the Sources and Uses of Funds

The purpose of this analysis is to determine how the company is using its financial resources from year to year. By comparing balance sheets from one year to the next, one may determine how funds were obtained and the way in which these funds were employed during the year.

To prepare a statement of the sources and uses of funds it is necessary to (1) classify balance sheet changes that increase cash and changes that decrease cash, (2) classify from the income statement factors that increase or decrease cash, and (3) consolidate this information on a sources and uses of funds statement form.

Sources of funds that increase cash are as follows:

1 A net decrease in any asset other than a depreciable fixed asset
2 A gross decrease in a depreciable fixed asset
3 A net increase in any liability
4 Proceeds from the sale of stock
5 The operation of the company (net income, and depreciation if the company is profitable)

Uses of funds include

1 A net increase in any asset other than a depreciable fixed asset
2 A gross increase in depreciable fixed assets
3 A net decrease in any liability
4 A retirement or purchase of stock
5 Payment of cash dividends

We compute gross changes to depreciable fixed assets by adding depreciation from the income statement for the period to net fixed assets at the end of the period and then subtracting from the total the net fixed assets at the beginning of the period. The residual represents the change in depreciable fixed assets for the period.

For the ABC Company the following change would be calculated:

Net property and plant (1988)	$1,175,000
Depreciation for 1988	+ 80,000
	$1,255,000
Net property and plant (1987)	− 1,155,000
	$ 100,000

To avoid double counting, the change in retained earnings is not shown directly in the funds statement. When the funds statement is prepared, this account is replaced by the earnings after taxes, or net income, as a source of funds and dividends paid during the year as a use of funds. The difference between net income and the change in the retained-earnings account will equal the amount of dividends paid during the year. The accompanying sources and uses of funds statement was prepared for the ABC Company.

A funds analysis is useful for determining trends in working-capital positions and for demonstrating how the firm has acquired and employed its funds during some period.

ABC CO.'S SOURCES AND USES OF FUNDS STATEMENT FOR 1988

Sources	
Prepaid expenses	$ 13,000
Accounts payable	100,000
Accrued federal taxes	250,000
Dividends payable	3,750
Common stock	1,200
Additional paid-in capital	195,500
Earnings after taxes (net income)	410,000
Depreciation	80,000
Total sources	$1,053,450
Uses	
Cash	$ 25,000
Accounts receivable	320,000
Inventory	175,000
Long-term receivables	165,000
Property and plant	100,000
Other fixed assets	20,000
Bank loans payable	75,000
Current maturities of long-term debt	8,500
Long-term liabilities	75,000
Dividends paid	90,000
Total uses	$1,053,450

Ratios and working capital	1984	1985	1986	1987	1988	Trend	Standard	Interpretation
Liquidity: Current								
Quick								
Leverage:								
(etc.)								
Working-capital position								

EXHIBIT 5.27 **A summary of the financial position of a firm.**

Conclusion

It is recommended that you prepare a chart such as Exhibit 5.27 so that you can develop a useful portrayal of these financial analyses. The chart allows a display of the ratios over time. The Trend column could include arrows to indicate "favorable" (↑), "neutral" (—), and "unfavorable" (↓) for the ratios over time. The Standard column could include the desired (or required) ratio. The Interpretation column can be used to describe the meaning of the ratios for this firm. The chart gives a basic display of the ratios as one aspect of the firm's financial condition.

REFERENCES

[1] Strategic Advantage Factors

Croon, P.: "Aids in Determining Strategy: The Internal Analysis," *Long Range Planning,* vol. 12, no. 4 (August, 1979), pp. 65–73.

Porter, M. E.: *Competitive Strategy: Techniques for Analyzing Industries and Competitors* (New York: Free Press, 1980).

Steiner, G.: *Strategic Factors in Business Success* (New York: Financial Executives Research Foundation, 1965).

Wirnerfelt, B.: "A Resource-Based View of the Firm," *Strategic Management Journal,* vol. 5 (1984), pp. 171–180.

[2] Analyzing Marketing and Distribution

Abell, D. F., and J. S. Hammond: *Strategic Market Planning* (Englewood Cliffs, N.J.: Prentice-Hall, 1979).

Kotler, P.: *Marketing Management* (Englewood Cliffs, N.J.: Prentice-Hall, 1980).

"Marketing: The New Priority," *Business Week,* Nov. 21, 1983, pp. 96–106.

[3] Analyzing R&D and Engineering

Boseman, B., M. Crow, and A. Link (eds.): *Strategic Management of Industrial R&D* (Lexington, Mass.: Lexington Books, 1984).

Gold, B.: "Strengthening Managerial Approaches to Improving Technological Capabilities," *Strategic Management Journal,* vol. 4 (1983), pp. 209–220.

Helm, L.: "The Big Two of Consumer Electronics," *Business Week,* Dec. 30, 1985, pp. 62–64.

Joseph, J., and A. Hall: "Japan Focuses on Basic Research to Close the Creativity Gap," *Business Week,* Feb. 25, 1985, pp. 94–96.

Mitchell, R.: "High Tech to the Rescue," *Business Week,* June 16, 1986, pp. 100–104.

"A Productivity Revolution in the Service Sector," *Business Week,* Sept. 5, 1983, pp. 106–108.

"Spending for Research Still Outpaces Inflation," *Business Week,* July 6, 1981, pp. 60–75.

[4] Analyzing Production and Operations Management

Buffa, E.: "Making American Manufacturing Competitive," in G. Carroll and D. Vogel (eds.): *Strategy and Organization: A West Coast Perspective* (Boston: Pitman, 1984).

Ignatius, D.: "Aging Mills: U.S. Steel Makers Fail to Modernize Quickly, Fall Behind Japanese," *Wall Street Journal,* Aug. 3, 1977.

Kiechel, W.: "The Food Giants Struggle to Stay in Step with Consumers," *Fortune,* Sept. 11, 1978.

"Quality: The U.S. Drives to Catch Up," *Business Week,* Nov. 1, 1982, pp. 66–69.

"Small is Beautiful Now in Manufacturing," *Business Week,* Oct. 22, 1984, pp. 152–156.

"Steel's Sea of Troubles," *Business Week,* Sept. 19, 1977.

[5] Analyzing Corporate Resources and Personnel

"Business is Turning Data Into a Potent Strategic Weapon," *Business Week,* Aug. 22, 1983, pp. 92–98.

Cushman, R.: "On Becoming a Billion Dollar Company," *Business Week,* May 19, 1980, p. 14.

Dobrzynski, J. H., J. P. Tarpey, and R. Aikman: "Small Is Beautiful," *Business Week,* May 27, 1985, pp. 88–90.

Ginzberg, E., and G. Vojta: *Beyond Human Scale: The Large Corporation at Risk* (New York: Basic Books, 1985).

"Hardware Wars: The Big Boys Might Lose This One," *Business Week,* Oct. 14, 1985, pp. 84–90.

Hoerr, J.: "Human Resource Managers Aren't Corporate Nobodies Anymore," *Business Week,* Dec. 2, 1985, pp. 58–59.

"Management's Newest Star: Meet the Chief Information Officer," *Business Week,* Oct. 13, 1986, pp. 160–168.

"Sony: A Diversification Plan Tuned to the People Factor," *Business Week,* Feb. 9, 1981, pp. 88–89.

[6] Analyzing Finance and Accounting

"Asset Redeployment," *Business Week,* Aug. 24, 1981, pp. 68–74.

Naylor, T. H.: "Management Is Drowning in Numbers," *Business Week,* Apr. 6, 1981, pp. 14–15.

Peavy, J. W.: "Modern Financial Theory, Corporate Strategy, and Public Policy," *Academy of Management Review,* vol. 9 (1984), pp. 152–157.

"The Q-Ratio: Fuel for the Merger Mania," *Business Week,* Aug. 24, 1981, p. 30.

"Seagram: Its Cash Hoard Is Spent, and Its Future Is Up in the Air," *Business Week,* Dec. 21, 1981, pp. 98–102.

[7] Techniques for Analyzing Strengths and Weaknesses

Ball, R.: "Physical Distribution: A Suitable Case for Treatment," *Long Range Planning,* vol. 13 (February 1980), pp. 2–11.

Dubin, R. A., and J. R. Norman: "The Airlines," *Business Week,* July 1, 1985, p. 22.

Hofer, C., and D. Schendel: *Strategy Formulation: Analytical Concepts* (St. Paul, Minn.: West, 1978), p. 149.

Lieberman, M. B.: "The Learning Curve, Diffusion, and Competitive Strategy," research paper #766a, Graduate School of Business, Stanford University, 1985.

[8] Descriptions of Internal Analysis

Day, G. S.: *Strategic Market Planning* (St. Paul, MN: West, 1984).

Hitt, M. A., and R. D. Ireland: "Corporate Distinctive Competence, Strategy, Industry and Performance," *Strategic Management Journal,* vol. 6 (1985), pp. 273–294.

Ohmae, K.: *The Mind of the Strategist: The Art of Japanese Business* (New York: McGraw-Hill, 1982).

Stevenson, H. H.: "Defining Strengths and Weaknesses," *Sloan Management Review,* vol. 17, no. 3 (Spring 1976), pp. 51–68.

[9] Diagnosing Internal Factors Strategically

Christensen, C. R., K. R. Andrews, and J. L. Bower: *Business Policy* (Homewood, Ill.: Richard D. Irwin, 1978).

"Fighting Back: It Can Work," *Business Week,* Aug. 26, 1985, pp. 62–68.

Kiechel, W.: "Three (or Four, or More) Ways to Win," *Fortune,* Oct. 19, 1981, pp. 181–188.

Porter, M. E.: *Competitive Advantage* (New York: Free Press, 1985).

Zakon, A.: Address to Business Policy and Planning Division, Academy of Management, New York, 1982.

CHAPTER OUTLINE

GENERIC STRATEGY ALTERNATIVES

OBJECTIVES

- To understand why strategists should consider several alternative strategies prior to making a strategic choice
- To review the major strategic alternatives available to firms
- To understand the advantages and disadvantages of various alternatives

INTRODUCTION

Chapter 6 begins a three-chapter unit on the strategic choice phase of the strategic management process. Let us now assume that you as the strategist have thoroughly analyzed the environment for opportunities and threats. You have prepared the environmental threat and opportunity profile (Chapters 3 and 4). You have done a good job assessing the enterprise's strengths and weaknesses. You have prepared the strategic advantage profile (Chapter 5). You have also reexamined ideal goals in light of the expected outcomes of pursuing the existing strategy (Chapters 1 and 2). As a result, you should be in a position to consider the underlying potential for a gap between expected and ideal performance outcomes.

As indicated in Exhibit 6.1, you have completed the analysis and diagnosis phase of the strategic management process and are ready to begin the choice phase. This phase consists of two activities:

1 The generation of a reasonable number of strategic alternatives that will help fill the gaps matching the environmental threat and opportunity profile with the strategic advantage profile (Chapters 6 and 7)

2 The choice of a strategy to reduce the gaps (Chapter 8)

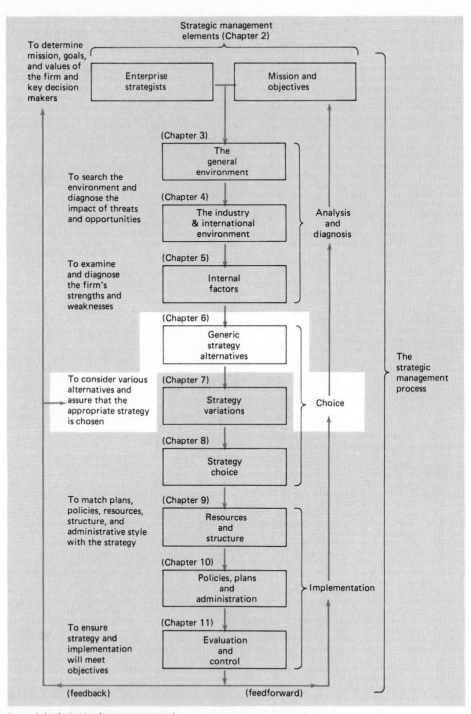

EXHIBIT 6.1   **A model of strategic management.**

This chapter and the next look at how the strategic decision makers generate alternative strategies to fill the gaps found when the results of the two profiles and the firm's goals are compared. Relative to the gap analysis, you start with the current strategy. If the gap is small or nonexistent (on the basis of analyses of goals, external factors, and internal factors), then we assume that current strategy is adequate and little or no change is required. As the gap increases (threats, opportunities, strengths, weaknesses, or goal changes create gaps), then strategy alternatives to close the gap need to be considered. By comparing the ETOP and SAP, you will acquire clues about the nature of strategic alternatives to close any gaps. For instance, if a substantial environmental opportunity exists with an internal ability to take advantage of it, expansion alternatives are most likely. If environmental threats seem most pressing, it may be that the way to improve performance is by retrenching. If no gaps are perceived (or if gaps are not significant, or if you believe they are out of your control), you are likely to pursue a stable approach. Note that at this stage, the alternatives for change are being generated with the perspective of improving performance by taking action to close performance gaps expected in the future.

As shown in Exhibit 6.2, in a corporation the primary generator of strategic alternatives is the top manager, and in a multiple-SBU firm, the primary generators are the SBU top managers and the corporate top manager. Lower-level managers are involved to the extent that they prepare proposals for consideration by top managers. For instance, an R&D unit may propose that additional resources be allocated for the development of a new product. Top managers need to analyze these proposals, taking into account strategic considerations that are broader than the merits of any single project. Functional-level managers are also involved to the extent that plans to implement strategies are considered as part of the strategy formulation process, and strengths and weaknesses coming from functional levels are evaluated by these managers as inputs to the total process.

EXHIBIT 6.2 THE ROLE OF STRATEGISTS IN CONSIDERING STRATEGY ALTERNATIVES

Strategists	Generate strategy alternatives	Analyze strategy alternatives
SBU-level managers	Regularly	Regularly
Top managers	Regularly	Regularly
Corporate planners	Occasionally	Regularly
Board of directors	Rarely	Occasionally
Consultants	Occasionally hired to advise	Rarely
Functional-level managers	Prepare proposals	Regularly

STRATEGIC ALTERNATIVES AND THE DEFINITION OF THE BUSINESS [1]

The central factor that is examined at the beginning of strategy consideration is the mission definition—the business the firm is in or wants to be in. We described this in Chapter 2. Here we start to get more specific. That is, the definition needs to clarify the products or services provided, the market niches served, and the functions performed.

The choice of products or services requires questions about the breadth and depth of the offering. Should the line be broad or narrow? This is part of the scope issue discussed in Chapter 2. How are the products or services to be differentiated? Can additional uses be found for them? Are they to be of high quality or low quality? Perhaps the fundamental question regarding products or services is, What is offered in the way of customer *utility?* Does the product or service provide time, place, form, or information utility or other utilities valued by customers? The business definition should clarify the nature of the product or service offerings initially. Alternative strategies can then be developed around the definition (or the definition can be changed).

The choice of markets basically involves territories, channels, and customer types. Do we serve local, regional, national, or international markets? Do we use wholesale or retail distributors, rely on direct sales, or consume outputs ourselves? Do we serve commercial or industrial firms, nonprofit enterprises, individual consumers, or military or governmental units? How do we segment customers into classes? Should we serve more markets or fewer? Do we go after a large share of submarkets (concentrate), seek a share of many markets (undifferentiated), or differentiate markets and customize programs for each?

The question of functions (or technologies) revolves around how the firm wishes to add value. It may create new ideas or plant seeds, locate resources or grow them, or extract or harvest, refine or process, manufacture, assemble, or pack, store, or distribute goods and services. These are usually thought of as the processes used to transform into inputs, beginning with creation and ending with delivery to the end user. Production is the stage most people usually think of. Here, of course, assembly lines are a common form. But other types of approaches are available. Craft-oriented job shops or teams of specialists can be used to produce goods. In addition, the organization can serve to link parties who desire to exchange goods, services, or money (banks, wholesalers, retailers, and employment agencies are examples). In this case, a physical transformation is not intended. At each stage from creation to delivery to the end user, choices include the processes used to add value. Further, the business definition needs to clarify which of the stages the firm will focus on, ranging from complete vertical integration at one extreme to specialization in only one stage at the other.

Once the initial choice of product, market, and function scope has been determined, strategic alternatives abound. A firm can accomplish strategic change by expanding or retrenching in any of or all these areas, or by stabilizing in some and expanding in others. It can do this simultaneously or over time, yielding a huge number of options for consideration. In effect, this is why firms can pursue so many different kinds of strategies which seem to be successful in attaining objectives.

For smaller firms, this business definition is simple enough. The product or service, market, and functions are usually limited to one category or a few categories. This is true for many medium-sized organizations as well. A majority of large firms are involved in multiple businesses. So their business definition is more complex.

Some firms are in so many businesses that it is hard if not impossible to describe the "business" they are in. In one study of three conglomerates (Litton, Indian Head, and Bangor Punta) it was found that their strategy making did not involve delineating specific businesses. Their definition of business involved only the specifications in detail of the corporate objectives in terms of growth rates, financial policies to guide their acquisition of funds and firms, and organizational policies.

Decisions regarding business definition and mission are made at the corporate level. Corporate-level strategies involve issues of which businesses to be in. Business-level strategies involve questions of what to do with those businesses—expand them, re-trench them, or stabilize them. At the functional level within business units, alternative plans and policies are set forth to specify ways in which the strategies will be made to work. Thus corporate-level strategic alternatives revolve around the question of whether to continue or change the business(es) the enterprise is currently in. Business-level strategic alternatives involve improving the efficiency or effectiveness with which the firm achieves its corporate objectives in its chosen business sector.

The central strategic alternatives to consider are the following:

1 What is our business? What should it be? What business should we be in 5 years from now? 10 years?

2 Should we stay in the same business(es) with a similar level of effort? (stability)

3 Should we get out of this business entirely or some parts of it? (retrenchment)

4 Should we expand into new business areas by adding new functions, products, and/or markets? (expansion)

5 Should we carry out alternatives 3 and 4, 2 and 4, or 2 and 3? Simultaneously or sequentially? (combination)

These strategic alternatives will be described shortly. Note that in all instances, the major reason for pursuing the strategy is to maintain or improve performance, or reduce gaps if they exist. Thus in all cases, question 1 is a beginning point. You have to know where you are and where you want to be before you can decide how you're going to get there from here. In this sense, the existing business definition prevents you from considering certain alternatives. Only in rare instances can you abandon your past.

THE GENERIC STRATEGY ALTERNATIVES

Whether dealing with corporate- or business-level strategy, there are four generic ways in which alternatives can be considered: stability, expansion, retrenchment, and com-binations. These are options for the pace or level of effort in the current business definition, or for changing the mission. Exhibit 6.3 shows a matrix of these basic options with some representative examples of approaches for carrying out the strategy. That is, the firm may decide to change its *business definition* by expanding or re-trenching the scope of its products, markets, or functions. If it chooses to maintain

EXHIBIT 6.3   GENERIC STRATEGY ALTERNATIVES

	Expand		Retrench		Stabilize		Combinations*
	Business definition	Pace	Business definition	Pace	Business definition	Pace	Definition and/ or pace
Products	Add new products	Find new uses	Drop old products	Decrease product development	Maintain	Make package changes, quality improvements	Drop old while adding new products
Markets	Find new territories	Penetrate markets	Drop distribution channels	Reduce market shares	Maintain	Protect market shares, focus on market niches	Drop old customers while finding new ones
Functions	Forward vertical integration	Increase capacity	Become captive company	Decrease process R&D	Maintain	Improve production efficiency	Increase capacity and improve efficiency

*Can include activities from across two or more of these cells simultaneously or sequentially over time: for example, "maintain stability of product offerings while expanding market territories at the same time," or "improve efficiency before later expanding into new products in a planned sequence."

its definition, it still may alter its strategy by changing the *pace* of effort within the stable business definition in order to become more efficient or effective in the way it carries out its mission. Of course, combinations of options are possible at the same time or over time. The rest of this chapter will describe some features of these generic options. Our next chapter explains some variations for carrying them out. Chapter 8 describes factors affecting the choice among alternatives.

STABILITY STRATEGIES [2]

A stability strategy is a strategy that a firm pursues when:

1 It continues to serve the public in the same product or service, market, and function sectors as defined in its business definition, or in very similar sectors.

2 Its main strategic decisions focus on incremental improvement of functional performance.

Stability strategies are implemented by "steady as it goes" approaches to decisions. Few major functional changes are made in the product or service line, markets, or functions. In an effective stability strategy, a company will concentrate its resources where it presently has or can rapidly develop a meaningful competitive advantage in the narrowest possible product-market-function scope consistent with its resources and market requirements.

A stability strategy may lead to defensive moves such as taking legal action or obtaining a patent to reduce competition. Stability usually involves keeping track of new developments to make sure the strategy continues to make sense.

Note that the stability approach is *not* a "do nothing" approach; nor does it mean that goals such as profit growth are abandoned. The stability strategy can be designed to increase profits through such approaches as improving efficiency in current operations. As suggested in Exhibit 6.3, the business definition may be stable (no change in products, markets, or functions), but the *pace* of activity may be changed in combination with this stable definition. By the same token, a stable pace may be pursued, but the management may try a competitive strategy to be sure desired performance outcomes are accomplished (such as making packaging changes or making pricing changes to protect market share). Such competitive changes are characteristic of a stable pace, but do not imply that management is sitting idle.

This strategy is typical for firms in a mature stage of development, or mature product-market evolution. Frequently, firms will segment markets or pursue product differentiation and seek to use assets efficiently. For a small firm, this strategy is frequently used to maintain a comfortable market or profit position. Or it can be used to bring control to a company experiencing wide swings in past performance. Usually, however, the level of goal attainment is not set as high as might be found in firms following expansion strategies. Or stability may be used in combination with expansion to provide a base of support for other strategic moves and an element of risk reduction.

Why Do Companies Pursue a Stability Strategy?

A number of explanations can be offered to support stability.

1 The firm is doing well or perceives itself as successful. Management does not always know what combination of decisions is responsible for this. So "we continue the way we always have around here."

2 A stability strategy is less risky. A high percentage of changes fail, whether we are talking about new products or new ways of doing things. So conditions must be really bad (or opportunities good) if a firm decides to take the additional risk. The larger the firm and the more successful it has been, the greater is the resistance to the risk.

3 Managers prefer action to thought. A stability strategy can evolve because the executives never get around to considering any other alternatives. Many of the firms that pursue this strategy do so unconsciously. They react to forces in the environment and will change their business definition only in extraordinary times.

4 It is easier and more comfortable for all concerned to pursue a stability strategy. No disruptions in routines take place.

5 The environment is perceived to be relatively stable, with few threats to cause problems or few opportunities the firm wishes to take advantage of.

6 Too much expansion can lead to inefficiencies. In effect, many decision makers do not perceive a significant gap between the future level of goal attainment they expect to reach and their ideal objectives.

A firm's executives may also believe that resources or other environmental changes prohibit the continuation of expansion in the business definition that may have occurred in the past. Here the analysis could suggest that continued expansion could actually

EXHIBIT 6.4   A NEW BABY FORMULA

Gerber Products Company had long dominated the U.S. baby food market. But a declining birthrate in the 1970s forced the firm to begin seeking growth elsewhere. Forays into marketing adult foods failed, and day-care centers were only moderately successful. But Gerber did begin to build the only national baby-products brand name, with more than 400 items ranging from bottles and toys to humidifiers and clothes. By 1978 the birthrate had begun to climb, and the strategy was "selling more to the same mothers."

Five years later, this stability strategy was still in force. Gerber's baby food market share stood at 71%, and merchandise sales were double the amount they had been 5 years earlier. Growth prospects look good. A small but positive 1% annual growth in births is expected until 1990, per capita use of baby foods is rising, and 40% of babies are first-born, the ones who get the most new accessories.

Gerber does not expect its market share to grow much, but planners believe the market will grow 3%. President Smith says the company "has a few ideas, but none of the projects we have under way have yet resolved themselves to a direction." And none is particularly innovative. One might simply be to revive an earlier product failure.

For Gerber, the formula is still to sell a little more each year to a few more mothers. Concentrating on slow, steady growth with a stability strategy seems to make sense when a firm is doing well in a moderately stable environment.

Source: Adapted from "Gerber: Concentrating on Babies Again for Slow Steady Growth," *Business Week,* Aug. 22, 1983, p. 80.

increase the *performance gap*. Thus stability in the *pace* of activity becomes desirable. Executives may realize that the consequences of expansion could become dysfunctional. For instance, expansion (for example, by some types of acquisitions) could lead to antitrust pressure from government or attacks from competitors or pressure groups. Or the firm may need a breathing spell. It may have expanded so fast that it must stabilize for a while or else become inefficient and unmanageable. Its costs may have gotten out of hand, especially if it appears that hard times are coming. This is a particularly difficult problem for aggressive entrepreneurs of successful small firms which have been expanding rapidly.

Stability is not the kind of strategy that makes news. It is news to say that 8 million are unemployed, and it is not news to write about 110 million employed. So articles and research usually do not focus on this strategy. However, we would have to infer that since most firms pursued this strategy at some point, stability is effective when the firm is doing well and the environment is not excessively volatile. Exhibit 6.4 provides an example. This means that for many industries and many companies and SBUs, the stability strategy is effective. As one owner of a successful private firm put it, "I've got only one egg in my basket and I watch that basket very carefully."

EXPANSION STRATEGIES [3]

An expansion strategy is a strategy that a firm pursues when:

1 It serves the public in additional product or service sectors or adds markets or functions to its definition.

2 It focuses its strategic decisions on major increases in the pace of activity within its present business definition.

A firm implements this strategy by redefining the business—either adding to the scope of activity or substantially increasing the efforts of the current business.

Again, Exhibit 6.3 shows some ways in which expansion is pursued. For instance, changes in business definition could lead to new product lines or new markets being added. Or a retailer might decide to supply its own goods and make, instead of just buy, its products (backward vertical integration). Even without a change in mission, many firms seek pace expansions. The most common approach is an effort to increase market share substantially, often accompanied by plant expansion (pace increase in functions).

This is often considered an "intrapreneurial" strategy, where firms are found to develop and introduce new products and markets or penetrate markets to build share. Small firms are often in the emergence stage of the life cycle or in introduction and growth stages of product-market evolution. High investment is implied, often with aggressive risk taking to finance new resources (plants, personnel, etc.).

Expansion is usually thought of as "the way" to improve performance. An increase in assets or size is thought by many to yield growth in profits or ROI. Several studies support this proposition. But the opinions and research of others suggest that short-run inefficiencies often result. As we pointed out in Chapter 5, greater size may lead to trade-offs in profits or returns. And as noted before, rapid expansion can lead to antitrust pressures or competitor reactions. In essence, strategists need to distinguish between desirable and undesirable expansion. Expansion which fails to make resources more productive is "excess fat." Volume, by itself, may represent a "cancer" which needs to be cut out. Nevertheless, expansion is popular in the literature.

Why Do Companies Pursue Expansion Strategies?

After reading the list of reasons for pursuing the stability strategy, it may be hard to imagine reasons for adopting an expansion strategy. Stability has a number of things going for it.

The reasons given for adopting expansion are as follows:

1 In volatile industries, a stability strategy can mean short-run success, long-run death. So expansion may be necessary for survival *if* environments are volatile.

2 Many executives equate expansion with effectiveness.

3 Some believe that society benefits from expansion.

4 Managerial motivation. It is true that there is less risk with stability. But there are also fewer financial and other rewards. There are many managers who wish to be remembered, who wish to leave a monument to themselves in the workplace. Who remembers the executive who stood at the helm for 5 years "steady as it goes"? Strategies may result from the power needs of many executives; the recognition needs are strong in these executives too. Thus these needs or drives encourage some executives to gamble and choose a strategy of expansion. Their companies also become better known, may attract better management, and often leads to higher pay.

EXHIBIT 6.5   HOW HIGH CAN YOU FLY?

Donald Burr, chairman-founder of People Express Airlines, is the epitome of the modern entrepreneur. A missionary, he seized the opportunity of deregulation to create a new kind of airline. People Express was founded on the belief that if all workers were owners, their commitment would assure success. Burr's buzzwords are "worker participation," "responsibility sharing," and "high growth."

Indeed, high growth has occurred, with 4000 current employees from the original 250, and from 3 planes to over 70. Yet the competition is getting rougher, and the explosive growth is straining the structure of the firm, which requires people to switch jobs depending on work needs (even pilots handle ticketing or baggage on occasions).

Some pilots refer to the strong leadership of Burr as evangelistic, referring to him as "Guyana Jones"—an allusion to the Jonestown incident where Jim Jones's followers blindly heeded instructions to drink poisoned

Kool-Aid. Unwillingness to delegate authority led to the resignation of the second-in-command for a high-level job at Pan Am in 1982. In 1985, the president and cofounder resigned, and another cofounder was dismissed.

In 1985, Burr acknowledged some of the problems of dramatic growth, saying, "We intend to pull back and consolidate. It's time for some fine-tuning." Yet the philosophy still appears to be "grow-grow-grow" and "Don't worry about profits, they'll come later." Indeed, in 1986 People acquired Frontier and another airline. But says another airline CEO, "There's a point where structure counts. It's great to be an entrepreneur and provide direction. But when you get big you've got to delegate." In many cases, entrepreneurs learn this lesson the hard way. Burr may learn he can only fly so high without making sure the "equipment"—his organization—can accommodate the pressures. Indeed, by mid-1986, trouble appeared and People Express was bought by Texas Air.

Source: Adapted from R. A. Dubin, "Growing Pains at People Express," *Business Week*, Jan. 28, 1985, pp. 90–91.

5 Belief in the experience curve. There is some evidence that as a firm grows in size and experience, it gets better at what it's doing and reduces costs and improves productivity.

6 Belief that growth will yield monopoly power.

7 External pressure from stockholders or securities analysts.

Perhaps the major reason for its popularity is the *belief* that rapid environmental change requires expansion. Further, there is a belief and some evidence that expansion results in performance improvements. However, some suggest that volatility is not as great as it seems, and others prescribe stability to avoid overreaction to change. Also, critics of expansion point to firms "engulfed in a growth syndrome"—expansion at any cost—which they believe leads to inefficiencies and a lower quality of life due to harm from the environment. We believe the jury is still out on these issues. Exhibit 6.5 is an interesting case in point.

RETRENCHMENT STRATEGIES [4]

A retrenchment strategy is pursued by a firm when:

1 It sees the desirability of or necessity for reducing its product or service lines, markets, or functions.

2 It focuses its strategic decisions on functional improvement through the *reduction of activities* in units with negative cash flows.

A firm can redefine its business by divesting itself of a major product line or an SBU. It could abandon some market territories. A firm could also reduce its functions. For example, a firm may choose to sell most or all of its output to a single customer (e.g., Sears). In effect, it has permitted another firm to perform its distribution function. This is known as a ''captive company.'' Of course, the ultimate redefinition is a write-off or total liquidation.

As for retrenching in pace, a firm could use layoffs, reduce R&D or marketing or other outlays, increase the collection of receivables, etc. Note that these efforts and those in redefining the business through retrenchment *can* improve performance. In fact, selling profitable assets to gain resources to be put to use elsewhere is not uncommon in combination with expansion. Retrenchment alone is probably the least frequently used generic strategy. Yet the mid-1980s witnessed huge write-offs because of overcapacity, obsolescence, failed strategies, and long-term structural change in some basic industries.

Retrenchment is frequently used during the decline stage of a business when it is considered possible to restore profitability. Or if prospects appear bleak, controlled disinvestment can be used. Firms might abandon market shares, reduce expenses and assets, prune products, and pursue maximum positive cash flows.

Why Do Companies Pursue a Retrenchment Strategy?

This strategy is the hardest to pursue; it goes against the grain of most strategists. It implies failure. Just as most business executives hate to cut prices, they hate a retrenchment strategy. Why do they follow it, then? A few reasons are as follows:

1 The firm is not doing well or perceives itself as doing poorly.

2 The firm has not met its objectives by following one of the other generic strategies, and there is pressure from stockholders, customers, or others to improve performance.

3 The environment is seen to be so threatening that internal strengths are insufficient to meet the problems.

4 Better opportunities in the environment are perceived elsewhere, where a firm's strengths can be utilized.

Any strategy, if chosen at the right time and implemented properly, will be effective. However, the retrenchment strategy tends to be reserved for dealing with crises, even though there can be positive reasons for its use. The retrenchment strategy is the best strategy for the firm which has tried everything, has made some mistakes, and is now ready to do something about its problems. The more serious the crisis, the more serious the retrenchment strategy needs to be. For minor crises, pace retrenchment will do. For moderate crises, divestiture of some divisions or units may be necessary. For serious crises, a liquidation may be necessary. Exhibit 6.6 describes a firm which believes that its crisis is serious enough to warrant a retrenchment in pace, which could lead to liquidation.

EXHIBIT 6.6   FROM A GREYHOUND TO A DACHSHUND

The Greyhound bus station, with its sleek figure of a swift dog, has been a part of the American landscape for years. But it appears that this familiar figure may need a new mascot—the stubby little dachshund.

In 1985, only 33 million Americans rode Greyhound, down from 64 million in 1979. Bus riders are switching to cheap airlines, and employees have rejected cost-cutting proposals.

President Teets has embarked on a significant pace retrenchment which could eventually become a retrenchment in business definition if Greyhound gets out of the bus business entirely. In 1985, terminal and route cutbacks were planned until labor leaders sought a substitute package that included a 3-year wage freeze and permission for outside operators to run empty terminals. This would have forced 3000 employees to work for less pay—or lose their jobs. The pact was rejected by 59% of the union's members; and Teets accelerated his retrenchment plans.

He will close at least half of Greyhound's 98 company-owned depots, and drop all bus service in a number of states. One-third of Greyhound's 10,000 workers may lose their jobs. In cities where service will continue but costly terminals will be shut, Greyhound will make deals with other bus companies—or just drop passengers off on a downtown street. Teets was also considering dropping charter service.

In late 1986, Teets was prepared to take another crack at labor, asking for major concessions on a new 3-year pact. He remarked, "If labor balks, it would be easy to walk away from the bus business. Our assets are liquid."

Shutting down an $800 million bus business would be drastic, but such a retrenchment may be the only prudent alternative for a company faced with stiff competition from substitute transportation, and a recalcitrant labor union.

Source: Adapted from S. Toy: "Labor Can't Blunt Greyhound's Ax," *Business Week,* Feb. 10, 1986, pp. 28–29.

The retrenchment strategy is the hardest strategy for the business executive to follow. It implies that someone or something has failed, and no one wants to be labeled a failure. But retrenchment can be used to reverse the negative trends and set the stage for more positive strategic alternatives. Many U.S. business firms began withdrawing from Europe in the early 1980s due to the stubborn recession, high labor costs, high taxes, and competition from government-subsidized industries. And in the mid-1980s many conglomerates began "asset redeployments" to get out of old businesses and into new ones, or to get back to basics.

Foreign managers appear more willing to consider retrenchment than U.S. managers. The first question the Japanese, German, or French strategist asks is likely to be "What are the old things we are going to abandon?" This provides resources for innovation, new products, or new markets.

COMBINATION STRATEGY [5]

A combination strategy is a strategy that a firm pursues when:

1 Its main strategic decisions focus on the conscious use of several grand strategies (stability, expansion, retrenchment) at the same time (simultaneously) in several SBUs of the company.

2 It plans to use several grand strategies at different future times (sequentially).

With combination strategies, the decision makers consciously apply several grand strategies to different parts of the firm or to different future periods. The logical possibilities for a simultaneous approach are stability in some areas, expansion in others; stability in some areas, retrenchment in others; retrenchment in some areas, expansion in others; and all three strategies in different areas of the company.

The same logical possibilities exist for time-phased combinations, but the number of possibilities is greater, especially when the products, markets, and functions are considered and when the choice occurs through changing the pace or the business definition. For instance, the sequential expansion in the pace of the business with some business redefinition later seems to be a common approach; it may be followed because of the recognition of risks and problems in rapid expansion or redefinition. Often a firm pursuing this strategy initially concentrates on one product or service line. It expands incrementally by adding greater market penetration, adding new products or services after extensive testing, adding new markets geographically, etc. Some firms even follow a strategy that allows them to seek a low market share in their industry as a whole. Much of the literature and PIMS data make it appear that this is suicidal. Yet it has been shown that firms like Crown Cork and Seal, Union Camp, and Burroughs achieved excellent return-on-invested-capital objectives through effective market segmentation, effective use of R&D, and a lowering of production and processing costs through increased efficiency. Firms pursuing combinations need to be especially alert to competitor reactions. For example, you may want to combine stability in one area to provide cash for expansion in another area. A shrewd competitor may attack the stable area in an attempt to divert your management time and resources away from the expansions to protect your "stable" base of operations. Such multiple-point competition is particularly problematic for the multiple-SBU firm trying a combination strategy.

Exhibit 6.7 shows how one firm has used a combination of strategies, although perhaps it didn't plan it that way.

Why Do Companies Pursue a Combination Strategy?

A combination strategy is not an easy strategy to use. It is much easier to keep a firm in one set of values or one strategy at a time. But when a company faces many environments and these environments are changing at different rates, and the company's products are in different stages of the life cycle, it is easy to visualize conditions under which a combination strategy makes sense.

Thus it is possible that when the economy is performing well, most industries are doing well. Therefore, the generic strategy might be expansion. But at the start of a recession, some industries begin to suffer, while others are still doing well. Thus a combination strategy makes sense for a multiple-industry firm at that time.

In the case of time-phased combination strategies, several scenarios come to mind. For example, a firm realizes that some of its main product lines are beyond the optimum point in the product life cycle and that it is not worth the investment to

EXHIBIT 6.7   A PICTURE IN TIME

1986 will be a year of retrenchment for Kodak. During the past few years, Kodak has followed all three of the generic strategies of stability, expansion, and retrenchment.

At one point, Kodak had been expansion-oriented, and a product development leader in the photographic business. After 1970, when it left the 35mm camera to the Japanese, the firm seemed content with a long period of stability. Up until late 1984, except for the imitative instant camera introduction long after Polaroid, the firm sort of slumbered in contentment. Its revenues became steady at about $10.5 billion, primarily in the photographic arena. But Kodak failed to see or ignored changes in its markets, customers, and competitors while it pursued its stability strategy.

In early 1985, it seemed as if Kodak was waking up, but it also became apparent that Kodak was just about to sleep through its final exam. Expansion was the initial instinct of the recently awakened giant. Kodak reorganized its photographic division into 17 "entrepreneurial" business units with the intention of making decisions easier to make. It also launched a barrage of new products to present an image of innovation. To help speed the introduction of these new products—such as 8mm video cameras, 35mm cameras, and an electronic publishing system for corporate documents—Kodak brought these products from Japanese firms already producing them and marketed them under the Kodak name. In effect, this approach represents product expansion combined with "retrenchment" in certain functions in that Kodak does not supply its own product needs. Competition in these new areas is tough and Kodak is finding them of little help in its attempts to improve its sales and profits. So it has also expanded by offering photofinishing in retail stores through "minilab" technology.

Kodak recently lost a patent suit with Polaroid, necessitating the write-down of $400 million in assets from its instant photography division. This, along with its already poor profitability, has caused the firm to announce the layoff of 12,900 workers in a program to cut costs. Kodak will also cut back in services and marketing. In a word, the company is also retrenching. Kodak, then, is simultaneously pursuing function retrenchment with product expansions after a long period of stability.

This rapid succession of generic strategies has not been properly planned, so it can't be considered an intentional time-phased combination strategy. However, retrenching at this time may be just what Kodak needs to give it time to wake up and develop an effective long-range strategy capable of eliminating the large gaps created by its expectations.

Source: Adapted from "Kodak Just Can't Get Its Giant Feet Moving Fast Enough," *Business Week,* Mar. 4, 1986, pp. 37–38.

"prop the product up." The firm may choose to retrench in this area and follow an expansion strategy in a new product area.

Most large firms such as *Fortune*'s 500 largest industrials are probably the most frequent users of combination strategies. Even here, it is the multiple-industry firm that is most likely to use them. The medium-sized firm that is multiple-industry-based is also a likely user. An example is NCR, which sold a unit to buy back some debt and then expanded.

All strategies can be effective. The question is, When is a combination strategy most likely to be effective? What should have become clearer in this section is that combination strategies are most likely to be effective for larger, multiple-SBU firms in periods of economic transition or periods of transition in the product-service life cycle. The combination strategy is the best strategy for a firm whose divisions perform unevenly or do not have the same future potential.

ALTERNATIVES AND PERFORMANCE [6]

Before we conclude our discussion of generic alternatives, it will be useful to recapitulate and reinforce our earlier statements about the relationship of strategies to performance. First, Exhibit 6.8 graphically presents the alternatives which are possible. Each dimension represents an overlay so that they *all intersect one another*. That is, expansion, stability, or retrenchment can be applied to products, markets, or functions. And combinations of these are possible. If change occurs, it may be in the pace or the business definition. Our intent is to convey the idea that there is overlap in how these strategic approaches can be put together for any given firm. The particular configuration of alternatives considered by any firm will not be this large, however. Managers are more likely to focus on a few of these for a detailed analysis.

Second, keep in mind that any alternative or combination has the potential to improve performance. One is not necessarily superior to another in all circumstances. As shown in Exhibit 6.9, advantages and disadvantages are associated with each. Naturally, if substantial growth in size is the objective, expansion is a more likely alternative. But this may come at the expense of other objectives, at least in the short run. Growth in profits could be enhanced by a retrenchment. For instance, financial theory suggests that if the net present value of a liquidation is greater than the expected value of continued operations, selling assets to gain funds to invest elsewhere will be a good alternative for the goal of improving cash value. The breakup value of some firms may be large due to "hidden" assets or unrealistic book values. So retrenchment may ultimately lead to growth (in terms of cash goals). Some tax laws give companies a reason to spin off subsidiaries to shareholders or sell assets and distribute proceeds, because companies liquidated within a year of an asset sale are exempt from taxation on related capital gains. Of course, such tax laws can change, and analysis of these

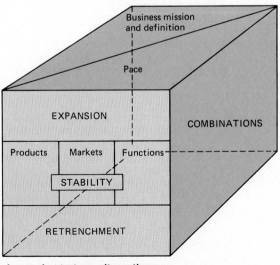

EXHIBIT 6.8   *Overlays of generic strategy alternatives.*

EXHIBIT 6.9   PROS AND CONS OF STRATEGY CHOICES AT IBM

All strategy alternatives have advantages and disadvantages. The options facing IBM are a case in point. Known as clones, company after company now produces a personal computer which is compatible with the IBM product. Frequently, these competitor products claim to be cheaper, faster, and more reliable while they offer similar hardware options and use the same software.

IBM has considered several strategy options, each of which has pros and cons, to deal with the competitive threat from clones.

Strategy option	Advantage	Disadvantage
A. Introduce a low-price replacement for the basic PC using newer, less expensive technology.	IBM would regain market share lost to clones and add a model ideal for the education market.	IBM might sacrifice gross margins, divert sales from more profitable models, and possibly hurt corporate earnings.
B. With new hardware and software, alter the PC to make cloning more difficult and to prevent clones from participating fully in IBM computer networks.	IBM would keep major corporate customers, rebuild market share as they shift to the new technology, reestablish control over prices and margins.	Consumers, especially small businesses, might stick with the current PC, for which there are thousands of software packages.
C. Bring out a steady stream of new PCs that include more features, while cutting prices on older models.	By continuously updating and improving the PC, IBM could quickly make most clones obsolete and improve prices for its products.	A rash of new models might make inventories of IBM PCs obsolete and could clog the dealer channel. With demand slackening, new models might not sell better than current ones.
D. Withdraw from the low-end, "commodity" PC market, leaving the clones to battle each other in a low-margin business.	IBM would be free to concentrate on selling more profitable versions of the PC to large corporations and, by linking those PCs into company data networks, would ultimately stimulate demand for mainframe computers to support them.	IBM would be walking away from as much as $3 billion in annual revenues. Such a move also would hinder its efforts to win big shares of the education and home markets.

Source: Business Week, July 28, 1986. In April 1987, IBM chose B.

These strategies range from product-line expansion (C), to market retrenchment (D), to stability (A and B involve product modification and improvement). The choice may come to repeating IBM's historical practice of sticking to high-margin businesses (D). In any case, important trade-off decisions usually arise when strategy alternatives are considered.

Source: Adapted from "The PC Wars: IBM vs. the Clones," *Business Week,* July 28, 1985, pp. 62–68.

EXHIBIT 6.10 STRATEGIC CHANGE IS A MEANS TO AN END

Change is frightening. It can paralyze powerful executives. It can cause entire organizations to drag their corporate feet. It's the stuff sleepness nights are made of. Not long ago, International Harvester was in the shadow of an even more frightening prospect. The reaper was already at our doorstep. We had to change. Or else.

We consolidated facilities. Eliminated five levels of bureaucracy. Doubled manufacturing productivity. Cut inventory by two-thirds. And orchestrated the largest private debt restructuring in history. An old company, set in its ways, changed. And was reborn as Navistar International Corporation.

In doing so, we learned a lession. Change is not a nemesis. It is vital to our organization. To any organization. Properly managed, change is progress. It's the road to improved quality, and to new products that will help our customers meet their changing needs. It's a competitive edge. Change helps us further strengthen our number one position. Yet we know we must never change merely for the sake of change. Change is not a goal. It's the means to a goal.

Today, we're still changing. Change, however, still keeps us awake at night. But these days it's because we're dreaming of new ways to accomplish it.

Source: Adapted from a Navistar ad, *Business Week*, July 7, 1986, p. 21.

laws should be an integral part of environmental analysis. If an entrepreneur's objective is to maintain control of a business, stability may enhance this more than expansion. If the goal is to spread risk, business definition changes may be in order. Thus it is inappropriate to necessarily equate "growth" with "expansion." And retrenchment should not be considered a sign of failure or pursued only when threats appear. Stability does not imply that goal improvements are not being accomplished. In other words, don't confuse the strategy, as a means to an end, with the objective. Exhibit 6.10 provides an example of an advertisement making just this point.

SUMMARY

We have just completed the first chapter that deals with the strategic choice part of the strategic management process. This chapter has discussed the generation of a reasonable number of generic strategy alternatives that will help fill the gaps faced by a firm.

The central factor that is examined at the beginning of the consideration of strategic alternatives is the business the firm is in. Business definitions will vary from the simple definition (for a one-product or one-service firm) to the very complex definition (for a large firm involved in multiple businesses). Products, markets, and functions need to be identified as part of corporate-level strategy. Once the business the firm is in has been defined, various questions (such as, Should we get out of this business entirely? Should we try to expand?) will help the strategist focus on the type of strategic alternative the firm should pursue.

The generic strategy alternatives are to expand, stabilize, or retrench with regard to the pace or the business definition of products, markets, or functions. Combinations of simultaneous activities or sequential options are included. All of these can be designed to improve performance, but several propositions are offered for when each is more likely to be successfully pursued.

> **Proposition 6.1**
>
> *Stability is more likely if the firm is doing well, the environment is not excessively volatile, and the product or service has reached the stability or maturity stage of the life cycle.*
>
> **Proposition 6.2**
>
> *Expansion is more likely in highly competitive, volatile industries, particularly early in the product-service life cycle.*
>
> **Proposition 6.3**
>
> *Retrenchment is more likely if the firm is not doing well, greater returns can be gained elsewhere, or the product or service is at a later stage of the life cycle.*
>
> **Proposition 6.4**
>
> *Combinations are more likely for multiple-SBU firms, in periods of economic transition, and during changes in the product-service life cycle.*

These are overall estimates, but a variety of reasons were suggested for why each strategy could be followed, and the advantages and disadvantages associated with each were stated.

Our next chapter elaborates on these generic strategies by providing you with variations on the themes of expansion, stability, retrenchment, and combinations. There are a number of approaches for carrying out these strategies. The approach will depend on various internal strengths and weaknesses, environmental threats and opportunities, and the value preferences of the strategists. Before concluding this segment with strategic choice, you should be aware of the many options for creatively carrying out these generic strategies.

REFERENCES

[1] The Starting Point of Strategy—Business Definition

Abell, D. F.: *Defining the Business: The Starting Point of Strategic Planning* (Englewood Cliffs, N.J.: Prentice-Hall, 1980).

Levitt, Y.: ''Marketing Myopia,'' *Harvard Business Review,* vol. 38 (July–August 1960), pp. 45–60; and *Harvard Business Review,* vol. 53 (September–October 1975), pp. 26–28.

[2] The Stability Strategy

Clifford, D. K., Jr.: ''Thriving in a Recession,'' *Harvard Business Review* (July–August 1977), pp. 56–65.

Fruhan, W.: ''Pyrrhic Victories in Fights for Market Share,'' *Harvard Business Review* (September–October 1972).

Ketchum, B. W.: ''Privately Held Companies in the U.S.,'' *INC.,* (December 1981), p. 39.

[3]   The Expansion Strategy

Drucker, P.: *Management* (New York: Harper & Row, 1974), chap. 60.

Guth, W. D.: "Corporate Growth Strategies," *The Journal of Business Strategy,* vol. 1 (Fall 1980), pp. 56–62.

Thompson, A.: "Corporate Bigness—For Better or for Worse?" *Sloan Management Review* (Fall 1975), pp. 36–61.

[4]   The Retrenchment Strategy

Bibeault, D. B.: *Corporate Turnaround* (New York: McGraw-Hill, 1982).

Ehrlich, E.: "Industry Cleans House," *Business Week,* Nov. 11, 1985, pp. 32–33.

Brand, D.: "U. S. Business Reduces Rate of New Investing in European Facilities," *The Wall Street Journal,* Aug. 12, 1982, p. 1.

Klein, H.: "Liquidations Are Growing More Popular," *The Wall Street Journal,* Aug. 12, 1982, p. 17.

Mingle, J. R.: *Challenges of Retrenchment* (San Francisco: Jossey-Bass, 1981).

Toy, S.: "Splitting Up: The Other Side of Merger Mania," *Business Week,* July 1, 1985, pp. 50–55.

[5]   The Combination Strategy

Ansoff, H. I.: *Corporate Strategy* (New York: McGraw-Hill, 1965).

Drucker, P.: *Management* (New York: Harper & Row, 1977), chaps. 56, 57.

Karnani, A., and B. Wernerfelt: "Multiple Point Competition," *Strategic Management Journal,* vol. 6 (1985), pp. 87–96.

[6]   Strategies and Performance

Buzzell, R. D., B. T. Gale, and G. M. Sultan: "Market Share–A Key to Profitability," *Harvard Business Review* (January–February 1975), pp. 97–106.

"The Latest in Tax Relief: Committing Corporate Suicide," *Business Week,* Jan. 14, 1985, pp. 116–117.

Rumelt, R. P.: *Strategy, Structure and Economic Performance* (Boston: Harvard University Press, 1974).

Weiss, S.: " 'Breakup Value' Is Wall Street's New Buzzword," *Business Week,* July 8, 1985, pp. 80–81.

Note: Also see Chapter 7 references.

CHAPTER OUTLINE

CONSIDERING STRATEGY VARIATIONS

OBJECTIVES

- To understand how generic strategies can be pursued and implemented in different ways
- To illustrate conditions under which strategy variations are considered appropriate
- To consider how strategy variations apply in the international setting
- To explain the advantages and disadvantages of mergers and diversification

INTRODUCTION

Numerous variations of the generic strategy alternatives outlined in Chapter 6 are possible for a given organization. Exhibit 7.1 provides examples to be discussed in this chapter. Consideration of these depends on the particular configuration of objectives, ETOP, SAP, and the generic strategy itself. It is convenient to think of these as possible dimensions which supplement the matrix outlined in Exhibit 6.3. The dimensions are internal and external, related and unrelated, horizontal and vertical (backward and forward), and active and passive. These may apply to one or more generic strategies. In each case, the dimension refers to various approaches for carrying out a generic strategy.

Exhibit 7.2 reminds us that we are trying to identify the alternatives from which to choose to close strategic gaps.

EXHIBIT 7.1   POSSIBLE STRATEGY VARIATIONS

	Expansion	Stability	Retrenchment	Combination
Internal	Penetrate existing markets; add new products; add new markets.	Seek production and marketing efficiencies; reorganize.	Reduce costs; reduce assets; drop products; drop markets; drop functions.	Subcontracting.
External	Acquisitions; mergers.	Maintain market shares.	Divest SBUs; liquidations; bankruptcies.	Cross-licensing. Joint ventures.
Related	Seek synergy from new products, markets, or functions (concentric diversification).	Improve products.	Eliminate related products, markets, or functions.	
Unrelated	Conglomerate diversification in products, markets or functions.		Eliminate unrelated products, markets, or functions.	
Horizontal	Add complementary products or markets.		Eliminate complementary products or markets.	
Vertical	Add new functions.		Reduce functions.	
Active	Innovative, entrepreneurial moves.			Grow to sell out.
Passive	Imitator in R&D, new products.	Reactive defense of position.		

INTERNAL AND EXTERNAL ALTERNATIVES

This dimension usually applies to expansion, but it may also apply to retrenchment. The basic question is whether the organization wishes to pursue a strategy independently (internal) or in conjunction with other parties (external).

Internal Expansion [1]

This is the most common approach. In effect, the firm tries to increase the sales and market share of the current product or service line faster than it has been. It is probably the most successful strategy for firms whose products or services are not in the final stages of the product-service life cycle. But Exhibit 7.3 presents the case of a firm using this strategy even though the main line is in decline.

Most of the approaches to internal expansion deal with product-market realignments. In fact, when growth in sales and profits is mentioned, most executives think of market share first. The usual approaches to internal expansion that are considered are as shown in Exhibit 7.4. In cell 1, firms try to expand sales by increasing primary demand and encouraging new uses for present products and services in the territories served now. This is often done by changing pricing and promotion. This strategy is effective for firms with small market shares, whether the product is in the high-growth

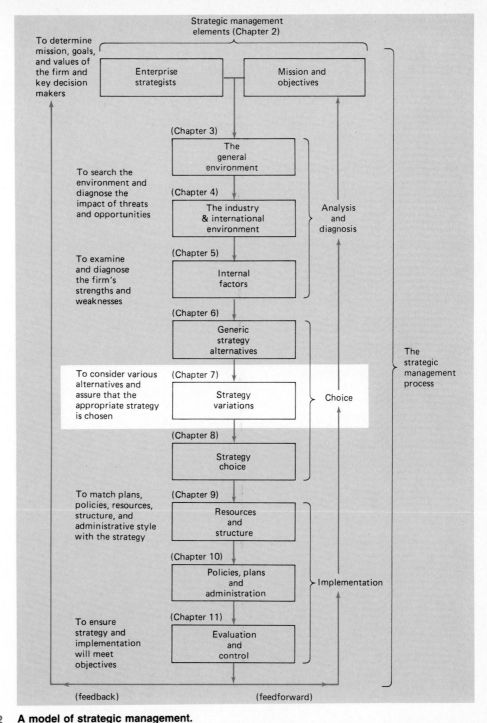

To determine
mission, goals,
and values of
the firm and
key decision
makers

Strategic management
elements (Chapter 2)

| Enterprise strategists | Mission and objectives |

To search the
environment and
diagnose the
impact of threats
and opportunities

(Chapter 3)
The general environment

(Chapter 4)
The industry & international environment

To examine
and diagnose
the firm's
strengths and
weaknesses

(Chapter 5)
Internal factors

Analysis
and
diagnosis

(Chapter 6)
Generic strategy alternatives

To consider various
alternatives and
assure that the
appropriate strategy
is chosen

(Chapter 7)
Strategy variations

Choice

(Chapter 8)
Strategy choice

To match plans,
policies, resources,
structure, and
administrative style
with the strategy

(Chapter 9)
Resources and structure

(Chapter 10)
Policies, plans and administration

Implementation

To ensure
strategy and
implementation
will meet
objectives

(Chapter 11)
Evaluation and control

The strategic management process

(feedback)   (feedforward)

EXHIBIT 7.2   **A model of strategic management.**
*(Robert H. Waterman, Jr., Thomas J. Peters, and Julian R. Phillips, "Structure Is Not Organization," Business
Horizons, June 1980, p. 18; Copyright © 1980 by the Foundation for the School of Business at Indiana
University. Reprinted by Permission.)*

EXHIBIT 7.3 LOOKING INWARD FOR EXPANSION

In the late 1970s, John M. Richman, Chairman of Kraft Foods, was convinced the company's performance could be improved by diversifying into higher-margin, nonfood items. This led to the 1980 merger with Dart Industries (Tupperware and Duracell). Hobart Corp. (Kitchen Aid) was acquired in 1981. But diversification proved to be a detour away from better profits. Newly acquired businesses had management problems and were vulnerable to the recession. When Esmark became available for purchase in 1984, analysts assumed Dart & Kraft would jump in because its product portfolio fit the collection of Dart & Kraft brands. Stated Richman, "We never intended to become a conglomerate, and we don't now."

Instead Dart & Kraft is looking for internal expansion by adding new products, extending existing lines, and spicing up slumping brand names with aggressive marketing to move the firm into the top 20% of the consumer products industry on return on capital. Says a rival, "Kraft was sleepy in the 1970s. Management was busy on the acquisition trail, and Kraft missed an opportunity to leverage its high-quality name by moving into new food categories."

Kraft commands 45% of the U.S. cheese market and strong shares of other foods with brand names like Miracle Whip, Sealtest, and Parkay. But these markets are mature, so Kraft is counting on product-line additions to boost sales. Kraft added eight new salad dressings under the Philadelphia Brand name, and is pushing hard for other new products. A new level of product manager was assigned to 20 top marketing people. Previously, R&D had concocted new concepts without close coordination with brand managers, who were mainly interested in existing products.

After the Dart merger, declines that hit several divisions have spurred new products and marketing efforts as well. Tupperware, a victim of social changes in women's working and life-styles, introduced a new line of stackable containers aimed at smaller families. And it planned to introduce a line of cookware for microwave ovens. Duracell introduced a new line of flashlights in 1983. And Hobart broadened its Kitchen Aid line of dishwashers and trash compactors.

While Richman does not rule out further acquisitions, he appears convinced that internal growth is best for his business, and food is targeted as the biggest growth sector.

Source: Adapted from "Dart & Kraft Turns Back to Its Basic Business," *Business Week,* June 11, 1984, pp. 100–105.

EXHIBIT 7.4 **Internal expansion through products and markets.**

PRODUCTS

	Current	New
Current	Penetrate existing markets with existing products (1)	Add new markets (2)
New	Add new products (3)	Add new products and new markets (4)

MARKETS

stage or maturity stage of the life cycle. The firm increases its pace of activity without changing its business definition.

This penetration approach implies that the firm specializes where it has, or believes it can obtain, a significant competitive advantage. The benefits from higher market shares are thought to come from cost savings due to the learning curve effect and economies of scale. However, short-run profit trade-offs are likely, as the expense of penetration can be high. Further, as greater shares are achieved, the firm is more likely to become a target of consumer groups, government agencies, and other competitors. Finally, the risks of specialization involve industry cycles or downturn.

Thus many firms segment markets or products to take advantage of opportunities. For instance, in cell 2, firms try to expand sales of the existing product or service by seeking additional types of customers or moving into additional geographic areas. In cell 3, firms may attempt to increase sales by introducing new products or services to the same markets served now. Other firms move to cell 4 by adding new products *and* markets or by introducing minor modifications in the product or service to new segments of the markets. Examples include new sizes or shapes and private labeling or brand labeling. These moves also entail risks, however. Moving into new areas may require new skills that the firm may be unfamiliar with. Failure rates are high. And the barriers to entry discussed in Chapter 4 can play a role here.

Internal Stability [2]

This is probably self-explanatory. However, an interesting approach is associated with the purpose for which it can be used in a multiple-SBU firm. When the main objective for an SBU is to generate more cash than it spends, the SBU is known as a "cash cow." It is "milked" while it maintains its position; if necessary, it may even sacrifice some market share. In effect, a stability business definition may be combined with an internal retrenchment in the pace of some activities. This will be discussed shortly.

Aside from the cash-cow use, a stability approach can be used by a firm trying to offset the risk of expansion in other SBUs by providing a stable base of operations. Internal stability can also be used as a "pause" between other strategies. A firm may have expanded, and now the organization needs a "break" period to catch up with itself. Or the executives may believe that conditions are unfavorable for further expansion at the present time, so they pursue stability. Thus internal stability is often a useful approach in combination with other plans.

Internal Retrenchment [3]

This is usually called an "operating turnaround" strategy. The emphasis is on improving internal efficiency, as the steel industry is attempting to do. The environmental conditions leading to turnaround strategies usually include recessions or depressions in the economy as a whole or in the industries the firm does business in.

The major approaches for turnaround strategies include:

1 *Reducing costs.* Examples include cutting the number of employees through attrition or layoffs, reducing less crucial maintenance costs, trimming the airline travel

expenses of executives, using less costly stationery, and leasing equipment instead of purchasing it.

2 *Increasing revenues.* Examples include better investment of cash and current assets, tighter inventory controls, better collection of receivables, and the use of *more effective* advertising, sales promotion, etc., to generate an increase in sales and profits without increasing expenditures.

3 *Reducing assets.* Some airlines sold 747s when the number of passengers decreased. A firm can sell land, buildings, and equipment no longer needed (obsolete) or those needed to implement expansion that now appears unrealistic. For example, Chrysler decided to build a plant in the eastern United States, but before the building was completed, Chrysler sold it to another firm.

4 *Reorganizing products and/or markets to achieve greater efficiency.* Operating turnaround involves mostly changes in pace. But internal retrenchments can also include dropping some products or markets or vertically integrating (discussed in a later section). These "strategic turnarounds" reverse the flow implied in Exhibit 7.4. Exhibit 7.5 provides an example of a firm attempting a strategic turnaround.

Internal retrenchment may be called for if many or most of these conditions are present:

- The unit's product is in a stable or declining market.
- The unit doesn't provide sales stability or prestige for the firm.
- The unit's market share is small, and it would be too costly to increase that share.
- The unit does not contribute a large percentage to total sales.
- The corporation has better uses for its funds.
- The decline in sales will be less rapid than the reduction in corporate support.
- The price or availability of raw materials presents problems.

EXHIBIT 7.5   A SMALLER CAT FOR ANOTHER LIFE

Caterpillar Tractor Co. is learning to think small in its quest for recovery. As the largest manufacturer of giant construction equipment, Cat historically focused on equipment for heavy mining, construction, and energy-recovery jobs. But demand began plummeting in 1982, and the firm lost over $1 billion in 3 years.

Although critics charge the crash of its markets caught Cat napping, the company began a retrenchment to bring expenses into line in 1982. Cat reached its goal of slashing costs by 22% by the end of 1985, a year ahead of schedule. It reduced its work force by one-third and increased the number of parts acquired from outside suppliers. Cat also reduced its debt by more than $1 billion, to 33% of total capitalization. And it intends to continue cutting, slashing manufacturing capacity by 25% through 1989.

Finally, Cat has turned its attention to marketing smaller equipment it already sells to large customers. Cat may be in for a dogfight here. The low end of the construction equipment market is more competitive and price-sensitive than the firm is used to, with well-entrenched competitors. And its legendary distribution system is not geared to selling to small contractors. Nor will small machines ever replace big earth-moving equipment for dollar volume. But, at least in the near term, such retrenchment appears to be a viable strategy.

Source: Adapted from K. Deveny, "Caterpillar Is Betting Big on Pint-Size Machines," *Business Week,* Nov. 25, 1985, p. 41.

Various policies can be used to achieve turnarounds. Selective price increases is one. Cost reduction without price reductions is another. Essentially, firms limit the amount of support they give the SBU, and perhaps over time they will provide no support at all.

Many firms have found that turnaround strategies require different kinds of experience, managerial focus, and leadership style. Sometimes they have "turnaround specialists," managers who are put in charge of units needing turnaround or who take charge at times when a turnaround strategy is required. They often get the reputation of being "head choppers" who are hired for 2 or 3 years to shape up an organization and then move on. Some turnaround specialists buy firms that are in trouble, "turn them around," and then sell them.

External Retrenchment [4]

This includes divestiture and liquidation. In these cases, other parties are involved in the strategy (usually as buyers). This approach is the reverse of a merger, which is an *external expansion* approach. (External expansion will be discussed later.) It is another, more serious form of strategic turnaround. A divestment strategy involves a selling off or liquidation of an SBU or a major part of an SBU by the strategists. Divestment is, in fact, a substitute for a turnaround strategy. It is often used after turnaround has not solved the problems it was expected to solve or as a way to change the business definition through the elimination of products, markets, or functions. Or it can be used as a combination with an internal retrenchment program. For example, the Bank of America divested its stake in 45 foreign operations and Finance America at the same time it was selling its headquarters building, closing 187 California branches, and dropping 1000 of its 3000 North America corporate clients.

Why do divestments take place? A number of reasons can be advanced. Some are inadequate market share or sales growth, lower profits than for other SBUs and the availability of better alternatives, technological changes requiring the firm to invest more resources than it is willing or able to invest, antitrust requirements, and the poor adjustment of some SBUs after mergers. Another reason is to slim down after an earlier attempt at acquisition. Many firms that failed to divest units became takeover targets, and the raiders followed up with a divestiture themselves. A final reason is a desire to "get back to basics." Many firms (such as General Mills) discover that a diversification strategy fails to accomplish its objectives. One-half to two-thirds of all mergers don't work; one in three is later undone. In 1985, for every seven acquisitions, there were three divestitures—many of which had once been high-hope acquisitions. Firms that had pursued unrelated (conglomerate) diversification found that they did not know how to effectively manage their new businesses. Divesting units unrelated to the basic business they *did* know how to run allowed these firms to improve their performance.

The decision to divest is a very difficult decision for management to make. Porter says that there are at least three sets of factors which work against this decision.

1 Structural factors: durable and specific assets, useful primarily to one company, one industry, or one location. The more durable and more specific the assets, the more difficult the divestment.

2 Corporate strategy factors. The more interrelated or complementary the SBUs within the corporation, the more difficult the divestment.

3 Managerial factors. These are as follows:

    a There is inadequate information about an SBU—management doesn't realize that the SBU isn't doing as well as it should be.

    b The divestment hurts the manager's pride and is seen as a sign of failure.

    c The divestment severs identification with a business and hurts specialized careers.

    d The divestment conflicts with social responsibility objectives.

    e Incentive systems for managers reward large size.

Divestment can be accomplished in one of several ways:

1 If the SBU is viable, it can be spun off as an independent firm. The parent may or may not continue an ownership interest.

2 If the SBU is viable, it can be sold to its employees.

3 The SBU can be sold to an independent buyer who would find it useful.

4 The SBU can be liquidated and its assets sold.

Most managers regard liquidation as the least attractive strategy and choose it only if the alternative is bankruptcy or if the stockholders would be better off with the result of liquidation than with an attempt to keep the firm going. The decision to liquidate is a decision that few are able to make. It implies failure. It is rarely made, except in extreme circumstances. However, as Exhibit 7.6 suggests, liquidation can be a successful strategy; it was growing more popular in the early to mid-1980s, as it offered a quick return on stockholder investment.

Of course, we should mention that bankruptcy is always an alternative which can be used. It does have the advantage of leading to a restructuring of the finances of the firm, which could allow the firm to start up again as a new entity, as happened with International Harvester (Navistar). In fact, if an attractive offer of liquidation is not found, other parties such as stockholders and debt holders may prefer this approach.

While many firms have criteria for evaluating acquisitions, few have developed criteria for making divestiture choices. It would seem prudent for firms to plan this ahead of time in order to reduce some of the emotionality involved in such decisions.

Just as there are specialist managers for turnaround strategies, there are consultants who are brought in to liquidate firms. Indeed, in all these forms of retrenchment, it is likely that the old CEO will be replaced, which is another reason why retrenchment is not viewed as an attractive strategy by many CEOs.[1]

---

[1] Nonetheless a few managers and individuals have used the bankruptcy laws in a proactive strategic manner, even though they were not insolvent. Wilson Foods Corp., Manville, and others have used Chapter 11 to shelter themselves against such threats as unfavorable union contracts or legal claims in asbestos-related diseases.

EXHIBIT 7.6   IT'S WORTH MORE DEAD THAN ALIVE

It is unusual for managers to recommend that their businesses be liquidated, particularly voluntarily as opposed to forced bankruptcy. Some of the reasons, of course, involve the problems of finding buyers of assets, loss of jobs, and confusion among suppliers and distributors. But the major reason for resistance is probably that managers want to deny defeat, assuming that selling out implies failure.

Yet liquidation need not be a sign of failure. A case in point is UV Industries, formerly number 357 in the *Fortune* 500. Through acquisitions, its sales had been increasing over a 15-year period from $31 to $600 million, with profits going from $2.3 to $40 million. Before liquidation plans were announced, its stock was selling for $19 a share; the price jumped to $30 after the announcement. One analyst estimates that the sales of assets will net stockholders $33 or more.

Of course, if a firm is not doing well, a liquidation may be justified also. An example here is the case of Overseas National. After running operating losses of over $2.7 million in 5 years, the airline sold its planes. Inflation and long waits for new jets in 1978 raised the price of used planes to the point where sales of the company's assets brought in $114 million, or $23 million over book value. In this case, the firm was controlled by investors rather than "airline types," and the investors doubled their equity value through the liquidation.

While some managers choose liquidation because they are pessimistic about the future, others believe that depressed stock prices understate the true value of the firm. Not surprisingly, top officers and directors owned large amounts of stock in many of the companies which chose liquidation.

Liquidation tends to be easier for smaller, less complex firms which have a few highly salable hard assets such as land and resource reserves. Firms whose operations are neatly packaged so that a sell-off doesn't disturb the rest of the business also have an easier time liquidating. The liquidation of giant Kaiser Industries, with stakes in aluminum, steel, cement, broadcasting, engineering, and aerospace, has been much more difficult; Kaiser's plan is now in its fourth year.

Perhaps more executives ought to consider the option of examining expected future returns against present value. They, too, may find that the company is worth more dead than alive.

Sources: Adapted from "Overseas National Exits in Style," *Business Week,* Oct. 2, 1978, p. 36; "When a Company Is Better Dead," *Business Week,* Mar. 26, 1979, p. 89; and P. W. Bernstein, "A Company That's Worth More Dead than Alive," *Fortune,* Feb. 26, 1978, pp. 42–44.

As you consider internal or external retrenchment or stability, you should keep in mind a particular phenomenon known as the "declining industry" [5]. Harrigan notes a number of conditions here, the most prevalent being saturation and a decline in the product life cycle. Under these circumstances, firms might use "endgame strategies."

The strategies used by the successful endgame players are (1) dominate the market (internal expansion), (2) hold the market share (internal stability), (3) shrink selectively (internal retrenchment), (4) milk the investment (internal stability or retrenchment), and (5) divest now (external retrenchment).

Corporate and industry strengths dictate which of these to follow, as indicated in Exhibit 7.7. Industry conditions that are favorable for an endgame include low uncertainty in the environment, low exit barriers, and relatively less rivalry among competitors. Strengths and weaknesses vary as discussed in Chapter 5. So some firms have successfully profited from careful management of products when most firms felt they were obsolete and left the industry. Exhibit 7.8 contrasts firms in the tire industry to highlight this.

EXHIBIT 7.7   CONDITIONS FOR USING ENDGAME STRATEGIES

	Possess relative corporate strengths	Have relative corporate weaknesses
Favorable industry traits for endgame.	"Dominate market" or "hold market share."	"Shrink selectively" or "milk."
Unfavorable industry traits for endgame.	"Shrink selectively" or "milk."	"Get out now!"

Source: Kathryn Harrigan and Michael Porter, "A Framework for Looking at Endgame Strategies," *Proceedings of the Academy of Management* (August 1978), p. 14.

External Expansion [6]

This is the flip side of divestiture or liquidation. Thus far in this section, the emphasis has been on retrenchment or expansion from *within* a company. But companies also expand externally, acquiring other firms or parts of firms which they feel would add

EXHIBIT 7.8   ENDGAME STRATEGIES FOR TIRES?

What strategy does a firm follow if it is a big business in a mature, marginally profitable industry? Some firms will try to dominate or hold on, some will shrink, and others will get out. The tire business is a case in point. Goodyear is expanding in tires. Many competitors are diversifying to shrink their emphasis on tires, and this is leading to less rivalry and some "exit" behavior. General seems to be reducing its diversification, and it seems likely that it will try to sell its tire operations.

Goodyear is betting $374 million that it can increase its market share. It announced plans to build a new technical center in 1978, and several new plants have come on stream or are being built. This expansion is happening precisely at the time when producers are facing 5 years of poor profits and low growth. The belief is that Goodyear has the marketing muscle to succeed where others can't. For example, Goodrich introduced an all-weather tire in 1965, and it bombed. Goodyear's introduction of the same "round, black tire" turned into a success. Its economies of scale are believed to be benefits in the competition with Michelin.

General is the most diversified of the tire and rubber manufacturers. It owns RKO and operates aerospace, plastics, and other businesses in addition to the tire and rubber businesses. The board was working on a plan in 1981 to spin these off into separate companies to achieve a higher stock price in a market that refuses to place a premium on conglomerates. The tire operations earned less than $10 million on $1.5 billion in sales, while Aerojet General and RKO earned over $40 million each on sales of $700 million and $529 million, respectively. After the spin-off, the tire business may be merged with another business—in effect, the tire business will be sold off.

Goodrich and Uniroyal reduced their tire operations by seeking high-profit niches. In 1980 Uniroyal closed two plants, trimmed its product line, and went private with a leveraged buyout. In 1985, Goodrich closed two tire plants. In 1986, these two formed a 50-50 joint venture to become the nation's second largest producer. The two companies have complementary strengths: Goodrich is strong in high-performance tires for the replacement market while Uniroyal is the preeminent tire supplier to General Motors. Many of the minor players are dropping out or switching to highly specialized products or selling to a single big customer.

Clearly a number of "endgame strategies" can be pursued in this declining industry.

Sources: Adapted from "Goodyear's Solo Strategy," *Business Week,* Aug. 28, 1978, pp. 67–78; "General Tire: Pondering Spinoffs to Make the Most of Its Assets," *Business Week,* Sept. 7, 1981, pp. 98–102; and "Can Goodrich and Uniroyal Keep Each Other Off the Skids?" *Business Week,* Feb. 10, 1986, p. 28.

to their effectiveness. Mergers have become increasingly popular. There are a number of terms used for external expansion: acquisitions, mergers (one company loses its identity), and consolidations (both companies lose their identity, and a new company arises). But one term will be used for all these: mergers.

A merger is a combination of two or more businesses in which one acquires the assets and liabilities of the other in exchange for stock or cash, or both companies are dissolved and assets and liabilities are combined and new stock is issued. Mergers can take place within one country or across national borders.

There are many reasons why a firm may desire to merge. They can be grouped under buyer's motives and seller's motives.

The buyer's motives for merging include the following:

• To increase the value of the firm's stock. Mergers often lead to increases in the stock price and/or price-earnings ratio.
• To increase the growth rate of the firm.
• To make a good investment. A firm may make a better use of funds by purchasing instead of plowing the same funds into internal expansion.
• To improve the stability of the firm's earnings and sales. This is done by acquiring firms whose earnings and sales complement the firm's peaks and valleys.
• To balance or fill out the product line.
• To diversify the product line when the current products have reached their peak in the life cycle.
• To reduce competition by purchasing a competitor (possible violation of the Sherman Act).
• To acquire a needed resource quickly—for example, high-quality technology or highly innovative management.
• For tax reasons. It may be desirable to purchase a firm with prior tax losses which will offset current or future earnings.
• To increase efficiency and profitability, especially if there is synergy between the two companies. (Synergy is discussed later in the chapter.)

The seller's motives for merging include the following:

• To increase the value of the owner's stock and investment in the firm.
• To increase the firm's growth rate by receiving more resources from the acquiring company.
• To acquire the resources to stabilize operations and make them more efficient.
• For tax reasons. If the firm is owned by a family or an individual, a merger makes it easier to deal with estate tax problems.
• To help diversify the owning family's holdings beyond the present firm.
• To deal with top-management problems such as management succession for an entrepreneur or dissension among top managers.

As can be seen from examining the two lists, there are a number of "matching" reasons. When there are enough matches, mergers are more likely to take place.

Recently, however, mergers seem to not necessarily rely on a "match." Indeed,

EXHIBIT 7.9   A FEW EXAMPLES OF MERGERS IN POST-1980 U.S. INDUSTRY

Brand-name mergers

Pantry Pride pays $2.7 billion for Revlon.
Proctor & Gamble acquires Richardson Vicks for $1.24 billion.
Monsanto buys G. D. Searle for $2.8 billion.
Greyhound buys Purex for $264 million.
Coca-Cola acquires Columbia Pictures, Embassy Communications, Merv Griffin Enterprises,
   Walter Reade Organizations, and joint ventures with Tri-Star Pictures (total = $1.5 billion).

Tobacco and food

R. J. Reynolds buys Nabisco for $4.9 billion and Canada Dry for $175 million.
Phillip Morris buys General Foods for $5.75 billion (which acquired six firms from 1982 to 1984).
Beatrice, going private in leveraged buyout, buys Esmark, which had bought Norton Simon, for
   $2.7 billion.
Nestle buys Carnation for $2.9 billion.
Quaker Oats buys Stokely Van Camp for $226 million.
Ralston Purina seeks ITT's Continental Baking for $475 million.

The oil and gas patch

Texaco is involved in a court battle ($11 billion judgment on appeal) for derailing merger of
   Pennzoil and Getty.
Exxon buys $4 billion of its own stock to ward off suitors.
Dupont pays $7.3 billion for Conoco.
InterNorth buys Houston Natural Gas.
Carl Icahn threatens Phillips Petroleum.
CSX buys Texas Gas Resources for $1.1 billion.
Chevron pays $13.2 billion for Gulf.
Phillips buys some R. J. Reynolds properties for $1.7 billion.

Exhibit 7.9 provides some evidence that merger mania—the corporate game of ''Let's Make a Deal''—has hit American business firms. In 1985 alone, firms acquired in whole or in part averaged 11 *per day*. Between 1969 and 1980, only 12 transactions valued at over $1 billion took place between U.S. firms. In 1985, 35 deals worth at least that amount took place. And megamergers are not just an American phenomenon. They have taken place in Britain, Japan, and a few other countries. What's going on?

For one thing, acquisitions have boosted stock prices of target firms an average of 30 percent. Corporate raiders have seen an opportunity to ''get rich quick''; with access to enough borrowed cash, they have put pressure on existing managers to ''get more value for the stockholder.'' Arbitragers, speculators who snap up stock when an acquisition play is announced, will take big risks in the hope of a rapid stock price rise. And with takeover artists on the prowl, managers may look for protection by seeking mergers instead of planning new products or considering new markets. Thus many recent mergers have been based more on issues of short-term financial gain or job protection (of top managers) than on strategic considerations.

The use, success, and implementation of mergers has been the subject of substantial research and writing. We include in the appendix for this chapter some technical

EXHIBIT 7.9   A FEW EXAMPLES OF MERGERS IN POST-1980 U.S. INDUSTRY (*Continued*)

The raiders

T. Boone Pickens goes after Gulf Oil, which finally sells out to Chevron for $13.3 billion.
Ted Turner tries to buy CBS; settles for MGM/UA Entertainment. [CBS buys back $1 billion
    (20%) of its shares to avoid takeover.]
James Goldsmith acquires Crown Zellerbach.
Carl Icahn buys TWA, then buys Ozark.

Airlines

United Airlines buys Pan Am's Pacific routes.
Southwest Air buys Muse Air.
People Express buys Frontier, then sells it.
Piedmont acquires Empire Airlines.
Northwest buys Republic.
Texas Air buys Eastern.

Others

Southern Pacific merges with Santa Fe, valued at $5.1 billion (under challenge).
GE buys RCA for $6 billion (largest non-oil merger to 1986).
Capital Cities buys American Broadcasting for $3.5 billion.
W. R. Grace buys back stock to ward off possible takeover.
GAF makes $4 billion takeover bid for Union Carbide.
GM acquires Electronic Data Systems and buys Hughes Aircraft for $5.2 billion.
CIT Financial (formerly owned by RCA) pays $1.5 billion for Manufacturers Hanover.
IBM pays $1.2 billion for Rolm.
Ameritech buys Applied Data Research.
Monsanto buys G. D. Searle for $2.7 billion.
LTV merges with Republic Steel.
Maytag merges with Magic Chef for $711 million.

Sources: Compiled from J. Greenwold, "Let's Make a Deal," *Time*, Dec. 23, 1985, pp. 42–51; "The New LTV Steel," *Business Week*, Apr. 16, 1984, pp. 129–133; C. Hawkins and A. Bernstein, "Airlines in Flux," *Business Week*, Mar. 10, 1986, pp. 107–112; "Why Nabisco and Reynolds Were Made for Each Other," *Business Week*, June 17, 1985, pp. 34–35; "Mainframe Software Makers Have Seen the Future, and It's Rugged," *Business Week*, Dec. 23, 1985, pp. 69–70; "The New Food Giants," *Business Week*, Sept. 24, 1984, pp. 132–138; P. B. Brown, "New? Improved?" *Business Week*, Oct. 21, 1985, pp. 108–110; "The Top 300 Deals," *Business Week*, Apr. 18, 1986, pp. 266–284; "Columbia Pictures: Are Things Really Better with Coke?" *Business Week*, Apr. 14, 1986, pp. 56–58.

details associated with mergers. We can sum these up here by making several observations:

1 Mergers must be carefully planned.
2 Human considerations are as important as financial ones.
3 The valuation of a merger candidate is an important process.
4 Legal factors must be carefully assessed.
5 Much of the research suggests that mergers are less successful than internal expansion.
6 Mergers which create synergy are likely to be more successful.
7 The acquiring firm's managers usually have more to gain than the stockholders of either firm or the acquired firm's managers.

Internal and External Combinations [7]

A firm may decide to cooperate with another firm (or firms) in a contractual agreement which allows each to remain independent, but which leads to gains for both. In effect, the firm pursues both an internal (independent) and external (cooperative) strategy simultaneously. There are many variations possible here. *Subcontracting* on a long-term or short-term basis may be done. *Cross-licensing* or technology sharing can lead to benefits from patents which might require substantial internal investments otherwise. Several firms in an industry may benefit from forming a *consortium* for research or development of standardization of production processes or technologies. *Franchising* allows a firm to grant exclusive rights to other firms, while still retaining the right to operate its own company-owned units. Probably the most common variant is the *joint venture* for expansion. A joint venture involves an equity arrangement between two or more independent enterprises which results in the creation of a new organizational entity. (There has been one joint venture to buy and manage an existing firm, but it is highly unique.) As noted in Exhibit 7.10, a joint venture is a combination of internal and external expansion.

There are three joint-venture strategies (sometimes called *strategic alliances*).

Spiderweb Strategy

A small firm establishes a series of joint ventures so that it can survive—and not be absorbed by its larger competitors. An example is an oil firm which jointly bids for drilling rights with five or six other firms. It may not have enough funds to bid on its own, or it may wish to spread resources to increase the chances of success or reduce the risk of a takeover.

Go Together–Split Strategy

In this strategy, the firms agree to a joint venture for a specific project or length of time. When the project is completed, they "split." Examples of this kind of strategy have been seen in many construction projects, such as the Alaska pipeline project and R&D projects. This strategy can also evolve as the two partners grow to the point where they don't need each other for economies of scale or efficiency reasons.

EXHIBIT 7.10 **Internal-external combinations.**
(S. Gullander, "Joint Ventures and Corporate Strategy," Columbia Journal of World Business, vol. 11, no. 1 [Spring 1976], p. 106.)

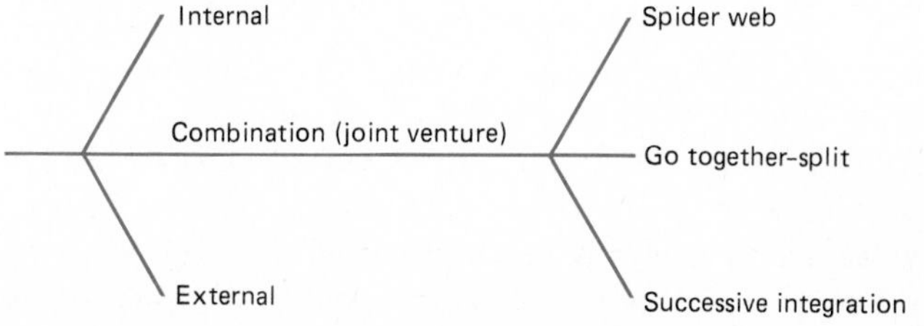

Successive Integration Strategy

A firm begins a relationship that is weak and then develops several joint ventures that can lead to a merger. In fact, joint ventures could become a laboratory setting prior to a merger, as happened with Conoco and Du Pont (see Exhibit 7.8).

The spiderweb strategy makes sense for small companies or large, undiversified firms organized into an oligopoly. Go together-split makes sense for firms that prefer independence but are financially unable to go it alone. Successive integration is chosen by firms whose management is risk-aversive regarding mergers but uses joint ventures to test the water.

Reasons advanced by advocates of joint ventures include the following: to reduce the high risk of new ventures; to help smaller companies to compete with giants; to introduce new technology or new products quickly; to save financial outlays, thus lowering costs for both parties; to increase sales, thus lowering production costs; to provide speedy channel acceptance, thus reducing marketing costs; to maintain the independence of both companies.

Joint ventures will be formed when firms cannot obtain strategic objectives on their own. If the need to cooperate comes from insufficient resources, lack of markets, or competitive timing advantages, joint ventures are highly opportunistic arrangements. For example, several highly publicized joint ventures between Japanese and American automakers have resulted in advantages for both parties. And Apple Computer set up a joint venture after it learned that Mexico was about to nationalize its manufacturing operations. Even AT&T has found joint ventures useful—for breaking into European markets which are highly protected. Nonetheless, many managers prefer to ''go it alone'' where possible. A number of studies indicate that larger firms may use joint ventures to control, influence, or reduce competition or as a means of influencing suppliers. And a joint venture may be used as a way to get into markets which would otherwise be restricted, without risking high investment. If these are true, then potential legal problems may be a possible drawback or trade-off. And many of these relationships have been too unstable to endure. For example:

• Financial troubles at McLouth Steel required its partners (Inland Steel, International Harvester, Cleveland Cliffs Iron) in a mine project to find a buyer for its share. They didn't, and $264 million of debt came due.

• Conoco was involved with a joint-venture partner in the construction of a prototype industrial boiler to cleanly burn high-sulfur coal. But due to a weak economy Conoco deferred capital investment and left its partner in a bind.

• Du Pont's purchase of Conoco created competitive problems that wrecked a joint venture between Conoco and Monsanto, which competes with Du Pont.

A number of crucial decisions must be made when setting up joint ventures, including decisions about the share of control and voting strength, the share of ownership, the share of ''rewards,'' and the choice of partners. Where the venture crosses national boundaries, these decisions can be particularly difficult because of differences in culture and economic development. As differences increase, joint-venture problems increase. However, joint ventures can provide a ''front-row seat'' in a new country.

Locals can interpret the industrial language and customs of the country, thus reducing the host government's nationalistic fear that foreigners are taking over.

RELATED AND UNRELATED ALTERNATIVES [8]

These approaches are usually found with expansion of the business definition either internally or externally. New products, markets, or functions that are added are "related" if they conform to or are very similar to the current business definition. The addition of related products, markets, or functions is termed a "concentric diversification." For instance, if a food company decided to sell kitchen equipment, the equipment could be considered either a product or a market-related addition (if sold through the same channels of distribution used for food). Major advantages of related expansion are thought to be the concentration of strength, the ability to act more quickly (than firms with unrelated expansion), exploitation of a market niche, and the development of synergy.

Synergy can be developed through internal expansion but is usually discussed in terms of external expansion (mergers). The argument is that the "whole is greater than the sum of its parts." Synergy exists when the strengths of two companies more than offset their joint weaknesses. *Sales synergy* arises from many products having the same salespeople, warehouses, distribution channels, and advertising. *Investment synergy* arises from many products having the same plant, inventories, R&D, and machinery. *Operating synergy* arises from many products making possible a higher utilization of facilities and personnel and the spreading of overhead. *Management synergy* arises from management experience in handling problems in one location or industry that helps to solve problems in another. Exhibit 7.11 indicates how an international news company wants to create operating and investment synergy in the services it provides.

Synergy can be negative too. In most mergers, at least one and possibly more of the factors can be negative. In theory, the concept of synergy is appealing. It should be pointed out that there has been little systematic proof that synergy actually exists. But the combined resources of two companies, if properly integrated, can create a stronger operation than stand-alone firms.

The "unrelated" approach is usually termed a "conglomerate diversification." There are a number of reasons why a firm might wish to diversify internally or externally. Only a few can be discussed here.

• The first is that the firm fears that its product or service line is in a business approaching market saturation or obsolescence. The firm may wish to stabilize its earnings and dividends in a cyclical industry. It does this by diversifying into an industry with complementary cycles. Or the market may be too small to allow the firm to achieve growth objectives efficiently. In sum, it feels uncomfortable being dependent on one product line.

• The current product or service is producing more cash than can be usefully reinvested. The opportunities with other products or services provide better returns.

EXHIBIT 7.11   CREATING SYNERGY

Reuters Ltd. is a London-based international news company that sells its services to publishers and broadcasters throughout the world. In 1981 its plan was to attempt to acquire United Press International from E. W. Scripps of Cincinnati. A Reuters-UPI network would form a news-gathering outfit with revenues about twice the size of those of the Associated Press.

Executives and industry observers noted that a remarkable synergy would be created by this merger. Reuters needed to fill a gap in its U.S. news bureaus. UPI's 78 overseas bureaus would augment Reuter's 81. In addition, UPI operates a new international telephoto service, and Reuters lacks this service. Further, UPI would give Reuters a base from which to invade North America with computerized data services—an area in which it has been developing expertise. About 15,700 subscribers are now linked to Reuters so that they can retrieve news and prices with regard to commodities, foreign exchange, securities, and financial instruments in global markets.

While Reuters faced possible opposition from National Public Radio (NPR), Scripps has few options if UPI is to remain intact, since it has been unprofitable for 25 years. From Reuters's point of view, the synergy obtainable in this horizontal merger would be worth the price it would have to pay to obtain UPI, despite its losses. But from Scripps's point of view, the tax deduction of a sale to NPR could have offset the annual losses. What is interesting is that a private consortium of investors bought UPI from Scripps. NPR did not have sufficient resources to compete with the consortium's offer. Clearly, buyer and seller goals in a merger are also important.

Sources: Adapted from ''Why Reuters Wants UPI on Its Wires,'' *Business Week,* Sept. 21, 1981, p. 33, and ''NPR Directors Vote to Consider Takeover of UPI Wire Service,'' AP news release, Jan. 16, 1982.

- Tax policy induces reinvestment in research and development at present. Diversification can arise when R&D develops a new product or service which is not in the present product or service line.
- Antitrust prohibitions appear difficult in the present industry.
- A firm may diversify, usually by means of a merger, to try to prevent a hostile takeover. For example, if the firm trying to take over is in the bread business, the target firm acquires a bread company. Such a merger may result in legal problems for the firm trying to take over, or the new combination might be too large to be acquired by the hostile firm.
- A firm may diversify, usually by means of a merger to acquire a tax loss.
- A firm may diversify, usually by means of a merger, to enter the international sector quickly.
- A firm may diversify, usually by means of a merger, to attain technical expertise quickly.
- A firm may diversify to attract more experienced executives and to hold better executives who may become bored in a single-product or single-service-line business.

Recognize, however, that unrelated diversification is not a panacea. Some old problems may not be solved through diversification. It can lead to spreading resources so thinly that no competitive advantage is obtained. And management may find it difficult to control and coordinate the increased activities which result. A section in the appendix on concentric and conglomerate diversification provides additional details and examples.

The unrelated-related dimension is most often associated with expansion, as we said earlier. But many conglomerates have not been successful due to past unrelated diversification and have pursued a strategy of divesting themselves of unrelated SBUs. Thus retrenching out of unrelated businesses is also an approach that is possible in this dimension.

HORIZONTAL AND VERTICAL ALTERNATIVES [9]

The horizontal dimension is quite similar to the "related" dimension. However, it usually applies to the addition of products, or services, and/or markets which complement the existing business definition. If this expansion occurs via a merger, the legal aspects must be carefully considered. Exhibit 7.11 is an interesting example (Reuters wished to expand horizontally).

Vertical integration is a strategy which expands or contracts the business definition primarily in terms of functions performed. As a firm takes some input and transforms it into output, it adds value in the form of utility to a buyer of its output. Exhibit 7.12 suggests that the value added varies at different stages in the chain of transformation. The vertical integration strategy question is whether to perform more or fewer functions than are now performed. There are two kinds of vertical integration. A *backward integration* is associated with strategies affecting the supply of a firm's inputs (toward the raw material stage). *Forward integration* refers to moves altering the nature of the distribution of the firm's output (toward end users). Note that expansion or retrenchment is possible. The firm can add or subtract functions. Vertical integration is the primary form of a make or buy decision.

Examples of vertical integration may help clarify these distinctions.

• Ashland Oil could integrate forward if it decided to sell its entire output of gasoline through its own service stations instead of most of it through distributors.

EXHIBIT 7.12   **The value added to a product at different stages in the production chain of raw material to consumer.**
(J. L. Bower, Simple Economic Tools for Strategic Analysis [Boston: Intercollegiate Case Clearing House, no. 9-373-094, 1972].)

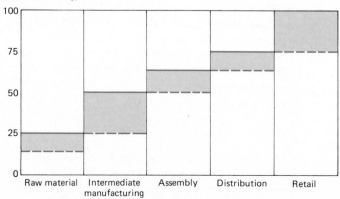

• Seven-Up vertically integrated backward when it bought its flavor supplier and the lemon groves which provided the raw materials for the flavor company and Seven-Up.

• Kellwood was formed through a backward vertical integration strategy when several suppliers of clothing were merged to produce most of their output for Sears. Instead of producing and distributing, they retrenched out of the distribution function, letting Sears market the products.

• Carter Hawley Hale has rediscovered customer service in its department stores after cutting corners by doing away with many salespeople.

Advantages of vertical integration are thought to be better control of suppliers or distributors and possible cost savings. Disadvantages may come in the form of increasing dependence on one industry or the risk of possible antitrust violations. Recognize that expanding forward or backward could result in the addition of new markets for products, and the firm may compete with former distributors or suppliers.

Perhaps these pros and cons can be seen more clearly if we examine the "captive-company" strategy—retrenching by means of vertical integration as in the Kellwood example. A captive-company strategy is followed when (1) a firm sells more than 75 percent of its products or services to a single customer and (2) the customer performs many of the functions normally performed by the independent firm.

The captive-company strategy may be chosen because of:

1 The inability or unwillingness to strengthen the marketing function or other functions.

2 The perception that this strategy is the best means for achieving financial strength. It will be rationalized as a security strategy but is in fact risky and costly to the prestige and independence needs of the manager.

In effect, when you become captive, your captor makes many decisions for you. Perhaps some of these decisions concern product design, production control, and quality control. The captor negotiates the price of the goods, usually from a position of strength, assuring for itself an adequate return much in the way a public utility and the public service commission of a state relate. It may be able to avoid cost squeezes from competitors in this fashion. But the captive becomes closely tied to the results of the actions of its major purchaser, and this can be risky. Still, the strategy is a way to assure adequate profitability, especially if the captive company competes with much bigger companies that can spend large amounts on advertising and marketing. Most captive companies are not well known, but they can be large.

This strategy requires a management that is able to develop good long-term relationships with its major customer. In a way, it is a strategy that can be as risky as doing most of your business with the military. But if the contractual relationship is a good one, the firm can prosper and hedge against the loss of business by developing its own line, as Whirlpool did very successfully. Still, many executives intuitively like to be relatively independent, and this strategy may be unrewarding to them. It may be one of the few choices a firm has at times. It is also a strategy which is easy to drift into unintentionally. A few large customers buy more and more of your output until you find yourself dependent on them for future business.

Retrenchment out of functions reaches an extreme when a firm becomes a "shell" corporation. Such firms may subcontract out manufacturing, marketing, and in some cases even collection functions. This vertical "disintegration" is seen as a way to reduce capital needs and add flexibility. However, these firms become vulnerable to their subcontractors and often have volatile earnings. Companies who use this strategy are Nike, Esprit, Emerson, and Schwinn Bicycle, among others.

ACTIVE AND PASSIVE ALTERNATIVES [10]

The last dimension refers to management's attitude and timing with regard to pursuing its strategy alternatives. Depending on the strategists, there may be a preference for active or passive strategies.

An *active,* or offensive, strategy is one in which strategists act before they are forced to react to environmental threats or opportunities. A *passive,* or defensive, strategy is one whose major characteristic is that strategists react to environmental pressures only when forced to do so by circumstances.

Active or passive approaches may occur with any of the generic strategies. Obviously, firms can develop strategies which are offensive (active) with regard to one part of the business definition and passive with regard to the other parts. In fact, a crucial characteristic determining the choice of active or passive strategies may be the relative size of the firm in its market. In general, large and dominant firms will be effective if they develop active strategic alternatives in their major market segments. Small firms will survive if they have passive strategies concerning the large firms' major market and if they have active strategies concerning market segments which are ignored by the dominant firm(s) and which they can develop.

The approach to research and the development of new products is another area where this dimension becomes important. Firms can be active or passive in this function in the following ways:

1 *Being innovative—the first to market.* This is an offensive, active approach in both research and development. In some instances, however, the firm is strong in research but weak in marketing products. It tries to make the environment accept its approach.

2 *Being a fast second.* There are firms which are active in development but passive in research. They need superior competitive intelligence and enough research to make sure that the gaps between them and innovators don't become too large.

3 *Being an imitator—a slow third.* Some firms emphasize applications engineering based on product modifications to fit particular customer segments. These firms tend to react to the needs they identify in the environment.

A typical prescription these days is that innovation is mandatory so that the firm can get "fast down the learning curve" and thus preclude competition. Other advocates argue that firms should seek to create barriers to entry in their industries by seizing the initiative and becoming the "first occupant" who can preemptively erect such barriers (see Chapter 4 for a discussion of barriers to entry). Yet some firms prefer to let others test the waters and make the mistakes which they can learn to avoid. A number of follow-up approaches such as the acquisition of inventions, securing licenses, and outright imitation are available to those who prefer passive approaches or who may have limited capital. Exhibit 7.13 presents some of the pros and cons of follow-up, or passive, approaches in the R&D area.

Interestingly, in some areas the large firms with more resources are those who are fast seconds or imitators, leaving innovation to smaller firms. And as discussed earlier in the book, as technological change occurs in the environment, strategic response patterns vary from stability in old technologies to expansion into new ones. Clearly, executives have different preferences for passive or active approaches, and these influence the alternative strategies which are likely to be considered.

A good example of an active approach to a sequential combination of expansion and retrenchment is known as a ''grow to sell out'' strategy. Here we find many entrepreneurs who plan from the start of their business to expand, but when it gets to the high-growth-rate apex of the product life cycle, they will sell out (usually for stock) to a larger firm. Typically, they take the proceeds in stock (for tax purposes) and stay on as consultants for 3 to 5 years. Usually they agree not to compete with the acquiring firm for a period. With this agreement they can maximize their return and retire early or build up another firm to be sold out. Many entrepreneurs have used this approach, but this combination strategy has not been studied in any depth. Note that the difference between the active approach and the passive approach here is the idea that the ''retrenchment'' was planned from the start, that it was not a reaction to ''unfavorable'' circumstances.

Of course, this dimension does *not* imply that flexibility is inappropriate. Active preplanning of ''contingency'' strategies does not suggest that the firm is merely

EXHIBIT 7.13   ADVANTAGES AND DISADVANTAGES OF PASSIVE RESEARCH AND DEVELOPMENT

Advantages	Disadvantages
• Involvement based upon calculable risk	• Difficulties involved with the search for suitable objects
• Quick availability of new technologies	• Payment of license fees
• Reduction of the high risk normally associated with R&D	• Reduced opportunity to train specialists for the future
• Cooperation with or financing by third parties easier to obtain	• Reduced opportunity to obtain knowledge for new ideas
• Effective way to achieve short-to-medium-range diversification	• No technological advantage over competitors
• Easy adaptation of the supply to the demand in different markets = flexible marketing strategy	• Increased risk to investments and ongoing programs from new developments not anticipated by a firm doing little exploratory research

Sources: Adapted from D. Altenpohl, "Acquisition of Technology as One Specific Way to Achieve Technology Transfer," in H. Davidson, M. Cetron, and J. Goldhar, *Technology Transfer* (Leyden, the Netherlands: Noordhoff, 1974), and D. Altenpohl, paper presented at the NATO Advanced Study Institute on Industrial Applications of Technology Transfer, Les Arcs-Bourg St. Maurice, France (June–July 1975).

passive. For example, many firms attempt to forecast product life cycles so that new-product introductions can be developed (see Exhibit 7.14). In effect, this is an *active, sequential combination* of *expansion, stability,* and *retrenchment* in *products.* It can be flexible in that the exact timing of stability and phaseout may be contingent on prespecified conditions; the firm does not have to passively await saturation or decline. In other words, it can plan for exit at the time of entry.

More typically, firms passively or unintentionally pursue different strategies as the product life cycle changes occur. During youth stages, new products and new markets are introduced. If they are successful, diversification, mergers and joint ventures, or vertical integration may be pursued during growth stages. At the maturity stage, stability or operating turnarounds may be pursued. At the stage of saturation and decline, strategic turnarounds, divestments, and other retrenchments are pursued. The prescription for active planned entry and exit is based on this idea, but it urges a greater degree of control instead of passive reaction to external conditions. Further, remember that endgame strategies need not be passive. Retrenchment is not preordained, and an active approach can be successful even in a declining industry.

Finally, whole typologies of firms' past strategies have been developed around the active-passive dimension. The best known is the Miles and Snow framework. Miles and Snow propose that, historically, firms have had four strategic postures:

Defenders. These are firms which penetrate a narrow product-market domain and guard it. They plan intensively, have centralized control, use limited environmental scanning, and are cost-efficient. This is the passive end of the strategic continuum.

Prospectors. At the active end of the continuum are the firms which use broad planning approaches, decentralized controls, and broad environmental scanning. They also have some underutilized resources. The prospectors seek new product/market segments.

Analyzers. In between the two poles are two choices, one of which is the analyzer. The analyzers have some of the characteristics of prospectors some of the time and some of the characteristics of defenders the rest of the time.

Reactors. The other in-between choice is the reactor. The firm that realizes that the environment is changing but cannot effect the necessary realignment of strategy

EXHIBIT 7.14   **A common product life cycle.**

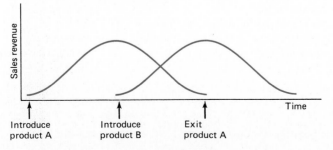

and environment fits in this category. Reactors must either become one of the other three choices or die. They have an unstable strategic posture.

Thus the active-passive dimension provides another approach to examining the pursuit of alternative grand strategies.

INTERNATIONAL STRATEGY VARIATIONS [11]

In Chapter 4 we noted threats and opportunities associated with the international environment. This leads to a special case of strategy variation. While the alternatives explained earlier apply here as well, it is useful to explore in more detail some of the strategies which firms can consider if they seek an international presence.

New Markets

Some firms seek to open up new markets in other countries when they face slower growth rates at home or a restricted domestic market. This has been a major reason for Japanese expansion, for example. Firms must identify a critical mass of GNP and population growth before exploring the international alternative further. Of course, other factors, such as competitor activity in the market, ability to produce domestically or in the foreign market, and so on, must be taken into account. For example, the firm's domestic competitors may not be located in selected foreign markets, possibly allowing the company to obtain a better price. On the other hand, competitors based in the foreign country may enjoy favored treatment by customers or the government. Whatever the circumstances, the prudent strategist must determine the firm's ability to compete effectively.

Some strategists have opened new foreign markets for diversification and risk-spreading purposes. When a domestic economy slumps, foreign economies operating in a lagged cycle may provide a way to stabilize sales and earnings. To the extent that a "global economy" begins to emerge, such a strategy could lose its appeal. Other factors, such as political considerations, may emerge as a reason to go into foreign markets. For example, some foreign firms may invest in the United States because it is seen as politically stable.

In some cases, the motivation to compete in domestic markets may be done to protect a position already secured in the multinational marketplace. A case in point was the strategy of Heinz in the 1960s and 1970s. The U.S. baby food division at Heinz was competing with Gerber for declining baby food demand in the United States. Heinz held only a 5 percent market share in the United States, yet it used low pricing as a primary weapon against Gerber. While its pricing policy led to marginal profitability in the United States, the Heinz strategy was designed to protect the high profits it reaped from control of an 80 percent share of the multinational baby food market. By keeping Gerber busy at home, Heinz sought to reduce Gerber's resource capability and direct management attention away from Gerber's interest in foreign expansion. Similarly, banks, accounting firms, market researchers, and so on have established operations in foreign locations to prevent competitors from gaining access to key customers in those locations.

New Products

Firms can sometimes introduce new products sooner into a foreign market than at home. This is especially so for U.S.-based pharmaceutical firms. FDA delays in approving new products have led some firms to develop and market drugs in foreign countries before introducing them in the United States. On the other hand, as more Americans have traveled overseas, they have returned home with a heightened awareness of the different products available. American marketers send buyers around the world to locate new products which they can import to meet the demand. Large retailers such as Sears and J. C. Penney have permanent foreign buying offices to identify products that can be successfully sold in the United States.

Functions

As we discussed in Chapter 4, firms can identify particular countries as *energy-rich, resource-rich,* or *labor-rich*. Any of these conditions can lead to the decision to produce goods in foreign locations to lower the cost of goods sold. And firms which have been exporting to a given country may find that producing in that location can yield benefits as well. For instance, a host government may prohibit imports to the country if there is a given level of ''domestic-content'' production in existence. Such protectionism serves as a trade barrier, but can benefit the firm which decides to open a production facility in such a country. In the Chilean market, General Tire was competing with a dozen or so exporters. But once General Tire began producing in Chile, it became the only supplier of tires for the entire market. Finally, some countries provide incentives (tax breaks, loans, grants, etc.) to locate there.

Protection of domestic markets may be another reason for locating production facilities abroad. If a firm faces lower-priced foreign imports, it may move part or all of its facilities to the source of its competition to take advantage of the lower costs of labor, materials, or energy. Strategists can manufacture selected components and assemble at home, or send components elsewhere for final assembly. For example, many U.S. clothing manufacturers have opened facilities in Mexico or the Far East to take advantage of lower labor costs. Some send cloth to be processed by foreign laborers, then ship finished goods back to domestic markets.

By the same token, suppliers will often locate new facilities in countries where their customers are locating. As Japanese car manufacturers moved to open U.S. plants, many Japanese suppliers began to consider opening facilities as well. Note, then, that there is both threat and opportunity for domestic suppliers when foreign manufacturers enter a market. Entry of new customers *and* competitors may go hand in hand.

Supply of raw materials or technology may also be a reason for choosing to locate production facilities in another country. Canadian firms, such as INCO, have invested in developing nations where new deposits of important ores or other resources have been found. And some foreign firms have located in the United States to gain knowledge of computers and semiconductors, areas in which the U.S. has held an edge in development.

Sequential Combinations

As we mentioned in Chapter 4, the movement toward international markets is frequently incremental. Most firms begin by exporting. This includes relatively low investment and risk. Depending on internal capabilities, firms may export directly (internal) or indirectly (external). That is, strategists may assign someone within the firm to handle this function or set up their own sales company in foreign locations. If the firm has no special expertise, export agents may be sought out. Depending on the nature of the business, franchising or licensing are other options by which a firm can begin to establish a presence in foreign locations.

The next stage for a firm may be to engage in a joint marketing venture with a foreign local who will act as its agent. In either the joint-venture or export case, issues of the need for product modification (to suit "local" tastes), different promotional tactics, control procedures, and so on will need to be considered. These are implementation issues which can affect the choice of entry.

EXHIBIT 7.15 TIME HORIZON OF SEQUENTIAL INTERNATIONAL STRATEGIES

Now	2 years	5 years
Market research—consider countries	Market research—study selected target markets	Continuing market analysis
Sell present product—no modification	Consider product modification	Consider new products
Limited penetration and promotion	Moderate penetration—special promotion	Full penetration and promotion
No servicing	Limited servicing	Full servicing
No new investment in production facilities	Add local investment of facilities to service foreign sales	Foreign investment
Use present supply sources	Contract manufacturing or possible overseas assembly in leased facility	Overseas manufacturing
Independent exporters	Overseas agents or representatives	Foreign sales branch or subsidiary
Correspondent relationships	Contractual relations or branch offices	Joint ventures or foreign subsidiary
No specialized personnel	Specialized personnel	Internationally oriented staff
No organizational changes	Minor organizational changes	Major organizational changes
Tight control	Loose control	Decentralized control

Source: Adapted from R. D. Robinson, *International Business Management: A Guide to Decision Making* (New York: Holt, 1973).

Once a foreign presence is obtained, the strategist may decide to expand the firm's activities. Specialized products may be developed, with new investments made in local manufacturing facilities. Or direct investment in the foreign economy may be made. This can be done a number of ways. A wholly owned subsidiary could be formed by building new facilities or acquiring a going concern in the foreign location. The factors affecting these choices are complicated by issues of personnel policies, legal requirements, and so on, which, as we suggested before, vary from country to country. Hence, many firms find it easier to use a successive-integration joint-venture arrangement which may eventually lead to complete ownership. Eventually a merger or buyout would occur if the joint venture became important to the company's core business.

Exhibit 7.15 indicates a number of the issues which can be involved over time as a strategist makes long-range plans for foreign involvement. Of course, the strategies given in this time line are implemented only if the firm is successful and expanding its presence, investment, and control. Retrenchment is possible if objectives are not being reached, or management finds better opportunities elsewhere.

SUMMARY

Various approaches to the generic strategies were identified. These are listed below in outline form.

1 Internal and External Dimensions
  a Internal moves suggest that the firm pursues its strategy independently.
    (1) Internal expansion can occur through the addition of products, markets, or functions to the business definition or through an increase in the pace of operations (through market penetration, for example).
    (2) Internal stability is used to maintain the pace or business definition.
    (3) Internal retrenchment in pace is an "operating turnaround" strategy that involves cutting costs, improving efficiency, reducing assets, or reorganizing. Internal retrenchment is a "strategic turnaround" strategy if it involves dropping products, markets, or functions.
  b External moves are those requiring the involvement of other entities.
    (1) External expansion involves a merger with another firm.
    (2) External retrenchment involves the divestment of SBUs or the liquidation of the entire business.
  c Internal and external combinations are usually in the form of a joint venture.
2 Related and Unrelated Dimensions
  a In related moves, changes in products, markets, or functions conform in some way to the current business definition. Related internal expansion can be used to create synergy.
  b Unrelated approaches imply a diversification into areas that do not conform to the current business definition.
3 Horizontal and Vertical Dimensions
  a Horizontal changes imply related moves which result in the addition of products or markets that complement or supplement the existing business definition.

    b Vertical changes expand or contract functions.

       (1) Backward integration is movement toward suppliers.

       (2) Forward integration is movement toward end users.

       (3) A firm which retrenches via backward vertical integration is known as a "captive company."

4 Active and Passive Dimensions

    a An active strategy is one in which strategists act before they are forced to react.

    b Passive strategies are defensive reactions to environmental pressures.

    c A "fast-second" strategy involves a simultaneous combination of active moves in one function (development) and passive moves in another (research).

    d A "grow to sell out" strategy is a sequential combination of expansion and retrenchment.

5 International Strategy Variations

    a New international markets may be sought for offensive or defensive reasons.

    b New products may be introduced in foreign markets for timing reasons or to import for domestic markets.

    c Foreign production may be done to take advantage of energy, resources, labor, or technology available elsewhere.

    d The movement to foreign activities is usually a sequential combination of a variety of strategies.

The advantages and disadvantages of these variations were described. In essence, any alternative or combination has the potential to improve performance. But we believe that the following proposition applies to many firms in moderately volatile environments.

Proposition 7.1

Firms with higher growth objectives are more effective if they expand their pace from a base of proven competitive abilities in the current business definition, organize divisions or departments to promote new opportunities in related fields, and take moderate risks.

This chapter has described various extensions of the generic strategy alternatives available to firms. The Appendix describes several expansion strategies in more detail. In Chapter 8, we will review how the manager chooses the strategy from the alternatives developed.

APPENDIX: Diversification and Mergers

Expansion through diversification and merger has received substantial attention in the literature. We chose not to bog you down in the chapter with the various technical matters associated with these strategies. Here we present some of the factors associated with these forms of expansion and review some of the research.

Diversification [12]

In and of itself, the term "diversification" can really refer to a host of different types of strategies. It can refer to changes in products, markets, or functions; it can be done internally or externally, horizontally or vertically; and it can involve related or unrelated changes. Although he uses slightly different terms, Ansoff has done the most theorizing on diversification strategies. Exhibit 7.16 presents one of his many mechanisms for analyzing diversification decisions.

This matrix can be used to plan the kind of diversification the firm should pursue insofar as nonfinancial aspects are concerned. But note that diversification is not *a* strategy; it is a number of kinds of strategies.

Drucker provides as good a list as any for why firms might pursue a diversification strategy. He lists the internal and external factors as follows:

1 Internal pressures
   a Psychologically, people get tired of doing the same things over and over again. They also believe that diversification will help them avoid the danger of overspecialization.
   b Diversification is seen as a way to balance the vulnerabilities due to one's wrong size.
   c Diversification is seen as a way to convert present internal cost centers into revenue producers.
2 External pressures (more important than internal pressures)
   a The economy (or market) the firm is operating in appears too small and confined to allow growth.
   b The firm's technology and research lead to the development of products which appear to have promise.
   c Tax legislation encourages reinvestment in research and development instead of the payment of dividends, and this leads to new products which are often a base for diversification.

Diversification is a much-used approach to strategy. Research has shown how single-product-line expansion has declined in relation to diversification for years in Europe, Japan, and the United States. Less than 1 percent of establishments are diversified (operate in more than one industry group). But this 1 percent employed 38 percent of the working people in the United States. The diversified firms are often concentrated in rapid-growth industries, with high increases in labor productivity and a high ratio of technical employees to all employees. It is

EXHIBIT 7.16   ANSOFF'S DIVERSIFICATION MATRIX

New functions	New products	
	Related technology	Unrelated technology
Firm is its own customer		Vertical integration
Same type of product		Horizontal diversification
Similar type of product	Marketing and technology-related concentric diversification	Marketing-related concentric diversification
New type of product	Technology-related concentric diversification	Conglomerate diversification

Source: H. I. Ansoff, *Corporate Strategy* (New York: McGraw-Hill, 1965), p. 132.

believed that firms diversify because they feel it is easier than trying to increase primary demand or market share. But diversifiers have not been found to reduce systematic risk.

Note that when we define diversified firms as those operating in more than one industry group, we are relying on a commonly used criterion of the numbers of different products produced. Thus as the number of different Standard Industrial Classification (SIC) definitions of products increases, diversification is thought to increase. Stated differently, diversity increases as *products* become *less related*. However, this definition ignores non-product-oriented aspects of diversification such as those in Exhibit 7.16.

A less precise but more strategically relevant measure of diversification has been developed by Rumelt. He established a set of categories defined largely in terms of "relatedness" and designed to capture important differences in the extent of diversity of a company as well as in the nature of the managerial relationships among the various businesses of a company. He examined the performance from 1949 to 1969 of 250 large U.S. firms in a very sophisticated research project. First he classified the firms into strategic categories at various points in recent years as shown in Exhibit 7.17. Then he examined the performance of these firms. Performance varied within each category (for example, single business), and subgroups performed differently. The *worst* performers were in the dominant (vertically integrated) and unrelated classes. The *highest* performers were in the related classes.

Rumelt did not separate those which diversified internally from those which diversified by means of a merger. However, several other researchers have done so, particularly in the examination of conglomerates. For instance, Berg has clarified some of the differences between diversified majors and conglomerates. He defined a conglomerate company as a firm which has at least five or six divisions which sell different products principally to markets rather than to

EXHIBIT 7.17 **ESTIMATED PERCENTAGE OF FIRMS IN EACH STRATEGIC CATEGORY**

Strategic category	1949	1959	1969
Major classes:			
Single business*	34.5	16.2	6.2
Dominant business†	35.4	37.3	29.2
Related business‡	26.7	40.0	45.2
Unrelated business§	3.4	6.5	19.4

*95% or more of business in one end-product business.
†*70 to 94% of business in one end-product business.*
‡Less than 70% in one end-product business, and diversification primarily in concentrically related products.
§Less than 70% in one end-product business, and diversification unrelated to primary product group.
Source: R. Rumelt, *Strategy, Structure, and Economic Performance* (Boston: Harvard Business School, 1974).

Acquisition type	Percentage of total	Percentage of failures
Vertical integration	3	0
Horizontal	25	11
Concentric marketing	13	26
Concentric technology	14	21
Conglomerate	45	42

each other. (If the divisions sell privately to each other, the firm is an integrated firm.) Berg says that conglomerates diversified quickly, primarily through mergers, and usually into product or service lines unrelated to their prior business. By "diversified majors," Berg means firms which developed their diversification over a long period of time primarily through internal expansion into products or services related to their prior business. Examples of diversified majors were Koppers, Borg Warner, and International Harvester.

Berg says that the conglomerate management style is different. He says that when you compare conglomerates with diversified majors, you find these differences:

- Conglomerates' central offices are much smaller than the central offices of diversified majors. Usually they have no staff officials (for example, for research and development).
- Conglomerates tend to place most major operating decisions at decentralized divisional levels. This is often because the central office has no one expert in making operating decisions in that business.
- Thus division managers are autonomous as long as the division "delivers."
- Diversified majors have better opportunities for synergy than conglomerates.

Berg and other advocates of conglomerates believe that by placing responsibility where it belongs—at the divisional level—conglomerates can evaluate the performance better and not become involved in operating decisions which prevent top management from performing the strategic planning and evaluation functions.

Conglomerates expand quickly primarily by purchasing other companies in exchange for stock when their own stock has a much higher price-earnings ratio than the target company's stock. Thus the conglomerate growth rate can remain high because of mergers and sometimes because of internal growth as well.

One other study we would like to highlight examined the performance of mergers (which we will explain in more detail later) for the purpose of diversification. Kitching studied 22 firms that merged over a number of years and examined 69 of the 181 mergers of 20 percent of the companies in the period studied (1960–1965). A number of his important findings are summarized below.

1 Nearly half of the mergers were of the conglomerate type. Horizontal acquisitions were the next most common type, followed by concentric technology, concentric marketing, and vertical integration. There is a relatively high risk of failure in concentric acquisitions and a relatively low one in horizontal mergers.

2 A "size mismatch" (where the acquired company's sales were less than 2 percent of the parent company's sales volume before the merger) occurs in 84 percent of the acquisitions considered failures.

3 In 81 percent of the failures, the organizational format (either the reporting relationships established after the merger or the extent of autonomy allowed) is disturbed at least once after the acquisition is first brought into the new "family."

4 Theoretically, synergy in mergers should be greatest where production facilities are combined because economies of scale are possible. Combinations based on technology (process know-how and R&D transfer), marketing, organization (personnel economies and productivity increases), and finance (additional and cheaper capital) should be of diminishing value, in that order. According to top managers, however, the ease with which synergy is actually realized improves in the reverse order; that is, synergy is most easily accomplished where financial resources are pooled, and it is most difficult to achieve where production facilities are combined. Furthermore, the dollar payoff is actually lowest, on the average, where production and technological resources are put together; it is highest where financial resources are combined.

5 Failure rates vary by type of merger:

Drucker agrees strongly with Kitching, especially with his fifth point. He says:

Never was the belief in diversification (especially diversification by merger) as a panacea more widely held than in the 1950's and 1960's. Yet the success stories of these years were not the businesses that diversified (by mergers) let alone the conglomerates. They were businesses with one central product or product line, one central market, one central technology.

Our next section discusses mergers at more length. What we wish to point out is that diversification, particularly of the unrelated conglomerate forms, appears to lack some justification on a performance basis. Indeed, there is a body of research to suggest that specialized and related firms are more profitable with respect to their portfolio of business activities. Further, only limited synergy seems to be obtained in conglomerate mergers. However, there may be other considerations, especially antitrust reasons, for the development of conglomerates. If a firm can't move to related areas because of the fear that it will reduce competition, it might choose entirely unrelated areas. However, the last part of our next section summarizes other research which supports our negative view of the conglomerate merger for diversification.

Mergers

This external approach to expansion has received more attention than any other single type of strategy. In the following sections, we elaborate on why companies merge, how they merge, and the financial, legal, and human considerations involved in mergers. Finally, we review some of the research on the effectiveness of mergers.

Why Companies Merge (See [6])

In the chapter we identified a number of *objectives* which might be accomplished by means of external expansion through a merger. There are also *strategic* reasons for a merger that are related to some objectives. Exhibit 7.18 shows how our active-passive dimension might intersect with this form of external expansion.

EXHIBIT 7.18   **Motivations to merge.**
(F. T. Haner, Business Policy, Planning, and Strategy [Cambridge, Mass.: Winthrop, 1976], p. 399.)

The defensive strategies are probably more often reasons why sellers might seek a merger. Offensive approaches are usually taken by the acquirers. But remember that when buyer and seller objectives are matched, a merger is more likely to occur.

How Companies Merge [13]

Before a successful merger can take place, there must be sound planning. There are various approaches to effective planning for mergers. One of the more useful summaries of this type of literature is that of Willard Rockwell. He has been personally involved in a number of mergers and gives these "10 commandments" on acquiring a company:

"Must" factors

1 Pinpoint and spell out the merger objectives, especially earnings objectives.

2 Specify substantial gains for the stockholders of both companies.

3 Be able to convince yourself that the acquired company's management is—or can be made—competent.

4 Certify the existence of important dovetailing resources—but do not expect perfection.

Other key considerations

5 Spark the merger program with the chief executive's involvement.

6 Clearly define the business you are in (for example, bicycles or transportation).

7 Take a depth sounding of strengths, weaknesses, and other key performance factors—the target company's and your own.

8 Create a climate of mutual trust by anticipating problems and discussing them early with the other company.

9 Do not let "caveman" advances jeopardize the courtship. Do not threaten the management that is to be acquired.

10 Most important of these latter six rules, make people your number 1 consideration in structuring your assimilation plan.

In effect, Rockwell is suggesting that the firm plan the merger well by profiling the two companies and comparing them. Thus you could prepare strategic advantage profiles and environmental threat and opportunity profiles for both companies and systematically compare them. He advocates good strategic management (commandments 1, 4, 6, and 7). Rockwell also believes that crucial to merger success are the human and financial considerations. We will address those next. In essence, a firm attempts to learn a great deal about a candidate so that the factors Rockwell talks about can be analyzed. In fact, some firms go to the point of hiring acquisitions specialists to manage the process.

Financial Considerations in Mergers [14]

Rockwell's number 1 and 2 "must" factors include establishing financial goals. And, of course, one of the important questions about strengths and weaknesses is the financial condition of a merger candidate. Two issues seem to be involved here: (1) How much is a company worth? (2) How does the acquirer pay for it?

The first issue—How much is it worth?—depends on your strategy and what you are looking for. Exhibit 7.19 suggests another set of strategic purposes for mergers. What you should realize is that the approach to *assessing the value* for each will emphasize different characteristics such as plant value, market opportunity, earnings potential, or stock value. However, a common procedure is to estimate the present value of discounted cash flows (DCF) and expected after-tax earnings attributable to the acquisition. Of course, establishing the required rate of return and cost of capital is important.

EXHIBIT 7.19   STRATEGIC APPROACHES TO ACQUISITION

Acquisition "play"	Strategy to achieve performance premium
1 Acquire synergistic product/market position.	Achieve scale economies of distribution, production, or technology.
2 Acquire position in key international markets.	Achieve scale economies for global production and technology investments.
3 Acquire a "beachhead" in an emerging high-growth market.	Anticipate high-leverage business growth equations by identifying market-forcing functions.
4 Acquire a portfolio of minority investments.	Apply pressure for improved short-term earnings and sell stock. Gain improved information on future potential.
5 Acquire a company with underutilized financial strength.	Use borrowing capacity or other financial strengths (e.g., underutilized tax loss carry-forwards or foreign tax credits) to achieve an immediate performance premium.
6 Acquire an underskilled company in a related industry.	Apply superior marketing, technology, or production expertise to enhance the competitive position and performance of the acquisition candidate.
7 Acquire an underexploited physical asset.	Anticipate shortages and price increases in the physical asset's value. Invest to exploit the resource, using distribution capacity.
8 Acquire an undervalued corporate portfolio.	Apply more aggressive portfolio management to restructure resource allocation and upgrade results.

Source: M. G. Allen, A. R. Oliver, and E. H. Schwaille, "The Key to Successful Acquisitions." Reprinted by permission from *The Journal of Business Strategy,* vol. 2, no. 2 (Fall 1981). Copyright © 1981 by Warren, Gorham and Lamont, Inc., 210 South St., Boston, Mass. All rights reserved.

In addition to estimating the present value of DCF, it is necessary to value existing assets, particularly if the assets are being liquidated. Capital asset pricing methods (CAPM) can be used here. But we would like to add a caution, because valuation can be tricky, depending on how you account for inflation and other factors. Inflation can greatly affect the true value of existing assets or outlays in five areas: (1) the proportion of assets in cash inventories, or fixed assets, (2) the inventory valuation methods used and the turnover rate, (3) the age of assets and the depreciation method used, (4) the composition of expenditures—such as for construction or energy, and (5) the capital structure—debt is more favorable assuming that the firm is facing inflation. In other words, it is highly unlikely that the book value is the same as the market value for either a liquidation or an ongoing firm, given that inflation affects the present value of assets. Even political factors can have an impact on value, as in the case of Exxon selling its oil and natural gas assets to the Libyan state oil company for "slightly less than book value."

The second major issue, once value has been determined, is the method by which the merger will be financed. Exchange of shares is one approach. In this case, the acquiring firms should also be valued. Of course, cash tender offers are possible. If the purchase price cannot be met with existing resources or direct borrowing, creative financing options are available. Firms can and do borrow on the target company's assets and cash, using techniques such as "leveraged buyouts" or "bootstrap acquisitions."

It is beyond our purpose to discuss the details of techniques such as DCF, CAPM, or leveraged buyouts. Entire volumes are available on ways to assess financial value. And many firms will call in consultants who specialize in acquisitions. But according to one finance specialist quoted in *The Wall Street Journal,* "about the best any investment banker can do in a price fairness opinion is to come up with a figure within 10 or 15 percent above or below true value. Negotiations or takeover strategy decide the rest."

Thus remember that sellers are involved also. Their approach to valuing their business might be different from the buyer's. And their interest in the type of offer can vary. For instance, reluctant merger participants might be tempted by preferred stock or subordinated, convertible debentures. Selling a company is an investment decision whose objective should be to increase the value of the owner's equity in the future. Frequently, the decision to divest is hasty, ill thought out, and dependent on the first buyer who offers or whoever the top executive feels will treat the company "right." Once the decision to divest is made, the company should decide what it is worth on the basis of its tangible assets, its management, its products, and all intangible assets. Skillful companies wishing to sell will select buyers as carefully as merger-bound companies seek acquisitions. They will evaluate offers in the same way they would consider a merger: they will discount the future flow of funds to the present value. Effective managers-owners choose to sell out or terminate business under three conditions: (1) when they perceive their firm is unable to compete, (2) when they wish to leave the business for personal reasons such as retirement, and (3) when they perceive that there are better opportunities for them in another business.

To conclude this section, we can state that the final negotiations between the buyer and the seller are what ultimately set the true financing value.

Legal Considerations in Mergers [15]

Another question to consider is, Will the relevant government body approve the merger? In the United States, the Antitrust Division of the Justice Department might get involved. And many states also try to prevent mergers. In the United Kingdom and the Common Market, there are monopolies commissions. Canada also has a "watchdog" to examine multinational mergers. However, in the United States the political climate is such that mergers are less likely to be challenged by the Justice Department. New guidelines include the Herfindahl index, which is used to determine market concentration—the percentage of the market held by each seller is squared, and the totals are added. If the index is less than 1000 after a proposed merger, the merger is not likely to be challenged. But antitrust laws are still used by competitors, as happened when some Big Eight accounting firms challenged the merger attempt between Price Waterhouse and Deloitte Haskins.

Many firms try to protect themselves from a takeover by increasing the percentage of shareholders who must agree to a merger. Some firms change corporate bylaws to prohibit partial tender offers; others use "poison pills" that raise the costs of a takeover to a buyer, or use "shark repellents," "white knights," or proxy fights to fend off unwanted suitors.[1] This can lead to lengthy legal battles.

---

[1]A "poison pill" is a tactic designed to make a company very expensive to take over. For example, shareholders (other than a hostile bidder) might be given certain rights or warrants to trade stock which, if exercised, would cost a takeover bidder substantial sums. "Shark repellents" include such things as requirements that a raider pay an equivalent price for all shares, or "supermajority" rules requiring control of substantial shares. A "white knight" is a friendly bidder who will buy a firm under more favorable conditions (to the existing managers) than are being offered by a hostile bidder, hence "rescuing" the firm from a takeover.

Tax laws are also relevant to the financial aspects of mergers. Some observers claim that changes in tax laws have given firms more reasons to use acquisitions than to expand internally.

Finally, legal considerations may prompt takeover attempts. For example, a flurry of moves by tobacco companies to acquire other firms in the mid-1980s (Philip Morris–General Foods; Reynolds–Nabisco; American Brands holding company) was seen as an attempt to use diversification as a way to protect corporate earnings against potential liability from smoking-related lawsuits.

Human Considerations in Mergers [16]

Although some of the literature might give you the impression that merging is primarily a financial question, more evidence is arising that the human factors are crucial to a merger's success.

For example, Ebeid examined one form of mergers: the cash tender offer. He studied 117 cash tender offers over a 17-year period. He really was interested in seeing whether there were more successful ways of bidding, better stock market times, and more advantages with regard to certain similar factors. One of his major conclusions was that a merger offer was most likely to fail when the management of the target firm opposed the merger offer. This made the merger more costly if it was consummated. But more important, a merger was less likely to be consummated. Mergers were more likely to be opposed because the executives involved didn't like each other than for financial reasons. Similar findings arose from other research.

The psychologist Levinson has studied merger failures. His major conclusion was as follows:

> There are many reasons for merger, including psychological reasons. Many mergers have been disappointing in their results and painful to their participants. These failures have been attributed largely to rational financial, economic, and managerial problems.
>
> I contend that some psychological reasons not only constitute a major, if unrecognized, force toward merger, but that they also constitute the basis for many, if not most, disappointments and failures. At least those that have turned sour, or have the most dangerous potential for turning sour, are those that arise out of some neurotic wish to become big by voraciously gobbling up others, or out of obsolescence. Such mergers flounder because of the hidden assumptions the senior partner makes, and the condescending attitudes toward the junior organization which then follow. These result in efforts at manipulation and control which, in turn, produce (a) disillusionment and the feeling of desertion on the part of the junior organization, and (b) disappointment, loss of personnel, and declining profitability for the dominant organization.

Many of the human problems develop when the executives of the acquiring company seem threatening to the target company, and the executives of the target company fear that they will have to leave the firm. In sum, human relationships may be a much more significant factor in a successful merger than most analysts realize. Indeed, the takeover battle involving Allied Corp., United Technologies, Martin Marietta, and Bendix in 1982 was characterized in *The Wall Street Journal* as follows:

> This epic struggle involving four big companies and more than four bankers and hordes of lawyers is not about economics, is not about using assets wisely, is not about economic growth. It's a struggle between a few ambitious men using public companies, in which they own a fractional share, for their own gain.

Aside from the premerger problems noted here, postmerger human difficulties often arise. Corporate cultures and policies can clash, as happened at IBM and Rolm. Top managers who are being counted on may leave the firm, as happened at Kodak after a recent acquisition. And the structure of relationships between the partners can create problems. Such implementation problems should be considered before a merger but often are not. Thus, after a merger is consummated, such pitfalls as low executive involvement in the postmerger integration process, breakdowns in reporting and control relationships between parent and acquired firm, changes in responsibility within the parent for overseeing the acquired firm's activities, and the attitudes of personnel in both firms can significantly affect the degree of success of the venture.

Effectiveness of Mergers [17]

Earlier we cited some research about the performance of firms that merged, particularly conglomerate or unrelated mergers. At this point, let us reflect on whether a merger or acquisition is an effective strategy. There are four perspectives to consider: namely, those of the stockholders, the executives, the employees, and society.

Exhibit 7.20 summarizes the findings of the research. In general, society and the noted stockholders lose because the earnings growth rate tends to decline as compared to when the two separate firms' growth rates existed. Stockholders of the acquired firm can gain in the short run if their stock is bid up and they sell it at high prices.

The acquiring company's executives tend to gain, since salaries tend to be correlated with corporate size. The acquired company's executives usually suffer a disadvantage in that they lose status, authority, and often their jobs. Sometimes the acquired company executive gains when the acquirer seeks specific executives for their experience or if a quid pro quo exists— that is, in exchange for "friendliness" in the takeover, certain executives of the acquired company are "taken care of." But employees of the acquired firms usually lose out, even in "friendly" takeovers. The results for the unrelated acquired firm (friendly or unfriendly) vary for this reason and depend on how the acquiring firm structures the acquisition. If it remains autonomous, the acquired firm can be better off if its performance was lagging and it receives an inflow of capital.

If the new management reorganizes or brings in new management, employees can lose. Society usually loses, since with a lower earnings rate, fewer job opportunities are created. Antitrust legislation also exists to prevent too much concentration of economic and political power, which can lead to higher prices or less variety in the products and services offered.

Can mergers ever be a benefit? Yes. As indicated, not all mergers lead to dire conditions. If the acquired firm is worth saving (is effective but may be failing for lack of financial support), a merger may save it. For instance, a firm might have a great product or service, but it lacks

EXHIBIT 7.20 EFFECTIVENESS OF MERGERS (EXTERNAL EXPANSION STRATEGIES)

	Related		Unrelated	
	Acquiring firm	Acquired firm	Acquiring firm	Acquired firm
Stockholders	Usually negative	Can be positive	More negative than toward a related merger	Varies
Executives	Positive	Negative	Less positive than toward a related merger	Varies
Employees	Neutral to negative	Usually negative	Neutral	Varies
Society	Negative	Varies	Negative	Varies

financial expertise or some other skill, and a bank can't or won't provide it. An acquiring company could provide needed resources. And some mergers may create specialized firms which are stronger and more productive. Some research concludes that firms that were taken over should have been taken over because their rates of return were low at the time, and therefore the stockholders stood to benefit from the takeovers. Low rates of return may be due to incompetent management and stockholders may gain from takeovers. This is the argument used by corporate raiders. Still, many firms deserve to fail. Banks and venture-capital firms can usually help out if a firm is viable.

Hermann offers an explanation for why conglomerate and nonconglomerate postmerger profitability may vary. He examined acquisitions criteria used in 96 companies. While both types of firms sought good returns, the major distinctions were that conglomerate acquirers wanted existing managers to continue, and they were more interested in the reduction of earnings risk than in increases in earnings per se. However, a large body of research suggests that diversifications have not reduced systematic risk and that risk spreading can be done better by individual stockholders than by corporations.

In sum, we believe that there are substantial disadvantages to mergers as compared with internal approaches for expansion or related diversification. We will cite two other studies to support this conclusion.

Gutman studied 150 firms in the period 1954–1958. The 53 firms whose growth rate was twice the rate of growth in gross national product in that time acted thus:

1 They chose industries whose sales increased more rapidly than the growth of the economy as a whole.

2 They chose the subsectors and submarkets within each industry which grew more rapidly than the industry and *concentrated* on these sectors, not on the whole industry.

3 They entered the subsectors earlier than competing firms.

4 More than 80 percent of the growth firms introduced new products for current customers.

5 About 40 percent introduced new products for new consumers. Only about 7 percent tried to sell existing products to new customers.

6 Two-thirds of the high-growth firms sold their products outside the United States.

7 Those whose growth included mergers did not outperform those that grew entirely by means of internal methods.

Recognizing that these firms operated in a favorable economic climate, let's look at Clifford's study. Clifford examined over 1800 companies between 1970 and 1975 in 32 different industries. During the 1974–1975 recession, he distinguished top performers as companies whose earnings per share grew by 33 percent on the average, while the earnings per share of the other firms declined by 23 percent annually. What were the main characteristics of these firms?

1 They focused unremittingly on limiting financial risk by maintaining price discipline, which they accomplished by
  a Pricing ahead of inflation.
  b Reducing response time to price changes.
  c Pricing to value.

2 They emphasized cost discipline to maintain margins.

3 They emphasized financial control over balance sheet items.

4 They emphasized product discipline by
  a Exploiting winners and getting rid of losers.
  b Redesigning products.
  c Raising the hurdle required for margins on new-product entry.

5 They stayed close to their market niche by
    a Building on the strength of their core product lines.
    b Avoiding excessive diversification.
    c Finding specialized niches for opportunity.

The main characteristic of the losers in this period was that they aggressively diversified, paying little heed to the markets or to the complex structures being developed. Many mergers fail because of the following "seven sins," which seem to be committed too often by those making acquisitions:

1 Paying too much
2 Assuming a boom market won't crash
3 Leaping before looking
4 Straying too far afield
5 Swallowing something too big
6 Marrying disparate corporate cultures
7 Counting on key managers staying

The findings of these studies and others provide the basic support for many of our propositions in Chapters 6 and 7.

REFERENCES

[1] Internal Expansion Strategies

Buaron, R.: "How to Win the Market Share Game? Try Changing the Rules," *Management Review* (January 1981), pp. 8–17.

Buzzell, R. D., and F. D. Wiersema: "Successful Share-Building Strategies," *Harvard Business Review* (January–February 1981), pp. 135–144.

Chakravarthy, B. S.: "Strategic Self-Renewal," *Academy of Management Review,* vol. 9 (1984), pp. 536–547.

Kotler, P.: *Marketing Management* (Englewood Cliffs, N.J.: Prentice-Hall, 1976).

Kuhn, R. L.: *Mid-Sized Firms: Success Strategies and Methodologies* (New York: Praeger, 1982).

[2] Internal Stability Strategies

Hambrick, D. C., and I. MacMillan: "Efficiency of Product R&D in Business Units," working paper SC #41, Graduate School of Business, Columbia University, New York, 1985.

Tavel, C.: *The Third Industrial Age: Strategy for Business Survival* (Homewood, Ill.: Dow Jones–Irwin, 1975).

[3] Internal Retrenchment Strategies

Hambrick, D. C.: "Turnaround Strategies," in W. O. Guth (ed.), *Handbook of Strategic Management* (New York: Warren, Gorham and Lamont, 1986).

O'Neil, H. M.: "Turnaround and Recovery: What Strategy Do You Need?" *Long Range Planning,* forthcoming.

————: "An Analysis of the Turnaround Strategy in Commercial Banking," *Journal of Management Studies* (March 1986), pp. 165–188.

"Steel Jacks Up Its Productivity," *Business Week,* Oct. 12, 1981, pp. 84–86.

[4] External Retrenchment Strategies

"B of A is Becoming the Incredible Shrinking Bank," *Business Week,* Jan. 27, 1986, pp. 78–84.

Dobrzynski, J. H.: "Inside a School for Dealmakers," *Business Week,* July 7, 1986, pp. 82–85.

Norman, J. R.: "What the Raiders Did to Phillips Petroleum," *Business Week,* Mar. 17, 1986, pp. 102–103.

Porter, M.: "Please Note Location of Nearest Exit," *California Management Review,* vol. 19 (Winter 1976), pp. 21–33.

[5] Endgame Strategies

Glaberson, W. B.: "The Bankruptcy Laws May Be Stretching too Far," *Business Week,* May 9, 1983, p. 33.

Harrigan, K. R.: "Strategic Planning for Endgame," *Long Range Planning* (December 1982), pp. 45–48.

————: "The Effect of Exit Barriers upon Strategic Flexibility," *Strategic Management Journal,* vol. 1 (1980), pp. 165–176.

————: *Strategies for Declining Businesses* (Lexington, Mass.: Heath, 1980).

————: "Exit Decisions in Mature Industries," *Academy of Management Journal,* vol. 25 (1982), pp. 707–732.

[6] External Expansion Strategies

Davidson, K. M.: *Megamergers* (Cambridge, Mass.: Ballinger, 1985).

————: "Looking at the Strategic Impact of Mergers," *The Journal of Business Strategy,* vol. 2 (1981), pp. 13–22.

"The Great Takeover Binge," *Business Week,* Nov. 14, 1977, pp. 176–184.

Greenwald, J.: "Let's Make a Deal," *Time,* Dec. 23, 1985.

Steiner, P. O.: *Mergers, Motives, Effects, Policies* (Ann Arbor: University of Michigan Press, 1975).

Note: Also see [12] to [17] below.

[7] Internal and External Combination Strategies

Bresser, R. K., and J. E. Harl: "Collective Strategy: Vice or Virtue?" *Academy of Management Review,* vol. 11 (1986), pp. 408–427.

"GM Moves into a New Era," *Business Week,* July 16, 1984, pp. 48–54.

Gullander, S.: "Joint Ventures and Corporate Strategy," *Columbia Journal of World Business,* vol. 11 (Spring 1976), pp. 104–114.

Harrigan, K. R.: "Integrating Parent and Child: Successful Joint Ventures," working paper SC #44, Graduate School of Business, Columbia University, New York, 1985.

————: "Coalition Strategies: A Framework for Joint Ventures," *Academy of Management Proceedings* (1985), pp. 16–19.

Helm, L.: "AT&T's European Invasion Finally Gains the High Ground," *Business Week,* Mar. 10, 1986, pp. 44–46.

"How Supron's Buyers Would Slice the Pie," *Business Week,* Mar. 1, 1982, pp. 23–24.

"What Made Apple Seek Safety in Numbers," *Business Week,* Mar. 12, 1984, p. 42.

"When Joint Ventures Come Unglued," *Business Week,* Apr. 26, 1982, p. 100.

[8] Related and Unrelated Strategies

Biggadike, R.: "The Risky Business of Diversification," *Harvard Business Review* (May–June 1979), pp. 103–111.

Harris, P. R.: "The Seven Uses of Synergy," *The Journal of Business Strategy,* vol. 2 (Fall 1981), pp. 59–66.

Leontiades, M.: *Strategies for Diversification and Change* (Boston: Little, Brown, 1980).

Steiner, G. A.: *Strategic Planning: What Every Manager Must Know* (New York: Free Press, 1979).

Note: Also see [12] below.

[9] Horizontal and Vertical Strategies

Bower, J. L.: "Simple Economic Tools for Strategic Analysis" (Boston: Intercollegiate Case Clearing House, No. 9-373-094, 1972).

"A Duel of Giants in the Dishwasher Market," *Business Week,* Oct. 9, 1978.

Dunkin, A.: "How Department Stores Plan to Get the Registers Ringing Again," *Business Week,* Nov. 18, 1985, pp. 66–67.

Harrigan, K. R.: "Vertical Integration and Corporate Strategy," *Academy of Management Journal,* vol. 28 (1985), pp. 397–425.

Jauch, L. R., and H. Wilson: "A Strategic Perspective for Make or Buy Decisions," *Long Range Planning* (December 1979), pp. 56–61.

Williamson, O.: "The Vertical Integration of Production: Market Failure Considerations," *American Economic Review* (May 1971), pp. 112–123.

[10] Active and Passive Strategies

Ansoff, W. I., and J. M. Stewart: "Strategies for Technology Based Business," *Harvard Business Review,* vol. 45 (November–December 1967), pp. 71–83.

Hambrick, D. C.: "Some Tests of the Effectiveness and Functional Attributes of Miles and Snow's Strategic Types," *Academy of Management Journal,* vol. 26 (1983), pp. 5–26.

Harrigan, K. R.: *Strategic Flexibility* (Lexington, Mass.: Lexington, 1984).

MacMillan, I.: "Preemptive Strategies," *Journal of Business Strategy,* vol. 4 (Fall 1983), pp. 16–26.

———, M. L. McCaffery, and G. V. Wijk: "Competitors' Responses to Easily Imitated New Products," *Strategic Management Journal,* vol. 6 (1985), pp. 75–86.

Miles, R. E., and C. C. Snow: *Organizational Strategy: Structure and Process* (New York: McGraw-Hill, 1978).

Windsor, D., and F. D. Tuggle: "The Role of Technological Innovation in a Firm's Strategy," *Human Systems Management,* vol. 2 (1981), pp. 306–315.

[11] International Strategy Alternatives

Ball, D. A., and W. H. McCullock, Jr.: *International Business* (Plano, Tex.: Business Publications, 1985).

Davidson, W. H.: *Global Strategic Management* (New York: Wiley, 1982).

[12] Diversification Strategies

Berg, N.: "What's Different about Conglomerate Management," *Harvard Business Review* (November–December 1969), pp. 112–120.

Bettis, R. A., and W. K. Hall: "Diversification Strategy, Accounting Determined Risks, and Accounting Determined Return," *Academy of Management Journal,* vol. 25 (1982), pp. 254–264.

Carter, J. R.: "In Search of Synergy: A Structure-Performance Test," *Review of Economics and Statistics,* vol. 59 (August 1977), pp. 279–289.

Drucker, P.: *Management* (New York: Harper & Row, 1974), chaps. 56, 57.

Kitching, J.: "Why Do Mergers Miscarry?" *Harvard Business Review,* vol. 45 (November–December 1967), pp. 84–101.

Pitts, R. A., and H. D. Hopkins: "Firm Diversity: Conceptualization and Measurement," *Academy of Management Review,* vol. 7 (1982), pp. 620–629.

Rumelt, R.: *Strategy, Structure, and Economic Performance* (Boston: Harvard Business School, 1974).

Steiner, G.: "How and Why to Diversify," *California Management Review,* vol. 6 (Summer 1964), pp. 11–18.

Note: Also see [17] below.

[13] How and Why Companies Merge

Ansoff, H. I., et al.: *Acquisition of U.S. Manufacturing Firms 1946–1965* (Nashville, Tenn.: Vanderbilt University Press, 1971).

Birley, S.: "Acquisition Strategy or Acquisition Anarchy?" *Journal of General Management,* vol. 3 (Spring 1976), pp. 67–73.

Kusewitt, J. B.: "An Exploratory Study of Strategic Acquisition Factors Relating to Performance," *Strategic Management Journal,* vol. 6 (1985), pp. 151–170.

"Poppa Tests His Golden Touch," *Business Week,* Jan. 18, 1982, p. 102.

Rockwell, W., Jr.: "How to Acquire a Company," *Harvard Business Review,* vol. 46 (September–October 1968).

[14] Financial Factors in Mergers

Aplin, R. D., et al.: *Capital Investment Analysis: Using Discounted Cash Flows* (Columbus, Oh.: Grid, 1977).

Cameron, D.: "Appraising Companies for Acquisition," *Long Range Planning,* vol. 10 (August 1977), pp. 21–28.

"Deciding How Much a Company Is Worth," *The Wall Street Journal,* Mar. 19, 1981, p. 29.

"Exxon Agrees to Sell Oil and Gas Assets in Libya to Government for Net Book Value," *The Wall Street Journal,* Jan. 6, 1982, p. 4.

[15] Legal Factors in Mergers

"A Bid to Stop Big Eight Firms from Getting Bigger," *Business Week,* Nov. 19, 1984, p. 49.

Blustein, P., and D. Rotbart: "Court Rulings on U.S. Steel and Mobil May Change Merger Game," *The Wall Street Journal* (Jan. 7, 1982), p. 19.

Clark, L. H., Jr.: "Are the Corporate Raiders Really White Knights?" *The Wall Street Journal,* July 16, 1986, p. 33.

Ehrlich, E., and J. R. Norman: "Getting Rough with the Raiders," *Business Week,* May 27, 1985, pp. 34–36.

Hertzberg, D.: "Poison Pill Defense No Longer Is Seen as a Sure Way to Repel Hostile Suitors," *The Wall Street Journal,* Oct. 31, 1985, p. 3.

"Justice Overhauls Its Rules on Mergers," *Business Week,* June 8, 1981, p. 55.

"A Loosening of Merger Rules," *Business Week,* May 17, 1982, p. 120.

"Specialist Says Mergers Zooming under Reagan," Associated Press release, July 15, 1981.

Taylor, R. E.: "U. S. Eases Merger Guidelines, Allowing Somewhat More Concentrated Markets," *The Wall Street Journal,* June 15, 1982, p. 3.

[16] Human Factors in Mergers

"Atex: An Editing System That Isn't Printing Out for Kodak," *Business Week,* Sept. 3, 1984, pp. 70–72.

Ebeid, F. J.: "Tender Offers: Characteristics Affecting Their Success," *Mergers and Acquisitions* (1976), pp. 21–30.

"IBM and Rolm Cope with Prenuptial Jitters," *Business Week,* Nov. 19, 1984, pp. 166–170.

Levinson, H.: "A Psychologist Diagnoses Merger Failures," *Harvard Business Review* (March–April 1970).

"The 4 Horsemen," *The Wall Street Journal,* Sept. 24, 1982, p. 1.

[17] Effectiveness of Mergers

Clifford, D. K.: "Thriving in a Recession," *Harvard Business Review* (July–August 1977), pp. 56–65.

Gutmann, P. M.: "Strategies for Growth," *California Management Review,* vol. 6 (1964), pp. 81–86.

Herrmann, A. L.: "Corporate Acquisition Criteria: A Study," *Mergers and Acquisitions,* vol. 8 (Summer 1973), pp. 4–11.

"How the New Merger Boom Will Benefit the Economy," *Business Week,* Feb. 6, 1984, pp. 42–54.

Ingrassia, L.: "Employees at Acquired Firms Find White Knights Often Unfriendly," *The Wall Street Journal,* July 7, 1982, p. 21.

O'Hanlon, T.: "Swinging Cats among the Conglomerate Dogs," *Fortune* (June 1975), pp. 114–119ff.

Prokesch, S. E., and W. J. Powell: "Do Mergers Really Work?" *Business Week,* June 3, 1985, pp. 88–91.

Samuels, J. M.: "The Success or Failure of Mergers and Takeovers," in J. M. Samuels (ed.), *Readings on Mergers and Takeovers* (New York: St. Martin's, 1972).

Note: Also see [12] above.

STRATEGIC CHOICE

CHAPTER OUTLINE

STRATEGIC CHOICE

OBJECTIVES

- To review the importance of strategic choice
- To learn how to focus on a few of the many alternatives
- To learn how managers make a choice among alternatives
- To learn some tools and prescriptions to aid in making the choice

INTRODUCTION [1]

Chapter 8 completes the three-chapter unit on choice of strategy, as Exhibit 8.1 indicates. That is, when the analyses of environmental and internal conditions (ETOP and SAP) are completed, potential strategies are considered. These include stability, expansion, retrenchment, a combination, and some strategic variation of these generic strategies. All the while, the strategists are asking themselves the crucial questions: What are our objectives? Are these being met by our strategy? By the business definition we've chosen? Will they be met in the future? In other words, the gap between expected and ideal outcomes is examined vis-à-vis the alternatives being considered. If the gap is negligible, a stability strategy is likely, and the process shifts to better implementation. If the gap is large and important, a new strategy is necessary.

> *Strategic choice is the decision to select from among the alternatives the strategy which will best meet the enterprise's objectives. The decision involves focusing on a few alternatives, considering the selection factors, evaluating the alternatives against these criteria, and making the actual choice.*

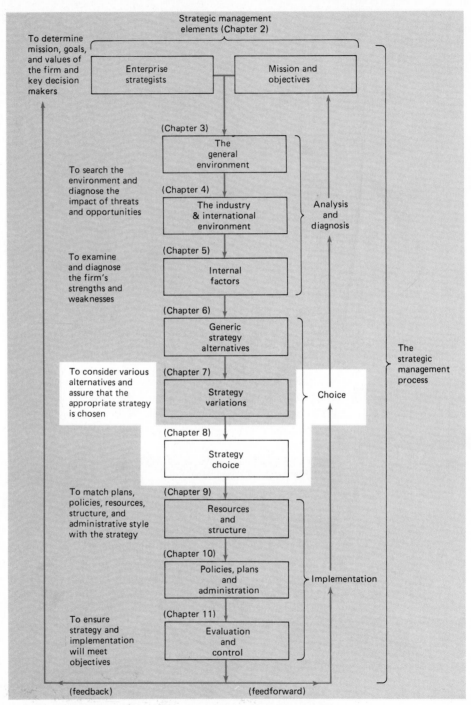

EXHIBIT 8.1 **A model of strategic management.**

Since strategic choice is a decision, all the things which were said in Chapters 1 and 2 about decision making apply to this decision. Remember that *descriptively*, managerial intuition and politics play a role. These pressures will constrain the choice process. *Prescriptively*, rational analytical models should aid the process of decision making.

We begin this chapter with a blending of these views. We suggest that the set of alternatives to choose from can be narrowed to a more manageable list. Then we discuss some prescriptive approaches to choosing from these alternatives. Next we discuss some of the managerial factors which constrain these "rational" models. Finally, we suggest an approach which attempts to integrate these perspectives to aid strategic decision making, and we conclude with a discussion of the need for contingency strategies in the choice process.

FOCUSING THE ALTERNATIVES FOR SELECTION [2]

If you reconsider Exhibit 7.1, you are immediately faced with a huge number of possible alternatives from which strategists can choose. Normative decision theorists will tell you to "consider all the alternatives." This is impossible because:

1 You do not know all of them and cannot know all of them. You are not omniscient. Using our simple classification system with only two sides to each dimension yields over 23,000 different possible strategies, to say nothing of various ways they can be implemented.

2 It would take too much time and energy. And so, if the situation appears to need moderate changes, you will probably consider a few strategies that make minor adjustments to your present strategy. If the situation appears to be serious or quite different from situations you have faced before, you will consider creative, brainstorming alternatives.

3 The managerial perception of risk, dependence, past strategy, and power will limit the number of alternatives considered. This will be discussed later in the chapter.

Why consider strategic alternatives at all? Why not just accept that first strategy that pops into the decision maker's mind? This is the opposite of the normative statement: Consider *all* alternatives. Our answer is that few decision makers are so bright or intuitive that they wouldn't be better off considering a few alternatives. Trying to generate several reasonable alternatives allows a systematic comparison of their trade-offs, strengths, and weaknesses. Thus the choice is likely to be a much better choice.

STRATEGIC CHOICE PROCESSES

Where do "reasonable" strategic alternatives come from? You do not consider alternatives out in the wild blue yonder. You begin to consider alternatives which you know about or which are proposed by subordinates, which you think will work, and which do not involve major breaks with the past (unless you have clearly diagnosed the situation as desperate).

So the alternatives you consider are incremental steps, usually small incremental steps, from your present pace and business. This is why a clear business definition is useful. You can choose alternatives by trying to work forward from the present to the future state and see how you can get there from where you are now.

This approach is implied by the use of the gap analysis described in Chapter 2. The purpose of strategic choice is to accomplish objectives. A strategy can be chosen to close the gaps in objectives. We think that the size of the gap, the nature of the gap, and whether or not management believes that it can be reduced will strongly influence the choice of some alternatives over others. For example, if the gap is narrow (small, not very important, or hard to reduce), certain dimensions are more likely to be considered than others, as shown in Exhibit 8.2. Thus, if the gap is perceived to be narrow, a stability choice is more likely; some pace changes may occur internally, but they are likely to be passive responses to minor external changes. For example, Mr. Coffee might offer a $5 rebate to maintain its market share.

Of course, the nature of the gap is also relevant. If the gap is large due to past or expected poor performance, retrenchment is more likely. If it is large due to expected environmental opportunity, expansion is more likely. If the gap is due to internal weakness, retrenchment is more likely. In Chapter 7, Exhibit 7.6 gives an example of a ''negative'' gap leading to retrenchment. Other case studies have illustrated ''positive'' gaps or opportunities leading to expansion.

We have no evidence to support these prescriptions. They are ways that we think managers can narrow and focus their choice of alternatives. The gap analysis in Exhibit 8.2 also reflects our ideas about the influences of managerial perceptions, which we will discuss later in this chapter and which we discussed earlier in Chapter 2. You can combine this analysis with our propositions in the summaries for Chapters 6 and 7 to construct a matrix showing which strategies to pursue under which circumstances.

We would like to carry you one step further in a prescription of how this sort of analysis can be combined with the diagnoses of internal and external conditions to narrow the list of alternatives. The gaps, of course, are coming from perceptions of desired and expected goal attainment along with the diagnoses. So the factors associated with your assessments of the decision makers, their values, their perceptions, and so on, play a role here, as discussed in Chapter 2. But as discussed in Chapters

EXHIBIT 8.2   Perceived gaps, strategic conditions, and alternative dimensions.

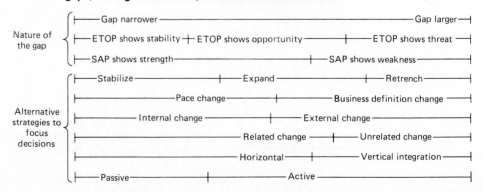

EXHIBIT 8.3 STRATEGIC SITUATION 1: IMPLEMENT STABILITY

ETOP		SAP	
Socioeconomic	0	Marketing and distribution	+
Technological	0	R&D and engineering	0
Competitor	0	Production and operations management	−
Supplier	0	Corporate resources and personnel	0
Government	0	Finance and accounting	0

3 to 5, the generation of reasonable alternatives can also be accomplished through a systematic comparison of the ETOP and SAP in relation to the gap. Exhibits 8.3 to 8.5 give several examples of this. There are a large number of possible combinations, but these three lead to suggestions of several strategies.

Exhibit 8.3 is for a firm that is likely to be considering a grand strategy of stability. It has its pluses and minuses, but the ETOP shows no significant threats or opportunities. The performance gap is likely to be small. This firm would probably focus on improving productivity in manufacturing. It would emphasize passive internal modifications. (See Proposition 6.1.)

In the case of Exhibit 8.4, however, the conditions may be right for expansion. Economic factors are positive, and perhaps the government is expected to deregulate the industry. This may open up the threat of new-competitor entry. However, the firm's marketing strengths may allow it to meet this threat or move into new markets which were closed to it before. To do this, however, the firm may be required to use its financial strength to improve the weaknesses in operations that exist, since it had not served these markets previously. Thus the timing of the firm's expansion may not allow the firm to fully take advantage of all the potential available immediately. The alternatives will focus on market and function dimensions; active approaches may be taken here, with perhaps external alternatives considered to improve production (e.g., a joint venture, subcontracting, or a merger with a manufacturer) if timing is important. If timing is less critical, internal development of operations may be considered more appropriate.

Suppose that the same ETOP is matched with another firm whose performance gap is negative, and the SAP indicates serious weaknesses as a result of deregulation. The firm represented by Exhibit 8.5 faces a situation in which a retrenchment may be useful for improving its performance (or increasing its chances for survival). For instance, this firm may be unable to compete effectively against new arrivals in many

EXHIBIT 8.4 STRATEGIC SITUATION 2: IMPLEMENT EXPANSION

ETOP		SAP	
Socioeconomic	+	Marketing and distribution	+
Technological	0	R&D and engineering	0
Competitor	−	Production and operations management	−
Supplier	0	Corporate resources and personnel	0
Government	+	Finance and accounting	+

EXHIBIT 8.5   STRATEGIC SITUATION 3: IMPLEMENT RETRENCHMENT

ETOP		SAP	
Socioeconomic	+	Marketing and distribution	−
Technological	0	R&D and engineering	0
Competitor	−	Production and operations management	0
Supplier	0	Corporate resources and personnel	+
Government	+	Finance and accounting	−

of its markets. One alternative is to abandon some territories so that resources can be focused where strength exists. The firm may be passive in some market areas, active in others. Good personnel in certain areas may be pooled to use advantages there and become more efficient.

Note that these comparisons are subject to substantial interpretation by the strategists doing the analysis. For instance, in view of the marketing strengths in strategic situation 1, more venturesome strategists may consider attempts to expand the market share as opposed to stability. In situation 2, less risk-oriented managers may believe that the operations weaknesses are severe enough to limit expansion; external possibilities are not considered. They may be satisfied to get whatever improvements come from their environment without making any changes in the pace or business definition. In effect, the gap in performance outcomes is not perceived to be so great as to require change. Optimistic or risk-oriented managers may look at situation 3 and believe that their strong personnel will be able to overcome marketing problems and take advantage of opportunities which will ultimately improve the firm's financial condition. They may not change the business definition, but they may try to increase employee output and effort to expand the pace of operations.

Thus perceptions of the environment and the internal need for change vary from case to case. This is clearly seen in the watch industry, where Japanese firms are pursuing rapid expansion while the Swiss and some American firms are trying turnarounds or retrenchments.

Of course, in situations where environmental factors are decidedly threats and where executives perceive weakness, a total liquidation may yield the greatest performance outcome possible. For example, Bayuk Cigars decided to liquidate for $28 million after declining a takeover offer of $15 million. It assumed that the industry was in a steady decline and that it "would have to become increasingly competitive to maintain its position."

Thus the search methods and diagnostic approaches described in Chapters 3 to 5 can be used by the strategists to search for strategic alternatives. Once a problem is perceived as a gap, the decision maker begins to generate alternative solutions. The decision maker can choose routine methods to generate alternatives (for example, looking at what the organization did before in such cases) or creative approaches. The latter can include such techniques as brainstorming. The alternatives may also be proposed from below. In this case, we would suggest that several others be generated for comparison and discussion on the basis of the gaps, ETOP, and SAP. But the ETOP and SAP are likely to show more than one threat or opportunity and weakness

or strength within each sector or factor. This would suggest that a number of options are usually available to a firm. But the approach suggested here can reduce the alternatives to a relatively limited number of reasonable possibilities.

Once a reasonable number of alternatives are generated, managers will have to decide which one should be used to close the gap. A number of "rational" approaches have been developed to guide the manager in this decision situation. Our next section outlines some prescriptions for the choice.

PRESCRIPTIONS FOR THE STRATEGIC CHOICE [3]

Aside from our prescriptions to guide the strategic choice in Exhibit 8.2, a number of techniques have been developed to help managers make strategic choices. The Boston Consulting Group product portfolio matrix shown in Exhibit 8.6 is one of the best-known examples.

Stars are products or SBUs which are growing rapidly, need large amounts of cash to maintain their position, and are leaders in their business and generate large amounts of cash. Cash flows will be roughly in balance (in and out) and represent the best opportunities for expansion.

Cash cows are low-growth, high-market-share products or divisions. Because of their market share, they have low costs and generate cash. Since growth is slow, reinvestment costs are low. Cash cows provide funds for overhead, dividends, and investment for the rest of the firm. They are the foundation of the firm, and stability is prescribed.

Dogs are products or divisions with low growth and a low market share and there-

EXHIBIT 8.6   **The business portfolio or growth-share matrix.**
(B. Hedley, "Strategy and the Business Portfolio," Long Range Planning [February 1977], p. 10.)

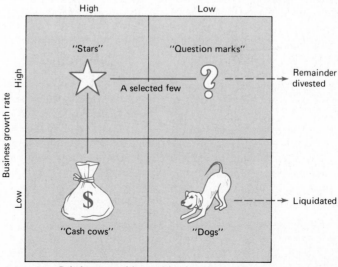

fore poor profits. They may need cash to survive. The dogs should be minimized by means of divestment or liquidation.

Question marks are high-growth, low-market-share products or divisions. Their conditions are the worst, for their cash needs are high, but cash generation is low. These, if left in this cell, become "cash traps." Since growth is high, market share should be easier to get for them than for dogs. So question marks should be converted into stars, then later into cash cows. This strategy will lead to a cash drain in the short run but positive flow in the long run. The other option is divestment.

The basic assumption of BCG analysis is that a high market share for faster-growing products or services normally leads to high profitability and stable competitive situations. On the other hand, if a firm has products in slowly growing markets, increasing the market share is normally costly. So the BCG recommends taking cash out of these businesses, even at the expense of market share. A firm will choose a strategy of expansion in market share if it has competitive strength, the funds to shift, and the estimated costs of gaining the share. The goal of all this is to have a balanced portfolio of products or divisions. This technique, then, usually applies to multiple-SBU firms making decisions about what SBUs should be expanded, maintained, or retrenched.

As Exhibit 8.7 suggests, firms can't always follow these prescriptions and might do better pursuing some other strategy. Further, some of the BCG prescriptions could ultimately lead to a lack of innovative product introductions, since, by definition, new products start as dogs or question marks.

EXHIBIT 8.7   ONE WAY TO CURE A DOG

General Host was a diversified firm with a problem. Its Cudahy Foods subsidiary represented 61 percent of sales but just 18 percent of its 24.2-million-dollar operating profit in 1979. The prescription for this SBU clearly called for selling off this operation and replacing it with high-margin expanding businesses to close the large performance gap. Clearly, Cudahy was a "dog," with a low market share in a mature market. The only dilemma in applying this formula was that the old-line meat-packing firm, faced with price and efficiency problems, couldn't find buyers for its business. How many firms want dog businesses?

General Host decided on a different tack—a forward vertical integration. It purchased Hickory Farms, the largest specialty food store in the United States. In addition to selling other products such as cheese, Hickory Farms sells processed meats from fresh cuts, which provide higher margins. Hickory Farms will be expected to switch purchases from archrival Armour & Co. and be supplied by Cudahy.

The purchase fit Host's strategy to reduce past diversification and reshape the business around specialty retailing and food processing. Over the last 6 years Host divested itself of a number of properties and added canned hams, frozen Italian foods, the Hot Sam pretzel shops, and Lil General convenience stores. Now Hickory Farms is seen as a centerpiece for internal expansion by Host.

Still, by getting rid of Cudahy, Host could put itself into a substantially higher return-on-equity position. But the president has set lower goals for returns because he does not expect to be able to sell Cudahy. Thus while some strategic prescriptions may be beneficial, barriers to implementation may be in the way. In this case, one way around the barriers was via vertical integration and a change in the size of the perceived gap due to the belief that nothing else could be done about it.

Source: Adapted from "General Host: Vertical Integration to Save a Subsidiary It Couldn't Sell," *Business Week*, Jan. 19, 1981, pp. 103–104.

Hofer criticizes the BCG approach because it inadequately represents new businesses in new industries that are just starting to grow and he offers an extension of BCG analysis that remedies that inadequacy. Hofer analyzed businesses in terms of their competitive position and stage of product-market evolution. Exhibit 8.8 outlines his suggestions. Circles represent the sizes of the industries involved. The pie wedges within the circles represent the market shares of the firms. He suggests that these be plotted for present and future businesses. Strategic choices based upon such a scheme might follow the logic below:

1 Business A appears to be an emerging star, and thus a target for excess resource allocation—especially to strengthen its competitive position in light of its strong market share.

2 Business B might follow much the same scenario as business A, but corporate resource allocation would probably be contingent on determining why B has been unable to obtain a higher market share, given its strong competitive position, and on the presentation of sound plans to rectify that deficiency.

3 Businesses C and D are question marks, though C is a strong candidate for retrenchment.

4 Business F and, to a lesser extent, business E represent cash cows within the corporate portfolio and would be key targets for corporate resource generation.

5 Business G appears to be an emerging dog, managed to generate short-term cash flow and targeted for eventual divestiture or liquidation.

EXHIBIT 8.8   Product-market evolution portfolio matrix.
(Adapted from C. Hofer, Conceptual Constructs for Formulating Corporate and Business Strategies [Boston: Intercollegiate Case Clearing House, no. 9-378-754, 1977], p. 3.)

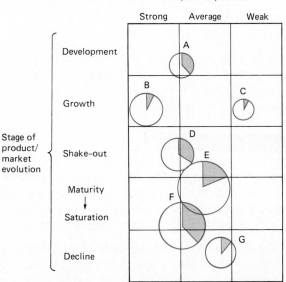

Hofer's approach can be a useful tool to aid the thinking of strategists in multiple-SBU firms who are considering alternative strategies for their various SBUs. Even within a single SBU with multiple products and/or markets, the approach can aid the thinking about the desired portfolio.

Another approach is to apply financial analysis to various alternatives. For example, what is the value added to the firm by pursuing a given alternative? Discounted cash flow methods could be applied to the expected financial outcomes of an alternative to assess the viability of a given strategic action or to determine whether an SBU is a dog or a star.

Finally, a new tool seems to be on the horizon. Spreadsheets, data bases, and various computerized management science techniques have been around for a while. But there is a new breed of decision-making programs designed to help executives use their personal computers in developing strategies and making qualitative decisions. Such programs allow the user to organize and evaluate a vast array of data and information. But they are, of course, only as good as the assumptions and criteria plugged in.

These programs have had an impact on the way business executives approach decision making. Many have in common the idea of setting up a matrix with internal factors (SAP) and external factors (ETOP) on the axes. Analyzing the matrix according to a prescribed formula leads to a recommendation of a particular strategic choice or choices. We suggest, however, that "choice by formula" should not and cannot replace strategic thinking. Computer programs can aid your thinking, but they should not replace the decision maker, especially since there is evidence that growth rates (the usually desired objective) do not always correlate with profitability. In effect, we agree with Seeger, who argues against oversimplification by suggesting: "We must remember that the dogs may be friendly, the cows may need a bull now and then to remain productive, and the stars may have burned themselves out."

Prescriptions for Choice of Business-Level Strategy

Most of the tools in the last section primarily apply to corporate or multiple-SBU activities as opposed to business-level strategies. Although some of those models are applicable to individual business units, there are other ways in which business-level strategic choices can be approached.

Expansion Prescriptions [4]

A large amount of work has been done to suggest how managers can accomplish growth goals. Expansion strategies are normally conceived as the best way to do this, and usually the focus is on gaining market shares. But there are other interesting suggestions for choosing various approaches to this strategy. One set of prescriptions (based on U.S. firms in relatively mature and stable industries) is as follows:

1 The first guide is to focus on products whose markets are growing. Never focus on slow-growth products unless there is technical or market know-how you can learn to apply to more promising markets. Or enter these markets only if you can produce a much simpler, much cheaper product when the dominant firms are not innovating.

2 It is better to be a big fish in a small pond if the pond (market segment) is growing. Get out of small nongrowth markets. Don't be a follower.

3 Choose feasible markets to compete in. Don't try to compete against larger firms with strong brand loyalty (in consumer goods) or large firms with strong financial capacity (in industrial goods).

4 In growing markets, it is easier to expand by combining a push for primary demand with a secondary demand push. Small firms with limited cash resources and a small market share should ignore primary demand. A major emphasis on secondary demand is optional when the objective is a limited market share in a very competitive market.

The strongest proponents of the value of market share come from the Profit Impact of Market Strategies (PIMS) studies. Essentially, PIMS is a cross-sectional study of the strategic experience of over 100 firms operating with over 1000 SBUs. The information has been gathered from the businesses in the form of about 100 pieces of data supplied by them in a standardized format. From this data models are generated using regression equations for ROI and cash flows.

Early results indicated that market share, investment intensity (ratio of total investment to sales), and product quality were the most important determinants of pretax return on investment. The PIMS studies also provided some interesting insights into the reasons for the link between market share and profitability. The results point to economies of scale and opportunities for vertical integration. High-share businesses (those with a share greater than 40 percent) tended to make rather than buy and tended to own their own distribution facilities.

The importance of economies of scale is also supported by the learning curve concept. The Boston Consulting Group (BCG) studied 24 products in seven industries longitudinally. Its focus was on the cost-to-price relationship which results from the experience curve (unit cost decreases as volume doubles). Its results suggest the following:

1 Get the biggest market share you can as early as you can.

2 Initially, the products will be sold below cost, but then as volume builds, the cost must be lowered. With the largest market share, this should be easy to do.

3 Hold costs and prices down. This will reduce the attractiveness of entrance to the market.

The prescriptions from these studies would seem to suggest that increasing the market share is almost a goal unto itself rather than one strategy to attain other objectives. Yet a variety of studies question whether this is so.

A study of the internal expansion of firms in the maturity or saturation stage of the product life cycle is that of Fruhan. He studied the relationship between market share and profitability and found that it was *not* economically worthwhile to increase the market share *if* (1) extremely heavy financial resources were required, (2) the expansion might have to be stopped before the firm reached its market share target, or (3) regulatory agencies might restrict the firm's activities. Other studies suggest that cash flow benefits may come at the expense of profits. As a result, some low-share SBUs may contribute cash to the overall firm even if, by themselves, they are not making high profit contributions.

Woo and Cooper, using the PIMS data, challenge the basic conclusion that a high market share is mandatory for a favorable ROI. Of particular importance is their finding that some successful low-share firms operate in very stable environments, characterized by high purchase frequency, high value added, and large numbers of competitors. What is interesting is that most of these firms sold *standardized industrial components and supplies.*

This key finding calls into question the validity of the product life cycle (PLC) concept as commonly understood, and on which much of the ''market share imperative'' is grounded. Indeed, Rink and Swan have reviewed the product life cycle research and concluded that ''investigators have focused almost exclusively . . . on nondurable consumer goods. Industrial items, as well as major product changes, have been nearly ignored.'' Moreover, they have identified *eleven* other PLC patterns which various researchers have uncovered for different kinds of products.

What do we conclude from these studies and their critics? Basically, we think that increasing the market share is not the only strategy alternative worth exploring. Even the supporters of the market share imperative point out that the explanation for the market/share-profitability relationship may reflect an underlying factor called ''quality of management''; that is, those who control costs get productivity from employees, and so on. So the implementation of a strategy may be just as important as the strategy itself.

A different matrix of alternatives, shown as Exhibit 8.9, suggests another way in which other factors can be brought into the choice process, particularly for the single-SBU situation. Here the idea is to consider a selected set of alternatives (changing the pace or business definition in products and/or markets) in relation to the ETOP, the SAP, and managerial values such as risk.

Position ①, expansion in the pace of present product and market development, would be prescribed if the SAP shows strength in the present products, the ETOP shows continued market opportunity, and management has relative low risk orientations. This penetration strategy also implies that there is a relatively small gap between desired and expected performance.

EXHIBIT 8.9   **A matrix of typical expansion alternatives.**

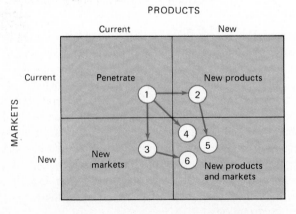

If the ETOP suggests that the market is saturated or that stronger competition or other threats to the market exist and the SAP shows weakness in distribution or strength in product development, position ② might be prescribed. This could be related or unrelated product development depending on the size of the gap or risk preferences. Other dimensions (such as internal or external expansion) might depend on financial strengths or timing; for instance, if speed is desired, a joint venture or merger could be used depending on financial ability.

Position ③ is similar to ②, but the SAP might suggest adding markets for existing products due to greater distribution strengths but production or product development weaknesses.

Position ④ is the combination alternative of simultaneously adding new products and new markets. The ETOP should indicate greater opportunity, the SAP should show greater strength, the gap should be larger, and the managers will probably have a higher risk propensity.

Positions ⑤ and ⑥ suggest that the long-range plan is to ultimately add new products and markets. But this is arrived at by a sequential combination of adding products (or markets) first, followed by markets (or products). In this case, strengths and opportunities are assumed to be as before, but new ones will be developed in the process. As opposed to their attitude in 4, then, managers are willing to accept a longer time horizon and are less risk-seeking. Exhibit 8.10 describes a firm which chose this approach.

EXHIBIT 8.10   STEADY AS SHE GOES

One way to reduce a performance gap is to set modest goals and work to achieve them slowly but surely. In the 1970s, President Duval of Hammermill Paper sought "average paper-company profitability," which itself was achieved with a struggle. Internal weaknesses at Hammermill included poor economies of scale, high costs of transportation between pulp and paper mills, antiquated equipment, and the inability to finance expensive new machinery.

Duval began in 1971 to make a gradual change in Hammermill's products and businesses to exploit its strengths and minimize its weaknesses. He decided to stick to specialized niches in papermaking with sustained expansion through acquisitions, primarily in paper distribution. He grabbed an early lead in making paper for photocopying and dropped products such as commodity-grade papers which Hammermill could not make efficiently. Duval also moved into the distribution of hardwood lumber. Paper distribution and lumber distribution are fragmented businesses where Hammermill can be a major competitor.

Hammermill's slow but steady progress has resulted in an improvement of financial position such that more aggressive expansion is about to start. Rebuilding of old equipment began a few years ago, and plans are to double the output of an Alabama pulp mill to help growth in its paper niches and to add the ability to export pulp as well. This will add risk, but opportunities are seen to be large. Duval's new goal is to raise Hammermill to the top quarter of the industry.

Hammermill has made steady progress, given its willingness to accept a moderate goal. It progressed by sequencing its moves over a period of time so that eventually it added new products and markets without taking large risks, given its internal weaknesses. Having accomplished this, it is changing its goal and risk orientations, largely due to moving from a position of greater strength.

Source: Adapted from "Hammermill Paper: A Slow but Sure Shift of Products and Businesses," *Business Week*, Jan. 11, 1982, pp. 119–120.

At any position, of course, retrenchment is possible if a firm moves in the opposite direction from the one that is suggested. Again, this would be prescribed depending on the gaps, the ETOP, the SAP, and risk orientation.

Retrenchment Prescriptions [5]

While less popular than expansions, there are some suggestions for when and how to choose retrenchment. A few of these suggestions follow. Break-even analysis can guide the turnaround approach, as shown in Exhibit 8.11.

Hofer's recommendations are to liquidate or sell assets if sales are less than a third of the break-even point. If sales are 30 to 60 percent of the break-even point, it is suggested that the firm increase revenues by focusing on existing products with price cutting, more advertising, or a more direct sales effort. In the 60 to 80 percent range, combinations of asset reduction, revenue increasing, and cost cutting are suggested. If the firm is below but close to break-even point and has high direct labor or fixed expenses, short-term decreases in costs are probably most effective.

Before a turnaround is attempted, the magnitude of the problem should be assessed. For instance, if the probability of bankruptcy is high or too much time is needed, the effort may be futile. (Beaver, Altman, and Wilcox have proposed several techniques which they claim can be used to predict failures well in advance.) In addition, for the turnaround strategies to be effective, existing managers will most likely have to be

EXHIBIT 8.11   **Deciding on the type of turnaround strategy to follow.**
(C. W. Hofer, "Turnaround Strategies," Reprinted by permission from The Journal of Business Strategy, vol. 1, no. 1 [Summer 1980]. Copyright © 1980 by Warren, Gorham and Lamont, Inc., 210 South St., Boston, Mass. All rights reserved.)

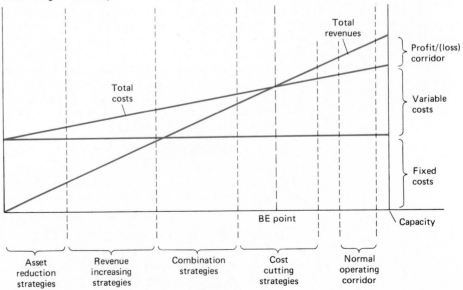

replaced, since they will be committed to existing strategy or will perhaps be seen as having to admit "defeat," leading to a belief that they are ineffective managers.

Empirical tests of these recommendations on turnaround with the PIMS data suggest that asset reductions occur with low levels of capacity utilization. Selective product-market pruning was pursued by businesses with high-capacity usage. In effect, this supports Hofer's prescriptions.

Bibeault studied the turnaround of 81 firms. He found that 88 percent of the firms used divestment of some sort during the course of the turnaround. And 37 percent shut down entire facilities. Sixty-six percent of these firms decreased staffing levels in selected functional departments, and 92 percent pursued a strategy of eliminating losers from the product line. An interesting sidelight is that the average turnaround cycle took 7½ years from the recognition of a problem to the resumption of healthy expansion. He also listed the following reasons for why a turnaround became necessary: bad luck (1 percent), external factors (23 percent), combination of internal and external factors (24 percent), internal problems (52 percent). In other words, sins of commission on the part of managers seems to be what gets most firms into trouble.

Retrenchments combined with other strategies have been prescribed for many old-line basic industries in the United States and elsewhere (mining, steel, etc.). Plants are outmoded and hobbled by low productivity, interest costs and low returns have precluded investment in new equipment, overcapacity has contributed to high overhead costs, labor rates are high, and markets must be fought for against new foreign competitors who aren't bothered by many of the domestic ills. To solve these problems, many firms will retrench by selling out or merging with cash-rich partners in an attempt to modernize factories. Others will abandon some traditional product lines to concentrate on specific market niches. A few will seek diversification to support a declining business; this strategy is riskier than others due to high expenditures and diversion of assets and attention from basic problems. Many firms pursue a strategy of stability, which has the effect of milking the business. Under these circumstances, prescriptions often heard include:

1 Reduce vertical integration; this reduces capital requirements, increases flexibility, and focuses effort. Disintegration means abandoning some functions. For example, many automakers now buy parts or even whole vehicles for sale in domestic markets.

2 Increase effective use of capital equipment. Add shifts or justify deviations from full use of capacity. Restructure labor contracts to add flexibility. (The steel industry has tried this with moderate success.)

3 Simplify product lines to become the low-cost producer in a specific niche to build competitive advantage. The trade-off here must be carefully considered vis-à-vis the risk of reducing volume, resulting in less effective use of capacity.

The dilemma is that managers are too often committed to past strategy, or signals of problems go unrecognized, and retrenchments are perceived as "failures." It took over 8 years, for example, for Mobil to finally admit that its acquisition of Montgomery Ward was a mistake. In 1985, a $500 million write-down was taken and Ward was retrenched in size, most likely to prepare it for a potential sale if Mobil could find a buyer.

Stability Prescriptions [6]

Business executives hear more and more people telling them to "stick to your knitting" and "do what you do best." This is sound advice, as long as it is done intentionally, with awareness of the alternatives. In an era of megamergers, firms see the allure of diversification, and too frequently follow the "ready, fire, aim" sequence. Yet more firms are following the recommendations of getting back to basics.

In some cases, the strategy is defensive—protection against loss. In others, gains are expected from an offensive strategy—using basic existing skills in new ways. While the business definition is stability, the prescription is pace expansion. Exhibit 8.12 provides an example of this.

Combination Prescriptions [7]

Our final section on prescriptions for business-level strategic choice deals with various combinations of alternatives for different settings. One set of prescriptions for SBU strategies comes from the Japanese director of McKinsey & Co.—Kenichi Ohmae. His argument is that you can classify businesses into four categories on the basis of the demand patterns of products, and he has prescribed strategies for each type.

• *Replacement demand.* This category includes industries where demand fluctuates in direct response to current economic conditions. Consumer durables (e.g., refrig-

---

EXHIBIT 8.12   A CHANGE OF PACE FOR AIRLINES

While airlines have diversified for some time, many into the hotel business, recent moves have been made to achieve greater productivity out of existing assets by sticking to what they know best. The "diversifications" now being considered involve developing revenues by finding new uses for the people, skills, and equipment basic to the central business of airline operations.

United Airlines takes in about $15 million a year training flight crews for other airlines. They formed a new subsidiary to go after a 5-year $250 million contract to train crews for the Air Force's C-5 transport program.

Computerized reservations systems in use by American, United, TWA, and Delta are currently leased to travel agents. In time, these systems are expected to be leased to cable companies for home computer users.

Firms which have grounded some fleets will lease those out and try to get more business servicing aircraft. Contract maintenance and ground-handling work are expected to allow some airlines to increase their pace of activities.

In effect, firms are being creative about the use of huge asset bases to develop new revenues where low costs are possible and the synergistic links are already in place. Such stable business definition together with expanded pace of functions allows for improved performance.

Source: Adapted from "New Airlines are Diversifying by Sticking to What They Know Best," *Business Week,* May 7, 1984, pp. 70–72.

erators) is one example. In this situation, Ohmae prescribes lowering the break-even point by increasing the ratio of variable costs to fixed costs.

• *International displacement*. Markets in this category have not experienced any major fluctuations, and there is no fear that demand will disappear. But costs have increased rapidly in the businesses. Examples are petrochemicals, textiles, and shoes. Top management here must seriously consider vertical integration, backward or forward, to gain some control over costs.

• *New economic order*. A heavy drop in demand for this set of businesses resulted from the price of oil. Producers of oil tankers and the electric power industry are in this category. In this situation diversification or retrenchment is mandatory.

• *Accelerated life cycle*. Industries here include those where product life cycles are progressively shorter. The microelectronics industry has required businesses which use its components to rapidly introduce new products to keep up with demand. To cope with this environment, firms need active and aggressive strategies with some restructuring of operations. For instance, R&D needs redirection into applied research, and some companies are shifting control over R&D to production or marketing. Others are using computer-aided design and manufacturing (CAD and CAM) to slash the turnaround time of product development. Markets must be treated as if they were part of the fashion industry.

Yet another strategy, one which gained favor in the mid 1980s, is private ownership through a leveraged buyout (LBO). This is prescribed for those who may wish to avoid a takeover, or for those who want control to manage for the long-term rather than the short-term expectations of Wall Street. Private ownership, however, when done with the LBO, is often a temporary resting place in a sequential combination strategy involving eventual sale of the firm. Otherwise, the new owners, usually the managers themselves and institutional investors, may not cash in. In effect, the business is being run to support finance, rather than finance being used to support the business. Hence, plans or decisions at functional levels may lead to strategic directions unintended by top-level executives.

In conclusion, different combinations of strategies are appropriate for differing circumstances. Thus decision makers must rely on the strategic processes of analysis and diagnosis, and then, with the appropriate prescriptions and tools in hand, ask several key questions when considering whether to accept each given alternative:

• Is the strategy responsive to the external environment?
• Does it involve a sustainable competitive advantage?
• How does it relate to other firm strategies?
• Does it provide adequate flexibility for the business and the firm?
• Is it consistent with the business mission and long term objectives?
• Is it feasible to implement?

The set of questions listed above is discussed in more detail in Chapter 11, since the final choice of a strategy should also take into account its plan for implementation. But, while we support the various analyses which can aid strategic thinking, we want you to be aware of another set of factors which influences and constrains managers as they make strategic choices. Our next section describes those factors.

DESCRIPTIONS OF MANAGERIAL CHOICE FACTORS [8]

While a planning staff or line executives often do provide analyses of various alternatives, there is some question as to whether executives pay much attention to them. And it is often difficult to pinpoint when the choice among alternatives is actually made. Many executives do not appear to use sophisticated decision-making techniques. They frequently rely on assumptions and the collective wisdom of the group. As a consensus begins to emerge, the CEO seems to ratify the emerging position. After an apparent pause, the consensus position with some modifications becomes policy. Thus policies or positions evolve from a process of creeping commitment.

You may ask, Why isn't a more rational process used? Is this any way to run a business? Why don't executives use the models and support data for "better" decision making?

Some argue that top management has little confidence in the data to support alternatives. Some techniques are unfamiliar, or the models are not trusted. Realistic assumptions may be violated in an attempt to find "optimal" solutions to problems. Besides, anyone can manipulate numbers to support a position. Others explain that power politics are involved, and model builders are weak power holders or naive politicians. But the creeping commitment approach to strategic decision making can also be traced to certain other managerial factors which limit the choice of alternatives. Remember our discussion in Chapter 1 about how several forces are at work in decision situations.

As a result of these forces a limited number of alternatives and consequences are considered. Positions are likely to be similar to or extensions of existing strategy. Executives will select targets of opportunity. Where events such as retirement, a scheduled review, or a major external threat or opportunity force a change, executives may take the opportunity to install modified programs, policies, and procedures. So let's examine the managerial factors that are crucial to an understanding of strategic choice.

Strategic choices are influenced by four managerial selection factors: (1) perceptions of external dependence, (2) attitudes toward risk, (3) awareness of past enterprise strategies, and (4) power relationships.

Managerial Perceptions of External Dependence [9]

Firms do not exist in isolation from the external environment. They depend on other units for their survival and prosperity. These units include the owners, competitors, customers, government, and community, as was made clear in Chapters 3 and 4. The more dependent a firm is on these other units, the less flexible its strategic choices can be. Thus the range of strategic choices is limited. Strategic choices result from interactions of the firm with its environment. Thus strategic choices are outcomes that are negotiated as various parties maneuver to reach their objectives. Propositions in the summary specify how.

These dependencies can be objectively measured. A stockholder who controls 51 percent of the voting stock clearly has more power, and the firm is more dependent on the wishes of the majority owner. But in addition to the objective phenomena there are the *subjective* views of the decision makers. Facts do not speak for themselves. Executives interpret these facts. Two firms of equal power (objectively measured in the environment) can be headed by executives who see the firms differently, as discussed in Chapter 2. One firm's executives can see their firm as weak and dependent, the other as strong (relatively). Thus the weights they put on the strategic alternatives can vary. For instance, a strategy requiring lower prices to gain market share may be rejected if managers believe that their union has the power to gain greater wages and benefits than their competitors offer.

Exhibit 8.13 suggests that diversification strategies are often used to reduce dependence. Of course, captive-company strategies have the opposite effect—they increase one firm's dependence on another.

Dependence does not necessarily always restrict alternatives, however. For instance, a firm can pursue active strategies to reduce dependence rather than allow it to dominate the choice process. For example, consider dependence on a supplier. If the gap in performance is unsatisfactory due to this factor, several approaches can be followed—new suppliers can be found, the firm can vertically integrate to make the input, or the firm can enter into a joint venture or merger with a supplier to reduce the dependence. Thus dependence (as well as the other factors to be discussed) is, in reality, only a constraint to the extent that it is *perceived* to be a limiting factor; i.e., managers believe that these variables are beyond their influence or control. In some cases they will be. But many managers sometimes limit themselves and their strategies unnecessarily.

EXHIBIT 8.13   WHAT'S BAD FOR GM IS GOOD FOR LOF?

For 50 years, the top priority at Libbey-Owens-Ford was to manufacture glass for General Motors. But in 1980, the first manufacturing executive in the history of LOF was appointed to head the glass operations, and the firm has restructured to make the automotive original-equipment group only one of three distinct business units. These changes and others revolve around a goal of "ending the days when General Motors drove what we built, where we built it, and what kinds of plants we built it in."

The nature of glass making leads to highly volume-sensitive production runs. So the relationship with GM made good sense when LOF could gear to GM's relatively predictable needs. However, GM's troubles and shifts in supply practices (giving more business to competitor PPG) has made the LOF dependence on GM's business a problem. Glass operations lost $6 million in 1980 due to huge plant operating costs and the lack of a diversified customer base to pick up the slack left by GM's decreased purchases.

The overdependence on GM in the past has also created problems for LOF in the sense that it must now catch up in the potentially lucrative architectural glass area. The irony is that the company invented insulating glass in the 1930s, but it tended to downplay the market for this product while it leaned on GM. Now the company is forced to diversify in markets due to its past dependence. Even diversification away from glass is not out of the question. While diversification is usually justified on the basis of spreading risk, it may also be a strategy of choice to reduce dependence. The dependence itself at LOF was a factor which influenced its choices in the past and now affects its future strategy.

Source: Adapted from "Turning Around Libbey-Owens," *Business Week,* Aug. 10, 1981, pp. 94–96.

Managerial Attitudes toward Risk [10]

As we suggested in our discussion of Exhibit 8.12, another factor influencing strategic choice is how much risk the firm, its stockholders, and management can tolerate. Managerial attitudes toward risk vary from comfort if not exhilaration with high risk to strong risk aversion. The risk averters probably view the firm as very weak and will accept only defensive strategies with very low risks. Three polar conditions with regard to risk can be conceived (Exhibit 8.14).

Risk attitudes can change, and vary by industry volatility and environmental uncertainty. In very volatile industries, executives must be capable of absorbing greater amounts of risk; otherwise, they cannot function. Exhibit 8.15 provides an interesting example of how risk attitudes can change and are important to strategic thinking in volatile conditions. You should also be aware that there is need to assess the "downside" risk of failure against the "upside" gains of opportunity from the environment. If executives' perception of an opportunity is overly optimistic, the risk of the opportunity may be overlooked.

Risk attitudes can also vary on the basis of the internal conditions discussed in Chapter 5. How much are you "gambling" on any given project? If you are betting the whole company, your risk assessment may be different than if you have little to lose. Similarly, how much can you afford to lose? And is it your money? Are you financially strong or weak? Past success also has an influence on the perception of risk. If you've won recently, you may see less risk in the future. (Also see Exhibit 8.10.)

Thus assessing the manager's perception of risk will help you understand the potential acceptability of a given strategic option. Insofar as they influence managerial attitudes, the risk attitudes of the managers and stockholders will eliminate some strategic alternatives and highlight others. For instance, if risk is being balanced, managers are likely to pursue stability in major parts of the business with expansion in one or a few SBUs. Note that this balanced risk position is assumed by the BCG product portfolio prescriptions. But if risk is seen as necessary, firms are likely to eliminate stability as a viable option.

EXHIBIT 8.14   RISK ATTITUDES AND STRATEGIC CHOICE

Managerial attitudes toward risk	Probable choice filters	Probable strategies
1 Risk is necessary for success. Optimistic; high risk leads to reward.	1 High-risk projects are acceptable or desirable.	1 Expansion
2 Risk is a fact of life, and some risk is acceptable.	2 Balance high-risk choices with low-risk choices (bet hedging).	2 Combination
3 High risk is what destroys enterprises; it needs to be minimized.	3 Risk aversion: risky projects are rejected.	3 Stability

EXHIBIT 8.15 THE RISKS AT GOULD

William T. Ylvisaker, chairman of Gould Inc., was initially successful in his first decade of running the company. Under his direction Gould went from being a battery maker with $100 million in sales to being a $2 billion conglomerate. The strategy responsible for this success was that of acquiring "old-line manufacturing companies and jolting their performance with stringent financial controls."

But later this strategy seemed to no longer be working for Gould Inc. Its profit margin had been slipping since it peaked in 1977. This caused Ylvisaker to take a look at the direction in which he was leading the company. Before the strategic change, Gould was into four businesses—electrical, battery, industrial, and electronics. Because Ylvisaker believes that electronics has by far the greatest growth opportunities in the 1980s and 1990s, that is where he decided to concentrate Gould's investment. This "strategic about-face" was also influenced by the high multiples that investors usually give high-technology stocks.

Gould has been divesting itself of many of its divisions and subsidiaries engaged in the electrical, battery, and industrial fields while at the same time investing more in the electronics field. It has also been emphasizing more internal growth in the future, and its acquisition targets will be smaller companies. (Gould acquired more than a few large companies in the past.) Eventually, Gould hopes to be the prime supplier for the systems that would provide not only computers and controllers but also electronic sensors, imaging equipment, and other products.

The move to electronics involves enormous risks. Gould is a newcomer to the fast-changing, highly competitive environment of high-tech products. This type of climate usually requires aggressive risk taking with less top-management control. Ylvisaker was known as a heavy-handed executive whose authoritarian manner led to high management turnover. But the setbacks Gould experienced apparently forced him to reconsider the direction and management style. It appears as though Ylvisaker does not intend to let his past management practices get in the way of his new strategy. He has completely reshaped the Gould hierarchy and has promised to take a less forceful role in managing the day-to-day affairs of operating units. Evidence already shows that top managers are listening more to middle managers than they did in the past.

Clearly, the risk implications and approaches to managing this business have changed along with the strategy.

Source: Adapted from "Bill Ylvisaker Bets His Company on Electronics," *Business Week,* Nov. 2, 1981, pp. 86–92.

Managerial Awareness of Past Strategies [11]

This factor's influence can be summarized very simply: Past strategies are the beginning point of strategic choice and may eliminate some strategic choices as a result. Recall that in the gap analysis it is assumed that the beginning point of the process is the present position of the firm. From there, the initial question is, Will the continuation of our strategy lead to the expected attainment of desired objectives? To the extent that the gap is small, past strategy will be continued. And to the extent that managers are committed to continuing the strategy, other alternatives will be ignored.

The corporate cultures built up to implement the past strategy also get in the way of choosing a new strategy. A corporate culture is the "personality" of an organization. As our chapters on implementation will suggest, changing a corporate culture represents new patterns of resource allocation, norms, communication, leadership, rewards, and so on. Such changes will be needed if a new strategy diverges very far from the past one. It is often difficult and time-consuming to change corporate culture, as GM found out when it acquired EDS. The cultures clashed, leading to some problems for both. Even the past image of the firm may make a new strategy harder to implement. For example, in attempts to avoid costly errors, conservative executives at Owens-Illinois moved cautiously into new product lines extending beyond their basic glass-container operation. But customers and analysts still believe that "the company's heart belongs to glass." So the values of management and perceptions of the firm from *outside* as a result of long commitments to past strategy are preventing the firm from moving rapidly into new growth areas. The same problem affected Dow Chemicals. In the era of the Vietnamese war, Dow was attacked as a supplier of napalm and Agent Orange. In 1985, Dow began a $50 million 5-year ad campaign featuring idealistic students and recent graduates working for Dow to make the world a better place. Executives believed this new image was needed to support a strategy aimed at reducing dependence upon commodity chemicals and a stronger move into consumer product lines.

On the basis of research into the longitudinal choice process in 10 separate businesses, Mintzberg and several colleagues have concluded that past strategic choices strongly influenced later strategic choices. Specifically, they found that:

1 The present strategy evolves from a past strategy developed by a powerful leader. This unique and tightly integrated strategy (a gestalt strategy) is a major influence on later strategic choices.

2 Then the strategy becomes programmed. And the bureaucratic momentum keeps it going. Mintzberg calls this the "push-pull phenomenon": the original decision maker pushes the strategy, and then lower management pulls it along.

3 When this strategy begins to fail because of changing conditions, the enterprise grafts new substrategies onto the old and only later gropes for a new strategy.

4 As the environment changes even more, the enterprise begins to consider seriously the retrenchment, combination, or expansion strategies previously suggested by a few executives who were ignored at the time.

In many cases strategic change is more likely to come about when new managers are brought in from outside the firm. Strategic change is less likely if new executives are promoted from within, and it is least likely if the existing management group remains in power. An interesting example of this was given in Exhibit 2.7. Thus the selection of a new CEO is one area where the board of directors has a particularly strong influence if strategic change is necessary or desirable. And policies of promotion from within need to be carefully considered. If insiders are committed to past strategy, policies, and people, and changes are needed, a new strategy may require an outsider.

Finally, expectations about the product life cycle can influence strategic change. In this sense, past strategic decisions regarding product introductions may influence future decisions. Where the firm's major products or services are in the product-service life cycle determines how critical it is if the firm is too heavily tied to past strategies. In the earlier stages, it is less critical if the firm is tied to historical strategies than in the maturity or decline stages.

Managerial Power Relationships [12]

Those with experience know that power relationships are a key reality in organizational life. In many enterprises, if the top manager begins to advocate one alternative, the decision to choose it is soon unanimous. In others, cliques develop, and if one clique begins to support an alternative, the other opposes it.

Sometimes personalities get involved in the strategic choice: whom the boss likes and respects has a lot to do with which strategic choice is made. And sometimes if "mistakes" are made, the powerful can shift the blame to lower-level executives. The power of the CEO plays a role, too. The manager's personal goals, ambitions, values, and motivation can affect the choice of strategy. If the CEO is very powerful, the organization's goals become intertwined with personal goals in the choice process.

No one doubts that power and politics influence decisions, including strategic decisions. The question is, How often is power a crucial factor in these decisions? We concluded in Chapter 1 that the significance of the decision, the degree of time pressure, the degree of uncertainty, and the style of the decision maker influence the relative roles of analytical, political, and intuitive approaches to decision making. Also, recall that external political pressures are involved in determining the trade-offs among objectives, as discussed in Chapters 1 and 2.

From all that we've said up to now, we would conclude that politics always plays a role, even to the extent of influencing objectives (criteria for choice) and the way the analytical approaches are used and interpreted. And politics seems to be an *overriding* factor in the strategic choice process about 30 percent of the time according to Mintzberg. Thus it is important to analyze the values and goals of the key managers, as we indicated in Chapter 2, if you are to understand the probability of acceptance of a given strategic recommendation.

Analytical purists no doubt abhor such a recommendation. Should the descriptions about *what is done* lead to a prescription that this is the way it *ought to be done?* Perhaps not. Yet from a pragmatic perspective, the strategy chosen has little chance of success unless it will be implemented effectively; it is unlikely that a politically unacceptable strategy will be carried out successfully.

Remember that the power of lower-level participants also plays a role in strategic decision making. We discussed this in Chapter 2 also. Of course, top managers make the strategic choices. But earlier strategic choices made by their subordinates limit the strategic choices usually considered. Recall that subordinates can choose to hold or submit proposals for strategic change. They can also influence the choice by providing analytical data which support their proposal (as opposed to "unbiased" pros and cons). Moreover, strategies must be implemented, and lower-level managers have the power to make or break a strategy.

Decision makers also have opportunities to select the type of environment within which they will operate. In large organizations, they have the power to influence conditions prevailing in the environments in which they are operating. According to Child, threats and opportunities perceived in the environment, which affect strategic choice, "are functions of the power exercised by decision makers in the light of ideological values." Hence, power constrains choices on the one hand, and expands choice opportunities on the other. The key is the *perception* of power and its use.

Finally, in Europe and elsewhere, sometimes workers' councils have an influence on strategic choices. This is true in Sweden, for example. Volvo's decision to open a plant in the United States was influenced by the demand of the workers' council not to close any operations in Sweden. German workers' councils have had an effect on Volkswagen's strategic choices in shifting its resources. Even in the United States, union leaders are sometimes "elected" to the board of directors. Thus, like the "dependence" variable discussed earlier, the power of "insiders" and "outsiders" can be a strong political influence on the strategic decision. Coalitions develop to influence the formation of objectives *and* strategies.

THE TIME DIMENSION AND STRATEGIC CHOICE [13]

The timing of decisions and time pressures were included among other decision factors we discussed in Chapter 1. We wish to expand on how this factor affects the strategic decision process and the quality of the decision.

The deadlines for making a strategic choice are often set not by the manager but by others. Consider the following strategic choice situation: Firm A (the Raider) offers a merger with a less than ideal set of conditions and a short response date, and it has another potential merger partner waiting if you do not accept now. Firm B (the White Knight) has not decided whether it will give you a merger offer or what conditions it will require. As you can see from this example, sometimes the strategist must make decisions in time frames set by others. In other cases, the strategist has more time to seek alternatives and choose among them.

When time pressures are significant, strategists may be unable to gather enough information or consider an adequate number of alternatives. Time pressures also affect the strategic choice process itself. For example, managers under time pressure put more weight on negative evidence than on positive evidence and consider fewer factors in making decisions.

Of course, these results could differ, depending on the alternatives being considered. For example, several studies indicate the following:

1 In making difficult decisions, managers take longer to select from two good alternatives and two poor ones than from four good alternatives.

2 In making easy decisions, managers take longer to select from four good alternatives than from two good ones and two poor ones.

Perhaps in the first case the job looks difficult when there are four good alternatives, and the managers impulsively pick one, whereas with two bad alternatives they feel competent in rejecting two and take their time choosing one of the remaining two. In the second case they feel capable of deciding that it takes longer to compare four alternatives than two.

Finally, the desire to accomplish certain objectives within a specific time frame will more naturally lead to the choice of some alternative strategies. For instance, expansion through active external approaches (e.g., mergers) may be chosen if the objective is to increase size rapidly. So time pressures and the time dimension influence some strategic choices.

SUMMARY OF THE CHOICE PROCESS [14]

The choice of a strategy is not a routine or easy decision. Strategic choice, like all decisions, is made in the context of the decision maker and the decision situation.

The manager's attitude toward risk and feelings about where the enterprise fits blocks out certain choices from view. Unable to follow the "rational model" of strategic choice because of a lack of ability, the lack of costly information, or fast-changing conditions, the strategist focuses on choices from alternatives which change the status quo by increments.

Exhibit 8.16 is one attempt to explain how the strategist focuses on less than all the possible strategic choices: Imagine that the whole rectangle represents all possible strategies. But the factors discussed earlier eliminate some possible choices. For example, time or resource limitations force us to ignore some possibilities. External dependencies won't allow certain strategies because they are not feasible. Risk aversion is such that other choices are viewed as too risky. Political problems within the firm screen out other choices, and the past strategy is the beginning point of the strategic choice. So these factors screen out many choices. And the strategist looks at and ranks only the new incremental choices within what we call the "choice zone" in Exhibit 8.16. This figure shows the small choice zone that is left after the risky, unfeasible, and unacceptable choices are eliminated. Well, how does the strategist decide within this choice zone?

Integrating Description and Prescription

We started this chapter by suggesting that some dimensions of strategy alternatives were more likely to be considered than others, depending on the size of the gap. Then we suggested that some prescriptive techniques could be used to aid in the choice. But we just finished saying that managerial factors will limit the size of the choice

EXHIBIT 8.16 **Strategic choice given factor overlays.**

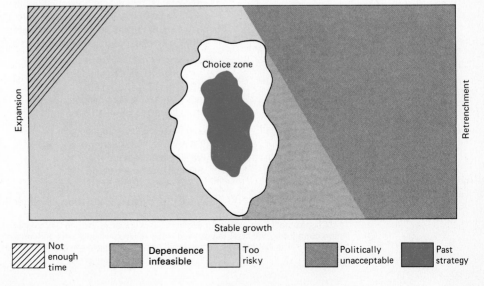

zone. In effect, these factors are what led us to hypothesize that some alternatives are more likely than others.

Now the decision maker is left with a narrower range of alternatives to choose from. But prescription suggests that we apply analytical tools to help us look at more alternatives. We think that the following procedure takes the prescription and description into account and can be used to guide the choice process.

First we begin with the past strategy, as noted in Exhibit 8.17. Note that as you move down the table, the strategies move further away from the past strategy, increase risk, alter dependencies, and probably become more unacceptable politically. So the arrangement of alternatives to be considered, in order, is based on the managerial factors and the size of the gap.

The procedure for making a choice is as follows:

1 First, analytically compare the present strategy with the next incremental change (e.g., 1 versus 2). Use the ETOP and SAP for analysis.

2 If the gap between expected objectives and desired objectives will be met by the present strategy, your choice is made; stay with the former strategy.

3 If the gap is not closed or the next strategy is expected to lead to the attainment of additional important objectives, proceed to compare the next two alternatives.

EXHIBIT 8.17   INCREMENTAL STRATEGIC CHOICE MODEL

Step	Choice*	Strategy
	1	Stable pace
1	2	Stable business definition: active pace expansion
2	3	Combination: passive, stable pace with active product or market change
		3A Internal expansion: horizontal, related
		3B Internal expansion: horizontal, unrelated
		3C External expansion: horizontal, related
		3D External expansion: horizontal, unrelated
3	4	Expansion of business definition
		4A Like 3A, without stable pace
		4B Like 3B, without stable pace
		4C Like 3C, without stable pace
		4D Like 3D, without stable pace
4	5	Vertical expansion in functions
		5A Internal, backward
		5B Internal, forward
		5C External, backward
		5D External, forward
5	6	Repeat of 2 through 5, but retrench rather than expand

*Choose the lowest numbered alternative that will close the gap unless analysis shows that the next alternative down the list will close the gap *and* result in substantially greater performance. If such a higher numbered alternative meets that criterion, proceed with pairwise analysis until gap is closed.

For example, you would start by comparing the stable pace strategy with pace expansion (e.g., increase market share in existing product-market segments). If the objectives (gap) will be achieved by a stable pace, your choice [of (1)] is made, unless expected outcomes will lead to attainment of new objectives which emerge in the analysis. If the latter is true, or if the gap is not closed, then compare the pace expansion with the first approach in step 2. That is, will a related, horizontal, internal expansion in part of the business (such as adding a related new product) combined with stability in the major parts of the business be superior to a pace expansion in terms of closing the gap in objectives? If so, you can then go on to compare 3A with 3B.

This process continues until the perceived gap is no longer significant or the strategist believes that nothing more can be done to close it. Remember that the gap can be created by internal and/or external conditions. In this sense, the SAP and ETOP provide the basic data for comparing pairs of alternatives. Also, remember that multiple objectives will probably require trade-offs due to external pressures. Thus a prescriptive analytical approach is implied but is limited to very few alternatives unless the gap is large. The matrix techniques discussed earlier could also be applied when paired alternatives are considered.

If you consider this procedure carefully, note that *if* the gap is large and due to an environmental opportunity, the comparisons will allow you to continue considering more alternatives, but they increase risk and require greater political acceptability for successful implementation. If the gap is large and due to a threat, you will probably begin considering retrenchments, although threats can be met by expansion. The retrenchment is placed where it is not because it is inferior but because it is considered less politically acceptable.

Also recognize that there is built-in efficiency of analysis. Each alternative step is usually only slightly different from the previous strategy. So the analysis in the previous stage is not wasted and can be used as the basis for considering additional factors if another pairwise comparison is necessary. Thus the time factor in the process is also incorporated in this procedure.

Finally, recognize that not all the possible combinations are considered here. These are our estimates of the more common alternatives. Further, timing (such as with sequential or simultaneous combinations) should be recognized as another factor to be incorporated. In this sense, more developed strategic plans will incorporate contingency strategies. This becomes more complex and deserves a bit more comment.

CONTINGENCY STRATEGIES [15]

The type of planning process used by a firm will influence the generation of alternatives. Strategists will choose to look at one set of strategic alternatives in first-generation planning and multiple sets of alternatives in second-generation or contingency approaches to strategic management. In more developed strategic management, managers also prepare alternative strategies that they can consider if conditions should change. When conditions change sufficiently, consideration of the contingency strategies is triggered. *Business Week* reported the following:

> Instead of relying on a single corporate plan with perhaps one or two variations, top management at more and more companies is now getting a whole battery of contingency plans and alternate scenarios. "We shoot for alternative plans that can deal with either/or eventualities," says the manager in charge of planning at du Pont.
>
> Companies are reviewing and revising plans more frequently in line with changing conditions. Instead of the old 5-year plan that might have been updated annually, plans are often updated quarterly, monthly, or even weekly. Arizona Public Service Company adopted a "dynamic" budget; changes in the price of a prime commodity can kick off a change in the company's cost models and the whole corporate plan may change accordingly. In the end, of course, that puts more pressure on top management, which must operate with an eye to numerous plans instead of being able to follow a single scenario. At Exxon Corporation, for instance, most-probable-case forecasts have been replaced by less definitive "envelopes" that include a range of possibilities. Says one corporate planning manager: "Today you still have to have a game plan. How do you get to that? Top management judgment and intuition. We don't really pin some things down anymore. There's a lot more thrown at the management."

Thus we can add one more dimension to our list of alternative approaches to strategic choice—a programmed or contingency strategy. A *programmed strategy* is a strategy which is planned in such a detailed and integrated way that it is difficult to change it once it has begun to be implemented. A *contingency strategy* requires the planner to choose the preferred strategy given the best estimate of conditions and other strategic choices. But it is flexible enough to allow for shifts in the thrust of the plan when conditions warrant it. In effect, programmed strategies emanate from first-generation planning. Second-generation planning leads to contingency strategy formation.

Programmed planning is suitable for stable environments with people who prefer well-defined roles. The contingency strategy is suitable for unstable environments with people who prefer variety and stimulation. Conditions change rapidly. Since 1972 large firms have chosen their strategies and have also developed plans B, C, and D on a "what if" basis. If the "what if" comes to be, plan C (or B or D) becomes the strategy. This requires that plan A include enough flexibility to allow the firm to recognize the need and then shift if necessary. In effect, the firm must provide for "anticipatory flexibility" with careful environmental monitoring and more frequent evaluation so that it can respond to signals as they become stronger.

Exhibit 8.18 describes a firm which practices contingency planning due to the mere complexity of its situation. Other firms have "disaster" contingency plans for continuing business if a disaster (such as a fire, a flood, a power outage, or the loss of computer records) strikes.

Most writers argue that moderately flexible strategies are the most effective. But those strategies are easier to advocate than pull off. In the period 1973–1974, the environment gave special problems to the auto industry. The energy crisis appeared to dictate a shift to compact cars. General Motors and others began to convert their factories to this strategy about the time that the crisis disappeared from motorists' minds and consumers began buying regular-sized cars again. Consumer preferences

EXHIBIT 8.18   CONTINGENCY PLANNING AT AMF

Attention to detail is a requirement at AMF due to its internal complexity. President York, who has a financial background, is in charge of an executive group that receives 1500 financial statements monthly. Then there are the 74 plants in distant nonurban locations using a variety of manufacturing technologies and distribution systems. After weeks of research, AMF concluded that it had either 41 or 54 SBUs in 1979, depending on how they were counted, organized within two industrial and five leisure-oriented divisions. Add to this the diverse environmental factors affecting these areas, and you have what is called "a killer" of a job managing the company.

In addition to an elaborate financial control system and bimonthly meetings with the seven groups, detailed strategic plans are required for each SBU. By themselves, these add complexity because of products which, at the time, ranged from sportswear (with short product life cycles) to motorcycles (with a long lead time for development calling for 10-year plans).

In 1978, the business units began providing contingency plans to "examine critical risks in achieving proposed profit objectives." The plans also required that steps be implemented if a specified event occurred. Many of the 1979 plans dealt with a possible recession and identified "trigger points" that would signal a need for certain steps. The proposed steps become more serious as successive trigger points are hit.

What is interesting is that many AMF executives don't believe that the contingency plans add much. "Many share the opinion 'Every good manager is thinking contingencies all the time.' " It is speculated, though, that the indifference has much to do with the vigor of their business in the late 1970s. Thus few of the plans faced a need to take the steps called for because the trigger points had not been reached by 1979. Further, the plans seemed to be defensive—the trigger points emphasized threats and defensive steps, not opportunities and offensive moves.

Just 2 years later, though, several contingency plans had been put into effect. The economic recession and inflationary gasoline prices cut heavily into recreational sales. Apparently these triggers were severe enough to lead to rather significant changes in the business definition, and the contingency plans provided some guidance for its direction. In 1981 AMF sold the Head Sports Wear Division and Harley Davidson and discontinued a number of product lines. After these moves, there was almost a 50-50 balance between leisure products and industrial products. Since then, the firm has expanded into electronic and energy-related areas, and it purchased a biotech subsidiary. York claims that the restructuring is designed to allow AMF to "grow some in bad times and a lot in good times."

Sources: Adapted from C. J. Loomis, "AMF Vrooms into Who Knows What," *Fortune,* Apr. 9, 1979, pp. 76–88, and *The New York Times,* Apr. 8, 1981, p. D1.

have changed again, of course. But once the equipment is purchased and plans are drawn to shift to compact cars, it is hard for a capital-intensive firm like General Motors to be flexible. Contingency strategies would have required several fallback strategies when conditions worsened. Moreover, if flexibility turns into vacillation, confusion in the marketplace and within the firm can lead to problems from a lack of consistency over time. So a balance needs to be struck between providing maneuverability and maintaining a thrust toward consistent objectives over time. This is why some firms are pursuing joint ventures, subcontracting, and "network" organizations—they add flexibility.

CHOOSING INTERNATIONAL STRATEGIES [16]

The decision to engage in international markets (or retrench from them) is similar to other strategic choices. However, because this is a more complex decision, it is useful to examine how strategists consider the various options we noted in Chapter 7. Both prescriptive and descriptive approaches exist.

As we discussed in Chapter 4, risk assessments are usually made for various countries in which the strategist considers doing business. In other words, an environmental analysis, considering threats and opportunities, is a requisite first step. But the usual internal assessment must incorporate the additional dimension of existing capabilities (personnel, production, management, and so on) from an international perspective. For example, what strengths and weaknesses exist in the firm for operating in foreign locations, and what are the abilities of the firm vis-à-vis domestic *and* foreign competition?

Once these factors are analyzed, tools similar to those described earlier can be applied. For example, Exhibit 8.19 shows a matrix used by Ford Tractor International to help it decide where to invest, divest, engage in joint venture, and so on. Such a matrix, which is a country portfolio, is similar to a product-portfolio matrix. Ford defined its country attractiveness scale as:

Market size [+] (2 [x] market growth) [+] (0.5 [x] price control/regulation [+] 0.25 [x] nontariff barriers [+] 0.25 [x] local content compensatory export requirements) [+] (0.35 [x] inflation [+] 0.35 [x] trade balance [+] 0.3 [x] political factors)

EXHIBIT 8.19 **Key country matrix.**
(G. D. Harrell and R. O. Kiefer, "Multinational Strategic Market Portfolio," MSU Business Topics [Winter 1981], pp. 5–15. Reprinted by permission.)

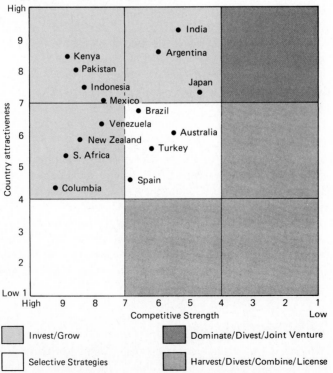

Ford defined its competitive strength as:

2 [x] (0.5 [x] absolute market share [+] 0.5 [x] industry position) [+] product fit [+] (0.5 [x] profit per unit [+] 0.5 [x] profit percentage of net dealer cost) [+] market support

Other techniques exist, of course, and vary with strategic requirements. As before, any tool is only as good as the assumptions which underlie it.

Recall from Chapter 7 that firms will often use a sequential strategy to enter foreign markets, and may seek foreign "partners" at some stage. In this case, the choice problem is compounded by the strategic desires of the foreign party. Davidson provides a way to help evaluate possible strategies when such negotiations become necessary. Exhibit 8.20 indicates that approaches will depend on whether the interests of the host country party are similar to or different from those of the focal firm. For example, if the focal firm has a declining product in domestic markets, but chooses to seek foreign markets, it is not likely to seek a joint venture or ultimately invest overseas. In such a case, it may want to license a foreign partner. But the nature of the license sought by the host country partner will vary according to whether it sees the business opportunity as one presently related to its core, or as one expected to become a related business in the future. The focal firm can usually expect nothing better than minority participation if its future business resides in the core businesses of the host partner. Empty cells for the focal firm in its core business mean that the firm would risk developing a wholly owned subsidiary (direct independent foreign investment or acquisition). While the tool illustrated in Exhibit 8.20 can be helpful, factors such as marketing expertise, technological emphasis, and relative financial strength between the parties are not considered, even though these can be important in determining which international strategic alternative is chosen. In effect, the com-

EXHIBIT 8.20   **Negotiating selected international strategic options.**
(William H. Davidson, Global Strategic Management [New York: Wiley, 1982], p. 58. Copyright © 1982 by Wiley. Adapted with permission from John Wiley & Sons, Inc.)

Host country partner

Focal Firm	Core	Related	Future	Unrelated
Unrelated declining businesses	Exclusive current and future license (4)	Standard license (5)	Agent contrast (9)	
Future businesses	Minority joint venture (3)	Co-owned joint venture (6)	Majority joint venture (8)	
Related businesses	Co-owned joint venture (2)	Majority joint venture (7)		
Core businesses	Majority joint venture (1)			

plexity of strategic choice increases as firms consider international options, because other parties often become involved. This is a major reason why many strategists prefer to pursue internal (independent) as opposed to external international strategies when the host governments allow it. Host governments, then, can also affect the choice of which foreign locations to enter (those allowing independent action being favored *ceteris paribus*).

You should not forget that the various managerial factors we described earlier in the chapter are also involved in international strategic choice. An interesting expansion of those concepts is illustrated in Exhibit 8.21. Note that this decision model incorporates many of the factors we described in earlier chapters which play a role in strategic decision making. Here external stakeholders are expanded to include *foreign* business groups and customers, foreign governments, and so on. Note that past foreign experience and strategy, and the involvement and interest of strategists, are key factors in the process. As with all strategic choices, managerial commitment plays an important role in international decisions.

SUMMARY

This chapter completed the three-chapter unit on choice of strategy. It is focused on the height of the drama of the strategic management process: the actual choice of the strategy. *Strategic choice is the decision to select, from among the alternatives, the strategy which will best meet the enterprise's objectives.* The decision involves focusing on a few alternatives, considering the selection factors, evaluating the alternatives against these criteria, and making the actual choice.

There are a number of useful tools to aid the decision maker's thinking about which alternatives are best. Many of these are matrices based on assessments of internal and external conditions, which, depending on circumstances analyzed, lead to prescriptions for choosing one strategy or another. Yet these techniques often fail to recognize the complexity involved, and sometimes ignore realities affecting managerial decision processes. And many techniques have been developed with only the multiple-SBU unit in mind.

Strategists will choose to look at one set of strategic alternatives in first-generation planning and at multiple sets of alternatives in second-generation or contingency approaches. Where will these strategic alternatives come from? Strategists begin with alternatives which they know about or which are proposed by subordinates and which they think will work and do not involve major breaks with the past (unless the situation is dire). Thus the size of the perceived gap in performance is likely to lead to a consideration of some strategies rather than others. Two propositions are offered here:

EXHIBIT 8.21 **Process by which a firm reaches a decision to commit resources to overseas projects.**
(R. D. Robinson, International Business Management: A Guide to Decision Making [New York: Holt, 1973].)

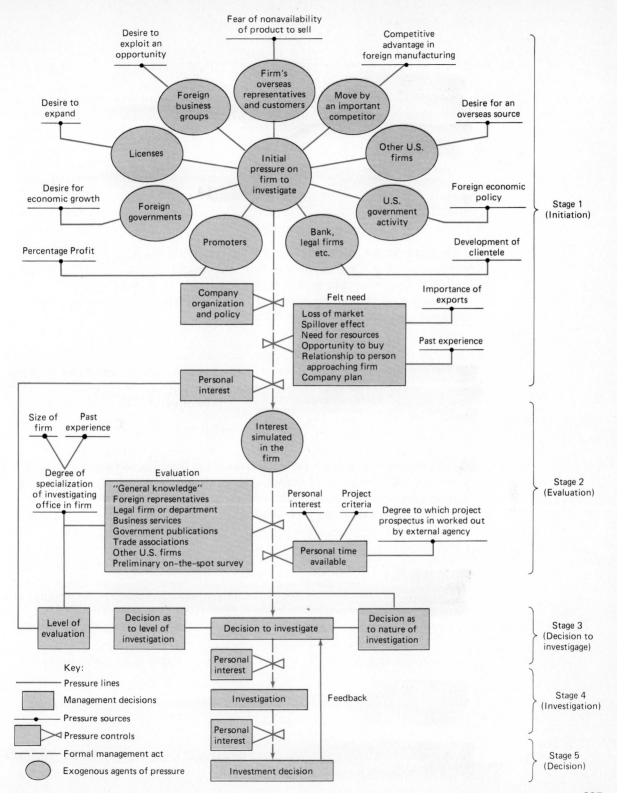

Fear of nonavailability
of product to sell

Desire to
exploit an
opportunity

Competitive
advantage in
foreign manufacturing

Desire to
expand

Desire for an
overseas source

Desire for
economic growth

Foreign economic
policy

Percentage Profit

Development of
clientele

Firm's
overseas
representatives
and customers

Foreign
business
groups

Move by
an important
competitor

Licenses

Other U.S.
firms

Foreign
governments

U.S.
government
activity

Initial
pressure on
firm to
investigate

Promoters

Bank,
legal firms
etc.

Company
organization
and policy

Felt need

Importance of
exports

Loss of market
Spillover effect
Need for resources
Opportunity to buy
Relationship to person
approaching firm
Company plan

Past experience

Personal
interest

Size of
firm

Past
experience

Interest
simulated
in the
firm

Degree of
specialization
of investigating
office in firm

Evaluation

Personal
interest

Project
criteria

"General knowledge"
Foreign representatives
Legal firm or department
Business services
Government publications
Trade associations
Other U.S. firms
Preliminary on-the-spot survey

Degree to which project
prospectus in worked out
by external agency

Personal time
available

Level of
evaluation

Decision as
to level of
investigation

Decision to investigate

Decision as
to nature of
investigation

Personal
interest

Investigation

Feedback

Personal
interest

Investment decision

Key:

Pressure lines

Management decisions

Pressure sources

Pressure controls

Formal management act

Exogenous agents of pressure

Stage 1
(Initiation)

Stage 2
(Evaluation)

Stage 3
(Decision to
investigage)

Stage 4
(Investigation)

Stage 5
(Decision)

295

> **Proposition 8.1**
>
> *If the performance gap is narrow, the alternatives considered will focus on stability and internal pace changes. If the business definition is altered, the change is likely to be passive and in a horizontal, related direction.*
>
> **Proposition 8.2**
>
> *If the performance gap is large, the alternatives will focus on expansion or retrenchment in the business definition. Active change in unrelated areas with external partners is likely. Occasionally, vertical integration will be considered.*

The nature of the gap and the types of environmental and internal conditions will determine which of the strategic alternative dimensions receives the most attention. The ETOP and SAP can be used to guide the focusing in the search for alternatives.

During the selection phase, corporate and SBU executives decide upon their preferred strategic choice. Proposition 8.3 applies here.

> **Proposition 8.3**
>
> *Effective companies hold formal meetings involving all or most of the top managers to make strategic choices and to record the criteria used.*

This is a prescriptive approach and implies the use of analytical techniques to compare alternatives with prioritized objectives. Descriptively, the actual choice may result from creeping commitment due to the influence of four managerial selection factors—dependence, risk, past strategy, and power.

> **Proposition 8.4**
>
> *The strategic choice is limited by the extent to which the firm is dependent for its survival on owners, competitors, customers, suppliers, the government, and the community.*

> **Proposition 8.5**
>
> *The more dependent the firm, the less flexibility it has in strategic choice except in crisis conditions.*

1 The more dependent the firm is on a few owners (or a family), the less flexible it is in its strategic choice.

2 The more dependent the firm is on its competitors, the less able it will be to choose an aggressive strategy. (''Dependent'' is defined as relatively weak in the competitive struggle.)

3 The more dependent the firm is for its success and survival on a few customers and suppliers, the more responsive the effective firm will be to their wishes.

4 The more dependent the firm is on the government and community, the less responsive it will be to market conditions and owner's desires.

Three polar conditions with regard to risk can be conceived: (1) risk is necessary for success; (2) risk is a fact of life, and some risk is acceptable; (3) high risk is what destroys enterprises—it needs to be minimized. Where the firm's managers fall along these attitudes about risk determines how innovative or risky the strategic choice will be. The manager's attitudes eliminate some strategic alternatives and highlight others. The volatility of the industry and the internal conditions of the firm affect the risk factor also.

Proposition 8.6

The strategic choice is affected by the relative volatility of the market sector the firm chooses to operate in. The more volatile the sector, the more flexible the strategic response needs to be in effective organizations.

Past strategies are the beginning point of strategic choice and therefore may eliminate some strategic choices.

In the next dimension of the strategic choice process, power relationships are a key reality in determining which choice is made. Personalities get involved—whom the boss likes and respects has a lot to do with which strategic choice is made. And lower level managers and workers' representatives can exert power within the firm to influence the choice process. Combined with the power aspects of dependence, then, internal and external coalitions serve to constrain choices and managerial discretion in decision making.

Finally, the timing of desired outcomes and the amount of time the decision maker has in which to make the strategic decision influence the final choice too.

Since the actual choice process is so complex, the model given in Exhibit 8.16 attempts to explain how the strategist focuses on less than all the possible choices. This model is used to suggest a procedure which attempts to integrate the managerial factors with the prescriptions for the use of analytical devices (Exhibit 8.17). In effect, the decision maker considers choices closest to the present strategy and incrementally moves from the most preferred strategies to the least preferred (riskier, less politically acceptable, and involving greater dependence). The decision maker stops when it appears that the gap has been closed.

Since conditions affecting the above process may change at any given moment, instead of relying on a single corporate plan with perhaps one or two variations, more and more top managers are getting a whole battery of contingency plans and alternate scenarios prepared. Anticipatory flexibility is urged as a response to the need for some consistency over time.

As with other strategies, the choice to engage in international activities is a difficult one. But added complexity is involved, since a wider range of external and internal characteristics need analysis, and since multiple parties are often involved. Various prescriptive tools can assist the strategist considering international options. But the managerial factors affecting commitment to this strategy must be carefully considered.

Now that the strategic choice has been made, what comes next? Chapters 9 through 11 describe the implementation of strategy. But our discussion of the role of past strategy and internal power relationships should make you realize that implementation may itself be a factor limiting the strategic choice. For convenience, it comes next sequentially. But the past strategy being implemented now affects the strengths and weaknesses of the firm, which in turn influence the new strategy. So remember that the model of the strategic management process requires a consideration of implementation as a component in strategic choice and the analysis stage. A strategy which can't be implemented would be a poor choice indeed.

REFERENCES

[1] Strategic Decision Making

Bateman, T. S., and C. P. Zeithaml: "The Context of Strategic Decision," *Academy of Management Proceedings* (1985), pp. 2–6.

Mintzberg, H., et al.: "The Structure of Unstructured Decision Process," *Administrative Science Quarterly,* vol. 21 (June 1976), pp. 246–275.

Shrivastava, P., and J. H. Grant: "Empirically Derived Models of Strategic Decision Making Processes," *Strategic Management Journal,* vol. 6 (1985), pp. 97–114.

[2] Focusing Alternatives

"Bayuk Cigars Inc. Holders Approve Liquidation Plan," *The Wall Street Journal,* Dec. 14, 1981, p. 11.

"Japanese Heat on the Watch Industry," *Business Week,* May 5, 1980, pp. 92–106.

Proctor, T.: "Theory of Search," *Journal of Management Studies* (February 1978), pp. 56–67.

[3] Techniques for Corporate-Level Strategy Choices

Allen, G.: "A Note on the Boston Consulting Group Concept of Competitive Analysis and Corporate Strategy" (Boston: Intercollegiate Case Clearing House, no. 9-175-175, 1976).

Emshoff, J. R., and A. Finnel: "Defining Corporate Strategy: A Case Study Using Strategic Assumptions Analysis," *Sloan Management Review,* vol. 20 (Spring 1979), pp. 41–52.

Field, A. R.: "Programs That Make Managers Face the Facts," *Business Week,* Apr. 8, 1985, p. 74.

Reimann, Bernard C.: "Strategy Valuation in Portfolio Planning: Combining Q and ROI Ratios," *Planning Review* (January 1986), pp. 18–45.

Staw, B. M.: "Knee-Deep in the Big Muddy: A Study of Escalating Commitment to a Chosen Course of Action," *Organizational Behavior and Human Performance,* vol. 16 (June 1976), pp. 27–44.

Wedley, W. C.: "New Uses of Delphi in Strategy," *Long Range Planning,* vol. 10 (December 1977), pp. 70–78.

[4] Prescriptions for Expansion—Market Share Imperatives

Anderson, C., and F. I. Paine: "PIMS: A Reexamination," *Academy of Management Review,* no. 3 (July 1978), pp. 602–612.

Cooper, A. C., G. Willard, and C. Woo: "Strategies of High-Performing New and Successful Firms," paper presented at the Strategic Management Society Conference, Philadelphia, 1984.

Fruhan, W., Jr.: *The Fight for Competitive Advantage: A Study of U.S. Domestic Trunk Airlines* (Cambridge, Mass.: Harvard University Press, 1972).

Hambrick, D. C., and D. Lei: "Toward an Empirical Prioritization of Contingency Variables for Business Strategy," *Academy of Management Journal,* vol. 28 (1985), pp. 763–788.

Perspectives on Experience (Boston: Boston Consulting Group, 1970).

Ramanujam, V., and N. Venkatraman: "An Inventory and Critique of Strategy Research Using the PIMS Database," *Academy of Management Review,* vol. 9 (1984), pp. 138–151.

Rink, D. R., and J. E. Swan: "Product Life Cycle Research: A Literature Review," *Journal of Business Research,* vol. 7 (September 1979), pp. 219–242.

Schoeffler, S., et al.: "Impact of Strategic Planning on Profit Performance," *Harvard Business Review* (March–April 1974), pp. 137–145.

Wensley, R.: "PIMS and BCG: New Horizons or False Dawn?" *Strategic Management Journal,* vol. 3 (1982), pp. 147–158.

Woo, C., and A. C. Cooper: "Strategies of Effective Low Share Businesses," *Strategic Management Journal,* vol. 2 (1981), pp. 301–318.

[5] Prescriptions for Retrenching

Bibeault, D. B.: *Corporate Turnaround* (New York: McGraw-Hill, 1982).

Ellis, J. E., W. Glasgall and A. Dunkin: "Mobil Tries to Make the Best of a Bad Buy," *Business Week,* May 20, 1985, p. 61.

Hamermesh, R. G., and S. B. Silk: "How To Compete in Stagnant Industries," *Harvard Business Review,* vol. 57 (September–October 1979), pp. 161–168.

Harrigan, K. R.: *Strategies for Declining Businesses* (Lexington, Mass.: Heath, 1980).

Hofer, C. W.: "Turnaround Strategies," *The Journal of Business Strategy,* vol. 1 (Summer 1980), pp. 19–31.

Platt, H. D.: *Why Companies Fail* (Lexington, Mass.: Lexington, 1984).

"Survival in the Basic Industries," *Business Week,* Apr. 26, 1982, pp. 74–84.

Willard, G. E., and A. C. Cooper: "Survivors of Industry Shake-Outs," *Strategic Management Journal,* vol. 6 (1985), pp. 299–318.

[6] Prescriptions for Stability

Peters, T. J., and R. H. Waterman, Jr.: *In Search of Excellence* (New York: Harper & Row, 1983).

[7] Combination Strategy Choice

Ohmae, K.: *The Mind of the Strategist: The Art of Japanese Business* (New York: McGraw-Hill, 1982).

Pauly, D., and T. Namuth: "The Pleasures of Privacy," *Business Week,* Mar. 19, 1984, p. 73.

[8] Managerial Choice Factors

Katz, D., and R. Kahn: *The Social Psychology of Organizations* (New York: Wiley, 1978).
Quinn, J. B.: *Strategies for Change: Logical Incrementalism* (Homewood, Ill.: Irwin, 1980).
Zeleny, M.: "Managers without Management Science?" *Interfaces,* vol. 5 (1975), pp. 35–40.
Note: Also see Chapter 1 references on Decision Making.

[9] Perceptions of Dependence Affect Choices

Murray, E., Jr.: "Strategic Choice as a Negotiated Outcome," *Management Science,* vol. 24 (May 1978), pp. 960–972.
Pfeffer, J., and G. Salancik: *The External Control of Organizations: A Resource Dependence Perspective* (New York: Harper & Row, 1978).

[10] Risk Attitudes and Strategic Choices

Anderson, C. R., and F. T. Paine: "Managerial Perceptions and Strategic Behavior," *Academy of Management Journal,* vol. 18 (December 1975), pp. 811–822.
Baird, I. S., and H. Thomas: "Toward a Contingency Model of Strategic Risk Taking," *Academy of Management Review,* vol. 10 (1985), pp. 230–243.

[11] The Influence of Past Strategy on Choices

Byrne, J. A.: "Should Companies Groom New Leaders or Buy Them?" *Business Week,* Sept. 22, 1986, pp. 94–96.
Jauch, L. R., T. N. Martin, and R. N. Osborn: "Top Management under Fire," *Journal of Business Strategy,* vol. 1 (Spring 1981), pp. 33–41.
Miles, R. E., and C. C. Snow: *Organizational Strategy: Structure and Process* (New York: McGraw-Hill, 1978).
Miller, D., and P. H. Friesen: "Archetypes of Strategy Formulation," *Management Science,* vol. 24 (May 1978), pp. 921–933.
———— and ————: "Strategy-Making in Context: Ten Empirical Archetypes," *Journal of Management Studies,* vol. 14 (October 1977), pp. 253–280.
Mintzberg, H., et al.: "The Structure of Unstructured Decisions," working paper, Faculty of Management, McGill University, Montreal, 1974. Mimeographed.
Mitchell, R.: "Dow Chemical's Drive to Change Its Market—And Its Image," *Business Week* (June 9, 1986), pp. 92–96.
"Owens-Illinois: A Cautious Venture beyond Glass," *Business Week,* July 4, 1983, pp. 84–85.
Schwenk, C. R.: "Information, Cognitive Biases, and Commitment to a Course of Action," *Academy of Management Review,* vol. 11 (1986), pp. 298–310.
Whyte, G.: "Escalating Commitment to a Course of Action: A Reinterpretation," *Academy of Management Review,* vol. 11 (1986), pp. 311–321.

[12] Power Relationships Impact Choices

Bower, J.: *Managing the Resource Allocation Process* (Boston: Harvard Business School, 1970).
Carter, E. E.: "The Behavioral Theory of the Firm and Top Level Corporate Decisions," *Administrative Science Quarterly,* vol. 16 (1971), pp. 413–428.
Child, J.: "Organizational Structure, Environment and Performance: The Role of Strategic Choice," *Sociology,* vol. 6 (1972), pp. 1–22.

MacMillan, I., and P. E. Jones: *Strategy Formulation: Power and Politics* (St. Paul, Minn.: West, 1986).

Mintzberg, H., and J. A. Waters: "Tracking Strategy in an Entrepreneurial Firm," working paper, Faculty of Management, McGill University, Montreal, 1980.

[13] The Impact of Timing on Choices

Jamieson, D., and W. Petrusic: "Preference and the Time to Choose," *Organizational Behavior and Human Performance,* vol. 19 (June 1977), pp. 56–67.

Toy, S., E. Ehrlich, A. Bernstein, and S. Crock: "The Raiders," *Business Week,* Mar. 4, 1985, pp. 80–90.

Wernerfelt, B., and A. Karnani: "Competitive Strategy under Uncertainty," *Academy of Management Proceedings* (1984), pp. 42–46.

[14] The Overall Strategic Choice Process

Berlin, V. N.: "Administrative Experimentation: A Methodology for More Rigorous 'Muddling Through,' " *Management Science,* vol. 24 (April 1978), pp. 789–799.

Braybrooke, D., and C. Lindblom: *A Strategy of Decision* (New York: Free Press, 1963).

Fredrickson, J. W.: "Effects of Decision Motive and Organizational Performance Level on Strategic Decision Processes," *Academy of Management Journal,* vol. 28 (1985), pp. 821–843.

McCall, M. W., and R. E. Kaplan: *Whatever It Takes: Decision Makers at Work* (Englewood Cliffs, N.J.: Prentice-Hall, 1985).

[15] Contingency Strategies

Ansoff, H. I.: "Managing Strategic Surprise by Response to Weak Signals," *California Management Review,* vol. 18 (Winter 1975), pp. 21–33.

Harrigan, K. R.: *Strategic Flexibility* (New York: Lexington, 1984).

"Piercing Future Fog in the Executive Suite," *Business Week,* Apr. 28, 1975, p. 56.

"When Computer Disaster Strikes," *Business Week,* Sept. 6, 1982, p. 68.

[16] International Strategic Decisions

Davidson, W. H.: *Global Strategic Management* (New York: Wiley, 1982).

Robinson, R. D.: *International Business Management: A Guide to Decision Making* (New York: Holt, 1973).

CHAPTER OUTLINE

CHAPTER 9

IMPLEMENTATION: RESOURCE ALLOCATION, ORGANIZATION, AND THE PLANNING SYSTEM

OBJECTIVES

* To understand why firms and SBUs must implement the chosen strategy
* To learn how implementation is related to strategy
* To understand the processes of resource allocation and budgeting as they affect strategy
* To learn how the organization structure evolves with strategy
* To understand the role of a planning system in linking strategies and plans

INTRODUCTION [1]

Some of you may think that the strategic management process ended with Chapter 8. The top manager(s) made the strategic choice. Now the enterprise knows how it is going to achieve its objectives. Exhibit 9.1 reminds us that we are not through yet. The choice does not mean that the enterprise will follow the decision.

Implementation is necessary to spell out more precisely how the strategic choice will come to be. Structural and administrative mechanisms which are compatible and workable need to be established to reinforce the strategic direction chosen and provide guides for action. A good strategy without effective implementation is not likely to succeed. Closing the gap between ideal and expected outcomes requires more than making a strategic choice.

Exhibit 9.2 is one consulting group's representation of the fact that strategy formation is but one component of a network of organization activities which must be integrated to accomplish objectives. The McKinsey framework suggests that the following components must fit together to make a strategy work effectively:

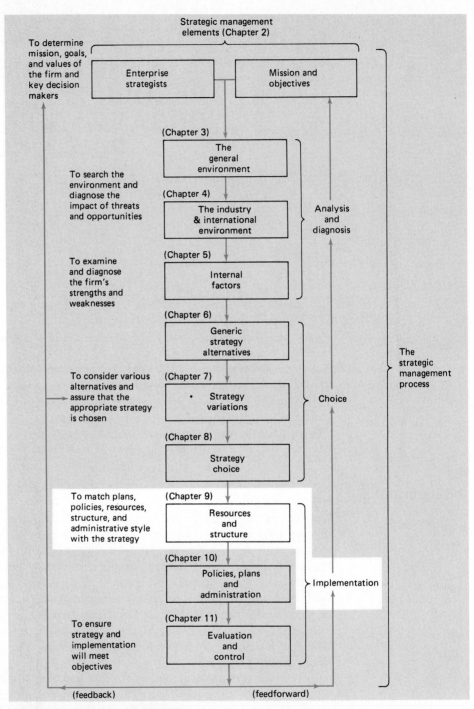

EXHIBIT 9.1   A model of strategic management.

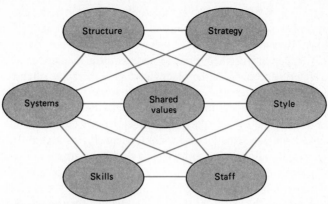

EXHIBIT 9.2   **McKinsey 7-S framework.**
(Robert H. Waterman, Jr., Thomas J. Peters, and Julien R. Phillips, "Structure Is Not Organization," Business
Horizons [June 1980], pp. 14–26.)

Final exam

1 *Strategy*. A coherent set of actions aimed at gaining a sustainable advantage over competition, improving position vis-à-vis customers, or allocating resources.

2 *Structure*. The organization chart and accompanying baggage that show who reports to whom and how tasks are both divided up and integrated.

3 *Systems*. The processes and flows that show how an organization gets things done from day to day (information systems, capital budgeting systems, manufacturing processes, quality control systems, and performance measurement systems all would be good examples).

4 *Style*. Tangible evidence of what management considers important by the way it collectively spends time and attention and uses symbolic behavior. It is not what management says is important; it is the way management behaves.

5 *Staff*. The people in an organization. Here it is very useful to think not about individual personalities but about corporate demographics.

6 *Shared values* (or superordinate goals). The values that go beyond, but might well include, simple goal statements in determining corporate destiny. To fit the concept, these values must be shared by most people in an organization.

7 *Skills*. A derivative of the rest. Skills are those capabilities that are possessed by an organization as a whole as opposed to the people in it.

Implementation involves a number of interrelated choices and activities. The resources of the enterprise must be allocated to reinforce the strategic choice, and the organization of the SBUs and corporation must reflect the strategy and objectives. The right strategists must be in charge of the SBUs and in key leadership positions to see that the strategy will work. The functional strategies and short- and medium-range policies must be developed such that they are consistent with the strategic choice. And some system is needed to link strategies with plans for implementation. Otherwise, the strategy that has been chosen will never see the light of day.

For example, joint ventures became an extremely popular strategy in the 1980s.

Yet 7 out of 10 of those ventures didn't meet objectives or were disbanded. One of the major problems has been that executive investment in implementation has been weak. Executives devoted 23 percent of their time to developing a joint venture, but only 8 percent of their time to setting up a management system to implement the strategy. Moreover, in the planning stages, there has often been inattention to making sure that the "parents" agree about how the "child" is to be operated.

We have split the implementation activities into the next three chapters. As with the rest of the model, they are in fact related closely to one another, and decisions about each are usually made simultaneously, as Exhibit 9.2 suggests. That is, resources are allocated to units which should be structured in such a way that they can effectively use the resources. At the same time, policies about the use of those resources are being established by managers in such a way, it is hoped, that the intended strategy will be accomplished. This chapter focuses on the resource allocation and organizational and planning system aspects of implementation, while Chapter 10 emphasizes the development of policies and administrative processes. Chapter 11 describes the control and evaluation system for integrating and following through on plans. As each topic is examined, however, remember that all the activities must be consistent if the firm is to operate effectively.

THE IMPLEMENTATION PROCESS [2]

In the conclusion for Chapter 8 we noted that there is a link between implementation and choice of strategy. That is, the chosen strategy must be put into action. Thus choice of strategy itself is constrained by the ability to alter past resource commitments, organizational structures, policies, and administrative systems. If the strategy calls for major alterations in these areas, strategists must be willing and able to change and make plans to do so. If the strategy choice process is to be effective, the implementation process must go hand in hand.

Exhibit 9.3 shows another way the process of implementation can be viewed. In the next three chapters we will discuss each of the topics identified in the flowchart. The "flow" itself is somewhat arbitrary in that there is not necessarily a *sequence* of activities. As with strategy formation, these aspects of implementation are interdependent. Also, note that implementation flows *from and into* the determination of strategy. Strategy formation and implementation are interdependent. Remember that in most cases, policies, structures, reward systems, and so on, are already in place. As such, this affects strategy formation.

Exhibit 9.4 indicates the roles various strategists usually play in the process of strategy implementation. For instance, the board would act if major organizational changes were needed, such as replacing a CEO or establishing different structures. The board would also be involved in approving major resource allocation decisions such as a merger or new-plant construction. Top managers are setting goals and strategies and negotiating with SBU managers, who will be pushing for the acceptance of their objectives and strategies and resource needs. However, SBU and corporate top managers have primary responsibility for deciding where to allocate resources,

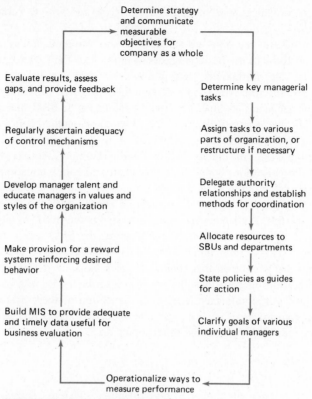

EXHIBIT 9.3 **Strategic implementation process.**

EXHIBIT 9.4 THE ROLE OF STRATEGISTS IN STRATEGY IMPLEMENTATION

Strategists	Resource allocation and organizing	Setting policies and administrative systems
Corporate top managers	Decide	Decide
SBU top managers	Decide for their units	Decide for their units
Corporate planners	Advise	Advise, and help manage planning system
Board of directors	Approves major changes	Rarely involved
Consultants	Occasionally hired to advise	Often hired to advise.

how to organize, what policies to establish, and how to coordinate and control the system.

Once basic decisions are made, of course, implementation takes place in a cascade fashion through the basic structural hierarchy of the organization. Choices are made at corporate headquarters and communicated to the SBUs. The SBUs then choose their specific strategies and implement them into their departments. For instance, major policy decisions are made by the top manager or SBU manager. These executives may ask the corporate planning staff to work out detailed policy changes in conjunction with affected line executives. If there is a small corporate planning staff or no corporate planning staff, consultants may be hired to help out. At that point, tasks are assigned to the organization, budgets are provided, and communications through the administrative system are designed to inform people of their responsibilities. Any personnel or organization changes which might be needed must also be made.

If the firm is a single-SBU firm, one step is removed. In more decentralized firms, the primary implementation takes place at the SBU level and lower. This process requires effective communication and negotiations among all the strategists concerned.

Our last section in this chapter focuses more on designing a planning system to facilitate the interrelationships we just described. The role of a planning staff takes on particular significance here. And the design of these systems helps other implementation processes such as resource allocation and is related to the way the firm is organized. So let's examine those topics first.

RESOURCE ALLOCATION [3]

Strategists have the power to decide which divisions, departments, or SBUs are to receive how much money, which facilities, and which executives. This is what we mean by resource allocation.

Recall that in Chapter 2 we suggested that there was a difference between official and operative objectives. The resource allocation decisions are very similar in that they set the *operative* strategy for the firm. Assume, for example, that resources are allocated to existing units on some formula basis (e.g., 10 percent above last year's budget). The implicit operative strategy is pace expansion. If the official strategy is expansion in some lines of business with stability in others, then greater resource flows to areas targeted for expansion are necessary to give force to the strategy. The formula approach (such as 10 percent above last year's budget for all lines of business) would *not* reinforce such a strategy. What is important to understand is that once the strategic choice is made, resources must follow the strategy, or we haven't put our "money where our mouth is." SBU and lower managers are smart. If a firm's strategists describe a strategy in words but do not shift money and executive talent and other resources to support it, the strategy will be considered a paper strategy. As with objectives, there can be a difference between "official" and "actual" strategy. So resource allocation decisions about how much to invest in which areas of the business reinforce strategy and commit the organization to its chosen strategy. Exhibit 9.5 shows an example of this.

EXHIBIT 9.5   REALLOCATING CAT'S RESOURCES

Caterpillar Tractor Company isn't used to bad news. But after a 48-year streak in continuous profits, worldwide demand for its giant yellow machines dropped like the rocks it was used to moving. Cat is faced with excess industry capacity, eroding overseas earnings due to the dollar's value, less construction in oil-rich countries suffering from lower prices and debt-ridden third world countries, and a Japanese competitor coming on strong.

To hold its market share, Cat is changing. And with the change, Cat is altering traditional resource allocation patterns. Cat slashed its dividend 2 years in a row, to a fifth of what it was in 1982. It is shrinking costs by lowering capital investment and allocating some production responsibilities to joint-venture partners overseas. Cat closed six plants and reduced its labor force by 19% from

its 1982 level. Cat's make-or-buy decisions have been changed to alter its resource allocations among procurement and manufacturing functions. From hardly any at all, Cat now purchases over 16% of its components from overseas firms, including some who are competitors. And it has moved the sales force out of Peoria into dealer districts to convert them from order takers to sales generators—a personnel resource reallocation. Further, Cat has allocated money to a new finance subsidiary to prop up its dealers and provide customer financing.

Clearly, Cat's strategy and resource allocation patterns among stockholders, labor, operations, and personnel have been dramatically reoriented to meet the requirements of a new environment.

Source: Adapted from "A Shaken Caterpillar Retools to Take On a More Competitive World," *Business Week,* Nov. 5, 1984, pp. 91–94; and "Even American Know-How Is Headed Abroad," *Business Week,* Mar. 3, 1986, pp. 60–74.

Let's consider how resource allocation is important to several strategic options. If new-product development is seen as the key to an active offensive strategy, more funds and personnel will be needed in research and development, with the possibility of longer-term capital expenditures for a new plant or new equipment. If the strategy calls for expansion in new markets, greater flows of funds for advertising, sales personnel, and/or market research will be required. If retrenchment is under way, resource allocation is of particular significance. Care must be taken to protect units which provide long-term competitive advantages. Unfortunately, the "easy way out" is often used—everyone is cut back equally, or resource flows are reduced for units which have a longer-term payout but are short-term users of resources without commensurate revenue generation. The usual example is to cut R&D or maintenance— the very places where long-term developments may be most critical for future competitive advantage. Thus shortsighted resource allocation decisions may come at the expense of the ability to pursue a long-term strategy. Exhibit 9.6 provides an example of this problem. It is instructive that in 1986, with collapsing export markets and falling profits, Japan's industrialists slashed capital spending budgets, but fattened their R&D budgets in the face of competition from the four tigers in Asia.

Of course, resource allocation decisions are linked to objectives through the strategies being implemented. Decisions about dividend policies, for instance, are important in relation to objectives and the long-term ability to attract sources of capital. Thus how to share expected profits among investors, management, and labor and whether to reinvest in the business are important resource allocation choices with long-term strategy implications. As we suggested in Chapters 2 and 3, many influences are at work during the formulation of objectives and strategies. External parties play a major

In October of 1979, it looked like Archie McCardell's turnaround plan for International Harvester was taking hold. A cost-cutting campaign had saved the firm $460 million in 2 years, helping the firm reach a 15-year high: an after-tax margin of 4.4% on earnings of $370 million. On November 1, 1979, the bubble burst when 36% of the work force went out on strike. McCardell chose to hold firm against the UAW and demanded work-rule concessions to further hold the line on costs. Union officials perceived this as "an outgrowth of McCardell's overzealousness in slashing costs." McCardell eliminated 11,000 jobs of the 15,000 he wanted to cut when he joined the company.

What is interesting is that the image of McCardell in the investment community caused problems in raising needed capital. He was "roundly criticized for cutting costs at Xerox at the expense of product innovation." His plan, despite the strike, was to forge ahead with increased R&D spending and a newly centralized team for new-product development. But reports of Harvester's troubles in late 1981 indicated that capital markets remained skeptical.

After a long strike, "McCardell may find his challenge not in cost reduction, research, or modernization, but in winning back customers taken by competitors." Indeed, the cost-cutting campaign in the interest of short-term gains did not result in the kind of turnaround required—one yielding longer-term benefits. McCardell lost his job in 1982. By 1985, IH had declared bankruptcy and Navistar emerged from the ashes as a very different firm from the old IH.

Source: Adapted from "International Harvester: When Cost-Cutting Threatens the Future," *Business Week,* Feb. 11, 1980, pp. 98–100.

role. For instance, government regulations may require a firm to invest large amounts of capital in "nonproductive" assets such as pollution-control equipment. Influential stockholders may force the firm to make greater dividend payouts. Thus the strategic agenda is partially set by the factors influencing the setting of objectives, since they will limit the resources available for implementing strategy as expressed in the allocation decisions. Finally, resource allocation is linked to the development of competitive advantage. In Chapter 5 we discussed some approaches to developing distinctive competence. It is presumed that those approaches were considered during strategy formulation. The key here is to make sure that preferential distribution of capital goes to the most critical units—the units where the strategy is directed at creating competitive advantages.

Tools for Allocating Resources [4]

In Chapter 8 we discussed the BCG product portfolio matrix. This is one tool that strategists can use to link resource allocation decisions to choices of strategy. If you recall, several prescriptions for investment and cash flow decisions were made depending on the type of SBU identified in the matrix. Thus "cash cows" are SBUs from which resources can be obtained for allocation to "question marks" or "stars." Of course, we suggested that there are several problems with this approach for strategic choice, and they apply here as well. For instance, resource allocation for new SBUs with initially low market shares might be overlooked. But for multiple-SBU firms this is one tool to aid thinking about how to allocate resources.

The primary approach to resource allocation in the implementation process is through the budgeting system. One system for budgeting resources within one firm is the product life cycle budgeting system used by Lear Siegler. This firm believes that the product life cycle of the product lines should influence its budgeting of resources. It believes that cash flow, departmental expenses, revenues, and capital expenditures should vary during the cycle. Therefore the balance sheets and income statements should look different at different stages of the cycle. The firm suggests adjusting resources accordingly. Thus to the extent that the product life cycle influences strategy, budgets tied to such a cycle will affect the product strategy. Others agree with this approach and suggest that zero-based budgeting is particularly useful when retrenchment strategies are being used.

From a long-term perspective, the capital budget is very critical. Here, plans for securing and distributing capital for large-scale investments are needed to accomplish strategy. Mergers, introductions of major new product lines, an increase in plant capacity, and vertical integrations are key mission changes which will require long-term capital investment decisions.

The more routine year-to-year allocation decisions are made within this context. But they are also important for making sure that the strategic direction of the firm is being followed, and they serve as a guide to future strategy. So let's look at this budget process in more detail.

Remember that resource allocation as expressed in the budget needs to be carefully linked to strategy. Exhibit 9.7 shows one explanation of how these can be linked in a multiple-SBU firm. Note that the process will involve planning at various levels in a back-and-forth fashion over time. In a series of negotiations among managers at the SBU and corporate levels, the strategy and plans to implement it are worked out. The final output is a set of budgets which give force to the overall plan. Let's look at these stages of the budgeting process in a bit more detail.

EXHIBIT 9.7   **A framework for the strategic budgeting process.**

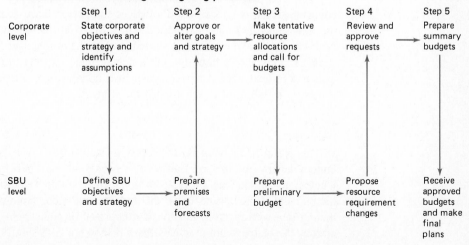

Step 1

Top management initiates the budgeting process. It does this by communicating the objectives of the firm for the period. It also announces the assumptions it uses—the predicted economic and competitive conditions, for instance—to set these objectives.

Of the various internal planning premises and assumptions which must be formulated, the sales forecast is clearly the most fundamental. Indeed, since anticipated product demand must be determined before budgets and plans for resource inputs are made, the sales forecast is typically cited as the basis or "key" for all internal planning. Among other things, the sales forecast is the basis for production planning, materials planning, capital planning, cash-flow analysis, personnel planning, and advertising and sales promotion planning. Moreover, projected sales, in whatever form—tax revenues for a city, dollar output for a company, or donations for a charity—constitute the revenue side of an organization's income statement. Thus on the basis of forecasted sales, an organization is able to project production requirements, establish what materials need to be purchased, determine the number of personnel to be recruited, estimate the level and timing of required financial resources, and decide what it can afford in the way of operating expenses (such as those for advertising and sales promotion) for the purpose of exacting a certain profit level.

Step 2

The budget department (in large firms) or administrator communicates information and offers advice to the units preparing the budgets. This unit prepares the forms and procedures for developing a budget. It helps those preparing budgets with technical problems and in the actual preparation. If there are budget specialists at the division level, it trains these persons and coordinates their work.

Step 3

Each unit prepares a preliminary budget for the next period. Normally the unit begins with the previous period's budget and performance against this budget. Next the unit states how the next period will differ from the current period. So the next year's budget that the unit proposes is based on the past budget plus or minus expected changes. This shows how the unit's management expects to achieve its objectives. This is a critical stage if strategic change is taking place. The unit must specify what resources it will need to accomplish the strategy.

Step 4

The preliminary budgets developed in step 3 are reviewed and approved. The budget department analyzes and reviews each unit's past performance and determines whether its projections are realistic given likely future conditions. After comparing the budgets of the various units, the budget department submits them to top management along with recommendations for approval or adjustment. Top management examines the budgets and approves them if they are consistent with past performance, anticipated revenues, and the firm's strategy.

This is the stage at which the resource allocation choice will be made. Who gets the money to hire more people, buy new furniture or machinery, or build a new building? In most enterprises resources are scarce, and not every unit can be given what it wants (and says it needs). The allocation of funds can be crucial to the success of a unit (and to the career of its manager). Loss of marketing funds for TV spots at a strategic time, for example, can wreck a unit's results. Because the decisions involved are so difficult, they are often made by a budget committee or a number of managers.

Step 5

At this stage summary budgets are usually prepared. Projected receipts and expenses are put together, and subsidiary budgets are developed—for example, the operating budget, financial budgets, the capital budget, and expense budgets. The operating budget specifies materials, labor, overhead, and other costs. Financial budgets project cash receipts and disbursements; the capital budget projects major additions or new construction. The expense budgets project expenses not covered in other budgets, such as marketing costs. Finally, in the summary budget (profit and loss or income statement), the total obtained by combining the subsidiary budgets is subtracted from the projected receipts. The remainder is a profit or loss. If the budgets meet objectives, approvals are made, and the budgets are enacted. If changes are needed, negotiations will take place.

The mechanics of preparing capital and operating budgets are beyond our purview. But this process is important, as it relates to the formation and implementation of strategy. Through the entire process, a variety of real problems of relevance to strategists often emerge. Estimating both revenues and costs is very difficult. In the case of an automaker, for example, how many new cars will the company sell? This depends on a number of factors, such as the economy, competitors' products, and how consumers evaluate its product in comparison with competing products. The company's pricing policy and marketing image affect this estimate, as do product quality, engineering, and the aggressiveness and reliability of dealers. Managers often handle this problem by making their best guesses—"ball-park" estimates. Sometimes they miss. The point is, the issues we addressed earlier affect budget preparation.

Moreover, the question of who gets the most money from the budget has a major effect on the work environment as well as on the careers of managers. If, as a manager, you "lose the budget battle," your employees will have to do more work with fewer helpers and less desirable equipment. They will feel that you have failed them, and they will treat you accordingly. This is one of the problems with using the product portfolio approach. Few managers want to have their units known as dogs or cash cows. It is also a problem affecting retrenchment strategies. Negotiations to protect a unit in the budget battle may come at the expense of pursuing a strategy in the best interests of the overall organization. Indeed, gamesmanship, overstatement of real budget needs, and even secrecy can lead to highly political budget battles across departments.

Another problem is that the usual budget process tends to be designed for allocating resources to existing departments or various investment proposals. These may or may not be tied to strategic changes desired by the organization; if they are not, then the budget process reinforces existing resource allocation patterns.

The budget process itself can lead to problems if it is not tied to the strategic direction of the firm. In fact, the process sets the operative strategy as we suggested earlier. So if lower levels are unaware of shifts in strategic direction, and if top managers fail to communicate strategic change or are weak negotiators, any intended strategy change is unlikely to take place.

Finally, you should note that the budget process is tied to the way units and divisions are arranged organizationally. New SBUs can be at a disadvantage if they are unaware of the "ins and outs" of the budget procedures used in their organization. And if truly major strategic shifts are occurring, the structure is likely to change along with the way resources are allocated. So let's turn to the second aspect of implementation—structuring for strategy implementation.

ORGANIZATIONAL IMPLEMENTATION [5]

Strategic management posits that the strategy and the organization structure used by the firm must match. In essence, the top manager looks at the organization now and asks, Do we have the right organization for our strategy? As Exhibit 9.8 suggests, structural change may be needed when organizations experience problems or are faced with strategic shifts.

Organization involves dividing up the work among groups and individuals (division of labor) and making sure that the parts are linked together in such a way that they will work together effectively (coordination).

EXHIBIT 9.8   THE GM OVERHAUL

General Motors has had a long presence in Europe. Vauxhall (Britain) was acquired in 1925, and Opel (Germany) was bought in 1929. GM operates in 17 European countries. Yet, recently, GM has had trouble wringing profits from those countries. Many blame its difficulties on its organization structure.

Prior to 1986, Opel executives were responsible for design and engineering functions throughout Europe, including Vauxhall. But there have been squabbles over investment and marketing decisions. General Motors poured $6 billion into automating its plants and bringing out new models. And it has increased its market share in Europe. Yet it still lags Ford in profits, and is fending off Japanese imports.

In effect, with the split between Vauxhall and Opel,

European operations suffered from the lack of "a coherent strategy and strong management." In 1986 GM determined it would end its European losses. It has created a European headquarters (GM-Europe) in Zurich. It has moved 100 executives from Opel Germany and about 100 from Vauxhall Britain and other European operations to its new headquarters. GM executives in Detroit believe this new approach will improve coordination and planning, and eliminate the country-by-country decision making on pricing, marketing, and cost cutting.

While critics suggest that merely moving key players to one location may not solve its woes, apparently GM is trying to foster a link between strategy and structure to accomplish its goal of improving profits.

Source: Adapted from "General Motors' Big European Overhaul," *Business Week,* Feb. 10, 1986, pp. 42–43.

Thus several basic questions are being addressed by the managers:

1 What tasks are needed to accomplish the strategy?
2 To whom should these tasks be assigned?
3 To what extent are these tasks interdependent?
4 How can we be sure that the tasks assigned will be performed?

The first two questions deal with dividing up labor. The latter two address issues of coordination and control. In this chapter we emphasize division of labor through resouce allocation and departmentation. Chapters 9 and 10 examine administrative systems for coordination and control. Again, our separation of these is "artificial" in that the structure and style must work together to be effective.

Basic Structures for Strategy [6]

The effective organizer tries to group duties into meaningful subunits while avoiding duplication of efforts or excessive specialization, which can lead to boredom or tunnel vision in the enterprise's executives. Cannon, a long-time consultant with McKinsey & Company, put it this way:

> The experience of McKinsey supports the view that neither strategy nor structure can be determined independently of the other. . . . Strategy can rarely succeed without an appropriate structure. In almost every kind of large-scale enterprise, examples can be found where well-conceived strategic plans were thwarted by an organization structure that delayed the execution of the plans or gave priority to the wrong set of considerations. . . . Good structure is inseparably linked to strategy.

There is a great deal of research which indicates that when the strategy is properly implemented with the right organization structure, the firm is more effective. For example, Chandler found that when firms shifted their strategies to diversification, they had to change their organization to a divisional form. In studying Swedish firms, Rhenman found that problems result from an inability or unwillingness to adapt the organization after strategic changes. Many other studies have found this linkage.

But the basic question has been raised: Which structure for which strategy? First let's review the kinds of structures which evolve. The emphasis here is on the horizontal division of labor, or forms of departmentation.

Department Evolution [7]

Organization structures evolve with changes in strategy. In the smallest enterprises, it is hard to determine much of an organization other than the boss and employees. As the enterprise develops and more and more employees are added, the first type of organization which arises is the functional type, as shown in Exhibit 9.9. In a firm organized by functional departments, the boss groups employees by the type of work the enterprise does: production and operations (goods and services), accounting and finance (money), personnel (people), research and development (ideas, new ways of doing things), and environmental relations (marketing, public relations, etc.). This

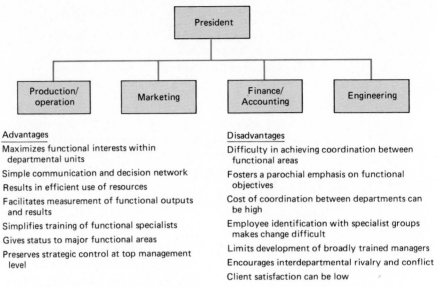

Advantages	Disadvantages
Maximizes functional interests within departmental units	Difficulty in achieving coordination between functional areas
Simple communication and decision network	Fosters a parochial emphasis on functional objectives
Results in efficient use of resources	
Facilitates measurement of functional outputs and results	Cost of coordination between departments can be high
Simplifies training of functional specialists	Employee identification with specialist groups makes change difficult
Gives status to major functional areas	Limits development of broadly trained managers
Preserves strategic control at top management level	Encourages interdepartmental rivalry and conflict
	Client satisfaction can be low

EXHIBIT 9.9   Firm organized by functional departments.

structure is believed to maximize economies of scale and specialization. However, the coordination and integration of units are often problems. Firms pursuing stability or pace expansions are quite likely to use the functional form.

If the enterprise grows by expanding the *variety* of operations it performs, then another level of management is inserted above the functional level, and thus the divisional (or multidivisional) structure is developed (Exhibit 9.10). It is thought that this structure maximizes the coordination of the subunits and increases the speed of response to changes in the environment. A basic problem, though, is that there tends to be less concern for efficiency and greater goal emphasis at the divisional level than in the overall system, as suggested by Exhibit 9.11.

Note that the divisional structure in Exhibit 9.10 is based on a product-oriented strategy. But the strategy could call for emphasis on markets, and thus divisions would be arranged by client type or territories. For instance, a firm might divide its operations into industrial, governmental, and retail sales divisions, as in Exhibit 9.12. Here, the strategy may be to rely on the internal ability to service specific customer needs.

Most large organizations which are geographically dispersed also specialize by territory. Exhibit 9.13 might represent a firm pursuing a multinational expansion strategy. In very large firms, especially multinationals, combinations of these forms are quite likely.[8]

Some very complex organizations can take one or both of two more steps. The first concerns the matrix organization. In firms whose products change frequently and are short-lived (especially defense firms), functional and divisional managers may form project groups. The purpose of project development and project implementation managers is to achieve speedier responses and better coordination. The project groups

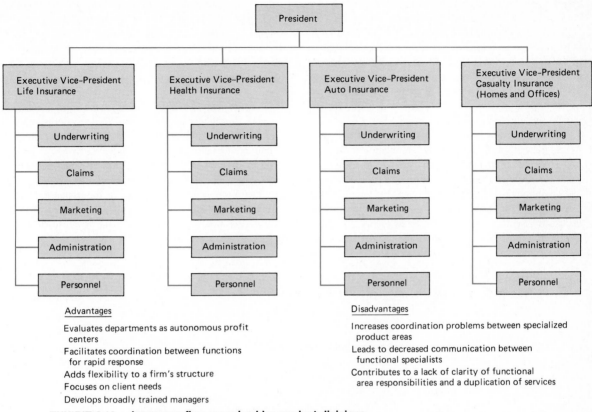

EXHIBIT 9.10   **Insurance firm organized by product divisions.**

are temporary and are scrapped when the project is completed. Exhibit 9.14 shows a firm whose strategy may involve several new venture projects.

In the most advanced organization, an innovative structure is used.[9] Fast-changing enterprises divide themselves into current business groups and innovation groups. The innovators invent and pretest products and services. Once the products and services are ready for the marketplace, they are transferred to the current business units. This amounts to creating a current business division and innovation divisions parallel to the current business division. With this form, an effort is made to combine the best features of the functional, divisional, and matrix forms of organization.

So, as the strategy changes from a single product or product line to a dominant product to related diversification to conglomerate unrelated diversification, the structure in effective organizations changes from primitive to functional to divisional or matrix. Note, then, that there seems to be a change in the forms of departmentation with the size and complexity which result from expansion strategies. But the exact way in which departments are put together needs to match the strategic direction of the firm. In this regard, many firms have begun to organize around their strategic business units, opting for a more product-oriented form of departmentation.

EXHIBIT 9.11   A PROBLEM OF INTEGRATION

In 1975 it appeared that 3M had positioned itself as a major competitor in the emerging office automation market. Acquisitions of a small word processing company with a leading edge in technology and a firm leading in facsimile devices added to 3M's already formidable base in the copier business. But 3M squandered its lead, and observers doubt that it can grasp much of a share of the $100 billion office equipment and supplies market. Fast-moving word processing firms overtook 3M, and in 1979 3M bowed out.

Some observers point to the structure and climate at 3M as the culprit. The company's reputation for innovation emanates from the autonomy granted to its 40 divisions. Each division has responsibility for its own research and development, manufacturing, and, for the most part, marketing. "But what works for Scotch tape does not necessarily work in the office." Sales to the "office-of-the-future" market seem to require a concerted, integrated "systems effort." The divisional lines giving 3M its en-

trepreneurial flair inhibit communication between product groups that would lead to the evolution of more complex office systems. The company did try to establish an office systems task force to coordinate divisional activities. But according to a former 3M executive, "the problem is 3M doesn't believe in strategic planning, so the task force really had no way to implement a plan across divisional lines."

It seems that 3M still wants to make some effort in this area through acquisitions. But the question remains as to whether it can buy companies that fit into its culture without losing its edge. Says one top executive, "If we're going to succeed in the office market, we may just have to do things like the rest of the world." If it does, will the integration of divisions come at the expense of the strengths established by its autonomous operations? Clearly, the structure at 3M will have much to do with its strategy in the future.

Source: Adapted from "3M's Problems in the Office of the Future," *Business Week,* Oct. 13, 1980, pp. 123–126.

EXHIBIT 9.12   **Firm organized by customer departments.**

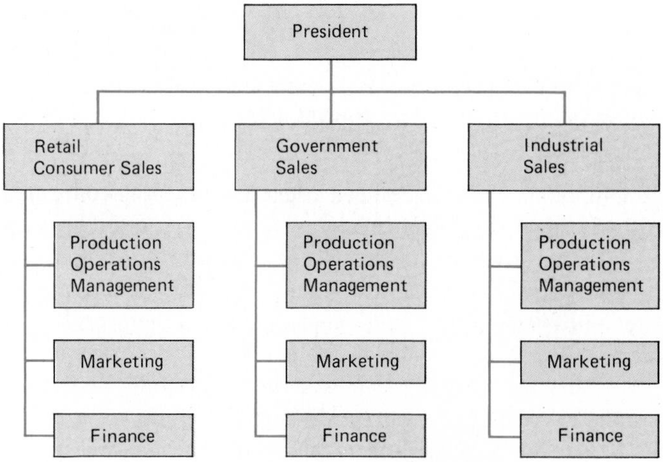

Advantages
Responds to customer needs
Ties performance to requirements of key market segments

Disadvantages
Increases difficulty of establishing uniform companywide practices
Leads to pressure for special treatment of various buyer segments
Contributes to customer groups developing at an unequal pace leading to underutilization of resources

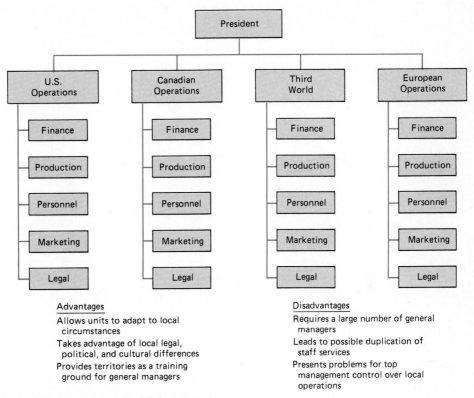

Advantages

Allows units to adapt to local
  circumstances

Takes advantage of local legal,
  political, and cultural differences

Provides territories as a training
  ground for general managers

Disadvantages

Requires a large number of general
  managers

Leads to possible duplication of
  staff services

Presents problems for top
  management control over local
  operations

EXHIBIT 9.13   **Firm organized by territorial departments.**

A few academics are promoting the idea that organization structures for the future will need to be very adaptive and open to the environment. Such structures would be more complex, with departments existing in many forms (some product-market, some limited-term-project, etc.). Decisions would need to be decentralized, and organizational structures more transitory. In effect, there is a call for structures to follow the strategic philosophy of anticipatory flexibility along several dimensions:

1 Operational flexibility—the ability to react efficiently to a change in production volume, as in the case of temporary decreases in demand

2 Strategic flexibility—the ability to change the product-market composition by means of product renewal, switching markets, acquisition, or divestment

3 Structural flexibility—the ability to change the existing structure in an easy way

Perhaps the innovative structure described before will be the next form to receive the plaudits of consultants as ''the best way'' to organize. Or perhaps the ''network'' companies now emerging will provide a new way to increase flexibility. Exhibit 9.15 indicates that some firms are becoming ''shell corporations,'' which contract out to other agents functions such as manufacturing, distribution, marketing, or even financial activities. In effect, such firms are retrenching by ''vertical disaggregation'' out

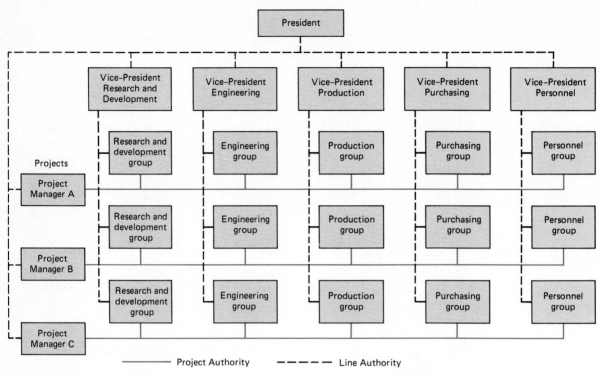

——————— Project Authority   — — — — — Line Authority

Advantages	Disadvantages
Adapts to fluctuating work loads	Places a premium on teamwork
Establishes one person as focal point for all matters pertaining to an individual project	Leads to possible conflict with existance of two separate operating systems
Permits maximum use of limited pool of functional specialists	Creates possible power struggle between project managers and functional area heads
Provides a home base for functional specialists between projects	Slows decision making and increases costs in certain instances
Makes it possible to respond to several environmental sectors simultaneously	Promotes narrow management viewpoint

EXHIBIT 9.14   **Matrix organization.**

of traditional functions, and the structures of the firms reflect this strategy. The structure comprises agents in various geographic locations linked by computer. This allows the firms to take advantage of lower-cost foreign labor and to pounce more quickly on new markets or new technologies, and offers a way to exploit some of the advantages foreign companies have. We believe the dictates of environmental and internal factors affecting strategy should be the determining factors in structural choice. Our next section explains this.

Which Organization Form Is Best? [10]

A lot of energy, blood, sweat, and tears has been spent in attempts to find the "best" organization form for all businesses. The results of all the research can be summarized

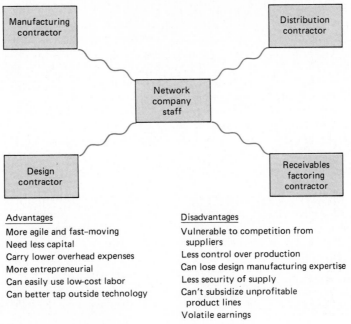

Advantages

More agile and fast-moving
Need less capital
Carry lower overhead expenses
More entrepreneurial
Can easily use low-cost labor
Can better tap outside technology

Disadvantages

Vulnerable to competition from
 suppliers
Less control over production
Can lose design manufacturing expertise
Less security of supply
Can't subsidize unprofitable
 product lines
Volatile earnings

EXHIBIT 9.15   Network organization.

as follows: An organization whose strategy has been implemented with an organization structure that fits its characteristics will be more effective than an organization whose structure does not fit its characteristics. There is no one "right" way to organize. Our previous descriptions of structures suggested that the "best" structure is related to the form of strategic advantages desired by management.

All organization forms work somewhere. So the analyses given here only represent general tendencies. In general, functional organizations work best in stable environments, with less need for cross-department coordination and communication and less need for innovation. The narrower the product line and markets, the better the functional structure works. Strategic choices determine whether products or markets are narrow or broad.

Divisional organizations work best in changing environments, which require faster adaptation, more coordination and communication, and innovation. Usually, the more complex the product line and markets, the better divisional (or even matrix) forms work. Always, strategic choices regarding complexity must be made. Exhibit 9.16 provides an example.

These guidelines should give you clues as to when a structural change is needed. For instance, if the strategy is rapid expansion through a merger, increased size may require new structures. If the strategy is to serve new markets or add unrelated products, the added complexity and diversity call for a changed structure. If the performance gap due to competition is such that retrenchment is needed, some SBUs may be dropped from the structure, or units may be recombined to gain greater

EXHIBIT 9.16   BANK OF AMERICA'S NEW STRUCTURE

Deregulation has affected the banking business dramatically. Those who could react fastest to changing customer needs and new competitors had the best chance to survive.

Bank of America has restructured in recognition that faster adaptation and better coordination and innovation are needed to face its environment. The Bank has created a new division to focus on more efficient handling of transactions. But the retail operations, including worldwide lending, deposit gathering, and other services, have not performed well enough as operating expenses have increased and some loans have gone sour.

Hence, Bank of America began reorganizing the retail bank operations in 1985. Under the new structure, the 220-person product development and marketing staff was split to focus on three market segments: individual customer accounts, personalized service for customers with sophisticated needs, and small business customers. And four newly independent sales and service units, including B of A's California branch network, national and international units, and an electronic delivery unit, will support each market group.

Under the old system, new product decisions were strictly made by senior management. And profit and loss controls were the responsibility of branch managers, who in fact had little control of overhead. The new approach attempts to spread decision-making responsibility to lower levels of the bank, and each market segment unit is responsible for profit or loss in its market. The new structure is expected to help make B of A more responsive to changes in its environment, and fits its strategic needs to reduce its image as a stodgy competitor.

Source: Adapted from "Bank America Hustles to Make Up for Lost Time—And Money," *Business Week,* Mar. 11, 1985, p. 38.

efficiency (a decrease in divisional structure). For example, General Mills divested its toy and fashion divisions, creating two new separate companies. This strategy was a function of the inability of the existing bureaucracy at General Mills to allow those divisions to quickly respond to the volatility of their markets. But many strategies can be accomplished through the existing anatomy with only fine-tuning or alterations in the administrative system which operates within the structure. Our next chapter will explore these aspects of implementation in more detail.

The final point we wish to make concerns the relationship between strategic choice and structural implementation. There is some debate about which comes first—strategy or structural change. As we indicated at the beginning of the chapter, we think that the process is circular. Structure constrains strategy to some extent. But if truly major strategic changes are made, structural change will be necessary. Exhibit 9.17 provides an example of how "misfits" between strategy and structure can create strategic problems. So the critical question is how the entire package of strategy and implementation is integrated to accomplish objectives.

Vertical Division of Labor [11]

Recognize that the emphasis here has been on forms of departmentation which tend to evolve as a strategy of expansion is put into place. Of course, the vertical structure is important also. That is, the number of levels in the hierarchy, the spans of control for managers, and the location of staff units can vary substantially. These can have an impact on strategy and vice versa. For instance, as the number of levels increases,

EXHIBIT 9.17   STRUCTURAL WOES AT DEC

Digital Equipment Corporation has more than Big Blue to contend with these days. A management reorganization has created other strategic problems for DEC.

Through 1982, DEC's structure was built around 18 separate groups that concentrated on selling to specific industries (e.g., education, engineering). This structure was originally a strength since it enabled the firm to respond quickly to customer needs. Even though most groups used the same products and components, each had discretionary funds for product development, and each handled its own market strategies, pricing, order processing, and inventories. Each group contracted with a central department for jobs needed done in manufacturing, field service, or engineering.

Eventually, these groups became fiefdoms that grew more and more protective of their own interests and lost sight of the company's long-range goals. They began fighting among themselves for limited central engineering and manufacturing resources. The process of new product development became so complex that it became difficult for DEC to move decisively.

In 1983, founder and president Kenneth Olsen per-

formed radical surgery to cut out the bureaucracy. He created 4 regional management centers to do the forecasting and sales support once done by the 18 headquarters-based groups. But the reorganization created a new set of headaches. "The corporate overhaul destroyed a delicate web of alliances that allowed people to get their jobs done in DEC's confusing matrix organization." As jobs were eliminated and reshuffled from headquarters to new jobs in regional centers, battles broke out over who was going to shoulder new responsibilities. Fifty managers from the old groups and six vice presidents left the company. Says one former manager, "The strategic direction at the top was not translated into job charters or communicated to us. It still is not clear."

As a result, forecasting, order processing, and production scheduling broke down. Manufacturing was putting out the wrong mix of products and too few disk drives rolled off the floor. Shipments to customers stalled, and inventories rose. Many customers received the wrong shipment, partial shipment, or none at all. Sales went flat.

Clearly, new strategic problems resulting from structural adaptation now face DEC.

Source: Adapted from "The Dark Side of DEC's Rebound," *Business Week,* Jan. 30, 1984, pp. 51–53.

communications become more difficult. Information needed about changes in the marketplace may take longer to reach the top. As spans of control become larger, decision making takes longer, since there is a tendency to involve more people. And as staff specialists (such as personnel, information systems, or legal specialists) or line units are centralized or decentralized, there is an impact on costs, the quality of decisions made, and the strategy itself.

The structure by itself doesn't tell you everything about how the organization functions. Mechanisms for control and coordination of units can vary within a given structure. And the power of a given subsystem manager to influence strategy or receive disproportional shares of resources may not be reflected by the organization structure, although centralizing units near the top usually gives them more clout. We will discuss some of these issues in more detail in Chapter 10. For now, it should still be clear that the structure itself can help or hinder the implementation of strategy. For instance, if departments are arranged so as to serve customer groups which are no longer significant to the future strategy of the firm, a mismatch is present, and the intended strategy is not likely to be accomplished without a reorganization. However, beware the "organization quick fix." Structural alterations are not always necessary or desirable. Our next section indicates when some changes might be needed, but don't assume that every strategy change requires an organizational accommodation.

PLANNING SYSTEMS TO IMPLEMENT STRATEGIC MANAGEMENT [12]

Exhibit 9.7 outlined one way to establish a planning system for linking the process of formulating a strategy with plans for its implementation. Of course, the assumption there was that a multidivision organization structure was in place. But mechanisms for planning differ from firm to firm. And the roles played by corporate strategists in the development of strategies, plans, and systems for integrating them also vary. In this section we will explore how planning systems have evolved and the role of planning departments in these processes.

Wrapp describes four ways in which companies organized for the planning function in the years when the use of strategic planning was gaining impetus:

1 There was a planning committee composed of top management which had responsibilities for both planning and operations; subcommittees undertook studies, while existing corporate staff groups were made available on request.

2 There was a central planning committee with subcommittees to plan specific projects; however, top-management members assigned to the committee became full-time planners with no operating responsibilities.

3 Planning was decentralized to a general manager in each division; home office staff personnel were available for assistance, but planning was primarily a divisional activity.

4 A special planning staff was charged with responsibility for developing long-range plans; this approach created the classic split between planners and doers, and the evidence indicated that line management seldom implemented completed plans.

This latter concern has prompted many firms to reduce the size of their planning staff and refocus their efforts. For example, GE slashed the corporate planning group from 58 to 33 in 1984, and purged scores of planners in various operating sectors, groups and divisions. Eaton reacted to a "rebellion against the 'planocrats' " and cut its staff from 35 to 16. The CEOs of the new generation coming to power believe they are "strategic thinkers," and think their key line operating people should be as well. Higgins puts it this way:

> To remove the planning function from the mainstream of organizational life, i.e., setting up separate staff groups, increases the probability that the planning effort will be attended to but also increases the likelihood that plans generated by such a process will be ill-suited for decision-making purposes.

Exhibit 9.18 indicates that planners can emphasize two kinds of tasks. One task is to contribute to substantive decisions about strategies and plans (*content*). The other is to perform an instrumental role in the design and implementation of a planning system (setting up the *process* in which substantive decisions are generated). Note that depending on the relative emphasis and tasks performed, planners might be viewed as catalysts (mostly involved with process), analysts, or strategists (mostly involved with content). Thus strategist roles of a planning staff could include making acquisition studies, identifying strategic options, narrowing down alternatives, and providing information about choices; or the planning staff could give advice on the relative merits of various planning documents submitted by SBU executives. The catalyst roles could

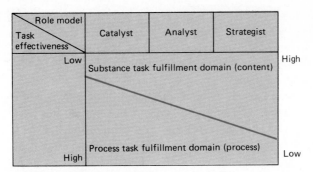

EXHIBIT 9.18 **Tasks and roles of planners.**
(P. Lorange, Corporate Planning: An Executive Viewpoint, p. 273. Copyright ©1980, Reprinted by permission of Prentice-Hall, Inc., Englewood Cliffs, N.J.)

include such activities as developing a conceptual framework for planning tailored to the needs of the organization, discussing the system with line executives, and assisting them in the use of the system (e.g., preparing planning manuals, disseminating planning calendars, distributing common planning assumptions, or arranging meetings to review interdepartmental plans).

We expect that recent changes and concerns about the "formula planning" approaches used by planning staffs, and the inability to gain commitment of the line to plans "dreamed up" by the staff, will lead to a greater focus on planning staff as catalyst for the line. This staff may perform analyses at headquarters, but the strategic decisions will be restored to those charged with implementing the plans.

SUMMARY

This is the first chapter on the implementation segment of strategic management. The implementation process involves an integrated set of choices and activities that are used to allocate resources, organize, assign key managers, set policies, and establish an administrative system to reinforce, control, and evaluate a strategy.

Proposition 9.1

A good strategy without effective implementation has a lower probability of success than if implementation decisions match strategic choices.

Strategists have the power to decide which divisions, departments, or SBUs receive what amount of money, which facilities, and which executives. These resource allocation decisions set the operative strategy of the firm.

The primary tool for making resource allocations is the budget process. A series of negotiations across organizational levels will result in final decisions about the operating budgets for SBUs or other units. Capital budgets, financial budgets, and

Final Exam

summary budgets prepared at corporate levels are established to give force to objectives and strategies intended to be accomplished. Several problems in budgeting were noted, indicating that this process can lead to unintended strategic directions if managers are not sensitive to the need to link resource deployment to activities needed to accomplish a strategy.

The second aspect of implementation discussed in this chapter is organizational implementation. Organization involves dividing up the work among groups and individuals (division of labor) and making sure that the parts are linked together to ensure that they will work together effectively (coordination).

Several propositions are useful in understanding organizational implementation, although not all would agree with these conclusions.

Proposition 9.2

As firms move from a single product to related products to unrelated diversification, effective firms move from a functional organization structure to a divisional organization structure.

Proposition 9.3

Organizations that operate in a stable environment, are small, and have a single product/ market scope will be more effective with a functional organization structure.

Proposition 9.4

Organizations which operate in a moderately dynamic environment, are large, and have diversified from a single product/market will be more effective with a divisional organization structure.

Proposition 9.5

Organizations which operate in a dynamic environment, are large, have technologically intense businesses where the economies of scale are not important, and have short-lived projects or products will be most effective with a matrix organization structure.

Proposition 9.6

Organizations which operate in a dynamic environment, are large, have intensive technologies and marketing where economies of scale are important, and assign a large percentage of the budget to innovation will be more effective with an innovative organization structure.

Which organization form is best? The best organization structure is one which fits the organization's environment and internal characteristics giving rise to a strategy. Effective strategic management suggests that the organization structure should change if strategy changes or if the organization experiences problems. We suggested some guidelines in this regard.

The last section of the chapter indicated the need to match the strategic planning system with the needs of the organization's structure and strategy. Planners tend to emphasize different roles depending on the evolution of the use of a formal planning system and the type of strategy and structure. As structure and strategy become more diverse and complex, corporate-level planners focus on catalyst roles. The line is expected to play a more significant role in the content of strategic planning in the future. The key to an effective planning system, though, is to make sure it is designed so that the strategy and implementation plans are closely integrated.

Our next chapter explores some outputs of the planning process—the policies and plans for implementing strategic choices—as well as some other administrative aspects of the strategic management system.

REFERENCES

[1] Integrating Strategy and Implementation

Bourgeois, L. J., and D. R. Brodwin: "Strategic Implementation: Five Approaches to an Elusive Phenomenon," *Strategic Management Journal,* vol. 5 (1984), pp. 241–264.

Bradford, D. L., and A. R. Cohen: *Managing for Excellence* (New York: Wiley, 1984).

Hrebiniak, L. G., and W. F. Joyce: *Implementing Strategy* (New York: Macmillan, 1984).

Levine, J. B., and J. A. Byrne: "Corporate Odd Couples," *Business Week,* July 21, 1986, pp. 100–105.

"The New Planning," *Business Week,* Dec. 18, 1978.

Note: Also see Chapter 10 references on Implementing Strategies [1]

[2] The Implementation Process

Lorange, P.: *Implementation of Strategic Planning* (Englewood Cliffs, N.J.: Prentice-Hall, 1982).

Vancil, R. F., and P. Lorange: "Strategic Planning in Diversified Companies," *Harvard Business Review* (January–February 1975), pp. 81–90.

[3] Allocating Resources

Bower, J. L.: *Managing the Resource Allocation Process: A Study of Corporate Planning and Investment* (Cambridge, Mass.: Harvard University Press, 1970).

Gluck, F.: "The Dilemmas of Resource Allocation," *The Journal of Business Strategy,* vol. 2 (Fall 1981), pp. 67–71.

Northcraft, G. B., and G. Wolf: "Dollars, Sense, and Sunk Costs: A Life Cycle Model of Resource Allocation Decisions," *Academy of Management Review,* vol. 9 (1984), pp. 225–234.

Treece, J. B.: "Companies Cut the Budget but Spare the R&D," *Business Week,* Apr. 14, 1986, p. 50.

[4] Budgeting and Other Tools for Resource Allocation

Camillus, J. C., and Grant J.H.: "Operational Planning: The Integration of Programming and Budgeting," *Academy of Management Review,* vol. 5 (1980), pp. 369–379.

Lorange, P., and R. F. Vancil: *Strategic Planning Systems* (Englewood Cliffs, N.J.: Prentice-Hall, 1977).

Savich, R. S., and J. A. Thompson: "Resource Allocation within the Product Life Cycle," *MSU Business Topics,* vol. 26 (Autumn 1978), pp. 35–44.

[5] Structuring for Strategy

Ansoff, H. I.: "The Changing Shape of the Strategic Problem," in D. E. Schendel and C. W. Hofer (eds.), *Strategic Management: A New View of Business Policy and Planning* (Boston: Little, Brown, 1979).

Chandler, A., Jr.: *Strategy and Structure: Chapters in the History of the American Industrial Enterprise* (Cambridge, Mass.: Harvard University Press, 1962).

Child, J.: "Organizational Structure, Environment and Performance: The Role of Strategic Choice," *Sociology* (January 1972), pp. 1–22.

Frederickson, J. W.: "The Effect of Structure on the Strategic Decision Process," *Academy of Management Proceedings* (1984), pp. 12–18.

Hall, D. J., and Saias M. A.: "Strategy Follows Structure!" *Strategic Management Journal,* vol. 1 (1980), pp. 149–163.

Kay, N. M.: *The Evolving Firm: Strategy and Structure in Industrial Organization* (New York: St. Martin's, 1982).

[6] Basic Structures for Strategy

Cannon, J. T.: *Business Strategy and Policy* (New York: Harcourt, Brace, 1968).

Child, J.: *Organization* (New York: Harper & Row, 1977).

Galbraith, J., and R. K. Kazanjian: *Strategy Implementation: Structure, Systems and Process* (St. Paul, Minn.: West, 1986).

Rhenman, E.: *Organization Theory for Long Range Planning* (New York: Wiley Interscience, 1973).

[7] Forms of Departmentation

Lawrence, P. R., and Lorsch J. W.: *Organization and Environment: Managing Differentiation and Integration* (Homewood, Ill.: Irwin, 1967).

Miles, R. E. and C. C. Snow: *Organizational Strategy, Structure and Process* (New York: McGraw Hill, 1978).

Sayles, L.: "Matrix Management: The Structure with a Future," *Organizational Dynamics,* vol. 5 (1976), pp. 2–17.

Thain, D. H.: "Stages of Corporate Development," *Business Quarterly* (Winter 1969), pp. 33–45.

"A U.S. Concept Revives Oki: Reorganizing into Strategic Business Units," *Business Week,* Mar. 1, 1982, pp. 112–113.

[8] Multinational Organization Structures

Brooke, M. Z.: "Multinational Corporate Structures: The Next Stage," *Futures,* vol. 11 (April 1979), pp. 111–121.

Daniels, J. D., R. A. Pitts, and M. J. Tretter: "Strategy and Structure of U.S. Multinationals: An Exploratory Study," *Academy of Management Journal,* vol. 27 (1984), pp. 292–307.

Harrigan, K. R.: "Managing Innovation within Overseas Subsidiaries," *Journal of Business Strategy,* vol. 4 (1984), pp. 4–19.

Rumelt, R. P.: *Strategy, Structure and Economic Performance* (Cambridge, Mass.: Harvard University Press, 1974).

[9] Innovative Forms of Structure

Burgelman, R. A.: "Managing the New Venture Division: Research Findings and Implications for Strategic Management," *Strategic Management Journal,* vol. 6 (1985), pp. 39–54.

Krijnen, H. G.: "The Flexible Firm," *Long Range Planning,* vol. 12 (April 1979), pp. 63–75.

Nord, W., and S. Tucker: *Implementing Routine and Radical Innovations* (Lexington, Mass.: Lexington, 1984).

Wilson, J. W., and J. H. Dobrzynski: "And Now, the Post-Industrial Corporation," *Business Week,* Mar. 3, 1986, pp. 64–71.

[10] Factors Affecting Structural Choice

Dewar, R., and J. Hage: "Size, Technology, Complexity and Structural Differentiation: Towards a Theoretical Synthesis," *Administrative Science Quarterly,* vol 23 (1978), pp. 111–136.

Horovitz, J. H., and R. A. Thietart: "Strategy, Management Design and Firm Performance," *Strategic Management Journal,* vol. 3 (1982), pp. 67–76.

[11] Vertical Division of Labor

Frederickson, J. W.: "The Strategic Decision Process and Organizational Structure," *Academy of Management Review,* vol. 11 (1986), pp. 280–297.

Osborn, R. N., J. G. Hunt, and L. R. Jauch: *Organization Theory: An Integrated Perspective* (New York: Wiley, 1980).

[12] Planning Systems

Camillus, J. C.: "Strategic Planning Systems in the Eighties: Challenging the Conventional Wisdom," paper presented at the Strategic Management Society conference, Philadelphia, 1984.

Dyson, R. G., and M. J. Foster: "The Relationship of Participation and Effectiveness in Strategic Planning," *Strategic Management Journal,* vol. 3 (1982), pp. 77–88.

Gottschalk, E. C., Jr.: "Firms Hiring New Types of Manager to Study Issues, Emerging Troubles," *The Wall Street Journal,* June 10, 1982, pp. 23, 28.

Lorange, P., and R. F. Vancil: *Strategic Planning Systems* (Englewood Cliffs, N.J.: Prentice-Hall, 1977).

"The New Breed of Strategic Planner," *Business Week,* Sept. 17, 1984, pp. 62–71.

"Sending the Staff Out to Solve Other Companies' Problems," *Business Week,* Jan. 16, 1984, pp. 54–56.

Wheelwright, S. C., and R. L. Banks: "Involving Operating Managers in Planning Process Evolution," *Sloan Management Review* (Summer 1979), pp. 43–59.

Wrapp, E.: "Organization for Long Range Planning," *Harvard Business Review,* vol. 35, no. 1 (January–February 1957).

CHAPTER OUTLINE

IMPLEMENTATION: PLANS, POLICIES, LEADERSHIP, AND INTERNATIONAL STRATEGY

OBJECTIVES

- To illustrate the major types of plans required to implement strategy
- To understand the process of policy implementation
- To indicate how executives handle leadership implementation
- To describe implementation aspects of international strategy

INTRODUCTION [1]

In Chapter 9 you learned how planning systems can be used as aids in the tasks of developing and implementing strategy. We also outlined what some of those tasks were—specifically, allocating resources and organizing jobs.

But there are other interrelated concerns that strategists must deal with if a strategy is to be effectively implemented. The organization requires some mechanisms to ensure that the activities are integrated and coordinated. Further, it is important that the plans developed be coupled with the strategies; otherwise, the plans may move the firm in an unintended direction. The importance of these efforts cannot be ignored, since field studies indicate that obstacles encountered by companies in implementing strategy are leading to executive disenchantment with strategic planning because "nothing happens, or what happens is not a consequence of planning." To close gaps created by internal conditions, plans must be made to accomplish the tasks assigned to functional areas.

The major way in which these aspects of implementation are accomplished is through the development of plans, policies, and administrative processes. Each functional area of the business needs a plan to give direction and timing to its activities and personnel in the use of resources consistent with the demands of the strategy. Policies are guides to action. They indicate how the tasks assigned to the organization might be accomplished and provide a basis for lower-level managers on which to make decisions about the use of the resources which have been allocated. The other major administrative process discussed in this chapter is leadership implementation. Managers need to be selected, developed, and motivated to accomplish the jobs assigned and interpret plans and policies which give force to the strategy.

We will defer a discussion of several other aspects of administrative processes to our last chapter. That is, a follow-through on implementation requires an effective control and information system to provide accurate, complete, and timely feedback for evaluating progress toward objectives. Exhibit 10.1 reminds you, then, that these aspects of the strategic management process are interrelated with one another.

PLAN AND POLICY IMPLEMENTATION [2]

Changes in strategic direction do not occur automatically. Operational plans and tactics must be established to make a strategy work. While middle managers in functional areas usually make such decisions, they need to be guided by the strategy so that the plans and tactics are geared to the accomplishment of desired objectives. Thus plans and policies for the functional areas of the business are established to assist in this process.

Our last chapter described the strategic planning function. We suggested that line managers need to be involved because they implement the strategy. In effect, functional managers make plans to use the resources allocated to them in specific ways. While some refer to these as functional "strategies," we prefer to regard them as *plans,* or *tactics,* for carrying out the business strategy. Such plans are drawn up within guidelines set at higher levels—policies.

An enterprise could develop hundreds of policies to cover the important areas of the business. But a policy does not tell the manager how to handle a specific promotion or add a specific product. It serves as a guide to middle and supervisory managers in making certain choices.

Plans and policies are developed to ensure that (1) the strategic decision is implemented, (2) there is a basis for control, (3) the amount of time executives spend making decisions is reduced, (4) similar situations are handled consistently, and (5) coordination across units will occur where necessary.

Development of Plans and Policies [3]

Creating plans and policies leads to conditions where subordinate managers will know what they are supposed to do and willingly implement the decision.

Managers create plans and policies to make the strategies work. Policies provide the means for carrying out plans and strategic decisions. The critical element is the ability to factor the grand strategy into plans and policies that are compatible, workable, and not just "theoretically sound." It is not enough for managers to decide to change the strategy. What comes next is at least as important: How do we get there?

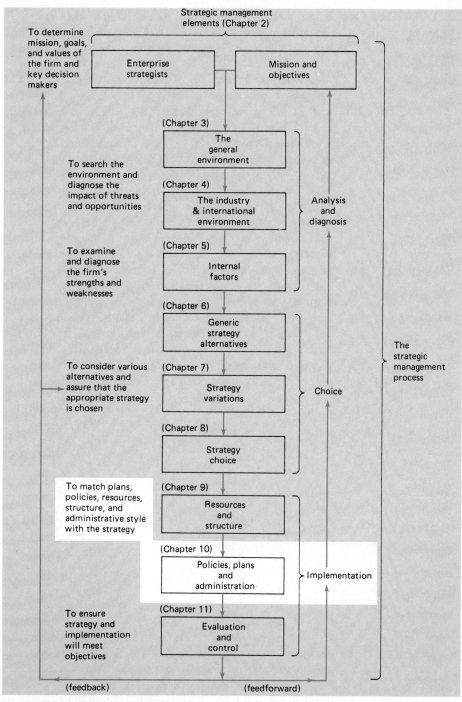

EXHIBIT 10.1   A model of strategic management.

When? and How efficiently? A manager answers these questions by preparing plans and policies to implement the grand strategy. For example, let us say that the strategic choice was to diversify. Now the executive must decide what to diversify into, where to diversify, how much money will be needed, where the money will come from, and what changes are needed in marketing, production, and other functions to make diversification work.

The amount of planning and policymaking in the formal sense will vary with the size and complexity of the firm. If the firm is small, or if it is a simple business, a few policies and plans will suffice. The plans and policies are generally understood and verbal. Larger and more complex firms find that policies and plans on every major aspect of the firm—marketing, finance, production and operations, personnel, and so forth—are necessary, for the competitive advantage of the large firm is its power, not its speed. That is where the smaller firm or decentralized division excels.

The processes involved in establishing plans and policies are quite similar to those influencing strategy formation and choice. That is, environmental factors can influence the choices; internal policies and the power of subunits jockeying for position play a role; etc. After all, these are going hand in hand with resource allocation decisions (see Chapter 9). Hence, resistance to change, conflict resolution techniques, and coalition building will all be at play in the development of plans and policies.

Without good plans and policies managers would make the same decisions over and over again. And different managers might choose different directions, and this could create problems. On the other hand, plans and policies should never be so inflexible as to prevent exceptions for good reasons. So criteria for judging the adequacy of plans and policies developed would include the following:

* Do they reflect present or desired company practices and behavior?
* Are they practical, given existing or expected situations?
* Do they exist in areas critical to the firm's success?
* Are they consistent with one another, and do they reflect the timing needed to accomplish goals?

As a result, policies and plans will:

1 Specify more precisely how the strategic choice will come to be—what is to be done, who is to do it, how it is to be done, and when it should be finished.

2 Establish a follow-up mechanism to make sure the strategic choice, plans, and policy decisions will take place.

3 Lead to new strengths which can be used for strategy in the future.

One example of a set of plans for several strategies is given in Exhibit 10.2. For each of these plans, a set of policies will have to be established for the appropriate area of the business. The policies will ensure that the plans are carried out as intended and that the different areas are working toward the same ends. Companies have plans and policies that cover nearly every major aspect of the firm. The example in Exhibit 10.2 illustrates only a few areas. The minimal plans and policies which must be developed are the key functional decisions for each area of the business. We will highlight some of the more important issues for each area in the rest of this section.

EXHIBIT 10.2   ALTERNATIVE BUSINESS STRATEGIES AND PLANS

Strategy	Marketing–product line plans	Manufacturing plans	Human resources plans	Financial plans	Timing
Retrenchment	Identify product lines for divestment—those with low sales or margins.	Identify plants to close on the basis of capacity utilization.	Reduce personnel on the basis of skills needed in the future and seniority.	Eliminate or reduce dividends, and manage cash flows.	Sell plants and reduce personnel in 1 year; cut dividends now.
Stability	Push the high-margin products in the line.	Defer plant and equipment investments over $200,000.	Invest in training programs to improve management skills.	Develop good bank relations, maintain steady dividends, and strengthen the balance sheet.	Continue for three years unless trends show high opportunity.
Expansion	Extend and improve product lines; volume is more critical than margins.	Expand plant capacity to support new products as necessary.	Hire additional sales, R&D, and production workers and managers.	Increase the debt-equity ratio by one-third. Consider the impact of dividend policy on cash-flow needs.	Evaluate market share position and financial condition after 2 years.

Then we will return to some questions about how these are to be integrated, since our criteria suggest that plans and policies need to be consistent, provide for coordination, and deal with timing issues.

As we discuss each area, recognize that we are not presenting an exhaustive list of issues. Specialists in each area develop plans and policies in much more breadth and depth than we can cover here. But the list indicates the types of major questions which need to be addressed if strategy is to be implemented effectively.

Financial and Accounting Policies and Plans [4]

Financial and accounting plans and policies are closely related to the resource allocation process discussed in Chapter 9. But financial policies may be set to provide guidelines in advance for where capital will come from, how capital may or may not be used, and how recurring needs will be met. Accounting policies will be established to deal with such questions as how to handle inventories, which accounts to capitalize, which tax approaches to use, and how to treat expenses and costs. These policies can make a huge difference in the firm's appearance of success or failure.

Capital

Long-term versus short-term plans are needed in relation to how to finance activities of the business. For instance, a policy is usually established with respect to the desired proportion of short-term debt, long-term debt, and preferred and common equity. Of course, philosophies regarding borrowing, the use of leverage, and control of the business, as well as such economic factors as the availability and cost of capital and tax implications, play a role in these decisions. For instance, in the 1980s many U.S. firms began replacing costly debt (due to high interest rates) with low-yielding stock. Policies regarding dividend payouts (e.g., regularity and rate) and reinvestment of profits in retained earnings are also related here and further reflect the impact of such factors as tax laws and owner influence and objectives. For example, tax benefits have enhanced the use of employee stock options (ESOPs) as a tool to raise capital or a means to become private in a leveraged buyout.

Lease or Buy

Sources of capital are related to uses of capital. A prime example is leasing versus buying fixed assets. A policy to lease classes of assets will change the nature of the need for funds over time and the nature of the balance sheet. Thus owning a building (say, the Pan Am building in Manhattan) versus leasing such space has an impact on working capital needs and the ability to finance other types of activities. Hence a strategy of rapid expansion, if funds are limited in the short term, might be accomplished through leasing rather than buying. Sale-and-leaseback arrangements became quite popular in the early 1980s because of the favorable tax benefits associated with such policies.

Risk

Other financial policies concern the evaluation of proposals for investing in certain projects. For instance, a "hurdle rate of return" may be specified as a policy guide before some strategic options will be considered. Hurdle rates may differ, depending on how risk is assessed. Another method for assessing potential investment alternatives includes a risk-adjusted discount rate in the net present value approach. A policy of a mix of investment risks is as useful as marketing-mix policies or planning a mix of basic and applied research. The investment-risk mix is related to strategic choice, of course. If expansion is the desired strategy, greater risks are acceptable. A mix of low-risk projects only may be an indication that retrenchment is on the horizon. In the mid-1980s, corporate treasurers made increasing use of "swap transactions" which allowed firms to trade interest rate payments and limit some exposure to risk of interest rate fluctuation. In addition, more and more firms sought to hedge foreign currencies as part of their financial plans.

The other area in which risk plans are needed is in the area of insurance. Corporate liability insurance in the mid-1980s was becoming very expensive, and in some instances difficult to get at all. Some firms were forced out of business because they did not believe they could expose themselves to the risk of doing business without insurance. Other firms chose a plan of in-house protection, but such plans require a large resource base. Still others joined consortia to pool resources as an alternative to traditional insurers. Another possibility is to change the nature of coverage for catastrophic risks and at the same time reduce or eliminate coverage for more common risks. Choices here can affect the strategy in terms of costs of doing business, or even lead to ultimate retrenchment (liquidation or sale).

Use of Assets

Specific targets for current assets and cash flows are also needed for items such as inventories (finished goods and raw materials) and accounts receivable and payable. Policies for the desired proportion of funds tied up in these accounts and the accounting treatment (e.g., LIFO or FIFO, or book or market value) are relevant here, as are rules for financial disclosure based on historical or ''inflation-related'' reporting. Some of these policies are mandated by the SEC or other government bodies, but managers should decide which approach provides them with the most useful information for decision making (as opposed to which treatment makes the books ''look better''). Alternative treatments of accounting data can lead to significant differences in the data upon which managers base their decisions.

Policies governing asset use have a direct impact on other components of strategy and cannot be made in isolation. For example, a policy with respect to maintaining a particular monetary value of safety stock of finished goods relates to marketing policy regarding customer relations and the ability to deliver outputs, as well as to production policy regarding lead times and the size of production runs. Or if an airline is trying to enhance relations with travel agents in a new territory, then extending the time for accounts receivable on the payment for tickets may be an important decision affecting marketing and finance.

Financial plans also become important in particular strategic actions such as mergers or liquidations or bankruptcies. In some cases, legal factors restrain choices. But there are usually several options which require a financial decision as to how to best implement the strategy. For example, the appendix for Chapter 7 suggested that a leveraged buyout was one option for financing a merger. Such an option would require a policy decision or would be made in relation to other plans associated with the desired financial structure of the business.

Exhibit 10.3 provides an interesting example of how some financial policies relate to the strategy of a firm. If a firm is divesting or liquidating, financial policies as well as other plans will need to be specified. For instance: How urgent is it? What will the cash flow look like? What will creditors get? Who are the potential buyers? What will the price be? How will we lay off people? In the early 1980s, many firms began to alter their plans to focus on debt reduction and increasing the cash flow due to stability strategies taken in response to disinflation.

Finally, some financial policies can have an indirect effect on strategy through the executive compensation system. For instance, firms which use stock options as a form of compensation may ultimately change the nature of control of the business or influence risk choices made by the executives involved. The implications could be positive or negative, and so such outcomes should be considered as these plans and policies are established.

EXHIBIT 10.3   TCI IS A MAMMOTH TAX SHELTER

Tele-Communications Inc. is the third largest cable company in the United States. Its strategy has been to buy existing small systems in small markets as opposed to competing for franchise rights in large cities. But it has steadfastly refused to invest in upgrading its systems, preferring to accumulate a large subscriber list by acquisition.

It uses some interesting financial policies. In fact, "it has so many subsidiaries and off-balance-sheet assets that it is hard to get a clear picture of what TCI owns." What is most interesting is that TCI seems to care little about earnings growth. The scheme is to go contrary to earning money, paying taxes, and issuing dividends. Says John Malone, president, "If TCI does not have earnings, it won't pay taxes, and that means more cash to buy systems." He expects that after-tax earnings will not be strong for the foreseeable future and prefers to keep TCI as "a mammoth tax shelter." Thus many of its acquisitions are based on sheltering income with expenses, and the firm has been aggressive in its use of accelerated depreciation.

TCI extends borrowing capabilities by creating non-consolidated operations that hold assets and can borrow for acquisitions and buy company stock. Another move to raise equity and avoid takeovers was to create a new class of common stock with 10 votes per share which management then took in exchange for old shares with one vote.

However, these financial approaches to implement expansion may also be a signal that the company is growing to sell out. While investing in existing systems offers economic stability for relatively long periods, franchise licenses may no longer offer a risk-free cash cow. Competition and demands from city councils may require heavy investment to upgrade systems. If that becomes a greater issue, TCI may be in a position where its large subscriber list makes it an attractive takeover target. So the financial policies to implement strategy may lead to a new strategy as well.

Source: Adapted from "How TCI Builds a Cable Empire," *Business Week,* Nov. 23, 1981, pp. 74–76.

Hence, some of the crucial financial questions needing implementation include:

- Where will we get additional funds to expand, either internally or externally?
- If external expansion is desired, how and where will it be accomplished?
- What will the strategy do to our cash flow?
- What accounting systems and policies do we use (for example, LIFO or FIFO)?
- What capital structure policy do we pursue? No debt or a heavily leveraged structure?
- How much should we pay out in dividends?
- How much cash and how many other assets do we keep on hand?
- Should we hedge our foreign currency exchange risk?

It is crucial that financial plans and policies are such that the funds needed are available at the right time and at the lowest cost.

Marketing Policies and Plans [5]

Some of the crucial marketing plans and policy questions include:

- Specifically, which products or services will be focused on, present ones or new ones?
- Which channels will be used to market these products or services? Will we use exclusive dealerships? Multiple channels?

- How will we promote these products or services? Is it our policy to use large amounts of TV advertising or no advertising? Heavy personal selling expenses or none? Price competition or nonprice competition?
- Do we have an adequate sales force?

In other words, marketing plans include the competitive tactics to use in the marketing mix. Specifically, how will we price, promote, and distribute, and what specific lines of products will we develop with what kind of quality?

Products and Markets

Assume, for example, that we have chosen a strategy of expansion in related products. Do we want a complete line? How many sizes or shapes? How many new products will we add, and when? How do we define quality (appearance, purity, durability, dependability)? Will we build in obsolescence? When will we introduce new products, or modifications?

Or assume that the strategy is to expand to new markets. Which specific customer groups are we going after? Do we want to limit the share of business we do with any given customer or class of customers? Which specific geographic territories will we enter? If we have chosen international markets, are we geared to meet different cultural needs and demands? These kinds of questions require decisions which should be guided by strategic intent. By the same token, product elimination as a retrenchment strategy is often neglected, but it is a viable plan for goals of long-term growth or survival.

Distribution and Promotion

Are there preferred channels of distribution for efficient and effective delivery? If there is a trade-off, what guideline should we use for choosing distributors? As we examine our customers, what is the preferred form of promotion? What sales approaches and media do we use? How much money will we allocate for advertising? Should we guarantee delivery? If we market in foreign countries, do our promotion policies account for cultural differences? More than one firm has failed to successfully enter foreign markets because advertisements, when translated, sent unintended messages.

Price and Packaging

Pricing and other marketing policies become particularly critical at various stages of product development and the firm's strategy. Price has become a primary weapon in tactical battles to secure a market share. For example, if rapid expansion is desired early in the development of a product, pricing may be below cost. (Of course, a desire to attract customers through loss leaders may be another reason for selling below cost.) Being a price leader or follower is a policy which managers need to address.

Here in particular you can see how the development of plans can be affected by managerial values. Offensive versus defensive strategists will view a particular pricing question differently. During periods of stable demand we would expect prices to remain relatively fixed (perhaps adjusted for inflation). If the strategy is retrenchment, price increases and a reduction in promotion and distribution costs would be expected if not outright abandonment. If the firm is retrenching out of certain areas as opposed to liquidating, an orderly withdrawal through various "demarketing" mechanisms would be necessary.

Packaging can be an alternative competitive weapon in the strategy of the firm. If product stability is the strategy, packaging changes (e.g., toothpaste in a pump, or shaving cream in a brush) can help expand the pace of market penetration.

Policies and plans must be made which interrelate several aspects of the strategy. For instance, a policy of different prices for different customers (or a one-price policy) is one which can have an impact on the product and market strategy. As you will see later, plans and policies must also be set in relation to other aspects of the business— for instance, price is particularly critical in relation to volume-cost-profit conditions, which affect production and the financial condition.

In Chapter 7 we indicated that firms can pursue active or passive strategies. If a firm pursues an active strategy, marketing "warfare" such as frontal attacks, flanking attacks, encirclement, a bypass attack, or guerilla warfare conjure up tactics for identifying competitors' weaknesses and for maneuvering using internal strengths. Conversely, passive alternatives can lead to marketing plans such as position defense, mobile defense, preemptive defense, counteroffensives, flank-position defense, or strategic withdrawal. Indeed, move and countermove can occur with the strategy as when Pepsi announced the purchase of 7-Up and Coke countered with a buyout of Dr. Pepper in a head-on battle for soft-drink market-share dominance. Exhibit 10.4 presents a picture of pricing warfare in the pharmaceutical business.

EXHIBIT 10.4   AT WAR WITH PRICES

What does a pharmaceutical company do if it is losing market share on an identical drug to a cheaper competitor, new over-the-counter drugs promise more competition, and cheaper generic versions are about to enter the battle when the patent runs out? Upjohn chose to cut the price by 30% of Motrin, its biggest seller arthritis pain killer. Upjohn hoped to preserve market share and give new product extensions a good start. They were willing to sacrifice present profits for future ones.

But Boots Pharmaceuticals, a British firm, cut the prices of its Motrin equivalent by 30% also, to preserve its advantage. Boots had licensed Upjohn to make and sell ibuprofen in the United States 10 years earlier. But it also retained its rights to sell the product in the U.S. market. Upjohn did not think they would be a serious competitor. At first, Boots' entry in 1977 had little im-

pact, so Upjohn raised the price of Motrin on two occasions. But the battle took another step. Boots licensed American Home Products to make an over-the-counter version of ibuprofen, and Upjohn agreed to let Bristol-Myers sell one that Upjohn makes. Both hit the market in 1983 and the battle was on. Many arthritic patients decided to treat themselves by taking more of the cheaper version.

The price war is likely to expand to a new front. Both Upjohn and Boots applied to the FDA for approval of a more powerful second-generation version of the drug. But Upjohn will continue to pay a license fee to Boots, giving the British firm a 15 to 20% cost advantage. Hence, the strategy at Upjohn on product extensions will be affected by past strategic choices and its pricing policies used to carry out strategy.

Source: Adapted from "Price Cuts That Backfired on Upjohn," *Business Week,* Aug. 6, 1984, pp. 23–24.

Again, if the marketing plans and policies don't mesh with the corporate strategy, and if marketing plans don't fit carefully with other functional policies, the objectives will not be met.

Production-Operations Management (POM) Policies and Plans [6]

POM is another area needing implementation plans and policies. Critical questions in this area include:

• Can we handle the business with our present facilities and number of shifts? Must we add equipment, facilities, and shifts? Where? Are layoffs needed? Should we subcontract?

• What is the firm's inventory safety level? How many suppliers do we need for purchases of major supplies?

• What level of productivity and costs should the firm seek?

• How much emphasis should there be on quality control and maintenance?

• How far ahead should we schedule production?

• How is the management of production and operations integrated with our strategy?

• Should we locate facilities in foreign countries, or exit countries where facilities are at risk?

Capacity and Utilization

Plans must be made for the levels of production or operations desired to fit the strategy. If rapid expansion is desired through internal means, does the firm have sufficient capacity to accommodate such expansion? Is the plant being used on overtime, double, or triple shifts? If retrenchment is under way, do we want to cut back production volume or keep the plant going and build inventories?

These questions may call for a plan for long-term production vis-à-vis marketing plans. Generally, three options exist for scheduling capacity usage: demand matching, operations smoothing, and subcontracting. If demand is seasonal, for example, demand matching calls for producing output with the season. Operations smoothing calls for continuous production to meet average demand levels. Subcontracting allows a firm to maintain steady minimal levels of output while meeting peak periods with output from subcontractors. Each of these approaches, of course, implies some trade-offs with respect to the costs of equipment, overtime, inventories, labor, maintenance, and subcontracting. When demand downturns occur, a plan to build inventory instead of retrenching becomes a major strategic decision.

As the plan is determined, there may remain a need or desire for longer-term capacity buildup. Here the options may include adding capacity, merging with another producer, or joint ventures. In any case, questions concerning the types of equipment, the amount of capacity, and the interface with existing units need to be addressed. Naturally, the overall size of a plant is of importance here and involves questions of economies of scale. This is partly determined by the technology employed but is also influenced by production scheduling and the basic marketing strategy. A large, "efficient'' plant may not be *effective* if it is not producing the kinds of outputs called for by the strategy. Capacity planning is also related to the policy question regarding scheduling. If demand matching is used, then plant size is geared to the production of peak output; otherwise, capacity can be smaller. Exhibit 10.5 indicates how production scheduling relates to decisions on plant capacity and broader strategic issues.

Location of Facilities

Assuming that a strategy of expansion is under way, another question of importance is where to locate plants or operations facilities. For instance, a major component in airline operations is the location of facilities for aircraft maintenance.

Of course, the critical elements of the firm's marketing and financial plans are relevant to the location decision. For instance, if new distribution approaches are a part of the strategy, locating plants near potential markets may outweigh factors such

EXHIBIT 10.5   A RADICAL PRODUCTION SCHEDULE?

True or False? The best way to maximize a plant's profitability is not to maximize its output. The "True" answer to this is anathema to traditional thinking; yet the optimized production technology (OPT) system argues for just such a policy in manufacturing.

Traditional cost accounting methods suggest that it is always better to run a batch of 1000 parts through a machine than it is to run 100 parts. Yet if 900 of those 1000 are going to sit in inventory, the OPT system suggests that such an approach is less cost-effective.

OPT is a two-part package: a simulated manufacturing program and radical shop-floor production rules. OPT enables companies to increase plant output while simultaneously lowering inventory and operating expenses. It forces managers and workers to coordinate their work and the flow of parts through a factory with one principle in mind: bottlenecks (lack of skilled labor, old machinery, etc.) ultimately constrain manufacturing output. By identifying bottlenecks in advance, and scheduling work flow with this in mind, manufacturing productivity can be increased dramatically. In fact, this is the basis of the "just in time" approach to inventory management popularized in Japan. By running bottlenecked operations at 100% of capacity while controlling the flow of materials into the bottleneck so they do not build up, inventories can be kept to the bare bones. In a just-in-time plant, managers tend to adjust production rates only after inventory build-

ups occur. But OPT simulations allow identification of bottlenecks in advance. Then managers schedule labor and machine hours so parts move continually through the system. Companies like Caterpillar, Bendix, and Westinghouse have used OPT to reduce work-in-process inventory, thus slicing weeks off lead times on customer orders.

Strategically, many companies investing in new factory automation systems may end up only boosting production costs. Hownet Turbine Components' plant used the OPT system instead of closing the plant during a downturn. Production in several operations was halted, and workers were transferred to shipping, where the bottleneck was identified. The firm managed to stabilize employment during a severe slump and cut delivery times. Hownet held its sales decline to 10% while the rest of the industry saw 50% drops in sales.

Consciously choosing not to run expensive machines flat out, or allowing workers to do nothing or transferring them, is an extraordinary leap of faith for manufacturing managers. It can be tough to sell the boss on the idea that lots of idle time is acceptable. Yet if such a system of scheduling production is effective, strategic choices on such things as plant expansion or new machinery for "productivity improvement" may result in money wasted.

Source: Adapted from B. Powell, "Boosting Shop-Floor Productivity by Breaking All the Rules," *Business Week,* Nov. 26, 1984, pp. 100–104.

as the availability or cost of raw material inputs. The financial trade-offs of locating facilities near sources of labor or energy versus customers also need to be examined. Naturally, the type of product and logistics costs of inputs versus outputs become relevant considerations.

Another factor of some importance is the degree of certainty associated with a new strategy. For instance, in the selection of a site for a new plant, the availability of land for further expansion later may be important if the decision is to plan for anticipated sales increases in the long run. And if the decision involves a move to foreign countries, social stability and tax conditions may play a role.

Finally, plants may be located near existing facilities to take advantage of economies of organization, purchasing, and the like. In some cases, the decision is to replace existing facilities (or equipment) with new ones to take advantage of new technologies that are replacing obsolete ones. In other cases, the decision is to add on to an existing plant or build nearby. In still others, the firm seeks to take advantage of lower-cost foreign labor by locating plants outside its home country. Again, factors such as labor, transportation, market location, and technologies play key roles in these determinations.

Processes

The types of processes to use are largely determined by the technology needed to produce given outputs. Still, some discretion or options may exist, particularly with respect to issues like the quality of the processing equipment and allowable tolerances. Many Japanese firms have gained significant competitive advantages by pursuing a policy of high-quality statistical control for their processing systems.

Equipment and Maintenance

Policies regarding investment to maintain or replace a plant and equipment can be important to the long-term ability of a firm to compete successfully and achieve objectives such as profits. Of course, the need for the maintenance of facilities varies from firm to firm. Maintenance at nuclear power plants or of aircraft is an absolute necessity. But there are often choices about whether to follow routine schedules (e.g., preventive maintenance) or whether to defer maintenance until there is a breakdown or replacement becomes necessary. Of course, keeping up-to-date, cost-effective equipment is a question of importance in creating a competitive advantage.

The overall quality component of a firm's strategy may determine the type of policy established for maintenance. But the criticality of prompt delivery of outputs may also play a role, and once again trade-offs with regard to inventory policies, the use of overtime, production schedules, and the like, become relevant.

Sourcing

Another key area in the operations of the firm involves sources of inputs or services important to the strategy. Choices about whom to purchase from involve more than a simple question of cost or availability. For instance, options may exist for shipping outputs by various forms of transportation (e.g., rail, airplane, ship). The speed of delivery versus costs may be important in the selection of the mode as well as the vendor. Further, whether to use one or more vendors or several sources for inputs and services is a question of some significance. Increasing dependence on one or a few sources may increase favorable treatment and cost savings but could come at the expense of flexibility.

Perhaps the key strategic issue involving sourcing is the make or buy question. In many instances, the decision is made by purchasing departments largely on the basis of the price to buy versus the cost to make. Yet such a policy is, in effect, a strategic decision regarding the development of competitive advantages. For instance, different financial needs are involved in making versus buying, and these can affect the capital structure. If quick delivery is important to the strategy, consideration must be given to the varying reliability of suppliers versus the control over components or supplies made in-house. If expansion strategies for new products are desired, a firm may opt for buying specialty products to round out a line or making these itself. Of course, plant capacity, personnel skills, and the financial condition all play a role in such a decision. Similarly, if retrenchment is the strategic choice, cost trade-offs of making versus buying can play a role here. In Chapter 9 we described the "network" organization. Network firms have gone to extreme vertical *dis*integration by choosing to eliminate control over internal production. Many use foreign suppliers as sources. In essence, the question of vertical integration as a strategy is implicit in make-or-buy decisions. Hence, internal and external factors as well as objectives involved in strategy formulation should guide the establishment of policies in this area; strategic choice should not be left to the purchasing department by default.

In Chapter 5 we discussed how flexibility might become an important strategic advantage in manufacturing. Here, policies such as relying on suppliers within 60 miles of a plant, or shipping finished goods immediately (instead of producing for inventory) can implement a just-in-time approach to accomplishing aggregate manufacturing flexibility. Similarly, personnel policies allowing the hiring of temporary or part-time workers for operations as necessary increase flexibility and can reduce costs. Allen-Bradley Company found that its highly automated assembly line increased flexibility, albeit at a cost of lower output. Yet the flexibility was seen as a higher-order priority than output, one that was essential to Allen-Bradley's future competitive ability.

POM is a crucial functional area in implementing strategies. Traditionally, marketing and POM have been rivals. But they must coexist and work together, and their tasks must be coordinated through appropriate policies and plans, if any strategy is to work.

Research and Development Policies and Plans [7]

Research and development is a function which straddles both POM and marketing. Crucial implementation questions for R&D include:

- Will we emphasize product or process improvements?
- Should we encourage basic research or focus on commercial development?

- Are we going to be leaders or followers?
- How much will we spend on R&D?
- Which technology should we pursue, and when should we pursue it?
- How can we manage the transition from one technology to another?
- How do we prepare the firm for technological change?

Products and Processes

Guidelines are needed to encourage the types of R&D efforts required for the strategy. For example, if new-product development is the basic strategic direction of the firm, then the research effort will be geared to focus on this activity. Of course, stability strategies which may call for product improvements would require a greater emphasis on modifications to the existing line. If a turnaround strategy is desirable, R&D efforts may be focused on improving production processes to reduce costs. Unfortunately, retrenchment strategies often are implemented by cutting R&D activities which may be needed for long-term improvements in the business. Such short-sighted policies provide an example of how the implementation of the current strategy may limit long-term strategy development.

The strategy of vertical integration (e.g., backward or forward expansion in functions) is another area where R&D policy becomes particularly relevant. The technologies involved in providing inputs or subsequent processing of outputs associated with changing functions would normally require policies to provide for resources and expertise in the new areas of activity.

Basic and Applied Research

Another area would include the relative focus of effort on performing basic or applied research. Few companies will authorize the research department to study anything its scientists may be interested in. But the extent of concern with short-term commercialization versus theoretical knowledge which may lead to major breakthroughs is an issue of some importance.

If a firm is going to undertake basic research, it must be prepared to accept certain financial outcomes and commitments: longer-term risk with potentially no payout or long payback periods, and enough capital to exploit discoveries if and when they are made. Of course, the firm may need to engage in some basic research if the nature of its business requires it (e.g., most pharmaceutical firms depend on basic research).

Offensive or Defensive Strategies

Some R&D options are available which reflect whether the strategy is offensive or defensive. That is, as with policies such as pricing, strategists can choose to be leaders or followers. If leadership is endorsed, greater emphasis will be placed on R&D in order to be "first to market." Of course, the costs and risk can be high. Others prefer to be fast seconds or followers who take basic research done by others and pursue product modifications. In the follower approach, another option is to buy the R&D efforts of others (such as university, government, or independent research labs). Buying patents or paying license or royalty fees may be another option for firms which do not have strengths in the R&D area or for firms which do not wish to make a commitment to or take the risks of building technological leadership. Another option is the joint-venture strategy, which combines internal and external approaches. Such strategies require policies for negotiating contracts and agreements, using outputs from research efforts, and deciding how the firm's own R&D departments will be involved in the joint efforts.

Allocating R&D Resources

Policies as to the amount of financial commitment in R&D can be based on the following guidelines:

- Maximum range—5 to 20 percent of gross profit, depending on the industry
- Minimum range—competitor actions

However, these figures provide a potentially wide range of discretion within which managers must subjectively determine how the R&D activity fits as a component of overall strategy. Perhaps more importantly, questions of how these funds will be used need to be addressed. Exhibit 10.6 suggests that changing policies on how R&D personnel use their resources can impact a firm's strategy.

EXHIBIT 10.6   POLISHING UP ITS R&D

Chesebrough-Ponds needs an innovation. Recent troubles included a costly stock repurchase and a $95 million bill for a firm it didn't want to buy. Both involved deals with Carl Icahn, and the moves boosted its ratio of debt to equity to 47%. At the same time, sales of its diverse product line (such as Prince tennis rackets, Ragu sauces, Bass shoes, and Vaseline) have plateaued. But recent moves to spur innovation may be just what the doctor ordered.

In late 1983, Chesebrough executives began allowing employees at its main lab to quit working on their assigned projects every Friday at noon to do experimental work of theirs—as long as it related to a business Chesebrough was in. As the director of R&D put it, "research efforts, especially in cosmetics, were often subservient to marketing." Marketers would identify a niche, and direct R&D to modify an existing product to fit it. As a result, breakthroughs were seldom achieved.

But the latest policy shift has resulted in a rare innovation in a business where "me-too" products are the rule. A "Polishing Pen" has been created whereby nail polish can be applied with a marking-pen-type applicator. Early users say the polish sometimes smudges and the tip eventually loses shape. But the ease with which the polish goes on and the speed at which it dries are expected to appeal to working women who will not sit still for lengthy manicures.

The researcher who made this breakthrough took Fridays at noon off to work on his idea, and soon weekends were devoted to the project. In 4 months, a prototype was developed. Chesebrough marketers ran the product by consumers and soon called for commercialization. A team of manufacturing, development, packaging, and marketing people planned to ready the pen for introduction in one year.

Chesebrough executives hope this will be just the beginning of a new product strategy resulting from the R&D policy changes they have made to spur innovation. Although they have actually cut back R&D with staff reductions, including firing 31 high-level managers, they have sharply focused efforts toward new product development.

Source: Adapted from "How Chesebrough-Ponds Put Nail Polish in a Pen," *Business Week,* Oct. 8, 1984, pp. 196–200.

Personnel, Legal, and Public Relations Policies and Plans [8]

Besides the four major line functions, major staff functions need functional policy implementation too. The crucial implementation questions for personnel include:

- Will we have an adequate work force?
- How much hiring and retraining are necessary?
- What types of individuals do we need to recruit? College graduates? Members of minority groups?
- How should we recruit—through advertising or personal contact? What methods of selection should we use—informal interviews or very sophisticated testing?
- What standards and methods are used for promotion? (For example, do we promote from within, or on the basis of seniority?)
- What will our payment policies, incentive plans, benefits, labor relations policies, etc., be?
- Is executive compensation tied to strategic objectives?

The basic questions for the *legal* staff include:

- Are the policies and plans in other areas legal?
- What are the implications of testing the law?

Finally, public relations policies deal with the presentation of the corporate image and involvement in community activities.

Personnel

As the strategy is developed, plans and policies for human resources need to be developed as well. Human resources must be recruited, allocated, developed, and maintained. Of course, questions about recruitment are similar to the "sourcing" issues. For example: Will the necessary work force be available? Where do the workers come from? Can we afford the cost? Personnel development is correlated with the "make versus buy" issue in the sense that policies of internal promotion and training may be preferred to recruiting from outside the organization. The allocation issue involves making sure that the tasks and resources distributed to various parts of the organization include the right people—those with appropriate skills and abilities to carry out the tasks effectively. Limitations on recruitment and allocation decisions may occur if there are legal restrictions or if the firm is unionized. Industrial relations policies need to be established which deal with such questions as affirmative action, work rules, etc.

With respect to maintaining the work force, policies regarding levels of pay, supplemental benefits, and systems for performance appraisal need to be established. Such policies can be critical, particularly in labor-intensive businesses, to the ability to carry out a strategy and compete effectively.

Perhaps one of the most difficult decisions regarding personnel occurs when a firm is pursuing a retrenchment strategy. At these times, questions usually include whether or not to lay off or terminate employees, how many, and who. Again, union contracts may establish some kind of policy here (resulting from earlier negotiations where a previous policy was laid down). But a firm may also attempt to protect labor and seek a shortened workweek or maintain the level of production for a time. Such policies relate to those in production and finance. A related matter is the relative proportion of managers and workers in line and staff functions. Several writers have suggested that the policies of many U.S. firms have stressed placing the brightest and best people in staff functions at the expense of the line, which does the basic work. This has been blamed for declining productivity, inadequate plant investment, marginal quality standards, and the like. As a result, many firms have begun a streamlining program by cutting the corporate level and other staff levels. Their goal is to pare overhead costs and gain some control over unwieldy, top-heavy structures. Of course, such trade-offs must be made with other objectives and considerations in mind.

Some firms incorporate a long-term human resource plan as an integral component of the strategic plan. Human resources managers have become an integral component in the strategic management activity, particularly as firms engage in mergers or major retrenchments requiring significant changes in the work force. This requires forecasts of human resource needs (labor and management) in conjunction with other changes going on in the planning effort.

Because policies and plans dealing with management personnel are such an important aspect of implementing strategy, the leadership implementation section of this chapter explores this area in greater detail.

Legal Issues

Policies and plans with respect to all the functions of a firm normally involve some questions of legality. For instance, a merger strategy to be implemented through the purchase of a competitor involves legal questions. A marketing policy to give exclusive territories to distributors may involve legal issues. Securing favorable price breaks on large purchases of materials or hiring certain classes of employees for the executive ranks also involves legal issues, and so on. Some firms may pursue a policy for the purpose of testing a legal issue, as Sears did when it challenged the Equal Employment Opportunity Commission. Other executives may delay implementing plans until "advice of counsel" is sought as to the legal ramifications of pursuing a given strategy in a certain way. Of course, implementing a strategy by moving into international territories compounds the difficulties and introduces the question of whether policies need to be established that are common to all SBUs or whether autonomy is to be granted to suit local conditions. The legal ramifications may have a great deal to do with a firm's policy on organizing such units. More firms appear to be increasing the size of in-house legal departments as problems connected with product liability, employee health and safety, employment practices, pollution problems, and so on have grown.

Once the legal issues are explored, there are still policy issues involved. In essence, a firm may have a policy of "let's follow the letter of the law," "let's follow the spirit of the law," or "let's test the law (if we're willing to pay the possible consequences)." Depending on the importance of the issue, the risks involved, and the values of management, these options are more or less likely for a given situation. The role of the legal staff is to lay out the implications so that managers can make a decision. Unfortunately, some managers let their lawyers determine policies themselves, and this can lead to the "tail wagging the dog."

Public Relations [9]

Somewhat related to policies concerning legal issues is the whole area of social responsibility. Policies in this area remain quite nebulous. A whole variety of issues can be involved, including advertising ethics, bribing government officials (foreign or domestic), and corporate philanthropy. Like legal policies, public relations policies can cut across all the functional areas. There may be ethical questions in developing certain areas of research (such as research on DNA) or in selling products that are unsafe to certain types of consumers (such as infant formula in Africa). Of course, some production processes may be designed to use state-of-the-art technology to prevent pollution, or there may be an option to continue the legal dumping of dangerous chemical wastes. The list of issues seems to be endless. As a result, the public affairs–government relations function has grown increasingly important, more staff members and resources are being allocated to this office, and more authority to make policies has been granted.

Policies here have an impact on the image the organization wishes to present. But some can also be seen as necessary to protect long-term economic interests. For example, many firms operating in South Africa under conditions of apartheid face critical policy questions. Thus some firms may choose to encourage employee participation in community activities, involve themselves in political action committees (PACs), or provide financial support for community development projects. In many instances, these policies may be a way to "manage the environment." Remember, strategies can be active or passive. More firms these days appear to exercise active approaches to influencing their environment to create opportunity or avert threat. In addition to involvement with PACs the public relations staff or high-level executives will monitor the progress of pieces of legislation in federal or state capitals. This involves watching committee assignments for bills, noting hearing schedules for bills of interest, and determining the action to be taken on each bill (testimony at hearings, speaking with committee members, attending the hearing, briefing key legislators regarding the issues, etc.).

Of course, the degree to which a firm attempts to exercise "influence" requires a policy on how far legal limits are to be stretched (e.g., should bribery be overlooked). This is a particularly difficult problem for the international firm. Should it behave as a change agent, or adapt to local customs? Should it follow the adage "When in Rome do like the Home Office"? The usual prescription is to strike a balance of constructive interaction, but this is often easier said than done.

Integrating Policies and Plans [10]

When all line and staff functions have developed plans and policies to aid implementation of the strategic choice, implementation is not necessarily complete. There is a need to be sure that there is internal consistency in the policies and plans developed for the line and staff. And these need to be related to the assessment of the role of strengths and weaknesses as they relate to the development of competitive advantage, as we suggested in Chapter 5. Let's consider an example to illustrate this key point.

Suppose that a furniture manufacturer pursues marketing plans calling for a narrow product line, a low price, and broad distribution. Various policies would probably include decentralized storage of finished goods, large-lot-size production, a low- or medium-skilled work force, and a limited number of large-scale plants.

On the other hand, a manufacturer of high-priced, high-style furniture sold through exclusive distributors might call for production to order, many model and style changes, well-trained and highly paid workers and supervisors, etc. While the operations and labor costs and policies in the second case might be seen as less efficient and a relative weakness, nonetheless they are consistent with and effective for the chosen strategy. If the manufacturer attempted to follow the usual prescriptions for "efficient" production (large-scale mass production of items), it probably would not be *effective* in carrying out its strategy.

As we discussed each area earlier, you may have noted that effective decisions cannot be made without regard to their impact on other areas of the business. Otherwise, suboptimization is likely to result. Trade-offs are generally required in this process. A policy of minimizing the inventory may come at the expense of satisfying customers. Exhibit 10.7 shows some of the common trade-offs which can result within certain areas. But this suggests where trade-offs occur across areas as well.

Hence, top executives must be involved with negotiations and policy formulation to assure that the plans that are developed are working together to accomplish the key tasks needed to carry out a given strategy. The extent of involvement needed relates to the strategy itself. That is, in some cases stronger linkages across units become more important. Consider, for instance, the need to link R&D, production, and marketing departments. If the strategy is to develop and produce products for specific customer needs, there will be a greater need to coordinate the activities of the three departments than if a "push" strategy in marketing is in use (selling whatever products are developed and produced). An example of this is Ford's "Team Taurus." Normally, the 5-year process of creating a new automobile is sequential—product planners define a concept, the design team takes over, and then engineering develops specifications that are passed on to manufacturing and suppliers. Such an approach was creating problems at Ford. The Team Taurus approach put together a group from planning, design, engineering, and manufacturing at the beginning of the process. The group asked assembly-line workers and suppliers for their ideas, at the same time doing extensive market research and back engineering on competitors' products to identify customer-desired features. Such integration was seen as necessary if Ford was to compete with foreign automakers.

If the business is highly capital-intensive with high manufacturing costs, then a stronger linkage between R&D and manufacturing is likely to be helpful for developing cost-saving process improvements. The idea is that policies can be developed to encourage the organization to maintain a desired liaison across units to effect the communication and coordination needed. In some instances, specialized formal units (e.g., expediters) may be set up in the organization to facilitate this coordination. The management information system may be used here for coordination and control. Chapter 11 discusses these topics.

EXHIBIT 10.7 SOME IMPORTANT TRADE-OFF DECISIONS IN VARIOUS POLICY AREAS

Policy area	Decision	Alternatives
Plant and equipment	Span of process	Make or buy
	Plant size	One big plant or several smaller ones
	Plant location	Locate near markets or locate near materials
	Investment decisions	Invest mainly in buildings or equipment or inventories or research
	Choice of equipment	General-purpose or special-purpose equipment
	Kind of tooling	Temporary, minimum tooling or "production tooling"
Production planning and control	Frequency of inventory taking	Few or many breaks in production for buffer stocks
	Inventory size	High inventory or a lower inventory
	Degree of inventory control	Control in great detail or in lesser detail
	What to control	Controls designed to minimize machine downtime or labor cost or time in process, or to maximize output of particular products or material usage
	Quality control	High reliability and quality or low costs
	Use of standards	Formal or informal or none at all
Labor and staffing	Job specialization	Highly specialized or not highly specialized
	Supervision	Technically trained first-line supervisors or nontechnically trained supervisors
	Wage system	Many job grades or few job grades; incentive wages or hourly wages
	Supervision style	Close supervision or loose supervision
	Industrial engineers	Many or few
Product design/ engineering	Size of product line	Many customer specials or few specials or none at all
	Design stability	Frozen design or many engineering change orders
	Technological risk	Use of new processes unproved by competitors or follow-the-leader policy
	Engineering	Complete packaged design or design-as-you-go approach
	Use of manufacturing engineering	Few or many manufacturing engineers
Organization and management	Kind of organization	Functional or product focus or geographical or other
	Executive use of time	High involvement in investment or production planning or cost control or quality control or other activities
	Degree of risk assumed	Decision based on much or little information
	Use of staff	Large or small staff group
	Executive style	Much or little involvement in detail; authoritarian or nondirective style, much or little contact with organization

The timing of these plans and policies must be designed so that they mesh correctly. For instance, a number of computer companies attempted to rush into new products with marketing programs promising more than could be delivered. Customers were anxiously awaiting the arrival of their new machines before production was capable of providing the necessary output. So lead times within each area of the business need to be considered in relation to one another before plans are implemented. Further, some policy decisions can be made and implemented immediately (e.g., change from LIFO to FIFO, hire unskilled workers). Others take long lead times to come to fruition (e.g., research and development, building new plants). For example, Genentech had a plan whereby it would hire sales force personnel contingent on approval of a new drug by the FDA, which takes some time.

Thus, in effect, firms create a cascade of plans and policies, with the long-range choices affecting medium- and short-range decisions.

Strategic choice	
	↓
Longer than 3 years	Long-range policies, plans, programs
	↓
1 to 3 years	Medium-range policies, plans, programs
	↓
Less than 1 year	Short-range policies, plans, programs

Policies also vary over time, shifting with strategic needs. One interesting perspective sheds some light on what may be one way to determine how plans need to change with certain strategies. Fox has shown how implementation will vary depending on where the firm's main product or service is in the product-service life cycle. Exhibit 10.8 presents his framework. Of course, a multiple-SBU firm may have a number of products, each of which is in a different stage of development. Hence specific guidelines are subject to some question as to their overall usefulness. Nonetheless, the exhibit does illustrate how policies can be meshed with different demands imposed by a strategy change.

Finally, it should be remembered that if contingency planning or second-generation planning is being used, alternative functional policies for each contingency plan must be developed.

These and many other functional plans and policies are needed to implement the grand strategy. Your ability to formulate these will be a good indication of your practical ability to make the strategy work. Research suggests that the success of a firm's strategy is dependent on proper implementation and balancing of resources, plans, and policies.

LEADERSHIP IMPLEMENTATION

As we mentioned, personnel plans and policies dealing with executive personnel are of crucial significance to the firm and its ability to implement (as well as formulate) strategy. The real test of a strategic decision is whether you put the right people in the job you've just identified as crucial. Here we focus on some of the key issues associated with providing for appropriate leadership skills as a critical component of the administrative system to implement strategy. These are important because leaders can help organizations cope with change, and people will not necessarily cooperate according to the policies or plans. Effective leaders are the major component in assuring that a follow-through of the policies occurs as planned.

Firms accomplish leadership implementation in several ways: (1) through changes in current leadership at appropriate levels, (2) by developing appropriate leadership styles and climates, (3) by getting involved in career development for future strategists, and (4) by using organization development techniques to effect changes.

Leader Choice and Assignment [11]

The first dimension of leadership implementation is to make sure that the right strategists are in the right positions for the strategy chosen for that SBU or firm. The questions pertaining to leadership implementation are as follows:

1 Who holds the current leadership positions?
2 Do they have the right characteristics to assure that the strategy will work well?
3 Who should be assigned which types of tasks?

Essential to examining leadership implementation is this question: Does the strategist have the right education, abilities, experience, and personality to implement the new strategy? For example, assume that a firm which has been handling a single product line in a stable industry has shifted to a strategy of expansion in a diversified set of product and service lines. Perhaps this firm's executive, with narrow experience in the marketing of the old product line alone, is not as qualified to head the firm as a strategist with wider experience. Or if a firm is heavily influenced by certain technologies, then education, ability, and experience relating to these would be highly useful for a strategist to have. Many CEOs have been replaced when it was discovered that they could not effectively deal with the demands of a changed environment or a new strategy. Of course, others are replaced because they are ineffective leaders or because their political skills are poor. Often, to implement a new strategy, executives tied to the past must be given the "golden handshake" of early retirement to allow the new strategy to work.

The firm must examine the match between the new strategy and the CEO. For instance, in a merger or acquisition, who will manage the new unit? Will the unit remain autonomous or be integrated into the existing structure? If it is integrated, do the skills and styles fit the current business? If a match between strategy and managers does not exist, serious problems of implementation could result. Indeed, Charles Brown succeeded John DeButts at AT&T, since he was in a better position to bargain

EXHIBIT 10.8   RELATIONSHIP OF IMPLEMENTATION TO THE PRODUCT LIFE CYCLE

	Functional focus	R&D	Production	Marketing	Physical distribution
Precommer- cialization	Coordination of R&D and other functions	Reliability tests Release blueprints	Production design Process planning Purchasing department lines up vendors and subcontractors	Test marketing Detailed marketing plan	Plan shipping schedules, mixed carloads Rent warehouse space, trucks
Introduction	Engineering: debugging in R&D production, and field	Technical corrections (engineering changes)	Subcontracting Centralize pilot plants; test various processes; develop standards	Induce trial; fill pipelines; sales agents or commissioned salespeople; publicity	Plan a logistics system
Growth	Production	Start successor product	Centralize production Phase out subcontractors Expedite vendors' output; long runs	Channel commitment Brand emphasis Salaried sales force Reduce price if necessary	Expedite deliveries Shift to owned facilities
Maturity	Marketing and logistics	Develop minor variants Reduce costs through value analysis Originate major adaptations to start new cycle	Many short runs Decentralize Import parts, low- priced models Routinization Cost reduction	Short-term promotions Salaried salespeople Cooperative advertising Forward integration Routine marketing research: panels, audits	Reduce costs and raise customer service level Control finished- goods inventory
Decline	Finance	Withdraw all R&D from initial version	Revert to subcontracting; simplify production line Careful inventory control; buy foreign or competitive goods; stock spare parts	Revert to commission basis; withdraw most promotional support Raise price Selective distribution Careful phaseout, considering entire channel	

Source: Reprinted by permission from *Atlanta Economic Review* (now *Business Magazine*). "A Framework for Functional Coordination," by Harold W. Fox, November–December 1973. Copyright © 1973 by the College of Business Administration, Georgia State University, Atlanta.

with the government to effect the company's new strategy. DeButts had made some enemies in Washington, D.C., and Brown was less rigid in his thinking about how to cooperate with the regulatory reformers.

As for determining areas of managerial responsibility, it has been suggested that

EXHIBIT 10.8   RELATIONSHIP OF IMPLEMENTATION TO THE PRODUCT LIFE CYCLE *(Continued)*

Personnel	Finance	Management accounting	Other	Customers	Competition
Recruit for new activities Negotiate operational changes with unions	Life-cycle plan for cash flows, profits, investments, subsidiaries	Payout planning: full costs/ revenues Determine optimum lengths of life-cycle stages through present-value method	Final legal clearances (regulatory hurdles, patents) Appoint life-cycle coordinator	Panels and other test respondents	Neglects opportunity or is working on similar idea
Staff and train middle management Stock options for executives	Accounting deficit; high net cash outflow Authorize large production facilities	Help develop production and distribution standards Prepare sales aids, sales management portfolio		Innovators and some early adopters	(Monopoly) Disparagement of innovation Legal and extra-legal interference
Add suitable personnel for plants Many grievances Heavy overtime	Very high profits, net cash outflow still rising Sell equities	Short-term analyses based on return per scarce resource		Early adopters and early majority	(Oligopoly) A few imitate, improve, or cut prices
Transfers, advancements; incentives for efficiency, safety, and so on Suggestion system	Declining profit rate but increasing net cash inflow	Analyze differential costs/revenue Spearhead cost reduction, value analysis, and efficiency drives	Pressure for resale price maintenance Price cuts bring price wars; possible price collusion	Early adopters, early and late majority, some laggards; first discontinued by late majority	(Monopoly competition) First shakeout, yet many rivals
Find new slots Encourage early retirement	Administer system; retrenchment Sell unneeded equipment Export the machinery	Analyze escapable costs Pinpoint remaining outlays	Accurate sales forecast very important	Mainly laggards	(Oligopoly) After second shakeout, only few rivals

the types of tasks and decisions should be assigned on the basis of criticality and urgency. Criticality refers to the strategic importance of decisions, while urgency refers to the timing needed for decisions. As decisions become more critical and urgent, they should be pushed to the highest levels (CEO). Division or functional managers would be held responsible for decisions that are urgent but less critical. The senior-level staff might deal with critical issues of less urgency. Typically, as issues move from analytical stages to implementation, they tend to become more urgent, but criticality may increase or decrease.

Style and Climate [12]

Leadership style is a crucial aspect of leadership implementation also. Essentially this aspect of leadership implementation relates to these questions:

1 Can the strategist lead the division effectively and relate well to peers, superiors, and subordinates with his or her present style?

2 Can the strategist change the leadership style if that is necessary to make the new strategy work?

3 Can the strategist develop the right climate and culture for the strategy?

The strategy needs to be reinforced with the right climate of managerial values and leadership style. This affects how willing the strategist is to delegate authority and develop the appropriate types and levels of controls.

As Exhibit 10.9 suggests, different management skills appear to be relevant depending on the job requirements for a given strategy or SBU. Thus an SBU that is a

EXHIBIT 10.9   **A suggested framework for strategy—manager matching.**

Strategy	Job Requirements	Matching Criteria	Managerial Skills and Behaviors	Person Attributes

Decision

Strategy

Growth

Defend

Maintain

Divest

Etc.

Job Requirements

1. Environmental scanning
2. Functional focus—source of job demands
3. Number and complexity of job related demands

---

1. Unit and interunit cooperation and collaboration
2. Number and importance of external contacts
3. Number and importance of internal contacts

---

1. Performance goals, standards and priorities
2. Need for control
3. Need for innovative behavior
4. Types of incentives and reward systems

Priorities

Matching Criteria

Knowledge

Integrative

Administrative

Priorities

Managerial Skills and Behaviors

1. Specific industry knowledge
2. Knowledge of organizational functions
3. Knowledge of overall company
4. Past performance

---

1. Number and quality of internal networks
2. Number and quality of external networks
3. Quality of interpersonal and communication skills

---

1. Quality of conceptual skills
2. Tendency toward innovative behavior
3. Type of control orientation
4. Flexibility in assignments
5. Preferred rewards and incentives

Person Attributes

Education

Family background

Personality

Needs

Intelligence

Matching Contingencies

Power

Structure

Culture

cash cow will require leadership styles and characteristics different from those appropriate for an SBU pursuing significant expansion in new product-market areas. Strategists will have to determine whether existing managers can adapt to new roles or whether they will need to be replaced.

The leader is responsible for developing a "climate" conducive to the mission of the business. There are a number of ways in which climate can be viewed. Here we mean the nature of leadership, motivation, decision, communication, and control processes and the development of a corporate "culture." Let's briefly review these aspects of the administrative system.

Leadership processes as a component of climate refer to the following types of questions:

1 To what extent do superiors have confidence in and trust subordinates? (No confidence to complete trust.)

2 To what extent do superiors behave in a manner that encourages subordinates to feel free to discuss important matters about their jobs? (No discussion to full discussion.)

3 To what extent do superiors try to get ideas and opinions from subordinates and use them constructively? (Never or seldom to always.)

Motivational processes as a component of climate can be represented by the following:

1 What types of motives are used? (Fear, threats, punishment, economic rewards, noneconomic rewards.)

2 How much responsibility do various managerial levels assume for goal achievement? (Attempts to sabotage at some levels to high responsibility at all levels.)

3 What types of interactions occur? (Little interaction and distrust to extensive friendly interaction with confidence and trust.)

4 To what extent is there a feeling of teamwork? (None or damaging competitiveness to substantial cooperation and cohesiveness.)

Decision processes as a dimension of climate can be characterized as follows:

1 At what level are decisions formally made? (Bulk at the top and centralized to decentralized spread of decision authority and delegation.)

2 To what extent are decision makers aware of lower-level problems? (Unaware to fully aware.)

3 To what extent is technical and professional knowledge used in making decisions? (No extent to great extent.)

4 To what extent do subordinates get involved in decisions related to their work? (No participation to high participation.)

The communication-process component of climate includes these questions:

1 In what manner are orders issued or goals set? (Orders issued from above to goals established by means of group participation.)

2 How does communication primarily occur? (Formal written memos to informal verbal exchanges.)

3 How does communication flow? (Primarily downward to laterally to primarily upward.)

The control-process dimension of climate is characterized as follows:

1 The extent to which review and control is concentrated. (Highly concentrated at the top to widespread responsibility for control.)

2 The extent of controls and standards. (Loose to tight.)

3 The extent to which control data are used for self-guidance. (Data used for policing to coordinated problem solving.)

Finally, the elusive aspect of corporate "culture" is a dimension of climate that leaders help develop. Here we are concerned with how the other aspects of climate interrelate to develop an informal organization which supports or opposes formal goals. A corporate culture might be defined as the overriding ideology and established patterns of behavior and norms which influence actions and decisions. There are forces which covertly or overtly resist the organization or fully support and accept the ways in which it operates. Also, the underlying values of the organization (its overall personality as distinct from the personalities of its members) constitute a dimension of some significance. It is important to be perfectly clear about your culture, so that new employees, customers, and shareholders know who you are and what you stand for. But it may also be necessary to change the culture, as is happening at Proctor & Gamble, whose past marketing prowess has become rusty. Such changes require revolutionary shifts and wholesale personnel replacements. The question of combining cultures when firms consider merger strategies is a factor that must be considered when choosing the strategy or determining the structure. Exhibit 10.10 illustrates these issues.

All in all, these aspects of leadership implementation are essential components of the administrative system which can make or break a strategy. They can be used to engender commitment and loyalty to the organization and its strategies. We should hasten to add that the character of these dimensions is *not* designed to suggest that one end of the continuum is necessarily better than the other end. As with other aspects of leadership implementation, the characteristics need to fit the needs of a given strategy.

Unfortunately, there is not much evidence suggesting which of these aspects is more appropriate for given strategies. However, the business press suggests that certain key aspects of excellence in management style and approach are appropriate regardless of the strategy: a bias toward action, a simple form and a lean staff, continued contact with customers, productivity improvement via people, operational autonomy to encourage entrepreneurship, stress on one key business value, emphasis on doing what one knows best, and the simultaneous use of loose and tight controls.

There is some evidence that suggests that chief planning officers recognize that problems in these areas can lead to frustration in translating strategy into operational terms. Some of the basic problems include difficulty in achieving goal consensus, communication breakdowns, ambiguity with regard to the roles of subunits, difficulty in obtaining commitment to a plan, lack of strategic thinking, and line-staff conflicts. Many of these problems are attributed to planners' lack of cognitive ability and the

EXHIBIT 10.10   MERGING TWO CULTURES

In late 1984, marketing giant IBM paid $1.3 billion for little engineering genius Rolm, its first acquisition in 20 years. Predictions were that the marriage wouldn't work due to cultural clashes. "It looked like a corporate Odd Couple." Rolm, a leading maker of computerized phone switchboards (PBX), was the epitome of Silicon Valley's freewheeling corporate culture. IBM, on the other hand, insisted on "buttoned-down decorum" from its huge work force. A year later, the pundits were still wondering when the marriage would go on the rocks.

Yet the informal atmosphere at Rolm—workaholic frenzy occasionally relieved by a dip in the company pool or a lunchtime barbecue—has not changed. "It's not the 'blueing' of Rolm that everyone expected."

The PBX is crucial to IBM in its effort to battle AT&T for the telecommunications markets. IBM does not want to botch its chance by alienating the engineering elite at Rolm. Top executives at Rolm have remained, and morale remains high. Rolm's management has avoided bureaucratic inroads. "The general manager of one sales unit who cut out free coffee in an effort to trim costs reversed the decision when employees blamed IBM."

IBM has maintained Rolm's unusual policy of granting employees a three-month paid sabbatical after 3 years, even though that has angered some IBM employees who don't receive the benefit. And stock options are more widely distributed at Rolm than at IBM. Combined sales efforts of IBM and Rolm sales forces have been effective, largely because IBM pays double commissions on many products.

Still, the merging of the cultures will likely lead to greater similarities if the long-term strategy is to be achieved. For example, Rolm is reorganizing its 5000-strong sales and service groups from 14 independent operating groups to 4 national units with centralized decision making. This smacks of IBM's style and portends a marriage of the two firms' sales forces that may alienate many in Rolm's entrepreneurial ranks. Some top performers left when a new compensation structure placed greater emphasis on base salary than commissions, and levied a cap on earnings.

So far, joint technical development consists of making existing products work together. Creating new ones from scratch could lead to friction. Further, since stock options at Rolm are vested after 2 years instead of 5, as they were under the old plan, many options leading to employee turnover may be exercised.

Thus, it remains to be seen whether the culture clash between two very different styles can lead to the accomplishment of IBM's strategic goals without some significant short-term pain.

Source: Adapted from J. B. Levine, "How IBM Is Getting the Most Out of Rolm," *Business Week,* Nov. 18, 1985, pp. 110–111.

quality of top-level administrators. Hence another aspect of leadership implementation is preparing managers to perform the appropriate tasks. This is the subject of the next section.

Career Development [13]

Because of the significance of leadership to the implementation of strategy in general, more attention is being devoted to the career development of strategists. Several elements are necessary to effectively plan for executive development: (1) the types and numbers of executives needed for the future strategy must be anticipated; (2) the current talent available must be reviewed; (3) promotion and recruitment schedules should be prepared; (4) plans for the development of individuals for promotion should be made; and (5) reward systems to attract and hold key managers must be established.

These are, of course, common human resource approaches. But to be a successful *strategist,* the executive must understand business function decisions, especially those concerning production-operations management, marketing, and financial management. It is also desirable to understand the impact of personnel, accounting, and legal staff functions on effective decisions. So some firms rotate potential strategists through experiences in as many of these functions as possible to develop multiple-ability strategists. Or, if international activities are important to the business, careers often include at least one foreign assignment. If there are significant differences in the characteristics of different SBUs, it is useful for the experiences to take place in the different SBUs. Thus the future strategists will realize that the functions and SBUs are mutually dependent upon corporate effectiveness. More firms are planning the careers of future strategists with these guidelines in mind, though the CEO may hinder these efforts. Many suggest that selection and placement of managers should be done in accordance with the needs of the strategy to which they are best suited. For example, one study found that greater willingness to take risk, higher tolerance for ambiguity, and stronger marketing experience by an SBU manager contributed to the effectiveness of expansion strategy but hampered the effectiveness of retrenchment strategy. However, there has been a lack of thorough analysis of how strategy implementation and managerial selection should work together.

Generally it is useful for a firm to reinforce the motivation to achieve strategic objectives by tying the strategist's compensation to strategic achievements. The nature of the incentive compensation used, the timing of incentive payments, and other dimensions can accomplish this mission. The key to such a system is to tie rewards to the type of performance required by the strategy and objectives. Hence if innovation is a key to performance in the future, then time horizons for judging performance will tend to be longer, and greater rewards for risk taking might outweigh short-term profitability in the incentive scheme. The reward system for executives is discussed in greater detail in Chapter 11.

Organization Development [14]

The final aspect of leadership implementation deals with change processes. That is, if new strategies or policies are being implemented, former policies and plans, people, and the climate are likely to undergo some sort of change. Typical reactions include denying, ignoring, accepting, adapting to, and embracing change. It is up to leaders to see that readiness for change and commitment to new activities will come about. This is easier said than done, as Exhibit 10.11 suggests.

To implement change, consultants and managers use a variety of activities and techniques. These include survey feedbacks, confrontation meetings, team building, transactional analysis, and various packaged approaches (e.g., Blake and Mouton's Grid or Lippitt's ITORP—implementing the organizational renewal process). Though studies vary as to the effectiveness of various approaches, most are designed to accomplish several things:

- Unfreezing—unlearning old behavior patterns or policies
- Learning—effecting the change desired
- Refreezing—institutionalizing new patterns and policies

EXHIBIT 10.11   CAN J&J CHANGE FROM BAND-AIDS TO HIGH TECH?

Johnson & Johnson's (J&J) new modernistic headquarters stands in stark contrast to the old brick building that was its home from the late 1890s until 1983. The new architectural facade is symbolic of the changes under way at this consistently successful company. Best known for such brands as Band-Aids and Baby Shampoo, J&J has accelerated its strategic moves toward more sophisticated medical technology. Success will depend on managing very different businesses from the past. And Chairman Burke is trying to change the management style and corporate culture that have been central to J&J's success. But he is having trouble.

For years, consumer products, prescription drugs, and hospital-supply lines have flourished under the marketing-dominated, decentralized management structure at J&J. People running its ''170 companies'' enjoyed substantial autonomy, with most divisions having their own boards. Corporate headquarters staff was small, and only one management layer separated division presidents from a 14-member executive committee.

However, the long-time dominance of marketing and sales executives and the insularity of the autonomous units could impede J&J's ability to push into new business and react swiftly to changing competition in health care. Yet attempts to gain greater coordination across units (such as centralized ordering and distribution to maintain a lead in hospital supplies) have been met with resistance and management turnover.

''General'' Johnson, CEO from 1938 to 1963, established the structure and style J&J used so successfully for so long. He wrote the corporate credo, which states that J&J's first responsibility is not to shareholders or employees, but to ''doctors, nurses, patients, mothers, and all others'' who use its products. This tradition helps explain why all 14 of the executive committee members have consumer-marketing or pharmaceutical backgrounds. That in itself portends problems of commitment to unfamiliar product lines and operating practices.

This tradition gets in the way of strategies to acquire and manage new medical equipment thrusts. Because of its financial and control system J&J has had trouble keeping entrepreneurs who built the acquired companies. And typical operating policies and practices have not been adapted to new needs. For example, soon after J&J acquired a dialysis business, prices for dialyzers (filters to clean blood) dropped as the government limited medicare funds. Cost-conscious customers began reusing dialyzers; but J&J was accustomed to selling products used once in a sterile environment: ''It was appalling to us to think that those things would become reusable.'' Hence, because J&J's culture prevented change, its competitors' products, which could be prepared for reuse more easily, gained a distinct advantage.

The cooperation and communication needed for the new strategy are also alien to the old culture. For instance, one J&J unit, so used to independence, refused to take managers from other J&J companies. And mixed signals from the top have confused managers about how committed their leaders are to cooperation. For instance, three separate units proposed that three of their products be packaged in a customized surgical kit. Headquarters failed to give approval. And, instead of creating formal structures to combine efforts in hospital services, units involved with this business will maintain separate sales forces.

Perhaps the two Tylenol capsule poisoning incidents in 1982 and 1986 are the least of J&J's worries. It may need some of its own medicine to cure the headaches of changing a corporate culture to meet the requirements of its new strategy.

Source: Adapted from ''Changing Corporate Culture,'' *Business Week,* May 14, 1984, pp. 130–138.

Specifically, with respect to implementing strategic change, Hobbs and Heany recommend six steps:

1 Before changing the strategy, make sure that serious functional overload does not exist; i.e., slack and balance are needed so that those involved in changes do not feel isolated or overburdened.

2 Contain strategic shock waves. Strategy change will upset the organization. So if you can, insulate the part of the business involved. (This is one reason why stability with expansion in one SBU is a favored strategy.)

3 Give personal top-management attention to changes.

4 If a strategic planning team is used, don't disband it until it identifies follow-through actions needed at the next operational level.

5 Communicate down about the reasons for the new strategy and the various roles needed to accomplish it.

6 Follow up 30 days after the new strategy change; ask a dozen managers at lower levels to write down the three most critical tasks needed which will determine the success or failure of the plan. Evaluation of the responses will give you an idea as to whether needed changes have been institutionalized.

For effectively accomplishing unfreezing, learning, and refreezing, the *nature of the change* may be as important as the techniques used. Here we are referring to the changes which are easiest to introduce and which generate less conflict and resistance (are more acceptable). A change is more likely to occur if it does not involve changing social roles or power configurations (if there are few organizational changes) and if people have sufficient ability to execute these roles. It is also easier to implement change if the change involved is not rapid—it usually takes time to introduce change. Thus workable targets or substrategies which don't affect the whole organization are easier to introduce. Finally, the nature of the change should include enough flexibility to accommodate later extensions. This means that attempts should be made to build in slack at the start and to provide for organizational learning over time.

Thus, as we suggested in Chapter 8, strategic choice must involve a consideration of implementation processes, among which change itself is included. These ideas argue that small incremental adjustments with anticipatory flexibility introduced over time have a higher probability of success. Again, the implementation factors discussed in Chapters 9 and 10 are the things we had in mind when we discussed limitations on strategic choice and which underlie the assumptions behind the incremental choice model we proposed. Hence you should see that the relationship suggested in Exhibit 10.1 between strategic choice and implementation involves a two-way flow.

IMPLEMENTING STRATEGY IN INTERNATIONAL SETTINGS [15]

As we have explored various aspects of implementation in this and the last chapter, we have identified selected issues of concern to strategists who operate in international arenas. Here we highlight some of the typical concerns affecting implementation due to the increased complexity for the firm pursuing an international strategy. We will follow the preceding scheme by exploring issues associated with the special case of international resource allocation, organization, plans, policies, and leadership.

Resource Allocation

International companies (IC) must find sources of capital and allocate them to domestic and foreign operations to support their strategies. This used to be a simple process of transmitting funds from the parent company to establish operations abroad. However, with greater availability of other sources in host countries and international capital markets (e.g., Eurodollars), and with the greater use of licensing and joint ventures, the corporatewide process of resource allocation is more complex. For example, global marketing systems can become a strength, providing sources of internal capital. Yet the firm engaged in foreign and domestic production must determine what funds should be allocated for maintaining older facilities (often in the home country where business was first started) and what should be allocated for investing in new capacity.

Organization

The resource allocation process will be affected by how the firm is organized. That is, resources will be allocated differently according to whether the firm establishes a global financial system or treats each foreign operation as a separate entity. In a unified system, excess cash from varied units can be allocated by central management for units that need it or to capital markets offering better returns. And new capital can generally be acquired from the lowest-cost sources. Because of differences between countries in tax rates, freedom to remit profits, risks, and so on, it is often beneficial to take a larger share of profit from business in one place than in another. A unified system has such a capability, as well as the ability to manage currency exchange rates more readily. This in itself can be a motivation for strategists to engage in foreign operations. For example, many U.S. filmmakers were shooting a third or more of their products in Canada in the early 1980s because favorable exchange rates (and more flexible unions) dramatically lowered production costs.

The international corporation can organize activities other than finance on a global basis. On the other hand, there are strong forces (e.g., economic and cultural differences as well as varying national interests) which operate against a unified organization system. For example, decision-making power held at corporate headquarters may be resented by the nation seeking to control the affairs of firms operating within its borders. Hence, the form of foreign involvement (wholly owned subsidiary versus joint venture versus licensing strategies, for example) will depend both on issues of organizational implementation and on the discretion of managers to choose the form they prefer.

Plans and Policies

As just indicated, a unified organization system can have an impact on plans and policies for implementing a strategy involving international activities. This section explores various planning and policy areas associated with an international strategy.

In the finance area, fluctuating exchange rates, currency controls, quotas, tariffs, and so on are problems the strategist must deal with if the firm operates internationally. Inflation, taxation, and fiscal and monetary policies will be affected by the domestic *and* (at least one) foreign government if the firm chooses an international strategy. Accounting principles vary from country to country. International debt crises and trade imbalances can impact the ability to move goods or services across boundaries. A unified financial system eases some of these problems. For example, the options for dealing with foreign exchange are greater because the capacity to shift funds among affiliates is easier and quicker. And centralized decision making to set exchange policy (and other financial policies) leads to greater consistency and responsiveness. As before, the disadvantages of centralization need to be considered in the context of the need to recognize different national needs and requirements.

In the marketing arena, one of the key issues is standardization of the product line across domestic and foreign markets. We noted in Chapters 7 and 8 that, at least initially, a firm usually enters foreign markets with identical products. Later, modifications or new products can be introduced. Yet, because of variations in local tastes, standards of living, climate, and so on, diversity is often desired. Incentives to move this way are strong, but the costs involve loss of the advantages of economies of scale for production and distribution on a "global" basis. Similarly, new promotion efforts designed to respond to differences in consumer attitudes and competitive conditions must be considered. Channels of distribution different from those traditionally used by the firm (before considering the international thrust) may also be required. For example, in less developed countries, wholesalers and retailers are generally more numerous, more specialized, and smaller. If the firm has traditionally distributed product through mass retailers, new marketing methods may discourage a strategist from entering certain territories. If new territories are entered, plans to establish new distribution methods will need to be made.

The area of research and development is a difficult one for some firms entering foreign markets. In some instances, the market is seen as a "dumping ground" for transfer of "obsolete" technology (in the domestic market). This may or may not be appreciated by the host country. Some governments will accept, or seek, such *intermediate* or *appropriate* technology if local skills and abilities are not developed enough to use more advanced technology. Yet some host nations seek economic progress through building technical capability, and these governments may require local R&D investment. For the IC, decentralization of R&D may duplicate effort, reduce communication, and make it more difficult to coordinate with global sales and manage production. In comparison with R&D of national companies, a unified global R&D effort allows costs to be spread over a larger base. On the other hand, responsiveness to local market conditions can lead some firms to develop multiple R&D units. As with all factors, the choice here involves an integration with other plans and policies.

Production, like marketing, is concerned with standardization to reduce costs and ease management. An ideal strategy would be a unified system in which a limited number of factories of optimum economic scale were located in sites with the lowest cost of labor and materials supplying markets all over the world. Nonetheless, volume or weight of products or breadth of product line may reduce the ability of the firm to set up such a system. And, while some processes can be transferred intact to foreign locations, others may have to be modified or replaced if new manufacturing facilities are to be set up. Furthermore, domestic legislation, the desire of labor unions to protect jobs, and so on may restrict the location of facilities to particular sites. Quite commonly, production is centralized on a regional basis, where transportation, labor, or governmental deterrents are minor compared to economics of scale. For example, the European Economic Community and other "fair trade" areas have been established to promote concentration of industrial activity in given regions. Company plans to locate facilities must recognize these conditions. Some international companies control raw materials which are used by themselves and other end-product producers in other countries. There may be internal pressures by some divisions to sell to competitors. Policies on inter- and intracompany transfer prices need to be established if such a strategy is to be pursued.

As mentioned above, labor unions may present a hurdle to a retrenchment strategy for a firm wishing to relocate in a foreign site. But labor is also a factor in plans for new sites. Asian firms opening facilities in the United States Midwest in the mid-1980s opted for locations where labor unions were weak or nonexistent. In any case, a plan for the use of labor needs to be established when an international strategy is chosen. Strategists need to determine the desired proportion of local and foreign workers and managers. When an economy slows, local citizens want jobs held by foreigners. Even in prosperity, ethnic conflicts between foreign employees and natives can occur. Benefit plans, pay scales, promotion policies, and so on will vary substantially from area to area, making a corporatewide standardized personnel system unlikely.

Leadership

Finally, managerial style is an issue which must be considered as the option of international strategy is considered. What managerial skills and techniques are appropriate given the development and culture of the host nation? For example, sophisticated consumer-behavior marketing skills may be appropriate in Europe, but may not work in Nigeria. Intensive superior-subordinate conferences using an MBO approach may work in Australia, but run counter to cultural patterns in Indonesia. The Japanese quality circle works well in some U.S. sites, but is not very effective where labor traditionally views managers as adversaries. The climate and culture of the "home office" may not fit the new setting.

The IC must also determine the importance of a foreign assignment to the career development of its managers. In making decisions on whether or not to transfer managers to a foreign location there is more to consider than the desire of host countries to have their people employed. Strategists transferring managers for an overseas assignment must also consider local living costs and expenses. Given the value of the yen, the cost of keeping an executive in Tokyo in 1986 was base salary plus at least $170,000 per year ($70,000 to rent a house, $12,000 for private schools per child, $9000 for a trip home, plus bonuses and cost-of-living allowance). Many Japanese firms have opened private schools for children of Japanese managers assigned to the United States.

It has not been our intent in this section to exhaustively cover all the various issues involved in implementing the strategies one can consider if "going international" is an option. Rather, we hope you begin to see that, as with the domestic firm, a multitude of implementation issues should be addressed before a final commitment is made to pursue an international strategy. Too many firms attempt an international strategy only to find that problems of implementation crop up which reduce chances of success. These implementation issues should influence the choice of strategies and how they are carried out. And we trust you now agree with our earlier statement that increased complexity is involved with the international set of strategies.

SUMMARY

Chapter 10 continues the discussion of the segment of the strategic management process concerned with implementing strategy. In addition to allocating resources and establishing an organizational structure, it is necessary to develop policies and plans and assign or reassign leaders to support the strategy and help achieve objectives.

Plan and policy implementation is designed to specify how the strategic choice will come to be. The firm creates plans and policies which are decisional guides to action, and these help make the strategies chosen work. The critical element is the ability to factor the grand strategy into plans and policies that are compatible, workable, and not just "theoretically sound."

The minimal plans and policies which must be developed are the key functional decisions necessary in the following areas:

1 Financial mix: (*a*) capital, (*b*) leasing versus buying, (*c*) investment risk, (*d*) use of assets, (*e*) accounting and tax treatment

2 Marketing mix: (*a*) products and markets, (*b*) distribution and promotion, (*c*) price and packaging

3 Production-operations mix: (*a*) capacity and utilization, (*b*) location of facilities, (*c*) maintenance and replacement, (*d*) sourcing

4 R&D mix: (*a*) products and processes, (*b*) basic and applied research, (*c*) offensive and defensive research

5 Personnel: (*a*) recruiting, (*b*) allocating, (*c*) developing, (*d*) maintaining

6 Legal issues

7 Public relations

Policies and plans developed for the operating and staff departments need to be consistent with one another and fit the strategic choice and timing needs of the strategy.

Proposition 10.1

Enterprises which prepare implementation policies and plans for strategic choices will be more effective than those which do not.

Leadership implementation is accomplished in several ways:

• Changes in current leadership at appropriate levels
• Development of appropriate leadership styles and climates

* Involvement in the career development of future strategists
* Use of organization development techniques to effect changes

Effective leadership implementation involves making sure the person has the right education, abilities, experience, motivation, and personality to enact the strategic choice. In proposition form:

Proposition 10.2

Enterprises whose strategists' abilities, experiences, and personalities match the strategy will be more effective.

The nature of the leadership style and the motivation, decision, communication, and control processes will determine how effective the leader is in developing a climate and culture conducive to making policies work. Propositions 10.3 and 10.4 summarize the last two aspects of leadership implementation.

Proposition 10.3

Enterprises which plan for executive career development will be more effective than those which do not.

Proposition 10.4

Leaders who apply organization development concepts will more effectively implement strategic change.

The processes of implementation described in Chapters 9 and 10 apply to firms following an international strategy. But an added level of complexity is involved. Essentially, strategists must decide whether to operate a unified system or try to keep foreign activities distinct and separate from domestic operations. Resource allocation, organization, plans, policies, and leadership will vary depending on the stage of development of the firm's involvement in foreign countries. As the strategy changes from exporting to direct investment in several countries, the implementation is likely to become more unified and integrated.

While detailed plans for each functional area need to be developed, top executives are interested in a summary of the strategic plan. Exhibit 10.12 provides an example. Note that the overall objectives are broken down into specific time-based targets, actions needed are specified, resource allocations are identified, and organizational responsibility is assigned. Such a summary is a useful way to portray the essence of a strategic recommendation which has been carefully thought through in terms of its requirements for successful implementation.

EXHIBIT 10.12 PLANNING SUMMARY FORM—A PAPER MANUFACTURER

STRATEGIC PLAN SUMMARY

PLAN TITLE: *Earnings improvement of the Y–Supplies Business*
PLAN PURPOSE: *Strengthen the profitability and defensibility of our position in the Y–Supplies market*

Objectives	Strategies	Tactical goals	Tactical actions	Resources required	Target dates Begin	Target dates End	Responsibility
Profitably commercialize new product YZ and achieve an annual sales rate of 1.5 million units by the end of 1990.	Introduce product YZ with a concentrated promotion campaign into the southeastern region at a premium price.	Annual sales rate of 400,000 units in southeastern region at a minimum price of $5 each by end of 1987.	Launch a 4-month direct-mail campaign at city engineers of all cities with population of 5000 or more.	$25,000 and 2 labor-months	June 1, 1987	September 30, 1987	Marketing manager of southeastern region
			Launch personal sales contact campaign at city engineers of all cities with 50,000 or more population.	$40,000 and 8 labor-months	August 1, 1987	November 1, 1987	Same
			Develop indirect sales channel by adding one distributor in Alabama and Georgia and two in South Carolina.	$100,000 cash investment for capital and 2 labor-months	April 1987	August 1987	Same
	Build a small initial plant in Birmingham with 1-million-unit capacity which can be doubled in capacity to 2 million units in 1989 if the market sustains a growth rate of 10% or more through 1989.	Construct original 1 million-unit plant within total cost budget of $1.3 million.	Use turnkey contract for speedy design and construction of the plant. Specify the X-11 vacuum-molding process in the design of equipment.	$1,300,000 and 20 labor-months	January 1, 1987	August 15, 1987	Project manager

Objective / Action	Resources	Start	Completion	Responsibility
Upgrade quality of products Y9 through Y15 and their acceptance in the market while increasing our average Y-gross margin to 35% by the end of 1989.				
Start up initial new plant and achieve a direct unit cost under continuous operation of $1.50 per unit by the end of September, 1987.	$50,000 and 15 labor-months	May 1, 1987	August 1, 1987	Plant manager
Complete training program of key personnel prior to completion of construction.				
Reorganize the purchasing department, and so forth.				
Reduce spoilage in raw material, and so forth.				
Other tactical actions, etc.				
Use national account purchasing as leverage for, and so forth.				

Source: Adapted from R. O'Connor, *Corporate Guides to Long-Range Planning*, Report No. 687 (New York: Conference Board, 1976), p. 81.

Chapter 11 discusses the last phase of the strategic management and implementation process: evaluation and control.

REFERENCES

[1] Implementing Strategies

Schleh, E. C.: "Strategic Planning—No Sure Cure for Corporate Surprises," *Management Review* (March 1979), pp. 54–57.
Note: Also see Chapter 9 references on Integrating Strategy and Implementation [1]

[2] The Policy Implementation Process

VanMeter, D. S., and C. E. Van Horn: "The Policy Implementation Process," *Administration and Society,* vol. 6, (February 1975), pp. 445–488.

[3] Developing Policies and Plans

Friend, J. K.: "The Dynamics of Policy Change," *Long Range Planning,* vol. 10 (February 1977), pp. 40–47.
Lindblom, C. E.: *The Policy-Making Process* (Englewood Cliffs, N.J.: Prentice-Hall, 1980).

[4] Policies and Plans for Finance and Accounting

Anders, G.: "Corporations Find Help for Balance Sheets: Swap Costly Debt for Low-Yielding Stock," *The Wall Street Journal* (June 30, 1982), p. 23.
"Companies Make Survival Their Strategy," *Business Week,* July 26, 1982, pp. 46–48.
Farrell, C., R. Welch, P. Houston, J. Hamilton, and V. Cahan: "The Insurance Crisis: Now Everyone's in a Risky Business," *Business Week,* Mar. 10, 1986, pp. 88–92.
"It Can Pay Off Big to Turn Common into Preferred," *Business Week,* July 2, 1984, p. 76.
"Matchmakers Heat Up the 'Swap' Market," *Business Week,* Nov. 5, 1984, p. 56.
"The Perilous Hunt for Financing," *Business Week,* Mar. 1, 1981, pp. 44–45.
"A Real-World Test for the New Inflation Rules," *Business Week,* Apr. 4, 1980, pp. 116–118.
"The Tax Magic That's Making Employee Stock Plans Multiply," *Business Week,* Oct. 15, 1984, pp. 158–160.

[5] Policies and Plans for Marketing and Distribution

Dunkin, A.: "Want to Wake Up a Tired Old Product? Repackage It," *Business Week,* July 15, 1985, pp. 130–134.
"Flexible Pricing: Industry's New Strategy to Hold Market Share Changes the Rules for Economic Decision Making," *Business Week,* Dec. 12, 1977, pp. 78–85.
Hise, R. T., A. Parasuraman, and R. Viswanathan: "Product Elimination: The Neglected Management Responsibility," *The Journal of Business Strategy,* vol. 2 (1982), pp. 56–63.
MacMillan, I., M. L. McCaffery, and G. Van Wijk: "Competitors' Responses to Easily Imitated New Products," *Strategic Management Journal,* vol. 6 (1985), pp. 75–86.
Ries, A., and J. Trout: *Marketing Warfare* (New York: McGraw-Hill, 1985).

[6] Policies and Plans for Production and Operations

"Alumax: Winning Big by Building Inventories during the Downturn," *Business Week,* Oct. 17, 1983, pp. 129–130.

"The Fully Automated Factory Rewards an Early Dreamer," *Business Week,* Mar. 17, 1986, p. 91.

Miller, J. G.: "Fit Production Systems to the Task," *Harvard Business Review* (January–February 1981), pp. 145–154.

Wheelwright, S. C.: "Manufacturing Strategy: Defining the Missing Link," *Strategic Management Journal,* vol. 5 (1984), pp. 77–91.

————and R. H. Hayes: "Competing through Manufacturing," *Harvard Business Review,* vol. 63 (January–February 1985), pp. 99–109.

[7] Policies and Plans for Research and Development

"A Call for Vision in Managing Technology," *Business Week,* May 24, 1982, pp. 24–33.

Ford, D., and C. Ryan: "Taking Technology to Market," *Harvard Business Review* (January–February 1981), pp. 117–126.

"TRW Leads a Revolution in Managing Technology," *Business Week,* Nov. 15, 1982, pp. 124–130.

[8] Policies and Plans for Personnel and Legal Activities

Baird, L., and I. Meshoulam: "Implementing Human Resource Strategic Management," working paper, School of Management, Boston University, 1983.

"Managing Company Lawsuits to Stay Out of Court," *Business Week,* Aug. 23, 1982, pp. 54–55.

"A New Corporate Powerhouse: The Legal Department," *Business Week,* Apr. 9, 1984, pp. 66–71.

"A New Target: Reducing Staff and Levels," *Business Week,* Dec. 21, 1981, pp. 69–73.

Patton, A.: "Industry's Misguided Shift to Staff Jobs," *Business Week,* Apr. 5, 1982, pp. 12–15.

Slocum, J. W., W. L. Cron, R. W. Hansen, and S. Rawlings: "Business Strategy and the Management of Plateaued Employees," *Academy of Management Journal,* vol. 28 (1985), pp. 133–154.

[9] Public Relations and Politics

Baysinger, B. D.: "Domain Maintenance as an Objective of Business Political Activity," *Academy of Management Review,* vol. 9 (1984), pp. 248–258.

———— and R. W. Woodman: "Dimensions of the Public Affairs/Government Relations Function in Major American Corporations," *Strategic Management Journal,* vol. 3 (1982), pp. 27–41.

Dickie, R. B.: "Influence of Public Affairs Offices on Corporate Planning and of Corporations on Government Policy," *Strategic Management Journal,* vol. 5 (1984), pp. 15–34.

[10] Integrating Policies and Plans

Andersen, T. A.: "Coordinating Strategic and Operational Planning," *Business Horizons* (Summer 1965), pp. 49–55.

Fox, H.: "A Framework for Functional Coordination," *Atlantic Economic Review* (November–December 1973), pp. 10–11.

Hamilton, J. O.: "Genentech Gets a Shot at the Big Time," *Business Week,* Oct. 28, 1985, p. 108.

Mitchell, R.: "How Ford Hit the Bull's Eye with Taurus," *Business Week,* June 30, 1986, pp. 69–70.

[11] Leadership Issues for Strategy Implementation

"Behind AT&T's Change at the Top," *Business Week,* Nov. 6, 1978, pp. 114–139.

Gerstein, R., and R. Reisman: "Strategic Selection: Matching Executives to Business Conditions," *Sloan Management Review* (Winter 1983), pp. 33–49.

Grant, J. H., and W. R. King: *The Logic of Strategic Planning* (Boston: Little, Brown, 1982).

Gupta, A. K.: "Contingency Linkages between Strategy and General Manager Characteristics," *Academy of Management Review,* vol. 9 (1984), pp. 399–412.

————and V. Govindarajan: "Business Unit Strategy, Managerial Characteristics, and Business Unit Effectiveness at Strategy Implementation," *Academy of Management Journal,* vol. 27 (1984), pp. 25–41.

Kerr, J.: "Assigning Managers on the Basis of the Life Cycle," *Journal of Business Strategy,* vol. 2, no. 4 (1982), pp. 58–65.

Smith, N. R., and J. B. Miner: "Type of Entrepreneur, Type of Firm, and Management Motivation," *Strategic Management Journal,* vol. 4 (1983), pp. 325–340.

Smith, K. G., and J. K. Harrison: "Hands on Leadership: A Key to Strategy Implementation and Organizational Excellence," paper presented at the Strategic Management Society Conference, Philadelphia, 1984.

Szilagyi, A. D., and D. M. Schweiger: "Matching Managers to Strategies," *Academy of Management Review,* vol. 9 (1984), pp. 626–637.

"Wanted: A Manager to Fit Each Strategy," *Business Week,* Feb. 25, 1980, pp. 166–173.

[12] Management Style and Climate

Byrne, J. A.: "Up, Up and Away?" *Business Week,* Nov. 25, 1985, pp. 80–94.

"Corporate Culture: The Hard-to-Change Values that Spell Success or Failure," *Business Week,* Oct. 27, 1980, pp. 148–154.

Kilmann, R. A., M. J. Saxton, and R. Serpa (eds.): *Gaining Control of the Corporate Culture* (San Francisco: Jossey, Bass, 1985).

"Life at IBM," *The Wall Street Journal,* Apr. 8, 1982, p. 1.

"Putting Excellence into Management," *Business Week,* July 21, 1980, pp. 196–205.

Schiller, Z., and A. Dunkin: "P & G's Rusty Marketing Machine," *Business Week,* Oct. 21, 1985, pp. 111–112.

[13] Managerial Career Development

Bartee, E.: "On the Personal Development of the Strategic Manager," in H. I. Ansoff et al. (eds.), *From Strategic Planning to Strategic Management* (New York: Wiley Interscience, 1976).

Murthy, K. R., and M. S. Salter: "Should CEO Pay Be Linked to Results?" *Harvard Business Review* (June 1975), pp. 66–73.

[14] Organizational Development

Argyris, C.: *Strategy, Change, and Defensive Routines.* (Marshfield, Mass.: Pitman, 1985).

Blake, R., and J. Mouton: *Building a Dynamic Organization through Grid Organization Development.* (Reading, Mass.: Addison-Wesley, 1969).

Hobbs, J. M., and D. F. Heany: "Coupling Strategy to Operating Plans," *Harvard Business Review,* vol. 55, no. 3 (May–June 1977), pp. 119–126.

Lippitt, G.: *Organization Renewal* (New York: Appleton-Century-Crofts, 1969).

Tushman, M. L., and E. Romanelli: "Organizational Evolution," in L. Cummings and B. Staw (eds.), *Research in Organizational Behavior* (Greenwich, Conn.: JAI Press, 1985).

[15] International Strategy Implementation

Ball, D. A., and W. H. McCullock, Jr.: *International Business* (Plano, Tex.: Business Publications, 1985).
Buell, B.: "Now It's the Land of Rising Rent," *Business Week,* July 7, 1986, p. 43.
Fayweather, J., and A. Kapoor: *Strategy and Negotiation for the International Corporation* (Cambridge, Mass.: Ballinger, 1985).
"Filmmakers Discover The Canadian Solution," *Business Week,* July 15, 1986, pp. 74–75.

CHAPTER OUTLINE

IMPLEMENTATION: EVALUATION AND CONTROL OF STRATEGY

OBJECTIVES

- To understand why firms evaluate and control strategy
- To understand how firms evaluate and control strategy
- To understand how evaluation and control fit into the strategic management process

INTRODUCTION [1]

We have come to the evaluation and control phase of the strategic management process as emphasized in Exhibit 11.1. Remember that this is an integral part of implementing strategy.

> Evaluation of strategy is that phase of the strategic management process in which managers try to assure that the strategic choice is properly implemented and is meeting the objectives of the enterprise.

We now assume that the infrastructure is in place. A plan to carry out the chosen strategy has been specified, and activities have been assigned to the organization; resources have been provided for doing these tasks; policies have been developed and communicated; and the leadership system and style have been formed so that the climate is geared to the strategy and plans. There are also several other crucial com-

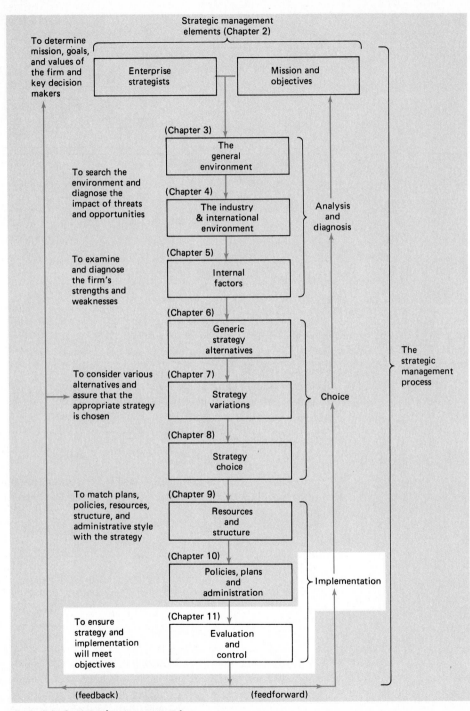

EXHIBIT 11.1 **A model of strategic management.**

ponents of an effective administrative system. These are needed to make sure that the other elements all work properly. A *follow-through* on strategy and its implementation requires a control system, an appropriate reward system, and an effective information system which provides managers with accurate, complete feedback in time so that they can act on the data. These are all integral elements of implementation and evaluation to be sure the plans *will work* and *are working*. The evaluation system is also needed as a way to recycle feedback as an input for new strategic planning and as a means for double-checking that the strategic choice is consistent, appropriate, and workable given internal and external analyses and the plan to implement it.

The *ways* in which subsystems perform their tasks, use resources, and interpret policy give meaning to the intended strategy. SBU and functional managers quite often have a fairly large range of discretion in interpreting policy and using resources. They may in fact work against an intended strategy. We might call this behavior a "sin of commission." Further, to the extent that these managers are protecting "their subsystem," new strategies or policies might never be considered. This could be tagged a "sin of omission." For instance, if a manager fails to forward information that is potentially damaging to the unit (e.g., if a sales manager hides the fact that a competitor's new product is hurting sales), a failing strategy might continue to be pursued. New alternatives would not be considered. Similarly, a manager may decide not to forward a proposal which is thought to run counter to the desires of top management, even though the idea may be a potentially useful alternative. (This type of manager is like students who write term papers based on what they *think* the instructor wants to see rather than on what is believed about a topic.) So the omissions and commissions of managers directly and indirectly affect the strategy of the organization as reflected in its action. In some cases, decisions are quite different from the intended strategy. Occasionally, there is feedback from clients that indicates that something is wrong. Or internal "whistle blowers" may come forth to challenge what is going on. Sins of omission and commission are two reasons why organizations establish control and evaluation mechanisms. Indeed a yawning gap in internal controls contributed to the cash management debacle at E. F. Hutton in 1985. Hutton is still trying to recover from strategic losses as a result of its guilty plea to fraud resulting from lack of control.

Control and evaluation processes help strategists monitor the progress of a plan. They seek to answer a number of questions, such as:

- Are the decisions being made consistent with policy?
- Are there sufficient resources to get the job done? Are the resources being used wisely?
- Are events in the environment occurring as anticipated? (For example, how are competitors reacting to our activities?)
- Are goals and targets being met, both short-term and long-term ones?
- Should we proceed with the plan as we have formulated it?

In effect, evaluation and control processes are set up to be sure the gap between expected and desired objectives will be closed according to the strategy.

In terms of our gap analysis approach, we want to determine whether the gaps between expected results and ideal outcomes *are being* (or will be) closed; and we want to know if any internal or external changes from the plan might alter our expectations regarding these gaps. The evaluation process should alert us to these conditions so that corrective action can be taken—getting back on track, changing the track, or changing our beliefs about the gaps and objectives. In other words, unless evaluation and control are integrated with a plan, strategic planning may be little more than pious hope rather than a means of achieving the desired future. So let's look at the components of a system which should lead to good control and follow-through.

THE CONTROL AND EVALUATION PROCESS [2]

The organization's administrative structure and style constitute the basic mechanism by which a firm attempts to control its activities. We discussed the basic elements of this in Chapters 9 and 10. Exhibit 11.2 shows how these factors are brought together for a follow-through on strategy.

The evaluation process is normally thought of as four interrelated activities:

A Establish performance targets, standards, and tolerance limits for the objectives, strategy, and implementation plans.

B Measure the actual position in relation to the targets at a given time. If outcomes are outside the limits, inform managers with discretion to take action.

EXHIBIT 11.2 COST CONTROL WITH A VENGEANCE

The systems of control at White Consolidated are essential to its strategy of competing successfully in the brutal major-appliances industry, where price competition is fierce. The doctrine of cost control has become a corporate religion, and the climate and structure are designed to control operations and achieve efficiency of plants, people, and equipment which the company acquires from larger firms that have given up.

After each acquisition, White makes massive cuts in the labor force (up to 40 percent) and takes a hard line with unions. It is willing to take strikes to get its way on other cost-cutting measures. Every product line and model is reviewed carefully, and many low-volume products are eliminated. Then the company streamlines operations; frequently it moves a given line to one plant for economies of scale in production.

There is also a decentralized management system for its 15 appliance plants. While the plant "presidents" can be overruled at headquarters, each has control over design, engineering, and product pricing as well as the manufacturing process. Managers can't blame success or failure on something else. But a tight financial reporting system is imposed by headquarters. Expense, manufacturing, and profit statements are collected *each day* from every department. And each month the plant "president" *and* the plant's controller send *independent* detailed operating statements.

The emphasis on penny-pinching at all levels of management is likely to lead to short-term gains, so White is concerned about productivity improvement. But the R&D staff favors production efficiency, not marketing innovation, and the research teams are clustered at the various plants whose operations they are trying to improve.

Given the nature of the appliance business, such a control system seems necessary, and White has turned around previously unsuccessful product lines. It took the company just 3 months to break even on a Westinghouse line of appliances which had been losing $2 million per month. But White's operating profit is about average for the industry.

Source: Adapted from "White Consolidated's New Appliance Bunch," *Business Week,* May 7, 1979, pp. 94–98.

C Analyze deviations from acceptable tolerance limits.

D Execute modifications if any are necessary and/or feasible.

This process can encompass a variety of dimensions of importance to strategic management. That is, a number of aspects of control need to be achieved, according to Rowe and Carlson.

1 Management control, which is based on past performance and historic data

2 Real-time control, which is concerned primarily with technical aspects of control so that information that is as current as possible is provided

3 Performance management, which is concerned with goal congruence and organizational effectiveness

4 Adaptive control, which has to do with determining the quickest and most effective way in which to respond to changes

5 Strategic control, which involves anticipating or developing ways to minimize potential deviations from desired outcomes

Our discussion of the reward system a bit later in the chapter touches on a number of these aspects, most particularly management control and performance management. We will discuss real-time control later when we discuss feedback systems. The first two aspects are mostly concerned with internal implementation questions, while the third involves questions of objectives. The last two are of more significance to questions of evaluating strategic validity and change. To effectively accomplish these types of control, it is necessary to modify the process so that it includes environmental as well as internal assessments.

1 Establish environmental assumptions basic to the strategy and plans.

2 Monitor these environmental factors to detect any significant deviation.

3 If extraordinary deviations occur, reassess goals, the strategy, and plans.

4 Execute new strategy formulation and implementation processes as needed.

Thus the strategic control and evaluation process also requires the monitoring and feedback of environmental conditions so that strategists can be sure that the assumptions on which the strategy and plans are based remain valid.

Exhibit 11.3 shows this modified process. Stages *C* and *D* are where strategists are required to actually perform evaluations. Standards or tolerance limits may not be met because they were too high or low, or the assumptions were possibly in error or had a great deal of uncertainty attached to them. In some cases, assumptions may have been pessimistic, and so the goals and objectives need to recognize new opportunities. Of course, the objectives may not be met because the choice was not properly implemented. Or it may be because the strategy chosen was not appropriate. Last but not least, the objectives may have been unrealistic or too high. The strategist must determine which of these cause-effect relationships might be operating.

Successful strategists are like physicians when they are treating illnesses. They look at symptoms and make the most probable diagnosis. Then they prescribe the best procedure or medicine. The diagnosis results from the analysis-diagnosis and choice stages of the strategic management process. The prescription is the implementation.

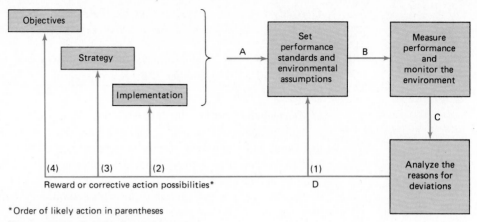

EXHIBIT 11.3   **The process of evaluation and control.**

If the prescription does not work, the physicians may believe that they made the wrong diagnosis (strategic choice), and then they may make another diagnosis. Just as physicians do not give up if the first choice does not work, so the strategists make another choice. The feedback system that they had developed showed that their strategy had failed. But they were ready, no doubt, with an alternative choice—a contingency plan. Exhibit 11.4 shows how General Mills has changed to address some of these issues.

The Role of the Strategist

The idealized evaluation process just described may not always work as effectively as you might think. Different organization levels and people are involved. The evaluation *should* take place at both the corporate level and the SBU level. If the SBUs do not take adequate steps soon enough, the corporate level may have to step in. The corporate-level executive evaluates the overall corporate strategy and also monitors the SBU-level evaluations. But here, too, problems can result.

As we mentioned in Chapter 9, the budget may often become a tool for control, since it interconnects the elements of a plan along common financial terms. This may not reflect some of the nonfinancial standards and key assumptions important to strategic control and evaluation. The *controller* at the corporate level may be in charge of the information system and budget control process as it relates to the preparation of various financial reports which are important inputs for executive decisions. This staff position, often located near the top of the structure with access to key executives, can thus lead to decision making without the assumption of responsibility. Therefore, it is important for top managers to recognize the informational role of the controller while they maintain authority over the control system as a major tool in the administrative system.

Of course, audit and executive committees of the board also play a role in evalu-

EXHIBIT 11.4   EVALUATING AND CONTROLLING DIFFERENT SBUs

For years General Mills maintained loose reins over a diverse group of entrepreneurial companies which it had acquired. Through its acquisitions the corporation got dynamic new businesses growing more rapidly than its core along with entrepreneurs to act as role models for existing managers. The entrepreneurs usually got fat contracts and access to staff support and seemingly limitless cash.

But within a few years relationships begin to chafe; the entrepreneurs deal with superiors who have little knowledge of their business; they may feel saddled with formidable reporting chores; and they may begin to compete with other SBUs for funds on the basis of standards alien to the particular business. The entrepreneur, often accustomed to an autocratic approach, may be reluctant to shift to a style stressing delegation, personnel development, and teamwork.

General Mills experienced these problems as it began to impose stringent financial controls on its nearly autonomous SBU chiefs. Says CEO Atwater, "We were so hands-off that we had little discussion of strategy and no discussion of people development." But he is concerned that he will cross the fine line between too much and too little control.

In 1980, sales at General Mills exceeded $1.1 billion. With such large numbers, stricter attention to financial control becomes necessary. Many of the new controls attempt to drive responsibility for managing capital deeper into the SBUs. "General Mills is imposing a hefty financial penalty on any subsidiary that exceeds existing working-capital guidelines unless the SBU head can prove that increased sales justify extra inventory building. It has increased internal working capital charges to 13% from 7%. And it has launched a study of the feasibility of taking a 'balance sheet' approach that would look at the cost of financing fixed assets, and would force each subsidiary to simulate intracompany dividends. It is even toying with the idea of assigning each company a debt-equity ratio based on an 'industry average.'" Subsidiary managers will also be asked to get strategic and budgetary goals approved by corporate headquarters. And General Mills has set up new positions, insisting that each SBU hire a controller trained by the corporation.

Reaction is mixed at SBU levels. Those used to autonomy are concerned, even though some heads suggest that headquarters is more forgiving than the general financial community would be if an SBU made mistakes. But others believe that common goals and targets are inappropriate, particularly the rules about tight, daily control of working capital. Says one, "I don't know if they realize that ours is a different industry. There is an absolute tradeoff in this business between holding down inventories and continuing growth."

General Mills's change in evaluating and controlling SBUs may result in the centralization of strategic planning and a reduction of the entrepreneurial spirit. To SBU heads, the answer depends on whether the corporate parent will be willing to accept variations in financial goals and performance. General Mills is sending its SBU managers through financial management courses "that it hopes will help them make better decisions on their own." And bonuses up to 50 percent of the base salary are still based on meeting SBU goals. But who sets those goals and standards may change the picture entirely. As one SBU manager put it, "When you're by yourself, you set the standards. Here the standards are set—and they're largely General Mills's standards."

Source: Adapted from "How to Manage Entrepreneurs," *Business Week,* Sept. 7, 1981, pp. 66–69.

ating and controlling top management, and external auditors can be used to evaluate the veracity of the financial system. Just as important, if the control system is to work effectively, managers must be motivated to use it, and rewards must be based on the standards established by the control system. These are the topics in our next section.

THE MOTIVATION TO EVALUATE [3]

If a control and evaluation system is to be used effectively, the top managers must want to evaluate the performance. This motivation develops if senior managers realize that the strategy can fail and if they are rewarded for their performance in relation to objectives.

Most senior managers have had failure experiences. Too many failures can stunt a career and may make the manager so cautious that few creative decisions are made. But experiencing no failures can be equally dangerous. Human beings can believe that they are omniscient when their history includes no failures and when they are surrounded by admiring assistants. A few failures remind us that we need to determine whether our strategies are working. One can think of many examples in political history of failures that resulted from an unwillingness to evaluate the strategy—for example, Great Britain's experiences in the Crimean and Boer Wars and in India, and the United States' experiences in Vietnam. Businesses can fail for lack of evaluation too. Perhaps the key is to allow for some failure if it is associated with appropriate levels of risk.

The Reward System

The second half of the motivation to evaluate is whether managers are rewarded directly for performance. If high performance in relation to meeting objectives was rewarded, the managers would be motivated to evaluate their strategies. There is little evidence that except in emergency times, this direct tie exists in most firms. Some evidence shows that rewards such as raises and promotions continue even when performance is lacking. Too often this is because the executives themselves make recommendations about salaries and promotions to the board for themselves and each other. To the extent that the chief operating officer and associates are held to performance before reward, they will be more motivated to evaluate the strategy. Exhibit 11.5 suggests that some better-managed firms have recognized this.

If the intent of the control process is to ensure that policies and plans are being followed and that the decisions which are made are consistent with the strategy, then rewards for the kind of performance or behavior intended will assist in this process. The demands of the strategy and plans should be what guides the reward system. If an SBU is in an early expansion stage where entrepreneurial moves are needed to develop new products and markets, the manager in charge might be motivated by rewards tied more closely to the performance of the SBU in finding new niches. If, on the other hand, a stability strategy is appropriate for a given SBU, the factors such as cost efficiency, the smoothness of production and distribution, or the degree of inventory control may be more relevant in an assessment of the manager's performance. While most managers don't like to think about it, retrenchment strategies for some parts of the business are a normal occurrence (assuming that the product life cycle concept is operating). Here, too, a plan for exit may be in place, and key warning signals that indicate the need to evaluate and abandon products or markets should be established *ahead of time*. Performance measures established at the time of entry may help a firm overcome problems such as the inability to admit mistakes or covering up problems to keep things going when they should stop. Unless managers are rewarded for alerting strategists about the possible value of retrenchment, it is unlikely that they will pass on data relevant to top decision makers.

EXHIBIT 11.5   REWARDING THE PERFORMERS

During the last two decades, compensation committees measured executive performance on the basis of earnings per share. Executive pay climbed at an unbroken pace during the 1970s. In 1960, only half of all CEOs received annual raises. By 1981, 90% received raises or bonuses. Boards used bonuses to reward performance and help managers with the rising cost of living.

More recently, the earnings per share measure has come under unfavorable scrutiny, because earnings can be manipulated (by selling assets, liquidating inventory, cutting out research and development, etc.). Yet such manipulations have long-term impact on the firm and its strategy. More and more corporate boardrooms are looking for other measures to reflect growth in stockholder value, and encourage strategic instead of short-term decision making.

Scores of companies, including Sears, Roebuck, Dow Chemical, and Dayton Hudson, are now measuring the performance of their business units on total operations and awarding incentive pay based on outperforming the competition. The intent is to force corporate leaders to rethink strategies focused on maximizing short-term earnings and revenues. Steel companies, for instance, have been notorious for justifying investments on the basis of immediate payback, without considering the viability of the entire business.

To close the connection between performance and reward, many firms have restructured to make managers identifiable and responsible for performance. But a compensation system geared to the performance of the organizational unit is an important motivational tool. And the system needs to be tied to different strategies of the organizational units. For example, GE and Westinghouse have both mature and young SBUs, with different missions. At GE's mature units, short-term incentives dominate the compensation packages of managers, who are charged with maximizing cash flow, achieving high margins, and retaining market share. In the younger businesses, where developing products and marketing strategies are most important, nonfinancial measures geared to the execution of longer-term performance dictate the major portion of a manager's remuneration. With 3- to 5-year plans, companies require managers to set priorities, such as attaining a market-share figure or establishing a sales network. Performance can be measured by success in achieving a portion of the goals each year.

Pay for performance is most difficult where a culture of teamwork is critical. Says Peter Cusack, vice president at ABC, "One of our challenges is to introduce greater sophistication into performance measurement without destroying the family concept. It's very hard to introduce dramatic change into a culture."

Yet the biggest challenge is to convince the CEO that compensation should be tied to long-term results, which are riskier and take longer to evaluate. Given the CEO's ties to board members on compensation committees, self-interest may yet take precedence over rewarding strategic thinking. But evidence suggests that raising the value of the company's stock is a reflection of changes in bonuses and compensation plans for executives.

Source: Adapted from "Executive Compensation: Looking to the Long Term Again," *Business Week,* May 9, 1983, pp. 80–83; and G. S. Becker, "Why Managers Have the Stockholder at Heart," *Business Week,* July 8, 1985, p. 14.

Care must be taken in developing a compensation system to be sure that the performance rewarded lies within the range of discretion of the manager. That is, some environmental or internal factors may exist over which the manager has little or no influence. If these play a large part in the performance of the unit, then penalizing the manager for poor performance due to events out of his or her control will only encourage the manager to attempt to lay the blame at the doorstep of these events. In such a situation, the proportion of incentives tied to overall unit performance should be smaller.

The reward system is also related to career development, which we discussed in Chapter 10. That is, job rotations and promotions to develop managers must be planned with the idea in mind that the time is sufficient to assess the performance of the manager in a given position. Holding a manager accountable for a situation inherited from another is not likely to be useful as a control or evaluation mechanism. And moving managers before the results of their activities can be properly assessed is only likely to encourage short-term decision making to show quick positive results, which may have negative long-term impacts.

Recognize that we have been *prescriptive* in laying out various aspects of ideal evaluation systems, though we did point out earlier that rewards often are not tied to performance. Part of the *descriptive* reason for this may be that it is very difficult to assess cause-effect relationships for unit performance. Further, managers will seek to protect their own interests in explaining performance. Experience suggests that if outcomes are positive, the wisdom and judgment of top management will be confirmed. But if plans fail, subordinates or external events may be blamed. In such cases, criteria for evaluation may be adjusted, positions may be reinterpreted, or top management may say that it was just sending up a "trial balloon." Even accounting changes may be used to provide the appearance of success. In other words, managers will try to rewrite history. As we noted in Chapter 2, objectives are often stated as vague generalities. Here's another reason—that makes it easier to rewrite history or claim success. Recognize also that the time horizon for performance evaluation is frequently short term. This pressures managers to consider short-term outcomes at the expense of long-term strategy.

There are many other potentially dysfunctional consequences of performance evaluation. Therefore, it is generally suggested that the use of a single criterion leads to undesirable or suboptimal results. For example, short-term profitability is not by itself an adequate measure of managerial performance. Return on investment is another potentially problematic criterion in that it can lead to the postponement of needed research or investment for upgrading facilities or equipment. As Christensen et al. point out,

> The management evaluation system which plays so great a part in influencing management performance must employ a number of criteria, some of which are subjective and thus difficult to quantify. It is easy to argue that subjective judgments are unfair. But use of a harmful or irrelevant criterion just because it lends itself to quantification is a poor exchange for alleged objectivity. [p. 644]

The remainder of the chapter explores the major issues in establishing the *content* of the control and evaluation system. The three major content areas in which strategic managers make decisions are (1) the criteria for evaluation, (2) the feedback system and tools to use in the control system, and (3) the outcomes of the strategic evaluation.

CRITERIA FOR EVALUATION [4]

The field of organizational effectiveness—defining and measuring evaluation factors—is very complex. It is not easy to choose the factors upon which to focus the evaluation. Evaluations can be based on objective and subjective factors. As suggested in our last section, different criteria may be appropriate depending on the purpose for the evaluation.

Further, we think that evaluation of the *content and process* of strategy and plans should play a role in the system. That is, evaluation is typically assumed to be an *after-the-fact* or real-time method of detecting whether the *content* of strategy *is working* or *has worked.* Quantitative measurement is quite appropriate here along with subjective judgments. But qualitative assessment can also be done to address the question *Will it work?* A qualitative check of the strategic management *process* can be done *before the fact* of activating plans for change. Let's examine these two approaches separately.

Quantitative Criteria [5]

In attempting to evaluate the effectiveness of corporate strategy quantitatively, you can see how the firm has done compared with its own history, or compared with its competitors on such factors as net profit, stock price, dividend rates, earnings per share, return on capital, return on equity, market share, growth in sales, days lost per employee as a result of strikes, production costs and efficiency, distribution costs and efficiency, and employee turnover, absenteeism, and satisfaction indexes.

The list is long, and many other factors could be included. Which factors should be used? Establishing the standards and tolerance limits is not as easy as you might expect. You need to first define the critical success factors—the factors which are most important to the strategy and to being successful in the business. Many of these were discussed in Chapter 5. Then the factors and plans developed need to be stated in terms of specific measures by which you can judge whether a success factor is being attained. An example for a contractor helps to illustrate some of the indicators which might be used to translate success factors into measurable performance criteria (see Exhibit 11.6).

EXHIBIT 11.6   SUCCESS FACTORS AND MEASURES FOR A CONTRACTOR

Critical success factors	Prime measures
Image in financial markets	Price-earnings ratio Orders-bid ratio
Technological reputation with customers	Customer "perception" interviews
Market success	Change in market share Growth rates of markets served
Risk recognition in major bids and contracts	Years of experience with similar products
Profit margin on jobs	Bid profit margin as ratio of similar jobs in this product line
Company morale	Turnover, absenteeism, grievances, etc. Informational feedback
Performance to budget on major jobs	Job cost, ratio of budgeted amount to actual amount

Source: Adapted from J. F. Rockart, "Chief Executives Define Their Own Data Needs," *Harvard Business Review,* (March–April 1979), p. 89.

Of course, success factors and measures may be quite different for other firms depending on objectives and strategies. For example, the typical way executives seek to monitor manufacturing often relies on a measure of inventory turnover. This is acceptable if the strategy relies on measuring output of long production runs. But quality of output may become important to the strategy. Here, control measures such as reject or rework rates redirect the emphasis in manufacturing to a concern with quality rather than output control.

Most of these measures are internal. The comparisons of achievement are made in relation to the standards established ahead of time. But objective assessments can also be made by comparing the firm's results with the results of similar firms. As suggested in Chapter 5 this is an important aspect of the assessment of strengths and weaknesses as an input for future strategy formulation to develop competitive advantages. Four sources of ''objective'' measures are as follows:

1 *Compustat* tapes provide data on *financial* results over the past 10 years (or sometimes longer) for large companies.

2 *Dun's* publishes (usually in November) its ratios of business. This is a quantitative guide to how a firm is doing financially in wholesaling, retailing, or the manufacturing sectors.

3 *Fortune* (in May and June) publishes the *Fortune* 1000 largest manufacturers and the *Fortune* 50s: the 50 largest retailers, transportation companies, utilities, banks, insurance companies, and diversified financial corporations. At that time, it also ranks the best and worst performers on financial aspects of the business such as return to investors, sales, profits, and sales per dollar of stockholder's equity.

4 Probably the best unbiased overall evaluation of the largest corporations is in the January 1 issue of *Forbes*. The issue is called *The Annual Report on American Industry*. *Forbes* ranks the firms all together and by industry on financial factors such as earnings growth, value, and profitability (e.g., growth in return on equity and return on investment). It also ranks the firms on sales growth, stock market performance, and performance compared with that of comparable companies and industries. Finally, it provides yardsticks of managerial performance. In these, *Forbes* combines all the indexes, and it rates the firms for the year, longitudinally, and assigns overall ratings to them.

There are no magic numbers to assign evaluation factors to. But outside assessments can help executives evaluate their performance and thus their strategic performance in an other than qualitative manner. Techniques such as sensitivity tests, risk analysis, the use of outcome matrixes, the use of models, and simulation can help managers evaluate results and the strategies.

Another approach is to ask ''experts'' which firms are the most successful. This is a subjective approach: *Dun's* description of the 5 or 10 best-run American companies is an example of this method.

Measurement comparisons become more difficult when more than one criterion is used to measure success. For example, efficiency and effectiveness can be measured on a number of dimensions. Efficiency isn't too hard to judge. However, a number of problems are involved in the measurement of effectiveness:

• *Stability of criteria:* A criterion emphasized at one point may not be valid later on.

• *Time:* Do we evaluate short-run or long-run effectiveness?

• *Precision and variety of measurement:* Not all measures are easy to compute, and there are different ways of computing measures.

It is a lot easier to measure success when a company shows consistent results on most of the measures in most years. In fact, research indicates that there is a high intercorrelation among organizational variables. If a firm is a "winner" on three measures, chances are it is a winner on all measures. To us the most critical problem is the trade-off among measures. Suppose, for example, that you are measuring effectiveness as shown in Exhibit 11.7. Admittedly, success is hard to measure, especially when you have eight performance measures and at the end of 1988 you see three up, three down, and two even. In such a case, success is declared if the three measures that are "up" are the critical success factors. Organizations feel that they are successful if the most important indicators are positive. It is easy to recognize success when most indicators are positive or negative but very hard when there are results like the ones in Exhibit 11.7.

Qualitative Criteria [6]

We have already suggested that "subjective" assessments can be included with after-the-fact evaluation. Some qualitative criteria can also be used for that purpose. Moreover, as we indicated before, subjective assessments of key environmental assumptions should be included with the quantitative measures of performance to be sure the strategy is resting on safe ground. But the criteria here tend to be more appropriate for examining a *plan in its entirety* before the organization is asked to change direction or put a strategy into effect. A series of qualitative questions can be developed for

EXHIBIT 11.7   AN EVALUATION OF RESULTS IN 1987 AND 1988

	Percentage of objectives achieved	
Criterion	1987	1988
Production effectiveness:		
Production output	110	105
Market share	12	13
Efficiency:		
Return on capital	6	7
Efficiency in utilization of equipment	95	90
Adaptiveness (rate of production innovation)	50	65
Satisfaction:		
Clients	80	75
Employees	75	75
Development (training investments)	90	90

each of three criteria. The basic questions are whether the integrated and comprehensive objectives, strategy, and plans are *consistent, appropriate,* and *workable.*

Consistency

Is the comprehensive, integrated plan consistent with objectives, environmental assumptions, and internal conditions?

1 *Objectives.* Will the plan probably close the gaps of importance to us? Are the standards of performance linked to critical success factors? Are there mutually inconsistent objectives where we have made trade-off decisions? Are the goal trade-offs consistent with our real priorities? Are the goals consistent with social responsibility needs to sustain our legitimacy?

2 *Environmental assumptions.* Are we making an adaptive response to critical changes that we might anticipate? Will the plan fully exploit domestic and international opportunities? Does it mitigate threats? Are marketing policies consistent with changes in the marketplace and financial policies consistent with changes in capital markets? Are R&D and production consistent with technological or supplier developments? Have staffing policies taken into consideration governmental changes? Are contingency plans in place so that we can respond flexibly to unanticipated change (anticipatory flexibility)?

3 *Internal conditions.* Are the policies, resource allocations, organizational structure, and administrative system coordinated with one another? Is there an integrated pattern of implementation which fits the strategy and develops needed competitive advantages? Does the strategy rely on weaknesses or do anything to reduce them? Have we clarified the inevitable policy trade-offs so that suboptimization is minimized? Are performance evaluation criteria and rewards tied to the policies we want to reinforce?

Exhibit 11.8 shows what can happen when strategy changes lead to inconsistencies over time.

Appropriateness

Is the comprehensive, integrated plan appropriate given our resource capabilities, risk preference, and time horizon?

4 *Resource capabilities.* Are critical resources in place? If not, does the plan provide for obtaining them when needed? Are the total resources available appropriate for what we want to accomplish? Are the policies providing for the development of raw materials, energy, workers, executives, facilities, equipment, competence, and expertise?

5 *Risk preference.* Does the strategy entail unnecessary risk? Is the degree of risk acceptable to top management? Is it too high or too low? Are we "betting the whole company"? Is that necessary? Does the plan depend on internal resources whose continued existence is not assured? Does it depend on environmental assumptions about which we are very uncertain?

EXHIBIT 11.8   THE INCONSISTENCIES AT RCA

A retrospective evaluation of the RCA Corporation leads us to a better understanding of why it merged with GE in late 1985.

In 1973, RCA earned $183.7 million on $4.2 billion in sales. Ten years later it earned $171.5 million on $9 billion in sales. On a total sales of $67.1 billion for the 10-year period, RCA posted profits of only $1.7 billion, or about a 2% long-term profit margin. The prime cause of such dismal performance can be summarized in a single word—inconsistency.

In the space of 10 years, RCA was led by four different CEOs, each of whom pursued a different strategy. The company has been diversified, divested, directed toward long-term goals, and redirected toward short-term goals; it was nearly done in by a massive acquisition, and diddled away dollars through huge employment and disemployment contracts.

Management problems began with the legendary General Sarnoff, whose passion was technological supremacy. Critics claim this diverted attention from management of the business. When Sarnoff's son took over, the labs were doing pioneering work, but management couldn't move ideas to the market. In the absence of new products, the younger Sarnoff made acquisitions ranging from car rental and book publishing to carpet-making and frozen foods.

Eased out in 1975, he was succeeded by a CEO whose 10-month tenure ended when it was learned that he had failed to file personal income tax reports. Next came Edgar Griffiths. His 6 years were marked by continual strife with the board, and hiring and firing of top aides, compensating them handsomely both on the way in and on the way out. Because he couldn't get quarter-by-quarter improvements, he began selling earlier acquisitions to "keep earnings up." With the board vocal in its disapproval, Griffiths went for an acquisition of CIT financial services in 1980. By the time interest rates had increased and other businesses began to sour with the recession, a board activist was given a $250,000 "consulting contract" to supervise operations and find a new CEO. Thornton Bradshaw replaced Griffiths in 1981. He put up Hertz and CIT for sale. CIT sold in 1984. As of April, 1984, analysts suggested that with its cash assets, NBC television, defense business, and Hertz, RCA was a sitting duck for raiders. Indeed, the company merged with GE a year later.

In effect, RCA failed the test of consistency over time. No well-defined mission or consistent strategy served to guide decisions and management, resulting in constant change in direction and policy making, personnel turnover, and poor results. No wonder RCA merged with GE.

Source: "RCA: Will It Ever Be a Top Performer?" *Business Week,* Apr. 2, 1984, pp. 52–56.

6 *Time horizon.* Are the objectives stated in terms of an appropriate time for achievement? Is rapid expansion appropriate given our capabilities? Have we committed resources for a sufficient period so that the strategy will have a chance to work? Are we making changes at frequent intervals or taking drastic leaps, or are we making steady, sustained progress? Which approach is appropriate for objectives? Are criteria for evaluation being measured in time so that appropriate adjustments can be made? Is now the right time to proceed with this plan, or will economic or other conditions change?

Workability

Is the comprehensive, integrated plan feasible and stimulating?

7 *Feasibility.* Does the plan overtax our resources and management capabilities? Does it create unsolvable subproblems? Is the strategy identifiable and clear? Is the strategy reasonable? Will there be unintended consequences that we can avoid?

8 *Stimulation*. Will managers be committed to making the strategy work? Is there a consensus among executives that the plan will work? Are reward systems designed to encourage effort in the desired directions? Are the personal aspirations of key strategists taken into consideration so that they are involved in decisions about the strategy?

Again, these are qualitative criteria to be addressed *before* a new strategy is activated. If "red flags" are raised by any of these issues, then the strategist is encouraged to reassess the strategy and plans to determine if other alternatives might be preferable or if adjustments and fine tuning are possible to resolve a possible problem area.

These criteria are useful for a mental double check to see that various aspects of the strategic management process have been comprehensively integrated. For instance, questions of internal consistency deal with whether the strategy, plans, and policies (Chapters 8, 9, and 10) reflect the internal assessments (Chapter 5) in relation to goals (Chapter 2). External consistency has to do with whether the strategy choice and policies (Chapters 8 and 10) relate to the environmental assessments (Chapters 3 and 4). Risk preferences and workability are concerned with how evaluation and other policies (Chapters 10 and 11) relate to assessments of the strategists (Chapter 2). And so on.

As we said in Chapter 1 and have stressed throughout, the various aspects of the strategic management process are ongoing, interrelated components. The evaluation system is a means for integrating these components into a unified whole. The criteria could be applied when a strategic choice is made (hence the feedback arrow pointing to "Choice" in Exhibit 11.1). In effect, this reinforces the idea that strategy implementation and formation need to be considered as a whole. The use of the evaluation criteria—consistency, appropriateness, workability—forces the strategist to make a strategic choice in light of the analysis *and* implementation phases of the strategic management process.

Recognize that managers may still proceed with their plan, even if the criteria raise significant questions about its validity. Exhibit 11.9 shows you how this happens. But if managers use these criteria before activating plans, the criteria can alert them to areas where closer control and tighter evaluation may be useful as progress is monitored.

MEASURING AND FEEDBACK

The previous section outlined what the standards might be. The next phase of control and evaluation is to measure performance and provide feedback for the managers involved. Here the questions are, When do we measure? and What do we report to whom?

Timing [7]

Assume that the qualitative evaluation has been made and that the decision is to "go" as planned. A crucial issue still remains: *When* should *results* be evaluated?

From a long-term strategy perspective, the problem of timing is particularly crucial.

EXHIBIT 11.9   CONFIDENCE AT A&P?

Outside evaluators of once mighty A&P believe that the firm is on its last legs. A strategy that was inappropriately timed given the economic recession of 1980–1981 has forced further store closings and changes in plans to renew and remodel old stores. Poorly sited stores, inefficient distribution, and stodgy management are other indications of internal conditions that are inappropriate for competing in the environment. Says one observer, "With their infrastructure, there is no way in the world that they will be able to compete in this industry."

Nonetheless, management *believes* that the plans for recovery are workable. CEO Wood is committed and confident that he can turn the company around, and he predicts profitability by 1983. The feasibility may depend on the resources and patience of E. K. Haub, the head of Germany's successful Tengelmann retail group, which owns over 50% of A&P. Says Haub, "If we had to do it

over again, we wouldn't do it. We reckoned it would take five years to return A&P to profitability when we bought it. But we're no longer so sure we'll make it by then. We believe, and I stress 'believe,' that we will still be able to make something out of A&P, but I still wouldn't call the outlook rosy."

It is important to note that Haub invested more than $100 million in A&P, and there would probably be few buyers. Also, liquidation and the elimination of 60,000 U.S. jobs would probably bring unwanted protests to the German firm. "Equally important, Haub is proud of his success as a food retailer in Germany, and he is not yet ready to admit defeat in the huge U.S. market."

So a variety of plans to bail out A&P are in the works, largely because of the belief that the plans are workable, regardless of the red flags raised by other evaluators.

Source: Adapted from "A&P Looks like Tengelmann's Vietnam," *Business Week,* Feb. 1, 1982, pp. 42–44.

Implementation may require some time before results can be expected. If standards are set to be achieved in, say, 5 years and measurement does not take place until the end of the fifth year, it will probably be too late to take action to correct deviations. On the other hand, if an evaluation is made too early, knee-jerk reactions could be made which will prevent the plan from having a chance to work. Many argue that if decision makers procrastinate, opportunities may pass them by. Still, it is often difficult to change direction quickly, particularly for large organizations.

As a result, in the establishment of the standards for measurement, the timing of expected or desired results must be specified. Benchmarks of progress are needed. Timing is not easy either. There are times when managers just do not know what events will lead to certain outcomes. But they must proceed with assumptions about the cause-effect relationships in the means-end chain. In effect, managers can establish the critical success factors as events along a critical-path network. Long-term targets can be broken down into intermediate steps for accomplishment. Periodically, then, measurements can be taken to compare intermediate progress. This can be done quarterly or annually, depending on the variable.

Ideally, top management should be alerted when there is significant deviation (positive or negative) from critical planned outcomes or assumptions. Two questions are important here: What is "significant deviation"? and What is meant by "critical"? Each management group must define these for itself and its strategy. Our earlier discussion suggested what some of the critical success factors might be. And in Chapter 1 we noted that the factors associated with the nature of the gaps are relevant to deviations. Further, as our earlier sections suggested, the qualitative criteria can indicate key areas where problems in a plan might exist.

Once criteria have been specified, we think that continuous versus periodic monitoring can be decided upon through the use of an analogy with the ABC system of inventory control. "A" factors are the few but most important critical success factors or environmental assumptions. These should have relatively narrow allowable variances and should receive constant monitoring and tight control (as in a perpetual inventory system). "C" items are the majority of variables. They provide advance warnings of environmental change or the firm's progress, but they are not on the critical path, so to speak. These can have wider tolerance limits for deviation and are measured periodically as suggested. They receive loose control. The "B" items are the factors which are important but take longer to become meaningfully evaluated. These should be measured as frequently as possible when the data make sense. For example, market share may be a critical success factor, but daily sales figures on a new-product introduction are probably not meaningful to most strategists for some time. This system is, of course, based on the concept of management by exception.

Feedback [8]

The foregoing implies that lower-level managers may receive some information that top strategists do not. Indeed, feedback needs for various types of information vary by manager. As far as strategic evaluation is concerned, information that is usable and timely is needed for the managers who have discretionary authority to make decisions about the critical success factors. That is, an effective management information system (MIS) is required, as well as honest and complete reporting of the results of the strategy. Of course, at many enterprises, the top managers do not want to hear bad news. So they hear what they want to hear until it is too late. The enterprise must encourage complete and accurate reporting so that top managers can react to reversals and reinforce progress. The MIS tool can assist in this.

Many early MISs were developed by staff specialists who knew how to use computer hardware. The reports that were printed out were in forms that few managers wanted or were able to use. Today, effective firms have a better system. MIS managers determine information needs and timeliness deadlines from all levels of managers. They then design the system so that it develops the required data and sends reports when the user can use them and in the form the user needs. Managers request and get reports measuring the current status in relation to each objective to be achieved. For example, reports on profitability, sales, market share, or efficiency can be delivered in time so that action can be taken. Some firms have advanced to the point where personal computers are appearing on the desks of many managers. Such a proliferation brings a greater need to manage information more closely. Thus the MIS can be used to help control the enterprise's outputs. A model of an integrated information system is illustrated in Exhibit 11.10.

However, managers can absorb only so much information, and they have only a certain amount of time for control. A manager who is not selective will be inundated with reports. Key strategic control items may be buried when this happens. Effective managers delegate the control of less significant items and objectives to subordinates. They receive MIS reports and use a strategic approach to control, concentrating only

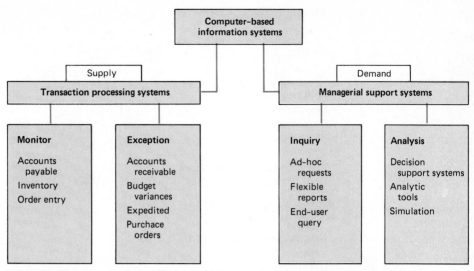

MONITOR The system monitors daily detail activity producing *standard* reports on a *fixed* schedule (daily, weekly, or monthly).

EXCEPTION The system processes detail activity reports where the *definition* of exception conditions is *fixed*.

INQUIRY The system provides a data base with flexible inquiry capability, enabling *managers* to design and change their own monitoring and exception reports.

ANALYSIS The system provides powerful *data analysis* capabilities (modelling, simulation, optimization or statistical routines) and the appropriate data base to support *managerial* decision-making.

EXHIBIT 11.10   A management information system model.

on those items necessary for meeting the most important objectives. Thus the MIS must be set up to provide the right information to the right people at the right time. It is a major tool for feedback and evaluation, and it can be a critical part of strategy implementation.

EVALUATION AND CORRECTIVE ACTION [9]

The final phase of evaluation and control is to use the timely information to determine the causes of deviations and take actions to correct these, or reward performance which remains ''in control.''

Let's assume that the MIS prepared a report for management such as the one in Exhibit 11.11. The critical success factors and measures are as indicated on the left. The report may represent progress 2 years into a 4-year plan of expansion into new product areas. At this stage managers will want to compare *progress to date* with *expectations to date*. Of primary interest are those factors where an existing deviation might lead to a *projected deviation* of some importance requiring corrective action. In this instance, competition appears to be making more progress in new-product development than was anticipated. The firm has not analyzed as many new-product ideas as it had planned, and it appears that the R&D effort is not leading to desired results. It is quite probable that this is due to the lag in recruiting senior engineers.

EXHIBIT 11.11   BENCHMARKS FOR EVALUATION

Key success factors	Overall objectives or assumptions	Expected performance at this time	Current performance	Existing deviations	Projected deviations
Financial:					
Reduce overhead cost	5%	2%	3%	+1%	+1%
Profit on sales	12%	5%	9%	+4%	+2%
Marketing:					
Analyze new-product proposals	10	4	2	−2	−3
Sales per employee	$7000	$6800	$6900	+$100	+$100
Personnel:					
Number of key managers needed	6	2	3	+1	+1
Ratio of indirect cost to direct cost	12%	14%	13%	−1%	0%
R&D:					
Recruitment of senior engineers	20	16	10	−6	−6
Increase R&D-sales ratio	5%	4%	3%	−1%	−1%
Operations:					
Increase production capacity	50%	40%	40%	0%	0%
Competitor reactions:					
Increased R&D	4%	3%	4%	+1%	+1%
Product changes	4	2	3	+1	+1

As a result of this information, managers are faced with several options. An assessment of the gaps may lead to the conclusion that internal factors account for discrepancies. Plans can be scaled up or down. For instance, greater efforts might be undertaken to place a higher priority on recruiting engineers to get new-product development back on track. On the other hand, the firm could decide to continue as planned, even though this may result in excess capacity, since plant expansion is on target. Of course, new plans to meet changed competitive circumstances might also be drawn up given projected deviations. In the example, another option is to change tactics; given the favorable profit deviation, a policy to lower prices may be feasible and could divert competitor attention on new-product development toward marketing, where the firm may have an edge.

Evaluations such as this can become much more detailed and can be done at SBU levels and at departmental budget levels in even more compressed time frames. For instance, the budget performances of units can be evaluated during the year. The budget department and line managers can review how well each unit has done in sticking to its budget. If a unit's performance in this regard is poor, then action can be taken to remedy the situation. After review and evaluation, if it is believed that the unit had a reasonable budget, the unit can be encouraged to meet the budget. In the unusual event that a unit's budget turns out to be unreasonable in practice—usually because of unforeseen difficulties—then the budget department can recommend a revised budget. Top management will approve or reject this revision just as it did for the entire current budget.

In any of these situations, care must be taken to make sure that short-term adjustments resulting from budgetary control procedures do not alter long-term plans. That is the reason for prescribing top-management approval. If adjustments will alter the plans, the strategic implications need to be assessed.

In more general terms, then, the "after-the-fact" evaluation and corrective action process should proceed as we outlined earlier in Exhibit 11.3.

Stage 1. Are the performance standards too low or too high, or are the environmental assumptions legitimate? If yes, alter by scaling up or down. If no, go to stage 2.

Stage 2. Is the implementation inadequate? Are policies, resources, or organization changes needed? If yes, alter accordingly. If no, go to stage 3.

Stage 3. Is the strategy inadequate? Has the environment changed unexpectedly? (Original assumptions are quite uncertain or faulty.) Is the contingency plan needed? If yes, use the contingency plan or begin to formulate a new strategy. If no, go to stage 4.

Stage 4. How can we alter our objectives or convince others that the gaps in performance will remain and are acceptable?

This order is established on the basis of the most likely (and easiest to change) prognosis of the conditions underlying performance gaps.

This brings us full circle to questions about the objectives of the organization. In Chapters 1 and 2 we discussed the establishment of objectives. Strategy formation and planning develops means to accomplish these and also contributes to their establishment. As we analyze gaps and set new strategies and plans, we begin to establish targets to accomplish long-term objectives. As we set up standards for measuring performance, we are getting to the real or operative objectives. As these are used as criteria for rewarding individuals, they give rise to behavior to accomplish them. If we discover that certain standards cannot be met as a result of our strategic planning process, then a reassessment of goals and objectives will result. As we suggested in our discussion about Exhibit 11.3 then, several options are available as managers analyze causes of gaps in performance.

Thus there is a feedback loop from evaluation to objectives in Exhibit 11.1. This means that through the reward and control system, management information system, and strategic planning evaluation, if managers become aware that the objectives are

- Too easily achieved, they should be raised.
- Impossible to meet, they should be lowered.

The ideal relationship is when objectives are attainable yet challenging. But remember that "success" is an elusive concept. Failure to achieve challenging goals should be considered in the light of evidence suggesting that even competent managers may have only about a ".300" batting average when it comes to innovative strategy.

Finally, through evaluation, feedback leads to the repetition of the ongoing strategic management process.

MANAGEMENT BY OBJECTIVES [10]

To sum up, we would like to suggest that the management by objectives (MBO) system in its *idealized* form is a management tool which can help managers accomplish the prescriptions we have been outlining. MBO can combine objective setting, planning, control, and reward systems, all of which are so crucial to the effective conduct of strategy formation and implementation.

An MBO system is designed to take the objectives determined during the strategic planning process. It then interprets these objectives (ends) in terms of the strategic choice (the means to these ends). Then for each subunit of the enterprise it leads to the development of a set of objectives. Implicit in the process is the involvement of those accountable for achieving objectives. Then a control and reward system is established so that progress is monitored and the achievement of objectives leads to positive outcomes for the individuals and the organization.

MBO systems found in practice tend to vary considerably from the prescriptive, idealized system. While some evidence suggests that such a system can be effective, other evidence suggests that so many things can go wrong that it is an idea whose time has gone. There has also been some criticism that MBO systems inappropriately encourage analytical decision strategies in settings which call for an "inspirational" strategy.

Like strategic management itself, the system is conceptually simple but difficult to use well. We can only hope that you will be able to apply the concepts while avoiding the inherent pitfalls. That is why we have tried to provide a blending of description and prescription throughout the book. With these ideas in mind, we hope you will be better prepared to manage in a superior fashion.

SUMMARY

The last phase of the strategic management process is evaluation. Evaluation of strategy is that phase of the strategic management process in which the top managers try to assure that their strategic choice is implemented properly and is meeting the objectives of the enterprise. This is necessary to assure that a follow-through on plans occurs, to provide information or needed corrective action, and to ensure the repetition of the strategic management process.

The control process requires multiple criteria, timely measurement and feedback, and an evaluation of performance deviations so that corrective action can be taken. Control and evaluation takes place at both the SBU level and the corporate level and may involve controllers, other top managers, and committees of the board.

Before evaluation will take place, the top managers must want to evaluate the performance. This motivation develops if they realize that the strategy can fail and if they are rewarded for their performance in relation to objectives. It is particularly critical to establish multiple standards of performance so that the reward system will encourage relevant strategic behaviors and decisions.

Evaluation of the content and process of strategy can be done by means of quantitative and subjective assessments for after-the-fact evaluations and qualitative criteria for assessing the comprehensiveness of a plan before it is activated.

Quantitative criteria are normally used for evaluating how the firm has done compared with its own history or with competitors' performance. Defining the critical success factors and the measures appropriate for these requires that managers consider the stability of criteria and the timing, precision, and variety of measurement.

Qualitative criteria can be used for examining the process of strategy. A variety of questions requiring subjective judgment can be asked to determine whether the integrated and comprehensive plan, strategy, and objectives developed are consistent, appropriate, and workable. These serve as a check on the nature of objectives, environmental assumptions, internal conditions, resource capabilities, risk preferences, timing, feasibility, and commitment.

Information in a usable form is necessary for evaluating the strategy. That is, an effective management information system is required, as well as honest and complete reporting of the results of the strategy. Also, information about the significant factors of environmental or internal change must be provided in time for managers to use the data to make decisions. An ABC system was suggested to guide the timing of the monitoring of success factors.

Corrective actions are needed if the evaluation shows actual and/or projected deviations from the plan as time goes on. In the order of priority, managers are more likely to consider changes in standards, then implementation, then strategy, and finally objectives themselves if performance gaps are found to exist. Thus the evaluation system provides feedback to the strategic management process in its entirety.

Since a follow-through of this type requires good objectives and standards, effective rewards, and accurate and complete feedback, a good MIS and a good MBO system can be useful tools for managers. But as with any system, effective application requires hard work.

As a way of illustrating the importance of effective evaluation to the strategic management process, the following proposition will suffice.

Proposition 9.1

Firms which systematically evaluate the results of strategic choice and control its implementation will be more effective than those which do not.

This summary is followed by a brief statement on the strategic management process in retrospect to help you focus on the overall process covered in Chapters 2 through 11.

STRATEGIC MANAGEMENT IN RETROSPECT [11]

We have discussed all the phases of the strategic management process. We have treated the phases in separate and distinct chapters. It is necessary to examine them one at a time. But we have stressed that the phases overlap and blend together in the world of work. They cannot be separated in actual strategic management. If you study the section on qualitative criteria in Chapter 11, you will quickly see why that is so.

We have tried to give you the reasons why strategic management makes good sense if managers really are interested in effectiveness. But the *irony,* the *supreme irony,* is that to perform other than superficially, the managers must do what they have never been rewarded for doing before: they must take time out from daily pressures and rewards, step back, and look at where the enterprise is now and what it is in for tomorrow. Then, they must anticipate future events and take steps to do something about them.

Strategic management requires the strategists to formalize objectives and formally assess events in the environment. It requires them to figure out formally where their firm's strengths and weaknesses are. Next, they are asked not to jump at the first solution that comes to mind but to compare several alternatives systematically. Then they must choose the best one, implement it, and take time to evaluate and make changes, if necessary, in the choice. This is hard work and requires executives with strong motivation.

These steps can be taken in many different ways. What has been presented here is a formal, normative way of going about strategic management. But we have also tried to present you with the evidence of how most executives undertake strategic management. So our formal, normative model has been tempered by descriptions of real problems in applying "rational" frameworks.

In the long run, we would still contend that our enterprises and societies would be better off if strategic management were comprehensive and formalized. We cited some of the evidence to support that belief in Chapter 1. And some other recent research hints that this is so. However, there is also nonempirical but subjective evidence about many of the ideas we have stressed. Throughout we have given examples of business firms which have succeeded and failed in efforts to apply strategic management concepts. Most of these have been from *Business Week.* The editors of that magazine summarized their impressions of enterprises in the United States. Among their conclusions are these:

> American managers have tried to maximize near term profits at the expense of long term objectives; they have catered to Wall Street resulting in shortsighted strategies; managers seem to refuse to take risks and overemphasize quantitative measures of success which reinforce short-term goals; they have resisted the winds of change, and have increased conflict with labor as they implemented their strategies.

Among their recommendations to resolve these problems are the following:

1 Reward long-range risk taking.
2 Promote young tigers who will take risks.
3 Keep research funds flowing.
4 Encourage employee differences.
5 Overhaul the business schools which stress analytical decisions at the expense of entrepreneurial strategies.

This predated the Peters and Waterman bestseller, *In Search of Excellence.* Both, however, stressed basic themes that U.S. enterprises suffer from paralysis of analysis, too much bureaucracy, too little innovation, and insufficient attention paid to customers and employees. Regaining a competitive edge is possible, however, if strategic thinking is followed and if managers stick to the skills and values they know best.

We hope our presentation of strategic management has alerted you to the need to consider many of the issues of importance to the future of organizations and societies. And we hope that further study of the ideas presented in our references will contribute to an understanding of the need for strategic management, how it is accomplished, and how it can improve organizational effectiveness.

Even as many firms are reducing the size of the planning staff, executives expect line managers to "think strategically." The process outlined here should prove helpful for performing this strategic thinking. We encourage you to apply it to your future endeavors.

REFERENCES

[1] Integrating Planning and Control through Evaluation

Bianco, A., S. Crock, and A. Beam: "Wall Street's Back Office Blues: Big Trouble Lies Ahead if Brokers' Controls Can't Cope with Growth," *Business Week,* Nov. 4, 1985, pp. 24–25.

Leonard, J. W.: "Strategic Control: Need for a New Definition," paper presented at the Strategic Management Society Conference, Philadelphia, 1984.

Merchant, K. A.: *Control in Business Organizations* (Marshfield, Mass.: Pitman, 1985).

[2] Strategic Control Processes

Daft, R. L., and N. B. Macintosh: "The Nature and Use of Formal Control Systems for Management Control and Strategy Implementation," *Journal of Management,* vol. 10 (1984), pp. 43–66.

Rowe, A. J., and J. Carlson: "Adaptive Control Systems for Operating Management," *Logistics Spectrum Journal* (September 1974).

Todd, J.: "Management Control Systems: A Key Link between Strategy, Structure and Employee Performance," *Organizational Dynamics,* vol. 5 (Spring 1977), pp. 65–78.

[3] Rewards in Evaluation

Berry, S. J.: "Performance Review: Key to Effective Planning," *Long Range Planning,* vol. 12 (December 1979), pp. 17–21.

Christensen, C. R., K. R. Andrews, and J. L. Bower: *Business Policy: Text and Cases* (Homewood, Ill.: Irwin, 1978).

"Executive Compensation: Looking to the Long Term Again," *Business Week,* May 9, 1983, pp. 80–83.

Matthews, W. E., and W. I. Boucher: "Planned Entry–Planned Exit," *California Management Review,* vol. 20 (Winter 1977), pp. 36–44.

"No Sign of Recession in Pay at the Top," *Business Week,* May 10, 1982, pp. 76–77.

Prasad, S. B.: "Top Management Compensation and Corporate Performance," *Academy of Management Journal,* vol. 17 (September 1974), pp. 554–558.

[4] Organizational Effectiveness

Steers, R.: *Organizational Effectiveness: A Behavioral View* (Pacific Palisades, Calif.: Goodyear, 1977).

Zammuto, R. F.: *Assessing Organizational Effectiveness: Systems Change, Adaptation, and Strategy* (Albany: State University of New York Press, 1981).

[5] Quantitative Evaluation Criteria

Argenti, J.: *Systematic Corporate Planning* (New York: Wiley, 1974), chap. 14.

Hofer, C.: "ROVA: A New Measure for Assessing Organizational Effectiveness," Graduate School of Business, New York University, 1979. Mimeographed.

[6] Qualitative Evaluation Criteria

Ferguson, C.: *Measuring Corporate Strategy* (Homewood, Ill.: Dow Jones–Irwin, 1974), especially chap. 6.

Rumelt, R.: "The Evaluation of Business Strategy," in W. F. Glueck, *Business Policy and Strategic Management* (New York: McGraw-Hill, 1980), pp. 359–367.

Steiner, G.: *Strategic Factors in Business Success* (New York: Financial Executives Research Foundation, 1969).

Tilles, S.: "How to Evaluate Corporate Strategy," *Harvard Business Review,* vol. 41 (1963), pp. 111–121.

[7] Timing in Evaluation

Ansoff, H. I.: "Managing Strategic Surprise by Response to Weak Signals," *California Management Review* (Winter 1976), pp. 21–33.

Slaybaugh, C. J.: "Pareto's Law and Modern Management," *Price Waterhouse Review* (Winter 1966), p. 27.

[8] MIS for Evaluation

Edstrom, A.: "User Influence and the Success of MIS Projects: A Contingency Approach," *Human Relations,* vol. 30 (1977), pp. 589–607.

"How Personal Computers Can Backfire," *Business Week,* July 12, 1982, pp. 56–59.

Wedley, W. C., and R. H. G. Field: "A Predecision Support System," *Academy of Management Review,* vol. 9 (1984), pp. 696–703.

" 'What If' Help for Management," *Business Week,* Jan. 21, 1980, pp. 73–74.

[9] Feedback for Control

Lawler, E., and J. Rhode: *Information and Control in Organizations* (Santa Monica, Calif.: Goodyear, 1977).

Nadler, D., P. Mirvis, and C. Cammann: "The Ongoing Feedback System," *Organizational Dynamics,* vol. 4 (Spring 1976), pp. 63–80.

Newman, W. H.: *Constructive Control: Design and Use of Control Systems* (Englewood Cliffs, N.J.: Prentice-Hall, 1975).

Rowe, A. J., R. D. Mason, and K. Dickel: *Strategic Management and Business Policy: A Methodological Approach* (Reading, Mass.: Addison-Wesley, 1982).

[10] Management by Objectives

Carroll, S. J., Jr., and H. L. Tosi, Jr.: *Management By Objectives: Applications and Research* (New York: Macmillan, 1973).
Dirsmuth, M. W., S. F. Jablonsky, and A. D. Luzi: "Planning and Control in the U.S. Federal Government: A Critical Analysis of PPB, MBO and ZBB," *Strategic Management Journal,* vol. 1 (1980), pp. 303–329.
Ford, C. H.: "MBO: An Idea Whose Time Has Gone?" *Business Horizons* (December 1979).
Migliore, R. H.: *An MBO Approach to Long Range Planning* (Englewood Cliffs, N.J.: Prentice-Hall, 1984).

[11] Strategic Management in Retrospect

Karatsu, H.: "The Deindustrialization of America: A Tragedy for the World," Report No. 31, Japan Institute for Social and Economic Affairs, October 1985.
Peters, T. J.: "On Political Books," *The Washington Monthly* (October 1983), pp. 56–58.
"Who's Excellent Now?" *Business Week,* Nov. 5, 1984, pp. 76–78.
Zucker, S., et al.: *The Reindustrialization of America* (New York: McGraw-Hill, 1982).

CHAPTER OUTLINE

CHAPTER 12

APPLYING THE STRATEGIC MANAGEMENT PROCESS

OBJECTIVES

* To learn about the case method
* To learn how to prepare a case analysis
* To learn how to present the findings of a case analysis

INTRODUCTION

The purpose of our final chapter is to help you apply the material you have learned. Case analysis is the most widely used method to help you understand the complexity of integrating strategic decisions from a top-management perspective. First we will briefly describe the case method. Then we will give you our suggestions for applying to cases the material in our first 11 chapters. Finally, we offer some ideas about how you might prepare reports and present analyses. Since you will eventually prepare analyses and make presentations to your peers and supervisors in organizations, it is useful to obtain some practical experience in doing this.

THE CASE METHOD [1]

A *case* is a written description of an enterprise (such as a business, an industry, a hospital, or an arts organization). A case usually contains information about numerous facets of the enterprise: its history, external environment, and internal operations. The cases used in *Business Policy and Strategic Management* are multifaceted, containing material on many aspects of the operations. Thus your analysis is expected to be comprehensive.

403

Cases are based on material gathered about real organizations. Most cases are undisguised; that is, the real names of the organizations are used. There are some disguised cases. The companies which are the subjects of these cases wish to remain anonymous, and so their names and locations are changed. This does not change the reality of their challenges and problems, and it serves no useful purpose for you to try to guess their identity.

Are Cases Complete?

There is no such thing as a *complete* case study. The amount of information required would make the case too long to read and too detailed to analyze. One reaction that frequently is heard is, "I don't have enough information." In reality, the manager *never* has enough information because some information is not available, some is not available at this time, or acquiring some kinds of information is too costly.

What does the manager do then? The manager makes the necessary decisions on the basis of the information at hand and after making reasonable assumptions about the unknowns. So with cases you must work with the information you have and make reasonable assumptions. A case contains enough information for the analyst to examine. Then the analyst can determine what the crucial factors are that confront management at the time. Acting on incomplete knowledge is the essence of the general manager's task. Since most cases are relatively complete, executives prefer that you do not call or write them for additional information on their companies.

Is All the Case Information Important?

When you get your mail, you may find that some of it is important, some is useless, and some is of minor interest. At work, managers are bombarded with information. It, too, is a mix of the relevant, the partially relevant, and the useless. So it is with cases. Indeed, instead of not having enough information, cases may have *too much* information, or some information which is not relevant. When the case writer gathers information, some of it will become crucial to analysis. Other pieces of information are not especially useful. Since you are training to be a manager, it is your job to do the manager's job: separate the wheat from the chaff. You also have to sort through sometimes conflicting evidence or opinions; hence, learn to deal with uncertainty.

Why Are Cases Used in Management Education?

Case studies allow a different kind of learning to take place. The approach that is used is close to a learn-by-doing approach. Cases are intended to simulate the reality of the manager's job. The material in a case provides the data for analysis and decision making. The cases become the laboratory materials that you use in applying what you have learned about how to be an effective strategist. Each case is a framework for a learning experience that goes far beyond the case facts. The discussion of the case partially simulates the emotional atmosphere in which managers must operate.

Cases require you to analyze situations, make decisions about the situations presented, and defend those decisions to your peers. In real decision making, you will need to persuade your peers and superiors that your analysis and solution are the best, and so communication and human relations skills are vital to success in management. Cases provide you with the opportunity to improve these skills too.

What Roles Do Students and Instructors Play in the Case Method?

Typically, the instructor encourages the students to analyze problems and recommend solutions. The instructor questions and criticizes and encourages the students' peers to do the same. At the end of class the instructor may summarize or simply walk away, refusing to answer questions such as, What would you do? or What did they do? That's because the relevant answer is the one which is proposed and logically defended by the analysts in class.

The student can play several roles. Some of the standard roles are the board chairperson, the president, and a consultant. We prefer the consultant's role. Thus the student can analyze a situation and recommend a solution, given the nature of the problem and the nature of the top executives. If the student feels that the suggestion is likely to be unacceptable to the president, he or she should discuss more than one solution or present a particularly convincing argument to make the recommendation acceptable and overcome objections. However, unlike consultants, internal executives cannot simply walk away from a situation. Therefore, some students are asked to play roles of executives at times.

The case method is interactive. Responsibility is placed squarely on the student to be prepared and to learn from the case experience. Just as managers must do, you will have to observe, listen, diagnose, decide, and intervene in group discussions. This will also involve competition, collaboration, compromise, and persuasion.

THE CASE PREPARATION PROCESS [2]

There are a large number of possible approaches to case preparation. This is one that has worked for some of our students.

1 Read the case. Underline and comment on parts that you think are important. Then you might try to determine what the major and minor problems are. You can jot down ideas about how you might analyze them. Then do some preliminary analysis to see if your impressions were correct. Identify the mission and strategy, and list the objectives of the firm. Put the case aside for a while.

2 Read the case again. This time prepare the environmental threat and opportunity profile and the strategic advantage profile. This will require an analysis of data (Chapters 3 to 5). At about this point, if you find it comfortable (and if your instructor allows it), you might sit down and discuss the case with several friends who have different interests or majors. You and your friends can help each other with the problem, and you can learn to understand your friends' points of view too. (We hope the instructor allows it, for in real life, if managers have a problem that has ramifications for other areas, they probably visit friends in those areas and get their points of view.)

You are then ready for real analysis. Examine your statements for implicit assumptions. Fill in areas where no ''hard'' data were presented with reasonable assumptions, and state them carefully.

3 Prepare a list of the major opportunities and problems. These should be rank-ordered in terms of importance. Prepare a list of alternative strategies (Chapters 6 and 7). Consider the advantages and disadvantages of the viable alternatives for this enterprise, using your previous analyses. Make recommendations which you have carefully thought through by asking such questions as, If I recommend that they do X in marketing, how will it affect finance, or Z company, or the sales manager?

4 Analyze the alternatives in terms of the problems and opportunities, and make a choice (Chapter 8) which seems to meet the objectives of the enterprise and reflects both the values of strategists and internal and external factors.

5 Clarify how the organization can implement your suggested strategy. Prepare a plan which specifies major resource needs, functional policies, organization design, and administrative systems supporting the strategy (Chapters 9 and 10).

6 Reevaluate your proposal in terms of the qualitative criteria in Chapter 11. Point out any possible problem areas, and state how and when they should be evaluated as the plan is put into effect.

7 Prepare notes for an oral presentation (and practice it), or prepare a final written report. Our last section of the chapter discusses these topics at more length.

It is equally easy to spend too much or too little time on case analysis. Plan to spend anywhere from 10 to 15 hours over a 4- or 5-day period in the analysis phases. Another 5 to 10 hours may be needed to prepare a report. You may spend more time if the case represents a real challenge to you. However, there is a danger that you may begin to lose perspective if you find yourself unnecessarily bogged down in detail.

Stages of Analysis

Our students seem to go through stages in handling cases. The amount of time spent in each stage varies with the student, but they all seem to go through these stages:

Stage 1: Factual Level

The first stage is characterized by the development of the ability to choose the pertinent facts from all the data in the case. In real life, managers are bombarded by cues and facts and information. In this stage of development, the students learn to separate the important facts from the unimportant ones and to see where the problem(s) is (are).

Stage 2: Preanalytical Level

This stage is characterized by rudimentary use of the tools of the trade. Thus, if in stage 1 the student perceived a problem in the financial area, they now say so and present a page of ratios, as well as various financial statements, cash budgets, etc.

Stage 3: Analytical Stage

Realizing that facts do not speak for themselves, the students enter a new stage. They now interpret the facts. They not only compute the ratios but also explain them meaningfully. They say, "The current ratio is 1:1. This is less desirable than the normal 2:1 ratio found in this industry [or risk class, etc.] and means that this firm . . ."

The students are now on the threshold of asking the right questions and establishing relationships (perhaps even cause-and-effect relationships) and can begin to apply their knowledge, experience, and judgment.

Stage 4: Problem-Solving Stage

The students have now reached the stage of "knowing" what the problem(s) is (are). What is to be done about it (them)? Usually, the students attempt to dream up potential ways of accomplishing what they want to do. They develop several potential solutions. They tell us about them, attempt to show what implications there are for each one, and weigh them as better or worse.

Stage 5: Decision-Making Stage

The students now must choose a solution to the problem. To do this, they need a weighing device. Normally, the students attempt to consider maximum goal achievement with the least effort. But there are many objectives for a firm, and sometimes, in fact oftentimes, these conflict with each other.

This final stage in the process is in many ways the least rational. In many of the earlier stages, the analysis can be fairly objective. Facts have been weighed as rationally as is possible through the use of tools that are as sophisticated as is appropriate. But at this stage, it is difficult to determine which alternative is best. Many of the alternatives have been based on estimates. Even with the use of decision trees, etc., there still exists the problem of setting probabilities of occurrence. The final stage, then, involves judgment. More emotional, more intuitive factors are used than in other stages. One value we have in our business society is rationality. We like to "stick to the facts." But these decisions have fewer hard facts to rely on. So the choice is based upon values and judgment and the experience of the executive, and we may as well face this openly. The executive also shows that his or her solution, strategy, or plan will solve the problem seen in the case.

Stage 6: Implementation Stage

After making a choice, the students now realize that they must implement the decision by adjusting the organization and setting up a control and evaluation system.

We hope that you will progress through all six stages, for they represent the kinds of processes we described in Chapter 1.

GUIDELINES FOR ANALYZING CASES

So far we have discussed the reason for and process of case analysis. Now let's look at the content of a good case analysis. Exhibit 12.1 repeats the model of strategic

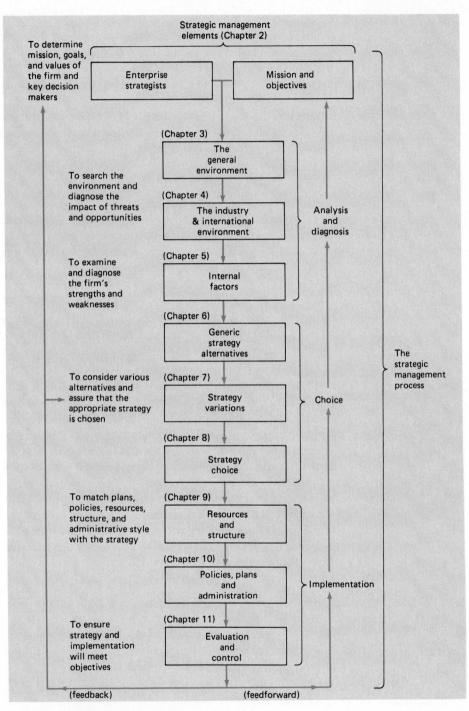

EXHIBIT 12.1   **A model of strategic management.**

management covered in the first 11 chapters. The purposes expressed in the exhibit for each aspect of the model should serve as a guide for the content of your analysis. That is, you should begin by identifying the past strategy and mission of the organization, as well as the key managers and their goals and values. Then you should analyze and diagnose the environment and the competitive advantages of the firm. From these stages, a determination of strategic gaps and alternatives to close them should be made. Next a strategy must be selected, and appropriate plans should be made for its implementation. Finally, you can apply some evaluative criteria to double-check your process and proposals.

At this point, you might want to review the summaries of the first 11 chapters, to refresh your memory of the high points of the process. In the rest of this section we will highlight a series of key questions and suggestions that you will want to address as you do your case analysis and apply the material in each of those chapters. For some cases, not all these questions may be directly applicable. In others, you may have to make some assumptions or do library research. The more of these questions you address, the more likely it is that you will do a good analysis.

The Strategic Problem

Our first chapter introduced you to the overall process of strategic management. In this regard, at all times in your analysis you need to keep in the back of your mind the ideas that you are ultimately trying to integrate. What is the current mission, and what are the objectives? What is the enterprise's business definition? What are its products and markets, and what functions does it perform? What is its environmental situation? What is its distinctive competence? Will the current strategy allow the firm to reach its objectives and meet the values and goals of its managers, or are there expected gaps with regard to accomplishing its mission in the future? Can the firm invent a creative solution to close those gaps? How can it organize and manage itself to the full advantage of its resources and implement its innovative solution? The whole thrust of your analysis should generally focus on those issues.

We also indicated in the first chapter some differences between single- and multiple-SBU firms. You will need to determine whether the case you are analyzing deals with the situation of a single SBU or whether several SBUs are involved. If the case involves a multiple-SBU firm, in your analysis you will have to examine more factors which influence different SBUs as well as the firm as a whole. And your recommendations may be different for various parts of the organization. You will probably need to recommend a corporate-level strategy and a strategy for each SBU. Similarly, if an international strategy is involved, the analysis may be more complex.

The Strategic Elements

Our second chapter described the roles of the mission and objectives and the strategists involved. Your analysis should include assessments of these elements.

Of course, one of the forces for change involves the values and goals of top management. Who are the key people with decision power in this case? What do they want? How do they make decisions? How much risk would they be willing to assume? Does the board support the CEO? If you are going to ultimately make realistic recommendations which have some probability of acceptance, you must have an understanding of who has the power (in the case) to implement your proposals. If you are playing the consultant role, you must convince the manager(s) with power that your recommendation will fit the managerial goals and values and be best for the organization. Otherwise, recommendations for changes in top-management personnel and/or implementation of planned cultural changes may be necessary.

What is the mission of the business? What is its business definition and past strategy? Prepare a statement which summarizes these elements. Exhibit 2.2 provided an example. The case itself may not state these clearly, but you need to attempt to determine this for yourself. In particular, look for synergies and utilities in the business definition (see pages 73 to 74). Also, try to make a list of objectives (the operative ones, not the official ones). Then ask if these objectives help define the organization, provide standards, and help to coordinate decisions, or if there is conflict. Since there are usually multiple objectives, how are they currently ranked? Are they long- or short-term? Are they specific or broad? Do they need to be more specific? Are they being achieved? What pressures are there to change them? Refer to Exhibit 2.10, and identify any forces which may be leading to changes in objectives. At this point, you may be able to do a gap analysis for objectives (see Exhibit 2.6).

Analysis and Diagnosis

The gaps between desired goals and expected attainment are caused by either external or internal changes. Thus the next stage of case analysis focuses on these factors.

The Environment

Chapters 3 and 4 indicated the importance of examining threats and opportunities coming from the environment. For the firm (and key SBUs if necessary), you need to analyze and diagnose the sectors of the general, industry, and international environments of importance. It is worthwhile to reexamine Exhibit 3.1, since that provides the key overall questions. What are the assumptions about the environment on which the current strategy is based? What predictions do you make for the future? Are there any gaps in those assumptions and predictions? If so, will they lead to changes in objectives or strategy?

Should this firm do more in the way of environmental analysis? What techniques do you recommend? More important for the case you are analyzing, which of your key predictions are creating threats and opportunities? You should focus your diagnosis on the critical areas—the sectors on which the firm is most dependent and where there is greater development, complexity, and volatility. In these areas, a much greater in-depth analysis should be done (see Exhibit 4.15). If the case data are insufficient, use the appendix for Chapter 4 to guide you in a search for information.

If you want to do a more sophisticated analysis, you can prepare several scenarios. These may ultimately lead to the preparation of contingency proposals. In any case, you should prepare an ETOP (see Exhibit 4.14) with a commentary based on your summary. That is, you should elaborate on data and estimates of revenue or cost implications and estimates of the likelihood of events and their timing. In the end, go back to the key questions: Where are the opportunities? Where are the threats? What strategic impact do they have? Reconsider the gap analysis for objectives if this is appropriate.

Internal Factors

Chapter 5 identified the areas within which you need to search for the firm's strengths and weaknesses. Like environmental factors, the internal factors may alter the gap between desired and expected outcomes.

You should reexamine Exhibits 5.3, 5.5, 5.9, 5.11, and 5.13. Which of these areas are in the "technical core" for the firm in the case? Those should receive your greatest attention. You need to identify distinctive competencies in these areas by asking key questions: What does the firm do well? Do these count? What does the firm do poorly? Does it matter? Remember that your analysis should focus on the data and indicators based on relative comparisons: How do current conditions relate to the past and future needs? How do the areas relate to one another? How do they relate to relevant competitors?

Prepare the SAP (see Exhibit 5.20). Also prepare any supporting documents and a commentary about distinctive competencies. At the very least you should prepare a summary of the firm's financial position (see Exhibit 5.27). The basic financial data need interpretation and point to other areas of the firm which may need to be examined. You might also prepare a resource-deployment matrix (Exhibit 5.16) and do a break-even analysis if the data are available. Your commentary should attempt to determine how the strengths and weaknesses have been used to develop competitive advantages and how they might be used later on (see Exhibit 5.22).

In the process of doing this, don't forget your ETOP. Begin to ask yourself whether the competitive advantages (the ones that exist or that could be developed) relate to the new opportunities that you identified earlier. Also, decide whether increased resources might be needed to offset any threats, and determine where those resources are now and where they need to be. In other words, how can the firm most effectively exploit the opportunities and meet the threats which the environment is presenting?

Strategy Alternatives and Choice

Before proceeding, reexamine your analyses and diagnosis in relation to the gap in the objectives of decision makers. Do the key strategists see a gap between where they want to be and where they will be if they continue with the existing strategy? Are there gaps that they should be made aware of which will result from the changes you expect in the environment or from changes in the internal condition of the firm?

Now review Exhibit 8.2 and our discussion there. Focus on the gap and the reasons for it. Focus on the generic strategy which is most relevant for the situation in the case. Also, compare this analysis with our four propositions in the summary for Chapter 6.

Next, prepare a summary of the advantages and disadvantages of following the generic strategy you are analyzing. Will it close gaps? Will it do a better job than the next alternative, which is more dissimilar than the current strategy? In other words, apply the strategic choice model (Exhibit 8.17).

If you have settled on a generic strategy, consider the various approaches for accomplishing this strategy. The summary in Chapter 7 presents the options in outline form. At this point you will want to consider the pros and cons of using one or more of these. For instance, will a particular option close gaps better than other alternatives? Does it use competitive advantages? Will it build new ones and allow the firm to develop a sustained, distinctive competence? Does it meet the challenges and opportunities in the environment? Does it change the pace or the business definition? Will that be acceptable to the power holders?

For a multiple-SBU firm, you will need to consider the portfolio of strategies of the firm as a whole. Then you will want to determine whether it is appropriate to apply a decision matrix to your case, such as Exhibit 8.6 or 8.8. Exhibits 8.19 or 8.20 might be used if international strategy options are involved.

Before recommending a choice, you should present two or three viable alternatives. Then consider managerial perceptions of dependence and risk, awareness of past strategy, and managerial power relations. Next, settle on a tentative choice for which you will develop a plan of implementation. Following that, the evaluation stage will be applied to confirm a final choice.

If you were doing a sophisticated analysis, you would compare several contingency strategies to go along with the scenarios that we suggested you prepare earlier. Hence you might have a worst case–best case–most likely set of strategies.

Implementation

Exhibit 9.3 outlines the major areas you need to consider for a plan to implement the strategy. For any given case, it is unlikely that you will be able to get to some of the details that are needed. However, several elements of a plan should minimally be included to "flesh out" your strategy recommendation.

What major changes in resource allocation are implied by your strategy? If a multiple-SBU firm is involved, will the firm need to shift resources from one SBU to another? Where will resources come from? Do you have a plan to secure needed funding? Will some functional areas need more resources? Where will they come from? If your strategy is to sell some assets, how much do you expect to get from the sale? If your strategy is expansion, will the firm use internal funds, debt, or equity, and what will the impact be on the balance sheet? If your strategy involves a joint venture, what kind of equity agreement do you recommend? A sophisticated analysis would present proforma balance sheet and income statement exhibits based on realistic assumptions of the plan based on the strategy.

A plan for implementation would also address key major changes needed in the organization structure. Usually in a case analysis, these would only occur if major redefinitions of the business resulted from your proposed strategy. However, some cases may focus on organizational issues. Here you would probably be provided with data on which to base more detailed recommendations. Depending on the recommendations, you may need to include a revised organization chart in your report. You should consider the strategic reason why any changes you propose would be necessary. For example, is the firm moving from related to unrelated product or market areas? If so, a change to the divisional form would probably be useful. Other characteristics of the firm and its environment which are related to the strategy should be considered as well (see Chapter 9, section [10]). In a few cases you may want to address the role of a planning staff as it relates to the future of the organization.

Of course, plans and policies for the functional areas need to be considered. Exhibit 10.2 suggests the kinds of issues you need to consider. Greater detail and more specifics for the case in question would be needed, but these are illustrations. The list in the summary for Chapter 10 suggests key functional decisions that you should make. Before drawing up your final proposal, look back over the decisions and ask yourself these questions: Are they consistent with one another? Are they consistent with the strategic choice?

Your plan should also consider leadership. Are changes needed in the current leadership? If yes, in what position? What kinds of changes are to be made? Is it feasible to recommend firing the president if it is the president who holds the power? Would a career development plan make sense? Can reward systems be set up to motivate managers to enact the strategic choice? How much effort will be needed to carry out your plan? If your strategy involves international moves, all these issues and others need to be considered. At the very least, issues raised by Exhibit 7.15 should be explained in the report.

Evaluation

After you have finished your analysis and prepared a plan to implement the tentative strategy, reevaluate the entire process—look at it as a whole. Is your plan comprehensive, unified, and integrated? Are the strategy and plans you developed consistent, appropriate, and workable? Will the plan close the gaps to a degree acceptable to the key strategists? If not, then you should rethink the plan for implementation. If there is no problem there but gaps are still not closed, you should consider another strategy. But if the strategy you developed is the best one available given your analyses and diagnoses, then you will have to convince the managers that their expectations about goal attainment will have to be modified (the only way left to close the gap).

If you are convinced that your proposals are the best you can come up with, complete your analysis by explaining how management can evaluate the performance of your plan over time. Set up benchmarks for evaluation (see Exhibit 11.11), and indicate when and how information should be delivered to the right managers at the right time.

Finally, if you are doing the more sophisticated second-generation planning, show how your plan is flexible enough to provide for contingencies. Indicate under what conditions and when a contingency strategy should be put into effect.

Problems in Analysis

We have taken you through our suggestions for a comprehensive basic case analysis. Remember that we have just summarized the highlights of more specific recommendations and prescriptions in the text chapters. If you really want to do a top-notch job, you will need to go beyond these basics. Some instructors may want you to supplement the case information with outside material, or expect you to relate your analyses to specific theoretical material.

In any event, we should also point out that not all questions we just raised for you to analyze will be directly addressed by most cases. In some cases, financial data are not available, or competitor data or other environmental data are lacking. In others, the focus may be on a more limited set of issues or problems. In these instances, you have several options:

- Do some library work to get additional data.
- Make assumptions and then proceed.
- Recognize that the case focus is limited, and apply the elements of the material you have learned which are most directly relevant.

Just as managers must do, you will often need to be creative; that is, you will often have to put together your own data and read between the lines to answer some questions and deal with significant strategic issues. We hope you will invest the time it takes to do that.

REPORTING YOUR RECOMMENDATIONS [3]

Each of us has our own style for presenting the results of an analysis. Now and in the future you will be asked to present, discuss, justify, and defend your recommendations. This is done in oral form and in writing. So we conclude by offering some suggestions for how you might make more effective presentations, assuming that those are backed up by the type of analysis we just outlined.

Written Presentations

Most written reports of case analyses tend to be relatively short (8 to 12 pages plus exhibits). Occasionally even shorter "management summaries" might be called for. In either case, a key guideline is to attempt to apply one principle: Keep it simple. Unfortunately, after hours of analysis and note taking, you will want to share your entire analysis to show what you have done. If you try that, it is likely that your report won't be kept simple. Keeping it simple and straightforward does not necessarily imply that you have done a sloppy job or that it lacks comprehensiveness. If the report is well put together, it will be apparent that it is based on good analysis.

In particular, if (as we suggested) you prepare and include supporting exhibits (such as an ETOP, an SAP, ratio summaries, break-even analyses, pro-forma financial statements, benchmarks for evaluation, and so on), you will be providing powerful evidence to justify your major arguments and recommendations and evidence that you have thought through the issues involved.

So do not be a "slave" to the particular format used in your analysis, such as a page on past strategy, another on the environment, and so on. Rather, when you begin to write, start writing from the *end* of your analysis. Sum up your major recommendations in one or two sentences or a paragraph. Then build a topical outline for the paper around these conclusions. What are the key messages from your analysis which support and build up to the recommendations? The commentary should be tightly integrated and have a logical flow from beginning to end so that the reader is led to agree with you. Remember, you are trying to convince your reader that your proposal should be adopted and that it will accomplish objectives of interest. The proper presentation of those exhibits will help. (Each exhibit should have a clear title, and there should be a source note so that the reader does not have to refer to the text.)

With regard to style, we prefer concise cases written in specifics. Generalities without a clear, precise meaning are not particularly helpful. For example, do not say that the firm's past performance has been poor and leave it at that. Indicate that specific objectives (such as an increase in sales growth or in profits as a percentage of sales) have not been reached or that the firm has missed the mark by a certain amount. Don't say "This firm needs more formal planning." If it does, indicate the types of planning it needs.

Finally, good writers do not turn in their first draft. Ask someone else to read it, or read it out loud to yourself. When you hear what you say and how you say it, you are likely to find rough areas to clean up, or you may find that you are not saying what you mean or that you failed to say something you need to say.

Oral Presentations and Discussions

You may have a chance to present your recommendations to a group that will question and challenge you. We hope that you do get such a chance, since it is good experience to stand up and justify a position and think on your feet.

Obviously, oral presentations are different from written ones. You should not just get up and read your written report. You will have to be even more precise, more specific, and more convincing. In a well-prepared written report, many of the facts you present speak for themselves. In an oral presentation, that can't happen, and the listeners do not have the time to digest exhibits which a reader might have. You should still use exhibits (handouts or material magnified by an overhead projector). But they will have to be less detailed and more to the point of summarizing key aspects of your presentation. As with the written presentation, you need to organize well in advance and prepare notes to yourself on the high points.

Guides for Oral Presentations and Discussion

Some suggestions for making more effective oral presentations are included below:

1 *Define your audience.* You need to gain audience attention and interest; consider the level of sophistication and preparation of your audience as you prepare your report. For example, if you assume the audience will follow a detailed technical explanation of a financial analysis, you would proceed differently than if you assume the audience

could not understand such an analysis. By the way, the attention span of most audiences is little more than 20 minutes or so; so plan accordingly.

2 *Prepare a complete outline.* Members of an audience may not understand the sequence or relationship of topics being discussed. The outline should help give an overview of the presentation so the audience does not get lost. Generally, oral presentations start with "telling the audience what you are going to tell them"; then you tell them the message; you conclude by "telling them what you told them." The outline helps your audience understand where you are going and how various topics are interrelated. In essence, the content of main sections and subheadings should say to the audience, "This is why this material is important, so keep listening; these are the topics we are going to discuss, in this order."

3 *Provide supportive detail.* To provide justification for a position, the audience must sense you know what you are talking about. Exhibits of supportive analysis help, but you cannot provide orally the detail contained in a written presentation. Thus describe supportive detail selectively. The two or three most important analytical conclusions should be presented with a brief description of the data and the assumptions and approach used to make calculations. Don't bore or irritate the audience with long, drawn-out descriptions of endless tables of numbers.

4 *Prepare clear visual aids.* Blackboards, flip charts, scale models, or overheads and slides should be prepared in advance. Wording should be brief; letters and figures should be legible when projected; numbers should be rounded; graphics and charts should be clear. The discussion about an exhibit should discuss the concepts; do not just read the statements, but explain their significance.

5 *Introduce your topic.* Explain the purpose of the presentation, present the agenda or outline, briefly describe the methodology (how you went about your analysis), and briefly summarize the major recommendations.

6 *Present material clearly and confidently.* Stand for the presentation; maintain eye contact with the audience; start without delay; maintain a steady pace; rehearse your presentation with note cards.

7 *Come to a natural conclusion.* Don't just end your presentation with, "Well, that's it." Restate the outline of the report, briefly. And restate the recommendations of the report and major rationale for the position.

8 *Respond to questions positively.* Expect aggressive or hostile attacks and be prepared for them. Don't hurry your response, but carefully consider the intent of the question. Don't ramble in your response; address the question directly without diverting to side issues. Don't try to bluff; if you don't know the answer, admit it. On the other hand, don't avoid direct confrontation—you may be able to answer the question with another question, asking the audience to respond or the questioners to present their point of view.

9 *Listen.* As a presenter, listen carefully to the question before answering. Furthermore, many times you will be asked to listen to someone else's presentation or participate in a group discussion of a case. Once again, full and complete analyses need to be done. But here, instead of a formal presentation, you are being asked to challenge the position of others and defend your own. Do this with facts, figures, assumptions, and logic. Do not attack a position unless you have a counterposition

with reasons to back it up. But do not be afraid to express your viewpoint if it differs. On the other hand, don't waste group time by repeating the same points and reasoning over and over.

10 *Avoid repetition*. In a case presentation or discussion, refrain from reviewing or rehashing the entire case background. Everyone (presumably) is familiar with that. What is of interest is your analysis of the material and your interpretations. Also, clearly distinguish between facts and assumptions.

11 *Go for it*. Take a defensible position and support it. Obviously there is some risk that you will be attacked, but don't be afraid to be criticized. You may as well learn what such criticism is like, and learn to deal with it. Different positions can always be taken based on the same facts. Since there is no one "right" answer to a case, discussion and criticism will help you hone your skills in justifying a position.

SUMMARY

The approach we have suggested is really a general approach to problem solving. Some might argue that it involves little more than common sense. That is not quite true. Hard analysis as we have suggested here may end up appearing to be "common sense" when it is all done. But the method is a specialized application of the scientific approach. And sometimes that method leads us to conclusions which are contrary to common sense but later appear to be quite natural. For example, our common sense tells us that the sun revolves around the earth. Our earthbound perspective and senses tell us that the sun "rises" in the east and "sets" in the west. And until science proved otherwise, people believed that the earth was stationary. So it is with elegant recommendations for strategy. The creative proposal is the proposal which in the end *appears* to be simple and *seems* to be based on nothing more than common sense. Yet it is likely to be the unique one which no one else ever dreamed of.

REFERENCES

[1] The Case Method

McNair, M. P. (ed.): *The Case Method at the Harvard Business School* (New York: McGraw-Hill, 1954).

Postman, N., and C. Weingarten: *Teaching as a Subversive Activity* (New York: Delacorte Press, 1969).

[2] Preparing Cases

Edge, A. G., and D. R. Coleman: *The Guide to Case Analysis and Reporting* (Honolulu: System Logistics, 1978).

Kepner, C. H., and B. B. Tregoe: *The Rational Manager* (New York: McGraw-Hill, 1976).

Raymond, R.: *Problems in Business Administration* (New York: McGraw-Hill, 1964).

Schnelle, K. E.: *Case Analysis and Business Problem Solving* (New York: McGraw-Hill, 1967).

[3] Preparing Recommendations

Hodgetts, R. M., and M. S. Wortman, Jr.: *Administrative Policy: Text and Cases in Strategic Management* (New York: Wiley, 1980).

Hosmer, L. T.: *Strategic Management* (Englewood Cliffs, N.J.: Prentice-Hall, 1982), especially chap. 14.

Ronstadt, R.: *The Art of Case Analysis: A Guide to the Diagnosis of Business Situations* (Needham, Mass.: Lord Publishing, 1984).

Turner, A. N.: ''The Case Discussion Method Revisited'' *Exchange,* vol. 6 (1981), pp. 33–38.

CASES

ACROSS, INC.

Laura Miller and
Joseph W. Leonard
Miami University

In the mid-1970's, the word for the future was "Plastics." Today, in 1984, as the plastics industry continues to boom, that prediction has been fulfilled. American industries are discovering new, more efficient uses for plastic products, thus increasing the demand for product suppliers.

In 1978, having anticipated the potential demand for plastics, specifically within the automotive sector, Ronald T. Noble incorporated a small manufacturing plant in his hometown of Bellefontaine, Ohio. His initial product was to be a plastic dust tube for shock absorbers. Noble best describes his corporate mission in a quote taken from the company's facilities list:

> We are dedicated to quality, service, and profit. Our goals are to grow in a diversified manner into a medium company with numerous fabricating and decorating secondary capabilities.

Noble chose the name of ACROSS, INC. with the help of his wife Pat, the corporate secretary-treasurer, whose

This case was prepared by Laura Miller under the direction of Joseph W. Leonard of Miami University as a basis for class discussion rather than to illustrate either effective or ineffective handling of organizational practices.

At the request of the company, the names of the corporation and the people who work for it have been disguised, but essential relationships have been preserved.

efforts enabled Ron to begin fulfilling his dream of self-employment.

COMPANY HISTORY

In March of 1978, Noble left his position as a marketing manager for Monte Plastics, Inc., in nearby Kenton, Ohio, to begin his own venture. Prior to his work with Monte, Noble had worked in sales for both the General Tire Company and Marmon Carbon Company. His education included a 1960 bachelor's degree in Chemistry from Wooster College and a few graduate courses in business administration that he took during his first years of employment.

Since Noble had spent all but one year of his life in the Bellefontaine area, his established reputation as an honest, hardworking businessman, his business contacts, and family contributions proved to be key factors in the establishment of the corporation. The immediate Noble family includes three children: a daughter who is a senior in college majoring in Accounting and two sons, one in college as a Pre-med major and one in high school. At the time of incorporation, all three children lived at home and, therefore, sacrificed Saturdays and summer vacation time to help with the production runs. Noble's father and father-in-law also volunteered help in running machines or in hand trimming products to meet customer specifications.

Through his past work experience, Noble learned not only how to successfully sell a product, but also of the increasing demand for plastics in the automotive industry. In 1978, the predominant Detroit manufacturers were switching from metals to plastics in order to reduce the weight of transportation vehicles and to comply with energy-saving regulations. Noble fabricated a mold for a dust tube and within several months, obtained a sufficient order from a supplier to one of these Detroit firms.

Acquiring sufficient bank loans to finance the corporation was a difficult process; the odds of Noble's success during the economy of the late 70's were slim. However, his persistence and confidence, as well as his contacts in the area, helped Noble to gain financial backing. With the funds, Noble installed production lines in a portion of a building which was situated in an area of the city with relatively low overhead costs. ACROSS leased a blow molding machine and various pieces of secondary equipment. Noble relied upon the expertise and advice of his long-time friends who also served ACROSS in the capacities of accountant, corporate lawyer, and insurance agent.

In 1978, Noble and his family had no idea of when or if ACROSS would prove a successful venture. Normally, survival for a firm such as this one through the first three years of incorporation would signify eventual success. The unanticipated effects of the 1980 and 1981 automotive recession delayed the company's profitable efforts a few years. However, the subsequent economic recovery extended to ACROSS. Today, in 1984, ACROSS claims 1.5 million dollars in sales and boasts a 1983 profit of $85,000.

PERSONNEL

In 1978, the ACROSS payroll consisted of two people: Ron, the president, and Robert Benson, the only other production worker. Noble served as "jack-of-all-trades" in fulfilling the roles of chief engineer, marketing manager, plant manager, personnel supervisor, financial planner, and president. His wife Pat worked out of their home as the secretary-treasurer on a volunteer basis.

ACROSS ran only one production shift in the first year of incorporation; Noble and Benson would alternate operating the main blow molding machine and hand finishing a product. Family members volunteered their time on those days when Benson didn't work or when three people were needed to meet production demands. Equipment breakdowns were a major concern; with merely two people in the plant and Noble being the only expert repairman, if equipment malfunctioned, production halted indefinitely.

Presently, management still consists of only a few individuals, thus making for a simpler and more timely decision-making process. Payroll includes 28 full-time employees, Benson being the only current employee hired before 1980. Twelve part-time workers remain on call as substitutes for full-time employees on vacation or as additional labor during the peak production months. Only three of the full-time personnel are salaried: Ron, Pat, and Steve Gilbert, the general foreman who has been with ACROSS since December of 1980. Gilbert has authority over the supervisors of each of the three production shifts. (As orders for shipment increased, ACROSS gradually added shifts of production.) The supervisors include Benson, Doug Clark, and Mark Curran. Clark and Curran joined ACROSS in July of 1981 and August of 1980, respectively. All three were hired without experience in plastics manufacturing or a college background.

Today, six years since the founding of ACROSS, Noble spends minimal time in the plant. He relies on his foremen to supervise labor and on Gilbert to help interview prospective employees. Yet, Noble remains committed to maintaining effective employee relations. (See Exhibit 1.) He has six month individual reviews with employees concerning bonuses, raises, and potential problems. When hired, each employee receives an employees manual which reflects ACROSS's committment to effective communication. (See Exhibit 2.) In this pamphlet, Noble expresses his and the company's enthusiasm in accepting the responsibility to provide good working conditions, good wages, good benefits, and fair treatment for all. ACROSS feels a union would be of no advantage to any of the employees; the business upon which each employee depends for his bread and butter should not be purchased by anyone who forces workers to pay dues. Accomplishment of expressing problems, suggestions, and comments need not be through a union, but through direct supervisors.

Office Personnel

ACROSS office personnel currently include Pat, who spends 3–4 days per week in the newly renovated secretary's office, and Julie Harden, whom Pat is training to

EXHIBIT 1   PRESIDENT'S TIME EXPENDITURES
(Per Month of Working Days)

Activity	Approximate percent of month
Production	10
Personnel & employee relations	20
Marketing	
Advertising	1
Entertainment & time with clients	29
Engineering	20
Financing	20
	100%

relieve the latter of her duties. Neither Pat, nor Harden, who joined ACROSS in 1982 as a production worker, have any significant business background. Because of the increased size of the payroll, ACROSS uses an outside EDP firm to process the payroll. Pat and Harden submit the ledgers and other pertinent work to a local CPA firm which quarterly compiles financial statements for ACROSS and offers Noble business and personal tax planning considerations.

Noble has investigated purchasing for the company a small business computer with a spreadsheet and word processing software. However, neither Pat nor Harden are able to find time to learn the system. They rationalize that the time lost in learning how to operate the computer and convert from a manual system is not worth the benefits to ACROSS, such a relatively young business. Noble re-

cently met with a systems consultant who estimates the cost for a complete spreadsheet system to be $18,000–20,000. This consultant feels adaptation of the system is a must.

Production Personnel

With the exception of the aforementioned office workers, all of the labor is employed in direct production, which operates in three 8-hour shifts. These workers are in the plant six days a week and receive overtime pay at time-and-a-half for hours worked exceeding 40 per week. Except for an employee who is hired into ACROSS as a foreman, workers begin at minimum wage. Full-time employees have seniority; when hired, Gilbert informs them as to their positions on the list of seniority. Part-time

---

EXHIBIT 2

EXCERPT FROM THE INTRODUCTION OF THE EMPLOYEE
WAGE AND POLICY MANUAL

Dear Fellow Employee:

Welcome to Across, Inc. I trust that this will be the beginning of a most beneficial association both for you and Across, Inc. I intend to maintain that "personal touch" through close communication with each of you. It has been our employees who through their outstanding efforts have made our Company a competitive and respected business . . . From time to time, new or revised policies will be developed to insure the continued common good and mutual interest of the Company and its employees, and to keep in step with modern trends and philosophies which perpetuate harmonious employee-management relationships. . .

workers stand in succession to full-time workers, a position to be desired for several reasons—better benefits, steady hours, and the opportunity to participate in the profit-sharing program. Noble outlined and, after consulting his lawyers, adopted the ACROSS Profit Sharing Plan in 1982. It extends to each employee after completion of 1 year of full-time hours.

In early years of production, employee turnover was a major concern. Often, Noble found himself working double shifts for workers who failed to report to duty. Now that ACROSS is "on its feet", this is no longer a major problem. If absenteeism becomes a concern, Gilbert takes responsibility; employees on the whole seem to be committed to a consistent schedule of working hours.

MARKETING

In 1978, ACROSS used *one* blow molding machine to produce *one* product sold to *one* supplier of *one* automotive company. In 1984, ACROSS operates *five* blow molding machines, produces *30* separate items, sells to *19* companies which represent *several* industries. Dust tubes comprise 49% of production and reflect purchase orders from 3 suppliers, in the U.S. and Canada, to 2 international automotive companies. Other products range from children's toys and plastic footballs to paint containers and birdfeeders. (See Exhibit 3.) Most customers

are based in the midwest. However, Noble anticipates that as the company's sales grow, ACROSS will need to find another location to not only house additional equipment, but also decrease freight costs. Having a balance of customers by industry has always been and will continue to be another concern for ACROSS.

Noble often finds himself traveling to home offices of customers to meet with purchasing agents, engineers, or quality control managers to discuss dissatisfactions of customers, to maintain relations, or to acquire new business. As a result of the previous 2 years of increasing production orders, Noble has employed 2 manufacturer's representatives who aid in the adoption of a contract between ACROSS and a customer. These men spend an insignificant amount of their time working with an ACROSS account; in fact, the growth in sales is attributable primarily to Noble's flexibility, reputation, and ability to undercut the larger bids of larger competitors.

After that initial visit to a customer's place of business, Noble will receive an oral or written option from a customer to quote on a product price per piece (i.e., a "piece price"), a mold price, and costs of necessary secondary fixtures. Sometimes, the customer will ask for a quote unexpectedly. In order to quote, Noble must consult several people: his moldmakers (2 independent contractors); his materials suppliers; and suppliers of secondary fixtures. He estimates for each job, the costs of raw materials, direct labor, and factory overhead based on standard

EXHIBIT 3   **Breakdown of ACROSS products.**

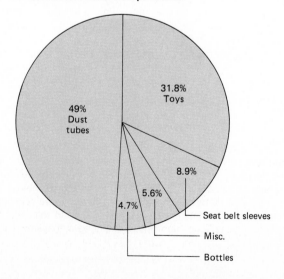

machine hours. Included in the overhead would be costs of operating ACROSS-owned equipment and secondary fixtures (i.e., drill presses, flame treaters, conveyors, table saws). All of these costs determine the piece price, which is expressed in price per thousand pieces and sent to the customer with a detailed print of the product matching customer specifications. Noble also must quote a mold and/or secondary fixture cost since the customer owns both his mold and a secondary fixture if the latter must be custom made for a particular job. Noble adds a markup to the cost of fabricating the mold which covers such potential mold and tooling expenses as repair and maintenance or trial runs. ACROSS does not attempt to make a profit on mold and tooling income, but merely strives to break even.

The fact that customers own their own molds and, often, the secondary fixtures installed at the ACROSS plant is not uncommon for the custom blow molding industry. (Noble does own one mold—the original dust tube design.) A blow molder may choose to own his molds and amortize their costs over several years; however, such companies run the risk of a customer not accepting the mold design. In fact, most customers demand unique mold specifications and prefer to have their own molds, despite the initial capital outlay of purchasing the mold. The majority of manufacturers such as ACROSS must anticipate the possibility of a customer's deciding to run production "in-house", i.e., not renewing an ACROSS contract, taking its molds and fixtures, and producing its own units.

PRODUCTION

The extent of the production process for each customer depends on that customer's specifications for dimension, color, and quantity. Dust tubes, for example, are of one color (black), and must be hand-trimmed once they are molded; toys come in various colors and must be hand-trimmed and flame-treated to pass quality inspections.

A 17,000 square foot building, purchased by Noble and subsequently leased to ACROSS, houses the production area. Originally, ACROSS rented one part of the building from an independent party. Now, however, with the need for increased office space, production area, raw material and finished goods storage, and employee lunch and break rooms, ACROSS leases the entire structure. It does rent a small portion of the building to a third party with the hopes of someday utilizing the complete floor space.

To meet production demands, ACROSS has leased 4 blow molding machines and last year purchased one used machine. Noble recently flew to New Jersey to inspect another machine being fabricated and to be delivered to Bellefontaine within a few months. The company also owns various secondary fixtures which it uses for several different jobs:

3 table saws;
1 radial saw;
3 conveyor belts; and
4 grinders.

Included in the production area are flame-treating stations, automatic handling equipment, and custom-made fabricating equipment. Raw materials are delivered to ACROSS via 40,000 lb. truckloads in the form of natural-colored pellets. To fabricate a colored product, a color concentrate is added to the process. A 45-gram product would contain 45 grams of resin and approximately 3% of concentrate, by weight. Raw material price is between 40¢ and 42¢ per pound.

All incoming materials or subcontracted parts are inspected for damages and flaws by the receiving department. They are then segregated by lots according to material and source.

When a sales order has been accepted, the production control department delivers the proper blueprint and program sheets to the foreman who controls the computerized channels of the complex blow molding machines. He also installs and approves the proper machine tooling. Machine tooling consists of a bushing and mandrel through which the molten plastic passes and is shaped.

Resin is poured into the machine where it is melted into an aluminum mold. Upon compression of the mold, air is injected into the cavity, thus "molding" the plastic to the shape of the cavity. Parts are, therefore, hollow. (Blow molding differs from another common plastics process, injection molding, the latter of which entails injecting *resin* into the mold in order to form a *solid* product.) Parts leave the machine via conveyor and move to a hand finishing station.

At the beginning of each new production run of either new or existing products, foremen conduct mandatory first-piece inspections to maintain compliance with predetermined dimensions and customer specifications. Once an hour, supervisors make sure these specifications are upheld; parts cannot proceed past any inspection station until accepted. If a discrepant part is discovered, the foreman and plant manager (Noble) review the item and either

EXHIBIT 4

August 23, 1983

QUALITY CIRCLES

Periodically over the past few weeks I have mentioned to many of you the desire to create "quality circles" amongst our people. What this means is that periodically each of our Class 1, Class 2, and Foremen groups would meet independently, the purpose of the meetings being to discuss ways to improve our operation. Anything can be brought up in these meetings and the only people attending would be the people in that particular job classification. The net result of these meetings should hopefully be to create a better channel of communication and to maintain or improve the quality standards of our products and company.

The meeting for our Class 2 workers, shift 1 and 3, would be at 3:15 PM on a designated day. Shift 2 Class 2 workers could meet before their shift time. Regular hourly rates would be paid for your attendance at these meetings.

I have asked Cindy Magoline to be the spokesperson for shifts 1 and 3 Class 2 job description, and Carrie Carroll for Class 2 job description 2nd shift. Todd Miller will coordinate the Class 1 job description meetings and be their spokesperson. Robert Benson will be the spokesperson for the Foremen and will coordinate their meeting.

The spokespersons mentioned above should let me know ahead of time about their meeting times so there are no conflicts of space, people, etc. The spokesperson should put in writing (a few words) the recommendations resulting from their meetings. Remember, we're all looking for ways to better the quality of our product and methods of our production.

This "quality circle" concept is experimental for us—we'll see how it works out. Thanks for your cooperation.

Ron

---

send it to a rework area or to the scrap area. Scrap may be successfully recycled into resin.

The impact on product quality of using recycled scrap depends on the type of product. Normally, a product may contain 20–30% scrap and still pass quality inspection. However, color may be one of the limiting factors—using recycled scrap may result in a color slightly lighter or darker than if pure resin were used. For some production runs of the black dust tubes, ACROSS has used 100% scrap and effectively maintained quality.

Finished products are boxed and tagged as one of the following:

1 Satisfactory and ready for shipment,
2 Held-over for reason on tag, or
3 Unsatisfactory for reason on tag.

These boxes remain in the finished goods storage area until shipment. Julie Harden maintains inventory control by indicating daily, through physical inspection, the finished goods status.

In order to enhance employee performance and participation, Noble recently implemented quality control circles. (See Exhibit 4.) Similarly, to maintain productivity and job performance, employees rotate positions every

4 hours. Through an extensive study, Noble concluded that 4 hours was the optimal rotational basis; shifting before 4 hours would only decrease product quality.

PLANT RENOVATION

One portion of the ACROSS building is allocated to office space, reception area, and an employee lunchroom. Casts, tools, and supplies are located in yet another room. Since July of 1982, ACROSS has undergone one-and-a-half phases of plant renovation. With the help of a local architect and long-time friend, Noble has divided renovation into 3 phases. (See Exhibit 5.) Phase I ended in early 1983; Phase II will extend through 1984. Pat is helping to furnish the offices and Noble's children help part-time to paint and wallpaper and upkeep the outside property, i.e., mow lawns, trim hedges.

CONCLUSION

Noble attributes the success of his venture to such factors as ACROSS' committment to uphold effective subordinate/superior relations, ideal quality control and Noble's

EXHIBIT 5

July 28, 1982

Dear Ron:

As we discussed previously:

A. To repair, remodel, and expand the existing building to provide for present and near future needs of Across, Inc. and three rental units (approximately 20,000 sq. ft.).

B. This cost is detailed as follows:

Phase I
New dock and silo area
Interior wall changes
Partial office area
Toilet facilities

	$43,500
Heating and ventilation	$ 3,500
New electrical power service—some plant and office lighting, service, etc.	$24,000
Contingency	$ 4,000
	$75,000

Phase II
Completion of office area, toilet area
Entry canopy and landscape

Parking pavement, etc.	$32,000
HVAC offices	$ 5,000
Electrical for offices and plant	$10,000
Contingency	$ 3,000
	$50,000

Phase III
Enclose additional storage space, dock, ramps, etc. at rear of bldg;

move fence, plumbing, etc.	$35,000
Heating and ventilation	$ 2,000
Electrical, lighting service, etc.	$ 9,500
Contingency	$ 3,500
	$50,000

Sincerely,

(S) R. Timothy James, P. E.

persistence and honesty in dealing with customers, bankers, accountants, and suppliers.

As the technology of the plastics industry continues to develop, Noble hopes to uphold the ACROSS image. His lifestyle as a member of top management is becoming more exclusive as he spends time entertaining clients, forecasting, long term planning, analyzing organizational changes, and investigating trends in technology. He recently has attended training seminars on employee relations and on Computer Integrated Manufacturing. The president only hopes his foremen reflect the leadership and authority, integrity, and discipline that he has attempted to instill in them.

ANHEUSER-BUSCH COMPANIES, INC. (B)

Neil H. Snyder
University of Virginia

INTRODUCTION

Originating in the United States during the 1840's, it did not take long for lager beer, a light beer with a mellow taste, to gain popularity and for the American beer industry to grow as consumers' tastes shifted away from heavy German beers. As the ability of beer manufacturers to produce beer in large quantities increased, a structural change took place in the beer industry that eventually led to the establishment of national as opposed to regional firms. Over the past 125 years, the realization of economies of scale by large producers has caused consolidation in the beer industry. Between 1860 and 1985, the number of breweries in the United States has declined from 1,269 to 85. As industry sales volume has grown and the number of firms in the industry has declined, advertising has become the primary tool used to differentiate between beers and to expand and maintain market share. Blind taste tests have shown that beer drinkers cannot consistently distinguish between brands.

Currently, the brewing industry faces two significant challenges that have the potential to reduce even further the number of producers in the industry: Saturation and changing consumer attitudes.

Saturation

Between 1975 and 1980, the beer industry expanded at an annual rate of approximately 4%, but in 1982 the growth rate was less than 1%. The year 1982 may have been the turning point for industry sales volume increases, and it was the first year in 25 years that domestic beer producers as a group experienced a profit decline. (Pierce and Robinson, *Strategic Management,* Irwin, 1985, p. 511) In 1984, beer industry sales declined 0.3% while other beverages were experiencing significant gains. For example, wine sales in 1984 were up 3.5%, and soft drink sales increased by an amazing 7.5%. To make matters worse, the industry had excess beer production capacity in 1983 estimated at 40 million barrels. Exhibit 1 shows total capacity and capacity utilization for six leading U.S. brewers.

The saturation problem has led many brewers to diversify. A-B has entered markets such as food products, industrial products and entertainment. Additionally, large brewers are becoming more vertically and horizontally integrated. According to Wall Street analysts, the beer

EXHIBIT 1   BREWING CAPACITY AND USAGE—1983
(Millions of Barrels)

Brewer	Capacity	% Utilization
Anheuser-Busch	66.5	91.0
Miller	54.0	69.4
Stroh	32.6	74.5
Heilman	26.5	66.0
Coors	15.5	88.4
Pabst	15.0	85.3

industry's sales volume has been, and will remain flat. A-B is the only firm in the industry that has been able to maintain annual growth while industry sales have been stagnant.

Changing Consumer Attitudes

"Domestic brewers are up against the campaign against drunk driving, a national trend toward health and fitness, and the presence of a small but growing foreign-beer segment." (Stevenson, "How Anheuser-Busch Brews Its Winners," *New York Times,* August 4, 1985)

The beer industry felt the first legislative blow in 1984 when Congress moved to establish a national minimum drinking age. Although this attempt failed, the federal government "black-mailed" most states into raising their drinking ages to 21 years by threatening to cut off highway funds if they did not. The problems with teenage drinking have been made clear by powerful lobbying groups such as Mothers Against Drunk Drivers (MADD). The industry responded to the threat of even more restrictive legislation by developing "low-alcohol" beers, but sales of these products have been disappointing. Although the pressure on Congress to regulate the producers of alcoholic beverages has declined somewhat lately, it has been proposed that television commercials displaying the consumption of alcohol should be banned.

Most industry analysts agree that the "fitness fad" has leveled off and that the introduction of light beers satisfied the demands of consumers concerned about fitness. However, imported beers remain a significant threat to domestic beer producers. Imports have achieved a 4% share of the U.S. market, and it is expected that future growth in import beer sales will be 10–12% per year. A-B is vulnerable to these and other threats to the consumption

of beer, because it produces most of its revenue from the sale of beer (see Exhibit 2).

A-B's POSITION WITHIN THE BREWING INDUSTRY

A-B's 1984 beer sales were up 5.8% over 1983 sales levels. The combined market share of A-B's products was 34.6% in 1984, up from 32.6% in 1983. Meanwhile, Miller Brewing reported no increase in sales for 1984 and a market share of only 20%. Utilizing segmentation strategies, international marketing, and new product development, A-B plans to continue its growth in the beer industry despite analysts' predictions of no aggregate domestic industry growth.

A-B believes that the international market can help it sustain its record of continuing sales growth. According to *Business Week,* it is nearly three times the size of the U.S. market. (*Business Week,* "Overseas Beer Market", October 22, 1984) John H. Purnell, chairman of Anheuser-Busch International, Inc., explains that "while we aren't out to conquer the world overnight, this (foreign beer sales) has the potential to become a significant profit contributor to the parent company." (*Business Week,* October 22, 1984) Emanuel Goldman, a securities analyst agrees with Purnell. He suggests that Anheuser-Busch's earnings from foreign markets could go to 15% of sales and 10% of earnings in ten years.

Success in the foreign market has come steadily for A-B but they have had setbacks, too. Budweiser is by far the best selling non-Japanese beer in the Japanese market with sales increasing from 500,000 cases in 1981 to an estimated 2 million cases in 1984, and Budweiser captured 6% of the Israeli market in only six months. However, attempts to enter the two largest beer markets in the

EXHIBIT 2   **Anheuser-Busch 1984 revenues.**

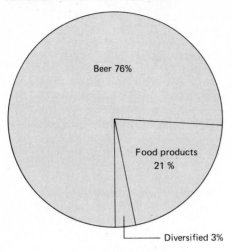

world have not been successful. A-B pulled out of the German market after being there only six months, and they worked for four years in the English market before joining forces with Allied Breweries, Ltd. According to *Business Week,* "If you are serious about the beer business, then you are going to have to participate in non-U.S. markets." (*Business Week,* October 22, 1984)

Segmenting the country by age, population, location, and even ethnic group and then targeting specific groups has enabled A-B to attract more consumers in the domestic market to its products, as well. As products gain name recognition and identity within a specific niche, product sales have increased. For example, Michelob has been marketed successfully to young mobile professionals, and Natural Light is targeted toward people who want a less-filling beer but would rather drink beer at home than at a bar or restaurant. With these marketing techniques, A-B has matched their competitors' sales efforts product for product.

Careful introduction of new products sets A-B apart from their competitors. One industry analyst compared the speed of A-B's test marketing efforts with the steady plodding of the Clydesdale horses—slow but steady. (*Fortune,* "Betting on Beer Without Buzz," June 25, 1984) When A-B enters a market, it utilizes its enormous advertising strength. For example, after waiting for four years before entering the light beer market, A-B now has three successful light beers (Natural Light, Michelob

Light, and Bud Light). Recently, A-B introduced a beer with less alcohol, LA, and it has provided significant advertising support to establish the product in the market. The company spends $47.40 per barrel to promote LA, but only $1.69 per barrel to promote Budweiser. One market in which A-B sees great potential for growth is the wine cooler market. Currently, it is developing a wine cooler through its new subsidiary, Anheuser-Busch Wines, Inc., and it plans to introduce wine for sale in stainless steel returnable kegs. Exhibit 3 shows A-B beer production by brand.

THE COMPETITION

Because of the shrinking domestic beer market, brewers must now take market share from competitors in each of the segmented categories. Thus, the industry is experiencing a proliferation of new products supported by enormous marketing budgets. It is reported that industry advertising spending was up 9% in the first half of 1984. (*Industry Surveys,* April 11, 1985) In addition to new brands, beers once sold regionally are now being marketed in broader distribution networks. For example, A-B has taken Busch national and Adolph Coors has expanded its market for its beers including Coors and Coors Light. The trend toward increased industry concentration seems destined to continue, and A-B and Miller are expected to hold 70% of the beer market by 1990. Addi-

EXHIBIT 3   1984 ANHEUSER-BUSCH
PRODUCTION BY BRAND
(Mil. Bbls.)

Budweiser	44.3
Michelob	6.7
Busch	4.3
Bud Light	4
Michelob Light	2.8
Natural Light	1.2
LA	0.4
Other	0.1

tionally, increased competition from imports has intensified the problem, and many brewers are seeking new products (i.e., Wine Coolers and non-alcoholic beers) and diversification into other areas.

Miller

Miller has been A-B's primary competitor since Philip Morris acquired them in 1970. During the 1970's, Miller moved from 7th to 2nd place in the brewing industry and surprised industry leaders with their successful introduction of "Lite" beer. A-B responded by increasing its advertising budget and taking Miller on in a head to head battle. In addition, A-B implemented a new strategic plan. The plan was to flank each Miller product in each category with two A-B products. For example, Budweiser and Busch flank Miller High Life in the premium category. (*New York Times,* August 2, 1985)

A-B won the battle with Miller, and its lead continues to increase. Despite the fact that A-B and Miller were the only two brewers to increase their volume in 1984, Miller's premium brands (Miller High Life and Lowenbrau) are not competing well, and the growth in sales for Lite is declining. To offset these declines, Miller has been rapidly introducing new products. In the past two and a half years, Miller has introduced at least eight new brands. Among these are two popular priced beers, Meisterbrau and Milwaukee's Best which were introduced to help support the faltering Miller High Life. They are also test marketing two bottled draft beers, Miller High Life Genuine Draft and Plank Road. Both are premium beers that will compete with Budweiser and Miller High Life.

Three prominent Wall Street beverage analysts have suggested that Miller's difficulties have arisen because of the decline of its flagship brand, Miller High Life. (*Beverage World,* "Is the Beer Industry Drying Up?", February 1985) They have speculated that, if Miller High Life sales do not stop eroding, it might be downgraded to a popular-priced product which could hurt A-B. According to the analysts, "Anheuser should be rooting for a mitigation of the erosion, something in that in-between land. What happens to High Life is very important to Anheuser." (*Ibid.*) Miller has recently changed ad agencies for the High Life account, indicating that they plan to turn the brand around. Additionally, Miller has excess capacity. This problem is exemplified by Miller's $450 million brewery recently constructed in Trenton, Ohio, which is not being used.

Heileman

In regional markets, Heileman has been very effective against A-B by using a strategy that entails acquiring struggling local brewers at low costs and then reintroducing their brands with aggressive marketing. A-B has responded with "heavy price competition from its Busch brand," and Heileman has halted their planned expansion in the southeast. (*Ibid.*)

Coors

Currently, Coors is expanding outside of its western markets, and their expansion drive has constrained their efforts to introduce new products. Additionally, Coors has met stiff opposition in the north where Strohs and Heileman are very strong. Some analysts have suggested that unless Coors can stop the erosion of their premium brands in their primary states (Texas, California, and Florida), they may become a takeover candidate. (*Beverage Industry,* "Brewers Fight for Share in a Declining Market," January 1985)

EXHIBIT 4   1984 PRODUCTION

	Top 6 brands (mil. bbls.)	Market share
Budweiser	44.3	24.2
Miller Lite	18	9.9
Miller High Life	14.5	7.9
Coors	8.7	4.8
Old Mil	7.1	3.9
Michelob	6.7	3.7

Stroh's

Stroh's, on the other hand, has the economies of scale and size (24 million barrels of capacity per year) to be an efficient national brewer. They have obtained modern brewing facilities nationwide through their acquisition of Schaefer and Schlitz. Their only weaknesses in comparison to A-B and Miller are their financial position and their distribution network. Stroh's is expected to play a major role in the future of the industry. (*Beverage World,* "Is the Beer Industry Drying Up?," February 1985)

Imported Beers

Imported beers are becoming more competitive in the U.S., and they are experiencing a growth rate of approximately 12% in the domestic market. Their growth is attributed to five factors: They are perceived to be of higher quality; because of the high value of the dollar, they are affordable; they have snob appeal; Americans are traveling abroad more and developing a taste for imported beers; and the American consumers are becoming more selective in their buying habits. (*Beverage Industry,* "Why Import Sales are Booming," July 1985) Topping the list of imports is Heineken with a 34% share followed by Molson with a 13.4% share. Becks and Amstel Light are expected to show particularly good growth, especially Amstel Light. (*Industry Surveys,* April 11, 1985)

Exhibit 4 shows production and market share statistics for the top six beer brands in the U.S. Exhibit 5 shows beer consumption in the U.S. between 1975 and 1983 by type of beer. Exhibit 6 shows the 1984 sales of the six leading producers of beer in the U.S.

MARKETING AND ADVERTISING

Over the past decade, A-B has, through massive marketing and ad campaigns, managed to transform Budweiser into one of the most familiar trademarks in the world. This is evidenced by the fact that Budweiser commercials have the best recall of beer ads nationally among consumers. Its aggressive marketing has already left the number two beer producer, Miller Brewing Company, far be-

EXHIBIT 5   BEER CONSUMPTION BY TYPE
(Mil. Bbls.)

Type	1975	1980	1981	1982	1983	% Chg. 1982–83
Popular	65.4	30	30.1	29.5	30.5	3.4
Premium	71.6	102.3	101.4	95.7	94.6	−1.1
Super-premium	5	11.5	11.2	10.6	10.1	−4.7
Light	2.8	22.1	26.2	32.5	34.1	4.9
Imported	1.7	4.6	5.2	5.8	6.3	8.6
Malt liquor	3.8	5.5	6	6.4	6.4	0
Ale	N.A.	1.9	1.8	1.8	1.7	−5.6
Total	150.3	177.9	181.9	182.3	183.7	0.8

EXHIBIT 6

Rank	Company	1984 Sales ($000)
1	Anheuser-Busch	5490000
2	Miller	2928000
3	Stroh	1600000
4	Heileman	1207394
5	Coors	937876
6	Pabst	752365

hind even though the two were close competitors just five years ago. A-B's growth is particularly dramatic when measured against the backdrop of a domestic beer market that has been stagnant for four years. August Busch, III gave much of the credit for A-B's strong showing to "aggressive advertising and merchandising surrounding the A-B sponsorship of the Olympic Games." (*Advertising Age,* "Anheuser-Busch Companies," September 26, 1985) Last year, A-B spent $245 million for advertising, $122 million on network sports events alone.

VERTICAL INTEGRATION AT A-B

A-B is a highly vertically integrated firm. Below is a list of A-B's vertically integrated components:

Metal Container Corporation: This subsidiary is a can and lid manufacturer with three metal container can plants.

Busch Agricultural Resources, Inc.: This subsidiary processes barley into brewer's malt. In 1984, this subsidiary supplied A-B with 32% of its malt requirements.

Container Recovery Corporation: This can recycling subsidiary functions in two ways — by collecting aluminum cans from consumers for recycling and by operating three container recycling process plants.

St. Louis Refrigerator Car Company: This transportation subsidiary has been in existence since 1878 and is involved in the maintenance of railroad cars as well as operating 650 specially insulated railroad cars for transportation of A-B's beer products.

Manufacturers Railway Company: This transportation subsidiary provides terminal rail switching services to St. Louis industries and operates a fleet of hopper cars and boxcars.

International Label Company: This company is a joint venture between A-B and Illochroma International, S. A. of Brussels, Belgium. The main function of this company is the production of metalized labels.

DIVERSIFICATION AT A-B

In addition to the brewing side of A-B's business, the firm has diversified into a number of related and unrelated businesses. Below is a list of A-B's diversified operations:

Busch Industrial Products: In 1984 this subsidiary was the leading producer and marketer of compressed baker's yeast in the U.S. This subsidiary also produces autolyzed yeast which is used for processed meats.

Busch Entertainment: This family entertainment subsidiary operates Busch Garden theme parks in Florida and Virginia. A water park called Adventure Island is adjacent to Busch Gardens in Florida. In addition, A-B owns Sesame Place in Pennsylvania, a 21st century play park oriented toward education and entertainment.

A-B International: This international licensing and marketing subsidiary formed in 1980 brews Budweiser in Canada, Japan, Israel, and the UK. A-B also exports to Hong Kong, Singapore, Guam, New Zealand, Panama, and Sweden.

Eagle Snacks, Inc.: In January of 1982 the Eagle Snacks Division was incorporated as Eagle Snacks, Inc., a wholly owned subsidiary of A-B. "In 1984, Eagle Snacks, Inc. began self-manufacturing virtually all of its snack products through the expansion of its Robersonville, NC plant and the start up of additional lines at the C-T (Campbell-Taggart) Fort Payne, Alabama plant." (1983 Annual Report) Eagle Snacks are distributed through A-B wholesaler and C-T distribution systems in

INCOME STATEMENTS

	Dec. 31, 1983	June 30, 1983	June 30, 1982	June 30, 1981	June 30, 1980	June 30, 1979
Sales	663,868	721,217	456,453	207,372	77,022	76,082
Cost of goods sold	493,682	442,193	228,552	118,734	56,076	68,147
Cross income from sales	170,186	279,024	227,901	88,638	20,946	7,936
Net mold and tooling income	17,714	10,241	258	4,628	8,568	15,986
Gross income from operations	187,900	289,265	228,150	93,266	29,514	(8,050)
Administrative and selling expenses	80,623	171,828	147,474	40,465	24,476	
Net income on operations	107,277	117,437	80,685	52,801	5,038	
Other income[1]	6,793	3,775	4,839	221	160	4,312
Other expenses[2]	(11,136)	(16,896)	(10,392)	(8,806)	(7,046)	(2,126)
Net income before tax	102,935	104,316	75,133	44,216	(1,848)	(5,864)
Provision for federal income tax	12,701	18,684	12,516			
Net income	90,234	85,632	62,617			

[1]Other income includes such items as dividends and interest on investments, rental income from sub-leased property, and gains on disposition of equipment.
[2]Other expenses include interest payments, penalties, and life insurance payments.

approximately 200 markets in the United States. They are available in restaurants, bars, hotels, supermarkets, convenience stores, airport lounges, and airlines.

Busch Properties, Inc.: This real estate subsidiary was established in 1970. It is currently involved in the development of a residential project in Virginia and the development of commercial properties in Virginia, Ohio, and California.

Busch Corporate Centers: A-B owns several business centers (Columbus, Williamsburg, Fairfield).

Civic Center Corporation: This corporation was acquired in 1981. It has redeveloped 43 blocks of downtown St. Louis. This subsidiary also owns Busch Stadium, St. Louis Sports Hall of Fame Museum and Gift Shop, Stadium Club, and four parking garages.

St. Louis National Baseball Club, Inc.: This subsidiary owns the St. Louis Cardinals baseball team.

Busch Creative Services Corporation: This communications subsidiary was formed in 1980. It offers a variety of multi-media, print, film, and other corporate and marketing communications material. In 1985 this subsidiary acquired Innervision Productions, Inc. which is a producer of TV commercials and industrial training films.

Campbell-Taggart (C-T): In 1982 A-B purchased C-T for $560 million. C-T is currently the nation's second largest bakery. C-T's subsidiaries are involved in the production and distribution of baked goods (mainly bread), refrigerated dough and salad products, frozen Mexican food, and packaged goods to food service companies. In addition to these operations, C-T also has manufacturing operations in Spain, France, and Brazil. The Spanish subsidiary is the largest baker in Spain.

FINANCES AT A-B

Below are A-B's consolidated balance sheet, statement of income, statement of changes in shareholders equity and convertible redeemable preferred stock, statement of changes in financial position, and notes to the consolidated financial statements:

SCHEDULE OF NOTES AND LEASES

Long-Term Debt

The long-term debt as of December 31, 1983 consisted of the following:

1) A note payable to Fifth Federal Bank in the amount of $7,672.35. Monthly payments which include interest computed at 10.5% amount to $419.16 and are due through August 23, 1985.

2) A note payable to Fifth Federal Bank in the amount of $11,625.30. Monthly payments which include interest computed at 10.7% amount to $258.34 and are due through September 5, 1987. The note is secured by an automobile.

3) A note payable to Wizard National Bank in the amount of $12,773.61. Monthly payments which include interest computed at 13.5%. The note is secured by a blow-molding machine.

4) A note payable to Wizard National Bank in the amount of $6,837.37. Monthly payments of $250.51 include interest computed at 11.9%. The note is secured by a pickup truck.

5) A capital lease obligation to Fifth Federal Bank in the amount of $26,529.05. Monthly payments of $998.05 include interest and are due through November 1985. A final payment of $5,570.00 represents the purchase price of the equipment at the expiration of the lease.

6) A capital lease obligation to Leasing Corporation in the amount of $70,267.10. Monthly payments of $1,406.68 include interest and are due through December 1, 1987. A final payment of $6,996.50 represents the purchase price of the equipment at the expiration of the lease.

7) A capital lease obligation to Brewer Leasing Corporation in the amount of $92,136.92. Monthly payments of $1,467.24 include interest and are due through October 1, 1988. A final payment of $7,027.00 represents the purchase price of the equipment at the expiration of the lease.

8) A capital lease obligation to Brewer Leasing Corporation in the amount of $87,626.98. Monthly payments of $1,510.81 include interest and are due through October 1, 1988. A payment of $7,027.00 will be made at the expiration of the lease to purchase the equipment.

9) A note payable to an officer of the corporation in the amount of $58,939.62.

Lease Commitments

The annual rent amounting to $38,400.00 during the first year of the initial lease is payable in monthly installments of $3,200.00. Annual rent for each year thereafter is subject to the percentage increase of the Consumer Price Index. The principal lease, which commenced May 1, 1983 and extends through April 30, 1993, is renewable for two additional five year periods subject to the same terms and conditions as the initial term.

CONSOLIDATED BALANCE SHEET
ANHEUSER-BUSCH COMPANIES, INC. AND SUBSIDIARIES

Assets (in millions) December 31,	1984	1983
Current assets:		
Cash and marketable securities (marketable securities of $69.3 in 1984 and $185.8 in 1983 at cost, which approximates market)	$ 78.6	$ 218.4
Accounts and notes receivable, less allowance for doubtful accounts of $2.8 in 1984 and $2.9 in 1983	275.6	283.6
Inventories—		
Raw materials and supplies	212.7	196.5
Work in process	65.7	61.1
Finished goods	37.5	41.2
Total inventories	315.9	298.8
Other current assets	106.2	96.8
Total current assets	776.3	897.6
Investments and other assets:		
Investments in and advances to unconsolidated subsidiaries	42.9	57.7
Investment properties	18.1	9.1
Deferred charges and other non-current assets	87.1	73.7
Excess of cost over net assets of acquired business, net	85.3	87.9
	233.4	228.4
Plant and equipment:		
Land	80.0	70.1
Buildings	1,398.1	1,303.6
Machinery and equipment	2,920.5	2,622.8
Construction in progress	395.3	311.6
Other real estate	6.7	5.8
	4,800.6	4,313.9
Less accumulated depreciation	1,285.6	1,109.7
	3,515.0	3,204.2
	$4,524.7	$4,330.2

Liabilities and shareholders' equity (in millions) December 31,	1984	1983
Current liabilities:		
Accounts payable	$ 338.2	$ 327.8
Accrued salaries, wages and benefits	150.3	142.5
Accrued interest payable	26.8	29.9
Due to customers for returnable containers	31.8	31.1
Accrued taxes, other than income taxes	43.6	64.3
Estimated income taxes	39.0	48.4
Other current liabilities	66.3	78.5
Total current liabilities	696.0	722.5
Long-term debt	835.8	961.4
Deferred income taxes	755.0	573.2
Minority shareholders interest in consolidated subsidiaries	—	20.6
Convertible redeemable preferred stock (liquidation value $300.0)	286.9	286.0
Common stock and other shareholders' equity:		
Preferred stock, $1.00 par value, authorized 32,498,000 shares in 1984 and 1983; none issued	—	—
Common stock, $1.00 par value, authorized 200,000,000 shares in 1984 and 1983; issued 48,641,869 and 48,514,214 shares, respectively	48.6	48.5
Capital in excess of par value	173.2	167.2
Retained earnings	1,829.3	1,555.4
Foreign currency translation adjustment	(6.6)	(3.7)
	2,044.5	1,767.4
Less cost of treasury stock (1,564,152 shares in 1984 and 119,552 shares in 1983)	93.5	.9
	1,951.0	1,766.5
Commitments and contingencies	—	—
	$4,524.7	$4,330.2

CONSOLIDATED STATEMENT OF INCOME
ANHEUSER-BUSCH COMPANIES, INC. AND SUBSIDIARIES
(In Millions, except per Share Data)

Year ended December 31,	1984	1983	1982
Sales	$7,158.2	$6,658.5	$5,185.7
Less federal and state beer taxes	657.0	624.3	609.1
Net sales	6,501.2	6,034.2	4,576.6
Cost of products sold	4,414.2	4,113.2	3,331.7
Gross profit	2,087.0	1,921.0	1,244.9
Marketing, administrative and research expenses	1,332.3	1,220.2	752.0
Operating income	754.7	700.8	492.9
Other income and expenses:			
Interest expense	(102.7)	(111.4)	(89.2)
Interest capitalized	46.8	32.9	41.2
Interest income	22.8	12.5	17.0
Other expense, net	(31.8)	(18.8)	(8.1)
Gain on sale of Lafayette plant	—	—	20.4
Income before income taxes	689.8	616.0	474.2
Provision for income taxes:			
Current	118.4	133.7	92.4
Deferred	179.9	134.3	94.5
	298.3	268.0	186.9
Net income	$ 391.5	$ 348.0	$ 287.3
Earnings per share:			
Primary	$ 7.40	$ 6.50	$ 5.97
Fully diluted	7.40	6.50	5.88

CONSOLIDATED STATEMENT OF CHANGES IN SHAREHOLDERS EQUITY AND
CONVERTIBLE REDEEMABLE PREFERRED STOCK
ANHEUSER-BUSCH COMPANIES, INC. AND SUBSIDIARIES

	Shareholders' Equity					Convertible redeemable preferred stock
	(In millions, except per share data)					
	Common stock	Capital in excess of par value	Retained earnings	Treasury stock	Foreign currency translation adjustment	
Balance at December 31, 1981	$45.6	$ 67.2	$1,094.9	$ (.9)		
Net income			287.3			
Cash dividends ($1.38 per share)			(65.8)			
Shares issued under stock option plans		1.0				
Shares issued in the acquisition of a company						$285.0
Shares issued upon conversion of the 9.00% convertible debentures	2.8	94.5				
Balance at December 31, 1982	48.4	162.7	1,316.4	(.9)		285.0
Net income			348.0			
Cash dividends:						
Common ($1.62 per share)			(78.3)			
Preferred ($3.60 per share)			(29.7)			
Shares issued under stock option plans	.1	4.5				
Accretion of preferred stock			(1.0)			1.0
Foreign currency translation adjustment					$(3.7)	
Balance at December 31, 1983	48.5	167.2	1,555.4	(.9)	(3.7)	286.0
Net income			391.5			
Cash dividends:						
Common ($1.88 per share)			(89.7)			
Preferred ($3.60 per share)			(27.0)			
Shares issued under stock option plans	.1	6.0				
Accretion of preferred stock			(.9)			.9
Shares acquired as treasury stock				(92.6)		
Foreign currency translation adjustment					(2.9)	
Balance at December 31, 1984	$48.6	$173.2	$1,829.3	$(93.5)	$(6.6)	$286.9

CONSOLIDATED STATEMENT OF CHANGES IN FINANCIAL POSITION
ANHEUSER-BUSCH COMPANIES, INC. AND SUBSIDIARIES
(In Millions)

Year ended December 31,	1984	1983	1982
Source of funds			
Net income	$ 391.5	$348.0	$ 287.3
Depreciation and amortization	203.4	187.3	133.6
Deferred income taxes	181.8	118.1	97.4
Total funds provided by current operations	776.7	653.4	518.3
Issuance of convertible redeemable preferred stock	—	—	285.0
Increase in long-term debt	7.8	32.7	259.8
Issuance of common stock on conversion of 9.00%			
debentures	—	—	97.3
Investment in unconsolidated subsidiaries	14.8	1.2	(12.1)
Disposition of Lafayette plant	—	—	20.6
Other, net	(2.6)	18.3	(79.4)
Total	796.7	705.6	1,089.5
Use of funds			
Capital expenditures	519.2	428.0	355.8
Dividends paid to stockholders	116.7	108.0	65.8
Decrease in long-term debt	133.4	40.3	108.1
Decrease in short-term debt	—	25.0	4.5
Installment purchase obligation	—	—	40.0
Acquisition of subsidiary	—	—	560.0
Acquisition of minority interests	20.6	—	—
Acquisition of treasury stock	92.6	—	—
Increase in investment properties	9.0	—	—
Increase (decrease) in non-cash working capital	45.0	(92.6)	27.4
Total	936.5	508.7	1,161.6
Increase (decrease) in cash and marketable securities	$(139.8)	$196.9	$ (72.1)
Non-cash working capital			
Increase (decrease) in non-cash current assets:			
Accounts and notes receivable	$ (8.0)	$ 40.1	$ 95.8
Inventories	17.1	(9.0)	79.4
Other current assets	9.4	(22.2)	49.4
Decrease (increase) in current liabilities:			
Accounts payable	(10.4)	(21.6)	(96.4)
Accrued salaries, wages and benefits	(7.8)	(11.4)	(49.7)
Accrued interest payable	3.1	(.1)	(2.5)
Due to customers for returnable containers	(.7)	(3.9)	(.9)
Accrued taxes, other than income taxes	20.7	(1.6)	(2.6)
Estimated income taxes	9.4	(22.0)	(21.2)
Other current liabilities	12.2	(40.9)	(23.9)
Increase (decrease) in non-cash working capital	$ 45.0	$ (92.6)	$ 27.4

NOTES TO CONSOLIDATED FINANCIAL STATEMENTS

1. Summary of significant accounting principles and policies

This summary of significant accounting principles and policies of Anheuser-Busch Companies, Inc., and its subsidiaries is presented to assist the reader in evaluating the company's financial statements included in this report. These principles and policies conform to generally accepted accounting principles and have been consistently followed by the company. The format of the Consolidated Statement of Changes in Financial Position at December 31, 1984 has been revised from a "working capital" format to a "cash flow" format. Accordingly, the format revision has been applied retroactively to all prior periods presented in the statement.

Principles of consolidation

The consolidated financial statements include the company and all its subsidiaries. Certain subsidiaries which are not an integral part of the company's primary operations are included on an equity basis. The Consolidated Statement of Income includes the operations of Campbell Taggart since November 2, 1982.

Foreign currency translation

Effective January 1, 1983 the company adopted Financial Accounting Standard No. 52, "Foreign Currency Translation." In the application of this statement, exchange adjustments resulting from foreign currency transactions generally are recognized in income, whereas adjustments resulting from translations of financial statements are reflected as a separate component of shareholders equity. The Consolidated Statement of Changes in Shareholders Equity and Convertible Redeemable Preferred Stock includes the foreign currency translation adjustment.

Inventories and production costs

Inventories are valued at the lower of cost or market. Cost is determined under the last-in, first-out method for substantially all brewing inventories and under the first-in, first-out method for substantially all food product inventories.

Plant and equipment

Plant and equipment is carried at cost and includes expenditures for new facilities and those which substantially increase the useful lives of existing plant and equip-

ment. Maintenance, repairs and minor renewals are expensed as incurred. When properties are retired or otherwise disposed of, the related cost and accumulated depreciation are removed from the respective accounts and any profit or loss on disposition is credited or charged to income.

Depreciation is provided principally on the straight-line method over the estimated useful lives of the assets (buildings 2% to 10% and machinery and equipment 4% to 25%).

Capitalization of interest

Interest relating to the cost of acquiring certain fixed assets is capitalized. This interest is included as part of the cost of the related asset and is amortized over its estimated useful life.

Income taxes

The provision for income taxes is based on elements of income and expense as reported in the Consolidated Statement of Income. The company has elected to utilize certain provisions of federal income tax laws and regulations to reduce current taxes payable.

Deferred income taxes are recognized for the effect of differences between financial and tax reporting. Investment tax credit is included in income when assets are placed in service or when the credit can be claimed under federal income tax laws relating to qualified progress expenditures.

Expenditures which provide possible future benefits

Research and development, advertising, promotional costs and initial plant costs are charged against income in the year in which these costs are incurred.

Net income per share of common stock

Primary earnings per share of common stock are based on the average number of shares of common stock outstanding during the respective years (52.9 million in 1984, 53.5 million in 1983 and 48.1 million in 1982). The convertible redeemable preferred shares are common stock equivalents; accordingly, these shares are assumed to have been converted into common stock at the date of their issuance and are included in the weighted average shares outstanding in computing primary earnings per share.

The company's 9.00% convertible subordinated debentures (issued in 1980) were called for redemption and converted into 2.8 million shares of common stock on April 29, 1982. Fully diluted earnings per share are computed on the assumption that these convertible securities and all outstanding stock options were converted into common stock as appropriate. Interest expense on the convertible subordinated debentures, net of income taxes, is added back to net income in the fully diluted earnings per share calculation.

2. Acquisition and disposition

On November 2, 1982 the company acquired all of the outstanding common stock of Campbell Taggart, Inc. (Campbell Taggart). Campbell Taggart, through its operating subsidiaries, is engaged in the production and sale of food and food-related products. The cost of the acquisition was $560.0 million, consisting of $275.0 million paid in cash for approximately 50% of Campbell Taggart's outstanding common stock and 7.5 million shares of Anheuser-Busch convertible redeemable preferred stock with an estimated fair value of $285.0 million issued in exchange for the remaining Campbell Taggart common stock.

The acquisition has been accounted for using the purchase method of accounting. Campbell Taggart's assets and liabilities have been recorded in the company's financial statements at their estimated fair values at the acquisition date. The excess cost of the acquisition over the estimated fair value of the net assets is being amortized on a straight-line basis over 40 years.

Assuming the acquisition of Campbell Taggart had occurred on January 1, 1982, the pro forma combined net sales would have been $5.6 billion for 1982. The pro forma combined net income and net income per share for 1982 would not have been materially different than that reported in the Consolidated Statement of Income.

In March 1982, the company sold its corn refining plant in Lafayette, Ind., resulting in a nonrecurring, after-tax gain of $13.3 million or $.28 per share (fully diluted). Sales and income from operations of this plant for the year ended December 31, 1982 were not material.

3. Inventory valuation

Approximately 75% of total inventories at December 31, 1984 and 1983 are stated on the last-in, first-out (LIFO) inventory valuation method. Had the average-cost method been used with respect to such items at December 31, 1984 and 1983, total inventories would have been $105.8 million and $94.9 million higher, respectively.

4. Credit agreements

In August 1982, the company entered into a ten-year revolving credit agreement with a group of eleven domestic banks. In December 1983, the agreement was amended to provide for a maximum borrowing of $400.0 million. Interest on the loans will be based, at the option of the company, on the prime rate, the domestic CD rate plus ½% or the Euro-Dollar rate plus 3/8% for the first five years, and at scheduled rate increases for periods thereafter. In addition, a negotiated sub-prime borrowing feature is available for the entire term of the agreement. At December 31, 1984 and 1983, the company had no outstanding borrowings under this agreement.

In June 1981, the company entered into a multicurrency revolving credit agreement aggregating $100.0 million or the equivalent amount in alternative currencies. This commitment extends through March 27, 1986. Interest on borrowings in Euro-Dollars and alternative currencies will be 3/8% over the Euro Basic Rate, as defined, and on United States currency borrowings, at the company's election, at either a floating rate equal to the prevailing Domestic Floating Base Rate, as defined, plus ¾% or at a fixed rate equal to the Domestic Fixed Base Rate, as defined, plus ½%. At December 31, 1984 and 1983, the company had no outstanding borrowings under this agreement.

Fees under these agreements and prior agreements amounted to $1.1, $3.3 and $3.7 million in 1984, 1983 and 1982, respectively.

5. Long-term debt

The only long-term debt issued by the company during 1984 was industrial revenue bonds. During November, 1984 the company redeemed all of its $100 million 16½% Guaranteed Notes due 1988. Pursuant to the early call provision of the notes, the redemption price was 101.5% of the principal amount, or $101.5 million. In October 1982, the company filed a shelf registration with the Securities and Exchange Commission covering up to $200.0 million of debt securities. On October 12, 1982, $100.0 million of 11⅞% sinking fund debentures due 2012 were issued under this shelf registration. The company has the option to issue the remaining $100.0 million of debt securities at such time as it considers appropriate.

Long-term debt at December 31 consists of the following:

	(In millions)	
	1984	1983
9.90% Notes due 1986	$100.0	$100.0
15.375% Notes due 1991	50.0	50.0
16.50% Guaranteed notes due 1988	—	100.0
11.25% Guaranteed bonds due 1990	100.0	100.0
Sinking fund debentures	449.6	472.3
Industrial revenue bonds	73.5	74.3
Other long-term debt	62.7	64.8
	$835.8	$961.4

The company's sinking fund debentures at December 31 are as follows:

	(In millions)	
	1984	1983
5.45% debentures maturing 1984 to 1991, less $11.8 in treasury in 1984 and $2.5 in 1983	$ 2.4	$ 13.9
6.00% debentures maturing 1984 to 1992, less $2.1 in treasury in 1984 and $3.4 in 1983	18.2	19.6
7.95% debentures maturing 1985 to 1999, less $10.0 in treasury in 1984 and $11.2 in 1983	83.5	88.8
9.20% debentures maturing 1986 to 2005, less $4.5 in treasury in 1984	145.5	150.0
8.55% debentures maturing 1989 to 2008	100.0	100.0
11.875% debentures maturing 1993 to 2012	100.0	100.0
	$449.6	$472.3

The aggregate maturities on all long-term debt are $15.9, $120.8, $20.2, $19.7 and $24.2 million, respectively, for each of the years ending December 31, 1985 through 1989.

6. Stock option plans

In December 1981, the company adopted an Incentive Stock Option Plan and a Non-Qualified Stock Option Plan for certain officers and key employees. These plans were approved by the shareholders in April 1982. Under the terms of the plans, options may be granted at not less than the fair market value of the shares at the date of grant. The Non-Qualified Stock Option Plan provides that optionees may be granted Stock Appreciation Rights (SARs) in tandem with stock options. The exercise of a SAR cancels the related option and the exercise of an option cancels the related SAR. The Stock Option Committee of the Board of Directors granted SARs under the 1981 Non-Qualified Stock Option Plan with respect to options for 48,800 and 81,800 shares in 1984 and 1983, respectively. At December 31, 1984 and 1983, 2,223,916 and 2,371,313 shares, respectively, were reserved for possible issuance under the 1981 plans.

Presented below is a summary of changes in stock options under the incentive Stock Option Plan and the Non-Qualified Stock Option Plan for the year ended December 31:

	1984	1983
Outstanding at beginning of year	1,543,864	1,279,739
Options granted	375,120	435,540
Options/SARs exercised	(189,825)	(139,937)
Options cancelled	(24,091)	(31,478)
Options outstanding at end of year	1,705,068	1,543,864
Options exercisable at end of year	1,099,264	765,055
Option price range per share	$40.81–$73.69	$40.81–$73.44

7. Pension plans

The company has pension plans covering substantially all of its employees and follows the policy of funding all pension costs accrued. Total pension expense was $71.9, $74.0 and $52.7 million in 1984, 1983 and 1982, respectively. In 1984, the company changed the actuarial investment rate of return assumption for funding purposes from 5½% to 6½% on several of the company's salaried and hourly pension plans. The effect of this change on net income was not material. A comparison of the actuarial present value of accumulated plan benefits and plan net assets, as of the most recent actuarial date, generally January 1, for the company's salaried and hourly paid pension plans combined, is presented below:

	(In millions)	
	1984	1983
Actuarial present value of accumulated plan benefits:		
Vested	$293.2	$265.6
Nonvested	34.4	34.2
	$327.6	$299.8
Net assets available for benefits	$497.7	$418.7

The weighted average assumed rate of return used in determining the actuarial present value of accumulated plan benefits was 8.5% in 1984 and 1983.

8. Income taxes

The provision for income taxes includes the following for each of the three years ended December 31:

	(In millions)		
	1984	1983	1982
Current tax provision			
Federal:			
Provision	$136.2	$156.4	$123.2
Charge in lieu of taxes	—	—	11.9
Investment tax credit:			
Normal	(35.1)	(32.5)	(35.0)
TRASOP	—	(6.8)	(7.6)
Safe harbor leases	—	—	(11.9)
	101.1	117.1	80.6
State and foreign	17.3	16.6	11.8
	118.4	133.7	92.4
Deferred tax provision:			
Federal	171.0	126.4	88.2
State and foreign	8.9	7.9	6.3
	179.9	134.3	94.5
	$298.3	$268.0	$186.9

In 1982 the company purchased tax benefits in the form of accelerated cost recovery allowances and investment tax credits under "safe harbor" leases as defined in the Economic Recovery Tax Act of 1981. The purchase price of these benefits is recorded as an asset which is amortized through a charge to the current tax provision during the initial years of the lease. That portion of the amortization related to the investment tax credit is recorded as a charge in lieu of taxes. In subsequent years of the lease, deferred income taxes are provided for the difference between the tax and the financial aspects of the lease. The effect of these leases on net income is not material.

The deferred tax provision results from timing differences in the recognition of income and expense for tax and financial reporting purposes. The primary differences are the calculation of depreciation for tax purposes using accelerated methods and shorter lives and expensing for tax purposes interest cost capitalized for book purposes. These timing differences had a tax effect of $178.5 million in 1984, $155.2 million in 1983 and $113.0 million in 1982.

The Tax Equity and Fiscal Responsibility Act of 1982 required the company to reduce the tax basis of depreciable property by one-half of the investment tax credit claimed on the tax return. The effect of the basis reduction is to reduce the financial impact of the normal investment tax credit to $31.1 and $26.4 million in 1984 and 1983, respectively.

The company's effective tax rate was 43.2%, 43.5% and 39.4% in 1984, 1983 and 1982, respectively. A reconciliation between the statutory rate and the effective rate is presented below:

	1984	1983	1982
Statutory rate	46.0%	46.0%	46.0%
Charge in lieu of taxes	—	—	2.5
Investment tax credit:			
Normal	(5.1)	(5.3)	(7.4)
TRASOP	—	(1.1)	(1.6)
Safe harbor leases	—	—	(2.5)
State income taxes, net of federal benefit	1.9	1.9	1.9
Other	.4	2.0	.5
Effective tax rate	43.2%	43.5%	39.4%

9. Common and preferred stock

In March 1984, the Board of Directors amended a 1982 resolution to authorize the company to purchase up to 4.8 million shares of its common stock. The shares will be used for the conversion to common stock of preferred stock issued in connection with the acquisition of Campbell Taggart. In 1984, 1,444,600 shares were purchased for $92.6 million.

In connection with the acquisition of Campbell Taggart, the company issued 7,500,766 shares of convertible redeemable preferred stock, par value $1. The convertible redeemable preferred stock has a redemption value of $40, requires dividend payments at a rate of $3.60 per year, is non-callable for five years and subject to mandatory redemption at the end of fifteen years. The preferred shares are also convertible into .645 of a share of the company's common stock and have voting rights in this ratio. The difference between the redemption value and the carrying value is being amortized over fifteen years.

10. Commitments and contingencies

In connection with the plant expansion and improvement program, the company has commitments for capital expenditures of approximately $489.5 million at December 31, 1984.

Obligations under capital leases are not material.

The company and certain of its subsidiaries are involved in claims and legal proceedings in which monetary damages and other relief are sought. The company is contesting these claims and proceedings. However, their resolution is not expected to occur quickly and their ultimate outcome cannot presently be predicted. In any event, it is the opinion of management that any liability of the company or its subsidiaries for such claims or proceedings will not materially affect its financial position.

11. Business segments

The company has identified its principal business segments as beer and beer-related, food products and diversified operations. The beer and beer-related segment produces and sells the company's beer products. Included in this segment are the company's raw material acquisition, malting, can manufacturing and recycling operations.

The food products segment consists of the company's food and food-related operations which include the operations of Campbell Taggart since November 2, 1982. In addition, this segment includes the company's yeast and snack food subsidiaries.

Diversified operations consist of the company's entertainment, communications, transportation and real estate operations.

Sales between segments, export sales and sales by geographic area are not material. The company's equity in earnings of unconsolidated subsidiaries has been included in other income and expense. No single customer accounted for more than 10% of sales.

The following summarizes the company's business segment information for 1984, 1983 and 1982 (in millions).

1984:	Beer and beer-related	Food products	Diversified operations	Eliminations	Consolidated
Net sales	$5,390.1	$1,353.5	$170.4	$(412.8)	$6,501.2
Operating income*	728.2	16.5	10.0		754.7
Depreciation and amortization expense	141.1	42.3	20.0		203.4
Capital expenditures	393.1	106.7	19.4		519.2
Identifiable assets	3,214.7	811.8	128.0		4,154.5
Corporate assets**					370.2
Total assets					4,524.7

1983:	Beer and beer-related	Food products	Diversified operations	Eliminations	Consolidated
Net sales	$4,907.7	$1,320.4	$150.2	$(344.1)	$6,034.2
Operating income*	649.9	47.3	3.6		700.8
Depreciation and amortization expense	129.5	40.3	17.5		187.3
Capital expenditures	348.1	54.8	25.1		428.0
Identifiable assets	2,994.1	768.6	143.7		3,906.4
Corporate assets**					423.8
Total assets					4,330.2

1982:	Beer and beer-related	Food products	Diversified operations	Eliminations	Consolidated
Net sales	$4,488.1	$282.8	$145.1	$(339.4)	$4,576.6
Operating income*	464.1	23.5	5.3		492.9
Depreciation and amortization expense	110.8	8.8	14.0		133.6
Capital expenditures	310.1	23.4	22.3		355.8
Identifiable assets	2,758.1	779.3	148.9		3,686.3
Corporate assets**					216.5
Total assets					3,902.8

*Operating income excludes other expense, net which is not allocated among segments. For 1984, 1983 and 1982 other expense, net of $64.9, $84.8 and $18.7 million, respectively, includes net interest expense, minority interests, other income and expense, equity in earnings of unconsolidated subsidiaries and a nonrecurring gain of $20.4 million on the sale of the Lafayette corn refining plant in 1982.

**Corporate assets principally include cash, marketable securities, investment in equity subsidiaries, goodwill and certain fixed assets.

12. Additional income statement information

	(In millions)		
	1984	1983	1982
Maintenance	$253.5	$261.4	$216.8
Depreciation and amortization	$203.4	$187.3	$133.6
Taxes, other than income taxes:			
Payroll	$ 90.3	$ 82.3	$ 44.7
Real and personal property	37.6	36.1	30.1
Franchise and other	16.2	14.2	7.8
Total	$144.1	$132.6	$ 82.5
Advertising costs	$480.2	$403.9	$322.3

13. Quarterly financial data (unedited)

	Net sales		Gross profit		Net income		Primary net income per share	
	1984	1983	1984	1983	1984	1983	1984	1983
First quarter	$1,468.8	$1,390.8	$ 459.1	$ 432.9	$ 77.7	$ 68.7	$1.45	$1.28
Second quarter	1,691.4	1,559.4	557.4	512.8	113.4	98.5	2.13	1.84
Third quarter	1,761.8	1,585.1	578.9	516.4	128.5	113.8	2.44	2.13
Fourth quarter	1,579.2	1,498.9	491.6	458.9	71.9	67.0	1.38	1.25
Total year	$6,501.2	$6,034.2	$2,087.0	$1,921.0	$391.5	$348.0	$7.40	$6.50

REPORT OF INDEPENDENT ACCOUNTANTS

One Centerre Plaza
St. Louis, Missouri 63101
314/425-0500

February 6, 1985

To the Shareholders and
Board of Directors of
Anheuser-Busch Companies, Inc.

In our opinion, the accompanying Consolidated Balance Sheet and the related Consolidated Statements of Income, Changes in Shareholders Equity and Convertible Redeemable Preferred Stock, and of Changes in Financial Position present fairly the financial position of Anheuser-Busch Companies, Inc. and its subsidiaries at December 31, 1984 and 1983, and the results of their operations and the changes in their financial position for each of the three years in the period ended December 31, 1984, in conformity with generally accepted accounting principles consistently applied. Our examinations of these statements were made in accordance with generally accepted auditing standards and accordingly included such tests of the accounting records and such other auditing procedures as we considered necessary in the circumstances.

Price Waterhouse

ASHLAND OIL, INC. (B)

M. Edgar Barrett
Southern Methodist University

EARLY HISTORY

In 1924, Swiss Oil, an oil and gas exploration and production company based in Lexington, Ky., bought a small refinery near Catlettsburg in Eastern Kentucky. Twelve years later the refinery was so successful it merged with Swiss to form Ashland Oil & Refining Company. Since then, Ashland's history has included a significant number of acquisitions. The company grew initially by acquiring refining capacity, pipelines and crude supply. Acquisitions included Allied Oil Company and Freedom-Valvoline Oil Company. In the 1960's, the company took its first step toward diversification by entering the chemical business. In 1962, it purchased United Carbon Company. This was followed by the acquisition of other chemical-producing companies. These chemical companies and Ashland's petrochemical operations were consolidated in 1967 to form Ashland Chemical Company.

During the 1960's, the company also expanded into highway construction and construction materials supply. In 1975, the construction company, later operated through

APAC (Ashland Paving and Construction), was formed to encompass all the company's construction activities.

By the 1970's, Ashland Oil, Inc., as the parent company was called, had grown into a large conglomerate. In 1985, Ashland was the 48th largest industrial corporation in the United States with operations in refining, transporting and marketing petroleum products; chemicals; coal; oil exploration; highway construction; and engineering services.

EXPLORATION ROLLERCOASTER

During the latter 1960's, under Chairman and C.E.O. Orin Atkins, the company diversified heavily into crude oil exploration and production. These activities required an initial investment of $43 million between 1966 and 1969. One of these early exploration efforts resulted in eight dry holes in the Santa Barbara channel and an $8 million write-off. Exploration success continued to elude Ashland in the 1970's, when more write-offs were taken for abandoned projects in Alaska, Iran and the Java Sea. Although it did drill some successful wells, by 1977 the company could supply only 20% of the crude oil requirements for its refineries. Citing high exploration costs (Ashland spent almost $900 million on exploration between 1972 and 1978) and lack of results, the company abruptly began selling much of its oil and gas producing property in 1978. The company sold its interest in Ashland Oil Canada Limited for $316 million in October of 1978. In March and April of 1979, the company sold various producing properties and leases in the Rocky Mountains, Southeast, Southwest, Mid-Continent and Gulf Coast regions of the U.S. for $731 million. In the same year, Ashland sold all its interest in North Sea producing properties for $94.5 million. Management decided that the more than $1 billion raised from these property sales would be used for retiring debt, repurchasing stock, paying higher dividends and making new acquisitions. In addition, funds were used to buy higher-priced crude and to pay an additional $256 million in taxes that resulted from the sale.

Following the property sales, Ashland became even more dependent on foreign sources of crude. Foreign supplies accounted for roughly 70% of the firm's crude requirements, most of this coming from OPEC countries. Iran in particular supplied more than 20% of Ashland's crude. (Crude supply from Iran was cut off entirely on November 12, 1979, when President Carter suspended imports of Iranian oil following a well publicized incident in which American citizens in Iran were taken hostage.) Less than 4% of Ashland's crude oil requirements in 1980 came from production owned by Ashland.

COMPANY OPERATIONS BY 1985

Refining

In 1985, Ashland was the nation's largest independent refiner of petroleum products. All refining operations were controlled by Ashland Petroleum Company, a subsidiary of Ashland Oil. It operated refineries in Catlettsburg, Ky.; St. Paul Park, Minn.; and Canton, Ohio, with a total daily capacity of 357,000 barrels. Ashland's refineries operated at 83% of capacity in 1985, running an average of 297,458 barrels per day (bpd) of crude. (By comparison, the nation as a whole had a refinery utilization of 76.0% in 1984.[1]) The company supplied 7.9% of this amount with its own crude (Table 1 shows Ashland's crude oil and gas production). The main refinery in Catlettsburg, Ky. included a recently completed 40,000 bpd Reduced Crude Conversion complex. This conversion process increased the yield of gasoline, diesel and jet fuel from heavy and high sulfur crude or allowed current production levels to

be maintained while using 20% less light crude.[2] In 1985, refining, wholesale marketing and transportation of petroleum products amounted to 48% of the company earnings.[3]

Marketing

Marketing was also under the control of Ashland Petroleum. The company marketed gasoline through 1,910 outlets located throughout the Midwest and Mid-Atlantic states. The company owned 520 of these outlets, including 347 SuperAmerica convenience stores. The remaining 173 of these Ashland-owned outlets were independently operated, but sold gas under the Ashland name.

SuperAmerica sold one-fourth of all Ashland's gasoline. These convenience stores, or "C-stores," were on a larger scale than most of Ashland's competitors. SuperAmerica stations often had as many as 36 pumps. The store operation inside was larger than most convenience stores, as well, and could be described as a mini-grocery store. SuperAmerica stations offered a wide variety of "non-gas" merchandise, which accounted for approximately half of the stores' total sales. In addition to food products, the stores carried their own brand of cigarettes and (in some outlets) liquor.[4] Outlets in the Minneapolis–St. Paul area offered fresh-baked goods under the SuperMom's brand name.

Also part of Ashland Petroleum was Valvoline Oil Company. A registered trademark since 1873, Valvoline brand motor oil was the third largest selling motor oil in the nation in 1985 (in a motor oil market which Ashland officials considered to be extremely competitive). Valvoline products were sold through 107,000 retail outlets (including SuperAmerica) and in more than 96 countries throughout the world.

Exploration and Crude Supply

The subsidiary in charge of exploration and production was Ashland Exploration, Inc. With the sale of most of

---

[1]*National Petroleum News 1985 Factbook,* p. 134.

[2]"Ashland Oil Begins Production at Facility for Crude Conversion," *Wall Street Journal,* April 12, 1983, p. 3.

[3]"Remarks by John R. Hall, Chairman and Chief Executive Officer Ashland Oil, Inc. at the Year-end Presentation to Security Analysts," November 6, 1985, p. 13.

[4]"Ashland Believes It Can Pump Out Earnings Despite Uncertainties Concerning Oil Refining," *Wall Street Journal,* February 26, 1985, p. 63.

TABLE 1   ASHLAND'S NET OIL AND GAS PRODUCTION
(Fiscal Year Ending Sept. 30)

	1985	1984	1983	1982	1981	1980
Crude oil (bpd)						
United States	2755	2500	2700	2700	2800	3100
Foreign	20,781	19,100	14,000	13,900	9500	9600
Total crude	23,536	21,600	16,700	16,600	12,300	12,700
Natural gas (mcf/day)						
United States	32,156	29,000	27,000	27,000	28,000	26,000

Source: Ashland Oil company documents.

its producing properties in 1978 and 1979, the company was left with only a fraction of its former production. By 1985, Ashland's domestic producing interests were concentrated in the Appalachian Region and the Illinois Basin. New drilling occurred primarily in the Houston Region, mostly in southern Louisiana, with offshore drilling planned for the Gulf of Mexico.

All foreign operations were located in Nigeria. Foreign reserves rose to 49.2 million barrels during 1984, up 29.5 million barrels from the previous year.[5] This increase was mostly due to development of the Akam field, offshore Nigeria. The division expected to complete a floating storage facility in early 1986 which would allow production to begin from eight development wells at the offshore Adanga field in Nigeria. The company's five-year production data is shown in Table 1.

Chemicals

Ashland Chemical Company, a wholly-owned subsidiary of Ashland Oil, engaged in the manufacture, distribution and sale of a wide variety of chemical products. It was divided into several specialty divisions.

One of these specialty divisions, Industrial Chemical and Solvents, was the largest distributor of industrial chemicals in the country. It sold its own products, as well as those of many other manufacturers, through 77 distribution centers located throughout North America. The division specialized in supplying mixed truckload and less-than-truckload quantities to the paint, oilfield, automotive, paper and rubber industries. This flexibility was said to allow them to sell to small, specialized companies that purchased in smaller quantities than large firms.

[5]"Nigerian Exploration Efforts Help Boost Ashland's Proved Reserves," *The Oil Daily,* November 9, 1984, p. A2.

Ashland manufactured and sold high-purity chemicals to the electronic and high-technology industries through its Electronic & Laboratory Specialty Division. These liquid chemicals and gases were used in manufacturing silicon chips.

The Petrochemicals Division marketed aromatic hydrocarbons, malic anhydride and other petroleum-based products.

Coal

The company was a major coal producer through Ashland Coal Inc., a 65%-owned subsidiary, and Arch Minerals Corporation, in which the company had a 50% interest. These firms mined coal in Alabama, Illinois, Kentucky, West Virginia and Wyoming, and sold to electric utilities and industrial users. Combined sales of these operations placed Ashland among the top coal producers in the nation.

Engineering and Construction

Ashland's Engineering and Construction unit was composed of the APAC construction subsidiaries and a group of companies known as the Engineering Services Group, which were acquired in 1981 as part of the purchase of U.S. Filter Corporation.

Ashland's APAC subsidiary manufactured construction material and performed contract construction work. This contract work included paving highways, shopping centers and parking lots. APAC operated in 13 Sunbelt states, with its administrative offices in Atlanta. The subsidiary owned 131 asphalt plants and 18 quarries.

The Engineering Services Group included several firms that were involved in architectural design, engineering services and project management. One of these subsidiaries, Holmes and Narver, had designed security systems for the Los Angeles Olympics. Williams Brothers Engineering Company, another firm within the Engineering Services Group, was a leader in the design of oil, gas and water pipelines and was a leading supplier of pipeline engineering services on the Alaskan North Slope. Projects of other firms included managing airport expansion and manufacturing pollution control equipment.

STRATEGY DECISIONS, 1980–1983

Diversification into Unrelated Businesses

In addition to retiring debt, repurchasing stock, and paying increased dividends, management targeted a major portion of the cash raised from the 1978–79 property sales for acquisitions in areas outside Ashland's normal operations. Ashland's 1981 annual report contained the following statement:

> Since the early 1970's, the climate for U.S. business in general and the petroleum industry in particular has been affected increasingly by events beyond the control of either individual companies or the U.S. government. To survive and prosper in such a volatile environment, companies must be willing to reappraise traditional operations and aggressively explore and develop new business opportunities.

These words came on the heels of two major acquisitions by Ashland. In the first of these, the firm entered the insurance business on January 1, 1981, with the purchase of the Integon Corporation for $238 million. (Payment was composed of $116 million in cash and $122 million of preferred stock. The excess $88,148,000 of the cost over the fair value of the assets acquired would be amortized over a 40 year period using the straight-line method.) Integon was an insurance holding company based in Winston-Salem, North Carolina. The company's primary business was the sale of life and health insurance; home protection policies; group life, annuity and health policies; and credit life and health policies. Through its subsidiaries, Integon also conducted a multiple line property and casualty insurance business, covering such risks as auto liability, fire, and workers' compensation. Integon Mortgage Guaranty Corporation, another subsidiary, was engaged in the mortgage guaranty business in the southeastern United States. Integon Realty Corporation invested in income producing projects such as motels and office buildings and provided mortgages in the form of construction loans for new projects. As of August 31, 1981, Integon had a total of $10.6 billion of life insurance in force.

In the second of its major acquisitions, Ashland purchased United States Filter Corporation on January 1, 1981 for $402 million. (Payment was composed of $376 million in cash and $26 million in 13.5% notes. Goodwill of $150,532,000 would be amortized over 40 years by the straight-line method.) U.S. Filter was the parent company of a number of foreign and domestic firms whose activities included engineering and project management services for the oil, mining, pipeline, and steam generation industries; design and manufacture of environmental control systems; production of steel castings for use in pumps, valves, turbines and compressors for the petroleum, chemical and power generation industries; production of specialty chemicals for industry and marine shipping; design and manufacture of industrial process instruments; coal mining; and cement production. In 1980, U.S. Filter earned nearly $28 million on sales of $865 million.[6]

Ashland immediately transferred the specialty chemical division (Drew Chemical) of U.S. Filter to Ashland Chemical. The remaining U.S. Filter units were placed into a new subsidiary called Ashland Technology. The catalyst and clay operations of U.S. Filter were sold for $99 million in late 1981. Ashland Technology was divided into four operating groups: 1) the Engineering Services and Power Generation Group; 2) the Process Instruments Group; 3) the Environmental Systems Group; and 4) the Metal Fabrication and Casting Group.

Ashland officials made the following comments concerning the acquisitions of Integon and U.S. Filter and their position in future strategy:

> . . . Ashland's strategy has been to further diversify its asset base, enhance its flexibility to adapt to changes and take advantage of new opportunities as they arise. In 1981, the strategy moved forward dramatically with the two largest acquisitions in Ashland's history. Through U.S. Filter the company has expanded its chemical operations and acquired a very solid base in the fields of engineering services for energy-related projects and environmental control systems for industry. Through Integon, the company has entered the vital and rapidly expanding insurance industry. These new fields promise to enhance Ashland's financial strength and tech-

---

[6]U.S. Filter Corporation, 1980 Form 10-K, p. F-4.

nological and engineering capability while at the same time opening doors for further growth into new areas of business.

Having made these two acquisitions, the company's strategic planning will now be concentrated in the following areas: 1) further strengthening of current operations and divestiture of any operations which do not hold strong prospects for growth, 2) continued reduction in operating costs, 3) further strengthening of the balance sheet, and 4) development of the company's many promising new technologies, such as the RCC process, as sources of income. Continuing diversification efforts will be highly selective and in areas compatible with existing core operations, to stimulate growth as well as new business opportunities.

With the addition of Integon and U.S. Filter, we now have strong positions in energy, chemicals, construction, engineering and technology, and insurance. These will be our primary areas for expansion in future years.[7]

Management Changes

In September of 1981, Orin Atkins unexpectedly retired as Ashland's chairman and chief executive officer. He was replaced by John R. Hall, a 24-year company veteran and, most recently, vice chairman.

The exact reasons for Atkins' retirement were not made public at the time. Several months later, however, rumors of impropriety involving Atkins began to surface.[8] In 1980, on his personal order, Ashland paid $1,350,000 to a wealthy Libyan middleman, Yehia Omar, in return for his securing a contract with the country of Oman to supply 20,000 barrels of crude a day to Ashland. Soon after, top Ashland officials met to discuss whether this payment was legal. (These concerns were raised because under the 1977 Foreign Corrupt Policies Act, corporate payments to foreign government officials were illegal.) Since Omar had at one time carried an Omani diplomatic passport, it was possible that Ashland, by making these payments, had broken the law. The company's directors commissioned an independent investigation to look into the matter. The findings of this investigation cleared Atkins and Ashland of violating any U.S. law because Omar had not been an Omani official at the time of the payment.

However, even though no law had been broken, the report criticized the impropriety of such payments.[9]

In early September 1981, Atkins met privately with several of Ashland's directors. It was reported that, at the meeting, the board voiced strong concerns regarding both Ashland's diversification moves and the nature of the Omani transaction.[10] "An element of the board thought we were doing too damn many things too damn fast," recalled F.H. Ross, a director and former Ashland executive.[11] Moreover, the company had just reported a 76% drop in profits for the nine months ending June 30, 1981. In a meeting on September 17, 1981, outside directors sought and received Atkins' resignation.[12]

Changing Economic Situation

The economic conditions that existed by the early 1980's were very different from what Ashland and many other U.S. firms had forecasted. Ashland's 1977 strategic plan had anticipated U.S. energy demand to increase steadily from 38.3 million barrels a day (mmbpd) of oil equivalent in 1978 to 47 mmbpd oil equivalent by 1990. In fact, actual U.S. energy demand was falling by the early 1980's. Real GNP growth was 1.3% annually instead of the 3% to 4% that had been expected. Interest rates were much higher than the company had anticipated. Furthermore, the U.S. economy experienced back-to-back recessions in 1980 and 1981–1982.

World crude prices, which had increased by this time to record levels, forced Ashland to use a greater portion of its cash flow on crude supplies for its refineries. At the same time, U.S. demand for petroleum products was falling. The national recession, high inflation, increased automobile fuel efficiency and individual conservation were all factors that led to a 6.4% drop in petroleum product demand in 1980.[13] The spread between crude and product prices had become so narrow that, in some instances, the

---

[7]Ashland Oil, Inc., 1981 Annual Report, pp. 7–8.

[8]"Ashland Oil Chief's Sudden '81 Departure Is Linked by Insiders to an Oman Payment," *Wall Street Journal,* May 16, 1983, p. 4.

[9]"Dubious Deals, Ashland Oil Criticizes Its Payments to Libyan To Get Oman's Crude," *Wall Street Journal,* May 24, 1983, p. 1.

[10]It was reported, for instance, that Ashland lost $2.3 million in a venture designed to produce re-usable sausage casings. ("Dubious Deals . . ." op. cit.)

[11]Ibid.

[12]"Ashland Oil Chief's Sudden '81 Departure . . ." op. cit.

[13]Ashland Oil, Inc., 1980 Annual Report, p. 11.

prices received for petroleum products were less than refiners' crude oil costs.[14]

Alternative Sources of Energy

The economic conditions which existed in the early 1980's led Ashland officials to make investments that would take advantage of the situation. Since low grade crude was cheaper and more readily available than light crude, the company converted some of its refineries so they could handle lower grades. In 1981, Ashland also began building a new 40,000 bpd refinery in Catlettsburg, Ky. that utilized its RCC process. The project cost was initially estimated at $190 million (though the final cost was $295 million).[15] The company justified the investment based on an estimate that the new refinery would increase pre-tax earnings by $10 million a month.[16]

With crude oil so expensive and in such short supply during the early 1980's, alternative methods for producing hydrocarbons became more attractive. One process, coal liquefaction, converted coal to liquid hydrocarbons. Ashland participated with the Department of Energy and other companies in building a coal liquefaction pilot plant near its main refinery in Catlettsburg, Ky. The company also planned a joint venture to build a commercial scale liquefaction facility. Under the proposal, Ashland and five or six other companies would each invest $100 million to $150 million in the project. The group would then negotiate guaranteed loans with the federal Synthetic Fuels Corporation. By 1982, Ashland had spent a total of $13 million on both projects.[17]

Hall's Initial Strategy

After Hall took office in late 1981, he outlined a new direction for the company, which included three major strategic goals.[18] The first goal was to strengthen the core business—refining. He proposed doing this by reducing

[14]Ashland Oil, Inc., 1981 Form 10-K, p. 3.

[15]Ashland Oil, Inc., 1983 Form 10-K, p. 1.

[16]"Ashland Oil Begins Production . . ." op. cit.

[17]"Ashland to Quit Role in Project For Synfuels," *Wall Street Journal,* November 23, 1982, p. 4.

[18]"Ashland Oil: Sequel To The Asset Redeployment Program," presented by John R. Hall at the Seminar For Senior Executives in the Oil & Gas Industry, Vail, Colorado, June 25, 1985.

the cost of raw materials used, namely crude oil. This was to be accomplished by becoming less dependent on foreign suppliers, which, as in the case of Iran, tended to be less reliable and more expensive than domestic sources. Hall also proposed reducing operating costs, mainly by improving refining efficiency. He wanted to put more emphasis on the marketing of Ashland's refined products as a way to strengthen the core business. This would involve increasing sales efforts and improving distribution of finished products. Reducing overhead was the final area in which Hall proposed strengthening the core business.

Hall's second major goal was to strengthen the financial situation of the company. Again Hall outlined several ways to achieve this. First, the company would try to maintain an "A" bond rating with the two major bond rating services. To do this it was felt that they would have to reduce the ratio of debt (plus preferred stock) to total capitalization to less than 40%. This was to be accomplished by repurchasing preferred stock and reducing long-term debt. Second, Hall wanted to achieve an overall return on equity of 17%, a return on assets of 12%, and a return on investment of 15%. Third, Hall hoped to reduce the dividend payout to 30–40% of normalized primary earnings. Fourth, he proposed improving the company's balance sheet by achieving real earnings per share growth. Finally, he desired to reduce corporate overhead. This could be accomplished, he asserted, by reducing G&A expenses through layoffs or realigning the corporate organization.

Hall's third major goal was defined under the broad heading of "diversifying profitability." For Ashland, diversification involved reducing dependence on the refining end of the business for earnings and cash flow. Hall stated that effective diversification could be achieved in two ways: 1) through investment in other segments of Ashland that had potential for profitable growth; and, 2) by acquiring outside businesses in either related or non-related fields.[19]

COMPANY DEVELOPMENTS AND DECISIONS

Refinery Closings

In 1980, Ashland operated seven refineries with a total daily capacity of 457,000 bpd. Throughout that year, its refinery system operated below capacity and processed an

[19]Ibid.

TABLE 2 ASHLAND OIL REFINERY CAPACITY AND UTILIZATION
(Barrels per Stream Day)

	1985	1984	1983	1982	1981	1980
Catlettsburg, Ky.	220,000	220,000	195,000	195,000	195,000	220,000
St. Paul, Minn.	69,000	69,000	69,000	69,000	69,000	69,000
Canton, Oh.	68,000	68,000	68,000	68,000	68,000	66,000
Buffalo, N.Y.	—	—	—	—	48,000	48,000
Louisville, Ky.	—	—	—	26,000	26,000	26,000
Findlay, Oh.	—	—	—	—	—	21,000
Freedom, Pa.	—	7000	7000	7000	7000	7000
Total	357,000	364,000	339,000	365,000	413,000	457,000
Crude oil refined (bpd)	297,000	301,813	285,029	312,200	321,499	363,427
Refinery runs/capacity	83%	83%	84%	86%	78%	80%

Source: Ashland Oil company documents.

average of 363,000 bpd. The Findley refinery in Ohio, with a capacity of 21,000 bpd, was closed in the spring of 1981. A little over a year later, operations were suspended at the Buffalo, N.Y. refinery. The company blamed an "unprecedented decline in the demand for petroleum products" and "bleak prospects for a rebound" for this latest closing.[20] A third refinery in Louisville, Ky. closed its doors in April 1983. The company planned to make up the 13,000 bpd that the Louisville refinery had been producing by increasing operations at its main refinery in Catlettsburg, which was operating at 70% of capacity.[21]

In April 1985, the company suspended crude oil processing operations at its 7000 bpd Freedom, Pa. refinery. The facility continued to operate as a product terminal and motor oil blending and packaging plant. The remaining refineries at Catlettsburg; Canton, Ohio; and St. Paul Park, Minn. were equipped to process a wider variety of crudes, including low quality crude.

Acquisitions

Late in 1982, the company bought the crude oil gathering and transportation system of Scurlock Oil of Houston for $80 million. Scurlock's system, mostly in Texas and Louisiana, included 2300 miles of oil pipeline (capable of moving 200,000 bpd of crude) as well as 2.5 million barrels of storage capacity. This system gave the company access to a significant amount of domestic crude, kept it in contact with major domestic producers, and allowed it to make offers to purchase the oil it transported. "We believe the acquisition will prove to be one of the most beneficial ever made," said Charles J. Luellen, president of Ashland Petroleum and senior vice president of Ashland Oil, "because it will substantially increase our supply of secure, economically priced U.S. crude oil."[22] "This was a very positive acquisition," echoed John Dansby, Ashland's vice president of planning. "It's hard to imagine a single decision that could have had a more decisive impact on the company."[23] Overnight, the Scurlock acquisition had increased Ashland's supply of domestic crude by 60,000 to 80,000 bpd.[24] Scurlock also had the advantage of posting the price it was willing to pay for crude. This allowed Ashland to adjust its purchasing price just like other majors did.

The company also acquired Tresler Oil Company in 1982. Tresler marketed oil products in the Ohio River Valley and operated a river front petroleum product storage terminal. Ashland officials believed this acquisition would strengthen the company's marketing and distri-

---

[20]"Ashland Oil Unit To Idle Refinery Near Buffalo, N.Y.," *Wall Street Journal*, May 11, 1982, p. 12.

[21]"Ashland Expects Loss In Fiscal 2nd Quarter, Mulls Dividend Cut," *Wall Street Journal*, March 18, 1983, p. 7.

[22]"A Troubled Ashland Banks On Chemicals," *Chemical Week*, June 23, 1982, p. 44.

[23]John Dansby, Vice President Strategic Planning, Ashland Oil, Inc. (December 3, 1985 interview, Ashland, Ky.)

[24]Ibid.

bution network for refined products in the Ohio River market.

Coal

In November 1982, Ashland pulled out of its proposed coal-liquefaction project. The company suspended participation because of uncertainty about crude prices, the massive capital investment necessary to construct the project, exposure to possible cost overruns, and tax law changes that reduced the tax benefits of the project. Ashland officials said costs of the project had been expensed as incurred, so the decision would not affect the company financially.[25]

In June 1981, Ashland sold a 25% interest in Ashland Coal to Saarbergwerke A.G. of West Germany for $102.5 million in cash. Saarbergwerke was 74% owned by the West German government. Proceeds from the sale were used to retire short-term obligations of Ashland Coal. Company officials said the deal provided Ashland Coal with a new export dimension in its overall marketing activity.[26]

The company sold an additional 10% of Ashland Coal in June of 1982 for $44.3 million to Carboex S.A., a coal supply firm owned by the Spanish government. This reduced Ashland's ownership of the coal subsidiary to 65%.[27]

Cost Control/Debt Reduction

In an attempt to promote efficiency and cost control in all operations, Ashland Oil, the parent company, was realigned along the lines of a holding company. A core group, made up of seven top parent company executives, monitored and reviewed the overall performance of the divisions. However, day-to-day operational decisions were turned over to divisional managers. This management structure was expected to give the divisions something close to the autonomy of separate companies.[28] By taking on their own administrative functions, the divisions were said to avoid a good measure of bureaucracy and to respond faster to market forces.[29] Through this process of realignment, Ashland was able to trim corporate staff by one-third.

Between 1981 and 1985, Ashland reduced debt and capitalized leases by $206 million. This included exchanging $23,167,000 of capital stock for long-term debt in 1983. During the same five-year period, the company reduced preferred stock by $109 million. In 1985 alone, the company reduced redeemable preferred stock by $54 million and long-term debt and capitalized leases by $41 million. As of Sept. 30, 1985, long-term debt, capitalized leases and redeemable preferred stock represented 39% of total capitalization, compared to 44% the year before. (Exhibits 2 and 3 provide greater detail on this subject.)

Earnings per share and dividends per common share paid by the company were as follows:

TABLE 3   SUMMARY OF EARNINGS PER SHARE AND DIVIDENDS PER SHARE
(In Dollars)

	1985	1984	1983	1982	1981	1980	1979
Earnings:							
From operations and investments	4.12	2.13	2.23	4.75	2.22	6.49	5.31
From divestitures and write-offs		(9.53)		.54		.31	10.24
From extraordinary gain from exchange of common stock for long-term debt			.23				
Total earnings per share	4.12	(7.40)	2.46	5.29	2.22	6.80	15.55
Dividends per share	1.60	1.60	2.20	2.40	2.40	2.20	1.80

Source: Ashland Oil company documents.

[25]"Ashland Drops Breckenridge H-Coal Project," *Oil & Gas Journal,* November 29, 1982, p. 43.

[26]"Ashland Nears Sale of Coal Unit Stake to West Germany," *Wall Street Journal,* May 28, 1981, p. 7.

[27]Ashland Oil, Inc., 1982 Form 10-K, p. 7.

[28]"A Troubled Ashland Banks On Chemicals," op. cit.

[29]Ibid.

Integon

To compete in the increasingly competitive deregulated insurance industry, Integon, in 1982, started selling a more flexible universal life policy that offered a higher yield to policyholders. During fiscal 1983, the insurance company sold most of its group accident and health business—reportedly because of rising costs of healthcare claims.[30] The following table shows Integon's financial results for 1981 through 1984:

TABLE 4   SUMMARY OF INTEGON FINANCIAL RESULTS
(In Millions)

	1984	1983	1982	1981
Net income	$ 9	13	14	8
Life insurance in force	$14,332	12,324	9,314	10,600

Source: Ashland Oil company documents.

For the six months ending February 29, 1984, Integon's profits declined 59% to $4.9 million (from $7.8 million in the year-earlier period).[31] At Ashland's annual meeting in January 1984, William Seaton, vice chairman and chief financial officer, said that Integon's income had decreased because of higher losses on property and casualty insurance. Further, he said, volatile interest rates and other available investment opportunities made Integon's ordinary life insurance policies less attractive to consumers.[32] Policyholders continued to surrender ordinary life insurance policies at higher than normal rates.

Ashland Technology

By late 1983, it was becoming clear, as well, that many units within Ashland Technology were not performing up to company expectations.[33] Most of the former U.S. Filter businesses were not market leaders and company officials conceded that "we probably paid too much" for U.S. Filter.[34] Segment data for Ashland Technology was as follows:

TABLE 5   SUMMARY OF ASHLAND TECHNOLOGY FINANCIAL RESULTS
(In Thousands of Dollars)

Fiscal Year Ending Sept. 30	1984	1983	1982	1981*
Sales and operating revenue	$677,239	633,123	817,727	588,786
Operating income	$ 21,916	700	22,506	8,798
Funds provided from operations	$ 34,863	18,720	20,100	22,522
Backlog of projects	$614,000	527,000	666,000	784,000

*Includes only nine months starting Jan. 1.
Source: Ashland Oil company documents.

[30]Ashland Oil, Inc., 1983 Annual Report, p. 30.

[31]"Ashland Oil Seeks Buyer for Integon, Its Insurance Unit," *Wall Street Journal,* May 22, 1984, p. 10.

[32]Ibid.

[33]"Ashland Oil: Trying to Cope With a Diversification Hangover and a Lingering Scandal," *Business Week,* November 7, 1983, p. 134.

[34]Ibid.

BACK TO BASICS

Divestiture and Redirection

In September 1984, Ashland announced plans to sell Integon and most of the U.S. Filter units (by now part of Ashland Technology) it had acquired just four years earlier.[35] The decision resulted in a one-time charge against after-tax earnings of $271 million in the fourth quarter of 1984. The write-down included the difference between the book value of the units to be divested and the $300 million after-tax proceeds expected to be generated from their sale in fiscal 1985.[36] It also included the write-down of an unprofitable methanol plant in Louisiana. After taking the charge, Ashland showed a net loss of $172 million for the year.

Ashland's 1984 "Letter to the Stockholders" justified the divestment and write-downs as follows:

> After careful study, we decided to reduce the scope of our activities in order to concentrate resources in growth areas which offer the greatest potential return to shareholders. We expect the divestiture to generate approximately $300 million which we plan to use to reduce outstanding preferred stock, retire debt and fund investments in growth businesses. Although the write-offs adversely affected the debt-equity ratio by reducing shareholders' equity, the balance sheet will be strengthened by our planned use of the proceeds. In addition, earnings per share will be improved as outstanding preferred stock is reduced. Despite the impact on 1984 earnings, we believe the divestiture and use of proceeds will be in the long-term best interest of shareholders.[37]

The company continued to pursue two of its three original major goals: strengthening the refining business and improving the balance sheet. However, the third goal, to diversify profitability, was altered. Ashland managers were determined they would no longer attempt to diversify by acquiring businesses in non-related industries. Rather,

they would attempt to reduce Ashland's reliance on refining by investing only in related non-refining businesses. Moreover, Ashland officials planned to divest unprofitable units and concentrate on ones which had proved consistently successful.

In particular, six of Ashland's existing businesses had been identified in late 1983 as growth areas which the firm would actively pursue. Management hoped these areas would provide increased profits as well as diversification away from refining. These areas were: (1) Valvoline Motor Oil, (2) SuperAmerica convenience stores, (3) chemical distribution, (4) specialty chemicals, (5) domestic exploration and production, and (6) engineering services.

In selecting these six areas, Ashland's management had particularly emphasized their firm's competitive position in each of the various businesses. Once these businesses were selected, they were analyzed under varying scenarios in an attempt to gauge their relative contributions to corporate income. In so doing, Ashland officials determined that these six areas might well be sufficient to meet the firm's financial goals.

Valvoline

Company officials believed success for Valvoline could be achieved through innovative marketing and product flexibility. The firm, for example, sponsored auto racing teams, which allowed the Valvoline trademark to be displayed on race cars during such races as the Indianapolis 500. They were also an active sponsor of NCAA basketball games.

The Valvoline division had recently introduced several new products, including FourGard Motor Oil (an oil specifically designed for small, four-cylinder passenger cars) and Turbo V (an oil designed for turbo engine cars).

Management intended to start packaging its Valvoline products in one-quart plastic bottles in 1986, as some other motor oil companies already had. By the summer of 1986, it expected all nine U.S. packaging plants to be able to produce the plastic bottles. Valvoline targeted the do-it-yourself consumer and sold its motor oil mostly through distributors, such as K-Mart, rather than through service stations. As the following table illustrates, do-it-yourself consumers constituted more than two-thirds of the motor oil market:

---

[35]As part of the divestment, Ashland sold all of Ashland Technology with the exception of the engineering services group, Riley-Beaird (which was part of the metal fabrication and casting group), and the recently acquired Daniel, Munn, Johnson & Mendenhall (an architecture and civil engineering firm).

[36]"Back to the Basics, with a $270 Million Loss," *Chemical Week,* September 26, 1984, p. 9.

[37]Ashland Oil, Inc., 1984 Annual Report, pp. 2–3.

TABLE 6 U.S. ANNUAL SHARE-OF-PURCHASES FOR ALL MOTOR OIL

	1984	1983	1982	1981	1980
Carried out by purchaser	69%	70	71	70	69
Installed where bought	31%	30	29	30	31

Source: 1985 National Petroleum News Factbook.

Valvoline was third in motor oil market share behind Quaker State and Pennzoil. Valvoline management foresaw growth for their product in further market share penetration, and expected to be the number two motor oil marketer by 1990.[38]

The Valvoline product line was expanded in September 1985 with the purchase of IG-LO Products Corporation. IG-LO was the nation's largest packager and marketer of refrigerant for automobile air-conditioners.

Operating results for Valvoline, included as a part of the entire Petroleum Company's results, are shown in the following table:

TABLE 7 ASHLAND PETROLEUM COMPANY FINANCIAL SUMMARY
(In Millions except Operating Information)

	1985	1984	1983
Sales and operating revenues	$5377	5678	5700
Operating income			
Refining, wholesale marketing and transportation	$ 180	40	138
Retail marketing[1]	$ 12	13	4
Valvoline	$ 43	40	39
Other	$ (22)	27	(5)
Total	$ 213[2]	120[2]	176

[1]Includes SuperAmerica.
[2]Includes $12 million in income from unusual items in 1985 and $46 million in 1984.
Source: Ashland Oil company documents.

SuperAmerica

Ashland officials planned to continue the rapid expansion of SuperAmerica by adding 50 new outlets each year. Many of these were planned in Southern Florida, which was outside SuperAmerica's established retail areas of the Upper Midwest (where SuperAmerica held a 20% share of the retail gasoline market in the Minneapolis–St. Paul area) and the Central Ohio Valley.

Each new store required an investment of approximately $1 million, including land. Start-up costs were expensed as they were incurred. Each SuperAmerica outlet pumped an average of 143,000 gallons of gas per month. (By comparison, the average U.S. gasoline outlet pumped 66,311 gallons per month in 1984.)[39] SuperAmerica also averaged $700,000 of non-gas sales per year per outlet. (The average C-store, meanwhile, had $460,000 of in-store annual sales in 1984.)[40] Whereas most C-stores attracted customers with lower gas prices and then took relatively high margins on food items, Ashland management stressed that SuperAmerica's food and

[38]"1984 Year-End Presentation," by John F. Boehm, Vice President Ashland Petroleum Co. and President Valvoline Oil Co., November 7, 1984, p. 14.

[39]*National Petroleum News 1985 Factbook,* p. 116.

[40]Ibid, p. 122.

merchandise were priced competitively with lower-margin traditional grocery stores.

Operating information for SuperAmerica is shown in Table 8.

TABLE 8   SUPERAMERICA FINANCIAL AND OPERATING DATA
(In Millions)

	1985	1984
Sales and operating revenues	$902	810
Operating income*	$ 12	13
Merchandise sales	$241	212
Number of stores	347	306
Average gallonage per store per month	143,000	142,000

*Includes other retail operations.
Source: Ashland Oil company documents.

Chemical Distribution

Chemical distribution was conducted in part by the Industrial Chemical and Solvents Division. Ashland management intended to increase the number of distribution centers and offer a greater variety of products. The IC&S Division added three new distribution centers in 1985. In addition, Ashland bought General Polymers National in 1983 for $10 million. General Polymers manufactured thermoplastic resins and had distribution centers in Ohio, Illinois, Minnesota and Texas. During 1985, General Polymers added two distribution centers, in Portland, Ore. and Seattle, bringing the total number of locations to 16. The company's goal was to have 20 locations by 1988.[41]

Specialty Chemicals

The specialty chemicals area of Ashland Chemical was seen by management as a means of establishing a niche in the chemical business. This division produced chemicals to fill a specific demand, such as the high-purity chemicals sold to the electronics industry. During 1983 and 1984, Ashland Chemical made several acquisitions and divestitures. The specialty chemical area acquired Scientific Gas Products, which produced and marketed equipment and high-purity gas to the electronics, medical, and industrial laboratory markets. It had facilities in Colorado, California, New Jersey and Texas.

Two other large acquisitions were made by Ashland Chemical during this time, as well. Goodyear's adhesive manufacturing facilities and technology were acquired in 1984. Goodyear officials claimed to have sold the line because it did not match its business objectives.[42] In October 1985, Ashland agreed to purchase J.T. Baker Chemical Company. Ashland officials said the acquisition would permit them to broaden the line of chemicals the company offered to the electronics, semiconductor, laboratory and other specialty markets. Baker's worldwide operations had annual sales of $80 million.

Data on Specialty Chemicals and Chemical Distribution is shown in the following table:

[41]Ashland Oil, Inc., 1985 Annual Report, p. 17.

[42]"Ashland Oil Acquisition," *Wall Street Journal*, February 2, 1984, p. 10.

TABLE 9   ASHLAND CHEMICAL FINANCIAL DATA
(In Millions)

	1985	1984	1983
Sales and operating revenues	$1499	1501	1208
Operating income (loss)			
Chemical distribution	$ 40	42	36
Specialty chemicals	$ 28	27	11
Commodity chemicals	$ 22	3	(20)
Other	$ (22)	(17)	(26)
Total	$ 68	55	1

Source: Ashland Oil company documents.

Domestic Exploration and Production

Though the company had moved increasingly back into exploration since the massive divestitures of the late 1970's, company officials stressed that their reasons were now entirely different. They claimed no longer to view exploration and production as a means of supplying crude to their refineries (as the major companies did). Instead, said officials, they viewed exploration and production as a source of profits. This time, said Hall and his administration, the company would limit its efforts to projects with high probability of success. In this way, the exploration segment of the firm would function much more like an independent producer.[43] The company's goal for exploration and production was simply to "create value for the shareholder."[44] In effect, said John Dansby, Ashland's vice president of planning, the company considered exploration and production just another non-refining segment whose profits would contribute to the diversification plan.

As part of this new effort, Ashland, in 1981, brought in the former chief geologist of Shell Oil Co. to head Ashland Exploration. Since then, E&P operations had been limited to Nigeria, the Eastern United States and the Gulf Coast area. (Only *domestic* exploration and production operations, however, were considered to be one of the six so-called growth areas.) Domestic exploratory drilling was carried out in Texas and Louisiana, and by 1985 had resulted mainly in natural gas discoveries. Additions to domestic oil reserves came primarily from developmental drilling in the Eastern United States (see Exhibit 6).

Engineering Services

The last growth area, engineering services, included the remaining units from the U.S. Filter sell-off and the Los Angeles-based Daniel, Mann, Johnson & Mendenhall (DMJM). DMJM's projects included joint management of the Los Angeles International Airport expansion and design of the Baltimore Metro System.

The combination of DMJM, Holmes & Narver, and Williams Brothers made Ashland one of the leading providers of architectural, engineering and other technical services. Holmes & Narver ranked sixth in total billings among the top 500 design firms ranked by *Engineering News-Record*. DMJM placed in the top ten, while Williams Brothers was in the top 50.[45]

According to company officials, the engineering services group required only limited capital expenditures. All firms within this growth area were heavily reliant on contracts from government entities.[46]

Results for engineering services are shown in the following table:

[43]"Ashland Oil: Sequel To The Asset Redeployment Program . . ." op. cit., p. 25.

[44]John Dansby interview . . . op. cit.

[45]Ashland Oil, Inc., 1984 Annual Report, pp. 27–28.

[46]"Remarks by John R. Hall . . ." op. cit., p. 12.

TABLE 10   ENGINEERING SERVICES FINANCIAL AND OPERATING DATA
(In Millions)

	1985	1984	1983
Sales and operating revenue	$396	336	287
Operating income	$ 14	7	4
Backlog	$345	466	492

Source: Ashland Oil company documents.

OVERALL GOALS AND OBJECTIVES

The stated overall objective of Ashland's late 1983 shift in strategy was to reduce the percentage of earnings coming from refining by substantially increasing the earnings from the six growth areas. The following table provides data on Ashland's stated 1990 goals regarding relative contribution to earnings. It also provides information on the firm's progress towards these goals.

TABLE 11   ASHLAND'S RELATIVE CONTRIBUTION TO EARNINGS

	1983	1985	Proposed 1990
Refining and wholesale marketing	51%	48%	25%
Six growth areas	37%	40%	60%
Other businesses	12%	12%	15%

Source: Ashland Oil company documents.

Management further stated that it would like the firm's non-refining businesses to be able to support earnings of $5 per share—even if refining should earn nothing.[47]

[47]"Ashland Oil: Sequel To The Asset Redeployment Program . . ." op. cit.

EXHIBIT 1 CONSOLIDATED STATEMENTS OF INCOME
(In Thousands except per Share Data)

Years ended September 30	1985	1984	1983
Revenues			
Sales and operating revenues (including excise taxes)	$8,183,733	$8,544,064	$8,108,169
Other	54,206	77,168	91,302
	8,237,939	8,621,232	8,199,471
Costs and expenses			
Cost of sales and operating expenses	6,745,700	7,214,937	6,960,088
Excise taxes on products and merchandise	292,510	291,500	255,870
Selling, general and administrative expenses	606,808	611,338	564,574
Depreciation, depletion and amortization (including capitalized leases)	202,174	212,547	192,006
Foreign exploration taxes	38,690	38,887	30,905
	7,885,882	8,369,209	8,003,443
Operating Income	352,057	252,023	196,028
Other income (expense)			
Interest income	20,309	19,723	31,821
Interest expense	(67,413)	(80,814)	(78,501)
Equity income	10,421	20,387	27,517
Other—net (including corporate administrative)	(57,014)	(67,446)	(72,807)
Divestitures and asset write-offs	(39,652)	(286,641)	—
Income (loss) before income taxes and extraordinary gain	218,708	(142,768)	104,058
Income taxes	71,986	29,710	7,421
Income (loss) before extraordinary gain	146,722	(172,478)	96,637
Extraordinary gain from exchange of common stock for long-term debt	—	—	6,196
Net income (loss)	$ 146,722	$ (172,478)	$ 102,833
Earnings (loss) per share			
Income (loss) before extraordinary gain	$4.12	$(7.40)	$2.23
Extraordinary gain	—	—	.23
	$4.12	$(7.40)	$2.46
Average common shares and equivalents outstanding	28,227	27,783	27,011

Source: Ashland Oil, Inc. 1985 Annual Report.

EXHIBIT 2   CONSOLIDATED BALANCE SHEETS
(In Thousands)

September 30	1985	1984
Assets		
Current assets		
Cash and short-term securities	$ 173,391	$ 132,111
Accounts receivable (less allowances for doubtful accounts of $27,409,000 in 1985 and $29,097,000 in 1984)	923,822	939,831
Construction completed and in progress—at contract prices	70,770	67,176
Refundable income taxes	—	33,837
Inventories	306,607	393,613
Deferred income tax benefits	62,360	59,605
Other current assets	58,782	50,799
	1,595,732	1,676,972
Investments and other assets		
Noncurrent net assets of operations held for sale	157,000	262,000
Investments in and advances to unconsolidated subsidiaries and affiliates	172,492	167,020
Cost in excess of net assets of companies acquired (less accumulated amortization of $4,626,000 in 1985 and $3,176,000 in 1984)	50,107	48,190
Advance coal royalties	58,366	55,157
Other noncurrent assets	77,932	80,643
	515,897	613,227
Property, plant and equipment		
Cost		
Petroleum	1,773,309	1,711,457
Chemical	335,154	305,428
Coal	180,503	185,631
Engineering and construction	379,132	353,325
Exploration	582,194	469,581
Other	8,037	8,089
Corporate	61,269	64,641
	3,319,598	3,098,152
Accumulated depreciation, depletion and amortization	(1,503,594)	(1,351,410)
	1,816,004	1,746,742
	$3,927,633	$4,036,941

EXHIBIT 2   CONSOLIDATED BALANCE SHEETS (Continued)
(In Thousands)

September 30	1985	1984
Liabilities and stockholders' equity		
Current liabilities		
Debt due within one year (including short-term notes of $1,200,000 in 1985		
and $726,000 in 1984)	$ 30,455	$ 49,644
Trade and other payables—	1,314,278	1,423,721
Contract advances and progress billings in excess of costs incurred	34,577	52,566
Income taxes	47,774	89,639
	1,427.084	1,615,570
Noncurrent liabilities		
Long-term debt (less current portion)	510,467	544,846
Capitalized lease obligations (less current portion)	105,519	113,204
Other long-term liabilities and deferred credits	268,675	225,980
Deferred income taxes—	380,240	331,783
Minority interest in consolidated subsidiaries	57,223	56,288
	1,322,124	1,272,101
Redeemable preferred stock (1985 redemption value		
$260,305,000)—	249,014	303,371
Common stockholders' equity		
Common stock, par value $1.00 per share		
Authorized—60,000,000 shares		
Issued—28,672,000 shares in 1985 and 28,264,000 shares in 1984	28,672	28,264
Paid-in capital	229,135	217,979
Retained earnings	690,621	619,373
Deferred translation adjustments	(12,682)	(14,506)
Common shares in treasury—at cost (285,000 shares in 1985 and 252,000		
shares in 1984)	(6,335)	(5,211)
	929,411	845,899
Commitments and contingencies		
	$3,927,633	$4,036,941

Source: Ashland Oil, Inc. 1985 Annual Report.

EXHIBIT 3 STATEMENTS OF CHANGES IN CONSOLIDATED FINANCIAL POSITION
(In Thousands)

Years ended September 30	1985	1984	1983
Funds retained from operations			
Income (loss) before extraordinary gain	$146,722	$(172,478)	$ 96,637
Expense (income) not affecting funds			
Depreciation, depletion and amortization[1]	209,102	212,547	192,006
Deferred income taxes	53,961	49,894	24,084
Equity income—net of dividends	(4,961)	(16,785)	(21,032)
Divestitures and asset write-offs—			
net of current income taxes	25,952	291,915	—
Other—net	16,452	12,356	1,547
Funds provided from operations	447,228	377,449	293,242
Decrease (increase) in working capital[2]	(69,541)	(64,405)	(26,799)
Dividends	(74,142)	(76,165)	(94,449)
	303,545	236,879	171,994
Funds provided from (used for) financing			
Issuance of long-term debt and capitalized lease obligations	63,417	59,623	7,827
Issuance of common stock	11,672	9,820	34,593[3]
Repayment of long-term debt and capitalized lease obligations	(123,706)	(57,315)	(91,633)[3]
Purchase, conversion and exchange of capital stock	(56,813)	(36,386)	(9,543)
Increase (decrease) in short-term notes	474	(15,057)	130
	(104,956)	(39,315)	(58,620)
Funds provided from (used for) investment			
Additions to property, plant and equipment	(290,371)	(279,675)	(322,074)
Net assets of companies acquired			
Working capital (excluding cash and short-term securities)	—	(996)	(5,373)
Property, plant and equipment	—	(18,445)	(1,808)
Investments and other assets	—	(42,019)	(2,621)
Noncurrent liabilities	—	2,060	—
Proceeds from sale of operations			
(including working capital of $44,900,000 in 1985)	$7,715	13,923	—
Net book value of property, plant and equipment disposals	23,717	51,970	55,874
Other—net	21,630	41,374	47,408
	(157,309)	(231,808)	(228,594)
Increase (decrease) in cash and short-term securities	$ 41,280	$ (34,244)	$(115,222)
Changes in components of working capital[2]			
Decrease (increase) in current assets			
Accounts receivable	$ (18,010)	$ (13,680)	$ 78,689
Construction completed and in progress	(3,594)	(6,477)	2,644
Refundable income taxes	$3,837	(8,366)	(25,471)
Inventories	56,123	(5,133)	(22,619)
Deferred income tax benefits	(10,912)	(43,949)	(4,098)
Other current assets	(9,218)	(7,829)	(2,281)
Increase (decrease) in current liabilities			
Trade and other payables	(84,068)	(24,950)	(17,068)
Contract advances and progress billings	(17,814)	(19,308)	(16,915)
Income taxes	(15,885)	65,287	(19,680)
	$ (69,541)	$ (64,405)	$ (26,790)

[1]Includes amounts charged to other income statement captions.
[2]Excludes changes in cash, short-term securities and debt due within one year and changes resulting principally from working capital at dates of acquisition or deposition for companies acquired or operations sold.
[3]Includes $23,167,000 of common stock issued and long-term debt repaid in connection with the exchange of common stock for long-term debt which resulted in the extraordinary gain of $6,196,000.
Source: Ashland Oil, Inc. 1985 Annual Report.

EXHIBIT 4 SIX YEAR SELECTED FINANCIAL INFORMATION
(In Millions except per Share Data)

	1985	1984	1983	1982	1981	1980
Summary of operations						
Revenues						
Sales and operating revenues (including excise taxes)	$8,184	$8,544	$8,108	$9,110	$9,506	$8,366
Other	54	77	91	94	75	64
Costs and expenses						
Cost of sales and operating expenses	(6,745)	(7,215)	(6,960)	(7,837)	(8,453)	(7,278)
Excise taxes on products and merchandise	(293)	(291)	(256)	(245)	(244)	(247)
Selling, general and administrative expenses	(607)	(611)	(564)	(570)	(564)	(370)
Depreciation, depletion and amortization	(202)	(213)	(192)	(171)	(153)	(131)
Foreign exploration taxes	(39)	(39)	(31)	(52)	(38)	(40)
Operating income	352	252	196	329	129	364
Other income (expense)						
Interest income	20	20	32	57	100	80
Interest expense	(67)	(81)	(79)	(79)	(98)	(89)
Equity income	11	20	28	13	23	11
Other—net (including corporate administrative)	(57)	(67)	(73)	(108)[1]	(34)[2]	(50)
Divestitures and asset write-offs	(40)	(287)	—	28	—	9
Income (loss) before income taxes and extraordinary gain	219	(143)	104	240	120	325
Income taxes	72	29	7	59	30	120
Income (loss) before extraordinary gain	147	(172)	97	181	90	205
Extraordinary gain from exchange of common stock for long-term debt	—	—	6	—	—	—
Net income (loss) (3)	$ 147	$ (172)	$ 103	$ 181	$ 90	$ 205
Balance sheet information						
Working capital						
Current assets	$1,596	$1,677	$1,630	$1,766	$1,867	$1,862
Current liabilities	(1,427)	(1,616)	(1,551)	(1,614)	(1,662)	(1,355)
	$ 169	$ 61	$ 79	$ 152	$ 205	$ 507
Total assets	$3,928	$4,037	$4,133	$4,210	$4,122	$3,358
Capitalization						
Long-term debt (less current portion)	$ 510	$ 545	$ 528	$ 585	$ 583	$ 462
Capitalized lease obligations (less current portion)	106	113	147	175	187	167
Deferred income taxes	380	332	290	252	206	123
Minority interest in consolidated subsidiaries	57	56	55	56	39	—
Redeemable preferred stock	249	303	344	353	358	245
Common stockholders' equity	929	846	1,085	1,047	972	907
	$2,231	$2,195	$2,449	$2,468	$2,345	$1,904
Cash flow information						
Funds provided from operations	$ 447	$ 377	$ 293	$ 380	$ 248	$ 339
Funds used for						
Additions to property, plant and equipment	290	280	322	423	281	79
Dividends	74	76	94	99	94	264
Common stock information						
Earnings (loss) per share	$ 4.12	$ (7.40)	$ 2.46	$ 5.29	$ 2.22	$ 6.80
Dividends per share	1.60	1.60	2.20	2.40	2.40	2.20

[1]Includes a loss of $26,000,000 from the write-off of investments in and loans to a foreign company and $22,000,000 in employee retirement, termination and relocation costs.

[2]Includes a gain of $23,000,000 from prepayment of long-term debt.

[3]Divestitures and asset write-offs did not have a material effect on net income for 1985, but resulted in a net loss of $265,000,000 in 1984 and net income of $16,000,000 in 1982.

Source: Ashland Oil, Inc. 1984 and 1985 Annual Reports.

EXHIBIT 5 FIVE YEAR INFORMATION BY INDUSTRY SEGMENT
(In Millions)

Years ended September 30	1985	1984	1983	1982	1981
Sales and operating revenues					
Petroleum (including excise taxes)	$5,377	$5,678	$5,700	$6,485	$7,044
Chemical	1,499	1,501	1,208	1,197	1,330
Coal	196	197	150	177	175
Engineering and construction	1,217	1,292	1,152	1,330	1,144
Exploration	287	276	226	241	190
Other	1	1	4	41	85
Intersegment sales	(393)	(401)	(332)	(361)	(462)
	$8,184	$8,544	$8,108	$9,110	$9,506
Operating income (loss)					
Petroleum	$ 213	$ 120	$ 176	$ 220	$ (6)
Chemical	68	55	1	28	41
Coal	15	19	—	16	15
Engineering and construction	54	45	2	36	38
Exploration (net of foreign exploration taxes)	5	15	20	39	42
Other	(3)	(2)	(3)	(10)	(1)
	$ 353	$ 252	$ 196	$ 329	$ 129
Identifiable assets					
Petroleum	$1,782	$1,831	$1,885	$1,775	$1,571
Chemical	496	503	423	402	463
Coal	220	226	195	244	209
Engineering and construction	433	503	602	675	672
Exploration	414	364	264	210	129
Other	7	15	8	11	117
Corporate	576	595	756	893	961
	$3,928	$4,037	$4,133	$4,210	$4,122
Funds provided from operations					
Petroleum	$ 242	$ 201	$ 224	$ 233	$ 59
Chemical	63	53	18	44	52
Coal	27	30	12	27	30
Engineering and construction	58	63	34	46	63
Exploration	67	66	49	69	40
Other	1	4	—	5	(2)
Corporate	(11)	(40)	(44)	(44)	6
	$ 447	$ 377	$ 293	$ 380	$ 248
Additions to property, plant and equipment					
Petroleum	$ 86	$ 87	$ 186	$ 214	$ 118
Chemical	39	22	20	27	35
Coal	7	26	11	43	23
Engineering and construction	30	26	20	26	28
Exploration	120	116	74	92	35
Other	—	—	2	1	4
Corporate	8	3	9	20	38
	$ 290	$ 280	$ 322	$ 423	$ 281
Depreciation, depletion and amortization					
Petroleum	$ 93	92	$ 80	$ 72	$ 64
Chemical	24	23	21	19	16
Coal	11	12	14	17	16
Engineering and construction	27	36	40	38	36
Exploration	47	42	28	13	11
Other	—	—	1	4	4
Corporate	7	8	8	8	6
	$ 209	$ 213	$ 192	$ 171	$ 153

Source: Ashland Oil, Inc. 1985 Annual Report.

EXHIBIT 6   CRUDE OIL AND NATURAL GAS RESERVES

Years ended September 30	1985			1984			1983		
	U.S.	Nigeria	Total	U.S.	Nigeria	Total	U.S.	Nigeria	Total
Crude oil reserves (in millions of barrels)									
Proved developed and undeveloped reserves									
Beginning of year	5.5	49.2	54.7	5.7	19.7	25.4	6.2	11.5	17.7
Revisions of previous estimates	(.1)	2.8	2.7	(.1)	—	(.1)	—	—	—
Extensions and discoveries	.6	4.3	4.9	.8	36.5	37.3	.5	13.5	13.8
Production	(1.0)	(7.6)	(8.6)	(.9)	(7.0)	(7.9)	(1.0)	(5.1)	(6.1)
End of year	5.0	48.7	53.7	5.5	49.2	54.7	5.7	19.7	25.4
Proved developed reserves									
Beginning of year	5.2	34.5	39.7	5.2	19.7	24.9	5.8	11.5	17.3
End of year	4.9	45.5	50.4	5.2	34.5	39.7	5.2	19.7	24.9
Natural gas reserves (in billions of cubic feet)									
Proved developed and undeveloped reserves									
Beginning of year	213.9			206.2			208.5		
Revisions of previous estimates	(4.6)			(.2)			4.6		
Extensions and discoveries	18.7			18.7			2.8		
Production	(11.7)			(10.8)			(9.7)		
End of year	216.3			213.9			206.2		
Proved developed reserves									
Beginning of year	161.6			155.2			151.6		
End of year	166.6			161.6			155.2		

Source: Ashland Oil, Inc. 1985 Annual Report.

EXHIBIT 7   SELECTED OPERATING INFORMATION

Year ended September 30	1984	1983	1982	1981	1980
Net proved developed and undeveloped reserves[1]					
Crude oil (millions of barrels)					
United States	5.5	5.7	6.2	6.3	6.2
Nigeria	49.2	19.7	11.5	10.8	12.7
Natural gas (billions of cubic feet)[2]	213.9	206.2	208.5	216.9	213.3
Net production					
Crude oil (barrels per day)					
United States	2,508	2,677	2,725	2,815	3,141
Foreign					
Nigeria					
Onshore	11,858	14,066	12,079	7,505	6,876
Offshore	7,222	—	—	—	—
Sharjah	—	—	1,761	1,927	2,660
Natural gas (thousands of cubic feet per day)[2]	29,483	26,715	27,360	28,359	26,321
Average sales price					
Crude oil (per barrel)					
United States	$28.84	$29.59	$32.68	$35.04	$32.90
Foreign	29.95	31.74	35.44	37.61	33.70
Natural gas (per thousand cubic feet)[2]	3.59	3.26	2.74	2.26	1.82
Net producing wells					
Crude oil					
United States	1,531	1,516	1,475	1,451	1,487
Foreign	24	16	16	11	13
Natural gas[2]	1,015	902	899	949	896
Net oil and gas acreage (thousands of acres)					
Producing					
United States	514	501	501	495	489
Foreign	174	75	98	98	98
Undeveloped					
United States	337	288	277	269	277
Foreign	—	99	99	99	99
Drilling activities					
Net productive exploratory wells drilled					
United States	20	4	8	7	—
Foreign	3	—	—	—	3
Net dry exploratory wells drilled					
United States	24	18	6	3	1
Foreign	—	3	—	—	—
Net productive development wells drilled					
United States	51	31	60	26	29
Foreign	6	7	5	2	2
Net dry development wells drilled					
United States	8	6	5	1	8
Foreign	1	1	—	—	—

[1]United States crude oil and natural gas reserves are reported net of royalties and interests owned by others. Nigeria crude oil reserves relate to reserves available to Ashland, producer, under a long-term production sharing contract with the Nigerian National Petroleum Corporation.

[2]Amounts relate to U.S. operations. Ashland has no material natural gas reserves outside the United States.

Source: Ashland Oil, Inc. Financial & Operating Supplement 1984.

EXHIBIT 8   SALES, PRODUCTION, AND PROCESSING DATA

Year ended September 30	Crude oil processed (in barrels)		Refined products produced (in barrels)				
	Total for the period	Average per day	Gasoline, jet fuel, aromatics & naphthas	Kerosine & distillates	Heavy fuel oils	Asphalt	Other
1984	110,463,493	301,813	68,993,847	25,415,162	3,880,719	6,222,736	3,108,061
1983	104,035,875	285,029	65,221,538	23,434,424	4,381,274	5,887,099	3,248,995
1982	113,953,033	312,200	66,945,886	28,036,535	7,629,663	5,866,136	2,320,887
1981	117,346,974	321,499	69,708,758	23,780,197	10,705,817	6,647,059	1,497,295
1980	133,014,201	363,427	76,205,915	27,133,078	12,851,355	9,243,840	3,805,802
1979	134,225,778	367,742	71,039,800	31,920,124	11,785,281	10,783,068	4,988,164
1978	128,827,589	352,952	71,898,241	29,153,321	11,839,621	9,829,217	3,763,301
1977	130,752,556	358,226	70,983,767	31,155,164	12,952,142	8,232,363	5,213,858
1976	127,425,451	348,157	69,181,740	31,027,020	12,172,167	7,746,326	5,895,269

Year ended September 30	Sales (in barrels)				
	Gasoline, jet fuel, aromatics & naphthas	Kerosine & distillates	Heavy fuel oils	Asphalt	Other
1984	79,942,401	29,492,890	13,386,085	7,335,784	7,409,397
1983	73,732,045	25,745,913	22,369,293	6,224,221	7,192,872
1982	75,601,370	29,894,597	28,791,680	7,009,221	6,768,048
1981	76,506,260	27,681,764	40,718,069	7,130,262	7,921,595
1980	82,832,857	29,714,190	52,830,738	9,851,572	6,946,309
1979	85,170,381	34,787,595	53,264,429	11,238,881	9,184,310
1978	82,729,048	35,199,381	48,496,000	10,654,214	8,634,643
1977	82,647,976	35,762,119	52,846,571	9,376,714	8,034,905
1976	80,962,190	34,337,810	47,721,071	8,902,286	8,238,500

Source: Ashland Oil, Inc. 1984 10-K.

EXHIBIT 9   DEBENTURE INFORMATION

Debenture		Trustee	Rating	
			Moody's	Standard & Poor's
4.725%	Sinking fund debentures, due 1988	Chemical Bank	A3	BBB +
4.875%	Sinking fund debentures, due 1987	Citibank, N.A.	A3	BBB +
6.15%	Sinking fund debentures, due 1992	Citibank, N.A.	A3	BBB +
8.00%	Guaranteed debentures, due 1987	Citibank, N.A.	—	—
8.20%	Sinking fund debentures, due 2002	Citibank, N.A.	A3	BBB +
8.80%	Sinking fund debentures, due 2000	Citibank, N.A.	A3	BBB +
4.75%	Convertible subordinated debentures due 1993	The Chase Manhattan Bank, N.A.	Baa1	BBB
11.10%	Subordinated debentures due 2004	The Chase Manhattan Bank, N.A.	Baa1	BBB

Source: Ashland Oil, Inc. Financial & Operating Supplement 1984.

BALDOR ELECTRIC COMPANY

Peter M. Ginter
Andrew C. Rucks
Linda E. Swayne
University of Alabama, Birmingham
University of North Carolina, Charlotte

In September, 1984, Gregory C. Kowert, Baldor's Vice-President for Strategic Planning, was reflecting on Baldor's distinctive position in the electric motor market. He listed the following comparative advantages achieved by Baldor:

• *Concentration on industrial electric motors.* By manufacturing only electric motors for industrial markets, Baldor has been able to focus its resources on a highly specialized market.

• *Energy-efficient motors.* Through the years, the Company has followed the strategy of providing better products at competitive prices. For Baldor, this has translated into better materials and superior engineering directed at durability and energy efficiency.

The research and written case information were presented at a Case Research Symposium and were evaluated by the Case Research Association's Editorial Board. This case was prepared by Dr. Peter M. Ginter and Dr. Andrew C. Rucks of the University of Alabama in Birmingham and Dr. Linda E. Swayne of the University of North Carolina at Charlotte as a basis for class discussion.

• *Availability.* Baldor attempts to sell as many items as possible as stock products and carries heavy inventories of these items positioned close to customers in 28 warehouses around the country. This inventory policy is unique in the industry.

• *Independent representative sales organization.* The Company sells all of its products through independent representatives. Many representatives derive most of their income from Baldor, and thus the selling task is accomplished by a group of semiautonomous entrepreneurs compensated by direct incentives.

• *Backward integration.* Baldor manufactures more of its component parts than the competition does.

• *Most committed to the industry.* Baldor has the largest percentage of its sales in electric motors. Many of the competitors are divisions of larger companies, and most compete with other divisions for allocations of resources.

Kowert felt that past strategies, particularly the emphasis on energy efficiency, had brought rapid growth to the Company. Baldor appeared to be making the transition from a small to a medium-sized company. However, the slight sales decline in 1982 was causing Kowert and the entire marketing team to closely monitor the 1983 plan and to carefully prepare the Company's 1984 plan.

BALDOR ELECTRIC COMPANY PROFILE

Edwin C. Ballman founded Baldor Electric Company in St. Louis, Missouri, in 1920. The Company opened a plant in Ft. Smith, Arkansas, in 1957, and subsequently moved the corporate headquarters to Ft. Smith. Today there are plants in six states, which employ over 2,200 people.

From the very beginning, Baldor's emphasis was on motors that deliver maximum output while consuming a minimum of energy. Kowert thought that the energy crisis in the early 1970s increased the awareness of energy efficiency, which led to rapid growth for the Company.

Baldor has been the fastest growing company in the electric motor industry. During the period between 1971 and 1981, Baldor's growth rate was approximately 22% annually, almost 80% faster than the industry as a whole. As illustrated in Figure 1, Baldor's market share increased about 15% during the 1975 recession, increased by 20% during the 1982 business contraction, and doubled in the period between 1973 and 1982.

Product Line

In 1982, Baldor Electric Company vigorously expanded its new-product development program. The program greatly increased the depth and breadth of the Company's product line. With the exception of 1976, more new motors were added to Baldor's product line in 1982 than during any previous period. All Baldor's motors are manufactured in accordance with industry standards supplied by NEMA (National Electrical Manufacturers Association).

Baldor reacted to the increased popularity of permanent-magnet direct-current motors used in a broad variety of adjustable-speed applications by expanding the line to a total of 15 stock models. In addition, Baldor supplies a broad variety of direct-current shunt wound motors, which also are used in SCR control (adjustable speed and torque) applications. Baldor's line of SCR control motors includes models ranging from 1/50 HP to 15 HP and is among the broadest in the motor industry. Exhibit 1 identifies the major product lines produced by the Company.

During 1983, Baldor introduced a new super-efficient line called the Baldor SUPER-E. As shown in Figure 2, the efficiency of the new SUPER-E line is considerably higher than that of "average premium motors." Despite its higher efficiency, the new line is priced competitively with other manufacturers' super-efficient models.

The introduction of the SUPER-E motors places Baldor in a unique competitive position. Baldor is the only motor manufacturer capable of offering a choice between competitively priced standard motors or competitively priced premium motors—both higher in efficiency than other manufacturers' comparable lines.

Promotion

Advertising and trade promotion traditionally have been important elements in Baldor's marketing mix, serving as direct lines of communication to an extremely broad and growing audience of customer and sales prospects. In ad-

FIGURE 1 **Baldor's market share (1973–1982).**

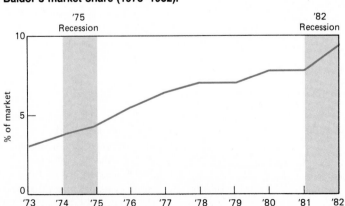

EXHIBIT 1   BALDOR'S PRODUCT LINES

• *Explosion-proof motors* The Company supplies explosion-proof motors ranging to 100 HP, including models with all the performance characteristics required for service on offshore drill rigs.

• *Agribusiness* Baldor's line of agri-duty motors traditionally has been considered one of the industry's broadest and most diversified. In order to further strengthen its position in this market, Baldor added a series of specialized models, such as centrifugal fan motors, confinement house motors, vacuum pump motors, aeration fan motors, and grain stirring motors.

• *Small motors* Baldor had been active in the development of "small" motors as well. The Baldor/Boehm line includes more than 70 different models in the subfractional horsepower range, and has a newly designed

mounting allowing for greater versatility. In addition, the Baldor/Boehm line includes permanent split capacitor AC motors in 18 different ratings and an expanded selection of permanent magnet motors.

• *Heavy-duty motors* The Company also markets a variety of heavy-duty cast-iron motors ranging in size from 1½ HP through 15 HP in their 300 and corrosion-protected lines.

• *SUPER-E series* The SUPER-E line (super-efficient) is designed primarily for applications where energy consumption is unusually high and motors are operated continuously for extended periods.

• *Additional lines* Other product lines include close-coupled pump motors and motors specifically designed for use with six-step and pulsewidth-modulated inverters.

dition, these efforts directly support the selling activities of Baldor representatives and distributors.

Advertising objectives are to develop brand recognition and brand preference. The investment in advertising and promotion during 1982 was over 20% higher than in 1981. The reasons for the increase were the introduction

of many new products and continued penetration of new markets. Much of the 1983 advertising has been directed toward promotion of the new SUPER-E motors. The efficiency savings is prominent in Baldor's advertising to the trade.

FIGURE 2   **Efficiency comparison: Baldor SUPER-E vs. "Average Premium" Motors.**

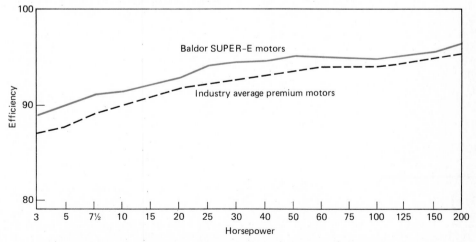

*Efficiencies of "Average Premium" Motors were determined by averaging the efficiencies of 10 leading competitive motors as reported in manufacturers' published data (includes 4-pole motors only).

Channels of Distribution

Baldor's products are marketed through a well-established network of distributors, as well as direct to OEM's. Figure 3 depicts these channels.

Motors and grinders flow through 34 district offices in the United States and Canada. Factory stocks of more than 1,800 different types of motors and grinders are maintained at 28 geographical points (Exhibit 2). Baldor maintains a sophisticated computer-based communication system, which links sales offices, plants, and corporate headquarters. The system makes it possible for the sales team to quickly determine the product status of motors and locate products needed to correct a temporary out-of-stock condition.

The industrial distributor is becoming more important in the motor industry. Better design, increased applications, higher speeds, and greater reliability have broadened the use of electric motors to various new industries. Distributors have greater familiarity with these new markets than Baldor's salesforce does.

Financial Position

While sales declined 6.3% in 1982 from 1981, the Company has maintained a strong financial position and liquidity. Exhibit 3 shows Baldor's consolidated earnings for the years 1980 through 1982 and Exhibit 4 presents Baldor's consolidated balance sheet.

Baldor's dollar and unit sales declined in 1982 for the first time in 22 years. However, during this period Baldor continued to gain market share. The cost of doing business increased in 1982 due to the rise in manufacturing expenses and a lower volume of sales. The increase in manufacturing expense results from increases in compensation, other manufacturing expenses including depreciation expense on new machinery acquired to improve quality and productivity, and engineering expenses due to the Company's commitment to research and development. Cost of goods sold, as a percentage of sales was lower for 1981 than for 1980, due primarily to lower raw material costs.

The Company has maintained a conservative capital position. Long-term obligations were 15% of total capitalization at December 31, 1982 (stockholders' equity plus long-term obligations) compared to 18% at December 31, 1981. Four and a half million dollars of industrial revenue bond financing was received in 1981. No new long-term financing was sought in 1982. Exhibit 5 presents a ten-year summary of important financial data for Baldor Electric Company. Exhibit 6 shows the changes in Baldor's

FIGURE 3   **Baldor's channels of distribution.**

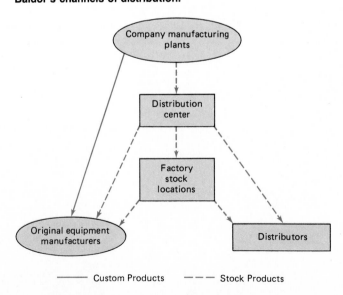

EXHIBIT 2   LOCATIONS OF BALDOR'S PLANTS, DISTRICT OFFICES, AND WAREHOUSES
(United States and Canada)

City	Plant	District office	Warehouse
Atlanta, Ga.		✓	✓
Auburn, N.Y.		✓	✓
Baltimore, Md.		✓	✓
Bethel, Conn.	✓		
Birmingham, Ala.			✓
Buffalo, N.Y.		✓	
Charleston, S.C.	✓		
Chicago, Ill.		✓	✓
Cincinnati, Ohio		✓	✓
Cleveland, Ohio		✓	✓
Columbus, Miss.	✓		
Dallas, Tex.		✓	✓
Denver, Colo.		✓	✓
Des Moines, Iowa		✓	✓
Detroit, Mich.		✓	✓
Edmonton, Alta.		✓	✓
Fort Smith, Ark.	✓	✓	✓
Grand Rapids, Mich.			✓
Greensboro, N.C.		✓	✓
Houston, Tex.		✓	✓
Indianapolis, Ind.		✓	✓
Kansas City, Mo.		✓	✓
Los Angeles, Calif.		✓	✓
Louisville, Ky.		✓	
Memphis, Tenn.		✓	✓
Midland-Odessa, Tex.		✓	✓
Milwaukee, Wis.		✓	✓
Minneapolis, Minn.		✓	✓
Montreal, Que.		✓	✓
New Milford, N.J.	✓		
New Orleans, La.		✓	✓
New York, N.Y.		✓	
Oakland, Calif.		✓	✓
Philadelphia, Pa.		✓	✓
Portland, Ore.		✓	✓
St. Louis, Mo.	✓	✓	✓
Salt Lake City, Utah		✓	✓
Tampa, Fla.		✓	✓
Vancouver, B.C.		✓	✓
Wallingford, Conn.		✓	✓
Westville, Okla.	✓		
Winnipeg, Man.		✓	✓

EXHIBIT 3   CONSOLIDATED EARNINGS OF BALDOR ELECTRIC COMPANY (1980–1982)
(In Thousands except Share Data)

	Year ended December 31		
	1982	1981	1980
Net sales	$ 150,031	$ 160,162	$ 146,454
Other income—net	1,405	1,546	270
	151,436	161,708	146,724
Costs and expenses			
Cost of goods sold	108,373	110,556	102,286
Selling and administrative	25,201	25,382	23,812
Profit sharing	2,067	3,024	2,399
Interest	927	843	868
	136,568	139,805	129,365
Earnings before income taxes	14,868	21,903	17,359
Income taxes	6,350	10,170	7,950
Net earnings	$ 8,518	$ 11,733	$ 9,409
Earnings per common share	$1.33	$1.84	$1.50
Weighted average common shares outstanding	6,426,256	6,376,052	6,284,229

financial position from 1980 through 1982, and Exhibit 7 provides a statement of stockholders' equity.

Penetration of International Markets

During 1982, Baldor completely changed its method of marketing to foreign countries. For many years at Baldor, international sales were handled by an export management company. Recently, Baldor brought this function ''in house.'' Each international market is studied individually, rather than collectively as in the past, to determine the best method of distribution. As a result, Baldor established representatives in many targeted countries and is seeking representation in others. Representatives recently have been established in such markets as Latin America, Australia, the United Kingdom, West Germany, the Middle East, and Singapore.

Baldor has also increased its product capability in the international markets by introducing motors with standards interchangeable with those outside the United States. In addition, Baldor is increasing international advertising and participation in foreign trade shows.

CURRENT SITUATION

The Company has been extremely successful in differentiating its products from those of competitors by offering energy-efficient motors at competitive prices. However, sales were down 8.2% in 1982, and Greg Kowert knew he had to make a recommendation to increase sales.

Several options were easy to identify. The electric motor market continued to offer opportunities since there were many small companies that had not been able to completely serve the market. New products could be developed to meet the needs of new markets, which have been projected to grow rapidly, and international markets presented good opportunities. The lines between motors, controls, and the devices they control have blurred; thus, Baldor could diversify into related areas of computers and/or robots.

Greg Kowert wondered which one or combination of opportunities he should recommend to continue the growth of Baldor. He supposed he should start with a thorough situation analysis of the electric motor industry.

INDUSTRY NOTE

Electric Motors

The U.S. electric motor industry can be divided into two primary segments: industrial motors and consumer, or appliance, motors. A few of the big manufacturers, like General Electric and Westinghouse, supply both markets;

EXHIBIT 4 CONSOLIDATED BALANCE SHEET FOR BALDOR ELECTRIC COMPANY (1982)
(In Thousands)

	December 31	
	1982	1981
Assets		
Current assets		
Cash and temporary investments	$ 17,252	$ 15,322
Receivables less allowances of $560,000 in 1982 and		
$490,000 in 1981	24,598	25,945
Inventories		
Finished products	20,901	17,758
Work in progress	8,762	10,731
Raw material	17,212	18,950
	46,875	47,439
LIFO valuation adjustment (deduction)	(16,712)	(16,406)
	30,163	31,033
Deferred income taxes		1,550
Other current assets	1,107	1,414
Total current assets	73,120	75,264
Other assets	2,663	2,767
Property, plant and equipment		
Land and improvements	1,316	1,289
Buildings and improvements	10,073	9,425
Machinery and equipment	34,889	26,624
Allowances for depreciation and amortization (deduction)	(15,996)	(13,093)
	30,282	24,245
	$106,065	$102,276
Liabilities and stockholders' equity		
Current liabilities		
Accounts payable	$ 8,043	$ 10,021
Employee compensation	2,035	2,388
Profit sharing	2,041	3,022
Anticipated warranty costs	2,950	2,850
Other accrued expenses	1,978	1,603
Income taxes	1,436	1,958
Current portion of long-term obligations	998	1,205
Total current liabilities	19,481	23,047
Long-term obligations	12,610	13,497
Deferred income taxes	3,130	2,262
Stockholders' equity		
Preferred stock, $.10 par value		
Authorized share: 5,000,000		
Issued and outstanding shares: none		
Common stock, $.10 par value		
Authorized shares: 25,000,000		
Issued and outstanding shares:		
1982—6,427,570: 1981—6,378,645 (less shares held in		
treasury: 1982—90,535: 1981—123,665)	643	638
Additional capital	11,243	10,340
Retained earnings	58,958	52,492
	70,844	63,470
	$106,065	$102,276

EXHIBIT 5   TEN-YEAR SUMMARY OF SELECTED FINANCIAL DATA FOR BALDOR ELECTRIC COMPANY
(In Thousands except Percentages and per Share Data)

	Net sales	Cost of goods sold	Net earnings	Per share data		Percent return on average equity	Stockholders' equity	Total assets	Long-term obligations	Working capital
				Net earnings	Dividends					
1982	$150,031	$108,373	$ 8,518	$1.33	$ .320	13%	$70,844	$106,065	$12,610	$53,639
1981	160,162	110,556	11,733	1.84	.290	20	63,470	102,276	13,497	52,217
1980	146,454	102,286	9,409	1.50	.240	20	52,448	81,973	10,318	43,733
1979	140,018	98,304	9,331	1.50	.193	24	42,985	74,112	11,210	36,310
1978	120,105	81,251	8,642	1.40	.140	29	33,929	60,466	7,427	28,462
1977	94,277	66,149	5,741	.95	.093	25	25,582	48,466	6,106	20,983
1976	70,832	49,405	4,043	.69	.070	24	20,258	36,348	4,458	17,769
1975	56,081	41,095	2,418	.50	.050	21	12,951	27,628	4,688	11,854
1974	51,123	39,651	1,285*	.26*	.033	13	10,632	25,214	5,041	9,826
1973	41,736	30,649	1,800	.37	.033	21	9,488	19,670	2,910	7,702
Compound annual growth rate (from 1972 base)										
10 Yr.	17%	22%		18%	27%					

*After decrease of $891,000 ($.19 per share) in 1974 resulting from 1974 change to last in, first out and full absorption method of inventory valuation.

480

EXHIBIT 6   CHANGES IN BALDOR ELECTRIC COMPANY'S FINANCIAL POSITION (1980–1982) (In Thousands)

	Year ended December 31		
	1982	1981	1980
Funds provided			
Net earnings	$ 8,518	$11,733	$ 9,409
Expenses not requiring outlay of working capital:			
Depreciation and amortization	4,113	3,410	2,732
Deferred income taxes	868	436	767
From operations	13,499	15,579	12,908
Issuance of treasury stock to employee profit-sharing plan	642	559	1,233
Additions to long-term obligations (less $1,500,000 unexpected proceeds included in other assets)		3,000	
Utilization of unexpended debt proceeds	377		1,733
Stock option plans	266	572	319
Total funds provided	14,784	19,710	16,193
Funds used			
Dividends	2,052	1,843	1,498
Additions to property, plant and equipment (including assets acquired in purchase of Nupar Manufacturing Company of $3,399,000 in 1981)	10,139	7,771	6,504
Reduction of long-term obligations	887	1,321	891
Other	284	291	(123)
Total funds used	13,362	11,226	8,770
Increase in working capital	1,422	8,484	7,423
Working capital at beginning of period	52,217	43,733	36,310
Working capital at end of period	$53,639	$52,217	$43,733
Changes in components of working capital			
Increase (decrease) in current assets:			
Cash	$ 1,930	$ 9,513	$ 4,045
Receivables	(1,347)	1,103	1,006
Inventories	(870)	2,776	676
Deferred income taxes	(1,550)	269	263
Other current assets	(307)	489	(45)
Increase (decrease) in current assets	(2,144)	14,150	5,945
Increase (decrease) in current liabilities:			
Accounts payable	(1,978)	3,563	(1,381)
Accrued employee compensation and other liabilities	(859)	1,572	(1,114)
Income taxes	(522)	241	867
Current portion of long-term obligations	(207)	290	150
Increase (decrease) in current liabilities	(3,566)	5,666	(1,478)
Increase in working capital	$ 1,422	$ 8,484	$ 7,423

EXHIBIT 7   STATEMENT OF BALDOR ELECTRIC'S STOCKHOLDERS' EQUITY (In Thousands)

	Common stock		Additional capital	Retained earnings	Total
	Shares	Amount			
Balance at January 1, 1980	6,167	$617	$ 7,678	$34,691	$42,986
Employee profit sharing plan	71	7	1,226		1,233
Stock option plans	47	5	314		319
Net earnings				9,409	9,409
Common stock dividends—$.24 per share				(1,498)	(1,498)
Balance at December 31, 1980	6,285	629	9,218	42,602	52,449
Employee profit sharing plan	31	3	556		559
Stock option plans	63	6	566		572
Net earnings				11,733	11,733
Common stock dividends—$.29 per share				(1,843)	(1,843)
Balance at December 31, 1981	6,379	638	10,340	52,492	63,470
Employee profit sharing plan	33	3	639		642
Stock option plans	16	2	264		266
Net earnings				8,518	8,518
Common stock dividends—$.32 per share				(2,052)	(2,052)
Balance at December 31, 1982	6,428	$643	$11,243	$58,958	$70,844

some producers, like Baldor, make only industrial motors; still others specialize in consumer motors.

The industrial/consumer distinction is ordinarily used to identify the difference between motors made in extremely high volume (usually fractional HP consumer market motors) and those usually manufactured in lower volume (higher HP motors designed for special and heavy usage). Generally, consumer motors are made with less durable, lower quality parts, while industrial motors are manufactured for greater durability and more rugged conditions.

Key Competitors

There are approximately 340 companies in the United States involved in the production of motors and generators. In 1981, the top three companies in the industry accounted for over 50% of the industry's sales, and the top eleven companies accounted for approximately 80% of the industry's sales. Exhibit 8 illustrates electric motor sales comparisons for the top eleven companies.

The electric motor industry is a growing industry with strong competitors including many of the best managed companies in America. To a great degree, the relative strengths of competitors help maintain high-quality products. One measure of this quality has been the industry's

ability to export four times as many motors as are currently imported. The financial position and operating results of most of the top companies in the industry are very strong (Exhibit 9).

• **General Electric** General Electric (GE) is the industry leader and the only company manufacturing a full line of electric motors. The company is also the single largest exporter of motors and generators, although its motor sales account for less than 10% of its production. General Electric is respected in the industry as a very well-managed company producing quality products.

• **Emerson Electric** Emerson Electric is second in terms of motor sales and has maintained a rapid growth rate over the last five years. Emerson's sales consist of approximately two-thirds consumer motors distributed through Emerson Motor division and one-third industrial motors sold through U.S. Electrical Motors.

• **Westinghouse** Westinghouse, third in sales among the motor manufacturers, has a broad line of electric motors. However, its growth rate has been below the average of other leaders in the industry. The lack of growth is probably due to a number of other concerns that have diverted management attention from motor sales in the last few years.

• **Reliance Electric** Reliance, a subsidiary of Exxon since 1979, has had problems with some new products.

EXHIBIT 8   ESTIMATED ELECTRIC MOTOR SALES FOR THE INDUSTRY'S LEADING FIRMS
(Dollars in Millions)

Company	1969 Sales (motors only)	Rank	1981 Sales (motors only)	Rank	1976–1981 Cagr Total	Cagr Motors	Percentage of total sales
General Electric	519	1	1200	1	11.7	8.7	4
Emerson (including USEM)	285	3	700	2	17.9	15.8	20
Westinghouse	353	2	450	3	8.8	8.4	5
Exxon (Reliance)	122	4	290	4	N/A	15.0	N/A
W. W. Grainger	75	5	265	5	16.8	13.6	25
Baldor Electric	18	11	151	6	17.6	18.0	94
Franklin Electric	30	9	150	7	11.1	10.8	94
Siemens-Allis (A-C)	70	6	125	8	6.1	10.8	N/A
Gould (Century)	60	7	120	9	8.5	5.9	7
Litton Industries (L/A)	40	8	100	10	N/A	N/A	N/A
Marathon Electric	25	10	80	11	N/A	N/A	N/A

Source: Baldor Electric Company

However, the company has maintained a good reputation regarding the quality of its electric motors, and continues to be a well-respected manufacturer of industrial motors and a tough competitor in the industry.

• **W. W. Grainger** Grainger's expertise has been as a distributor of products to industry through its stores, its catalog ("the Blue Book"), and direct sales to original equipment manufacturers (OEM's). Motors represent about 25% of Grainger's sales.

• **Baldor Electric Company** Baldor focuses on en-ergy-efficient industrial electric motors and sells to distributors and OEM's. Since 94% of its sales are electric motors, Baldor is committed to the electric motor industry.

Electric Motors

Rather than being used for one purpose by a single market, electric motors are used in many types of machinery

EXHIBIT 9   1981 OPERATING RESULTS FOR SELECTED ELECTRIC MOTOR FIRMS
(Dollars in Millions)

	Total assets	Total net worth	Current ratio	Long-term debt to total capital	Net earnings to total sales	Return on average total assets	Return on average equity
General Electric	$20,942	$ 9,128	1.2	.104	.061	.083	.190
Emerson	2,201	1,386	2.4	.106	.080	.130	.210
Westinghouse	8,316	2,837	1.0	.180	.047	.058	.163
Exxon	62,931	28,517	1.3	.153	.049	.093	.206
W. W. Grainger	472	335	2.2	.041	.065	.119	.180
Franklin Electric	98	53	2.3	.263	.041	.074	.141
Baldor Electric	103	63	3.3	.175	.073	.127	.202
Siemens-Allis (A-C)	1,594	656	1.5	.305	—	—	—
Gould (Century)	1,597	810	2.3	.299	.052	.061	.119

Source: Annual reports of companies listed.

and equipment by both consumers and industrial users throughout the world.

The electric motor markets can be segmented into five major product categories:

• Fractional horsepower motors (motors under 1 horsepower)
• Integral horsepower motors and generators
• Prime mover sets (internal combustion engine/generator combinations)
• Motor generator sets (electric motor/generator combinations)
• Other equipment (servos, synchros, resolvers, parts, and accessories)

The electric motor is a rotating machine used for the conversion of electrical energy to mechanical power. Motors can meet a variety of service requirements such as running, starting, holding or stopping a load.

Electric motors are the sole method of converting electrical energy to mechanical power. No matter what the source of energy—coal, oil, gas, or nuclear—an electric motor is utilized for conversion of the electrical energy to mechanical power. Advantages of electrical power are ease of transportation over great distances and ease of control compared to other forms of energy. Currently, 30% of all energy is converted to electrical power, and 64% of that generated electricity is used to power motor-driven equipment.

The basic science used in the operation of the electric motor has remained the same since its invention early in the nineteenth century. There have, however, been substantial refinements in manufacturing processes and size of the components. Figure 4 summarizes the different types of AC powered and DC powered motors.

Induction motors account for approximately 90% of the sales in the fractional and integral horsepower ratings. This type of motor is the simplest and most rugged. The stator "induces" an electric current in the rotor (which has no wiring) resulting in a motor that is less expensive and less subject to failure than other types of motors. The major variations for induction motors relate to the construction of the rotor (squirrel cage or wound rotor) and the operating current (single-phase or poly-phase). Most industrial systems use 3-phase AC current, and most consumer applications use single phase. However, the motor can be designed to run on either single-phase or poly-phase current.

Squirrel cage rotors utilize a laminated steel core fitted with slots into which conductors are placed as the rotor.

Wound rotor units employ a copper winding in the rotor assembly. Wound rotor units are more expensive and usually limited to variable-speed applications (electronic control devices).

• **Synchronous motors** are used in applications where constant operating speed is required—the AC motor operates in perfect synchronization with the frequency of the line current. They can be constructed to run on single-phase or polyphase current. Integral horsepower synchronous motors are constructed with a rotor, which must be supplied with DC current from an external source.

• **Commutator motors** produce rotary motion through the interaction of two stationary electromagnetic fields. The commutator functions as a rotating switch, which reverses the direction of current flow to the armature coil (or rotor) every half revolution of the motor. Commutator motors can be run on either AC or DC current, although most are of the DC type.

• **DC motors** have quick signal response, can be easily operated at different speeds, and can be given precise speed-torque relationships. Applications using DC motors include those that have precise control characteristics—instrumentation, material handling and automation equipment, computer output devices, and word-processing equipment.

Electric Motor Market Growth

Electric motors are fundamental to a modern industrialized society. The 1980s appear to hold many changes for the United States as well as for all world economies. Specifically, there will be increased emphasis on factory automation, electronics, and conservation of resources, which suggests greater demand for efficient electric motors. Thus, it appears that the pace of change in the electric motor industry will accelerate.

Sales of motors and generators increased from 107 million units in 1963 to over 300 million in 1978—an annual growth rate of over 7%. This growth exceeded the less than 5% growth in U. S. production of motors because of expanding mechanization and use of motorized equipment in all sectors of the economy. While the prices of electric motors declined during this period due to improved designs, materials, and manufacturing processes, price increases have been rapid since the mid 1970s primarily because of higher rates of inflation. Growth patterns for electric motors by motor type and by selected industries are summarized in Exhibits 10 and 11.

Projected growth by motor type indicates that projected real growth is largest for integral horsepower mo-

FIGURE 4 **Summary of motor types.**
(Motors and Generators: Predicasts Industry Study No. 272, Cleveland, Ohio: Predicasts, 1982.)

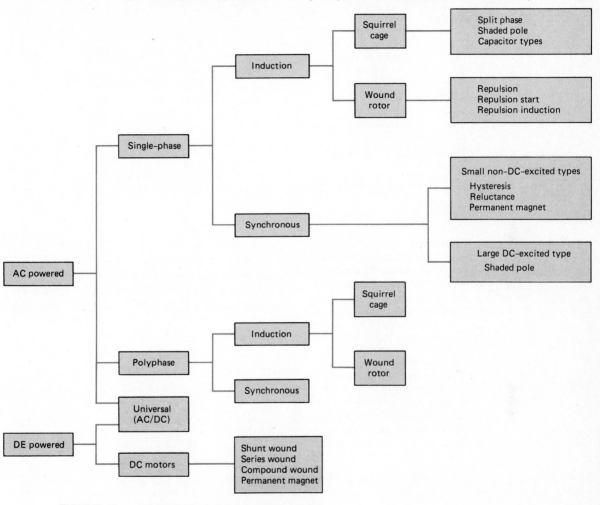

EXHIBIT 10   MARKET GROWTH BY MOTOR TYPE

	Average annual growth (as a percentage)		
	1970–1975	1975–1980	1970–1980
Fractional horsepower motors	5.7	16.1	10.8
Integral horsepower motors, excluding land transportation	11.5	9.6	10.5
Land transportation motors	12.1	10.3	11.2
Prime mover generator sets, except steam or hydraulic turbine	16.3	12.2	14.2
Motor generator sets and other rotating equipment	−0.4	12.5	5.9

Source: Business Trend Analysts.

EXHIBIT 11 GROWTH IN THE PURCHASES OF MOTORS BY SELECTED INDUSTRIES
(Dollars in Millions)

Industry	1972	1977*
Refrigeration and heating equipment	$344.5	$593.9
Household laundry equipment	94.1	141.8
Household refrigerators and freezers	76.8	98.7
Construction machinery	29.2	88.5
Electric housewares and fans	40.8	58.6
Electric computing equipment	34.1	55.2
Motor vehicle parts and accessories	9.0	41.3
Blowers and fans	23.4	37.9
Special industry machinery, NEC	25.1	37.4
Mining machinery	12.4	35.4
Machine tools, metal-cutting types	20.6	33.3
Household appliances, NEC	20.5	31.0
Household vacuum cleaners	7.6	28.3
Office machinery and typewriters, NEC	6.0	28.2
Shipbuilding and repair	9.8	26.0
General industrial machinery, NEC	12.5	23.5
Conveyors and conveying equipment	9.2	22.1
Industrial trucks and tractors	10.6	19.3
Printing trades machinery	8.0	16.5
Woodworking machinery	8.6	16.1
Household cooking equipment	6.5	15.9
Machine tools, metal-forming types	7.1	15.3
Measuring and controlling devices, NEC	2.2	14.6
Hoists, cranes, and monorails	8.4	13.6
Lawn and garden equipment	1.6	12.2
Elevators and moving stairways	11.7	12.0
Radio and TV sets	13.0	11.7
Power-driven hand tools	10.3	11.6
Engineering and scientific instruments	5.1	11.0
Food products machinery	11.2	10.6
Metal working machinery, NEC	4.0	10.1

*Preliminary figures.
Source: Business Trend Analysts, Census of Manufacturers.

tors (approximately 10% annual growth), while growth for fractional horsepower is projected to be flat and other motor type segments are expected to have moderate growth (Exhibit 12).

Exhibit 12 may underestimate the growth rate for servo motors and other motors used in factory automation. Currently small markets, these segments are expected to grow to approximately $200–$400 million in the 1980s.

Demand for electric motors is projected to increase across all categories. Relative growth for selected electric motor markets is illustrated in Exhibit 13.

Industry Dynamics

The electric motor industry is capital-intensive with substantial investments required in facilities, machinery, and tooling. The required high investments create formidable entry barriers. In addition, the industry is of a technical nature, requiring complex engineering skills. As a result, only one new company has entered the top eleven companies in the industry over the last 15 years. (This company was founded by a past owner of another one of the top companies.) Finally, the sunk costs of electric motor

EXHIBIT 12   PROJECTED GROWTH IN MOTOR SALES BY MOTOR TYPE (1980–1990)*

Fractional horsepower motors	9.9%
Integral horsepower motors, excluding land transportation	19.3
Land transportation motors	17.2
Prime mover generator sets, except steam or hydraulic turbine	15.0
Motor generator sets and other rotating equipment	7.8

*Includes estimated 10% annual inflation.
Source: Business Trend Analysts.

production also make it difficult for a company to exit the market.

Major factors currently affecting the electric motor industry include rising energy costs, electric vehicles, factory automation, and technological evolution.

Rising energy costs have resulted in an increased emphasis by customers on product quality and energy efficiency. Energy cost increases are projected by the federal government to continue for the foreseeable future. Many manufacturers are offering higher efficiency electric motors at premium prices to meet this demand. It is estimated that energy-efficient motors now account for 11% of the 5–20 HP market, compared to 1% in 1977.

The difference of a few percentage points in energy efficiency can result in a complete payback of the motor's purchase cost within the first year for larger horsepower units. Exhibit 14 illustrates the possible savings using an energy-efficient 50-HP motor rather than an average standard motor for different hours of operation. Because of such cost savings, many users are considering replacing their less efficient motors with new, energy-efficient electric motors.

EXHIBIT 13   RELATIVE GROWTH FOR SELECTED ELECTRIC MOTOR MARKETS

Item	1978	1985	1990
Mfg. production index	147	193	230
mil motrs/index pt	1.82	1.99	2.12
Motor, generator sales (mil)	267.2	383.5	488.0
Fabricated metals	4.5	5.8	6.6
Machinery and equipment	34.5	40.5	45.9
Electrical and electronics	42.0	62.7	73.3
Transport equipment	34.4	40.7	46.2
Instruments	5.6	8.1	10.1
Toys, games, other mfg.	43.3	64.0	76.4
Interplant transfers	102.8	161.7	229.5
$/unit	16.5	26.5	42.6
Motor, generator sales (mil$)	4,403.9	10,170	20,780
Fabricated metals	101.9	203	290
Machinery and equipment	1,823.1	3,864	5,856
Electrical and electronics	620.5	1,427	2,250
Transport equipment	455.7	1,266	6,772
Instruments	158.2	320	485
Toys, games, other mfg.	145.6	270	392
Interplant transfers	1,098.9	2,820	4,735

Source: Baldor Electric Company.

EXHIBIT 14   POSSIBLE SAVINGS FROM ENERGY-EFFICIENT MOTORS
(Annual Savings with 50-HP Motor at 50 Weeks of Use per Year)

Power cost (per KWH)	40-hr week (1 shift)	80-hr week (2 shifts)	168-hr week (continuous)
$.02	$ 72.07	$144.15	$ 302.71
.04	144.15	288.30	605.42
.06	216.22	432.45	908.14
.08	288.30	576.60	1210.85
.10	360.37	720.74	1513.56

Source: Baldor Electric Company.

Forecasts are for electric vehicles to be used increasingly for consumer and industrial transportation. Increased usage will result from rising costs of fossil fuel, improved battery technology, and improved operating efficiencies of electric vehicles.

Factory automation is creating a whole new market for electric motors. This new field (electronic motors) includes the servo motors and controls used for the movement and precise positioning of robots, machine tools, and factory vehicles. This particular portion of the industry is in its infancy and includes many small companies. The most successful of these small electric motor companies will be subject to acquisition by the larger firms in the industry.

Technological evolution has become important not only to the markets served but also to the individual companies within the industry. Automation of the electric motor manufacturers' factories, thus taking advantage of the newer production technologies, will be critical to the companies' abilities to compete as low-cost producers.

Key Factors for Success in the Electric Motor Industry

Several factors are essential if a firm is to have long-term success in the electric motor industry. The key factors appear to include:

- market share,
- product differentiation,
- product quality and reliability,
- price/low-cost production,
- distribution,
- research and development, and
- financial strength.

Market Share

Market share is an important factor for success in the electric motor industry because the industry is maturing and consolidation is quite likely. Firms that do not command a significant share of the total market or are not firmly entrenched in a particular segment of the market may be subject to acquisition as competition becomes more intense.

Product Differentiation

Many of the larger firms attempt to compete in a number of distinct markets, while the smaller firms generally tend to concentrate on developing a special niche. Most of the highly successful firms in the industry have segmented the market and have developed different products to serve as many of the segments as possible. Examples of successful market segmentation include:

- Franklin Electric—submersible pump motors
- W. W. Grainger—unique distribution through a catalog and company-owned stores
- Baldor—product availability and energy-efficient motors

While it is possible (even essential) to be successful in the short run by serving specialized markets, broad market coverage may better assure long-term success since the company is not dependent on the contingencies of a single market.

Product Quality and Reliability

Because much of the industry produces motors for the industrial market, durability and reliability are quite important. Quality issues include the mechanical and electrical functions, raw materials used, durability, efficiency, and care of manufacturing. Company image concerning quality is important in the consumer market as well.

Price/Low-Cost Production

In a mature industry, the low-cost producers are usually the most successful. As an industry matures, competition increases (the electric motor industry has 340 companies), and it becomes more difficult to provide a unique product. Therefore, as the technology of market segments stabilizes and products become relatively standardized, price becomes a major consideration. In order to offer low prices, manufacturers must be low-cost producers.

Distribution

The electric motor producer must have well-established distribution systems in order to meet customer needs. Important factors in electric motor distribution are

* availability—the ability to deliver immediately from stock
* delivery reliability—the ability to consistently meet delivery lead times
* service—a close, friendly relationship with customers (primarily OEM's)

Research and Development

In today's environment, modernized manufacturing methods and technical product developments will be needed to remain competitive. Therefore, firms in the industry will have to seriously engage in both process and product research and development.

Financial Strength

Adequate financial strength is required for companies in the industry to remain competitive and to respond to possible strategic moves by other companies. Financial support is necessary for quality assurance programs, distribution system needs, and research and development requirements.

BRITISH AIRLINES

**H. Landis Gabel and
Robert Levy**
INSEAD

THE PRIVATIZATION OF BRITISH AIRWAYS

In September 1984, Mr. Nicholas Ridley, Secretary of State for Transport in the UK Government, faced what must have seemed to him an unwinnable situation. In June 1983, Mrs. Thatcher's Conservative Party, elected for a second term with a large parliamentary majority, had announced plans for the sale of the nationalized British Airways (BA) to the private sector. Since then, an acrimonious debate both within and outside the Conservative Party had developed and intensified about the future structure of the British airline industry as well as the government's general industrial policies of privatization and competition. (For a summary of the main events of the BA controversy, see Exhibit 1.) Mr. Ridley had recently been appointed chairman of a Cabinet Committee with the objective of resolving the debate over BA and the airline industry.

Paradoxically, this period of policy uncertainty coincided with the successful turnaround of BA from a loss-making airline into what has since been heralded "the world's most profitable airline." Indeed, the prospect of this streamlined, efficient and profitable BA entering the

This case was written by Associate Professor H. Landis Gabel and Robert Levy, MBA candidate, INSEAD.

private sector was causing much of the debate. Sir Adam Thomson, Chairman of British Caledonian Airways, Britain's largest independent airline, expressed the concern he and other relatively small operators felt about the future.

> If I were chairman of a privatized BA, it would be my duty to the shareholders to maximize profits. If I could kick a competitor, however small, out of business and so make more profits for myself and the shareholders, fine I'd do it.[1]

Sir Adam's fear was, however, mitigated by the opportunity the situation presented to him. If BA shares were to appeal to the private financial community, the regulatory framework within which the UK airline industry operated would have to be firmly set for the foreseeable future. Thus, Sir Adam had a chance to influence the policymaking bodies of the government to try to challenge the domination of BA—domination which had long been sustained by government policy.

The Background of Privatization

BA was not an isolated example of the sale of public assets to the private sector. By late 1984, eight large

[1]*The Daily Mail,* August 16, 1984.

EXHIBIT 1   MAJOR EVENTS IN THE PRIVATIZATION OF BRITISH AIRWAYS

Date	Event
May 1979	Conservative Government elected to power under the leadership of Mrs. Margaret Thatcher, with commitment to sell into private ownership many of Britain's major nationalised industries, including British Airways.
1981	Lord King appointed as Chairman of British Airways, with specific mandate to prepare the airline for privatization. King appoints Mr. Colin Marshall as CEO.
1981–1983	Major program of cost reduction and efficiency improvements, involving cutting employment from 59,000 to 37,000.
1983	British Airways announces profit of £180 million.
June 1983	Conservative Government elected for second term with promise to sell British Airways in this Parliament.
1 November 1983	John Moore, Financial Secretary to the Treasury, emphasizes in a major speech that privatization must go "hand-in-hand" with increased competition.
3 November 1983	British Caledonian Chairman, Sir Adam Thomson, proposes to the Government that his airline should buy British Airways' routes and assets to ensure fair competition in UK aviation.
4 November 1983	British Airways announces half-year profit of £160 million and declares that it will be ready for privatization in 11 months.
16 November 1983	Prime Minister tells Lord King that BA privatization will have to wait until after the massive floatation of British Telecom, i.e. 1985–1986.
12 December 1983	Secretary of State for Transport, Mr. Nicholas Ridley, announces in the House of Commons that British Airways will be privatized as soon as possible, probably early in 1985.
	In the same speech, Mr. Ridley announces that he has asked Mr. John Dent, Chairman of the Civil Aviation Authority, to conduct a major review of the airline industry to determine if changes might be needed in the licensing structure.
1 February 1984	Final submissions to CAA review, including BCal proposals thought to suggest transfer of a third of BA's routes to independent airlines.
3 February 1984	BCal announces that if its proposals for route transfers from BA are accepted, it is likely to offer a share issue for between £100–£150m before the floatation of BA. This would be BCal's first quotation on the stock market.
15 February 1984	CAA announces that it has granted to BCal the right to fly from London to Riyadh, Saudi Arabia, in preference to BA. BA keeps rights to Jeddah and Dhahran.
3 March 1984	BA announces appointment of stockbrokers and merchant bankers to manage its public floatation.
18 April 1984	CAA publishes interim report declaring that airline competition is beneficial, but will remain impossible as long as BA controls 81% of its services.

EXHIBIT 1   MAJOR EVENTS IN THE PRIVATIZATION OF BRITISH AIRWAYS *(Continued)*

Date	Event
1 May 1984	Sir Adam Thomson proposes that privatization of BA should be delayed to give time for changes in the structure of UK civil aviation.
5 May 1984	Lord King declares that he would regard transfer of routes from BA to BCal as "a resignation issue".
6 June 1984	BA publishes its accounts showing bank borrowings of more than £900 million.
	Full-year profits for BA revealed to be £294m before interest and tax.
12 June 1984	BA begins of £2 million advertising campaign to counter the claims of the independent airlines.
12 June 1984	Nine independent airlines write to the CAA asking that a legal interpretation of BA's position in the industry be sought from the Monopolies Commission.
16 July 1984	Civil Aviation Authority review of "Airline Competition Policy" published, proposing significant route transfers from BA, and increasing the strength of independent airlines.
	BA declares the proposals "disastrous" and "unacceptable".
3 August 1984	A Cabinet Committee, consisting of Norman Tebbitt, Nigel Lawson, Nicholas Ridley, Lord Cockfield and John Wakeham, set up in an attempt to resolve the dispute over British Airways' routes—a decision deferred until "late Summer". Deadline set for 13 September.
September 1984	Continued negotiations throughout September between Cabinet Committee, Lord King and Sir Adam Thomson.

formerly nationalized companies had been privatized in the UK, and legislation was enacted to enable the privatization of twelve more (including BA and British Telecom). The policy of privatization reflected a change in mainstream Conservative thinking in the 1970s. The free market, not government intervention, was now to be the preferred medium for achieving the government's economic goals.

As Nigel Lawson, Chancellor of the Exchequer and the man with Cabinet responsibility for the privatization program, said,

The Conservative Party has never believed that the business of government is the government of business.[2]

The policy was, of course, in sharp contrast to that of the post-World War II Labor Governments which had

[2]Quoted in D. Healä and D. Steel, "Privatizing Public Enterprise: An Analysis of the Government's Case, *Political Quarterly*, July 1982, pp. 333–349.

nationalized many industries with the objective of using them to influence the economy. The post-war nationalizations created some of the biggest organizations in the UK economy—organizations that in 1983 accounted for approximately one-tenth of the UK's gross domestic product, one-seventh its total investment, and employment of 1.5 million people. Three public enterprises had been established in the airline industry—BOAC, BEA, and BSAA. Each was granted a monopoly in a different market. In 1949, BSAA was merged into BOAC, and in 1970, BOAC and BEA were consolidated to form BA.

To Mrs. Thatcher's Conservative Party, public enterprise looked inherently less efficient than private enterprise because it was insulated from the discipline of the capital and product markets. BA was taken as a case in point. In 1981, when Mrs. Thatcher appointed Lord King Chairman of British Airways with a mandate to prepare it for privatization, BA was practically bankrupt. Only an immense program of government-guaranteed loans kept BA in the air. (See Exhibits 2 to 4 for BA's financial reports.)

EXHIBIT 2   BRITISH AIRWAYS FINANCIAL SUMMARY—1983

	£m
Airline traffic revenue	2,044
Other earnings	453
Group turnover	2,497
Operating costs	
Airline operating expenditure comprised:	
Staff costs	
Wages and salaries	412
Pension contributions	63
National Insurance	37
Aircraft fuel and oil	531
Landing fees and en route charges	163
Amortisation of capital expenditure	105
Commission on traffic revenue	154
Other airline operating expenditure	405
	1,870
Non-airline operating expenditure	437
	2,307
Group operating surplus	190
Associated companies, trade investments and other income	20
Profit before cost of capital borrowings and taxation	210
Interest	(120)
Currency losses on capital borrowings	(28)
Profit before tax	62
Taxation and minority interests	(11)
Profit before extraordinary items	51
Extraordinary items	26
Balance transferred to reserves	77
Internal cash flow	
Profit after extraordinary items	77
Less profit on fixed asset and investment disposals	(36)
Add back non-cash items	
Amortisation—airline activity 105	
—other 6	
	111
Currency losses	28
Other	3
Cash generated from operations	183
Net proceeds from asset disposals	110
Movement in net current liabilities	(86)
Total cash generated	207
Capital expenditure	(172)
Net cash generated	35
Capital borrowings repaid	(99)
Capital borrowings raised	(64)

	£m
Balance sheet	
Net assets	
Fixed assets	978
Investments	18
Net current liabilities	(164)
	832
Financed by	
Shareholders' funds	(221)
Capital borrowings	1,053
	832
Current cost accounts	
The change in the result from the historic cost accounts to the current cost accounts is explained below	
Current cost operating profit	133
This is the historic cost result before other income of £196m, less £63m additional depreciation resulting from the revaluation of assets in current cost terms.	
Other income	12
This is the historic cost amount of other income less an adjustment of £1m to the historic cost surplus on disposal of fixed assets and investments.	
Current cost profit before cost of capital borrowings and taxation	145
Cost of capital borrowings	(100)
This is the historic cost figure of £148m reduced by the gearing adjustment of £48m which reflects the burden of inflation borne by lenders who have helped to finance net operating assets.	
Current cost profit before taxation	45
Taxation and minority interests	(11)
Current cost profit before extraordinary items	34
Extraordinary items	22
Current cost profit attributable to British Airways	56

EXHIBIT 3   BRITISH AIRWAYS BALANCE SHEET—1983

	Note	Group 1983 £m	Group 1982 £m	Board 1983 £m	Board 1982 £m
Net assets					
Fixed assets					
Fleet		773.7	751.5	721.6	696.2
Property		123.9	132.2	110.1	112.9
Equipment		80.0	88.8	72.2	73.3
	10	977.6	972.5	903.9	882.4
Interests in					
Subsidiaries	11a			77.7	79.0
Associated companies	12a	15.0	15.0	.2	—
Trade investments	13a	3.6	6.2	.5	.4
Net current liabilities	15	(163.8)	(237.1)	(211.0)	(283.3)
		832.4	756.6	771.3	678.5
Financed by					
Public dividend capital	16	180.0	180.0	180.0	180.0
Reserves	17	(325.4)	(402.0)	(386.2)	(472.2)
Exchange equalisation account	18bii	(75.7)	(34.7)	(75.7)	(34.7)
Deficiency of assets over liabilities		(221.1)	(256.7)	(281.9)	(326.9)
Capital borrowings	18a	1,053.2	1,010.6	1,053.2	1,005.4
Minority interests		.3	2.6		
Deferred taxation	19	—	.1		
		832.4	756.6	771.3	678.5

BA's return to profitability under Lord King was felt to be attributable in good part to the massive cuts "in overmanning in BA which could not have been achieved if the intention to privatize had not already been expressed."[3] The Conservative Party's beliefs seemed to be validated.

A second justification for the planned privatizations was stated in a major policy speech in November 1983 by John Moore, Financial Secretary to the Treasury and guiding hand behind the privatization program.

The primary objective of the Government's privatization policy is to reduce the power of the monopolist and to encourage competition.[4]

A third justification for the privatizations was that they would permanently remove nationalized firms' future

credit demands from the government's public sector borrowing requirement. Despite its recent successful performance, BA in 1984 still owed its creditors 863 million pounds. About half of the estimated 1 billion pound proceeds of BA's sale would be used to reduce the company's outstanding debt—debt which might not otherwise be repaid. (So serious was BA's financial situation that the airline was not considered saleable with its existing debt.)

Finally, the Treasury had an obvious financial motive to sell nationalized companies like BA—and to sell them as dearly as possible.

(Other justifications occasionally referred to include a reduction of state power in order to increase individual freedom, making the civil service more efficient by streamlining it and eliminating its regulatory mentality, broadening equity markets, and breaking the power of the civil service unions which had long been particularly troublesome in the UK.)[5]

[3]M. Beesley and S. Littlechild, "Privatization: Principles, Problems and Priorities," *Lloyds Bank Review*, July 1983, pp. 1–20.

[4]Addressing a conference of stockbrokers, November 1, 1983.

[5]Mrs. Thatcher was at the time trying to privatize all nonmedical services in the National Health Service where unionized cleaners, porters, and catering personnel had led bitter nationwide strikes.

EXHIBIT 4   BRITISH AIRWAYS TEN YEAR RESULTS AND STATISTICS

Years ended 31 March	1974	1975	1976	1977	1978	1979	1980	1981	1982	1983
Results										
Scheduled services										
Revenue—passenger & baggage (£m)	444.3	526.6	660.0	898.6	965.1	1,191.4	1,409.9	1,489.5	1,608.7	1,770.9
Revenue—mail (£m)	21.1	22.3	23.6	32.7	33.0	36.2	39.8	41.0	33.7	35.7
Revenue—freight (£m)	68.4	83.8	82.1	105.3	115.3	131.4	152.7	161.7	148.1	151.0
Revenue—total (£m)	533.8	632.7	765.7	1,036.6	1,113.4	1,359.0	1,602.4	1,692.2	1,790.5	1,957.6
Total Airline operations (including Airtours)										
Revenue (£m)	566.1	663.5	801.5	1,073.9	1,156.1	1,403.3	1,654.4	1,749.8	1,861.0	2,043.5
Operating expenditure (£m)	512.9	665.3	798.8	978.1	1,099.3	1,327.3	1,638.4	1,854.0	1,855.1	1,869.5
Operating result (£m)	53.2	(1.8)	2.7	95.8	56.8	76.0	16.0	(104.2)	5.9	174.0
British Airways Group										
Profit before interest and tax (£m)	64.1	5.0	11.6	115.8	79.0	109.8	54.9	(69.9)	10.8*	209.8*
Average net assets (£m)	502.3	511.7	529.7	558.7	639.1	745.3	879.8	1,043.2	938.1	794.5
Return on net assets (%)	12.8	1.0	2.2	20.7	12.4	14.7	6.3	(6.7)	1.2	26.4
Turnover (£m)	647	748	916	1,248	1,355	1,640	1,920	2,061	2,241	2,497
Ratio of turnover to net assets	1,288	1,462	1,729	2,234	2,120	2,200	2,182	1,976	2,389	3,143
Statistics										
Scheduled services										
Revenue passenger km (m)	24,803	24,171	27,280	30,143	29,751	36,366	42,144	40,076	38,521	36,394
Available seat km (m)	41,703	41,126	44,816	48,576	49,637	56,387	62,534	64,043	57,752	54,710
Tonne km—mail (m)	109.4	119.1	128.0	140.2	155.7	165.5	171.5	165.0	150.0	151.8
Tonne km—freight (m)	746.5	721.1	679.4	716.2	818.4	883.2	995.8	995.8	884.9	833.7
Tonne km—total (m)	3,061	2,997	3,249	3,607	3,711	4,417	5,036	4,812	4,503	4,307
Revenue per passenger km (p)	1.79	2.18	2.42	2.98	3.24	3.28	3.35	3.72	4.17	4.87
Revenue per RTK (p)	17.4	21.1	23.6	28.7	30.0	30.8	31.8	35.2	39.8	45.5
Available tonne km (m)	5,528	5,388	5,856	6,233	6,408	7,164	7,797	7,930	7,147	6,786
Passenger load factor (%)	59.5	58.8	60.9	62.1	59.2	64.5	67.4	62.6	66.7	66.5
Break-even passenger load factor (%)	52.4	59.0	60.6	55.4	56.4	60.3	66.6	67.0	66.6	60.0

EXHIBIT 4   BRITISH AIRWAYS TEN YEAR RESULTS AND STATISTICS *(Continued)*

Years ended 31 March	1974	1975	1976	1977	1978	1979	1980	1981	1982	1983
Overall load factor (%)	55.4	55.6	55.5	57.9	57.9	61.6	64.6	60.7	63.0	63.5
Break-even overall load factor (%)	49.9	55.8	55.3	52.5	55.0	58.2	64.0	64.5	62.7	57.8
Punctuality (% within 15 mins)	76	81	80	79	64	65	68	81	78	84
Number of passengers carried (000)	14,361	13,349	13,792	14,510	13,370	15,768	17,319	15,918	15,231	14,635
Average distance travelled (km)	1,727	1,811	1,978	2,077	2,225	2,306	2,433	2,518	2,529	2,487
Tonnes of mail carried (000)	31.2	30.5	29.8	33.2	34.9	38.0	39.0	39.0	35.0	38.3
Average distance carried (km)	3,509	3,908	4,304	4,223	4,466	4,355	4,399	4,230	4,288	3,960
Tonnes of freight carried (000)	237.0	219.7	170.1	167.9	192.0	209.9	225.5	203.4	170.2	161.1
Average distance carried (km)	3,150	3,283	3,993	4,265	4,262	4,208	4,415	4,897	5,200	5,176
Total Airline operations (including Airtours)										
Available tonne km (m)	6,077	5,832	6,247	6,555	6,793	7,557	8,153	8,243	7,522	7,208
Revenue hours flown (000)	543.5	490.7	454.8	440.6	431.8	469.0	492.5	447.0	405.5	386.2
ATK per hour	11,181	11,885	13,735	14,876	15,733	16,112	16,553	18,440	18,551	18,664
Revenue aircraft km (m)	321.3	289.4	273.1	267.2	265.7	288.5	307.3	283.1	253.5	244.7
Average speed (km/hr)	591	590	600	606	615	615	625	633	625	634
Revenue stage flights (000)	284.3	267.1	237.3	225.9	212.2	230.4	239.4	211.1	195.6	189.3
Average sector (km)	1,130	1,083	1,151	1,183	1,252	1,252	1,283	1,341	1,296	1,293
Average length of flight (hr)	1.91	1.84	1.92	1.95	2.03	2.04	2.06	2.12	2.07	2.04
Operating expenditure per ATK (p)	8.4	11.4	12.8	14.9	16.2	17.6	20.1	22.5	24.7	25.9
Average staff—Airline activities	54,600	54,861	53,977	54,362	55,438	55,985	56,140	53,616	47,753	39,693
ATK per employee (000)	111.3	106.3	115.7	120.6	122.5	135.0	145.2	153.7	157.5	181.6

*Profit before interest, tax and extraordinary items

The Civil Aviation Authority Report

It was in the context of the privatization program that Nicholas Ridley first declared in a speech on December 12, 1983 that BA would be privatized with a target date of early 1985. In the same speech he announced that he had ordered the UK air transport regulatory body, the Civil Aviation Authority (CAA), to carry out a major policy review of the airline industry.

The CAA played a role in the UK airline industry that would normally be reserved for the UK Monopolies Commission. The Fair Trading Act of 1973 exempted airlines from the authority of the Monopolies Commission, and a separate act of Parliament assigned its duties to the CAA. Since the CAA had earlier concluded that BA's dominance brought it under the Fair Trading Act's definition of "monopoly," it could hardly avoid using this opportunity to try to increase competition in the industry.

After receiving submissions from 105 interested parties, the CAA reported in July 1984. Proclaiming its principal objective to be correcting "the underlying imbalance of competitive advantage in the airline industry,"[6] the CAA proposed to reduce the relative size of BA for the sake of other airlines. In particular, it recommended

1 replacement of BA by BCal on routes to Saudi Arabia and Zimbabwe,

2 the transfer of BA's scheduled routes from Gatwick and its European routes originating from provincial airports to independent UK airlines, and

3 access to Heathrow by other UK trunk airlines, at the expense of BA if necessary.

These proposals were estimated to reduce BA's operating revenues by about 7%. No compensation was planned.

The CAA also requested additional powers to promote a more even balance among the competing UK airlines. This request included the power to transfer routes between carriers solely to redress an imbalance and thus to promote competition—a power the CAA did not at the time possess.

> Route licenses are not property. . . . Insofar as the State, through the licensing of air services, gives airlines an opportunity to operate profitably, these opportunities remain at the disposal of the State.[7]

[6]CAA, "Airline Competition Policy," July 1984.

[7]*Ibid*.

BA categorically rejected the CAA's proposals, and amidst intensifying lobbying, a Cabinet Committee chaired by Mr. Ridley was set up in August 1984 with a deadline of September 13 to report. This deadline now faced Mr. Ridley.

Competition in the UK Airline Industry

The airline industry can be divided into three major market segments. Exhibit 5 shows the CAA's estimate of the shares of the segments by carrier in 1983.

(1) The Charter Market

This is the largest sector of the UK market with 42.2% of passenger-trips and is essentially a competitive market. The market is not regulated by bilateral agreements, tariff fixing, or revenue pooling. But since most charter flights are taken as part of package holidays and are subject to schedule restrictions, this market is effectively isolated from the international scheduled market. BA's subsidiary, British Airtours, held a 12.6% share of the market.

(2) The Domestic Scheduled Market

BA held a 50% share of the domestic scheduled market—a market which comprised 20.7% of the UK airline industry output. Approximately one-sixth of BA's revenue came from its domestic routes.

On a formal basis, the domestic market is regulated, but it is relatively competitive nonetheless. Entry controls exist which give BA monopoly rights to many routes where its only constraint is the competition from ground transport. Flight capacity is not controlled on the competitive routes, but fares are set by the CAA. In general, the situation is similar to that in the US before the period of deregulation.

A CAA's policy of *ad hoc* liberalization (such as its grant of Heathrow-Glasgow/Edinburgh routes to British Midland Airlines) has made the domestic market increasingly competitive. BA's heavily discounted "Super Shuttle" flights to various UK cities are a manifestation of the aggressive competition from the smaller independents.

(3) The International Scheduled Market

This market segment (36.1% of all passenger-trips in the UK) was the core of BA's business, and most of the

EXHIBIT 5   AIRLINE SHARES

Airline	Passengers
Airline shares of United Kingdom charter services	
Air Europe	10.4%
Britannia	31.4%
British Airtours	12.6%
Monarch	8.9%
Orion	7.3%
Airline shares of United Kingdom domestic scheduled services	
British Airways	50.0%
British Midland Airways	16.4%
British Caledonian	8.6%
Air UK	6.6%
Dan-Air	6.2%
Others*	12.2%
Airline shares of United Kingdom international scheduled services	
British Airways	81.8%
British Caledonian	11.1%
Others	7.1%
	100.0%

*Sixteen other airlines are involved in domestic passenger services and a further two in providing cargo carriage.
Source: CAA Airline Statistics.

company's routes were international. The Continental routes constituted slightly more than one-quarter and the North American routes slightly less than one-quarter of BA's revenues.

As the traditional UK flag carrier, BA had 82% of the British end of this market. It was on the basis of this market share that the CAA reported,

BA's dominance of the British airline industry in terms of scale brings it firmly within the meaning of a monopoly situation.[8]

Yet regarding the CAA's estimate of BA's market power, Lord King said, "it is ridiculous to claim that the airline is a monopoly."[9]

Commenting on the origins of BA's dominant share of the international scheduled market, the CAA said,

[8]*Ibid.*

[9]Lord King, in a letter to *The Times,* July 6, 1984.

BA has become overwhelmingly dominant in the UK airline industry as a result of historical accident and government policies rather than commercial power.[10]

BA's two overwhelming competitive assets—assets it controlled "as a result of historical accident and government policies"—were its route structure (about which more will be said below) and its exclusive use of Heathrow Airport for international flights.

Heathrow was not only the biggest international scheduled service airport in Britain, it was also the greatest international air service hub in the world. Approximately 80% of BA's flights either originated or terminated there. In January 1984, BA served 108 cities in 63 foreign countries from Heathrow. By contrast, that same month British Caledonian served only 30 cities in 23 countries from its Gatwick base. To quote the CAA,

[10]CAA, *op. cit.*

Differences of scale and activity between Heathrow and Gatwick . . . have a significant impact on the effectiveness of competition between British carriers.[11]

To illustrate its point, the CAA referred to the case of British Midland Airlines which, when given government permission to fly from Heathrow to Glasgow, gained in a week the same market share it had taken BCal fifteen years to develop flying from Gatwick to Glasgow.

Allocation of capacity at British airports was the responsibility of the British Airports Authority (BAA). It charged a price for landing and takeoff rights, but the price was less than the true market value as evidenced by excess demand. This was a consequence of the BAA's policy of pricing to cover costs rather than to make a profit or to use pricing as a rationing mechanism. Since rationing was not done by price, the BAA had to use non-price methods of rationing. For example, charters were forbidden to use Heathrow. As recently as 1970, any scheduled carrier could use Heathrow if it wanted. As capacity utilization rose, new carriers were sent to Gatwick and some

[11]*Ibid.*

of the flights previously to or from Heathrow (such as BA's Spanish operations) were moved to Gatwick. (For data on the UK airports, see Exhibits 6 and 7.)

Heathrow's capacity was 330,000 air traffic movements (ATMs),[12] but a new terminal was soon to open with an annual limit of 275,000 ATMs. Gatwick had only one runway, and the construction of a second would have led to considerable opposition from environmentalists.

Post-War Evolution of the World Airline Industry

The structure of the world airline industry is based on the Chicago Conference of 1944 which stated in Article 1,

> The contracting states recognize that every state has complete and exclusive sovereignty over airspace above its territory.[13]

The principal objective of the Conference was to achieve a multilateral system of exchanging air rights. The Con-

[12]An ATM is a takeoff or landing of an aircraft engaged in transporting commercial passengers or cargo.

[13]Quoted in A. Sampson, *Empire of the Sky,* London, 1984, p. 69.

EXHIBIT 6   INTERNATIONAL TRAFFIC

UK Airport	Scheduled	Charter
United Kingdom airlines' share of international traffic at certain airports		
Heathrow	39.3%	—
Gatwick	60.7%	81.7%
Manchester	35.6%	88.2%
Birmingham	61.2%	84.7%
Glasgow	26.4%	83.4%
Luton	—	89.6%
United Kingdom TOTAL	43.0%	81.0%
Percentage of total United Kingdom international traffic served at London area airports		
Heathrow	79.1%	0.2%
Gatwick	13.9%	41.5%
Luton		9.2%
Stansted	0.2%	1.7%
Southend		0.2%
	93.2%	52.8%

Source: CAA Airline Statistics.

EXHIBIT 7   **Uses and capacities of London Airports (thousands of ATMS).**

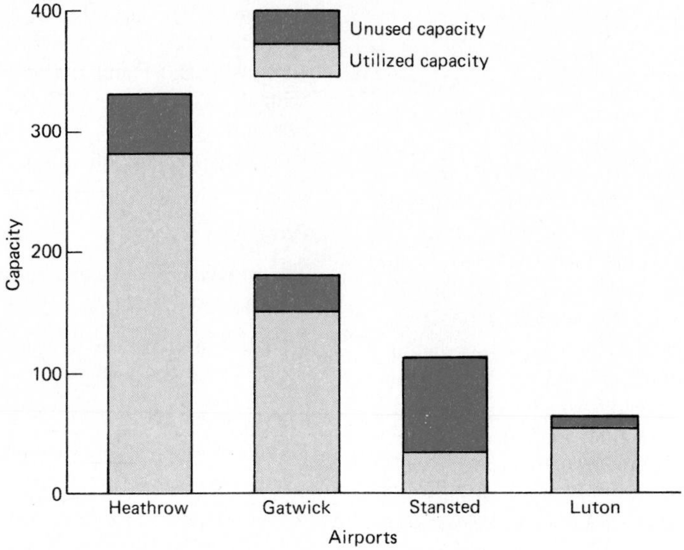

ference failed to achieve this, and instead concluded with a system of bilateral international agreements over landing rights, gateways, and "freedoms." (See Exhibit 8.) Each government designated one of its airlines (its nationalized "flagship" in most instances) as one of the two airlines (the other being the opposite country's designated airline) entitled to share what was in effect a two-firm cartel on each route. On occasion, a country would designate multiple airlines as joint operators of its half of the cartel. In the case of the UK, the favored airlines were the three nationalized predecessors of BA. By 1984, there were 23,000 bilateral agreements between 200 countries involving 16,000 airports.[14]

In 1945, a further pillar of the post-war aviation industry was established at the Havana Conference where thirty one nations approved the articles of a revised International Air Transport Association (IATA).[15] In 1946, the two countries most responsible for the Chicago Agreement, the USA and Britain, signed what was to become the prototype for all other bilateral agreements—the Bermuda Agreement. One of the most important clauses of the agreement delegated the question of whether and how

to set fares to the IATA. As one critic of the industry noted,

> As more nations joined the fare-fixing, IATA became both the instrument and the scapegoat for the natural tendencies of the airlines to restrict competition.[16]

IATA also coordinated the growing network of flight routes and timetables. Via its clearing house, IATA created a means whereby travelers could freely transfer from one airline to another using the same ticket (called "interlining"). It also set up and controlled common safety and navigational standards, engineering cooperation, and pilot training programs.

In Europe, an international agreement in 1967 by the European Civil Aviation Conference (ECAC) set procedures to regulate competition on the Continent. The procedures relied heavily on IATA rules. Under ECAC rules, entry, capacity, route structure, and tariffs were all controlled. An additional method by which the ECAC restricted competition was the "pooling agreement." The bilateral negotiations referred to above usually concluded with two designated national airlines flying the same route with equal frequency at a fare above the cost of the high-cost carrier. It was only natural then to establish and share

[14]*International Herald Tribune*, May 3, 1985.

[15]IATA's predecessor had supervised European air travel in the 1930s.

[16]Sampson, *op. cit.*, p.74.

EXHIBIT 8

THE SIX FREEDOMS

1st Freedom:	the right of a carrier to fly over the territory of another country without landing. (E.g., a PanAm airplane can fly over France.)
2nd Freedom:	the right of a carrier to land on the territory of another country for a non-commercial purpose. (E.g., the PanAm airplane can make a refueling stop in Paris.)
3rd Freedom:	the right of a carrier to disembark passengers from its home country in another country. (E.g., PanAm can leave Americans in Paris.)
4th Freedom:	the right of a carrier to take passengers from another country and to disembark them in its home country. (E.g., PanAm can take French travelers to New York.)
5th Freedom:	the right of a carrier to land and takeoff from a second country and embark and disembark passengers travelling to or from a third country. (E.g., the PanAm flight can pick up German travelers in Berlin, land in Paris and disembark a few of them, then continue on to New York.)
6th Freedom:	the right of a carrier to embark and disembark passengers travelling wholly within the boundaries of another country. (E.g., the PanAm flight from Berlin can stop in Paris, embark and disembark any passengers, then continue to Marseilles to do the same before leaving for New York.)

---

a single pool of revenues. For example, on the Paris-London route, Air France and BA would fly the same number of flights between the two capitals and put their receipts into a pool which would be divided between the two airlines. Fares were fixed by IATA (under the ''double approval'' principal by which both governments and both airlines had to agree on the fares), and any service competition (e.g., competition over meals, drinks, movies, etc.) was forbidden. Thus, there was virtually no scope for seeking competitive advantage, and the rewards of any competitive advantage (won, for example, by introducing new aircraft on a shared route) would have to be shared. The only way a carrier could increase its profits relative to its duopoly partner was through relative cost efficiency.

(The situation in Europe contrasted with that in the US where a similar system of fare-fixing by the Civil Aeronautics Board (CAB) prevented price competition, but where there was no revenue pooling and less control of non-price competition. In particular, there was no control of competition over flight frequency. Thus, US carriers rapidly introduced more and more scheduled flights—and more and more excess capacity—as the principal means of winning customers from other airlines.)

By the early 1980s, very little had changed in Europe. Some international routes had changed hands but only when the national flag carriers declined to exercise their rights to fly the routes.

The US Regulatory Revolution

US airline policy in the late 1970s was an ominous harbinger of change for what Sir Adam Thomson called Europe's ''network of cosy cartels''[17] President Carter appointed Alfred Kahn, economics professor and ardent deregulator, to head the CAB with a mandate to deregulate the industry and eliminate the agency. This policy was formalized in 1978 with the passage of the Airline Deregulation Act which laid down a six year timetable (ending in January 1985) for the return of the US domestic

---

[17]Sir Adam Thomson, quoted in *The Sunday Telegraph*, August 12, 1984.

airline industry to the discipline of the free market and for the abolition of the CAB.

The 1978 Act phased out entry restrictions and progressively allowed airlines more and more freedom to fly the routes they wished with frequencies and prices they wished. The airlines, previously prohibited from trading routes, began to exchange them to establish efficient networks. Complete freedom to set airfares came on January 1, 1983.

These new freedoms led to the rapid entry of "instant airlines," principally on local routes where their flexibility was an advantage. By January 1983, 22 wholly new airlines had entered service. This compares to the 28 trunk airlines which existed without change between the time of the last chartered entrant (1938) to the time of deregulation. Over those forty years of no entry, there was a several thousand percent increase in airline service demand! The new entrants and expanding regional airlines that came with deregulation took 12% of the major trunk airlines' market share by 1983.

With relevance to the situation facing the UK in 1984, the new entrants to the US market following deregulation found their expansion hampered by their inability to obtain landing rights at the most popular (and most congested) US airports. Allocation of these rights had been negotiated in scheduling committees made up of the older carriers under antitrust immunity. Thus, the established airlines maintained a significant market advantage vis-a-vis the newcomers. But in June 1984, the US Department of Transportation approved an experimental policy of encouraging a market for landing rights at four major US airports (Washington, Chicago, and two in New York City). In approving this experiment, the Department of Transportation rejected a proposal to auction the landing slots to start the market. Thus, landing rights now worth millions of dollars were granted for free to their traditional holders. (It was estimated that a 08.00 departure slot from LaGuardia would be worth hundreds of thousands of dollars in a free market.)

The initial period of US deregulation coincided with record airline profits as the economy boomed and airlines were unable to adjust their capacity. This brief period was followed by the fuel price increase and recession at the end of the decade which resulted in record losses. In 1982, the US industry lost $733 million. But since 1982 the results have been largely positive. Load factors increased, prices fell, price discrimination became less common, and route structures shifted to an efficient "hub and spoke"

system with fewer multistop flights and greater reliance on smaller narrow-bodied jets. As Nicholas Ridley noted,

> Fares are generally lower, the variety of services is enormous. . . . There have been extraordinary improvements of air productivity, and the restructuring of air networks more closely reflects what passengers want.[18]

Further studies of the American experience have concluded that "economies of scale appear to be small or non-existent."[19] Although most routes in the US continue to be served by only a few carriers (rarely more than two or three), potential entrants make the markets contestable even if their structure is not perfectly competitive.

While it would appear that on the whole the economy benefitted from deregulation, there were adverse consequences for some groups including particular consumer groups. Some small communities previously benefitting from local air service which was cross-subsidized by longer distance flights lost service or faced higher fares. (Traditionally the CAB set fares in direct proportion to distance. Since cost per mile declines with distance, long distance flights earned relatively high margins which supported short low-margin flights.)

Other clear losers have been the employees of some of the older established airlines whose salaries had been much higher than those offered outside the industry or by newer entrants to the market. For example, in 1980, airline typists in America earned forty-one percent more than other typists for the same work.[20]

> Under regulation, airline employees had been able to capture a significant share of the gains of lower-cost technologies by obtaining restrictive work rules and progressively higher wages.[21]

Deregulation changed this dramatically. New airlines were not tied to these historical high-cost wage agreements, and they hired their staff at much lower salaries. For example, they employed pilots at $40,000 per year rather than the typical $80,000 and stewardesses at $15,000 rather than $35,000. Overall, average annual em-

[18]*Hansard*, May 5, 1984.

[19]P. J. Forsyth, "Airline Regulation in the US: The Lessons for Europe," *Fiscal Studies*, November 1983.

[20]Sampson, *op. cit.*

[21]D. Graham and D. Kaplan, "Competition and the Airlines: An Evaluation of Deregulation," CAB Staff Report, 1982.

ployee compensation in 1983 was $22,000 for the new-comers compared to $42,000 for the older carriers. Labor costs for the former were 18% of operating expenses whereas for the latter they were 37%. This enabled the "no frills" airlines to compete very effectively with the established airlines. The latter, in turn, sought to cut their labor costs by renegotiating standing contracts. Some, such as Continental Airlines, filed for bankruptcy to force renegotiation of labor agreements. In 1983, Continental eliminated two-thirds of its workforce and halved the wages of the remainder.

Further casualties of deregulation were those airlines that did not manage to adjust in terms of cost or route structure to the increasing competition that came with deregulation. At least nine airlines went bankrupt. Furthermore, the charter market virtually disappeared after deregulation since its economic justification rested almost entirely on the regulatory restriction of competition in the scheduled market.

Pressure on the European Cartels

Although the CAB only had unique authority over intra-US flights (where two-fifths of all flights in the world took place), the American experiment constituted a major change in the international environment. The channel through which US policy was transferred to Europe was the North America-Western Europe route network. In 1977, the British and Americans signed a new "Bermuda 2" agreement to liberalize fares across the Atlantic. When the British tried to maintain some control over price competition, the CAB (with what was to become a familiar tactic) turned to Britain's rival Holland and offered the Dutch more American destinations if they accepted the offered agreement. The Dutch agreement was a truly precedent setting one. There were no restrictions on entry, capacity, or number of designated carriers, and tariffs were to be set unilaterally (with only a control over predatory pricing). No mention was made of IATA. The Dutch agreement forced Britain into a liberal interpretation of "Bermuda 2" to allow Heathrow and Gatwick (i.e., BA and BCal) to compete with Holland's Schiphol Airport.

In 1982, the US and the members of the ECAC signed the US-ECAC "Memorandum of Understanding" which led to partial deregulation of all the North Atlantic routes to the US and to dramatic fare reductions. The understanding was reached after the CAB threatened to file an antitrust suit in the US against the airlines for their fare-fixing. The understanding established minimum and maximum fares within which competition would be allowed.

Intensified competition over the North Atlantic led to the entry of low price "no frills" airlines such as Sir Freddie Laker's "Skytrain". In granting Laker a permit, the CAB hailed Skytrain as "a golden opportunity to encourage imagination and innovation in the North Atlantic air travel market." Sir Freddie's innovation was to bring to the scheduled market the low prices of the charter market.

Laker quickly touched off a price war in which the older airlines such as BA and BCal dropped their prices to match or undercut those of Laker. (Sir Adam Thomson described Laker as "the most disruptive airline on the North Atlantic.") The price war (or the predatory pricing, as was believed by Sir Freddie) and Laker's overexpansion led to the company's bankruptcy in 1982 with a debt of nearly half a billion dollars. In that year, BA set record losses caused in good part by its losses on the Atlantic routes.

Laker's bankruptcy prompted an antitrust investigation by the US Department of Justice which focused on three issues. The first was the allegation that 10 major airlines[22] threatened to end all business with McDonnell Douglas unless the airplane producer pulled out of a reported plan to rescue Laker. The second was the question of whether the companies used predatory pricing to drive Laker out of business. The final issue was whether Laker was harmed by a general conspiracy of the 10 to fix prices.

In May 1984, the Department of Justice dropped its investigation of the threats to McDonnell Douglas. As of the fall of 1984, it was still investigating the final two issues, but there were rumors that the predatory pricing charge would also be dropped.

The bankruptcy also prompted an antitrust suit in the US by Laker's creditors. The defendants and the charges were the same as those in the US government's investigation. Although this case was civil rather than criminal, the damages for which the defendants could be proven liable were estimated to be about $1.7 billion. In the fall of 1984, the case hung like a pall over BA's privatization. The UK government made no move to offer indemnification to BA's future private sector owners for any legal obligations, and BA's efforts to negotiate an out-of-court settlement with Laker's creditors had been unsuccessful.

---

[22]The prospective defendants included BA, BCal, Pan AM, TWA, Lufthansa, Swissair, Sabena, KLM, UTA, and SAS.

Liberalization over the Continent?

Deregulation of the North Atlantic routes has left its impact. Over the last ten years, full economy and budget transAtlantic fares have fallen by 40% in real terms. (By contrast, business fares in Europe doubled in real terms from 1978 to 1984.) The number of passenger-trips has more than doubled from 3 million to 6.4 million annually.

The fervor of deregulation and price competition now seems to be regularly reflected in UK policy statements. To quote Nicholas Ridley,

> The government stands firmly as the champion of the consumers. We are the flag carriers for lower air fares.[23]

How far price competition can be introduced into Continental markets is unclear, however. In the Summer of 1984, the UK and Dutch governments negotiated a "sixth freedom" agreement between their countries[24] which nearly halved the lowest price round trip fare. The agreement allowed each country to set fares independently of the other, it abolished revenue pooling, and it permitted any carrier from one country to have access to any route to the other with as much capacity as it wanted. An obvious objective was to divert passengers away from routes where the traditional cartel arrangements left uncompetitive prices. Subsequent fare reductions in West Germany, Switzerland, and France can be directly attributed to the agreement. Pressure on Continental European countries to liberalize may thus appear due to the indirect competition of nearby routes. (The process is a repetition of what the US did to induce a liberal UK interpretation of Bermuda 2.) There is a population of 180 million within a radius of 250 miles of Schiphol allowing the airport to siphon traffic from uncompetitive carriers for both UK and intercontinental trips. (Indirect competition can also originate from fifth freedom carriers such as Singapore Airlines which flies the London-Frankfurt route. But fifth freedom rights apply to only about 1% of scheduled intra-ECAC flights.)

Consumer complaints are another source of pressure for liberalization. Again quoting Mr. Ridley,

It will be very difficult to tell the citizens of Paris that the Dutch can have fares lower by two-thirds than they have.[25]

Over the years, IATA has lost influence as the industry price fixing body as well. In 1960, IATA members carried 90% of the world's scheduled passenger traffic. By 1983, that share had fallen to 70% as a result of the growth of non-IATA members such as Singapore Airlines, People Express, and Virgin Airlines. And IATA officials admit that only about 60% of their official fares are complied with.

Nonetheless, there is considerable resistance to an extension into Europe of the American experience with a free market in airline services. Deregulation US-style would necessitate the agreement of different nations since, by contrast to the US, most intra-European flights are international. (For example, 80% of West German air service demand is international, and the country has 11 international airports.) And whereas liberalization obviously looks attractive to a country like Britain with a low cost carrier and with only ship service to the Continent as an alternative to air service, it looks much less attractive to the large Continental countries with high cost carriers, relatively large internal markets, and fast international train service. Change is obviously feared by countries with high cost carriers. The differences in costs across airlines and countries can be extremely large. According to IATA reports, European operating costs are 67% higher than US costs. More costly fuel and landing fees, lower volumes, and shorter average stage lengths account for part of this difference, but salary and other productivity differences are also pronounced. Whereas BA's labor costs are 27% of sales, such costs are only 13% of sales for all US carriers and 5% of sales for People Express. Salary costs of Lufthansa and Swissair are three to four times higher than those of BA.[26] Competition would thus have a dramatic impact on the relative fortunes of different employee groups, carriers, and countries. (See Exhibit 9 for airline cost comparisons.)

Furthermore, all airlines, European and non-European, will need to make heavy investments in the new generation of aircraft now entering service. The 135 airlines which are members of IATA will need $150–$200 billion over the next decade to buy 2,000 new aircraft. (Ironically, much of the demand for new aircraft, especially for a new 150-seater, is due to the changes in route structures

---

[23]*Hansard*, June 22, 1984.

[24]This means, for example, that a traveler could book a ticket in Glasgow on a KLM flight via Amsterdam to the Far East without going through London. Such a prospect of selling long-haul fares over another airline's home base is clearly advantageous for efficient airlines from small strategically placed countries.

[25]*Hansard*, May 5, 1984.

[26]*International Herald Tribune*, February 15, 1985.

EXHIBIT 9   AIRLINE COST COMPARISONS*

Carrier	Cost index
British Caledonian	0.91
Pan American	0.94
TWA	0.99
KLM	1.15
Air France	1.18
SAS	1.21
British Airways	1.24
Alitalia	1.25
UTA	1.25
Lufthansa	1.27
Sabena	1.28

*The figures shown are based on an index and derived from 1980 data. Note that this is prior to BA's cost-cutting.
Source: Findlay and Forsyth, "Competitiveness of Internationally Traded Services: The Case of International Airlines".

and densities caused by the regulatory changes discussed here.) Yet 1984 will be the first year since 1977 in which they will show a combined profit—of only $1.2 billion! Competition, it is claimed, will prevent the necessary profit levels.

The EEC is categorically in favor of liberalizing the European market, but it has not yet had the political power to influence events. In 1974, the European Court of Justice stated that the objectives and rules of the Treaty of Rome (such as non-discrimination and the prohibition of cartels) should apply to the airline industry. Yet it was not until 1984 that the Commission initiated action. Its "Memorandum No. 2," issued in February 1984, contains proposals for minimum and maximum fares within which airlines would fight it out. (This Memorandum is patterned after that of the US and the ECAC.) The price minimum is intended to prevent "destructive" price wars detrimental to all carriers but especially small ones. It also recommends ending the revenue sharing cartels, forcing the 50/50 capacity sharing agreements to vary up to 25/75, and easing entry of small airlines. Yet Memorandum No. 2 has provoked such criticism from European airlines and governments that its future is uncertain. It is estimated to be a couple of years before anything with legal standing comes out of the EEC, and even then the final policy is expected to be a weak one because it requires the unanimous approval of the Council of Transport Ministers.

In testifying against Memorandum No. 2 before the EEC, Karl-Heinz Neumeister, Secretary-General of the Association of European Airlines, asked,

> Are antitrust laws applicable to air transport, when governments in Europe already control or own the airlines? Obviously, antitrust laws are a method of protecting the consumer from the potential or real excesses of private enterprise.[27]

The Cabinet Committee's Impending Report

All parties involved directly or indirectly in the Cabinet Committee's decision had reason to fear its outcome.

BA feared that the original position of the CAA would be sustained by the Committee and thus strengthened. Any transfer of routes would be perceived as a betrayal of BA's employees who had suffered so much in the previous few years to improve the company's position. It would also be perceived as a personal betrayal of Lord King whose only fault (apparent to the company) was to have been too successful. And from the purely commercial viewpoint, a loss of routes would reduce the value of BA to the private financial community to whom the airline was soon to be offered.

BCal feared that a privatized BA would be a menace to the rest of the industry and particularly to BCal. Summing up his concern, Sir Adam Thomson said,

[27]*International Herald Tribune,* November 21, 1984.

Endowed with profitable routes and public funds, rescued from bankruptcy by a benevolent government, and operating from a virtually impregnable position at Heathrow, the world's busiest international gateway, BA in private hands would be in a position to stifle us.

Perhaps a more subtle fear was that unless the regulatory environment of the industry were changed before the BA sale, it would effectively remain unchangeable for the foreseeable future.

The other independent airlines feared a BA-BCal duopoly. From their point of view, the only thing worse than a BA monopoly was a BA-BCal duopoly implying twice the resistance to the growth of the smaller independents. The fate of Laker and the other 13 independent British airlines to have gone out of business since 1974 was a stark memory.

The CAA feared that rejection of its comprehensive report would destroy its credibility vis-a-vis the airline industry in general and particularly vis-a-vis its biggest regulatory client—BA. And if the CAA's proposals were rejected, BA would constitute an even more obdurate adversary. The CAA specifically cited this problem in its July report.

If British Airways were to become the sole British operator of international services, it would be the more difficult for this Authority to bring effective pressures to bear upon it. [28]

In terms of the political background to the Cabinet Committee's deliberations, Mrs. Thatcher was thought to favor Lord King to whom she had apparently made a promise of an untouched BA for sale to the private market. Lord Whitelaw—the Deputy Prime Minister—was a personal friend of Sir Adam Thomson. The Treasury wanted BA privatized as soon as possible at the highest price. The Trade Secretary, Norman Tebbitt, was a former BOAC pilot whose personal leaning was towards BA.

Nicholas Ridley's situation as he faced the September 13 deadline was aptly summed up by *The Observer*.

Whichever way he jumps, he now faces political embarrassment. Either he will break up BA—thus delaying its privatization plans indefinitely—or he will leave BA's route network intact and be seen to have ignored the CAA's most searching policy review for 20 years. [29]

---

[28]CAA, *op. cit.*, p. 2.

[29]*The Observer*, July 22, 1984.

BRITISH AIRWAYS

British Airways' market power is a major national asset where the British industry is in competition with foreign operators. [30]

British Airways is in favor of competitive solutions where competitive opportunities are available and where the result of adopting them is the overall strengthening of the UK civil aviation industry and the national interest. [31]

When Lord King (then Sir John King) was appointed Chairman of British Airways (BA) in 1981, there seemed to be little likelihood that BA would be a serious candidate for privatization in the foreseeable future. The company was over-manned, saddled with very heavy debt and losing money. (See Exhibits 2 to 4 for BA's financial results.) The whole airline industry was in the midst of one of the worst recessions in its history.

The year 1981 saw Lord King and his newly appointed Chief Executive, Colin Marshall, assessing the damaged state of the company and writing off all potential losses to start the next years afresh. The poor operating results for the first few years were exacerbated by huge redundancy payments, but by 1984 BA had reduced its workforce from 59,000 to 37,000, saving 200 million pounds in annual wages. It cut its aircraft fleet by a third to eliminate old high-cost equipment, and it abandoned 62 routes. At the same time, in a demonstration of the government's confidence in BA's new leadership, the airline became one of the first in the industry to place heavy orders for the new generation of fuel-efficient aircraft regarded as essential to long-term profitable operations. BA invested 400 million pounds to acquire 17 Boeing 757s, the most economical aircraft the company ever operated. More recently, it committed a further 200 million pounds to lease 14 smaller Boeing 737s with an option on a further 17.

By 1984, Lord King and Colin Marshall could claim that on the basis of operating results, BA was the world's most profitable airline!

This remarkable reversal in BA's fortunes—at great sacrifice from the existing workforce—was accomplished with the specific objective of preparing BA for privatization. And it was reported that Lord King had received assurances from his personal friend Mrs. Thatcher (who had appointed him) and from various ministers that the

---

[30]CAA, "Airline Competition Policy," July 1984.

[31]British Airways' submission to the Civil Aviation Authority, May 11, 1984.

company would be kept intact in the process of privatization. These implied or explicit assurances were, in turn, communicated to BA's employees.

Now, however, BA was threatened by a proposal from the Civil Aviation Authority (CAA) to transfer routes worth about 7% of its operating revenues to its rival, British Caledonian Airways (BCal). (See "The Privatization of British Airways".) As a BA spokesman put it,

> It would be a poor reward for BA and its staff if the consequence of its efforts were to be the arbitrary removal of a share of its business. . . . It would be ironic not to say unfair, if BA were now to be penalized for its increased efficiency.[32]

Lord King himself echoed the same sentiment.

> The dismemberment of BA would be a breach of faith to the Board which engineered the turnaround in its fortunes and the workforce which made sacrifices enabling the turnaround to become a reality.[33]
>
> I would regard it as a resignation issue, but whether I would resign, I don't know. My philosophy is that I accept resignations, I don't submit them.[34]

A likely consequence of implementing the CAA's proposals to transfer routes from BA to BCal was suggested in an article in the *Financial Times.*

> If the CAA proposals were approved, the Board would not resign, but would publicly refuse to accept any such transfers. . . . That in turn would almost inevitably force Mr. Nicholas Ridley . . . to sack the Board.[35]

British Airways' Case for Competition

Beyond the political and possibly ethical points noted above, BA argued that to remain competitive in world markets, it could not afford to lose routes to other UK carriers. The company's case was expressed by one of its powerful supporters, Industry Secretary (and former airline pilot) Mr. Norman Tebbitt.

> I think that the strongest case for maintaining a large British Airways is that it's existing in competition with a lot of other giants—Pan Am, TWA, Lufthansa, . . . When there is enor-

mous international competition and the competing companies are giants themselves, we need big companies to compete.[36]

Lord King himself also insisted that any transfer of routes from BA to BCal would not enhance competition but would rather "weaken BA's ability to compete with other international airlines such as Pan Am and TWA."[37]

The basic argument was that on most international routes, one British airline (BA or BCal) would be competing with a single foreign airline, and any diminution of the market share of the stronger UK airline (presumably BA) would only help the relative position of the foreign carrier. So righting a competitive imbalance between BA and BCal would be no policy success if it created a competitive imbalance between BA and some foreign carriers. In fact, a former BA chief executive, Roy Watts, suggested that a single major British airline be established which would match the power of foreign competitors. The obvious suggestion was that BA should buy BCal after privatization. The suggestion was reportedly made with the knowledge of Lord King.

One specific threat to the UK's national interest, a threat acknowledged by the CAA, was that a transfer of international routes from BA to BCal would also transfer arrivals and departures from Heathrow to Gatwick. Travelers unwilling to accept the move to the less popular Gatwick had the option of flying on a foreign carrier based at Heathrow. Going beyond this, Heathrow competed with overseas airports like Schiphol in The Netherlands which advertised itself as London's third airport. Any weakening of the attractiveness of Heathrow could transfer passengers out of the UK altogether.

BA was willing to accept dual designation on routes where there was sufficient demand (see Exhibits 10 and 11 for data on route densities), but even the CAA reported that this was not often the case. (Monopoly efficiencies start to become exhausted at about 2,000 passengers daily.)

> It seems fairly clear that only a very limited number of intercontinental markets could support additional competing British services based predominantly on end-to-end traffic.[38]

Since there was so little scope for new route entry, the CAA proposal only amounted to substituting one UK car-

---

[32]British Airways spokesman, quoted in the *Financial Times,* February 2, 1984.

[33]Quoted in *The Observer,* September 9, 1984.

[34]Quoted in *The Times,* May 2, 1984.

[35]*Financial Times,* September 10, 1984.

[36]Quoted in *The Daily Telegraph,* January 9, 1984.

[37]Quoted in *The Observer,* September 23, 1984.

[38]CAA, *op. cit.,* p. 43.

EXHIBIT 10 PRINCIPAL UNITED KINGDOM AIR TRAVEL MARKETS

Market		Passengers (millions)
United Kingdom	Spain	9.6
	USA	5.8
	France	3.3
	Germany	3.2
	Italy	2.5
	Greece	2.0
	Netherlands	1.8
	Eire	1.6
	Switzerland	1.7
	Canada	1.4
	Portugal	1.1

Source: CAA Airline Statistics.

EXHIBIT 11 LONDON/EUROPE SCHEDULED PASSENGERS (1983)—ROUTES EXCEEDING 100,000 PASSENGERS PER ANNUM

Route	No. of passengers	Route	No. of passengers
Paris*	2,132,000	Stockholm	238,000
Amsterdam*	1,076,000	Munich**	238,000
Dublin*	878,000	Nice	222,000
Frankfurt*	723,000	Malta	203,000
Brussels*	610,000	Malaga	193,000
Zurich*	533,000	Lisbon	184,000
Geneva*	525,000	Barcelona	179,000
Copenhagen	392,000	Cork*	157,000
Rome	379,000	Rotterdam	147,000
Dusseldorf	371,000	Cologne**	143,000
Athens	366,000	Vienna**	139,000
Milan	353,000	Stuttgart**	127,000
Madrid	336,000	Helsinki**	127,000
Oslo	293,000	Shannon**	124,000
Hamburg**	292,000	Berlin	116,000
Larnaca	258,000	Hanover**	106,000

*Competing Heathrow and Gatwick services operated by British carriers.
**Competing Heathrow and Gatwick services licensed to British carriers but not operated from both airports.
Source: CAA Airline Statistics.

rier for another with no obvious reason to expect increased competition. As a BA spokesman summarized it,

> There is a major fallacy in the argument that to transfer routes from one British airline to another would create more competition.[39]

All of BA's arguments have to be seen in the context of its hopes for privatization. Colin Marshall was explicit about the threat that the policy debate posed for BA's stock floatation.

> From our perspective, any conclusion other than a continuation of the status quo is going to call into question the whole issue of privatization—and certainly the timing of our floatation.[40]

A transfer of some routes to BCal would not only deprive BA of some of its most valuable assets, but it would also set a precedent which could threaten the security of BA's hold on any of its routes. One logical long-term implication of the CAA's proposed policy to "improve the balance" between BA and BCal was that opportunities for future growth would be directed to the smaller airlines. In addition, a policy of favoring the development of Gatwick would benefit only the smaller airlines since the CAA proposed to move BA out of that airport. The financial market would surely incorporate the implications of any CAA policy changes in its valuation of BA shares.

All these threats risked causing an indefinite postponement of BA's privatization. And this postponement, in turn, could jeopardize the credibility of a government committed to increasing the scope of the private sector.

BRITISH CALEDONIAN AIRWAYS

British Caledonian Airways (BCal) is Europe's largest privately owned scheduled-service airline and operates more than 700 passenger and cargo flights each week. The company was created in 1961 and reached its current form in 1970 following a takeover of British United Airways. BCal has subsequently grown to become Europe's ninth largest airline (larger than some national carriers) and the 28th largest airline in the free world. In 1983 it was designated the "Business Executives' Airline of the Year." Of perhaps greater significance, the Caledonian

Aviation Group was generally profitable at a time when most airlines lost money. (See Exhibits 12 and 13 for financial data.) The Group is very strongly committed to aviation-based activities, and its only non-aviation subsidiaries are in the travel industry (such as travel agencies and hotels).

The success of BCal is a personal tribute to its founder, Sir Adam Thomson. A 58 year old Scotsman, Sir Adam has been described as "a canny Scot, a very shrewd operator who plays his cards close to his chest".[41] A British Airways (BA) executive put it differently. "Give Adam something now and he will be back for more".[42] He is reputed to be obsessively single-minded and determined when he perceives his airline's interests to be threatened. For example, when Laker Airlines was about to collapse, McDonnell Douglas (the American aircraft manufacturer) was rumored to be planning a rescue by taking a share in the ailing airline. Sir Adam was described as "incoherent with anger," calling Laker "the most disruptive airline on the North Atlantic." He allegedly informed McDonnell Douglas that if the rumor were true, he would cancel all further business dealings with the manufacturer.[43] (This threat became an element of both the US government's antitrust investigation and the antitrust case that Laker's creditors filed in the US against BCal, BA, and eight other large airlines.)

This determination characterized Sir Adam's opposition to the privatization of British Airways in its current form. Specifically, Sir Adam feared that the UK government would relieve BA of most of its debt and would offer the firm to the private sector with no change in its route structure or airport usage. As *The Sunday Telegraph* put it,

> Competing with an overblown, inefficient, uncanny and unprofitable state-owned airline is one thing. Flying against a slim, motivated, private, and—most important of all—decently financed airline, which is what BA could become by this time next year, is another.[44]

This threat and the fact that privatization would necessitate setting and then guaranteeing for the foreseeable future British aviation rules to the satisfaction of the in-

---

[39]BA spokesman, quoted in the *Financial Times*, February 2, 1984.

[40]Quoted in *The Times*, March 7, 1984.

[41]Graham Bright, MP, quoted in *The Times*, August 16, 1984.

[42]*Ibid.*

[43]*Ibid.*

[44]*The Sunday Telegraph*, November 13, 1983.

EXHIBIT 12 BRITISH CALEDONIAN CONSOLIDATED PROFIT AND LOSS ACCOUNT—1983

	1983 £'000	1982 £'000
Turnover	428,484	400,556
Cost of sales	(344,334)	(326,065)
Gross profit	84,150	74,491
Marketing costs	(31,998)	(27,387)
Administration expenses	(34,965)	(30,260)
Other operating income	513	340
Operating profit	17,700	17,184
Profits/(losses) on disposal of tangible fixed assets and investments	1,851	(178)
Income from shares in related companies	116	94
Income from fixed asset investments	20	19
Net interest payable	(16,350)	(15,577)
Profit on ordinary activities before taxation	3,337	1,542
Tax on profit on ordinary activities	(1,211)	(811)
Profit for the financial year attributable to shareholders	1,126	731
Earnings per share	10.7p	3.7p

vesting public prompted Sir Adam to issue his "Blue Book" on November 3, 1983. In this report, he outlined his ideas for the future structure of the British aviation industry and offered to buy routes from BA which constituted 20% of BA's profits. (For details, see Exhibit 14.)

Tactically, Sir Adam's timing was perfect. Sir John Moore, Financial Secretary to the Treasury, had delivered a major speech only two days earlier stating that the principal objective of privatization was to increase competition in the industry. And in December 1983, the Minister of Transport, Nicholas Ridley, announced that the Civil Aviation Authority (CAA) would carry out a major review of the UK airline industry.

BCal's Public Relations Offensive

In a carefully orchestrated and expensive public relations offensive, BCal took its case to the public and, more specifically, to the powerful conservative back-bench MPs.

The core of BCal's argument was that competition in the UK aviation industry only existed to a very limited degree. Over the years, the government had granted BA approximately 80% of the UK-originating international scheduled market—a market characterized by cartel pric-

ing and revenue pooling. Furthermore, BA's exclusive right to Heathrow Airport for international departures was a major competitive advantage which, like its international market share, was granted to it by government policy rather than won competitively. From this protected market base, BA would be able to cross-subsidize its operations in the more competitive domestic and charter markets to the detriment of smaller carriers.

The CAA's report was issued in July 1984 and endorsed this argument.

> BA is therefore very well placed to use international route profits to support expansion in other markets. Despite regulatory constraints, it could deploy this market power, almost at will, in any particular market where it chose to compete aggressively with other British airlines. It is this potential for exploiting its market power which frightens many respondents. . . . It is often difficult to distinguish between normal competitive behavior and behavior that is predatory in character.[45]

As part of its public relations campaign, BCal attempted to refute some of BA's arguments, including

[45]CAA, "Airline Competition Policy," July 1984, p. 5.

EXHIBIT 13   BRITISH CALEDONIAN CONSOLIDATED BALANCE SHEET—1983

	1983		1982	
	Group £'000	Company £'000	Group £'000	Company £'000
Net assets employed				
Fixed assets				
Intangible assets	1,861	—	2,674	—
Tangible assets	242,782	5,391	227,948	5,216
Investments	3,088	48,036	453	48,836
	247,731	53,427	231,075	54,052
Current assets				
Stocks	19,168	—	17,725	—
Debtors	85,419	16,926	73,768	12,679
Cash at bank and in hand	69,118	81	56,364	1,457
	173,705	17,007	147,857	14,136
Creditors—amounts falling due within one year				
Trade and other	(155,937)	(9,417)	(138,871)	(6,978)
Working capital	17,768	7,590	8,986	7,158
Loans & term finance	(34,336)	(413)	(24,278)	(1,000)
Net current assets/(liabilities)	(16,568)	7,177	(15,292)	6,158
Total assets less current liabilities	231,163	60,604	215,783	60,210
Creditors—amounts falling due after more than one year				
Loans & term finance	(160,297)	(4,372)	(158,773)	(4,785)
Deferred income	(1,633)	—	(1,585)	—
	69,233	56,232	55,425	55,425
Represented by				
Capital and reserves				
Called up share capital	19,807	19,807	19,807	19,807
Revaluation reserve	24,381	962	13,798	981
Profit & loss account	25,045	35,463	21,820	34,637
	69,233	56,232	55,425	55,425

BA's claim that it competed "fiercely" with the other airlines of the world.

It is nonsense for BA to suggest that it competes with hundreds of foreign airlines. Their system is rigged with a network of cosy cartels.[46]

BCal also ridiculed BA's offer to let BCal compete alongside it on any international route BCal chose. As BCal pointed out, the offer sounded fair, but under the current system of bilateral agreements any entry of BCal onto an international route would require the approval of a foreign government—an unlikely prospect.

Competition cannot exist unless the contestants have equal access to the market place. . . . Plainly BA is saying that it is all for competition so long as it can have the High Street supermarket while its competitor must be happy with corner grocery stores.[47]

BCal's exclusion from most international routes due to the bilateral cartel structure of the route system led to BCal's offer to buy routes from BA. When Lord King, Chairman of BA, called BCal's offer "a smash and grab raid,"[48] Sir Adam replied that at least it would be a golden brick that would come through Lord King's window.

[46]Sir Adam Thomson, quoted in *The Sunday Telegraph*, August 12, 1984.

[47]BCal, "The Historic Opportunity."

[48]*The Observer*, November 13, 1983.

EXHIBIT 14 BRITISH CALEDONIAN PROPOSALS

In November 1983, Sir Adam Thomson, Chairman of BCal, made public his bid to secure the transfer of a significant proportion of BA's routes and related assets at what he considered a fair market price. His detailed proposals were never published, but knowledgeable sources indicated that they fell into three major categories:

1 BA should transfer to BCal licenses to fly routes in the following five categories:

• All BA routes to Spain, Portugal, Bologna, Naples, Copenhagen, Stockholm, originating from Gatwick.
• All BA flights to eight Caribbean destinations.
• The North Pacific routes including Tokyo, Beijing and Seoul.
• Low-frequency BA flights to Turkey, Cyprus, Greece, Malta, Austria and Finland.
• BA routes to the Arabian Gulf, including Abu Dhabi and Kuwait.

2 On the transfer of these routes, BCal should reimburse BA at their estimated market value of £200–£250 million.
3 In order to serve these routes, BCal would purchase from BA seven Boeing 747 jumbo jets and nine Boeing 737 narrow-bodied jets, worth about £300 million.

These proposals formed the basis of BCal's submission to the CAA early in 1984, although it is understood that

BCal proposed an even more substantial set of route transfers. As they stood, the November 1983 proposals envisaged the transfer of 20% of BA's profits, and a significantly higher proportion of its revenues. In addition, Thomson also proposed that BA's domestic German routes, its feeder domestic UK traffic, and the charter subsidiary, British Airtours, be sold to other independent airlines. This represented another £230 million in revenues and £20 million in profit. Thomson couched his proposals in the following terms:

> The time has never been more opportune for the Government to take a visionary initiative to create a really strong and highly competitive civil aviation industry in wholly private ownership and to lay down a framework for long-term growth.

He added that:

> Routes have never been sold before, but I'm happy to talk about it to the right people.

Lord King of BA, who presumably was one of "the right people", responded that BCal's proposals were a "smash and grab raid" and declared:

> The boarding party they have in mind might well have been more successful when we're on our backs.

Again, BCal's case had the endorsement of the CAA.

> There is a need for an alternative airline, which although relatively smaller than BA, would nonetheless be capable of operating as a world-class airline and could replace BA on a major international route should the need arise. BCal is the only airline which the UK has that is immediately capable of filling that role."[49]

The CAA also sought to encourage indirect competition between BA and BCal. It granted BCal a license to fly to Riyadh in Saudi Arabia in February 1984 while allowing BA to continue scheduled services to Jeddah and Dharan.

> The CAA concluded that the interests of users would be better served if more than one British airline operated services to

Saudi Arabia. . . . Indirect competition is likely to be beneficial and users will gain from the enhanced service and wider choice.[50]

While BCal's campaign emphasized the need for greater competition, stressing that this was the principal declared objective of privatization, it introduced other issues as well. BCal was based at Gatwick Airport while BA was based at Heathrow, Europe's busiest airport. In 1983 Heathrow accounted for nearly 80% of total UK scheduled international traffic and Gatwick only 14%. Any transfer of routes from BA to BCal would mean a corresponding movement from Heathrow to Gatwick and would further the government's objective of reducing the discrepancy between the two airports. Quoting the CAA,

[49]CAA, *op. cit.*

[50]CAA, quoted in the *Financial Times*, February 15, 1984.

Present airports policy . . . has not yet been wholly success-ful either in developing Gatwick's full potential or in provid-ing the infrastructure for a fully competitive British airline industry.[51]

When asked what would happen if BCal were not granted some new routes, Sir Adam replied, ''We would have to apply for a transfer to Heathrow.''[52] It was not clear to observers whether Sir Adam hoped (or threatened) to move all or only some of his flights to Heathrow, but there would be important employment and capacity utili-zation implications of any significant shift.

BCal emphasized that it did not intend to reduce sub-stantially the size of BA. Even if all the route transfers asked for by BCal were effected, BA would remain the dominant British airline with about 70% of international scheduled services. In BCal's view, this would leave BA ''still a most attractive privatization candidate.''[53]

BCal's strongly voiced opinion that the entire industry was threatened by a privatized and unfettered BA mo-nopoly was shared by all the other independent airlines. However, BCal's additional opinion that ''except in spe-cial circumstances, there is only room for two interna-tional airlines from the UK''[54] led to cynical press com-mentary.

Monopolies are like small babies. You may think they are really unattractive—but just wait until you have one of your own![55]

[51]CAA, *op. cit.*, p. 6.

[52]*The Observer*, September 16, 1984.

[53]*Financial Times*, September 12, 1984.

[54]Sir Adam Thomson, quoted in *The Daily Mail*, February 28, 1984.

[55]*The Daily Mail, op. cit.*

COMPAQ COMPUTER CORPORATION

Sexton Adams
Adelaide Griffin
North Texas State University
Texas Woman's University

The classic way for entrepreneurs to break into technology-based businesses is with dazzling innovations and leapfrogging the best products offered by established competitors. Yet, COMPAQ Computer Corporation, one of the most successful newcomers in United States corporate history, did it assiduously holding innovations in check.

The company's record is a credit to its co-founder and chief executive, J. R. "Rod" Canion, a 40-year-old engineer from Texas Instruments so unswashbuckling that even a top aide admits he "lacks sizzle." Canion's game plan has served the company well and made it a serious contender in the personal computer market.

Can Canion keep this up? The question sends Benjamin M. Rosen, the venture capitalist who is COMPAQ's chairman, into fits of frustration. Will investors, security analysts, and other fascinated observers, he asks, never give this company its due?

BRIEF HISTORY OF THE COMPANY

COMPAQ Computer Corporation was incorporated in Delaware on February 16, 1982, to engage in the development, manufacture, and sale of personal computers. During 1982 the company was in the development stage, and its activities mainly involved the design and development of a portable computer, establishment of manufacturing facilities, and development of a dealer network.[1]

The first product was the 28-pound COMPAQ Portable Computer; product shipment did not begin until January 1983. Within a period of ten months, in October 1983, the second product, COMPAQ PLUS Portable Computer, was introduced. This was a more powerful version of the first product.[2] In yet another eight months—in June 1984 the company introduced its first non-portable computer line known as the COMPAQ DESKPRO family, which had four models.[3]

Although such growth seemed impossible for a company that started only in 1982, it was not at all surprising in the light of the following statement of Rod Canion, President and Chief Executive Officer, and the brain be-

This case was prepared by Danny Duncan, Medar Sevintuna, Raj Shaw, and Beverlee Polzin under the supervision of Professor Sexton Adams, North Texas State University, and Professor Adelaide Griffin, Texas Woman's University.

[1] Annual Report 1983, COMPAQ Computer Corporation.

[2] Ibid.

[3] Second Quarter Report 1984, COMPAQ Computer Corporation.

hind this phenomenally successful company. Canion stated that "when we formed the company in 1982, we viewed it as a major company in the formative stages, rather than a small company with big plans."[4] The personnel hired had experience and could not only do their initial jobs, but could also manage a large organization as the company grew. The best people were located and hired and took the company from zero to $111 million in sales in the first year, and as Canion proudly points out they did it "profitably and under control." Sales tripled and were $325 million in 1984.[5]

MANAGEMENT PHILOSOPHY AND STRATEGY

The company took advantage of three key trends in the personal computer field:[6]

1 The establishment of the IBM Personal Computer architecture of the industry standard for software and hardware for 16-bit personal computers

2 The rapid growth and widespread acceptance of personal computers for business and professional use

3 The emergence of the portable computer as the fastest growing segment in the personal computer market

In pursuing these trends the company followed some very basic principles which are the backbone of management's philosophy.[7] First, the company decided to hire an exceptional management team. As explained above, this resulted in record-breaking performance by the company.

The second principle was to achieve true compatibility with industry standards. The company believed that an industry standard existed for software, peripherals, option boards, displays, and keyboards; and it made its computers compatible with this. Many other companies believed that such standardization would thwart innovation.

Development of a widely-accepted family of products was the third principle. This was based on the belief that to be successful, the company must have a product family that solves the real needs of the market; a commitment to short development cycles in order to grow and prosper.

Fourth, rapid achievement of high-volume manufacturing was considered important. Management foresaw a

strong demand for its products and planned and achieved an extremely rapid buildup in manufacturing capacity and shipped at an annualized rate of more than $200 million worth of computers by the fourth quarter of 1983.

Fifth, establishing a high-quality dealer network was a major ingredient for success. One of the most important steps that the company took during its formative period was to listen to dealers and to examine both the successes and failures of competitors. As a result of this, the company established a strategy based on very close, noncompetitive relationships with its Authorized Dealers.

Last and very important, it was imperative to raise substantial financial resources. The company decided from the very outset that it would raise capital before needs occurred, thereby enabling it to conduct planning and operations without financial constraints. Seeing opportunities materializing in the near future and need for significant additional capital, the company went public in December 1983 and raised approximately $61 million in the initial offering of its common stock. The company was, therefore, in a strong working capital position.

The foregoing philosophy was responsible for the formulation of a unique strategy. The game plan that brought COMPAQ to this enviable position in 1985 was a strategy of piggybacking on IBM rather than leapfrogging it. The company's aim was to stay compatible with IBM because most software was made for them. However, COMPAQ ensured that it was not relegated to the position of a mere IBM-knock off by a strategy which was highly sophisticated.

This strategy was zealously pursued by a team of closely knit professionals put together by Rod Canion. It included acknowledged stalwarts in the PC industry. (Refer to Exhibit A.) Their enthusiasm, determination, and hard work had enabled COMPAQ to take on the giants of the computer industry, and to emerge as a true industry leader.

Compatibility was the operative word, and everything else centered around it. Careful planning went into ensuring compatibility despite being in an industry which was innovation oriented. All "innovation" at COMPAQ was geared to compatibility, and programmers were firmly indoctrinated into the desired mold. So successful was this strategy that the industry gurus were hard-put to name another company that had earned respectable profits over the long run. However, COMPAQ understood that such a path was fraught with dangers because IBM was known to make unexpected moves: it could cut prices or come out with machines so tough to copy that emulators

---

[4]Annual Report 1983, COMPAQ Computer Corporation.

[5]Ibid.

[6]Ibid.

[7]Ibid.

EXHIBIT A COMPAQ COMPUTER CORPORATION OFFICERS and DIRECTORS

Officers

President and Chief Executive Officer: Joseph R. Canion,
  Senior Vice President, Corporate Operations: James M. Eckhart
  Senior Vice President, PC Division: B. Kevin Ellington
    Vice President, Corporate Resources: Wayne F. Collins
    Vice President, Corporate Communications: James D. D'Arezzo
    Vice President, General Counsel and Secretary: Wilson D. Fargo
    Vice President, Systems Engineering: J. Steven Flannigan
    Treasurer: John M. Foster
    *Vice President, Telecommunications and
     President, COMPAQ Telecommunications Corporation:* Murray Francois
    Vice President, Finance and Chief Financial Officer: J. F. Gribi
    Vice President, Engineering: James M. Harris
    Vice President, Corporate Marketing: William H. Murto
    Vice President, Human Resources: Cecil C. Parker
    Vice President, Europe: Eckhart Pfeiffer
    Vice President, Product Marketing: Michael S. Swavely
    Vice President, Sales: Max E. Toy
    Vice President, Manufacturing: Robert E. Vieau
    Corporate Controller: Daryl J. White

Directors

President, CEO of COMPAQ Computer Corporation: Joseph R. Canion
General Partner: L. John Doerr III, Kleiner, Perkins, Gaufield & Bryers II and III
Chairman: Benjamin M. Rosen, Sevin Rosen Management Company
President: L. J. Sevin, Sevin Rosen Management Company

  Source: Compaq Annual Report/1984.

---

would get left in the lurch. In the summer of 1984, IBM slashed prices of the PC just before COMPAQ came out with its first non-portable line. In August of the same year, IBM introduced the IBM PC AT, a computer that was not fully compatible with its own PC, and hence not with COMPAQ's PORTABLES or DESKPROS.

Even so, making a computer compatible was not easy. Microsoft Corporation had written the operating system for the IBM PC, software that established the playing field for word processing, spread sheets, and other application programs to operate on. COMPAQ was able to buy some of the Microsoft Operating system and the INTEL 8088 microprocessor chip that was the PC's brain. But special instructions copyrighted by IBM were built into a microchip to make the operating system run. COMPAQ's engineers had to mimic the program, flaws and all, without

violating the copyright. A team at COMPAQ worked for nine months and succeeded after an expenditure of $1 million.[8]

Once the "hardware compatibility" was established and Canion felt they had a saleable computer, COMPAQ moved quickly to position the computer with retailers. It lined up Sears and the large computer chain—Computerland. COMPAQ's distribution strategy was a key major computer maker that sold solely to retailers; it did not have its own direct sales force skimming off business with large corporations, even though direct sales accounted for 25% to 35% of all micros sold. In addition, the products were priced to dealers so that they could gross 36% on

[8]*Fortune*, February 18, 1985, pp. 286–287.

sales made at the suggested retail price versus 33% on sales of IBM computers.

To ensure good relations with retailers, COMPAQ hired away a key member of the IBM team that developed the PC. H. L. ''Sparky'' Sparks, who developed IBM's network of authorized dealers, didn't come cheap. Canion offered him options on 98.906 shares @ $.53, a $100,000 up-front bonus, and salary of $150,000, which was $30,000 higher than his own at that time.[9]

The result of all these efforts was that COMPAQ became one of the few companies other than IBM and Apple to command a vast swath of shelf space in stores. COMPAQ took advantage of its dealers' loyalty by using them in market research. The company brought key dealers together several times a year and relentlessly quizzed them on why products were selling or what customers were asking for in the stores. Dealers were cooperative in the quest of COMPAQ to know the pulse of the market. Although some dealers felt exhausted after a full day of grilling, others felt that COMPAQ's ''success (was) not from the latest technology or a lot of razzle-dazzle but from coming out with what dealers want(ed).''[10]

Consequently, when COMPAQ introduced its first line of nonportable computers in mid-1984—the DESKPRO family—it was a hit. There was no razzle-dazzle, but just some new features that reflected what COMPAQ learned from talking to dealers and from other market research. Three months before the DESKPRO was released, dealers complained that their stockrooms would have trouble accommodating four new models. COMPAQ promptly redesigned the line. Though it was priced from $2,500 to $7,200, the same DESKPRO chassis could accommodate all four models. Instead of four different models, dealers could simply plop in extra disk drives or hard disks and whip up whatever the customer ordered.

The demands of the dealers were, however, accommodated after careful filtering through the astuteness and cool tenacity of Rod Canion, who had proved a master of both the technology and the marketing of micro-computers. The introduction of the IBM PC AT is a case in point. The PC AT was a truly powerful computer, was faster than the DESKPRO, and was a multi-user machine. This reflected a strategic shift by IBM and some dealers wanted a ''COMPAQ AT.'' But Canion said no and explained that ''the PC market (was) absolutely not going to multi-user machines; the basic reason for the PC's success (was) that it (gave) you flexibility you (couldn't) get in multi-user environments. With multi-user machines you have to share computing power and the storage capacity. If only one of the users (ran) software with bugs in it, that (would) shut down the entire machine.'' Having made the decision not to emulate the multi-user machine, Canion got high points from the dealers like CompuShop who agreed ''100%'' and added that ''in the old days you went multi-user to share processors or expensive peripherals like data-storage disks and printer. . . . All those (were) so absurdly cheap (in 1984) that there was no technological or economic reasons for multi-user machines.'' There was a feeling that IBM would introduce a single-user AT later and Canion didn't rule out copying the new AT.[11]

RESEARCH AND DEVELOPMENT

With a keen eye for the future, a subsidiary called COMPAQ Telecommunications Inc. was formed and made responsible for the development of ''telecomputers''—machines that would combine the functions of computers with those of telephones, clocks, calculators, and calendars into one desktop console. The subsidiary had already developed an IBM-compatible machine that would carry both data and voices. The product was aimed at upper level executives who didn't need a lot of spreadsheet calculating power but wanted something to help manage the hectic schedules. The President of COMPAQ Telecommunications felt that upper level executives had avoided computers because they were perceived as too difficult to master. There was, therefore, an emphasis on software, some of which COMPAQ wrote, that would make the machine easy to use. A device to turn a COMPAQ computer into a Telecomputer was expected to be introduced.[12]

MARKETING STRATEGY OF THE CORPORATION

COMPAQ has received high marks from all around for its sophisticated marketing strategy. Forbes[13] said that ''Compaq's marketing strategy is first rate.'' And this

---

[9]Ibid.

[10]Ibid.

[11]Ibid.

[12]*Forbes*, January 14, 1985, pp. 286–287.

[13]*Christian Science Monitor*, April 5, 1984, pp. 16–17.

opinion seemed to reverberate throughout the industry. The company had the most successful first year of sales in American business history with revenues of $111 million—and it proudly celebrated this fact in its advertisements.

"Our success was not luck," said an officer of the company in April 1984 and explained that the marketing strategy of the corporation was oriented towards the market's needs and does not try to push new technology on a market that isn't ready for it.[14] To stay constantly in touch with the "needs of the market" the company stayed in constant touch with its dealers and "listened" to them. As explained earlier, dealers were invited to Houston and grilled for a whole day.

Realizing early on that a strong dealer network would be the key to compete in an IBM-dominated marketplace, COMPAQ moved early to develop a strong network in the United States. As soon as the design of the basic computer was over, the prototype of the COMPAQ Portable was unveiled at a big national computer show for

retailers in November 1982.[15] The prototype won over the acceptance of Sears (the largest retailer) and ComputerLand. The network grew—continued to expand from there—and soon included major national and regional chains. Many other major dealers with multi-store operations also carried COMPAQ products. Exhibit 1 shows the geographical spread of the dealer network as of December 1983.[16]

Demand for COMPAQ computers from outside the United States prompted management to expand its marketing activities throughout North America and Western Europe. The company appointed a vice president, and was selling through 330 retailers in Europe by the end of 1984.

The dealers in both North America and Europe were selected on the basis of their financial strength, their ability to provide quality sales and service, and their commitment to producing a high level of consumer satisfaction. To provide support to the dealers, the company set up sales and service support centers in Atlanta, Boston,

[14]*Fortune*, February 18, 1985, pp. 74–83.

[15]Annual Report 1985, COMPAQ Computer Corporation.

[16]*Forbes*, January 14, 1985, pp. 286–287.

EXHIBIT 1   Unit shipments of leading office personal computers (worldwide—1983).
(March 1984, Future Computing Incorporated, 900 Canyon Creek Center, Richardson, Texas 75080).

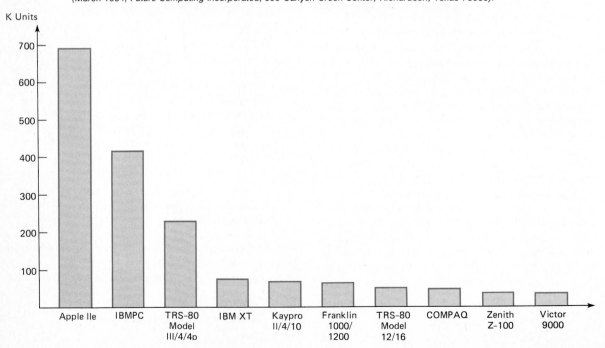

Chicago, San Francisco, and Santa Ana, California, to work closely with the Authorized Dealers and to concentrate other resources of the company. The staff at the regional locations was composed of professional sales people who were highly knowledgeable about personal computers for business and professional use.

Further support for the dealer network came in the form of the "COMPAQ in Major Accounts Program" in 1984. This plan was designed to aid dealers in the sale of COMPAQ Personal Computers to major industrial companies and other large organizations. Another program was the "COMPAQ in Schools," which encouraged Authorized Dealers to sell COMPAQ Personal Computers to high schools, colleges, and universities.

In addition to this, the company gave its dealers discounts that were higher than IBM and also higher than the industry average.[17] Its products were priced to dealers so that they could gross 36% on sales made at the suggested retail price, versus 33% on sales of IBM computers.[18] This helped dealers in an industry in which manufacturers' price cuts usually came out of retailers' share. Unlike most IBM-compatible machines, COMPAQ did not have to be sold by price cutting.

COMPAQ had made itself even more attractive to the dealers because it did not compete with them in any way. COMPAQ was the only major computer maker that sold directly to retailers and did not have a separate sales force selling directly to end users. Although COMPAQ was aware that direct sales accounted for 25% to 35% of all micros sold, it decided against skimming off such business because it would be to the detriment of its relationships with retailers.

COMPAQ looked upon its dealers as business partners and supported them totally. Such support, it hoped, would be reciprocated to total commitment from the dealers to its products; it paid off handsomely. The result of all these efforts was that COMPAQ's computers were one of the few, other than IBM's and Apple's computers, to command a vast swath of shelf space in computer stores.

Although dealer support was a very important part of the marketing success, it was not the only one. The products it made and marketed were excellent. As Canion claimed, "on every model we've sold we've always offered a little more than IBM—faster speed, more memory,

a bigger screen, words and graphics on the same screen. . . ."[19]

Compatibility with the IBM PC had been the mainstay and its products were better mated with the IBM than any other manufacturer's. But the company's strategy did not stop there. The company was committed to fulfilling needs in the market through its products. Sometimes, to its good fortune, the "market need" was a shortage of IBM PC's.

COMPAQ's early growth was propelled by shortages of the IBM PC. Said Seymour Marion, Chairman of Computer Works chain of dealerships, "when IBM PC's were first introduced and were in short supply you could safely buy a COMPAQ and know that every single IBM PC program you were using would also work without modification. . . . That made it a very comforting purchase."[20] The product was good, and the quality control program was indeed impressive. Components were tested for quality before arrival at the plant. Finished products were self-tested for 48 hours. Various manual and electronic checkpoints were set up along the production line. To demonstrate the quality of the product, a COMPAQ Portable loaded with software was dropped on the floor at COMPAQ's Sales Training Course. It was then picked up from the floor and everything was still in one piece and running. Mr. Homes, an attending salesman, felt that if an IBM PC were dropped on the floor "a lot of pieces would be sitting at your feet."

"This is all true," said Tom Kruchaway, a research director at the Yankee Corporation, a Boston firm specializing in high-tech research and consulting, "COMPAQ's products beat the new IBM portable in weight, size, and graphic capabilities, but people in large corporations tend to prefer IBM when it's available." [21] Even Ben Rosen, Chairman of COMPAQ, knew that IBM's reputation won the sales battle over COMPAQ.[22] The company therefore decided to spend $20 million in 1984 on an advertising campaign to overcome this handicap. The company wanted to stress that it was a serious player in the market and wanted to distance itself from other industry comets that had quickly burned out like OSBORNE computers.

The company's image as a serious player improved,

[17]*Fortune,* February 18, 1985, pp. 74–83.

[18]*Forbes,* January 14, 1985, pp. 286–287.

[19]Ibid.

[20]*Christian Science Monitor,* April 5, 1984, pp. 16–17.

[21]*Fortune,* April 16, 1984, pp. 60.

[22]Ibid.

and in 1984 COMPAQ's share of the PC market doubled to 10% (up from 5% in 1983—its first year of selling) compared with 20% for Apple and 50% for IBM. Within its market share, the company showed strength at the high end. Sales of COMPAQ's DESKPRO had begun to take hold, and it was selling better than Apple's Macintosh and IBM's PC AT and XT, the three machines closest in performance and market.

The company's record was praiseworthy and analysts wondered whether it could keep it up. Wall Street found it hard to believe that any PC start-up could play in the same league with IBM and Apple. The degree to which COMPAQ had tied its fortunes to the IBM PC was also discomforting to its investors. IBM compatibility was not accepted as a long-term business plan for COMPAQ.[23]

In implementing COMPAQ's strategy, both Canion and Ben Rosen, Chairman of COMPAQ Computers, all but ignored the threat that IBM could abandon its "open architecture" policy in micro-computers. They did not think IBM would close off the architecture, but even if it did, they believed the new machines would be compatible with the old ones and, therefore, with COMPAQ. "There are two million people out there that have bought IBM PC's," said COMPAQ's Chairman, Ben Rosen. ". . . The company cannot abandon those machines."[24]

INDUSTRY AND TRENDS

The PC market was expected to reach $38 billion in 1985[25]. Looking back, many companies left the market due to the very competitive market situation. By the 1990's it was expected to be served by only big names such as IBM, Apple, etc.

Before the IBM PC's announcement in July 1981, Digital Research's Control program for microcomputers "CP/M" was the favored operating system in offices that used microcomputers. But IBM not only forced a change to MICROSOFT's MS-DOS but also "legitimized" business computing and created new groups of personal computer users. The competition was from Apple, OSBORNE, XENIX, and others. But, by underproducing the IBM PC and its hard disk drives, the PC XT, IBM created the demand that spawned the IBM PC–compatible industry and companies such as COMPAQ, EAGLE, COLOMBIA, DATA GENERAL, as well as new MS-DOS- or PC-DOS-compatible products from Texas Instruments, FUJITSU and most recently, TANDY[26].

Apple was clearly the king of personal computer hill in 1980. It took the company nearly five years, though, to repeat the success it had with the Apple II. In 1984, the arrival of the $2,500 Macintosh redefined the minimal user requirements of nearly every personal computer to follow. IBM strode into the scene surrounded by skeptics. In the early months, software was scarce, but the PC offered the stability software producers were lacking, modest enhancements in the way of processing power, and leaps in random access memory. With the help of Lotus 1-2-3, which required more memory than Apple II could provide, the PC quickly took the place of the Apple II on many office desks. Then followed the PC XT, the PC 3270, the PC IX, and finally the PC AT[27].

Other players of the game: HEWLETT-PACKARD showed a computer with touch screen, and EPSON flirted with economically designed keyboards. The mouse scurried out of the lab and onto the desk of America[28]. AT&T showed an OLIVETTI designed PC clone and readied a Convergent-Technologies bred UNIX machine.[29] Computer size became a big deal. Adam Osborne was the first to fit the essential components into a package that fit under an airline seat. Following the attempts by EPSON and Radio Shack, the industry embarked on a campaign to put everything into a box that fit in a briefcase or on one's lap.

"What-if" software remained the most powerful tool produced for personal computer users in the last five years. Five years ago the hottest selling program was VisiCalc for the Apple II Computer—the first spreadsheet program which allowed managers and financial analysts to conduct complex "what-if" scenarios quickly. In 1980, Apple sold school markets while IBM and its imitators geared up with Lotus 1-2-3 dominating the business market. The second most significant kind of software for microcomputers, word processing, did sell a lot of PC's. In the last year, programs that caught the eye included

[23]*Forbes*, January 14, 1985, p. 286–287.

[24]Ibid.

[25]*Fortune*, February 18, 1985, pp. 74–83.

[26]*Time Magazine*, February 5, 1985.

[27]*Fortune*, "Macro Wonders from the Latest Micros," December 10, 1984, Vol. 110, No. 12, pp. 115–128.

[28]*Infoworld*, February 5, 1985.

[29]*Infoworld*, February 5, 1985.

sophisticated graphics programs, such as MacPaint and Filevision, "idea processors," such as Thinktank and Framework, which turn outlines into pages of finished text; expert systems, which turn the accumulated knowledge of a human specialist into a "black box" that users can ask questions of; and natural languages programs that not only understand English commands but also ask users for classifications and expanded vocabulary according to new trends.

Printers got quicker, faster, and cheaper. Slow, 300-baud modems have given way to 1200-baud modems in the office. Monitors and televisions got better more quickly than some of the computer technology. The last, and latest, big push in new technology was networking. Now a new generation of 32-bit microprocessors was emerging that would give low-cost desktop workstations and personal computers the power they need to tackle big jobs formerly reserved for expensive minicomputers and mainframes. Few products incorporate 32-bit microprocessors now, but the chips would lead to desktop computers that would transform office work and to cheap, but powerful, workstations for design shops and factories. Many computer scientists consider the 32-bit a natural unit for data because that is enough to handle everything from word-processing to precise scientific calculations.

The earliest microprocessors could nibble only four bits of information at a time, barely enough to run a calculator or time a turkey in a microwave oven.[30] Then the chips doubled and redoubled the number of bits they could handle, to 8 and then 16, without becoming much more expensive. The first personal computers were made possible by 8-bit microprocessors. Most of today's desktop computers, including the various IBM PC models, incorporate 16-bit chips.

INTEL, whose 16-bit chips power IBM's PC's and COMPAQ's PC's, insists that 16-bit chips were powerful enough for most applications. "We dominate the office," said INTEL Vice-President David House, referring to IBM's PC and their clones, "and the office is not going to move to 32-bits quickly."[31] Following IBM's lead, hundreds of other companies stampeded to incorporate INTEL's chips in their products.

OFFICE PC ENVIRONMENT

In 1984 worldwide unit shipments of office personal computers totaled over 6 million units[32]. This was a gain of 3.6 million over 1983 shipments of 2.4 million. The U.S. market accounted for under 75% of worldwide shipments. By 1990 unit sales for office computers in the United States will represent under 60% of the worldwide total market as the European and other markets expand.[33] Exhibit 1 shows the top 10 office personal computers for 1983 according to Future Computing's survey. Exhibit 2 shows the unit sales of U.S. computer stores as the percent of market.[34] Personal computer sales could be broadly categorized by the operating system they employed: CP/M, MS-DOS, Apple-DOS, TRS-DOS, and 68000 based systems.

Functionally compatible computers refer to computers positioned to the same workload, whereas data operation–compatible computers refer to some degree of either for data files or systems/application software compatibility. The installed base of key office personal computers is shown in Exhibit 3.[35] The IBM PC+ XT total over 690,000 units installed, and the combined IBM PC and PC-compatible installed base was 950,000 to 960,000. At the end of 1983, more functionally, data- and MS-DOS-compatible computers were installed than those that were operationally compatible. The increasing number of operationally compatible models would change this relationship in 1984.

The Apple II- and IIe-installed base reached nearly 1.5 million units worldwide in 1983. Although it was not growing as quickly as the IBM PC–compatible base, its sheer size still made it an attractive target for software developers.

Estimated monthly shipments during the first quarter of 1984 for key office personal computer systems are shown in Exhibit 4.[36] The IBM PC+ PC Jr XT totaled nearly 100,000 units per month. More manufacturers were introducing products that were operationally compatible, and several with data- and MS-DOS-compatible products were moving them over to be an operationally compatible

---

[30]Ibid.

[31]*Fortune*, December 10, 1984, pp. 115–128.

[32]Ibid.

[33]*Officeviews*, 1984 Future Computing Incorporated 084-3.

[34]Table 5.

[35]*Fortune*, "Compaq's Grip on IBM's Slippery Tail," February 18, 1985, Vol. 111, No. 4, pp. 74–83.

[36]*Forbes*, January 14, 1985, p. 286.

EXHIBIT 2 **Installed base of office personal computers (year end 1983).**
(March 1984, Future Computing Incorporated, 900 Canyon Creek Center, Richardson, Texas 75080.)

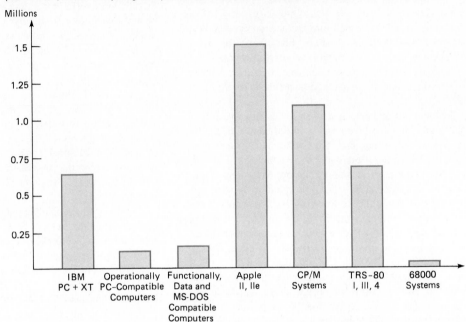

category. Shipments of all varieties of CP/M systems totaled approximately 40,000 units per month. Future Computing's survey of computer specialty stores showed Apple's Macintosh doing well. This product would begin to take the place of the Apple IIe at the low end of the office market for Apple, with total sales expected to reach 250,000 to 300,000 during 1984.[37]

THE IBM PC–COMPATIBLE ENVIRONMENT

IBM held 60% of the 1983 IBM PC–compatible hardware market as shown in Exhibit 5.[38] IBM PC–compatible manufacturers captured 27% of the total $2.4 billion market, and third-party hardware manufacturers accounted for 12% of the total.[39] Third-party manufacturers included companies such as HERCULES, TECMAR, and EPSON America, which manufactured add-on boards, mass-storage systems, and printers.

According to Future Computing, a Dallas-based company, IBM increased its share of the office personal computer market from 18% to 40% in 1982 to 1984.[40] PC-compatible manufacturers with products that were operationally, functionally, or data-compatible captured 27% of the PC-compatible market in 1983 for a total of $650 million in worldwide revenues. Excluding IBM, COMPAQ captured 17% of the PC-compatible market with approximately 56,000 units sold in 1983 for a total of $111 million in revenues. Zenith scored second in the PC-compatible arena, with 15% or approximately $100 million in sales recorded for the Z-100 in 1983 (sale was a large party shipment to Pentagon). The Texas Instruments Professional was next in line with 12% of approximately $80 million in sales for 1983. WANG captured 3% of the PC-compatible market in 1983, with Fortune 1000 companies being WANG's primary customers.

In 1984 AT&T entered the market with its IBM PC–compatible machine 6300. AT&T was expected to introduce a new model by mid-1985. TANDY Corpora-

---

[37]*Officeviews,* 1984 Future Computing Incorporated 084-3.

[38]Ibid.

[39]Ibid.

[40]Ibid.

EXHIBIT 3   **Unit sales at U.S. computer stores percent of microcomputer market.**

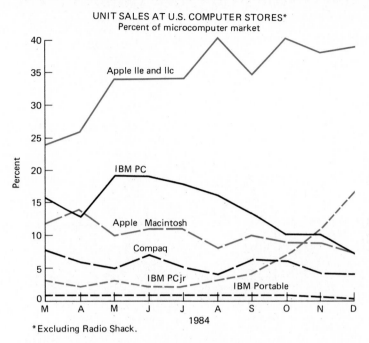

UNIT SALES AT U.S. COMPUTER STORES*
Percent of microcomputer market

*Excluding Radio Shack.

WHAT JUNIOR ATE

● IBM feared that its PCjr—announced in late 1983—would steal business from the PC itself. But Junior wasn't much of a cannibal; its design was so badly flawed that IBM had to overhaul the machine last summer. After that, the new machine fullfilled IBM's hopes and fears: as the PCjr took off, the PC's dropped. Compaq's machines, compatible with the PC, haven't suffered nearly as much. Last year was great for the Apple II line, nearly eight years old, whose newest member, the IIc, was introduced last April.

tion also followed IBM by introducing TANDY 1000 line, an IBM PC–compatible machine, in 1984.

COMPAQ PRODUCT LINES

When IBM went on the market in 1982, a few months later COMPAQ introduced a 28-pound portable personal computer which was as close to a clone of the PC as the law allowed. COMPAQ manufactured personal computers in two categories: "PORTABLE and DESKTOP." All COMPAQ products run all the popular software written for the IBM PC and XT. This compatibility also applied to industry-standard peripherals, printers, plotters, and expansion boards.

COMPAQ Portable Computers:

COMPAQ PORTABLE line came with two PC's, "COMPAQ PORTABLE" and "COMPAQ PLUS." COMPAQ PORTABLE was a 28-pound PC with 128K bytes of storage as standard primary memory (256K standard on dual-drive model, with up to 640,000 optional for others), 9-inch dual-mode display, and true software and peripheral compatibility with IBM PC and XT. COMPAQ PLUS increased the computer capacity further with a 10-megabyte hard disk. (See Exhibit 6 for technical specifications.)[41]

[41]*Officeviews,* 1984 Future Computing Incorporated 084-3.

EXHIBIT 4 **Monthly sales rates of office personal computers: 1Q 1984.**
(March 1984, Future Computing Incorporated, 900 Canyon Creek Center, Richardson, Texas 75080).

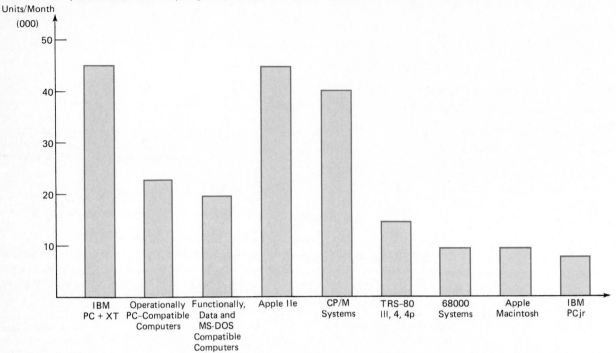

EXHIBIT 5 **1983 PC-compatible hardware market shares (worldwide factory value).**
(March 1984, Future Computing Incorporated, 900 Canyon Creek Center, Richardson, Texas 75080).

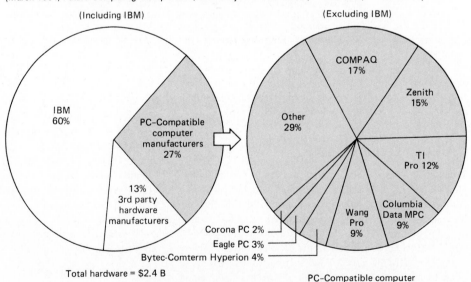

EXHIBIT 6   COMPAQ Specifications

	Portable	PLUS
Software	Runs all the popular programs written for the IBM PC.	Runs all the popular programs written for the IBM PC/*XT*.
Storage	One 320K-byte diskette drive, second drive optional.	One integrated 10-MB fixed disk drive. One 360K-byte diskette drive.
Expansion board slots	Three IBM-compatible slots.	Two IBM-compatible slots.
Memory	128K bytes RAM, expandable to 640K bytes.	
Display	9-inch dia. monochrome (25 lines by 80 characters). Upper- and lowercase high-resolution text characters. High-resolution graphics.	
Interfaces	Parallel printer interface. RGB color monitor interface. Composite video monitor interface. RF modulator interface.	
Physical specifications	Totally self-contained and transportable. 20″W × 8½″H × 16″D.	

Desk Computers:

COMPAQ DESKPRO was COMPAQ's first non-portable office computer. COMPAQ DESKPRO Series was four models designed for continued expandability and compatibility. COMPAQ offered more performance than IBM PC or XT at a comparable price.[42] COMPAQ DESKPRO, which employed PC-DOS version 3.0 as a primary operating system, also ran UNIX-based operating system in order to offer the capability and flexibility for networking, multitasking, multiuser environment, and tape-backup.[43] DESKPRO series run two or three times faster than IBM PC or XT.[44] (See Exhibit 7 for specifications.)[45]

[42]Ibid.

[43]*Officeviews*, 1984 Future Computing Incorporated 084-3.

[44]*Fortune*, "Compaq's Grip on IBM's Slippery Tail," February 10, 1985, Vol. 111, No. 4, pp. 74–83.

[45]*Officeviews*, 1984 Future Computing Incorporated 084-3.

COMPAQ Telecommunications:

COMPAQ's year-old COMPAQ TELECOMMUNICATIONS subsidiary aimed to introduce a new level of competition into the industry with its TELECOMPAQ model. The computer-cum-telephone, based on the powerful DESKPRO, is designed for a market the personal computer industry has yet to tap: telephone equipment buyers.

TELECOMPAQ represents a considerable gamble for COMPAQ. TELECOMPAQ combines the innards of an IBM PC–compatible DESKPRO, based on the INTEL 8086 chip, with a built-in HAYES modem, telephone, speakerphone, two phone lines, three disk drives, and a set of utility programs that stays in RAM when other programs are running. TELECOMPAQ would cost from $4195 to $6395.[46] ROLM Corp. of Santa Clara, California, now an IBM subsidiary, introduced a similar $4295 machine called the CEDAR in November 1984.[47]

COMPAQ had announced marketing agreements with BELL operating companies and with NORTHERN TELECOM, among others. "This is anything but a personal computer with a telephone attached," says H.L. "Sparky" Sparks, COMPAQ TELECOMMUNICATIONS's Vice President for sales. "The most important aspect about it is the integration of the computer and telephone functions, with one-button access to and from any function."

COMPETITORS

IBM:

IBM's success in personal computers was legendary: it entered the market late with a hastily designed product in 1981, and by 1984 captured 40% of the market. IBM, which used basic software any company could license, established an industry standard. Except for Apple, which already locked in enough users so that every major company eventually had to embrace some degree of IBM compatibility. Yet, being fully compatible with IBM was also dangerous. Over the last three years, IBM has launched five versions of its PC and cut the price by half.[48]

IBM's total revenues reached 46 billion in 1984, of which the revenues from the PC market constituted only

[46]Annual Report 1984, COMPAQ Computer Corporation.

[47]Infoworld, April 8, 1984.

[48]Ibid.

EXHIBIT 7   **The "have it all" personal computer.**

The "have it all" personal computer.

Specifications

Model 1   128K bytes random-access memory (RAM)
One diskette drive
12-inch green or amber dual-mode monitor
Six compatible expansion slots

Model 2   256K bytes random-access memory (RAM)
Two diskette drives
12-inch green or amber dual-mode monitor
Six compatible expansion slots

Model 3   256K bytes random-access memory (RAM)
One diskette drive
One 10-megabyte fixed disk drive
12-inch green or amber dual-mode monitor
Four compatible expansion slots
Asynchronous communications/clock board

Model 4   640K bytes random-access memory (RAM)
One diskette drive
One 10-megabyte fixed disk drive
One fixed disk drive backup (tape)
12-inch green or amber dual-mode monitor
Four compatible expansion slots
Asynchronous communications/clock board

Standard Features

Processor	16-bit 8086
Software	Runs all the popular programs written for the IBM PC and *XT* using the MS-DOS Version 2 operating system. Also runs PC DOS Version 3.0, and UNIX-based operating systems.
Memory	128K bytes RAM at entry level. Expandable up to 640K bytes on system board.
Keyboard	Standard 83-key PC layout. LED indicators on cap-lock & num-lock keys. Six-foot cable connects at front of system unit.
Interfaces	Parallel printer interface. RGB (red, green, blue) color monitor interface. R.F. modulator interface. Composite video monitor interface.
Physical specifications	System unit—19.8″W × 5.8″H × 16.5″D Keyboard—18.0″W × 1.5″H × 7.0″D
Power Supply	120 volts AC, 60 Hz, 200 watts

Options

☐ 30M-byte fixed disk drive
☐ 10M-byte fixed disk drive (one or two)
☐ Fixed disk drive backup (tape)
☐ Backup tape cartridge (10M-byte capacity)
☐ 8087-2 co-processor
☐ MS⁻-DOS/BASIC Version 2 diskette and reference guides
☐ 12-inch amber or green dual-mode monitor

☐ 128K-byte memory
☐ 512K-byte memory
☐ Diskette drive
☐ Asynchronous communications/clock board
☐ Desk-Saver
☐ Tilt & Swivel monitor stand

a small portion. In a watershed strategic statement four years ago, Chairman John R. Opel, the CEO, decreed that IBM should match or beat the information processing industry's growth in all segments—increases ranging from up to 12% per year for large mainframes to 40% for PC's and software.[49] By 1990, IBM planned to double its revenue to $10 billion annually; by 1984 revenues should nearly double again, to at least $185 billion. The responsibility for making IBM the largest company in history was passed to John F. Akers, president and new chief executive.[50] IBM, a 395,000-employee leviathan with sales in 1983 of $46 billion, so far had managed to meet these goals.[51] In the last five years, IBM spent $13 billion

[49]Ibid.

[50]Ibid.

[51]Ibid.

on land, buildings, and equipment and an additional $15 billion on Research and Development and engineering—amounting to 70% of its current assets.[52] In the next five years, IBM planned to invest at least $56 billion and turn over yet another 70% of its assets.[53]

The IBM PC ranked second after Apple in shipments of office personal computers for 1983. Over 400,000 units were sold worldwide with approximately 80% being sold in the United States. IBM PC was being sold by about 700 dealers during the first quarter, and IBM added over 500 more dealers during 1983. At the beginning of 1983, an average of 20 IBM PC's were sold per store carrying them.

IBM's PC hardware and software revenues totaled approximately $1.6 billion worldwide in 1983.[54] Of that, more than $1 billion was generated by PC hardware sales, putting the PC ahead of Apple IIe in terms of revenue.[55] The IBM PC+ XT placed fourth with about 80,000 unit shipments during 1983. The IBM PC Jr was categorized as a home/office product and was selling 10,000 units per month in 1983.

IBM also offered 16% discount if the customer bought 20 IBM systems over 18 months. If the deal was big enough, IBM even offered 40% off, sometimes even 50%. IBM also offered PC AT, which was specially designed for multi-user and network applications. PC AT was setting another standard in the industry in respect to speed and power.

While software accounted for about 10% of IBM's sales in 1984, management was aiming for a torrid 35% growth rate in the years ahead.[56] By the 1990's, said Krowe, spokesman for IBM, "software may represent up to a third of our business."[57] Another area that IBM was concentrating its efforts on in 1984 was communications. "The focus is on work stations and communications," said C. Mitchell Armstrong, the senior vice president who leads the Information Systems and Communications Group.[58]

"It's obvious the machine is new and has the same kinds of capabilities to grow as the PC and XT had at their introductions," said Rick Scott, spokesman for Big Blue.[59] In terms of its technical capabilities, Scott said, the IBM PC AT was a new start and new direction.

The INTEL 80286 chip was the heart of the PC AT. XENIX, which was MICROSOFT's version of AT&T's UNIX operating system added another dimension to the PC AT multi-user capability. It would strengthen the AT's role in networks and allow networking in greater numbers. XENIX also opened the doors, letting programs and users go beyond the 640K of RAM that was the maximum usable amount under PC-DOS or MS-DOS.

TANDY:

In 1985, Radio Shack presented a complete line of MS-DOS-based machines designed toward being IBM-compatible. The philosophy behind the new line emphasized a high degree of hardware and software compatibility with the IBM PC line of computers. This move signified the growing realization in the computer industry that a firm must become IBM-compatible to survive and grow. TANDY had shown such a change in its marketing strategy by positioning itself to attack the fast-moving IBM PC market. This showed a clear shift in emphasis by TANDY from its own operating system (TRS-DOS) and the in-house development of its own software to the building of machines compatible with the large software libraries available for IBM PC. TANDY had followed a strategy of branded software and tried to corner the market on software for its own computers. Due to this strategy, TANDY became one of the largest software suppliers in the business, but as its software sales grew, its lucrative hardware sales plummeted in lost growth by about $3.00 of every $1.00 increase in software sales.[60]

In an attempt to remedy such problems, TANDY decided to try to concentrate more on hardware production and allowed more third-party software support for its products. This translated into building machines that were running MS-DOS operating systems and were compatible with the IBM PC. Radio Shack continued its support for its own line of TRS-80 Model computers, but shifted its marketing emphasis to its new MS-DOS-based machines.

---

[52]Ibid.

[53]*Businessweek*, "IBM: More Worlds to Conquer," February 18, 1985, No. 2881, p. 84.

[54]Ibid.

[55]Ibid.

[56]Ibid.

[57]*Officeviews*, 1984 Future Computing Incorporated 084-3.

[58]Ibid.

[59]*Infoworld*, "Highgrowth Potential for AT," February 11, 1985, p. 34.

[60]*Businessweek*, "IBM: More Worlds to Conquer," February 18, 1985, No. 2881, p. 84.

Radio Shack also attempted to break into the business computer systems by opening a new line of TANDY stores designed to carry only TANDY's new line of business computers. This was a strategy designed to penetrate the business market by trying to break away from the "personal computer image" associated with Radio Shack stores. TANDY's new business was a new line of large business machines based on the MOTOROLA 32-bit chip, the 68000. AT&T's UNIX operating system was used in the machines, thereby allowing the computer to support more than one user at a time through multi-tasking capabilities available in UNIX.

Along with its new computers, TANDY also developed a local area network system which allowed businesses to link together their computers into a large network, thereby allowing users within the network to share hardware peripherals, programs, and data. Developing such LAN's was seen as a key in the development of business computer products.

TANDY had also developed hardware and software protocol packages which allowed its machines to emulate the IBM 3270 terminal,[61] thereby allowing TANDY's business computers to communicate with large IBM mainframe systems. TANDY had also developed large libraries of business software for its new business systems. By linking its new UNIX, MS-DOS-based machines together with its LAN's, TANDY provided its users with the capability to construct large networks of computers with the ability to link such systems with large mainframes so that information can be uploaded and downloaded back and forth. With its new line of computers and its new marketing strategy, TANDY had positioned itself to attack the computer business market.

AT&T:

The breakup of AT&T could have been the big event in PC systems, but somehow it never was. AT&T showed an OLIVETTI-designed PC clone, PC 6300. PC 6300, which was based on the INTEL 8086 chip, was faster than the IBM PC, but lacked the glitter to make it a big success. In 1984, the most-asked question was "where is AT&T's much anticipated competition?"

AT&T's long-awaited answer to IBM's PC AT, the AT&T 7300, was being built by Convergent Technologies

in 1984.[62] It was based on the MOTOROLA 68010 microprocessor. It would come with a version of the UNIX System V OS, as well as UNIX extension for creating windows and pull-down menus. It had a built-in modem, two telephone lines, and communication software. It also had an expansion board that would allow it to run MS-DOS or PC-DOS software, but was not confirmed since March 1984.[63]

The key question in 1984 was how AT&T PC 7300 would be sold against IBM PC AT. Prediction was that it would be positioned as an alternative to PC AT and priced similarly; it would be marketed to large to medium size businesses. Also, AT&T would make UNIX System V as its standard for a multi-user world, whereas IBM used UNIX System III. PC AT running XENIX supported only two additional terminals; 7300 would allow many people to use the same terminal.[64]

On the other hand, telecommunication's great AT&T was not abandoning its roots as it reached out to touch a myriad of microcomputer markets with a promised "plethora of products" in 1984.[65] Among them, there was graphics software that takes the concept of popular painting programs a step further, communications software, scheduled to appear in mid-1984, to go with the AT&T modem introduced in September 1984. All emphasized AT&T's telecommunication talents.

KAYPRO:

KAYPRO followed in the steps of Adam Osborne Company and built a budget 8-bit CP/M-based portable computer that was bundled with a large selection of software. This marketing strategy was highly successful in that it allowed a consumer to pay one price and receive all the hardware and software needed.

KAYPRO has extended this strategy into building an inexpensive clone of the IBM PC XT that is portable and includes some interesting bundled software. The bundled software includes a spread sheet, word processing, database, graphics, and communication packages.

KAYPRO's forceful move into the IBM market rep-

---

[61]*Infoworld*, "Kaypro New Portable," March 25, 1985, Vol. 7, Issue 12, p. 34.

[62]*Infoworld*, "Kaypro Introduces First of the PC AT Clones," March 4, 1985, Vol. 7, Issue 9, pp. 15–16.

[63]*Infoworld*, "Convergent/ and New President," February 4, 1985.

[64]Ibid.

[65]Ibid.

resented an attempt to recover from a disastrous inventory buildup that caused the firm to have in 1984 its first unprofitable year since its inception. Perhaps the biggest shift in the KAYPRO blueprint was its move to sign up office supply dealers. In 1984, more than 150 office supply stores have agreed to carry KAYPRO products, in addition to its substantial base of more than 1000 independent dealers. KAYPRO has geared its machines for price-conscious consumers wanting the performance of IBM.

ATARI:

The new ATARI XL was introduced as competition for the Macintosh and PC Jr. ATARI also offers rock bottom prices. 130ST with 128 K and 520 ST with 512 K are being offered at prices of $399 and $599, but not including monitor and disk drives. The operating system used is Digital Research's GEM (graphics environment manager) and T.O.S. (Tramiel Operating System). ATARI will produce 200,000 ST units per month. It is also called the "poor man's Macintosh." ATARI users are 16–26 years old. ATARI was trying to start a national school program by March 1, 1985.

FINANCE

COMPAQ's initial year of operations was financed by private investment and venture capital. Canion approached Sevin-Rosen in January 1982 in an effort to raise $200,000 to develop the product. In the following 12 months, Sevin-Rosen raised an additional $30 million to fund COMPAQ and become its largest investors.

The initial public offering of the Company's common stock was in December 1983. The common stock was traded in the over-the-counter market and was quoted on the NASDAQ National Market List. The high and low bid prices during the period of entry were 12½ and 11, respectively.[66] Within the next six months, the price tumbled to 4 3/8, down from a high of 14 5/8 and was trading at about 7 by July 1984. This period was marked by a general market decline, investor nervousness, and IBM price cuts.[67] On February 27, 1985, the price was up to $8.50.

Gross margins have increased in each period since the introduction of COMPAQ's first product. As production increased, various economics of scale came into play. Quantity discounts associated with volume purchasing and the spreading of fixed manufacturing overhead has reduced unit costs and increased gross margins. (Refer to Exhibits I and II.)[68] Based on average common shares of 27,205,000, earnings per share were $0.22 as of September 1984 compared to a deficit of 0.16/share a year earlier.[69] As of September 1984, profitability was impaired by substantial expenditures for the expansion of facilities and marketing and the increased production of the COMPAQ DESKPRO.[70] Research and development costs remained relatively stable during the first three quarters of 1983 but gradually rose the third quarter of 1984.

Marketing and sales expense increased in absolute dollar amounts in each quarter. This pattern was due to the high initial promotion and advertising costs necessary to introduce and establish new products.[71] General and administrative expenses increased in 1983 but remained relatively stable in 1984. General and administrative expenses have declined as a percentage of sales.[72] (Refer to Exhibits IV, V, and VI.)

During an interview in March 1985, Mr. Sevin, director of COMPAQ, disclosed a convertible debenture offer to reduce a bank debt, which had risen from 25% in 1983 to 52% by the end of 1984. COMPAQ offered $75 million of convertible debentures priced at par to yield 9.25%. The securities, due June 1, 2005, were convertible at a rate of $11.50 of debenture for each common share.

Looming over COMPAQ's success was a lawsuit filed by Texas Instruments in January 1984, charging COMPAQ with "pirating trade secrets and infringing Texas Instruments patents" to build its computer. Neither side will comment on the suit, but COMPAQ has countersued, asserting that Texas Instruments was trying to destroy the company.[73]

---

[66]Ibid.

[67]COMPAQ Computer Corporation Form 10K, Year ended December 31, 1983.

[68]Ibid.

[69]1983 Annual Report, COMPAQ Computer Corporation, p. 19.

[70]Standard OTC Stock Reports, Volume 50, Number 128, Section 12, November 7, 1984.

[71]Ibid.

[72]"Three Makers of Computers Post Rise in Net," *Wall Street Journal*, April 24, 1984, p. 10.

[73]Annual Report 1983, COMPAQ Computer Corporation, p. 19.

EXHIBIT I   COMPAQ COMPUTER CORPORATION
QUARTERLY STATEMENT OF OPERATIONS—1983
(In Thousands)

	Quarter ended			
	March 31, 1983	June 30, 1983	September 30, 1983	December 31, 1983
Sales	$4,895	$18,051	$36,032	$52,243
Cost of sales	4,734	14,130	25,331	38,246
	111	3,921	10,701	15,907
Research and development costs	777	720	305	1,429
Marketing and sales expense	1,318	2,707	2,865	4,650
General and administrative expense	1,240	1,940	3,184	4,434
Interest expense (income) net	(63)	(216)	38	6
	3,727	5,151	6,892	10,519
Income (loss) before provision for income taxes and extraordinary item	(3,161)	(1,230)	3,809	5,478
Provision for income taxes				2,296
Income (loss) before extraordinary item	(3,161)	(1,230)	3,809	3,182
Extraordinary item: Utilization of net operating loss carryforward				2,102
Net income (loss)	($3,161)	($1,230)	$ 3,809	$ 5,284

EXHIBIT II   **Quarterly statement of operations—1984.**

Quarterly Sales Revenue

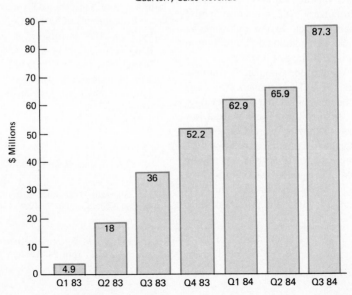

EXHIBIT III   COMPAQ COMPUTER CORPORATION
QUARTERLY STATEMENT OF OPERATIONS—1984

	Quarter ended		
	March 31, 1984	June 30, 1984	Sept. 30, 1984
Sales	$62,879	$65,936	$87,547
Cost of goods sold	43,954	46,147	64,398
Gross margin	18,925	19,789	23,149
Research and development costs	1,986	2,384	3,056
Marketing and sales costs	7,265	10,315	11,847
General/administrative costs	5,213	4,629	5,351
Interest cost (income), net	(1,183)	1,385	592
Income before tax	13,281	18,713	20,846
Income (loss) before provision for income tax	5,644	1,076	2,303
Net income (loss)	3,274	892	1,879

EXHIBIT IV   COMPAQ COMPUTER CORPORATION
CONSOLIDATED STATEMENT OF OPERATIONS
(Unaudited)
(In Thousands, except per Share Amounts)

	Nine months ended September 30,		Quarter ended September 30,	
	1984	1983	1984	1983
Sales	$216,362	$58,978	$87,547	$36,032
Cost of sales	154,499	44,245	64,398	25,331
	61,863	14,733	23,149	10,701
Reseach and development costs	7,426	2,302	3,056	805
Marketing and sales expense	29,427	6,890	11,847	2,865
General and administrative expense	15,193	6,364	5,351	3,184
Other (income) expense, net	794	(241)	592	38
	52,840	15,315	20,846	6,892
Income (loss) before provision for income taxes	9,023	(582)	2,303	3,809
Provision for income taxes	2,978		424	
Net income (loss)	$ 6,045	($ 582)	$ 1,879	$ 3,809
Earnings (loss) per common and common equivalent share	$ 22	($ 16)	$ 07	$ 19
Shares used in computing earnings (loss) per common and common equivalent share	27,205	3,735	27,186	20,127

EXHIBIT V COMPAQ COMPUTER CORPORATION
CONSOLIDATED BALANCE SHEET
(Unaudited)
(In Thousands)

	September 30, 1984	December 31, 1983
Assets		
Current assets:		
Cash and short-term investments	$ 32,465	$ 51,797
Accounts receivable	65,436	27,773
Inventories	78,262	25,396
Prepaid expenses	741	379
Total current assets	176,904	105,345
Property, plant and equipment, less accumulated depreciation	30,788	12,662
Other assets	3,311	3,099
Total	$211,003	$121,106
Liabilities and Stockholders' Equity		
Current liabilities:		
Notes payable	$ 54,000	
Accounts payable	44,514	$ 24,878
Other current liabilities	10,321	5,534
Total liabilities—all current	108,835	30,412
Stockholders' equity:		
Preferred stock: $.01 par value: 10,000,000 shares authorized: none issued and outstanding		
Common stock: $.01 par value: 149,000,000 shares authorized: 26,178,295 and 25,371,029 shares issued and outstanding	262	254
Serial common stock: $.01 par value: 1,000,000 shares authorized: none outstanding		
Capital in excess of par value	95,759	90,338
Retained earnings	6,147	102
Total stockholders' equity	102,168	90,694
Total	$211,003	$121,106

EXHIBIT VI   COMPAQ COMPUTER CORPORATION
CONSOLIDATED STATEMENT OF OPERATIONS
(In Thousands, except per Share Amounts)

	Inception through December 31, 1982	Year ended December 31, 1983
Sales		$111,221
Cost of sales		80,491
		30,730
Research and development costs	$ 1,506	3,731
Marketing and sales expense	760	11,540
General and administrative expense, including start-up costs in 1982	2,592	10,798
Interest income, net	(258)	(235)
	4,600	25,834
Income (loss) before provision for income taxes and extraordinary item	(4,600)	4,896
Provision for income taxes		2,296
Income (loss) before extraordinary item	(4,600)	2,600
Extraordinary item: Utilization of net operating loss carryforward		2,102
Net income (loss)	($4,600)	$ 4,702
Per common and common equivalent share:		
Income (loss) before extraordinary item	($1.48)	$.13
Extraordinary item		.11
Net income (loss)	($1.48)	$.24

FUTURE

According to Future Computing Inc., a private firm that monitors the industry,

> . . . even rising stars are not immune to the forces of gravity. Analysts note that the success of COMPAQ and scores of other high tech companies depends largely on their ability to avoid the price cutting excess inventories now plaguing manufacturers of inexpensive (under $500) home computers and video games.[74]

[74]"COMPAQ will offer $75 million of debt," *Wall Street Journal*, March 7, 1985, p. 46.

CONTACTS

1   Mr. Sevin, President of Sevin Rosen Management Corporation.
2   Future Computing Inc., Dallas, Texas

CONSOLIDATED RAIL CORPORATION (Conrail)

George S. Vozikis
Timothy S. Mescon
Memphis State University
Salisbury State College

Freight transportation has never been a very popular area with business school graduates. Manufacturing has dominated the career choices of many business majors. The railroad merger movement, however, as well as the new rules of the game promised by deregulation, points to the transformation of a once-routine freight transportation industry into a new stimulating, competitive, and active business.

THE INDUSTRY

The freight transportation industry has six major components: trucking, railroads, oil pipelines, great lakes shipping, rivers and canals, and air freight. The economic recovery of 1984 produced a strong rise in freight traffic. Because of industrywide discounting however, volume increases did not translate into significantly better profitability. Aggressive pricing and successful pricing strategies forced freight rates down, especially since deregulation of the trucking industry in 1980. Large publicly owned common carriers have been scrambling ever since for market share, holding down railroad rates. More than half of the railroad lines in the railroad surface transportation subgroup, were unable to reach their five-year return on equity averages in 1984, as Exhibit 1 shows. The exceptions generally have been firms largely dependent on hauling coal, such as Burlington Northern, especially since utilities started stockpiling coal in anticipation of a mine workers' strike that never came (*Forbes*, January 14, 1985).

A HISTORY OF THE RAILROADS UNTIL 1980

The railroad as it is known today originated in England in the first quarter of the 19th century. The development of mechanical traction to replace horsepower may be said to mark the emergence of the modern railroad. Interest in railroads in the United States developed almost as soon as in England. In 1815, John Stevens received from the New Jersey legislature the first charter for a railroad ever granted in America. By February 28, 1827, the Baltimore & Ohio Railroad Company was chartered as a common carrier of freight and passengers. Subsequently, the company expanded, both by new construction and acquisition of other railroads, until it reached Chicago, St. Louis, and the Great Lakes.

Almost simultaneously, other American railroads emerged. On December 25, 1830, the five-foot-gauge line from Charleston to Hamburg, South Carolina became the first line in the U.S. to start scheduled passenger operations using a steam locomotive. Ultimately, this line became part of the 10,000-mile Southern Railway System.

EXHIBIT 1 SURFACE TRANSPORTATION YARDSTICKS OF MANAGEMENT PERFORMANCE 1985

Company	% in segment— sales/profits	Profitability: Return on equity — Rank	Return on equity — 5-year average	Return on equity — Latest 12 months	Debt as % of equity	Net profit margin	Growth: Sales — Rank	Sales — 5-year average	Sales — Latest 12 months	Earnings per share — Rank	Earnings per share — 5-year average	Earnings per share — Latest 12 months	Earnings stability
Railroads													
CNW	•/•	1	23.2%	def	165.7%	def	8	1.1%	-2.3%		NM	P-D	NM
Kansas City Southern	70/77	2	16.0	15.7%	43.0	13.0%	3	11.2	1.7	1	11.4%	52.1%	high
American Standard	22/17	3	14.7	12.6	44.6	3.5	7	1.8	10.2	8	-17.9	20.7	average
Norfolk Southern	•/•	4	13.5	10.9	19.2	13.5	6	2.3	2.8	5	-2.1	2.8	very low
Burlington Northern	46/65	5	12.8	13.4	50.4	7.2	1	16.7	7.8	2	7.6	7.9	average
Union Pacific	50/61	6	11.9	10.8	41.0	6.5	2	15.0	-2.6	7	-6.6	47.5	low
Santa Fe Southern	74/32	7	10.9	7.6	28.9	6.7	5	3.7	-0.8	3	0.8	-1.6	very low
CSX	63/64	8	10.8	8.3	46.8	5.6	4	10.3	-5.1	4	-1.6	-19.5	very low
Amsted Industries	30/26	9	9.6	7.9	0.0	4.2	11	-10.1	11.9		NM	20.2	NM
IC Industries	24/30	10	8.6	7.9	92.2	2.8	9	0.6	12.9	6	-3.9	-33.8	very low
GATX	25/63	11	4.1	def	276.1	def	10	-2.8	-13.9		NM	D-D	NM
Medians			11.9	8.3	44.6	5.6		2.3	1.7		-3.9	2.8	
Truckers													
Roadway Services	•/•	1	20.7	14.6%	0.0%	5.5%	3	5.1%	9.5%	2	11.5%	-13.9%	very high
IU International	59/DP	2	18.8	def	119.8	def	4	-1.7	5.9	5	-33.7	P-D	low
Ryder System	•/•	3	18.4	15.4	142.5	4.5	1	11.5	-1.7	1	11.8	-11.0	high
Consol Freightways	•/•	4	17.7	14.2	11.3	4.2	5	-1.7	16.1	3	2.7	15.9	very low
Leaseway Transport	•/•	5	14.8	8.7	122.8	1.8	2	8.4	8.7	4	-7.5	-25.3	average

•90% or more. DD: Segment deficit, total deficit. DP: Segment deficit, total profit. DP: Segment profit, total deficit. PD: Segment profit, total profit. D-D: Deficit to deficit. P-D: Profit to deficit. def: Deficit. NA: Not available. NM: Not meaningful. †Four-year growth. ‡Three-year average. ‡‡Three-year growth.

By 1840, there was 2,800 miles of line in the U.S., and America had entered the first great era of railroad building. As a result, in 1860 the U.S. had 30,000 route miles of track.

As a general rule, early railroads were designed mainly to promote the commercial interests of the local communities and areas. Progress, however, brought the consolidation of small roads, forming through routes that served fairly large territories. This led new railroad projects, such as the Pennsylvania Railroad Company (Penn Central), to become more ambitious. Due to their growth, efficiency and time related factors, railroads had an immediate and often catastrophic effect on other forms of land transportation, mainly the stagecoach and the canalboat. Newspapers and mail soon began to be moved by rail with dramatic time savings.

The economic impact of railroads came mainly from freight traffic, which increased almost as fast as passenger travel. Railroads made it unnecessary for some types of factories to be located near canals or rivers. In addition, farmers could find a more ready market for their crops, and coal and ore could be moved longer distances more economically. Furthermore, in the U.S., the railroad was a major means of opening up new territory such as the West.

Railroad construction slowed during the Civil War, but it resumed on a large scale soon afterwards. During the decade of the 1880's, more than 70,000 miles of track were built. Construction continued at a relatively high level through the 1900–10 decade. The growth and construction of railroads was not only a result of private enterprise, but also of government assistance. By the end of the Civil War, railroads had received in total about 131,000,000 acres for about 18,000 miles of line.

In the period 1900 to 1930, several developments were made: 1) the first practical and reliable diesel-electric locomotive was in operation, 2) the perfecting of centralized traffic control, 3) a highly efficient system of controlling train operations, and 4) the use of continuous welded rail which contributes to a smoother track that costs less to maintain. After World War II, the diesel locomotive completely superseded the steam locomotive in the U.S., allowing railroads to continue under private operations due to their profitability.

Although most U.S. railroads were privately run, they soon came under relatively intense regulation due to their far reaching influence on the domestic economy. The government passed railway acts prescribing such things as signal brakes, track standards, and employee training. Also, the Interstate Commerce Commission was orga-

nized to regulate interstate surface transportation, and to regulate railroad rates and fares while exercising licensing power over mergers and other financial operations. Furthermore, the post World War II era brought competition from other transportation modes.

GOVERNMENT REGULATIONS

Rail Rates

From their ascendancy in the post-Civil War years, the U.S. railroads rapidly established a virtual monopoly on inland transportation. Their power, even where it was not abused, was so great that demand for public regulation became a major political issue which culminated in the passage of the *Interstate Commerce Act of 1887*. Thereafter, all aspects of the railroad industry—new construction, operating practices, conditions of service, and rates—were subject to official scrutiny. Detailed regulations governed everything, especially the complex determination of fair rates. A cumbersome procedure emerged and remained in place until highway and air competition made it clear that it was no longer necessary to maintain the railroads as a regulated monopoly.

When railroad managements began to respond to competitive conditions, albeit slowly, they found archaic regulations standing in their way. New rules appeared to be in order. Culminating in the *Railroad Revitalization and Regulatory Reform Act (the 4R Act) of 1975,* new legislation was focused on the physical improvement and rationalization of the railroad network. Loans were made available for the rehabilitation of plant: joint use of physical assets was encouraged. The ICC was directed to "make a continuing effort to assist carriers to attain (adequate) revenue levels . . . to cover total operating expenses . . . plus a fair, reasonable, and economic . . . return on capital employed in the business."

The principal effect of the 4R Act was to slow the decline of maintenance, to retain capacity, and to give the concept of "revenue adequacy" a central role in the rate-making process. But rehabilitation depended upon regaining a substantial market share, in addition to physical improvements and adequate rates.

The *Staggers Rail Act of 1980* is considered to be the most important piece of railroad legislation in 100 years. It suspended the regulation of rates for all traffic in which competition was deemed effective. As defined therein, competition was deemed effective when a carrier set rates in which the ratio of revenue to variable cost did not exceed 160% *and* was shown not to enjoy "market dominance.'' The effect of this legislation was the exemption from rate setting of many classes of traffic, notably fresh fruit/vegetables and trailers on flatcars (TOFC)—the ''piggyback'' business. Subsequently, joint rates were curtailed; each railroad sought the longest possible haul over its own lines. Mergers were encouraged as a means to extend the scope of an individual system; market dominance shifted.

A case in point is the Orange Blossom Special, a freight train named after a long-since discontinued luxury passenger train that carried wealthy travelers between the northeastern U.S. and Florida. Today it carries citrus products in refrigerated highway trailers mounted on railroad flatcars—a scheme that could not have existed before deregulation, since railroads were not permitted to change rates daily as the market moved. As a result, truckers simply charged slightly less than the published railroad tariff and, thereby, dominated the perishable market segment. If the railroads wanted to compete, they had to initiate lengthy proceedings with the ICC to change the tariffs. Today, CSX Corporation, which operates the Orange Blossom Special, can change rates at will to meet changing conditions.

In 1978, the ICC initiated its *Western Coal Investigation—Guidelines for Railroad Rate Structure* to set coal transportation rates on a case-by-case basis and to solve the issue raised in the 4R Act regarding the establishment of adequate railroad revenue levels. In February, 1983, no restraint was placed upon the right of a carrier to fix rates in markets which it did not dominate, the beneficial effect of competition being assumed. Pricing of coal traffic in dominated markets became subject to four constraints:

1 No shipper could be charged more than the ''standalone'' cost of serving its traffic, i.e., the cost of providing service for a single shipper as an upper limit.

2 Captive shippers could not be required to bear the cost of obvious management inefficiency (not so well defined).

3 Carriers could not increase their rates on captive traffic by more than 15% per year (after inflation), but were free to do so, until ''revenue adequacy'' had been achieved.

4 After achieving ''revenue adequacy,'' a carrier became free to adjust its rates uncapped, as long as it did not violate constraints 1–3.

Of 21 Class I railroads, the ICC found that 17 could achieve revenue adequacy, defined as return on investment equal to 13.4% of the current cost of capital. By assuming competitive pipelines to come into the picture over the medium-term, the ICC forecasted that the restraining of further rail rate escalation would occur naturally.

In September, 1983, export coal was exempted from rate regulation, leaving the railroad and the shipper free to reach an agreement in the marketplace. The protection of regulation was deemed unnecessary, due to sufficient competition in the marketplace assumed to guarantee fair market determined rates. And even though many mines would appear captive, the market theoretically provided protection. The ICC based its concept of competition upon the world market, asserting that U.S. coal was in competition not only with coal produced in other nations, but with all other forms and sources of energy.

However, 60% of the coal exported is handled by only two rail groups—Norfolk Southern Corporation (Norfolk and Western Railway and Southern Railway) and the Chessie System railroads of CSX Corporation—and rail rate regulation is expected to return. In fact, a federal appeals court decision, being hailed as a milestone by the U.S. coal industry, recently (September, 1984) overturned the ICC decision to deregulate rail transportation rates and service on export coal, based on the unsubstantiated assumption that world competition would force railroads to keep tariffs reasonable. The coal exporters interpreted the reversal as the court's recognition 1) to attempt to balance the needs of shippers and the needs of the railroads and 2) to suggest that the ICC improperly interpreted the Staggers Act. ''While competition certainly exists,'' the court said, ''the ICC did not prove that the world market would act as an effective restraint on the ability of the railroads to raise rates exhorbitantly.''

An industry official (Association of American Railroads) warns that rail rates for export coal could become less responsive to market conditions, if the appellate court decision takes effect. In fact, export rail rates for coal have declined since the passage of the 1980 Staggers Act. If regulated, rates may not be reduced in slack times, due to the process, burden, and expense to the rail carrier.

Railroad/Barge Line Mergers

The merger of the nation's largest barge line ACL, and the nation's second largest railroad, Chessie System Railroads, has raised concern among shippers and consumers of reduced competition and even higher transportation costs. According to the Edison Electric Institute, ''barge transportation offers one of the few remaining opportunities available to electric utilities to help restrain the growing market power of the dominant railroad systems in the U.S.'' CSX, as the parent company of Chessie System Railroads and Seaboard System Railroad, is the nation's largest rail shipper of coal, accounting for 31% of the national traffic. Texas Gas, acquired by CSX Corporation in June, 1983, owned ACL, whose primary commodity hauled is coal.

Opponents of the merger claim it violates the *Panama Canal Act,* which prohibits railroads from owning, operating, controlling, or having any interest in a ''water common carrier or vessel carrying property or passengers on a water route with which it does or may compete for traffic'' unless it can be shown that such an acquisition is in the public interest and that competition will be maintained. According to Hays T. Watkins, Chief Executive Officer of CSX Corporation, the merger will maintain competition and is in the best interest of the public because it will result in greater rail/barge cooperation and better service. ''In my opinion, it is time to stop talking of rail or truck or barge or pipeline transportation in isolation and to start talking about transportation,'' Watkins told the ICC. ''The fact is that our customers are interested in only one thing: making sure that their products arrive at their destinations safely and efficiently.'' With an integrated system, storage costs are expected to become eliminated while waiting for barge or rail connections.

In October, 1984, the sixth US Court of Appeals (Cincinnati, Ohio) lifted the stay it had imposed on the merger, allowing the merger to become effective while it considers the merits of the case. The court gave barge lawyers 30 days to prepare their arguments for their protest of the ICC approval to the merger.

Due to the increase in merger activity since the Staggers Act of 1980, the railroad industry has become more and more concentrated. As a result, there are nine major railroads in the U.S., mainly in the business of hauling freight. (See Exhibit 2.) There is a freight railroad, Consolidated Rail Corporation (CONRAIL), which is owned mainly by the federal government. Also, there is one major survivor of the passenger railroad sector which is the government owned and operated National Railroad Passenger Corporation (AMTRAK).

THE CONRAIL SALE

At about 2:15 p.m. on February 5, 1985, Transportation Secretary Elizabeth H. Dole telephoned Norfolk Southern Corporation Chairman Claytor to announce that his railroad was her choice to buy Consolidated Rail Corp. (CONRAIL). Conrail is the U.S. government's freight rail system in the East, which was formed in the mid 1970's out of the bankrupt Penn Central and five other ailing Northeastern railroads. The U.S. government owns 85% of Conrail while the other 15% is owned by its employees.

The efforts to sell Conrail began in 1981 when a piecemeal sale of the railroad was considered but abandoned as the carrier became profitable. Conrail's turnaround was attributed to extensive track and equipment improvements, line abandonments, tax breaks, wage concessions, drastic layoffs, and marketing efforts that took advantage of loosening regulation. In fact, to date, the railroad's cash reserves have grown to $800 million.

The Conrail turnaround has been termed ''extraordinary.'' After losing $1.5 billion during its first four years in operation (1976–80), Conrail netted a $39 million profit in 1981. In 1982 profits were $174 million, while in 1983 they were $313 million representing an 80% increase from the previous year ('82). To add to this picture, net income in 1984 was a little over $500 million. But this has been a slow and sometimes painful growth. Conrail's first four years were mainly ones of rebuilding through a federally-funded multi-billion dollar effort presided over by Edwards Jordan (the railroad's first CEO).

When the Staggers Act of 1980 came along, Conrail was ready to take advantage of its opportunities with a trimmed-down, rebuilt plant and an aggressive marketing team headed by James A. Hagen and the new CEO L. Stanley Crane. More help for Conrail came in 1981 through such factors as wage concessions, the passage of the Northeast Rail Service Act giving Conrail additional latitude in closing down uneconomic lines, and authorized federally-funded, one-time separation payments to displaced workers. All of these things, along with the economic recovery of 1983–84, have helped to continue Conrail's profitable performance.

In 1984, Conrail operated a weekly average of 3,653 through freights, 187 Trail Van Lines, and 1,570 local freights. On time performance: dock-to-dock (within 24 hours of schedule) 81.1 percent; trailvan (within one hour of schedule) 86.3 percent; unit trains (within one hour of schedule) 94.9 percent. Furthermore, its piggyback operations are considerable since it handles nearly 16% of all piggyback traffic in this country.

However, since 1984, the U.S. government had intensified its search for a sound and viable prospect to acquire Conrail. For months, the Transportation Department has negotiated with the finalist bidders, among which were

EXHIBIT 2   INDUSTRY PARTICIPANTS: MAJOR RAILROADS

	Gross revenue ($ mill)	Operating profit margin	Net income ($ mill)	Return on equity	Net profit margin
Burlington Northern					
1980	$ 3,953.6	10.6%	$ 222.9	8.8%	—
1981	4,935.8	9.7%	272.2	10.4%	—
1982	4,197.6	6.6%	178.0(1)	6.3%	—
1983	4,508.2	16.8%	413.2	11.0%	—
Canadian Pacific Limited (2)					
1980	$ 9,984.5	—	$583,157	—	5.8%
1981	12,636.3	—	485,600	—	3.8%
1982	12,604.4	—	188,294	—	1.5%
1983	12,259.3	—	143,000	—	1.1%
Chicago & North Western					
1980	$ 935.7	—	$ 39,034	—	—
1981	981.8	—	45,104(1)	—	—
1982	803.8	—	19,088	—	—
1983	859.9	—	33,819	—	—
CSX Corporation					
1980	$ 4,841	10.4%	$ 281.6	9.8%	—
1981	5,400	11.2%	367.7	11.7%	—
1982	4,900	6.9%	338.4	10.0%	—
1983	5,800	10.8%	271.6	6.0%	—
Kansas City Southern					
1980	$ 323.5	15.5%	$ 30.6	15.0%	—
1981	368.2	17.9%	38.7	16.6%	—
1982	384.3	15.6%	33.3	12.8%	—
1983	404.9	18.7%	41.8	11.4%	—
Norfolk Southern					
1980	$ 1,576.3	—	$232,416	—	—
1981	1,807.7	—	291,063	—	—
1981 (3)	3,592.3	—	500,291	—	—
1982	3,360.0	—	411,400	—	—
1983	3,148.1		356,500		
Santa Fe Southern					
1980	$ 3,215.0	14.2%	$ 301.8	13.1%	—
1981	3,366.9	10.5%	242.2	10.0%	—
1982	3,159.6	9.0%	180.2	7.3%	—
1983 (4)	5,976.0	10.5%	333.4(1)	5.8%	—
Union Pacific					
1980	$ 4,872.3	25.4%	$ 404.5	14.3%	—
1981	6,380.7	23.2%	410.7	13.3%	—
1982	5,880.0	21.8%	326.8	7.7%	—
1983	8,517.0	9.5%	441.0(1)	10.9%	—

(1) From continuing operations
(2) Includes Soo Line Railroad
(3) Proforma for merger with Southern Railway Co.; Prior year figures for Norfolk & Western.
(4) Combined results of Santa Fe Industries and Southern Pacific Corp.
Source: Moody's Handbook of Common Stocks
Winter 84–85, Moody's Investors Services, New York, New York, 1985.

Norfolk Southern (NS), the Alleghany Corporation of New York City, and an investor group led by hotelier, J. Willard Marriott, Jr. As was mentioned previously, NS was chosen as the finalist bidder, only needing the approval from Congress. The NS bid consists of at least $1.2 billion for the government's 85% stake in Conrail, plus $375 million for the employees' 15% interest. Although Conrail's 1984 profits of $500 million would be a 32% return on its purchase price, there are important conditions attached to the sale. To ensure NS would not be receiving a tax windfall, NS would give up $2.1 billion in tax-loss carryforwards and $275 million in investment tax credits belonging to Conrail. In addition, NS has agreed to divest 1,500 miles of track to two smaller railroads to resolve potential antitrust problems arising from the purchase of Conrail.

Under the divestiture plan, Guilford Transportation Industries Inc., a Massachusetts-based railroad holding company, would acquire track or the right to use track from Buffalo, New York, to Cleveland and on to Chicago and St. Louis. It would also get lines linking tracks it already owns to Toledo, Ohio and to Indianapolis. Separately, the Pittsburgh & Lake Erie Railroad would get tracks from Pittsburgh to Cleveland and Toledo.

Other commitments made by NS are: 1) NS must maintain Conrail's business "substantially as it is now being conducted" for the next five years, 2) NS must refrain from taking dividends out of Conrail for the next five years unless a cash balance of at least $500 million would remain afterwards, 3) unionized workers, who have been paid 12% less than industry norms since April 1981, would be brought up to par retroactive to last July 1, and 4) any workers laid off as a result of the merger would receive full pay for six years.

Secretary Dole chose NS because it was the only railroad among the finalists, and the only finalist with $1.2 billion in cash. Mrs. Dole argues that the purchase by NS would leave Conrail in the strongest possible financial position after the sale. This is important to many government officials since the first rescue in 1976, which formed Conrail, cost taxpayers more than $7 billion. Moreover, despite Conrail's improvements over the last two years, the railroad's carloadings in 1984 were only 64% of its traffic in 1977. But final approval of the sale must come from Congress which initiated hearings on the matter on February 27, 1985. Although NS has been given the "OK" by the Transportation Department, many industry experts believe there will be a tough controversy surrounding the decision due to both the positive and negative resulting effects and the various interest groups involved.

The combined railroads would significantly and directly affect the 76,000 employees at the two railroads, the tens of thousands of shippers served by them and those using products hauled on them, and the major eastern competitor, CSX Corporation, NS's chief rival, who vehemently opposes the merger.

If the merger is finalized, it would create the largest railroad in the U.S., a 31,500-mile network stretching from Jacksonville, Florida, to Boston and from New York City to Kansas City. The possible monopolistic effects would be felt most strongly in the Midwest, where the railroads overlap. The tight hold that this combined railroad might have on eastward moving traffic could push up the prices of automobiles and electricity in the Northeast, but new efficiencies in moving north-south traffic could lower the prices of paper and beer. "The toast on Northeast breakfast tables might become more expensive, the orange juice cheaper."

The American Iron and Steel Institute, noting that 75% of the steel made in the U.S. is produced within Conrail's territory, worries that more steel plants would become captive shippers. U.S. Steel estimates that 15% of the price of its products are attributable to transportation costs. Thus, higher rail rates could ultimately increase the prices of automobiles and appliances. Even Amtrak, the government subsidized passenger service, could feel negative effects from the merger. Heavier north-south freight traffic on Amtrak's Northeast corridor could result in congestion, slower passenger travel and heavier maintenance bills. But this same freight traffic could also bring more revenues to Amtrak from the fees collected when railroads run freight trains on Amtrak lines.

For the most part, labor at Conrail is divided on the acquisition issue. First labor had voted to support Alleghany, the only bidder behind which 19 unions could unite. The Brotherhood of Railway and Airline Clerks, the largest union at Conrail, had favored a public offering of Conrail (the most likely alternative if Congress does not approve the sale to NS). However, the head of the United Transportation Union seems to be leaning towards a merger with NS. But the union's main fear is the layoffs, since the merger would result in the loss of 2,530 jobs. Rail labor's contribution is crucial in this merger.

But the benefits and efficiencies resulting from the merger are many.

The combined rail system might bring back beer makers whose Southeastern breweries have been giving more of their northbound traffic to trucks. The new railroad could put together long hauls on a single line and thus avoid interline rate disputes, switching fees, and loss, damage or delay of freight. This is especially important since the synergistic effects of piggyback operations and intermodalism would be greatly enhanced through the Conrail acquisition. In addition, the merger would counterbalance CSX's dominance in the East. The combined railroad would hold 42.1% market share of the total business while CSX would hold 39.2 percent. Most important, in an industry where economies of scale are important, this merger can bring lower rates for shippers and long-term survival for the railroads involved. Consequently, these lower rates for shippers through longer hauls and single rail service is transmitted to the consumer via lower prices.

A consolidated system can:

1 shorten circuitous or roundabout routings
2 establish through-rates that guarantee more reliable service
3 effect economics by reducing the number of freight yards, interchange points and other facilities
4 cut freight rates more readily than two railroads sharing a shipment that one originates and the other delivers.

Despite the advantages created from such a merger, controversy during Congressional hearings will be heated. As of April 19, 1984, the Senate Panel has delayed the Conrail-sale vote due to pressure from small rival roads, especially Chicago & North Western. Several Midwestern railroads, including Chicago & North Western, Illinois Central Gulf Railroad, and Grand Trunk Western Railroad, fear that Norfolk Southern, through its acquisition of Conrail, will lure away some of their freight business. Although Norfolk Southern has reached an agreement with Kansas City Southern Railway, other Midwestern rails are opposing the merger. The main fear at Chicago & North Western is that Norfolk Southern could carry much of the eastbound traffic that it (C&NW) now carries directly through Kansas City, and thereby leaving C&N out of the picture. The problem for Norfolk Southern is that the longer Congress delays in reaching a decision, the more viable a public sale of Conrail becomes to both Congress and the administration.

In addition, many analysts are concerned with the financing of this purchase. Three weeks after Dole announced NS as the winner of the bid, NS's stock price was little changed from its 66¾ just before the announce-

ment. This merger could quickly drain NS's cash reserves and push its debt up from the current 18% of capital. Furthermore, NS plans to close its $315 million purchase of North American Van Lines Inc., by mid-1985; and the Conrail deal alone would require a $1.2 billion in new debt.

HISTORY (See Exhibit 4)

The federal government began work in 1970 on what was to be the largest consolidation in U.S. history until then. The idea was to merge the bankrupt Penn Central and other northeastern railroads into one line called Consolidated Rail Corporation (Conrail). Conrail's creation would offer competition in the northeast region thus reducing the chance for a monopoly.

The federal government previously had established the United States Railway Association (USRA) which conducted the study to consolidate six railroads, then in bankruptcy. The USRA became the holding company for Conrail. Its function is to receive subsidies from the government for Conrail operations and to monitor Conrail's progress.

Consolidated Rail Corporation (Conrail) is a private, for profit corporation chartered in the Commonwealth of Pennsylvania. It was created by an Act of Congress (Regional Rail Reorganization Act of 1973, as amended) to acquire and revitalize most of the freight operations previously provided by six bankrupt carriers: Central of New Jersey; Erie Lackawanna; Lehigh and Hudson River; Lehigh Valley; Penn Central; and Reading. Conrail began operations on April 1, 1976.

Just seven weeks before this start date, Conrail learned that it was going to be a 17,000 mile railroad, not 15,000 miles. Conrail gained this extra 2,000 miles of track when the Chessie and Southern Railways backed out of their deal with the Ford Administration to acquire the 2,000 miles of the Penn Central Line when labor disputes could not be solved with their unions. This increase in track would cost the government an additional $185 million in order to start up Conrail.

In June, 1978, the company acquired from the Lehigh Coal and Navigation Corporation, its lease hold interest in the Lehigh and Susquehanna Railroad for cash consideration of approximately $5,200,000.

Conrail is not a nationalized railroad, a government corporation or public agency. The federal government has authorized the investment of $3.3 billion in Conrail to help the corporation fulfill its congressional mandate to

EXHIBIT 3 HOW NOT TO SELL A RAILROAD

Transportation Secretary Elizabeth Dole says her choice of a buyer for Conrail is "imminent." The Washington rumor mill is working overtime and Norfolk Southern is the handicappers' favorite, in part because it has courted Conrail's unions for help in getting congressional approval. That key consideration tells you why selling a government-owned railroad, even at a sizable markdown from total investment, is no simple deal and is likely to be no bargain for the taxpayers.

Selling Conrail should never have been complicated. In the best of all possible worlds, you would call in the underwriters and tell them to prepare a secondary offering of all the stock the government holds. Then you would agree on a price, and sell it. That's it. The Treasury gets the money, and from that day forward there's that much less interest to pay on the national debt. The $7 billion in tax money squandered on the government's decade-long experiment in railroad ownership would be nothing but a bad memory. Arguments that Conrail is too big to be sold that way aren't impressive when you consider how easily little Britain managed to peddle an even larger British Telecom offering.

But Congress couldn't do this simple thing without muddling it up. In response to the 1981 Reagan administration proposal to sell Conrail, Congress naturally concocted a law. It required the Department of Transportation to come up with a "plan," but the plan must meet certain requirements. We'll spare you the mind-boggling details, but here's an idea: If the U.S. Railway Association determined that Conrail could be profitable, it could be sold only as a single entity until Oct. 31, 1983. Then there would be a second USRA profitability determination and employees would have a shot at buying it. But if the road were sold piecemeal, 75% of its service would have to be maintained. And on and on, with each covenant and restriction reducing the government's chances of getting rid of the darn thing with even a minimal recovery of taxpayer losses.

This process has been lumbering along for 3½ years. Mrs. Dole, looking at the situation when she came into the DOT, decided that the best way to go would be to find a qualified suitor, get that suitor to meet certain obligations to please Congress, and then marry off Conrail to this eligible and willing bridegroom. The three finalists appear to be Norfolk Southern, Alleghany Corp. and an investors group led by hotel executive J. W. Marriott Jr.

If Norfolk Southern is to be the choice, it has some things to recommend it. It is a large, profitable, experienced railway operator. The two systems would meld together into a regional network. But its strength is also its weakness. The Justice Department is looking at the antitrust implications and its findings will have some bearing on the final outcome. CSX Corp., Norfolk Southern's big competitor, is not at all pleased; it has argued that Conrail should be sold piecemeal.

Conrail's management still is pushing for a public stock offering. It contends that the road, which has piled up some cash reserves in today's freer regulatory climate, is worth more than the $1.2 billion that seems to be the limit any suitor is willing to pay. But, no doubt with an eye on keeping control in the hands of existing employees—who already own the 15% of Conrail not owned by the government—the managers want a restriction that no buyer or buyer group could acquire more than 10% of the company.

So everyone wants restrictions. And everyone has his eye on how the forces will line up in Congress. (Congress, by the way, is now theoretically prohibited by a Supreme Court decision from exercising the legislative veto it has provided itself with, but anyone who wants to test that ruling in the present case would be merely asking for further protracted delay.) If Conrail is ever to be pried out of the public domain, there is indeed much to be said for managing the politics carefully, just as they were managed carefully by the people who manipulated it into the public domain a decade ago.

It remains to be seen whether Mrs. Dole has managed them carefully enough. Our own worst fear is that the wrangling will go on and on and Conrail will continue to be the political medicine ball it has been for a decade. If Mrs. Dole can't make her deal stick, whatever it turns out to be, let's hope that she calls in the underwriters and has a go at doing it the simple way.

The Wall Street Journal, Tuesday, January 15, 1985

EXHIBIT 4   THE EVOLUTION OF CONRAIL
(Start-up Dates of Predecessor Railroads and Steps toward Conveyance Day)

History

October 7, 1826
Conrail's oldest segment, Granite Railway Co., built to carry granite blocks for the Bunker Hill Monument from a quarry in West Quincy, Mass. Through successive mergers became part of New York, New Haven & Hartford Railroad, a predecessor of Penn Central

June 6, 1829
Schuylkill Valley Navigation and Railroad Co., oldest segment of Reading Company

August 9, 1831
Mohawk and Hudson Railroad, oldest portion of New York Central Railroad, a Penn Central predecessor

October, 1832
Camden & Amboy Railroad & Transportation Co., earliest segment of Pennsylvania Railroad, a predecessor of Penn Central

January 1, 1842
Elizabethtown & Somerville Railroad Co., oldest line of Central Railroad Co. of New Jersey

May 14, 1851
New York & Erie Railroad, oldest segment of Erie Railroad, a predecessor of Erie Lackawanna Railroad

October 15, 1851
Lackawanna & Western Railroad, original line of Delaware, Lackawanna & Western Railway Co., an Erie Lackawanna predecessor

June 11, 1855
Delaware, Lehigh, Schuylkill & Susquehanna Railroad, earliest line of Lehigh Valley Railroad Co.

August 14, 1882
Lehigh & Hudson River Railway Co. stock held by other five predecessor railroads in Conrail

1880s–1920s
Railroads, as America's primary mode of freight transportation, prospered, as a whole

1930s–1960
Competitive modes, supported in part (directly and indirectly) by enormous government financial resources, severely cut into railroads profitability and traffic; railroads capital resources declined (especially in the Northeast Quadrant of America); maintenance expenditures were deferred

October 17, 1960
Erie Lackawanna Railway Co. formed by merger of Erie Railroad and Delaware, Lackawanna & Western Railroad

Bankruptcies

March 22, 1967
Central Railroad of New Jersey entered bankruptcy

February 1, 1968
Penn Central Transportation Co. created by merger of Pennsylvania Railroad and New York Central Railroad

December 31, 1968
New York, New Haven & Hartford Railroad included in Penn Central

June 21, 1970
Penn Central entered bankruptcy

July 24, 1970
Lehigh Valley Railroad Co. declared bankruptcy

November 23, 1971
Reading Company entered bankruptcy

April 18, 1972
Lehigh & Hudson River Railway Co. filed for bankruptcy

June 26, 1972
Erie Lackawanna Railway Co. entered bankruptcy

(Continued)

EXHIBIT 4   THE EVOLUTION OF CONRAIL *(Continued)*
(Start-up Dates of Predecessor Railroads and Steps toward Conveyance Day)

Government action

February 8, 1973
One-day labor strike shuts down Penn Central; government intervention ends strike, setting in motion process of government participation to resolve dilemma of rail bankruptcies in Northeast

January 2, 1974
President Nixon signed Regional Rail Reorganization Act into law, calling it a turning point in history, following Congressional passage on December 21, 1973

May 2, 1974
Penn Central, Reading Central Railroad of New Jersey and Lehigh Valley ruled unreorganizable by their respective bankruptcy courts

December 16, 1974
Supreme Court found RRRA Constitutional by 7-2 vote

February 26, 1975
United States Railway Association's Preliminary System Plan for restructuring bankrupt lines released. Called for 15,000 route-mile system, including 3,400 miles of light density lines, and expanded Norfolk & Western and Chessie System to provide competition.

April 16, 1975
Special Appeals Court in Washington upheld Erie Lackawanna Reorganization Court decision to allow late inclusion of EL in Conrail

November 9, 1975
USRA's Final System Plan for Conrail (filed with Congress on July 28, 1975) is accepted by Congress

January 28, 1976
Railroad Revitalization and Regulatory Reform Act passed Congress (signed by President Ford on February 5) amending the RRRA

March 12, 1976
Financing Agreement between USRA and Conrail concluded. Conrail has access to government investment funds up to $2,025 billion to launch operations.

Conrail begins

April 1, 1976
Rail properties conveyed to Conrail at 12:01 a.m.

Source: Company's lines.

restore reliable freight service to the region at a profit, and seek its goal of economic self-sustainability in the private sector. Through March 31, 1980, $2.775 billion of federal funds had been invested in Conrail.

During this same period (through Conrail's first four years of operations) the corporation invested more than $2.43 billion in improvements to physical assets and obtained more than $850 million in financing from the private sector for new equipment.

Since its formation, Conrail has been rationalizing its rail system and has become a profitable company despite the severe recession of 1982. The rail systems inherited by Conrail in 1976 were too large to serve the traffic base of the Northeast and Midwest region on a profitable basis. Moreover, the assets had been undermaintained and required significant overhaul to raise freight service levels to acceptable standards. The federal government's $3.28 billion in Conrail between April 1976 and June 1981, together with Conrail's revenues, provided funds to eliminate the deferred maintenance of the predecessor railroads which plagued Conrail in its early years. Conrail has ad-

dressed all of these problems in the past few years. Costs have been reduced substantially, the rail system has been rationalized, and the assets have been rebuilt or replaced. In addition, Conrail has benefited substantially from the deregulation of the railroad industry. By applying the marketing freedoms granted by the Staggers Act, Conrail established itself as an independent competitive influence in our markets and a leader among railroads in adapting to an era of deregulation. In 1984, Conrail led the industry in developing deregulated pricing strategies and the computer technology to implement those strategies.

At the present time, Conrail is experiencing one of the most dramatic events in its history. After the government put Conrail for sale, and Transportation Secretary Elizabeth Dole declared Norfolk Southern the winner of the bid for Conrail, Norfolk Southern's chairman, Bob Claytor quickly stepped up lobbying to head off Norfolk Southern opponents. Among them were Conrail's management, at least some shippers and labor union officials, and representatives for CSX railroad. Dole stated why she did not prefer a public stock offering, "You've got an uncertain situation vs. a done deal. You have all the downside risks and virtually no upside.''

In spite of the decision by Dole bids still kept coming in. In particular a bid by Morgan-Stanley and Company caught the attention of the unions. Norfolk Southern repeatedly threatened to withdraw its bid if Congress didn't hurry up and end the increasingly testy rivalry (*Business Week*, January 13, 1986).

Eventually, during the first week of February 1986, the Senate cleared the sale of Conrail to Norfolk Southern on a 54–39 vote. Lawmakers first turned back a proposal to sell Conrail to Morgan-Stanley and then rejected several attempts to scuttle the sale to Norfolk Southern. This vote gave Norfolk Southern an advantage over competition but they still face a major battle in the Democratic-controlled House. Norfolk Southern got the deal through by resolving problems in relation to competition. They agreed to divest various stretches of track to competitors. Critics said the sale would so hurt competition that the government would have to reverse its policy of deregulating railroads.

MANAGEMENT

Conrail technically is a private corporation but will remain under control of a government-dominated board of directors until it becomes profitable and sufficiently repays its government debt (*Public Utilities Fortnightly*, 1976, p. 16).

Of the eleven members of Conrail's board of directors, elected by security holders, USRA as the holder of the debentures and Series A Preferred Stock is entitled to elect six directors; the voting trustees for Series B Preferred Stock, three directors; and the voting trustees for common stock, two directors. As required by the Railroad Revitalization & Regulatory Reform Act, the chairman and the president of Conrail are also directors of the corporation.

The list on page 546 shows the directors and corporate officers of Conrail.

From its inception until mid-1980, Conrail was under the direction of Chairman Edward G. Jordan. He is the former president of a Los Angeles insurance-services company. The only railroad experience he had before he took the Conrail job was two years as president of the United States Railway Association.

Complementing Jordan's experience was Conrail's president, Richard D. Spence. He was vice president for operations at Southern Pacific prior to joining Conrail. However, in mid-1978, Spence was replaced by Stuart M. Reed. He came from American Motors Corporation with a reputation as a cost-cutter and tough labor negotiator (*Business Week*, March 12, 1979, p. 20).

In May, 1980, Jordan accepted a new position with Cornell University, thus, providing an opening for a new chairman (*Business Week*, June 2, 1980, p. 33). Jordan was replaced by L. Stanley Crane, one of the industry's most respected figures, formerly of Southern (*Railway Age*, January 26, 1981, p. 65). Mr. Crane is receiving less pay at Conrail. His three-year contract calls for an annual salary of $265,000 without any bonuses, when Southern's compensation was $278,000 plus $53,000 in bonuses, and an abundance of other lucrative fringe benefits. During his 43-year railroad career he developed a reputation of taking a firm stance toward the unions but without going out of his way ''to pick a fight.''

Crane is liberal in delegating authority and responsibility to Conrail's employees. He has initiated joint labor-management programs and has quality circles now working in 12 cities. Management has implemented a massive information management system which improves communications and helps in the analysis of problems. Additionally, several other computer-based systems are used to monitor and control critical phases of operations.

MARKETING

The passage of the Staggers Act in 1980 opened many doors for marketing. Emphasis has been on competitive pricing options for shippers and the signing of several thousand contracts. Additionally, contracts with alternative modes of shipping have been let in order to facilitate more intermodal traffic. Multimodal shipping has expanded market potential and has become a major new market for the company. Rail market share of intercity freight dropped from 80 percent in 1925 to 37 percent in 1975. Marketing strategies emphasize the regaining of some of this market share. Tailored contracts, service plans, and transportation packages offered to freight customers have improved market share considerably already. Another incentive, which is particularly attractive to manufacturing firms, is that of warehousing. Conrail provides low-cost storage of commodities which are shipped on their lines. To expand markets, they increasingly have handled multimodal freight shipments under the ''Conrail umbrella''. The customers are served a comprehensive

EXHIBIT 5

DIRECTORS AND CORPORATE OFFICERS OF CONRAIL

Board of Directors

WILEY A. BRANTON, ESQ.
Partner
Sidley & Austin

DANIEL B. BURKE
President and Chief Operating Officer
Capital Cities Communications, Inc.

L. STANLEY CRANE
Chairman and Chief Executive Officer
Consolidated Rail Corporation

WILLIAM R. DIMELING
President
Great Eastern Coal Corporation

SAM HALL FLINT
Retired Executive of
The Quaker Oats Company

HENDRIK J. HARTONG, JR.
General Partner
Brynwood Partners
Investment Partnership

ROGER S. HILLAS
President—PNC Financial Corp
and Chairman—Provident National
Bank

STANLEY E.G. HILLMAN
Former Trustee of the
Chicago-Milwaukee Railroad

JUDITH RICHARDS HOPE, ESQ.
Partner
Paul, Hastings, Janofsky & Walker

L. CHESTER MAY
Vice President Finance and
Director—Standard Oil
Company of Indiana (Retired)

STUART M. REED
President and Chief Operating Officer
Consolidated Rail Corporation

JOHN E. ROBSON
Executive Vice President
and Chief Operating Officer
G.D. Searle & Company

RAYMOND T. SCHULER
President and Chief Executive Officer
The Business Council of
New York State, Inc.

Corporate Officers

L. STANLEY CRANE
Chairman and Chief Executive Officer

STUART M. REED
President and Chief Operating Officer

H. WILLIAM BROWN
Vice President and Treasurer

RICHARD W. GARBETT
Vice President—Public Affairs
(Deceased December 20, 1984)

JAMES A. HAGEN
Senior Vice President—Marketing and Sales

RICHARD B. HASSELMAN
Senior Vice President—Operations

CHARLES N. MARSHALL
Vice President—Marketing

ALFRED A. MICHAUD
Vice President—Sales

WILLIAM B. NEWMAN, JR.
Vice President and Washington Counsel

CLIFFORD W. OWENS
Vice President—Engineering and Staff

ROBERT H. PLATT
Executive Vice President—
Finance and Administration

ALLAN SCHIMMEL
Corporate Secretary and
Assistant to the Chairman

MICHAEL D. SIMS
Vice President—Information Systems

RICHARD C. SULLIVAN
Vice President—Resource Development

DONALD S. SWANSON
Vice President—Transportation

ROBERT E. SWERT
Vice President—Labor Relations

ROBERT V. WADDEN
Vice President and Controller

JEREMY T. WHATMOUGH
Vice President—
Materials and Purchasing

BRUCE B. WILSON
Vice President—Law

EXHIBIT 6   **Expanding or relocating?**

Expanding or relocating?

ANNOUNCING CONRAIL'S 3-POINT SITE SELECTION GUARANTEE

Now you can take the risk out of site selection or expansion with Conrail's 3-point guarantee that includes assistance in capital financing, delivery-as-promised, and multi-year rate and service commitments

Never before has the Northeast-Midwest region been so attractive for manufacturing and distribution. You already know it contains the country's largest concentration of industrial capacity, and industrial and consumer markets. But did you know the Northeast-Midwest has an exceptionally high proportion of skilled, educated workers?

Now Conrail will make this territory even more attractive to you, because we want your business. Our Regional Market Development Team is ready to roll up its sleeves to help you build your business with these three ironclad guarantees:

Map of the Northeast-Midwest region showing cities including Montreal, Grand Rapids, Lansing, Detroit, Buffalo, Syracuse, Albany, Boston, Chicago, Elkhart, Toledo, Cleveland, Newark, New York, Streator, Harrisburg, Philadelphia, Peoria, Columbus, Pittsburgh, Hagerstown, Wilmington, Baltimore, Indianapolis, Cincinnati, Washington D.C., East St. Louis, Charleston, Louisville

*HEADQUARTERS CITY
— PRINCIPAL CONRAIL ROUTES ONLY
···· TRACKAGE RIGHTS

1 Guaranteed assistance in capital financing for rail access

Conrail will guarantee its new partnership with you through aid in capital financing for rail access. If your contracted carloadings are above a minimum threshold, we'll cover your switch and connecting track installation costs.

Why is Conrail making this guarantee?

It's proof of our commitment to your investment. Our Regional Market Development Team, maintaining full confidentiality, works with you and a network of development specialists to tailor a site and service package that minimizes your logistics costs and maximizes long-term productivity.

We'll gather critical data on utilities, taxes, energy, sewerage and other factors which affect your costs. Contact us *early* in your facility planning to find the site which offers the best access to supply sources, markets, and services.

2 Guaranteed delivery-as-promised

We'll guarantee 100% delivery-as-promised for your origin-destination pairs that meet an established volume. If our performance falls below 100%, you're guaranteed a free carload for every one that brought us below that percentage.

Why is Conrail making this guarantee?

We have a great service record in meeting the demands of our customers who operate on just-in-time inventory schedules. And we intend to keep that record. Can you afford to settle for less when you're looking for a new site?

3 Guaranteed multi-year rate and service contract

Conrail will tailor a transportation contract with built-in rate and service commitments to meet your needs. This will allow you to control your future transportation costs.

And because we want you to locate on Conrail, we'll negotiate the lowest rates possible to put you on our system.

Why is Conrail making this guarantee?

We've pruned away unprofitable routes, and invested nearly five billion dollars in physical plant improvements. Today, Conrail's service and competitive spirit are second to none.

Don't wait—get Conrail's help early in your planning. Please call us, or mail the coupon for more information.

Free Site Inspection Tour by Rail for the first 100 qualified callers. Call 1-800-3-NUSITE (1-800-848-SITE in Pennsylvania). In Canada, call collect, 0-215-893-6029.

G.M. Williams, Jr.
AVP Regional Market Development
Conrail, 1528 Walnut Street
Suite 1600, Philadelphia, PA 19102

☐ I want Conrail to call me about locating in the Northeast-Midwest. Call me directly at _____ .

☐ Send me a new Site Selection Brochure containing more valuable information to help me select a site.

Name _____

Firm _____

Address _____

City _____

State _____ Zip _____

CONRAIL

We won't be satisfied until you are

package combining long-haul rail service with other modes of transportation, other railroads, warehouses, leasing companies, transportation terminals and any other port or facility that can participate in the movement of freight. To protect export coal producers hampered in their markets by competition from Europe and South Africa Conrail has reduced prices. They did this by blending different qualities of coal and delaying price increases allowed by the Staggers Act. Other marketing incentives include a money-back guarantee to new customers if their first shipment does not arrive on time and "Three Point Site Selection Guarantee". The program offers guaranteed assistance in capital financing for rail access to new plants, guaranteed Conrail delivery schedules, and guaranteed multi-rate service contracts (Exhibit 6).

OPERATIONS

Conrail's system consists of 13,443 route miles spawning 15 states in the Northeast and Midwest. This territory is the source of nearly half the nation's industrial output, and encompasses some of the keenest competition in the transportation marketplace. Conrail handled about 190 million tons of freight in 1984. Their tonnage includes more than 35 major commodities—including coal, coke and ore, automobiles and automotive parts, farm and food products, chemicals, pulp and paper products and general merchandise. To handle this freight, Conrail runs an average of 760 trains a day, drawing on an equipment fleet of about 94,000 freight cars and 2,800 locomotives.

Conrail is in its best physical plant condition ever. 1984 expenditures totaled $556 million used to optimize opportunities in the marketplace. Productivity between 1980 and 1983 has increased by 45 percent in terms of ton-miles per freight employee. Significant improvements in maintenance have made Conrail one of the most efficient in the industry. Since 1980, total transportation costs per car handled has dropped by 29 percent. An automated quality control system has been installed which provides information that enables further improvements on operations efficiency. On-time performance of freight trains climbed from 32 percent in 1976, when Conrail began operations, to 86 percent in 1984. Average transit time was also decreased 20 percent. Further, Conrail's total transportation cost per car handled has dropped by 29 percent. Beginning in 1982, Conrail was one of the first railroads to start "just-in-time" service for the auto industry, a premium service that helps reduce inventory

costs for American auto manufacturers so they can compete more successfully with foreign manufacturers. Both the productivity and quality of Conrail's maintenance of way efforts have increased tremendously. Largely as a result of converting from single to dual rail gangs in 1982, rail gangs can now install as much rail in one eight-hour day as they installed in three days in 1976. Tie gang productivity has improved by 129.5 percent since 1976, and surfacing gangs have improved their output by 147 percent. Work quality ratings have gone up 27 percent and tie surface quality ratings have gone up 31 percent.

See Exhibit 7 for productivity measures.

LABOR

Since 1976, Conrail has made significant progress in relations with unions representing its employees. Conrail negotiates with its unions outside the national rail union bargaining process, being the only major railroad to do so at the present time. As a result of wage concessions from the May 5, 1981 Agreement and other agreements that have enabled Conrail to reduce its work force and labor costs permanently, the ratio of labor costs to revenues has become competitive with other railroads.

In February 1985, Conrail reached a new contractual agreement with most of its unions and, was working toward reaching a similar agreement with the remainder under which union employees were returned to industry wage levels retroactive to July 1, 1984. Conrail 1984 financial results include provision for the restoration of employee wages to industry standards since employees have been paid about 12% below the national scale since mid-1981. Also as part of the wage restoration agreement, Conrail management joined with the national railway labor conference (representing rail management) to enter into national bargaining with rail labor.

FINANCE

Conrail's operations for 1984 resulted in net income of more than $500 million—the highest ever achieved in the company's nine year history, representing an improvement of 60% over the $313 million net income in 1983. In 1982, Conrail's net income was approximately $174 million.

Operating results for 1984 reflect substantial benefits from modest traffic growth, coupled with marketing and

EXHIBIT 7   **Productivity measures for Conrail.**

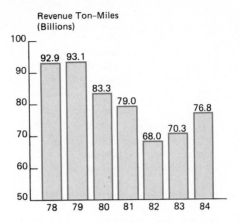

Revenue Ton–Miles
(Billions)

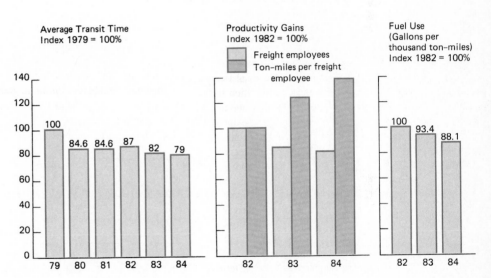

Average Transit Time
Index 1979 = 100%

Productivity Gains
Index 1982 = 100%

   Freight employees
   Ton-miles per freight
   employee

Fuel Use
(Gallons per
thousand ton-miles)
Index 1982 = 100%

customer service improvements, and continued company-wide efforts to increase productivity and trim costs.

Operating expenses of $2,913 million in 1984 were $125 million higher than similar expenses of $2,788 million in 1983. Labor costs, including payroll taxes and fringe benefits, increased $93 million as a result of applicable rate increases. Volume related cost increases of $55 million were primarily associated with train and engine crew labor, freight car inspections and repairs, diesel fuel consumption and equipment rental requirements. Material, supplies and other costs increased $17 million over

1983. Partially offsetting these cost increases were net savings of $40 million associated with productivity improvements and efficiency programs.

Exhibits 8 through 12 present financial statements and other pertinent financial information for Consolidated Rail Corporation.

EPILOGUE

The Reagan Administration's moribund plan to sell the government-owned Consolidated Rail Corp. may soon

EXHIBIT 8 CONSOLIDATED RAIL CORPORATION CONSOLIDATED STATEMENTS OF INCOME FOR
THE YEARS ENDED DECEMBER 31
(In Millions except per Share)

	1984	1983	1982
Revenues (1982 includes $618.0 from passenger operations)	$3,379.4	$3,076.4	$3,616.6
Operating expenses			
Way and structures	490.5	473.2	619.0
Equipment	775.9	771.0	910.9
Transportation	1,357.9	1,274.0	1,746.3
General, administrative and other	289.1	270.0	291.8
Total operating expenses	2,913.4	2,788.2	3,568.0
Income from operations	466.0	288.2	48.6
Other income, net	34.2	24.8	125.6
Income before income tax and extraordinary credit	500.2	313.0	174.2
Charge equivalent to federal income tax	27.8	14.9	
Income before extraordinary credit	472.4	298.1	174.2
Extraordinary credit resulting from utilization of net operating loss carryforward	27.8	14.9	
Net income	$ 500.2	$ 313.0	$ 174.2
Income per common share			
Income before extraordinary credit			
Primary	$ 17.46	$ 11.16	$ 6.82
Fully diluted	17.46	11.16	6.59
Net income			
Primary	18.50	11.73	6.82
Fully diluted	18.50	11.73	6.59

CONSOLIDATED STATEMENTS OF DEFICIT FOR THE YEARS ENDED DECEMBER 31
(In Millions)

	1984	1983	1982
Balance, beginning of year	$1,043.5	$1,352.2	$1,522.8
Net income	(500.2)	(313.0)	(174.2)
Accretion to redemption price of Series A preferred stock	5.0	4.3	3.6
Balance, end of year	$ 548.3	$1,043.5	$1,352.2

EXHIBIT 9   CONSOLIDATED BALANCE SHEETS, DECEMBER 31
(In Millions)

	1984	1983
Assets		
Current assets		
Cash and temporary cash investments	$ 846.0	$ 533.4
Accounts receivable, less allowances of $34.9 in 1984;		
$34.7 in 1983	494.2	485.9
Material and supplies	161.0	142.1
Other current assets	14.8	9.0
Total current assets	1,516.0	1,170.4
Investments in and advances to affiliated companies	33.9	37.0
Property and equipment, net	4,614.5	4,399.8
Other assets	72.0	95.6
Total assets	$6,236.4	$5,702.8
Liabilities and stockholders' equity		
Current liabilities		
Accounts payable	54.9	58.9
Wages and employee benefits	257.6	189.8
Current maturities of long-term debt	120.3	115.8
Casualty reserves	110.0	111.7
Accrued and other current liabilities	386.3	383.3
Total current liabilities	929.1	859.5
Long-term debt, less current maturities	1,711.1	1,679.1
Casualty reserves, less current portion	80.7	97.1
Other liabilities	76.7	98.5
	1,868.5	1,874.7
Preferred stock with mandatory redemption		
(liquidation and redemption value in 1984, $2,554.6)	2,316.8	2,311.5
Preferred stock with mandatory redemption and common stock		
Series B preferred stock (liquidation value $1,587.0)	31.7	31.7
Common stock	29.4	29.4
Additional paid-in capital	1,613.6	1,644.8
Deficit	(548.3)	(1,043.5)
	1,126.4	662.4
Stock held by subsidiary	(4.4)	(5.3)
	1,122.0	657.1
Total liabilities and stockholders' equity	$6,236.4	$5,702.8

EXHIBIT 10 CONSOLIDATED STATEMENTS OF CHANGES IN FINANCIAL POSITION FOR THE YEARS
ENDED DECEMBER 31
(In Millions)

	1984	1983	1982
Funds provided by operations			
Income before extraordinary credit	$472.4	$298.1	$174.2
Non-cash charges (credits)			
Depreciation and amortization	239.3	244.8	240.6
Charge equivalent to federal income tax	27.8	14.9	
Provision for casualty losses, noncurrent	(16.4)	(7.6)	12.7
Other, net	(20.0)	.6	16.6
Changes in working capital	703.1	550.8	444.1
Accounts receivable	(8.3)	34.2	202.6
Material and supplies and other current assets	(24.7)	32.6	62.1
Accounts payable	(4.0)	(14.8)	(24.0)
Wages and employee benefits	67.8	(36.5)	(36.4)
Current maturities of long-term debt	4.5	(5.3)	(39.1)
Casualty reserves	(1.7)	(2.6)	(10.7)
Accrued and other current liabilities	3.0	(38.2)	(98.9)
Total funds provided by operations	739.7	520.2	499.7
Funds provided by (used for) financing activities			
Issuance of long-term debt	156.8	117.7	54.0
Current portion of long-term debt	(124.8)	(126.4)	(168.3)
Redemption of 7.5% debentures		(3.5)	(60.6)
Other	.3	.3	12.1
Total funds provided by (used for) financing activities	32.3	(11.9)	(162.8)
Funds provided by (used for) investment activities			
Property and equipment additions	(555.7)	(454.7)	(367.0)
Sales and other property transactions	101.7	50.7	78.3
Other, net	(5.4)	(17.8)	(4.1)
Total funds used for investment activities	(459.4)	(421.8)	(292.8)
Increase in cash and temporary cash investments	312.6	86.5	44.1
Cash and temporary cash investments			
Beginning of year	533.4	446.9	402.8
End of year	$846.0	$533.4	$446.9

EXHIBIT 11   **Conrail Corporation selected financial data.**

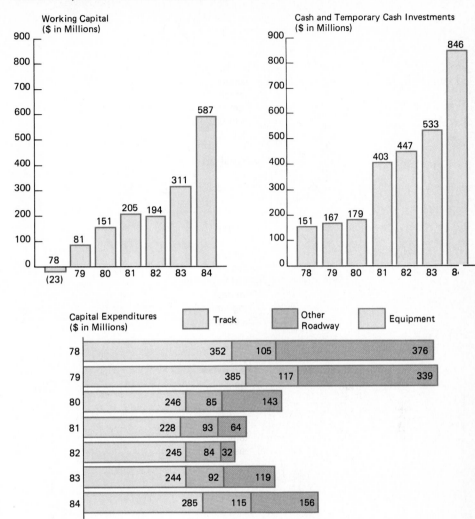

Working Capital
($ in Millions)

Year	Value
78	78
	(23)
79	81
80	151
81	205
82	194
83	311
84	587

Cash and Temporary Cash Investments
($ in Millions)

Year	Value
78	151
79	167
80	179
81	403
82	447
83	533
84	846

Capital Expenditures
($ in Millions)   Track   Other Roadway   Equipment

Year	Track	Other Roadway	Equipment
78	352	105	376
79	385	117	339
80	246	85	143
81	228	93	64
82	245	84	32
83	244	92	119
84	285	115	156

EXHIBIT 12   **Conrail Corporation operating expense and revenue distribution.**

Uses of 1984 operating expense dollar
Total operating expenses (in millions) $2,913

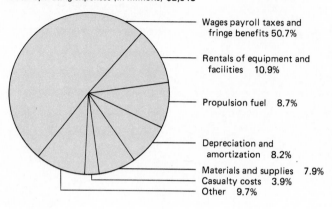

Wages payroll taxes and
fringe benefits 50.7%

Rentals of equipment and
facilities   10.9%

Propulsion fuel   8.7%

Depreciation and
amortization   8.2%

Materials and supplies   7.9%
Casualty costs   3.9%
Other   9.7%

1984 revenue distribution by commodity

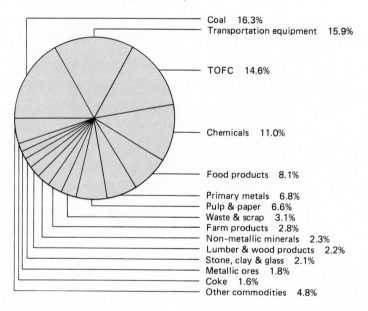

Coal   16.3%
Transportation equipment   15.9%

TOFC   14.6%

Chemicals   11.0%

Food products   8.1%

Primary metals   6.8%
Pulp & paper   6.6%
Waste & scrap   3.1%
Farm products   2.8%
Non-metallic minerals   2.3%
Lumber & wood products   2.2%
Stone, clay & glass   2.1%
Metallic ores   1.8%
Coke   1.6%
Other commodities   4.8%

come back to life. White House Chief of Staff Donald T. Regan will urge Transportation Secretary Elizabeth H. Dole to propose a public offering of Conrail stock. Dole's plan—selling Conrail to Norfolk Southern Corp.—has been blocked by the opposition of House Commerce Committee Chairman John D. Dingell Jr. (D-Mich.). Din-gell wants Conrail sold to the public, and, sources say, he has now persuaded Regan to go along. Wall Street analysts say a stock offering could bring as much as $2 billion in cash, worth considerably more to the government than the complex $1.9 billion deal Norfolk Southern has offered (*Business Week,* June 30, 1986, p. 47).

THE DANNON DECISION

Danny G. Kinker
Washburn University

Mr. James L. Dutt, Chairman and Chief Executive Officer of Beatrice Foods Company, faced a "very difficult decision." The company had been approached by a party offering to buy their Dannon yogurt subsidiary at a very attractive price. Should he recommend to the Board of Directors that the offer be accepted or rejected?

BEATRICE FOODS COMPANY: A PROFILE

In 1894, Beatrice Foods Company had two products to sell—butter and eggs. Today, Beatrice is highly diversified, producing and distributing more than 9,000 products worldwide. The 1981 Annual Report notes that Beatrice posted records for sales, earnings, and earnings per share for the twenty-ninth consecutive year. Sales rose 6 percent, from $8.3 billion in fiscal 1980 to $8.8 billion in fiscal 1981. Net earnings increased to $304.2 million, a

The research and written case information were presented at a Case Research Symposium and were evaluated by the Case Research Association's Editorial Board. This case was prepared by Danny G. Kinker of Washburn University of Topeka as a base for class discussion.

Distributed by the Case Research Association. All rights reserved to the author and the Case Research Association. Permission to use the case should be obtained from the Case Research Association. Used by permission of Danny G. Kinker and the Case Research Association.

5-percent gain from the $290.1 million recorded in fiscal 1980. Primary earnings per share rose 5 percent, from $2.81 in fiscal 1980 to $2.94 in fiscal 1981. Fully diluted earnings per share were $2.79, up 4 percent from the $2.67 posted in fiscal 1980.

Much, if not most, of the spectacular growth of Beatrice occurred during the twenty-four-year reign of William G. Karnes. This was for the most part accomplished during the late 1960s and early 1970s when the market rewarded acquisitive firms with high P/E ratios. A corporate officer explained that "firms were purchased for a price representing, say, 8 times earnings with stock trading at a multiple of around 20." When asked to describe the acquisition "strategy" of this period, Mr. Dutt said, "They would buy just about anything that came along." While this may have been true, a large portion of their acquisitions had similar characteristics. They were relatively small, local or regional in scope, entrepreneurially managed, and profitable. After acquisition, the firms remained quite autonomous and the entrepreneurial ex-owner remained at the helm. See Exhibit 1 for a depiction of the growth of Beatrice under the leadership of Mr. Karnes.

Mr. Karnes retired in 1976 and was succeeded by Wallace N. Rasmussen, who continued an acquisition strategy. Upon the retirement of Mr. Rasmussen in 1979, Mr. Dutt was appointed Chairman and Chief Executive

EXHIBIT 1   **Twenty-four consecutive years of growth.**

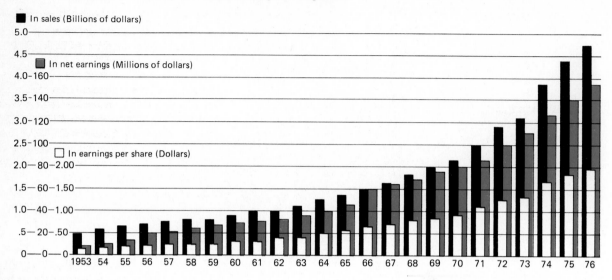

Officer. It was soon noted that under the leadership of Mr. Dutt, a significant change had occurred in Beatrice's strategy. The Wall Street Journal called it "a quiet revolution." With all the attention placed on acquisition, a few of Beatrice's 430 autonomous businesses or "profit centers" had turned into "profit losers."

The significant change in strategy was the fact that Beatrice had begun selling businesses as well as acquiring them. For example, in 1979 Beatrice sold its Southwestern Investment Co. and used the proceeds to buy Fiberite Corp. While Southwestern's earnings were growing at 8 percent per year, Fiberite's were growing at about 30 percent. Mr. Dutt said, "Before, we had companies coming in, but now, we'll have companies going out as well." Walter L. Lovejoy, president of the industrial division, explained that (under Mr. Rasmussen), "If we weren't doing well in a business, it was because we weren't managing properly. Mr. Dutt believes there are some things maybe we just shouldn't be in." Mr. Dutt also said, "We're not going to let companies die on our vine."

By 1981, Mr. Dutt's strategy had crystalized. The 1981 Annual Report contained the following discussion of "asset redeployment."

Beatrice has made great strides in its asset redeployment program over the past three years. During that time, the company has divested operations that generated approximately $500

million in sales in 1979. This is a managed program over time, and an ongoing review is conducted of all operations to ensure an optimum mix of companies.

Within that diverse mix, Beatrice looks for operations to exhibit the following characteristics: they should be able to achieve a real growth rate of 5 percent: *or* they should be achieving a return on net assets equal to or in excess of 20 percent: *or* they should be generating cash to be invested in operations which are growing in real terms.

When redeploying assets, Beatrice looks to profit centers or acquisition candidates that are generating returns that are higher than the corporate average.

Net sales and earnings by major lines of business, 1978–1981, are shown in Exhibit 2, and abbreviated income statement and balance sheet data for the company are shown in Exhibit 3.

DANNON YOGURT: A PROFILE

The history of Dannon yogurt begins in 1919, when a Spaniard named Carasso created the product. He then named the product after his son, Daniel, and Danone yogurt came into existence. The Danone operation was subsequently moved from Spain to France and eventually sold to BSN. Dannon yogurt came into existence in 1942 when

EXHIBIT 2 NET SALES BY MAJOR LINES OF BUSINESS
(In Thousands)

	1981	1980	1979	1978
Food and related services				
Dairy and soft drinks	$2,297,068	$2,027,639	$1,925,631	$1,809,811
Grocery	1,313,026	1,220,735	963,184	707,623
Food distribution & warehousing	1,292,254	1,131,771	976,689	827,129
Specialty meats	677,826	688,948	657,983	548,483
Confectionery & snack	602,140	522,260	467,750	415,112
Agri-products	450,086	461,346	391,311	348,289
Manufactured and chemical products				
Institutional & industrial	843,886	872,561	753,325	678,382
Travel & recreational	503,325	513,017	496,751	437,507
Housing & home environment	390,216	530,293	572,765	522,440
Chemical & allied products	402,977	321,939	273,636	227,636
Net sales	$8,772,804	$8,290,509	$7,479,025	$6,522,467

NET EARNINGS BY MAJOR LINES OF BUSINESS
(In Thousands)

	1981	1980	1979	1978
Food and related services				
Dairy & soft drinks	$122,499	$109,948	$106,610	$102,708
Grocery	125,190	113,997	82,353	50,064
Food distribution & warehousing	67,991	60,335	50,217	43,546
Specialty meats	53,224	50,009	44,964	44,520
Confectionery & snack	75,288	66,203	59,510	47,704
Agri-products	34,225	38,677	33,191	24,943
Manufactured and chemical products				
Institutional & industrial	106,485	126,616	111,126	106,188
Travel & recreational	54,082	47,823	45,816	38,053
Housing & home environment	22,435	22,148	42,470	53,215
Chemical & allied products	52,410	46,812	37,693	29,517
Total operating earnings	713,829	682,568	613,950	540,458
Less*	409,618	392,428	351,783	313,740
Net earnings	$304,211	$290,140	$262,167	$226,718

*Non-operating expenses, interest expense, and income taxes

EXHIBIT 3 STATEMENT OF CONSOLIDATED EARNINGS YEAR ENDING
LAST DAY OF FEBRUARY, 1981
(In Thousands of Dollars)

Income	
Net sales	$8,772,804
Interest income	40,198
Other income	25,590
	8,838,592
Costs and Expenses:	
Cost of sales, excluding depreciation	6,510,782
Selling, administrative and general expenses excluding depreciation	1,457,158
Depreciation expense	155,373
Interest expense	96,403
	8,219,716
Earnings before income taxes and minority interests	618,876
Provision for income taxes	301,700
Earnings before minority interests	317,176
Minority interests in net earnings of consolidated subsidiaries	12,965
Net earnings	$ 304,211

CONSOLIDATED BALANCE SHEET AS OF LAST DAY OF FEBRUARY, 1981
(In Thousands of Dollars)

Assets

Current assets:	
Cash	$ 132,420
Short-term investments	285,108
Receivables	834,480
Inventories:	
Finished goods	507,807
Work in process	138,371
Raw materials and supplies	325,854
	2,224,040
Prepaid expenses and other current assets	72,573
Total current assets	2,296,613
Investments in affiliated companies	57,021
Plant and equipment:	
Land	70,171
Buildings	592,544
Machinery and equipment	1,252,049
Capitalized leases	202,745
	2,117,509
Less accumulated depreciation	803,587
	1,313,922
Intangible assets	463,363
Noncurrent receivables	80,570
Other assets	25,060
Total assets	$4,236,555

EXHIBIT 3   STATEMENT OF CONSOLIDATED EARNINGS YEAR ENDING
LAST DAY OF FEBRUARY, 1981 *(Continued)*
(In Thousands of Dollars)

Liabilities and stockholders' equity	
Current liabilities:	
Short-term debt	$ 122,410
Accounts payable	521,061
Accrued expenses:	
Taxes (other than income taxes)	30,252
Other accruals	243,880
Income taxes	112,792
Current portion of long-term debt	28,813
Current obligations of capitalized leases	15,563
Total current liabilities	1,074,771
Long-term debt	564,710
Long-term lease obligations	126,728
Deferred items:	
Income taxes	90,963
Investment tax credits	31,870
Other	23,368
Other noncurrent liabilities	89,293
Minority interests in subsidiaries	53,407
Stockholders' equity:	
Preference stock	259,567
Common stock	180,850
Additional capital	106,930
Retained earnings	1,634,098
Total stockholders' equity	2,181,445
Total liabilities and stockholders' equity	$4,236,555

Daniel Carasso persuaded a friend, Juan Metzger, to come with him to the United States. They intended to produce and market yogurt. Dannon is an Americanization of Danone, and Daniel Carasso was the same Daniel for whom the yogurt was named. The initial operation was set up in the Bronx and produced 200 bottles of plain yogurt a day. Juan Metzger recalled, "Anything would have been easier to sell than yogurt in those days." Their customers were mostly recent European immigrants.

In 1947, a daring attempt was made to enhance the product by placing strawberry preserves in the bottom of the bottle. This seemed to appeal to customers and, eventually, the product line was to contain 16 flavors.

In 1952, Daniel Carasso returned to Europe to tend to his yogurt business there but Juan Metzger remained to cultivate the yogurt business in the United States. So successful was Metzger that, realizing its potential, Beatrice sought and acquired Dannon in 1959. After the purchase by Beatrice, Metzger remained at the helm of Dannon and

eventually became a member of the Board of Directors of Beatrice. With the resources of the larger company available, much faster growth was possible for Dannon. Automated equipment was installed which dramatically increased volume and the old glass bottles were replaced by waxed cups, but basic technology remained the same. The yogurt was made by keeping pasturized lowfat milk at temperatures around 100 degrees Fahrenheit while bacteria (good ones) converted the milk's sugar into lactic acid. This caused the milk to thicken and take on the tart taste of yogurt. Beatrice also invested heavily in marketing, expanding the geographic base until it became national.

THE DECISION

The offer to buy Dannon came from a not-unfamiliar source. It was in fact from BSN-Gervais-Danone and the offer was $84.3 million in cash. The amount surprised many food analysts because it was nearly 23 times Dannon's profits the previous year. Dannon's recent earnings had been depressed and the previous year's sales of nearly $130 million had produced net earnings of only around 53.5 million. Income statement and balance sheet data for Dannon are presented in Exhibit 4.

Three reasons can be cited for Dannon's recent drop in performance. First of all, anxious to tap the West Coast market, distribution to this area was initiated prior to acquiring a production facility in California. The area was served by the Ft. Worth, Texas, plant, sharply increasing distribution costs. Production in California had just recently commenced. Second, to counter the threat posed by Dannon, West Coast regional brands significantly increased their promotional spending. Third, Dannon encountered a new national competitor. Yoplait, a French style yogurt, was introduced under license by General Mills.

There was one other market factor of some importance. Beatrice believed that the yogurt market was achieving maturity at about 1.3 billion containers per year. Of this 1.3-billion-container market, over 30 percent

of it belonged to Dannon. Additionally, Dannon had introduced its own French style yogurt, Melange. It was estimated that this product category represented roughly 15 percent of yogurt sales. See Exhibit 5 for annual production and per capita consumption of yogurt.

Production in California joined the network of plants in New York, New Jersey, Florida, Ohio, and Texas. The Texas plant had recently been enlarged as well. Dannon had considerable experience in the yogurt industry and the dominant market share. While Dannon appeared to be related to Beatrice's other dairy operations (Meadow Gold, VIVA, etc.), synergies had never been realized. Metzger was quoted as saying, ''We will not depend on anyone else for storage or shipping or handling our product. Yogurt is perishable and the minute you let it get out of your sight, someone might get careless.''

Dannon's growth potential was uncertain, but **Metzger's** position was, ''We have been a one-product company for a long time. It's time to diversify.'' Also, Dannon's future as a cash generator was uncertain, but the sale would result in an estimated after-tax gain of over $45.0 million. What should Mr. Dutt recommend to the Board of Directors?

EXHIBIT 4 SELECTED DATA FROM DANNON'S 1981 FINANCIAL STATEMENTS

	1981	1980	1979	1978	1977	1976
			Income data			
Total sales	$129,385	122,552	113,426	100,897	76,681	55,449
Gross margin %	43.42	44.05	42.79	43.44	44.31	44.34
Earnings (pre-tax)	$ 6,789	6,590	5,634	10,705	9,765	6,436
Interest chg. (intercompany)	(118)	(126)	98	121	130	147
	$ 6,671	6,464	5,732	10,826	9,895	6,583
Margins (pre-tax):						
After int. %	5.28	5.40	5.01	10.79	12.86	11.62
Before int. %	5.19	5.30	5.09	10.91	13.03	11.89
Employees	1,201	1,310	1,270	995	804	613
			Asset data			
Acct. rec.	$ 9,647	9,121	9,597	9,521	6,951	5,234
Inventory	$ 2,325	2,296	2,192	1,787	1,206	839
Acct. pay.	$ (6,187)	(5,989)	(4,160)	(4,277)	(4,048)	(2,615)
Net assets	$ 19,450	21,533	23,760	22,670	17,977	12,538

Note: All dollar amounts expressed in thousands.

EXHIBIT 5   TOTAL U.S. PRODUCTION AND CONSUMPTION OF YOGURT

Year	Pounds (millions)	% Chg.	Sales (pounds per capita)	% Chg.
1960	44	—	.26	—
1961	49	11.4	.28	7.7
1962	45	−8.1	.25	−10.7
1963	51	13.3	.28	12.0
1964	53	3.9	.29	3.6
1965	61	15.1	.32	10.3
1966	70	14.8	.37	15.6
1967	90	28.6	.47	27.0
1968	124	37.8	.63	34.0
1969	169	36.3	.85	34.9
1970	172	1.8	.86	1.2
1971	236	37.2	1.16	34.9
1972	284	20.3	1.38	19.0
1973	318	12.0	1.52	10.1
1974	343	7.9	1.63	7.2
1975	445	29.7	2.09	28.2
1976	482	8.3	2.24	7.2
1977	534	10.8	2.45	9.3
1978	566	6.0	2.57	4.9
1979	567	0.2	2.54	−1.2
1980	589	3.9	2.61	2.8
1981	582	−1.2	2.55	−2.3

Note: 1980 figures were preliminary and 1981 figures estimated.
Source: USDA, Production and per capita consumption of yogurt. 1960–1981.

DIAGRAPH CORPORATION

Lawrence R. Jauch
Northeast Louisiana University

Diagraph Corporation is in the industrial marking business. Diagraph manufactures and distributes a full line of stencil cutting machines, stencil oil boards, inks, duplicator marking equipment, conveyor line and hand coders and free hand marking devices. Approximately 170 people are employed at Diagraph's office and factory located in the Ordill area near Crab Orchard Lake in Southern Illinois. Other than the Ordill facility, approximately 40 more persons are employed in St. Louis. Additionally, Diagraph has 72 branch offices and distributor locations around the world which employ about 300 more people.

HISTORY

Diagraph began operations in the late 1800's. Andrew Jackson Bradley, somewhat of an inventive genius, is responsible for the very first stencil cutting machine. Bradley, also responsible for the patent and manufacture of a paper cutter, became cognizant of the need for stencil cutting machines as a direct result of witnessing huge piles

Nancy Owens made a significant contribution to this case study while a graduate assistant to Dr. Jauch at Southern Illinois University at Carbondale.

The Company requests that students do *not* contact the firm for additional information. The case provides all the information necessary for study.

of boxes always blocking the streets when he traveled to and from work. He learned these boxes were awaiting marking and their huge accumulation was the result of the marking being such a slow process. He conceded that there had to be a faster way.

The drop forge stencil machine character and invention of the stencil machine was recognized by the Franklin Institute in Philadelphia in 1900 as the outstanding invention of the year. The Bradley Machine also received the highest award at the 1904 World's fair in St. Louis.

During its first year of operation, 1894, nine machines were sold. During this period of continuing growth, Stephen Hartog, one of Bradley's first employees, presented to Bradley a new idea for improving the stencil machines. Bradley, unimpressed, dismissed the idea in addition to relieving Hartog of his job.

Hartog decided to try to make it alone. He fell upon hard times in this solo effort but not before he had introduced his idea to Theodore Remmers, a well-known St. Louis pattern maker. Remmers then interested several families in the product and with their contributions of capital formed the Diagraph Company.

In 1913 a young man by the name of J. W. Brigham went to work for Remmers. By 1915 he had assumed full responsibility for sales and then in 1928 purchased the company from Remmers.

In 1936, Brigham saw an opportunity to expand sales

by buying out the old Bradley Stencil Company, which had a larger plant capacity and many established customers. It was at this point that the company of Diagraph Bradley was formed.

World War II stimulated Diagraph Bradley's operations dramatically, with sales increasing from 75 per month to 500 per month and the majority of sales going to the government. During war times a great demand for industrial marking exists. Soldiers' duffel bags were marked with names and identification numbers and additionally defense related industries had an increased need for marking systems due simply to the increase in demand for defense products.

In 1948, the company sensed a need for diversification due to the war ending. A plant was purchased in Southern Illinois to manufacture recreation equipment. These efforts failed miserably. However, the Korean War came along just soon enough to preclude the company's total demise. In the words of J. R. Brigham, current Chairman of the Board, "The war in Korea actually saved the company, because there was a spurt in demand for stencil cutting machines which brought revenue, and that helped a great deal."

One might expect that the end of the Korean War would mean an end to Diagraph. However, 1954 marked the first real product innovation for the company. This new technique was a method of applying a mark to a roller and using a roller as opposed to a brush or stencil. It was seen as a tremendous improvement for the company.

Additionally, the competition stayed out of that business for about 5 years because they didn't think customers would accept paying the high prices Diagraph was charging for the ink. This new technique was approximately eight times more expensive than the previous technique of applying the ink with a brush. The product's name was Rol-It-On. Rol-It-On was the breakthrough that the company needed to develop domestic and export sales organizations, improved manufacturing facilities and other new products.

Also during this period, Diagraph became a qualified supplier of aircraft components for the United States Air Force. Production of assemblies for the Boeing Airplane Company greatly improved Diagraph's overall situation, and solidified the firm as a machine-tool oriented business.

In 1958, two new products, the Mark X Marker and Rol-Flo stencil applicator, were introduced. These products resulted in further growth for the company.

The sixties marked a period of continuing expansion for Diagraph. During the mid-sixties, the duplicator product line was introduced and in 1968 the first model of the DiPrinter was introduced along with a line of label paper. Additionally, Diagraph started manufacturing coders and introduced the first models of the DiCoder in March of 1969. The nature of these products is explained later in the case. By this time domestic sales had strengthened, as well as sales to foreign countries.

The seventies was a period of diminished expansion for the firm. Five product lines were firmly established and the firm concentrated its efforts on refining these products. These products included the following systems: stencil cutting, label printing, duplicator marking, in line coder, free hand marking, label gumming and adhesives.

TRADITIONAL DIAGRAPH PRODUCTS AND THEIR OUTLOOK

Included here is a brief discussion of each of Diagraph's traditional product lines as well as management's assessment of their potential.

Stencil Cutting Machines

As mentioned earlier, stencil cutting machines are the original product line of the Diagraph Corporation. Although the machine has been through some minor modifications, it is still very much like the original model.

Diagraph's management feels that this product has reached the maturity stage in the domestic markets. However, a great potential for growth does exist in the international markets. No significant decline is expected, as the mature stage for the stencil cutter life cycle will continue for many years.

The demand for supplies associated with this system such as stencil oil boards and inks will continue to be related to the level of industrial activities. The current strength of the U.S. dollar is held responsible for keeping demand low in the international markets.

Hand Duplicator and Stencils

Related to the stencil cutting machine is a product line of hand duplicators and stencils. Like the stencil cutting machine these products are part of the original product line of Diagraph.

The hand duplicator is a small device for marking packages. The product consists of an ink pad, stencil and an ink bottle which is used to make markings on a variety of industrial products. While these products have provided stability for Diagraph, it seems that they are approaching the final stage in the product life cycle. The market for duplicators is shrinking while the market for stencils is flat or slightly declining.

Conveyor Line and Hand Coders

A coder is a machine that prints a code on an item such as a box, bag, bottle, spool, can, intricate metal or plastic parts. A good example of the use of coders is the marking of expiration dates on the side of a milk jug. In addition to date coding, these products are useful for product identification, inventory control and production control. These products can either be used by hand, or integrated into a mechanical production line network.

This product is seen as one where numerous opportunities for growth exist.

Mechanical Label Printing

These machines print labels for a variety of industrial uses including product identification, shipment addressing, inventory control and production control to name just a few.

The September 1982 release of Diagraph's 8000 DiPrinter was one of the most successful new product introductions Diagraph has seen. Demand for these products reached a peak of 10 a week, but sales in 1983–84 were not able to maintain that level. Diagraph would like to see an increase in its share of the market for these products. However, implementation of bar code requirements for automotive suppliers is likely to cause an additional 30–40% decline for these printers.

Markers

Diagraph produces a variety of marking pens such as the Mark-X, GP-X and Jumbo Insta Marker. Refillable markers are also a part of this product family.

The Mark X is mature but should not be declining. Sales have been affected by quality problems and lack of sales time and emphasis. Refillable markers are continuing to decline. Diagraph has achieved rapid growth and reasonable penetration with the GP-X for opaque colors. Competition and price pressure continues with numerous imports from Japan. The Jumbo Insta Marker is a quality product but offers no special advantages. Growth and

profit potential in the marker line is minimal according to management.

Diagraph's major new products will be described later. Suffice it to say for now that dramatic sales expansion in domestic markets is expected to result from newer product lines. Before describing that strategic change, we take a look at Diagraph's operational areas.

OPERATIONAL ACTIVITIES AT DIAGRAPH

This section explains the ways in which marketing and production operate at the company.

Marketing & Distribution

Management at Diagraph believes that strong sales support and distribution systems together represent one of Diagraph's major strengths. The company's first branch office opened in 1949. Between 1954 and 1964, the financial success of three items, namely the Rol Flo, Mark X and the duplicator line, permitted the acquisition and financing of general distributorships. Two distributorships were acquired, taking on subsidiary status, while other distributorships were set up by providing financial assistance in a geographic territory. Diagraph's sales and distribution network is currently made up of more than 300 sales and support personnel in 14 company-owned branch locations and 22 independent stocking distributors. (See Exhibit 1, Branch & Distributor Locations in the U.S.)

The distribution system at Diagraph has evolved from one where a predominance of independent distributors handled its products to a situation of tightly controlled company owned branch offices. According to Mr. James Brigham, Chairman of the Board, experience has shown him that the best means of handling his product has been a tightly controlled situation.

Over the years, the company has replaced non-productive distributors which were independent business people with company-owned branches. While this strategy has proven to be effective, according to Brigham, there is no plan to replace productive and committed independent distributors who are achieving the sales objective of the company.

In the early days at Diagraph, management couldn't expect distributors to sell only Diagraph products. The product line was really not wide enough for a distributor to sell Diagraph exclusively. Distributors also had to sell

EXHIBIT 1 DIAGRAPH BRADLEY—BRANCH AND DISTRIBUTOR
LOCATIONS IN THE UNITED STATES

State	# Distributors	# Branches
Alabama	1	0
Arkansas	1	0
California	0	2
Colorado	1	0
Florida	1	0
Georgia	1	1
Hawaii	1	0
Illinois	0	1
Indiana	1	0
Kentucky	1	0
Louisiana	0	2
Maryland	1	0
Massachusetts	0	1
Michigan	1	1
Minnesota	1	1
Missouri	0	1
Nebraska	1	0
New Jersey	0	1
New York	0	1
Ohio	3	0
Oklahoma	1	0
Oregon	1	0
Pennsylvania	0	2
South Carolina	0	1
Tennessee	1	0
Texas	1	1
Virginia	1	0
Washington	1	0
Wisconsin	1	0

staples, tape machines and tapes in order to make a living. According to Brigham, the distributors lacked loyalty to the Diagraph product line.

As a part of this controlled distribution system, Diagraph has spelled out explicit terms in its arrangements with distributors and branches. Both have certain quotas to fulfill in various Diagraph product lines. Additionally, distributors are precluded from selling competitors' products.

Diagraph also spells out the conditions for a sale if the distributors have reached retirement age or simply want out of the business. According to John McKevitt, Senior Vice President, these contractual arrangements have evolved in response to Diagraph's pursuit of control.

As part of Diagraph's continuous commitment to ef-fective branch and distributor arrangements, the following objectives have been identified:

- Establish sales quotas by Branch & Distributor location and for branch salesmen
- Develop performance reviews for AMS Representatives (Advanced Marking Systems is described later)
- Develop criteria for measurement of Branch Manager's performance
- Evaluate territories based on potential for maximum return
- Establish goals by units for major equipment
- Monitor and report quota achievement performance
- Develop performance criteria and review for individual distributors

• The 1984–85 overall goal was a 10% sales increase in basic products.

The organization of marketing at Diagraph has gone through a variety of changes in the past few years. Once an umbrella organization with areas as diverse as Engineering and Customer Service reporting to it, the Sales/Service organization now operates differently with fewer people reporting. This change has been a result of the growth taking place at Diagraph since 1982.

The marketing organization was under the direction of John McKevitt until a major restructuring took place in 1986. Mr. McKevitt's experiences prior to coming to Diagraph included retail sales, sales of class rings for a company called Jostens, and even a brief stint in the signal department for a railroad. Mr. McKevitt came to work for Diagraph in 1963 as a manager in the New Orleans office. He also worked in both the Houston and Birmingham offices. In 1974 he became Vice President of Sales, in 1982 Vice President of Marketing and Sales, and Senior Vice President in 1986. This new position makes him responsible for developing alternate distribution methods for traditional products, managing the U.S. Government and Postal Service business, managing key vendor rela-tionships, advising on pricing and handling special projects. In addition to his responsibilities as Senior Vice President, McKevitt also serves on the Board of Directors. (The Board consists of nine members, with five outsiders who are described in Exhibit 2.)

Mr. McKevitt has seen many changes since his early days at Diagraph. He is optimistic about the new direction the company is taking. McKevitt sees Diagraph's strengths as coming from a variety of areas. For example in the past, Diagraph tended to be a market driven operation. Customers' needs were gathered from distributors and branches and this information was then channeled to upper level management to be acted upon. Currently Diagraph has taken a more aggressive approach. It is paying more attention to its competitors and perhaps of even greater importance, Diagraph is focusing energy on applications of both its traditional and new product lines. Diagraph objectives with respect to corporate sales and marketing communication include the following:

• Improve corporate identity—image (packaging, literature, trade shows, support material, advertising)
• Increase market awareness of Diagraph products
• Strengthen salesman recognition program

EXHIBIT 2   OUTSIDE MEMBERS OF THE DIAGRAPH BOARD OF DIRECTORS*

William C. Martinez **(65, St. Louis)**

Retired executive vice-president of the St. Louis based Sunnen Products, a $60 million industrial and automotive machine tool manufacturer. Became associated with Diagraph in 1944 when he started to operate as an independent exporter. Diagraph was his first client.

Richard K. Holt **(66, Hilton Head Island, South Carolina)**

CPA, management consultant, and entrepreneur whose association with Diagraph began in 1960 when his Centralia, Illinois, auditing firm performed the company audit.

Richard E. Fister **(48, St. Louis)**

A financial consultant and entrepreneur who became associated with Diagraph in the early 1970's when he was president of the Tower Grove Bank of St. Louis. A graduate of St. Louis University Law School, he is the only attorney on the board of directors.

Hal E. Kroeger, Jr. **(41, St. Louis)**

President of Distribix, a regional marketer and distributor of fine and industrial papers with nine divisions in five states. A graduate of Princeton and the Harvard Business School, Mr. Kroeger serves as a national director of the Young Presidents Organization.

Thomas K. Hill **(39, New York)**

Joined the Diagraph Board in 1978 to replace a retiring director. Hill, an independent marketing and communications consultant, graduated from the University of Texas and the Wharton School of Business. He has been a business associate of J. R. Brigham, Jr., since 1970.

*It is unusual for a company of this size and type to find a majority of the Board composed of outside Directors. These Directors have served Diagraph an average of 12 years' duration, and Mr. Brigham, Sr., indicates that they do not serve in a typical "rubber stamp" role. Mr. Brigham, Sr., Mr. Brigham, Jr., Mr. McKevitt and Mr. Patterson are the "inside" Board members; their backgrounds are described elsewhere in the case.

* Establish groundwork to develop market research
* Enhance and monitor lead management
* Encourage field reporting on quality and product problems
* Continue to enhance products (AMS and traditional products)

Management attributed its success in marketing its products to factors like these and its compensation of field representatives. Based on gross profit, the compensation of the sales force relative to competitors in industrial marking has contributed to profitable sales growth over the years, and longevity of the sales force is high on average.

Production

Production at Diagraph can generally be thought of to resemble a job shop operation except that products are made for stock rather than to order. Products are bench assembled as opposed to the typical "assembly line" operation.

The production facilities at Diagraph (as with the rest of the company) are currently in the throes of change. The biggest change has been the implementation of MAPICS.* Management estimates that MAPICS has cost the firm nearly one-half million dollars.

The Manufacturing Organization in 1985 was broken down into three areas: Materials Control Group; Industrial Engineering Group; and the Engineering Group (at one time the only group). The Materials Control Group was responsible for the company's Inventory Control, Stockrooms and Shipping Department. The Engineering Group was responsible for product design and manufacture.

The Industrial Engineering Group is the latest addition to the Manufacturing organization. This group's functions are many and varied, ranging from time-motion studies to efficiency tests on set-up time, machine run time and labor time. This group also prepares quality reports about actual vs. standard costs. The Industrial Engineering Group also does shop floor reporting, and monitors indirect labor in an effort to keep costs under control. This group has recently taken on the responsibility of tool designing. In the past, the tool and die makers were not just making the tools (their presumed actual function) but were also designing them. The many production processes at Diagraph call for numerous tools. The design of the tools

is a critical component of the manufacturing process and better tool design should result in improved factory productivity.

The vast array of production processes at Diagraph make for a seemingly inefficient production system. For instance, the pouring of ink is just one such example. The company sells a substantial amount of black ink. However, they also sell limited quantities of red, green and blue inks. Since these colors are produced in small quantities they are more costly to the firm. However, Diagraph's philosophy has been to be a "full-line" manufacturer. While it may at first seem that some low margin items are not extremely profitable, usually they are consumed by a customer who might buy a huge volume of black ink. The idea is to provide good customers with products for all their needs, not just those with high margins. In effect, the production process appears driven by Diagraph's efforts to service the needs of its customers.

The wide array of production technologies in use at Diagraph also reflects the historical tendency towards vertical integration. Management has elected to integrate various manufacturing areas in order to gain control over product quality. Examples of this include ink production and stencil fabrication related to the basic stencil product line. Indeed, management views the business in terms of the "razor-razor blade" relationship where the "follow-on" products contribute greatly to volume and profits.

The entire production process in 1985 was headed up by *Roger Hopkins,* then *Vice President of Manufacturing.* Prior to taking the position of Vice President, Hopkins was Director of Engineering for approximately one year. Before that he served 10 years as Manager of Engineering for Diagraph. He joined the company as product manager in the Engineering Department in 1969.

Hopkins is a graduate of Southern Illinois University with a Bachelors degree in Industrial Technology. Prior to joining Diagraph, he was employed by Aurora Pump Company in Aurora, Illinois.

The Labor Force at Diagraph

Diagraph is unique in terms of demands placed on its labor force. The job shop processes of Diagraph's products require much more skill than a normal assembly line operation. The work is not repetitive in nature. In fact at some point employees are required to read blueprints, set up their own machinery, and measure and check parts. When Diagraph hires new employees, consideration must

---

*The actual function of MAPICS will be explained later.

be given not only to the employee's immediate job responsibilities but also to what the company will be demanding of that employee in the future.

Mr. Hopkins described the labor force as fairly stable. Few layoffs occur. On the other hand, even with sales expansion, few new hires have resulted in the manufacturing area.

Currently, employees at Diagraph belong to the International Association of Machinists and Aerospace Workers Union. Approximately 85–90 employees belong to the union.

On November 4, 1982, the first meeting of a newly formed joint Labor/Management Committee was held. The purposes of the committee are "to improve the labor/management relationships, to insure and promote the success of Diagraph in meeting the challenges and demands of the competitive marketplace within a framework of the best possible labor/management relationship, communications, mutual goals and objectives and general harmony." The committee is made up of five representatives of the union, five representatives of management and a recording secretary. The chairmanship of the committee alternates between labor and management. Some issues which have been addressed include a need for greater concern regarding product quality, a need for better communications and the ability to obtain decisions with regard to the work process.

RECENT STRATEGIC CHANGES

Diagraph Corporation has recently undergone a series of changes with respect to overall corporate strategy and structure. Once a basically market driven operation, Diagraph has progressed from a policy of stable growth to one of intensely competitive and aggressive growth.

According to Jim Brigham, Sr., up until about 1981, Diagraph had a nice comfortable business. The company wasn't doing much in the way of innovations. Then, top management decided it was time for some major strategic changes. The company had two choices: either milk the company and its existing product lines or adopt a goal of aggressive growth. They chose the latter. Brigham describes this choice as being a result of basic entrepreneurial instincts. As mentioned earlier, Diagraph is a family-owned operation, with James Brigham as Chairman of the Board and James Junior as President. Some background follows.

James R. Brigham, Chairman of the Board, was born in St. Louis, Missouri. He attended Duke University in Durham, North Carolina, for three years until WWII interrupted his studies. He later returned to his native St. Louis completing his bachelor's degree at Washington University.

He worked for IBM in St. Louis for several years but was lured to Southern Illinois to help salvage the family-owned business. Mr. Brigham, Sr., has been with the company since 1948. He became President in 1965 and held that position until 1983 when his son, James Brigham, Jr., became President. Mr. Brigham, Sr., is currently Chairman of the Board.

Throughout Mr. Brigham's career, he has found time to give his talents to Southern Illinois by serving on the Southern Illinois Inc. (SII)[1], Board of Directors and as Chairman of the Chief Executives Council and Co-Chairman of the Union/Management Council. He has served as a director of the Illinois Manufacturer's Association and the Herrin Chamber of Commerce, and as a former member of the U.S. Department of Commerce Export Expansion Council.

Mr. Brigham served as Chairman of the Southern Illinois University (SIU) Foundation from 1974 through 1985 and also serves on the Board of Directors of the Commerce Bank of St. Louis.

James Brigham, Jr., joined the staff of Diagraph Corporation in July of 1981 as Vice President, Corporate Development. Brigham Junior was elected President of the Corporation in November of 1983.

Brigham Junior served as Budget Director for New York City from February, 1978 to August, 1981, during the administration of Mayor Edward O. Koch. Brigham has been credited with saving the city of New York from financial disaster. Koch was quoted as saying of Brigham just prior to his leaving the Budget Directorship:

> "He is leaving behind two consecutive balanced budgets, a revitalized capital spending program, and an investment grade rating for our long-term bonds. This is the most prestigious position in municipal finance in the United States."

A graduate of Carbondale Community High School, Brigham received his Bachelors degree in History from Duke University and his Masters Degree in Business from the University of Chicago. Mr. Brigham also serves as an Advisor for long-range planning to Marsh and McClennan Companies, Inc., an insurance brokerage company with headquarters in New York, where he resided until 1985. The new Diagraph President divides his time among New

---

[1] SII is a regional economic development organization.

York, St. Louis, Southern Illinois, and branch office locations, but moved to St. Louis in February 1985.

Like his father, James Junior is involved in a variety of business, civic, fraternal and cultural activities. He is a Director of the Menasha Paper Corporation, Menasha, Wisconsin, New York Botanical Gardens and New York Shakespeare Festival.

As mentioned previously, Diagraph adopted a new growth goal in 1981–1982. The result of this has been the development of an expansion strategy into two new major product lines, namely The Advanced Electronic Label Printing System and Telemark, a powerful and flexible ink-jet marking system.

The nature of these products was so very different from Diagraph's traditional product line that Diagraph created a new support organization specifically for these products, called Advanced Marking Systems, which is based in St. Louis.

In addition to developing Advanced Marking Systems, Diagraph has increased its international/export operations and has also implemented a new inventory/production system known as MAPICS. These strategic changes in products, markets, and functions are described below.

Advanced Marking Systems (AMS)

Advanced Marking Systems is a newly formed group which basically represents two product lines for Diagraph—an ink-jet printing system (Telemark) and the Electronic Label Printing System. Telemark is a unique system of marking in the factory. Through keyboard entered messages, automatic date and time coding and sequential numbering, a user can mark packages and products on an assembly line. See Exhibit 3 for an illustration of Telemark.

The Electronic Label Printing System is a system which links an IBM personal computer with a printronix printer. The result is a system which prints professional looking labels that help control inventory and speed up shipping and handling. Bold legible labels can be created in a variety of shapes, sizes and styles with the added versatility of printed bar codes and customer graphics at the touch of a button. Powerful label management software gives the flexibility to recall, modify and track an unlimited number of label formats. See Exhibit 4 for an example of the Electronic Label Printing System.

Both Telemark and the new Electronic Label Printing System represent a significant investment by the company in providing new growth areas to keep Diagraph a leader in industrial marking. They also created the need for increased support for the field sales force.

In response to these needs, Diagraph created the AMS organization, headquartered in Earth City, with the Diagraph Technical Center near St. Louis. AMS's function is to provide the marketing coordination and sales support needed by the field sales force in order to sell this new family of high tech products while maintaining sales volume in the more mature traditional product lines. Regional AMS Representatives have been selected to work with branch offices and distributors in these supportive and coordination functions.

As part of the development of the Electronic Label Printing System, Diagraph recently acquired G&G Systems. This company is responsible for development of the software which enables the label printing device to link up with the IBM PC. This is only one example of the aggressive stand Diagraph has taken to meet its competitors head on.

Export

The export trade has become an increasingly important part of the Diagraph business. Ms. Sarah Fetter, J. R. Brigham's daughter, is responsible for the export business at Diagraph. She cites control as a very key element to succeeding in the export arena.

Sarah Brigham Fetter, President of Diagraph International, began her career at Diagraph as export administrator in 1977. Her major accomplishment has been to strengthen distributor relationships and provide a strong foundation for international expansion.

Besides her responsibilities in the International Department, Sarah was the Chairperson of Diagraph's Labor/Management Committee. She was promoted in 1986 to Vice President to head a new department of Human Resources in charge of job classification and employee benefits, labor-management relations, evaluation and incentive compensation, and employee education, training, communication, and recruiting. Sarah served for several years as an Executive Vice President of Southern Illinois Inc. and chaired a committee at Southern Illinois University to explore Government/Industry/Labor/Education partnerships to promote international trade. She has appeared on regional television and has addressed various business and government bodies to stimulate interest in international business. In 1982 she was selected as an "Outstanding Young Woman of America."

Before Sarah joined the firm in 1978, the export business was handled through an export management firm in

EXHIBIT 3 **The Telemark System.**

Printhead and
Photocell

Printhead
Controller

Portable
Terminal

System
Console

Ink/Power
Supply

The Telemark Difference

Advanced Technology

Non-contact ink-jet marking is part of the technological revolution reshaping the factory environment. It brings the benefits of keyboard-entered messages, automatic date and time coding and sequential numbering to a broad range of package and product marking applications. But all ink-jet systems are not created equal.

Only Telemark incorporates a fully interactive "building-block" approach in its microprocessor design.

This advanced electronic architecture (a distributed microprocessor network governed by a true multi-tasking operating program) gives Telemark its flexibility and remarkably improved performance. It's why Telemark is the fastest, friendliest, most productive ink-jet system you can buy.

Telemark's technical superiority even extends to its ink ejectors. The unique one-piece Diajector® design achieves precision ink-drop formation while it virtually eliminates clogging.

It means Telemark can handle the widest range of marking inks specially formulated for both porous and non-porous surfaces.

Advanced product engineering should make life easier for the user. Telemark measures up to this rule. A simple question-and-answer program guides you as you write and edit messages, call up system status reports and select character size and spacing. Installation and maintenance procedures have been reduced to the minimum. Telemark's tough enclosures are sealed and secured against environmental hazards.

EXHIBIT 4   The Electronic Label Sorting System.

The Diagraph system links the easy-to-use and powerful IBM Personal Computer with the compact Printronix printer with its patented printing mechanism.

DIAGRAPH introduces the Perfect Package for Electronic Label Printing

Now there is an electronic label printing system that combines the speed and efficiency of advanced technology with Diagraph's 90 years of experience in the field. With Diagraph's electronic label printing system you print professional looking labels that help control your inventory and speed up shipping and handling. *PLUS* —— enhance your company image. We make the Diagraph system different to give you the competitive advantage.

- Increase productivity
- Improve shipping and handling
- Reduce label inventory
- Enhance company image
- Reduce operating costs.

IBM is a registered trademark of International Business Machines Corporation.

St. Louis. There were only three full-time employees in the export department until recently. Today the division is known as International Operations and consists of eight employees. The export business has doubled since Ms. Fetter joined the firm and Diagraph began controlling its own exports.

Besides distributing its products in all 50 states, Diagraph also has distribution centers throughout Canada and in at least 25 foreign countries including markets in Australia, Japan, Europe, Southeast Asia, Africa, South America, and the Scandanavian countries.

Australia has the potential to be a real growth market with expectations that market share will double in the near future. China is a second major area with growth potential since Premier Deng Xio Ping has moved to open the country to more business.

The South American market also holds growth potential for Diagraph. However, language is a problem. In the Japanese and European markets, most customers speak English. But doing business in South America, Southeast Asia and China is much more difficult since English is not as prevalent in those countries. Of course, the products are available to make package markings in the various languages. But communicating with distributors and customers is more difficult.

Recent staff additions may help resolve some of these problems. For example, *Mr. Juan Bergoudian* became *Vice President of International Operations* in 1983 and is working closely with Ms. Fetter at the new offices in St. Louis. A graduate of Milton College and Marshall University, Juan is fluent in five languages, an ability which further enhances his role in international operations.

Mr. Bergoudian has more than 16 years of experience in international sales and marketing. Before joining Diagraph, he was the Director of International Marketing for Alvey, Inc., a leading manufacturer of conveyors, palletizers, and distribution systems all directly related to the packaging industry. He is comfortable working with a distributor organization, having established a worldwide network of over 70 exclusive distributors for a manufacturer of industrial products.

Juan, in response to an invitation of the U. S. Department of Commerce, is currently a member of the Missouri Export Council. He has actively participated in numerous trade shows throughout the world and has worked directly with distributors, their salesmen and their customers.

In addition to staffing additions, the export business is being developed with the help of foreign representatives. For example, the Union Packaging Company is the firm which represents Diagraph in all of Japan and Southeast Asia with offices in the Japanese cities of Osaka, Tokyo and Nagoya. This firm is also actively pursuing the Chinese market. Mr. T. Hori, President of Union Packaging's Tokyo office, participated in the Food Packaging Expo in Guangzhow. Union Packaging feels that the Chinese market has great potential for industrial marking equipment.

In addition to distribution, part of Diagraph's commitment to international operations was the opening of their own overseas office, namely Diagraph GmbH. Located in Hamburg, West Germany, Diagraph GmbH was established to provide a European technical service center for Telemark, as well as central warehousing for distribution of Diagraph's traditional products throughout Europe.

Wolfgang Dede of Hamburg and Sarah Brigham Fetter are the general managers of Diagraph GmbH. Peter Wade, an electronics specialist and native of Bavaria, is the Telemark technician.

However, the "bread and butter" lines for exports appear to be the more traditional product lines of stencil cutting machines, inks, Rol-It-On, etc. While these products have in some cases saturated the domestic markets or reached the end of their growth life cycle, many opportunities continue to exist for these products in the foreign markets. While export sales may only account for about 7% of total Diagraph business, management expects exports to eventually reach 20% of total sales of the corporation.

MAPICS

Diagraph Corporation is currently in the process of implementing a formal manufacturing system. The one which top management has selected is known as "Manufacturing Accounting & Production Information Control Systems" (MAPICS). The generic name for such a system is Manufacturing Resource Planning, or MRP. MRP is a system to effectively plan the resources of a manufacturing company. The system gathers and dispenses information to all departments of the organization so that these departments will be working with the same figures.

At Diagraph Company in particular, capacity and materials are two problem areas which prevent the firm from achieving its established goals. MAPICS includes the information required to forecast the material and capacity needed. This information will come from all departments. For example, the marketing department will be required to provide as accurate a forecast as possible. Manufacturing will be required to supply the lead times needed for purchased and manufactured parts. Engineering will be required to input the correct Bill of Materials and the routing (or steps) in the manufacturing process. The overall plan establishes the priorities for the capacity and materials needed and then controls those priorities once set.

A well-managed master schedule driving the Material Planning System may help to overcome many of the shortages Diagraph has experienced in the past. Good shop floor control and a capacity requirements system will give management the visibility into future problems long before they occur. A dispatch list and input/output reports will provide updated priorities to manufacturing and the ability to pinpoint problem areas. As priorities change due to customer orders or schedule changes, the system will reschedule work in process due dates to reflect the new schedule.

Management also hopes to greatly reduce back orders and missed shipping dates, which periodically had been a problem at Diagraph. Salespeople will have the information to go to their customers, in advance of the promised delivery date, tell them what has happened and give them a revised shipping date at that time. Management has achieved customer fulfillment levels of 95% and the back order problems have become the exception. Management is also hoping to obtain the following goals with its new system:

95% + Inventory Accuracy

98% + Bill of Material Accuracy
98% + Routing Accuracy

Management at Diagraph is devoting a great deal of time and energy and money to the undertaking of MAPICS. It is hoped that this system can help to make Diagraph a dominant force in the industry.

Executive Perception of Strategic Change

While Diagraph is enjoying substantial growth from these new strategic changes, this growth has perhaps come at the expense of stability in many of its operations.

According to Roger Hopkins, substantial changes in

EXHIBIT 5   Diagraph Corporation table of organization.

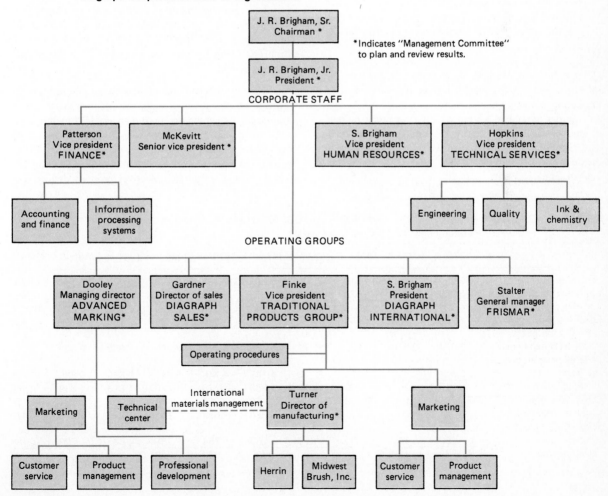

many areas have occurred simultaneously at Diagraph. The introduction of a MAPICS system alone would account for enough change to occupy management for one or two years. In fact when the system was beginning its implementation phase, advisers to Diagraph suggested making no other strategic changes while developing MAPICS. The implementation of MAPICS is a very major undertaking, particularly for a firm like Diagraph with so many production processes. Even James Brigham, Jr., describes the situation as being a "bit too ambitious" and terribly difficult on a lot of people with the move to new high-tech products, the export thrust, a new president, new production planning and controls and a new sales/support organization.

Other members of management see the changes at Diagraph as simply a necessary move for survival of the firm. Although it may seem as though management has taken on quite a bit already, it doesn't seem to have quelled their zest for future growth. According to James Brigham, Sr., Diagraph hopes to expand again in another five years. They would like to do this internally with no reliance on going public with a stock issue. James Junior has also said that going public would only be a last resort since the family wishes to maintain close control.

In order to prepare for growth, a major organizational change was instituted in early 1986. According to President Brigham, Jr., this change would provide a "foundation for growth into the 1990's." Exhibit 5 portrays the new structure.

Five corporate profit centers were established, three with responsibility for manufacturing, and marketing to the sales and distribution organization.

• Traditional Products Group includes all Herrin manufacturing operations and the marketing of all the traditional products.

• Advanced Marking Systems Group includes the marketing of the Telemark ink-jet and electronic labeling systems and associated materials. Manufacturing operations are housed at the Technical Center in St. Louis.

• Frismar, Inc., operates as a subsidiary responsible for the manufacture and marketing of stencil tissues and mimeograph stencils.

• Sales/Service Group includes all branch offices, sales offices, and regional warehouses with responsibility for direct customer sales and service of all products.

• Diagraph International continues to be responsible for marketing all products and managing distributor relationships outside the U.S., including management of GmbH in Germany and a new venture to be established in Hong Kong.

President Brigham noted that the organization was founded on objectives of being customer oriented, profit motivated, integrated and entrepreneurial. A memo to all staff noted that "the proper role of management is to coordinate and lead rather than to direct and control. We believe our managers are capable of managing themselves within a set of corporate objectives properly defined and

EXHIBIT 6   DIAGRAPH CORPORATION CONSOLIDATED AUDITED STATEMENT OF INCOME AND EXPENSE
(For 10 Years Ended May 31, 1983, in Thousands)

	1974	1975	1976	1977	1978	1979	1980	1981	1982	1983
Net sales	$9,990	$10,559	$11,719	$13,483	$15,399	$17,196	$18,705	$20,332	$23,173	$23,002
Less cost of goods sold	5,666	6,055	6,374	7,245	8,358	8,883	9,514	10,545	12,288	12,357
Gross profit	4,324	4,504	5,345	6,238	7,041	8,313	9,191	9,787	10,885	10,645
Less direct selling exp.	1,250	1,288	1,460	1,466	1,608	1,849	2,101	2,154	2,390	2,381
Profit after direct selling expense	3,074	3,216	3,885	4,772	5,433	6,464	7,090	7,633	8,495	8,264
Less other operating exp.	2,557	2,847	3,125	3,713	4,147	4,746	5,291	5,820	6,836	7,796
Net operating profit	517	369	760	1,059	1,286	1,718	1,799	1,813	1,659	468
Other expenses	96	106	89	48	66	65	44	38	81	39
Income before taxes	421	263	671	1,011	1,220	1,653	1,755	1,775	1,578	429
Provision for fed. inc. taxes	190	145	300	476	563	758	785	845	729	84
Net income	$ 231	$ 118	$ 371	$ 535	$ 657	$ 895	$ 970	$ 930	$ 849	$ 345

EXHIBIT 7 DIAGRAPH CORPORATION COMPARATIVE CONDENSED STATEMENT OF FINANCIAL CONDITION
(For 10 Years Ended May 31, 1983, 000's Omitted)

Balance sheet	1974	1975	1976	1977	1978	1979	1980	1981	1982	1983
Current assets	$3,444	$3,571	$4,026	$4,375	$5,276	$5,719	$6,086	$7,027	$7,867	$7,829
Current liabilities	1,267	1,220	1,469	1,519	1,729	1,735	1,844	2,393	2,440	2,536
Working capital	2,177	2,351	2,557	2,856	3,547	3,984	4,242	4,634	5,427	5,293
Property & equipment	349	342	331	355	651	1,099	1,577	2,035	2,455	3,041
Other assets	278	296	302	289	283	273	273	333	280	311
Deferred taxes	(14)	(16)	(16)	(24)	(60)	(93)	(129)	(194)	(316)	(378)
Net assets	$2,790	$2,973	$3,174	$3,476	$4,421	$5,263	$5,963	$6,808	$7,846	$8,267
Financed by:										
Long-term debt	$ 796	$ 880	$ 760	$ 596	$ 967	$ 962	$ 763	$ 841	$1,162	$1,348
Stockholders' equity	1,994	2,093	2,414	2,880	3,454	4,301	5,200	5,967	6,684	6,919
Total long-term debt & capital	$2,790	$2,973	$3,174	$3,476	$4,421	$5,263	$5,963	$6,808	$7,846	$8,267

EXHIBIT 8   SALES IN UNITS AND DOLLARS BY MAJOR PRODUCT LINES[1]

	Unit sales					Projected	Dollar sales			Projected
Product lines	78–79	79–80	80–81	81–82	82–83	83–84	81–82	82–83	83–84
Stencil machines	2,050	1,999	1,614	1,909	1,528	1,325	$1,447,327	$1,231,157	$1,262,775
Label printers & paper	316	317	347	339	555	419	2,618,484	3,036,225	3,902,983
Coders	2,699	2,767	3,407	4,248	4,581	4,850	2,010,684	2,188,714	2,344,571
Rol-It-On/Rol-It-On ink/									
Rol Flo	166,317	171,505	152,177	162,280	138,065	165,597	2,314,305	1,944,405	2,348,156
Brushes & markers	1,200,727	1,092,260	1,001,286	963,297	985,584	1,068,675	716,109	703,783	798,034
Duplicators	19,402	20,709	18,296	16,777	13,093	15,068	507,488	374,402	384,094
Stencils	38,188,600	39,962,700	35,827,400	38,472,400	33,817,700	36,822,202	1,285,623	390,571	465,717
Telemark[2]							138,524	126,689	126,359

[1]Schedule is not all-inclusive—Does not include all product categories in units or sales.
[2]Sales in units not available.

communicated.'' Brigham Junior believes that the organization will reduce layers of management and allow for rapid decision-making and problem-solving.

Finance and Accounting

Mr. Roger Patterson, Financial Vice President and Corporate Treasurer, has been employed at Diagraph for approximately 7 years. He manages all accounting and financial functions as well as the Information Processing Department. Several of his senior staff will serve as controllers of the operating groups for purposes of budgeting, financial reporting, and planning.

Mr. Patterson is a native of Southern Illinois. Prior to coming to Diagraph he spent approximately 6 years in public accounting. Patterson received a Bachelors degree in accounting from Eastern Illinois University and shortly after his graduation joined the Chicago office of Arthur Anderson. Mr. Patterson spent 3 years in Chicago achieving the status of Certified Public Accountant and also reached a supervisory level position on the audit staff. After his 3 years at Arthur Anderson, Mr. Patterson joined a local accounting firm in Centralia, Illinois. It is here that Mr. Patterson became acquainted with Diagraph when his CPA firm served as auditors for Diagraph. Mr. Patterson spent about 3 years with the local firm before joining the staff of Diagraph as Treasurer.

According to Mr. Patterson, Diagraph has positioned itself for the 1980's and beyond by investing significant amounts of resources in the development of four projects as follows: Telemark, Electronic Label Printing System,

Advanced Marking Systems Group to support high-tech products and IBM's MAPICS. Specifically, for the year ended May 31, 1984, Diagraph invested $1.6 million in operating expenses toward the implementation of these four major projects. In addition $2.2 million of roughly $10 million in assets relating to these four development projects are reflected on the year end balance sheet.

One other significant effort which Diagraph has maintained for some time is the aggressive pursuit of the latest ''state of the art'' technology for financial recordkeeping. One of the early adoptees of computers, the firm uses this technology to deliver accurate information on time when management needs it.

The following financial statements reflect the financial position and related activities of Diagraph Corporation for the 10 years ended May 31, 1983. Also included is an exhibit of sales by major product lines.

As evidenced by the comparative condensed statement of financial position, the company's financial condition continued to strengthen, with almost all working capital needs and equipment additions being financed with reinvested profits. In 1984, with additional significant outlays being required both in operating expenses and capital expenditures as noted above for the development projects, profits were down, necessitating increased borrowing for working capital needs and equipment additions.

Mr. Patterson expects that beginning in 1985 and beyond, profits will return to their historical levels. Diagraph's position in the marketplace will expand, affording gradual reductions in long-term debt through reinvested profits.

DONALDSON COMPANY, INC.

Shannon Shipp
University of Minnesota

Donaldson Company Inc. (DCI), Bloomington, Minn., learned in 1983 that the rules of the industry in which it had been a dominant force worldwide for over sixty years were changing. DCI weathered the Depression, World War II, numerous recessions, and major changes in technology and manufacturing processes while maintaining a steady stream of profits. In 1983, however, it experienced its first loss in 50 years. Sales decreased from $262 million in 1982 to $203.6 million in 1983. Earnings declined from $7.2 million, or $1.40/share in 1982 to a loss of $3.5 million, or −$.68/share in 1983. Chairman of the Board Frank Donaldson II began his annual letter to DCI stockholders in 1983 by saying, "A year ago we said that business was lousy. Well, it got worse. We learned first-hand about a profit *and loss* economy". Although 1984 yielded some improvements over 1983, DCI began a critical look at its worldwide operations, with the goal of returning the company to its previous performance levels.

This case was prepared by Shannon Shipp as a basis for class discussion rather than to illustrate either appropriate or inappropriate handling of an administrative situation. The U.S. Department of Education funded the preparation of this case under Grant #G00877027.

THE COMPANY

History

In 1915, Frank Donaldson, Sr., the original chairman of the company, invented the first effective air cleaner for internal combustion engines. Air is a necessary ingredient for the combustion process to occur. Prior to this invention, engines were extremely susceptible to "dusting out," or becoming inoperative due to excessive accumulation of dust entering the engine from unfiltered air.

In subsequent years, DCI led the industry in introducing new products, such as oil-washed filters, mufflers, multi-stage air cleaners, and high-tech hydraulic filters. DCI became the world's largest manufacturer of heavy-duty air cleaners and mufflers, and established a worldwide reputation for high-quality, reliable products which were at the leading edge of filtration technology. Facilities grew from 200 square feet of manufacturing space in 1915 in St. Paul, Minn., to more than 3 million square feet of manufacturing and office area worldwide in 1980.

Mission

By 1984, the company had broadly defined its mission as to design, manufacture, and sell proprietary products which "separate something unwanted from something wanted.'' The company's product line included air cleaners, air filters, mufflers, hydraulic filters, microfiltration equipment for computers, air pollution equipment, and liquid clarifiers. These products were developed, sold, and serviced by the organizational structure appearing in Exhibit 1. According to this exhibit, DCI has a functional organization structure, with the nine worldwide support groups responsible for product development, manufacturing, and administration and finance, while the four business groups are responsible for selling and servicing products to their respective markets. The 1980 to 1984 sales of the four major business groups are listed in Exhibit 2. The fifth group listed, Microfiltration and Defense Products (MFD) was a part of the Business Development Group until 1984, when it was spun off to form a new business group.

The 1983–84 Situation

In 1983, a peculiar set of circumstances combined to downgrade DCI's performance. Sales of medium/heavy duty trucks, buses, tractors and combines, construction equipment, and aftermarket replacement elements simultaneously hit five-year or all-time lows. These markets constituted the majority of sales for both the Original Equipment Group (OEG) and International. Although soft demand had been experienced in one or two of these markets before in one year, never had all businesses declined so precipitously in the same year.

Both external and internal causes were proposed to explain the decline of each market. External causes included slow construction and agricultural equipment sales. Construction equipment purchases slowed as major

EXHIBIT 1   **DCI organization chart (1983).**
(Internal company documents.)

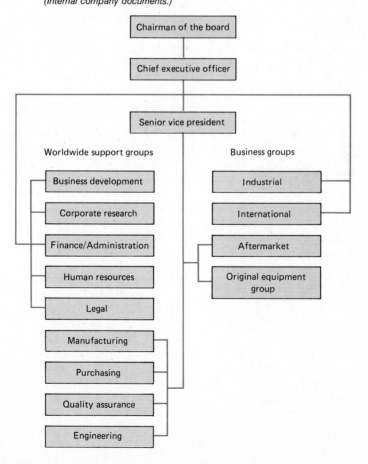

EXHIBIT 2   DCI'S FOUR MAJOR BUSINESS GROUPS 1980–84 ANNUAL SALES (IN MILLIONS)

	1984	1983	1982	1981	1980
Original equipment group	$102.2	63.9	101.3	104.6	101.6
Aftermarket	22.6	17.6	20.5	20.1	17.0
Industrial	32.2	32.0	41.3	37.0	35.0
International	71.2	68.7	81.4	87.0	69.4
MFD	26.0	21.4	17.4	15.1	11.4
Total	$254.2	203.6	261.9	263.8	234.4

Source: DCI 1984 Annual Report

projects accounting for the majority of new equipment purchases, such as the interstate highway system, neared completion. Also, developing nations (especially oil-producing), a major market for construction projects in the 1970s and early 1980s, were curtailing construction, based on declining oil revenues. Caterpillar, DCI's largest customer, experienced a devastating seven-month strike by workers at its U.S. production facilities, that produced the bulk of Caterpillar's heavy-duty mobile equipment. Agricultural equipment sales were slowing because of generally depressed conditions in the agricultural industry, particularly in the United States. Purchases of new equipment by U.S. farmers, squeezed by high fixed costs and low market prices, were at a five-year low. Finally, the strength of the dollar in 1982–84 was making DCI's customers less competitive in foreign markets. This, in turn, affected DCI's sales of replacement parts.

Some of the internal problems included an inability to coordinate customer service to multinational customers, inability to provide accurate cost figures for given production quantities, and especially for its small customers, "being difficult to buy from." Each of these problems will be explained in greater detail below.

DCI found it difficult to coordinate customer service efforts for those customers with multiple purchasing or production facilities in different countries. Although DCI had offices in all of the countries, such as West Germany, Brazil and Mexico, where high sales potential existed, lack of coordination among the offices caused spotty customer service. For example, customers were known to "shop" for the best prices among DCI offices, since each office was free to set prices according to local conditions. Unfortunately, with its customers willing to look worldwide for the lowest DCI price, different offices were competing against each other for the same business, to the detriment of DCI performance overall.

DCI was also unable to provide accurate cost figures for production of small amounts of product. This hampered salespeople's efforts to quote prices which would cover DCI's costs and yield profits. For example, set-up costs in switching from producing one product to another were not factored into the cost of production runs. As a result, DCI salespeople were willing to promise delivery of low quantities of products (sometimes as low as one or two units) based on the actual production cost, without taking into account the changeover costs borne by manufacturing small quantities. Order costs, estimated at $35 per order processed, were also not taken into account when salespeople quoted prices for small lots. Lastly, account executives were measured primarily on sales rather than profits, thereby encouraging them to devote less attention to the costs of actually filling an order.

Finally, DCI had a reputation for being "difficult to buy from." Although relationships with its largest customers were strong based on its ability to work with those customers in solving problems, smaller customers complained to salespeople of slow response for engineering drawings and price quotes. They also complained of slow responses to questions about billing or order status. Very small customers (under $25,000 in annual sales) were not vocal with complaints about DCI because they were seldom contacted by DCI representatives.

Although these internal problems existed to an extent in all divisions, it was crucial to DCI's success for OEG to address them promptly. Exhibit 2 shows that OEG is the largest of the four major business groups. OEG also suffered the largest absolute and percentage loss from 1982 to 1983. For DCI to regain its former performance levels, OEG must perform more strongly.

In 1984, DCI's operating results began to return to pre-1983 levels (see Exhibit 3). One reason was a success in the wet filtration area, particularly with high-tech lube

EXHIBIT 3   DCI OPERATING RESULTS (IN 000'S)

	1984	1983	1982
Net sales	$254,052	203,608	262,018
Cost of sales	157,257	131,548	169,816
Gross earnings	96,795	72,060	92,202
Earnings (loss) before income taxes	20,238	(1,738)	12,805
Income taxes	10,546	1,800	5,572
Tax rate	52.1%	—	43.5%
Net earnings	9,692	(3,358)	7,233
Depreciation	7,694	8,320	8,518
Interest	2,670	2,076	2,345
Financial position			
Current assets	97,425	81,668	82,109
Current liabilities	45,022	32,796	35,574
Current ratio	2.2	2.5	2.3
Working capital	52,403	48,872	46,535
Long-term debt	19,549	21,791	18,752
Shareholder's equity	90,232	84,880	91,637
Capitalization ratio	22.1	22.1	21.2
Return on average shareholder's equity	11.1	(4.0)	7.9
Return on average invested capital	9.0	(3.3)	6.4
Property, plant and equipment (gross)	118,663	118,182	14,465
Property, plant and equipment (net)	55,045	59,694	63,739
Total assets	160,613	148,083	151,160

Source: DCI 1984 Annual Report

filters which were designed to protect mechanical components in high-stress environments. The primary reason, however, was that DCI's worldwide markets, particularly heavy-duty truck, began to return to pre-1983 levels. Because of the external causes listed previously, however, DCI management thought it unlikely that its market opportunities would return to pre-1980 levels. To minimize the effects of the decline in worldwide demand for DCI's products, attention was placed on internal problems that also affected 1983 results. For DCI to return to its steady pattern of consistent growth, those internal problems must be rectified.

ORIGINAL EQUIPMENT GROUP (OEG)

Products and Markets

OEG constitutes the bulk of DCI's traditional businesses, such as heavy-duty trucks, and construction, mining, industrial and agricultural equipment. It sells air and hydraulic filters, acoustical products (mufflers) and re-

placement elements to manufacturers and end-users of heavy-duty mobile equipment. OEG has not typically sold oil filters, as they are a commodity item and require much higher production runs than OEG traditionally makes. OEG is reviewing its position on producing oil filters as its customers seek a single source for all their filter needs. North America constitutes about one-half of the annual worldwide sales of these products.

Current Organizational Structure for OEG

OEG is currently organized around the markets it serves. The construction, agriculture, industrial, and truck-bus markets have their own market director and support staff. Each market is headed by a market director, responsible for all planning and administration, as well as maintaining good relations with the largest customers in the market. Each market group has outside salespeople who call directly on customers, as well as inside salespeople responsible for routine orders and customer service. A manager of marketing support includes order entry personnel and clerks and two special projects. The first special project manager coordinated the efforts of the worldwide action teams responsible for gathering information on competitors and customers. The second special project manager developed a marketing program aimed at gaining understanding of small OEs. A chart showing the executive level positions under the market-based organizational structure appears in Exhibit 4.

Within each market, customers were served by size. Large accounts (more than $250,000 in annual sales) were served by market directors or salespeople assigned to that account. Mid-sized customers (between $25,000 and $250,000 in annual sales) were called upon by a salesperson responsible for that territory. Small OEs were served, if at all, by inside salespeople or order-entry personnel in the marketing support services group.

Organization by market area offered a number of advantages to OEG. For example, with a market-based organization, it was easy to track marketwide changes in demand or customer usage characteristics. This helped OEG in product development and allocation of application engineering resources. Furthermore, a market-based organization in OEG mirrored similar organizations in Engineering, which facilitated communication across functional divisions, since marketers and engineers worked on products and programs for the same markets.

Organization by market area also had some problems. Some customers straddled markets, making it difficult to assign the costs and profits from serving that customer to a specific market. One large customer, for example, manufactured both agricultural and construction equipment. Instead of having one salesperson from each market area call on the account, one salesperson from the agricultural division maintains customer contact to reduce overlap in customer service. In charging the market areas for the sales, however, agriculture is fully responsible for the salesperson's salary and expenses, while the construction market area enjoys the benefits of the sales to that customer without incurring any selling expenses. Another problem was the occasional inability to coordinate the engineering support for those customers who straddled market areas. Engineers were assigned by market, not customer. If a customer had a problem with applications in two markets, the tasks were assigned to two engineers, even if the actual parts were very similar.

OEG's Position Within DCI

OEG had primary worldwide responsibility to serve manufacturers of mobile heavy equipment. Other divisions within DCI served or competed with those customers. For example, the Aftermarket group sold heavy equipment replacement elements under the Donaldson name through fleet specialists, heavy-duty distributors and other sources. These elements competed with the products sold through manufacturers' dealers supplied by OEG. Engineering, a staff group, was also an important part of OEG's selling function. Engineering helped customers design filters and other products for specific applications. Since OEG's reputation depended on Engineering's

EXHIBIT 4   **OEG's market-based organizational structure.**
(Internal company documents.)

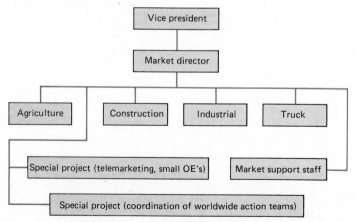

service to its customers, this group was important in maintaining close customer relations. The International division sold OEG's products in markets outside the U.S. Communication between OEG and International was particularly crucial in providing high levels of customer service for multinational customers, as the responsibilities for these customers were split geographically.

OEG's Proposed Strategies for Regaining Former Performance Levels

In 1983, Tom Baden was appointed the new vice-president of OEG. Baden had 35 years experience with the company. He began at DCI as a draftsman while still in college, and over the years held posts in Engineering and Fluid Power (a division later absorbed by the OEG business group) before assuming leadership of OEG. Baden's task was simply stated; he was to return OEG to financial performance levels of the 1975–79 era and establish a base for long-term consistent growth in the markets served by OEG. Baden was also responsible for maintaining and reinforcing DCI's corporate image as a high-quality, high-service provider of state-of-the-art products.

To reach those goals, Baden instituted a year-long strategic development process that involved Finance, Human Resources, Engineering, Manufacturing, International and all units within OEG. Several studies that evaluated markets and identified customer needs provided input for developing strategy. These studies were undertaken with a worldwide focus. Reports were prepared by worldwide action teams, composed of members from DCI offices around the world. These reports and activities were coordinated by a market director at OEG headquarters.

Some of the studies performed included: 1) research on telemarketing and global account management as alternatives to personal selling in reaching customers; 2) in-depth analyses of customers and competitors; and 3) definition of pricing, promotion and distribution policies. These studies and analyses of current OEG operations were the basis for meetings designed to solicit suggestions for changes that would allow OEG to meet the demands of its customers. These meetings included all OEG executives, as well as various functional specialists who presented information from related studies. The schedule of meetings is presented in Exhibit 5. The stated purpose of the meetings was to develop overall marketing strategies and derive specific supporting strategies in promotion (including advertising, trade promotion and personal selling), organizational design, distribution, pricing and product management. OEG executives used the results of the worldwide action team reports and the analyses of current OEG operations to suggest changes in OEG's marketing policies and organizational structure.

WORLDWIDE ACTION TEAMS REPORTS AND ANALYSES OF CURRENT OPERATIONS

OEG's Customers

OEG had over 600 customers, divided into three groups: large, mid-sized and small.

EXHIBIT 5   MEETING SCHEDULE FOR THE STRATEGIC DEVELOPMENT PROCESS

Activity	Week
Preparation/meetings within market area groups and worldwide action teams	0
Opening meetings/all OEG executives —Presentations of worldwide action team reports —Presentation of market area reports	1
Development of options	2–3
Present/analyze options	4
Refine/Reanalyze options	4–5
Review alternatives/all OEG executives	6
Refine/test against resources/constraints	7–10
Present and review final recommendations—all OEG executives	11
Prepare final recommendations for DCI executives	12

Source: Internal company documents

Large Accounts

OEG's large customers, consisting of 46 accounts and their dealers, constituted more than 90 percent of OEG sales and more than 50 percent of DCI sales. Thirty of these customers were headquartered in the U.S., eight in Europe and eight in Japan. A partial list of these customers appears in Exhibit 6. These customers were all large, and most had sales offices and production facilities in more than one country.

The competitive environment for large original equipment manufacturers (OEs) was undergoing rapid change. Some large OEs, such as Caterpillar, were experiencing increasing competition from non-U.S. manufacturers. Increasing competition from other manufacturers, coupled with the strength of the dollar against other currencies, forced Caterpillar to reduce costs to remain competitive. Caterpillar announced a three-year program beginning in 1983 and terminating in 1985 that required its suppliers to maintain stable prices even though inflation was predicted to increase 22% for that period. In 1984, Ford announced a similar program, that required suppliers to reduce costs by 10 percent per year for the next five years. Other manufacturers were considering similar programs.

The implications for DCI of these announcements were profound. Caterpillar, for example, was DCI's largest single customer, accounting for between 10 and 12 percent of annual revenue. As a result, the squeeze on DCI's margins brought about by Caterpillar's announcement could strongly impact DCI's performance. The emphasis by large customers on cost containment was a major change from the 1960s to the 1970s, which emphasized product performance.

According to meetings among salespeople and account executives, DCI's largest customers had common needs for filtration equipment. At a minimum, large customers desired state-of-the-art products at the lowest possible prices for products meeting specifications. Recent demands by large customers included:

1 just-in-time deliveries;*
2 long-term fixed source contracts;
3 drop-ship arrangements to customers' dealers and/or manufacturing facilities for OE parts;
4 worldwide availability of product;
5 the OE brand name on the product; and
6 electronic system tie-ins for improved order placement/followup and customer service and support.

These recent demands were concomitant with OE's efforts to consolidate their purchases to achieve stronger positions vis-a-vis their suppliers.

ORIGINAL EQUIPMENT DEALERS

Large customers also perceived sales opportunities for replacement element sales through their distributor networks. In North America, the large OEs had 21,000 outlets, or original equipment dealers (OEDs) through which DCI could sell replacement elements. OEDs represented a different market opportunity for DCI. Traditionally, DCI had sold replacement elements to OEs imprinted with the OE's brand. Once the OE took title to the products, DCI expected the OE to provide the necessary training and support to its distributors through which the products would be sold. Within the past three to five years, OEDs

*Just-in-time deliveries occur when the supplier and customer have devised a schedule to ensure the next shipment of parts or supplies is delivered when the customer is about to use the last unit from the previous shipment.

EXHIBIT 6   SOME LARGE CURRENT OR POTENTIAL CUSTOMERS FOR OEG

North America	Europe	Japan
Allis-Chalmers	Daimler-	Hitachi
Caterpillar	Benz	Isuzu
Champion	IVECO	Komatsu
Clark Equipment	Leyland	Kubota
Cummins	Lister	Mitsubishi
Detroit Diesel	Lombardini	Nissan
	MAN	

Source: Internal company documents

were more actively looking for product lines to improve cash flow and profitability. Part of the impetus for the search for additional products was slow equipment sales. Service parts provided a logical line extension and source of steady cash flow for OEDs. To capitalize on the market in service parts, however, OEDs needed extensive support in terms of sales training, product knowledge, product literature and merchandising. They also needed full lines of filters to service all makes of equipment, not just the lines they represented. To increase their share of the service parts business (currently at 20 percent, with the remainder held by independent dealers), OEDs would have to rely on greatly increased OE and filter manufacturer support.

Mid-Sized and Small Customers

Smaller OEs (usually under $250,000 in annual purchases) were offered only standard products from the OEG catalog. Custom engineering was rarely provided to these customers, unless they were willing to bear its full cost.

Smaller OEs had different needs than large OEs. In general, they desired state-of-the-art products, but were willing to wait for a large OE to install a new product first. They also desired consistent contact with DCI salespeople to keep abreast of changing filter fair prices (while realizing that they did not have the volumes to command the lowest available prices) and good product quality. Small OEs often requested the DCI name on the filters used in their equipment as a marketing tool, capitalizing on DCI's reputation for high quality among end-users.

Major Competitors

DCI was the traditional heavy-duty mobile equipment market leader. Major competitors included Fleetguard, Fram, Nelson and Mann and Hummel. Other firms, such as Wix, Baldwin, Purolator and AC/Delco competed in certain market segments. In general, all of the competitors were on sound financial footing. Fleetguard and Fram had very healthy parent organizations (Cummins Engine and Allied/Bendix Corporation, respectively). Mann and Hummel and Nelson were healthy from good internal financial management. Research and development costs were generally lower for these organizations than for DCI because they tend to follow DCI's technological breakthroughs.

Each competitor was strong in a particular market or through a particular channel. AC/Delco and Fram, for example, were very strong in the automotive aftermarket, which required good merchandising skills and emphasizes high volume production. Fleetguard promoted directly to end-users. It recently began a program aimed at educating end-users on the total costs of maintaining equipment. To serve users with a variety of filter replacement patterns, it brought out different lines of filters. For users demanding maximum protection because of extended use in high-stress environments, a high-priced filter with high filtration specifications was introduced. For fleet users, or those on scheduled maintenance, a cheaper filter was introduced to provide protection between replacement periods, without providing unused capacity. Mann and Hummel targeted German and Scandinavian manufacturers, particularly at their corporate headquarters, with extensive technical support and high-quality products. Wix and Baldwin were known, particularly in the truck and construction markets, for providing inexpensive replacement elements. All of these manufacturers, except Nelson, offered a full line of air and oil filters. A full line helps both customers and distributors meet all their filter needs through one source.

MARKETING STRATEGIES

Product and Price

DCI was known throughout the industry for its conservative management style. Its strategic moves occurred slowly, based on careful planning. OEG was no exception. OEG preferred serving selected, high-margin markets where customers were beginning to demand higher performance levels than those available from the products currently available. OEG's strengths were its quality design and engineering capabilities. It preferred pursuing markets where those capabilities demanded a price premium. Price-cutting was not a major component of OEG's market strategies.

Distribution

Distribution of OEG's products occurred through two primary channels. The first was directly to OEs, who purchased products for installation on new equipment. DCI's management philosophy and strengths in technology reinforced its position as an "OE house." In some markets, such as heavy-duty trucks and construction equipment, more than 70 percent of all new units shipped were factory-equipped with DCI products. OEs depended on DCI as a reliable supplier of state-of-the-art products. DCI encouraged its major customers to think of it as their filter and acoustic products design group. DCI's engineers often worked closely with its customers' engineers to design products for special applications or environmental conditions.

The second major channel was for replacement elements. These elements were often packaged and sold under the manufacturer's logo and distributed through its dealer network. OEG provided replacement elements for Caterpillar, International Harvester, J.I. Case, Freightliner, Volvo and several other OEs.

Promotion

OEG products are promoted several ways, including advertising, direct mail, trade shows and promotional literature. A distribution of OEG's promotional expenditures for 1984 appears in Exhibit 7. DCI encourages direct communication between OEG engineers and technicians and their customer counterparts. While this is not reflected in the promotional budget, it is an important element in OEG's communications with its customers.

Other off-budget promotional expenses include sending OEG engineers to attend professional meetings and guiding customers on tours of the research and testing facility. At professional meetings, engineers talk to customers to detect changing trends in customer demand or areas where DCI's technical expertise can be brought to bear. The engineers also act as informal ''good-will ambassadors,'' reminding customers that OEG is monitoring their concerns. OEG also uses its facility as a selling tool, bringing customers' representatives to corporate headquarters in Bloomington, Minn., for a tour of its engineering and research facilities. Some of the most modern, state-of-the-art filtration research facilities in the world, at DCI's headquarters, constitute a potent selling tool.

Selling Methods

OEG has traditionally relied on face-to-face selling to provide information to and solicit orders from customers. Two major problems existed with heavy reliance on personal selling. First, it was not cost efficient for OEG to serve mid-sized and small customers unless a standard product already existed to fit the customer's application. Service to these customers was provided primarily by local distributors or through DCI's Aftermarket Group. As a result, OEG's knowledge of these customers' needs was minimal, leading to possible missed market opportunities. Second, for large customers with multiple purchasing and usage sites, it was difficult to coordinate the activities of salespeople assigned to customers geographically. This problem became acute when the customer had purchasing or usage sites overseas, served through the International division. This meant that salespeoples' activities had to be coordinated across geographic regions as well as across divisions within DCI. Two selling methods, telemarketing

EXHIBIT 7   PROMOTIONAL BUDGET (1984)

Item	Percent of budget
Advertising	55%
PR	2
Sales literature	13
Other sales materials	1
Advertising specialties	1
Trade shows	16
Photography	2
Coop advertising	4
Audiovisual materials	1
Other	5
	100%

Source: Internal company documents

and global account management, are being considered as substitutes or supplements to the current selling method.

Telemarketing

Telemarketing involves organized, planned telephone communication between a firm and its customers. Telemarketing ranges from salespeople simply calling prospective customers to set appointments to complex systems with different employees responsible for different parts of selling, such as prospecting or customer service.

One special projects manager explored the feasibility of telemarketing to small OEs. The study's objective was to profile the small OEs to understand their needs. The subjects were small OE's that had purchased OEG products. These firms were questioned about their use of OEG products, needs for additional OEG support, and overall satisfaction with OEG products and services. Four hundred and sixty-one small OEs were contacted during the month-long study, none with more than $25,000 in purchases from OEG the preceding year. Some study results appear in Exhibit 8.

Global Account Management (GAM)

GAM is a method of assigning salespeople to accounts. Sellers use GAM when customers are large, with multiple purchase or use points. Under a GAM system, an account executive is responsible for all the communications between the customer and the seller, including (but not limited to) needs analysis, application engineering, field support, customer service and order processing. Depending on the account size, the executive might have several subordinates provide necessary services. GAM's major advantage is communication coordination. Since all seller and buyer contact is monitored by the account manager, uncoordinated communication is unlikely.

Implementing GAM would involve assigning teams to OEG's largest customers to improve support. Account teams would be composed of salespeople and applications engineers, with the number of people on the account proportional to its annual orders. Each team head, or account manager, would coordinate communications between all customer buying locations and OEG. Account managers would have worldwide P&L responsibility for their assigned customers. Sales representatives in district offices in other countries would report their customer activities to the lead account executive. Account executives are responsible for the subsidiaries of global customers in their geographic area. Account executives and sales representatives typically have multiple reporting relationships. A sample organizational chart appears in Exhibit 9. The boxes do not all represent people assigned full time to that account. A brief example may clarify Exhibit 9. The account manager in Europe for Daimler-Benz would report to the Sales Manager in Europe. The Daimler-Benz account manager for Europe might also be a subsidiary account executive for Caterpiller in Europe, reporting to an account manager in the U.S.

MAKING THE DECISION

After attending the worldwide action team and OEG operations presentations, OEG executives split into two groups. Each group prepared a presentation explaining its vision for OEG's future corporate structure and marketing

EXHIBIT 8   TELEMARKETING STUDY RESULTS

	Number	Percent of responses
Quotes	8	2%
Follow-up phone calls	17	4
Literature requests	211	46
Not qualified as customers	58	13
Satisfied customers	102	22
Terminations	5	1
Orders	9	2
Unavailable, not listed, duplicates	51	11
	461	100%

Source: Internal company documents

EXHIBIT 9   **Global account management sample organization chart.**
(Internal company documents.)

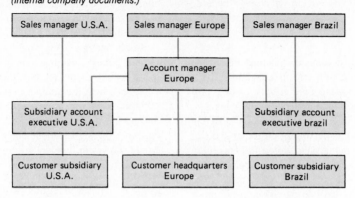

strategy. One group maintained that the current organization structure (see Exhibit 4) would adequately meet the challenges posed by current external and internal problems. The other group proposed a different organizational structure, explained below.

Proposed New OEG Corporate Structure

Based on the results of the strategic development process, the second group made several suggestions to improve OEG's performance. Two suggestions, global account management for large OEs and telemarketing for small customers were key features of the proposed organizational structure.

To incorporate these selling methods into OEG operations, the second group proposed the organizational structure appearing in Exhibit 10 to replace the structure in Exhibit 4. The major difference was the replacement of the market groups (truck, agriculture, industrial and construction) with the large customer and mid-sized and small customer groups. The product/technical group is added to improve communication between engineering and marketing. Although this is a change from the current organizational structure, it is not a basis on which to accept or reject the new structure, since it could be appended to the current structure with little ado.

The suggested organizational structure would offer a number of advantages. Service to multinational customers

EXHIBIT 10   **Proposed structure—EOG.**
(Internal company documents.)

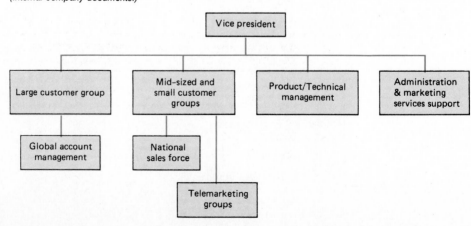

would be coordinated under a single account manager. Current problems with lack of coordination among DCI offices could be minimized. Small OEs would receive more attention. Although little deviation from standard products would be permitted these customers, they would be contacted more frequently under telemarketing. Service to mid-sized accounts would not change.

The proposed plan has several disadvantages as well. With fewer managers at the market director level, the number of workers each must supervise would increase. For the director of large accounts, that would involve 10 to 13 account managers for 30 to 40 accounts (some managers would be responsible for more than one account). Second, the reporting relationships (see Exhibit 9) grow rather complex under a GAM structure. This can obscure good and poor performance, making it more difficult to reward outstanding performance or detect poor performance. It could also make the salesperson's job more ambiguous as orders come from a variety of bosses. Third, new product development would be centered around applications for specific customers. With all salespeople focusing on specific customers, no one would be charged with maintaining a perspective on the market as a whole. Without a broad perspective on changing market conditions, it would be possible to miss a trend in customer usage characteristics, DCI missing a chance to be technology leader in a new market. Narrow focus on a single customer's needs might also cause the salesperson or applications engineer to miss similar work performed for another account, duplicating effort.

SUMMARY

Baden must choose one of the two organizational structures to present to corporate management. He can, of course, modify the structures as he deems necessary, but three issues preclude much tinkering with the two structures as presented. First, the strategic development process ensured that all OEG executives, including Baden, had the same information on which to suggest changes in OEG organizational structure. As a result, Baden was not likely to develop a change because he had information unavailable to other executives which made their suggestion untenable. Second, the executives suggesting changes were responsible for implementing the plan. Modifying their approaches too much might lose their commitment to implementing whichever organizational structure was selected. Finally, there was a corporate urgency that something must be done to improve OEG's performance. This required that a decision be made soon on the appropriate organizational structure so that OEG personnel could work on bringing OEG's performance back to previous levels.

Baden is aware that any organizational change inevitably causes staff upheaval, and wants to ensure that the OEG structure chosen will remain in place for a long time. In deciding, he also must remember that the current organizational structure has been successful for many years, and that any changes must be supported by sound reasoning. To help decide, he prepared the following questions to organize his presentation on the appropriate organizational structure to top DCI management.

1 How will customers react to both plans?

2 Which plan comes closest to solving the problems OEG faced in 1983?

3 Other than the alternatives presented, what organizational structures exist to accomplish the same goals?

4 Analyze the major strengths and weaknesses of each alternative. What conclusions can be drawn from the analysis?

5 Assuming the new organizational structure is selected, how should it be implemented?

DYKINS LIMITED

**Bill Blake and
Henry W. Lane**
Western Management

In the spring of 1982, Bert Dykins was spending a large part of his time considering the future growth of Dykins Industries. In the five short years since its inception, Dykins had moved from its Montreal base to participation in a number of joint ventures in the developing world as well as a recently completed venture in England. Bert knew that his company was short on top management and that it was becoming increasingly difficult for him and his partner to attend to the needs of the Montreal plant and the overseas opportunities. The joint ventures would soon be reaching the stage where even more management time would be required. He remained convinced that international markets, and developing countries in particular, were the key to Dykins future success but was wondering what the next step should be.

BERT DYKINS

Bert Dykins was a born innovator, a man who was "always starting something new". During World War II, Bert was a flight engineer in the Royal Air Force. After the war he went to work for General Electric as an in-

dustrial engineer and helped to develop the first printed circuit board manufactured in the United Kingdom. In 1957 Bert moved to Canada as a manufacturing engineer for Canadian Aeronautical Engineering (CAE). He subsequently became general manager of CAE's Utica, New York subsidiary, and for three years was involved in producing communications systems for the American Armed Forces. From CAE Bert moved to the Radium Dial Corporation, quickly boosting their sales of printed circuits from nothing to over $1 million annually. He was next employed by Sperry Gyroscope where he worked on the design of numerical control prototypes and from there moved to Marconi Corporation. In 1973 Bert was appointed General Manager of Presto Corporation, an automotive parts manufacturer. When Bert arrived, Presto had $300,000 in gross sales annually, and when he left two years later the company was generating $300,000 a year in net income. Bert's next move was to become general manager and part-owner of Monarch Tool, a company involved in producing shock absorbers, caulking guns and exercise bikes.

In 1975 Bert was hired as General Manager and consultant for B.K. Products, a company involved in importing and manufacturing bicycles for the Canadian market. B.K. Products was owned by B.K. Gupta, an Indian entrepreneur. The company was sourcing the bulk of its components for the bicycles abroad and was having trouble including sufficient Canadian content to benefit from lower tariff rates. In 1978 Gupta proposed to build a frame plant to increase Canadian content and suggested that Bert take on the added responsibility. When Bert protested that this would be too much to handle in addition to his normal duties, Gupta asked him to give up his other responsibilities and concentrate on setting up a frame plant to supply B.K.

The previous year Bert had been on a tour of thirty companies in Japan and Taiwan that manufactured bicycles and had found the competition "cut-throat". He felt that while Canada could produce spokes, nipples, rims, and other components, it would be very hard for Canadians to be competitive in producing the frames of the most popular tenspeed bikes. Nonetheless Bert felt that there was profit to be made in the production of certain frames. No one in Canada was producing frames for exercise and Junior bikes and Bert agreed to set up a manufacturing plant to produce these for Gupta.

START-UP

Although Dykins Industries Limited was created to produce frames for junior and exercise bikes, Bert hoped to generate some fast cash flow through the sale of sporting goods. To this end he hired three salesmen to sell a broad product line of sporting goods. After three months it became apparent that the sporting goods were not going to generate any profit and Bert laid off the salesmen and dropped the lines. This move left the company engaged exclusively in producing frames for Junior tricycle and exercise bikes for B.K. Industries. One year later B.K. was sold to Action Traders, who immediately cut the level of orders for frames. The reduction in orders hurt Dykins badly, and in the summer of 1979 Bert started to sell Weider weight benches and equipment to help pay the rent on the premises. At this point in time, with Dykins future doubtful, CCM approached Bert.

CCM was the largest producer of bicycles in Canada, and for many years had been the dominant force in Canadian sporting goods sales. During the preceding years the company had been driven almost to the point of bankruptcy and new management had recently been hired to try and turn the company around. These managers liked the Dykins product and offered to make Dykins the sole supplier for frames for all CCM junior bikes if Dykins would produce an exclusive design for CCM. The initial order was set at 25,000 frames and Dykins was told to

be prepared to supply a total of 50,000 frames if CCM was pleased with the initial product.

The CCM order was the key to the future for Dykins and Bert knew it. He also knew the company needed more senior management and decided to call on an old friend, Bob Sage. Bob had been a customer of Monarch Tools when Bert was General Manager and had recently gone into semi-retirement. Nonetheless when Bert called he immediately agreed to fly to Montreal to discuss the possibility of his involvement with Dykins.

BOB SAGE

Bob Sage was also an entrepreneur. He had been a Merlin Engine technician during the war and following demobilization he enrolled at McGill where he completed two years of the Commerce program before withdrawing to join Trans-Canada Airlines. Bob completed a five year apprenticeship program for air engineers with TCA and became a roving technician and failure investigator. Although his future with TCA was secure, it seemed dull and when Curtis Wright began operations in Canada, Bob was among the first to apply for a job. Within three months, he was heading the service group, responsible for planned maintenance of spare parts valued at $30 million. By 1960, Bob was Vice President of the Aerospace Division and, as Curtis Wright became increasingly diversified, was sent on the Harvard Business School course in acquisitions. Although he was subsequently named Vice President of the Industrial Division, Bob was becoming increasingly frustrated by his inability to sell his ideas to head office. He could see no order in the acquisitions that Curtis Wright was making and when the company decided to divest the aerospace division, Bob resigned.

Although he agreed to continue as a consultant for Curtis Wright, Bob had decided that there were not enough Canadian manufacturers and that he would become one. At this point, he was approached by Wally Wild, a Toronto entrepreneur. Wally had been producing jacks for Curtis Wright and now asked Bob if he would like to come and run a jack-manufacturing facility for him. It was to be a 50–50 partnership, with Wally supplying the equipment and the premises. Bob accepted the offer and the company was soon making money. One of Bob's customers was a direct-mail marketing group and Bob became increasingly involved with the group's marketing philosophy. His interest and ability were soon recognized and he was hired as a technical consultant for products sold by the group.

When Wally Wild died, Bob decided to sell his half of the manufacturing plant but continued consulting. He was in no hurry to get a new job and considered himself in a state of semi-retirement. A few weeks later, Bert Dykins called. Despite the CCM order, Dykins Ltd. was financially tight. Bob flew down to Montreal to discuss the situation with Bert and at the end of their meeting, offered to "help out for an indefinite period in any way at all". Because Dykins was short of working capital, Bob initially focused on improving the company's finances. His real interest, however, was in overseas marketing. He felt that the Canadian market was saturated and that the opportunities and money were offshore. This opportunity to help Dykins develop overseas operations had attracted him to the company.

During his initial months with the company Bob Sage concentrated on developing a comprehensive financial overview. He moved quickly to clear up gaps in Dykins' financing and then, to allow monitoring of the ongoing financial condition he developed a simplified seven line profit and loss statement to be filled out on a weekly basis. He also broke down production costs so the company could keep track of expenses and make better pricing decisions. As a result of these efforts, management developed the ability to monitor ongoing expenses and revenues and plan the company's financial needs.

The key personnel of the new company were now in place. Both men had extensive senior management experience and both were first-rate machinists who liked to get their hands dirty. Of more importance to the future of Dykins Ltd., both were entrepreneurs who shared a common philosophy:

"Let's get this thing going or close it."

DE-SKILLING THE PRODUCTION PROCESS

The production of frames for the standard bicycle is a complex operation which requires skilled tradesmen and the use of sophisticated brazing techniques. The brazing process involves the bonding of tubular steel using a thin bead of solder which is applied while one of the tubes is red hot. To produce frames for the junior and exercise bike market, Bert had introduced a radically different philosophy. He decided to simplify the skill requirements for frame production by using mig welding techniques and developed a series of jigs which allowed the production of strong, inexpensive, welded frames by unskilled work-

ers with minimal training in welding, often no more than one day's instruction. The introduction of this process had resulted in the production of a much stronger frame, a particularly important factor in the rapidly growing junior bike market.

The resulting frames were not as aesthetically pleasing as those of the ten speed bikes but Bert did not consider this an important factor in the junior market. More important to him were the savings involved which made it impossible for conventional manufacturers to compete in price with Dykins. Because all of his competitors had well-established facilities which utilized the brazing technique, Bert did not expect any of them to make the capital expenditure necessary to change over to the Dykins process in the near term.

The next step in the simplification process was the introduction of powdered paint.[1] Bert first became aware of the potential of this process while recuperating in hospital. He noticed that his bed frame was painted, and asked a friend about the health hazard from lead in the paint. He was told that powder paint had no lead content, was easy to apply and was virtually unchippable. Bert immediately saw the potential for bicycles and arranged to acquire the necessary equipment for Dykins. This process, like the welding allowed the use of unskilled workers and the resulting paint surface was hard, durable and inexpensive. The final step in the simplification process had been the design of a cleaning system for tubular steel. Conventional processes required a seven step process which Bert now reduced to one through the introduction of a spray gun system using liquid detergent.

The introduction of the new systems allowed Dykins to produce an inexpensive, durable bicycle frame. This factor won them the CCM contract and the company hoped that the process would be the means by which it would grow.

DOMESTIC DEVELOPMENTS

In the fall of 1980, Dykins and Sage visited Pro Cycle and Universal, two of CCM's largest competitors, and were surprised when they were told: "We thought CCM owned you." The partners were quick to point out that they were, in fact, open to offers and that the exclusive clause with CCM was strictly for design and not for sup-

---

[1]Powdered paint is applied electrostatically with no liquid involved.

ply. In the bicycle business, orders were placed once a year for production throughout the subsequent months; therefore both Pro Cycle and Universal were committed for the following year. However, both told Dykins to return the following fall.

Even without additional business from Pro and Universal, Dykins was finding it hard to meet demand. CCM was happy with the quality of the product it was receiving and had increased its total order to 50,000 frames. By November 1980, the plant was running two and sometimes three shifts a day and was still unable to keep up with demand. The partners realized there was a need to improve productivity, but were unsure how to do so. They felt that a raise was not a good incentive, as the resultant increase in the standard of living inevitably led to the need for a further raise. "Keep in mind, it's a boring job. On a nice day people take the day off. There's no pressure in production, just boredom."

After considerable discussion with the shop foreman, Bob Sage decided to introduce a quota incentive system. Under his plan, daily quotas would be set for each worker and, when the quota was reached, the worker would be paid his daily wage and an $8 bonus and be permitted to go home. The plan was made even more attractive by allowing the worker to stay on after meeting his quota and earn more pay at the regular hourly rates. At the time the plan was introduced, Dykins was employing 75 workers and the factory was working two or three shifts per day. Within a few weeks the number of employees was under 50, the remaining employees were working a one-shift day and were saying themselves that the quota was too low. The plan was obviously a resounding success, although as Bob said, it was "contrary to any union thinking in this world."

The new system had a number of important features. In addition to being perceived as fair by the production workers, it made cost estimation very easy for management which made the pricing procedure easier. During the high demand periods in the fall and winter, workers made much more than normal pay, while in the summer slow demand period they seemed not to object to the low rate paid them. Not all the Dykins employees were on the incentive plan, however. Office staff and assembly workers who were unskilled and tended to be transient were paid a straight hourly rate and it was considered essential that these employees not be aggravated by any perceived injustice in the incentive plan.[2] For this reason, the shop

foreman considered that problems might arise if quota employees were seen going home early by hourly workers. To prevent a problem, the plan was modified and he encouraged the incentive workers to work a full eight hours, providing additional work for them to do when their quotas were reached. In his words: "They love it. I have never seen people more satisfied."

Bicycle sales were booming in Canada and CCM was unable to assemble enough bicycles to meet the demand. To fill the gap CCM asked Dykins to assemble bicycles for them. Because there is little profit to be made in assembly the partners initially hesitated to undertake this operation; however, to maintain their relationship with CCM they decided they should comply. While they were hiring assembly workers the partners were approached by a social worker who asked if they would hire some slow learners under an incentive plan in which the Provincial Government paid a percentage of their wage. The partners agreed and five of the twenty-five new workers hired were slow learners. These workers never seemed to get bored and in the words of Bob Sage, "You should have seen the looks on their faces when they got their first pay cheque. Keep in mind that these people had never received a pay cheque in their lives!" The slow learners were among the most productive assemblers.

THE MOVE OVERSEAS

During the summer of 1980, the partners had spent considerable time planning the company's growth. Although their frame production process was innovative, they both realized that in the limited Canadian market competitors would eventually learn and adopt the Dykins process. Of more immediate concern, CCM was beginning to adopt the process and the unions at CCM had been demanding that the production of frames be "transferred in" with the end goal of producing all frames internally. This was the result of a slow down in the Canadian economy and the desire of the unions to maintain as high a level of employment as possible. The partners were very concerned about the coming recession. Although sales had grown by $100,000 to $1,800,000, they foresaw a sharp drop in the demand for bicycles in the Canadian market as the recession worsened. This possibility led the partners to consider other markets. The U.S. market was considered highly competitive, with high entry costs and low profit potential. Accordingly, it was decided to look for new markets overseas.

At this point, the markets of the developing world were first discussed. The partners foresaw great potential for

---

[2]These workers in total represented about 20 percent of Dykins employees.

their product in these countries and expected little competition from established manufacturers. The bicycle manufacturing business was very secretive and on his trip to Japan Bert had been unable to view any but the simplest production procedures. This was true for all large manufacturers and Bert believed that Dykins was the only company in the world that would go into a developing country and offer to share all its knowledge with a local partner. Should they get into local production, there was always the possibility of government protection through the introduction of tariff barriers.

Because of the financial constraints of their developing business, the partners hoped to explore offshore at minimum cost. Accordingly, they decided to investigate the availability of Government assistance.

While he was working at Curtis Wright, Bob Sage had spent much time dealing directly with various levels of government. As a result of this experience, he knew people who could direct him to the appropriate government department for assistance. In June of 1980, Bob visited Ottawa and after discussions with Industry, Trade and Commerce was sent to see Maurice Hladik at the Industrial Cooperation Division of the Canadian International Development Agency (CIDA-ICD). Following their meeting, Hladik sent ICD employees to the Dykins plant in Montreal to assess the operation. CIDA was impressed with their operation and according to Bob Sage, "We did virtually nothing after that." Shortly thereafter Hladik returned to Dykins with an invitation to attend the Technology For The People Show to be held in Geneva that September. The Industrial Cooperation Division was sponsoring the participation of 19 Canadian companies in the show and was subsidizing the firms to a maximum of $10,000 per company. According to Sage "without their incentive we would never have gone." While they were planning their display, the partners received another call from ICD. Industrial cooperation was very interested in promoting joint ventures in the Cameroons and was wondering whether Dykins would be interested in going on to the Cameroons following the Geneva fair. Sage readily agreed and the stage was set for Dykins' first overseas venture.

The organization of the Geneva fair was faultless. The Dykins booth was ready on arrival and all the administrative details had been taken care of in advance. Despite the efficiency, the partners were in some ways disappointed. They felt that the delegates were too senior to be interested in their level of technology and found that they learned more from other exhibitors than they did from interaction with the delegates.

"We needed to connect with the guy at the grass roots level who would actually build bikes."

Despite their disappointment with the delegates, however, the trip was by no means wasted. The partners made a number of important contacts, notably meeting Michael Deale, a doctorate of engineering in bus and truck transmissions who was at the fair displaying his prototype automatic transmission system for ten speed bikes. The partners were excited with Deale's invention; however, they felt that the transmission was far too expensive to be competitive. Nonetheless, they felt that they could apply their simplification procedure to the transmission just as they had to the production of bicycle frames. A rapport and mutual respect quickly developed and after extensive discussion, they signed a contract with Deale. Under the terms of the agreement, Deale was to leave his position on the faculty of a British engineering school and move to Montreal where he would be subsidized by Dykins while he worked full time developing the transmission. Dykins would receive the Canadian rights to the transmission and, upon completion of the simplification process to Deale's satisfaction, the world-wide rights. Deale would receive 6% of gross sales of the transmission.

The second important contact Dykins made at the show was with an Englishman named Nichols. He was in the boat business but was very interested in bicycles. He discussed the problems of bicycle production in the United Kingdom with the partners and indicated that he would like to go into business with them. During the discussion it was revealed that Raleigh, the dominant bicycle manufacturer in the United Kingdom, was grossly inefficient and, with a badly overstaffed work force of 12,000 men, was producing bikes at 2½ times the equivalent Canadian cost. Nichols felt strongly that there was a place for the Dykins junior bicycle in the English market and left Geneva with the understanding that he would conduct a feasibility study on that market as soon as practical, and communicate the results to the partners as a preliminary step to serious discussions on a possible joint venture.

The Cameroons

On their arrival in the Cameroons, the partners immediately missed the efficiency they had grown accustomed to in Geneva. They had been scheduled to arrive on a Saturday; however, an air controllers' strike kept them stranded at Orly airport in Paris for an extra day. They were unable to inform the Canadian High Commission in Yaounde of the delay and, as a result, there was no one to meet them when they arrived in the Cameroons at 0300 Sunday morning. Because the partners had left local arrangements to the embassy staff, they had no idea where they would be staying and left that space blank on their entry card. An amazed customs officer said:

> "You're coming into this country and you don't know where you're going to stay."

The customs officer sent them to the back of the line. After talking to a stewardess, the partners wrote in the name of the local hotel and waited patiently as the line inched forward.

The next encounter was even worse. Neither man had been aware of the requirement for a visa and when the customs officer realized they didn't have one he ordered them to a nearby bench with a curt

> "You can't get into this country."

For the next five hours the two men were kept under armed guard, awaiting the arrival of the Commissioner of Police. They couldn't use a phone, were escorted by armed guards to get a coffee and were not allowed to approach the airline reservations desk. The men found the experience "harrowing" and commented that it was lucky they had been kept away from the airline counter. As Bert put it:

> "If there was any way I could have got to a counter I would have gone right home."

Happily, the problems were finally resolved by the arrival of the Police Commissioner. After listening to their story, he grudgingly issued them a visa, good for seven days, and warned that if they were found to be in the country after that time, they would be thrown in jail. Tired and disheveled, the partners arrived at their hotel a little wiser in the ways of the developing world.

The local Industry, Trade and Commerce (ITC) representative had done a very effective job of preparing for the partners. At their request he had arranged interviews with four local businessmen in "generic" manufacturing trades, either bending tubes or welding steel. The caliber of these businessmen impressed Dykins and Sage. After five long days of discussions they felt they could have worked with three of the four groups; however, they realized they had to choose one. Their decision was essentially a technical one and they chose the most advanced of the four. This man was already in the bicycle fabrication business; however he knew he needed technical assistance to progress further, and the partners knew they could help him to expand. Following two more days of discussion a letter of understanding was signed which, it was hoped, would lead to the signing of a joint venture agreement.

The partners had discussed the joint venture process at length before leaving Canada. Dykins was a young company, and despite their optimism they had neither the resources nor the inclination to invest money overseas. While they were not prepared to put cash into joint ventures, the partners were expecting to supply them with custom made jigs and fixtures, a contribution worth approximately $40,000. They saw the technology transfer as a three year process.

Year One   —Bicycles shipped "knocked-down" from Dykins plant and assembled by the
            local partner.
            —Foreign personnel visit Canada for three weeks training in assembly
            processes.

Year Two   —Continuation of training program with emphasis on basic fabrication.
            —Partial frame fabrication in the host country.

Year Three —Technology transfer complete. All systems internalized by the local partner.
            —Dykins provides managerial advice only.

The partners expected to have effective control of the venture through technology and new developments and were satisfied with a minority equity position which would allow them to stay out of the day-to-day management. In the case of the Cameroons the partners agreed to the local partners' offer of a 40% equity position in return for their jigs, fixtures and knowledge.

The local partner was currently producing 60 bicycles a day. At this level he could not meet local market demand and the agreement reached with Dykins was designed to improve both production and management efficiency. The partners' goal was to keep the same number of staff and by improving productivity increase production to 200 bicycles a day. The end product would be a standard single gear bike which would be better and cheaper than the current product. The key to the plan would be a total shutdown of the Cameroons plant for a three-week period. During this time key personnel would be flown to Canada for extensive training in Dykins' Montreal facility. They would then return to the Cameroons with a Canadian technical advisor who would spend three months directing the rebuilding of the plant and installation of the new machinery to produce an exact duplicate of the Montreal layout. To meet market demand during the shutdown and startup phase Dykins negotiated a contract, contingent upon signing the overall agreement, to sell $500,000 worth of bicycles to the new venture. This order would cover the cost of the bicycles, the jigs and fixtures to be installed, and provide a profit.

Both Dykins and Sage were impressed by the potential of the people they met in the Cameroons. They were highly motivated and appeared to have a tremendous learning capability. The biggest gap appeared to be in the area of middle management, which would be addressed with an ongoing training program and periodic working visits to the plant.

Although their potential partners were ready to sign a deal on the spot, Bert and Bob felt that they should follow CIDA advice and have the project evaluated by experts. At CIDA's suggestion they hired a consulting firm to carry out a feasibility study on the local market and evaluate the proposed venture. Despite repeated prodding from Dykins over the succeeding year, by the summer of 1981 the consulting firm had still not released its final feasibility study and Bert and Bob were having serious misgivings about whether the local partner would still be interested when it was released.

By the fall of 1981, Bob and Bert were very impatient with the consultant. Confident from their previous discussions that their local contact was a man they could trust, they let the consultant go and made plans for a return visit to the Cameroons. In assessing their potential risk, Bob said: "If you are the catalyst that will make them money they won't dump you".

Sri Lanka

Shortly after their first visit to the Cameroons, Dykins was again contacted by CIDA and invited to display at the Sri Lanka fair to be held the following spring. The partners had learned a lot about the needs of the developing world, both by talking to the exhibitors at the Geneva fair and from their visit to the Cameroons. For the Sri Lanka fair they changed their display to present third-world delegates with bicycles that they felt would be more appropriate for their countries. In particular, they had learned that in the third world bicycles were often used more for transporting heavy goods than for recreation, as was common in the developed world. The focal point of their Sri Lanka display, therefore, was a carrier bike not unlike those used by grocery store delivery boys in North America, except that this bike had both front and rear carriers. This configuration would allow the bike to be used for heavy loads when travelling on narrow jungle or undeveloped trails. The financial terms for participating in the Sri Lanka fair were similar to those at the Geneva fair and once again CIDA asked if Dykins would be interested in visiting other countries after Sri Lanka. Following the completion of the Sri Lanka fair CIDA representatives would escort Dykins and 18 other Canadian companies on a tour of three or four more countries.

The Sri Lanka fair was very successful and Dykins signed a letter of intent with the Mercantile Bank of Colombo for a joint venture in Sri Lanka. Dykins was to receive 40% of the equity in the new company in return for jigs, fixtures and training; a similar proposal to that of the Cameroons venture. In their discussions with the Bank, the partners emphasized the nature of their three step plan to joint venture self sufficiency and their desire not to be involved in the management process.

India

Following the fair, the companies visited India. Neither of the partners liked the method of doing business in India: "We had the feeling that these people were acting as agents for other people." They also felt that the trade commission was introducing them to people who were too high ranking for their needs. They were not meeting the small businessmen that they liked to deal with and felt that they were having their brains picked by the engineers who attended the meetings.

While in India the partners met with B. K. Gupta, Bert's former employer. Gupta told them that he wanted to form a company to manufacture their most labour intensive product. This was the frame for the exercise bicycle. Gupta calculated that he could land an exercise bike in Canada for $50 as compared to the Canadian price of

$85. Although the opportunity appeared interesting to the partners, they had some concerns about Indian workmanship as India had a terrible reputation for bikes throughout the world. Bert felt that this problem could be surmounted, but only if the plant were laid out as a Canadian plant. "It's got to be a Canadian plant operating in India." After further negotiations a letter of interest was signed. It was hoped that this would be followed by an agreement for Bert to spend two months in India making sure the plant was properly set up and the quality assurance was at acceptable levels. The partners would also hire a Canadian to work full time in India. "A Canadian will check every bike off that line." As in the other ventures the partners had entered into, there would be no cash input by Dykins to the new venture. Dykins would supply jigs, fixtures and training and would have the rights of acceptance on every frame produced. This would ensure those frames that landed in Canada would meet Dykins rigid standards for quality and would be acceptable in the Canadian market. Shortly after their return to Canada the partners heard of used tooling appropriate to the needs of the plant, on sale for $6,000. They relayed this information to Gupta in India. In the summer of 1981 the partners were waiting to hear whether or not Gupta wished to purchase the tooling.

Singapore and the Philippines

The next stop on the tour was Singapore. The partners met some potential suppliers; however they discovered that the level of technology was generally too high and that there was little opportunity for their type of operation. From Singapore they moved on to Manila where they talked to a number of businessmen from the ASEAN block at a trade fair where they displayed their bicycles. Because these contacts had not been prescreened by the staff at the High Commission, the partners were less willing to trust them and in all their discussions they didn't meet a man they felt they wanted to work with. This feeling, combined with the awareness that they were spreading themselves thin, led the partners to decide to finalize their other negotiations before pursuing any opportunities in S.E. Asia.

In June, 1981 the outlook for Dykins seemed rosy indeed. Although CCM had reduced its orders for the subsequent year, new orders from Pro Cycle and Universal promised to make the domestic operation very profitable. Although none of the new ventures in the developing world had yet been formalized, the partners had

recently signed an agreement with a group in the United Kingdom.

United Kingdom

The United Kingdom developments were the work of Nichols, the British delegate the partners had met at the Geneva technology fair. Nichols, a naval architect by training and an intense salesman, ran the Impex Southern Limited Group (ISL). On his return from the Geneva fair, he had done a thorough analysis of the U.K. market and had decided that the cost and overheads in Raleigh and the other major manufacturers were excessive. Nichols felt that the Dykins junior bike had a very good potential in the British market and after obtaining price quotations from the partners managed to obtain an order for $140,000 worth of bikes. The buyer also indicated a willingness to buy a further $560,000 worth of product if the initial shipment proved successful.

Nichols now contacted the International Technology Transportation Limited Division of the Intermediate Technology Group (ITT). ITT had contracted with Oxfam to produce the "Ox Bike"[3] and had some experience in the design of bicycles. The proposal was that ITT would build the bicycles in England and Impex would do the marketing. Dykins would provide the initial frames and eventually supply jigs, fixtures and training to allow a plant to be built in England to produce the whole bicycle there.

The only missing ingredient in the partnership was financing. Nichols managed to find a prospective partner who, after meeting Bert and discussing the potential of the project with him, agreed to put up $250,000. The only difficulty arose from the fact that the financing partner wanted control of the new enterprise. Bert would not agree to this condition. In the developing world his knowledge and the ability to provide ongoing managerial and technical assistance gave him effective control even with a minority equity position. In the UK operation the Dykins name would be used on the final product and Bert didn't want anyone else to be able to direct the operation. Bert countered with an offer which gave the backer preference shares to allow him to make a larger proportion of the profits. The backer agreed to this counteroffer and a

---

[3]Oxfam was a charitable organization, active in the developing world. The ox bike was a simplified bicycle that had been designed for the developing world but which, for lack of a strong sponsor, had never been produced in quantity.

partnership agreement was signed. Under the terms of the agreement the financing partner put up £88,000 in return for 40% of the equity and 55% of the profits. ITT, Impex and Dykins each put up £4,000, for which they each received 20% of the equity. In the initial years the new company, Dykins U.K., was to generate a very small profit of 2½% of sales, while ITT would receive £15,000 or 5% of Value Added and Impex would receive £30,000 or 5% of sales. Dykins supplied the jigs, fixtures and initial inventory and was given a retainer of $25,000 per year for management advice.

The buyer in England would be GUS, a catalogue store with annual sales of $1.5 billion. GUS intended to buy the bicycle from Dykins U.K. for $110 and sell it for $200. Both Bert and Bob felt that the U.K. venture was one of the most potentially profitable. Nonetheless, they still felt the potential for market development was in the developing countries and were planning to display at the Second Annual Technology for the People Conference, to be held in Mexico City in November 1981.

Tunisia

Following their second visit to the Cameroons in the fall of 1981, the partners flew to Tunis. The ITC representative there had given their name to a local businessman who then indicated that he wanted to talk. The meetings proved to be "a total flop". The contact was a hard "Mafia type" who showed them through three plants staffed by "frightened-looking people". Their contact proposed a deal, saying "You put up the money, take the exports and we will get cheap labour". Bob felt strongly that the whole deal had a "slave labour" flavour to it and both men agreed they wanted nothing to do with it. They returned to Canada cutting short their planned visit.

Morocco

The partners' next venture was the result of another CIDA sponsored trip. Eight Canadian companies, including Dykins, were preselected by the Moroccan government to visit that country and meet with local businessmen. After listening to three days of very dry talks from Moroccan bankers, Sage finally met the owner of a local bicycle parts plant. Upon accompanying him to the plant, the men were shown a modern facility with automatic equipment and the services of a first-class French tool and die maker.

The plant produced seats, bearings, pedals and other parts and Bob was at a loss as to how he and Bert could provide any useful input to the operation.

Their contact then took them to his frame factory, a decrepit plant with antiquated equipment. After one look the partners knew that they could help develop a new frame plant, but expressed some surprise at the radical difference in the appearance of the two operations.

The explanation was understandable to anyone familiar with government bureaucracy. Funds were available at 10% interest for the construction of a new plant, but these rates did not apply to money borrowed for expansion and updating. As a result, the frame plant was being run into the ground and every possible drop of profit was being squeezed from it to provide funds for a modern facility. Their contact was now at the stage where he was prepared to write off the old plant completely and open a new operation and for this he wanted Dykins' help. The partners liked their contact and were eager to come to some agreement with him. During the tour of his plant he had demonstrated an intense interest in and knowledge of his employees and the production processes. He was the "hands-on-type" of manager the partners were comfortable with and they saw great potential in dealing with him. It was eventually decided that Dykins would receive 15% of the equity in return for supplying technology and helping with layout and marketing for the new plant. In addition Dykins would become the North American distributor for the high quality parts that were being produced in the modern facility. Once again the partners had negotiated the type of deal they preferred, minimum financial exposure and an opportunity to be involved in designing and starting up another frame plant.

While events had been unfolding in Cameroon and Morrocco little had been heard from their potential partner in India, B.K. Gupta. Dykins had managed to obtain $18,000 worth of used equipment for only $6,000 on Gupta's behalf, but the money had not been forthcoming and they were unwilling to ship without the funds. They did, however, have a man in Casablanca willing to buy the equipment and they sent an ultimatum to Gupta stating that if no funds were forthcoming they would sell the equipment elsewhere. The telex sent, the partners settled back to wait for a reply.

In addition to these operations significant new developments were taking place. The joint venture in the United Kingdom had been signed and a plant was to be set up in March 1982 to produce the junior trail bike. Interest in Dykins had been shown by a Jamaican group,

EXHIBIT 1   LESSONS LEARNED AT DYKINS

Third World Situation

In Dykins estimation, there is money to be made in the "Third World" over the next few years. Company executives caution, however, that one make out a check list concerning certain parameters prior to entering into such ventures.

A Analyze Yourself
  1 Are you really an entrepreneur?
  2 Are you psychologically equipped to withstand the frustrations of airport immigration problems, open sewage, extreme climate, and little sleep?
  3 Do you have the basics of another language (preferably French)?
  4 Do you realize that overseas travel is expensive and negotiations are slow?

B Who Should Go
  Only decision-making management; contracts and letters of intent are usually signed on the spot.

C Before You Go
  1 Make a conscious decision that you want to be in the international market place and that you belong there.
  2 Recognize that developing business in the Third World is a long-term proposition and investment. You cannot be impatient.
  3 Most important—You have to structure your company to give yourself the time to spend in the other countries.
    (a) Do not go at all unless your plant at home is staffed with good middle management who are decision-makers; you cannot function properly if you are worried about the home situation.
    (b) When you return home and you have to run the day-to-day activities of the company, you tend to ignore your Third World opportunities.
    (c) If you do not divorce yourself from the daily routine, you do not have the time to make yourself available in the other countries and follow-up on your opportunities.
  4 Contact the Trade Commissioner at Canadian embassies to prescreen your potential joint venture partners.
  5 Ensure that the Trade Commissioner's staff set up only meetings with potential partners that are in a generic type industry. A lot of time and effort can be wasted on nongeneric potential partners who have money, but an inability to effect the transfer of technology.

D When You Get There
  1 After you select a potential partner, do *not* act as a consultant. Start working with him in his plant as if you were part of his staff. This is the only way that you will gain his confidence.
  2 Remember successful negotiating will depend on developing mutual trust.
  3 Recognize that the type of information and statistics you normally use for your decisions in Canada may not be available in Third World countries. Canadians often get put off when the local people do not have the numbers.
  4 Be fully aware that you are no longer in Canada, nor governed by Canadian civil or corporate law.
  5 Don't get too legal, but do have a local lawyer check out your contract.
  6 Contact the local banks and the embassy to confirm that you can take money out of the country.

E Marry an understanding woman!

---

and a starter study[4] had been submitted to further investigate opportunities in Sri Lanka.

In November, Dykins took part in a "Technology for the People" fair in Mexico City. Prior to their departure, they were contacted by the Bank of Montreal in Toronto.

[4]Starter studies are grants up to $10,000 provided by the Industrial Cooperation Division of CIDA to allow Canadian companies to explore market opportunities in the developing world.

An associate bank in Mexico had equity in a plant producing 300,000 bicycles per year on three lines and wanted to add one "Dykins line". During talks at the fair, it developed that the company wanted to buy the machinery from Dykins and sign a contract to have Dykins install it.

The speed of the international developments turned the partners' attentions once more to an ongoing concern, a strong desire to restructure the organization to allow them to withdraw completely from the day-to-day management of the Montreal manufacturing facility. As a first step, a new plant manager and a new accountant were hired.

While this left the partners more time to develop offshore operations, Bert was unsure as to what the ideal structure for the company would be. What was clear was that the move offshore had ensured their financial viability. Canadian sales had dropped from $1,800,000 to $1,400,000 as the recession deepened; however, offshore sales to England and more recently Jamaica, had grown from zero to $600,000. Bert was hoping to double that figure the following year and hoped to hold the line in Canada. As he reflected on the move offshore Bert thought of the lessons he had learned (Exhibit 1). The real key to success was the local partner and Bert had decided on the criteria that were necessary for a successful relationship: the local partner must be in a generic enterprise, he must have an entrepreneurial orientation and mutual trust must be developed. Using these guidelines, Bert hoped to see Dykins expand through the developing world.

GENICOM CORPORATION

Per V. Jenster
John M. Gwin
David B. Croll
University of Virginia

Curtis W. Powell, President of GENICOM Corporation, faced the morning of June 18, 1985 with uncertainty. His upcoming meeting with the labor union at the firm's Waynesboro, Virginia facility was one which raised some disturbing questions about the company's future, and even its past.

Prior to today's meeting, GENICOM had proposed wage and benefit reductions, which resulted in increasing confrontation with union representatives. Mr. Powell pondered what strategic alternatives the company should pursue if the union did not accept the proposed reductions. And even if the union did make the concessions needed, what strategy should GENICOM follow in the competitive computer printer market over the next 3 to 5 years?

BACKGROUND

GENICOM was founded in June 1983, as a result of a leveraged buy-out of General Electric's (GE) Data Communication Products Business Department in Waynesboro, a relatively self-contained entity which produced

This case was used in the fifth McIntire Commerce Invitational (MCI V) held at the University of Virginia on February 13–15, 1986. We gratefully acknowledge the General Electric Foundation for support of the MCI and the writing of this case.

computer printers and relay components. The department operated as one of GE's strategic business units.

GE came to Waynesboro, a small town in Central Virginia, in 1954 as part of a major decentralization effort which also included establishing facilities nearby in Lynchburg and Salem, Virginia. Between 1954 and 1974, the Waynesboro plant produced a wide variety of highly sophisticated electro-mechanical devices such as process controls, numerical controls, and aircraft controls, many of which are now produced by other GE divisions.

Products once manufactured in the Waynesboro facility accounted for several hundred million dollars in annual sales revenues for GE. As a result, the Waynesboro factory had a long-standing reputation for its skill in electro-mechanical design and engineering and for its ability to solve difficult design tasks in its highly vertically integrated facilities.

The first electro-mechanical printer was created by GE in Waynesboro as a result of the firm's own dissatisfaction with the performance of the Teletype 33 printers. The new GE printer was three times faster than the Teletype 33 and gained quick popularity. In 1969, a send-receive printer was introduced with such success that it evolved into one of GE's fastest-growing product lines. Other products were added using the same technology, and by 1977 the business in Waynesboro had attained annual revenues of $100,000,000 while being very profitable.

In 1980, GE changed corporate leadership. The new GE Chairman, John F. Welch, initiated a major review of the corporation's businesses to determine which ones were critical to GE's future strategies. Businesses with products which did not rank number one or number two in their served industries or did not have the technological leadership to become first or second required special review. The Waynesboro products did not rank number one or number two in their served industry, nor were they critical to GE's long-term strategies, and in 1981, the department's Strategic Planning process investigated the possibility of divestiture as an alternative course of action.

During 1981, the then current General Manager resigned and Curtis Powell, the Financial Manager and long-time GE employee, was appointed the new General Manager.[1]

During the same time frame the printer business' line of reporting was dismantled; the General Manager, the Division Manager and his superior, the Group Vice President, left GE and the Executive Vice President and Sector Executive retired. As a result, there were no administrative levels between the Waynesboro facility and a newly appointed Sector Executive. Mr. Powell received the dual task of (1) positioning the business for divestiture and (2) making it viable if no acceptable buyers could be found. To accomplish these two objectives, Mr. Powell implemented programs to improve the competitiveness of the Department's printer products and productivity programs to reduce the cost of operations. To support aggressive new product design efforts, funding of research and development activities were increased by $1.0MM per year. The first product, the new 3000 Series printer, was introduced in the latter part of 1981. By 1982, the 3000 Series product had received an excellent reception in the marketplace. Variable cost had been reduced by 28%, primarily as a result of the relocation of 300 jobs from Waynesboro to the Department's Mexican facility, fixed costs had been reduced by 25% and net assets in the business had been reduced by $14.0MM. Despite the successful introduction of the new printer product and rapidly increasing orders, GE was still interested in divesting the business.

After several months of meetings with potential acquirers, GE had not received an acceptable offer. During

[1] In this respect, it is important to understand GE's organizational structure. GE was organized as follows: The chairman, three vice-chairmen, seven industry sectors, numerous groups and divisions, each containing many departments. The Waynesboro factory was a department.

the fourth quarter of 1982, Mr. Powell and a group of plant managers offered to purchase the Waynesboro based business from GE.

THE BUY-OUT OF GENICOM

During early 1983, GE agreed to sell the business as a leveraged buy-out, but required a substantial cash payment. In order to complete the transaction, the Management team was joined by two New York based venture capital firms who provided the financial resources needed to purchase the business.

The price agreed upon for the business was net depreciated value plus $8.0MM (note that the business had been in Waynesboro since 1954 and the net depreciated value was significantly less than the appraised value). The purchase price amounted to less than six months sales revenue.

The assets purchased included every printer ever designed by the Waynesboro facility, all customers and contracts, all patents and cross licenses, tools, and buildings, as well as the Relay business. The purchase agreement was signed October 23, 1983, at which time GE received approximately 75% of the purchase price in cash and subordinated notes for the balance. The purchase amount was financed through sale of shares to the venture capital firms and to local management (approximately 45 of the top managers received stock or stock options). Twelve million dollars were borrowed against fixed assets in the business, and a revolving credit line was secured against equipment leases, receivables, and selected inventory. Given the assessed value of the firm, GENICOM had not exceeded 65% of its borrowing capacity.

THE GENICOM CORPORATION

By 1983, GENICOM was one of the larger independent computer printer companies which manufactured teleprinters (i.e., keyboard send/receive units), dot-matrix printers, and line printers. These printers were primarily industrial grade, and thus were not widely used for personal computer output. They served a wide variety of data processing and telecommunication needs, with printing speeds ranging from 60 cps (characters per second) in the teleprinter version to 400 lpm (lines per minute) in their line printer series. GENICOM was also the industry leader in crystal relays sold to defense, space, and other industries where there was a need for highly reliable electrical switches.

GENICOM was also a multi-national company with production facilities in Waynesboro (1300 employees) and Mexico (700 employees). Approximately 20% of the 1984 sales revenue of $140.0MM was derived from International customers, primarily Original Equipment Manufacturers (OEM's). GENICOM was in the process of establishing its own sales affiliates in the United Kingdom, France, Germany, and Sweden in order to further serve its foreign customers.

Prior to the change in ownership, Genicom's management negotiated a comprehensive benefits package which was essentially the same as GE's. Furthermore, a new agreement with the Union was settled, and customers and suppliers were briefed. All but fifteen current employees were offered positions with GENICOM at the same salary and similar benefits as provided by GE and all accepted.

According to Mr. Powell, "Everything considered, the buy-out went extremely well. 1984 was an excellent year, a very successful year for GENICOM. We are still trying to change the culture we inherited from GE, where people feel they have unlimited resources to a small company climate, a climate in which costs must be contained. Some of our people in Waynesboro believe that the success we had in 1984 will continue forever. They don't realize that in our industry product life cycles are short and even if your products are doing well today, you need to prepare for tomorrow. This transition from GE to GENICOM has been difficult."

"When we were a part of GE all employees were paid GE wages and salaries. Other firms in our industry and other firms in Waynesboro paid considerably less than GE rates." As part of the two largest employers in Waynesboro, GENICOM's actions when dealing with its employees became public very soon. "We have a very quality conscious work force in Waynesboro and quality has always been extremely important to us. But in our competitive market quality is not enough, we must be cost competitive also."

MANAGEMENT AND STRUCTURE

Genicom's management inherited an organizational structure and an information system which reflected GE's standards and procedures. Consequently, GENICOM was probably the most vertically integrated printer company in the world (largely encouraged by GE's capital budg-

eting and performance evaluation system), making almost everything in-house from tools to printer ribbons to sales brochures. This high degree of vertical integration enabled GENICOM to respond quickly to specific requests for redesign of products to suit individual customer needs.

The firm's information system was also aligned with GE's reporting system, which led one outside observer to conclude that he "had never seen an organization with such a sophisticated information system which used it so little." As an illustration, Exhibit 1 shows GENICOM's MIS budget *vis-a-vis* industry averages. Exhibit 2 compares GENICOM's data processing department with a similar organization in the industry. According to Coopers and Lybrand, a consulting firm retained by GENICOM, the cost problem, highlighted in these two exhibits, could also be found in other areas: Finance, Materials, Shop Operations, Manufacturing Engineering, Quality Control, Marketing, Product Engineering, and Relays.

The management team of GENICOM (April 1985) consists of the following members:

Curtis W. Powell, President/Chief Executive Officer: Mr. Powell graduated from Lynchburg College, Lynchburg, Virginia in 1961 with a BA Degree in Business Administration-Economics. Prior to the purchase of the Waynesboro business by GENICOM, Mr. Powell had served 22 years in various General Electric assignments; the last two as Department General Manager of the Waynesboro business.

John V. Harker, Executive Vice President: Mr. Harker was responsible for the Sales and Marketing functions, including Product Planning, Market and New Business Development, Marketing Administration, Customer Service, Domestic Sales and International Operations. He formerly held positions as Senior Vice President for Marketing and Corporate Development at Dataproducts, Vice President of Booz, Allen, and Hamilton, Inc., a Management Consulting firm, and with IBM in various Marketing capacities. Upon joining GENICOM, he initiated the hiring of six new Marketing and Sales Executives from the computer peripherals industry.

Robert C. Bowen, Vice President & Chief Financial Officer: Mr. Bowen has served in various financial capacities with GE since 1964, and with GENICOM's predecessor for the past ten years.

W. Douglas Drumheller, Vice President of Manufacturing: Mr. Drumheller joined GE's Manufacturing Management Program in 1970 and was appointed Vice President at GENICOM in 1983.

EXHIBIT 1   COMPARISONS WITH INDUSTRY AVERAGES

	Manufacturing (electronics, electrical)			GENICOM		
	($1,000)*	% of revenue	% of MIS budget	($1,000)	% of revenue	% of MIS budget
Total revenue	$75,590	100	N/A	$165,000	100	N/A
MIS operating budget	723	1.01	100	2,567.4[1]	1.56	100
Personnel	308	.43	42.5	1,271.0	.77	49.5
Hardware	208	.29	28.4	400.6[2]	.24	15.6
System software	21	.03	3.1	27.5	.02	1.1
Application software	36	.05	4.9	76.5	.05	3.0
Supplies	57	.08	7.8	110.3	.07	4.2
Outside services	36	.05	7.8	559.0	.34	21.8
Communications	21	.03	3.3	19.8	.01	0.8
Other	36	.05	5.0	102.7[3]	.06	4.0

Sources: Infosystems 25th and 26th annual salary surveys, June, 1984 and June, 1983. Survey of 642 firms conducted for *Datamation,* and published March 15, 1985 shows that firms averaging $200 million in revenue employ an average of 20.1 people in data processing (equivalent to IS&S at GENICOM without office services). This provides an index of average revenue of $19,950,200 per data processing employee.

1. GENICOM's IS&S actual expenses January—May 1985 have been annualized and have been modified to (1) remove office services expenses and to (2) add estimated hardware depreciation expense and estimated occupancy expense in order to correlate to survey figures.

2. This category includes equipment rental, maintenance and depreciation expense. Depreciation expense is drawn from GENICOM'S fixed asset register and includes annual depreciation (book) for all assets acquired through December, 1984.

3. This category includes occupancy expense estimated at 4% of total MIS expense budget.

*Represents average amounts reported in source survey.

EXHIBIT 2   SAVINGS . . .

Listed below is a personnel information comparison for a data processing department with some similarities to GENICOM

	GENICOM	Other firm
Hardware	5 H-P 3000's	4 H-P 3000's
Number of data centers	1 current 1 planned	2
Annual revenues of organization	$165,000,000 (1985 budget)	$500,000,000 (1985 budget)
Type of business	Manufacturing	Manufacturing
Number of employees in MIS	34 (includes staff at one data center)	44 (includes staff at both data centers)
Salary expense	$1,051,300	$1,075,200 (1984 + 5%)
Processing characteristics	In-house plus heavy use of remote computing service	In-house plus heavy use of remote computing service
Company revenues per MIS employee	$4,852,900	$12,500,000

Comparisons with industry averages

Dennie J. Shadrick, Vice President of Engineering: Mr. Shadrick recently joined GENICOM after seventeen years with Texas Instruments, where he served in a variety of Engineering and Management positions in the terminal and printer business unit.

Charles A. Ford, Vice President of Relay Operations: Mr. Ford has had a long career with GE and GENICOM serving in the areas of Manufacturing, Engineering, and General Management.

Robert B. Chapman, Treasurer: Mr. Chapman has been with GENICOM since 1984, after holding positions with Centronics Data Computer Corporation, Honeywell, Inc., and the Datapoint Corporation, where he was Assistant Treasurer.

Part of our GE heritage was a strong Engineering and Manufacturing orientation and this is a valuable asset. However, as a new and independent company, we needed to establish a Marketing presence, we needed a new and aggressive approach to our Marketing and Sales Activities. One of our first

EXHIBIT 3   GENICOM CORPORATION AND SUBSIDIARIES CONSOLIDATED BALANCE SHEET

(Amounts in thousands)	December 30, 1984	January 1, 1984
ASSETS		
Current assets:		
Cash	$ 451	$ 3,023
Accounts receivable, less allowance for doubtful accounts of $958 and $483	21,224	22,459
Inventories (Note 3)	26,917	24,343
Prepaid expenses and other assets	1,368	356
Total current assets	49,960	50,181
Property, plant and equipment (Note 3)	27,821	27,314
Other assets	239	180
	$78,020	$77,675
LIABILITIES AND CAPITAL		
Current liabilities:		
Current portion of long-term debt	1,600	11,841
Accounts payable and accrued expenses (Note 3)	16,104	15,682
Deferred income	1,519	1,359
Income taxes (Note 8)	5,579	
Total current liabilities	24,802	28,882
Long-term debt, less current portion (Note 4)	36,400	44,500
Deferred income taxes	1,590	504
Redeemable preferred stock, $1 par value; 32,000 shares issued and outstanding at January 1, 1984; stated at liquidation value of $100 per share		3,200
Stockholders' equity (Note 11):		
Common stock, $.01 par value; 20,000,000 shares authorized; shares outstanding: December 30, 1984—10,995,500 and January 1, 1984—8,575,000	110	86
Additional paid-in capital	9,297	772
Retained earnings (deficit)	5,821	(269)
	15,228	589
	$78,020	$77,675

The accompanying notes are an integral part of the financial statements.

action items was to recruit the best Marketing and Sales executives we could locate. GENICOM's strategy for developing marketing strengths has been to bring experienced and capable people from other firms in the computer peripherals industry.

FINANCIAL STATEMENTS

The 1984 financial statements and footnotes are included in Exhibits 3–7. Due to the time period constraints associated with any financial statements, GENICOM's balance sheet for December 30, 1984 did not include the subsequent private placement of stock that took place on January 3, 1985. GENICOM sold 353,000 shares of its unissued common stock for $5 per share. If these shares had been issued at December 30, 1984, unaudited *pro forma* stockholders' equity would have been $16,993,000.

The two period comparisons used in the financials entitled "December 30, 1984" and "January 1, 1984" are not true comparisons since the time periods covered are not equal. The first column for the year ending December 30, 1984 represents a 12-month period, but the second column for the year ending January 1, 1984 represents only a two-month, ten-day period.

The remaining statements and ten footnotes are complete and self-explanatory. The strong financial orientation of the management is evident in the statement presentation.

COST ACCOUNTING

A major cost accounting issue was that GENICOM's product costs were well above those of their competitors. GENICOM's willingness to customize their products to meet their customers' individual needs allowed them to charge a premium price. The costs that seemed disproportionately high were salary and hourly wages. GENICOM's salary and wage structures were established over many years while it was a part of GE. General Electric

EXHIBIT 4   GENICOM CORPORATION AND SUBSIDIARIES CONSOLIDATED STATEMENT OF INCOME

(Amounts in thousands, except per share data)	Year ended December 30, 1984	October 21, 1983 to January 1, 1984
Net sales	$136,661	$26,752
Cost of goods sold	90,647	20,403
Gross profit	46,014	6,349
Expenses:		
Selling, general and administration	22,442	3,965
Engineering, research and product development	4,795	890
Interest	6,900	1,386
	34,137	6,241
Income before income taxes	11,877	108
Income tax expense (Note 8)	5,787	377
Net income (loss)	$ 6,090	$ (269)
Net income (loss) per common share and common share equivalent:		
Primary	$.61	$(.03)
Fully diluted	$.59	$(.03)
Weighted average number of common shares and common share equivalents:		
Primary	9,967	8,753
Fully diluted	10,292	8,892

The accompanying notes are an integral part of the financial statements.

EXHIBIT 5 GENICOM CORPORATION AND SUBSIDIARIES CONSOLIDATED STATEMENT OF CHANGES IN CAPITAL ACCOUNTS

for the year ended December 30, 1984 and the period from October 21, 1983 (commencement of operations) to January 1, 1984

(Dollar amounts in thousands)	Redeemable preferred stock	Common stock	Additional paid-in capital	Retained earnings
Issued in connection with acquisition:				
32,000 shares of redeemable preferred stock	$3,200			
8,000,000 shares of common stock		$ 80	$ 721	
Issuance of 525,000 shares of common stock		5	47	
Exercise of stock options		1	4	
Net loss				$ (269)
Balance, January 1, 1984	3,200	86	772	(269)
Issuance of 1,297,000 shares of common stock		13	5,288	
Redemption of preferred stock	(3,200)	6	3,194	
Exercise of stock options		5	43	
Net income				6,090
Balance, December 30, 1984	—	$110	$9,297	$5,821

The accompanying notes are an integral part of the financial statements.

traditionally provided its employees with both a generous base salary and a generous fringe package. As wages and benefits were negotiated with the union on an overall corporate basis, the printer department had avoided serious conflicts with the union.

Consultants from Coopers and Lybrand were hired by GENICOM to evaluate the firm's cost structure. Although the study was not completed, preliminary research had focused on this labor cost problem. The preliminary findings suggested that most areas of the firm seemed overstaffed and salary and wage levels exceeded both industry norms and local community standards (e.g., see Exhibits 1 & 2).

An interesting point was that GENICOM's wage and salary differential over other local companies was so great that it proved detrimental to some laid-off employees. Other companies in the region had reported that they were hesitant to hire a laid-off GENICOM employee knowing that, as soon as an opening existed, the employee would be lost back to GENICOM.

UNION NEGOTIATIONS

Negotiations with Local 124 of the United Electrical Radio and Machine Workers (UE) of America started on April 23, 1985. Management's primary goal was to reduce the average costs of an applied direct labor hour by four dollars. Included in the employee benefit package were vacation (five weeks maximum), holidays (ten days), comprehensive medical benefits, life insurance, temporary disability, overtime premium, pension, breaks, night-shift bonus, paid sick days/personal time, and job structures which included seventeen pay grades. Appendices 1–6 provides a picture of the negotiations as the confrontation grew.

Earlier in April, a different local of UE in a nearby Virginia town had been involved in an almost identical situation. A former department of Westinghouse which had been sold to outside interests, confronted with wage and benefit structures originally negotiated at the national level, attempted to win major financial concessions from

EXHIBIT 6   GENICOM CORPORATION AND SUBSIDIARIES CONSOLIDATED STATEMENT OF CHANGES IN FINANCIAL POSITION

(Amounts in thousands)	Year ended December 30, 1984	October 21, 1983 to January 1, 1984
Sources of working capital:		
From operations:		
Net income (loss)	$ 6,090	$ (269)
Charges to income not affecting working capital:		
Depreciation	4,664	630
Amortization	49	
Deferred income taxes	1,086	504
Working capital from operations	11,889	865
Issued or assumed in connection with acquisition:		
Redeemable preferred stock		3,200
Common stock		801
Long-term debt		57,841
Proceeds from issuance of common stock	8,501	52
Exercise of options	48	5
Other, net	357	(189)
Total sources	$20,795	$62,575
Applications of working capital:		
Additions to property, plant and equipment	5,636	918
Noncurrent assets purchased in acquisition		27,017
Reduction of long-term debt	8,100	13,341
Redemption of preferred stock	3,200	
Total applications	$16,939	$41,276
Analysis of working capital components:		
Increase (decrease) in current assets:		
Cash	(2,572)	3,023
Accounts receivable	(1,235)	22,459
Inventories	2,574	24,343
Prepaid expenses and other assets	1,012	356
Totals	(221)	50,181
Increase (decrease) in current liabilities:		
Current portion of long-term debt	(10,241)	11,841
Accounts payable and accrued expenses	422	15,682
Deferred income	160	1,359
Income taxes	5,579	
Totals	(4,080)	28,882
Increase in working capital	3,859	21,299
Working capital, beginning of period	21,299	
Working capital, end of period	$25,158	$21,299

The accompanying notes are an integral part of the financial statements.

EXHIBIT 7 GENICOM CORPORATION AND SUBSIDIARIES NOTES TO CONSOLIDATED FINANCIAL STATEMENTS

1 *Incorporation and Acquisition:*
GENICOM Corporation (the "Company") was incorporated on June 1, 1983 and had no activity other than organizational matters until October 21, 1983 when it acquired substantially all of the net assets of the Data Communication Products Business Department and all of the outstanding common stock of Datacom de Mexico, S.A. de C.V., both wholly owned by General Electric Company ("GE"), a related party. These entities together functioned as a single business unit and were acquired in a purchase transaction for consideration totaling $62.1 million. The consideration was financed by (a) borrowing $41.0 million under a revolving credit and term loan agreement, (b) issuing $16.8 million in subordinated notes to GE, (c) assuming $340,000 of liabilities and (d) selling $800,000 of common stock and $3.2 million of redeemable preferred stock.

The consideration was allocated to working capital ($35.1 million) and property, plant and equipment and other assets ($27.0 million). The allocation of the purchase price to assets acquired and liabilities assumed is subject to adjustment resulting from refinements in the application of purchase method accounting.

If the acquisition is assumed to have been made as of January 1, 1983, unaudited pro forma consolidated net sales, net loss and net loss per share (computed by adjusting historical operations for acquisition financing and purchase method accounting) would approximate the following for the year ended January 1, 1984 (dollar amounts in millions, except per share amounts): net sales—$113.5; net loss—$3.4; net loss per common share and common share equivalent: primary—$.42 and fully diluted—$.42.

2 *Summary of Significant Accounting Policies:*
The Company, one of the largest independent computer printer companies, is a manufacturer and leading supplier of teleprinters, serial dot matrix printers, and line printers serving a wide variety of data processing and telecommunication markets. Additionally, the Company is a recognized leader in the manufacture and supply of high quality, crystal/can relays, which are used in the Aerospace and Defense industries.

(*a*) Principles of consolidation: The consolidated financial statements include the accounts of the Company and its wholly owned subsidiaries. All significant intercompany accounts and transactions have been eliminated.

(*b*) Fiscal year: The Company's fiscal year ends on the Sunday nearest December 31. Accordingly, the Company is reporting on the period October 21, 1983 (commencement of operations) to January 1, 1984 and for the 52-week period ended December 30, 1984.

(*c*) Inventories: Inventories are stated at the lower of cost or market. Cost is determined on a first-in, first-out basis.

(*d*) Property, plant and equipment: Property, plant and equipment is stated at cost. Depreciation is computed using the straight-line method for financial reporting purposes based on estimates of useful lives at their acquisition date (generally 15 to 25 years for buildings and 3 to 8 years for machinery and equipment). Significant improvements and the cost of tooling are capitalized, while repairs and maintenance costs are charged to operations.

(*e*) Income taxes: Timing differences exist in the computation of income for financial and tax reporting purposes which give rise to deferred taxes. The principal reason for these differences is the use of alternative methods for computing depreciation. The Company accounts for investment tax credits as a reduction of current taxes in the year realized.

(*f*) Research and development: Research and development costs are charged to operations as incurred. The costs were $3,367,000 for the year ended December 20, 1984 and $475,000 for the period October 21, 1983 to January 1, 1984.

(*g*) Foreign currency translation: Through its subsidiary, Datacom de Mexico, S.A. de C.V., the Company operates in a country considered to have a highly inflationary economy. As such, translation adjustments, which are not material, are included in results of operations. The consolidated financial statements of the Company include foreign assets and liabilities of $2,643,000 and $526,000 at December 30, 1984 and $1,291,000 and $96,000 at January 1, 1984.

(h) Employee benefit plans: Substantially all of the Company's employees are eligible to participate under the Company's employee benefit plans described in Note 5. These plans are contributory and each employee must elect to participate and make contributions to the plans. Employee contributions vest immediately.

(i) Net income per common share and common share equivalent: Primary net income (loss) per share was computed by dividing net income (loss) by the weighted average number of common shares and common share equivalents outstanding during the period. Common share equivalents include the weighted average number of shares issuable upon the assumed exercise of outstanding stock options and warrants after assuming the applicable proceeds from such exercise were used to acquire treasury shares at the average market price during the period.

Fully diluted net income (loss) per share was based upon the further assumption that the applicable proceeds from the exercise of the outstanding stock options and warrants were used to acquire treasury shares at the market price at the end of the period if higher than the average market price during the period.

3 *Supplemental Balance Sheet Information:*

Inventories consist of:

(Amounts in thousands)	December 30, 1984	January 1, 1984
Raw materials	$10,110	$ 9,897
Work in process	9,781	9,708
Finished goods	7,026	4,738
	$26,917	$24,343

Property, plant and equipment consist of:

(Amounts in thousands)	December 30, 1984	January 1, 1984
Land	$ 709	$ 709
Buildings	5,383	5,268
Machinery and equipment	25,628	21,760
Construction in progress	1,291	207
	33,011	27,944
Less accumulated depreciation	5,190	630
	$27,821	$27,314

Accounts payable and accrued expenses consist of:

(Amounts in thousands)	December 30, 1984	January 1, 1984
Trade accounts payable	$ 6,297	$ 7,881
Accrued liabilities:		
Compensated absences	2,801	2,532
Payroll and related liabilities	1,589	808
Interest	1,337	1,426
Employee benefits	1,830	332
Other	2,250	2,703
	$16,104	$15,682

EXHIBIT 7 GENICOM CORPORATION AND SUBSIDIARIES NOTES TO CONSOLIDATED FINANCIAL STATEMENTS *(Continued)*

4 *Long-Term Debt:*

Long-term debt consists of:

(Amounts in thousands)	December 30, 1984	January 1, 1984
Revolving credit notes	$21,000	$27,500
Term loan	12,000	12,000
Subordinated notes payable to GE	5,000	16,841
	38,000	56,341
Less current portion	1,600	11,841
	$36,400	$44,500

On October 21, 1983, the Company entered into a financing agreement with several banks which provides the Company with $31 million of revolving credit and a $12 million term loan.

The revolving credit and term loan bear interest at the prime rate (10¾% at December 30, 1984) plus 1½%, payable quarterly. In addition, a commitment fee of ½ of 1% is payable quarterly on the average daily unused portion of the revolving credit borrowing base. The Company is also required to maintain compensating balances of at least 5% of the total outstanding revolving credit and term loan. Withdrawal of the compensating balances is not legally restricted and any deficiency in maintaining such balances is subject to a fee based upon an average borrowing rate on amounts outstanding under this agreement.

The initial revolving loan base of $31 million decreases by $1.55 million beginning on October 1, 1986, and continues to decrease by $1.55 million each quarter thereafter and expires on October 1, 1991.

The term loan is payable in quarterly installments of $600,000 beginning October 1, 1985.

All borrowings by the Company under the agreement are collateralized by liens on all of the Company's assets. The agreement requires the Company to meet certain financial ratios related to indebtedness, net worth and current assets and current liabilities. The agreement also limits additional borrowing, purchase of property and equipment, the sale or disposition of certain assets, and restricts the payment of dividends to 50% of retained earnings. Under the most restrictive covenant $2.9 million of retained earnings was available for payment of dividends at December 30, 1984.

In connection with the acquisition, at October 21, 1983, the Company issued subordinated notes to GE in the amount of $16.8 million. These notes bear interest at the prime rate, payable quarterly. During 1984 in accordance with the terms, the Company paid $11.8 million of the notes. The remaining $5 million is payable as follows: October 21, 1985—$1 million; October 21, 1986—$2 million; and October 21, 1987—$2 million.

Maturities of long-term debt for the five fiscal years subsequent to December 30, 1984 are (in millions): 1985—$1.6; 1986—$4.4; 1987—$4.4; 1988—$6.4; and 1989—$8.6.

5 *Employee Benefit Plans:*

Effective January 1, 1984, the Company established a defined benefit pension plan for hourly employees. Employees must elect to participate and the plan is contributory. Employee contributions are 3% of compensation in excess of $12,000 per year. The Company makes contributions to the plan and records as pension expense an amount that is actuarially determined to be sufficient to provide benefits provided for under the plan, including amortization of unfunded liabilities over a maximum of 30 years. For the year ended December 30, 1984, pension expense was $408,000. Details of accumulated plan benefits and net plan assets as of the initial valuation date (January 1, 1984) are as follows:

EXHIBIT 7   GENICOM CORPORATION AND SUBSIDIARIES NOTES TO CONSOLIDATED FINANCIAL STATEMENTS *(Continued)*

Actuarial present value of accumulated plan benefits are:

Vested	$ 74,777
Nonvested	28,067
	$102,844
Market value of assets	$ 49,969
Rate of return assumed	7½%

Certain hourly employees have the additional benefit of receiving Unemployment Supplemental Income if their employment is terminated due to reductions in the Company's workforce.

Substantially all salaried employees are eligible to participate in the Company's deferred compensation and savings plan. The plan provides for contributions to be made by employees through salary reductions. The Company makes certain matching contributions which are allocated to the participants and vest as called for by the plan. For the year ended December 30, 1984, the Company's expense under this plan was $1,002,000.

6 *Warrants and Redeemable Preferred Stock:*

In connection with the acquisition the Company issued to GE stock purchase warrants to acquire 2,500,000 shares of the Company's common stock at a price of $.50 per share. The warrants are currently exercisable and expire October 21, 1988.

On December 20, 1984, the Company redeemed all of the outstanding redeemable preferred stock ($3.2 million) by issuing 640,000 shares of common stock. Holders of the redeemable preferred stock waived payment of the cumulative preferred stock dividends for all periods the stock was outstanding.

7 *Restricted Stock Purchase and Incentive Stock Option Plans:*

Under the Company's restricted stock purchase plan, the Company may offer to sell up to 975,000 shares of common stock to employees of the Company at a price per share equal to 100% of the fair market value as determined by the Board of Directors on the date of offer. Purchased shares vest to the employees as provided for under the agreement and, in certain cases, is dependent upon the attainment of annual financial objectives. Shares issued under the plan which are not vested at an employee's termination are subject to repurchase by the Company at the lower of original issue price or their then fair market value.

At December 30, 1984, 200,000 shares of common stock are reserved for future grants under this plan. The following table summarizes the activity of the plan during the respective fiscal periods (fair market value as determined at date of purchase):

	Year ended December 30, 1984		October 21, 1983 to January 1, 1984	
	Number of shares	Market value	Number of shares	Market value
Unvested shares outstanding, beginning of period	525,000	$ 52,500		
Shares issued	250,000	95,000	525,000	$52,500
Shares vested	(175,000)	(17,500)		
Unvested shares outstanding, end of period	600,000	$130,000	525,000	$52,500

EXHIBIT 7   GENICOM CORPORATION AND SUBSIDIARIES NOTES TO CONSOLIDATED FINANCIAL STATEMENTS *(Continued)*

Effective October 21, 1983, the Company adopted an incentive stock option plan whereby 1,300,000 shares of unissued common stock was reserved for future issuance. The plan was amended on October 20, 1984 to reduce the number of shares available under the plan from 1,300,000 to 1,025,000. Stock option activity for the respective fiscal periods is as follows:

	Year ended December 30, 1984			October 21, 1983 to January 1, 1984		
		Option price			Option price	
	Number of shares	Per share	Total	Number of shares	Per share	Total
Outstanding, beginning of period	780,000	$.10	$78,000			
Granted	82,500	$.20–$1.00	46,500	830,000	$.10	$83,000
Exercised	483,500	$.10	48,350	50,000	$.10	5,000
Cancelled	65,000	$.10–$.20	7,250			
Outstanding, end of period	314,000		$68,900	780,000		$78,000
Options exercisable, end of period	5,000	$.10	$ 500			
Options available for future grants	177,500					

The plan provides for the exercise of the outstanding options at 20% per year beginning five years from date of grant. The Company accelerated the exercising provisions of 475,000 options granted, and these options were exercised prior to December 30, 1984. Of these shares issued, 425,000 shares are restricted and subject to certain vesting provisions related to annual financial objectives. Additionally, under the plan, other options granted also become exercisable at earlier dates if these same financial objectives are attained. During the year ended December 30, 1984, such objectives were attained and 45,000 shares of those restricted above accrued to the benefit of the holders and 63,500 options became exercisable of which 58,500 were exercised and shares of common stock issued. The Company must continue to attain certain financial objectives annually in order to continue to have accelerated exercise dates (with respect to options) and continue to vest (with respect to restricted shares). In the event of employee termination prior to full vesting in these shares, the Company may purchase such shares at the lower of fair market value at date of termination or the original option price.

EXHIBIT 7 GENICOM CORPORATION AND SUBSIDIARIES NOTES TO CONSOLIDATED FINANCIAL STATEMENTS *(Continued)*

8 *Income Taxes:*

Income tax expense consists of:

(Amounts in thousands)	Year ended December 30, 1984	October 21, 1983 to January 1, 1984
Current:		
Federal	$4,788	
State	936	
Foreign	(72)	
	5,652	—
Deferred:		
Federal	73	$302
State	1	75
Foreign	61	
	135	377
	$5,787	$377

Total tax expense amounted to an effective rate of 48.7% for the year ended December 30, 1984 and 44.9% for the period October 21, 1983 to January 1, 1984. Income tax expense was different from that computed at the statutory U.S. Federal income tax rate of 46% for the following reasons:

Tax expense at statutory rate	$5,463	$ 50
Increases (decreases) related to:		
Investment tax credits	(249)	(56)
State income tax, net of federal income tax benefit	515	40
Purchase method accounting for inventories	103	370
DISC income	(70)	
Other, net	25	(27)
Actual tax expense	$5,787	$377

Deferred income tax expense results from timing differences in the recognition of revenue and expense for tax and financial statement purposes. The sources of these differences and the tax effect of each are as follows:

(Amounts in thousands)	Year ended December 30, 1984	October 21, 1983 to January 1, 1984
Depreciation	$ 728	$ 497
Inventory valuation	(668)	
Other, net	75	(120)
	$ 135	$377

9 *Leasing Arrangements:*

As Lessee

The Company leases certain manufacturing and warehousing property. Rent expense included in the consolidated statement of income amounted to $740,000 for the year ended December 30, 1984 and $120,000 for the period October 21, 1983 to January 1, 1984.

Annual future minimum lease commitments for operating leases as of December 30, 1984 are immaterial.

EXHIBIT 7 GENICOM CORPORATION AND SUBSIDIARIES NOTES TO CONSOLIDATED FINANCIAL STATEMENTS *(Continued)*

As Lessor

The Company has rental plans for the leasing of printers. Operating lease terms vary, generally from one to 60 months. Rental income for the year ended December 30, 1984 and for the period October 21, 1983 to January 1, 1984 was $18,139,000 and $3,807,000, respectively. Minimum future rental revenues on noncancellable operating leases with terms of one year or longer at December 30, 1984 are (in thousands): 1985—$2,900; 1986—$500; 1987—$400; and 1988—$300.

At December 30, 1984 and January 1, 1984, the cost of equipment leased was (in thousands) $4,087 and $4,040, which is included in property, plant and equipment, net of accumulated depreciation of $1,072 and $131, respectively.

10 *Related-Party Transactions:*

The Company presently utilizes GE for various services, such as repair services for customers and data processing, under contracts expiring generally in 1985. The Company also purchases various raw materials from GE. The cost of these materials and services for the year ended December 30, 1984 and the period October 21, 1983 to January 1, 1984, totaled $8.4 million and $1.1 million, respectively.

Sales to GE were $12.4 million for the year ended December 30, 1984 and $3.3 million for the period October 21, 1983 to January 1, 1984. In addition, sales to GE affiliates, who serve as distributors to third party customers in certain markets, and sales of parts for maintenance services to customers amounted to $14.4 million for the year ended December 30, 1984 and $1.7 million for the period October 21, 1983 to January 1, 1984. Accounts receivable from GE were $4.6 million at December 30, 1984 and $5.2 million at January 1, 1984; accounts payable to GE were $.8 million at December 30, 1984 and $.9 million at January 1, 1984.

its workforce in order to become cost competitive in its market. The local refused to accept any cutbacks in its package and, after several months of negotiation, went on strike. Two days later the company announced it would begin hiring permanent replacements for the striking workers on the following Monday and placed help wanted ads in the local newspapers. On Sunday afternoon, in a close vote, the union members voted to end the strike and accept management's proposals.

THE PRINTER INDUSTRY

The demand for printer hardware is derived from the demand for computing machinery. As the demand for computing capability shifted from mainframe computers to minicomputers to microcomputers, so did the demand for printing capacity shift from output capability to output quality. Similarly, the attributes of printers which determined their success in the marketplace changed from reliability and performance when dealing with mainframe applications to price and capability when dealing with microcomputer applications. At the same time, as business applications of microcomputers moved into networking situations, where a number of microcomputers are linked to a central database and a single printer, the demands placed on the printer hardware changed from the demands of a stand-alone microcomputer.

In addition to the changes that took place in the printer industry as a result of changes in the computer industry, there was change in the competitive structure of the marketplace. The presence of the Japanese manufacturers had altered the competitive nature of the industry. As had been the strategy in other industries, Japanese manufacturers entered the market at the bottom of the price structure. Because of lower labor rates and efficient production capability, the Japanese products forced extreme price pressure into the market. Once established, the Japanese manufacturers then began to "trade up" through product improvement and brand extension. As a result, the Japanese printer manufacturers became a formidable force in the marketplace, particularly in the microprinter (for personal computer use) segment. This set of competitors was a force all U.S. manufacturers of printers must have accounted for in the formulation of new product introductions and pricing strategies. A number of U.S. manufacturers had licensed "off-shore" (Mexican, Korean, Taiwanese, and Japanese) manufacturers to produce price competitive products under the U.S. manufacturer brand names as a means of competing with the Japanese manufacturers.

THE MARKET

The total market for printers of all types was predicted to be $10.44 billion in 1986. The breakdown of sales by printer type is shown in Exhibit 8. The market was segmented by impact (printers which use a printhead that actually strikes the paper) and non-impact (printers which do not strike the paper, but apply ink in some other fashion). Within the impact market, printers were also segmented by dot-matrix (printers which use dots to form the characters printed) and fully formed (printers which print an entire character at once, such as a "daisy wheel" printer). This market was further segmented according to whether a printer was a serial printer (one which prints character by character in a serial fashion) or a line printer (one which prints an entire line at a time—in general, line printers are called "high speed" and print faster than serial printers, but often at a lower quality); finally, the impact market segment was subdivided according to speed of printing. The non-impact printers were also segmented as page printers (those which print a complete page at a time). All non-impact printers were considered to have fully formed characters. A schematic representation of the complete market for printers is shown in Exhibit 9.

Besides print quality, different classes of printers had advantages and disadvantages for end users. Fully-formed character printers, whether daisywheel or band line, offered no graphics capability since they were limited to alphanumeric characters. These printers also were very noisy while printing unless special quietized enclosures were used to surround them. Additionally, daisywheel printers, which were found almost exclusively in offices for word processing applications, were extremely slow.

The primary drawback to dot matrix printers was perceived print quality, although a number of technological developments had improved their performance. These printers, however, supplied excellent adaptability to applications needs—graphics, spreadsheets, data and word

processing, for instance—and prices had been dropping very rapidly in this market segment.

Non-impact printers offered much of the best aspects of performance—quiet operation, flexible application, and outstanding print quality—but drawbacks included high prices, inability to print multiple copies simultaneously (i.e., continuous multipart forms printing), higher cost of operation because of their utilization of consumable supplies such as toner, and some perception on the part of users that non-impact printers, like the copiers their technology was derived from, were less reliable.

As advances in technology decreased the cost of non-impact printers, the growth of sales in these segments was expected to increase. The prices of nonimpact printers were still high relative to impact offerings, and the impact printers still enjoyed a speed advantage. However, the non-impact printers were much quieter than their impact counterparts, and the quality of their output was at least as high as the best fully-formed impact output. Exhibit 10 shows the characteristics of printer types, as compared against the "ideal" printer.

GENICOM PRODUCT LINE

By April of 1985, GENICOM primarily produced dot matrix impact printers, though $6,000,000 in 1984 revenue was derived from a 300 lpm fully formed character line printer. The company produced line and serial printers which could print from 60 cps in an office environment to 600 lpm in a high speed line printer used for volume production. Most of the GENICOM product line also offered letter-quality printing at slower speeds, so the machines were flexible, depending on the user's needs. GENICOM offered branded printers as peripheral devices, and produced OEM printers for a number of major customers. GENICOM's products generally were more expensive than those of their major competitors, but had higher performance capabilities and greater durability. GENICOM sales by product for 1984 are shown in Exhibit 11.

GENICOM COMPETITORS

GENICOM had a number of major competitors in each of the market segments it served. Its two major U.S. competitors were Centronics and Dataproducts, both competing essentially "head on" with GENICOM in almost every market segment. There were other, smaller com-

EXHIBIT 8 THE U.S. PRINTER MARKET

	1983			1986		
	# of units	(% share)	$ value	(% share)	# of units	(% share)	$ value	(% share)
Serial daisy wheel	712,000	25	1.37 billion	25	2,000,000	24	2.4 billion	23
Serial dot matrix	1,857,000	66	2.28 billion	41	4,600,000	54	4.14 billion	40
*Serial nonimpact	132,000	5	162 million	3	1,600,000	19	990 million	9
**Nonimpact page printers	5,200	0	222 million	4	150,000	2	1 billion	10
Fully formed line printers	86,000	3	1.13 billion	21	100,000	1	1.4 billion	13
Dot matrix line printers	31,000	1	318 million	6	55,000	0	510 million	5
Total:	2,823,000		5,482 billion		8,505,000		10.44 billion	

*Inkjet and thermal transfer printers.
**Laser and similar printers.
Source Datek Information Services Inc.

EXHIBIT 9 **Electronic printer market breakdown.**

Source: DATAQUEST, Inc.

petitors for special applications and certain of GENICOM's market segments. Exhibit 12 offers market share estimates for major competitors in each major segment.

END USER

The end user for GENICOM products was faced with a complex decision process in the choice of a printer. The current products operated faster, printed more legibly, and cost less than those of a few years ago. However, there were more machines to choose from, so the choice needed to be carefully made.

GENICOM MARKETING STRATEGY

GENICOM's general marketing strategy had been one of improving current products and expanding product lines rather than developing entirely new products or diversifying into new technologies. The strategy could have been characterized as "evolutionary" rather than "revolutionary." GENICOM's main distinctive competencies in the market had been flexibility in production and the quality of its products. They had traditionally been on the upper end of price points for similar products and had sought to gain market share by stressing the advantages their machines offered relative to the competition. Each of GENICOM's products offered some distinct advantage—speed, print quality, quietness, or flexibility—which was thought to offset price disadvantages.

GENICOM had an important presence in the OEM market, offering those customers a wide variety of choices regarding specifications for products. The GENICOM presence in the branded printer market was not so strong, though efforts were underway to increase the importance of that market.

EXHIBIT 10   **Personal computer printer trends: characteristics by technology.**

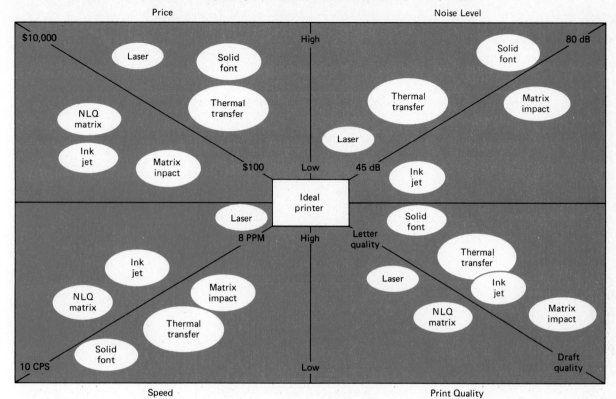

EXHIBIT 11   GENICOM 1984 SALES

Printers	$(000)		Units
340/510	5980		1749
200	8564		4016
2030	6131	}	
		}	9623
2120	5011	}	
3000	30924		20495
3014/3024	3879		5036
4000	—		—
Other	399		—
Subtotal	$ 60888		31296
Parts	16962		
Ribbons	7846		
Lease	18140		
Service	9380		
Printer Business Total			
	113216		
Relays	23426		
Company total	$136642		

EXHIBIT 12   MARKET SHARE DATA

Country of manufacture	Manufacturer	% share	Fully-formed	Dot matrix
	Market share (Units) U.S. serial impact printer market—1984			
Japan	Epson	20.1		X
	C. Itoh (TBC)	13.9		X
	Okidata	11.4	X	X
	Star	3.2		X
	NEC	2.4	X	X
	Brother	2.0	X	X
	Ricoh	2.0	X	
	Toshiba	1.1		X
	Canon	0.9		X
	Juki	0.9	X	
	Fujitsu	0.6	X	X
	Subtotal	58.5		
United States	Xerox	3.2	X	
	IBM	3.0	X	
	Texas Instruments	2.2		X
	DEC	2.2		X
	Teletype	2.0		X
	Qume	2.0	X	
	Centronics	1.6		X
	GENICOM	1.1		X
	Anadex	0.6		X
	Datasouth	0.4		X
	Dataproducts	1.6	X	X
	Subtotal	19.9		
Europe	Mannesmann	0.9		X
	Facit	0.5	X	X
	Philips	0.3		X
	Hermes	0.2		X
	Subtotal	1.9		
Other		19.7		
	Market share (Units) U.S. line impact printer market—1984			
United States	Dataproducts	31.0	X	
	IBM	23.0	X	X
	Teletype	8.0	X	
	Centronics	7.0	X	
	Hewlett-Packard	6.0		X
	Printronix	6.0	X	X
	GENICOM	1.5	X	
	Subtotal	82.5		
Japan	NEC	4.1	X	
	Fujitsu	1.6	X	
	Hitachi	0.7	X	X
	Subtotal	6.4		
Europe	Mannesmann	2.1	X	
Other		8.0		

EXHIBIT 12   MARKET SHARE DATA *(Continued)*

Market share (Units) U.S. non-impact printer market—1984		% share		Page	Thermal	Inkjet
Japan	Canon	17.3		X		X
	Okidata	17.0			X	X
	Star	12.8			X	
	Sharp	8.5			X	X
	Brother	4.5			X	
	Subtotal		60.1			
United States	IBM	8.0		X	X	X
	Hewlett-Packard	4.5			X	X
	Xerox	3.6		X	X	X
	Texas Instruments	2.5			X	
	Subtotal		18.6			
Europe	Siemens	3.5		X		X
	Honeywell	1.0		X		
	Subtotal		4.5			
Other			16.8			

EXHIBIT 13   **Domestic distribution channels.**

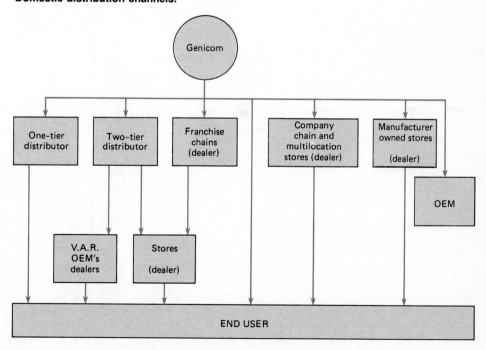

The product positioning of the GENICOM line had been for the professional user. Both for data processing and for word processing, the strength of GENICOM's product line had been in the commercial rather than the personal segments. The current product line was more durable, had more capability, and was more expensive than the bulk of the personal printer market. The GENICOM products could be compared to IBM office typewriters; they were generally considered "over-engineered" for the home market. GENICOM was giving some consideration to the personal printer market, to compete with Epson, Okidata, Toshiba and others. It recognized that among other factors a new product line, rather than modification of an existing product, would be necessary to compete in this highly price-competitive market.

Distribution

In early 1985, GENICOM products were distributed through a distributor network which focused on industrial users and on wholesale/retail distributors who serviced end user needs. Consideration was given to entering retail distributorship relations with large companies or with independently owned and franchised chains.

The GENICOM distribution system was not vertically integrated at that time. Although GENICOM had been contemplating expanding the distributor network slightly to effect better geographic coverage of markets, other plans suggested that they develop recognition of authorized dealers through the current distributor network. A schematic representation of the GENICOM distribution system is presented in Exhibit 13.

While prices and margins for dot-matrix impact printers had been dropping as market pressures grew, the future could be said to be nothing but certain. Curtis Powell considered the union negotiations a critical turning point in the firm's history.

Appendix 1: The United Effort

Negotiations Report

On Tuesday afternoon the negotiating committee met with Relations and a lawyer to start contract talks. Right away, without putting any paperwork on the table, this lawyer wanted us to tell him ways management can cut *four dollars an hour* off the cost of labor. According to him, the cost per hour, including wages and benefits, is fourteen dollars an hour and this is "significantly higher" than other workers are making in Waynesboro and must drop to ten dollars total of wages and benefits. He was even so helpful as to offer selections, like a smorgasbord, if you will, of items from which *we* could decide where to make the cuts.

For our consideration he laid out: rate cuts, night shift differential pay, vacation time cuts and other paid time off, give up bump rights, retraining, premium pay for some overtime, call in pay, medical benefits and the list goes on. All he wants *us* to do is decide where to cut to come up with a four dollar price cut. He pointed out that the wages in the lower job rates are much too high and will have to be cut to make us more comparable with other wage earners in Waynesboro.

Based on the claim that GENICOM needs for us to cough up four dollars worth of wages and benefits, we naturally figured the company was going broke so we asked a question about the financial condition of the business. The reply was contrary to what you might suspect based on them wanting cost cuts. It turns out that the company is *making* money but wants to make *more* money and in order to do that they want to get into our pockets.

Just as we figured, when the word got out in the plant, you became furious to think that the company would be so greedy as to come after the wages and benefits you have worked years for and some of you even walked a picket line for a hundred and two days in 1969 to get. There is a growing demand from the union membership to hold work stoppages to protest these unrealistic demands by management and it appears the time will come for that kind of action! The next meeting with management is scheduled for May 6th and Boris "Red" Block will be here for that meeting. We will have a full membership meeting the next day, Tuesday, May 7th, to let you know what is going on and how negotiations are progressing. At that time we will be *led by the membership* about what action you want to take.

After we listened to what management had to say about their thoughts we laid out our proposals and informed them that the list was only a partial list of what we think is needed in a new contract. Some of what we are looking at includes strong job security language, improvement in pensions and downward adjustments in our contributions to the pension plan, a better severance pay clause, insurance coverage to be nothing less than we now have, improvements in S&A benefits, cost of living clause, contract language improvements and a general wage increase. And, as we pointed out, there are other things we are looking at which we will lay on the table later. What happens in negotiations and what we are able to do is directly dependent on you and how much support you are willing to give.

It's your Local and "The Members Run This Union!"

Appendix 2: The United Effort

The Members Decide

At the end of the second session of negotiations management still insists on demanding a $4.00 an hour wage and benefit concession from you. They set the record straight so there would be no mistake in anyone's mind we were told "we are taking it." We asked time and time again what they would do with the $4.00 if they can take it and we were told rather matter of factly, "we are going to put it in our pockets." It's not that GENICOM didn't make a profit last year, it's just plain and simple they just want to add an additional $3200.00 an hour to their pockets (300 employees × $4.00 per hr. = $3200.00 an hour) at your expense.

At a full house special membership meeting, 1st and 2nd shift, the committee was instructed to take a secret ballot strike vote. We normally keep the meetings to one hour but due to the number of members who wanted to speak, the meeting lasted well over the normal length of time and then a vote was taken, which was in favor of a strike action. As we have said before, this local doesn't have a history of strike action but the workers at GENICOM feel they have no choice but to fight on the issues of wages and working conditions in this plant. Management some time ago decided to cut the rate of the mold machine operators from R13 to R9 and it seems this only whet their appetite to want to take even more. We filed a grievance and processed it through the required steps of the grievance procedure and we will be taking action on that grievance at the proper time of which you will be notified.

We don't need to tell you how important it is for everyone to support the strike action. The issue is over a rate cut on one job but remember, the bigger issue is now management is saying they are going to cut $4.00 off of everyone in wages and benefits. Whether they can get away with it or not depends on you and everyone in the plant. The stakes are high and it's up to you to decide. Do you just fork over the $4.00 in wages and benefits or do you join your fellow workers and fight?

Shop Steward Election

There will be a meeting at Jim Durcin's desk today, five minutes before the end of lunch break, to nominate and elect a shop steward.

Appendix 3: GENICOM Printer Flash

To All Employees:

In response to the excessive amount of publicity in the local press concerning GENICOM's negotiations with the UE Local 124, the following advertisement will appear in tomorrow's Waynesboro News-Virginian and Sunday's Staunton News Leader. We felt you, as GENICOM employees, should be the first to have this information.

What's Really Happening at GENICOM

GENICOM and its negotiations with Local 124 have been the subject of much discussion in our community and among GENICOM employees in recent weeks. All the information to this point has come from the Union. Since so much is at stake for GENICOM, its employees, and our community, we believe management should do its best to assure that the people who may be affected understand what is happening—and why.

GENICOM is a Waynesboro company that is dedicated to remaining a Waynesboro company. That dedication is reflected in GENICOM's proposals to UE Local 124 to establish a wage and benefit program that will allow GENICOM to meet competition while providing GENICOM workers with wages and benefits in line with community standards.

As part of the negotiations process, GENICOM provided wage survey data to Local 124 on both GENICOM's national competition and its Waynesboro neighbors. Reflecting that data, GENICOM's proposal includes job rates from $6.50 to $12 per hour, three weeks paid vacation, eight holidays, medical and dental insurance at a cost of $4 per week to employees, a defined benefit pension plan with limited contributions by employees, as well as company paid life and disability programs.

Starting in 1954, and for nearly 30 years, General Electric Company conducted manufacturing operations at the current GENICOM facility in Waynesboro. Under General Electric, wages were negotiated on a national basis. As a result, Waynesboro wage and salary costs reached levels which are out of line with the electronics industry and with the Waynesboro community. GENI-COM Corporation was formed to operate the Business purchased from G.E. GENICOM is now managed by people who are committed to establishing and maintaining a successful and profitable business—because it is our only business. In the 19 months since GENICOM acquired its business, it has been operated on a profitable basis. This was particularly true in 1984, when the market for computers and related equipment was robust. The Business is less profitable now that its market has become much softer and competition for sales of electronic products such as GENICOM's has become very intense. GENICOM management is determined and committed to reducing costs and competing.

These cost reductions can be accomplished either by moving operations to GENICOM's existing lower cost locations or by lowering costs in Waynesboro. GENI-COM has decided to stay in Waynesboro. The wage and benefit concessions requested will make Waynesboro a competitive manufacturing location—a manufacturing location with a future. These concessions will not be easy or insignificant for GENICOM workers to accept, but they are not unreasonable. Competitive wages will make operations in Waynesboro much more economically attractive for GENICOM and increase GENICOM's incentive to maintain and expand those operations, thus offering more job security to Waynesboro workers and greater stability to the Waynesboro community.

C.W. Powell
President and chief executive officer
GENICOM Corporation

Appendix 4: The United Effort

GENICOM Should Tell It Like It Is, Instead of Wanting To Pocket 6½ Million Dollars of Its Employees and the Community

That's what Genicom wants in concessions from the hourly workers. Genicom said that's not all. They are going to get a like amount from the lower paid salary workers and supervisors.

Not once have they said they are going to cut top paid Genicom employees such as Mr. Powell.

Genicom says they are dedicated to remaining in Waynesboro. If that is so, why have they moved over 600 jobs to Mexico, and continue to move jobs out of Waynesboro. They say they need concessions from their employees to do this. But they refuse to put in writing to the Union that these concessions will keep jobs in Waynesboro.

Instead the Company tells us they want to "put the money in their pockets". They go on to say they will use some of this money to buy other plants in other states. This will not bring jobs to Waynesboro. The Company is going to run the plants where they buy them. Not once has the Company said they would bring jobs back from Mexico with the $4 per hour concessions that they want.

The Truth Is!

The Company proposal to the Union means 2 less paid holidays per year, it means that most employees would lose 2 weeks paid vacation per year. All employees would take pay cuts. So Genicom families would take cuts of $12,000 per year. As for the pensions and the insurance, the proposal is to leave it as it is now. The Company proposal would take away all of the night shift bonus, the few sick days workers have now, and would do away with rest breaks.

If the company really means that they will bring more jobs to Waynesboro, they should be willing to put it in writing.

If the Company really means to have greater stability for the Community they should reinvest the extra profits in the Genicom Waynesboro plant. Not take the money and buy plants in other states.

Genicom would like the Community to believe that GE negotiated the last Union contract. *THAT IS NOT SO. GENICOM NEGOTIATED THE LAST CONTRACT.* Mr. Stoner of Genicom Management was part of the last negotiations and he is part of this negotiations. Mr. Stoner plays a big part in negotiations.

The Company admits in their paid ad that they made money with the last Union Contract. They could make money with the new contract that has no cuts.

It's time for Genicom to put in writing to its employees that the Company will keep jobs in Waynesboro. Genicom is making a profit. They should let the employees keep what they have. There should be NO CUTS. Workers should keep their 6½ Million Dollars. This would keep the money in the Community. Not take it to other States and Mexico.

If Genicom takes this money and "puts it in their pockets," merchants will lose, taxes for other people in the Community will go up and everyone in the Community will lose.

Only top management like Mr. Powell will gain when they line their pockets with our money at Community expense.

Appendix 5: GENICOM

June 13, 1985

This letter was mailed to all hourly employees on 6/14/85. This copy is for your information.

TO: OUR GENICOM EMPLOYEES AND THEIR FAMILIES

I would like to take this opportunity to express my appreciation for the patience being displayed by the majority of our employees during a very difficult time in which we are negotiating a new labor agreement.

GENICOM and its Management team remain dedicated to the resolution of differences with UE Local 124 and the adoption of a new collective bargaining agreement through the negotiation process. Nevertheless, in reflecting on Local 124's recent newsletter concerning strike preparations, we feel compelled to offer our thoughts on some questions and other appropriate subjects that should be addressed by the Union's lawyer at Sunday's meeting.

Question: Is the Company required to pay wages to strikers during an economic strike?

Answer: No, the Company is not required to pay wages to economic strikers.

Question: Is the Company required to pay the premiums to continue health insurance, life insurance and other benefits for strikers during an economic strike?

Answer: No, the Company is not required to continue payments for benefits to economic strikers.

Question: Are economic strikers eligible for Virginia unemployment benefits during an economic strike?

Answer: No, state law disqualifies employees involved in a "labor dispute."

Question: Is it possible for the UE to guarantee that GENICOM will change its proposals because of strike action?

Answer: No, negotiations are a give and take process that may remain unchanged in the face of employee strikes or Company lockouts.

Question: If there is no agreement for a new contract by June 23rd, is the Company required to keep the current contract in effect?

Answer: No, at that time the Company may unilaterally implement its final proposal.

Question: Can economic strikers be permanently replaced by new workers if the Company decides to continue operations without them?

Answer: Yes, federal law allows a company to continue operations with new employees. The law also does not require the Company to discharge those employees to allow returning strikers to resume their jobs. Replaced strikers who indicate they wish to return to work on the Company's terms may fill open positions if any exist or be placed on a hiring list ahead of non-employees.

Once again let me say we, as GENICOM's Management team, remain dedicated to reaching agreement with UE Local 124 *without* any strike action. However, we are also dedicated to continue the growth of a viable business in Waynesboro. In order to accomplish this, we *must* reduce our cost structure to a level that will allow GENICOM to meet our competition.

Currently, the demand for our printers is poor due to a downturn in the computer market and foreign competition. This market situation, and GENICOM's decision to maintain Waynesboro as our primary production location, demand the changes we have proposed to the UE.

We have furnished wage data on Waynesboro and our national competition to the Union negotiating committee establishing that our proposals are competitive with both Waynesboro and national rates.

Under one proposal, wages would run between $6.00 per hour and $11.50 per hour and benefits would remain at current levels or slightly better. In recognition of the economic impact that such concessions may have, we have offered alternative proposals such as eliminating sick days, night shift differential and afternoon breaks. These reductions would increase the wage proposal to between $6.50 and $12.00 per hour. All other benefits would remain the same or slightly better.

We hope that our employees, their families and their collective bargaining representatives will consider all these factors before taking any action that could be injurious to both the Employees and the Company.
Sincerely,

Curtis W. Powell
President/Chief Executive Officer

Appendix 6: Genicom seeks workers; union claims 'a threat'

By Sergio Buston
Staff Writer

WAYNESBORO—Genicom's advertisement in area newspapers seeking immediate applications for production and maintenance workers was seen as "a threat" Monday by a union representative as negotiations between both sides continue toward a June 23 contract deadline.

The company advertised in two newspapers, including The Daily News Leader today, seeking immediate applications for production and maintenance employees "to fill regular, full-time positions."

The company is advertising "an excellent compensation package, including competitive pay rates, beginning at $6.50 per hour, up to $12 per hour . . ." It also offers medical and dental benefits as well as up to three weeks paid vacation.

"We figure it's a threat—a form of intimidation." said George Stevens, the union representative for United Electrical Radio and Machine Workers local 124. He said he was "not surprised" by management's action.

"We are still a long way apart in negotiations." added Stevens, who said Monday's negotiations saw no changes in management's position.

"It's still the same basic proposal of a $4 cut in wages and benefits," said Stevens.

Genicom management officials would not comment when reached Monday.

William Freeman, union president, however, said management's latest move would "intimidate workers" and result in their not joining further work stoppages. He added it "was a definite threat" and "was not expected."

"I imagine it (management's action) would work," said Freeman, who said Monday's negotiation session between the two was "terrible."

"I'm amazed that each offer (from management) is worse than the one made before," said Freeman.

Management's action is similar to the action taken by the McQuay division of Snyder General in April when its workers went on strike.

Following six days of striking, however, McQuay union workers agreed to a three-year contract after management threatened to hire non-union workers.

Negotiations between Genicom management and the union began late in April and will continue until June 23, according to Stevens.

HARDY AND JUNCKER, INC. A CORPORATION OF CERTIFIED PUBLIC ACCOUNTANTS

Jeffrey A. Barach
Tulane University

INTRODUCTION

"Since graduating from Trinity University and starting my own business, I have wanted to recount my experiences for a case study," Kenneth Juncker explained. "This happens to be a particularly tumultuous period for my business and a time of personal dilemma. I hope to obtain valuable feedback concerning the future viability of my firm and the effect the firm's status will have on my personal options."

KENNETH JUNCKER

Kenneth Juncker was an accountant in his early thirties. Although born in Chicago, his family moved to San Antonio, Texas, while he was a child. He was raised in a middle-class suburb which mushroomed in the '50's and '60's. Juncker attended a suburban public high school. He was a fraternity brother of Clement Hardy's at Trinity University, and, after serving in the military, he by coincidence worked at the same local office of a "big eight" accounting firm that Hardy had initially joined.[1]

CLEMENT HARDY

Clement Hardy was also an accountant in his early thirties. He had been born in San Antonio, Texas, and raised in a typical white middle-class environment. Hardy had attended a large central-city Catholic high school. He had continued his education at Trinity University. After graduation he had worked at the local office of a "big eight" accounting firm until he decided to establish his own business.

ENVIRONMENTAL BACKGROUND

San Antonio, Texas, was a metropolitan area of one million plus population located approximately 125 miles from Mexico and the Gulf coast. Over the last 25 years San Antonio had experienced nearly a three-fold growth in population and now ranked tenth among U. S. cities. The population comprised approximately 51% Mexican-

[1]The "big event" in order of generally agreed size ranking were Peat, Marwick, Mitchell & Co., Arthur Andersen & Co., Coopers & Lybrand, Haskins & Sells, Touche Ross, Price Waterhouse & Co., Ernst & Ernst, and Arthur Young & Co.

American, 40% Caucasian, and 9% mixed racial minorities, many of whom were bilingual. Three of the fifteen radio stations and one of the five television stations broadcasted in Spanish.

The city of San Antonio was governed by a city-manager-council form of government. The nine council members were the only elected officials in the city government. The Mexican-American segment of the community was gaining political control and having an impact on the tax structure and redistricting efforts. Contained within the city limits of San Antonio were five incorporated cities with a population of approximately 22,000.

There were nine independent public school districts serving metropolitan San Antonio. In addition there were Catholic, Protestant, non-denominational and military private schools. San Antonio boasted eight institutions of higher learning; five universities, two junior colleges, and a permanent extension of the National University of Mexico. The total college and university population of San Antonio was in excess of 33,000.

Although there was 8½% unemployment, there were approximately 400,000 people employed in San Antonio. The major employers included five military installations (Kelley Air Force Base being the largest single employer in San Antonio), a fast growing medical industry, diverse manufacturing (executive aircraft, church furniture, storage batteries, stained glass windows, clothing, food processing, steel forms, food handling equipment, commercial refrigeration, electronic data processing, leather, cement, chemicals, and paper), tourism, trade, and service industries. San Antonio was also a leading livestock center and one of the largest produce exchange markets in the U. S. These factors had made San Antonio the banking, transportation, and trade center of south central Texas.

Within the accounting profession San Antonio was served by 35 accounting firms employing approximately 300 Certified Public Accountants. The 35 firms ranged from entrepreneurial ventures through Alexander Grant & Co. and Seidman & Seidman which had branches in many other cities but did not have "big eight" stature to four offices of the "big eight": Peat, Marwick, Mitchell & Co., Haskins & Sells, Touche Ross & Co., and Ernst & Ernst.

The accounting profession like other service professions in San Antonio was characterized by a low key, low pitch atmosphere. Social contact played an important role. It was thought to be difficult for a newcomer to succeed in a new service business.

There were approximately 50 businesses which provided tax return preparation services in addition to five branches of Beneficial Finance Company and 14 offices of H&R Block Company. Many of these businesses provided year round tax and bookkeeping services. Twenty per cent were owned and operated by Mexican-Americans.

San Antonio offered a variety of cultural attractions that included a symphony orchestra, institutes of Texan and Mexican culture, the Witte Museum, and the McNay Modern Art Institute. There were professional sports teams: the National Basketball Association "Spurs," the North American Soccer League "Thunder," and the minor league baseball "Brewers." The social event of the year was Fiesta, held for nine days each spring.

FIRM FORMATION: AUGUST 1974–DECEMBER 1974

In August, 1974, Clement Hardy began practice as an independent CPA. Hardy's office was in his home. His initial business consisted of 40 accounts, of which 30 were individual tax clients. Three of these accounts were major accounts acquired through referral from a local office of a "big eight" accounting firm.

Business grew faster than Hardy anticipated. He was interested in finding someone to share the expanding work load. Although Hardy and Kenneth Juncker had not kept in close touch since college, they met occasionally at social gatherings. On several occasions Hardy mentioned to Juncker his increasing business and the need for a partner. Juncker was currently employed at a "big eight" accounting firm as a Senior Assistant managing small audits and working as staff on large audits.

By October, 1974, Hardy and Juncker became serious about forming a partnership. In assessing their present positions, they concluded that Hardy could contribute:

1 CPA.

2 Seven years experience (2 years part-time, 5 years full-time) with a "big eight" accounting firm.

3 Five months experience as an independent accountant.

4 Forty current accounts.

5 Professional library.

6 Office equipment.

7 Office space in his home.

8 Cash.

And Juncker could contribute:

1 CPA.
2 Two and a half years experience with a "big eight" accounting firm.
3 General business experience from military service.
4 Client development skills.
5 Superior technical ability.
6 Cash.

Both were confident they could handle a wide variety of business from write-ups[1] to tax accounting, audits, and management consulting. Hardy had demonstrated expertise in the area of tax, which he particularly enjoyed. Juncker favored auditing and management consulting. However, they were both anxious to work in all areas of accounting during the formative stage of their new venture.

Forecasts for the potential new firm were made. Hardy formulated annual revenue projections by multiplying the industry's standard number of working hours per year by an acceptable fee (Exhibit 1). Hardy's projections in-

cluded a couple of expected annual "biggies" along with routine work. Juncker felt these projections were too optimistic. He thought it was more realistic to project below capacity with a growth factor added for expansion. However, when Juncker weighed their relative business experience, he deferred to Hardy's judgment.

Before leaving his current job, Juncker wanted assurance of a reasonable probability of 1) firm survival, 2) salary, 3) future growth potential, and 4) management responsibility. Based on his projections, Hardy assured Juncker on these points.

The men decided to form a firm with Hardy and Juncker each holding 50% ownership. The option to incorporate under Subchapter S of the Internal Revenue Code was not elected.[2]

In December, 1974, Hardy and Juncker gave a Christmas party for friends and business acquaintances to an-

---

[1]Basically bookkeeping and supporting functions.

[2]Election to be taxed under the provisions of Subchapter S would have allowed the losses (as well as profits) from operations to pass through directly to the income tax returns of the shareholders rather than losses being "locked in" (or profits taxed) at the corporate level as they would be in the conventional to incorporation which was chosen.

EXHIBIT 1

HARDY'S FORMULA FOR PROJECTED ANNUAL REVENUE

$$\frac{\text{Number of hours}}{\text{able to work}} \times \frac{\text{Reasonable}}{\text{rates}} = \frac{\text{Projected annual}}{\text{revenue}}$$

Hardy's projected annual revenue:
    2080 hours/year × $25/hour = $52,000

Juncker's projected annual revenue:
    2080 hours/year × $20 hour = $41,600

Total projected annual revenue:	$93,000
*Billing: Approximately 85% of total possible revenue (93,600 × .85)	$79,560
**Collection: Approximately 90% of total billings (79,560 × .90)	$71,604
Net annual projected revenue	$71,604

*85% of time billable as work done for clients. 15% of time devoted to administrative and development work.
**10% estimate for write-off for goodwill development and bad debt.

EXHIBIT 2 *THE AMERICAN INSTITUTE OF CERTIFIED PUBLIC ACCOUNTANTS CODE OF PROFESSIONAL ETHICS CONTAINS A SECTION ON ADVERTISING.*

Rule 502—*Solicitation and Advertising.* A member shall not seek to obtain clients by solicitation. Advertising is a form of solicitation and is prohibited.

Some methods within bounds of Accounting ethics which could promote new business are:

1 Join national and local accounting organizations (i.e., National Accounting Association).

2 Produce quality work which yields satisfied clients.

3 Talk to old and new friends (there are definite and strict limitations about what can be said—i.e., it is prohibited to suggest that a friend leave his current accountant and bring his business to you).

4 Publish articles in professional journals. (This method enhances professional stature more than it develops new business.)

5 Teach courses in Accounting.

6 Join civic and social organizations.

nounce, promote, and celebrate the new corporation. On January 2, 1975, Hardy and Juncker, Inc., officially opened for business in Hardy's home.

FIRM DEVELOPMENT: PART I
JANUARY 1975–SEPTEMBER 1975

Hardy's current accounts formed the core of the new firm's business. The two men agreed that their present strategy for acquiring new business should be to accept "anything and everything" that was not absolutely unreasonable. Eventually they envisioned the luxury of selectivity. They then hoped to provide a greater proportion of such services as total revamping of antiquated accounting systems which would require full use of their skills and potential future facilities. Hardy and Juncker thought many firms in the city needed this type of accounting service.

At the present time they felt that ongoing development of new business from all possible sources was important to the survival and growth of the firm. Hardy thought the best promotion was through excellent work which would yield repeat clients and new clients by word-of-mouth. Juncker concurred with this idea but also wanted to pursue a more active strategy within the constraints of accounting ethics (Exhibit 2). Business lunches and dinners at reasonably priced restaurants and an occasional play or sports event with bankers, attorneys, and personal friends were Juncker's ideas of effective and ethical development. Hardy and Juncker decided to adopt and pursue both approaches.

The developmental strategy and other heavy demands

on Juncker's time were taking a toll at home. Marital problems which existed prior to the firm's formation were increasing during January and February 1975. Juncker and his wife separated briefly in March 1975, attempted a reconciliation in April, and then separated permanently in May 1975.

Although Juncker was distracted by personal problems, he and Hardy felt the firm's prospects looked good and they enthusiastically discussed expansion. There was enough routine business to require assistance for the current staff,[3] and new accountants could participate in development.

Additional financing was necessary for expansion. During February and March 1975, Hardy and Juncker negotiated with their bank. A developing relationship with officers of the bank and the firm's expansion potential enabled them to obtain $15,000 in cash and a $10,000 open line of credit. The loan required Hardy and Juncker to sign notes as owners of the firm and to sign personal continuing guaranties for the debt.[4]

Concurrently with the bank negotiations, Hardy and Juncker actively searched for additional accountants. A friend of Juncker's, Roberto Buras, who was working at the "big eight" accounting firm Hardy and Juncker had

---

[3]Staff: 1 part-time junior staff (35 hours per week)
1 part-time junior staff (student)
1 part-time secretary/junior staff (student)

[4]The usual requirement by the banking industry for persons entering into entrepreneurial ventures was that the entrepreneur must personally countersign any notes of the entrepreneurial corporation.

recently left, was interested in the job. Both men liked Buras, knew his qualifications, and felt that a Mexican-American would add a new dimension. On March 16, 1975, Buras joined the firm.

At the same time, Hardy and Juncker were talking to Sidney Bays, with whom they had also previously worked. Bays declined their offer because of personality differences and because he questioned the short term viability of the firm.

A full-time secretary was hired to augment the staff.

Besides the routine work, Hardy and Juncker, Inc., had four large accounts in the spring of 1975. The largest was a motel chain client acquired in April 1975 who they expected to generate cash flows of $15,000 for at least one year. A financial planning consulting firm appeared to have the greatest growth potential and was a significant factor in Hardy's and Juncker's expansion decision. The three referrals from a large accounting firm had promise, and a small construction company audit had growth pos-

sibilities. Projections of revenue from these clients, the bank financing, and the cash flow from anticipated new business was expected to more than cover their expenses. Hardy and Juncker planned to continue to draw full salaries as they had from the beginning (Exhibit 3). A move to larger quarters also appeared feasible now.

Both men felt a better and more spacious location was appropriate for their rapidly developing firm. Negotiations were begun for the rental of one fourth of a floor in a below-capacity occupancy office building with a good location. A favorable contract was concluded whereby Hardy and Juncker, Inc., occupied a portion of the floor immediately and the landlord was restricted to leasing the remainder on an annual basis. This arrangement allowed Hardy and Juncker to review annually the decision to expand their office space.

Hardy and Juncker spent considerable time arriving at the final office design which included detailed plans for expansion. A current client in the office furniture business

---

EXHIBIT 3

PROJECTIONS FOR HARDY AND JUNCKER, INC.—MAY 1975

1 Routine revenue
  a Retainer work:
    approximately $1000/month
    projected average growth $250/quarter

2 Contracts
  a Motel chain
  b Financial planning consulting firm
  c Small construction company

3 Negotiations
  a $11,500, cash flow expected to begin June 1975

4 Tax season
  a $11,500, cash flow February through August

5 Bank loan
  a $15,000 cash
  b $10,000 line of credit

Gross receipts minus expenses (excluding salaries) for next twelve months:

	Optimistic	Pessimistic
Net:	$85,000	$72,000
Staff salaries:	$33,000	$33,000
	$52,000	$39,000

gave the firm a "good deal" on furnishings. Each man had his own office and personally selected his color scheme, draperies, and wall coverings. The final touch was a large double oak entrance door.

The new quarters exuded feelings of confidence and success. Clients appeared to react favorably, which gratified everyone. Hardy was especially pleased that former fellow workers could witness concrete evidence of his recent achievements.

FIRM DEVELOPMENT: PART II
SEPTEMBER 1975–OCTOBER 1977

During the fall of 1975 Buras, who had participated in development work since joining the firm, increased his efforts in this area. With Buras as a member of the firm, Hardy and Juncker, Inc., qualified as a minority small business,[5] and the city government and a federal minority manpower agency were happy to have Hardy and Juncker, Inc., bid for small government contracts. Hardy and Juncker, Inc., got one small "trial balloon" contract which gained them entrance into the Mexican-American business community in San Antonio. Hardy and Buras saw enormous growth potential in contracts for federally funded programs, contracts for minority small businesses, and the growing Mexican-American business community. Buras had personal contacts within the city government and several federally funded agencies which could facilitate such development.

The future was full of potential, but during the fall of 1975 there was a cash flow problem. Hardy was worried. Juncker was out of town on business three days per week from September 1975 to January 1976. Hardy felt the best solution to the cash flow problem was to work diligently on current accounts. He was averse to any other kind of developmental work during this period, and he discouraged Juncker and Buras from doing development work at the expense of servicing current clients. He often said, "We can't afford a developing partner and accountant who sell and do not work." Moreover, Buras was becoming ineffective in development and work because of marital problems that soon led to separation. Hardy was managing the firm. He resolved the cash flow problem by not

remitting to the IRS money withheld from employees. At the time, no operating statements were routinely prepared for internal use. Juncker asked for internal operating information, but due to the work load and his personal problems, he did not insist on the information.

By January 1976 the firm was managing by crisis. To alleviate the immediate cash flow problem, Hardy and Juncker decided to 1) delay payment of their debts, 2) apply pressure on those who owed the firm, 3) complete current work in a timely manner to realize immediate revenue. Still, their operating plan was vague. Bankruptcy of the motel chain client delayed expected revenue from this source for several months. Ultimately, the firm collected all but a small percentage of the total fee.

Hardy and Juncker each continued to draw full salaries of $1665 per month, although occasionally between January and November 1976 they had to defer their salaries for thirty days.

The tax season of 1976 helped the firm get by. During the summer of 1976 a "walk-on client" brought in $12,000 for an audit, and the award of a $26,000 city contract brought the largest contract ever. Even with these contracts, there was just enough business to squeak by, but the cash flow was not there.

In June 1976, Hardy negotiated with the IRS for payment of $13,000 in back payroll withholding taxes. An agreement was reached whereby Hardy and Juncker, Inc., would pay $1000 per month. While Juncker concurred with Hardy's initial decision not to remit the withholding taxes, he did not feel that Hardy negotiated a realistic settlement. In fact, the firm paid $1000 per month for only two months.

Throughout the spring and summer of 1976, Buras' marital problems had a detrimental effect on the firm; in September, he took a job out of town. He assumed the status of a part-time employee with Hardy and Juncker, Inc., which provided him occasional income and allowed the firm to maintain the minority small business classification. He realized the firm could not support him full-time. Also, Buras was in the midst of a difficult separation from his wife.

By November 1976, the cash flow crisis was acute. Hardy and Juncker could no longer draw their monthly salary. Instead, irregular "loans to the shareholders" in the average amount of $400 per month each were paid.

A government contract in February 1977 for $10,000 and the tax season of 1977 kept the firm viable. By June 1977, the tax revenues ran out and work on the government contract was neglected while revenues from the con-

---

[5]Because Hardy and Juncker, Inc., had a Mexican-American accountant in the firm, they qualified as a minority small business. This was an advantageous situation because it made them eligible for certain government contracts that were, for all practical purposes, available only to such businesses.

tract were accelerated. The possibility of imminent bankruptcy faced the firm. Juncker stopped servicing clients and pursued development in an effort to determine the possibility of keeping the business going. Hardy preferred to plug away at the meager work available. In May 1977, Juncker decided to personally borrow money to live on rather than bankrupt the firm. He thought his development work would start to yield adequate cash flows by the fall of 1977.

In September 1977, Juncker renegotiated with the IRS for payment of $16,000 in back withholding taxes. A settlement was reached whereby Hardy and Juncker, Inc., would pay $400 per month through May 1978. A renegotiation was planned at that time with the expectation of increasing payments to a maximum of $600 per month.

In October 1977, Juncker also renegotiated with the bank for a realistic payment schedule on the loan secured in March 1975 to aid in the corporate expansion. The agreement called for the signing of a new demand note of $32,000 payable June 1, 1978. Monthly payments of $600 ($320 in interest, $280 in principal) were due until May 1978 when renegotiation was scheduled.

At the same time, Juncker prepared extensive cash flow projections for the next twelve months (Exhibit 4). These figures represented Juncker's best estimate of the short term viability of the firm.

During September and October 1978, Juncker devoted 75% of his time to negotiations, projections, and development. Only 25% of his time was spent servicing clients. Hardy suggested to him in late October that he "better get back to work." Juncker replied, "If I hadn't been doing all this, we wouldn't have any work to get back to."

KENNETH JUNCKER: BACKGROUND AND PERSONAL GOALS

"You now know the background and the current situation of Hardy and Juncker, Inc.," Kenneth Juncker continued. "However, before you can offer any constructive suggestions to help me assess the situation and make my decisions, I think you need to know more about me."

Juncker characterized himself as a "communicator." He eagerly sought interactions with others. There were many occasions now for social interactions in his professional life, and Juncker particularly enjoyed this. His sociable nature and penchant for marketing made development work easy and enjoyable.

Juncker taught accounting at the permanent extension of the National University of Mexico because he desired to contribute to the academic community, and he enjoyed teaching. His exposure to the Mexican-American community was beneficial to development, and the salary at this point was useful.

In the short term, Juncker was willing to work an inordinate number of hours. However, this willingness was founded on the belief that an investment of time and the foregoing of the consumption of time today would result in a greater ability to consume time in the future. This consumption would satisfy personal needs of teaching, family, and leisure.

Where Juncker would invest his time was dependent upon certain decision criteria. He valued time more than money. The future return of time would influence where he invested his present time. Another criterion was that an activity be intellectually challenging and interesting.

The physical location of his work was also important. The regional climate, recreational opportunities, potential life style, professional associates, and personal relationships would be factors to consider.

Juncker lacked a burning desire to become "top man" of an organization. He did not want the responsibilities, work load, and time commitment this achievement entailed. He was willing to allow someone else to be the managing partner if he was competent and if Juncker maintained equal status.

Juncker was not willing to "eat, sleep, and live" a business venture. However, he was willing to shoulder a certain amount of risk as he expressed, "I am young and smart and could easily start over."

KENNETH JUNCKER: PERSONAL DILEMMA

What action should Juncker take to realize the personal goal he has set for himself? These personal goals were of paramount importance and the motivation behind his professional aspirations.

Should Juncker remain with Hardy and Juncker, Inc.? This could be a conditional decision influenced by the probability of success of Hardy and Juncker, Inc., or it could be an absolute decision. Until he reached a decision on his future with the firm or the firm failed, Juncker had to have a means of support. His personal sources of income (savings and personal loans) were totally exhausted. He felt justified in determining to take $1250 per month out of Hardy and Juncker, Inc., as salary.

EXHIBIT 4 HARDY AND JUNCKER, INC. REVENUE AND EXPENSE PROJECTIONS
September 1977–August 1978

	Sept.	Oct.	Nov.	Dec.	Jan.	Feb.
Routine:						
Write-ups	1700	1800	2200	2300	2900	3100
Special projects	2000	1500	1500	1000	1500	1000
Total	3700	3300	3700	3300	4400	4100
Tax	—	—	—	—	—	500
City contracts:						
Contract #1	—	600	—	—	—	—
Contract #2	—	800	—	—	—	—
Contract #3	—	3000	3000	3000	3000	3600
Contract #4	—	—	—	—	—	—
Federal government projects						
Project #1	—	2600	—	—	—	—
Project #2 (?)	—	—	—	—	—	—
Independent company projects						
Project A	—	—	—	—	—	—
Project B	2300	3500	2500	1000	500	500
Total	6000	11200	11800	7300	7900	8700
Carryfwd. from prior mos.	—	1200	5100	8900	8000	7700
Total	6000	12400	16900	16200	15900	16400
Expenses:						
Routine operating	—	4400	4600	4800	4800	4800
IRS	—	400	400	400	400	400
Bank (principal only)	—	—	500	500	500	500
Total	4800	4800	5500	5700	5700	5700
Partner draws	—	2500	2500	2500	2500	2500
Monthly excess carryfwd.	1200	5100	8900	8000	7700	8200

A major, if not the pivotal point that influenced Juncker's short term decision to remain with the firm was Hardy's house. Hardy had obtained a second mortgage on his home in order to secure the firm's major debt. Initially, Juncker felt morally obligated to do everything possible to prevent Hardy from losing his home through the bankruptcy of the firm. Although he considered Hardy's home an extraordinary risk that he did not share in kind, he was embittered by the events of the past year. Juncker felt Hardy lacked compassion by equally dividing the business proceeds when he (Hardy) had considerably greater outside income. Hardy's other sources of income, including his wife's salary, totaled $23,000 annually. Juncker's total income for the twelve month period, November 1976 to October 1977, derived from the firm, personal loans and savings was $8,000. Juncker had concluded that a house was only "sticks, stones, and mortar and could always be replaced."

The dissolution and bankruptcy of Hardy and Juncker, Inc., would have a definite impact on Juncker's ability to achieve his personal goals. Since Juncker personally undersigned the debt of the corporation, a corporate bankruptcy would result in a personal bankruptcy. This stigma would be difficult if not impossible to erase. Of greater consequence could be $13,000 in outstanding "trust fund" payroll taxes withheld that had not been paid to the Internal Revenue Service. These obligations would not be erased by bankruptcy, but would become the personal responsibility of the corporate officers. Each person would be liable for 100% of the amount due (agreement of equitable sharing would be valid only among the officers).

If Juncker decided to leave Hardy and Juncker, Inc.,

EXHIBIT 4 (*Continued*)	Mar.	Apr.	May	June	July	Aug.	Year total
Routine:							
Write-ups	3300	3500	3600	3700	3800	3900	
Special projects	1000	1500	1500	1000	1000	1000	
Total	4300	5000	5100	4700	4800	4900	51300
Tax	1500	3500	1500	1000	500	500	9000
City contracts:							
Contract #1	—	—	—	—	—	—	600
Contract #2	—	—	—	—	—	—	800
Contract #3	—	—	—	—	—	—	15600
Contract #4	—	—	3000	3000	3000	3000	12000
Federal government projects:							
Project #1	—	—	—	—	—	—	2600
Project #2 (?)	—	—	—	—	—	—	—
Independent company projects:							
Project A	500	500	500	500	500	500	3000
Project B	500	500	500	500	500	500	13300
Total	6800	9500	10600	9700	9300	9400	108200
Carryfwd. from prior mos.	8200	6700	7700	9800	11000	11800	
Total	15000	16200	18300	19500	20300	21200	
Expenses:							
Routine operating	4900	5100	5100	4900	4900	4900	
IRS	400	400	400	600	600	600	
Bank (principal only)	500	500	500	500	500	500	
Total	5800	6000	6000	6000	6000	6000	68000
Partner draws	2500	2500	2500	2500	2500	2500	27500
Monthly excess carryfwd.	6700	7700	9800	11000	11800	12700	12700

he had identified the following potential options: 1) controller and part owner of a small California corporation that supplied wearing apparel on a sub-contract basis to a major labeler, 2) manager or partner in one of two existing medium-sized CPA firms, one in San Antonio, the other out of state, 3) member of the internal audit section of an international firm based in New York City, 4) financial analyst for a large firm in New York City. All of these positions offered annual salaries in the $20,000 to $30,000 range. Some of these opportunities were available only for a short time, others were available for a longer period.

Juncker had also identified two small companies in need of a turnaround that were looking for a chief operating officer. Each offered approximately $30,000 salary and part ownership. In addition, Juncker had sent a resume to a professional "head hunting" firm in New York City with a request for a survey to identify firms searching for someone like himself. Included in this material were general statements concerning Juncker's personal goals, company goals, business environment, and lifestyle that Juncker felt were important.

Efforts to develop Hardy and Juncker, Inc., into a viable ongoing concern would be beneficial even if Juncker decided to later leave the firm. He would be able to leave from a position of strength without feelings of guilt and would be better able to sell his share of the business.

CONCLUSION

"You now know Hardy and Juncker, Inc.'s predicament. You also have information about my personality, background, and personal goals and are aware of my personal dilemma," Kenneth Juncker stated.

"One obvious course of action for me would be to leave Hardy and Juncker, Inc., face the chain of bankruptcies, let the chips fall where they may, and start over somewhere else doing something else. But I could never and would never do this now.

"In reality I am looking at a decision point one year from now. At that time, I think the firm will begin to turn around, and I could leave without the severe repercussions of today. Or alternatively, I could stay.

"Deep down inside I want Hardy and Juncker, Inc., to be the success I envisioned it would be when we began. But is this wish possible? And does it suit my personality?

"What action needs to be taken so that Hardy and Juncker, Inc., can succeed? Where did we go astray initially? What pitfalls of the past should we avoid in the future? What strategy do you recommend and what tactics should be employed—both for the short term survival/development of the firm and for long term development of a career suited to my personality and perceived lifestyle?"

HONEYWELL, INC. IN BRAZIL

Delbert C. Hastings
University of Minnesota

"How can we stay in Brazil?" was the question put rhetorically by John May, Honeywell's Vice President and General Manager for Latin America one day in early 1981 at the firm's Minneapolis headquarters. "Their informatics policy and protectionist exclusions are driving us into Guanabara Bay."

"Yes, but we've got to hang on," responded Edson Spencer, Chairman and CEO of Honeywell. "The long-run prospects are still very promising and I doubt we could get back in if we withdraw."

Brazil's actions of 1979 and succeeding years had indeed made Honeywell's situation in that country precarious. In 1979 Brazil had established regulations and a regulatory body aimed at boosting quickly Brazil's position and capabilities in a field they called "Informatics." The term covered anything having to do with computers, chips and their applications, all sizes and varieties of hardware and components, software, and digital telecommu-

This case was prepared by Delbert C. Hastings (with the assistance of Esra Gencturk) as a basis for class discussion rather than to illustrate either appropriate or inappropriate handling of an administrative situation. The U.S. Department of Education funded the preparation of this case under Grant #C00877027.

nications, digitalized equipment and instruments in many lines. The regulatory bodies, the regulations and their applications were developed and extended year by year in the 1980s.

The Informatics product lines were at the heart of Honeywell's business, and Brazil's computer development policies might therefore have been expected to benefit Honeywell in Brazil. But aims of the regulations were highly restrictive. *Domestic* development of technology in these lines was the keynote: Brazilian firms, Brazilian products, Brazilian technical expertise. The ultimate aim was to put Brazil's computer technology, skills and products on a level with the leading countries of the world.

Brazil's development strategy in this field involved making selective use of foreign firms and technology. The regulations were designed to impede international and foreign firms that were operating or seeking to operate in Brazil in the product lines in which Brazil wanted domestic expertise. Foreign firms were permitted to operate in Brazil only to the extent that technological knowledge, skills and productive capabilities were transferred to or built up in Brazil.

Foreign and international firms were controlled by issuance or denial of licenses to operate in a desired product or service line. Denial of a license forced the firm out of that product line and perhaps out of Brazil. This was the situation that Honeywell found itself facing. The situation had become increasingly difficult as the regulations and regulatory bodies were developed and modified in the early 1980s, and as the regulatory bodies denied a series of Honeywell's carefully prepared applications but approved arrangements with selected competitors.

In part Brazil's government policies were *defensive,* owing to endemic problems of capital shortage, inflation and shortages of foreign exchange. In part they were *forward-looking,* as Brazil sought to boost its people's welfare by speeding economic development. And in part they were *aggressive,* as Brazil sought the capability of keeping up with world technology.

Honeywell's top managers were convinced that Brazil was a country that would repay strenuous efforts to "stay in." Brazil is a major country, with a huge area and a large and growing population. It has vast resources, even now not fully explored, and it is well along in industrialization. Though Honeywell's annual revenue in Brazil had never exceeded $15 million, Brazil's promise as a future industrial power could not be ignored.

Honeywell had operated in Brazil since 1958. It built its business on selling control products and systems, made or assembled in its São Paulo plant from imported or locally made parts. The business itself and the importation of parts were now being severely threatened. A complex web of factors involving Honeywell and its Brazilian subsidiaries, the Brazilian government agencies enforcing the Informatics policy, and the history, culture and politics of Brazil must be grasped in order to understand the situation fully.

THE COMPANY: HONEYWELL'S CORPORATE ORGANIZATION AND OPERATIONS

Organization

Honeywell, operating in 85 country-markets in its centennial year of 1985, has been an international company at least since 1930, when it acquired an office in Toronto, Canada (though it had begun exporting a decade earlier). In recent decades it has become one of the world's leading business firms, providing computer, control, and communication systems and services to customers around the globe. Its main business falls into four industry segments. These segments constitute the firm's macro organizational structure. Honeywell's 1984 Annual Report describes them as follows:

Aerospace and Defense includes the design, development and production of guidance systems and controls for

military and commercial aircraft, space vehicles, missiles, naval vessels and military vehicles.

Control Products includes microelectronic and electromechanical components and products for residential, commercial and industrial applications which are marketed on an individual product basis to wholesalers, distributors and original equipment manufacturers.

Control Systems includes sophisticated commercial building and industrial systems, both analog and digital-computer based, which are designed for data acquisition, monitoring, control and management of customer processes and equipment.

Information Systems includes products and services related to electronic data processing systems for business, governmental and scientific applications.

In addition to these four, the organization includes an International Controls unit, operated as a separate unit but related in products to both the Control Products and the Control Systems units. International Controls is subdivided into four geographic divisions, as noted in Exhibit 1 (facing). The Information Systems has its own International Group, and the Aerospace and Defense division also handles its own international matters. Numerous foreign subsidiaries exist. Thus the skeleton organizational structure of Honeywell Inc. is set out in Exhibit 1.

Honeywell High-Tech Trading Inc. is a recent (1984) addition to the International Controls division. Organized as an export trading company under recent U.S. law, it exports products of clients, engages in various forms of countertrade and represents Honeywell products in countries not otherwise covered.

In 1984 the International Controls Division operated plants in 33 locations, had offices in 40 countries around the world and had distributors in 52 additional countries. Its factories are located in Australia, Belgium, Brazil, Canada, France, Germany, Japan, Mexico, the Netherlands, Singapore, Spain, Switzerland, Taiwan and Thailand. In 1984 the International Controls division had 14,934 employees out of a Honeywell corporate total of 93,514. International Controls is headed by J. E. Chenoweth, an Executive Vice President of Honeywell.

International Controls, Latin America division, is of special interest here since it includes Brazil. The division has plants in São Paulo, Brazil, and Chihuahua and Mexico City, and also operates 100-percent-owned subsidiary companies in Argentina, Brazil, Mexico, Puerto Rico, Venezuela and Uruguay.

In this case it is necessary to distinguish carefully be-

EXHIBIT 1   **Honeywell, Inc.'s corporate structure.**

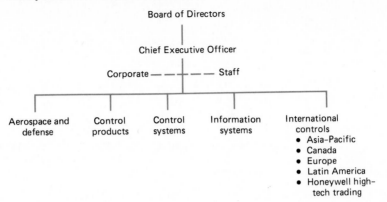

tween Control Products and Control Systems, as well as between the commercial and industrial applications of such products.

Control Products manufactures high-unit-volume individual products and markets them through direct sales or through distributor networks. These products become Original Equipment in many applications. The catalog of Control Products' MICROSWITCH division lists over 50,000 sensors, switches and controls, used in manufacturing, materials handling, automotive ignition, commercial products, business machines, aerospace, ordnance and marine equipment. Control Products' Energy Products division specializes in controls and systems for retail stores, offices, restaurants and supermarkets (referred to as "light commercial" applications). The Residential division specializes in air-quality-and-comfort controls and systems for homes. Thus Control Products markets individual products both to industrial users and to commercial and residential applications. Control Products does not in general sell systems for heavy industrial use.

In contrast, Control Systems emphasizes systems rather than individual parts. This division commonly contracts with buyers to provide complete custom-designed control systems for large industrial and commercial uses. A control system might be a complex set of sensors, valves, meters and communications lines to a central microprocessor to control a complete steel mill as well as to display and record results, or to provide controls over heating and cooling, air purification, fire detection, security and other aspects of a major office building or building-complex. Process control and process manage-ment functions are major industrial applications. Control Systems has been expanding into communications systems, including internal telephone, telecommunications and computer network systems. This division includes the Honeywell/Ericsson Development Company, an R&D joint venture with the Ericsson Group of Stockholm, Sweden. Control Systems is thus centrally involved in investments to increase efficiency and quality and to effect technological improvement in both industrial and commercial operations. Thus the Control Systems division also markets to both industrial and commercial users, but is more involved in industrial process control and in large projects.

Both Control Products and Control Systems (and hence International Controls) depend for their main markets on their buyers' capital investment projects (though the replacement market is also important). Hence the investment climate and availability of investment capital in their market areas are highly important.

Honeywell's Financial Performance

Honeywell's 1984 revenues totalled $6.074 billion, moving the firm into 56th place among Fortune 500 U.S. industrial companies, up from 60th in 1983. Exhibit 2 provides a financial and operating overview by line of business from 1980 through 1984. Exhibit 3 gives data by major geographic areas. Both exhibits are taken from Honeywell's 1984 Annual Report.

EXHIBIT 2 HONEYWELL, INC. CONSOLIDATED CORPORATE FINANCIAL AND OPERATING DATA BY MAJOR
PRODUCT LINES, 1980–1984
(Millions of U.S. Dollars)

	1984	1983	1982	1981	1980
			Revenue		
Aerospace & defense	$1,608.0	$1,540.0	$1,258.3	$1,103.5	$ 996.3
Control products	1,024.5	890.4	822.0	854.7	888.1
Control systems	1,615.8	1,570.8	1,622.1	1,529.4	1,351.2
Information systems	1,825.3	1,666.1	1,684.7	1,773.7	1,634.1
	$6,073.4	$5,667.4	$5,387.1	$5,261.3	$4,869.7
			Operating profit		
Aerospace & defense	$ 116.2	$ 109.0	$ 87.4	$ 77.2	$ 62.1
Control products	141.1	83.0	79.3	82.1	132.9
Control systems	135.9	134.9	187.2	175.0	150.4
Information systems	179.7	130.8	79.8	158.3	183.5
Operating profit	572.9	457.7	433.7	492.6	528.9
Gain on sale of interests in Cii-Honeywell Bull & GEISCO	—	—	90.8	—	—
Unallocated items	(142.0)	(100.2)	(133.5)	(135.9)	(119.7)
Income before income taxes	$ 430.9	$ 357.5	$ 391.0	$ 356.7	$ 409.2
			Assets		
Aerospace & defense	$ 800.5	$ 701.8	$ 674.4	$ 478.1	$ 367.1
Control products	671.3	661.5	584.6	584.3	600.2
Control systems	1,074.1	972.9	930.7	899.7	815.0
Information systems	1,310.4	1,322.6	1,369.1	1,371.4	1,340.6
Corporate	841.9	885.3	769.8	893.8	701.5
Discontinued operations	61.6	119.6	126.8	86.7	60.4
	$4,759.8	$4,663.7	$4,455.4	$4,314.0	$3,884.8

Honeywell's Corporate Policies

Honeywell's business philosophy is rooted in the marketing concept. Its 1984 Annual Report states, "Honeywell is an international corporation whose mission is to work together with customers to help them achieve their goals through leadership in automation and control."

Honeywell's commitment to leadership in its product lines and market areas is firm. As stated in its 1983 Annual Report, Honeywell intends to participate in market segments only where it can serve the needs of its customers as leader or—at worst—sharing leadership. A statement to a prospective joint-venture partner set this out as follows: "Honeywell is willing to take risks in new products, new businesses, and new markets, but always with the long-range objective of leadership in mind. After a period of time operating in the risk mode, if such a goal is unattainable, we may withdraw from such segments."

The company's long-term financial objectives include an 18 percent return on equity and a 14 percent return on investment, with a debt ratio not to exceed 30 percent.

Guided by this philosophy, Honeywell believes that its long-term success can be assured only through the effectiveness of its products, through cost controls, and through continuously developing new technology so as to insure maintenance of its leadership position.

Achievement by Honeywell of its leadership in Brazil has been put in question in recent years. Persistent infla-

EXHIBIT 3　HONEYWELL, INC. CORPORATE FINANCIAL INFORMATION BY GEOGRAPHIC AREAS
1984, 1983 AND 1982
(Millions of U.S. Dollars)

	1984	1983	1982
External revenue			
United States	$4,514.6	$4,179.9	$3,885.3
Europe	1,059.7	1,059.0	1,022.4
Other areas	499.3	428.5	479.4
Totals	$6,073.6	$5,667.4	$5,387.1
Transfers between geographic areas			
United States	$ 265.3	$ 220.6	$ 241.9
Europe	29.9	22.9	16.6
Other areas	19.5	24.7	14.1
Totals	$ 314.7	$ 268.2	$ 272.6
Total revenues			
United States	$4,779.9	$4,400.5	$4,127.2
Europe	1,089.6	1,081.9	1,039.0
Other areas	518.8	453.2	493.5
Eliminations	(314.7)	(268.2)	(272.6)
Totals	$6,073.6	$5,667.4	$5,387.1
Operating profit			
United States	$ 417.9	$ 320.9	$ 259.7
Europe	108.0	80.6	128.8
Other areas	54.9	50.9	30.9
Eliminations	(7.9)	5.6	14.3
Operating profit	572.9	457.7	433.7
Gain on sale of interests in Cii-Honeywell Bull and GEISCO			90.8
Unallocated items*	(142.0)	(100.2)	(133.5)
Income before income taxes	$ 430.0	$ 357.5	$ 391.0
Identifiable assets			
United States	$2,900.2	$2,794.4	$2,675.1
Europe	812.8	783.7	791.2
Other areas	363.7	357.1	356.9
Corporate	841.9	885.4	769.8
Eliminations	(158.8)	(156.9)	(137.6)
Totals	$4,759.8	$4,663.7	$4,455.4

*Interest expense, and general corporate income and expense.

tion, devaluations, currency shortages and the emergence of protectionist regulations implemented through Brazil's "Informatics" Law have made it hard, if not yet impossible, for Honeywell to continue its business operations there. Some background in Brazil's history, culture and political development is useful for understanding Honeywell's strategic moves during the first half of the 1980s and their ill-fated outcomes.

THE COUNTRY: BRAZIL

Brazil has been transforming itself from a primarily agricultural into a major industrial nation, producing iron and steel, heavy machinery, automobiles, weaponry, electronics, food products and consumer goods. It is now the eighth largest free world economy (GNP equal to about U.S. $250 billion or $2000 per capita in 1981, a recession year). Its estimated 131 million people made it the world's sixth most populous country in 1985. In area, its 3,286,000 square miles make it just smaller than the U.S. (3,615,000 sq. mi.), and fifth largest in the world. It extends 2965 miles north-south, 2691 east-west, occupies nearly half of the South American continent, and borders every South American country except Ecuador and Chile (see Exhibits 4 & 5). It has vast quantities of minerals, agricultural land, forests and fisheries as well as human resources.

1968 to 1974—The "Economic Miracle" Years

With these vast human and natural resources, Brazil has been portrayed by many as the land of the future. Such contentions were further reinforced between 1968 and 1974, referred to in Brazil as the "Economic Miracle" period, when Brazil's GNP increased at the impressive annual rate of 11.5 percent and manufacturing output rose at the even higher rate of 18.9 percent. These high rates resulted in part from expansionary government policies and from reemployment of manufacturing capacity idled in 1967. In addition, a substantial expansion of world trade and a high level of capital inflow created a favorable international environment. Brazil's exports increased an average of 27 percent a year while exports of manufactured products rose 38 percent annually. Moreover, this rapid economic growth was accompanied by declining inflation and only a modest rise in external debt.

Brazil's current situation is best understood in terms

EXHIBIT 4   **Map of Brazil.**

EXHIBIT 5   **Map of South America.**

of history and political background. Brazil's (as the U.S.'s) history starts in Europe in the 1400s.

Historical and Political Background

The discovery of Brazil occurred as part of the "Age of Exploration" of the late 15th and early 16th centuries, with the discovery of sea routes around Africa, Columbus' voyage to the Caribbean, and extended exploration of the New World. The original chief participants were rivals, Spain and Portugal. Potential and actual conflicts in territorial claims between the two countries were settled in 1494 by the Treaty of Tordesillas which gave Portugal the lands east of and Spain the lands west of a dividing line 370 leagues west of the Cape Verde Islands. This treaty made Brazil the only Portugese-speaking country in the New World.

In 1500 Admiral Pedro Cabral discovered and claimed for Portugal the territory of Brazil (its coast lay east of the Tordesillas line). Early development by a system of "captaincies" was followed by crown colony status under a royal governor-general. A sugar industry based on African slave labor soon flourished; by 1600, 120 sugar mills were operating in Brazil. The native Indians were also enslaved, but their numbers were soon decimated by disease. Jesuit missionaries sent to convert the Indians soon became their advocates in both Brazil and Portugal. Inflow of Europeans began.

Exploration of the interior continued, especially by the legendary Bandeirantes of São Paulo. Their explorations and settlements pushed Brazil's western boundary to the Andes foothills, far beyond the Tordesillas dividing line. A frontier economy based largely on cattle-raising developed. The sugar plantations and cattle ranches gave rise to the typical elite owner class and working/slave class.

French, Dutch, English and Spanish incursions into Brazilian territory were fought off. When the conflicts were finally settled, the recognized territory of Brazil extended to the Andes foothills on the west, the River Plate on the south, and nearly the entire Amazon basin on the north. Spain ruled Portugal from 1580 to 1640. Afterward conflict with Spain over territory in Brazil's south continued until a final division created the country of Paraguay. This conflict recurred sporadically for years.

Gold and diamonds, discovered and mined since 1693 in Minas Gerais state enriched Portugal's royal coffers. The Jesuits, opposing Indian enslavement, were judged too influential and were expelled in 1759. Cotton and coffee became important exports during the 1700s. Immigration from Europe continued.

The year 1789 (notable in the U.S. and Europe as well) brought initial stirrings for independence in Brazil. The Portugese royal family fled to Brazil in 1807 during Napoleon's invasion of their kingdom. When the royal court was able to return to Lisbon in 1820, it sought to reestablish Brazil's former colonial status. The Brazilians again sought independence and achieved it peaceably in 1822. A constitution adopted in 1824 legitimated Dom Pedro as emperor but also set the precedent, continued in all Brazilian constitutions, of indirect election (via "electors") of some officials, diluting popular participation and now much disputed.

Brazil remained an empire until 1889. The first emperor, Dom Pedro I, authoritarian and unpopular, was soon forced to abdicate. The second, Dom Pedro II, ruled well and popularly for his first 25 years. However, a disastrous war with Paraguay put him in a bad light and had the unexpected effect of raising the Brazilian army as a permanent political force. Slavery was abolished in 1888, but the process weakened Dom Pedro's standing. His deposition in 1889 ended the empire. A republic was then set up, and a constitution modeled on that of the United States was adopted in 1891. But strife continued and the government was under military dictatorships until 1893. A revolt then permitted a civilian president to take office;

this form of government endured until 1930. During that period, Brazil sided with the Allies in World War I.

In 1930 Getulio Vargas overthrew the civilian government and set up a dictatorship which lasted until 1945. After several Brazilian ships were sunk by German submarines, Brazil entered World War II on the allies' side. Brazil lent airfields and naval facilities, and Brazilian troops fought valiantly in the Italian campaign.

Vargas was deposed by the military in 1945. A succession of elected presidents then held office until 1964. Pressures toward more effective mass participation in the political system continued. The latter three presidents—Kubitschek, Quadros and Goulart—were increasingly leftist, and a socialist revolution of uncertain variety seemed imminent. In 1964 the military forces and two state governors, acting to forestall such an outcome, declared a (nonviolent) revolution and deposed Goulart. These nonradical "revolutionaries" undertook to restore economic and financial order, to remove Communists from government and to bring about "moral regeneration." Union officers, mayors, governors, bureaucrats, legislators and former presidents were arrested. Democracy, respectability and legal status of government were, however, stated goals of the military revolutionaries.

This military government lasted 21 years, from 1964 to 1985, with five army generals ruling in turn. But the economic troubles of the 1970s, skyrocketing oil prices, increasing foreign debt and intractable inflation ended confidence in military leadership. In the later years, the military did aim at restoring civilian rule (under the term "abertura" or "opening") and ultimately planned and carried out an election. With the decisive Electoral College vote of January 15, 1985 Tancredo Neves was elected president, to succeed General Figueiredo. Jose Sarney was chosen vice president. But Neves, aged 75 and in poor health, was hospitalized on inauguration day (March 15, 1985), and died on April 21, 1985. He was quietly succeeded by Sarney.

Observations Arising from Brazil's History

1 Brazil's political-cultural background has been elitist. Adhering to a strict class system, Brazilians follow the tradition of honorable, generous and responsible behavior associated with high rank on both. The country has slowly evolved toward democratic political structure, with impulses toward rapid and extreme political change mediated by the guiding presence and frequently the overt

action of the military forces. The social conflicts implicit in this process are important factors in the continuing instability of the Brazilian political system.

2 The all-important military has long had and continues to have a special position, role, and ideology in Brazil. Under the constitutions of 1891, 1937, 1946 and 1967 the military was recognized as a guardian of Brazil not only externally but internally. After 1889 the military asserted their role as guarantors of constitutional government, in the name of the people, even though often violating constitutional status in the guarantee process. Meanwhile, the military forces evolved (primarily in the officer corps) from elitist toward middle class (but significantly not lower class). Officer training and schooling is thorough and rigorous. The process has produced many able officers and, through a system of selective attendance at upper level military schools by civil officials, has strongly influenced the higher levels of the civil administration also.

3 The military governments have stood for both stability and change, pushing economic development perhaps more successfully than do civilian governments. The extended military intervention from 1964 to 1985 may have forestalled conversion to some form of socialism. While accompanied by a modest level of resistance and strife, this special military role is accepted in Brazil more than in other Latin American countries.

4 Strong government interventions in and guidance of the Brazilian economy, including government establishment and continued ownership of significant firms is also of long standing, and is considered normal. Current interventions in the economy are in no way unusual. For a "nonsocialist" country, the list of government-owned firms is extensive, but not unusual for Latin America.

5 Prohibitions against foreign firms in specific operations or industries have been present since colonial times. Thus current prohibitions against multinationals are not unusual.

6 While Brazil has tremendous natural resources, it has had and continues to have a concomitant tremendous need for capital to develop these resources. Because of the country's vastness and lack of significant petroleum deposits, its transportation system (railroads, roads and highways) and its energy and power sources are insufficient for current operations and future development. Consequently it has put its capital into large infrastructure projects—electric power, development of alcohol production as a substitute for petroleum, development of offshore oil fields, development of iron mines for exports—all

holding significant promise for the future but not yielding immediate increases in needed consumption goods or exports (except in the case of iron ore).

7 Internally generated capital has met only a fraction of the country's needs. Forced to draw on external sources, Brazil has accumulated large foreign debts. Debt service requirements bring the inevitable shortages of foreign exchange, import restrictions (even when imports of capital and capital goods would be to its great advantage) and export campaigns (even when its lower classes need homes and food). These forces have rendered Brazil highly vulnerable to world economic downturns such as that of the early 1980s.

8 Throughout its history, Brazil has suffered successive boom-and-bust swings in sugar, cotton, cocoa, rubber and coffee. Capital has been accumulated in such industries only to be dissipated in the downswings. Economic stability has been a stranger to Brazil.

9 Despite all these difficulties, Brazil has achieved major industrial growth in recent decades, especially in iron ore, steel, automobiles, machinery, soy beans and military goods.

10 Population growth has been rapid during the past 50 years (2.47 percent in the early 1980s; U.S. under 1 percent). The 1980 census showed Brazil, with a population of 119 million (U.S. 228 million), to have 17 million wage earners (U.S. employment of 101 million) out of a work force of about 50 million (U.S. 108 million). Brazil's population is skewed to pre-working age children and young adults. While Brazil has large areas to be populated, its economic development has lagged, yielding high unemployment and inadequate housing, education and social services. High infant mortality and illiteracy continue. This imbalance between population growth and economic development is perhaps Brazil's greatest enduring problem and, with the political features cited above, the source of much of its continuing instability.

11 An estimated 90 percent of the population is baptized Roman Catholic; Brazil is the largest Roman Catholic country in the world. The clergy has been a force for amelioration of the conditions of the poor but, with a few notable exceptions, has not been highly active politically.

12 By at least the 1930s Brazil perceived itself as having a "manifest destiny" to become a leading nation. Its size and resources, and its able people and significant accomplishments have led outside observers to the same conclusion. Although achievement has been difficult, the goal strongly influences current Brazilian public policy.

13 Brazil's national pride runs high. Brazil seeks self-

development and independence of foreign countries, institutions and firms.

> "In Senator [Roberto] Campos view, support for the [1984 Informatics] protectionist legislation was so overwhelming because of Brazilian national pride and the country's anger at its dependence on foreigners.
>
> " 'When our country feels it has suffered external humiliation, for instance, bankers at the door, the IMF imposing austerity measures, the result is an outburst of nationalism—an outburst against those imposing the humiliation.' " (*Financial Times,* November 5, 1984)

But this understandable pride and self-confidence runs counter to Brazil's needs for capital, for economic development, and for the technology available only in the more highly developed industrial countries. These conflicting and emotionally charged goals have created major internal stresses in government policy-setting as well as restrictions laid on foreign and multinational firms. In external affairs the same conflicts recur with foreign banks, with the IMF, and with multinational enterprises striving to operate in Brazil.

14 Despite the facts that Brazil's development runs perhaps a half century behind that of the U.S. and that its southern European flavor creates significant contrasts to the stronger northern European influences in the U.S., Brazil and the United States share distinct similarities. The two are sibling New World countries of European parentage, with large areas and great natural and human resources, with admixtures of African and native American racial stocks and cultural attributes. Both adopted the goals of industrialization and, broadly speaking, of democracy. Brazil's constitutions and military organization have been patterned significantly on those of the U.S. Both performed on the Allied side in two world wars. It is little wonder that ties between the two countries have been and continue to be strong.

Current Economic Conditions in Brazil

Brazil's five and one-half years of miracle growth came to a sudden halt during the latter part of 1974. Economic problems beginning then (and still continuing) stemmed in large part from the quadrupling of oil prices, which induced general world recession and financial problems in many countries of the world. These problems were most severe in underdeveloped countries and in those without domestic oil sources. World inflation resulted, since oil was so important an input to all economies. The grossly higher oil prices caused oil-poor Brazil immediate difficulties in paying for its imports.

(NOTE: About half of Brazil's imports have been of crude oil and products, since Brazil had very low oil production until the offshore developments of 1983 to 1985. *Financial Times* data of November 5, 1984 show that in 1973 total Brazilian consumption of crude oil ran at 790,000 barrels per day and domestic production was about 175,000 b/d, 22 percent of consumption. By 1984 consumption was about 960,000 b/d and domestic production was 460,000 b/d, 48 percent of consumption. Thus Brazil is gradually improving its oil situation.)

Thus, in the mid-1970s Brazil's balance of payments stringencies imposed constraints on growth while inflation accelerated to unprecedented levels. The major recourse to sustain growth was to borrow from abroad. Brazil's foreign indebtedness increased sharply in the 1970s, expanding nearly fourfold between 1973 and 1978. Gross external medium- and long-term indebtedness equalled U.S. $53.8 billion in 1980.

The Second Oil Crisis and the 1980–81 Recession

The second-round (1979–1980) oil crisis, coupled with high interest rates accelerated Brazil's already mounting debt. Each year more loans were rolled over rather than repaid. Brazil suddenly developed a need for new earning power for foreign currencies, a need not yet fulfilled by late 1982. The total medium- and long-term external debt stood at U.S. $61.4 billion at the end of 1981. This trend continued at an accelerated rate: Brazil entered 1983 with a foreign debt of over U.S. $83 billion; it rose in 1984 to $90 billion, and in early 1985 to about $100 billion, the largest foreign debt of any Third World country.

Brazil was not alone. An international financial crisis loomed at this time, since other Third World countries such as Yugoslavia, Poland, Mexico and Argentina were also deeply in debt. International aid was required, with the IMF, BIS and groups of developed countries striving to avoid breakdown of the world monetary system and debt repudiations. A "cartel of debtors" was proposed. But with global private and public cooperation debts were stretched out, payments postponed, and a crisis was averted. IMF credits were arranged, but reduced government spending and other austerity measures were enforced as a prerequisite to the actual advance of funds to countries.

Brazil's Debt Management Problems

The country's growing foreign debt, balance of payments difficulties, and economic instability planted the seeds of its current austerity program and import curbs. In 1974, at the end of Brazil's miracle growth period, the trade balance turned sharply negative by U.S. $4.7 billion. Restrictions on imports and export incentives were implemented. In 1980 the nominal average tariff on manufactured imports was boosted from 47 percent to a range of 23 to 203 percent, averaging just above 100 percent. As a result, Brazil's trade deficit was reduced to U.S. $2.8 billion by 1980. In 1982 a trade surplus of $775 million was achieved because of government policies that further restricted imports, encouraged exports, and induced domestic recession.

In the same year, President (General) Figueiredo reaffirmed the government's commitment to a $6.0 billion foreign trade surplus in 1983. The goal was overmet by 1984's trade surplus of $13 billion. But by 1985 Brazil had been in a severe recession for five years and its debt problems persisted.

"Brazil is scheduled to resume talks with bankers early next month on the package to stretch over 16 years some $45 billion in principal foreign debt payments falling due between 1985 and 1991. The current democratic government inherited . . . the pact from the previous military regime.

"More pressing is an agreement with the IMF on an economic austerity program that must underpin any bank accord. The IMF suspended emergency credits to the country last February, after Brazil repeatedly failed to meet economic targets stipulated by its three-year, $4 billion IMF agreements."

Inflation, just under 100 percent at the end of 1982, was again in triple digits in 1983. The consumer price index rose by 210 percent in 1983, 220 percent in 1984 and an estimated 250 percent in 1985. Brazil continued indexation of wages, prices, and interest rates to offset the effects of inflation.

Brazil's currency is nominally tied to the U.S. dollar. But inflation required a policy of weekly mini-devaluations of the cruzeiro, averaging 2.5 percent and with occasional larger devaluations.

Exhibit 6 gives summary figures on Brazil's balance of payments for the period 1977–1980 while Exhibit 7 gives estimates for Brazil's balance of trade for the years 1982–1985.

Role of Government in the Brazilian Economy

Brazil's near hyperinflation noted above traces to the public finance imbalance of its miracle growth years. In striving for faster growth than permitted by domestic capital and resources, the government had run high budget deficits. Part arose from subsidies required to cover losses of the 500 or so companies (called "parastatals,") wholly or partly owned by the federal government. Some states (similar to the U.S.) also formed companies, particularly banks, to aid the steer development in their areas. Governments at various levels also took over and frequently subsidized other firms so as to provide essential goods and services at low cost. But curbing hyperinflation called for even greater reductions in government expenditures. Thus, the 1982 austerity measures included reductions in credit and subsidy programs, fixed interest rates and changes in the Salary Law, which had indexed salaries to inflation.

The parastatals, however, still played a dominant role in Brazil's economy. Of the top 200 Brazilian firms in 1980, 82 were under partial or total government control. Furthermore, these parastatals accounted for 76 percent of the total net worth of the top 200 firms. These firms accounted for a large part of Brazil's new investment and many private Brazilian firms depended heavily on them for business.

Foreign firms also continued to find that their largest customers were among the nearly 500 parastatal bodies. Hence while the austerity program was designed to reduce the investment spending by the Brazilian government in 1981, the parastatals were responsible for about one-half of the nation's foreign debt and 29 percent of fixed investment. The public sector deficit, which Brazil expected to reduce to 8.8 percent of GDP in 1983, was nevertheless continuing at the 1982 level of 15.5 percent. As noted above, many of the public firms were unprofitable (steel, nuclear energy), and their subsidies added to the public deficit.

Investment by private Brazilian companies and multinational firms was expected to dampen the recession caused by the austerity program. However, private investment slowed during the mid-1980s because of the eco-

EXHIBIT 6   BRAZIL'S BALANCE OF PAYMENTS, 1977–1980
(Millions of U.S. Dollars)

(A + sign in parentheses indicates a source of foreign exchange,
a − sign indicates a use.)

	1977	1978	1979	1980
Current account				
Exports (+)	$12,120	$12,659	$15,244	$20,132
Imports (−)	12,023	13,683	18,084	22,961
Balance on merchandise trade	97	−1,024	−2,840	−2,829
Interest payments (net) (−)	2,462	3,344	5,347	7,150
Other payments for service (net) (−)	1,672	1,647	1,834	2,200
Balance on current account	−4,037	−6,015	−10,021	−12,179
Capital account				
Direct foreign investment (net inflow) (+)	810	1,071	1,491	1,202
Brazilian loans abroad (net)	−267	−357	−610	568
Medium- and long-term loans (net inflow) (+)	940	988	759	1,011
Financial credits (net inflow)	3,690	7,857	4,606	4,440
Other capital movements	−506	718	560	1,459
Balance on capital account	4,667	10,277	6,806	8,680
Change in currency reserves	630	4,262	−3,215	−3,499

Source: Adapted from *Brazil, A Country Study,* U.S. Army, 1983.

nomic and political uncertainties. Net direct investment inflow into Brazil, $1.5 billion in 1979, was down to $1.2 billion in 1980 and was estimated to be under $500 million in 1983.

Brazil's stated policy was to encourage foreign investment for its impetus to growth, industrial development, and contribution to the balance of payments. The policy has favored joint ventures, and gave additional advantages (e.g., in credit arrangements) to joint venture firms with majority local capital. This policy line had induced a number of multinational firms to take on Brazilian partners.

However, the austerity measures and the growing distaste for direct foreign participation and investment in high technology industries created political uncertainty for foreign firms. In 1983, the third year of Brazil's recession, the economic and politically hostile environment created major concerns among the multinationals in Brazil.

EXHIBIT 7   BRAZIL'S EXPORTS AND IMPORTS 1982–1985
(Millions of U.S. Dollars)

	1982	1983	1984e	1985e
Exports	$20,175	$21,900	$26,500	$26,000
Imports	NA	15,400	13,500	14,500
Balance on merchandise trade	NA	6,500	13,000	11,500

Sources: 1982, 1983, International Monetary Fund, *Financial Times,* Nov. 5, 1984
1984, 1985 estimates, *Wall Street Journal,* April 19, 1985

Brazilianization

The austerity program also included various measures to lessen foreign participation in markets considered priority industries for the growth of a modern Brazilian economy. Before 1979 industries reserved for Brazilian firms only included the merchant marine, information media and petroleum refining and exploration. Foreign firms were also legislated out of banking, petrochemicals, mining and, in 1979, "informatics." Since it hit their major area of business, closure of the informatics sector was seen as potentially fatal by most multinationals in Brazil.

INFORMATICS

The term "informatics" is used in Brazil in a very broad sense, referring to virtually any product with an electronic digital component, as well as to the software and services involved. Semiconductors, electronic instruments, computer and telecommunications equipment and the software associated with this equipment were included. As Henry V. Eicher, president of Burroughs Electronica put it, "This ban would theoretically apply even to digitalized toys and watches."

History of the Current Policy

The Brazilian government first became involved in the informatics sector in 1972 by creating CAPRE (Coordinating Commission for Electronic Processing Activities) under the Planning Ministry (SEPLAN; see Exhibit 8) CAPRE was expected to contribute to managing Brazil's severe balance of payments problems.

EXHIBIT 8   **Brazil government organization (as of 1984).**

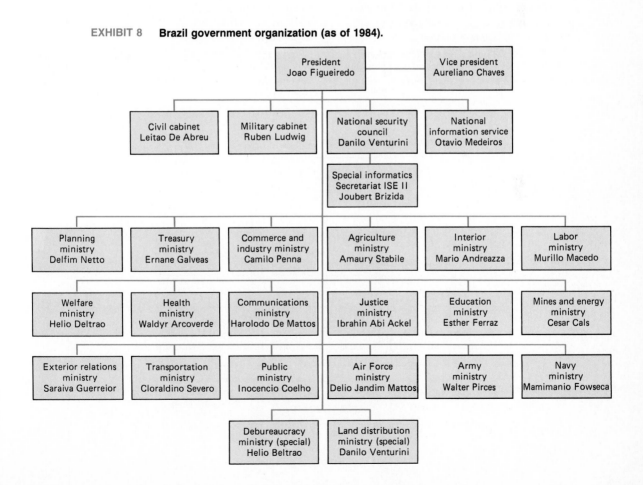

However, with the late 1970's economic slump, the Brazilian government decided that a national informatics industry was a prerequisite for the country's modernization. This initiative originated in the Brazilian Navy's inability fully to utilize British ships it had purchased, for lack of domestic computer expertise. The Informatics policies and programs have since had a strong military and national security component, an impediment to the flexibility needed for economic and technological development. Thus the Government's overall objectives, to serve both military-political and economic objectives, were to create indigenous technological design and production capabilities.

Government authorities further believed that technologically and financially dominant foreign firms—most multinationals in Brazil—even though operating as joint ventures, controlled the national informatics industry via their control over technology. Hence regulation of informatics and other high technology was rooted in three needs: (i) to modernize the entire Brazilian industrial base; (ii) to maintain national security; (iii) to insure that scarce currency reserves were not expended on technologies either inappropriate for Brazil or remaining under foreign control.

Viewing informatics in strategic (with a large military component) rather than economic terms, in late 1979 the Brazilian government created the Secretaria Especial de Informatica (Special Secretariat of Informatics or SEI) to replace CAPRE. Underlining this concern, rather than remaining in the Planning Ministry SEI was placed directly under the National Security Council, with a direct reporting line to the (military) president. SEI's early-1984 organization chart appears as Exhibit 9.

Though formulating and administering Brazil's informatics policy since 1979, SEI's outlook became much more protectionist and nationalistic in May 1984 when Colonel Edison Dytz replaced Colonel Joubert Brizida as Executive Secretary. Dytz served in this post until Sarney became president in 1985. Dytz had long advocated and defended 100-percent-Brazilian ownership of computer firms. To meet the objectives of the new Brazilianization campaign, SEI imposed and continued to expand a wide array of restrictions that limited foreign investment and participation in informatics.

This policy became known as "Market Reserve." In July 1981 as SEI announced its strategy, it reserved to national firms (defined as 100-percent-Brazilian ownership, public or private) the exclusive right to manufacture

EXHIBIT 9　　**SEI organizational chart (as of 1984).**

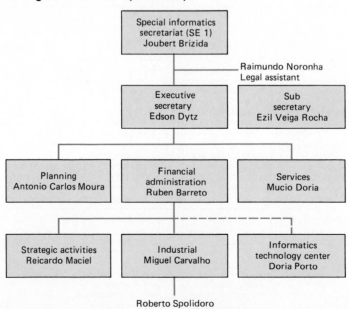

and sell products within 18 high technology categories. In 1983 the market reserve list was extended to five additional product categories. Exhibit 10 lists these product categories under market reserve.

The market reserve policy was implemented by requiring all import license applications and manufacturing proposals involving market reserve products or products with electronic features or end-uses to be submitted to SEI for approval or disapproval. SEI had full authority to deny production by foreign firms or importation by either foreign or domestic firms of any product within its mandate if it believed that the product or a close substitute was or could be available from a Brazilian source. A product was considered a substitute if it could accomplish the same task regardless of cost or loss of efficiency.

Technology transfer through licensing was also dependent on SEI approval. Such transfers were controlled by constraints on royalty payments. Foreign firms operating in Brazil were not allowed to sell informatics products in the country unless they satisfied the "no national substitute" rule. Thus, SEI expanded its coverage to sectors related to informatics.

In May 1985, shortly after Jose Sarney became President of Brazil, Colonel Dytz was replaced as Executive Secretary of SEI by Jose Rubens Doria Porto, former leader of the Informatics Technology Center. Colonel Dytz endorsed the new head as representing "continuity of the former team."

"Pirating" Intellectual Property

Brazil has avoided having laws or international agreements protecting "intellectual property"—patents, copyrights, trademarks—and does not act to prevent "counterfeiting" of packaging, corporate, professional or brand names, or making use of trade secrets. A U.S. government publication, *Business America,* in early 1985 stated: "Disrespect for intellectual property rights is firmly entrenched in Brazil. . . . There is little support for copyright protection of software." A bill introduced

---

EXHIBIT 10   PRODUCT CATEGORIES UNDER MARKET RESERVE IN BRAZIL

Original List (1981)
- Minicomputers, microcomputers
  Electronic cash registers
- Electronic data processing machines
  Electronic accounting machines
  Financial terminals and controls
  Electronic authenticators, ticket preparers
  Analog and digital equipment, modems
  Video terminals
  Remote access terminals for data banks
  Data entry equipment
  Electronic communications processors
- Digital multiplexers for data communications
- Digital concentrators for data communications
  Teleprinters
  Facsimile equipment
- Process control instrumentation; programmable controllers
- Numerical control equipment
  Secrecy and crypto-technological equipment

Added in 1983
- Microcomputer software
- Biomedical instrumentation
- Analytical instruments
- Measuring and testing instruments
  Superminicomputers

---

*Affecting Honeywell most directly

in the Brazilian Congress would require all software brought into the country to be listed in a public registry, with source codes included.

A *Financial Times* story of Nov. 5, 1984 reported that certain Brazilian firms simply disregard international patents. Twenty firms were making counterfeit Apple IIs and three IBM PCs. In the absence of law and regulations, these Brazilian firms' operations were quite open and seemed to enjoy the implicit blessing of SEI. Both Apple and IBM were rebuffed when they sought to register their products with SEI for protection.

An Exception

One Brazilian firm operating legitimately appeared to have promise. Itautec of São Paulo, subsidiary of the important Banco Itau, spent four years from its founding in 1979 developing its staff and its technology. It sold 270 of its own-design microcomputers in 1984 and projected sales of 6000 in 1985, with revenues going from U.S. $5 million to U.S. $50 million. Its workforce grew from 400 to 1900, and it expects to export soon to Third World countries.

Effects of Informatics Policies on Foreign Firms

In general, Brazil's informatics policy either excluded foreign firms from markets or restricted them to licensing technology. Denial of import requests and manufacturing proposals forestalled their new product lines. These adverse effects pushed some foreign firms to divert investment to other countries. On the other hand, Philco (Ford Motor's consumer electronics subsidiary), closed its $30 million plant barely two years after it started producing chips in Brazil. Similarly the German firm Siemens announced its intention to close its Brazilian subsidiary and withdraw from Brazil since its major business—digital controls—was reserved by SEI. Others, including IBM and Burroughs, chose to "dig in" for the duration of market reserve, believing that withdrawing from this key Third World market would be irreversible.

As its policies bit, Brazil apparently began paying a high price, in cutoff of foreign capital inflows, in technological lag and in higher consumer costs. A 1984 U.S. government publication states, "Brazilian firms are generally not able to supply state-of-the-art technology at competitive prices." And "Foreign experts view Brazilian technology in the computer area as being outdated by

at least five years. . . . [A]dvances in technology are so rapid in this industry that it will be difficult for Brazil to make the major leaps required to make its industry competitive on a global basis."

Despite these costs, foreign firms, large or small, lost ground in Brazil regardless of their strategies. Even if not yet forced to leave, they found their survival more and more challenged. Even the most tenacious felt their survival unlikely without changes in informatics policy.

The 1984 Informatics Legislation

On October 3, 1984 the Brazilian Congress passed a national informatics law which institutionalized the existing system. *Business America* (December 10, 1984, p. 44) explained as follows:

"The law's provisions will continue to limit foreign access to Brazil's informatics market by extending market reserve for eight years and by broadening product coverage.

"The law transfers policymaking authority from the Special Secretariat for Informatics (SEI), which is controlled by the National Security Council, to a new organization—the National Council for Informatics and Automation (CONIN). CONIN will be comprised of representatives from ten Executive agencies and eight members from the private sector. This membership should balance the interests of the national security-conscious SEI with commercial and economic concerns of other government agencies and industry. CONIN will be required to develop a three-year national informatics plan that will require Presidential and Congressional approval. Furthermore, the Congress has been vested with annual oversight responsibility involving the plan's implementation.

"For the first time, 'national company' is officially defined. The definition is essentially unchanged from the practical definition that has been in place for several years, i.e. 100 percent Brazilian ownership. 'Effective' national control is required, meaning autonomy of the firm from foreign sources of capital and technology, and full voting control by resident Brazilians. Although this represents a change in language from 'exclusive' Brazilian control, the Brazilian government has already indicated that it will prohibit joint ventures . . . .

"Although the restructuring of informatics policymaking to include representatives from the executive branch and private industry, and vesting Congress with oversight authority, could lead to a more flexible and practical application of market reserve, it is unlikely to lead to the policy's demise. Market reserve has strong, broad-based domestic support, demonstrated in part by the virtually unanimous Congressional approval of the new law. Brazil is likely to keep market reserve in place and accommodate demands by modifying its application in areas where there is a strong domestic constituency for change, such as industrial process controls and digital input for unrelated industries (e.g. automotive industry). Much will depend on the implementing regulations that are now being developed, on the inclination of the new Brazilian government that takes office next March 15 [1985], on the national informatics plan proposed by CONIN, and on the evaluation of that plan by the Congress. However, the outlook for imports and foreign direct investment is not likely to improve in the short- to medium-term.

"Some U.S. firms already in Brazil are prepared to 'dig in' for the duration of market reserve, in the hope that the policy will be abandoned, or at least modified, in the 1990s. They view the new legislation as simply a codification of the existing system, which they have learned to live with. Others think the new legislation 'regularizes' the current system, and suggest that this may result in application of more objective standards to government investment/import decisions. Still others see the legislation as an indication that restrictive policies will be more effectively enforced.

"Looking back over the past several years at the application of informatics policy, apparent inconsistencies between policy and practice are evident. For example, in spite of restrictions on foreign equity investment, foreign and national companies actively court each other as potential partners, in anticipation of SEI eventually allowing joint ventures. SEI is regularly receptive to project proposals that include foreign participation, and some have been approved. SEI tends to look more favorably on proposals that: 1) link small manufacturers with strong financial institutions; 2) propose establishing R&D centers in Brazil; and/or 3) indicate a positive trade balance. Follow-up is essential because SEI's small staff is frequently unable to review detailed proposals thoroughly. In addition, although SEI originally argued that only two Brazilian firms would be authorized to produce super-minicomputers, eight proposals were ultimately approved. The super-minicomputer will be produced by three Brazilian firms which intend to develop their own technology based on previously acquired foreign know-how, and four additional Brazilian firms using newly licensed foreign technology. This market has been estimated at $1.5 billion over the next five years."

The *Financial Times* commented on the October 1984 Informatics law as follows in its Nov. 5, 1985 addition:

> "Colonel Edison Dytz, of the SEI government agency agrees: 'The fact that you import foreign products does not mean that you learn the technical expertise yourself.' "

> "Not surprisingly, ABICOMP, the Brazilian association of computer manufacturers, totally supports the legislation."

HONEYWELL'S OPERATIONS AND STRATEGIES IN BRAZIL

Honeywell first entered the Brazilian market in 1958 on the belief that Brazil would be a key economy in the world by the end of this century. As is common, it entered by forming a subsidiary under Brazilian law. As it turned out, use of organizational alternatives became a central feature of Honeywell's Brazilian strategy.

Honeywell Controles, Limitada and Its Operations

With the establishment of a wholly-owned control systems subsidiary in 1958—Honeywell Controles LTDA, (HCL)—the company made substantial investments in Brazil to develop a leadership position. HCL concentrated on four product categories: (i) Residential Controls, (ii) Commercial Building Systems, (iii) Components and (iv) Process Control Instruments.

Residential Control's business included safety, environmental and energy conservation systems for residences and apartment buildings. This line accounted for 9 percent of HCL's 1981 sales. Since the Brazilian residential controls market was not yet developed, only a limited number of burner safety devices and gas controls could be marketed locally, the majority being exported.

Commercial Building Systems covered instruments, systems and services for comfort controls, security, fire protection and energy conservation in large buildings such as hotels, airports, offices and hospitals. This line represented 14 percent for HCL's 1981 sales. Again, without a fully developed Brazilian market for these systems, the majority sold by HCL were imported, with local manufacturing of only control valves, flow switches, electromechanical temperature controls, and panels. The market for these products was largely limited to simple, unsophisticated applications that could be supplied by local manufacturers or imported by small distributor compa-

EXHIBIT 11 SALES OF HONEYWELL CONTROLES, LTDA (BRAZIL), 1981
(100 Percent Owned by Honeywell, Inc.)

Business lines		Sales (U.S. $ millions)		Percent of total
Residential controls		$1.05		9
Commercial building systems		1.70		14
Components		1.62		13
Industrial process controls		7.66		64
Sold through HCL	3.73		31	
Imported by customers	3.93		33	
Total		$12.03		100

nies. Lacking a local market for its imported advanced systems, HCL was not able to import solid state spare parts, microchips or printer circuit cards, or to capitalize on its technology to differentiate its products from those of local firms.

The Components business, accounting for 13 percent of HCL's 1981 sales, included electric and electronic switches and components. These products were used by manufacturers of consumer and capital goods and were also sold through authorized distributors and replacements. Some of the component products were assembled from U.S. imported parts.

Process Control Instruments had been HCL's biggest and fastest growing product line, accounting for 64 percent of 1981 sales. This line included analog and digital control systems and control panels. The engineering and services accompanying these products were directed at petrochemical industries, steel plants and mineral process-

ing, electric utilities, and most of the smaller direct user manufacturing and processing plants in Brazil. An overview of HCL's business is presented in Exhibit 11.

Of HCL's four business lines, only Components and Process Control Instruments concentrated primarily on local needs since they served well developed markets in Brazil.

THE COMPONENTS AND PROCESS CONTROLS MARKET IN BRAZIL

The Brazilian economy offered a substantial market for components and industrial process controls, with sales totaling some $85 million in 1979 and $89 million in 1980 (but declining in 1981) as set forth in Exhibit 12.

While estimates of the number of Brazilian producers of process controls ranged from 44 to 200, trade sources indicated that 17 leading firms accounted for 95 percent

EXHIBIT 12 BRAZIL: THE TOTAL MARKET FOR INDUSTRIAL PROCESS CONTROLS* SELECTED YEARS, 1974–1981
(Millions of U.S. Dollars)

	1974	1977	1979	1980	1981
Production	$28	$64	$24.8	$27.4	$30.5
+ Imports	50	73	62.0	63.5	53.2
− Exports	1	4	1.4	1.6	2.0
= Domestic market size	77	133	85.4	89.3	81.7

Source: "Industrial Process Controls: Brazil," Country Market Survey, 1979, 1984. U.S. Department of Commerce.
*Figures include process control valves (36 percent of total in 1981) which are locally manufactured and whose importation is prohibited.

of production in 1980. Seven local subsidiaries of U.S. companies supplied about a third of this total while three operations owned by other foreign manufacturers (two German, one Japanese) contributed 17 percent.

Domestically-owned companies including Engematic and Fujinor, together supplied 20 percent of locally built instruments, and Encil, Engro, Hiter, IEF and Transmitel, each supplying for about 5 percent. A number of U.S. firms either had technology licensing agreements with local companies or operated Brazilian subsidiaries. In addition to Honeywell, other American firms with Brazilian factories included Bailey, Bristol and Babcock, Fisher and Porter, Foxboro, Masoneilar, and Taylor. Other competitors were manufacturers from Japan, Germany, France and the United Kingdom.

The high concentration and dominance of foreign firms in the industrial process controls and components market were largely attributed to Brazil's need for upgrading its process industries. Improved process controls and components that increased efficiency were essential if Brazil was to boost exports and generate revenues to meet the country's whopping debt service and oil bills. Hence, process control sales were projected at $112 million in 1987, a 5.4 percent annual growth rate. Exhibit 13 summarizes expected growth by product categories.

HONEYWELL AND SEI REGULATIONS

Despite anticipated growth, SEI questioned the role of foreign firms in the industrial process control and components industry. Considering it critical for national security and local technology, in 1981 SEI brought industrial process controls and components under Informatics market reserve. Foreign firms were thus banned from making and selling or importing such control products, and Brazilian firms were required to obtain SEI licenses in order to import foreign equipment. Predictably, the number of local firms and domestic production increased at the expense of imports and local manufacturing by multinationals. HCL's components and process controls business was hard hit.

HCL's components business was severely hurt by SEI's import restrictions since HCL imported most components from Honeywell USA. SEI nearly choked off all such imports. It was the closing of the process control sector to foreign firms that endangered HCL's survival.

In 1979, before SEI's rulings, HCL's sales of process control instruments reached $8.2 million, while in 1981 they were down to $7.7 million, and have steadily declined since. Banned from selling its most profitable line—advanced digital process controls—which would have given it leadership in Brazil's process control market, HCL's financial position deteriorated. HCL's exclusion from the digital controls market reduced it to offering only outmoded analog systems. Demand for these high cost–low efficiency systems was shrinking as government policy encouraged automation and digital technology. Consequently, HCL incurred a one-time write-off loss in 1982 (though it broke even every year thereafter). By 1984 HCL's total sales were down to $4 million compared with the $12 million of 1981.

As a 100-percent-foreign owned company, HCL was of course the very type of firm that SEI policies and regulations were intended to affect. While Honeywell had anticipated emergence of a protected market for informatics on SEI's establishment in 1979, the consequences of SEI restrictions were unexpectedly severe.

EXHIBIT 13　BRAZIL: THE MARKET FOR SPECIFIC INDUSTRIAL PROCESS CONTROLS 1981 AND 1987 (Millions of U.S. Dollars)

	1981	1987
Control valves	29.8	37.5
Nonelectric/nonelectronic instruments	23.4	31.5
Electric/electronic instruments	28.5	42.9
Total	81.7	111.9

Source: U.S. Department of Commerce, International Trade Administration, Office of Trade Information Services Research Report
(Note: This information is in chart form in the original.)

Honeywell Transcontrol Automacao, Limitada

During SEI's initial days in 1979, when the Brazilianization campaign was just beginning, Honeywell formed a 55-percent-Brazilian-owned (45-percent-Honeywell-owned) joint venture called Honeywell Transcontrol Automacao, Ltda (or HTAL). This strategic step was part of Honeywell's response to uncertainty about SEI's future policy actions. Honeywell planned to use HTAL to enter the protected markets by having the joint-venture recognized as a company with majority national capital and ownership.

In 1980 four firms were selected and approved by SEI as Registered Manufacturers to provide selected analog (old technology) control instruments in Brazil. The chosen firms (and the technology they were to employ) were Engematic (Hitachi, Japan); Bristol (Bristol & Babcock, U.S.); Fujinor (Fuji, Japan); and Ecil (Leeds & Northrup, U.S.). In exchange for agreeing to Brazilian majority ownership and to the requirement that they manufacture (i.e. assemble) in Brazil 95 percent of the controls sold locally, the four were to be assured import licensing for all necessary components, an 80 percent reduction in import duties, exemption from the 15 percent tax levied on duty-paid value, and exclusive access to the 50–70 percent of the market controlled by the Government. (Later, observers found these firms to be less than successful.)

Honeywell's joint venture HTAL was thus not included on the 1980 list. But the expected lockout of all other importers did not occur; despite the rules some rejected manufacturers were given import licenses at times. And in 1981 a government commission reported that process controls required by major Brazilian industries were beyond the capabilities of domestic manufacturers.

Until 1981, HTAL existed very nearly in name only, having little business of its own. However, in 1981 when SEI further restricted imports and foreign manufacturing in informatics, it became impossible for Honeywell to operate in the reserved process control market through its wholly-owned subsidiary HCL. But the Brazilian process control market offered too large an opportunity for Honeywell to abandon it, especially when the company had achieved modest growth and had invested effort and money in this sector for 20 years.

With no opportunity to operate in the industrial process controls market through either HCL or imports, Honeywell decided to seek SEI approval through its joint venture HTAL. In 1981 HTAL prepared several proposals for SEI's review. However, even by 1982 SEI had yet to issue its appraisal. SEI views regarding such joint ventures were not encouraging either. SEI's Colonel Brizida had made clear SEI's stand.

> "Whenever foreign capital, which holds technology control, participates in joint-ventures (even with only 10 percent ownership) the technology is not effectively transferred to Brazil. SEI makes clear its disapproval of the participation in 'reserved market areas' by companies where foreign investors hold any kind of equity, even nonvoting capital."

Greatly discouraged but still reluctant to leave the Brazilian market, in 1982 Honeywell began closing down HCL's local Process Control business, trimming its local personnel and investment and redirecting its analog process control business to a new Brazilian distributor firm formed by its former process control-division employees.

Honeywell then tried one more organizational alternative in the attempt to stabilize its position.

The Digidata Licensing Arrangement

In late 1981, with HTAL's proposals languishing in SEI's files, Honeywell opened negotiations toward a licensing agreement with a small Brazilian company named Digidata in another attempt to get its advanced digital control systems into Brazil. Honeywell's strategy was to license its advanced digital control technology to this 100-percent Brazilian company which would then perform final assembly sale and installation of the systems.

The negotiations were successful. In early 1982 SEI announced an important action, in which it would select Brazilian producers of advanced digital process control instruments incorporating licensed foreign technology. Digidata-Honeywell prepared a proposal and presented it to SEI. Despite its previously failed attempts, Honeywell was optimistic about this proposal. First, Digidata met SEI's 100-percent ownership and control requirement for participation in this reserved market. Also, Honeywell's advanced digital process control technology was acknowledged to be the world's leader.

SEI's evaluations took over a year. Finally, in July 1983 SEI announced the firms to which it was granting permission to manufacture control instruments with licensed foreign technology. The chosen firms with proposed foreign technology source were Electronica Brasileira (Leeds & Northrup, U.S.); Ecil and P&D-Sistemas Electronicos (Yokogawa, Japan); Unipar, Unipar Quimica, and Brascontrol Industria e Comercio (Fisher, U.S.);

Prologo (Asea); and Industrias Villares (Hitachi, Japan). Digidata's name was not on the list.

With this latest outcome, Honeywell found itself virtually locked out of both licensing and import privileges, and out of the reserved markets in which it once had had the majority of its Brazilian business. And in 1982, Professor Jose de Jesus Mendez' statement in front of Colonel Dytz was pointed: "We want Honeywell's technology for the next two or three years, but after that we expect Honeywell to get out of Brazil."

Honeywell entered 1984 with greatly scaled down Brazilian operations, having adjusted as best it could (largely during the year 1982) by several drastic changes in its Brazilian operations:

• Dissolution of the joint-venture firm Honeywell Transcontrol Automacao, Ltda (HTAL).
• Closing down the local process control business of Honeywell Controles, Ltda (HCL), and turning the remaining business over to HCL's former process control division employees.
• Scaling down local personnel, with more than 50 percent of its employees already laid off.
• "Fire Sale" of all inventory of products in the reserved markets.

With these steps, which flowed from both SEI's regulations and Brazil's continuing economic problems, Honeywell's early 1984 presence was reduced to a bare minimum. The company was represented by a small corps of support personnel for economically feasible import sales and services not specifically regulated or prohibited by government decrees. While Honeywell still believed in Brazil's long-range future, the five years of continuous struggle and deteriorating conditions since 1979 forced the question whether Honeywell would have a place in Brazil's future. Thus Honeywell was faced with hard choices regarding further operations in Brazil.

THE FUTURE

SEI's actions over the five years, 1979–1984, were marked by continuously increasing restrictions on imports and production by foreign firms of products within the 23 reserved product areas. Continuation of discrimination against manufacturing and service firms companies not qualifying as "national firms" was expected. Strong approval of SEI's policies by the Brazilian Congress in 1981 and 1984 pointed to possible future expansion of SEI's activities and broadening of its product and market restrictions. Brazil's historic regulatory and protectionist philosophy left no sector immune from potential future decrees.

Yet there were a few rays of hope, if only hope, remaining. Brazil's foreign debt situation, though still shaky, had not deteriorated into abrogation of foreign debt, though Brazil chafed under IMF restrictions. A transition of government from the 1964–1985 military regime to a civilian president had occurred quite smoothly, though the president-elect's untimely death had thrust the vice-president-elect precipitately into the presidency. Brazil had showed that it could change a negative trade balance into a positive one by pushing exports and restricting imports, though the balance of payments problem remained, owing to high debt service requirements. And the continued import restrictions underlay much of Honeywell's problem. Finally, the change to the civilian-dominated policy board, CONIN, overseeing the Informatics program and SEI, as well as the Congressional oversight program, both set up by the 1984 Informatics Law, offered the possibility of a more sympathetic view of involvement of foreign firms in the lines of business served by Honeywell. But government actions during 1985 indicated that an unbending stance was still the politically most rewarding attitude.

In view of the expected economic and political conditions in Brazil and the magnitude of losses already incurred, Honeywell knew that the problem would not work itself out. The situation required immediate and forceful action, and Honeywell's top management in Minneapolis, together with its international and South American executives, began a critical examination of Honeywell's options in Brazil.

THE HONOLULU ARMED SERVICES YMCA (B)

James C. Makens
Wake Forest University

INTRODUCTION

On July 30, 1980, the board of directors of the Honolulu Armed Services YMCA were assembled in the blue room to discuss future courses of action for their aging downtown building. Before each director was a copy of a feasibility study on alternate uses for the building, which had been compiled by a professional consulting firm. The report analyzed each alternative and provided five-year cash flow statements for each of the following uses for the building:

1 Status Quo—leave the building as is.
2 Convert to a moderately-priced commercial hotel.
3 Convert to a commercial office building—renovated and operated by the ASYMCA.
4 Lease entire building to a professional development-management company.

Mike Ellis, director of the local ASYMCA, called the meeting to order, then read a letter to the board which he had recently received from the national director of the

This case was written by Peter Gammie, Graduate Assistant of the School of Travel Industry Management of the University of Hawaii, and James C. Makens, of the Babcock Graduate School of Wake Forest. It was not designed to present an illustration of either effective or ineffective handling of administrative problems. Copyright © the authors.

ASYMCA. The letter urged the local board of directors to maintain the downtown building as a conventional 'Y' building, complete with physical fitness facilities and rooms for rent. It was not an unexpected sentiment from the national director, as he had voiced similar opinions in the past. However, the local board of directors felt compelled to explore alternate uses for the building, and as a result, proceeded to approve a motion to evaluate each of the alternatives on their own merit. Whatever course of action the local board of directors decided upon would need to be economically sound and justifiable to the National Board of Directors of the ASYMCA.

THE ARMED SERVICES YMCA

The primary mission of the Armed Services YMCA was to serve the needs and interests of military personnel and their dependents. The program was initially started to meet the temporary housing needs of low-ranking servicemen—those that could least afford to stay elsewhere. The ASYMCA was able to open its facilities or extend its program and services to the civilian population in communities which lacked ASYMCA facilities, when in so doing it would not lessen or conflict with its services to military personnel and their families.

Although the central building for the Hawaii branch

of the ASYMCA (one of 26 in the world) is located in downtown Honolulu, most of its interaction with military personnel was accomplished through five satellite locations on the island of Oahu. Located in various military bases, the structures for the satellite installations were provided by the armed services, but the ASYMCA provided the programs and staffing necessary to operate the programs. Various programs such as child abuse counseling, parent interaction groups, support groups for women in the armed services, prenatal assistance and counseling, homemaking classes, and information referrals were offered through the satellite facilities.

THE ASYMCA BUILDING

In 1917, the Royal Hawaiian Hotel, located at the corner of Richards and South Hotel Streets, was purchased and converted into an ASYMCA facility. This building, due to functional obsolescence, was demolished in 1925. Two years later, the current ASYMCA facilities were completed at a cost of $305,000.

The building stood five stories tall and contained approximately 83,000 square feet of space under the roof. The architectural flair was Mediterranean, from the red tile roof to the stately Romanesque arches that lined the front of the building. The glazed tile floors, wrought iron banisters and railings, and thick concrete walls were in good condition after more than 60 years, attesting to the quality of construction in earlier years.

The ASYMCA building was listed on the National Register of Historic Buildings and was nominated for the Register of Historic Buildings in the State of Hawaii. Between the new judiciary building and the State Capitol, the 'Y' was centrally located in downtown Honolulu. Zoning statutes placed their 87,471 square foot parcel within the capital district, limiting the types of exterior building modifications permissible.

Although the building was well preserved, there were problems that arose with the passage of time. The electrical and plumbing systems required substantial maintenance to keep them operational and the archaic hot water boiler required custom-made replacement parts which were quite expensive. The Spanish tile roof, as old as the building itself, was deteriorating rapidly and would probably need to be replaced within ten years. Estimates for reroofing the building were roughly $450,000. The wooden window frames in the building were suffering from dry rot and termites, and also needed to be replaced.

PRESENT SITUATION

The ASYMCA building served a variety of uses. Parts of the first two floors were rented out to various entrepreneurs as office space at varying rental rates. The ASYMCA also maintained a swimming pool, gymnasium, locker facilities, and their offices on the first two floors. Floors 3–5 contained 244 rather small rooms for rent and a recreation room located on the third floor. The rooms were sparsely furnished and contained no kitchen facilities. Communal bathrooms were located on every floor. The majority of rooms were rented by pensioners and transients who lived on very limited budgets. The managerial ability of Mr. Ellis had been instrumental in directing the ASYMCA building operations through a decade of profitability. These profits were used to operate the various satellite facilities maintained by the ASYMCA on Oahu, resulting in the island-wide entity retaining its nonprofit status. However, rapidly escalating expenses were causing Mr. Ellis to become increasingly concerned about the future availability of profits from the downtown building. Determined to maintain the downtown location as a profit center, Mr. Ellis and the ASYMCA board of directors identified four alternate uses for the building. A brief look at each of them follows.

STATUS QUO

This alternative merely continued the operating pattern which already existed at the ASYMCA. No major marketing plans or capital expenditures were included in the analysis. The two primary assumptions in the status quo which would have a major impact on cash flows were energy costs and room rate increases.

Natural gas, fuel oil, and electricity were consumed at the 'Y' building. Of these, electricity accounted for the highest utility cost, averaging $5,000 per month in early 1980. These costs were assumed to increase by 50% in the beginning of 1981, then at 20% per year after that. Utility payments were included within the current lease rates and none of the rental units were individually metered for electrical usage.

Room rates had periodically been increased by Mr. Ellis to cover rising costs. Aware of the price elasticity of demand for rooms, the consultants suggested a rate increase ceiling at 8%, despite a 10% assumed inflation rate. The degree of elasticity, however, was not fully ascertained by the consultants. Whether this rate increase would be tolerated by the guests was questionable.

TABLE 1   YMCA ROOM OCCUPANCY RATES

	Rooms sold			% of house occupancy		
	1978	1979	1980	1978	1979	1980
January		242	242	95	99	99.1
February	229	242	241	95	99	99
March	227	241	241	95	98.8	99
April	217	238	224	90	97	92
May	213	230.5	207	89	94	85
June	208	221	195	87	90	80
July	210	210	189	82	86	77.5
August	218	218		77	89	
September	227	227		86	93	
October	216	216		88	89	
November	215	215		94	88	
December	228	228		97	93.5	
	215	227		89.5	92	

Most expense items were assumed to increase with the rate of inflation (assumed to be 10%), given that their usage remained relatively constant. Being a nonprofit organization, the ASYMCA enjoyed an exemption from property taxes, which would have amounted to $75,000 otherwise. Minimal taxes were paid on the space used for office rentals, but the payments were the responsibility of the lessees.

Occupancy rates at the 'Y' averaged 90% for the two years prior to the feasibility study. Seasonal fluctuations were noticeable, but not excessive, with the winter months being the busiest time of the year. Occupancy patterns at the 'Y' roughly followed those of the Hawaiian hotel industry. Therefore, it was not surprising that occupancy rates at the 'Y' were down to the 70–80% range in the May–July segment of 1980 (See Table 1). Many of the local hotels were experiencing much lower occupancy rates, the cause of which had generally been attributed to a nationwide recession combined with an unprecedented 20% prime rate in the first quarter of 1980. Of course, occupancy rates affected projected profitability, as shown in the cash flow statements.

MODERATE PRICE HOTEL

A marketing study prepared for the Honolulu Downtown Improvement Association indicated that a downtown hotel could indeed be a viable concern, but it should not attempt "to mirror Waikiki properties in style, facilities or clientele."[1] This study was not conducted for the ASYMCA and did not deal with the subject of the ASYMCA building. There were no reputable downtown hotels in existence at the time of the feasibility study, leading the ASYMCA board of directors to think that their facility could, if renovated, become a successful moderately priced hotel. As a moderately priced hotel, the ASYMCA building would be geared towards a target market of visitors whose primary business was associated with the downtown area. It was felt that this market would consist of middle income business travelers who viewed the room primarily as a place in which to sleep rather than as a center for vacation, leisure, or entertainment.

Waikiki Beach and its assortment of hotels lay only 5 miles from downtown Honolulu, presenting formidable competition for any downtown hotel. The lure of the ocean and white sand beaches at Waikiki would have to be offset by convenient, comfortable, and affordable accommodations in a downtown hotel. The aforementioned study also indicated that a downtown hotel should be in the 300–400 room range.

The idea of conversion to a hotel facility had been previously discussed by the local board of directors and a set of preliminary conversion figures was compiled by

[1]*Summary Statement, Downtown Hotel Marketing Study,* August 25, 1978.

a local architectural firm. The original plan had been to convert only the two top floors to hotel rooms, leave the third floor as a recreational facility and meeting area for 'Y' groups, and continue to rent out offices and operate their physical fitness facilities on the first two floors. A small coffee shop would also remain on the first floor.

In the feasibility study, the hotel concept was modified to a certain degree by suggesting that the top three floors be converted into hotel rooms. Each floor would contain a combination of regular rooms (roughly 300 sq. ft.) and suites (roughly 600 sq. ft.), each with private bathroom facilities. The resulting configuration of rooms would allow for 33 rooms per floor or 99 rooms altogether. The athletic facilities on the first floor, except for the gymnasium, would be leased to a private health fitness club, and the rest of the first two floors would remain as office and shop rental space.

Renovation costs were estimated on a square foot basis, with cost estimates approximated through discussions with various developers in Honolulu. An average renovation cost of $60 per square foot was decided upon. Other costs included room furnishings at $4,000 per room and plumbing fixtures (toilets, shower stalls, etc.) at $2,000 per room.

The restaurant facility on the first floor presented a special problem. In order for the ASYMCA to attract a reputable restaurateur into the building it would have to significantly upgrade the facility, at an estimated cost of $80 per square foot, or $264,000. This problem arose because the location of the restaurant made it difficult to attract large numbers of people walking by, and the restaurant operator would be hesitant to invest a significant amount of money in such a risky venture. Of course, the restaurant could have remained as it was—a coffee shop with a limited menu and clientele. This would have required no additional capital investment.

Revenues from room rentals in 1981 would be quite limited because of the renovation process and were projected to be nil in the first half of 1982. Renovation was estimated to take 1.5 years, with work progressing a floor at a time. The hotel would be officially opened in mid-1982, following a $25,000 advertising campaign. Projected occupancy rates averaged 80% and room rates varied from $17 to $40 per night in 1982. These rates were assumed to increase with inflation.

A minimum operating staff of 23 (including 4 ASYMCA staff members) employees would be needed to operate the hotel. Although it would be preferable to have a nonunion shop, the payment of union wages was assumed for purposes of the cash flow. In order to attract and maintain a reliable work force, it was felt that wages on the local union scale should be paid (See Table 2).

TABLE 2   WAGE EXPENSES—1980 LEVEL—ALTERNATIVE 2

Job	No. of employees	Hourly wage	Yearly wage incl. paid vacation (2080 hrs)
Housekeeper—working supervisor	1	$5.64	$ 11,731
Housekeepers	4	4.52	37,606
Maintenance—foreman	1	8.97	18,657
Maintenance—utility	2	5.23	21,756
Gardener	1	5.24	10,899
Front office working supervisor	3	6.30	39,312
Sr. reservations clerk	1	5.95	12,376
Bellboy	1	4.25	8,840
Laundry attendant	1	4.80	9,984
Sr. accounting clerk	1	6.30	13,104
Jr. front office clerk	1	4.95	10,296
General manager	1	Salary	24,000
Secretary	1	Salary	10,000
YMCA management & staff	4	Salary	59,000
Total	23		$287,561

Renovation costs were assumed to be roughly $3.6 million, as shown below:

Renovation expenses:

Construction (@ $60/sq. ft.)	$2,581,770
Furnishings (@ $4,000/rm.)	396,000
Plumbing fixtures ($2,000/rm.)	198,000
Gymnasium ($35/sq. ft. × 4816 sq. ft)	168,650
Restaurant ($80/sq. ft. × 3,300 sq. ft.)	264,000
Total	$3,608,420

It was highly improbable that the national board would be able to loan the local 'Y' this amount of money, as it was itself experiencing financial difficulties. The only option available, therefore, lay in borrowing from commercial banks. Besides requiring statements showing the financial ability to repay the loan, the commercial bank would also require proof that experienced, competent management operate the hotel. The commercial bank would provide an interim loan to cover the costs of construction during the construction period. The long-term portion of the loan would then be transferred to an interested institutional leader such as an insurance company, pension fund, or trust company.

For a loan of the size necessary for ASYMCA renovation, the bank would probably charge a floating rate set at roughly two points above prime, plus a one-time charge of two points. The prime was at 12.5% at the time of the study, so the interim loan rate would be 14.5% plus two points. It was assumed that a prime rate of 12% would be in effect in 1981 and would not fluctuate too widely from that figure.

The long-term portion of the loan might be picked up by a small life insurance company on the West Coast or a local pension or trust fund. It was assumed that 14% interest, plus two points, would be appropriate.

No provisions for roof or boiler replacement were made in this alternative. These could require replacement before the end of five years. Expenses relating to the operations of the ASYMCA office were included, as it would remain in the building under this alternative.

CONVERT TO OFFICES OPERATED BY ASYMCA

The market for office space in downtown Honolulu was extremely tight in early 1980. The information in Table 3 reflects the fact that occupancy rates ranged between 93–100% in the first quarter of 1980. A subsequent article in the *Honolulu Advertiser*, May 30, 1980 indicated that available office space in Honolulu was 1.5%.

Predictions by those interviewed were for a continuing tight market for downtown office space through 1981. There was also concern that office building projects underway at the time could reverse the situation by 1982. The planned introduction of new and renovated office space, if combined with a continuing business recession, could reverse the present situation and lead to price stability in the office-lease market as well as increase options for lessees concerning the type of property they were willing to lease as early as 1982.

It was not unusual for the market for downtown office space in U.S. cities to exhibit periods of tight and slack occupancy. It was considered unrealistic to expect that the market in Honolulu would reflect a continuing high occupancy without periods of slack demand.

Being located between the state capitol and the new judiciary building, the ASYMCA building offered great potential as a centrally located office building. Under this alternative, the ASYMCA would demolish the existing interior walls, rewire the building, refinish the ceilings and add a second elevator. Space in the building would then be offered for lease, with the lessees performing the work necessary to transform their individual spaces into offices.

The ASYMCA would continue to manage the building but it would be converted to full use as a profit center. All areas of the building would be converted to their highest yield use without consideration of traditional uses as an ASYMCA. The highest yield use would be dependent upon investing as little capital as possible in the renovation of the building. The building would not be equipped with central air conditioning but, instead, individual air conditioning units would be used.

The timing of estimated cash flows considered the leases already existing on office and retail space on the first two floors. As soon as existing leases expired, the 'Y' would increase leases on a basis that reflected market conditions at the time.

In order to more equitably distribute operating costs of the building, a triple net leasing system would be used. Relatively new to Hawaii, but prevalent in many mainland cities, triple net leases meant that the lessees paid all the operating costs of the building, besides their lease payments. The basis for allocating these costs varied, but a system based on square footage occupied would be used

TABLE 3   OCCUPANCY SURVEY OF DOWNTOWN
HONOLULU OFFICE SPACE
First Quarter 1980

40 Buildings	
Total	5,179,022 sq. ft.
Occupied	5,002,473
Occupancy	96.6%
100,000+ square feet	
Total buildings	16
Total	4,048,734
Occupied	3,910,785
Occupancy	96.6%
40,000–100,000	
Total buildings	8
Total	537,511
Occupied	499,681
Occupancy	93.07%
Under 40,000	
Total buildings	8
Total	139,181
Occupied	139,181
Occupancy	100.0%
Over 25 Years	
Total buildings	8
Total	453,596
Occupied	453,826
Occupancy	99.8%

Source: Building Owners and Managers Association, Suite 206, 677 Ala Moana, Honolulu, Hawaii 96813

by the 'Y'. Depending upon the location, projected monthly rental rates (not on existing leases) would range from $.60 to $.90 per square foot in 1981.

It was generally agreed by realtors, developers and others interviewed that a strong but limited market existed for renovated older buildings. Among the type of individuals most commonly listed as prospective clients for these buildings were:

Lawyers—especially younger ones
Architects
Planners
Independent businesspeople—i.e., manufacturers, representatives
Consultants
Advertising agencies

It was generally felt that these individuals somehow seemed more attuned to the nostalgia of older buildings

and were willing to live with the natural problems inherent in old buildings even after renovation. They also seemed particularly willing to adapt their furnishings to match the natural theme of the building.

A few novel ideas were introduced as possible sources of increased revenue generation. The parking lot, comprising 7,578 sq. ft., was leased out on a monthly basis to a rental firm which rented stalls on a daily basis. Raising their rental rate by 20% in 1981 would generate a total of $1,895 in rental income per month. However, should they revamp the system by managing the lot themselves and renting out stalls for $75 per month, monthly income of $5,700 was felt to be possible in 1981. This rate was comparable with similar parking locations in downtown Honolulu.

Another idea was to lease out the unused lanai and patio areas (5,316 sq. ft.) on the second floor to an entrepreneur who would establish a wine and cheese food and beverage operation. The ASYMCA already held a liquor license for the building which could be applied to the wine and cheese operation. At a monthly rental rate of $.30 per sq. ft. in 1981, the ASYMCA could conceivably gross $19,140 from the lease payments.

Labor costs would be significantly reduced if the building were converted to offices. Wages for employees engaged in ground and building maintenance would be paid for by the tenants of the building through the triple net arrangement. Utility costs would also be passed along to the tenants. The ASYMCA would be responsible for paying all expenses accruing to their office in the building, but would be relieved of most other costs.

All the area currently used for physical fitness training would be converted into office space, including the gymnasium. The time necessary to prepare the building for offices was assumed to be one year, and two cost figures were examined in the cash flow analysis. At $40 per sq. ft., total renovation costs to the 'Y' were roughly $2.5 million. This increased to roughly $3.5 million at a $60 per sq. ft. renovation cost (See Table 4). As in the hotel scenario, short and long term (20 year loan) financing were 14% plus two points to each lender.

The final result with this alternative could well be a hodge-podge of office styles and quality. The exterior landscaping and building facia would remain the same, but the interior results would depend upon the whims of the lessees. As manager of the building, the ASYMCA would assume all the risks and problems associated with such a project. Filling every space at the projected rental rates would be necessary to generate the revenues projected in the cash flow statement.

ALTERNATE IV. COMPLETE BUILDING LEASED TO AND OPERATED BY A PROFESSIONAL DEVELOPMENT-MANAGEMENT COMPANY

The fourth alternative stipulated that the entire property be turned over to a professional development-management company on a long-term lease (40 years). The board of directors of the ASYMCA would select the lessee on the basis of (a) Net return to the ASYMCA, (b) Reputation and professional expectations of the lessee, (c) Understanding that the building would be used only for mutually agreeable purposes, (d) Other conditions and considerations agreeable to both parties.

The purpose of the option of arranging a long-term lease with a professional firm would be to allow the ASYMCA to continue to use the building as a source of income without the necessity of renovating and managing the property. The resources and energy of the current building staff and the revenues from its lease could be used to improve services at the various satellite facilities that provide direct services to armed forces personnel and their dependents.

Several developers contacted by the consultants expressed interest in the prospect of leasing the building on a long-term basis. After viewing the building there was general agreement that it offered excellent potential as an office building for the following reasons: (1) well situated—good location; (2) sound structure; (3) aesthetically pleasing; (4) possibility of State Historic Registry—although this offered positive and negative factors, it appeared to generally be considered as desirable.

There was also general agreement that the building would need extensive and costly renovation to enable it

TABLE 4   RENOVATION COSTS—ALTERNATIVE 3

Floor	Sq. ftg.	$40/sq. ft.	$60/sq. ft.
1	4,816	$192,640	$288,960
2	4,816	192,640	288,960
3	14,624	584,960	877,440
4	14,624	584,960	877,440
5	14,624	584,960	877,440
Sub-total		2,140,160	3,210,240
Add:			
Gym floor ($35/sq. ft.)		168,650	168,650
Elevator #2		150,000	150,000
Total		2,458,810	3,528,890

TABLE 5   DIA SUMMARY OF POTENTIAL DOWNTOWN DEVELOPMENT PROJECTS

Project name developer	Location	Principal use/cost	Parking	Configuration	Status
Grosvenor Center 2nd office tower Grosvenor Internat'l	Bishop/Queen/Nimitz/ Alakea	Office-rental 275,000 sf $32 million	786 already built	20 floor office tower on existing 10 floor garage. First floor commercial	To begin in next few months. Completion about mid-1981.
The HK Building Office Building Hasegawa Komuten (USA), Inc.	Mililani/Halekauwila	Office-rental	221	8 floor office tower with first floor commercial	In construction completion late 1980
Central Pacific Bank Headquarters office Central Pacific Bank	King/Alakea	Bank building office-rental	390 subject to design change	25 floor office tower over 6 floors of parking. Ground for bank operations	In design. To begin sometime during 1980. Revised certificate of appropriateness OK'd.
Super block-Phase 2 Office Building Campbell Estate + Robinson Estate(?)	Fort/Bethel/Hotel mauka of new LH	Office-rental Commercial $25 to $30 million	600 total—4444 already built over LH	Tower above parking and commercial	In design and feasibility study
Century Square Convertible condo L. Robert Allen	Beretania/Bishop/Fort- Lady of Peace Cathedral	360 unit office— condominium $35 million	362 in four levels underground	37 floor tower. Underground garage	Announced— construction soon. Completion about Spring 1981.
Executive Center Commercial/Convertible Condo. L. Robert Allen	King/Hotel/Fort/Bishop (excludes Gasco & Bishop Trust)	300 office units 160 one br apts. 76 luxury apts. 33 townhouses $120 million	900 above grade	Two 40 floor towers 13 floors of other commercial includes new Longs and Woolworths.	Announced. Completion about mid-1982.
Pacific Trade Center Phase II NW Mutual Life	Bishop/Hotel/King Alex. Young site	—	—	—	In design and feasibility study
Honolulu Tower Condominium Charles Pankow, Inc.	Beretania/Nuuanu/ Maunakea Block F makai	396 apts. condominium $45 million	484 in ten story garage	Tower on parking building. Park area dedication of 77,000 sf	In design. Will announce soon. Completion about Fall 1981.
Unnamed project apartment building Charles Pankow, Inc.	Smith/Beretania City parking lot	596 rental apts. day care unit public parking	202 public, other for tenants	Honolulu Tower park part of package	In negotiation with City and in design and feasibility study

665

TABLE 5   DIA SUMMARY OF POTENTIAL DOWNTOWN DEVELOPMENT PROJECTS *(Continued)*

Project name developer	Location	Principal use/cost	Parking	Configuration	Status
Unnamed project	Bethel/Hotel/Nuuanu City parking lot	—	—	—	Three proposals under study by City
Unnamed project	Richards/Hotel/Alakea City parking garage	—	—	—	Possible call for proposal by City
Unnamed project	Bethel/Nimitz/Merchant City parking garage Kaahumanu	—	—	—	—
Unnamed project office building City Bank	Alakea/Queen/Richards	Office-rental	—	—	In preliminary design
Governor's Mansion Condominium Hadley	Beretania/Pali/Queen Emma Block J	Condominium apartments	—	—	—
Unnamed Rental Apts. Hadley	River/Vineyard Mortuary site	Rental apartments for elderly	—	—	—
Stangewald/Security Title Bldgs. Historic properties	119 Merchant and 121 Merchant	Office-rental Commercial	None	Restoration	In execution
Royal Queen Emma Convertible Condo Park and Kam	222 Vineyard Street	24 residential/ commercial	24 tenant 20 guest	6 floor convertible condo over ground floor commercial	Requesting Certificate of Appropriateness for Construction in HCD
Armed Forces YMCA	Beretania/Richards/Hotel	Upgrading of some hotel rooms	—	Renovation	In design and feasibility
District Courts Bldg. State of Hawaii	Hotel/Alakea	Courts and Offices	—	Tower on Courts and parking underground	In construction completion about mid-1982

Source: Downtown Improvement Association, 602 Bishop Trust Bldg., 1000 Bishop Street, Honolulu, Hawaii 96813. William A. Grant, Executive Director.

to be rented at the highest possible rates. Although there were differences in opinion concerning what could be done with the building, there appeared to be a general concensus concerning the following:

a Building should retain its 1920's theme inside and out.

b Central air conditioning would be needed.

c New wiring, flooring and ceiling would be needed. Plumbing might also need to be replaced.

d Other extensive repairs would probably be necessary in terms of roof and windows.

e Outside landscaping would be needed.

f Second elevator would be needed.

It was generally felt that with extensive renovation the building could continue to enjoy high occupancy in spite of new offices which would be placed on the market. However, there was fear that if renovation was less than first class, there could be future difficulties in leasing the space for the highest possible yield. Lessees could be attracted to some of the new properties coming on line, a list of which is shown in Table 5.

With extensive renovation the ground floor space could become attractive to boutique shops, a quality restaurant and other retail services. This area could then command higher per square foot rental rates than the office space, and this consideration was built into the cash flow statement. It was possible that areas of the second floor which were used for offices might also be developed as retail space although the only consideration in the cash flow

analysis was for a wine and cheese food and beverage outlet on that level.

The total renovation period was projected to be 1.66 years (20 months) and the consultants made some important assumptions affecting the cash flow statements:

1 It was assumed that all existing leases would be legally circumvented, allowing the building to be renovated. No monetary considerations for circumvention of the leases were included in the cash flow statement.

2 It was assumed that each floor would be fully occupied as it became available, and would remain fully occupied for 5 years. Because of the discomforts of being a tenant during the renovation period (i.e., noisy, dusty, air conditioning not hooked up, etc.), it was further assumed that rents would be held at 50% of their full price until the end of 1982 (when renovation was to be completed).

Three rental rates were examined, as were three expense rates for construction. The rental rates, based on 1980 figures, were $1.00, $1.25 and $1.50 per month for office space, and $1.75, $2.00, and $2.25 per month for retail space. Rental rates were assumed to increase at 10% per year, which was not an unusual clause in many Honolulu office rental contracts. As in the previous alternative, a triple net arrangement would be made, forcing lessees to pay all operating costs of the building in proportion to the square footage they occupied. For purposes of the cash flow statement, rule-of-thumb operating costs were used, amounting to 40¢ per sq. ft. for office and

TABLE 6   RULES OF THUMB CONCERNING PRESENT OPERATING COSTS FOR OFFICE BUILDINGS— DOWNTOWN HONOLULU (EARLY 1980)

	Per square foot
Janitorial	3–5¢
Air conditioning and electricity	12–15¢
Taxes	2–2½¢
Security	2¢
Insurance	1–1½¢
Elevator maintenance	2¢
Water and sewage	1–2¢
Management	3–4¢
Repairs and maintenance	3–4¢
Parking	1–2¢
Total	30–40¢ per month

TABLE 7   RENOVATION COSTS—ALTERNATIVE 4

	$60/ft.	$80/ft.	$100/ft.
Main renovation	$5,249,960	$6,952,260	$8,654,560
Elevator #2	150,000	150,000	150,000
Gym floor ($35 × 4816 ft.)	168,650	168,650	168,650
Totals	$5,568,610	$7,270,910	$8,973,210

retail space (See Table 6) and $.60 per sq. ft. for restaurant space in 1980, which was assumed to increase at 10% per year.

Renovation costs were very difficult to estimate in such an old building, so a variable cost schedule was drawn up. Renovation estimates of $60, $80, and $100 per sq. ft. were examined, resulting in total expenditures of $5.57 million, $7.27 million, and $8.93 million, respectively (See Table 7). Finance charges were assumed to be 14% interest on both the interim and long-term loans, as well as 2 points to the lender of each loan. Cash flow statements were constructed in such a way that the low construction cost estimates were paired with the low rental rates, medium to medium and high to high. (See Appendices.)

APPENDIX IA   TOTALS—CASH FLOW ANALYSIS—STATUS QUO OPTION—90% OCCUPANCY

	1981	1982	1983	1984	1985
Cash inflow	898,110	969,338	1,047,511	1,131,503	1,222,289
Cash outflow	826,293	911,378	1,007,034	1,116,007	1,238,698
Positive (Negative)	71,817	57,960	40,477	15,496	(16,404)

	85% occupancy					75% occupancy				
	1981	1982	1983	1984	1985	1981	1982	1983	1984	1985
Revenues:										
Membership dues	12,941	15,099	17,256	19,413	21,570	11,419	13,322	15,226	17,129	19,032
Resident fees	582,379	628,969	679,227	733,582	792,251	513,864	554,973	599,318	647,278	699,045
Other income	267,770	287,384	309,996	334,164	360,524	267,770	287,384	309,996	334,164	360,524
Total income	863,090	931,452	1,006,479	1,087,159	1,174,345	793,053	855,679	924,540	998,571	1,078,601
Expenses:										
Fixed										
Prof. fees, etc.	14,300	15,730	17,303	19,033	20,937					
Office supplies	5,750	6,612	7,604	8,745	10,056					
Rec. & voc. supplies	3,750	3,063	2,376	1,689	1,000					
Food & beverages	1,000	500	—	—	—					
Misc. purch. for resale	1,100	1,210	1,331	1,464	1,610					
Telephone	17,078	18,102	19,188	20,340	21,560					
Postage & shipping	3,450	3,000	4,140	3,600	4,968					
Maint. (bldg & grds.)	27,000	29,700	32,670	35,937	39,531					
Real estate taxes	11,000	12,100	13,310	14,641	16,105					
Insurance (bldg & grds)	19,300	21,231	23,354	25,689	28,258					
Equipment (maint & rent)	10,000	11,000	12,100	13,310	14,461					
Media, printing	1,000	1,100	1,210	1,331	1,464					
Meals, lodging	2,500	2,750	3,025	3,327	3,660					
Transport, fares	1,120	2,240	1,254	2,509	1,405					
Company vehicles	2,090	2,299	2,529	2,782	3,060					
Vehicles insurance	525	577	635	699	769					
Conf., conv., mtg.	1,450	1,200	1,200	1,200	1,200					
Org. & indv. mbr. dues	235	258	284	313	344					
Property & maint. res.	13,190	13,190	13,190	13,190	13,190					
World service support	1,800	1,980	2,178	2,396	2,635					
New equipment	3,000	3,300	3,630	3,993	4,392					
Total fixed costs	140,638	151,142	162,511	176,188	190,605	140,618	151,142	162,511	176,188	190,605
Variable										
Salaries & wages	403,446	435,722	470,580	508,226	548,884	384,489	415,248	448,468	484,346	523,093
Employee benefits	34,293	37,063	39,999	43,199	46,655	32,681	35,296	38,120	41,169	44,463
Payroll taxes	26,829	31,293	36,517	42,574	49,674	25,568	29,823	34,801	40,574	47,340
Supplies—misc.	520	572	629	692	761	458	504	554	610	671
Janitorial supplies	9,988	10,987	12,086	13,294	14,624	9,149	10,064	11,070	12,177	13,395
Laundry, linen, housekpg.	8,810	9,867	11,051	12,377	13,863	8,049	9,015	10,097	11,308	12,665
Utilities	154,690	183,121	216,884	256,994	304,658	143,940	170,396	201,811	239,134	283,486
Fair share	26,066	28,276	30,711	33,340	36,193	23,965	26,004	28,252	30,682	33,321
Total variable costs	664,642	736,901	818,457	910,696	1,015,312	628,299	696,350	773,173	860,000	958,434
Total expenses	805,280	888,043	980,968	1,086,884	1,205,917	768,937	847,492	935,684	1,036,188	1,149,039
Profit (Loss)	57,810	43,409	25,511	275	(31,572)	24,116	8,187	(11,144)	(37,617)	(70,938)

APPENDIX IC — PROJECTED CASH FLOW—(CASH INFLOW) 90% OCCUPANCY—STATUS QUO OPTION

	1980 (est)	1981	1982	1983	1984	1985
Membership dues	9,800	13,703	15,986	18,270	20,554	22,838
Resident fees	554,709	616,637	665,968	719,245	776,785	838,927
Vending machines	5,500	6,050	6,655	7,320	8,052	8,858
Ancillary services	3,000	3,150	3,308	3,472	3,647	3,829
Rental income—offices	114,596	121,101	132,183	145,652	160,085	176,056
gym	4,000	4,000	4,000	4,000	4,000	4,000
Telephone	18,519	19,630	20,808	22,057	23,380	24,783
Physical education	90,500	95,025	99,776	104,765	110,003	115,503
Sales—mdse. & services	2,700	2,970	3,267	3,594	3,953	4,348
Subtotal		882,266	951,951	1,028,375	1,110,459	1,199,142
Add:						
Property tax		11,000	12,000	13,310	14,641	16,105
General excise tax		4,844	5,287	5,826	6,403	7,042
Total revenues		898,110	969,338	1,047,511	1,131,503	1,222,289

APPENDIX ID — PROJECTED CASH FLOW—(CASH OUTFLOW) 90% OCCUPANCY—STATUS QUO OPTION

	1980 (est)	1981	1982	1983	1984	1985
Salaries and wages	384,720	412,100	445,068	480,673	519,127	560,657
Employee benefits	32,701	35,028	37,831	40,857	44,126	47,656
Payroll taxes	23,583	27,405	31,965	37,300	43,487	50,739
Prof. fees & contr. svcs.	17,000	14,300	15,730	17,303	19,033	20,937
Supplies—misc.	500	550	605	665	732	805
Office supplies	5,000	5,750	6,612	7,604	8,745	10,056
Janitorial supplies	10,386	10,400	11,440	12,584	13,842	15,227
Rec. & vocational supplies	8,800	3,750	3,063	2,376	1,689	1,000
Food & beverages	1,650	1,000	500	—	—	—
Laundry, linen, housekeeping	8,200	9,184	10,286	11,520	12,903	14,451
Mdse, purch, for resale	1,000	1,100	1,210	1,331	1,464	1,610
Telephone	16,111	17,078	18,102	19,188	20,340	21,560
Postage and shipping	2,500	3,450	3,000	4,140	3,600	4,968
Utilities		159,969	189,371	224,285	265,764	315,055
Maint. (bldg. & grds.)	27,515	27,000	29,700	32,670	35,937	39,531
Real estate taxes	10,000	11,000	12,100	13,310	14,641	16,105
Insurance (bldg. & grds.)	17,546	19,300	21,231	23,354	25,689	28,258
Equipment (maint. & rental)	12,800	10,000	11,000	12,100	13,310	14,641
Media, printing, promo.	1,500	1,000	1,100	1,210	1,331	1,464
Meals & lodging	2,000	2,500	2,750	3,025	3,327	3,660
Transportation fares	2,000	1,120	2,240	1,254	2,509	1,405
Company vehicles	1,900	2,090	2,299	2,529	2,782	3,060
Vehicles—insurance	800	525	577	635	699	769
Vehicles—leasing cost	700	—	—	—	—	—
Conf., conv., meetings	810	1,450	1,200	1,200	1,200	1,200
Organ. & indiv. member dues	550	235	258	284	313	344
Fair share	24,100	26,175	28,383	30,813	33,435	36,281
Prop./maint. reserve	13,190	13,190	13,190	13,190	13,190	13,190
World service supp.	1,200	1,800	1,980	2,178	2,396	2,635
Misc. loan repayments	5,000	—	—	—	—	—
Improvements	—	—	—	—	—	—
New equipment	1,000	3,000	3,300	3,630	3,993	4,392
General excise tax (4%)		4,844	5,287	5,826	6,403	7,919
Total expenses		826,293	911,378	1,007,034	1,116,007	1,238,698

APPENDIX IE   UTILITIES—90% OCCUPANCY—STATUS QUO OPTION

	1980	1981	1982	1983	1984	1985
Water	8,400	9,492	10,725	12,120	13,696	15,476
Sewer	4,320	4,882	5,516	6,233	7,044	7,959
Natural gas	10,752	12,365	14,220	16,352	18,805	21,626
Oil	13,800	19,320	22,218	25,550	29,383	33,790
Electricity[1]	62,269	113,910	136,692	164,030	196,836	236,204
Total		159,969	189,371	224,285	265,764	315,055

[1]Breakdown—electricity

1/80–12/80 @ .064 per KWH	61,440	Base rate, Jan '81 @ .10 per KWH	
2.1% Rate ↑, June 1980	614	1/80–12/80 @ .115 per KWH	110,400
2.1% Rate ↑, Nov. 1980	215	4.77% Rate ↑, May 1981	3,510
(results in base rate of .0667 KWH)			

APPENDIX IIA   MODERATE PRICE—HOTEL OPTION*

	1981	1982	1983	1984	1985
Cash inflow	659,226	656,281	1,185,439	1,307,914	1,427,895
Cash outflow	840,989	1,198,879	1,542,095	1,662,804	1,794,119
Surplus (deficit)	(181,763)	(542,598)	(356,656)	(354,890)	(366,224)
Accumulated deficit	(181,763)	(724,361)	(1,081,017)	(1,435,907)	(1,802,131)

*This set of figures assumes no renovation to restaurant facilities, resulting in lower rental revenues from restaurant and lower loan repayment schedule. Triple net revenues not included.

APPENDIX IIB   MODERATE PRICE HOTEL OPTION—CASH FLOW—REVENUES*

	1981	1982	1983	1984	1985
Room revenue	436,920	338,232	755,917	815,191	880,382
Office rental	182,436	253,576	322,600	373,762	417,228
Telephone	8,738	13,676	33,823	37,796	40,759
Vending machines	3,327	3,660	7,320	8,052	8,858
Laundry		8,760	19,272	21,199	23,319
Sub-total (taxable)	631,421	617,904	1,138,932	1,256,000	1,370,546
Add:					
Collected from rentees:					
Share of prop. taxes	20,508	28,234	33,603	36,964	40,660
4% Excise taxes	7,297	10,143	12,904	14,950	16,689
Total	659,226	656,281	1,185,439	1,307,914	1,427,895

*This set of figures assumes no renovation to restaurant facilities, resulting in lower rental revenues from restaurant and lower loan repayment schedule. Triple net revenues not included.

APPENDIX IIC MODERATE PRICE HOTEL OPTION—CASH FLOW—HOTEL* OUTFLOW

	1981	1982	1983	1984	1985
Salaries and wages	193,010	213,650	362,244	391,223	422,521
Employee benefits	13,380	19,868	25,035	27,358	29,899
Payroll taxes	12,835	15,628	29,148	34,627	41,138
Prof. fees and contr. serv.	51,631	10,340	11,374	12,511	13,762
Security	22,082	24,290	26,719	29,391	32,323
Supplies:					
Office	5,750	12,612	10,573	11,630	12,793
Janitorial	7,111	6,776	11,713	12,884	14,172
Laundry-linen-housekpg	4,080	8,500	5,500	6,050	6,655
Telephone	12,455	13,962	29,599	31,375	33,258
Marketing		24,617	40,587	45,355	48,911
Utilities	115,624	142,510	237,504	281,948	334,848
Maint.—bldg. & grounds	15,400	10,890	13,310	14,641	16,105
Equipment—maint. & rental	10,000	11,000	12,100	13,310	14,641
Taxes—bldg. & land	79,234	87,157	95,873	105,460	116,006
Insurance—bldg. & grounds	19,300	21,230	23,354	25,689	28,258
Trans. fares	1,120	1,254	1,405	1,573	1,762
Conf., conv., mtgs.	1,200	1,200	1,200	1,200	1,200
Organiz. & indiv. mbr. dues	250	797	877	965	1,061
Fair share support	18,943	16,596	31,784	35,902	39,161
Prop. maint. reserve	13,188	13,188	13,188	13,188	13,188
World service support	1,800	1,980	2,178	2,396	2,635
Loan repayments	217,340	508,485	499,062	499,062	499,062
Credit card pmt	—	6,222	15,389	17,197	18,546
General excise tax (4%)	25,256	22,127	42,379	47,869	52,214
Equipment purchases		4,000			
Totals	840,989	1,198,879	1,542,095	1,662,804	1,794,119

*This set of figures assumes no renovation to restaurant facilities, resulting in lower rental revenues from restaurant and lower loan repayment schedule.

APPENDIX IID MODERATE PRICE HOTEL OPTION—UTILITIES*

	1981	1982	1983	1984	1985
Water	5,828	11,732	13,257	14,981	16,929
Sewer	2,880	5,798	6,552	7,404	8,366
Natural gas	9,929	8,479	13,002	14,952	17,195
Electricity	82,497	103,171	184,253	221,104	265,325
Oil	14,490	13,330	20,440	23,507	27,033
Total	115,624	142,510	237,504	281,948	334,848

*This set of figures assumes no renovation to restaurant facilities, resulting in lower rental revenues from restaurant and lower loan repayment schedule.

APPENDIX IIIA   CASH FLOW—TOTALS* MODERATE PRICED HOTEL

	1981	1982	1983	1984	1985
Revenues	674,545	731,985	1,322,303	1,493,937	1,633,386
Expenses	847,808	1,238,255	1,581,490	1,702,199	1,833,514
Surplus (deficit)	(173,263)	(507,270)	(259,187)	(208,262)	(200,128)
Accumulated deficit	(173,263)	(680,533)	(939,720)	(1,147,982)	(1,348,110)

*This set of figures assumes restaurant renovation of $264,000, resulting in higher loan repayment schedules and higher lease revenues to the YMCA. Triple net revenues also included.

APPENDIX IIIB   CASH FLOW—REVENUES* MODERATE PRICED HOTEL

	1981	1982	1983	1984	1985
Room revenue	436,920	338,232	755,917	815,191	880,382
Office rental	182,436	274,090	390,428	434,602	483,672
Net/net revenue (offices)	43,124	93,567	115,543	177,097	196,396
Telephone	8,738	13,676	33,823	37,796	40,759
Vending machines	3,327	3,660	7,320	8,052	8,858
Laundry		8,760	19,272	21,199	23,319
Total	674,545	731,985	1,322,303	1,493,937	1,633,386

*This set of figures assumes restaurant renovation of $264,000, resulting in higher loan repayment schedules and higher lease revenues to the YMCA. Triple net revenues also included.

APPENDIX IIIC   MODERATE PRICE HOTEL OPTION—CASH FLOW—HOTEL* OUTFLOW

	1981	1982	1983	1984	1985
Salaries and wages	193,010	213,650	362,244	391,223	422,521
Employee benefits	13,380	19,868	25,035	27,358	29,899
Payroll taxes	12,835	15,628	29,148	34,627	41,138
Prof. fees and contr. serv.	51,631	10,340	11,374	12,511	13,762
Security	22,082	24,290	26,719	29,391	32,323
Supplies:					
Office	5,750	12,612	10,573	11,630	12,793
Janitorial	7,111	6,776	11,713	12,884	14,172
Laundry-linen-housekpg	4,080	8,500	5,500	6,050	6,655
Telephone	12,455	13,962	29,599	31,375	33,258
Marketing		24,617	40,587	45,355	48,911
Utilities	115,624	142,510	237,504	281,948	334,848
Maint.—bldg. & grounds	15,400	10,890	13,310	14,641	16,105
Equipment—maint. & rental	10,000	11,000	12,100	13,310	14,641
Taxes—bldg. & land	79,234	87,157	95,873	105,460	116,006
Insurance—bldg. & grounds	19,300	21,230	23,354	25,689	28,258
Trans. fares	1,120	1,254	1,405	1,573	1,762
Conf., conv., mtgs.	1,200	1,200	1,200	1,200	1,200
Organiz. & indiv. mbr. dues	250	797	877	965	1,061
Fair share support	18,943	16,596	31,784	35,902	39,161
Prop. maint. reserve	13,188	13,188	13,188	13,188	13,188
World service support	1,800	1,980	2,178	2,396	2,635
Loan repayments	224,159	548,861	538,457	538,457	538,457
Credit card pmt	—	6,222	15,389	17,197	18,546
General excise tax (4%)	25,256	22,127	42,379	47,869	52,214
Equipment purchases		4,000			
Totals	847,808	1,239,255	1,581,490	1,702,199	1,833,514

*This set of figures assumes restaurant renovation of $264,000, resulting in higher loan repayment schedules and higher lease revenues to the YMCA.

APPENDIX IIID   MODERATE PRICE HOTEL OPTION—UTILITIES*

	1981	1982	1983	1984	1985
Water	5,828	11,732	13,257	14,981	16,929
Sewer	2,880	5,798	6,552	7,404	8,366
Natural gas	9,929	8,479	13,002	14,952	17,195
Electricity	82,497	103,171	184,253	221,104	265,325
Oil	14,490	13,330	20,440	23,507	27,033
Total	115,624	142,510	237,504	281,948	334,848

*This set of figures assumes restaurant renovation of $264,000, resulting in higher loan repayment schedules and higher lease revenues to the YMCA.

APPENDIX IVA   CONVERSION OF BUILDING TO OFFICES—RENOVATED AND OPERATED BY YMCA

	1981	1982	1983	1984	1985
$40/sq. ft. renovation cost					
Revenues	752,627	1,088,576	1,276,116	1,473,910	1,636,687
Expenses (except loan pmt.)	566,537	643,521	722,750	811,215	908,477
Loan payments	307,349	416,085	366,909	366,909	366,909
Surplus (deficit)	(161,219)	28,970	186,457	295,786	361,301
$60/sq. ft. renovation cost					
Revenues	752,627	1,088,576	1,276,116	1,473,910	1,636,687
Expenses (except loan pmt.)	566,537	643,521	722,750	811,215	908,477
Loan payments	441,110	597,167	526,589	526,589	526,589
Surplus (deficit)	(255,020)	(152,112)	26,777	136,106	201,621

APPENDIX IVB   CONVERSION OF BUILDING TO OFFICES—RENOVATED AND OPERATED BY YMCA—REVENUES (100% OCCUPANCY)

	1981	1982	1983	1984	1985
Room rentals	68,000	—	—	—	—
Office rentals	393,852	623,039	724,948	833,230	910,021
Parking	68,400	72,960	77,520	82,080	86,640
Net-net revenues:					
Property taxes	54,456	85,837	94,421	103,863	114,249
Excise taxes (4%)	15,754	24,921	28,789	32,828	35,934
Utilities	67,218	131,766	170,873	214,934	260,247
Maintenance	84,947	150,053	179,565	206,975	229,596
Totals	752,627	1,088,576	1,276,116	1,473,910	1,636,687

APPENDIX IVC   CONVERSION OF BUILDING TO OFFICES—RENOVATED AND OPERATED
BY YMCA—EXPENSES (Renovation Cost of $40/Sq. Ft.)

	1981	1982	1983	1984	1985
Salaries and wages	133,320	143,986	155,504	167,945	181,380
Employee benefits	9,075	9,905	10,836	11,842	12,941
Payroll taxes	8,866	10,341	12,067	14,069	16,415
Prof. fees and cont. services	14,300	15,730	17,303	19,033	20,937
Supplies—misc.	550	605	665	732	805
Office supplies	4,600	5,290	6,083	6,996	8,045
Janitorial supplies	6,240	6,864	7,550	8,305	9,136
Security	52,998	58,298	64,127	70,540	77,594
Yard maintenance	4,800	5,280	5,808	6,389	7,028
Telephone	1,800	1,800	1,800	1,800	1,800
Postage & shipping	3,450	3,000	4,140	3,600	4,968
Utilities	132,320	157,314	187,095	222,591	264,909
Maint.—bldg.	18,040	16,698	19,699	21,668	23,835
Real estate taxes	79,234	87,157	95,873	105,460	116,006
Insurance (bldg. & grds.)	19,300	21,230	23,354	25,689	28,258
Equipment (maint. & rental)	15,280	16,808	18,488	20,338	22,371
Media, printing, promo	1,000	1,100	1,210	1,331	1,464
Meals & lodging	2,500	2,750	3,025	3,327	3,660
Trans fares	1,120	2,240	1,254	2,509	1,405
Conf., conv., meetings	1,450	1,200	1,200	1,200	1,200
Organ. & indv. mbr. dues	235	258	284	313	344
Fair share	22,579	32,657	38,127	43,841	48,751
Prop./maint. reserve	13,190	13,190	13,190	13,190	13,190
World service support	1,800	1,980	2,178	2,396	2,635
Loan repayments	307,349	416,085	366,909	366,909	366,909
Excise tax (4%)	18,490	27,840	31,890	36,111	39,400
Totals	873,886	1,050,606	1,089,659	1,178,124	1,275,386

APPENDIX IVD   CONVERSION OF BUILDING TO OFFICES—RENOVATED AND OPERATED
BY YMCA—UTILITIES

	1981	1982	1983	1984	1985
Water	4,560	5,153	5,823	6,580	7,435
Sewer	2,160	2,441	2,758	3,117	3,522
Gas	20,000	23,000	26,450	30,417	34,980
Electricity	105,600	126,720	152,064	182,477	218,972
Totals	132,320	157,314	187,095	222,591	264,909

APPENDIX VA   CONVERSION OF BUILDING TO OFFICE WITH COMPLETE BUILDING LEASED AND OPERATED BY PROFESSIONAL DEVELOPMENT COMPANY*

	1981	1982	1983	1984	1985
Revenues:					
Room rental	272,000				
Physical fitness club	90,000				
Existing office rental	113,820	20,992			
New offices ($1/f)	70,194	279,700	790,324	869,356	956,292
Rest., shops ($1.75/f)		61,628	203,372	223,710	246,080
Wine and cheese area		8,504	28,063	30,869	33,956
Storage area		6,212	20,450	22,550	24,805
Net—net revenues	88,113	399,949	570,409	633,348	696,682
Prop. tax and excise-tax revenues	15,844	2,895			
Total revenues:	649,971	779,880	1,612,618	1,779,833	1,957,815
Expenses:					
Operating Expenses	475,011	517,498	570,409	633,348	696,682
Loan payments ($60/f)	510,918	740,624	942,334	830,962	830,962
Total expenses	985,929	1,258,122	1,512,743	1,464,310	1,527,644
Surplus (deficit):	(335,958)	(478,242)	99,875	315,523	430,171

$60/sq. ft. renovation and $1.00/sq. ft. for space plus $1.75/sq. ft. retail space.
*Low estimate (revenues and expenses)

APPENDIX VB   CONVERSION OF BUILDING TO OFFICE WITH COMPLETE BUILDING LEASED AND OPERATED BY PROFESSIONAL DEVELOPMENT COMPANY*

	1981	1982	1983	1984	1985
Revenues:					
Room rental	272,000				
Physical fitness club	90,000				
Existing office rental	113,820	20,992			
New offices ($1.25/sq. ft.)	87,741	349,613	987,914	1,086,705	1,195,376
Rest., shops ($2.00/sq. ft.)		70,432	232,425	255,668	281,235
Wine and cheese area		8,504	28,063	30,869	33,956
Storage area		6,212	20,450	22,550	24,805
Net—net revenues	88,113	399,949	570,409	633,348	696,682
Prop. tax and excise-tax revenues	15,844	2,895			
Total revenues:	667,518	858,597	1,839,261	2,029,140	2,232,054
Expenses:					
Operating expense	475,011	517,498	570,409	633,348	696,682
Loan payments ($80/sq. ft.)	644,242	924,650	1,230,401	1,084,983	1,084,983
Total expenses	1,119,253	1,442,148	1,800,810	1,718,331	1,781,665
Surplus (deficit):	(451,735)	(583,551)	38,451	310,809	450,389

$80/sq. ft. and $1.25/sq. ft. office lease space and $2.00/sq. ft. retail space.
*Middle estimate (revenues and expenses)

APPENDIX VC CONVERSION OF BUILDING TO OFFICES WITH COMPLETE BUILDING LEASED
AND OPERATED BY PROFESSIONAL DEVELOPMENT COMPANY*

	1981	1982	1983	1984	1985
Revenues:					
Room rental	272,000				
Fitness club	90,000				
Existing office rental	113,820	20,992			
New offices ($1.50/f)	105,291	419,531	1,185,478	1,304,027	1,434,429
Rest., shops ($2.25/f)		79,236	261,479	287,627	316,389
Wine and cheese area		8,504	28,063	30,869	33,956
Storage area		6,212	20,450	22,550	24,805
Net—net revenues	88,113	399,949	570,409	633,348	696,682
Prop. tax and excise-tax revenues	15,844	2,895			
Total revenues	685,068	937,319	2,065,879	2,278,421	2,506,261
Expenses:					
Operating expenses	475,011	517,498	570,409	633,348	696,682
Loan payments ($100/f)	823,291	1,193,436	1,518,469	1,339,005	1,339,005
Total expenses	1,298,302	1,710,934	2,088,878	1,972,353	2,035,687
Surplus (deficit):	(613,234)	(773,615)	(22,999)	306,068	470,574

$100/sq. ft. renovation and $1.50/sq. ft. office space and $2.25 for retail space.
*High estimate (revenues and expenses)

CONSIDERATIONS

Before they even read the feasibility study, Mr. Ellis and the board of directors were well aware of the following areas:

1 Members of the armed forces rarely used the ASYMCA as a lodging place when they were in Honolulu. Some of the cheaper hotels in nearby Waikiki weren't much more expensive than staying at the 'Y', especially if two or more people shared the cost of a room. The depressed tourist market at that time had caused many of the hotels with low occupancy levels to lower their rates, hoping to increase their occupancy levels, in order to defray a portion of their fixed costs. One fear expressed by a banker knowledgeable in the industry was that a full-blown rate war amongst the hotels could develop if the tourism market didn't reverse its downward trend.

2 Electricity rates would be increasing dramatically at the end of 1980. Hawaiian Electric Company would be ending its favorable long-term oil contract at that time, causing its oil costs to immediately increase by at least 75%. Price gouging by various OPEC countries and the lack of price stability within the cartel itself also had Mr. Ellis worried about the future cost of energy.

3 Maintaining the old ASYMCA building was getting much more expensive as it got older and labor and parts costs continued to increase. Inflation of at least 10% was expected for the next few years meaning prices would continue to rise.

4 Inflationary pressures affect people on fixed incomes most severely, and the majority of occupants at the Y were on fixed incomes. This made it very difficult for Mr. Ellis to raise the rent while maintaining high occupancy rates (90% occupancy rates had been standard for the past few years).

HOUSTON MARINE TRAINING SERVICES, INC.

Tulane University

In January of 1984, Brant Houston, President of Houston Marine Training Services (HMTS), Inc., was considering alternative solutions to a problem that had plagued his company for the past five years. The problem was that his company had historically experienced a low return on operations outside of the Louisiana area. Increased competition and high overhead had exacerbated the problem. He had to find a way to make operations outside of Louisiana more profitable or discontinue them.

Since 1972, HMTS had served the marine industry by conducting license preparation courses for Coast Guard required licenses. Over 17,000 people in the charter fishing, towing and offshore oil industries had received Coast Guard licenses after completing an HMTS course. HMTS trained 3305 students in 1983, 72% of whom were trained outside Louisiana.

Geographic expansion started in 1978 in response to existing demand. Sales grew rapidly from $450,000 in 1978 to $780,000 in 1979. By the end of 1983, sales were $1.3 million. Profits, however, peaked in 1978 at

$55,000, a level not exceeded until 1983. (See Exhibits 1 and 2 for current financial data.)

During the period from 1979 to 1984, Brant tried numerous measures to increase the profitability of the firm. The first of these measures was an attempt to isolate the revenues and costs of conducting courses outside Louisiana. According to Brant, ''The revenues and costs for each of the two geographic markets were so different that we began asking how much of our money is coming in from these different sources and how much is being used to support them? We didn't know at that point. We just knew that we had a pile of money coming in and a pile going out, and when we subtracted the two we had some left. That's about all we knew. We analyzed the situation and learned what we knew instinctively—that we were making more money inside Louisiana than we were outside Louisiana. But, we had no idea how drastic the difference was.'' That was in 1980.

In 1983, the problem persisted; 70% of HMTS courses were offered outside Louisiana, and the profitability of these courses had to be increased somehow. Brant considered several options, including: partnerships between the company and individuals, joint ventures, strong management incentive programs for local managers, and the hiring of a full-time sales manager. After revealing reservations with regard to these alternatives, Brant reflected on the problem. ''Whatever option we choose, it has to

This case was prepared by Mr. James F. Simpson under the direction of Associate Professor Jeffrey A. Barach, Graduate School of Business Administration, Tulane University, as a basis for class discussion and not to illustrate either effective or ineffective administrative practices. Copyright © 1984 by the School of Business, Tulane University

EXHIBIT 1   HOUSTON MARINE TRAINING SERVICES
INCOME STATEMENTS

Revenues	6/1/80– 5/31/81	6/1/81– 5/31/82	6/1/82– 5/31/83
Gross sales	$1,293,580	$1,536,548	$1,842,128
Total revenues	1,293,580	1,536,548	1,842,128
Direct expenses			
Sales	$	$ 15,305	$
Salaries and benefits	74,465	317,799	389,254
Commissions & contract services	318,454	76,839	271,733
Rentals—classrooms	52,865	116,056	146,680
Advertising	40,506	86,714	97,120
Entertainment	1,137	1,828	3,860
Travel & transportation	85,650	89,787	96,082
Phone	48,834	14,613	50,302
Postage	11,849	6,418	9,184
Supplies		6,947	16,423
Registration		88,775	
Cost of goods sold		98,020	123,516
Training support		34,904	63,904
Marketing			153,600
Miscellaneous	33,013	14,414	3,988
Intra company transfers			(49,418)
Total direct expenses	$ 666,773	$ 968,419	$1,376,228
Gross profit	$ 626,807	$ 568,129	$ 465,900
General and administrative expenses			
Equipment expense	$ 47,098	$ 48,167	$ 56,545
Salaries & benefits	10,773	22,524	12,925
Salaries & wages	225,397	330,776	311,511
Professional services	39,865	68,671	34,390
Promotional/marketing	22,410	16,019	20,512
Contributions/subscriptions	2,882	4,123	4,212
Taxes, fees, licenses	1,715	3,678	9,157
Telephone	3,542	54,788	23,917
Travel and transportation	1,912	13,368	9,361
Supplies	25,974	35,325	34,852
Postage (office-Kenner)	6,489	13,415	10,509
Janitorial and utilities	3,712	17,505	13,306
Insurance	12,094	8,569	18,565
Entertainment	2,528	3,147	4,987
Depreciation	19,718	56,924	55,715
Miscellaneous operating expenses	6,853	9,053	6,739
Office rent	8,640	26,100	18,804
Applied overhead		(274,887)	(320,072)
Total	$ 446,602	$ 457,265	$ 326,435
Other income (expenses)			
Miscellaneous other income	(1,527)	(76,241)	5,514
Interest	34,749	1,569	(49,677)
Bonuses	21,088	3,752	
Accelerated depreciation expense	(63,624)		
R&D write off			(32,985)
Contributions	4,270		
Bad debts	8,704		
Taxes	11,371	(262)	
Profit and sharing expenses	31,000	15,000	
Total operating expenses	$ 622,989	$ 553,565	$ 403,583
Net income	$ 3,818	$ 14,564	$ 62,317

EXHIBIT 2   HOUSTON MARINE TRAINING SERVICES, INC.
BALANCE SHEETS

	5/31/81	5/31/82	5/31/83
Assets			
Cash	$ 53,051.48	$ 48,655.34	$126,731.63
Accounts receivable	30,320.35	52,837.19	94,346.38
Inventory	11,044.15	15,465.31	27,860.16
Prepaid expenses	1,145.00	16,157.64	55.65
Total current assets	$95,560.98	$133,115.48	$238,993.82
Building	$368,696.60	$396,323.75	$412,706.68
Furniture, fixtures & equipment	36,164.00	51,431.56	75,277.60
Autos	27,569.16	32,235.16	45,293.14
Leasehold improvements (Larose)	63,656.40	69,652.55	69,652.55
Less accumulated depreciation	(54,093.00)	(106,690.00)	(160,157.00)
Net property & equipment	$441,993.16	$442,953.02	$442,772.97
Other assets[a]	$ 53,242.80	$ 3,283.87	$ 15,629.20
Total assets	$590,796.94	$579,352.37	$697,395.99
Liabilities			
Student liabilities	-0-	-0-	$41,192.67
Accounts payable	$33,547.80	$11,110.32	$30,585.66
Taxes payable	$16,214.68	(818.25)	775.22
Bonus & profit sharing payable	39,088.31	18,752.30	6,000.00
Notes payable (current)	50,000.00	3,645.44	97,114.00
Total current liabilities	$138,850.79	$ 32,689.81	$169,667.55
Notes payable (net)	$274,607.79	$354,759.73	$273,508.58
Total liabilities	$413,458.58	$387,449.54	$443,176.13
Common stock	$ 100.00	$ 100.00	$ 100.00
Retained earnings	173,420.65	177,238.36	191,802.80
Net income	3,817.71	14,564.47	62,317.06
Total stockholders' equity	$177,338.36	$191,902.83	$281,662.53
Total liability & equity	$590,796.94	$579,352.37	$697,395.99

[a]Other assets (investments, deposits, investments in & amounts due from [to] affiliates)

work,'' he said. ''If it doesn't, we can hang it up as far as our business outside Louisiana is concerned.''

BACKGROUND

Brant Houston graduated from the U.S. Coast Guard Academy in 1967. For the next three years, he served aboard Coast Guard cutters in Vietnam and the Atlantic. After sea duty, Lieutenant Houston was selected to attend the Coast Guard Marine Safety School. From there he was assigned to the Marine Inspection Office in New Or-

leans, Louisiana. During the next two years, he worked in the Coast Guard's investigation, vessel inspection, and marine personnel licensing departments.

Brant observed first-hand the rapid expansion of the towing and offshore oil industries on the Gulf Coast. He was aware of the industries' many safety problems. He knew companies had a hard time obtaining trained and licensed personnel to operate vessels in a manner that complied with Coast Guard requirements. He also knew many people wanted these jobs, but they did not know how to qualify themselves.

After identifying these opportunities, Brant resigned

from the Coast Guard and founded Houston Marine Training Services, Inc. in suburban New Orleans. His personal skills and reputation gave him a distinctive competence to solve these problems. Establishing his name with potential customers was critical, because customers could not prejudge quality due to the simultaneous creation and delivery of services. Making a go of the business wasn't easy. Often a wrong decision would have meant serious losses and inability to support his wife and children.

For the first year, Brant worked out of a bedroom at home. From 1973 through 1976 he rented a two-room office suite, and in 1977 he rented two additional rooms. Later that same year, HMTS moved into a modern office/classroom facility located along a highway in a commercial strip near the Mississippi River about nine miles from downtown New Orleans. In 1980, Brant purchased an 8000 square foot building in Kenner, LA, adjacent to the New Orleans International Airport. This location was selected because it was accessible to students and clients; it was convenient to motels and restaurants for out-of-town students; and because its administrative and classroom spaces were adequate to serve the company's needs.

In addition to the headquarters building, the company had a branch office located in Larose, LA, approximately 50 miles southwest of New Orleans. Until 1982, HMTS sold charts, books, course materials, and nautical gifts through the Captain's Locker, Limited, a subsidiary corporation which was a Hallmark Gift Store also located in Larose, LA. The Captain's Locker was no longer an ongoing business.

INDUSTRY BACKGROUND

HMTS served people in the marine industry who required a Coast Guard license for employment. The company had found that it actually served two separate groups. One category was comprised of people needing a license to gain employment in the oil exploration industry and the towing industry. They enrolled in such courses as Able Seaman, Tankerman, Towing Vessel Operator, and Master/Mate. The other category consisted of individuals who owned their own boat and who wanted to use it to carry "passengers for hire." These people enrolled in the Passenger Vessel Operator (PVO) Course.

Federal Regulations required that any individual who carried "passengers for hire" must be properly licensed. The "passenger for hire" definition covered a wide variety of vessel operators, and crew boat operators. There were a number of court cases which had stretched the definition of "passengers for hire." Boat owners had been found to have been carrying "passengers for hire" if they accepted food or beer from otherwise non-paying passengers.

Getting a Coast Guard license was not easy. Both passing a written examination and experience on the water were required. Any person over 18 years of age with at least 365 days on the water using any size motor vessel could qualify for the Motorboat Operator license if he completed the required Coast Guard forms, a medical exam, and passed the license exam. This license authorized the holder to carry a maximum of six passengers for hire on motorboats 65 feet or less in length. To carry more than six passengers, the Ocean Operator license was required. This license also authorized the holder to operate a vessel inspected by the Coast Guard. For this license, two years' experience on the water was required. The experience had to be in the deck department (deckhand, mate, etc.) of a motorboat or small motor vessel on oceans or coastwise waters.

The number of newly licensed personnel was directly related to industry supply and demand. More boats were operated during times of economic prosperity, and licensed personnel were in heavy demand. However, according to Brant, his company's fortunes to some extent worked the opposite of the industry. He explained that when the towing industry was booming, a towing company had more boats, hence more notes to pay. An owner would operate his boat even if he didn't have the proper number of licensed seamen. He could operate his boat illegally because the Coast Guard had insufficient personnel to adequately enforce the licensing laws. It was relatively easy for a seaman to find employment even if he didn't have the proper license.

When the economy was bad, the industry laid people off. The last employee to be laid off was the one with a license. Job security became important and a license, in many cases, was the key to job security. This was also a time when many people upgraded their licenses. These factors partially insulated HMTS during downturns in the economy.

Still, demand varied seasonally and from port to port depending on economic conditions. Despite built-in insulations described in the last paragraph, HMTS had suffered from the recession in the oilfield and towing industries. Decreased sales and increased operating costs created dangerously weak cash positions as the company entered slow seasonal periods.

Brant was encouraged by predictions of turn-arounds in the industries he served. One industry newsletter, *Marine Management Newsletter,* reported in July of 1983:

"Many observers of the rig charter market, both foreign and domestic, believe the rig market has, in fact, reached bottom. That should signal the beginning of a turn-around for the offshore service vessel market as well—at least as far as the number of available jobs is concerned."

In another issue of the same newsletter it was reported that:

"Gulf of Mexico Market could show an upturn by late 1983 according to some observers. As a result of the recent central Gulf lease sale, as many as 50 of the 71 idle rigs located in the Gulf could be back at work by the end of 1983. This would raise the rig utilization rate in the Gulf from the present mid 60% level to about 90%."

If the oilfield and towing industries recovered from the recession as expected, Brant estimated increased demand for qualified marine personnel could result in net operating income of as much as $400,000.

COMPETITION

Although the Coast Guard promoted self study, it could not offer license prep courses because its responsibility in this area was limited to certifying the competence of marine personnel. Competition did exist among a variety of individuals, state schools, and other commercial schools.

The individuals who taught license prep courses did so on a part-time basis; most were charter boat captains who had a knowledge of the exams. They were interspersed along the Gulf and Atlantic coasts. They advertised in local telephone books, posted notices at marinas, and placed ads in local newspapers. They also found customers through word of mouth or through customer contact established in the normal course of their businesses.

A number of small schools taught license prep courses in Louisiana. Almost all students in these schools were employed in the offshore oil or towing industries. Two state vocational training schools offered license prep courses at no charge to state students and only a token charge for non-residents. These schools were similar to vocational schools in that their courses covered a longer period of time. Because the courses were substantially longer in duration, these schools did not compete directly with HMTS. Another school offering license prep

courses, Page Navigation, was located in downtown New Orleans. This school specialized in classes for higher level licenses, and there was little overlap with HMTS courses.

There were two commercial schools competing directly for HMTS customers. Both schools were owned by former HMTS instructors or sales agents. One, located in New Orleans, competed primarily for mineral and drilling customers. The other school, headquartered in St. Petersburg, FL, competed for PVO customers in Florida, Alabama, and New Orleans. The success of these schools had caused Brant to re-evaluate his pricing and promotional strategy. Although competition was costly, he maintained that competition had been good for his company in that it had caused exploration of new areas (computer-assisted instruction, e.g.) and new strategies to recapture market share.

COMPANY HISTORY

Houston Marine Training Services began as Houston Marine Consultants, Inc. Brant perceived a need for training in 1972, but he believed the greatest need in the oil exploration industry was for a consultant who could advise clients how they could best prepare for Coast Guard inspection of their vessels. He felt that his knowledge of federal regulations and his familiarity with Coast Guard policies with respect to enforcing these regulations qualified him for consulting. He soon found that consulting was less profitable than he anticipated, so he turned to a lucrative market that was not being served—the Coast Guard license prep market.

Growth during the early history of the company was slow. It had all the problems faced by new businesses: under capitalization, no proven track record, and inexperienced management. Brant freely admitted that he didn't know what direction he was headed and that energy was wasted shifting the company's emphasis from consulting to training.

In 1977, revenues were $221,000. HMTS still had a consulting division, but its contribution to total revenue was minimal. Total revenue in 1978 was $455,000, and Brant estimated that only five percent had been generated by consulting activities. License prep courses accounted for 90% of the revenue. Courses offered included: Passenger Vessel Operator (Motorboat Operator, Ocean Operator, and Inland Operator), First Class Pilot, Uninspected Towing Vessel Operator, Chief/Assistant Engineer (Mineral and Oil), Able Seaman, Third Class

Radio-Telephone Operator, Tankerman, 300 Ton Master/ Mate of Mineral and Oil vessels, Master/Mate—Freight and Towing (1000 Ton), Loran C, and Celestial Navigation.

A portion of the revenue in 1978 had been provided by a retail operation, the Captain's Locker, Ltd. This was a subsidiary corporation which became a Hallmark Gift store located in a Larose, LA shopping center in 1980. HMTS sold charts, books, course materials, and nautical gifts through the Captain's Locker. In 1981, this venture fell victim to a recession in the oil exploration industry which hit severely the Larose area and the Captain's Locker's shopping mall.

Brant believed that his success in the license prep market could be attributed to many factors including: few competitors, delivery of a quality product, respect for students, and a loyal and experienced corps of instructors. (See Exhibits 3 and 4 for a description of HMTS philosophy and instructors.)

In 1979, the training division had eighteen full-time salaried instructors. Most instructors taught two classes per month, occasionally traveling to nearby areas where eight or more students enrolled in a course. At the time, Brant estimated that five students in an out-of-LA course covered out-of-pocket costs, and 12 covered its full costs.

EXHIBIT 3   HOUSTON MARINE TRAINING SERVICES
The Ten Commandments of Houston Marine

---

1 The STUDENT is the most important person at Houston Marine.

2 The STUDENT is not an outsider—he is the reason for our existence.

3 The STUDENT is not an interruption of our work—he is the purpose of it.

4 The STUDENT does us a favor when he calls, we are not doing him a favor—nor are we doing a favor when we serve the STUDENT.

5 The STUDENT is not a cold statistic but a human being with feelings and emotions like our own. He does not like to be referred to as a PVO, Master/Mate, UTV, etc.

6 The STUDENT is not someone to argue or match wits with.

7 The STUDENT is a person who brings us his needs. It is our job to assist in the meeting of those needs.

8 The STUDENT is deserving of the most courteous and attentive treatment that can be given.

9 The STUDENT is often dependent on us and we are equally dependent on the STUDENT.

10 The STUDENT is the life blood of Houston Marine.

Between 1979 and 1984, the number of courses conducted annually and the number of instructors increased, but in the pursuit of profitability, the company relied less on full-time salaried instructors and more on contract instructors and training representatives, both of which will be discussed later.

HMTS served two distinct geographic markets—a Louisiana market and a market outside Louisiana. The study confirmed what Brant already knew intuitively: the company was making 60% gross profit on sales in Louisiana and 20% gross profit on sales outside Louisiana.

"My initial reaction was to terminate operations outside Louisiana," remarked Brant. "I couldn't do that because sales outside Louisiana were contributing to overhead and the contribution was significant. So, I began to look for ways to make this aspect of the business more profitable."

One of the first things he did to improve the profitability of operations outside Louisiana was to create a new and experimental position: Area Manager. The area manager was a salaried instructor who liked the challenge of organizing his own business territory and performing the administrative functions required to get a student his license.

The first area manager, Tom Webb, was responsible for operations in Florida. His responsibilities included handling local problems with instructors, resolving problems with Coast Guard officials in his territory, teaching courses himself, and promoting Houston Marine Training Services.

The area manager concept was successful in Florida because of the concentrated sales of courses. Other areas of the country had pockets of activity which warranted expansion into these areas, but could not support an area manager. Coordination in these areas was done through headquarters. Full-time salaried instructors, mostly residents of the areas where there was a demand for courses, were used to conduct the courses, but the cost of travel and lodging for the instructors made this unprofitable. This led to another experimental concept: the training representative.

The training representative concept was designed and implemented in 1981. Pursuant to an agreement entered into by the company and the training representative, the training rep agreed to promote and organize classes in a designated protected territory. He was responsible for conducting all classes. This included all classroom instruction, locating and paying for the classroom, handling all attendant paperwork, and paying for local promotion

EXHIBIT 4   HOUSTON MARINE TRAINING SERVICES
SELECTED PERSONNEL: QUALIFICATIONS AND FUNCTIONS

Name	Year came to MTS	Background	Function	Location
Bill Clark	1983	Retired Coast Guard Captain, Graduate U.S. Coast Guard Academy	Profit Center Mgr; Instructor: (1) Towing (2) Master/Mate	New Orleans
Baba Cullen	1976	Holds 100 Ton Captain's License	Training Rep:VI, PH	St. Thomas, USVI
Terry Southerland	1983	Retired U.S. Navy; Graduate U.S. Naval Academy	Instructor: Master/Mate	New Orleans
Heinz Hickethier	1982	Retired U.S. Navy; NROTC Instructor, Univ. of PA	Manager, Larose, LA Profit Ctr; Instructor	Larose, LA
Paul McElroy	1982	Great Lakes Charter Captain; (Accomplished Author & Publisher)	Training Rep, Great Lakes	Hoffman Estates, Il.
Greg Szezurek	1975	Former Coast Guard Officer	Vice Pres., Profit Center Manager	New Orleans
George Bishop	1982	Graduate U.S. Naval Academy; 3rd Mate License	Training Rep	Pelham, NJ
Ken Woods	1978	Retired, U.S. Navy (24 years); Graduate U.S. Naval Academy	Profit Center Mgr. Instructor: Capt's C.	New Orleans
Tom Webb	1977	Holds Lie-Master upon Oceans on Steam or Motor Pass. Vessels & Master Frt & Towing Vessels	Profit Center Mgr. Instructor	Key Largo, FL
Mike Ellison	1983	Graduate U.S. Naval Academy; M.B.A. Navy Post Graduate School, Monterey, CA; 3 yrs. management consulting.	Profit Center Mgr., Marketing Manager	New Orleans

when required. Each training rep was responsible for his lodging, travel, and food expenses. These costs were non-reimbursable.

The training rep provided the company with collections and itemized reimbursable expenses (such as: local advertising, classroom rental, etc.) for each class. The net of gross receipts less reimbursable expenses was split between the training rep and the company. For its part, the company provided marketing and administrative support, and validated review questions similar to those appearing on actual Coast Guard examinations.

The training representative concept was highly successful in selected geographic areas and significantly improved the overall profitability of operations outside Louisiana. This was done primarily because particular training reps had been able to increase their class sizes. See, for example, Maryland (Conklin) and the Great Lakes area

(McElroy) in Exhibits 5 & 6. There were several problems, however. Specific problems included:

1 The training representative was limited to a relatively small territory because of the same expense and control problems HMTS had experienced when trying to do business on the road. Because the market was so specialized, there were only a limited number of territories that would support a sufficient number and size of classes to make the proposition attractive to a potential training rep. Many of the courses offered in New Orleans were not marketable because a given territory would not produce enough students at any given time to make a profitable class.

2 The initial recruiting and training costs were high and might be lost if the potential training rep changed his mind during the training process.

EXHIBIT 5   HOUSTON MARINE TRAINING SERVICES
NUMBER OF CLASSES SCHEDULED AND CONDUCTED, BY STATE AND YEAR

State	1979		1980		1981		1982		1983	
	Schd*	Cond*	Schd.	Cond.	Schd.	Cond.	Schd.	Cond.	Schd.	Cond.
VT	0	0	0	0	0	0	0	0	0	0
ME	9	4	4	1	2	1	0	0	4	3
NH	1	1	3	3	2	0	4	0	3	0
MA	10	6	7	7	11	11	7	7	7	7
RI	10	8	5	5	3	3	4	4	4	4
CT	12	7	11	11	4	3	9	8	5	4
NY	15	9	11	7	11	10	8	8	8	8
NJ	23	15	22	17	20	19	21	18	18	16
PA	4	2	4	4	8	8	6	4	4	4
DE	4	2	2	1	3	3	0	1	2	1
MD	1	1	3	1	0	0	8	8	8	8
DC	0	0	0	0	0	0	1	1	0	0
VA	3	0	5	2	0	0	1	1	3	2
NC	12	7	10	6	3	2	7	5	9	8
SC	1	1	2	1	0	0	0	0	4	3
GA	0	0	0	0	0	0	0	0	0	0
FL	64	48	51	42	39	38	42	33	45	39
VI	4	4	7	6	4	2	5	5	6	5
PR	1	1	1	1	0	0	0	0	2	2
AL	7	6	3	3	1	1	9	9	17	17
MS	2	2	3	3	0	0	3	3	5	5
LA	76	76	79	78	78	78	96	96	132	109
TX	15	13	13	13	23	23	32	28	41	34
IN	0	0	0	0	0	0	1	0	2	2
IL	1	1	0	0	1	1	3	3	4	4
OH	0	0	0	0	0	0	0	0	4	4
MI	0	0	0	0	0	0	0	0	6	6
WI	0	0	0	0	1	0	0	0	3	3
CA	1	1	1	1	3	3	3	2	0	0
WA	0	0	0	0	0	0	2	2	4	3
OR	0	0	0	0	0	0	0	0	1	1
Total	276	213	247	213	217	208	273	249	353	302

3 Once trained, the training rep needed little in terms of ongoing services from HMTS. Should he leave the company, he would be a formidable competitor in an area that he had developed.

Another change which had reduced fixed costs was the addition of contract instructors. They were paid a base for each course, plus a commission for each student. The contract instructor was required to teach the course and collect the tuition from each student. If he failed to get the minimum number of students, HMTS could cancel the class no later than the seventh day before the class

was to commence. The use of contract instructors was a recent development, and its profitability was still being evaluated.

The greatest change in operations was in 1980 when the company grouped all products and services offered by Houston Marine into profit centers. Each profit center had a profit center manager who was accountable to Brant. Responsibilities of profit center managers included scheduling of classes, teaching courses, supervising instructors assigned to that profit center, promoting and selling courses. Instructors of all kinds (full-time, part-time, contract, and training reps) reported to their respective profit

EXHIBIT 6   HOUSTON MARINE TRAINING SERVICES
NUMBER OF STUDENTS BY STATE AND COURSE

State	1979 PVO[1]	1979 Other[2]	1980 PVO	1980 Other	1981 PVO	1981 Other	1982 PVO	1982 Other	1983 PVO	1983 Other
VT	0	0	6	0	0	0	0	0	5	0
ME	39	0	6	0	18	0	0	0	16	0
NH	10	0	35	0	13	0	33	0	30	0
MA	90	0	115	0	101	0	83	0	131	0
RI	93	0	66	0	51	0	61	0	48	0
CT	44	0	90	0	28	0	76	0	24	0
NY	76	0	83	0	99	0	59	0	85	0
NJ	202	0	194	0	172	0	180	0	200	0
PA	25	0	45	0	76	0	53	0	49	0
DE	14	0	3	0	36	0	0	0	8	0
MD	5	0	29	0	0	0	104	0	128	0
DC	0	0	0	0	0	0	13	0	0	0
VA	0	0	14	0	0	0	12	0	22	0
NC	45	0	50	0	3	0	31	0	50	0
SC	9	0	6	0	0	0	21	0	13	0
GA	0	0	0	0	0	0	0	0	0	0
FL	489	0	510	0	441	0	412	0	381	15
VI	119	0	158	0	31	0	32	0	22	0
PR	8	0	9	0	0	0	0	0	87	11
AL	69	0	26	0	9	0	62	0	32	59
MS	18	0	31	0	0	0	31	0	37	0
LA	573	315	891	543	860	491	618	592	188	752
TX	136	0	154	0	178	0	174	0	249	0
IN	0	0	0	0	0	0	29	0	64	0
IL	0	0	0	0	3	0	44	0	123	0
OH	0	0	0	0	9	0	24	0	139	0
MI	0	0	0	0	0	0	0	0	199	0
WI	0	0	0	0	0	0	17	0	75	0
CA	0	0	6	0	0	0	0	0	0	0
WA	0	0	0	0	0	0	0	4	0	52
OR	0	0	6	0	0	0	24	0	0	11

[1]PVO included—Ocean Operator, Inland Operator, and Motorboat Operator
[2]Other included—Tankerman, Towing Vessel Operator, Master/Mate, Able Seaman, First Class Pilot, Loran C, and Celestial Navigation.

center manager. Profit centers were organized by product line. In 1983, they were changed to geographic organization, as the company became more market oriented.

OPERATIONS

In 1984, HMTS operated in 25 states, Puerto Rico, and the Virgin Islands. Most of its operations were directed at assisting otherwise qualified individuals prepare for Coast Guard examinations. The company offered day courses and night courses in 50 locations to make courses convenient for students. This sometimes resulted in conducting classes with as few as five students (see Exhibits 5 and 6) when a minimum of six students was required to cover variable costs. In 1983, HMTS conducted 302 courses and prepared 3305 students for Coast Guard examinations.

Students were taught material they needed to know to obtain licenses required for employment in the marine industry. They were also taught how to take the exam and what tricks to watch for in questions. Great care was taken in structuring courses so students covered all relevant material needed to pass the exam.

HMTS acted as a liaison between companies, students, and the Coast Guard in assisting with paperwork, photographs required for documents, application problems, medical examinations (using contract physicians), and testing arrangements. Whenever possible, the company arranged for Coast Guard exams to be administered in its classrooms immediately following the period of instruction. This allowed students to test in a convenient and familiar environment, resulting in improved pass rates.

A recent change in HMTS operations was the addition of multilevel courses. Market research had shown that HMTS customers were of two basic types. One type wanted to increase his professional knowledge while preparing for the examination. The other type only wanted a license, and he wanted to learn nothing beyond what was absolutely necessary to obtain a license. Two levels of courses were being given in Kenner in 1984: self-paced and professional development. These are described in Exhibit 7.

In 1983, courses were taught by five full-time, salaried instructors; four half-time salaried instructors; seven contract instructors; and six training representatives. Salaries for full-time instructors ranged between $17,000 and $24,000. Because instructors were crucial to the success of the firm, Brant Houston recruited new instructors himself. The process was both long and difficult, sometimes taking a month to hire a new instructor. Once hired, Ken Woods supervised the instructor's two month training period. Mr. Houston felt that if an instructor stayed for three years, the training effort was worthwhile. Typically, instructors did stay two and a half to three years. Classes in New Orleans were conducted at the company's Kenner location which had three classrooms and computer terminals for the self-paced courses. In Larose, LA classes were held in classroom/office space leased by HMTS. Self-paced courses were also offered in Larose. Courses conducted outside the New Orleans area were held in rented classrooms, usually motel conference rooms. Net profit for operations varied depending on the location of the course and whether the course was taught by a salaried instructor, contract instructor, or a training representative (see Exhibit 8).

To provide control over operations, all products and services offered by HMTS were grouped into profit centers, with each profit center manager reporting directly to

the director of marketing, Mike Ellison, or to the president, Brant Houston. Responsibilities of profit center managers included scheduling of classes, promoting, teaching, and selling.

The profit center manager's primary objective was to maintain a profitable operation and to insure that the product delivered met the standards set by HMTS and those expected by the customer. He had sales agents, instructors, and headquarters support personnel working to help him achieve these objectives. In addition to managing these resources, the profit center manager was also responsible for formulating and executing the budget for his profit center.

In 1984, the company had 38 employees: two in Florida, one in North Carolina, one in Texas, two in Larose, LA, and the remainder (instructors and administrative employees) at the headquarters location in Kenner, LA. The company was divided into six separate areas with the head of each area reporting directly to Brant. The six areas were: Administration, Finance, Training Support, Electronic Data Processing, Research & Development/Special Products, and Marketing (See Exhibit 9 for Organization Chart).

Administration was headed by Mrs. Jeanne Roy. She served as Administrative Assistant to the President and as HMTS's Personnel Officer. In addition, she was also the business office manager, and plant/property manager.

The Vice President of Finance was Robin Houston. Besides performing the duties of that job, she also managed the accounting department.

Ken Woods was manager for the Training Support and Training Representative Profit Centers. As Training Support manager, he was responsible for maintaining and updating course materials, and supervising the Distribution Center Manager. His duties as Training Representative Manager included providing guidance and answering questions they had concerning changes in regulations affecting their courses. Ken was also responsible for ensuring courses conducted by Training Reps met the standards set by HMTS. This sometimes required that he attend classes given by a Training Rep who was having problems as evidenced by poor student evaluations. Ken would make suggestions for improvements, and if the course did not improve, he would recommend the termination of the Training Rep. In addition to Training Reps, Ken also supervised 12 Sales Agents.

Data processing had become such an integral part of HMTS that it had been removed from the Accounting Department. It was now an independent department man-

EXHIBIT 7

HOUSTON MARINE TRAINING SERVICES
SELF-PACED/PROFESSIONAL DEVELOPMENT

So you want your license? Well Houston Marine Training Services now offers you a choice in courses. You can take our Professional Development Course or our Self-Paced License Prep Course. The choice is yours!

Self-Paced License Prep

Houston Marine has developed the surest and easiest way to get your Passenger Vessel license in as little as three days! Combining the latest in technology and personalized instruction, we can give you what you want in a license prep course: your license in as little time possible! The course can be scheduled when you want it—call for your appointment today!

How It Works

You learn the course material from a concise study manual based on our lectures. It's written in plain English that is easy to understand. A Houston Marine instructor is on hand to answer your questions and explain any difficult concepts. Once you feel comfortable with the material, you test your knowledge with a computer-assisted review. When you and the instructor are satisfied with your scores on the computer, you take the Coast Guard exam.

No Pressure

This is a SELF-PACED course! There's no pressure to keep up with the fastest guy in the class. And if you do your homework, you can have your License in as little as three days! Call today to set up your appointment!

Tuition: Self-paced $295

Professional Development

Houston Marine's Professional Development Captain's Course is designed to improve and broaden the student's maritime skills and knowledge. The course is taught by an experienced instructor who covers the material in depth while making difficult concepts and regulations covered on the Coast Guard exam easy to understand. This is for the mariner who wants more than just a license!

Course Date & Times

Location: Houston Marine
           1600 20th St.
           Kenner, LA 70062

Dates: April 25–May 1
        May 15–22
        June 5–June 12

Time: 8:00 am–5:00 pm

Class Size is Limited

Enroll now! A $50 registration fee will reserve a seat for you. When we receive your fee, we will send you the necessary Coast Guard applications and instructions on how to fill them out. We accept certified checks, money orders, cashier's checks, VISA, Mastercard and American Express. The tuition covers everything you need for the course.

Tuition: Prof. Dev. $495

Our eleven years of professional maritime training experience makes it easy for us to say: Your success is guaranteed—or your money back!

aged by Robert Andre. He worked for Brant, for the Marketing Department, and for any other department requiring data processing support.

Greg Szczurek was manager of the Research and Development Custom Courses, and Special Projects Profit Centers. He developed course materials (books, videotapes, and study guides) to improve the quality and reduce the costs of HMTS courses. Greg also developed custom courses tailored to the needs of a particular company. He was a member of and actively involved in a number of professional trade associations.

Custom courses were developed for companies covering the subject matter of any of HMTS's standard courses. These courses offered several advantages for a

EXHIBIT 8   HOUSTON MARINE TRAINING SERVICES
            REVENUE/COSTS COMPARISONS

I Company salaried instructor (inside Louisiana)

	Students				
	6	8	10	12	15
Revenue	2970	3960	4950	5940	7425
Less direct costs					
Instructor salary	648	648	648	648	648
Travel/transportation	0	0	0	0	0
Lodging/meals	0	0	0	0	0
Classroom rental	1000[1]	1000	1000	1000	
Materials	240	320	400	480	600
Direct advertising	128	128	128	128	128
Total direct expenses	1976	2096	2176	2256	2376
Gross margin	994	1864	2774	3684	5049
Less indirect costs					
Training support	154	154	154	154	154
Marketing	412	412	412	412	412
Admin/accounting	82	82	82	82	82
Total indirect expenses	648	648	648	648	648
Net income per course	346	1216	2126	3036	4401

[1]Allocated cost of headquarter's classroom.

II Company salaried instructor (outside Louisiana)

Revenue	2970	3960	4950	5940	7425
Less direct costs					
Instructor salary	648	648	648	648	648
Travel/transportation	200	200	200	200	200
Lodging/meals	360	360	360	360	360
Classroom rental	600	600	600	600	600
Materials	240	320	400	480	600
Commissions	180	240	300	360	450
Direct advertising	128	128	128	128	128
Total direct expenses	2356	2496	2636	2776	2986
Gross margin	514	1464	2314	3164	4439
Less indirect costs					
Training support	154	154	154	154	154
Marketing	412	412	412	412	412
Admin/accting	82	82	82	82	82
Total indirect expenses	648	648	648	648	648
Net income	(34)	816	1666	2516	3791

EXHIBIT 8   HOUSTON MARINE TRAINING SERVICES
REVENUE/COSTS COMPARISONS *(Continued)*

III Contract instructor

	Students				
	6	8	10	12	15
Revenue	2970	3960	4950	5940	7425
Less direct costs					
Instructor salary[1]	680	740	800	860	950
Travel/transportation	200	200	200	200	200
Lodging/meals	360	360	360	360	360
Classroom rental	600	600	600	600	600
Materials	240	320	400	480	600
Commissions	0	0	0	0	0
Direct advertising	128	128	128	128	128
Total direct expenses	2208	2348	2483	2628	2838
Gross margin	762	1612	2402	3312	4537
Less indirect expenses					
Training	154	154	154	154	154
Marketing	412	412	412	412	412
Admin/accting	82	82	82	82	82
Total indirect expenses	648	648	648	648	648
Net income	114	964	1814	2664	3939

[1]Instructor salary is $500 + $30 per student.

IV Training representative

Revenue	2970	3960	4960	5940	7425
Less direct costs					
Classroom rental	600	600	600	600	600
Materials	240	320	400	480	600
Direct advertising	128	128	128	128	128
Total direct expenses	968	1048	1128	1208	1328
Gross margin	2002	2912	3822	4732	6097
HMTS gross income (50%)	1001	1456	1911	2366	3048.50
Less indirect costs					
Training support	154	154	154	154	154
Marketing	412	412	412	412	412
Admin/accting	82	82	82	82	82
Total indirect costs	648	648	648	648	648
Net income	353	808	1263	1718	2400.50

EXHIBIT 9   **Organization chart.**

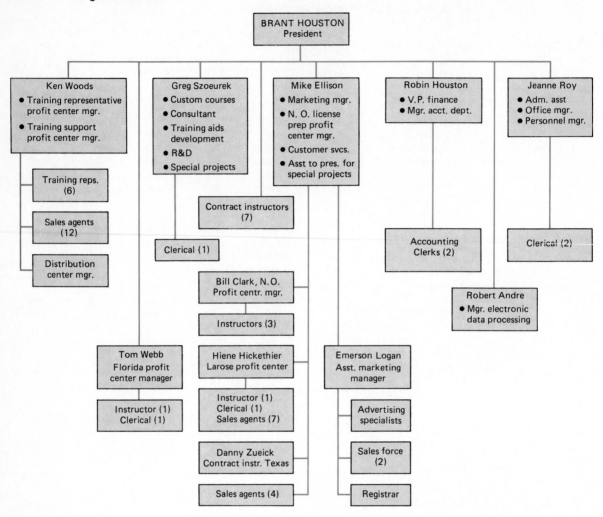

company. The material was specifically tailored to the company's needs. Training could be held at the company location. Courses could be scheduled to fit the company's work schedule.

Greg also produced and sold training aids such as books, videotapes, slides, and outlines (see Exhibit 10 for a description of books published). Most of the sales of training aids had been to the Coast Guard, Navy, and students enrolled in HMTS's courses. Books were sold through *Hooked-Up* (the Houston Marine Newsletter), and by direct mail, but were sold primarily to students by their instructors.

Mike Ellison was Marketing Manager. The Marketing Department consisted of an assistant manager, an advertising specialist, a sales force, and a registrar. All courses conducted in New Orleans were promoted and sold through the Marketing Department. In addition, it provided national advertising and marketing support to training reps and other license prep profit center managers. This department also conducted research and feasibility studies for new markets and new courses. Mike was also Profit Center Manager for License Prep Courses in Louisiana and Texas, and had two other profit center managers and the contract instructor for Texas reporting directly to

EXHIBIT 10   HOUSTON MARINE TRAINING SERVICES
BOOKS PRODUCED AND SOLD BY HMTS (PARTIAL LIST)

Unified Rules

- study guide and reference book
- fulfills requirement that vessels over 39 feet carry a copy of Rules aboard
- chosen as textbook at U.S. Naval Academy
- cost: $10.50 plus shipping

COLREGS

- study guide and reference books
- easy guide to International Collision Prevention Regulation (COLREGS)

- chosen as textbook of U.S. Naval Academy
- cost: $9.50 plus shipping

Licensing Procedures Manuals

- contains most Coast Guard licensing policies and procedures
- only book available that offers one easy to read source
- used by personnel managers and Coast Guard personnel

---

him. He also supervised four Sales Agents. In addition, Mike was the Profit Center Manager for Customer Services, which was responsible for arranging for photographs and physical examinations required for students' licenses. Finally, Mike served as Special Assistant to the President.

MARKETING

The marketing department assisted each profit center manager in developing his marketing plan and budget. Functions performed by the company's marketing group included:

- telephone sales—handled incoming calls from prospects and actively solicited new business.
- maintained sales/prospect files.
- maintained master company course schedule (tally boards, status boards).
- used and updated computer information for possible leads.
- developed advertisements, promotional materials, schedules, etc., at request of profit center managers.
- placed advertisements.
- maintained contact with agents and training reps regarding all marketing functions.
- market research—questionnaire development and implementation.

The marketing department was responsible for coordinating sales force activities, advertising programs and other promotional activities for each profit center and for the company overall. Additionally, the marketing department conducted surveys to measure the student's perception of courses and the overall services provided by

HMTS. It also monitored trade journals to follow industry trends and recommended new courses or modifications to existing courses when it appeared that there was a demand that would justify the addition or change. Finally, in this area, the marketing department researched and presented demographic data to help management keep abreast of its customer bases in the various markets and geographic areas it served.

As a part of the marketing department, there was a local sales force of two people who made telephone calls throughout the country. These individuals also handled all incoming calls from prospective students. After a student was "sold" he or she was referred to a profit center for registration, processing, teaching, etc. The sales section did not handle incoming calls for custom courses, videotapes, or books.

Outside of Louisiana there was a network of 31 sales agents. These agents were not HMTS employees. Rather, they were part-time salespeople, most of whom were employed in the marine industry, who sold courses on a commission basis per student. The agents promoted and sold courses in their local areas.

The agent had been, and continued to be, the weakest link in the HMTS service chain. Ironically, he was often the only personal contact a prospective student had with the company. Service by the agents was inconsistent according to Jeanne Roy, who had coordinated the activities of sales agents before they were assigned to profit center managers.[1] The biggest problem was motivating them. She said the company had initiated a number of incentives (bonuses, an "early bird" program providing a higher

---

[1] Sales agents reported to profit center managers in Headquarters, Florida, and Larose, LA

commission for filling classes early, and an agent newsletter), but had failed to find one that worked satisfactorily.

The third method of sales management was with training representatives in locations outside Louisiana. This method had built-in motivation. If the training rep didn't sell, he didn't teach, which meant less income. If he did not watch his expenses, he made less money. An advantage of this method was that the training rep had face-to-face contact with the prospective student. He could hire a sales agent, but he had to pay the commissions.

Mass advertising at HMTS was used most extensively for the PVO classes. Advertisements were placed regularly in the classified or boating sections of boating magazines and local newspapers. Also, regional and national fisherman publications were used, as were national magazines like *Yachting*. Radio had been used on a limited basis, and outdoor billboards were used in the Bayou Lafourche area of Louisiana. Additionally, for all courses, advertising consisted largely of direct mail flyers, course schedules, brochures, etc. These were sent to former students and practically anyone who had expressed an interest in an HMTS course. Other targeted advertising efforts included postal routes with flyers and brochures in marine stores, personnel offices, yacht and fishing clubs, etc.

Course prices were initially established by executive management, with gradual increases of roughly $25 twice a year. Prices did vary by geographic area with courses taught in Louisiana priced at $50–$100 lower than other regions with the exception of Florida. (See Exhibit 7 for PVO course prices in Louisiana.) Tuition in Florida had been lowered in response to strong competition. Training reps set the price of their courses generally at equal or slightly lower costs than the home office. Course prices were largely relative to the length of the course, averaging $350–$450 per week. Customized courses or products were priced to return 30–50% gross profit depending upon the specifics.

There were companies and schools in the marketplace that provided license preparatory courses or home study materials. For the most part, these schools or companies were lower priced than HMTS. While the services provided were not comparable, they could be used as substitutes for the HMTS products. Home study packages ranged from $14.95 up, and the Captain's Course could be had for as little as $99, or were available free from the Louisiana state schools. Basically, much of the competition, aside from the "free schools," looked to HMTS for a standard, and priced their courses accordingly to offer a price advantage. One of the competitive schools

stressed that license prep was license prep, and why spend $100–$150 more, and why go to school longer, as their program was only five nights, four hours each, for the PVO test. They saved time and still achieved excellent pass rates by stressing test preparation rather than teaching navigation.

According to an in-house marketing report, clients almost never expressed the opinion that HMTS prices were too high. Most recognized the product as worth the price. Also, for many, the company picked up the cost of the course. For a great many who travelled from outside Louisiana to take courses at Kenner, tuition was just a part of the overall cost including hotel, transportation, meals, etc. To an individual, price mattered, but the goal was to obtain a license as cheaply and as quickly as possible. Thus, high pass rate and scheduling dates could become deciding factors, rather than price.

There had been some sense among agents that HMTS's prices were too high. While Mike Ellison recognized that this might have been a fair reflection of resistance in the marketplace, he felt that the agents should have recognized and communicated that the product was worth the price.

Ellison said that there were two basic groups which made up the customer base for HMTS. The target market varied depending on the course content.

For PVO classes, customers fell into the following categories:

• Individuals who wanted to charter their boat for hire;
• Individuals who were currently operating illegal charters;
• Recreational boaters who wanted to learn more about their boats for safety and interest; and
• Professionals seeking tax deductions and insurance benefits.

Until recently, fishing had been the backbone of the charter industry, but sailing charters, sightseeing, waterskiing, etc., were growing as individuals sought ways to increase their incomes or pay for the boat's expenses. Also, using the boat to transport passengers for the drilling industry was a lucrative charter.

For other license prep courses, the market included:

• individuals employed or seeking employment on towing vessels, supply boats or in the drilling industry;
• companies owning or managing towing vessels or supply boats;
• drilling company personnel or management.

Clients with all levels of experience were eligible for different courses. A large part of this market was involved in the offshore drilling industry, but many worked on the Mississippi River transporting coal, grain, etc., as well as in the oil-related fields.

Jobs on boats appealed to young and independent people who preferred being out on the water to a regular job. The river and offshore oil boat operators often alternated seven days on board ship and seven days off. In good times, turnover was high, because the men switched jobs often to suit their own individual schedules, and because they upgraded their licenses and advanced to larger vessels. Still others left the industry or were promoted to jobs on shore. Among deckhands, turnover typically had been 300–500% a year. Although not as high, the turnover among licensed officers and operators had often run in excess of 100%. Mr. Houston estimated that 20 percent of this turnover was from people who left the industry permanently. Therefore, even if demand remained constant, many new jobs requiring licenses became available every year. The recent recession in the industry had reduced personnel turnover.

Companies were often the target while individuals were the direct consumer. Many times companies paid for or encouraged an individual employee to obtain a particular license. Thus, company management played a large part in the decision-making process by either recommending a particular school or making all the arrangements and requiring attendance at that school. When the supply of licensed personnel was less than companies needed to meet their Coast Guard requirements, companies were more likely to send their employees to school.

For training aids, consulting and special seminars, the target market included the same individuals and companies interested in the license prep courses, as well as Navy, Coast Guard or Air Force training classes and others involved with or affected by Coast Guard regulations who may be in need of expert advice.

Custom courses were marketed to companies involved in the maritime or drilling industry. Custom courses were less likely to be oriented to license prep and more likely to be focused on safety issues such as stability, hazards on the rig, firefighting, etc.

The marketing department had been able to develop customer profiles of its students. A majority of HMTS students were between the ages of 20–45, males, white, married, high-school educated or less, outdoor oriented, and had a maritime occupation. Incomes varied widely, from $8,000–$10,000 as unlicensed deckhands coming for their first license to $25,000–$35,000 when they got an advanced license.

For the PVO classes, students tended to be fishermen, shrimpers, charter boat captains or those hoping to be charter boat captains, and a small group of professional people—doctors, lawyers, airline pilots, etc.—looking for tax write-off. PVO students tended to be somewhat older than students in Able Seaman, Mate or Tankerman classes, with a majority 35–50 years old, male, white and high school educated.

In addition to developing a customer profile, the marketing department had identified reasons individuals engaged HMTS' services. It had found that, among other reasons, customers were motivated to take courses because:

• They were required by the Coast Guard to have a license for the job they had or a job they wanted;
• They wanted a license so that they could legally hire out their vessel for a part-time source of income;
• They wanted a license for prestige, tax deductions or insurance benefits; or
• They were interested in the knowledge and benefits obtained from taking a course, rather than the license itself.

Those who wanted to obtain their Coast Guard license took a course because they knew, or had heard, how difficult it was to qualify without the course. Their objective was usually to get the license in as short a time as possible and return to work. Many had tried on their own and failed, and some had tried the "free" state schools and failed. They saw HMTS as the quickest way to their desired end.

Factors that were considered to affect an individual's decision to study at Houston Marine rather than elsewhere were:

• scheduled dates for classes—class scheduled during time off or availability to start immediately
• class location
• recommendations from friends, captains or company personnel officers
• previous experiences with HMTS or other schools
• good pass rate
• their company made the decision
• advertising
• sales pitch from marketing department or agent
• only school the individual knew of was HMTS
• price

BRANT HOUSTON, CHIEF EXECUTIVE OFFICER

When Brant founded HMTS, he was pretty much a one-man show. By 1979, the company had matured, and while he occasionally taught a course, most of his time was spent doing high level consulting, selling, working with industry groups, and managing the organization. The pace was typical for an entrepreneur, hectic. Appendix A presents a week in Brant Houston's life in 1979.

Commenting on what had happened since then, Brant remarked that the more things change, the more they remained the same. He did no teaching now, and his direct involvement in consulting had diminished considerably. Industry groups, key customers, and other ''outside'' matters still took much of his time, but more and more of his time was devoted to working with his management team. The ever-expanding computer system commanded constant attention, as it did in 1979. Running had replaced racquetball because it could be done in less time and at any hour. He still got to take his wife to lunch, though she was now Vice-President of Finance.

His biggest challenge was in developing middle level managers who could take the load off him in managing the various departments and profit centers. An enormous amount of his time was taken up interacting with these individuals. If a manager had been promoted from within, he usually had been hired because of his technical or teaching experience and skills and had to learn the marketing and business aspects of the job. If a manager had been hired from the outside, he had an equally formidable task of learning the company's organization, products, philosophy, etc. Brant wanted to delegate more but felt like he was abdicating his responsibility if he did so before the manager was ready to take on more responsibility.

Personally, Brant's family had grown from no children when the business was founded to three. The family needed more and more of his time. Although he still enjoyed his work immensely, he had begun to realize that the day would come when he would want to have the option to retire or at least decrease his day to day involvement with the business.

FUTURE

In an in-house document, Brant described Houston Marine as a company on the move. It had thrived for the first year of the national recession in spite of the fact that the oilfield and towing industries were particularly hard hit. The company had upgraded its management, marketing, and operating personnel; improved its marketing tools and techniques; and had developed several innovative new products. These changes were part of a strategic plan that established an annual increase in net operating income of 20% and predicted gross sales to be $5 million in 1988.

Several factors were to contribute to this growth. Brant was particularly excited about two product innovations. A computer-assisted course had been developed and had been successful in New Orleans and Larose. Plans to expand it to other locations were being considered. This new method of preparing students for examinations was expected to not only reduce operating costs, but it was believed that it would be more attractive to a larger segment of the market and would help increase the company's market share.

Another development that had been successful was a ballast control simulator program. The course was intended for anyone responsible for maintaining and monitoring stability on mobile offshore drilling units. Tuition ranged from $600 for the two-day course to $1200 for the full five-day course.

The success of these and other recent developments had fueled Brant's optimism for the future. He anticipated these factors to increase net operating income by more than $200,000 by 1985. If the oilfield and towing industries recovered as predicted from the recession, the increased demand for qualified marine personnel could result in net operating income of $400,000.

Over the next several years, Brant planned to diversify within the training business to offer training prep courses outside the marine industry. He felt that, with slight modifications, his organization was excellently suited to offer GMAT, SAT, LSAT, and GRE review courses.

Other potential sources for growth were not the products or services offered, but the manner in which they were distributed. Franchising was being considered. Brant believed that operating costs would be decreased and revenues would be increased by going to a self-paced, computer-assisted series of courses offered by local individuals with full control over advertising, sales, and operations under the Houston Marine Training Services name in defined territories. Because of the advent of videotaped instruction materials requiring constant updating, the company would have something substantial to offer franchisees, in addition to the HMTS name, to keep the franchisee paying a percentage to HMTS rather than becoming a competitor.

However profitable franchising might prove to be, Brant did not see it as an immediate solution to the problem associated with geographic expansion. He was considering two or three alternatives to increase the profitability of operations outside Louisiana. One alternative was

APPENDIX A

HOUSTON MARINE TRAINING SERVICES, INC.
WEEK IN THE LIFE OF THE PRESIDENT*

Monday

5:50 a.m.	— Leave home for racquetball courts.
6:00 a.m.–7:00 a.m.	— Play two games of racquetball.
7:00 a.m.–7:45 a.m.	— Sauna, whirlpool, shower & dress.
8:15 a.m.	— Arrive at office.
8:15 a.m.–8:30 a.m.	— Coffee, check with key personnel for any crises.
8:30 a.m.–1:30 p.m.	— Approve 10 expense reports; take telephone complaint from employee in Florida whose paycheck did not arrive; write letter to government agency to straighten out snafu caused by government personnel changes; discuss personnel and licensing problems in Mass. with area manager; read mail, assign various tasks of responding; meet with insurance agent on ramifications of new Federal regulations on maternity leave; politely get rid of Chamber of Commerce salesman; brief customer on Coast Guard Industry Day meeting which he could not attend; discuss Coast Guard policies with personnel manager of a customer.
1:30 p.m.–2:00 p.m.	— Lunch (can of Sego); discuss progress of computer installation with DP manager and programmer.
2:00 p.m.–5:00 p.m.	— Review new policy from Coast Guard HQ on license renewal for special licenses, compare with conflicting regulations, develop strategy to tactfully point out the error to the CG; review sales strategy with marketing manager; revise drafts of sales letter to drilling companies; miscellaneous phone calls; work on rough draft of letter to US Senate Foreign Relations Committee explaining the adverse impact of an international convention scheduled for ratification hearings.
5:00 p.m.–5:30 p.m.	— Supervise and generally get in the way of secretary, DP manager and programmer learning how to type letters into the new computer.
6:00 p.m.	— Arrive home.
6:00 p.m.–9:00 p.m.	— Eat with family.
9:00 p.m.–10:30 p.m.	— Listen to home study tape course on computers; read computer user guide.

Tuesday

6:00 a.m.	— Arrive at office.
6:00 a.m.–8:30 a.m.	— Continue drafting letter to Congress on international convention.
8:30 a.m.–12:30 p.m.	— Review computer insurance proposal; review marketing letters; make last-minute check of air conditioning modification plans for computer room; take 15 minutes for public relations with old customer to show him our facility and discuss his problems; read mail, assign responses; discuss international convention with former delegate for 30 minutes on telephone (promised a copy of 1975 drafts which had been "impossible" to obtain); discuss payroll problems with bookkeeper; miscellaneous phone calls.

*Source: Aronson, Dale A. and Barach, Jeffrey A., "Houston Marine Consultants, Inc. (New Orleans, LA: School of Business, Tulane University, 1980), pp. 28–30

APPENDIX A *(Continued)*

12:30 p.m.–1:30 p.m.	— Took bookkeeper (wife) to lunch.
1:30 p.m.–5:00 p.m.	— Supervised air conditioning work; discussed results of morning exams with CG; discussed relocation plans with an employee; approved payables; wrote two letters; proofread international convention draft letters; developed strategy on mail campaign.

Wednesday

8:30 a.m.	— Arrive at office, check with key personnel.
8:45 a.m.–noon	— Meet with assistant to finalize agenda for OMSA manning and licensing committee meeting to be held at our facility on Thursday; plan handouts and strategy in general for meeting; review mail; handle miscellaneous calls.
12:00 noon–1:00 p.m.	— Have lunch with training director.
1:00 p.m.–5:30 p.m.	— Continue preparing for committee meeting.

Thursday

8:00 a.m.–8:30 a.m.	— Work with key personnel to be sure that office work and meeting will go smoothly for the day.
8:30 a.m.–9:00 a.m.	— Greet arriving committee members.
9:00 a.m.–noon	— Conduct meeting.
12:00 noon–1:30 p.m.	— Have lunch with several committee members (who are also customers).
1:30 p.m.–5:30 p.m.	— Catch up on morning's work, assign tasks of following up on morning meeting.

Friday

7:00 a.m.–9:00 a.m.	— Meeting with training director to review resumes of prospective instructors.
9:00 a.m.–9:15 a.m.	— Check with key personnel for any problems.
9:15 a.m.–noon	— Prepare for afternoon meeting of Marine Education Association in Thibodaux; agree to work on United Fund campaign in a weak moment; review mail.
12:00 noon–1:00 p.m.	— Enroute to Thibodaux; eat hamburger on the way.
1:00 p.m.–4:30 p.m.	— Attend meeting.
5:00 p.m.–6:30 p.m.	— Attend cocktail party.
6:30 p.m.–8:00 p.m.	— Dinner with OMSA Executive Secretary, M & L Committee member, and House of Representatives minority and majority counsels to discuss status of impending legislation (last-minute happening—had planned to be home by 7:00 p.m.).
9:30 p.m.	— Arrive home.

to increase the number of training reps wherever possible. Over 18% of HMTS students in 1983 were trained by the Great Lakes training representative. His compensation for 1983 approached $100,000. HMTS had benefitted too. Until 1982, only 12 students had trained in this area. Increasing the number of training reps would mean less supervision required by HMTS, although extra care would be required to safeguard course quality. Brant felt that if he could locate highly motivated, qualified instructors he could negotiate an incentive plan that would increase the company's profits. However, he also knew that this was the kind of individual who was most likely to leave the company, and at the expiration of the non-competing clause of his employment contract, would become a formidable competitor.

Another alternative was to leave the organizational structure as it was. (See Exhibit 9 for organization chart.) The profit center concept was new; perhaps he should give it time to work. He could use the computer to isolate costs, and he could rid the company of marginal areas. Brant felt that if he could get costs in line, motivate sales agents, and increase the average number of students per class, he might make more money (with less risk of loss of control and creating competition) with his existing mix of full-time, part-time, and contract instructors than by turning more territory over to training reps.

Brant wasn't sure which alternative—existing organization or increased training reps—would solve his problem. He had even entertained the idea of hiring a sales manager. Maybe he could use a sales manager even if he decided to increase the number of training reps. This thought led to another problem; whom should he hire as sales manager?

Mike Ellison came to mind, but Brant wondered whether he could handle the extra duties. Since coming to HMTS, Mike had sought and had been given increased responsibility. He now had full control of marketing activity and supervisory responsibility for the marketing staff. He was also responsible for exploring and assessing the marketability of new courses for HMTS. In addition, as profit center manager for license prep courses, he had two other profit center managers and one contract instructor reporting to him. They were: Bill Clark (New Orleans License Prep), Heinz Hickethier (Larose License Prep), and Danny Duzick of Houston, the contract instructor for Texas.

Brant was not sure what he should do. There was one thing of which he was sure, however; whatever he did had to work.

HUMANA, INC.

George S. Vozikis
Timothy S. Mescon
Memphis State University
Salisbury State College

Michael M. LeConey, security analyst for Merrill Lynch, Pierce, Fenner and Smith, has said, "With Humana, investors are dealing with what I believe may be the most aggressive and smartest major company in the U.S. That's a lot to say about any company, but Humana's success, and the absolutely uncanny accuracy of its corporate strategy, make it a supportable statement" (*Wall Street Transcript,* June 9, 1980).

HISTORY

Humana, Inc. was begun in 1961, when David A. Jones and Wendell Cherry, two young lawyers, built their first nursing home. Humana, Inc. was incorporated in Delaware, on July 28, 1964, as Extendicare Inc. It became the successor to Heritage House of America Inc., which commenced operations in 1961.

By 1967, government health programs such as Medicaid and Medicare had been implemented by Congress, and Humana, Inc. was running eight nursing homes. In 1968, a flu epidemic struck New Haven, Connecticut, and a hospital placed its overflow in their local nursing home.

The "Gold Dust Twins," as business associates sometimes call Jones and Cherry, discovered that hospitals earned six times as much from Medicare and Medicaid as nursing homes did.

In 1968, a boom year for nursing home stocks, they took their company public. Humana began to buy up existing private hospitals at a rate of one per month, and by selling their nursing homes and mobile home parks (and by borrowing heavily), in 1972 and 1973 embarked on a $300 million dollar hospital construction program, completing some 39 hospitals in the South and Southwest by 1976. The National Health Planning and Resources Development Act was passed in 1974, which prohibited the renovation, construction, or purchase of equipment costing more than $100,000.00, unless state and local health planning agencies approved it as necessary. Humana, Inc. was convinced that this law would practically halt new construction, and they began to supplement hospital purchases by buying out competitors such as American Medicorp, number two in the industry in 1978 when it was purchased by Humana.

Little cash was used. The acquisitions were accomplished by exchanging stock with doctor-owners. Success in acquisition efforts precipitated an internal growth strategy of construction of additional hospitals, coupled with a divestment of the nursing homes. By 1977, this strategy increased revenues to $316 million from $85 million in 1971, and long-term debt to $224.3 million from $87.8 million.

In 1980, Humana's revenues increased to $1.1 billion from 1977's $316 million, and profits from $11.8 million to $64.6 million. Significantly, Humana's 10-year compounded growth rate of 32 percent exceeded all but eight companies in *Financial World* magazine's annual ranking of 10-year performance by companies with revenues above $500 million.

Humana views the pursuit of medical excellence as its most important task. The company's Mission Statement is the focal point of its commitment: "The mission of Humana is to maintain an unequaled level of measurable quality and productivity in the delivery of health services that are responsive to the needs and values of patients, physicians, employers and employees."

In an era where the continued demand for quality health care is matched by the need to control costs, Humana provides an integrated system of high quality, cost efficient health care services through its three operating divisions: Hospital Division; Health Services Division; and Group Health Division.

Hospital Division

Humana owns and operates 86 hospitals containing approximately 17,700 beds in 21 states, England, Switzerland, and Mexico. (See Exhibit 1.)

As a reflection of Humana's commitment to medical excellence, the Centers of Excellence program was established at Humana hospitals in 1982 to support practicing physicians who excel in their specialty so that they can undertake clinical research and medical education programs in conjunction with their private practices. A Center of Excellence is a medical referral and consultation

EXHIBIT 1   EXISTING HOSPITAL LOCATIONS, THEIR CAPACITY, AND HOSPITALS UNDER CONSTRUCTION (AS OF AUGUST 1985)

State	# of hospitals	Total bed capacity	Hospitals or additions under construction	Add. beds
Alabama	6	983	—	
Alaska	1	199	1	39
Arizona	2	434	—	—
California	5	938	—	—
Colorado	2	450	—	—
Florida	17	3,820	5	138
Georgia	4	718	—	—
Illinois	2	556	—	—
Indiana	1	150	—	—
Kansas	2	510	—	—
Kentucky	7	1,861	1	61
Louisiana	8	833	—	—
Mississippi	1	101	—	—
Nevada	1	670	—	—
North Carolina	2	198	—	—
Tennessee	4	472	—	—
Texas	11	2,990	2	35
Utah	1	110	—	—
Virginia	3	650	—	—
Washington	1	155	—	—
West Virginia	2	201	—	—
England	2	265	—	—
Mexico	1	200	—	—
Switzerland	1	242	—	—
Total	87	17,706	9	273

center at a Humana hospital that provides the surrounding region with the highest quality of care in a given clinical specialty. Currently 15 Centers of Excellence have been designated in the clinical specialties of burn care, cardiovascular disease, diabetes, neurosciences, women's medicine, orthopedics, spinal injury, pulmonary medicine, and ophthalmology.

Humana is recognized as a leader in the hospital industry in providing high quality, cost efficient health care services. Through centralized purchasing, computer services, and flexible staffing techniques, the cost per admission at Humana's hospitals averages 19.4% less than other hospitals in the same communities with the same types of patients according to the *1985 U.S. Industrial Outlook*.

Health Services Division

In 1981 Humana began developing a network of freestanding, extended-hour, medical treatment centers called MedFirst. More than 147 MedFirst units provide consumers with primary medical care at least 12 hours a day, 7 days a week. The number of Humana MedFirst offices is expected to grow to approximately 260 by September 1986, according to George Atkins, Vice-President of Public Affairs.

MedFirst is a cooperative effort between independent physicians in a given community and a Humana subsidiary. Humana builds an office, provides equipment and supplies, and hires, trains, and employs the support staff. The physicians control all medical aspects of their private practice.

In addition to the continued expansion of the Humana MedFirst office network, the company's Health Services Division is exploring new health care services including freestanding breast diagnostic centers and home health care services.

Group Health Division

In September 1983, Humana introduced Humana Care Plus, an innovative group health benefit plan that gives employers, for the first time, the controls they need to keep the cost of employee health care in line with other normal costs of doing business. Humana can offer guaranteed caps on an employer's health care costs because of its ability to control hospital costs.

Humana Care Plus offers employers a variety of flexible benefit plans to meet the individual needs of companies. All plans allow employees to keep their own doctors. If hospital care is required, plan members are given economic incentives to use Humana Care Plus' participating hospitals. Humana has added a number of participating hospitals from outside the Humana system in order to ensure comprehensive coverage in its service areas. In addition members receive benefits at non-participating hospitals when emergency services are needed, or if an elective service is not available at a participating hospital.

During its first year, approximately 65,000 Humana Care Plus members were enrolled in 11 metropolitan areas. By August, 1985 Humana health plans were available in approximately 53 metropolitan areas across the U.S. and total plan members numbered more than 359,000.

INDUSTRY TRENDS

The health care industry is a complex one. There are many distinct categories of products and services and a corresponding range of company types in business to provide them. In most references the industry is defined as those companies/institutions which directly interface with patients and those which supply medical products/services to the directly interfacing companies.

The major categories of companies/institutions involved are hospitals, physicians, dentists, drug manufacturers, medical device manufacturers, medical supplies manufacturers, nursing homes, and miscellaneous services (professional, cleaning, management, etc.).

Health care expenditures have grown dramatically, both in absolute dollars and as a percent of the GNP over the last twenty years and will continue to do so through 1990. (See Exhibit 2.) The sources and uses of health care funds are shown in Exhibit 3.

Several factors accounted for the quantum leaps in health care expenditures over the years:

a General inflation in the economy, especially over the seventies.

b Enactment of Medicare and Medicaid by Congress. A key ingredient of this legislation was its cost plus reimbursement scheme, which encouraged increased expenditures by all providers. (See Exhibit 4.)

c Growth in the use and per capita expenditures of third party insurers. (Ford Motor Company spent $22 per car for health insurance in 1965 and $275 in 1985.)

EXHIBIT 2   TOTAL HEALTH CARE EXPENDITURES 1965–1990

Year	Total health care dollars (in billions)	Percent of GNP
1965	$ 41.7	6.0
1970	74.7	7.8
1975	132.7	8.6
1980	249.0	9.3
1984	392.7 E	10.9 E
1987	529.8 E	11.8 E
1990	690.4 E	12.3 E

Source: Standard & Poor's Industry Surveys, Health Care, January 17, 1985, p. H13.

d A general aging of the population, especially in the over 65 age group. (See Exhibit 5.)

e Development and expanded use of expensive medical equipment and procedures (CAT scan, kidney dialysis, organ transplants, etc.).

The tremendous growth in health care costs has alarmed all those parties who must pay for it. For all levels of government these costs are budget busters (especially for the federal government) at a time when deficits are a major national issue. For the insurance and general business sectors these cost increases mean significant increases in the cost of doing business, tending to make them raise prices and become, thereby, less competitive. Members of the general public who have to pay some or all of their health care bills are also concerned.

In 1984 hospitals accounted for $17.2 billion in revenues. Within the industry, Humana had revenues of $2.6 billion, or 15.1% of the total hospital revenues for the year. Increase for the industry from 1983 was 8.3%.

On April 20, 1983, President Reagan signed P.L. 98-21 (the ''Act'') into law. Title VI of the Act substantially changed Medicare payments to acute care hospitals for inpatient hospital service by creating a prospective

EXHIBIT 3   NATIONAL HEALTH EXPENDITURES BY SOURCES AND USES OF FUNDS

	1970	1984 E	1990 E
Sources			
Patients	34.8%	28.8%	27.8%
Federal government	23.7%	29.0%	30.4%
Health insurers	22.9%	27.8%	28.8%
State & local	13.5%	12.7%	11.5%
Other	5.1%	1.5%	1.5%
Uses			
Hospital care	37.2%	42.2%	43.8%
Physician's services	18.1%	19.4%	19.3%
Drugs & medical sundries	10.7%	6.8%	6.3%
Nursing home care	6.3%	8.3%	8.5%
Administration, prepayment, public health activity, research & construction	12.7%	11.0%	10.4%
Dentist's services	6.3%	6.0%	5.8%
Other personal health care	7.7%	6.3%	5.9%

Source: Standard & Poor's Industry Surveys, Health Care, January 17, 1985, pp. H14–H15.

EXHIBIT 4   **Medicare expenditures for hospitals.**

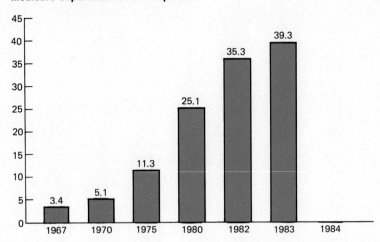

form of payment based on 470 diagnostic related groups ("DRGs") whereby hospitals are paid a fixed amount per patient for operating costs regardless of their actual operating costs attributable to such patient. DRGs are a system of classifying illnesses according to the estimated intensity of hospital resources necessary to furnish care for each diagnosis. If the hospital's costs to treat the patient exceed the DRG payment, the hospital will generally not be entitled to any additional amount. Furthermore, the hospital is precluded from charging the patient any costs beyond the co-insurance and deductible required under Medicare. The method of payment provided for in the Act became effective for most of Humana's hospitals on September 1, 1984. Although it would appear that this newly imposed payment system would have an adverse effect on Humana's revenue, it did not. In fact, the company ex-

EXHIBIT 5   **Elderly population projections, 1980–2000.**
(U.S. Census Bureau, "Projections of the Population in the U.S.," Series P-25, No. 952, May 1984.)

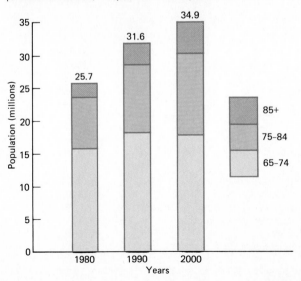

perienced a significant increase in net revenue per Medicare admission compared to the amount it would have received under the prior cost-based reimbursement system.

This increase is primarily attributed to the fact that the DRG payment is a fixed amount rather than a reimbursement of cost. Humana's operating costs and annual increases in operating costs are, on the average, generally lower than those of most other hospitals. This type of cost containment measure has finally slowed down the dramatic rise in health care costs whose annual rate of increase has abated, as Exhibit 6 shows.

COMPETITIVE STRUCTURE

In many areas served by Humana's hospitals, there are other hospitals, some of which are larger and more established than the hospitals operated by Humana. In addition, certain hospitals located in the areas served by Humana are special service hospitals which provide medical, surgical and psychiatric services not available at Humana or other general hospitals. Certain hospitals which compete with Humana's hospitals are operated by not-for-profit, non-taxpaying or governmental agencies, which can finance capital expenditures on a tax-exempt basis, and which receive funds and charitable contributions unavailable to Humana's hospitals.

The competitive position of a hospital is to a large degree dependent upon the number and quality of its staff physicians. Although a physician may at any time terminate his connection with a hospital, Humana seeks to retain physicians of varied specializations on its hospital staffs and to attract and maintain high ethical and professional standards. Humana's competitive position and hospital pricing policies are increasingly affected by the development of facilities which provide, on an outpatient basis, services that have traditionally been provided in hospitals. Health care delivery and financing systems such as (HMOs) Health Maintenance Organizations, which attempt to direct and control utilization of hospital services and obtain discounts from hospitals' established charges, also affect the competitive position of a hospital.

The occupancy rate of a hospital is affected by a number of factors, including the number of physicians using the hospital, the composition and size of the population, general economic conditions of the area serviced by the hospital, variations in medical and surgical practices in local communities, the degree of outpatient use of hospital services, the length of patient stay (Exhibit 7), the number, type and quality of other hospitals in the area and its competitive position. The decrease in occupancy rates during the last four fiscal years (as well as the decreasing rate of increase in the number of hospitals in general) was caused primarily by cost containment efforts by federal and state governments, third party payers and private in-

EXHIBIT 6   **Health care cost increases are slowing down.**
(Bureau of Labor Statistics.)

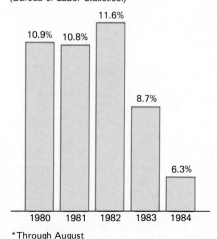

*Through August

EXHIBIT 7 **Average length of hospital stays (all patients).**
(American Hospital Association.)

Patients are leaving hospitals sooner, as hospitals
turn to more outpatient and home care and business
encourages alternatives to inpatient care.

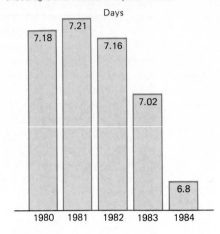

Days

7.18 — 1980
7.21 — 1981
7.16 — 1982
7.02 — 1983
6.8 — 1984

*Through June

dustry, whose efforts resulted in fewer admissions and shorter lengths of stay. These efforts include pre-hospital admission authorization, increased deductibles and co-payments in employee health benefit plans and incentives which encourage increased use of outpatient services. The decline in occupancy rates in 1983 and 1984 at certain hospitals was also influenced by general economic conditions.

It is estimated that investor-owned hospitals account for approximately 13% of the total number of community hospital beds in the country. Approximately 52% of those investor-owned beds are owned by four hospital companies. Humana ranks third in number of hospital beds owned.

GENERAL ORGANIZATION AND MANAGEMENT

By the end of 1984, the CEO, David A. Jones, and the President, Wendell Cherry, had put together a management team "second-to-none." The top levels of management are young and energetic executives that bring together many years of experience in marketing, management and innovation (Exhibit 8).

The day-to-day administrative operation of each hospital is under the supervision and direction of a full-time professional administrator. Three regional Executive Vice Presidents and one Senior Vice President are responsible for operations in their designated geographic areas.

Centralized management services are supplied to each hospital by the Company's headquarters. These services include financing, recruiting, personnel development, accounting, data processing, legal advice, public relations, marketing, insurance and purchasing. Each hospital is responsible for developing its own competitive strategy within the area it is located. However, the company operations have enough autonomy within the regions to have a voice in the corporate and regional decision-making process.

MARKETING

Humana ranked second in the amount of revenue generated for FY 1985 among the major hospitals. They accounted for 17.3% of the revenue generated by all hospitals during that period.

With the clampdown on health care spending by both the employers and the government, marketing among hospitals has become big business. With occupancy rates at an average of 66% for the industry, the lowest in two decades, hospitals are fighting for patients. Traditionally, hospitals have been unable to use the word 'marketing.' Those days are gone. Humana Hospital Phoenix recently

EXHIBIT 8   HUMANA, INC. ORGANIZATION AND MANAGEMENT

Directors

William C. Ballard Jr., Executive Vice President—Finance and Administration, Humana Inc.

Hilary J. Boone, Jr., Owner-Operator, Wimbledon Farm, Thoroughbred horse farm, Lexington, Ky.

Wendell Cherry, President and Chief Operating Officer, Humana Inc.

Michael E. Gellert, Executive Director, Drexel Burnham Lambert Incorporated, Investment bankers, New York, N. Y.

J. David Grissom, Chairman of the Board and Chief Executive Officer, Citizens Fidelity Corporation, Bank holding company, Louisville, Ky.

David A. Jones, Chairman of the Board and Chief Executive Officer, Humana Inc.

Antonie T. Knoppers, M.D., Business Consultant, Summit, N. J.

John W. Landrum, Owner, Executive Flight Service, Harrodsburg, Ky.

Carl F. Pollard, Senior Executive Vice President, Humana Inc.

David C. Scott, Chairman of the Board, Allis-Chalmers Corporation, Manufacturer of processing, agricultural and electrical equipment, Milwaukee, Wis.

Charles L. Weisberg, Chairman of the Board, Bass & Weisberg Realtors, Real estate and property management, and President, Charmar Galleries Limited, Antiques and art gallery, Louisville, Ky.

William T. Young, Chairman of the Board, W. T. Young, Inc., Public warehousing, Lexington, Ky.

Executive committee

| William T. Young, Chairman | Wendell Cherry | Carl F. Pollard |
| | David A. Jones | |

Audit committee

| David C. Scott, Chairman | J. David Grissom | Charles L. Weisberg |
| | Antonie T. Knoppers, M.D. | William T. Young |

Compensation committee

| Michael E. Gellert, Chairman | Hilary J. Boone, Jr. | William T. Young |
| | Charles L. Weisberg | |

Officers

| David A. Jones, Chairman of the Board and Chief Executive Officer | Wendell Cherry, President and Chief Operating Officer |

(Continued)

EXHIBIT 8 HUMANA, INC. ORGANIZATION AND MANAGEMENT *(Continued)*

Staff management

William C. Ballard Jr., Executive Vice President, Finance and Administration

Thomas J. Flynn, Executive Vice President and General Counsel

H. Linden McLellan, Senior Vice President, Facility Management

H. Herbert Phillips, Senior Vice President, Administration

Fred Pirman Jr., Senior Vice President, Information Systems

David G. Anderson, Vice President and Treasurer

George L. Atkins, Vice President, Public Affairs

W. Roger Drury, Vice President, Finance and Control

Michael A. Hendricks, Vice President, Real Estate

John V. Kessler, Vice President, Insurance

Gail H. Knopf, Vice President, Information Systems

Patrick B. McGinnis, Vice President, Finance and Planning

Paul B. Powell, Vice President, Purchasing

Richard A. Schweinhart, Vice President and Controller

Michael R. Smith, Vice President, Human Resources

Kenneth E. Snyder, Vice President, Information Systems

Robert B. Steele, Vice President, Taxes

Charles E. Teeple, Vice President, Investor Relations

James J. Walters, Vice President, Design and Construction

Tyree G. Wilburn, Vice President, Internal Audit

Alice F. Newton, Secretary

Operating management

Carl F. Pollard, Senior Executive Vice President

Hospital division

Paul A. Gross, Executive Vice President and Division President

Jack Clark, Executive Vice President, Mid-South Region

Lee R. Ledbetter, Executive Vice President, Florida Region

Wayne T. Smith, Executive Vice President, Central Region

James D. Bohanon, Senior Vice President, Pacific Region

Gary W. Metcalf, Senior Vice President and Controller

F. David Rollo, M.D., Ph.D., Senior Vice President, Medical Affairs

Philip B. Garmon, Vice President, Central Region

Donald L. Maloney II, Vice President, Florida Region

Kathryn M. Mershon, Vice President, Nursing

Larry H. Montgomery, Vice President, Mid-South Region

Thomas D. Moore, M.D., Vice President, Medical Affairs

George G. Schneider, Vice President, Pacific Region

(Continued)

EXHIBIT 8   HUMANA, INC. ORGANIZATION AND MANAGEMENT *(Continued)*

Group health division

Henry J. Werronen, Senior Vice President	Richard M. Mastaler, Vice President, Sales and Marketing	John H. Morse, Vice President, Operations	Joseph E. Shiprek, Vice President, Group Administration
W. Larry Cash, Vice President, Finance, and Controller			

Health services division

Randolph G. Brown, Senior Vice President	Savas G. Mallos, Vice President	Donald L. Stewart, Vice President

took out ads promoting "special rates" in local newspapers to drum up business.

Kenneth Abramowitz, an analyst at Sanford C. Bernstein & Co., emphasized in an interview with *USA Today*, February 26, 1986, that "Health care is moving from a provider-controlled industry to a consumer-controlled industry. That means companies are going to have to start appealing to the needs of consumers." Humana threw the first punch in early 1986 when it opened a $20 million advertising campaign featuring Olympic gymnast Mary Lou Retton in order to establish a national brand image. Retton underwent arthroscopic surgery performed on her knee at a Humana hospital six weeks before the 1984 Olympic Games. "Instead of saying 'take me to the hospital,' we want consumers to say 'take me to a *Humana* hospital,' " says George Atkins, spokesman for Humana.

Humana has also placed increased emphasis on promoting its Humana MedFirst medical centers, which maintain extended hours, including evenings and weekends, with independent physicians providing medical care to their ambulatory patients. Humana is also promoting Humana Care Plus, which offers an indemnity type health insurance and prepaid health care. These products gen-erally permit individuals the freedom to choose any physician or hospital facility, but provide incentives to use the Company's hospitals.

Marketing and advertising as a whole has been expensive for Humana since the summer of 1983, with the promotion of Humana Care Plus and Humana MedFirst. However, MedFirst and Care Plus have been industry trendsetters since their inception. Humana has also made its name a household word since Dr. William DeVries implanted the first successful artificial heart into William Schroeder in 1984.

OPERATIONS

Humana enjoys a strong position in its three operating divisions. The three operating divisions include the Hospital Division, Group Health Division and Health Services Division. The principal source of the Company's revenues (approximately 96% in fiscal 1985) is provided by the Hospital Division, which as of August 31, 1985, operated 87 hospitals containing 17,706 licensed beds. The Company's hospitals are located in 21 states, two hospitals in England, one in Mexico, and one in Switzerland.

EXHIBIT 9   HUMANA, INC.—OPERATIVE DATA

	1985	1984	1983	1982	1981
Hospitals:					
Revenues	$2,785,435	$2,578,106	$2,284,151	$1,920,130	$1,702,077
Number of hospitals in operation at end of period	87	91	90	89	89
Licensed beds at end of period	17,706	18,242	17,248	16,286	16,431
Weighted average licensed beds	17,853	17,360	16,767	16,165	16,655
Patient days	3,142,400	3,454,900	3,579,300	3,548,600	3,723,300
Humana Care Plus patient days	44,500	3,400	—	—	—
Admissions	525,400	549,500	566,700	561,300	579,500
Humana Care Plus admissions	9,300	700	—	—	—
Occupancy	48.2%	54.4%	58.5%	60.1%	61.3%
Length of stay	6.0	6.3	6.3	6.3	6.4
Humana Care Plus:					
Revenues	$89,126	$7,893	—	—	—
Number of operational markets at end of period	50	10	—	—	—
Number of members enrolled and committed at end of period	359,200	40,900	—	—	—
Humana MedFirst					
Revenues	$37,960	$23,128	$14,457	$3,398	$1,520
Number of operational units at end of period	148	68	65	45	5
Hospital revenues paid by Humana Care Plus (eliminated in consolidation)	$37,381	$2,712			

[Note: As used in the above table, the term "licensed beds" is the maximum number of beds permitted in the facility under its license regardless of whether the beds are actually available for patient care. The term "weighted licensed beds" is the number of licensed beds after giving effect to the length of time the beds have been licensed during the period. "Patient days" is the total number of days of patient care provided by the Company's hospitals. Occupancy rates are calculated by dividing average patient days (total patient days divided by total number of days for the period) by weighted licensed beds.]

The day-to-day fiscal and administrative operation of each hospital is under the supervision and direction of a full-time professional administrator. Three regional Executive Vice Presidents and one Senior Vice President are responsible for operations in their designated geographic areas.

Centralized management services are supplied to each hospital by the Company's headquarters. These services include financing, recruiting, personnel development, accounting, data processing, legal advice, public relations, marketing, insurance and purchasing. As of August 31, 1985, Humana had under construction the following major projects, nearly $230 billion in new construction for fiscal 1985.

EXHIBIT 10 HUMANA, INC.—DESCRIPTION OF PROJECTS UNDER CONSTRUCTION

2 new hospitals (138 beds)	$ 14,402,000
Replacement of 1 hospital (net reduction of 78 beds) and renovation and expansion of 2 hospitals (47 net additional beds)	61,144,000
Renovation of 24 hospitals	68,174,000
12 new medical office buildings, 14 condominium office buildings	77,383,000
12 medical care centers	7,952,000
Total	$229,055,000

PERSONNEL

One of the Company's major strengths is in the capability, experience and leadership of the executive and management team personnel. At August 31, 1985, Humana hospitals had approximately 32,500 full-time and 11,300 part-time employees, including approximately 16,800 registered nurses and licensed practical nurses. Approximately 28,000 licensed physicians are members of the medical staffs of the hospitals, approximately one-half of whom are members of the active staffs. With minor exceptions, physicians are not employees of the hospitals. However, some staff physicians provide ancillary services in Humana hospitals under contract. Any licensed physician or dentist may apply to be admitted to the medical staff of any of the Humana hospitals, but admission to the staff must be approved by the medical staff and the Board of Trustees or the Board of Directors. Members of the medical staffs of Humana hospitals may also serve on the medical staffs of other hospitals.

All hospitals have generally experienced satisfactory labor relations. Approximately 560 employees at 4 hospitals are represented by labor unions. The Company experiences union organizational activity in its hospitals from time to time. Humana promotes from within whenever feasible. Several of the personnel now occupying executive and managerial positions came in at lower levels out of college. Their maturity and growth in their job performance has been rewarded through promotions and other recognition. This in turn provides incentives for the new and lower level employees to recognize that they too will be rewarded for their diligent and loyal services to Humana, Inc.

FINANCE

The following exhibits present the consolidated financial statements for Humana, Inc.

EXHIBIT 11 HUMANA, INC.—CONSOLIDATED STATEMENT OF INCOME
FOR THE YEARS ENDED AUGUST 31, 1985, 1984 AND 1983
(Dollars in Thousands Except per Share Results)

	1985	1984	1983
Revenues	$2,875,140	$2,606,415	$2,298,608
Provisions for contractual allowances and doubtful accounts	686,750	645,226	533,485
Net revenues	2,188,390	1,961,189	1,765,123
Operating expenses	1,546,128	1,420,429	1,310,424
Depreciation and amortization	147,337	120,560	94,665
Interest	118,825	87,950	71,252
	1,812,290	1,628,939	1,476,341
Income before income taxes	376,100	332,250	288,782
Provision for income taxes	159,880	138,909	128,133
Net income	$ 216,220	$ 193,341	$ 160,649
Earnings per common share	$2.19	$1.96	$1.63

EXHIBIT 12 HUMANA, INC.—CONSOLIDATED BALANCE SHEET
AUGUST 31, 1985 AND 1984
(Dollars in Thousands except per Share Amounts)

	1985	1984
Assets		
Current assets:		
Cash and cash equivalents	$ 82,255	$ 260,954
Accounts receivable less allowance for loss of		
$63,415-1985 and $59,215-1984	365,851	257,675
Inventories	50,904	45,249
Other current assets	39,501	41,428
	538,511	605,306
Property and equipment, at cost		
Land	181,160	165,413
Buildings	1,449,565	1,228,701
Equipment	791,669	681,756
Construction in progress (estimated cost to		
complete and equip after August 31, 1985-		
$132,000)	91,177	160,079
	2,513,571	2,235,949
Accumulated depreciation	562,300	452,641
	1,951,271	1,783,308
Other assets	230,112	189,233
	$2,719,894	$2,577,847
Liabilities and stockholders' equity		
Current liabilities:		
Trade accounts payable	$ 85,261	$ 88,323
Salaries, wages and other compensation	55,001	52,292
Other accrued expenses	117,945	97,936
Income taxes	48,972	59,956
Long-term debt due within one year	57,817	53,720
	364,996	352,227
Long-term debt	1,205,559	1,286,526
Deferred credits and other liabilities	246,489	195,909
Common stockholders' equity		
Common stock, 16⅔¢ par; authorized 200,000,000		
shares; issued and outstanding 97,299,419		
shares—1985 and 96,848,643 shares—1984	16,217	16,141
Capital in excess of par value	223,392	219,218
Translation adjustments	(16,076)	(19,340)
Retained earnings	679,317	527,166
	902,850	743,185
	$2,719,894	$2,577,847

EXHIBIT 13 HUMANA, INC.—CONSOLIDATED STATEMENT OF CHANGES IN FINANCIAL POSITION
FOR THE YEARS ENDED AUGUST 31, 1985, 1984 AND 1983
(Dollars in Thousands)

	1985	1984	1983
Funds provided:			
From operations:			
Net income	$ 216,220	$193,341	$160,649
Items which did not require working capital:			
Depreciation and amortization	147,337	120,560	94,665
Deferred income taxes	39,785	7,404	21,876
Other	1,281	3,593	(16,374)
	404,623	324,898	260,816
Additions to long-term debt	207,198	358,811	316,795
Issuances of common stock	4,236	9,695	116,967
Increase in allowance for professional liability risks	23,707	22,032	18,808
Disposition of properties	97,233	55,442	72,183
Other	19,959	22,869	13,553
	756,956	793,747	799,122
Funds applied:			
Additions to property and equipment	400,855	445,741	514,776
Reduction of long-term debt	285,216	137,067	108,094
Redemption of preferred stock	—	62,277	188
Payment of cash dividends	64,055	60,217	50,609
Insurance subsidiary's investments	30,769	23,566	22,621
Additions to goodwill	18,066	1,017	—
Additions to deferred charges	18,276	7,862	10,965
Other	19,283	19,989	27,526
	836,520	757,736	734,779
Increase (decrease) in working capital	$ (79,564)	$ 36,011	$ 64,343
Increase (decrease) in working capital consists of:			
Cash and cash equivalents	$(178,699)	$ 10,906	$ 40,530
Accounts receivable	108,176	57,222	32,671
Inventories	5,655	3,735	7,152
Other current assets	(1,927)	11,884	14,686
Trade accounts payable	3,062	(5,938)	(14,842)
Salaries, wages and other compensation	(2,709)	2,890	(8,666)
Other accrued expenses	(20,009)	(16,577)	(22,923)
Income taxes	10,984	(25,094)	26,569
Long-term debt due within one year	(4,097)	(3,017)	(10,834)
	$ (79,564)	$ 36,011	$ 64,343

EXHIBIT 14 HUMANA, INC.—CONSOLIDATED STATEMENT OF COMMON STOCKHOLDERS' EQUITY
FOR THE YEARS ENDED AUGUST 31, 1985, 1984 AND 1983
(Dollars in Thousands except per Share Amounts)

	Common stock		Capital in excess of par value	Translation adjustments	Retained earnings	Total
	Shares	Amount				
Balances, August 31, 1982	90,630,107	$15,105	$ 93,474	$ (9,424)	$286,057	$385,212
Net income					160,649	160,649
Cash dividends on common stock ($.46⅞ per share)					(44,364)	(44,364)
Cash dividends on preferred stock ($2.50 per share), and $216 provision for redemption value					(6,461)	(6,461)
Unrealized translation losses				(3,369)		(3,369)
Public offering of common stock, net of expenses of $3,891	4,800,000	800	112,684			113,484
Stock options exercised and related tax benefits, net of 11,562 shares tendered in partial payment therefor	315,095	52	3,113			3,165
Other	69,847	12	306			318
Balances, August 31, 1983	95,815,049	15,969	209,577	(12,793)	395,881	608,634
Net income					193,341	193,341
Cash dividends on common stock ($.57½ per share)					(55,541)	(55,541)
Cash dividends on preferred stock ($1.875 per share), and $162 provision for redemption value					(4,838)	(4,838)
Unrealized translation losses				(6,547)		(6,547)
Stock options exercised and related tax benefits, net of 16,280 shares tendered in partial payment therefor	1,008,644	168	9,551			9,719
Redemption of preferred stock					(1,559)	(1,559)
Other	24,950	4	90		(118)	(24)
Balances, August 31, 1984	96,848,643	16,141	219,218	(19,340)	527,166	743,185
Net income					216,220	216,220
Cash dividends on common stock ($.66 per share)					(64,055)	(64,055)
Unrealized translation gains				3,264		3,264
Stock options exercised and related tax benefits, net of 71,071 shares tendered in partial payment therefor	281,398	47	3,514			3,561
Other	169,378	29	660		(14)	675
Balances, August 31, 1985	97,299,419	$16,217	$223,392	$(16,076)	$679,317	$902,850

EXHIBIT 15   THE FUTURE: "TEXAS OUTLAWS 'DUMPING' POOR PATIENTS; CONGRESS MAY DO SAME"

Private hospitals across the country that routinely send indigent emergency patients to public hospitals could soon face stiff penalties if Congress follows Texas in outlawing such transfers.

Congress is considering legislation making it a civil offense to transfer to another hospital any patient whose medical condition has not been stabilized. Under the proposed law, hospitals violating the regulation could be denied medicare funding, and physicians approving the transfers could face up to $25,000 in civil penalties.

Last year Texas became the first state to approve regulations prohibiting the transfer of patients for economic reasons. The Texas rules, stronger than those now being considered by Congress, go beyond emergency cases to include all patients, and allow transfers only for medical reasons, and only if the receiving hospital has agreed to accept the patient. In December, the state Board of Health approved the regulations as part of an indigent health-care package.

"Dumping," the practice of sending patients who are poor financial risks to public hospitals, has received growing attention as beleagured public hospitals have publicized glaring examples of abuse. The problem is centered primarily in urban areas, where large public institutions, and many of the poor, are concentrated.

A force behind the proposed federal regulations is Rep. Fortney H. Stark (D) of California, whose San Francisco-area east bay district was the site of a Harvard University study of dumping. An aide to Representative Stark said the rules would allow patients, as well as hospitals, to sue in federal court the hospitals and physicians accused of dumping. Stark is chairman of the House Ways and Means Committee's subcommittee on health.

The Texas rules were originally proposed by state Board of Health Chairman Ron Anderson, who is also the chief executive officer of Parkland Memorial Hospital, a large county-operated hospital in Dallas where dumping had become a regular occurrence.

According to Parkland spokesman Gregory Graze, the problem is exacerbated in Texas because of the state's low medicaid funding. Texas has very stringent rules for determining who is eligible for medicaid and thus covers only the poorest of the poor. (Texas ranks 48th among the 50 states in the level of payments under the federally mandated program.)

The Legislature last year approved $70 million to help counties pay for care for the poor but turned down a proposal for broader indigent health-care coverage.

Emergency physicians are unhappy with the federal proposal because they feel it "singles them out," according to Virginia Pitcher, director of the American College of Emergency Physicians' Washington, D.C., office.

She continues, "The real problem that has yet to be addressed is indigent health care. . . . The reason the dumping is going on is that these patients have no source of funding."

Mr. Graze agrees but says that because there is no national indigent health care plan on the horizon, all hospitals should share the financial burden of providing care to the poor.

Dennis Andrulis, director of research for the National Association of Public Hospitals, says the proposed federal law would put those hospitals that routinely dump patients on notice that they will be subject to penalties.

He says, "It's important we make this clear now, because as the screws continue to tighten on the financial spigot, the temptation for other facilities to divest themselves of individuals who are financial liabilities will increase."

The Christian Science Monitor, Howard LaFranchi, staff writer of *The Christian Science Monitor*, Tuesday, January 14, 1986, p. 3.

JOHN HANCOCK MUTUAL LIFE INSURANCE COMPANY

Raymond M. Kinnunen
Northeastern University

John G. McElwee, Chairman of the Board and Chief Executive Officer of the John Hancock Mutual Life Insurance Company,[1] asked himself three questions in the Spring of 1984 as he prepared the company for the 1990s and beyond: What is it you want the institution to be? What do you think the world will be like? How do we prepare for that in terms of what business the company will be in and what it will need in terms of talent? A move to financial services came out of that analysis and, more specifically, an analysis of what McElwee saw as his six criteria: economy, demographics, attitudes and lifestyles,

This case was prepared by Ramond M. Kinnunen, Associate Professor of Business Administration, with the assistance of L. Jake Katz, Research Assistant, with the cooperation of the John Hancock Mutual Life Insurance Company and its Chairman, John G. McElwee and the support of the Instructional Development Fund at Northeastern University. It is intended to be used as the basis for class discussion rather than to illustrate either effective or ineffective handling of an administrative situation.

The research and written case information were presented at a Case Research Symposium and were evaluated by the Case Research Association's Editorial Board.

Distributed by the Case Research Association. All rights reserved to the author(s) and the Case Research Association. Videotapes featuring John G. McElwee are available from Northeastern University's Department of Management in Boston.

[1]See Appendix A for biographical sketches.

competition, technology, and government action. In McElwee's view, however:

> Nobody *really* knows what the financial services industry will be. We all admit to that. We are all trying to be flexible. We know we all are not doing everything right, and the jury is still out as to which companies will have the right combination and the wisdom and courage to remedy the situation as it evolves. When will this happen? When will the paradigm of the new FSI be in place? In my view it won't be before 1990.

The John Hancock Mutual Life Insurance Company began its move into financial services in 1968. This case offers some background on the financial services industry (FSI), the insurance industry, and the nature of the issues and problems facing the company in 1984.

TRENDS IN THE INDUSTRY

The late 1970s and early 1980s saw a significant trend toward the provision of fuller financial services being offered by institutions:

> The FSI is a huge amalgam of firms ranging in size from the CitiCorp with well over $130 billion in assets to many small credit unions with a few hundred thousand dollars of assets. In 1980, there were over 40,000 individual firms competing

in the FSI with a mix of products including savings accounts, life insurance policies, pension management services, and stock brokering. The size of the FSI as measured by financial assets under control was nearly $4 trillion in 1980, and was experiencing nearly 11% annual growth.

Historically, the various segments of the FSI have been primarily defined by government regulation. In fact, this is the reason many firms in the FSI are considered institutions rather than firms in the economic sense. The institutional segments of the FSI have been controlled and defined by their relationships to regulatory agencies. For example, banks are regulated at the federal, state, and local levels by various agencies. Securities firms are regulated only at the federal level by the Securities and Exchange Commission (SEC). Insurance companies, since 1946, have been regulated by state agencies. The result is an industry where products have been defined by regulation and customer markets have been given access to those products only through specific institutions. Until fairly recently, a customer went to a bank for a loan, to an insurance company for an insurance policy, and to a securities firm to trade stock. In this regulated environment, which defined the channels between customers and the financial products, the FSI was on average, very profitable. Between 1975 and 1980, the banking industry reported annual profit growth of 18%, the life insurance industry reported 30% annual profit growth, and the securities industry reported 7% profit growth (for a scale of measurement, all U.S. industry reported 12% profit growth during that time) . . . .

Competition in the FSI has not been very intense compared to other industries; in fact, the common view of many financial institutions has been that the main objective is not to compete, but to provide public services. This view has been allowed and reinforced by: a) the regulatory environment, b) the web of relationships among financial institutions which required a large degree of coordination and cooperation and c) the historical values and culture which preside in most financial institutions. (The "lean and mean" operation has not been the role model for most financial organizations.) Regulations, severely limiting the dimensions of competition, have sought to create a sort of economic DMZ (demilitarized zone) between the customers and the financial markets, reasoning that unlimited competition, by nature, causes behavior and results which are not in the best interest of the customer. The regulatory thinking assumed that unbridled competition would certainly mean more failures of weak and poorly run institutions. This would, over time, create a more efficient marketplace, but the result on the customer of a failing in-

stitution could be devastating. Also, it was expected that competition would drive institutions to more predatory and less benign behavior towards their customers and competitors as the scramble for profits intensified.

Traditionally, different types of institutions offered different types of products and services. Banks have concentrated on offering transaction products, and many kinds of loan products to individuals and corporations. Savings and loans (thrifts) have provided savings products and specialized mortgage lending to individuals. Securities firms have tended to specialize to a degree with different firms offering "wholesale" products to corporations such as underwriting and other investment banking activities (e.g., Goldman Sachs and Salomon Brothers) and other firms specializing in "retail" brokerage and trading for consumers (e.g., Merrill Lynch, Shearson and E.F. Hutton). Insurance companies have generally specialized in either life insurance products (e.g., Prudential, Metropolitan and New York Life), or property and casualty insurance (e.g., State Farm, AllState, INA). To a degree they have also been involved in mortgage and commercial lending. Traditionally, most insurance companies have served both individual and corporate customers. Finance companies have concentrated on consumer lending and mortgage lending primarily to individuals. As noted above, a dominant reason in the traditional product/institution relationship has been regulation but institutional thinking has also greatly influenced how the industry has defined itself.[2]

While the level of merger and acquisition activity within the financial services industry over the last decade seemed to suggest an inevitable fusion of services under one roof, companies found that sales personnel trained to move one service were not necessarily well suited at uncovering client needs for another. For example, Merrill Lynch, the largest marketer of securities, found it inefficient to have their stockbrokers selling insurance policies. "Meanwhile, Merrill has begun experimenting with a more specialized approach to selling. Convinced that the average broker is unable to sell insurance, Merrill last June began installing life insurance specialists in 32 branches. It plans to hire 100 more this year."[3]

[2]From Gregory L. Parsons, The Evolving Financial Services Industry: Competition and Technology for the '80's, 9-183-007, pp. 1–3. Copyright © 1982 by the President and Fellows of Harvard College. Reprinted by permission of the Harvard Business School.

[3]"Merrill Lynch's Big Dilemma," *Business Week*, 16 January 1984, p. 62.

David Koehler, president of Financial Learning Systems, a firm training both securities and insurance personnel to sell new products and to prepare for licensing exams, cites five major barriers insurance agents face when selling noninsurance products. These barriers include: (1) licensing (state licensing exams are relatively easy for the insurance industry but fairly rigorous exams for securities); (2) product knowledge (the level necessary for life agents to be comfortable selling securities may be underestimated); (3) skills to sell the product (different skills are required to sell a life insurance policy than a mutual fund); (4) commissions (to get a similar dollar-for-dollar commission, an agent has to sell a fund possibly fifty times the "value" of a life policy); and (5) attitude (life agents are accustomed to selling "guaranteed" products).[4]

Others in the industry acknowledge these barriers but conclude that the lines between agents and brokers are becoming blurred. Because of competition, the agent has diversified his product line while the broker has added more service through financial planning.[5]

To make matters more complex, some feel that both agents and brokers will be competing with other brokers selling products based more on price than on service.[6] The vast majority of consumers' liquid assets are held in depository institutions which gives the banking industry an advantage. One way for insurance companies to compete with banks is to offer transaction accounts. To do this, however, they must acquire a bank image.[7]

Standard and Poor's Industry Surveys note the following in regard to the trend toward full service.

The emergence of alternative products, along with general deregulation of the financial industry, has intensified competition in the life insurance industry. The successful life insurance company will be one that adapts quickly to the changing environment. The competitiveness of life insurance will increasingly depend not only on innovations in products and services, but also importantly on the quality of marketing and distribution systems.

Insurers are aware of the need for more effective marketing strategies and some already are making changes. One approach that is taking hold is the combination of insurers and other major financial institutions to form broad-based financial services conglomerates. The goal here is to bring together a variety of financial products and services, provide one stop access to the consumer, and allow cross-marketing of product and service combinations as financial services packages. This approach to market expansion is evidenced by such recent acquisitions as Bache Group Inc. by Prudential Insurance Co. of America and Shearson Loeb Rhoades by American Express (which owns Fireman's Funds Insurance Co.) among others.[8]

Theodore Gordon, president of the Futures Group, summed it up this way:

The whole marketplace for insurance is becoming very dynamic. It will be increasingly difficult in the future to tell the difference between a brokerage house, an insurance company, a bank, and a large-scale credit card company. To some degree, the functions of these institutions already overlap.[9]

A May 1982 article in *Institutional Investor* questions the effects of mergers that result in extended financial services.

While it is too early for a verdict on that, however, there's another critical question at stake here. These firms have also been trumpeting the *synergistic* benefits that are supposed to flow from these mergers. American Express, for example, hopes to sell a wide variety of financial services through its credit cards, opening up vast new vistas for Shearson. Sears can envision its millions of customers buying Dean Witter products at its stores. And the Pru can look forward to its agents selling Bache products nationwide. Bache chairman Harry Jacobs Jr. perhaps best sums it up when he says, "We expect the merger to extend the range of services both firms provide."

Yet, amid all the euphoric talk, no one has really stopped to ask whether these future synergistic wonders will actually come to pass, whether synergy on such a grand scale can really work in the financial services business. Will the vaunted synergy ever materialize to any *significant* extent? Will the diverse parts of these financial services conglomerates truly mesh and spur each other on to new heights—

[4]Stephen Piontek, "Securities Products Face Agents with Problems," *National Underwriter, Life and Health Insurance Edition*, 17 July 1982, pp. 28–36.

[5]Ibid., p. 3.

[6]Ibid., p. 43.

[7]Barbara E. Casey, "Customer is Key to Insurance-Banking Rivalry," *National Underwriter, Life and Health Edition*, 17 July 1982, pp. 8–9, 36.

[8]*Standard & Poor's Industry Surveys*, 7 July 1983 (Vol. 151, no. 27, sec. 1), *Insurance & Investments Basic Analysis*, p. 155.

[9]Theodore J. Gordon, "Life Insurance Companies in the 80's: A Quiet Revolution," *Resources*, July/August 1981, p. 3.

boosting sales, cutting costs and adding up to more than the sum of the parts?

Actually, there's plenty of evidence to suggest these companies may be in for a tougher time of it than most people suspect. For one thing, there's the nagging fact that dozens of previous attempts to create synergy in the financial services industry have, at best, been somewhat disappointing. It was fashionable in the early 1970s, for example, to suppose that retail brokers could sell life insurance as a sideline, thereby increasing their earnings and those of their firms. As it turned out, however, these brokers either lacked the skills to sell insurance or were too busy with stocks to bother with it. No precise figures are available, but Securities Industry Association statistics indicate that Wall Street firms gathered revenues of less than $500 million from insurance in 1980, compared with their total revenues of $16 billion.[10]

The article goes on to detail the experience of Continental Insurance.

Continental Insurance made little progress toward the synergy that was supposed to accrue from its consumer finance subsidiary and its Diners Club credit card operations—both of which have since been sold. Other than the relatively minor business of travel life insurance, Continental found it difficult to sell policies via the credit card. It was hard, says one Continental official, to design a home insurance application form to mail out with bills because it entailed asking so many detailed questions. Nor was it really feasible to sell insurance through consumer finance outlets—local Continental agents would have been annoyed by the competition. Reports Continental chairman John Ricker sadly: "One-stop financial shopping is a buzzword returning to our vocabulary. I am skeptical, not by nature, but by experience. Continental has tried the full financial services approach, and it didn't work.[11]

Robert Beck of Prudential is quoted later in the same article with this view:

"I don't think previous attempts have *all* been failures," is the way Prudential chairman Beck shrugs it off. Or perhaps a better way of putting it is that they're persuaded that times have changed dramatically since their previous efforts to achieve financial services synergy were made. Notes American Express chairman Robinson, "The environment today is 100 percent different than it was when those [previous]

relationships were formed." For one thing, he notes, "there's a trend toward constructing hybrid financial products," begun by Merrill Lynch's CMA account—a trend Robinson thinks multifaceted houses may be able to exploit.[12]

The customer base is also an important factor when it comes to offering financial services.

Sears Roebuck and Company, American Express Company and Prudential Life Insurance Company currently sell their services to some 50 million Americans. The three companies intend to bombard these clients with new financial services products. But according to conventional wisdom in the financial services business, it's not really the quantity of customer that counts, but the quality—how rich the customers are . . . . it's generally assumed that servicing well-heeled folk will be more profitable in years to come than pushing financial products at people of moderate means.[13]

"Well-heeled" is typically defined as meaning an annual family income of $50,000 or more; there are an estimated 3.2 million households in this group. Some experts fear that, with a large number of big as well as small institutions competing, few will make a profit. Given those estimates "the supercompanies plan to concentrate on the vast middle market of families earning $20,000 to $50,000 a year.[14]

The supercompanies (Sears, Roebuck and Company, Prudential-Bache Securities, Bank America Corp., American Express, Citicorp, and Merril Lynch and Co.) continue to expand into new businesses as fast as the law and technology permit (Table 1 compares some financial and product data on the supercompanies with those of the John Hancock). Some large insurers are acquiring small securities firms, money managers, and mortgage bankers. Alexander Clash, President at New York's John Alden Insurance Company, expressed one view that acquisitions are a cheap form of R&D and added, "Buying a foothold in every conceivable financial service is a way of participating in every business because no one is sure what the hot areas will be in 1990."[15]

Obviously, there are considerable mixed feelings in the financial services community concerning recent changes. Movement continues to take place even in light

---

[10]Neil Osborn, "What Synergy," *Institutional Investor*, May 1982, p. 50.

[11]Ibid., p. 52.

[12]Ibid., p. 52.

[13]Ibid., p. 54.

[14]Arlene Hershman, "The Supercompanies Emerge," *Dunn's Business Month*, April 1983, p. 46.

[15]Ibid., p. 47.

TABLE 1   COMPARISONS

	American Express	BankAmerica	Citicorp	Merrill Lynch	Prudential	Sears	John Hancock
Financial data (all figures in millions of dollars)							
Revenues	7,800	13,112	18,258	4,590	13,200	29,180	4,422
Net income	559	425	774	220	not comparable	735	NC
Assets	27,700	120,496	128,430	20,940	62,500	34,200	*23,174
Customers' deposits	5,700	93,208	77,359	3,930	—	2,300	—
Customers' credit balances	1,200	—	—	2,700	740	200	—
Money market funds	17,200[1]	—	—	48,900	5,000	9,000	1,125
Commercial loans	4,200	48,800	60,411	400	1,560	—	2,000
Consumer loans	1,000	25,100	22,029	5,000	3,900	4,250	1,900
What they do							
Securities brokerage	•			•	•	•	•
Securities trading	•	•	•	•	•	•	•
Cash management services	•			•		•	•
Investment management	•	•	•	•	•		•
Commodities brokerage	•			•	•	•	
U.S. corporate underwriting	•			•	•	•	
International corporate underwriting	•	•	•	•	•	•	
U.S. commercial banking		•	•				
International commercial banking	•	•	•	•			
Savings & loan operations			•			•	
Small loans offices		•	•			•	
Credit card, charge cards	•	•	•				
Traveler's checks	•	•	•				
Foreign exchange trading	•	•	•	•	•	•	
Leasing	•	•	•	•			•
Data processing services	•	•	•	•			•
Property-casualty ins.	•				•	•	•
Life, health insurance	•			•	•	•	•
Mortgage insurance						•	•
Mortgage banking	•	•	•	•		•	•
Real estate development	•				•	•	•
Commercial real estate brokerage				•		•	
Residential real estate brokerage				•		•	
Executive relocation services				•		•	

[1]Total assets under management $37 million
*Not including subsidiary assets
Sources: The New Financial Services, Alliance of American Insurers, Shaumburg, Ill., 1983 (reprinted with permission of Prudential-Bache Securities); John Hancock internal documents

of the questionable results companies may achieve when they offer one-stop financial services, in effect becoming financial supermarkets (see Exhibit 1). Part of the reason for this trend may be the estimated $200 billion that Americans spent on financial services in 1982, reportedly earning suppliers of those services $42 billion.[16]

The decade of the 1980s promises to be an exciting one for the huge American financial services industry, which has, until now, been fragmented. Some uncontrollable factors, such as interest rates, the economic climate, the regulatory climate, and the role of technology, will also affect the industry. Many experts believe that technology (especially computers and telephones), with its costs and unpredictable product breakthroughs, will play such a large part in product cost and delivery that the big competition to worry about may be not other companies in the financial services industry but AT&T and IBM.[17]

THE JOHN HANCOCK MUTUAL LIFE INSURANCE COMPANY[18]

The John Hancock Company began in 1862 when John Hancock started selling life insurance. By 1864 the company had over half a million dollars of insurance in force. In less than ten years, the company's insurance in force grew to nearly twenty million dollars. In the early part of the twentieth century, the company pioneered a number of products, including group life insurance. The John Hancock Company prospered during the boom years following World War I and continued to grow through the Depression. As late as the mid 1960s the company was still primarily a seller of insurance. A hundred years after its founding, the company's pool of capital had been invested in nearly every imaginable sector of the economy, both private and public.

In December 1983, in an internal bulletin to all home office employees, the John Hancock Mutual Life Insurance Company announced a definitive merger agreement with the Buckeye Financial Corporation of Columbus, Ohio. The merger agreement provided for the acquisition of Buckeye by the John Hancock subsidiary for approximately $28 million in cash, equal to $13.50 per share of

Buckeye common shares on a fully diluted basis. Buckeye, a savings and loan holding company in Columbus, Ohio, is the parent of Buckeye Federal Savings and Loan Association. Buckeye Federal, a federally chartered savings and loan association, conducts its business through nineteen offices located throughout central Ohio. With assets of approximately $1.2 billion as of September 30, 1983, Buckeye Federal is one of the largest savings and loan associations in Ohio and is the largest mortgage lender in central Ohio. In April 1982, less than two years prior to this merger agreement, the Hancock had acquired Tucker Anthony Holding Corporation, the parent of Tucker Anthony and R.L. Day Inc., a regional brokerage house with thirty offices in the Northeast.[19] These two announcements were the latest of a number of financial services subsidiaries (most developed internally) that had been added since 1968. In a letter dated December 23, 1968, and addressed to home office associates, then President Robert E. Slater discussed the concept of subsidiaries:

> We think of them (the subsidiaries) as a device through which we can develop markets and new products and, as a corollary, other new avenues toward increased compensation for our sales forces. They also provide investment vehicles to enhance the return on total investable funds. Life insurance is still our main business—by a very wide margin—but in the larger view we can use these subsidiaries to augment or supplement our life insurance sales with the marketing of a wide array of financial services.

BACKGROUND ON THE INSURANCE INDUSTRY

Today in the United States the insurance industry is divided into three major categories: life, health, and property and casualty. The life and health areas are further divided into group and individual categories. In 1981 new purchases of life insurance in the United States amounted to $812.3 billion.[20]

Commercial life insurance companies are divided into two categories: stock and mutual companies.[21] A com-

---

[16]Ibid., p. 44.

[17]Ibid., p. 50.

[18]Historical facts on the company were taken from *A Bridge to the Future; One Hundreth Anniversary 1862–1962*, copyright 1962, John Hancock Mutual Life Insurance Company, Boston, Mass.

[19]"Hancock to Acquire Tucker Anthony at Up to $47 Million," *Wall Street Journal*, 15 April 1982, p. 16.

[20]Sources of factual data on the insurance industry were *1983 Life Insurance Factbook*, American Council of Life Insurance, Washington, D.C., 1983, and S.S. Hubner and Kenneth Black, Jr., *Life Insurance*, 9th ed., Prentice Hall, Inc., Englewood Cliffs, N.J., 1976.

[21]For data on the top ten insurance companies, see Exhibit 2.

pany that has stockholders is a stock company, whereas a mutual company is owned by its policyholders. Just over 2,000 life insurance companies were doing business in the United States in 1982; 135 were mutual companies, while 1,900 were stock companies. Although mutual companies represent only 7 percent of the total they own 57 percent of the assets of all life insurance companies in the United States and accounted for 43 percent of the life insurance in force in 1982.

Stock companies seek to earn the highest possible profits for their shareholders. Policy owners do not benefit from any gains the stock company enjoys nor are they hurt by any losses the company suffers. Because they are not directly affected by the company's financial experience, their policies are called nonparticipating. Because no dividend is expected the premium paid by a stock company must meet capital and surplus requirements as well as other requirements established by its home state. Having met these requirements and having had its stock subscribed, a stock company may begin doing business. Because a stock company is owned by its shareholders, the first responsibility of the directors is to those shareholders. Because stockholders can vote on major issues and elect the Board of Directors, control of the company rests with the owners of a majority of the stock. Shareholders may sell their stock or buy more shares at prevailing market prices.

Mutual insurance companies are owned by policyholders. Management's first obligation is to create profit for policyholders, who have the right to vote for directors. When funds available exceed solvency requirements, the directors may pay policyholders a dividend, although such payment is not mandatory. The cost of a policyholder's premium less the dividend paid determines the final cost of the insurance coverage. Because the policyholder may benefit from the favorable financial experience of a mutual company, that policy is called participating. Owners of mutual companies are numerous and scattered and have proportionately small ownership positions. For these reasons, control of a mutual company remains largely with management.

By the end of the 1960s, the rising inflation rate caused a number of people to seek new investment vehicles that offered higher returns than life insurance. The public's attention turned to the stock market. Many viewed life insurance as a high opportunity cost versus returns they imagined were available through stock market investments. A number of investment firms answered that market's desire by offering mutual fund shares. The public

sank dollars into a new breed of mutual fund called money market funds. Securities firms (such as Merrill Lynch) and fund operators (such as Fidelity) invested billions of dollars in low-risk securities offering record levels of income. Banks began offering certificates of deposit (CDs) with very high returns. The insurance industry found itself fighting not only for new business but to retain the reserves that they already held.

To grow and, indeed, to survive, traditional insurance institutions like John Hancock found themselves forced to compete with higher yielding instruments offered by the federal government, municipal governments, and brokerage houses.

JOHN HANCOCK SUBSIDIARIES, INC.

In 1980, the structure of the John Hancock Company was changed to incorporate the existence of ten subsidiaries in the form of a downstream holding company (see Exhibits 3 and 4). Table 2 describes the products and services offered by the subsidiaries. Selective financial data on the parent company and the subsidiaries can be found in Exhibits 5 and 6.

Stephen Brown, Executive Vice President of Financial Operations of the John Hancock Mutual Life Insurance Company and President and Chief Executive Officer of John Hancock Subsidiaries, Inc., had worked for the Hancock for twenty-two years when he became President of the Holding Company in 1981. Brown offered the following explanation on the origins of the Holding Company and its operations. Initially when the individual companies were started (the first in 1968), they became part of an existing department of the company. For example, Hanseco, which offered a line of casualty insurance, operated as a part of the Marketing Department and was expected to attract more revenue to the company by giving insurance agents a larger package of securities to offer. At that time the major objective of a new addition was synergy—or—as Brown described it, "putting more dollars in the agency force." Profit and growth were secondary.

In January of 1980, when the holding company (John Hancock Subsidiaries, Inc.) was established, management was charged with the responsibility of overseeing the subsidiary companies and reporting to the Board of Directors of the Life Company. As control mechanisms, the Holding Company was to submit to the Board quarterly financial statements and yearly presentations on its overall strategy. In addition, various Board committees on or-

TABLE 2

SUBSIDIARIES OF JOHN HANCOCK MUTUAL LIFE INSURANCE COMPANY (JH)

John Hancock International Services S.A., Brussels, Belgium
1968 Incorporated in Belgium. Established to enable the International Group Department of John Hancock to perform the international employee benefit services expected by multinational companies that participate in the John Hancock International Group Program (IGP).

Maritime Life Insurance Co., Halifax, Nova Scotia
1969 Acquired by JH. Reports to Life Company through JH Subsidiaries, Inc. for management reporting purposes. Offers a full range of life insurance products in Canadian markets.

John Hancock Servicos Internacionais S/C, Ltda., Sao Paulo, Brazil
1973 Organized in Brazil. Established to enable IGP to deliver the same financial results to clients with subsidiaries in Brazil as in all other IGP countries, and to enable funds to be transferred out of Brazil.

John Hancock Variable Life Insurance Co., Boston, MA
1979 Incorporated in Massachusetts. Provides a vehicle for John Hancock agents to sell individual variable life and universal life insurance products.

John Hancock Overseas Finance N.V., Curacao, Netherlands Antilles
1982 Incorporated in Netherlands Antilles. Raises funds outside the United States and lends such funds to John Hancock and its affiliates.

John Hancock Subsidiaries, Inc., Boston, MA
1979 Incorporated in Delaware; commenced business in 1980. A downstream holding company organized to provide a means of centralizing the reporting responsibility for the following subsidiaries as a group to coordinate their financial planning and the development of unified policies and strategies.

Subsidiaries of (JHSI)

Herbert F. Cluthe and Co., Springfield, NJ
1968 Acquired by JH.
1980 Acquired by JHSI. Develops total financial plans and group and pension programs for business and trade associations.

John Hancock Advisers, Inc., Boston, MA
1968 Incorporated in Delaware.
1980 Acquired by JHSI. Manages the portfolios of six open-end investment companies: John Hancock Growth Fund, Inc.; John Hancock U.S. Government Securities Fund, Inc.; John Hancock Bond Fund, Inc.; John Hancock Tax-Exempt Income Trust; John Hancock Cash Management Trust; and John Hancock Tax-Exempt Cash Management Trust, shares of which are sold by its subsidiary broker-dealer, John Hancock Distributors, Inc.

John Hancock Realty Services Corp., Boston, MA
1968 Incorporated in Delaware.
1980 Acquired by JHSI. Invests in income producing real estate; provides commercial real estate brokerage, mortgage placement and servicing, and appraisal services through its subsidiary, John Hancock Real Estate Finance, Inc. Operations are conducted nationwide through a series of regional offices.

TABLE 2 *(Continued)*

Profesco Corporation, New York, NY
1968 Acquired by JH.
1980 Acquired by JHSI. A nationwide organization of franchised specialists providing complete financial services to the professional and business communities.

HANSECO Insurance Co., Boston, MA
1971 Incorporated in Delaware.
1980 JH ownership transferred to JHSI. In addition to providing a vehicle for John Hancock agents to sell personal lines of Sentry Insurance, the company is actively involved in the reinsurance business through three wholly owned subsidiaries.

Hancock/Dikewood Services, Inc., Albuquerque, NM
1979 Incorporated in Massachusetts.
1980 Acquired by JHSI. Provides data processing and systems analysis services to health care providers. The company also offers a full range of management services to health maintenance organizations and associations.

John Hancock Financial Services, Inc., Boston, MA
1980 Incorporated in Delaware. Provides equipment leasing and financing (tax- and nontax-oriented) and related financial services to the agricultural, professional and general commercial markets on a national scale.

Independence Investment Associates, Inc., Boston, MA
1982 Incorporated in Delaware. Provides investment management and advisory and counseling services, principally to pension funds and other institutional investors.

John Hancock Venture Capital Management, Inc., Boston, MA
1982 Incorporated in Delaware. Serves as general partner and manager of the John Hancock Venture Capital Fund, a limited partnership with $148,000,000 of committed capital.

Tucker Anthony Holding Corp., Main Offices: Boston, MA and New York, NY
1982 Incorporated in Delaware. A holding company offering through its subsidiary Tucker Anthony & R.L. Day, Inc., a broad range of financial services, including stocks and bonds, money management, corporate finance, and tax-advantaged investments.

---

ganization, finance, compliance, conflict of interest, and auditing could also ask for reports. The individual subsidiaries submitted strategic plans to the Board of the Holding Company. In 1980 the objectives for the subsidiaries had become first profit followed by growth and then synergy, and the subsidiaries were expected in the long run to return 15 percent on investment. Brown noted that before this time "profit and return on investment" were not commonplace expectations in the company.

In Brown's view, the major reasons for changing the structure to a holding company were for tax purposes (some subsidiaries were profitable and others were not) and to form more consistent planning and control systems throughout the subsidiaries. Although there were some in

the company who felt that various departments should continue to control the subsidiaries, the outcome of the restructuring, according to Brown, was that "there are now clear controls in place with the subsidiaries operating autonomously from day to day."

Each subsidiary has its own Board of Directors. The Holding Company decides on the directors and reviews the minutes of meetings. Major capital requirements and any significant change in the type of business performed by a subsidiary also requires approval by the Holding Company. Personnel selection and compensation are left completely to the subsidiaries. Subsidiaries are welcome, but not required, to use the staff facilities at the Life Company (for example, EDP, Accounting, Public Relations). Brown stated that, on the average, he visits the subsidiaries once a month. With the major objectives of profitability, growth, and synergy clearly stated, the approach used to run the subsidiaries is, according to Brown, "Now, go do it!"

Mr. Brown commented on the future of the John Hancock:

> Profit and return on investment were not common words in the company. In the long run I see us adopting GAAP instead of statutory accounting and defining profit centers throughout the Life Company as we do in the Holding Company. This is a step toward becoming in the long run a stock company where we can purchase with stock as opposed to cash and offer stock incentives to management and tie a bonus to profits and growth. If in the long run this is where we are headed, the only way to do it is the profit center concept.

The addition of the Holding Company in 1980, along with the different systems used to measure performance, added a new dimension to the John Hancock and its way of operating. This became clear as people discussed the changes that had taken place inside the Hancock over the past sixteen years and the future in the changing financial services industry.

STRUCTURE, CULTURE, AND SYSTEMS

A major focus in the Company was the fact that two different entities operate under the name John Hancock Mutual Life Insurance Company. Furthermore, two distinct cultures evolved as a result of defining the subsidiaries as profit centers in 1980 and evaluating them based on profit and return on investment. That change in structure and systems in essence created a new way of operating and, to some extent, a new breed of manager.

Phyllis Cella was President and Chief Executive Officer of Hanseco, a subsidiary spawned in 1971 from within the Hancock and staffed originally with Hancock employees. The expressed purpose of starting Hanseco was to provide products for the Hancock agents. In 1983, Hanseco had approximately $750,000,000 in assets under its management. Up until 1980 they had operated within the Hancock structure. Cella described some of the thinking that went on inside Hanseco as the subsidiary grew. In the beginning

> Hanseco was run according to the Hancock style, and we were all on the Hancock payroll. As we got bigger and began to understand our own business, we began to change that. Having grown up in it you learn how to deal with it, but you

also understand how time consuming it is and that you don't always get the answer you want because it is a bureaucracy. Even before the Holding Company officially was formed, we saw ourselves as running a company that was now different from and, in our own minds, separate from the John Hancock, even though we were still on the John Hancock payroll. In our minds the paycheck was the only connection. When the world turned [introduction of the subsidiary structure] and the primary objective now became profit, it strengthened the fact that you really are a completely separate entity—it has now been blessed—and you are your own employer."

In 1984 Hanseco had its own payroll that was processed not on the John Hancock computers but by the First National Bank of Boston. The subsidiary set its own salaries and had its own retirement plan. According to Cella, the attitude at Hanseco was: "If I can get it cheaper downtown, then I'm going to do that—it's my bottom line. There are still people in the organization that don't understand or accept the fact that maybe we will buy their services—but maybe we won't. There is no question that there now exists two different cultures."

Hanseco's 40th-floor offices are a modular arrangement as opposed to the traditional open concept of the Hancock. Cella's office was on the outside corner of the glass building overlooking the Charles River and the Boston Common. She remarked that she had consciously chosen the modular design and had had to fight for it.

> Once you get a taste of it [the profit center concept], I don't think it would be possible to go back and work in the other framework—not at this level or an officer level. Partly because of the size—we still have only 225 employees but are growing every day—but partly because of the need. We all participate very heavily in this organization—all of the officers. We have eight officers, so it is not hard to get eight people together, hammer things out, let everyone have his say, have everyone really go at it, and wide open. How do you do that in the Hancock? You don't—it is impossible. It is much more fun here. A bigger challenge, a lot more sleepless nights than you ever had in the other big organization, but you cannot match the excitement and satisfaction of it and the gratification when it works.

Although officers of the Life Company were quite aware of the differences, some, like Frank Irish, Vice President Corporate Analysis and Planning, viewed the subsidiaries "as indistinguishable from the parent company from the point of view of management control. Standards should be applied equally to subsidiaries and parent company. A lot of my efforts have been designed to achieve this goal, and I think we are close to that.''

In response to the issue of transforming units of the Life Company into profit centers, Irish went on to say: ''I can only say that we are very seriously considering it. We obviously can. We know we can.'' He also had some doubts, however, as to whether the change would accomplish what the Hancock wanted and if, in fact, that change was consistent with their policyholders. ''When managing a participating insurance business you are not supposed to be profit maximizing—so why have a profit center concept. There is a conflict.''

Phyllis Cella felt as Steve Brown did: ''Theoretically, they [the units of the Life Company] ought to be profit centers and have a bottom line.'' There was some concern, however, from a practical point of view as to the difficulty of actually getting to the bottom line of some of the units within the Life Company that really do not have income.

There was also some concern among middle managers within the Life Company concerning the somewhat different nature of the business conducted within the Holding Comnpany and the way the Holding Company managers were being compensated. As Irish commented:

> What is at this point different about the subsidiaries is their attitude toward things like personnel policies, tenure, compensation, that sort of thing. Not only have they been decentralized, but in theory the subsidiary personnel are working in a more highly rewarded, more risky business than the parent company. . . . I'm not sure how top management views it—and I usually know top management. I know how many middle managers view it—very critically. Subsidiary managers are paid better and have more freedom and have greater opportunities. That's how some people view it, and it's a problem we are going to have to work with. I don't know what the answer is. . . . The other side is that you are generally dealing with kinds of operations where you need risk takers. . . . I think the problem is perhaps made worse by the obvious fact that, despite the statements about profit responsibility, some of the subsidiaries have not produced an adequate rate of return.

A related issue was the Hancock's financial restructuring to a stock company. Although this issue was much broader, it related directly to the existing culture within the Hancock. As noted previously, Steve Brown saw the Hancock in the long run, taking on the structure of a stock company. On that particular issue, Frank Irish pointed out that the thinking had been dominated in the past by having to generate capital internally and that that way of doing things takes away certain possibilities in the way of financial dealings. However, there is less pressure in a mutual company to sacrifice long term objectives for short term profit growth.

Irish went on to say that there are other advantages and disadvantages to both forms of business. Some feel mutual companies have more leeway in pricing their products. By adjusting the dividends, mutual companies may more closely reflect the actual cost of the service provided than their stock company counterparts. Stock companies are constrained to charge whatever the market will bear to achieve the highest possible level of profit for their stockholders.

As insurance companies extend themselves into broader areas of financial service, there is a tendency for firms to make use of holding companies for the management of their subsidiaries. Stock companies typically employ upstream holding companies. An upstream holding company is perched at the top of a corporate organization. The shareholders own it and it owns the subsidiaries. Mutual companies are constrained to use downstream holding companies. A downstream holding company is positioned midway down the corporate hierarchy and is wholly or partially owned by the mutual company. Because the parent mutual company is governed by state insurance laws, the management of a downstream holding company is often more complex than that of an upstream holding company.

As noted earlier, a stock company can raise capital by selling stock. A mutual company does not have this equity option. It may earn revenue from its operations, receive income from its investments, and acquire debt. A stock company may use its stock to acquire other organizations and in merger situations. Frank Irish contends that many of the older and larger mutual companies were able to experience immense growth because at their outset they were not pressured by shareholders to achieve high levels of profitability. Instead, management chose to pursue growth as the company's main objective.

It is possible for a mutual company to convert into a stock company and vice versa. Both processes are complicated, time-consuming and expensive. Conversion from a mutual company to a stock company would typically require the calculation of a policyholder's share of the company and transference of that share to shares of stock. In some instances a stock company, usually motivated by the fear of a takeover, may attempt to mutualize. This conversion would require approval by the company's board, the state insurance commissioner, the stockholders, and the policyholders. All the stock must be purchased and cancelled by the company before it can mutualize. According to the *1983 Life Insurance Fact Book,* "In the past 16 years, five companies have converted from the status of a mutual company to a stock company and two stock companies have converted to mutual."[22]

Phyllis Cella commented on moving from a mutual to a stock company:

> I think that it is essentially a good idea, because then the whole company has to have a bottom line. Right now mutuals do have a net gain from operations. A stock company has a very different attitude and culture because they have the stockholder that wants a rate of return. But just doing it is not the answer. Just because you become a stock company doesn't suddenly make everything perfect. The old culture is still there.

THE FUTURE

Given the recent announcement of a merger agreement with Buckeye Financial Corporation and the 1982 purchase of Tucker Anthony in addition to the other ten subsidiaries, the Hancock took some major steps toward competing in the FSI. The strategic thrust behind such moves was that they would result in synergies along such dimensions as offering more products for the sales force, developing multiple service relationships with individual customers, and management synergy—they "knew how to manage financial services."

A major question, however, for Frank Irish, among others, was "Can you really expect, once you have developed all of these capabilities, that any large percentage of your customers is going to come to you for all of them? We don't know. We are intensely aware of the question and have to be prepared to jump both ways. I hate to say that about strategic questions, but sometimes it is true."

To attract customers in this way, others felt that the Hancock would have to act differently than it had in the past. In the past, when the company started something it stuck with it and never gave up. The major question now appeared to be that if the time comes when the financial

[22]*1983 Life Insurance Factbook.* The American Council of Life Insurance, Washington, D.C., 1983, pp. 88–89. Of the seven companies that converted, the Council has identified six. Those converting from mutual to stock were: National Heritage Life Insurance (1966), Brookings International Life Insurance (1966), Viking Life Insurance (1972), West States Insurance Company (1973), and Equitable Beneficial Mutual Life Insurance Company (1977). Farmers and Traders Life Insurance converted from stock to mutual in 1974.

services dimension is not working, can the company change the way it functioned rapidly enough and bow out.

There had also been some thought given to management needs in the future based on the changing nature of the company and the industry. Currently, top management at the parent company was to a large degree made up of people who had risen to those positions from actuarial backgrounds. Frank Irish noted:

> New technical types are coming in who are not actuaries and they are going to become stronger and stronger. Market research and that sort of thing is going to bring in a whole host of specialists who maybe once would have been actuaries but are no longer going to be. There once was a time when actuaries were the only technical people around (besides lawyers). That is a day we are well rid of as far as I'm concerned.

Phyllis Cella looked at the question of future management needs somewhat differently.

> I think what we need more of is what I would call businessmen. We do not have enough people who know what it is like to take a business risk and not come out with an actuarial model that has 900 assumptions. They can't function unless they do it all with numbers always having to prove that everything is lovely.

Although the move to the profit center concept in the Holding Company was a conscious choice, there still remained the question of how to measure similarly the performance of the various units within the parent or Life Company. "We don't know of any mutual company that knows how to do this yet—learn with the learner! It is going to be an interesting experience," remarked Jack McElwee.

For E. James Morton, President and Chief Operations Officer and Vice Chairman of the Board, the question of measuring performance in the life company was at the heart of what he considered one of the Hancock's major problems. What had been done in the past could not be readily identified as bottom-line. They essentially had no measures of profit and inconsistent measures of growth. Size as indicated by assets under management had also become difficult to measure. According to Morton: "We have always had some kind of measures that we have tried to be tough about. But I'm not sure they have been the right ones and the ultimate kinds of measures. And they haven't been the kinds of measures that you can really compensate people on."

Morton had some reservations about moving to the profit center concept. He noted that at times they had the feeling that they were a generation behind and that the profit center idea was becoming outmoded. He referred to management journals that indicated that managers spent too much time worrying about short-term results, thus sacrificing long-term objectives.

Part of the problem of moving to the profit center concept was the method of accounting used in mutual life insurance companies. Morton felt, however, that another big piece of the problem was attitude.

> Maybe the attitude was not so bad in the days when all we were was a mutual life insurance company being operated with the primary purpose to supply insurance at cost to our policyholders. But now that we are trying to compete in a broader financial services industry we can't do that anymore. We have to operate with the same kinds of efficiencies as our competition.

Morton felt that they had to change the way management and essentially all of the employees of the company look at what the objectives are.

> If we do that, we are going to benefit our policyholders a lot more than perhaps we have in the past. We will be forced to cut costs, run things efficiently, be market driven, and expand the base that expenses can be spread over, resulting in lower consumer costs. We think we are headed in the right direction. But that is not to say that for the first 100 years things were done the wrong way. The times have changed.

De-mutualizing or moving to a stock company, is a very complex issue because of having to deal with fifty state insurance commissions and agreeing on whether a mutual company has equitably treated its existing policyholders. For Jack McElwee, it was also a complex issue but one that he related to the future environment of the Hancock.

> A lot of people feel that it is too complex but you can't possibly afford to feel that way. If the reality of the future is that only a corporation which is in the form of a stock company will be able to survive, then you'd better find a way to be a stock company, or at least have all the legal and regulatory characteristics that a stock company has.

Even though the future of the FSI is questionable, there should also be all kinds of opportunities. McElwee noted that capitalizing on those opportunities means "managing ourselves properly. That's what this exercise is all about—it's called management."

Jim Morton expanded on the role of the John Hancock in the FSI:

> I am not sure what one-stop financial shopping means. What we hope to do is attract clients. If we attract a client in one piece of the organization, we hope to make that client a target for the other pieces of the organization. I think it would be unrealistic to think that there are going to be a lot of people that get all their financial services from us. We want to see a lot of cross selling. We want to have plenty of clients in all the sectors and hopefully the rest will take care of itself.

Morton felt that to succeed in the FSI, the important step is to fill out the product line. He went on to say, "That is why we so badly need a bank. If we can't buy the bank, let's find that out in a hurry because we have to make other arrangements. There is no way we can be a large financial services organization without offering banking services. If you can't do it by owning a bank, you have to do it some other way."

Morton went on to discuss the future of the John Hancock:

> We want to end up with an organization that when people look at it they say, "That's a financial services organization." And if you ask the man on the street, "What is the John Hancock?" he will say that it is a financial services organization where I can go to do almost anything. I can buy stocks and bonds, house insurance, securities, and tax shelters. I can also get a mortgage for my house and banking services. Furthermore, I get a statement on everything once a month . . . that is what we would like to be in 1990, and I think we have a reasonably good chance of doing it. There will be maybe fifty large financial organizations at that time and that is the list we want to be in. In order to do that we have to internally become customer-driven, profit-oriented, entrepreneurial, and all those good things you are supposed to be if you are a healthy, growing business. We know what we need to do. The trick is to do it.

It was also clear to Jim Morton that in the next five to ten years the composition of the businesses of the Hancock is also going to change. The assets in the non-traditional ventures are going to become bigger than those in the traditional ventures. According to Morton, "If we succeed in buying the bank that is another billion dollars of assets. Clearly, the non-traditional ventures are where the growth is."

To complicate management tasks in the environment of an evolving FSI, McElwee also had to deal with what he considered an intriguing question, namely, "What is beyond the financial services industry?" To this end he recently put together a study group focusing on the time-frame of 2025 and the major questions of "What are the directions that the Hancock should move?" and "To what extent do those directions influence what we do in the way of financial services today?"

EXHIBIT 1   FINANCIAL SERVICES ANNOUNCEMENTS
              THE FIRST HALF OF 1983

"Travelers owns Securities Development Corporation (securities clearing subsidiary).

President of American Express joins Travelers (hiring said to be influenced by his financial services background).

Equitable Life and First National Bank of Chicago to market cash management services.

Prudential to buy Capital City Bank of Hopeville, Georgia.

Sears to have Dean Witter offices in 100 stores by the end of 1983, 150 by end of 1984 and eventually 400.

CIGNA buys automatic Business Centers, commercial payroll processing centers.

Kemper's regional brokerage houses earned $8.3 million in 1982.

Nationwide to offer insurance in offices of Banc One.

John Hancock's Independent Investment Associates to offer financial services for corporations and institutions.

Prudential to have 30 joint offices with Bache by the end of 1983.

Travelers to offer insured cash management services through its trust company.

Hartford to buy 24% of Minneapolis brokerage firm.

Aetna Life & Casualty buys majority interest in Federal Investors.

Mutual of Omaha plans to acquire investment banking and brokerage firm of Kilpatrick, Pettis, Smith, Polian, Inc.

J.C. Penney to buy First National Bank of Harrington, Delaware.

Merrill Lynch to buy Raritan Valley Financial Corporation, a New Jersey savings and loan.

Kemper announces intention to buy a savings and loan.

Chairman of Manufacturers Hanover says much of the euphoria about financial supermarkets may be exaggerated.

Source: "Insurance and the Financial Services Industry," Robert A. Bull, *United States Banker*, August 1983, p. 118.

EXHIBIT 2   ASSETS

Company	Dollar amount of total assets*
Prudential	66,707,209
Metropolitan Life	55,731,371
Equitable Life of N.Y.	40,285,559
Aetna Life	28,551,098
New York Life	22,549,386
John Hancock	21,710,494
Travelers	17,440,305
Conn General	15,660,054
Teachers Ins & Ann	13,519,897
Northwestern Mutual	13,252,835

*Figures do not include assets of subsidiaries.
Source: Best's Insurance Management Reports, October 1983.

EXHIBIT 3   **Organization chart effective April 1, 1983.**

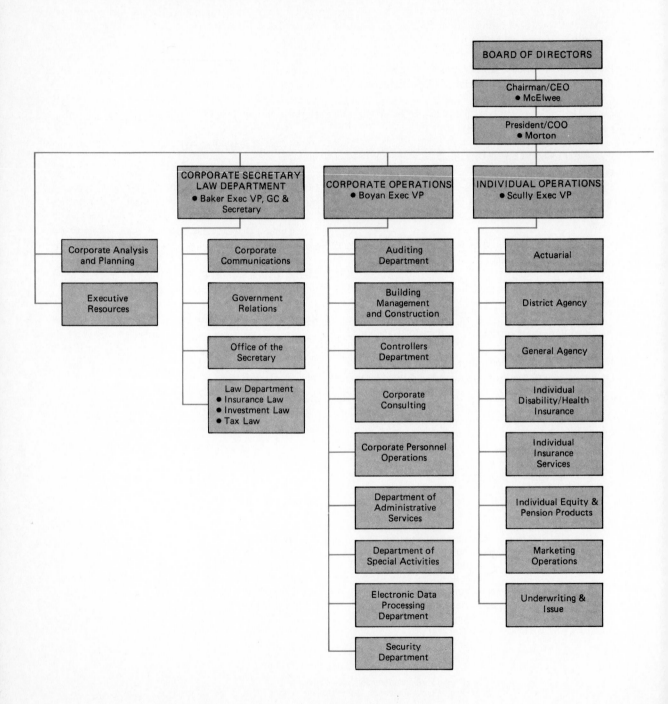

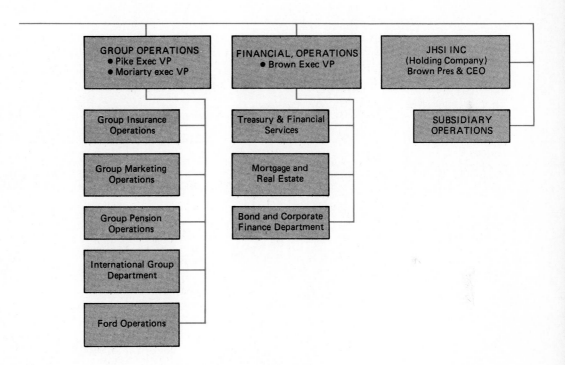

EXHIBIT 4   Subsidiary organization chart.

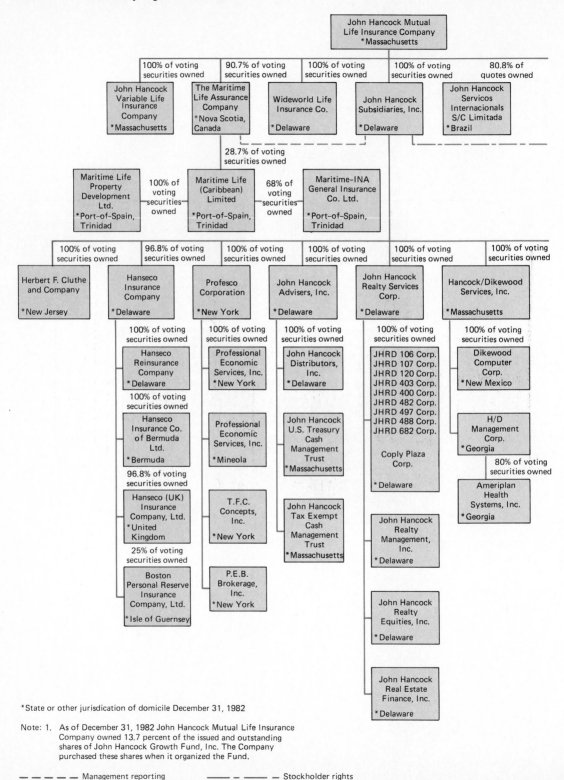

John Hancock Mutual Life Insurance Company *Massachusetts

- 100% of voting securities owned — John Hancock Variable Life Insurance Company *Massachusetts
- 90.7% of voting securities owned — The Maritime Life Assurance Company *Nova Scotia, Canada
- 100% of voting securities owned — Wideworld Life Insurance Co. *Delaware
- 100% of voting securities owned — John Hancock Subsidiaries, Inc. *Delaware
- 80.8% of quotes owned — John Hancock Servicos Internacionals S/C Limitada *Brazil

28.7% of voting securities owned

Maritime Life Property Development Ltd. *Port-of-Spain, Trinidad — 100% of voting securities owned — Maritime Life (Caribbean) Limited *Port-of-Spain, Trinidad — 68% of voting securities owned — Maritime-INA General Insurance Co. Ltd. *Port-of-Spain, Trinidad

- 100% of voting securities owned — Herbert F. Cluthe and Company *New Jersey
- 96.8% of voting securities owned — Hanseco Insurance Company *Delaware
- 100% of voting securities owned — Profesco Corporation *New York
- 100% of voting securities owned — John Hancock Advisers, Inc. *Delaware
- 100% of voting securities owned — John Hancock Realty Services Corp. *Delaware
- 100% of voting securities owned — Hancock/Dikewood Services, Inc. *Massachusetts

Hanseco Insurance Company branch:
- 100% of voting securities owned — Hanseco Reinsurance Company *Delaware
- 100% of voting securities owned — Hanseco Insurance Co. of Bermuda Ltd. *Bermuda
- 96.8% of voting securities owned — Hanseco (UK) Insurance Company, Ltd. *United Kingdom
- 25% of voting securities owned — Boston Personal Reserve Insurance Company, Ltd. *Isle of Guernsey

Profesco Corporation branch (100% of voting securities owned):
- Professional Economic Services, Inc. *New York
- Professional Economic Services, Inc. *Mineola
- T.F.C. Concepts, Inc. *New York
- P.E.B. Brokerage, Inc. *New York

John Hancock Advisers, Inc. branch (100% of voting securities owned):
- John Hancock Distributors, Inc. *Delaware
- John Hancock U.S. Treasury Cash Management Trust *Massachusetts
- John Hancock Tax Exempt Cash Management Trust *Massachusetts

John Hancock Realty Services Corp. branch (100% of voting securities owned):
- JHRD 106 Corp.
  JHRD 107 Corp.
  JHRD 120 Corp.
  JHRD 403 Corp.
  JHRD 400 Corp.
  JHRD 482 Corp.
  JHRD 497 Corp.
  JHRD 488 Corp.
  JHRD 682 Corp.
- Coply Plaza Corp. *Delaware
- John Hancock Realty Management, Inc. *Delaware
- John Hancock Realty Equities, Inc. *Delaware
- John Hancock Real Estate Finance, Inc. *Delaware

Hancock/Dikewood Services, Inc. branch:
- 100% of voting securities owned — Dikewood Computer Corp. *New Mexico
- H/D Management Corp. *Georgia
- 80% of voting securities owned — Ameriplan Health Systems, Inc. *Georgia

*State or other jurisdication of domicile December 31, 1982

Note: 1. As of December 31, 1982 John Hancock Mutual Life Insurance Company owned 13.7 percent of the issued and outstanding shares of John Hancock Growth Fund, Inc. The Company purchased these shares when it organized the Fund.

– – – – – Management reporting   ——— – ——— Stockholder rights

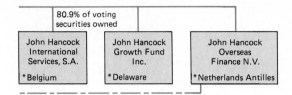

80.9% of voting securities owned		
John Hancock International Services, S.A. *Belgium	John Hancock Growth Fund Inc. *Delaware	John Hancock Overseas Finance N.V. *Netherlands Antilles

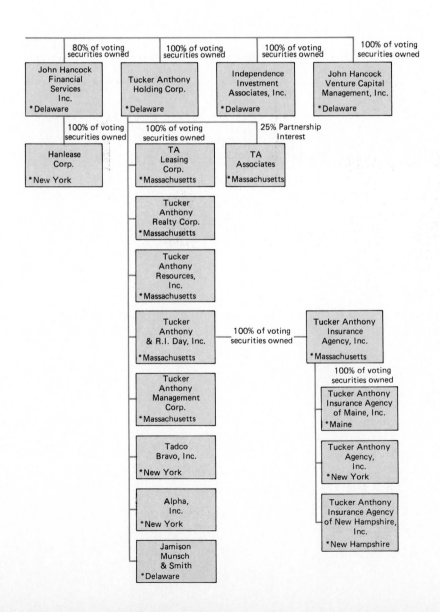

80% of voting securities owned	100% of voting securities owned	100% of voting securities owned	100% of voting securities owned
John Hancock Financial Services Inc. *Delaware	Tucker Anthony Holding Corp. *Delaware	Independence Investment Associates, Inc. *Delaware	John Hancock Venture Capital Management, Inc. *Delaware

100% of voting securities owned	100% of voting securities owned	25% Partnership Interest
Hanlease Corp. *New York	TA Leasing Corp. *Massachusetts	TA Associates *Massachusetts

Tucker Anthony Realty Corp.
*Massachusetts

Tucker Anthony Resources, Inc.
*Massachusetts

Tucker Anthony & R.I. Day, Inc.
*Massachusetts

— 100% of voting securities owned —

Tucker Anthony Insurance Agency, Inc.
*Massachusetts

100% of voting securities owned

Tucker Anthony Insurance Agency of Maine, Inc.
*Maine

Tucker Anthony Agency, Inc.
*New York

Tucker Anthony Insurance Agency of New Hampshire, Inc.
*New Hampshire

Tucker Anthony Management Corp.
*Massachusetts

Tadco Bravo, Inc.
*New York

Alpha, Inc.
*New York

Jamison Munsch & Smith
*Delaware

EXHIBIT 5   JOHN HANCOCK COMPANIES—ASSETS UNDER MANAGEMENT
($ In Millions)

	1972	1973	1974	1975	1976	1977	1978	1979	1980	1981	1982	1983
General account	$10,377	$10,737	$11,232	$12,071	$13,098	$14,101	$15,212	$16,207	$17,263	$17,824	$18,336	$18,708
Separate account	818	710	591	730	898	937	1,016	1,111	1,377	1,448	1,754	2,066
Guaranteed benefit separate account	0	0	0	0	0	0	0	0	121	671	1,633	2,766
Subsidiaries (estimated)*	283	488	462	633	708	838	1,014	1,269	1,625	2,365	5,400	6,013
Pension advisory accounts	0	0	0	0	19	24	83	133	161	203	269	398
Total assets under management	$11,478	$11,935	$12,285	$13,434	$14,723	$15,900	$17,325	$18,720	$20,547	$22,511	$27,392	$29,951

*Subsidiary assets are net of Hancock parent equity holdings and contain estimated components.
Source: John Hancock Mutual Life Insurance Company Annual Reports.

EXHIBIT 6   CONSOLIDATED SUMMARY OF OPERATIONS AND CHANGES IN POLICYHOLDERS' CONTINGENCY RESERVES
John Hancock Mutual Life Insurance Company and Subsidiary

Year ended December 31 (*In millions*)	1983	1982	1981
Income—			
Premiums, annuity considerations and pension fund contributions	$2,489.5	$2,573.4	$2,435.6
Investment income	1,818.1	1,668.1	1,491.2
Separate account capital gains (losses)	118.4	132.9	(106.9)
Other	(346.1)	(562.6)	(552.5)
	4,079.9	3,811.8	3,267.4
Benefits and Expenses—			
Payments to policyholders and beneficiaries:			
Death benefits	513.3	447.0	405.1
Accident and health benefits	423.9	444.5	496.4
Annuity benefits	182.9	25.0	11.6
Surrender benefits	248.9	90.1	79.1
Matured endowments	15.2	11.6	11.3
	1,384.2	1,018.2	1,003.5
Additions to reserves to provide for future payments to policyholders and beneficiaries	1,560.2	1,599.3	1,187.6
Expenses of providing service to policyholders and obtaining new insurance:			
Field sales compensation and expenses	308.9	292.5	285.6
Home office and general expenses	310.6	279.0	262.5
State premium taxes	30.5	32.2	30.2
Payroll and miscellaneous taxes	27.6	25.2	22.7
	3,622.0	3,246.4	2,792.1
Net gain before dividends to policyholders and federal income taxes	457.9	565.4	475.3
Dividends to policyholders	390.5	326.7	314.2
Federal income taxes	36.0	70.1	50.2
	426.5	396.8	364.4
Net gain	31.4	168.6	110.9
Net capital gain or loss and other adjustments	(52.6)	(50.2)	40.4
Less amounts allocated for:			
Increase (decrease) in valuation reserves	(1.2)	(1.2)	1.2
Additional provision for prior years' federal income taxes		13.9	30.0
Other adjustments	16.0	7.0	15.8
Increase (decrease) in policyholders' contingency reserves	(36.0)	98.7	104.3
Policyholders' contingency reserves at beginning of year	1,002.8	904.1	799.8
Policyholders' contingency reserves at end of year	$ 966.8	$1,002.8	$ 904.1

APPENDIX A: OFFICERS

John G. McElwee

John G. McElwee was elected chairman and chief executive officer of John Hancock Mutual Life Insurance Co. effective January 1, 1982. McElwee entered the John Hancock administrative training program in 1945 and subsequently served as administrative assistant and in a series of line management responsibilities prior to his election as second vice president in 1961. He became executive vice president and secretary in 1974. McElwee then served as president and chief operations officer from January 1, 1979, to his election as chairman. He has been on the Board of Directors since March 1976.

E. James Morton

E. James Morton was elected President and Chief operations officer of John Hancock Mutual Life Insurance Co. effective January 1, 1982. Morton entered the company as an actuarial student in 1949. He subsequently held a variety of line assignments within the actuarial area prior to his election in 1967 as vice president and actuary. In 1971, he was elected senior vice president, technical operations, and in 1974 executive vice president, corporate operations. Morton has been on the Board of Directors since March 1976.

Stephen L. Brown

Stephen L. Brown was elected executive vice president of financial operations of the John Hancock Mutual Life Insurance Company in December 1981, to the Hancock Board of Directors in January 1982, and served as President and Chief Executive Officer of John Hancock Sub-sidiaries, Inc. until February 1984. Brown joined the company in 1958. He subsequently held various assignments within the actuarial department and was elected second vice president in 1970 and vice president in 1973. In 1975, he became vice president at the treasury department and in 1977 was named senior vice president and treasurer.

Phyllis A. Cella

Phyllis A. Cella of Boston is president, chief executive officer, and director of Hanseco Insurance Co., a subsidiary formed for the reinsurance of Sentry Insurance Co. policies sold by John Hancock representatives. She is also chairman of the board of Hanseco (U.K.) Insurance Company Ltd. and a director of John Hancock Subsidiaries, Inc. Cella joined the parent company as a statistician. She advanced to statistical consultant in 1963 and served as assistant to the senior vice president of field management and marketing from 1968 to 1970, when she was named general director of special projects and research. Cella was elected second vice president in January 1972, vice president in February 1975, and senior vice president in December 1979.

Frank S. Irish

Frank S. Irish was promoted to vice president, corporate analysis and planning, at John Hancock Mutual Life Insurance Co. in January 1979. Irish joined the company in 1963 as an assistant actuary. He was promoted to associate actuary in 1966 and in 1971 joined the corporate analysis and planning department in that capacity. Irish was elected second vice president, corporate analysis and planning, in 1972.

KOOR TRADE

Joseph Ganitsky
Tulane University

In April 1984 Mr. Joseph Berenthal, Managing Director of Koor Trade (KT), and Mr. Amir Segev, his assistant, wondered whether the firm should make any additional strategic modifications. Recently they decided to make some critical changes in order to cope with the firm's challenges and opportunities (See Exhibit 10). Among others, they had:

- Simplified KT's organisational structure;
- Placed heavy emphasis on new products, preferably those with high gross margins;
- Stressed the strategic importance of those markets requiring professionalism, technical expertise and support service; and
- Promoted joint ventures with local and foreign entrepreneurs.

These decisions were taken so as to achieve the firm's main objectives, namely:

- To secure KT's proper position in the market;
- To increase its profitability; and

- To achieve long-term commitments with its suppliers,

and effectively cope with:

- The forecasted more competitive environment of the mid and late 80's on the international trade scene;
- The very difficult economic conditions in the Israeli economy; and
- The limited resources and weakened motivation of Israeli businessmen who had been negatively affected by the previous trends.

Government officials were interested in overcoming the country's economic hurdles. For that purpose they considered it imperative for Israel to increase both the local value added on exports, and total export turnover.

Mr. Berenthal and Mr. Segev held that these imperatives would have to be achieved despite Israel's increasing uncompetitive cost structure which was further affected by rampant inflation.[1]

KT is Israel's largest international trading firm. 'International trading firms' are those involved in supplying international trade services to manufacturers and consumers around the globe. As these firms grow they take strategic decisions in three dimensions, namely:

[1]Israel's inflation rate was about 200% in 1983 and it was expected to reach 400% during 1984.

• the degree of diversification in the products (and suppliers),

• the extensiveness of their market networks, and

• the set of functions they perform (from the original import/export ones to related others, such as information gathering, transporting, distributing, financing and insuring).

Eisenberg Trading, Israel's second largest trading firm, is privately owned, and mainly specialises in defence markets. Its export turnover is estimated to be only between a tenth and a fifth of KT's. CLAL Trading, the third largest, has developed strengths throughout Latin America, where some of its initial partners run their business. In total there are more than 100 export trading firms in Israel, most of them with marginal turnover.

In 1983 KT handled more than 6% of Israel's total industrial exports, excluding diamonds.[2] KT is one of the six Groups in which its parent company, Koor Industries (KI) is divided (see Exhibit 1 for an overall perspective of KI). In turn, KI is one of the bodies controlled by Hevrat Ha'Ovdim—the Histadrut Enterprises holding company, which is the economic arm of the General Federation of Labour in Israel (see Exhibit 2 for Hevrat Ha'Ovdim's overview).

The remainder of this case presents a review of the firm's strategic developments starting from its early inception.

KT'S FIRST TWENTY YEARS

KT's origins date from 1952, the year in which Solcoor Marketing and Purchasing Co. was established by KI, then part of Solel Boneh, for the direct handling of imports and exports of these concerns. Export volume picked up very rapidly reaching $5.4 million in 1956, $16.8 million in 1961 and $22.1 million in 1966. Meanwhile, the Israeli government established in the late 50's and early 60's four independent wholly owned trading subsidiaries, each one promoting exports to a different region:

ASTRACO   (Asia)
LAMISCO   (Latin America)
DIZENGOFF   (West Africa)
AMIRAN   (East Africa)

The government's trading firms were losing money in the early 60's so it decided to merge them into a single

[2]See Israel's exports, by economic branch, in Exhibit 13.

one (ALDA—Israel Foreign Trade Co.). The new firm covered the same regions through 14 branches with a common centralised management team. ALDA gained considerable experience in Africa (Ethiopia, Ghana, Ivory Coast, Kenya, Nigeria, Tanzania and Zambia) and Asia (Singapore, Thailand and Hong Kong).

Yet it kept losing money. In 1968 the government decided to sell it. KI, then under the new leadership of Meir Amit, was the highest bidder. For KI this was an excellent opportunity to rapidly expand abroad, specially taking into account that until then, London and New York were KI's only foreign branches. It was also an opportunity to broaden its local base of suppliers. These two features permitted KI to transform its import-export companies into a conglomerate of much broader trading firms.

ALDA, under the new ownership, became profitable and was further expanded to include several European markets. ALDA and Solcoor operated independently and in parallel, under a common roof, each one specialising in separate markets. In 1971 this common roof took the divisional form of Koor Inter-Trade Ltd. (KIT). Their joint export turnover reached $43 million (almost twice that of Solcoor in 1966 and 9% of Israel's industrial exports). Mr. Moshe Alpan was appointed Managing Director of both KIT and ALDA in 1971.

In 1972 Koor International Projects Ltd. (KIP) was established with the purpose of promoting sales and operating major integrated and/or turn-key projects abroad. KIP also reported to KIT. Similarly, several of KI's foreign joint ventures in the pharmaceutical, chemical, electric and agri-business fields ended up reporting to KIT. Also new trading branches were opened in Japan and Canada, reporting directly to KIT, rather than to ALDA. Finally, domestic trading activities were also incorporated into KIT. The emerging structure became too large (more than 20 branches) and too complex (see Exhibit 3).

As more products were handled it became necessary to appoint in Tel Aviv more purchasing specialists by product class (such as building materials, agricultural inputs, technical equipment. . . .). Their main function was to support foreign branches in all their dealings with their suppliers and vice versa. By doing so the organisation gradually evolved a cadre of professional product managers who established strong links with suppliers.

Since that time KT carries out its foreign trade activities according to three different trading modes:

1 As an *agency* the company takes customers' orders and obtains a sales commission after goods are delivered.

It is the simplest method as the firm is not responsible for all the risks involved in the operation. Consequently, it gets the lowest margin.

2 In other instances after the customer's order has been obtained KT prefers to:

—purchase the corresponding goods,

—perform all the necessary trading functions until goods are delivered, and

—take the additional risks involved (financial, compliance with quality and delivery schedule, etc.).

This trading mode, called *Presold*, carries higher gross margins and, in many instances, is more profitable.

3 Finally, in other instances the company decides to carry stocks of the product abroad even before it has customers' orders on hand. This is the *stock trading* mode which has the highest risks and, also, the potentially highest benefits.

The responsibilities of each branch manager increases as its branch's activities rise from agency to presold, and from the latter to stock trading. Similarly, they increase as the breadth of its product line broadens. A branch may carry simultaneously some products as an agency, others as presold, and yet others from stock. The business decisions associated with the breadth of product line and trading mode are influenced by, among others, local market conditions, the capacity of the local manager, and KT's willingness to support the activity. Hence the characteristics and performance differ widely among branches, despite possible corporate efforts oriented to develop a common pattern.

In 1972 Mr. Schlomo Steinfield was appointed Managing Director of ALDA with the dual purpose of easing Mr. Alpan's burden and of obtaining better results from the foreign branches' managers.

BLUMENTHAL'S ERA: 1973–1982

Mr. Naphtali Blumenthal, then head of the Finance Department and Vice President of KI, held that KT's operation be organised around geographic areas, rather than along the professional lines in which it had been structured; that is to say around foreign customers rather than local suppliers. There were strong arguments within Koor's management around which organisation was the appropriate one. As Naphtali's ideas prevailed and were supported by Koor's Board, Mr. Alpan resigned in 1973. In order to replace him Mr. Blumenthal was appointed

V.P. for Finance and Trade of KI, and Managing Director of KT.

In 1974 a new organisational structure based on four independent regional companies and an Israeli based export house was adopted. Each one of them, and also each branch, started to operate as a separate profit center. The regional companies supervised several branches from the following locations, where they were based:

Regional company	Head office	Manager
Koor Inter-Trade ASIA Ltd	Hong Kong	Former manager of Japan branch
Koor Inter-Trade EUROPE Ltd	Amsterdam	Outsider
Koor Inter-Trade Ltd AMERICA Ltd	New York	Mr. Steinfeld (ALDA)
Koor Inter-Trade AFRICA Ltd	Amsterdam	Amsterdam

At the same time, it was decided to transform ALDA in Tel Aviv from a holding company into a supply house. Its new purposes were to purchase and to handle the relations with suppliers; to bill; to export; and to provide all the pertaining logistic and administrative backing in Israel that the new regional companies required. Agreements were signed between ALDA and the branches. These agreements stated the scale of commissions that were recognised for ALDA by each branch for the services rendered. These scales varied in accordance with the product class and volume involved. The agreements were a tool used in order to activate the new profit center concept.

An additional characteristic of the new structure was that each regional company was allowed to establish its own small support referent office in Tel Aviv. The financial, administrative and operations control activities were handled by three staff departments in Tel Aviv. Therefore, the Foreign Trade Division of KT was composed of eight separate units. Finally, the Domestic Trade division was charged with the marketing in Israel of locally made and imported goods (see Exhibit 4).

Mr. Blumenthal appointed Mr. Michaeli manager of the Domestic Trade Division. As no person was appointed manager of the Foreign Division, the Managing Director of KT was always directly involved in the discussion of plans, organisation, staffing and control of each one of the eight units within the Foreign Division. He spent most of his time establishing the new companies, recruiting the new managers, building new communication channels and developing Management Information, Planning and Control Systems (MIPCS). The main element of the firm's MIPCS is the annual work plan. It is composed of:

- a set of basic assumptions (see Exhibit 5 for an outline of the suggested topics), and
- projected Cash Flow, P & L and Balance Sheet Statements.

Its purposes are:

1 to define the objectives for the branch's operations during the forthcoming year, in coordination with the overall activities of the concern;
2 to control its execution,; and
3 to learn from experience.

The planning process starts from the bottom of the organization. Each branch submits for discussion its detailed work plan in October. After review and approval by KT's top management this work plan serves as a yardstick for assessing the success of the subsidiary in promoting the interests of the concern. For this purpose each branch reports its sales and inventory levels monthly and its P & L bimonthly. The Balance Sheet Statement is reported each semester. MIPCS have gradually improved and become more sophisticated.

As a result of the new efforts, KT's network of suppliers and customers increased and export volume boomed (reaching US$ 120 million in 1976 more than twice that in 1972). However, a new set of problems implicit in the new organisational structure started to emerge and gradually became more evident. As the new structure implied two decision centers (ALDA and the Regional/Branch managers) it was necessary to define which of the two prevailed in what decisions. This was in order to avoid confrontations between them and achieve the delegated responsibility that KT was aiming for. Unfortunately it had not been defined from the very beginning and already many confrontations between them had occurred. Two types of conflicts were observed, namely those relating to:

- the evaluation-reward mechanisms associated with the profit sharing scheme (in regard to the amount of the commission to be recognized to ALDA), and

- their responsibilities (who makes a business decision, who a transaction, who defines the supplier and who the breadth of product line for a branch/region).

In order to avoid these confrontations some branches had decided, independently, to do business directly with their suppliers (and through their referents) thus weakening the lines of communication.

Though the Managing Director had attempted to maintain effective informal lines of communications, in order to avoid possible bottlenecks through a formal and more hierarchic method, it was clear that some changes had to be made. Thus, in 1977 the following decisions were made:

- ALDA stopped debiting for its services to the branches.
- The business decision making process was formally shifted to the regional companies.
- Negotiations with each supplier were done on a country basis rather than worldwide, as formally conceived.

Meanwhile, Mr. Naphtali Blumenthal's responsibilities were growing at a very rapid pace. In 1976 he was appointed Acting Chairman of Bank Hapoalim, and a year later President of KI, as Mr. Meir Amit became Knesset Member and Chairman of KI's Board of Directors. However, it was not until mid 1978 that Mr. Moshe Balla was appointed Managing Director of KT. Mr. Balla had previously served as General Manager of Soltam, one of Koor's (and Israel's) leading industrial metal companies.

In turn, Mr. Balla appointed Mr. Joseph Berenthal as head of KT's Domestic Division, so that Mr. Balla was able to devote most of his time to KT's Foreign Division. His efforts were oriented to effectively exploit the organisation's infrastructure and Israel's growing capacity to manufacture traditional and more sophisticated goods. During his tenure several organisational changes took place. One was the establishment in 1981 of a fifth regional company based in Mexico (Koor Inter-Trade Am Lat Ltd.) as the number and turnover of that region's branches increased. In January 1982 the formerly International Projects department (within ALDA) became an independent division with the purpose of selling, financing and in some instances managing large integrated projects and systems. Mr. Amir Segev, who had been ALDA's Managing Director for five years, became its first Managing Director. In 1982 KT's Domestic Trade Division was reorganised into seven subsidiaries (see Exhibit

6). By doing so KT took advantage of the excellent business opportunities for imported goods in the booming local market. These opportunities were a direct result of:

a the changes introduced by the government in the country's economic policies, and

b the more frequent usage of KT's local marketing services by many firms owned by KI. These firms had developed and manufactured new items which also satisfied the needs of some segments of the domestic market.

In 1981 KT's export turnover reached US$ 275 million, more than twice that of 1976. This period was a very profitable one for KT. Yet, a new set of problems emerged as both the foreign and local environments went through significant changes.

In the early 1980's the international arena was characterised by a world recession which caused general trading conditions to become much tougher. While more competitors actively participated in each market, customers demanded more services (after sales service, long-term finance, bartering . . .) and growing financial costs consumed most of the diminishing trading margins. In addition, some developing countries started to experience lack of liquidity in their foreign reserves. This implied not only that they could not meet their prior obligations but that they wouldn't buy a fraction of what they used to, at best. In 1981 trading activity with African nations experienced a mild decline, and with Europe a sharp one. Meanwhile, exports to the US market grew rapidly. Trading based on foreign sources stabilised at a much lower level than the one previously reached (see Exhibit 7).

In the local arena other changes took place which were even more significant from KT's perspective. The composition of the goods being exported changed. Agricultural and wood products became less important while chemicals, electronics and products with mixed technologies exhibited a continuous growth pattern. The proportion of suppliers of more sophisticated goods increased. Also, KT's sales originated by Koor affiliated firms increased from 28.7% in 1976 to 47.8% in 1981 (see Exhibit 8). This was at the expense of private suppliers. This phenomenon partially reflected KI's gradual growth through acquisitions.

It should be observed, however, that not all KI's subsidiaries export through KT. Each one is free to choose its most appropriate export arrangement. For example, Tadiran handles directly most of its huge export volume (see Exhibit 1). This follows KI's definition of management's autonomy and responsibility. According to its pol-

icy managers are given free hand, and the corresponding responsibility, for all their activities, except in two areas where they must follow a common approach, namely: a) wage and salary policies, and b) centralised financial control. As a result, all KI's financial activity is channelled through a central financial clearinghouse.

KT's management noticed that as each supplier increased its export volume it:

1 learned more about the basics of the export business;

2 required less from KT in terms of its traditional know-how, while it expected a more sophisticated backing abroad;

3 was willing to pay proportionally less for KT's services, since it was less costly for him to put up his own export marketing activity; and

4 communicated directly with KT's branches. This disrupted KT's information and control systems, which in turn diminished KT's central bargaining power with them.

In summary, suppliers were moving from kindergarten to university very fast. KT's strategy was oriented to encourage their development, yet KT was also breeding its future competitors as it did not provide adequate responses to the changing needs of its suppliers. This deficiency was further aggravated by the fact that during the early 80's Israel's economy and terms of trade deteriorated. Hence, export profitability was greatly damaged.

In response to these simultaneous phenomena some exporters, mainly those more developed, started examining the possibility of exporting directly to the larger and most profitable markets. This approach implied that KT would be left with the smaller and less profitable ones specially as many of them required a tremendous effort in order to establish a beachhead. As some suppliers moved from analysis to action KT lost some valuable customers and thereby its revenues also diminished. To the best of KT's management's knowledge, none of KT's former suppliers exported afterwards through other trading firms. In 1982 KT's export turnover reached only US$ 227 million. Yet KT's share of total Israeli industrial exports remained approximately constant, as compared to that of 5 years earlier.

The Foreign Trade Division's revenues were also negatively affected by the fact that inflation had exceeded devaluation by more than 10% annually during the early 80's. This difference was not covered by the foreign currency insurance. It did not protect foreign trade services.

In addition to the environmental changes, KT's structure, after almost ten years of operation, had expanded and become difficult to operate and slow to respond. The end result was that KT's suppliers were dissatisfied. Under these threatening circumstances KT's management recognized that it had to introduce significant changes in its strategy and structure if it wanted to regain an upward pattern on its export turnover and be profitable.

RECENT DEVELOPMENTS

In late 1982 Mr. Naphtali Blumenthal was elected member of the Knesset. As a result he was promoted to KI's Chairman of the Board and Mr. Yeshayahu Gavish became KI's President. Mr. Gavish joined KI in 1970, after retiring from active army service with the rank of Lt. General, in order to serve as Managing Director of KI's Metals Division. Then, he became Managing Director of Koor Steel & Metals Group and afterwards executive vice-president of KI (deputy to Blumenthal). They worked very closely for more than six years.

Mr. Gavish had won his reputation for achieving results by stressing the examination firstly of objectives to be accomplished, and secondly of motivational and organisational factors associated with their implementation. Above all, though, he centered his actions around people. Consequently, almost as soon as he became KI's President he talked to people at different levels of KI's organisation. This way he got a firsthand impression, well beyond the figures, of what was happening in terms of problems, opportunities, strengths, weaknesses and human factors. He also asked for their opinions, ideas and action plans to cope with them.

As a result of this process, Mr. Gavish decided to appoint different people in KI's key positions. Mr. Joseph Berenthal was appointed, in April 1983, Managing Director of KT and was directed to focus his energies on transforming KT into a more aggressive and attractive marketing organisation for its suppliers and at the same time a more profitable one.[3] In other words, KT should give equal service at a lower cost, or at the same cost a better service. In turn, Mr. Berenthal appointed Mr. Segev as his assistant. In June 1983, a major reorganisation was put in motion, once Mr. Berenthal moved to his new position. The following decisions were taken:

---

[3]It should be pointed out that even after the recent difficulties KT had managed to be profitable both in its domestic and foreign operations.

1 to reorganise KT's former five regional companies into two regional divisions (Afro-Asia and Euro-America) whose headquarters are located in Tel Aviv;

2 to form an International Trade Division that would also include the activities previously performed by the International Projects Division and the shipping unit;

3 to discontinue ALDA as a separate purchasing house;

4 to concentrate the imports to Israel in the Domestic Trade Division;

5 to make each one of the four divisions a separate accounting unit responsible for its profit and loss statement; and

6 to centralise in two units (finance, and management and manpower) KT's staff (see Exhibit 9).

All these measures were oriented to make KT's structure one having:

1 very simple and clear lines of business and financial responsibility;

2 more professional attitude in its international trade operations;

3 an effective integration between the Domestic Division and the foreign branches in regard to imports to Israel; and

4 better communications between suppliers and branches.

In summary, KT was swinging back into a simpler organisation. After half a year of implementation 27% of KT's former employees at its headquarters in Tel Aviv had been transferred to other companies within KI, or had resigned. Thus, KT had become also a lower fixed cost operation, with greater flexibility, and a more competitive one. Branch managers were encouraged to negotiate directly with suppliers, agreeing on lower commissions for higher turnovers, and to take decisions within limits of risks already pre-defined. Furthermore lines of communication and control were shortened and all those possible duplications between ALDA and the branches were eliminated. Branches were not allowed to purchase from sources other than Israel without obtaining approval from headquarters. A significant change that took place was the relocation of key personnel within KT. It implied that new blood and fresh approaches would be superimposed throughout the emerging organisation. The following is a list of the changes in crucial personnel, in addition to those that have been already mentioned:

New manager	Previously manager of
Afro-Asia division	Africa
Euro-America division	Asia
Solcoor (N.Y. + Lat. Am.) (Under Euro-am.)	KT's M.D.
Domestic division	New York
International division	ALDA

After everyone had moved into his new position, Mr. Berenthal and Mr. Segev were very concerned how to implement the managerial changes that would allow KT to achieve its two ultimate objectives. Furthermore, they thought that there might be additional ideas or approaches in defining KT's scope, strategy and managerial process. Hence, they decided to prepare a working paper which they submitted in September '83 for analysis and discussion to the members of KT's Top Management Committee.[4] They also invited KI's long-term planning manager to this four day closed door brainstorming meeting. As a result of these discussions KT's new Policy Directives were agreed upon (as summarised in Exhibit 10).

Of particular significance among these guidelines was the fact that KT recognized an urgent need to move away from mainly a commission merchant basis to mainly a controlled risk-taking policy. For that purpose the firm was encouraging more presold and stock trading; joint commercial and manufacturing ventures both with local suppliers and foreign customers; and whatever other steps could be taken in order to narrow at the branch level the firm's product line, so as to develop local distinctive expertise. This expertise would gradually become a unique service that suppliers would find very difficult and expensive to replace, thus creating a mutual long-term commitment beneficial to all parties involved. Branch managers were directed to implement this strategy without losing the short-term profit perspective.

It was already inevitable that 1983's performance

[4]This was composed of 8 people in addition to themselves: KT's four divisional managers, KT's heads of finance, and management and personnel units, and KI's Financial and Operations Control managers.

would not be changed by these new policies. Indeed, total export turnover for the year only reached US$ 216 million, a figure which was below the previous year's performance and well below what had been planned a year earlier as the firm's reasonable goal (US$ 258 million). Exhibits 7 and 8 indicate the firm's sales performance for the last two years as well as 1984's sales target. This difference in turnover represented a difference in contribution to fixed costs of about US$ 1 million. Yet, this reduction also reflected a condition which they considered incidental rather than structural. Indeed the drastic drop in exports to Africa had been prompted by Nigeria's overall reduction in imports to a third of its previous level, as well as by its Central Bank's inability to meet its obligations to foreign suppliers (see Exhibit 11).

The collapse of the African market as well as the inherent weakness of other markets in developing regions underlined the strategic importance that more developed markets were already acquiring in KT's strategy. However, these more developed markets demanded more sophisticated products which in turn implied heavy financial-technical-human investments. These demands in turn originated two sets of new problems, namely:

• How to create reliable professional marketing units in very narrow and specific fields. For example, unless competent staff in the electronics and systems engineering fields were to join the company and demonstrate that they could also perform the required marketing functions, KT would not be able to tap some of the largest and fastest growing markets around the globe.
• How to develop the required after sales service network in order to back up KT's marketing activity.

Traditionally, trading firms had not been involved in these fields. Hence, KT projected a "lack of competence" image. This, in turn, rightly inhibited Israeli manufacturers of sophisticated goods even to consider KT as a potentially effective marketing alternative. And as a result of this behaviour, it remained so. KT's management decided to break this self-defeating and reinforcing cycle by:

1 Hiring several specialists, such as electronics and systems engineers with marketing experience, to develop key target markets. Their availability was communicated to the relevant audience of manufacturers of high-technology products.
2 Forming joint marketing ventures with some Israeli manufacturers for specific foreign markets. Under them,

manufacturers were encouraged to a) professionally manage them, and b) provide all their technical expertise, while KT supplied its logistics, trading and financial strengths. Both parties shared the risks and profits on an equal basis. In early 1984 such agreements had been finalized, for example, with Raphael valves in West Germany and the U.S., and Telrad telecommunications products in the U.K.

3 Becoming partners with, or taking over existing foreign professional marketing organisations. For example, Koor recently acquired 50% of a marketing firm specialising in irrigation equipment in Spain.

4 Carrying out, with external advice, studies oriented to identify investment opportunities in small Israeli firms manufacturing new high technology products with high foreign market potential. Their final purposes were: a) to become in these firms a small shareholder, and b) to secure their long-term export commitments and their own future growth. These studies were only in their initial stages in early 1984.

The U.S. market was, in the early 80's, KT's largest one (see Exhibit 7). It also seemed to be towards the future the most attractive one. However KT's top executives were puzzled, as they did not know which were their best options there. KT operates in this market from two lo-

cations: New York with more than 100 people, and Los Angeles with 15. Despite this market's huge potential not all suppliers are attracted or can afford to put together the resources to serve it as required. Others are discouraged by its complexity, competitiveness and/or distance. KT's management considered that precisely the latter reaction represented a tremendous business opportunity. In order to take advantage of it they had to design viable marketing instruments. Apparently this could be the case in those instances where several manufacturers of competing and complementary products were to agree on developing joint integrated marketing strategies. In such a case, KT would act as a catalyst satisfying the needs and constraints of all those involved.

In late 1983 KT's top management decided to call in an external consultant. He was required to examine the U.S. market situation, its alternatives, and come up with a specific plan of action. In particular, they wanted him to analyse about 50 groups of products in terms of their relative advantage (from Israel's viewpoint vs the rest of the world) and in terms of their market attractiveness (i.e., market conditions, trends and potential) (see Exhibit 12). The consultant had agreed to present his conclusions and recommendations within a few months. Meanwhile, they wondered if they should take any additional actions concerning this market.

EXHIBIT 1   KOOR IS . . . R&D

- Israel's major industrial complex
- 175th in Fortune's 1982 listing of the world's largest industrial concerns (outside the U.S.A.)
- a unique organization skillfully combining national, social and economic objectives
- a producer of 11% of the nation's industrial output and 14% of industrial export (excluding diamonds)
- a diversified industrial complex encompassing 250 companies—manufacturing, commercial and financial
- a labor-owned organization, whose shares are held by the workers of Israel
- an international concern active on six continents through 45 offices in major marketing centers
- the country's leader in workers' profit-sharing, participation in management and social welfare
- a major factor in the industrialization of outlying development areas

- a successful joint venture, participant with both local and overseas investors in more than 50 enterprises
- a profit-oriented corporation, whose profits are reinvested in the company's further development
- Israel's leading industrial exporter, who, with its trading arm Koortrade, accounts for 20% of the country's industrial exports.

Koor's principles

Reflect the Company's national, social and commercial objectives:

- To spearhead the development of Israel's industry.
- To promote national goals: increased exports, industrialization of development areas and industrial research and development.
- To safeguard the principles of the Histadrut and to ensure their practical application.

EXHIBIT 1   KOOR IS . . . R&D *(Continued)*

• To channel profits into continued development.
• To provide improved working conditions and social benefits and to promote workers' welfare.
• To maintain high productivity and profitability levels and sound financial structure.

Organizational structure

Hevrst Ha'ovdim Board of Directors

Management

Groups	Metals
	Mechanics & Systems
	Chemicals
	Food & Consumer Goods
	Tadiren
	Trade
Divisions	Electric & Electronics
	Ceramics
	Glass
	Cement

General data

	1980	1981	1982	forecast 1983
Sales turnover, $ bil.	2.40	2.80	2.90	3.10
Industrial exports, $ mil.	390	450	470	520
Investments, $ mil.	90	90	130	160
Employees, in thousands	28.2	29.6	32.1	32.9

Koor's share in Israel's Industry in 1982 excluding diamonds

Sales—11%; exports—14%; Investments—18%; Employees—10%.

Industrial sales, $ million

	1982	1983 forecast
Steel & metals	369	411
Food & consumer goods	272	295
Chemicals	204	207
Tadiren	384	460
Electric & electronics	108	126
Ceramics & glass	56	66
Cement	154	152
Alliance tires	87	98
Others	36	37
Total	1670	1852

Sales by markets

Percent of sales turnover	1981	1982	1983 forecast
Exports	31	30	30
Construction	19	19	18
Defense	10	12	13
Industry & intrastructure	7	6	6
Telecommunications	5	5	5
Food	8	9	9
Consumer goods	7	7	7
Transportation	4	3	3
Agriculture	4	4	4
Others	5	4	5

Exports by industrial branches, $ million

	1982	1983 forecast
Steel & metals	88	92
Chemicals	95	95
Tadiren	157	190
Food and consumer goods	49	40
Electric & electronics	18	34
Glass and ceramics	9	10
Alliance tires	39	43
Others	16	16
Total	470	520

The share of exports in Koor's total sales increased from 17% in 1970 to 30% in 1982. In 1990, exports are projected to reach 50% of total sales.

R & D

Koor places great emphasis on industrial research and development, which is directed toward

• diversifying product mix
• integrating new technologies

Products developed in-house form an increasing portion of Koor's product range.

About 50% of Koor's exported products are based on company-originated R & D.

Over the past few years, R & D projects have included electronic exchanges, communication systems, military and medical electronic equipment, plant protection chemicals, algae cultivation, solar energy, etc.

EXHIBIT 1 KOOR IS . . . R&D *(Continued)*

In the foreseeable future, priority will be given to the development of export-aimed products in electronics, telecommunications, agromechanics, weapon systems, medical applications and biotechnology.

R & D expenditures by the end of the decade will reach $600 million.

R & D projects, some of which have been declared national projects, are carried out on both group and plant levels, often in cooperation with the Israeli universities and research institutes.

Investments

Koor is Israel's largest industrial investor, with the rate of investment increasing yearly. Company policy is to direct investments toward export-oriented industries.

Two-thirds of these investments are concentrated in the field of electronics and chemicals. 35% of the $160 million investment budget for 1983 in being allocated to development areas.

Investments, % of sales
1977—6.5%
1978—7.0%
1979—8.5%
1980—10.0%
1981—11.0%
1982— 8.0%
1983— 9.0% (forecast)

The Koor worker

The worker is Koor's most valuable natural resource.
The worker represents the key to the fulfillment of corporate goals.

He and She are partners in all that Koor accomplishes.
This has been achieved through workers' participation in profits, and in management, which was first introduced in Israel by Koor.

Worker participation in management implies:

• better communication between management and employees.
• involvement in shaping the future development of the plant and the worker's position within it.
• stronger worker identification with the plant.

One third of Koor's Board of Directors are workers' representatives. Additionally, a member of the Executive Management is a delegate of the workers.

Joint-management committees have been formed in 25% of the plants, with this trend continuing until all units are included.

Workers' participation in profits

Koor employee profit-sharing plan is:
• a concrete symbol of the employee's contribution to his enterprise's success
• a means of increasing identification with the plant's activities
• an incentive towards higher profitability through greater productivity.

Employee profit-sharing has been steadily increasing in Koor since 1970.

20,000 employees shared the profits of 1981.

EXHIBIT 1   KOOR INDUSTRIES LIMITED AND SUBSIDIARIES COMPREHENSIVE CONSOLIDATED
BALANCE SHEET AT DECEMBER 31, 1982 *(Continued)*

	$ In Thousands		%
	1982	1981	Increase
Current assets:			
Cash	50,327	41,609	21
Fixed-term deposits	269,515	209,262	29
Government compulsory loans	10,713	9,560	12
Accounts receivable	585,935	491,513	19
Inventories and contracting work in progress	519,947	460,511	13
Total current assets	436,437	1,212,455	18
Investments and long-term receivables:			
Associated companies	36,883	19,561	89
Other investments and receivables	197,300	186,711	6
Total investments and long term receivables	234,183	206,262	14
Property, plant and equipment:			
Cost	1,202,146	1,070,122	12
Less—accumulated depreciation	604,139	535,491	13
Total property, plant and equipment	598,007	534,631	12
Other assets	1,584	3,561	(56)
Total assets	2,270,211	1,966,909	16
Current liabilities:			
Short-term loans and credits	332,086	320,777	4
Accounts payable and accruals	468,520	401,784	17
Customer advances	236,603	221,248	7
Total current liabilities	1,037,209	943,809	10
Long-term liabilities:			
Loans from banks and others	372,244	253,641	47
Other	121,214	124,118	(2)
Total long-term liabilities	493,458	377,759	31
Reserve for equalization of taxes on income	16,044	9,822	63
Accrued severance pay and retirement grants	5,235	1,914	174
Total liabilities and reserve	1,551,946	1,333,304	16
Investment grant	39,449	30,061	31
Interest of outside shareholders in consolidated subsidiaries	245,160	205,773	19
Long-term loans convertible into shares	2,143	2,143	—
Shareholders' equity:			
Share capital	24,292	24,292	—
Receipts on account of shares	8,868	8,868	—
Capital surplus	12,063	9,420	28
Retained earnings	386,290	343,048	13
Total shareholders' equity	431,513	385,628	12
Total liabilities and shareholders' equity	2,270,211	1,956,909	16

EXHIBIT 1   KOOR INDUSTRIES LIMITED AND SUBSIDIARIES COMPREHENSIVE CONSOLIDATED
STATEMENT OF INCOME FOR THE YEAR ENDED DECEMBER 31, 1982 *(Continued)*

	1982		1981	
	In $ thousands	%	In $ thousands	%
Income:				
From sales work performed and international transactions	2,231,926	117.90	2,299,114	125.20
Less—agency sales and international transactions	338,818	17.90	462,755	25.20
	1,893,108	100.00	1,836,359	100.00
Other income—net	64,847	3.43	30,571	1.66
Total income	1,957,955	103.43	1,866,930	101.66
Cost and expenses:				
Cost of sales and work performed	1,586,856	83.80	1,542,702	84.01
Selling and administrative expenses	229,628	12.16	220,976	12.03
Financial expenses—net	24,866	1.31	16,694	0.91
Total cost and expenses	1,841,350	97.27	1,780,372	96.95
Income before taxes on income	116,605	6.16	86,558	4.71
Taxes on income	33,783	1.79	17,745	0.97
	82,822	4.37	68,813	3.74
Share of outside shareholders in net income of consolidated subsidiaries	39,437	2.08	30,005	1.63
Net income for the year	43,385	2.29	38.808	2.11
Earnings per share— I.S.—1. par value—in dollars				
Primary	9.65	—	8.61	—
Fully diluted	3.43	—	3.07	—

EXHIBIT 1   COMPREHENSIVE CONSOLIDATED STATEMENT OF CHANGES IN FINANCIAL POSITION
FOR THE YEAR ENDED DECEMBER 31, 1982 *(Continued)*

	In $ Thousands	
	1982	1981
Source of funds:		
Operations	144,765	120,386
Long-term liabilities	181,802	121,522
Proceeds from realization of fixed assets and others	36,479	21,714
Other	33,240	15,487
Total source of funds	396,286	279,109
Application of funds:		
Investments in fixed assets	142,268	103,512
Repayment of long-term liabilities	55,003	34,688
Other	67,407	115,441
Increase in working capital	131,608	25,468
Total application of funds	396,286	279,109
*Include depreciation and amortization	78,204	60,394

EXHIBIT 2   HEVRAT HA'OVDIM, THE LABOUR-OWNED SECTOR OF THE ISRAELI ECONOMY

The organization was set up at the second Histadrut convention in 1923 to supervise all the economic activities—then more of a hope than a reality—of the labour movement.

Although all Hevrat Ha'Ovdim members are also members of the Histadrut, it is not a formal part of the Histadrut. Rather it is a parallel organization with the Labour Federation.

Nevertheless, the Histadrut and Hevrat Ha'Ovdim are run by the same people at the highest levels. They meet both as the Histadrut or Hevrat Ha'Ovdim councils, with the secretary-general of the Histadrut also being chairman of Hevrat Ha'Ovdim. But at the executive level, entirely different people take over.

The bodies within Hevrat Ha'Ovdim can be broken down into two main divisions.

The first are those in which Hevrat Ha'Ovdim controls 51 percent of the shares. These include Bank Hapoalim (one of the two largest banks in Israel); Koor, the largest manufacturing conglomerate in the country with more than 150 industrial plants as well as about 100 service branches; Hassneh, the country's largest insurance group; Solel Boneh, the country's largest construction company; *Davar,* the Histadrut's newspaper; Am Oved, its publishing company, and many others.

The second major divisions are the cooperatives. These are owned and run by their members.

These cooperatives can be subdivided into three main groups.

The first is the rural cooperatives such as the kibbutz networks and the moshavim. These rural cooperatives own national groups, such as Tnuva and Hamashbir Hamerkazi. The kibbutzim also own many organizations which perform regional functions.

The second sub-division is the consumer cooperatives. Here the members usually don't do the work but enjoy the services provided. These consist mainly of the Zarchaniot supermarket chains and Hamashbir Le'zarchan (which is owned jointly by Hamashbir Hamerkazi and the five regional groups of the Zarchaniot supermarkets).

The third sub-division consists of about one hundred urban "producers' cooperatives" where the principle "all

EXHIBIT 2 HEVRAT HA'OVDIM, THE LABOUR-OWNED SECTOR OF THE ISRAELI ECONOMY *(Continued)*

work is of equal value'' is still a way of life. These include bakeries, printing shops, metal factories, with the best known being the Dan and Egged. If Hevrat Ha'Ovdim did not exist, it would have to be invented. ''It fulfils an indispensable role in the country's economic life which no other body can, or has, undertaken.'' So says Danny Rosolio, secretary of the organization, which provides about one-quarter of the country's gross national product.

''At present, we see three things wrecking the national economy: non-growth, inflation, and social and labour unrest. The worst feature is that youngsters are deserting the development areas for the cities to find work.''

Rosolio believes that Hevrat Ha'Ovdim can help solve these problems, if its potentials are developed and tapped.

''Today,'' said Rosolio, ''92 per cent of the funds flowing into the Histadrut pension must be invested in government index-linked bonds. Of the rest, nearly all goes for loans to members. Nothing is left for development.''

Rosolio thinks that if only 30 percent (''of course we would like more'') of Histadrut pension funds were used for development, several hundred million dollars could be funneled every year into the productive sector.

He admits that this would deprive the government of the same amount of income, ''but then the government is using these funds to finance its own activities. It wouldn't hurt the government to trim its budget. After all, the future of the country lies in constant economic development, not in frittering away the funds in unneeded governmental expenses.''

As for Hevrat Ha'Ovdim, it is taking certain specific steps to ride out the economic storm. ''Our very structure helps us. For example, take Koor. It is a concern, composed of many companies. If one Koor company runs into difficulties, another one can help it.''

Despite this, Hevrat Ha'Ovdim has taken steps to prevent a crisis from developing within these concerns.

The first step is to intensify cooperation between member companies.

The kibbutz industries are working closer with each other. They are also working much closer with Koor and with regional cooperatives.

Hevrat Ha'Ovdim is also going ahead with its own economic development plans.

And finally, Hevrat Ha'Ovdim is intensifying its social

and educational programmes.

Hevrat Ha'Ovdim is a flexible socialist organization whose philosophy is not only to change gradually with the times but also to change the times gradually.

This is how Ben Rabinovitch, 44, director of its economic department, describes the organization.

''Thus, we have different grades of carrying out social values. In the kibbutzim, the equality is higher than in an urban cooperative, yet it is higher in an urban cooperative than in an organization like Bank Hapoalim and it is higher in Bank Hapoalim than in any commercial bank in the private section.''

Considerable benefits accrue from these various forms of organization—even if all have the same objective of social advancement through economic activity. ''And not being actively controlled by Hevrat Ha'Ovdim encourages democracy to function as well as entrepreneurial initiative.''

Nevertheless, Hevrat Ha'Ovdim's long range planning encourages all its groups to be more responsive to the needs of the public.

Hevrat Ha'Ovdim fights unemployment. It sets up plants in development areas. It establishes retail outlets in areas where no profit-minded individual would go.

''Our structure is poised to withstand economic shocks better than any private organization. Our stronger members help our weaker ones. A good example is Koor. Instead of closing down a failing plant, Koor takes steps to find a way to keep the men employed. Sometimes it retools the plant, sometimes it merges it with another.''

But Rabinovitch warned: ''Strong as we are, there is a limit to what we can do. We can't guarantee endless help to a failing plant and we cannot always provide employment.''

Change means progress, and a sign of Hevrat Ha'Ovdim's ability is the industrialization of the kibbutzim. Today, about half the income of some kibbutzim comes from industry. And at present, Koor is now studying ways and means of setting up industry in the moshavim.

Hevrat Ha'Ovdim is big enough to take a long view of the future. For example, during the past few years, when private investment in industry dropped, Hevrat Ha'Ovdim saw that its groups maintained investments at the same level.

Source: The Jerusalem Post Hevrat Ha'Ovdim Supplement, December 28, 1983.

EXHIBIT 3 Koor Inter-Trade Ltd. organizational chart (1972).

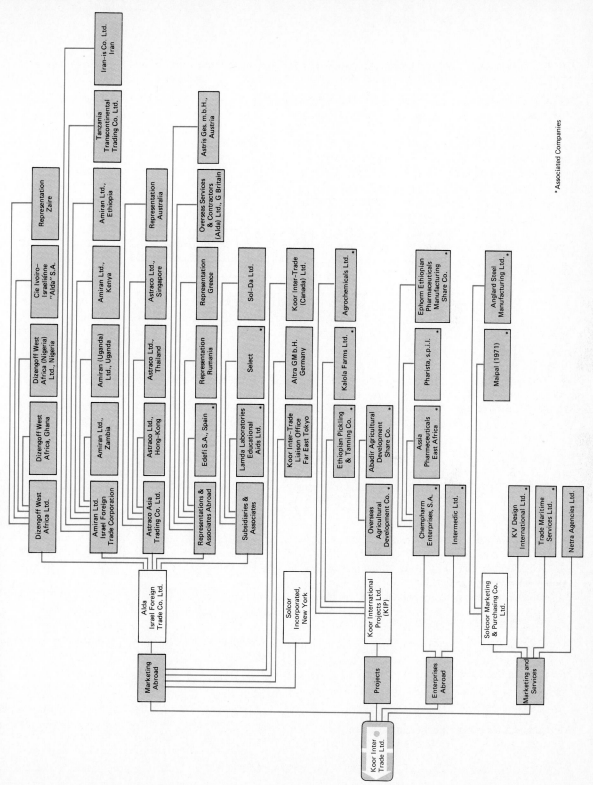

* Associated Companies

EXHIBIT 4 **Koor Trade's organizational chart (1974).**
(Casewriter's drawing based on descriptions by K.T.'s management.)

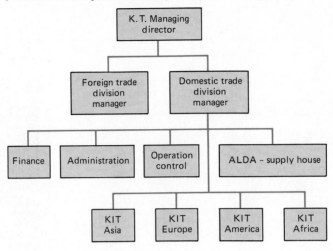

EXHIBIT 5 FORM 2.00, BASIC ASSUMPTION FOR THE ANNUAL WORK PLAN

A document for this purpose will be prepared by the subsidiary's manager on subsidiary's letterhead with contents as follows:

Reporting subsidiary's letter head

   TO: 1 (General manager, company in-charge)
       2 (Concern's H. O.)
   Re: Basic assumptions for the annual work plan

A. Political and economic developments

   Short review of the political situation, government policies on developments, projects, defense & social welfare, on inflation, currency stability and rate exchange, import duties, income tax and taxation in general, emphasizing the effect on subsidiary's operations.

B. Subsidiary's main objective for planned year

C. Turn-over & profits

   Factors that are expected to affect turn-over or profits, either in volumes, in product mix or source of goods, should be reviewed.

D. Man-power

   Expected changes in man-power, and salaries.

E. Investments

   Review of required new investments or disposal of same.

F. Trading terms & financing

   The credit terms of the subsidiary's purchases and sales. Overdrafts available, details of collateral, rates of interest on credit lines and on funds drawn. Details of overdrafts should be given for each bank separately.

EXHIBIT 6   **Koortrade Ltd. Domestic Trade Division.**

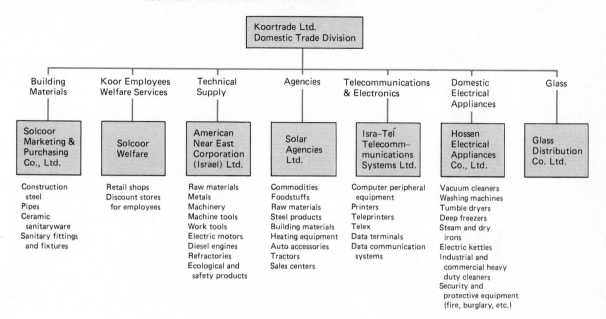

EXHIBIT 7   KT'S SALES VOLUME ABROAD (IN MILLIONS U.S. $) (1976/1984)

	1976	1977	1978	1979	1980	1981	1982	1983	1984[F]
By source									
From Isreal	131	163	197	207	273	269	227	216	287[2]
From abroad	69	93	108	56	68	69	48	41	87
Exports to									
Asia	29	39	51	45	53	55	52	36	53
Africa	29	38	49	52	79	69	49	31	43
Europe	9	30	41	56	77	47	42	45	55
North America	45	54	53	50	59	87	97	97	114
Latin America	—	1	1	2	4	9	6	6	7
Total	131[1]	163	197	207	273	269	227	216	287[2]

[1]This total includes $18 million which represents that year's turnover of American Near East Corporation, ANEC, (a second purchasing house acquired by Koor and which later was integrated into KI and KT). ANEC devoted most of its export activity to processed food, which is carried out nowadays by Koor Foods Ltd.
[2]includes $13 m of barter deals of the International Trade Division which have not been allocated by region/supplier/product line.
(F) = Forecasted
Source: Company records

EXHIBIT 8   KT'S SALES VOLUME BY TYPE OF SUPPLIER AND PRODUCT LINE (IN MILLIONS U.S. $) (1976–84)

	1976	1977	1978	1979	1980	1981	1982	1983	1984[F]
By type of supplier									
Affiliated to Koor	35	41	51	51	108[1]	128	124	119	128
Kibbutzim	17	28	30	36	46	45	33	30	49
Private	79	94	115	119	118	95	74	67	96
Total	131	163	197	207	273	269	227	216	287[2]
By product line									
Agricultural	24	25	29	32	40	15	10	10	n.a.
Wood & by-products	17	5	3	4	3				
Chemical industry	27	43	49	63	68	78	83	80	n.a.
Electric/onics & optics	9	14	15	16	24	41	40	45	n.a.
Metals, machinery	20	28	41	34	56	47	33	27	n.a.
Plastic, rubber & paper	23	39	41	41	53	44	32	41	n.a.
Mixed technologies[3]	6	5	8	4	16	25	13	7	n.a.
Miscellaneous	3	3	9	10	9	14	14	6	n.a.
Total	131	163	197	207	273	269	227	216	287[2]

[1]Two important exporters (Sefen—Formica manufacturers, and Alliance—in tires) were acquired by KI this year.
[2]includes $13 m. of barter deals of the International Trade Division which have not been allocated by region/ supplier/product line.
[3]includes technical goods, engineering supplies, transport equipment and various building materials.
(F) = Forecasted; n.a. = not available. Plans were revised by supplier and market, but were not consolidated by product line.
Source: Company records

EXHIBIT 9   **Koor Trade's organizational chart (1983).**
(Company records.)

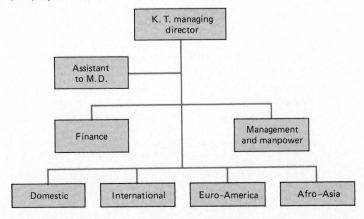

EXHIBIT 10   SUMMARY OF KOOR TRADE'S POLICY DIRECTIVES

As a result of the reorganisation, the management of Koor Trade set up a series of discussions concerning relations between its activities and the organisational structure.

In the discussion that took place on 1st September 1983 it was decided to adopt, with some changes, the plan presented, the main details of which are as follows:

A EXPORTS FROM ISRAEL

1 Products

To reclassify the product offerings handled by the company, the aim being to cut down the range and to handle its depth with a specialised professional approach.

2 Suppliers

2.1 The relations between the branch and its supplier will be based on a directly connected working system.

2.2 Working agreements which will be signed with suppliers, will take into account the turnover's volume, type of product, and the duration of the relation. Commission levels will be fixed accordingly.

2.3 A list of preferred suppliers will be drawn up to which special attention will be paid.

2.4 The branches will have to find in the markets products suitable for production by those suppliers connected to Koor Trade.

3 Sales and Marketing Systems

3.1 The company should encourage a wider range of marketing methods by adopting selling methods from stock, presold, as well as representation as an agent.

3.2 The company encourages the setting-up of joint professional marketing units with those manufacturers in which we are interested, and to invest accordingly in the necessary marketing systems.

3.3 The motivation and incentive methods will be used as a lever to broaden marketing and sales, and to increase profits.

3.4 Additional service systems will be built up in order to serve suppliers in the commercial and marketing areas.

3.5 The company will use the financial systems of Koor Industries and Koor Trade as a tool to achieve its commercial and marketing goals. The financial department of Koor Trade will be organised accordingly.

4 Markets

4.1 Non-profitable branches, which are unlikely to become profitable in the near future, will be closed and instead a replacement marketing system will be developed through local companies and local agents.

4.2 Regional centers will be set up to serve various countries simultaneously.

B INTERNATIONAL TRADE AND IMPORTS TO ISRAEL

1 An international network for trading and projects will be set up. The International Division will, with the help of the branches, make joint ventures with foreign firms, both in trade and in projects.

C MANAGEMENT AND ORGANISATION

1 The group will organise all its activities by means of four trading divisions and two staff departments.

2 All trading divisions will be managed from the centre in Israel. The management of the divisions will be responsible for determining policy, planning, reaching overall agreements with suppliers, and control. The branches will give backing and services to the field units.

3 The authority and responsibility of the branch's manager will be increased, and tasks that in the past were assigned to management in Tel Aviv will be transferred to them.

4 The control and administration of the divisional managers over branch managers will be increased in order to prevent deviations from company policy.

5 An instrument for evaluation of manager's performance will be created, as an incentive in achieving the firm's objectives. In parallel, the company will encourage the use of local sales forces which, in the long range, will be integrated in the branches.

6 The manpower dealing with marketing and sales will be helped by, and combined with, the parallel systems of Koor Industries, Kibbutz Industries and private factories connected with Koor Trade. All this will ensure the orderly rotation of marketing people.

D Summary

The management of Koor Trade feels that the above mentioned methods and the selected tools will enable the company to achieve the objectives set for it by Koor Industries. These tools and methods will more than meet the demands made by markets in the 1980's from a modern trading firm and will put Koor Trade on the right tracks.

EXHIBIT 11 CUSTOMERS IN LATIN AMERICA AND AFRICA DEFAULT ON PAYMENTS: ISRAEL MAY LOSE $60M. IN BAD DEBTS

TEL AVIV—Israeli companies stand to lose a maximum of $60 million in Latin America and Africa. "But the actual losses will in all likelihood be much smaller, and eventually we hope to recover all sums owed us by foreign importers," says Amior Kamir, general manager of the Israel Foreign Risks Insurance Corporation, a government-sponsored company.

"And the losses, no matter whether large or small, could have been five times as big if we had not taken preventive steps in time," he adds.

Kamir notes that three years ago the entire situation regarding trade with South America and Africa took a new turn. Some of these countries, like Venezuela, Mexico and Nigeria, derived a considerable part of their income from petroleum.

"We saw a new trend emerging in international trade. The price of oil was stabilizing and beginning to fall; on the other hand, the oil-importing countries, such as the U.S. and many European countries, were mounting huge export drives to sell their products in order to recover part of the sums they had to lay out for oil. And the oil-producing countries, still under the illusion that their revenues would remain high, were buying and buying, although their political and financial problems were steadily growing."

Israel could have sold five times as many goods as it was shipping. "But we began warning manufacturers that the future was not as bright as it looked." Industry Minister Gideon Patt used all his influence to temper exports, and it was finally decided to export only enough to maintain our foothold in these markets. Something akin to an export quota system was actually formulated.

Exports were divided into two categories: to Africa—mainly Nigeria—it was consumer goods and semi-capital goods, such as equipment and sprinklers; to Latin America it was mainly capital goods generally sold on long-term credit.

Some time ago, when the financial situation of the importing countries got worse, they no longer allowed funds to be taken out of the country, since they faced a severe shortage of foreign currency as oil and other revenues dropped off.

At present, importers in the various countries owe Israeli exporters the following sums: Nigeria, about $40m.; Argentina, Mexico, Venezuela, Peru, and Brazil, each $10m., with Ecuador owing about $5m.

The Latin American countries went to what was called the Club of Paris, which drew up a rescheduling of their debts. Nigeria, probably for prestige reasons, refused to join this "club" and tried to arrange consolidation loans in England. Negotiations are still continuing.

"What is apparent now," Kamir notes, "is that the financial situation of both Argentina and Mexico is improving steadily, and there is every reason to believe that they will soon be able to honour most of their debts. We hope that their improved situation will have a beneficial influence on the other Latin American countries. But the situation is worse in Venezuela."

Nigeria presents a serious problem. Even if she arranges loans leading to the rescheduling of payments, it seems apparent now that she will declare a two-and-a-half year moratorium on her debts; but then there is every likelihood that she will be able to pay within the following three-and-a-half years. "Even if we recover the entire debt, we will certainly lose interest payments, and this also is a considerable sum."

Yeshayahu Gavish, general manager of Koor Industries, said recently that Koor had filed a claim with the Foreign Trade Risks Corporation for a $20m. debt owed it by importers in Nigeria. Gavish said that 80 per cent of the debt would be covered by the corporation.

At present, the authorities are discussing export strategies to all the countries which owe Israel money. "We must never forget that they all are very important markets, and that once they get back on their feet, their importance as customers will continue to grow."

So far, the corporation has had to pay out to Israeli exporters about $25m. for losses incurred in former years. Of this, $5m. was lost in Iran and the remaining $20m. in Uganda. "The latter case went to arbitration, and the arbitrator ruled in Israel's favour. Therefore we have hopes of recovering most of the monies owed us by Uganda."

By Macabee Dean, *Jerusalem Post* reporter, *The Jerusalem Post*, Wednesday, April 11, 1984, p. 6

EXHIBIT 12 EXCERPTS FROM CORRESPONDENCE BETWEEN KT AND THE CONSULTANT
(a) from the letter of KT to the consultant

16th November 1983

Dear Sir:

Re: Research in the USA.

Further to our conversation and the suggestion you made to us in October 1983, I wish to define the research aims, as we see them:

General

To examine the range of products with which KT will be dealing in America during the next 5 years, and the organizational-economic conclusions to be drawn from the findings.

Time range

We will be guided by the results of the research in the near future—1984, and the more distant future—the next 5 years.

Population to be researched

1 Product range and group of suppliers having existing connections with KT-America.

2 Products ranges and groups of producers not connected with KT-America's system; evaluations of them will be used in the research, indicating whether connections with them, and investing in their exports to the U.S., are worthwhile.

Technique

Subject will be examined in two parallel directions:

1 Examination of ability and extent of future exports of those product ranges checked, together with a check on their relative advantage in the American market.

2 Examination of potential American markets, suitable for these products; is it strategically worthwhile to invest in their penetration.

The technique of the actual examination will be made in accordance with your proposal.

EXHIBIT 12 EXCERPTS FROM CORRESPONDENCE BETWEEN KT AND THE CONSULTANT
(a) from the letter of KT to the consultant *(Continued)*

Application of the conclusions

In accordance with the presented results, it will be possible to progress to the recommendations stage, which will deal with the following fields:

1 Recommended marketing methods for each range/market

2 Recommended organization/preparation for the KT-America system

3 Necessary resources for the KT-America system

Implementation

2 teams will simultaneously collect data, one in the USA and the other in Israel. Final data processing and report-writing will be done in Tel-Aviv.

Time-table

We hope that the entire project be completed by the end of February 1984, so we can start its application during the year. I would ask you, therefore, to present the findings as progress is made, and the next stage will be decided upon in mutual discussions.

Summary

We would like to receive a system of practical data enabling us to rapidly translate the report terms into terms of action. We should avoid "deteriorating" into the preparation of an in-depth "pure research" report involving an analysis of the "Whither Israeli Exports?" type. We perceive KT's enormous variety as hampering the achievement of our aims, but in spite of this, I believe we can guide our teams in the correct spirit.

Good Luck!

Yours sincerely,
Amir Segev

EXHIBIT 12   *(Continued)*
(b) from the proposal of the consultant to KT
A PROPOSAL FOR STRATEGIC MARKETING ANALYSIS

Planning Stages

The overall planning effort can be divided into the following three stages:

1 *Strategic choices*
1.1 Evaluation of existing and potential product groups based on two dimensions:
(a) Industry Attractiveness
(b) Comparative Advantage
1.2 Strategic decision-making about each product group with respect to four alternatives:
(a) Investment
(b) Maintenance
(c) Skimming
(d) Divesting

2 *Operational Planning*
2.1 Marketing research projects for specific product groups designed to explore alternative penetration and expansion options.
2.2 Development of marketing plans for all major product groups.

3 *Organizational planning*
Review and possible adjustment of the organizational structure and systems needed to accomplish the marketing plans.

Methodology (stage 1)

The following methodology is proposed for the evaluation process of Stage 1

1 Identification of product groups, from a marketing point of view, including both existing groups and potential additions. Approximately fifty product groups will be identified.

2 Evaluation of each product group based on two composite measures: Market Attractiveness and Comparate Advantage.

Market Attractiveness consists of such factors as: market size, rate of growth, competitive intensity, technological risk and stability of demand.

Comparative Advantage consists of factors such as current market share, profit potential, technological advantage, product quality, price competitiveness, investment in R & D production capacity, market knowledge and relations with suppliers.

Estimates about these factors will be developed both in Israel and in the U.S., based on secondary sources and on a survey of knowledgeable individuals in Koortrade and in the supplier firms. We anticipate the development of about five independent estimates for most factors. The independent estimates will be consolidated into one measure by weighted averaging. Each of these factors will be given a mutually agreed-upon weight for calculating the composite measures of Market Attractiveness and Comparative Advantage.

3 Two presentation matrixes will be prepared based on the axes of Market Attractiveness and Comparative Advantage, one for existing product groups and one for potential additions. The relative position of each product group in the matrix will serve as a product classification system designed to assess its strategic implications. This matrix has been developed by General Electric as a "strategic business screen" and has been used extensively in recent years.

4 A joint meeting will be called to discuss the strategic choices that have to be made and the priorities for marketing action in the short and long term.

EXHIBIT 13A: EXPORTS, BY ECONOMIC BRANCH

Economic branch	$ million						
	1982	1981	1980	1979	1978	1975	1970
Grand total	5,281.5	5,670.1	5,537.5	4,546.3	3,921.3	1,940.7	778.7
Agricultural exports—total	*553.0*	*599.6*	*555.7*	*555.6*	*455.3*	*277.6*	*129.6*
Citrus fruit	185.6	246.3	231.1	254.6	202.7	176.1	86.1
Other	367.4	353.3	324.6	301.0	252.6	101.5	43.5
Industrial exports—total	*4,606.2*	*4,945.3*	*4,880.4*	*3,916.1*	*3,400.2*	*1,610.6*	*637.7*
Mining and quarrying	189.1	194.4	158.4	102.0	78.3	86.5	40.8
Food, beverages and tobacco	332.4	333.6	298.1	253.9	211.1	125.3	62.9
Textiles	92.5	109.7	152.9	112.5	77.0	52.3	44.4
Clothing and made-up articles	255.4	277.0	313.3	226.9	169.5	104.1	53.6
Leather and leather products	6.5	8.4	7.2	9.8	8.2	5.4	3.5
Wood and its products	22.9	27.7	43.2	37.9	33.1	12.8	9.6
Paper and its products	6.4	7.6	14.8	9.4	4.2	2.8	3.2
Printing and publishing	19.9	20.7	21.3	16.4	14.3	18.3	5.9
Rubber and plastic products	107.2	107.7	128.2	84.9	72.1	44.7	23.5
Chemical and oil products	580.1	653.0	647.5	498.6	338.7	183.3	52.9
Non-metallic mineral products	14.5	17.1	16.1	10.0	14.2	6.5	3.0
Basic metal	35.5	58.6	97.4	38.6	29.1	26.1	7.9
Metal products	514.6	463.6	377.3	316.8	330.7	103.1	28.2
Machinery	112.0	116.6	91.4	79.6	58.0	30.9	18.1
Electrical and electronic equipment	465.7	387.1	287.1	168.3	137.2	97.7	12.8
Transport equipment	439.9	513.3	398.0	364.1	240.1	40.1	9.1
Diamonds, polished—gross	1,157.7	1,397.1	1,615.1	1,418.8	1,477.4	640.7	244.6
Thereof: net	904.7	1,067.2	1,409.1	(1,224.0)	(1,317.6)	(548.6)	(202.0)
Miscellaneous	253.9	252.1	213.1	167.6	107.0	30.0	13.5
Other exports—total[1]	*122.3*	*125.2*	*101.4*	*74.6*	*65.8*	*52.5*	*11.6*
Thereof: bunkers and stores for foreign ships and aircraft	83.9	88.9	75.1	41.4	34.0	18.1	8.1
Returned exports	*−264.7*	*−341.2*	*−245.6*	*−232.9*	*−205.2*	*−106.2*	*−45.1*
Net exports—total	5,016.8	5,328.9	5,291.9	4,313.4	3,716.1	1,834.5	733.6

[1] Incl. also industrial goods which are not included in "Industrial exports—total" above.
Source: Statistical Abstract of Israel, 1983, p. 232.

EXHIBIT 13B: PERCENTAGE BREAKDOWN OF VALUE OF EXPORTS BY AREA OR COUNTRY

	(Sept.) 1983	1982	1980	1975	1970	1960	1950
Europe	43.9	42.2	52.1	52.1	54.3	69.9	72.7
Common Market	34.4	33.1	38.3	37.4	37.5	47.8	48.7
Germany	7.0	6.9	9.8	8.3	8.6	9.7	
United Kingdom	8.0	7.9	8.4	8.7	10.5	16.7	31.6
France	5.1	4.9	5.4	5.8	5.1	2.1	0.6
EFTA	6.8	6.4	9.3	8.7	7.9	11.0	14.8
Switzerland	3.3	3.0	5.5	4.2	4.3	5.5	3.1
Other European countries	2.7	2.7	4.4	6.0	9.0	11.1	9.1
Asia	11.0	10.0	11.0	18.9	14.0	6.1	1.1
Hong Kong	3.0	3.4	4.5	5.8	4.8	3.5	
Japan	3.7	3.7	4.2	5.1	4.2	0.9	
Singapore	1.0	0.7	1.3	1.5	0.5	0.4	0.3
Iran	—	—	—	4.8	2.9		
Africa	3.0	3.6	3.5	3.8	5.3	4.9	0.3
South Africa	1.8	1.5	1.4	1.8	1.4	0.9	
Nigeria	0.5	0.8	0.8	0.7	0.5	0.9	
North and South America	27.1	24.3	19.5	20.0	22.5	16.4	25.4
U.S.A.	25.4	21.2	16.0	15.8	19.2	13.6	23.7
Australia and New Zealand	1.0	1.3	0.9	1.0	0.7	0.6	0.3
Other countries	14.0	17.0	13.0	4.2	3.2	2.1	0.2
	100.0	100.0	100.0	100.0	100.0	100.0	100.0

MANVILLE CORPORATION (A)

Arthur D. Sharplin
Bentley College

Asbestos is an insidious poison. Microscopic fibers, as small as a human cell, cause progressive, irreversible, incurable disease. Asbestos causes scarring of the small airways and further scarring of the lung tissue itself, parenchymal asbestosis. Asbestos causes scarring, thickening and calcification of the lung linings, pleural asbestosis. Asbestos causes an always fatal cancer, mesothelioma, in the tissue surrounding the lungs. Asbestos causes lung cancer. Asbestosis causes an abnormally high level of lung infections which are unusually hard to treat.

For eight years in the boiler rooms of the USS Santa Fe, the USS Antietam and the USS Thomas F. Nickel, Ed Janssens used and repaired thermal insulation. He never knew he was planting a time-bomb deep within his lungs. Twenty years passed before he first felt its toxic effects. He was sick, but he didn't know why.

Ed Janssens has asbestosis. To be more specific, his asbestos exposure from 1943 through 1951 has caused thickening and calcification of the lining of his lungs, small airways disease, complication of his asthma, life threatening lung infections, and a progressive decrease in lung function. He will require close medical surveillance forever. If Ed Janssens, an asbestotic, does not die soon of cancer, mesothelioma or massive lung infection, the inexorable march of asbestosis will eventually block his blood flow, swell his heart and cause death by coronary pulmonale.

In 1981, 30 years after his last exposure to its asbestos, Ed Janssens brought Johns-Manville to trial. For ten years, his asbestosis has been stealing his breath, complicating his asthma, retarding treatment for lung infections, keeping him out of work, making him lonely and reclusive, causing him depression and frustration, reducing the length of his natural life, and keeping him from sleeping in even the same bedroom with his wife, Patsy, the mother of his eight children. For years, he had to sit up in a chair to get any sleep; now, under more effective medical care, he can sleep lying down—sometimes.

It was 1978 when Ed Janssens, 35 years too late, first learned of the asbestos hazard. Who knew the death-dealing hazards of the asbestos fibers? Johns-Manville knew. Who knew in 1929, when Ed Janssens was just five years old? Johns-Manville did. Who exercised editorial prerogative over Dr. A. J. Lanza's 1935 United States Public Health Service report entitled "Effects of Inhalation of Asbestos Dust on the Lungs of Asbestos Workers"? Johns-Manville did. And who rushed on Christmas Eve 1934, to make sure "additions, omissions or changes . . . beneficial from the industry viewpoint" would be included in Dr. Lanza's official report? Johns-Manville did.

When an asbestos manufacturer's health credo was "our interests are best served by having asbestosis receive the minimum of publicity," it is no surprise to learn that no hazard warning besmirched [Manville's] asbestos bags and boxes until 30 years after Dr. Lanza acceded to his benefactor's demands; and, even then, only because Dr. Irving Selikoff had "held the smoking gun aloft"—publicly in 1964.

Wayne Hogan
Counsel for Asbestos Victims

The Janssens filed suit in 1979 and were eventually awarded $1,757,600 in compensatory and punitive damages. But Manville moved for a judgment, notwithstanding the verdict, then for a new trial, and then for a return of part of the adjudged damages (none of which had been paid). When all these motions were denied in December 1981, Manville initiated the formal appeal process. The appeal had not been heard—and Ed Janssens had not been paid—when the Manville board of directors met secretly on August 25, 1982, to decide whether to file for protection under Chapter 11 of the U.S. Bankruptcy Code.

Manville Corporation (Johns-Manville until 1981) is a diversified mining, timber, and manufacturing company. In 1982, the company employed about 30,000 people at more than 125 facilities (plants, mines, and sales offices), mostly in the United States. For many years, the company had been the world's largest producer of asbestos and asbestos-based products. In 1976, sales of asbestos fiber alone (mostly to manufacturers outside the United States) provided 52 percent of Manville's income from operations, although it constituted only about 11 percent of sales. In addition, asbestos was used by the company in making hundreds of products such as floor tile, textiles, filters, pipe, and roofing materials. Altogether, asbestos and asbestos products clearly accounted for more than one-half of Manville's sales and probably for three-fourths of its operating profit. The ruled insert below describes asbestos.

In 1957, the Industrial Health Foundation proposed a study on asbestos and cancer to be funded by the Asbestos Textile Institute (made up of asbestos manufacturers).

WHAT IS ASBESTOS?

This is taken from the *Encyclopaedia Britannica:*

> *asbestos,* mineral fibre occurring in nature in fibrous form. It is obtained from certain types of asbestos rock, chiefly the chrysotile variety of the serpentine groups of minerals, by mining or quarrying. Valued since ancient times for its resistance to fire, asbestos fibre achieved commercial importance in the 19th century.
>
> The fibre is freed by crushing the rock and is then separated from the surrounding material, usually by a blowing process.

This is from an article by Bruce Porter in *Sunday Review of the Society:*

> Perhaps no other mineral is so woven into the fabric of American life as is asbestos. Impervious to heat and fibrous—it is the only mineral that can be woven into cloth—asbestos is spun into fireproof clothing and theater curtains, as well as into such household items as noncombustible drapes, rugs, pot holders, and ironing-board covers. Mixed into slurry, asbestos is sprayed onto girders and walls to provide new buildings with fireproof insulation. It is used in floor tiles, roofing felts, and in most plasterboards and wallboards. Asbestos is also an ingredient of plaster and stucco and of many paints and putties. This "mineral of a thousand uses"—an obsolete nickname: the present count stands at around 3,000 uses—is probably present in some form or other in every home, school, office building, and factory in this country. Used in brake linings and clutch facings, in mufflers and gaskets, in sealants and caulking, and extensively used in ships, asbestos is also a component of every modern vehicle, including space ships.

The proposal was rejected by Manville and the other manufacturers at the March 1957 meeting of the institute. The minutes reported, "There is a feeling among certain members that such an investigation would stir up a hornets' nest and put the whole industry under suspicion."

In 1963, Dr. I. J. Selikoff of Mt. Sinai Medical Center in New York completed an extensive study of asbestos and health. The minutes of the Asbestos Textile Institute's Air Hygiene Committee meeting of June 6, 1963, noted Selikoff's forthcoming report:

> The committee was advised that a Dr. Selikoff will read at the next meeting of the AMA in about 30 days a paper on a study he has made of about 1,500 workers, largely in asbestos insulation application, showing a very large incidence of lung cancer over normal expectations.

Dr. Selikoff's report and the symposia and publications which followed revealed, for the first time to those outside the industry, the magnitude and character of the asbestos problem: Thousands had already died of asbestos-related diseases, and hundreds of thousands more would become disabled and die in the decades to follow. Breathing asbestos dust causes progressive thickening and stiffening of lung tissue (asbestosis) and sometimes causes the always fatal asbestos cancer (mesothelioma); either of these diseases may disable the victim twenty to forty years after exposure.

The dangers of ingesting asbestos fibers began to be widely publicized in the 1960s and 1970s. Beginning in 1978, there were hundreds of newspaper stories, magazine articles, and television documentaries concerning the problem. Joseph Califano, Secretary of the Department of Health, Education and Welfare (HEW), estimated that between 8.5 and 11 million workers had been exposed to asbestos since World War II. In April 1978, HEW announced that it was warning present and former asbestos workers and their doctors about the hazards of asbestos, and the U.S. Surgeon General sent 400,000 warning letters to the nation's doctors. In June, the Environmental Protection Agency established limits for airborne asbestos resulting from building demolition. Then, in December, 1978, the Environmental Defense Fund claimed that millions of school children had been exposed to cancer-causing levels of asbestos because of use of the product in school construction.

MANVILLE'S LEGAL DEFENSES WEAKEN

The dozens of asbestos injury lawsuits against Manville in the twenties and thirties, scores during the forties and fifties, and hundreds in the sixties and early seventies became thousands in the late seventies. Although the asbestos litigation was not mentioned in Manville's 1977 annual report, it was described, as the law required, in the company's 1977 Form 10K, submitted to the Securities and Exchange Commission in April 1978. This form reported 623 asbestos lawsuits against Manville, some of them multiplaintiff cases involving many claimants. The claims for which amounts were given totaled $2.79 billion.

For nearly fifty years, Manville had been able to hide the fact that company executives knew the dangers of breathing asbestos dust from about 1930 onward and sup-

pressed research and publicity concerning asbestos-related diseases. But, in April 1978, plaintiffs in a South Carolina asbestos tort case obtained the so-called Raybestos-Manhattan papers. These documents consist of asbestos industry correspondence and reports from the 1930s and 1940s. Coupled with the publications of Selikoff and other researchers, the Raybestos-Manhattan papers made a compelling case. The ruled insert on page 765 gives excerpts from a few of the papers.

In ordering a new trial, the South Carolina judge wrote:

> The Raybestos-Manhattan correspondence reveals written evidence that Raybestos-Manhattan and Johns-Manville exercised an editorial prerogative over the publication of the first study of the asbestos industry which they sponsored in 1935. It further reflects a conscious effort by the industry in the 1930s to downplay, or arguably suppress, the dissemination of information to employees and the public for fear of the promotion of lawsuits. . . .
>
> On two separate occasions, September 1977, pursuant to subpoena duces tecum, and December 1977, pursuant to a Request to Produce, plaintiff sought to discover the Raybestos correspondence in question. . . . it is uncontroverted that the same documents were produced in April 1977, in a New Jersey asbestos lawsuit. . . .
>
> It is also clear that the defendant, Johns-Manville, upon whom the December Request to Produce was also served, had in its possession since April 1977, the Raybestos correspondence, which also involved its corporate agents.

During the late seventies, asbestos plaintiff lawyers were able to obtain depositions from a number of retired Manville executives. Dr. Kenneth W. Smith (mentioned in the Raybestos-Manhattan excerpt) had been Manville's physician and medical director from 1945 to 1966 (except for one year). In a 1976 deposition, Dr. Smith testified that he became "knowledgeable of the relationship between the inhalation of asbestos fibers and the lung condition known as asbestosis" during his internship in 1941–1942, before he went to work for Manville. Following are other excerpts from Dr. Smith's testimony:

Q. Did you [tell other employees of Johns-Manville] of the relationship between the inhalation of asbestos fiber and the lung condition known as asbestosis?

A. Many people at Canadian Johns-Manville in su-

EXCERPTS FROM THE RAYBESTOS-MANHATTAN PAPERS

From a December 15, 1934, letter from George Hobart, Manville's chief counsel, to Vandiver Brown, Manville's corporate secretary and legal vice president:

> . . . it is only within a comparatively recent time that asbestosis has been recognized by the medical and scientific professions as a disease—in fact, one of our principal defenses in actions against the company on the common law theory of negligence has been that the scientific and medical knowledge has been insufficient until a very recent period to place on the owners of plants or factories the burden or duty of taking special precautions against the possible onset of the disease in their employees.

From a 1935 letter to Sumner Simpson, president of Raybestos-Manhattan Corporation, from Anne Rossiter, editor of *Asbestos,* an industry trade journal:

> You may recall that we have written you on several occasions concerning the publishing of information, or discussion of, asbestosis. . . . Always you have requested that for obvious reasons, we publish nothing, and, naturally your wishes have been respected.

From an October 3, 1935, letter from Vandiver Brown to Sumner Simpson, commenting on the Rossiter letter:

> I quite agree that our interests are best served by having asbestosis receive the minimum of publicity.

From a report by Dr. Kenneth Smith, Manville physician and medical director, on a 1949 study of 708 men who worked in a Manville asbestos mine (The report shows that only four of the 708 were free of lung damage and that those four had less than four years' exposure to asbestos dust):

> Of the 708 men, seven had X-ray evidence of early asbestosis. . . . They have not been told of this diagnosis. For it is felt that as long as the man feels well, is happy at home and at work, and his physical condition remains good, nothing should be said. . . . The fibrosis of this disease is irreversible and permanent. . . .
>
> There are seven cases of asbestosis and 52 cases in a "preasbestosis group." These 59 cases are probable compensation claims. . . . There are 475 men with [fibrosis extending beyond the lung roots] all of whom will show progressive fibrosis if allowed to continue working in dusty areas.

pervisory positions already knew about the association of inhalation of asbestos fibers and disease. I just amplified that [and] made much more explicit the disease process.

Q. Did you or did you not have discussions with Mr. A. R. Fisher with respect to the relationship between the inhalation of asbestos fiber and the pulmonary lung condition known as asbestosis, both with respect to employees of Johns-Manville and what you defined as the civilian population? [Mr. Fisher had been involved in the asbestos litigation in the 1930s and was president in the 1950s and 1960s.]

A. Definitely, we discussed the whole subject many times, about dust and what it does to people, whether they are employed or not employed . . . . The good Lord gave us all the same breathing apparatus and if the asbestos fiber is present and the housewife, and the asbestos worker, and the fireman, and the jeweler, and doctor, and everybody else are all in the same room, they all going to breathe the same dust . . . .

So wherever there is dust and people are breathing dust they are going to have a potential hazard.

Q. Did you at any point . . . make any recommendations to anyone at Johns-Manville in respect to the utilization of a caution label for the asbestos-containing products?

A. Hugh Jackson and I sat down with many people in other divisions suggesting that similar caution labels should be put on products which when used could create airborne dust that could be inhaled.

Q. When did you sit down with Hugh Jackson and come to that conclusion?

A. It would be late 1952 and early 1953.

Q. What was the reason . . . the asbestos-containing products were not labeled with a caution label back in 1952?

A. It was a business decision as far as I could understand. . . . application of a caution label identifying a product as hazardous would cut our sales. There would be serious financial implications.

Q. Did you at any time recognize the relationship between the inhalation of asbestos fibers and pulmonary malignancies, as you phrased it, or lung cancer, or pleural cancer?

A. Yes, I have recognized the alleged and sometimes factual association of malignancy with the inhalation of asbestos fibers.

Q. When would that have been, Doctor, for the first time?

A. The first time would be in the late 1940s.

Q. Had there not been studies in Britain and perhaps even in the United States prior to the beginning of the Saranac Lake Laboratories studies [1936] which had indicated [that fibrous asbestos dust caused lung disease]?

A. Very definitely. As I recall, Merriweather and his cohorts studied the effects of the asbestos textile dust many years prior to 1935 and their publications are well-documented and available world wide.

Dr. Smith died in 1977. In 1981, a Manville lawyer (appealing a $1.9 million damage award to asbestos victim Edward Janssens), argued that the Smith deposition should not have been admitted in court. The attorney said, "J-M made a conscious policy decision not to cross-examine Dr. Smith as fully as it otherwise would have. For example, Johns-Manville decided against examining Dr. Smith regarding the fact that he was an alcoholic and under psychiatric care."

Another Manville executive, Wilbur L. Ruff, who had worked for Manville from 1929 through 1972, much of the time as plant manager at a number of Manville plants, gave an extensive deposition in 1979. Excerpts follow:

Q. Do you know whether in fact, abnormal chest findings ever were discussed with any employee of the Johns-Manville plant?

A. I know of no specific cases.

Q. Was there a policy at that time not to talk to the employees about chest findings, findings that suggested asbestosis, pneumoconiosis, or mesothelioma [asbestos cancer]?

A. That was the policy.

Q. When did the policy change?

A. In the early 1970s.

Q. Have you on other occasions, Mr. Ruff, referred to this policy that we have been discussing as a hush-hush policy?

A. Yes.

Q. Were you aware that it was company policy

back in the late forties that if a man had asbestosis or industrial lung diseases that nothing would be said to him until he actually became disabled?

A. That's the way it was done.

Q. You were aware that was the company policy?

A. Whether it was policy or not, it was somebody's decision.

In 1964, Manville placed the first caution labels on its asbestos products. The labels read:

This product contains asbestos fiber.

Inhalation of asbestos in excessive quantities over long periods of time may be harmful.

If dust is created when the product is handled, avoid breathing the dust.

If adequate ventilation control is not possible, wear respirators approved by the U.S. Bureau of Mines for pneumoconiosis producing dust.

In upholding a landmark 1972 district court decision against Manville and other asbestos defendants, the New Orleans U.S. Court of Appeals stated:

Asbestosis has been recognized as a disease for well over fifty years. . . . By the mid-1930s the hazard of asbestos as a pneumoconiotic dust was universally accepted. Cases of asbestosis in insulation workers were reported in this country as early as 1934. . . . The evidence . . . tended to establish that none of the defendants ever tested its product to determine its effect on industrial insulation workers. . . . Indeed the evidence tended to establish that the defendants gave no instructions or warnings at all.

The court quoted Manville's caution label (above) and continued:

It should be noted that none of these so called "cautions" intimated the gravity of the risk: the danger of a fatal illness caused by asbestosis and mesothelioma or other cancers. The mild suggestion that inhalation of asbestos in excessive quantities over a long period of time may be harmful conveys no idea of the extent of the danger.

NEW DIRECTIONS FOR THE 1970s

By the 1960s, several of Manville's older directors had died or retired. Among them were A. R. Fisher and E. M. Voorhees, senior Manville officials since before 1930. (Both Fisher and Voorhees were involved in the early asbestos lawsuits. Also, Fisher was chief executive in the fifties and early sixties.) Compared to the 1966 board of directors, the 1969 board contained a majority of new members. Departing from a tradition of promotion from within, in 1969 Manville brought in an outsider, psychologist Richard Goodwin, to fill a top management position. The next year, the board of directors voted to move long-time president C. B. Burnett to the position of chairman and to install Goodwin as president and chief executive officer. Goodwin led the company through at least twenty acquisitions and several divestitures, increasing the company's profit and sales but also increasing its long-term debt—from zero in 1970 to $196 million in 1975.

Goodwin arranged to purchase the 10,000-acre Ken-Caryl Ranch near Denver in 1971, moved the company there from New York, and made plans to build a luxurious world headquarters. The first phase of the project was to cost $182.2 million, 45 percent of Manville's net worth. The magazine *Industrial Development* called the Manville plan "a study in corporate environmental concern." *Fortune* magazine quotes Goodwin as saying, "A company's headquarters is its signature. I wanted a new signature for J-M that, frankly, would attract attention—that would tell everybody, including ourselves, that things were changing."

Things did change. When the asbestos problem grew out of control and the company lost the first of many asbestos lawsuits, Manville turned back to one of its own—its chief legal officer—for leadership. In what *Fortune* magazine called "the shoot-out at the J-M corral," the board of directors deposed Goodwin without explanation and installed J. A. McKinney as president in September 1976. McKinney charted the new course in his 1977 "president's review":

> We believe we can further improve the fundamental economics of a number of our operations and we will be working toward that end in the year to come. . . .
>
> Asbestos fiber, while contributing substantially to earnings, has assumed a less important position with the earnings growth of our other basic businesses. Although its profitability is expected to improve in the long term with reviving European economies, we do not expect asbestos fiber to dominate J-M earnings to the extent that it has in the past. . . .
>
> We have also consolidated and repositioned some businesses for more profitable growth and phased out others not important to the future direction of the company. . . .
>
> We have begun aggressively to seek out opportunities for growth. One example is the previously announced $200 million capital expansion program which will, by 1980, double

U.S. fiber glass capacity over the 1976 levels. . . . We continue seeking still other growth possibilities that would markedly change the Johns-Manville profile, possibly through substantial acquisitions. . . .

> Our main thrust in 1978 will be to continue improving profitability by maintaining our expense control and pricing vigilance, by adding volume to below-capacity businesses, by better utilizing existing capacity and by adding capacity in sold-out businesses.

By that time, Manville had already begun to seek a large merger candidate—a "substantial acquisition"—employing the services of the Morgan Stanley investment banking firm to assist in the search. Manville quickly identified Olinkraft Corporation, a forest products manufacturer and timber company (owning 580,000 acres of timberland), as a likely prospect. After a brief bidding war, Olinkraft and Manville completed their merger agreement. The purchase price was $595 million. This was 2.24 times Olinkraft's June 1978 book value and over twice the average total market value of Olinkraft's stock in the first half of 1978.

Approximately half of the purchase price was paid in cash, and the other half with preferred stock. The preferred stock was described in the 1978 annual report:

> On January 19, 1979, the Company issued 4,598,327 shares of cumulative preferred stock, $5.40 series, to consummate the acquisition of Olinkraft. . . .
>
> Under a mandatory sinking fund provision, the Company is required to redeem the $5.40 preferred series between 1987 and 2009 at $65 per share plus accrued dividends. The annual redemption requirements will consist of varying percentages applied to the number of outstanding shares on October 20, 1986, as follows: 5% annually from 1987 through 1996, 4% annually from 1997 through 2007, and 3% in 2008. All remaining outstanding shares are required to be redeemed in 2009.

While the Olinkraft merger was being negotiated, Manville common stock declined in market value to a low of $22.125, a total decrease of over $225 million. Olinkraft's stock rose, approximating the proposed acquisition price of $65 a share.

The merger was consummated on January 19, 1979. The purchase method of accounting was used. Essentially, the book values of Olinkraft's assets were adjusted upward by the amounts by which the purchase price exceeded the net worth. The adjusted and unadjusted balance sheet values for Olinkraft are shown in Table 1.

TABLE 1   PURCHASE METHOD MERGER ACCOUNTING:
OLINKRAFT BALANCE SHEETS

	Adjusted	Unadjusted
Current assets	$137,557	$119,610
Investments in and advances to associated companies	6,886	6,078
Property, plant, and equipment	700,633	372,761
Deferred charges and other assets	799	3,513
	$845,857	$501,962
Current liabilities	$ 83,912	$ 67,793
Long-term debt	141,258	141,295
Other noncurrent liabilities	25,159	26,678
	$250,329	$235,766
Net worth	$596,546	$266,196

Source: December 31, 1978, Manville-Olinkraft joint proxy statement and Manville 1978 annual report.

After the mergers and divestitures engineered by Goodwin and McKinney, Manville's mix of businesses (as described in the 1978 and 1979 annual reports) was as follows:

Fiberglass products: Residential insulations account for the largest portion of the product line, with commercial and industrial insulations and fiber glass making up the rest. . . . New home construction represented 55 percent of the total market while [insulation for existing homes] accounted for 45 percent. . . .

Non-fiberglass insulations: This business segment includes roof insulations, refractory fibers, calcium silicate insulation, and a broad range of other commercial and industrial insulating products. . . .

Pipe products and systems: Major products in this business segment are polyvinyl chloride (PVC) plastic pipe and asbestos cement (A-C) pipe. . . .

Roofing products: The roofing products segment includes residential shingles and built-up roofing for commercial and industrial structures. New construction accounts for 40 percent of sales. Reroofing represents 60 percent. . . .

Asbestos fiber: Asbestos fiber is sold in markets throughout the world. A major portion of the fiber sold is used as a raw material in products where the fiber is locked in place by cement, rubber, plastics, resins, asphalts, and similar bindings. Products include asbestos cement products, brake linings, resilient flooring, roofing, and other products that require strength and fire protection, heat resistance, dimensional stability, and resistance to rust and rot. . . .

Industrial and specialty products and services: A diverse group of businesses that has as its principal areas: Holophane lighting systems, filtration and minerals [comprised of diatomite, perlite, and fiber glass filter products] and industrial specialties. . . . Perlite is . . . used by J-M in the manufacture of Fesco Board roof insulation. Other uses are in acoustical ceiling tile, horticultural applications, and in cryogenic insulations.

Forest products: Forest products include clay-coated unbleached Kraft and other paperboards: corrugated containers; beverage carriers and folding cartons; Kraft bags; pine lumber, plywood, and particleboard; and hardwood veneer and flooring.

STRATEGIC MANAGEMENT IN THE 1980s

After Richard Goodwin was expelled, top management continuity was maintained through the late seventies and eighties. The chairman of the board and chief executive officer, J. A. McKinney, the president and chief operating officer, Fred L. Pundsack, and all ten senior vice presidents listed in the 1981 annual report, were also listed in the 1977 annual report. In fact, the five most highly paid executives of Manville, as shown on the March 1982 proxy statement, had all been with the company for twenty-nine years or more. Only three of Manville's outside directors joined the board after the sixties. Except for John D. Mullins, former president of Olinkraft, who performed brief service, no new director was added after

1976. Then, in May 1982, the existing directors were renominated.

Manville's asbestos-related health costs were relatively insignificant (less than 0.5 percent of sales through 1981). But asbestos use, especially in the United States, declined sharply after 1978. The U.S. Department of the Interior reported a 36 percent drop from 1979 to 1980 alone. With a virtual U.S. monopoly of asbestos sales, Manville was hardest hit. The loss of asbestos profits was compounded by a deep recession in housing and other construction which began in mid-1978 and was to last through 1982.

Attempts to expand and diversify Manville had begun in 1970, when net sales totaled $578 million. The sixties had seen only a 1.5 percent real rate of growth, less than the rate of gross national product (GNP) growth. Because of the purchases of businesses by Goodwin and Mc-Kinney, the company had surpassed $1 billion sales in 1974 and $2 billion in 1978. However, on an inflation-corrected basis, sales declined from 1978 onward, despite the contribution of $500 million in annual sales by Olin-kraft. Figure 1 illustrates Manville's sales and earnings patterns from 1976 through 1982. The corresponding fi-

nancial statements and a record of Manville's common stock prices appear in the financial tables at the end of this case.

Six pages of Manville's 1978 annual report and over half of J. A. McKinney's "chairman's message" were devoted to the personal injury lawsuits. Excerpts from these documents follow:

> During the past year a great deal of publicity has appeared in the media about asbestos health hazards—most of it attacking the corporation and nearly all of it needlessly inflammatory. Your corporation has acted honorably over the years and has led the asbestos industry, medical science and the federal government in identifying and seeking to eliminate asbestos health problems. . . .
>
> Individuals exposed to asbestos-containing insulation materials are particular victims of the incomplete knowledge of earlier years. . . . It was not until 1964 that the particular risk to this category of worker [insulation workers] was clearly identified by Dr. Irving J. Selikoff of Mt. Sinai Hospital in New York City. . . .
>
> Media representatives and some elected officials have

FIGURE 1   Manville Corporation sales and earnings, 1978–1982.
(Annual reports.)

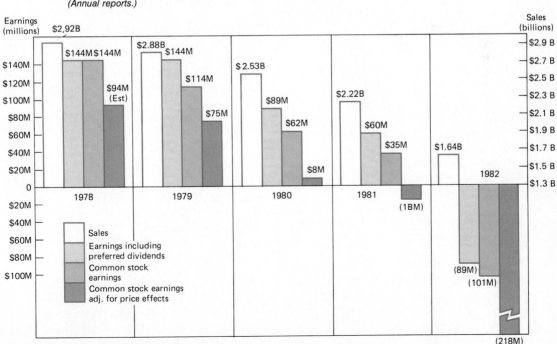

consistently ignored J-M's intensive efforts to solve asbestos health problems and, in fact, have untruthfully portrayed those efforts. . . .

Litigation is based upon a finding of fault, and with respect to asbestos-related disease, there simply is no fault on the part of J-M, a fact increasingly recognized by juries throughout the nation. Litigation is, of course, favored and fostered by lawyers in search of lucrative fees and by "media personalities" in search of sensational stories. . . .

Despite the worsening financial situation and though beseiged by thousands of asbestos victims seeking billions of dollars in damages, Manville was publicly optimistic. The 1979 annual report stated, "Johns-Manville has a strategy for the early 80's . . . and the commitment to succeed. . . . J-M's strategic plan embraces three major goals." The goals were described as follows:

Goal 1: To rebuild our financial reserves. . . . As expected, the Olinkraft acquisition burdened our financial resources. . . . For this reason, our most immediate short-term goal is to improve and increase the financial strength of J-M's balance sheet. We will accomplish this by increasing productivity and using the better levels of cash flow that result to provide for most of our new capital needs.

Goal 2: To improve productivity and cost efficiencies. . . . We will look for ways to increase the output of our manufacturing processes, concentrating first on those projects promising the shortest payback periods. . . .

Goal 3: To reaffirm J-M's position as a technological leader in terms of product performance and cost of production. . . . to increase the effort and money spent on improving manufacturing methods, enhancing the competitive strengths of present product lines and developing new products.

In 1981 Manville accelerated efforts to avoid the asbestos claims. McKinney wrote to his shareholders, "You can be assured that we will continue to be aggressive in asserting our defenses." By spending millions on the defense efforts, Manville was able to avoid or delay payment of most tort judgments and to settle many for cents on the dollar. The company was reorganized into a parent corporation and a number of operating subsidiaries, with the asbestos businesses in one subsidiary.

THE DAY OF DECISION APPROACHES

It quickly became apparent that courts would see through the new corporate structure and treat the companies as one for asbestos liability purposes. Further, as the number

and amounts of asbestos tort judgments skyrocketed, Manville's ability to avoid paying them grew increasingly questionable.

Manville's mid-year 1982 form 10Q (submitted to the Securities and Exchange Commission) described the worsening situation with regard to the asbestos injury claims:

During the first half of 1982, J-M [Manville] received an average of approximately 425 new cases per month brought by an average of approximately 495 new plaintiffs per month. . . .

J-M was, for the first time in 1981, found liable by juries for punitive damages in five separate asbestos-related actions. [Punitive damages are payments above the actual damages sustained—intended to punish defendants.] All of these cases are presently subject to post-trial motions or appeals filed by J-M. The average of the punitive damages awarded against J-M in these five cases (one of which involved eleven plaintiffs) and the five cases decided during the first half of 1982 and discussed below is approximately $616,000 per case. . . .

Hansen v. Johns-Manville. $1,060,000 in compensatory damages and $1,000,000 in punitive damages were assessed against J-M. . . .

Bunch v. Johns-Manville Corp. A jury verdict of $420,000 in compensatory damages and $220,000 in punitive damages. . . .

Dorell v. Johns-Manville Corp. The jury awarded the plaintiff $100,000 in compensatory damages and $1,000,000 in punitive damages. . . .

Jackson v. Johns-Manville. A jury verdict of $195,000 in compensatory damages and $500,000 in punitive damages. . . .

Cavett v. Johns-Manville Corp. The jury awarded the plaintiff $800,000 in compensation damages and $1,500,000 in punitive damages.

Aside from actual and anticipated tort claims, Manville was in much worse condition in 1982 than the financial statements indicated. This was true for four reasons. First, $340 million of Manville's net worth resulted from purchase method accounting in the Olinkraft merger. Second, the $300 million in "preferred stock" shown on the balance sheet was essentially equivalent to a 16 percent long-term debt. Third, Manville had endured several years of negative cash flow requiring certain cash-producing strategies which tended to reduce asset values. For example, the 580,000 acres of timber farms obtained in the Olinkraft purchase were converted to a thirty-year planned life from a forty-year life. This rationalized immediate cutting of about one-fourth of the timber and continuing removal of one-thirtieth of that remaining each year instead of one-fortieth. Finally, the desire of Manville executives to show profits each year had resulted in "creative accounting" which tended to inflate reported earnings. The following are examples from the 1981 annual report: (1) a $9 million increase in "other revenues" which resulted largely from the sale of mineral exploration rights on 580,000 acres of timberland, (2) a $2.7 million increase in reported earnings due to the "reversal of a portion of the litigation reserves established at the time of the Olinkraft, Inc., acquisition," (3) a $9.8 million increase in reported earnings because of a new way of reporting foreign currency transactions, (4) an unspecified amount due to "the sale during 1981 of eight container plants [which] occurred as part of [the] asset management program" and (5) an $8.4 million increase in reported earnings brought about by "changes in certain actuarial assumptions in computing pension expense."

If Manville were to fail, not only would managers and directors lose their salaries, benefits, and perquisites, but they would also lose their corporate indemnification against personal liability for the asbestos injury claims. Undoubtedly each one would then be subject to hundreds, perhaps thousands, of tort lawsuits.

In December 1981, Manville formed a ten-member committee of inside and outside lawyers, the litigation analysis group (LAG), to study the firm's situation with regard to the asbestos injury liabilities. LAG employed a number of consultants to research various aspects of the issue and met each month to hear reports and discuss developments. The conclusion of LAG, arrived at in mid-1982, was that Manville would eventually have to pay about $2 billion to present and future asbestos injury victims.

In a subsequent lawsuit it was alleged that the $2 billion figure was contrived so as to be high enough to justify a filing for reorganization under Chapter 11 of the U.S. Bankruptcy Code but not high enough to appear to require liquidation of the company. At a meeting of the board of directors on August 4, 1982, J. A. McKinney (chairman of the board and chief executive officer) appointed four outside directors to a special committee to determine what Manville should do. Members of the special committee were briefed on Chapter 11 by company executives. A limited overview of the practical effects of a Chapter 11 reorganization is provided in the lined insert below.

A special meeting of the board of directors was called for August 25, 1982. The special committee was expected to present its recommendation at that meeting.

USUAL EFFECTS OF FILING FOR REORGANIZATION UNDER CHAPTER 11

All debts are stayed until a "plan of reorganization" is confirmed or special approval of the bankruptcy court is obtained.

The bankrupt corporation, with prefiling management, is declared to be the "debtor in possession" (DIP).

The DIP can carry out the "ordinary course of business," e.g., hiring and firing employees, incurring and repaying debts, making and executing contracts, selling and buying assets.

The DIP is allowed to enforce all claims against others, by filing lawsuits if necessary.

Lawsuits against the DIP are stayed.

Unsecured creditors and common and preferred stockholders are represented by committees appointed by the bankruptcy judge.

The DIP is allowed to cancel contracts, including collective bargaining agreements and leases, to the extent that they have not been carried out.

The DIP is allowed 120 days to file a plan of reorganization and 60 days to seek the required approval of each creditor class (half in number holding two-thirds in amount) and equity class (holders of two-thirds in amount), either of which periods may be extended.

The plan of reorganization typically provides for:

1 Payment of postfiling debt, including costs of administering the case

2 Payment of secured prefiling debt up to the value of the liened property

3 Payment of some or all of unsecured debt over some period into the future, with or without interest

4 Discharge of all claims not provided for in the plan

EXHIBIT 1 MANVILLE CORPORATION INCOME STATEMENTS
(Amounts in Millions)*

	1982 6 mos	1981	1980	1979	1978
Sales	$949	$2,186	$2,267	$2,276	$1,649
Cost of sales	784	1,731	1,771	1,747	1,190
Selling, gen., and admin. exp.	143	271	263	239	193
R&D and engineering exp.	16	34	35	31	33
Operating income	6	151	197	259	232
Other income, net	1	35	26	21	28
Interest expense	35	73	65	62	22
Total income	(28)	112	157	218	238
Income taxes	2	53	77	103	116
Net income before extraordinary items	(25)	60	81	115	122
Div. on preferred stock	12	25	25	24	0
Extraordinary item	0	0	0	0	0
Net income available for common stock	$ (37)	$ 35	$ 55	$ 91	$ 122

Revenues and income from operations by business segment						
	1981	1980	1979	1978	1977	1976
Revenues						
Fiberglass products	$ 625	$ 610	$ 573	$ 514	$ 407	$ 358
Forest products	555	508	497	0	0	0
Nonfiberglass insulation	258	279	268	231	195	159
Roofing products	209	250	273	254	204	171
Pipe products and systems	199	220	305	303	274	218
Asbestos fiber	138	159	168	157	161	155
Industrial and spec. prod.	320	341	309	291	301	309
Corporate revenues, net	12	9	11	20	12	(22)
Intersegment sales	(95)	(84)	(106)	(94)	(74)	(56)
Total	$2,221	$2.292	$2,297	$1,677	$1,480	$1,291
Income from operations						
Fiberglass products	$ 90	$ 91	$ 96	$ 107	$ 82	$ 60
Forest products	39	37	50	0	0	0
Nonfiberglass insulation	20	27	27	35	28	18
Roofing products	(17)	9	14	23	14	8
Pipe products and systems	0	(5)	18	26	24	(3)
Asbestos fiber	37	35	56	55	60	60
Industrial and spec. prod.	50	55	43	36	25	19
Corporate expense, net	(23)	(38)	(23)	(23)	(24)	(49)
Eliminations and adjustments	3	11	(2)	1	3	2
Total	$ 198	$ 223	$ 280	$ 260	$ 212	$ 116

*Totals may not check due to rounding.
Source: Annual reports and June 30, 1982, Form 100.

EXHIBIT 2 MANVILLE CORPORATION BALANCE SHEETS
(Amounts in Millions)*

	June 30 1982	1981	1980	1979	1978
Assets					
Cash	$ 10	$ 14	$ 20	$ 19	$ 28
Marketable securities	17	12	12	10	38
Accounts and notes receivable	348	327	350	362	328
Inventories	182	211	217	229	210
Prepaid expenses	19	19	20	31	32
Total current assets	$ 576	$ 583	$ 619	$ 650	$ 645
Property, plant, and equipment					
Land and land improvements		119	118	114	99
Buildings		363	357	352	321
Machinery and equipment		1,202	1,204	1,161	1,043
		$1,685	$1,679	$1,627	$1,462
Less accum. depreciation and depletion		(525)	(484)	(430)	(374)
		$1,160	$1,195	$1,197	$1,088
Timber and timberland less cost of timber harvested		$ 406	$ 407	$ 368	$ 372
	$1,523	$1,566	$1,602	$1,565	$1,460
Invest. and adv. to assoc. cos.		0	0	0	0
Real est. sub. invest. and adv.		0	0	0	0
Other assets	148	149	117	110	113
Total assets	$2,247	$2,298	$2,338	$2,324	$2,217
Liabilities					
Short-term debt	$	$ 29	$ 22	$ 32	$ 23
Accounts payable	191	120	126	143	114
Comp. and employee benefits		77	80	54	45
Income taxes		30	22	51	84
Other liabilities	149	58	61	50	63
Total current liabilities	$ 340	$ 316	$ 310	$ 329	$ 329
Long-term debt	499	508	519	532	543
Other noncurrent liabilities	93	86	75	73	60
Deferred income taxes	186	185	211	195	150
Total liabilities	$1,116	$1,095	$1,116	$1,129	$1,083
Stockholders' equity					
Preferred ($1.00 par)	$ 301	$ 301	$ 301	$ 299	$ 299
Common ($2.50 par)	60	59	58	208	197
Capital in excess of par	178	174	164	0	0
Retained earnings	642	695	705	692	643
Cum. currency translation adj.	(47)	(22)	0	0	0
Less cost of treasury stock	$ (3)	$ (3)	$ (4)	$ (4)	$ (6)
Total stockholders' equity	$1,131	$1,203	$1,222	$1,196	$1,134
Total liab. and stockholders' equity	$2,247	$2,298	$2,338	$2,324	$2,217

*Totals may not check due to rounding.
Source: Annual reports and June 30, 1982, Form 10-Q.

FIGURE 2   Manville Corporation monthly common stock trading range, 1976–July 1982.

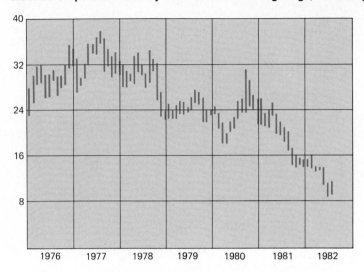

MARQUIS HOTELS AND RESORTS, INC.

James C. Makens
Wake Forest University

In January of 1984, Mr. Michael B. Peceri, President of Marquis Hotels, Inc. was concerned with the future expansion of his company. Marquis Resorts and Hotels had built a strong reputation in the management of resorts, condominiums and commercial properties in Florida. The company had recently acquired a consulting contract for a ski resort in Steamboat Springs, Colorado which would mark its entrance into a new area of resort management. Now, there was serious discussion conerning the advisability of entering the commercial hotel segment of the hotel industry within cities of 100,000–200,000 in population.

HISTORY OF COMPANY

Marquis Hotels, Inc. was a division of Mariner Properties, Inc., a holding company with headquarters in Fort Myers, Florida. In addition to Marquis Hotels and Resorts, the parent company also owned CMI, a general construction company, VIP Realty, a firm that specialized in com-

This case was written by James C. Makens, Associate Professor in the Babcock Graduate School of Management of Wake Forest University. The author retains the right to copyright privileges. Copyright © 1985 by James C. Makens. This case was not designed to present an illustration of either effective or ineffective handling of administrative problems.

mercial and residential real estate, Robb and Stuckey, a retail furniture company, that sold furniture for resorts and other commercial properties in southern Florida through five stores, Guardian Title Insurance, a title insurance company and other financial service companies.

Marquis Hotels and Resorts was started as a resort-hotel management company and added a property management division to the company. Marquis managed five time share complexes, seven resort hotel properties, 1400 condominium units, an office complex, two utility service companies, two shopping centers and a country club in Southwest Florida.

MIKE PECERI

Mike Peceri had served as the first president of Marquis Hotels and Resorts incorporated in 1980. He had previously held the position of Executive Vice President of Marquis' flagship property, South Seas Plantation. This was located on Captiva Island off the coast near Fort Myers. This luxury resort included a beautiful old plantation house which had been converted into a hotel, resort villas, tennis villas, beach villas, bayside villas and beach cottages. It also contained twenty tennis courts, fifteen swimming pools, and a 9 hole golf course as well as many restaurants including Chadwick's which was considered to be one of South Florida's finest.

775

Marquis Hotels and Resorts consulting agreements

KEY BISCAYNE HOTEL AND VILLAS
Key Biscayne, Florida
DEERHURST INN AND COUNTRY CLUB
Huntsville, Ontario
Canada
NAPLES BEACH AND GOLF CLUB
Naples, Florida
PORT OF THE ISLANDS RESORT AND MARINA
Marco Island, Florida
JUPITER BAY RESORT AND TENNIS CLUB
Jupiter Bay, Florida
WILS LANDING RESTAURANT
Sanibel Island, Florida
ISLAND HARBOR RESORT
Cape Haze, Florida
RAVINES RESORT
Middleburg, Florida

Marquis operates these fine resort facilities:

South Seas Plantation Resort & Yacht Harbour
Captiva Island, Florida
Beach Best Western
Ft. Myers Beach, Florida
Boathouse Beach Resort
Ft. Myers Beach, Florida
Eventide-on-the-Beach
Fort Myers Beach, Florida
Seawatch-on-the-Beach
Ft. Myers Beach, Florida
Eagle's Nest Beach Resort
Marco Island, Florida
Casa Ybel Resort
Sanibel Island, Florida
Dunes Golf & Tennis Club
Sanibel Island, Florida
Hurricane House
Sanibel Island, Florida
Sanibel Cottages
Sanibel Island, Florida
Song of the Sea Resort
Sanibel Island, Florida
Sundial Beach and Tennis Resort
Sanibel Island, Florida
Tortuga Beach Resort
Sanibel Island, Florida
Regime Resort (under development)
Steamboat Springs, Colorado

The following is a list of the condominium and homeowner projects managed by Marquis Property Management.

Association Name

Bayside Villas Condominium Association
Beach Cottages Condominium Association
Beach Homes Condominium Association
Beach Homesites Homeowners Association
Beach Villas I Condominium Association
Beach Villas II Condominium Association
Beach Villas III Condominium Association
Caper Beach Condominium Association
Casa Ybel Beach & Racquet Club (Interval Ownership)
Casa Ybel I, J, K (Interval Ownership)
Cottage Colony West Condominium Association
Cottages at South Seas Plantation Condo. Association (Interval Ownership)
The Dunes Home Owners Association
Eagle's Nest (Interval Ownership)

Estero Island Yacht & Racquet Club Condominium Association
Gulf Cottages Homeowners Association
Harbour Cottages Homeowners Association
McGregor Woods Homeowners Association
Moorings Point I Condominium Association
North Shore Place Condominium Association
Plantation Beach Club I Condominium Association (Interval Ownership)
Plantation Beach Club II Condominium Association (Interval Ownership)
Plantation Beach Club III Condominium Association (Interval Ownership)
Sanibel Cottages Condominium Association (Interval Ownership)
Seawatch Condominium Association (Interval Ownership)

Snug Harbor Condominium Association (Sanibel)
South Seas Club (Interval Ownership)
Sunset Captiva Homeowners Association
Sunset Captiva Condominium Association
Tennis Villas Condominium Association
TerraMar Condominium Association
Tortuga Beach Club (Interval Ownership)
Villa Sanibel Condominium Association
Windward Point Condominium Association

Shopping Centers
Cypress Square Shopping Center
Periwinkle Place Shopping Center
Cross Trails Shopping Center

Utilities
South Seas Sewer System
Sanibel Sewer System

Michael B. Peceri, CHA
President

Michael B. Peceri, president of Marquis Hotels and Resorts, is one of the hospitality industry's most prominent executives. He has been affiliated, for the past 11 years, with The Mariner Group, a nationally recognized leader in the development of resort and timeshare projects. Prior to joining The Mariner Group he served for 20 years in the Diplomatic Service of the United States.

In his present role as president of Marquis Hotels and Resorts, a Mariner Group company, he leads a team of professionals in the management of over 10 resorts, hotels and timeshare properties in Florida, including the nationally recognized South Seas Plantation Resort and Yacht Harbour on Captiva Island.

Mr. Peceri is a member of the Governor of Florida's Tourism Advisory Council and is president of the Florida Hotel and Motel Association. He has also earned the designation of Certified Hotel Administrator from the American Hotel and Motel Association.

He is a member of the Governing Board of the National Timesharing Council and national chairman of the council's Management and Operations Committee. He has addressed the National Timesharing Council's conventions held in Miami, Atlanta and Chicago. He addressed the International Council of Management Companies at a meeting held in Vancouver, Canada and the Australasian Timeshare Council in Sydney, Australia.

Mr. Peceri has been named to "Who's Who Among Innkeepers" and "Who's Who in the South and Southeast United States."

More recently, Mr. Peceri has been instrumental in the success of the Lee County Tourist Development Council, and holds a director's position on this council.

He holds a Master of Science in Management from George Washington University and is also a graduate of the Harvard Business School's Program for Management Development.

Mike had not been trained in hospitality management and had joined the Mariner Group after twenty years with the U.S. Diplomatic Service where he had held important posts in several parts of the world including Vienna and Moscow. The experience of working with diverse types of people and understanding the requirements of wealthy and influential people had proven to be of particular value in the leadership of Marquis Hotels and Resorts.

His entrance into the company was accidental rather than a planned career move. The owners of the company had been attempting to purchase a thirty unit luxury motel on Sanibel Island near Fort Myers. The owner, a Frenchman, had refused to sell to anyone who had not lived in Europe as he felt that most American owners would not appreciate the solid oak furnishings, French draperies and other European appointments.

Mike agreed to write a report for Mariner concerning the property on a consulting basis. Upon receiving the report, the owners of Mariner asked Mike to run the hotel after acquisition. Mike replied he would assume the position of manager if he could acquire partial ownership. He also admitted that the challenge was accepted without understanding how to make a hotel reservation. The principle guiding him then and later was to serve the guests as he would want to be served if he were the guest.

Suddenly, after twenty years of chauffeur driven service and dining with world leaders, Mike found himself cleaning toilets and picking up cigarette butts. Occupancy in the motel was running at 60–70% when it was acquired, but operated at 95% when Mike moved on to manage South Seas Plantation. This was achieved by a combination of continuously striving for excellence and a targeted marketing strategy. Mike personally went to major east coast cities which former guests at the hotel had listed as home. Upon arriving he checked into the finest hotel in town and obtained a map of the most affluent areas of the city. He then took a cab to the travel agencies in those sections and began the process of convincing the owners and managers that his hotel met the requirements of their clients.

From this hands-on experience in the hospitality industry, Mike progressed to his current position as President of Marquis and President of the Florida Hotel and Motel Association.

EXPANSION OBJECTIVES

The management of both Marquis Hotels and the parent company desired for Marquis to become a national hotel and resort management company. To promote this objective, the company had recently signed a consulting contract with a group of developers in Steamboat Springs, Colorado to eventually manage a new ski resort. The

Steamboat Springs venture seemed to fit the three criteria established by Marquis for the management of any resort property. These were (1) the property must be in a popular resort area, (2) the property must be well conceived and (3) there must be sufficient capital behind the property.

In addition to the ski lodge business, Mr. Peceri said that Marquis was looking at the commercial hotel market in second tier cities throughout the sun belt of the United States. It was the feeling of those in Marquis that major sun belt cities in the U.S. were suffering from an over-expansion of hotels but many second tier cities of 100,000–250,000 population had a scarcity of quality hotels with 150–200 rooms to serve the up-scale market. Second tier cities with well known medical facilities were felt to be excellent targets since they would attract a steady group of visitors.

MANAGEMENT OF TIME SHARE RESORTS

The management style of Marquis Hotels and Mike Peceri was exemplified in the management of the company's time share resorts. Marquis managed five different time share resorts with a total of 240 units.

Marquis maintained a policy of not accepting management contracts for time share projects which were in trouble. The company philosophy maintained that most of these had been ill planned and probably had little likelihood of long range success. Mr. Peceri personally believed that a major shakeup in the time share industry was coming and that many existing projects would fail.

The Marquis policy was to begin working with the developers of a time share resort at the beginning of the project. It was felt that developers have a short run viewpoint but a management company must think of the long run.

The Marquis policy was to become involved in the entire planning process of the project including blueprints and interior decorations. If a developer refused to cooperate, Marquis would remove itself from future management. The management of Marquis believed that a time share project differed considerably from a conventional hotel or resort development.

a A time share project has hundreds or thousands of owners. A conventional hotel or resort has one or a few.

b Time share projects receive high intensity use with 95% occupancy being normal. Furniture, carpeting and other furnishings can wear out in one third the time.

Therefore, rules of thumb developed for hotels would often not apply in time share.

c The guest assumed a proprietary interest in time share. Guests were extremely critical since they viewed the unit as theirs and would complain about things that a hotel guest would accept.

d A great deal of hype went into the sales of a time share unit and guests arrived with extreme expectations. Marquis had to bring reality into the dreams that the sales department created.

e The long run success of a time share unit depended upon attracting the same guests each year for as long as twenty years or more. If guests became dissatisfied and enough guests decided to drop their ownership, resales would be very difficult and the entire project could be in jeopardy.

Several management practices had been developed by Marquis to deal with these complexities.

Owner Feedback

Owner comment sheets were distributed to each owner-guest upon each visit. Mike took pride in the fact that he personally read each one. These sheets covered a variety of areas from general appearance of the unit to any evidence of insects and rodents. If the comments were particularly bad, a member of management including Mr. Peceri would personally contact the owner and report on the steps that had been taken to correct the problem.

Feedback was also received in "owner coffees." These weekly meetings with owners included attendance by one or more members of management. These could include the resort owner, the head of housekeeping, the director of internal management or others including Mike.

A quarterly newsletter was published by Marquis Hotels and sent to all owners. In addition to information of a general nature such as changes in air fares to the resort, the newsletter was personalized to the extent it reminded all owners of their vacation week.

Recreation Management

Marquis believed that even the most beautiful and best maintained resort could eventually become boring. To insure that guests would find something new each year, a recreation program was established with a full-time professional in charge. Programs were designed for all ages. These employed some of the successful concepts of "Club Med."

Supervised programs for children allowed parents a freedom they could not enjoy at most resorts. Hot dog parties, beach parties, tennis competition, sea shell classes and many other programs offered a variety of recreational and educational pursuits. Each recreational program was monitored as to attendance and guest satisfaction and weak ones were eliminated. A dominant feature of all the programs was the opportunity for interaction among guests. Mike believed that a guest at the average resort could spend a week and never develop new friendships. The recreation programs hopefully allowed friendships to develop.

Housekeeping and Maintenance

The turnover of a majority of the guests one day and the mass arrival of an equal number the next, provided special housekeeping and maintenance problems for the time share projects.

A full time maintenance crew was employed and a large inventory of replacement furnishings was carried. If a TV or electric range had a problem it was immediately replaced rather than sending a repairman. With only one vacation week, Mike felt that a guest did not want to share it with a repairman.

Housekeeping was performed for the time share resorts under contract with an independent housekeeping company. The housekeeping managers of Marquis were responsible for personally examining each room and insuring that corrections immediately followed discovery of a problem.

The Marquis Image and Philosophy

"All Marquis properties must be first class, there is no room in this corporation for mundane or second class properties." This statement by Mike Peceri summed up the company's philosophy. Although the name Marquis was considered to be public domain, the name Marquis Hotels and Resorts was not.

The philosophy concerning quality had led the management of Marquis Hotels and Resorts to change its policy concerning the new properties it would manage. The company started without holding an equity position in the properties it managed but had decided to hold an equity

position in all future properties. This decision was made for two reasons. First, an ownership position would allow Marquis Hotels to have a stronger voice in the development and management of properties and would help to insure quality. Second, Marquis Hotels had no interest in "bringing up" properties to a desired quality and performance level only to find that the managers had decided not to renew the management contract.

This concern led Marquis Hotels to believe that the company's interests would best be satisfied if the ownership of a property consisted of a syndicated general partnership in which Marquis Hotels held a sufficient equity position to have a strong voice.

Corporate Objectives

The management and ownership of Marquis Hotels and Resorts desired for the company to be recognized as a strong national resort and commercial hotel management company within ten years. It was felt that resort properties offered limited growth opportunities since the most desirable locations had been developed by others.

The best strategy for the next five years seemed to lie in the development of first class commercial properties within sun belt cities of 100,000 to 200,000 people. It was felt that the development of three new properties per year in this market was realistic.

Sun belt cities were felt to offer the best potential for growth because of the scarcity of 150–200 room quality hotels. These second tier cities remained important industrial and agricultural centers and in many cases did not offer truly first class hotel accommodations. In many cases, a respected medical complex had been developed in these cities and it was felt that this factor alone would serve as a magnet for visitors.

Developing an Appreciation for Quality and Service

Mike believed that the success and reputation enjoyed by Marquis had been the direct result of developing the right mentality within all employees. It was his belief that owners and managers of a hotel chain often developed a bricks and mortar mentality and forgot the factors that really mattered. To emphasize this, he was fond of telling new employees at South Seas Plantation a hypothetical story about the employees of the resort who did not show up for work in mass. He would then suggest to them that his phone had just rung and his secretary had informed him that the entire staff did not show up for work that morning. It meant that only the people in the room with him were available to run the resort that day. Hypothetically then, each of them would have to plan and operate all departments of the resort that day. All tried to do a good, but impossible job; and of course, they failed. He suggested, moreover, that within a few hours, the last guest would leave, angrily shouting that "South Seas Plantation was a lousy resort!"

Nevertheless, their efforts to meet the simulated crisis had been sincere, and it was important to recognize the valiance of their attempts. So he invited them to the other end of the property for a reward of refreshments.

As they moved through the resort, they passed the "beautiful grounds;" "the excellent restaurant;" "the 14 tennis courts and 20 swimming pools;" and "beautiful accommodations."

There were all the things the employees had described that made South Seas Plantation a success. Yet, the last hypothetical guest had made the environs seem insignificant. Why? Because South Seas Plantation was not just those things; rather, South Seas Plantation was its employees. How effectively they did their jobs was impor-

tant; and they were, in effect, the resort. They clearly understood this and this understanding played a very important part in relating the employees to the roles they were expected to fill and did.

"The problem for us will be how to maintain that perspective as we grow. We want our employees to think first about serving the guests rather than their bosses," stated Mike.

Mike believed that the proper role of top management should be to serve as coaches. "It is our role to take a bare wall and a felt tip pen and design a scenario. It is the job of the General Managers and their teams to fill in the blanks and make the scenario come alive."

In the past Mike had observed that the managers of some properties did not operate their properties in a manner he felt was according to accepted methods and yet they had achieved results. "We can't build this company with purple cows but neither do we want to stifle creativity. It is the responsibility of top management to remain flexible and to investigate why a General Manager doesn't go by the book. If conditions are truly different for that property we need to rewrite the manual to suit those needs. The problem is, how to do this without creating anarchy."

EXHIBIT 1   **Marquis employees.**

Loraine G. Maroon, CHA
Executive Vice President

As Executive Vice President, Loraine G. Maroon is responsible for the overall operations of the accounting, marketing, operations, property management and recreation departments of Marquis. Her thorough knowledge of real estate development and construction, resort management and

marketing qualifies her for this senior management position.

Her experience most recently included a post as Executive Vice President and partner in Vistana Resort Management, Inc. In that capacity, she supervised the construction, refurbishing and opening of Vistana as a resort in Lake Buena Vista, Florida. Under her direction, from 1978 to 1984, this project became a highly successful resort/interval property.

For 15 years, she held key management positions including Chief Executive Officer of Manor Park Realty and Development Company and Executive Vice President of Northwestern Construction Company, both of Bloomingdale, Illinois. In these business ventures, Mrs. Maroon was heavily involved in the development, construction and management of mid-rise, multi-family apartment complexes, condominiums and luxury homes.

In 1981, Loraine G. Maroon was awarded the distinction of Certified Hotel Administrator from the American Hotel and Motel Association.

Mrs. Maroon serves on the Governor of Florida's Tourism Advisory Council and was one of the founders of the Central Florida Hotel and Motel Association and served as board member and Secretary/Treasurer. She is past president of Women in Travel and a member of the American Land Development Association's management committee, a board member of the Community Association Institute, Orlando chapter, and a board member of the Travel and Tourism Research Association, is a trustee and Vice President of the Orlando chapter of the Leukemia Society and is a member of Florida Executive Women. She has also served on the board and was Secretary of the Orlando Area Tourist Trade Association.

Jack M. Smith, CHA
Vice President of Finance

Mr. Smith is responsible for the operations of the accounting, finance and data processing departments for Marquis. His years of diversified financial expertise, as well as accounting controls, qualify him for this newly created position.

Prior to joining Marquis' corporate staff, Jack Smith was Vice President of Finance at their South Seas Plantation Resort, Captiva Island, Florida. He held a similar position with Island Gem Ltd. Management Company for the Mullet Bay Resort and Caravanseri Resorts on St. Maarten Island, N.A. For four years, he served as Controller for the prestigious Breakers Hotel in the Palm Beach area. His island resort experience also includes Controller of the Montague Beach and Pilot House Resort Hotels in Nassau. His early career began at the Emerald Beach Hotel, also in Nassau.

Mr. Smith is a member of the National Accounting Association. In January, 1983, he received the designation CHA as Certified Hotel Administrator, conferred by the American Hotel and Motel Association.

G. Scott Siler
Vice President and General Manager
Sundial Beach & Tennis Resort

Mr. Siler's knowledge of resort operations, combined with an adroitness for generating both rental and food and beverage profits, qualify him for the position of Vice President and General Manager of Sundial Beach & Tennis Resort.

Since assuming this position, Scott Siler has initiated and supervised an extensive remodeling of food and beverage facilities, has implemented a refurbishing program aimed at completing 75 percent of the resort's units and has expanded the existing rental program inventory.

An original member of the Mariner Group of Affiliated Companies, he has held various executive positions with Mariner, including Director of Food and Beverage for South Seas Plantation, Vice President, Food and Beverage, for Mariner Properties, Inc., Vice President, Food and Beverage, and Acting President for Marquis Hotels and Resorts and Vice President, Operations, for Marquis Hotels and Resorts.

Mr. Siler attended Cornell University's School of Hotel Administration, where he received a Bachelor of Science degree. He is a member of the Cornell Society of Hotelmen, Les Amis du Vin and La Chaine des Rôtisseurs.

Austin L. Mott, III, CHA
Executive Vice President and General Manager South Seas Plantation Resort

Austin L. Mott, III is Executive Vice President and General Manager of South Seas Plantation on Captiva Island, Florida. Recently he was elected to the position of Vice President for Marquis Hotels and Resorts of Fort Myers, Florida.

Prior to coming to South Seas, Mr. Mott was General Manager of the Elbow Beach Hotel in Bermuda for two years, and was with Sea Pines Plantation on Hilton Head Island, South Carolina, for five years as Vice President and General Manager of Hilton Head Inn and Villas and the Plantation Club. Mott spent seven years at the Hotel Hershey,

Pennsylvania; three years as General Manager and four years as Manager and Director of Sales. Additionally, he has been the Vice President and General Manager of the Don CeSar in St. Petersburg Beach, Florida, and Sandestin in Destin, Florida.

He received his Bachelor of Science degree in Business Administration in 1964 from the University of Denver in Colorado.

Dale R. Homan, CPM
Vice President
Property Management Division

As head of the property management division, Marquis Property Management, Rob Homan is responsible for ongoing management, accounting functions, communications, and physical maintenance of over forty resort condominiums, interval ownership projects, upper scale shopping centers and office complexes.

Prior to his current position, he was the Director of Corporate Security and Personnel for The Mariner Group, the parent company of Marquis Hotels and Resorts.

Rob Homan began his career as a local law enforcement officer

at the age of 21, and progressed to a position with the Federal Bureau of Investigation as a Special Agent. He has obtained the professional designation of Certified Property Manager.

Mr. Homan is a graduate of Ferris State College where he obtained a Bachelor of Science Degree, and is also a graduate of Biscayne College, where he received an MBA.

Philip H. Schlegel, III, CHA
Director of Operations

With 12 years of extensive hotel/motel management experience, Philip Schlegel specializes in resort operations, ensuring that each of our properties functions as smoothly and efficiently as possible. Mr. Schlegel supervises resort managers, carefully examines and monitors front desk and reservation systems, food and beverage procedures and energy and cost saving measures at all properties.

Phil Schlegel joined Marquis in 1982 as a resort General Manager and shortly thereafter, became Marquis' Operations Manager. His previous hotel management experience includes positions as General Manager and Director of Sales at

the Gainesville Hilton and Assistant Manager and Sales Director at the Flagler Inn in Gainesville, Florida.

Mr. Schlegel received a Bachelor of Arts degree from the University of Connecticut, and also graduated from the American Motel School in Roanoke, Virginia.

He has served on the board of directors of the Florida Hotel and Motel Association and is a member of the employee relations committee of the American Hotel and Motel Association.

Phil Schlegel has recently obtained the designation Certified Hotel Administrator from the Educational Institute of the American Hotel and Motel Association.

Joseph Mandarano, CHA
Chief Financial Officer

With over 17 years of diversified financial experience in the hospitality industry, Joe Mandarano is a valuable asset to the Marquis accounting team. As Chief Financial Officer, his responsibilities include financial and operational controls and budgetary and forecast analyses.

Mr. Mandarano's knowledge of finance has derived from such positions as Senior Auditor with the international public accounting firm of Laventhol and Horwath, as Controller with the Sheraton Corporation, supervising all accounting and financial activities of several multi-unit Sheraton properties, and as Vice President, Controller with Heritage Management Services, Inc., a hotel management company operating in five states.

He received his accounting degree from the State Institute of Commerce in Siderno, Italy and is a Certified Accountant and Commerce Expert by the State of Italy in Europe.

Budgeting

The budgeting process employed by Marquis Hotels was described as a bottoms up approach. Each level of management within each property was required to prepare a budget and submit it to their general manager. The general managers then submitted budget requests to top management where they were reviewed and either accepted or returned for modification.

Monthly expenditures were projected for each property and were reviewed against results. Deviations in projected cash flow for each property were also reviewed. General managers were held accountable for continuing deviations in cash flow and budget.

It was Mike's belief that Marquis' top management should not directly interfere in the management of a property. "There are properties where I am disappointed with the sales manager and have told this to the general manager. So far he has decided not to replace this person. If it were up to me I'd change that sales manager tomorrow but I don't feel I should directly interfere and force the general manager to act. If I do, the manager is likely to say, 'Okay, if you want to run the hotel do it all and just send me my check.' "

Recruiting

Originally Marquis Hotels hired general managers directly from other hotels. This proved to be unsatisfactory as the majority of them could not adapt to the environment at Marquis. This led to a policy of seeking individuals with some hotel and restaurant background and grooming them for positions as general managers in 2–3 years.

Mike indicated that each week he received an average of ten unsolicited resumes and personally responded to each. These were kept on file and many were updated after six months.

Each year the company hired one graduate from the hotel school at Florida International University. It was felt that it would be impractical to hire and train more than one inexperienced hotel school graduate per year.

A few individuals had been hired from outside the hotel and restaurant industry such as the Vice President of Property Management who had worked for the Federal Bureau of Investigation, but in most cases prior experience in the industry was required.

Although Mike felt this policy paid off, it also had limitations. The company attempted to update all management people and keep them informed of technological changes in the industry by subscribing to a weekly executive news tape which was sent to each.

A broader problem was that many members of management seemed uninterested in anything that didn't directly apply to what they were doing. Mike saw this as a limiting factor as he felt his own broader background and wide range of interests had served him well in the hotel business. He felt that the company would need individuals who were able to think and act beyond narrow bounds to enable Marquis to become a national organization.

EXHIBIT 2   **Organizational chart, 1-2-85.**

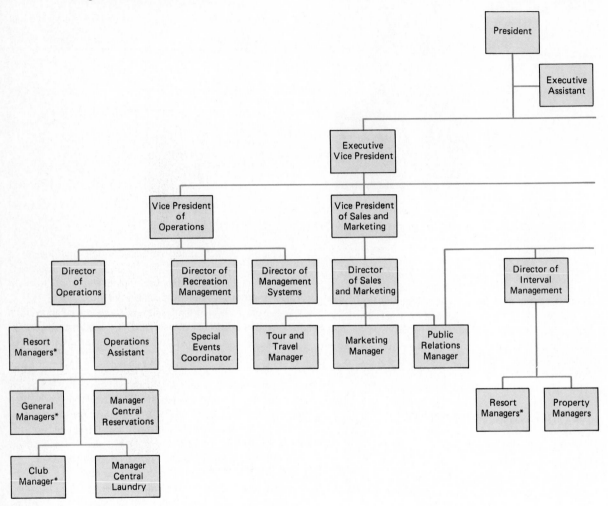

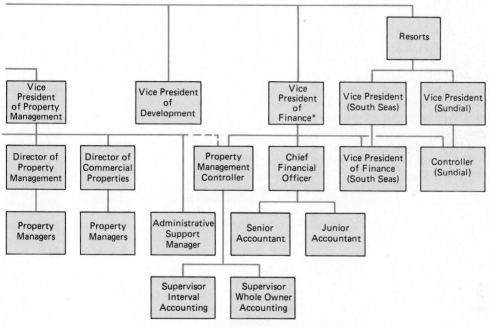

*All Resorts Financial and Accounting
functions have a dual reporting relationship
to that property's Resort Manager and the
Vice President of Finance. All Resorts
Marketing functions have a dotted line
reporting relationship to the Vice President
of Sales and Marketing.

THE FUTURE

With 1000 employees and annual sales of $150 million, Marquis Hotels and Resorts was no longer a small company yet neither could it be ranked with Marriott, Sheraton and others.

The company had grown by doing all things internally that could be done well. Architectural planning was a strength of the company and the parent company of Marquis had its own architectural firm. The parent company also owned a furniture store. This store supplied the properties with furnishings. Yet there were areas such as housekeeping for time share properties that were contracted to outside firms, as the company felt it could only be marginally profitable.

Although management felt that the best opportunities for growth existed in the development of commercial hotels it was also recognized that alternative growth paths were available. For instance, increased vertical integration was possible. This would place Marquis on a path of acquiring and operating more of the services which were needed to operate a chain of hotels and resorts.

Marquis Hotels and Resorts is a member of the following professional associations

Accredited Management Organization
American Hotel and Motel Association
American Land Development Association
American Society for Personnel Administration
Building Owners and Managers Association
Building Owners and Managers Institute
Club Managers Association of America
Community Associations Institute
Florida Hotel and Motel Association
Florida Timeshare Council
Fort Myers Board of Realtors
Fort Myers Metropolitan Chamber of Commerce
Hotel Sales Marketing Association, International
Institute of Real Estate Management
International Council of Hotel-Motel Management Companies
Motel Brokers Association of America
National Association of Mortgage Brokers
National Association of Realtors
National Restaurant Association
Personnel Association of Southwest Florida
Professional Golf Association
Sanibel-Captiva Islands Chamber of Commerce
Society of Real Property Administration
Southwest Florida Timeshare Council
United States Tennis Association

MULTIQUIMICA DO BRASIL

M. Edgar Barrett
Southern Methodist University

"I'm really concerned about our position in Brazil. Our pharmaceutical products are being hurt by both local and foreign producers and our foreign exchange policies may well be to blame." So said Don Howard, controller of the foreign operations of the pharmaceutical group of Multichemical Industries, Inc. "Look at Levadol, for example, our sales are falling while those of Hoffman et Cie are up."[1]

This conversation took place in February 1983 as Don was reviewing the 1982 results of the foreign operations of the pharmaceutical group with the group's general manager, Paul McConnell. The men were in the company's corporate offices in Houston, Texas.

BACKGROUND

Multichemical Industries, Inc. sold 75 different products in over 50 countries during 1982. Sales for the year were

---

[1]Hoffman et Cie was a large, multinational firm based in Bern, Switzerland.

$3.1 billion (see Exhibit 1 for financial data). The company's principal product groups were: pharmaceuticals; industrial chemicals; agricultural chemicals; and petrochemicals. Multichemical's overseas subsidiaries accounted for 35% of sales in 1982; with the majority of the activity taking place in Europe.

Multiquimica do Brasil (MB) was responsible for all sales and manufacturing which took place in Brazil. Thus, its managers had responsibility for products in several of the firm's product groups. Sales during the year were $65 million, 6% of foreign sales. This wholly-owned subsidiary was formed in 1977 with the initial purpose of establishing manufacturing facilities for agricultural chemical, industrial chemical and pharmaceutical products in Brazil. Prior to that time, Multichemical had been active in Brazil through export sales. In other words, products which were manufactured in the United States had been sold in Brazil through local, independent importers. Multichemical did not operate either manufacturing facilities or a division office in the country until 1977.

The new subsidiary began manufacturing and selling herbicides in 1977. MB did not show a profit until 1980. The losses which were incurred were primarily attributable to two factors: the large startup costs associated with a new business and a weak economic period in Brazil. As a result of the losses sustained during the 1977 to 1980

EXHIBIT 1 FINANCIAL DATA: CONSOLIDATED CORPORATE RESULTS
(Millions of Dollars)

	1982	1981
Income statement		
Sales		
Agricultural chemicals	$ 658	$ 600
Industrial chemicals	583	513
Petrochemicals	652	585
Pharmaceutical products	1,210	1,086
Subtotal	$3,103	$2,784
Cost of goods sold	1,300	1,169
Selling and administrative expense	884	793
Depreciation	296	262
Research expense	292	250
Subtotal	$2,772	$2,474
Operating income	$ 331	$ 310
Interest expense	45	42
Other income—net	41	30
Subtotal	$ 4	$ 12
Income before taxes	327	298
Income taxes	126	110
Net income	$ 201	$ 188
Balance sheet		
Current assets	$1,016	$1,001
Net property, plant and equipment	1,536	1,338
Other assets	241	139
Total assets	$2,793	$2,478
Current liabilities	363	297
Long-term debt	394	309
Deferred income taxes	140	124
Stockholders' equity	1,896	1,748
Total liabilities and stockholders' equity	$2,793	$2,478

Source: Multichemical Industries Inc. 1982 Annual Report.

period, MB was entitled to a substantial amount of tax loss carryforwards on its Brazilian tax return.[2]

In late 1979, the company installed a manufacturing plant to process Levadol, an aspirin-free pain reliever. Such facilities were included in the original operating plans for MB. They were scheduled, however, for the early 1980s. They went onstream sooner than originally planned due to an increase in the amount of duty on imports.

[2]The term "tax loss carryforward" refers to the fact that net operating losses, to the extent that they exceed taxable income of the preceding three years, can be carried forward, thus reducing future taxable income.

The manufacture of this product involved shipping the raw materials in bulk form from the United States. The raw materials were formulated, converted into tablet form, and packaged in the Brazilian plant and then sold to distributors. MB sales of Levadol in 1982 were $6.8 million.

PRODUCT AND PRICING FLOW FOR LEVADOL

The raw materials for Levadol were shipped from a domestic subsidiary of Multichemical to MB. The invoiced price for the transferred goods during 1982 averaged $60/case equivalent. The invoice was denominated in U.S. dollars.

The cost of goods sold on MB's books for Levadol averaged $131/case. This figure included the $60/case raw material costs, plus $31/case for import duty and $40/case to formulate, convert, and package it.

The product was sold to wholesalers serving both drug stores and chain stores, usually on 90 day payment terms, for a price of approximately $218/case. The $87/case difference between the sales price and the cost of goods sold consisted of marketing costs (roughly 20% of sales), administration, distribution, and interest expenses and approximately a 5% profit margin before taxes. The distributors, in turn, usually added a 10–20% margin. This was designed to both cover their costs and provide a profit margin.

DOLLAR LINKAGE BILLING

On their tax and fiscal books, MB benefited from a system known as dollar linkage billing. A statement on the invoice which was sent from the domestic subsidiary to MB said, "payable at the exchange rate in effect on the date of the receipt of goods." (Management books, on the other hand, were kept on the assumption that the invoice was to be paid in dollars—thus, effectively, using the exchange rate in effect at the time of payment.)

Brazilian law, at the time, required 180 day payment terms on imports. Since the Brazilian cruzeiro lost value in relation to the dollar on a more or less continuous basis, a foreign exchange loss would normally show up on a Brazilian firm's cruzeiro denominated books. Given the above mentioned system, however, the foreign exchange loss showed up on the U.S. tax books.

DOMESTIC SALES WITHIN BRAZIL

Even within the context of the Brazilian domestic market, MB's reported profit in dollar terms was affected by the more or less continuous devaluation of the cruzeiro. The major problem here was tied to the fact that competition had forced MB to offer 90 day payment terms to their customers. Given the fact that the cruzeiro was formally devalued approximately once every 10 days, any domestic subsidiary with terms of 90 days was faced with a translation loss whenever its books were translated back into dollar terms.[3]

[3]This "translation loss" would be caused by the fact that the *dollar value* of the original *cruzeiro denominated* sale would exceed the *dollar value* of the actual *cruzeiro denominated* collection of the account receivable some 90 days later.

In an attempt to deal with the situation, MB put into place a method known as "forward pricing." Under the assumptions of this method, MB's management predicted the amount of cruzeiro devaluation which would occur during the forthcoming 90 days. This estimate then served as the basis for raising the then current sales price. In other words, they passed along the expected loss due to the devaluation of the cruzeiro to the customer. As a result of this policy, product prices were revised at least monthly.

HEDGING POLICIES

From 1977 to 1979, the annual inflation rate in Brazil was in the general range of 30 to 50%. In 1979, however, Brazil—which imported the vast majority of its crude oil—began to feel the effects of the increasing price of crude oil. As a result, the domestic inflation rate took off *and* the cruzeiro was devalued by 30% during the year. MB reacted by pushing up its prices, a policy which it continued to adhere to throughout 1982.

Beginning in late 1979, the corporate treasurer's office of Multichemical began to "encourage" MB to borrow locally. Such a policy was designed to match assets and liabilities in cruzeiro terms and thus offset the translation loss on assets with a translation gain on liabilities. By having the subsidiaries borrow locally, the corporate treasurer was hoping to eliminate the risk of having to report large translation losses on the corporate income statement. Local borrowing, in essence, helped to smooth the corporation's reported income stream by substituting a periodic interest expense for less frequent, but presumably larger, losses due to translation. There was a cost, however. The nominal interest rate in Brazil in 1982 was approximately 160%. (See Exhibit 2 for foreign exchange and inflation rate data.)

PERFORMANCE MEASUREMENT POLICIES

Multichemical had recently changed its internal reporting system. Previous to the change, operating managers had been held responsible for the performance of their units as measured by the "operating income" figures. This meant that items such as other income, other expense, interest expense, and translation gains and losses were not focused upon in the quarterly business results review meetings. Over time, the senior management at the corporate level had come to feel that this system of per-

EXHIBIT 2 YEAREND FOREIGN EXCHANGE RATES
(Per U.S. Dollar)

	Brazilian cruzeiro	Swiss franc
1976	12.34	2.45
1977	16.05	2.00
1978	20.92	1.62
1979	42.53	1.58
1980	65.50	1.76
1981	127.80	1.80
1982	252.67	1.99

Source: International Financial Statistics, International Monetary Fund.

CONSUMER PRICE INDEX NUMBERS AND YEARLY PERCENTAGE CHANGES

	Brazil		Switzerland		U.S.	
1976	254.3		147.3		146.6	
1977	357.3	.41	149.2	.01	156.1	.06
1978	494.2	.38	150.8	.01	167.9	.08
1979	742.5	.50	156.2	.04	187.2	.11
1980	1321.2	.78	162.5	.04	212.4	.13
1981	2584.9	.96	173.1	.07	234.1	.10
1982	6394.7*	1.47	182.8	.06	248.2	.06

*Estimated.
Source: Monthly Bulletin of Statistics, United Nations, February 1983, p. 200.

formance measurement ignored the impact of some business decisions which could (or should) be taken by some of the operating managers in question.

After a thorough study of both the then existing internal reporting system and a set of alternative systems, a new system was designed and introduced. "Full Responsibility Accounting," as the new system was called, was made effective with the 1983 data. Under the terms of this new system, both individual product managers and product group managers were to be held responsible for the relationship between their profit after tax figures and the net assets under their control on both a world-wide and a "major" country basis. The term "net assets" for a particular sub-unit of the overall corporation was defined as net property (gross property less accumulated depreciation) plus net working capital. Thus, both individual product managers and product group managers now bore some of the responsibility for such items as interest expense, translation gains and losses, and the amount and composition of both short and long term assets.

The new system was designed with the intention that it would, among other things, force top management to delegate expansion and curtailment decisions to lower levels. The individual product managers and their superiors (the product group managers), sometimes in conjunction with an (geographic) area manager, were to have total responsibility for the assets which they employed in the process of producing, distributing and selling their particular product. The firm's capital budgeting and operational budgeting systems were to be altered such that the full year's capital expenditures would be approved at once and there would be agreement reached during the operational budgeting cycle as to the appropriate levels for inventories and receivables for the budget year in question.

While the new system was very focused upon a return on assets figure, two other measures were to receive emphasis under the terms of the new program. Both net income and cash flow were to be measured and monitored. The former would be measured against a budgeted target and the latter would be assessed in respect to an understanding of the underlying strategy for the sub-unit. Thus a sub-unit with a growth strategy might be expected to generate little or no cash (or indeed, even use cash) over a short to medium term time period.

Of particular concern to product group managers, such as Paul McConnell, was the fact that he was now responsible for both translation gains and losses *and* interest expense, the latter of which could be very high in the case of local borrowing. Fortunately, the translation losses that were to be reported were to be highly specific in nature. That is, they were to be directly traced to specific items on the local subsidiary balance sheets and, thus, would be tied to items directly related to the pharmaceutical group's products. Interest expense and translation gains, on the other hand, were not easily identified with such specific items. This lack of easy identification was caused by the fact that the corporate treasurer would sum all of the Brazilian borrowings and then allocate both translation gains and interest expense to each product group based on a formula tied primarily to sales.

COMPETITION

MB had been able to successfully position Levadol such that a significant amount of the population asked for Levadol when they wanted an aspirin-free pain reliever. This had become an important issue as the product became more widely stocked by the various grocery chains and cooperatives (with their open, free standing shelves). Every year MB sold a greater amount of Levadol through grocery stores than it had the year before. During 1982, it was estimated that 60% of the retail sales of all aspirin-free pain relievers in Brazil took place in grocery stores, while the remaining 40% were sold through some type of drug related outlet.

During 1982, MB lost both volume and market share on Levadol. Over 36,000 cases of Levadol were sold in 1980. Less than 32,000 were sold in 1982 (see Table 1 for volume and market share data). Although it was considered a premium product, an increasing number of distributors were reacting to the recession by substituting lower cost products.

MB's primary competition during 1982 was the Swiss firm Hoffman et Cie which sold a similar, but not identical, product. Hoffman's product was priced slightly lower than Levadol. The Swiss Franc (in relation to the cruzeiro) had not revalued as fast as the U.S. dollar over the most recent two year period (see Exhibit 2). Thus, the apparent incentive for Hoffman to raise its price to cover a translation loss was not as great at MB's. Also, Hoffman had been known to be somewhat more concerned with market share than with short term reported profit.

Other reasons for Hoffman's strength had to do with the company's size in Brazil. In addition to having a large percentage of the pharmaceutical market, it also had a very large share of the market in agricultural chemicals. Its field sales force was about three to four times the size of MB's. Also, Hoffman gave somewhat longer payment terms. Hoffman's management apparently felt that they could squeeze the profit margin in pharmaceuticals a bit because of their strong position and high profits with agricultural chemicals.

In addition to Hoffman and other foreign based firms, two local producers sold a generic substitute. The raw materials for the generic product were sourced in Brazil. The local patent covering this product had already expired. One result of this was that the industry was currently afflicted with an overcapacity of manufacturing facilities for products such as generic brand pain relievers. The price of the generic aspirin-free pain reliever had risen

TABLE 1   ASPIRIN-FREE PAIN RELIEVERS
(Percentage of Market Share by Major Competitors)

	MB	Hoffman	Generic	All other	Total volume (thousands of cases)
1977	3%	7%	31%	59%	125
1978	8	12	25	55	152
1979	9	17	21	53	202
1980	15	25	17	43	240
1981	13	32	13	42	287
1982	10	32	15	43	320

TABLE 2   AVERAGE WHOLESALE PRICE OF ASPIRIN-
FREE PAIN RELIEVERS
(U.S. Dollars per Case)

	MB	Hoffman	Generic
1980	$182	$180	$172
1981	201	198	187
1982	218	212	200

16% in the past two years. On the other hand, the price of Levadol had risen 20%, making the price difference $18/case (see Table 2).

CONCLUSION

"My greatest fear at this moment in Brazil is that we're being finessed by firms with a better knowledge of international business. Levadol should not be losing market share to Hoffman," said Paul McConnell. "I could understand some loss of market to the locals, but even there we should be able to sell the customer on our product superiority. Hoffman has a premium product. But it's not as good as ours."

PAMARK, INC.

William Aussieker
Rauf A. Kahn
California Polytechnic State University

"1979 was my twenty-fifth year in business. In those twenty-five years, we have become a 75 million dollar firm and the dominant machine shop and metal products firm in the Kansas City area," said Mark Willard, founder and chairman of the board of Pamark, Inc. "We acquired a Wichita firm last year, and this could be the beginning of many similar acquisitions, or we could be acquired by a large firm, and I could move to Palm Springs and retire. I know we've achieved about as much as possible in our immediate area."

HISTORY OF PAMARK—PAM, NAM AND SPAM

Pamark, Inc. can be traced to the year 1954 and Willard Machine Shop where Mark Willard began to provide general machine work and precision machining services to manufacturers in the Kansas City area. Willard quickly established a reputation for providing diverse and high quality machine work, and by 1963, sales and profits for Willard Machine Shop exceeded $250,000 and $25,000 respectively. In 1964, a slowdown in the local economy created a serious working capital problem for Willard who

had relied heavily on short-term credit to support expanding sales. Amounts payable and other current expenses accumulated, and suppliers threatened to cut off Willard's credit and refer the debts to collection agencies. As a result, Willard sought a short-term loan from his bank, but the bank routinely rejected the loan because of lack of collateral. The officer assigned to process the loan was Pamela Day, a 28-year old MBA who had been with the bank for five years. Day became quite interested in the machine shop. Aware of Willard's plight, she offered to buy one-half interest in the machine shop for $20,000 in cash and another $20,000 to be deducted from her salary as business manager of the newly formed Day and Willard Company.

Day and Willard Company prospered from an improved local economy, increased defense spending for the Vietnam War, and Day's business acumen. According to her description of the early days of Day and Willard Company,

Accounting records were kept in neatly stacked shoe boxes in one broom closet. Mark had thirty different machines, all with unique capabilities, and some were used only once a month. There were no sales policies or personnel as Mark relied on word-of-mouth and customers coming to him for business. The first six months were spent setting up an accounting system, rearranging a rather large debt, and soliciting new business, especially machine shop work that would better utilize the equipment.

By manufacturing bomb casings for ordinance manufacturers and machining parts for ammunition trailers, Day and Willard benefited as a subcontractor from increased defense spending for the Vietnam war. The company was incorporated as Pamark, Inc. in 1970 and employed over 100 people and had a net income of $500,000 with sales of about $10 million.

Rapid growth in sales continued into the 1970's. In 1972, Pamark had sales of 40 million and net income of more than $2 million. Despite more than 60 million in sales and four million in profits for 1973 trouble loomed for Pamark in 1974 as 80 percent of Pamark's sales were defense-contract related. According to Day:

> Both Mark and I exhorted the sales force to go after the nondefense business, but defense contractors were like shooting ducks in a barrel. We had machining services that they needed, and we were always available.

As a subcontractor, Pamark was the first to feel the reduction in defense spending as prime contractors anticipated the decline and reduced subcontracting. In the first six months of 1974, sales decreased to 12 million, and defense related sales dropped to less than six million or about one fourth for the same period in 1973. In retrospect, Day was able to refer jokingly to "the saga of 74":

> We were in serious trouble, and in order to avoid laying off all the employees, we began to solicit machinery repair and reconditioning work from the local food-processing manufacturers. Maintenance was a problem to these manufacturers since the food processing equipment manufacturers were in Chicago or New Jersey. Meatpacking and processing manufacturers were most of our early customers, and our first real breakthrough occurred when we showed a meatpacker how retooling three parts and slightly changing the assembly operation could improve production on a machine used in making spam. In the second half of 1974, maintenance sales were only four million, but I think that they kept us afloat.

1975 TO 1978

Sales and profits figures for Pamark for 1974 to 1978 are shown in Table 1.

The recovery of Pamark can be attributed to growth in the machinery repair or maintenance, machine shop work, and parts and equipment for manufacturers and retailers. Pamark's sales for repair or reconditioning machinery in meatpacking and processing, printing, grain milling, and farm, industrial, food processing and construction equipment industries expanded rapidly in 1975 and 1976. Custom machine shop work sales, 12 million in 1974 increased about a million a year because of the aggressiveness of the sales force in obtaining nondefense-related business. In 1976, Pamark began furnishing a national chain of retail stores, headquartered in Kansas City, with automotive parts and supplies. Total sales to this retail chain reached four million in 1978. Production and sale of machinery parts for equipment manufacturers began in 1977 and accounted for three million in sales in 1978. Sale of parts to automobile, truck and bus assembly plants in the area amounted to three million a year from 1975 to 1978.

By 1978, the composition of Pamark's sales had changed significantly from 1973. The percentage of Pamark's total sales for major product groups for 1978 in comparison to 1974 and 1973 are presented in Table 2.

In 1978, Pamark also reached agreement on the purchase price of Harman Machine and Tool, a Wichita firm specializing in machine work for aircraft and aerospace manufacturers, with sales of 12 million. Harman Machine and Tool provided Pamark with specialized machinery, engineering and metallurgical knowledge needed for sales in the aerospace and aircraft industry. The Wichita location provided Pamark a base for not only maintenance of the large meatpackers and food processors in the area with estimated sales of three million, but also machine shop work for equipment manufacturers and a refinery with estimated sales of four million. Harman had been coveted by Day and Willard for seven years. The acquisition oc-

TABLE 1

Year	1974	1975	1976	1977	1978
Sales	26,000	30,000	39,000	45,000	55,000
Profits	(4,000)	(1,000)	1,000	2,000	3,000

Sales and profits in thousands, ( ) net losses.

TABLE 2

Product group	1973	1974	1978
Machine shop	95	85	50
Defense	80	38	5
Nondefense	15	47	45
Maintenance	3	15	27
Meat	2	13	9
Grains	*	*	7
Printing	*	*	4
Equipment	*	*	4
Other	*	*	3
Parts and equipment	0	0	22
Automobile			12
Other transportation equip.			3
Manufacturing equipment			9

curred after Harman became overextended as a result of purchasing land and a new plant too large for its operations. Harman was purchased for $1 million in cash, assumption of 50,000 in current liabilities, and $4 million in long-term debt.

ORGANIZATION IN 1979

The organization chart for Pamark, Inc. is presented in Figure 1. The firm was organized along functional lines of operations, marketing, personnel and accounting. The organizational structure emerged from the financial difficulties of 1974 when lenders strongly recommended several organizational changes. First, Mark Willard became chairman of the board and stepped down as president. Second, Pamela Day became president. Third, Day's former position of business manager was abolished, and controller and personnel director positions were established and staffed with professionals from outside the organization. Fourth, Willard was retained as a consulting engineer in order to better utilize his technical and engineering skills. Fifth, the manager of marketing was brought under the direct control of Day.

In staffing the position of controller, Pamark was fortunate to land Ralph Kaan, 56, a CPA with twenty-five years experience as an accountant, auditor and controller of a large mid-western based aerospace company. The personnel director was Jennifer Hensley, 28, with degrees in psychology and industrial relations and six years experience with Pamark as personnel assistant, analyst and

administrative aide. Hensley was appointed director on December 1, 1979. The two other functional heads of Pamark units were Chick Snow and Bob Borst. Snow, the first machinist hired by Willard in 1954, was appointed manager of operations in 1970. Before his appointment, he was head machinist from 1960–66, and machine shop supervisor from 1966–70. His education did not extend beyond trade school, but he possessed many certificates in management and supervision from local community colleges. Borst was Pamark's first salesperson, and was appointed manager of marketing in 1969. He had a bachelor's degree in psychology and a Master's of Business Administration. Richard Harman was the President of Harman Machine and Tool since 1975, and was the son of the former owner. Educated as a mechanical engineer with a bachelor's degree in metallurgy, Harman was the company's metallurgist for twelve years after receiving his master's of mechanical engineering degree in 1957.

Though Day and Willard each owned one-half of Pamark, policy decisions were reached by a vote of the executive committee which consisted of Day, Willard, Borst, Snow, and Kaan. Weekly production and marketing plans were set at Monday morning meetings attended by the executive committee, the machine shop superintendent, maintenance manager and metal products manufacturing manager. These meetings facilitated coordination of production and marketing. Cooperation among the departments was extensive as close working relationships had developed among top, middle and supervisory personnel after many years of working together. Four of

FIGURE 1 **Organization chart, Pamark, Inc., December 1979.**

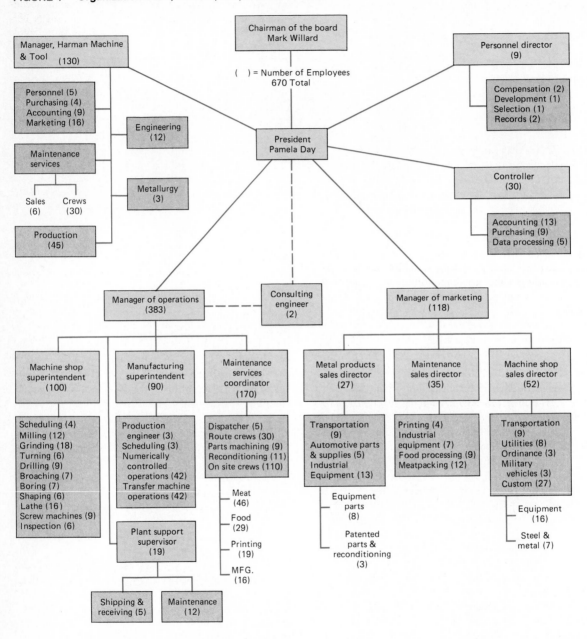

six top managers of Pamark had worked together for fifteen years or more, and all seven of Pamark's middle managers had worked together for ten or more years. Pamark's policy of promotion from within, a salary bonus plan that rewarded years of service, and liberal fringe benefits, including fully-paid health, dental, retirement and paid vacations encouraged supervisory and managerial employees to stay with Pamark.

OPERATIONS

The operations department of Pamark was organized into three separate production units (maintenance, machine shop and manufacturing) and two support units (plant support-custodial and maintenance services, and shipping and receiving). The machine shop was headed by the machine shop superintendent who was aided by a scheduling department that determined machine runs. The superintendent supervised nine machine supervisors who in turn supervised machinists on specific metal transforming machinery (milling, lathe, grinding, drilling, boring, broaching, shaping, turning, and screw machines). The manufacturing department produced large batch runs of metal products on numerically controlled or transfer machines. The largest runs were made on the transfer machine which involved assembling several pieces of machinery and programming the machines to perform several operations. The production engineer and his assistants arranged the sequencing process of the transfer machines. The maintenance services consisted of 10 on-site crews who worked full-time at one site for customers under long-term contract, and 15 route crews who serviced machinery of several customers on a periodic basis under monthly service contracts or provided maintenance on an on-call basis. One of the on-site crews numbered eighteen, and the smallest on-site crew had at least seven full-time maintenance personnel. The on-site crews performed all maintenance work on the site, except for machining of parts or assemblies which were sent to Pamark's machine shop.

Some organizational problems plagued the maintenance services. First, there was a 20 percent turnover rate among maintenance service personnel, most quitting to become in-house maintenance personnel for customers. Second, the crews were assigned routes to service monthly contract customers. They also were required to perform emergency repair for monthly contract customers and service new customers who may call for machinery repair only once. The maintenance service personnel were generally skilled machinists, and maintenance was frequently a routine and unchallenging job. Machine reconditioning, somewhat more challenging, was usually performed by the reconditioning unit personnel. Third, maintenance crews were important in communicating maintenance problems about machinery, but were not given credit for their role in engineering new parts or operations that reduced maintenance or improved production. Last, there was considerable disagreement between maintenance operations, marketing and Day about the area to be serviced by the maintenance crews. Day wanted the maintenance service representatives not to solicit service and maintenance contracts beyond a sixty-mile radius of Pamark's facilities. The restriction was imposed because of the necessity of the crews to drive to the maintenance sites and return. According to Day:

> It's not economical for us to have a crew drive for three hours for a $250 maintenance job. Also, if a part must be machined, we may be talking a six-eight hour delay. Even our on-site crews can get a part machined in less than four hours.

The other organizational issue concerned Harman Machine and Tool. During 1979, the first year after Harman was purchased, Pamark treated Harman as an autonomous subsidiary, and the only change in Harman's structure was the transfer of 30 Pamark employees to Wichita to start maintenance services for local manufacturers and solicit machine work for Pamark. Harman's personnel were somewhat edgy about the "outsiders" and possible loss of their identity as Harman Machine and Tool. Uneasiness was also present among Pamark's employees as some felt that transfer to Wichita or loss of job would result from the acquisition. Richard Harman was also unsure about his future:

> As part of purchase agreement, Pamark agreed to pay me $150,000 for ten years if I remained as Manager of Harman, and $1 million upon termination, death or age 65. So far, Pamark's top management has not interfered, and the maintenance and sales personnel have helped utilize about half of the excess space in the plant. But, it could all change tomorrow.

MARKETING

Pamark's sales for 1979 were 75 million. 1979 sales and gross margins for Pamark's products and services are presented in Table 3.

TABLE 3

	Maintenance	Machine shop	Metal products	Harman machine	Harman maintenance
Sales*	16	30	13	13	3
Margin**	5	27	25	20	7

*in millions
**Sales − cost of goods sold + selling expenses/sales

On the 1979 sales, marketing manager Borst stated:

Except for Harman and the Wichita maintenance sales, which we knew about in 1978, we did not increase our penetration in any market, but held our own. Increased sales in maintenance, machine shop and metal products were deceptive since they are mostly price increases. I don't expect our present markets to grow much more than 3 percent a year in real terms. Of course, if the inflation rate is 12 percent a year, we may have total sales increasing at 15 percent a year.

As shown in Figure 1, the marketing department of Pamark was organized on a product and industrial basis, and some members of the marketing department did not share Borst's assessment of sales growth. The most senior salesperson in the defense sales unit was quite critical of the company's treatment:

There is over $100 million a year in defense work in the Kansas City area, and we could capture 15 percent in subcontracting work. Day won't give us the budget or the personnel because of 1974.

In response, the machine shop sales director replied:

Defense and other government contract possibilities are well publicized, and we talk to all the prime contractors about our capabilities. But, most of the defense contracts today do not require machine work but electronics and guidance. The 3.5 million in defense sales in 1979 are for ordinance casings and military vehicle parts, both have a margin of 20 percent. In contrast, sales by the transportation, public utilities and custom machine sales amounted to 6, 8, and 14.5 million respectively, and margins are all about 30 percent. Besides, railroads, bus companies and automobile repair businesses have been doing business with us for years and are likely to continue for many years in the future.

The custom machine shop sales representatives were the elite of the marketing department of Pamark. Most were machinists by training and easily conversed technically with custom's production engineers or other line managers. Of the approximately 14.5 million in 1979 custom machine shop sales, about half of the sales were

machine work that involved 10 or fewer final pieces with an average price of $300 per piece. The average number of pieces was six. According to the custom sales supervisor:

Our rule of thumb is no job will be taken unless it is at least a thousand dollars. It costs about $100 to set up each job, and the machine time runs about $30 per hour per machine. In addition, there is a $10 per machine cost that includes moving the piece, setting up the machine, and so on. Material costs about 20 percent of the sales.

The other half of the sales were for longer runs of up to 200 final pieces. Average price per piece was $20, and the average number of pieces was 80. If the run was more than 200 final pieces, it was viewed as a part, and it was more economical to program the numerically controlled machines in the parts department. The cost to program a run is about $300. Because coordination between the customer and the machine shop was critical, custom-machine sales representatives were assigned to specific industries. The custom sales supervisor assessed the prospects for his unit:

The best sales people drifted to machine shop sales after the 1974 drop in defense sales. We have aggressively solicited machine work for the past five years in the Kansas City area, and of the $100 million a year in potential sales, we have 26.5 million which makes us about five times larger than the next largest shop. It will be hard to hold onto our market share over the next five years, and real sales growth can only occur if we move into new areas.

(Some of the problems with maintenance were described in the organization and operations section.) The maintenance sales personnel were mostly service representatives who served as a liaison between the maintenance service crews and the customer. After five years of soliciting maintenance work in the Kansas City area, including Atchison, Topeka and St. Joseph, maintenance sales personnel were fortunate to make one new contact a month. According to the marketing manager:

We perform reconditioning and/or maintenance work for 40 percent of the potential customers in our area. On a potential sales basis, we have over 60 percent of the business, and we are at least twelve times larger than our nearest competitor. Except for price increases and economic growth of about three percent a year, maintenance in the Kansas City area is not a good prospect for growth, in fact, it will be very difficult to hold on to our share. Actually, we are our strongest competitor. In the past two years, thirty maintenance personnel have left Pamark, mostly to work for former customers or start their own services. Smaller firms would rather have an individual rather than a firm that services 200 other firms.

The maintenance services marketing manager was more optimistic in his suggestions:

If Day would relax her policy and we moved into other areas, maintenance sales could double in two years. We obtained in one year sales of three million in Wichita, and Springfield, Missouri; Pittsburg, Kansas; Omaha; Cedar Rapids and Council Bluffs could be at least 15 million in sales.

The marketing manager was less buoyant in his projections:

If we moved into those markets, we could achieve 15 million in sales, but we would be overextended. Maintenance is at least 70 percent labor, add selling, equipment and overhead, and there might be a 1 percent profit margin. Twenty percent of the sales are for reconditioning with a margin of about 15 percent. We hope that with a large maintenance sales volume, it would result in parts and equipment sales, or at least reconditioning work.

Pamark's maintenance operations had developed five patentable parts for food processing equipment that could be adapted for use on five different types of meatpacking machines. The company charged $300 for installation and once installed about $100 per year in replacement parts could be expected beginning with second year of operation. The food processing equipment manufacturers representing five million per year in potential sales were reluctant to buy these parts because the installation costs were greater than their own. Because of the failure to sell directly to the manufacturers, these parts and assemblies were marketed by the maintenance service representatives as part of maintenance or equipment reconditioning. By the end of 1979, Pamark had installed its patented parts on 900 pieces of meatpacking equipment in the Greater Kansas City area. It was estimated that nine out of ten pieces of equipment had Pamark's parts. Total sales of these parts amounted to $150,000 in 1979 with a profit

margin of 40 percent. To date, Pamark had not marketed the parts in the Wichita area where there were 300 meatpacking machines suitable for adaptation.

In 1979, 13 million in metal products sales were distributed as follows: 4.5 million to a national chain of automobile parts and supplies stores; 4.5 million auto, bus and truck manufacturers in the Kansas City area; and 4 million to equipment manufacturers. A total of six customers accounted for 12 million of the metal products sales. According to the metal products sales manager, the market for metal products was not expected to grow at more than 2 to 3 percent a year, but Pamark expected to easily maintain its present sales without fear of competition.

The sales of Harman Machine and Tool consisted of 7 million in aluminum and light-metal machine work for three aerospace and aircraft manufacturers in the Wichita area. Six million were for custom machine work for an industrially diverse group of local manufacturers, transportation companies and public utilities. No single custom machine work customer accounted for more than half a million in sales.

In summarizing Pamark's developing marketing strategy, Bob Borst said:

We have specialized for the past fifteen years in high quality metal transforming work which required skilled labor and advanced equipment. Economical utilization of expensive machinery requires greater sales volume, and quantity sales involves competitive pricing and expanding markets. Maintenance was intended to utilize skilled labor, slack machine time and develop products for an expanding metal products' sales. It was a good concept, but the limited growth potential presents a problem.

PERSONNEL

As of December, 1979, Pamark employed a total of 670 employees, including 130 employees of Harman Machine and Tool. The personnel department maintained personnel records on all Pamark employees, performed wage and salary surveys, contracted for benefit programs, recruited and selected employees, conducted safety, supervisory training and management development programs, supervised the performance evaluation, training and orientation of employees, and handled employee relations. These functions were performed by a staff of five professional personnel analysts, three clerical support employees and the personnel officer. None of Pamark's or Harman's employees were unionized, Pamela Day and Mark Willard have always maintained that they will sell out if unionized.

Fear of unionization has dictated many of Pamark's personnel policies. A machine-piece rate pay plan in which employees were compensated according to a standard time work measurement system was abandoned in 1976 in favor of hourly wage rate for six different machinist classifications. Similarly, a straight piece rate compensation plan for semiskilled operatives in the metal products manufacturing section was also abandoned in favor of straight hourly wage rates. In addition to all government mandated insurance programs, Social Security, Workers Compensation, Unemployment and Disability, Pamark paid 20 percent of each worker's average hourly wage rate in fringe benefits: savings bonds, health, vision, dental, life or auto insurance, or a deferred annuity. Pamark has no employee retirement plan. Partly as a consequence of its compensation plan for production workers, Pamark's labor costs were about 10 percent greater than other machine shops in the area. According to Jennifer Hensley, Pamark's Personnel Director, "We're the biggest, why not be the best paying!"

Pamark's production supervisors were on a straight salary ($2,000/month or 15 percent greater than highest paid full-time machinist) with an annual bonus equal to one percent of annual salary for each year of service. The same fringe benefits program was offered production supervisors. Clerical, sales and managerial personnel also received the same fringe benefits and received monthly salaries. Clerical salaries were competitive with local employers, but not as high relatively as machinists and production workers. Sales personnel received a $500 a month salary plus expenses. Metal products sales people (average monthly compensation of $3,000) received a one percent commission on all sales, and custom machine shop sales people (average monthly compensation of $3,500) received 5 percent of the operating margin on all their sales. Maintenance services sales personnel received one percent commission on all monthly contracts, and as a group, received $50 a month for each one million maintenance contract. Pamark's managers were on a straight salary ranging from $20,000 for the personnel director to Pamela Day's $200,000 a year salary.

Until 1974, Pamark had been quite conservative in its financing of operations. No new debt was incurred from 1964 to 1969, and in the last quarter of 1973, Pamark's only long-term debt was a $5 million mortgage on building and land. However, about 9 million in long-term debt was required in 1974 and 1975 to finance maintenance services, increased parts manufacturing and a shortage of cash due to a severe drop in defense sales. Because the acquisition of Harman Machine and Tool required the payment of $1 million in cash during 1978, Controller Ralph Kaan began an aggressive working capital and cash management program in late 1977, but despite his efforts, the company was somewhat strapped for funds in late 1978. According to Kaan, "Our cost of labor increased 15 percent with the change to straight hourly wages which, of course, reduced operating income by about $500,000 a year."

Pamark is still a privately held company, and Kaan feels that going public was one alternative to raising funds for further expansion or acquisition. Kaan was rather pessimistic about further expansion through internally generated funds.

> For two years, we have deferred purchase of new equipment to use funds for purchasing Harman. I estimate that over the next five years about five hundred thousand must be allocated each year to purchase equipment for present operations. Possibly, there may be a savings of $300,000 a year by centralizing some accounting, marketing, personnel, and purchasing operations from Harman. I instituted an excellent cost control system, and I do not see many areas where cutting costs would be effective.

STRATEGIC CONSIDERATIONS

In 1979, 19 million of Pamark's sales were from maintenance services, 12 companies with long-term contracts accounted for 12 million in maintenance sales. Of these sales, meatpacking and processing companies contributed 8 million. The two largest maintenance contracts were from two meatpacking companies located in Kansas City, four million in 1979 sales. It was rumored that the companies may close these 90-year old plants in favor of relocating closer to feedlots in Nebraska, Iowa, Western Kansas, or Eastern Colorado. In contrast, nonmeat, food processing had become more concentrated, but regional grain milling and vegetable processing companies in Kansas City area had lost business to Minneapolis and Chicago. In 1979, Pamark had sales of four million in maintenance contracts with nonmeat, food processors.

Pamela Day regards the next five years as critical to Pamark, Inc.:

> We could continue along the same course, or Mark and I could cash out. Several firms have expressed an interest in Pamark, and a Minnesota based conglomerate has offered ten million in cash and 200,000 shares at present market price of $35 to 40.

Another alternative is to expand the maintenance and reconditioning services to other areas: Cedar Rapids-Quad Cities, Omaha, Des Moines, Minneapolis or Chicago. Any of Nebraska or Iowa locations would allow Pamark to provide maintenance services to a dozen meatpackers and processors that have more automated equipment. 12 million in sales were estimated for each location, and to set up a maintenance center would cost about two million. A Minneapolis or Chicago location represented a significantly larger potential market, but the competition was also much greater. Thus, estimated sales were less than ten million in either location, and the cost of a maintenance center was about the same as for a Nebraska or Iowa location.

A second alternative was to purchase another metals processing company. One particularly attractive company was a Chicago based public corporation involved in casting, forging and other metals processing services. The company also owned two aluminum forging facilities in California. The company earned $250,000 in net income with 40 million in sales in 1979. At the end of 1979, it had 12 million in assets and four million in long-term debt. Presently, about two million of the company's shares were outstanding, and were traded on the American Exchange. Price ranged between $5–9 a share.

On a recent trip to California, Mark Willard investi-gated two metal processing firms that he thought were ideal. First, an Oakland firm had eight million in sales, and net income of $100,000. The firm had three million in assets and no debt. The Oakland location would provide Pamark with good access to a potential 12 million in maintenance sales to a large number of food processing companies in the Bay Area. The second potential acquisition, located in Downey, dealt in tool and die making and powder metallurgical processes. With $4 million in assets and $1 million in debt, the company has sales of about ten million and net profit of $400,000. The price of either of the companies would be about three million.

A fourth alternative was to expand Harman's aluminum and alloy machine work for aerospace and aircraft companies outside of the Wichita area. Day and Borst estimated about 100 million in potential sales in Kansas, Texas, Missouri and Oklahoma from machine work for aerospace and aircraft manufacturers. At the present time, Harman's marketing department was not soliciting sales outside the Hutchinson-Wichita area. About $100,000 must be allocated for additional marketing costs to obtain $1 million in sales. Harman felt that a 5 percent share of the potential sales could be achieved within two years, but there was 50 percent chance that less than $1 million in actual sales could be obtained in a two-year period.

PAMARK, INC.
STATEMENT OF INCOME
(Year Ended December 31, 1979 in Thousands)

Sales		$75,000
Cost of goods sold		$64,000
Gross profit (margin)		11,000
Operating expenses:		
Selling	$2,500	
Administration	1,000	
General	1,500	
Depreciation	2,000	
Amortization of goodwill	30	7,030
Net operating income		$ 3,970
Interest expense		1,320
Net income before taxes		$ 2,650
Income taxes (50%)		1,325
Net income		$ 1,325
Retained earnings at beginning of year		$21,500
Net income		1,325
Retained earnings at the end of the year		$22,825

Note A: Amortization period for goodwill was determined to be 30 years. This does not violate provisions of APB opinion 17.

HARMAN MACHINE AND TOOL
STATEMENT OF INCOME TO PREVIOUS ACQUISITION BY PAMARK
(Year Ended December 31, 1978)

Net sales	$12,000
Cost of goods sold	9,500
Gross profit (margin)	$2,500
Operating expense:	
Selling & administrative expense	1,000
General expense (includes depreciation)	1,000
Net operating income	$500,000
Interest expense	420,000
Net income (loss)	80,000
Income taxes (50%)	40,000
Net income	40,000

PAMARK INC.
COMPARATIVE BALANCE SHEET

(Thousands)		December 31, 1979		December 31, 1978
Assets				
Current assets				
Cash		$ 2,500		$ 2,000
Marketable securities		2,030		2,000
Accounts receivable—net		7,525		7,000
Inventories		7,500		8,000
Total current assets		$19,555		$19,000
Fixed assets:				
Land		3,000		1,000
Plant & equipment	55,100		46,600	
Less accumulated depreciation	22,600	32,500	17,000	29,600
Intangible assets:				
Goodwill		870		
Total fixed assets		$36,370		$30,600
Total assets		$55,925		$49,600
Liabilities and owner's equity				
Current liabilities				
Accounts payable		$ 7,100		$ 6,400
Notes payable		5,800		5,600
Accrued wages and salaries		1,200		1,200
Accrued taxes		1,000		900
		$15,100		$14,100
Long-term debt		18,000		14,000
Total liabilities		$33,100		$28,100
Owner's equity		22,825		21,500
Total liabilities & owner's equity		$55,925		$49,600

Note A: Goodwill was determined in accordance with APB opinion 17.
Note B: Contingent liability of $1,000,000 payable to Harman, upon his termination as the Manager, his death, or retirement at age 65.

HARMAN MACHINE AND TOOL
(ACQUIRED BY PAMARK, INC. JANUARY 1,
1979) BALANCE SHEET AT DECEMBER 31,
1978

Assets	
Current assets	
Cash	$ 25,000
Receivables	50,000
Inventories	175,000
Total current assets	$ 250,000
Fixed assets	
Land	$1,000,000
Plant & equipment	6,500,000
Less depreciation	3,600,000
Total fixed assets	$3,900,000
Total assets	$4,150,000

Liabilities and equity	
Current liabilities	
Accounts payable	$ 20,000
Accrued wages	30,000
Total current liabilities	$ 50,000
Long-term debt	$4,000,000
Total liabilities	$4,050,000
Equity	100,000
Total liabilities and equity	$4,150,000

SHARPCO, INC. (1985)

Arthur D. Sharplin
Bentley College

In 1972, James Sharplin and two brothers decided to open a welding and steel fabrication shop in Monroe, Louisiana. The Sharplins formed a corporation, Sharpco, Inc., bought a parcel of land at the eastern edge of Monroe, and built a small shop building. Most of the initial equity investment was in the form of welding machines, tools, and other items contributed by the three owners. James worked full time at Sharpco while his brothers pursued other interests. The company was profitable from the first year. Sales grew steadily and the shop was expanded several times during the 1970s. In the early 1980s, James exchanged his interest in some commercial property the Sharplins owned for his brothers' shares of Sharpco stock.

Sharpco is engaged in four distinct business areas—all related to heavy equipment, especially crawler tractors (often called "bulldozers" or "caterpillars"). First, the company makes and sells a number of welded steel items for heavy equipment. Second, Sharpco markets new and used crawler tractor parts. Third, James and his workers provide repair service for heavy equipment owners. Finally, Sharpco does high strength repair welding for heavy equipment. Each of these business areas will be discussed further under the heading "Operations."

In January 1985, the business was moved to a new 30,000 square foot facility in what had become a rapidly expanding commercial and industrial area along Interstate Highway 20. Among the more than twenty firms on high-way I-20 near Sharpco are heavy equipment dealers representing Deere and Company (makers of John Deere equipment), Case Power and Equipment Company, and Fiat-Allis, Inc. (successor to Allis Chalmers, Inc.). Dealers for the other two major brands of heavy construction equipment, International Harvester and Caterpillar, are located about three miles away. Figure 1 shows the location of the new Sharpco plant. Table 1 provides geographic and demographic data relevant to Sharpco's main trade area.

PERSONNEL AND ORGANIZATION

In recent years, the workforce at Sharpco has varied from as many as thirty down to its 1985 level of eleven. As a general rule, Sharpco keeps a cadre of experienced workers and fills in with temporary welders and mechanics during busy periods. The company has no formal organization chart. However, the organizational chart on page 806 was drawn by James Sharplin to represent the organization as it existed in 1985.

The lines of authority at Sharpco are not rigidly followed. James routinely bypasses each of his direct subordinates and deals directly with workers. "The managers all work as a team," says James. "Any one of us can make a major or minor decision—or write a $10,000

FIGURE 1 **Sharpco's location.**

Monroe, Louisiana and surrounding region

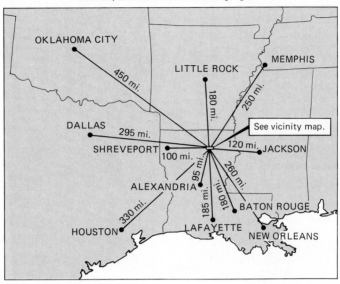

Sharpco vicinity

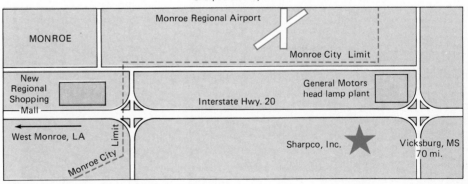

check.'' Everyone in the organization is expected to pitch in wherever there is a need for extra help and to accept direction from whoever knows most about the particular job being done. The insert below provides brief comments made by James Sharplin concerning each of the key employees.

There is no formal performance appraisal at Sharpco and no written compensation policy. Sharpco furnishes medical insurance for James, Jerry, and Tim (Peggy is covered under her husband's policy furnished by his em-

ployer). The company also pays about one-half the cost of insurance for each worker. The managers are paid on a salary basis. Hourly paid workers make from $6 to $9 an hour, about average for the area. Every year, James says, he ranks the employees in order of what he considers to be their contribution to the company. Then he adjusts the pay of any whose pay seems inequitable. Practically all hiring and firing is done by James personally, although Jerry Thompson has authority to terminate any of his workers.

TABLE 1 GEOGRAPHIC AND DEMOGRAPHIC DATA

	Monroe	Ouachita parish (county)	Northeast Louisiana (16 parishes)	Louisiana (entire state)	United States
Population, July 1982 (thousands)	57	141	434	4,373	230,000
Per capita income, 1981	$6,973	$7,486	$5,897	$8,113	$8,917
Change in population 1980–82 (percent change for entire period)	−0.9	1.2	1.4	4.0	2.8
Change in *real* per capita income, 1979–81 (percent change for entire period)	−5.1	−3.1	−2.9	1.0	−0.4
Value of agricultural production, 1982 (millions)	n/a	$14	$48	$1,407	$158,700
Personal income, 1982 (millions)	n/a	$1,380	$16,010	$44,000	$2,578,600
Workforce employed in manufacturing, 1982 (percent)	n/a	18.1	14.9	14.6	20.0
Workforce employed in construction, 1982 (percent)	n/a	8.6	5.7	9.6	5.8
Workforce employed in farming, 1982 (percent)	n/a	1.2	6.6	3.2	2.0
Approximate land area, 1982 (thousands of acres)	n/a	401	6,519	28,494	2,264,960
Proportion of land area in farms, 1982 (percent)	n/a	23.4	40.7	31.3	46.0

EXHIBIT 1 **Organizational chart.**

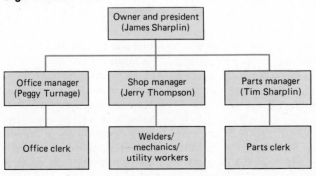

JAMES SHARPLIN DISCUSSES SHARPCO'S KEY PEOPLE

Jerry is thirty years old. He is my mother's grandnephew. Jerry is dedicated to Sharpco. He has a great deal of ability to get the job done. He is a good welder and the best mechanic we have. The men respect him and that helps make him a good manager. Customers like him; they ask for him. They know they can depend on what he says. During the move, when we were all running just to keep up, Jerry sold two excavator buckets. He worked right through a weekend, even though he had the flu, to get the buckets built. He has a good memory, too. He can usually tell a customer if we have a part without even checking the computer. Jerry's main recreation is hunting. I try to make sure he has some time off during hunting season. When I decided to furnish him a company pickup, I made sure it was something he has always wanted but never felt that he could afford—a four-wheel drive "mud hog."

Peggy is in her forties. She has taken a number of college courses. Although Peggy does not have a degree, she knows much more than most college graduates. She is as dedicated as any employee I have. She is the most cost conscious person in the whole organization, including me. After just a year of working with computers she knows more about them than the computer "expert" who sold us the machine. Somehow, Peggy and the computer were an instant match. Peggy is a highly religious lady. I think this accounts in some degree for her diligence and I know I can trust her with anything I have. There has never been the slightest need for me to check up on her.

Everyone here respects her and her presence helps keep foul language and rowdy behavior at a minimum. Peggy is usually miles ahead of me with any information I need—like sales statistics. She put the used parts on the computer without any guidance. And the information was in a form she knew I could use. If things move too fast she just works nights and Saturdays. She does all the advertising better than any ad agency could. She comes up with the ideas, does the copy, and just runs it by me for approval. Peggy is a perfectionist.

Tim is 25 years old. He is my nephew. Tim is strictly work, family, church, and school. He attends Northeast Louisiana University part-time studying business. Tim has a good number of outside obligations, including school. But whenever I need him he is here. He asked me if he should let his school wait while we get over the move and get things back on an even keel. I told him that he might take one course instead of two, only if he thought it best, but I felt he should continue his education without a break. He works hard—wants to do things right. He grew up on a farm, where he often had neither the time nor the equipment to do quality work. Tim is learning fast. In the long term I think he will be one of our most important people. In fact, he is now. He had to come almost from ground zero—learning welding, learning crawler tractors, learning fabrication. He has done remarkably well in the two years since he came to work here.

OPERATIONS

Figure 2 shows a typical crawler tractor with the main relevant parts labeled. Practically all of Sharpco's mechanical repair work and most of the parts sales are related to tractor undercarriages, final drives, and steering clutches. The undercarriage is that part of the tractor nearest the ground, including the heavy steel tracks along with rollers, sprockets, and structural members designed to pull the tracks and keep them in alignment. The final drive is a large closed gearbox which transmits power to the track. In Figure 2 the final drive is hidden from view behind the sprocket. The steering clutches are located above the final drives. They allow either the left or right final drive to be disengaged so that the brake can be applied on the respective side, causing the tractor to turn.

The tracks and related components cannot be insulated from the sand, dirt, and gravel in which a tractor usually operates. Consequently, all of the moving surfaces wear away steadily, especially those which are in contact with one another. The track chain is similar to a large bicycle chain. As the track is pulled by the sprocket around the idler and rollers, the pins wear mainly on just one side. Each pin fits into a bushing which also wears in the direction of the stress. A typical undercarriage will require major repair after 3000 hours of use and overhaul after 1500 additional hours. Major repair consists of removing the tracks and turning each pin and the respective bushing half around so that the least worn surfaces are in contact. To do this, a portable hydraulic press is used to press out one of the pins. This may require 200 tons of force. Then the tracks, weighing as much as 3,000 pounds each, are

FIGURE 2   **A typical crawler tractor.**

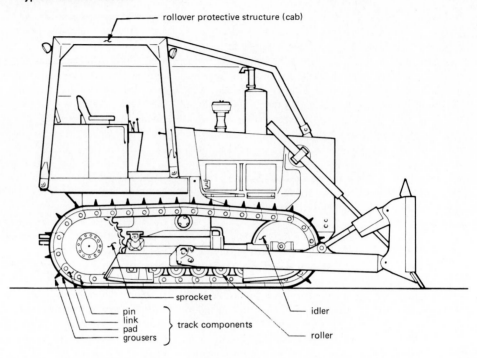

moved to the track press, where the remaining pins are pressed out, along with the respective bushings. All parts are then inspected and the tracks reassembled with the pins and bushings in their new positions. While the track is off, all undercarriage components are inspected for cracks, leaking oil seals, excessive wear, and other defects. Of course, any needed repairs are made before the tractor is reassembled.

When major overhaul is due, pins and bushings are replaced, idlers and rollers exchanged or reconditioned, and new sprockets are installed. With about every second major overhaul, worn grousers have to be cut off and new ones welded onto the track pads. The entire track chain may also have to be replaced. Less frequently, final drives and steering clutches require repair.

Among the items Sharpco manufactures are rollover protective structures (cabs) such as that shown on the tractor in Figure 2. Many of Sharpco's customers are involved in land clearing. The tractors they use must have heavy steel screens welded or bolted around the cabs to protect the operator from tree limbs. Sharpco makes and installs those screens as well. The cabs and screens are made from ordinary steel. However, most of the items the company makes involve the use of high strength steel, about three times as strong and hard as ordinary steel (and more than twice as costly). Several of these items are shown in Figure 3.

The special steel is used for cutting edges and strength members on the blades and buckets. This steel is purchased from major steel distributors and stocked in eight foot by twenty foot sheets, ranging in thickness from three-eighths of an inch to two inches. A portable acetylene cutting torch which runs on a small track is used to cut the steel to shape. Pieces which are to become cutting or digging edges are clamped in a vertical position and the edge beveled at a steep angle using the same kind of automatic torch. Curved pieces of mild steel (used for non-critical parts of digging buckets) and the steel pins and bushings used to attach the buckets to hydraulic excavators and backhoes are furnished by a local machine shop.

After the parts of a digging bucket or land clearing blade are cut and shaped they are welded together just enough to hold them. Then they are carefully inspected

FIGURE 3   **Items Sharpco makes using high-strength steel.**
(Drawn by Joy Kight.)

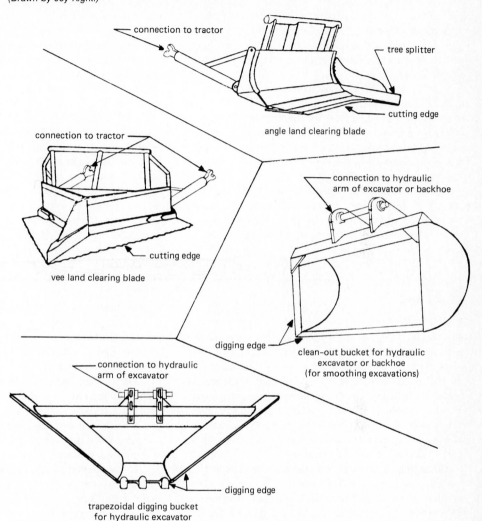

connection to tractor

tree splitter

cutting edge

angle land clearing blade

connection to tractor

connection to hydraulic
arm of excavator or backhoe

cutting edge

vee land clearing blade

digging edge

clean-out bucket for hydraulic
excavator or backhoe
(for smoothing excavations)

connection to hydraulic
arm of excavator

digging edge

trapezoidal digging bucket
for hydraulic excavator

prior to final welding. To ensure against failure, Sharpco workers weld all critical points manually, allowing components to cool between layers of weld material. This process requires special high strength electrodes (welding rods). Less critical welds can be made with semi-automatic machines, which are much faster and easier to operate than manual ones and which use large rolls of wire instead of individual welding electrodes.

Sharpco digging buckets range in size from small standard buckets weighing only 300 pounds to trapezoidal buckets weighing over a ton and measuring seventeen feet across. A trapezoidal bucket is designed to dig a complete drainage canal as the hydraulic excavator or backhoe to which it is attached slowly drives along the intended canal path, scooping out as much as three feet of new ditch with each stroke and laying the dirt aside. Sharpco land clearing blades and rakes weigh up to eight tons. The largest Sharpco vee-blade has two serrated cutting edges, each twenty feet long. Pushed by the largest production model tractor made by Caterpillar or Fiat-Allis, one of these blades clears a swath sixteen feet wide through timber up to thirty inches in diameter.

Blades and buckets require replacement of cutting edges and other wearing surfaces after extended use. Each item is designed so that the worn parts can be cut loose and new ones installed through a procedure similar to the original manufacture.

All of the items Sharpco reconditions or manufactures are painted at the Sharpco plant. Rollers and small parts are simply dipped into a paint vat. Larger items are spray painted. In addition, practically all of the equipment that comes in to be repaired is covered with dirt and mud. Cleaning is accomplished in the wash area using a special high pressure washer. Construction machinery and components to be repaired are usually brought to the Sharpco plant on customer trucks, although Sharpco does keep several trucks of varying sizes to make pickups and deliveries when necessary. The layout of the new Sharpco facility is shown in Figure 4.

MARKETING

Sharpco's customers include contractors, large farmers, and other heavy equipment owners, as well as equipment dealers who purchase Sharpco products and services for resale. Several equipment dealers employ Sharpco to repair tracks and recondition rollers and idlers for them.

Sharpco subscribes to a computerized used parts dealer network whereby subscribers exchange price and availability information on needed parts. As a result, the company ships an increasing number of parts, especially used ones, to dealers around the country.

Although the customer list totals more than 1,000, 100 contractors accounted for two-thirds of Sharpco's 1984 cash flow. For example, one land clearing contractor, with just four tractors, was billed $86,000 during 1984. Eighty percent of Sharpco's 1984 sales were to customers within a 100-mile radius of Monroe. "That is changing rapidly, though," said Peggy Turnage. "We are getting inquiries from all over the country because of the dealer network." For the months of August, September, and October 1984, 90 equipment owners, mostly contractors, were billed $342,742 out of Sharpco's total sales of $416,557. Shown this list of customers, James Sharplin identified 57 of them as having been regular customers for at least three years.

Sharpco's overall pricing policy, as expressed by James Sharplin, is "whatever the traffic will bear." For new tractor parts, he says, this is normally about 80 or 85 percent of dealer retail price. For used parts, it ranges from 25 to 60 percent of retail, depending upon whether the part in question is a frequently needed one or one which seldom fails. Sharpco prices its digging buckets at or above dealer list prices. According to James Sharplin, this is justified because the Sharpco buckets have a significantly lower failure rate than those equipment dealers furnish. When repair jobs are priced in advance, parts and labor are usually combined. Sharpco tries to stay just below usual original equipment dealer prices on such work. This often results in the loss of jobs to smaller independent service shops, which often price well below what major tractor dealers charge. About one-third of Sharpco's repair work is done on a time and materials basis. Under this kind of billing procedure, customers usually bargain on major components to be installed. But minor items (such as bolts, steel plate for welding reinforcement, and replacement track pads or links) are priced at 90 percent suggested retail, while labor is billed at standard billing rates, currently $26 per hour (local new tractor dealers charge an average of $28 an hour).

Prices are also used to keep Sharpco concentrated in its main businesses. When a customer insists that the company repair a transmission or engine, for example, the price for that work is intentionally elevated. Price changes are also used to control the overall level of work activity. When spurts in demand occur, hourly rates and markups on materials are increased, both for time and materials work and for work which is priced in advance. When demand slackens, workers are laid off until the crew is down to the ten or twelve person cadre of experienced workers. Only then are prices and markups sacrificed to sustain sales volume.

The primary means of promotion is direct mail. A typical mail out is illustrated in Figure 5. Currently the mailings are sent to all customers once a month. James has made plans, however, to program the company's computer to segment the mailing list along several dimensions and to mail more personalized advertisements to differing customer groups. Sharpco also spends about $700 a month on telephone yellow pages advertising. This provides for one-fourth page under "Contractors Equipment and Supplies," one-fourth page under "Welding," and a business card type advertisement briefly listing Sharpco's businesses under "Tractor Equipment & Parts." About once a quarter, Sharpco inserts a series of three two-page advertisements in consecutive issues of *The Contractor's Hotline,* a national weekly newspaper offering heavy equipment and parts for sale to about 5,000

FIGURE 4 **Sharpco plant layout.**

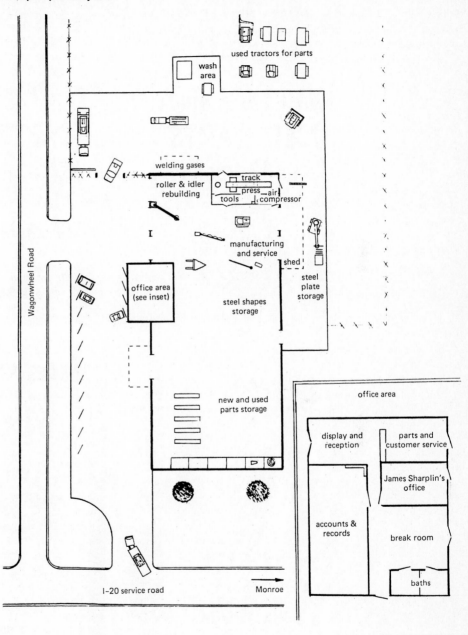

FIGURE 5   Typical direct mail advertisement.

Inside

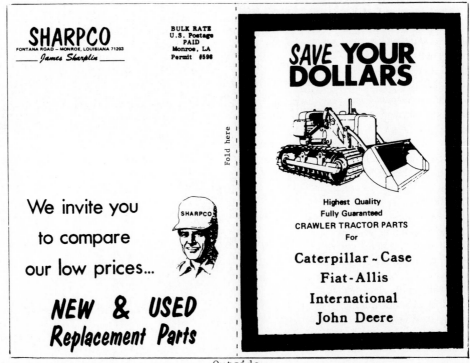

Outside

equipment owners and dealers. These advertisements cost about $1400 for each three week sequence. James, Jerry Thompson, and Tim Sharplin make infrequent sales calls within about 50 miles of Monroe.

FINANCE AND ACCOUNTING

Summaries of Sharpco's recent financial statements are provided in Appendix A. The short-term borrowings shown on the 1984 balance sheet are represented by 180-day notes held by a small bank in Delhi, Louisiana, the Sharplin family's hometown. These notes are secured by mortgages on Sharpco's inventories and the Sharpco plant. As they mature, accrued interest is paid and principal refinanced as needed. James has signed continuing guarantee agreements with regard to all present and future Sharpco debt at the bank.

The bank has agreed to convert the short term debt to a single five-year loan with fifteen-year amortization and interest established annually at the bank's prime rate, normally about $1\frac{1}{2}$ percent above New York prime. In addition to the five-year loan, the bank has agreed that it will provide Sharpco a $150,000 credit line for any needed additional working capital.

The long-term debt on the 1984 balance sheet includes a $200,000 purchase money obligation on the new Sharpco plant and the land on which it sits. The purchase-money mortgage is subordinated to the bank debt mentioned above. Sharpco's old plant with related long-term debt attached was given in part payment to the developer who built the new plant. By prior agreement with the developer, James Sharplin designed the office area and mechanical features (piping and electrical systems, cranes, etc.) of the new plant and constructed them using Sharpco workers and several subcontractors. This effort was financed with short-term bank borrowing. Upon completion, the new Sharpco facility was appraised at $760,000.

In early 1984, Peggy Turnage computerized the company's accounting records. The computer in use is a Dynabyte featuring 20 megabytes of hard disk storage, a 16-bit microprocessor, and three interactive terminals. The two extra terminals are located in James Sharplin's office and on the customer service counter. The new parts inventory of about 1500 items is carried on a first-in, first-out basis. When a used tractor is purchased for parts the cost of the tractor, plus all labor required to disassemble it, is added to used parts inventory. When a used part is sold, the entire selling price of the part is subtracted from the inventory line item representing the tractor from which it came. A subsidiary file is kept for each tractor, indicating which parts have been sold. So anyone inquiring at one of the terminals can easily determine which used parts are available for sale. James Sharplin has been advised that the accounting procedure he is following significantly understates the used parts inventory. Despite a recommendation from the company's CPA, he has not authorized changing the procedure.

Sharpco's steel inventory is taken at the end of each year and priced at current costs. The steel consists of plates (rectangular flat pieces four or more feet in both width and length) and shapes (long, straight pieces of various cross-sectional configurations—e.g., rounds, angles, beams, and channels). No plate or shape is included in inventory if any part of it has been used. In addition, a large quantity of steel, all entirely usable but of slow-selling shapes and sizes, is not counted because it has been declared "obsolete." As a result of these practices, the steel inventory is shown on company books at perhaps one-half its current market value. In addition, Sharpco owns many land clearing blades, digging buckets, and tractor parts which were "traded in" or abandoned by customers but for which no actual credit was given. Many of these items were later restored to usable condition during slack periods. Total value of these, as estimated by James Sharplin, is $15,000.

A job record is prepared for each customer order requiring shop work. One copy is kept in the office and another in a rack in the shop. Each worker is responsible for entering time worked on respective jobs. Parts and other materials issued to jobs are recorded on the office copies of job records. When a job is finished the shop copy of the job record is brought to the office and an invoice is completed.

Several years ago Peggy Turnage compared the time applied to customer jobs to the total time for which employees were paid. She found that fully one-third of employee time was unaccounted for. After telling of that experience, she said, "As soon as I can get the right computer program, I will set up a control system to charge every hour for which we pay employees to a customer job or to cleanup and maintenance."

INTERVIEW WITH JAMES SHARPLIN

The following are excerpts from an interview conducted on February 5, 1985.

Q James, what do you think is your most important business area?

A Well, I'd say used tractor parts are going to be our biggest money maker in the long run. When you can buy a D7E [a mid-size Caterpillar tractor] for $10,000, sell $25,000 worth of parts off it, and still have two-thirds of it left, that's got to be a good situation. More and more people are looking at saving that ten or fifteen percent, or whatever it is. They don't really care if the part is used or not as long as it is not hurt. The major tractor dealers have done a really good job, but their prices have just continued to climb. We're able to offer the customer a good part at fifty or sixty percent off dealer list. Customers are looking for that. They also know they can depend on us to install the parts we sell and to stand behind them. There is no question, also, that we are better at providing parts and undercarriage service for the whole list of crawler tractors—John Deeres, Caterpillars, Cases—than the average dealer is for just one brand of tractor.

Q What do you think are the major attributes that you or Sharpco has that will allow you to be successful—just in a general way?

A We know a great deal more about any undercarriage than dealers do. Of course, dealers have to know the whole tractor and we limit our mechanic work to the undercarriage. The various undercarriages are quite similar, of course, and we've just had a world of experience in that particular area. Also, there's not a better high quality welding shop, especially for construction equipment, in North Louisiana. We know that business. We're good at it.

Q What do you think about your crew right now, James? How does it stack up?

A On the whole, they're the best group of workers for this type of business in the Monroe area. We have to pick and choose the jobs that we put individual workers on but we put them on the jobs they're best at doing. Gene Lowe, for instance, is probably the best layout man and general welder that we've got. We use him just for that. But look at Jerry Hodges, who is our fastest welder. We'll let him weld the project out after Gene has cut out the pieces and tacked them together. Charlie LaBorde is real good with customers. So we like to send him out on field jobs, where he'll be in direct contact with the customer. Rodney Gee is another excellent man. He's a kind of handyman. He takes care of our tractor-trailor rig like it was his own. He's a good welder and a good mechanic. He just generally has a great attitude about anything Sharpco wants him to do.

Q What about the production things you do, the track press, for example, and the roller and idler shop?

A We run our track press operation quite differently from the way dealers do. We arranged the track press in a room by itself with all the necessary equipment—the turntable, all the tooling. We have it where one man can run the whole operation. It's a two-man job at most dealers. We've kept real good account of the number of hours it takes to do a job and we've steadily improved on that. The track press operator we have now, Juan Hernandez, has run the press for six years. He's by far the best I've ever seen. About a year ago, Juan hurt his back and Jerry Thompson and I filled in for him until he recovered enough to work again. He had major surgery. For at least a month or a month and a half after he came back we wouldn't let him lift anything. Just having him here during that time was a great help because he knew so much about how to set up the machine. We rebuild idlers by building up [with an automatic welder] the wear surfaces and replacing the seals—and they are as good as new. We do not weld on the rollers, though, like some dealers do. To get "new" quality, we replace the worn outer shells of rollers and reuse the shafts, bushings, and collars if they are not hurt. This costs more, and we lose some sales when customers just look at price. But I can't think of a single failure on one of our re-shelled rollers.

Q Why is the crew so small right now, James?

A I prefer to keep it small and work just a bit of overtime in order to keep a good steady crew over a long period of time. Besides that, it's so much easier to manage ten people compared to twenty people. I know all these people. I know their problems. I know what makes them tick. I know what will motivate them. When I had twenty or thirty people, I couldn't say that.

Q What are your long term plans now for Sharpco, James?

A Just to continue doing what we're good at and to keep our eyes open for any area where we can do a good job and make money: Grow if it will; but the big thing is to stay profitable and get it to where we can take just a little more time off.

Q Do you mean where *you* can take a little more time off?

A No. I mean the key people—Peggy, Jerry, Tim—and myself, of course.

Q What problems concern you most?

A Well, the problem is always the same: How to keep expenses down and jack up revenue. I do not ignore human costs but I have to focus mainly on dollars. There seems to be a conspiracy out there to keep us from making money. Besides, if we are profitable enough, I can handle most of the other problems that crop up. One thing I'm going to do, as soon as we get over the move, is to spend most of my time for two or three months with the computer and the accounting system, just getting on top of the numbers. I want to know where the sales and profits are coming from—geographically, of course; but also, what kinds of customers; what parts and services. I want to know where the costs are, too. We already know a lot of that. I just need to study it and set up the reporting system a little better. I also want to figure out the best ways to promote sales of parts, especially used ones, and digging buckets. The farm economy is down and land clearing is about dead. But there is always some construction work going on and people are tending to fix their old equipment rather than buy new stuff. We are broadening our market area, too.

Q James, how do you feel about your customers? Just tell me what your feelings are.

A Quite often, in dealing with them in the past from the place we had built over the years and which was at best just adequate for the job, I felt a little inferior. From the instant we moved into our new place I have felt better. For one thing, I'm not apologetic about a price, not timid at all about giving a man a price quick. I offered no apology yesterday when Charles Brooks said, "You're

killing me." I sense a new attitude on the part of customers. They seem to be more favorable towards us.

Q The question I was asking, James, had more to do with whether you develop any kind of personal relationship with your customers.

A Absolutely, with every one that I possibly can. Any way we can get interaction, joking or talking about common interests, we do. These things help me to remember the customer, of course. But it also gives us something to talk about and ask about the next time we see them. We've developed relationships with people that go back to when we first went in business. Take the Costello brothers. We're able to deal with them and do a great deal of business. Certainly, we give them prices, but I think the work—most of it anyway—would be ours regardless of the price. We know not to get ridiculous and they trust that we won't. Other customers, like Tom Fussel, have just become real close friends over the years. Tom came by here last week and said, "I'm gonna send you a picture of Sharpco when you first went in business. You had three blades in your only building. You didn't even have a door in the back. The shop was so small those three blades completely filled it." He said, "From there to here, you've come a long way—and during that time all the dealers seem to have gone downhill." And he just looked at me and said, "I wonder why that is?"

Appendix A: Financial Summaries

SHARPCO, INC., BALANCE SHEETS

	1981	1982	1983	1984
	Assets			
Current assets				
Cash	$ 49,420	$ 8,760	$ 10,205	$ 8,108
Accounts receivable	58,791	56,887	148,531	114,320
Reserve for bad debts	(9,974)	(19,702)	(22,311)	(20,659)
Notes receivable, stockholder	49,427	61,604	79,221	87,637
Inventory	177,322	95,308	144,499	315,108
Total current assets	$324,986	$202,857	$360,145	$504,514
Fixed assets				
Building and improvements	120,766	120,766	188,668	294,491
Machinery and equipment	141,897	141,897	113,444	113,444
Office furniture and equipment	15,856	15,856	13,464	27,943
Vehicles	54,431	62,556	104,021	95,896
Total	332,950	341,075	419,597	531,774
Less accumulated depreciation	163,271	197,074	194,408	138,219
Net depreciated assets	169,679	144,001	225,189	393,555
Land	34,010	47,770	55,530	95,000
Total fixed assets	$203,689	$191,771	$280,719	$488,555
Other assets				
Utility deposits	500	500	950	1,180
Total assets	$529,175	$395,128	$641,814	$994,249
	Liabilities and stockholders' equity			
Current liabilities				
Accounts payable	$ 28,458	$ 5,839	$ 48,487	$ 23,124
Accrued expenses	19,819	12,587	13,860	12,602
Withheld and accrued taxes	6,171	5,391	1,467	1,252
Accrued payroll	—	—	—	1,163
Accrued income taxes (overpayment)	11,636	(4,533)	(318)	6,430
Notes payable	171,600	81,281	185,872	268,505
Deposit from customers	9,000	—	—	—
Total current liabilities	$246,684	$100,565	$249,368	$313,076
Long-term liabilities				
Notes payable	21,293	8,094	59,390	259,009
Stockholders' equity				
Common stock	33,582	33,582	33,582	33,582
Less treasury stock	(11,316)	(11,316)	(11,316)	(11,316)
Retained earnings	238,932	264,203	310,790	399,898
Total stockholders' equity	$261,198	$286,469	$333,056	$422,164
Total liabilities and stockholders' equity	$529,175	$395,128	$641,814	$994,249

SHARPCO, INC., INCOME STATEMENTS

	1981	1982	1983	1984
Revenue				
Welding shop	$278,101	$ 297,547	$ 219,137	$ 268,366
Undercarriage shop	289,344	568,378	642,610	577,298
Direct parts sales	145,304	144,971	197,098	312,915
Steel	82,115	53,460	42,188	44,924
Miscellaneous	10,819	9,048	8,194	17,447
Total revenue	$805,683	$1,073,404	$1,109,227	$1,220,950
Direct costs				
Materials	327,829	565,993	559,097	570,100
Labor	80,117	100,499	112,259	118,684
Subcontractors	5,548	11,339	16,846	13,756
Freight	5,813	5,422	6,757	8,007
Other direct costs	238	77	50	560
Total direct costs	$419,545	$ 683,330	$ 695,009	$ 711,107
Gross profit	386,138	390,074	414,218	509,843
Indirect costs	318,779	359,336	361,599	408,125
Profit before taxes	67,359	30,738	52,619	101,718
Income taxes	11,636	5,467	6,032	12,610
Net profit	$ 55,723	$ 25,271	$ 46,587	$ 89,108

SHARPCO, INC. INVENTORIES,
DECEMBER 31, 1984

Steel	34,685
New parts	162,995
Used parts	100,152
Supplies	548
Finished goods	12,120
Work in process	4,608
Total	315,108

SHARPCO, INC. SALES BY MONTH (UNADJUSTED)

	1981	1982	1983	1984
Jan	55,974	73,463	60,666	51,492
Feb	67,743	91,547	82,996	74,689
Mar	78,002	111,144	69,295	41,780
Apr	73,360	79,510	52,365	70,196
May	85,944	126,957	45,374	151,595
Jun	32,936	77,153	94,390	142,620
Jul	65,898	108,988	137,806	142,505
Aug	69,470	138,695	138,878	116,862
Sep	66,891	95,743	87,621	183,710
Oct	77,054	83,119	149,283	115,987
Nov	76,967	56,725	105,716	49,168
Dec	51,325	24,812	76,682	64,228

SOLARTRON (A)

R. W. P. Blake
Henry W. Lane
The University of Western Ontario and Memorial University
The University of Western Ontario

Andre Marcil was elated. In five short years Solartron had grown from nothing to become one of the largest solar companies in Canada (see Exhibit 1). Now, with the awarding of the domestic hot water systems for 400 houses in Algeria, the company had taken its first significant move in developing its international market. As he sat contemplating the next move in his company's rapid expansion, Andre reviewed the events that had brought Solartron to its present position.

ANDRE MARCIL

Andre Marcil grew up in Hull, the eldest son of a wealthy Quebec businessman. Life in the Marcil household was hectic. The two boys and two girls competed constantly in almost any event involving speed. They were all competition calibre water and snow skiers and loved to drive fast. The purpose of life was to push and test oneself, to be constantly "on the edge".

Andre studied at the polytech in Hull where he completed a five-year mechanical engineering degree in three years. As one of two scholarship recipients in his graduating class, he moved to France to study for a Masters degree in nuclear engineering. During his 2½ years in Grenoble, Andre spent his summers working at Odelillo, site of the huge solar furnace. Andre worked on heat transfer and nuclear systems in the same building where solar engineers worked on solar heat transfer. Ongoing interaction between the groups made Andre think about the potential of solar energy and its application in Canada. When Andre returned to Canada in 1974, he was converted:

"I had specialized in nuclear engineering, but when I came back I knew that this was not what I was going to do in the long term."

Andre took a job in Ottawa, working on nuclear power plant design, engineering, and construction, but maintained his interest in solar, and continued the dialogue with his colleagues in France during regular visits to that country.

In 1974, total sales of solar systems in Canada were less than $18,000. In that year, the National Research Council (NRC) started a system of grants to promote research in the solar field. Andre's co-worker, Henri Char-

Case material of the Western Business School is prepared as a basis for classroom discussion rather than to illustrate effective or ineffective handling of an administrative situation. The names of people, places and organizations have been changed. The case was prepared by Research Associate Bill Blake under the supervision of Associate Professor Henry Lane.

Copyright © 1982, The University of Western Ontario.

818

EXHIBIT 1   SOLARTRON INC. STATEMENT OF INCOME 1978–1980

		Pro-forma	
	For the year ended Dec. 31, 1980	For the year ended Dec. 31, 1979	For the year ended Dec. 31, 1978
Sales and other operating revenues	$ 2,193,358	$ 950,490	$ 705,323
Cost of sales	1,499,853	651,839	428,868
	693,505	298,651	276,455
Other income			
Interest	150,491	26,618	27,250
Dividends	—	2,280	5,820
Gain on sale of marketable securities and other income	26,273	10,832	14,763
	870,269	338,381	324,288
Expenses			
Selling	289,975	115,384	118,486
Administrative	451,644	264,751	196,865
Interest and bank charges	4,009	11,594	24,504
Depreciation and amortization	35,347	24,089	7,469
	780,975	415,818	347,324
Loss before undernoted items	89,294	(77,437)	23,036
Write-off of mining properties and rights and deferred mining exploration and development expenditures	—	(779,464)	—
Equity loss of an affiliated company	(4,659)	—	—
Income taxes deferred	(39,800)	29,717	3,417
Profit (loss) before extraordinary items	44,855	($ 827,184)	($ 26,453)
Extraordinary items			
Gain on sale of marketable securities net of income taxes	445,282		
Reduction of income taxes on application of prior years' losses	39,800		
Net profit (loss)	$ 529,917		
Net profit (loss) per share before extraordinary items	$0.01		
Net profit (loss per share)	$0.15	($0.25)	—

est, believed that he could design a solar house and began doing systems designs with Andre.

Henri had a background in mechanical engineering and architecture. He too, had a long-standing interest in solar energy and it seemed natural for Andre and Henri to work together to build a solar house. Henri produced the plans for the house and the two men, working together, designed all the internal systems. Included in the house were solar air collectors for space heating and year-round solar heated hot water.

Media and public response to the house was overwhelming. Andre and Henri were proclaimed "the solar boy-wonders"; articles appeared in numerous magazines and newspapers and Andre was interviewed on radio and television about their home of the future. During the next few years the house was used as a laboratory by NRC and the Centre de Researches Industrielles du Quebec (CRIQ) to establish performance and operating characteristics of the system.

SOLENG

Andre and Henri were gratified and encouraged by the unexpected acknowledgement of their efforts. Both men wanted to be in business for themselves and on July 28, 1976, they incorporated "Soleng" along with Andre's brother, Alain, a marketing expert, as the third partner. Andre and Henri felt they could improve on the "Sunworks"[1] collector they had used in the house, and, working out of Henri's garage, they proceeded to develop their own systems.

Shortly after the incorporation of Soleng, the NRC announced a three-phase commercial, residential, industrial solar program. Soleng responded to a call for proposals in the monthly R&D bulletin, and received a contract to build three air and three liquid systems for six townhouses being built under a program known as NRC Phase II.

> "We just happened to hit the nail on the head and the timing was just right. We formed the company and immediately got a research grant to install solar systems in six townhouses."

Early in 1976, Andre left his job to work full time at Soleng. Later that year, he was joined by Henri and the two men worked together to build the young company.

In late 1976, the partners were approached by Trevor Duncan, Chairman of Metalfab, a manufacturer of mining equipment. He had read about Soleng in a newspaper article and wanted to meet the personnel involved in the company. Andre and Henri knew they needed cash to expand, but had found solar was not a sufficiently-developed concept to attract private investment capital. Duncan liked what he saw at Soleng and negotiations for Metalfab to buy into the company began.

Soleng was owned 50-25-25 by Andre, Henri, and Alain, and the partners now agreed to sell Metalfab 50%. In return they received 81,000 shares of Metalfab stock, $80,000 to buy equipment, access to a line of credit of $250,000 and a directorship on Metalfab's board for Andre. The major condition of the agreement was that Soleng enter into an agreement to license a known technology. To fulfill this condition, Soleng entered into a

---

[1]Sunworks, a large American solar company had supplied the collectors used in the solar house.

working agreement with Sunworks. Under the terms of the agreement, Soleng acquired the right to the use of technology, if it desired, based on payment of royalties. Although this agreement fulfilled the requirements of the sale to Metalfab Soleng did not exercise the option with Sunworks.

In 1977, Soleng had two basic products. The company was assembling flat-plate, air-cooled collectors at the rate of 100 per month, and was distributing low temperature swimming pool collectors. Although they were licensed to produce a Sunworks liquid high-temperature collector, this option was not being exercised. Andre and Henri had designed their own version of the liquid collector using fin and tube, as opposed to flat-plate surfaces. The fin, coated in black chrome over a nickel base, allowed much greater flexibility in the size of collectors produced. The fin and tube were being purchased in the United States as there was no machine in Canada capable of producing the sophisticated collector but Soleng executives were hoping to install a machine of their own shortly.

On July 4, 1978, the Minister of Energy, Mines and Resources (EMR), announced a 5 year, $380,000,000 program to promote the development of renewable energy technology in Canada. The plan called for implementation of the following programs for solar energy:

1 PUSH
  Purchase and Use of Solar Heating
  Public Works Canada to oversee the expenditure of $125,000,000 over 5 years for solar systems on government buildings.
2 PASEM
  Program of Assistance to Solar Equipment Manufacturers
  $3,100,000 to be distributed to private firms by the Solar Programs Office of Public Works Canada to increase their design and manufacturing ability (later increased to $4,100,000).
3 LENDA
  Low Energy Building Design Awards
  $350,000 for a design competition to encourage the use of passive solar heating.
4 Federal provincial demonstration agreement
  $114,000,000 to demonstrate promising conservation and renewable energy technologies
  10% to be spent on solar.
5 Research and development
  $14,000,000 for solar research and development.

The key to the future for Soleng was the PASEM program. The Solar Programs Office of Public Works Canada sent PASEM application forms to any company it felt might be interested in solar. Of the 152 firms responding, 24 were awarded grants of between $8,000 and $10,000 to prepare detailed proposals. On May 3, 1979, ten of these companies, including Soleng, were selected to receive grants ranging upwards from $200,000 for product development and marketing and production advances. The contract stipulated that PASEM could cover up to 50% of capital expenses and 75% on non capital expenses.[2] At the end of the 14 month contract, firms were to deliver their production prototypes of new products developed under PASEM for independent testing.

Because the Canadian Solar industry was dependent on government funding in all areas other than swimming pool collectors, the PUSH program was a critical part of the continued stability of virtually all of the Solar companies. A delay in the implementation of the PUSH program threatened the revenue source on which many companies were counting. To prevent the possible collapse of the industry, a further $1,000,000 was added to the PASEM funding.

As one of the ten companies selected to receive a grant Soleng was awarded $335,045. Of this amount $150,901 was spent on equipment such as test benches, hydraulic presses, dies, punches, and saws. Money was also allocated to technical and design developments.

In 1979, the PUSH program finally began to function effectively. The program was to spend $125,000,000 over 5 years on the installation of solar systems in government buildings. Of this amount, approximately $20,000,000 would accrue directly to the manufacturers of the solar equipment.

The process by which new contracts were awarded was complex. Any government agency or department could submit a preliminary feasibility study through Public Works to Treasury Board. If approved at this level, $8,000 could be allocated for an engineering study and final design preparations, to be carried out by a private engineering company. If Public Works approved the design and Treasury Board approved construction funds, the originating agency would place a call for tenders for construction. These tenders would be submitted by mechanical contractors and would be awarded on the basis of

lowest price meeting the specifications. Because the mechanical contractor was the selector of the technology utilized, Alain Marcil's main job, as marketing manager, became the establishment and maintenance of a relationship with the approximately 100 contractors who might submit bids on various contracts. The company also sought to develop good working relationships with the consulting engineers in the hope that they might influence the specifications chosen for the collectors/systems for a particular project.

FINANCING EXPANSION

By mid 1979, Andre had done a considerable amount of thinking about the future of solar energy in Canada. He realized the company was overly dependent on government support and would not be commercially viable without that support. His conclusion was that the company would have to expand and eventually seek markets outside the country in order to survive. Such an expansion would require more planning and much more money. Financing was the key to Andre. He had ambitious plans: "I didn't want to stay a small Ontario company in Solar and was afraid Soleng was going to run out of cash." Exploratory feelers for $1,000,000 over two years from Metalfab evoked the response that the industry was unproven and had no track record; Metalfab was unwilling to put up more money and Andre would have to raise it elsewhere.

At this point Andre first considered the idea of selling stock. No solar company in Canada had gone public and Duncan thought the industry was too new for Soleng to be listed on the Toronto Exchange through normal procedures. After seeking advice from lawyers in Toronto, Andre decided to become a public corporation by buying a majority interest in a listed company and changing its focus to solar. A search began for an energy company with few assets and an inactive stock.

The search yielded three names and it was finally decided to bid on the open market for shares of Fick Holdings, a company involved in small scale oil and gas exploration. There were 4,466,000 shares outstanding and Andre estimated that he would need over $1,000,000 to buy the shares necessary to gain control of Fick and to finance future expansion. To raise the required funds, he sold six blocks of Soleng treasury stock totalling 835,000 shares at $1.15 a share. This resulted in a net to the company of $893,000 after a 7% sales commission. Andre then purchased 1,200,000 shares of Fick Holdings at $.25

---

[2]This was subsequently increased to cover 100% of capital expenses and between 75% and 100% of non-capital expenses.

share. Following this transaction Fick merged with Soleng on the basis of 4 shares of Fick for one share of Soleng.

Following the amalgamation, all shares of Soleng were converted into shares of "Solartron", a new name for a company that would be involved in oil and gas exploration and in all forms of renewable energy. To raise money for Solartron, 500,000 Treasury shares were sold at $3.25 each. This established a value for the new company, and over the subsequent weeks, the stock price rose rapidly to $5.25, at which point, the TSE ordered a "stop trading" to identify the cause of the sudden jump. After the stop trading was removed, the stock value drifted down and stabilized around the $3.00 level.

The restructuring left Metalfab as the largest shareholder in Solartron with 29%, and Andre as the largest individual shareholder with 10%. The 3,259,860 shares were held as follows:

Soleng Management	653,344
Metalfab	980,016
Private Placement Purchase	835,000
Fick Holdings Shareholders	791,500

Giving up control didn't bother Andre who knew his knowledge and ability were the heart of Solartron.

"I don't give a damn about having control because I control with 10% anyway."

ENTER PAUL SHAW

In 1980 Paul Shaw joined Solartron as general manager for Ontario. Paul had been in solar since 1972 and had been one of Andre's major competitors. He had a B.Sc. from the University of Kentucky and had built his own land development corporation after graduation. In 1972, in an attempt to develop a solar collector for his swimming pool he built nineteen prototypes, none of which worked. Paul decided to visit Redwood, California, home of Fafco, the largest solar company in the world. Paul developed a close relationship with the company and bought five swimming pool collectors to bring back to Canada. He took them to the pool and patio show in Toronto "strictly for fun" and easily sold the collectors. The Fafco collector was the first collector displayed in Canada and the Ontario Research Foundation monitored the collectors for the remainder of that year. The following year Paul sold 50 of the systems and decided he should go into solar

full-time or drop the concept. He elected to go with solar and in 1975 sold $100,000 worth of solar pool systems. By 1978, sales had reached $800,000 and Paul sold 80% of the company to Tamas Investments with a buyback clause which allowed him to repurchase the shares on each anniversary of the sale. The company's name was changed to Solont with Paul as vice-president. The main reason Paul sold out was that Tamas Investments promised to fund his ongoing research. In 1973 when financial problems caused Tamas to sharply curtail R&D spending, Paul exercised his option and bought the company back.

Paul still held the Fafco Canadian licence and Soleng was his largest customer and Quebec distributor. He and Andre had met numerous times and had developed a strong mutual respect.

When the PASEM program was announced, Anston Industries, a $400,000,000 company, bought Solont and merged it with Sunpower and Cansun, producers of high temperature collectors, under the new name, Sunpower. Sunpower received a PASEM grant and found itself in direct competition with Solartron with whom it fought vigorously for market share. Sunpower had hoped to manufacture the Fafco collector in Canada and Paul estimated a $100,000 start-up cost. Sun Glow and Poolwarmers were already producing similar products in Canada and Paul recommended buying out Poolwarmers, a small company based in Chatham, Ontario.

Paul was not the only one looking at Poolwarmers. Solartron was also interested and Andre was first to move.

At this time the majority of Solartron sales were in two basic products, the flat plate collector and the swimming pool collector. The latter was being purchased from Poolwarmers and Andre now purchased a 50% interest in that company in exchange for 12,500 shares of Solartron, then valued at $3.10 a share. Solartron was the largest supplier of pool-heating systems in Canada and had developed an excellent distribution network across the country. Working with the basic Poolwarmer product, a black co-polymer collector, Solartron personnel added a corrugated co-polymer sheet as glazing and created an airspace between the glazing and the collector. The result was a low-cost, medium temperature collector which gave Solartron an even stronger position in the pool market.

When the PUSH program was delayed, swimming pool collectors were the only profitable solar business in Canada. Shaw wanted to compete head-to-head with Solartron and when his Board said no, he resigned, leaving the company early in 1980.

In subsequent discussions with Andre, Shaw stated his intention to go into private consulting. He also told Andre he would be interested in working with Solartron if he received shares in the company. Joining Solartron as general manager for Ontario he started to develop operations in that province.

Solartron had not faired well in obtaining PUSH contracts in Ontario largely because, despite its Ottawa base, most of the business was in Quebec and it tended to be regarded as a Quebec company. The two men now pursued a strategy which saw Solartron develop enough of a facility in Hamilton to be viewed as an Ontario company which, combined with Shaw's reputation and his knowledge of key people in the Ontario industry, allowed Solartron to compete successfully for a number of contracts. In 1980 Solartron's Ontario sales were $150,000 but the following year this figure jumped to over $1,000,000.

Paul Shaw and Andre Marcil enjoyed a relationship of mutual respect. Shaw believed they were unbeatable in their connections and their knowledge of operation, engineering and the business in general. His personal desire was to reduce the company's dependence on the government and to this end he worked on setting up a Biomass Division and the acquisition of Ensave[3] with its energy audit capability. On the solar side however, he continued to work with government to identify projects, as well as engineers to lock-in structural design and with mechanical contractors on the job. Shaw hoped to direct the eventual move of Solartron into the American market and hoped to make the company the largest solar company in the United States.

SOLARTRON

With the merger with Fick Holdings and the purchase of an interest in Poolwarmers complete, Solartron was now structured into two divisions. The petroleum division was to concentrate on the acquisition of oil and gas lands in North America for the purpose of exploiting proven resources and carrying out wild-cat drilling. The Soleng division would offer a full range of solar products and services for residential, commercial and industrial applications (see Exhibit 2).

[3]Ensave produced differrential solar controls and offered an engineering energy audit service.

With cash available for expansion, Solartron turned to the international market. Andre had already concluded that Solartron would have to seek markets outside Canada in order to survive but considered the American market as too large and expensive to penetrate. In addition, the 200 manufacturers in the United States made for an extremely competitive environment.

Andre felt more comfortable in France than in the U.S.A. His wife was French and he had developed an affection for the country during his student days. Andre believed that a Canadian company in Europe would be perceived as part of "North American technology" and receive better acceptance and respect than it would receive in the States. He also felt that there would be more "return for effort overseas". His first tentative move offshore had been to license a low-temperature pool collector to Sogen, a French company, for a straight fee of $25,000. He recognized however that a well thought out strategy would be required for further expansion. Because Energy, Mines and Resources was the focus for government solar programs, Andre went to them to solicit information on government assistance for international expansion. He was referred to Industry, Trade and Commerce, who in turn suggested the Canadian International Development Agency's (CIDA) Industrial Co-operation Division for work in the third world (Exhibit 3). Since the "sun belt", where solar was most feasible, encompassed many third world countries, and because these countries were being crippled by the soaring oil prices, the third world seemed a logical market to pursue.

Shortly after the initial discussions with CIDA, Solartron was involved in its first international tender. An Algerian agent visiting Ottawa suggested Solartron bid on a contract to supply 1,000 solar hot water heaters for the "Bondu Authority Project". Fifty-two companies from 35 countries submitted bids on the project and Solartron was one of three to make the short list. At this point, the Canadian Government agencies moved to support Solartron and Industry, Trade and Commerce, Export Development Corporation and CIDA all got involved in final negotiations.

Notification of the tender award had just been made and Marcil was elated. Solartron had received a contract for 400 of the 1000 domestic hot water systems to be installed and Andre was sure that this opportunity would open the door to further international expansion. Even as he started to plan the steps necessary to fulfill the contract, he was wondering what Solartron's next step should be.

EXHIBIT 2 SOLENG DIVISION PRODUCT LINE

Low-temperature solar thermal collectors

Pool heating systems are the only true consumer market for solar products. Solartron uses a conventional network of 125 distributors/dealers each of which has its own sales and installation force. Solartron provides marketing and technical services material and offers a bi-annual two-week installation course. Dealers normally split their sales force in two ways. Account reps call on contractors and pool builders while salesmen focus on retrofit sales, (the selling of the systems to pool owners who presently have an oil or gas heating system). While the dealer/distributor offers a full range of thermo-solar products, sales are almost exclusively in pool collectors.

The basic pool collector is made of extruded black plastic composed of hundreds of small squared tubes extruded side by side with a sub manifold and header pipe, heat welded on at each end.

The collectors are hooked up in series as required with systems selling in the $1500–$3000 range. Payback is approximately two years.

A glazed version of the basic collector can pre-heat process water to 50 degrees centigrade.

Soleng also sells pool blankets which act as a heat insulator at night and under cloudy conditions.

Medium-temperature collectors

Because of high costs and the climate in northern latitudes, domestic hot water collectors are still not economically viable in Canada although federal and provincial governments are subsidizing a number of pilot studies. Since most sales are government contracts, selling in this market requires close contact with government officials, design engineers and mechanical contractors. Internationally the domestic hot water "thermo-syphon" system is a key product. This low cost package is in high demand for new housing projects and for energy poor countries. Marketing in these countries involved tendering on projects and having a superior product at a competitive price. For this reason, price and quality are the key success factors.

Soleng produces four sizes of medium temperature collectors. These are flat plate copper collections with a black chrome over nickel selective surface. Unique features allow up to 25 collectors to be hooked up in parallel and a very low installation cost.

Medium temperature collectors are suitable for domestic hot water and certain commercial and industrial applications.

Industrial and high-temperature collectors

Sales in this area are almost exclusively through government-financed projects. Factory authorized representatives are used and are assigned geographic territories. Through regular calls on engineers, designers, architects, government agencies and mechanical contractors, they try to get Soleng products specification used in technical specifications in the contracts. Agents work on commissions ranging from 7 to 12%.

There are two major types of high temperature collectors. The evacuated tube concept is used for process water and low pressure steam while concentrating collection, using flat plate track and mirrors focusing on a single evacuator tube, can be used for high temperature processed water and low pressure steam for power generation.

Other products and services

Sun stock

Sun Stock is a flexible "mat" collector used to heat and cool greenhouses. This polyethelene/polypropolene flexible type collector is deposited on the ground of greenhouses, with flowers or vegetables growing through the collector mats.

Black chrome fin tubes

These modular copper fin tubes selectively coated with the exclusively black chrome over nickel electroplating process, are available for the manufacturing Solartron license.

Computer programs

Solartron in close cooperation with Sunworks, developed a complete set of software computer programs aimed at sizing solar systems and simulating collector performances on an ongoing daily basis in different geographical locations as well as environmental conditions. This computer service is offered to representatives and to several chosen designers and government agencies in order to help them determine the comparative thermal performance of the different solar collectors available in the market.

EXHIBIT 3   CIDA'S INDUSTRIAL COOPERATION PROGRAM[1]

The need

Strengthened economic ties between Canada and rapidly industrializing nations of the Third World.

Development assistance tailored to the changing needs and priorities of developing countries.

The response

Mutually profitable business relationships between Canadian companies and their developing country counterparts, e.g.:

- joint ventures
- direct investments
- management contracts
- licencing agreements
- co-production arrangements
- technical cooperation
- technology transfer
- project preparation studies
- information development and dissemination

The program

For Canadian Companies wishing to investigate industrial cooperation opportunities in developing countries:

- funding for travel, profitability and risk analyses, product/technology testing;
- funding for project preparation studies as a lead-in to large capital projects;
- funding for demonstration/test projects as a lead-in to technology transfer;
- leads and information on opportunities, and on local conditions and business practice;
- assistance in locating qualified Canadians to work abroad;
- specialized training of local employees;
- professional services to cope with special situations, such as complex tax or legal problems;
- investment missions to developing countries.

For developing countries seeking Canadian private sector participation in their economic development:

- investment-seeking missions to Canada;

- information on Canadian technology and expertise;
- trade facilitation;
- business training in Canada and in home country;
- linkages between Canadian and local business and manufacturing organizations;
- public sector institution building in cooperation with Canadian counterpart institutions;
- technical assistance to businesses requiring short term experts;
- long term credits for the use of Canadian consultants or experts to assist in delineating industrial development priorities, promoting and managing exports, and providing direct, continuing expert advice to all segments of the economy, private and public.

The recipient

Canadian business and industry, defined as businessman, proprietorships and limited companies subject to Canadian law.

Preference will be given to small and medium size companies;

most developing countries

STARTER AND VIABILITY STUDIES

Background

The need for developing countries to industrialize is self-evident as is the need for Canada to develop closer economic ties with these trading partners of the future. Long term, mutually beneficial business relationships between Canadian companies and local entrepreneurs can assist in fulfilling both needs.

Purpose

To reduce the front-end costs a Canadian company must incur to investigate opportunities in developing countries for joint ventures, direct investment, licencing agreements, co-production arrangements, long term management contracts, etc.

Coverage

Starter studies   (preliminary analyses of opportunities) Up to $10,000 per project for:

---

[1]This information is reproduced from the pamphlet "CIDA's Industrial Cooperation Program" published by the Canadian International Development Agency, Ottawa, Ontario.

EXHIBIT 3   CIDA'S INDUSTRIAL COOPERATION PROGRAM (*Continued*)

a return economy air fare for approved personnel (may include nationals of the country concerned) between Canada and the site(s) of the proposed project;

b accommodation and living expenses at $95 per day; and

c reasonable support services.

Viability studies   (detailed evaluation of projects)
Up to $100,000 on a matching basis as follows:
100% reimbursed
a return economy airfare for approved company personnel from Canada to the site(s) of the proposed project;
b accommodation and living expenses at $95 per day.
50% reimbursed:
a fees and expenses paid to outside consultants, lawyers and accountants and other necessary services. Travel costs will be accepted at economy class and accommodation and living expenses at $95 per day;
b expenses for testing to determine product, raw material, or process suitability; and
c economy class travel to Canada by approved personnel from the developing country, and accommodation and living expenses at $95 per day.

Criteria

Following discussions with CIDA, the company must submit an application outlining:

a the nature and scope of the project
b the company's ability to implement it, i.e. its financial, managerial and technical resources, as well as its record of business achievements to date;
c the contribution of the project to the particular country's development priorities, e.g.:

use of local labour
upgrading of skills
use of local materials
export or import substitutions potential

Eligible applicants
Canadian firms

CANADIAN TECHNOLOGY TRANSFER FACILITY (CTTF)

Background

Access to Canadian technology could significantly improve the development of many of the world's less advantaged nations. However, the cost of proving that the technology is appropriate in a developing country environment often restricts its availability and prevents companies from taking advantage of its potential for application overseas.

The CTTF is intended to apply to both process and product technology on two bases:

a traditional or stable technology in which the pace of change is relatively slow but for which refinements or adaptations may be required to meet particular environmental considerations;
b state-of-the-art or unstable technology in which the pace of change is so rapid that new generations of technology occur frequently and are often remarkably different than their immediate predecessors, but nevertheless at each stage may offer significant advantages for implementation or replacement of previous technology.

Purpose

To enable Canadian firms to test and adapt their technology in developing countries as a lead-in to long-term cooperation with their developing country counterparts.

Coverage

Up to $250,000 per project for up to 75% of the net costs of a test/demonstration in an eligible developing country.

Frequency

a for stable technology, generally one test in each of Latin America/Caribbean, Africa and Asia;
b for rapidly evolving technology, generally one test at any discrete stage in the technological development.

Criteria

Following consultations with CIDA, the company must submit a proposal outlining:

a the type of process/product technology; its level of development in Canada and its appropriateness to the developing country;
b its intention to engage in long-term cooperation in the country concerned;
c its intention to transfer all or part of the technology to the country concerned via mechanisms such as joint ventures, licencing, co-production, etc.
d the need for and scope of the test;
e the estimated costs of the test;
f the ensuring benefits to the developing country and to Canada;
g the track record of the applicant and the company's ability to follow through.

Eligible applicants

Canadian firms

TENNESSEE VALLEY AUTHORITY (TVA)

George S. Vozikis
Timothy S. Mescon
Memphis State University
Salisbury State College

INTRODUCTION: HISTORY OF TVA

The Tennessee Valley Authority (TVA) is a federally owned but largely self-financing corporation. Its three-member board directs a multi-faceted program of approximately $5 billion that profoundly affects the lives of more than six million people in a 7-state region (Figure 1), and over the years TVA has attracted worldwide attention as an example of "integrated regional development" (Neuse, 1983: 492).

Background

This anomaly among U.S. government agencies was created by the Tennessee Valley Authority Act of 1933 to provide decentralized administration removed from Washington that would have the management flexibility of a private corporation. From the perspective of half a century, TVA can now be seen as the convergence of "unique circumstances . . . , unique times . . . and unique personalities . . ." (Callahan, 1980: 362). A century of complex issues preceded the founding of TVA, but the unique immediate circumstances were the necessity of the federal government to dispose of its two World War I nitrate plants and partially completed Wilson Dam at Muscle Shoals, Alabama, and the willingness of polit-

ical Conservatives and Progressives to unite against powerful alleged private power trusts. The unique time was the Depression in which the largely rural and already poverty-stricken Tennessee Valley area was hard hit. The unique personalities were President Franklin D. Roosevelt and Senator George Norris, who were able to gain approval for an idealistic experiment for the unified development of the resources of a whole region. The TVA Act assigned broad responsibilities to provide navigation and flood control, reforestation and the proper use of marginal lands, agricultural and industrial development, and aid to national defense by the operation of the Muscle Shoals properties (Tennessee Valley Authority Act, 1933). The original three directors had equal votes. Given a broad charter, they essentially assumed direction of the areas in which they had most interest annd expertise.

The generation and sale of electrical power was not a significant point in the TVA Act, although the corporation was allowed to sell excess hydro power. An early struggle over the course TVA should take ensued among the directors and eventually culminated in the dismissal of one and the assumption of dominant direction by the electrical power advocate. Therefore, although regional development has remained an important part of TVA's management philosophy, the power program has dominated TVA operations almost from the beginning, and now accounts for 95 percent or more of its total budget.

827

FIGURE 1   **The region served by the Tennessee Valley Authority.**

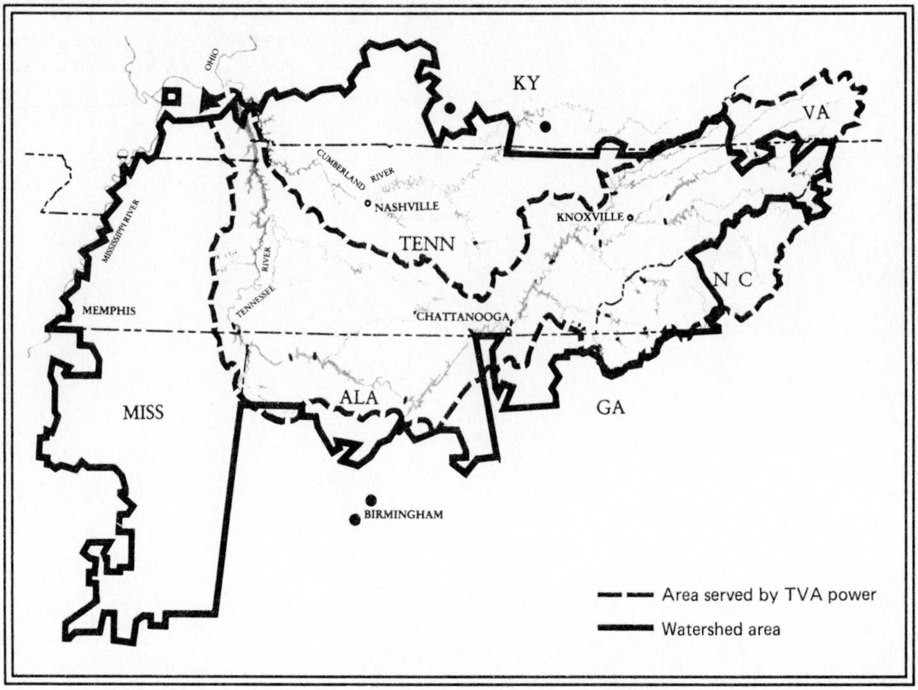

Development of TVA

The evolution of TVA has been marked by periodic struggles—usually with Congress—that resulted in redefinition or clarification of its role primarily as an electric utility. This evolution resembles a classic organizational life cycle (Figure 2):

The Creation and Construction Phase, 1933–1939, saw the start of construction on most of the high dams on the main river (Owen, 1973). This was also a period of protracted litigation in which private utilities challenged the constitutionality of the TVA Act and TVA's right to sell electric power. The issue was finally settled by a U.S. Supreme Court ruling in 1939, allowing TVA to begin consolidating its power system (Hobday, 1969).

The Consolidation Phase, 1940–1949, was marked by the acquisition of more customers, beginning with municipal utility corporations and ultimately negotiating for the transmission lines and facilities of private utilities. Also, as a result of increased power demands for the World War II effort, especially for the Manhattan Engineer District at Oak Ridge (Owen, 1973), dam construc-

tion was stepped up and one steam plant was built and others purchased. The excess power capacity after the war was not a serious problem because demand soared. After a bitter congressional debate, TVA was allowed in 1949 to construct the first in a series of large coal-fired steam plants that would become the backbone of the TVA power generating system.

The Expansion Phase, 1950–1959, achieved greatly increased generating capacity through the addition of large steam plants to meet the power demands of residential consumers and the Atomic Energy Commission. As a result, however, the issue of continued public financing of TVA's capacity to meet a steadily growing demand for cheap electricity became highly controversial, resulting during the Eisenhower administrations in renewed opposition from private utilities and suggestions for selling off parts of TVA. In 1959 amendments to the TVA Act made the power program totally self-financing from power revenue and the sale of bonds (Droze, 1983; Leiserson, 1983). In addition, the TVA power distribution area was limited essentially to its then existing boundaries.

The Growth Phase, 1960–1973, was one of cheap

FIGURE 2   **TVA organizational life cycle.**

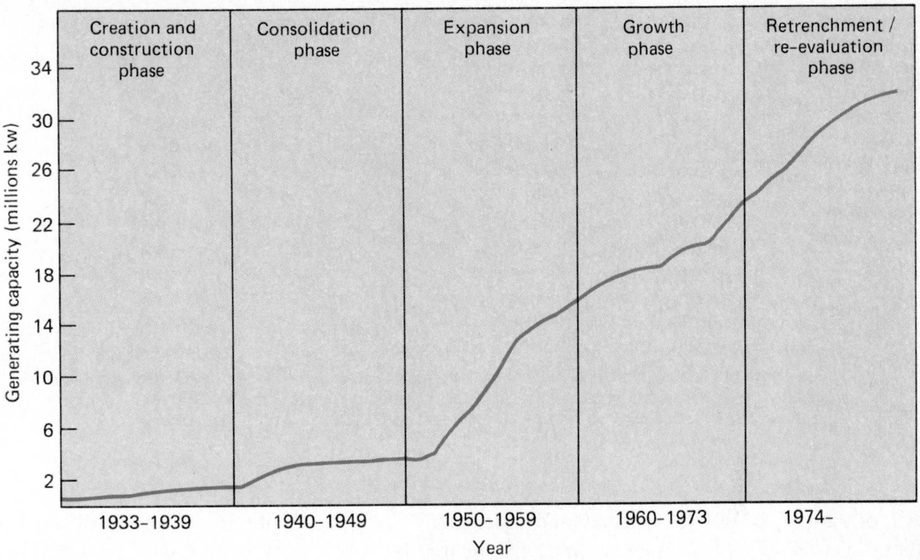

electricity in which the size of TVA's power program grew rapidly and TVA residents became highly dependent on electric power, achieving the highest average consumption of electricity in the nation (Chandler, 1984: 120). The demand for electricity increased by 170 percent in this period (Dean, 1985a: 2). Projections of continued demand growth, rising costs for coal and its environmental problems, and the availability by the mid-1960's of nuclear equipment of a scale competitive with steam plants made, as the current TVA chairman explains, "the nuclear option increasingly attractive" (Dean, 1985a). By the time of the oil embargo that created a major energy crisis in late 1973 and 1974, TVA was committed to seven construction projects involving 17 nuclear reactors, a program that would be the largest nuclear power system in the Western world.

The period from 1974 to today has been one of Retrenchment and Re-evaluation. Inflation, skyrocketing coal prices, high interest rates, nuclear accidents, increased regulations, and costly construction delays and changes made a shambles of the TVA forecasts and long-range plans. Rising utility rates led to decreased demand and necessitated higher rate increases in a vicious cycle. The region over which TVA had won so much control began to spin out of control as its ratepayers, citizen action groups, and others became vocal critics, some criticizing

not merely rates but the total concept of TVA (Chandler, 1984).

Current Issues

The major problems of TVA today come from two related sources. The first is related to the unusual relationship between TVA and the people of the TVA area that stems from the "grassroots" theory of TVA's beginnings, i.e., that the people own TVA (Cheuse, 1983; Neuse, 1983). The TVA ideology has become both a blessing and a curse. Because it is a government agency in a representative democratic society, TVA must, like other businesses, attempt to satisfy its customers. Their desires are clear: adequate power, cheap rates, *and* clean air and water. The "owners" were content to be passive when TVA power rates were extremely low; but, now that rates are rising steeply, they are attempting to exert more control. In attempting to achieve its objectives, TVA is facing increasing public and political pressure, as evidenced by its disfavor with Congress which has been aired frequently in the media recently (*Huntsville Times,* 1985a; 1985d).

Thus, one major issue facing TVA today is how to operate effectively, and perhaps even how to survive in this environment. The second and related issue is how to best adjust operations to recover from the devastating ef-

FIGURE 3   PROJECTED U.S. GENERATING CAPACITY[1] BY FUEL TYPE
(Megawatts)

Fuel	1982		1987		1992	
	Capacity	% of total	Capacity	% of total	Capacity	% of total
Coal	252.227	43.0	293.803	43.9	325.909	45.5
Nuclear	55.662	9.5	101.657	15.2	113.508	15.5
Hydro	80.475	13.7	85.157	12.7	87.487	12.2
Oil	76.797	13.1	67.810	10.1	66.982	9.3
Gas	43.296	7.4	42.677	6.4	39.850	5.8
Dual fuel	75.989	13.0	73.299	10.9	70.255	9.8
Other	1.696	0.3	5.520	0.8	12.906	1.8
Total	586.142	100.0	669.923	100.0	716.897	100.0

[1]Installed generating capacity at time of (noncoincident) system peak. Note nuclear and total capability (1987 and 1992) have been adjusted to reflect utilities' current projections of operating dates for nuclear units under construction.
Source: Standard & Poor's, 1984: U18, from North American Electric Reliability Council

fects of the nuclear power construction disaster that TVA shares in common with a number of other electric utilities. Therefore, before attempting to evaluate TVA's position, it is necessary to examine the utilities industry in order to place TVA in proper perspective.

THE POWER INDUSTRY

Industry Structure

The power industry currently is a regulated monopoly. The wholesale portion of the industry is federally regulated, and the retail portion is regulated by the states. Previously highly predictable, blue-chip stocks are now unstable, and many companies are diversifying to broaden their business base. Until recent years, pricing was determined by the various public service commissions on the basis of whatever was needed for adequate profit for the company, but this practice is no longer automatic.

The electric utility industry comprises about 3,000 companies supplying more than 92 million households, commercial businesses, and industrial operations. There are four distinct ownership segments: investor-owned firms, public systems owned by the federal government, public systems owned by states and municipalities, and cooperatives (Fenn, 1984).

The industry today is quite different from the approximately 2,000 private utility systems that existed in the 1920's. About 200 investor-owned utilities now dominate the industry. They generate 78 percent of the power and

supply 76 percent of all retail customers. The six federal systems account for almost 10 percent of generating capacity. Although the 2,000 municipal, state, and regional systems generate only about 9 percent of total electricity, they account for about 15 percent of total electricity sales. In 1980 the 900 rural co-ops accounted for only 2.8 percent of power generation, but this represented significant growth from 1.7 percent in 1970 and 0.7 percent in 1960. In addition to building their own generating plants, the co-ops in recent years have become involved in numerous generating project joint ventures with investor-owned utilities.

In many areas of the country, utility systems are highly interconnected through formal or informal coordination agreements. These interstate "power pools" account for over 40 percent of the nation's generating capacity (Fenn, 1984).

Trends

Forecasters are split over whether power demand will increase or decrease over the next 20 years; the majority see a small increase. In either case the utilities will have to deal with competition, for the first time for most of them.

The major sources of competition at present are (1) conservation and cogeneration, (2) other utilities, and (3) other energy forms. Conservation reduces demand in the same way as losing business to another supplier. Conservation competition ranges from efficient light bulbs to generators; e.g., General Electric sells big turbines to utilities and small ones to users. The Japanese may be shipping small residential cogenerators by 1988. Conservation to date has barely scratched the surface of potential savings.

Excess capacity has resulted in competition in wholesale marketing, to the extent permitted by federal regulations. Utilities are using rates to lure industrial users to relocate to their service areas. New municipal power companies are being set up to replace investor-owned utilities, sometimes offering 40 percent rate savings. An excess capacity of electric power in Canada is being dumped as far south as Maryland and Pennsylvania.

Natural gas is aggressively trying to regain markets lost to electricity in the past, especially in consumer appliances, heating, and industrial processes, and also is now moving into the electricity market via gas-fueled generators. Solar heating continues to erode usage of electricity, as do other renewable sources, such as wind-powered generators and wood heaters.

Regulations

Regulations have caused most of the electricity price increases—e.g., periods when oil and gas were banned as fuels, and the burdening of coal and nuclear plants with environmental controls. In the past, utilities have been allowed to pass along all costs to consumers, but they are meeting increasing resistance.

The current proposals range from complete deregulation to government ownership of utilities. None of the proposals is acceptable to all of the affected parties. The deregulatory proposals rest on the premise of fostering competition that in the long run will promote efficiency and benefit consumers. An important assumption of most deregulation proposals is that the major functions of today's vertically integrated utilities—generation, transmission, and distribution—are distinct from the economic standpoint. Almost all proposals assume that distribution of electricity remains a natural monopoly and should continue to be regulated. Most of them assume an independent transmission stage that, regardless of ownership or regulation, would purchase and sell power on a fair and nondiscriminatory basis. The major areas of difference in deregulation proposals thus far have been in degree and timing of deregulation of the power generation portion of the industry (Fenn, 1984).

Deregulation, however, faces formidable obstacles. First, there is no industry consensus on the desirability of deregulation or whether it would solve the financial problems that are at the core of the debate on regulatory reform. Second, the legal and economic problems for vertical disintegration of utility companies would be difficult. Third, the more comprehensive deregulation proposals raise concerns about reliability, coordination among systems, overall efficiency, and financing. Finally, political problems are compounded by state regulation. The electric power industry, unlike the airline, trucking, and railroad industries, cannot be deregulated by abolition of a federal agency or modification of rules governing interstate commerce (Fenn, 1984).

Despite monumental obstacles to deregulation, efforts to introduce competition into electricity markets, at least in a limited way, probably will continue. One consultant advises utilities to consider deregulation at a 20 to 25 percent chance in their planning (Fenn, 1984).

Besides the various forms of deregulation, there are also proposals for the federal government to preempt the regulatory function from the states to various degrees, but such proposals face major political opposition.

Industry Problems, Issues, Threats and Opportunities

As a result of the dramatic shift in the electric utility industry's traditionally stable operating environment after 1970, the industry is in a state of flux today, with some firms (those with extreme operating flexibility or not heavily committed to nuclear projects) in strong positions and others in such weak positions that their survival is questionable.

Electric utilities is an industry particularly vulnerable to uncertainty and miscalculation on the input side. Because of the high cost of large fixed capital assets, the necessity for maintaining sufficient (usually 20 to 25 percent) redundant capacity, and the long lead time for construction projects, firms must base today's commitments and actions on where they need to be 10 years or more in the future.

The unanticipated energy crisis of the early 1970's exposed a fact that had been concealed by the "grow and build larger" philosophy: that the electric utilities industry is at a very advanced stage. Decreased demand coupled with new plants coming into operation has created a saturated market.

The availability of material resources affects the industry both in the short and long term. In the short run, the price of such resources as coal, gas, oil, and uranium is crucial because the industry itself consumes more than one-third of the U.S. total primary energy (U.S. Department of Commerce, 1985; see (Figure 4), and is expected to consume 42 percent by the end of the century (Fenn, 1984). Although current fuel prices have moderated slightly, they remain high and subject to rapid change. This may be a problem depending on a firm's ability to influence supplier price, based on order size and purchasing/negotiation skills. Control over fuel supplies presents an opportunity for cost savings for those firms in a position to diversify; for example, by going into fuel exploration or mining operation. In the long term, the industry is threatened by scarcity of materials since there is a finite supply of nonrenewable fossil fuels. As supplies decrease, this threat will become an opportunity for firms that now have the foresight, flexibility, R&D commitment, and means to develop advanced nonrenewable or renewable energy sources.

The industry as a whole is experiencing a growing shortage of power engineers (Fenn, 1984). Nowhere is the importance of appropriately qualified labor better illustrated than in the nuclear portion of the industry where human errors have contributed to accidents (Lyman, 1980) and where proven project management expertise is in extremely high demand (Cook, 1985).

Financing is vital to the electric utilities industry; it is the most capital intensive in the U.S. Many firms are near bankruptcy today because of the extremely high interest rates prevailing at the time they undertook large nuclear construction projects that went awry. Those not heavily committed to nuclear programs or who have building programs successfully behind them and are beginning to generate more internal funds are in a favorable financial position because their stocks and bonds are attractive. Those with heavy indebtedness who are struggling to resolve construction problems face a threat because of declining stock values and bond ratings (Magnet, 1985).

Maturing technology is a threat, evidenced by the lack of significant increases in thermal efficiency since the early 1960's. Energy conservation, such as cogeneration, is still low on the learning curve and is a threat to conventional power sources when markets are saturated (Myers, 1985). Nuclear technology has considerable potential for advances that are being exploited in other parts of the world, but the present social climate is not favorable for taking advantage of it (*Electrical World,* 1981a; Cook, 1985).

Because of the electric utility industry's significance for national security and the health of important industries, it is highly regulated from three aspects: health, safety, and environmental impact. As a measure of regulatory impact, the nuclear regulations since 1970 have doubled the cost of labor, materials, and equipment, and have tripled the designers' effort (Fenn, 1984). Regulations and popular resistance often restrict the ability of utilities to build long-distance power lines that would enable them to sell surplus electricity to other areas (Brody, 1985).

On the other hand, deregulation is a continuing threat for firms vulnerable to strong competition. For small gen-

---

FIGURE 4   PRIMARY ENERGY CONSUMPTION BY CONSUMING SECTOR: 1960 to 1983

Sector	1960	1970	1974	1975	1976	1977	1978	1979	1980	1981	1982	1983
Total consumption (quad. Btu)	43.7	66.4	72.5	70.5	74.3	76.2	78.0	78.8	75.9	73.9	70.8	70.6
Residential and commercial	8.7	12.1	11.8	11.6	12.3	11.9	11.9	11.5	10.7	10.1	10.1	9.6
Industrial and miscellaneous	16.2	21.9	22.6	20.3	21.4	21.8	21.8	22.7	21.0	19.7	17.4	16.9
Transportation	10.6	16.0	18.1	18.2	19.1	19.8	20.6	20.4	19.7	19.5	19.0	19.0
Electricity generation	8.2	16.3	20.0	20.4	21.6	22.7	23.7	24.1	24.5	24.8	24.3	25.0
Percent of total:												
Residential and commercial	20.0	18.3	16.2	16.5	16.5	15.6	15.3	14.6	14.1	13.6	14.2	13.6
Industrial and miscellaneous	37.0	32.9	31.1	28.8	28.8	28.6	28.0	28.8	27.7	26.6	24.6	24.0
Transportation	24.1	24.2	24.9	25.8	25.6	25.9	26.3	25.9	25.9	26.3	26.9	25.9
Electricity generation	18.8	24.5	27.6	28.9	29.0	29.8	30.4	30.6	32.3	33.5	34.3	35.4

Source: U.S. Department of Commerce, *Statistical Abstract of the United States,* 1985: 556, from U.S. Energy Information Administration, *Annual Energy Review*

erating firms and those with successful advanced technology methods and strong markets, deregulation presents an opportunity for growth (*Wall Street Journal*, 1985).

The social and political climate has a significant bearing on the utility industry. The tendency of public service commissions to hold rate increases to a minimum means that the average return on equity is often held lower than competing investments and below the firm's cost of new capital.

The industry's decision-making power is also subject to increasing public participation and public veto power through organized ratepayer groups, pressure on legislatures, and public referendum. Another trend that is significantly shaping the industry is the influence of special interest groups such as anti-nuclear activists and environmental and consumer movements. These groups can pose a dilemma because of their conflicting interests.

GENERAL ORGANIZATION AND MANAGEMENT OF TVA

The powers of the TVA "corporation" are vested in the three-member Board of Directors appointed by the President, with Senate approval, to 9-year terms, although the average term is less. The Board establishes policies and programs (including electricity rates), reviews and appraises the results, approves the budget and authorizes major capital projects, approves staff appointments, and establishes the basic organization for execution of programs (Tennessee Valley Authority, 1984a). TVA differs from most investor-owned utilities in that the TVA directors exercise more direct operational control.

Officially the Board reports to the President and Congress. The relative autonomy in running TVA, originally intended to provide management flexibility, is currently being attacked. Increasing dissatisfaction with TVA's responsiveness to Congress and its ratepayers led 12 TVA region congressional representatives to introduce bills calling for a presidentially appointed inspector general to monitor TVA in order to strengthen it "by trying to improve its accountability" (*Huntsville Times*, 1985b; 1985h). Within three weeks (on October 18, 1985), the TVA board approved hiring its own inspector general (*Huntsville Times*, 1985n). The inspector is to aid in solving what TVA Chairman Dean freely admits are problems "in running the bureaucracy tightly enough to meet detailed inspections by such agencies as the Nuclear Regulatory Commission."

The administration of TVA operations is coordinated by the General Manager, who serves as liaison between the Board and the offices and divisions and originates or approves administrative controls to achieve integration of the total TVA program.

Administrative and management support activities are divided among three offices responsible primarily for budget, personnel, and corporate services (Figure 5). The TVA functional operations are carried out by the other four offices: Coal Gasification, Natural Resources and Economic Development, Agricultural and Chemical Development, and, most important, Power and Engineering.

The TVA organization has been attempting to solve serious communications problems in the recent past. Last year TVA undertook a major reorganization to "clearly focus responsibilities and accountability for nuclear operations" by assigning site directors to individual nuclear power plants and having them report directly to the deputy manager of TVA power operations. To shorten communication lines and avoid duplication, numerous employees were also transferred from a centralized Office of Nuclear Power to the individual plants to which they were assigned (*Electrical World*, 1984). TVA has recently taken a further step by consolidating all responsibilities related to nuclear power, which were dispersed among four separate divisions of Power and Engineering, under a separate office with its own management called "Power and Engineering (Nuclear)" (Sheppeard, 1985). These changes should prove beneficial to the troubled nuclear program.

External communication has also been troublesome. In addition to recent quarrels with congressmen, communication with the people in the TVA region (particularly educating the public to the realities of utility operations today) is a persistent problem that TVA shares to some extent with other utilities. Criticism of management for withholding information from the public, and even from TVA's own public relations people, has frequently arisen. Former chairman David Freeman established a Citizen Action Office (located in the Office of the General Manager) to provide programs ensuring a fair review of public concerns. Through toll-free telephone service and open board meetings TVA management seeks to provide for citizen participation and understanding of its operations (Citizens Guide to TVA, 1984). The effectiveness of the program remains debatable (Gwin, 1984). Despite current chairman Charles Dean's objectives, educating the public to TVA's problems and goals remains a problem (*Electrical World*, 1981b; Holden, 1984).

FIGURE 5   **Organization of the Tennessee Valley Authority.**

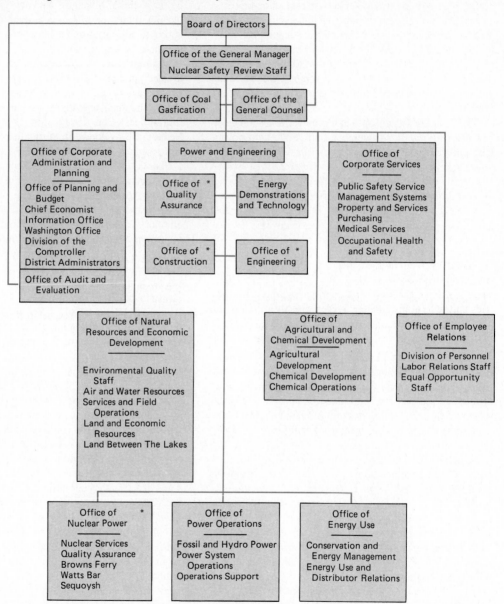

* In July 1985 all responsibilities relating to nuclear power were placed under a separate organization with its own management, called "Power and Engineering (Nuclear)"

MARKETING

TVA is a wholesaler of power through 160 local distributors and, thus, does not have direct contact with most consumers. However, TVA is required to meet the service standards of the 1978 Public Utility Regulatory Policies Act (PURPA) and to see that its distributors have compliance policies for such things as furnishing information to consumers, collecting deposits, and billing. This has some disadvantage for TVA in putting it into a regulatory role not previously assumed and certainly unusual for most utilities in the industry. In addition, its role in setting electrical rates for the region can place it in the position of judge in public disputes with distributors. In principle TVA is integrated only at the generation and transmission level. However, in practice it resembles a typical industry utility that is vertically integrated because of its complex 20-year, full-requirements contracts with independent distribution companies.

TVA's market consists of three major groups: 2.6 million residential consumers and more than 300,000 commercial consumers served by distributors, and 50 industries and federal installations served directly by TVA. In addition, through contractual arrangements, TVA can sell excess power to regional utilities. However, as a result of nuclear plant shutdowns, TVA has more frequently been a purchaser of outside power during the last year or two.

TVA's product is wholesale electric power, but it is marketed at variable rate mixes (Tennessee Valley Authority, 1981; 1982). Because the TVA Act provides that the economic benefits of power projects are intended first for the people, with use by industry secondary, the TVA pricing structure since 1981 has allocated lower cost hydro power to residential consumers based on initial blocks of 1250 kilowatthours of electricity. At the same time, declining block rates for commercial and industrial customers were replaced with flat rates. In addition, time-of-day rates are imposed for large industrial consumers. The ratemaking policy is intended to send a conservation message to consumers and, thus, allows TVA to have some influence on demand. Like many other utilities, TVA sometimes uses phase-in of rate increases to aid consumer adjustment and probably also aid TVA public relations, although this practice does negatively affect cash flow.

Until the last decade or so, TVA had traditionally kept to one of its original purposes—i.e., to serve as a "yardstick" for measuring public utilities—by maintaining comparatively low and efficient rates. TVA claims that its ultimate consumers still have lower rates than typical

areas in the country (Steffy, 1985). However, the fact that TVA region consumers in the 1950's and 1960's were encouraged to become such high users of electricity now works to TVA's disadvantage. As TVA rates began to climb in the early 1970's, the cost to the consumer increased dramatically because of the average amount of power consumption per household in the TVA area. Figures 6 and 7 compare average TVA electricity use, rates, and cost with the national average, as well as customer statistics.

Promotional activities since 1973 have been directed toward encouraging conservation of electricity rather than selling more. TVA average consumption is gradually approaching the national average as rates continue to rise. In addition, TVA offers a variety of free services, such as energy audits and inspection and approval of energy-efficient homes. Other services, when provided for by statute, have included low-interest installment loans for energy conservation improvements. These measures have the advantage of holding down supply costs by reducing load requirements and contributing to a positive corporate image.

However, if TVA reaches full operation with current nuclear plants, its projected excess capacity may be in conflict with its conservation policies. As Figure 8 indicates, TVA will be in a similar situation to that anticipated for the industry in that the most probable scenario indicates excess capacity for TVA until about the year 2000.

OPERATIONS

Nonpower Operations

Although about 95 percent of TVA's total budget is accounted for by its self-supporting power program, TVA is also directly involved in the total development of the human and natural resources of the Tennessee Valley region (Figure 9). Congressionally appropriated funds are used for the nonpower activities mandated by the 1933 TVA Act.

President Reagan's proposed 1986 budget, which recommended an appropriation of $33.6 million compared to $129.5 in 1985, would have eliminated almost all natural resource, economic, and community development programs, leaving only enough money to operate the reservoir system and a small part of the fertilizer program (Tennessee Valley Authority, 1985a). However, Congress declined to make such a drastic cut and, at this time,

FIGURE 6 REVENUE FROM ELECTRIC SALES
(Thousands of Dollars)

Fiscal year	Total	Residential	Commercial and industrial	Federal agencies	Outdoor lighting
1984	$5,022,329	$1,740,914	$2,570,478	$638,655	$72,282
1983	4,642,597	1,615,581	2,294,939	665,648	66,429
1982	4,674,745	1,603,349	2,323,721	685,175	62,500
1981	4,225,171	1,446,096	2,231,218	492,143	55,714
1980	3,576,533	1,222,042	1,864,468	441,463	48,560
1979	3,235,762	1,090,813	1,718,399	381,555	44,995
1978	2,747,716	1,015,406	1,379,852	312,328	40,130
1977	2,324,976	873,061	1,087,537	328,237	36,141
1976	1,978,805	724,011	915,431	308,071	31,292
1975	1,448,320	559,439	672,806	189,187	26,888
1974	1,138,887	442,644	545,319	126,544	24,380
1973	992,421	398,253	465,323	107,154	21,691
1972	860,669	352,116	412,374	76,685	19,494
1971	796,426	332,544	381,299	65,010	17,573
1970	667,418	277,153	312,574	62,459	15,232

Source: Tennessee Valley Authority. Power Engineering Report, 1984c: 47

RESIDENTIAL STATISTICS

Fiscal year	TVA average annual use, kWh	TVA average annual bill	TVA average annual rate ¢/kWh	U.S. average annual use, kWh	U.S. average annual rate ¢/kWh
1984	13,990	$668.32	4.78	8,968	7.09
1983	13,580	631.42	4.65	8,796	6.84
1982	13,760	635.18	4.62	8,903	6.34
1981	14,250	579.24	4.07	8,816	5.44
1980	15,130	498.49	3.29	8,944	4.78
1979	14,680	454.81	3.10	8,834	4.24
1978	16,190	434.03	2.68	8,828	3.98
1977	16,400	380.34	2.32	8,730	3.70
1976	14,370	325.35	2.26	8,209	3.33
1975	14,540	255.92	1.76	8,068	3.05
1974	14,480	209.37	1.45	8,019	2.54
1973	15,080	196.07	1.30	7,882	2.32
1972	14,040	179.92	1.28	7,496	2.25
1971	14,400	175.53	1.22	7,243	2.14
1970	14,560	150.39	1.03	6,810	2.09

Federal agencies include only TVA's direct service and interdivisional sales. To avoid overstating the number of customers in the region, the number of outdoor lighting customers excludes the customers who supplement regular service with the special outdoor lighting fixture. Only public street lighting and athletic field lighting customers are counted. However, the energy sales and revenue figures under outdoor lighting do include data for the special features.

Beginning with fiscal year 1977, data for TVA and U.S. average are for 12 months ending September. Prior years for TVA are for 12 months ending June each year.

Source: Tennessee Valley Authority. Power Engineering Report, 1984 c: 47

FIGURE 7   CUSTOMER STATISTICS*

Fiscal year	Total	Residential	Commercial and industrial	Federal agencies	Outdoor lighting
			Ultimate customers		
1984	2,968,490	2,633,892	327,360	12	7,226
1983	2,911,644	2,585,276	319,651	11	6,706[a]
1982	2,857,529	2,543,983	309,982	11	3,553
1981	2,826,882	2,519,709	303,716	11	3,446
1980	2,784,675	2,481,545	299,744	11	3,375
1979	2,722,984	2,425,623	294,041	11	3,309
1978	2,664,412	2,371,064	290,132	11	3,205
1977	2,601,415	2,316,414	281,906	11	3,084
1976	2,521,956	2,248,475	270,532	11	2,938
1975	2,458,822	2,192,972	263,056	11	2,783
1974	2,401,581	2,139,476	259,417	11	2,677
1973	2,325,134	2,068,150	254,423	11	2,550
1972	2,236,153	1,987,724	245,965	11	2,453
1971	2,158,423	1,919,208	236,687	11	2,517
1970	2,096,544	1,863,578	230,654	11	2,301
		Electricity sales, millions of kilowatthours			
1984	104,272	36,430	55,200	11,552	1,090
1983	101,409	34,715	49,207	16,353	1,134
1982	103,854	34,727	50,964	17,022	1,141
1981	110,152	35,568	58,169	15,285	1,130
1980	115,007	37,093	59,509	17,317	1,088
1979	113,438	35,212	60,511	16,667	1,048
1978	113,418	37,874	57,522	17,018	1,004
1977	117,764	37,648	56,552	22,582	982
1976	104,925	31,985	49,884	22,143	913
1975	102,778	31,785	50,117	20,027	849
1974	102,618	30,602	53,125	18,050	841
1973	99,670	30,637	50,557	17,694	782
1972	87,333	27,474	46,005	13,138	716
1971	85,930	27,291	45,553	12,427	659
1970	86,380	26,835	45,200	13,743	602

*In the tables, the sales and related statistics for TVA and for the local distributors have been combined to portray total sales to ultimate customers.

[a]Initial reporting and counting of individual outdoor lighting customers with no other service began in July 1983.

Source: Tennessee Valley Authority. Power Engineering Report, 1934c: 46

appears likely to approve a budget only 13 percent less than last year (*Huntsville Times*, 1985c; 1985i). The 70 percent reduction requested by the President would represent a fundamental change in TVA's role and could set the stage for its elimination as a government agency.

Figure 10 lists the 1983 and 1984 expenses for major nonpower programs. These figures are important and should be taken into consideration, even though they are not part of "TVA-the power company", because they do affect the overall bottom line and because other utilities

are also diversifying, though to a lesser extent. Some of them are into mosquito control, building hiking trails, promoting local hog production, and archaeological excavations.

Power Operations

TVA's power program operates very much like any other electric utility. It buys its equipment and supplies and hires its employees on the open market and is subject to

FIGURE 8   **Long-term load requirements and supply medium forecast.**
(Load Forecast, Tennessee Valley Authority, 1985b.)

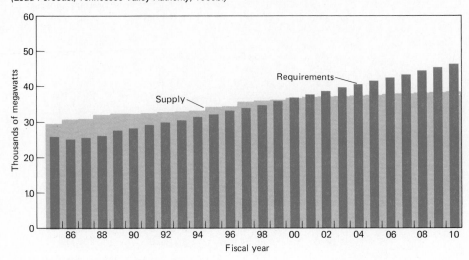

FIGURE 9   **TVA budget by program.***
(Chandler, 1984: 6.)

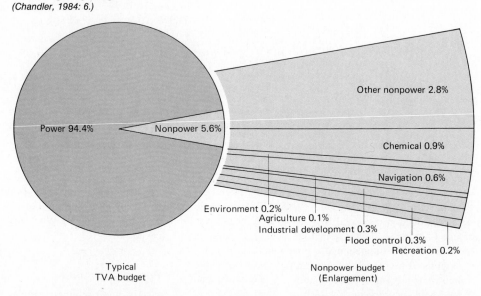

*Typical budget based on data available at the time (1982–1983). Subsequent reductions in congressional
appropriations for nonpower programs have reduced the nonpower percentage further; for example, a 13%
reduction from 1985 is anticipated in 1986.

For the years ended September 30, 1984, 1983	1984	1983 (thousands of dollars)
General resources development		
Navigation operations	$11,097	$ 8,637
System flood control operations	10,000	9,229
Recreation development	15,989	7,933
Community preparedness	2,529	3,450
Regional water quality management	2,216	1,674
Fisheries and wildlife resources development	3,105	1,794
Environmental protection of public lands and water	1,049	964
Environmental education	927	625
Valley agricultural development	5,817	5,303
Renewable fuels research	2,635	1,970
Forest resources development	1,721	1,505
Acidic precipitation assessment	503	308
TVA lands planning	765	728
Townlift	788	1,179
Industrial skills development	6,202	2,152
Economic development and analysis	3,184	3,198
Waterway development and engineering assistance	4,571	1,744
Special opportunities cities and counties program	1,182	2,204
Minority economic development	549	2,245
Floodplain management	1,109	2,579
Regional water and wastewater supply	1,273	—
Land Between The Lakes operations	9,639	8,514
Valley mapping and remote sensing	1,021	1,047
Other general resources development projects	688	592
Net expense of general resources development	88,559	69,574
Fertilizer development		
Research and development	24,380	18,336
Fertilizer introduction		
Fertilizer industry demonstrations	3,624	3,552
Farm test demonstrations outside the Valley	1,486	1,878
Net expense of fertilizer introduction	5,110	5,430
Developmental production		
Cost of products distributed	$40,413	$36,680
General expenses		
Loss on retirements of manufacturing plant and equipment, net	126	145
Gain on sale of phosphate reserves, net	—	181*
Removal of obsolete facilities	3,507	—
General and administrative	1,175	926
Other	1,549	1,724
Total general expenses	6,357	2,614
Total production expense	46,770	39,294
Less transfers and sales of products		
Transfers to other TVA programs, at market prices	24,426	20,312
Direct sales	434	362
Total transfers and sales	24,860	20,674
Net expense of developmental production	21,910	18,620
Net expense of fertilizer development	51,400	42,386
National energy demonstrations	297*	32
Other expense, net	1,022	1,451*
Net expense	140,684	110,541

*Deduct
Source: Tennessee Valley Authority, Power Engineering Report, 1984c: 32–33

the same regulations as other companies. In fact, because it *is* associated with the government, it is often expected to follow a higher standard than for-profit firms. One way in which TVA differs from most other power producers, however, is in distribution: TVA does not sell power directly to consumers, with the exception of about 50 large industrial firms and government installations. The great majority of TVA's power is wholesaled to 160 municipal and rural co-op distributors who route it to almost 3 million customers in seven states. Their markup accounts for the difference between the almost 5 cents per kWh that TVA charges for power and the cost shown in Figure 11, which summarizes fiscal year 1984 power operations.

TVA's objective is to keep electric rates as low as possible in order to encourage the region's economic development. The key to this stability is control of operating and capital costs. The primary means used recently to accomplish this end have been radical reorganization to increase efficiency and accountability, and the cancellation and amortization of most of the planned system of nuclear plants. Both of these decisions were unpopular with large numbers of voters and campaign contributors, and TVA has lost much of its political support as a result (*Huntsville Times,* 1985d; 1985e).

Because utilities are so capital-intensive, power companies cannot match supply and demand as easily as most other industries. It can take 15 or more years and billions of dollars to get a new facility on line, and there is no

guarantee that the anticipated demand will ever materialize to justify its existence. Because of this supply-side inertia, TVA has taken measures to modify demand. Conservation and energy management programs have reduced peak demand by about 1000 megawatts, almost as much as a nuclear power unit produces when in full operation. At the same time, to obtain revenue from idle excess capacity and preserve jobs, TVA is offering "interruptible" power to its large industrial customers at up to 30 percent less than the usual rate until the generators are needed for full-rate users. Customers are also encouraged to generate their own electricity and feed the excess back into the power network (cogeneration), thus decreasing both their own energy bills and TVA's need to build new power plants.

A power company's raw materials are its energy sources. TVA's first power supply was the hydroelectric by-product of flood control dams, and 18 percent of the utility's power still comes from this renewable source. In 1984, 60 percent of the electricity was produced by coal-fired plants and 22 percent by nuclear plants. (Gas and oil combustion turbines produced 0.04 percent, mostly during unexpected load peaks.) Figure 12 compares current TVA energy sources with available industry actual (1982) and projected (1987) energy sources. For 1985 the percentage of nuclear power generated will be down considerably, since all the nuclear units are presently off line. As the table of fuel statistics in Figure 13 shows, this will

FIGURE 11   SUMMARY OF TVA POWER OPERATIONS

	Fiscal year	
	1984	1983
Sales (billion kWh)*	109	106
Revenues (millions)	$ 4,453	$ 4,114
Payments in lieu of taxes to states and counties (millions)	$ 170	$ 165
Total operating expense (millions)	$ 2,775	$ 2,485
Net interest charges (millions)	$ 1,026	$ 992
Net income or (loss) (millions)	$ (134)	$ 439
Increase or (decrease) in retained earnings (millions)	$ (228)	$ 332
Total payments to U.S. Treasury (millions)	$ 114	$ 127
Total assets (millions)	$19,028	$18,807
Average annual residential use (kWh)	13,990	13,580
Average cost per residential kWh (cents)	4.78	4.65

*Represents total TVA sales at the delivery point to distributors, industries, and Federal agencies. The 1984 total sales to ultimate customers is 104 billion kWh. For 1983 total sales to ultimate customers was 101 billion kWh. The difference between TVA sales and sales to ultimate customers is the power lost in distribution facilities.
Source: Power Engineering report, Tennessee Valley Authority, 1984c: 1

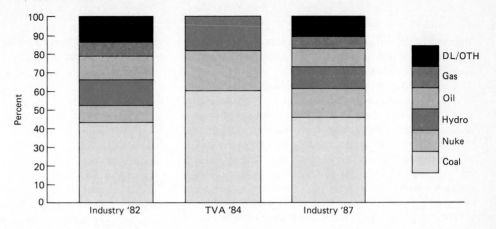

FIGURE 12   **Energy sources.**

FIGURE 13   FUEL STATISTICS

	1984	1983	1982	1981	1980
Fuel burned					
Coal-fired plants					
Coal—tons	29,334,992	27,466,097	28,802,494	35,645,302	35,825,904
Oil—gallons[1]	15,284,725	13,176,131	14,040,429	14,055,379	13,774,837
Total fuel expense	$1,199,179,689	$1,215,135,920	$1,207,486,733	$1,359,923,340	$1,236,906,202
Coal expense per ton	$40.452	$43.772	$41.341	$37.757	$34.134
Oil expense per gallon[1]	$0.818	$0.977	$1.192	$1.000	$1.018
Nuclear plants					
Total fuel expense	$162,493,974	$142,462,127	$111,964,362	$83,011,913	$55,797,057
Combustion turbine plants					
Oil—gallons	4,757,126	1,315,672	4,156,971	7,087,328	9,884,880
Gas—MCF	93,746	233,264	31,873	919,407	1,234,082
Total fuel expense	$3,229,159	$1,989,114	$2,784,380	$6,507,422	$7,631,419
Oil expense per gallon	$ .532	$ .530	$ .540	$ .531	$ .479
Gas expense per MCF	$3.415	$3.915	$5.122	$2.984	$2.350
Fuel ratios					
Fuel expense per net kWh—mills					
Coal-fired plants	17.34	18.50	17.72	16.53	14.98
Combustion turbine	72.22	122.79	85.48	49.72	42.38
Nuclear plants	6.54	5.06	4.06	3.95	3.00
Cents per million Btu burned					
Coal-fired plants	172.07	186.05	178.81	165.07	140.60
Combustion turbines	423.06	468.08	453.28	336.83	286.74
Nuclear plants	61.29	48.10	38.02	37.24	28.22
Coal received					
Tons	29,362,079	28,186,571	33,557,025	29,284,209	37,310,507
Mine cost plus transportation	$1,089,907,876	$1,165,403,602	$1,379,817,780	$1,153,106,637	$1,300,533,045
Cents per million Btu	157.82	175.69	175.96	169.70	150.60

[1]Oil fired for light-off of coal-fired boilers and auxiliary uses.

increase the total cost of generating electricity because, even though its cost has been rising, nuclear power is still cheaper than any of the other sources.

The efficiency of coal-fired steam plants (as a whole) has not improved significantly in the past 25 years. Although some individual TVA units rank among the most efficient in the country, the mature technology has generally had difficulty keeping pace with the demands of pollution control regulations. For any real change to occur, a breakthrough in technology will be needed. TVA may have found it in fluidized bed combustion, a process of burning pulverized coal in a bed of limestone that simultaneously provides efficient power production and efficient pollution control. TVA is currently arranging for funds to build a 160 megawatt demonstration plant, scaled up from the successful 20 megawatt pilot plant at Paducah, Kentucky.

TVA's most visible problem area is its nuclear program. TVA's original plan to build 17 reactors was based on the best estimates of future power demand available at the time. Its problem was compounded by its responsibility to supply power to the government's uranium enrichment plants. These plants expected their power requirements to increase by the equivalent output of five nuclear units by the mid-1980's, to produce fuel for 500 generating units. When the utility industry began jumping the nuclear ship after Three Mile Island, TVA's plans were dramatically impacted. Besides having more nuclear plants in the works than they could use, the cost of the plants had increased to the point that one of them would have cost more than the entire present TVA power system, from the 1930's dams to the already completed nuclear plants. When the construction projects were cancelled, TVA had to write off the $4 billion in sunk costs it had already invested in them and terminate the 20,000 people working on them. The cost of the cancelled projects will be amortized over the next 11 years, while TVA tries to use more accurate forecasting techniques. For example, more refined input to forecasting is now used, including such information as the impact of conservation on power load requirements (Freeman, 1985).

TVA's nuclear plants are currently off line for a variety of reasons, mostly related to changes in Nuclear Regulatory Commission (NRC) regulations and, in the case of Browns Ferry, to age and accumulation of required maintenance. TVA seems to be taking strong measures to ensure that all units will be safe to operate and fully compliant with regulations before they are brought back on line. In the meantime, 1985 and 1986 will each see a $40 million increase in cost to replace the power these plants would have produced.

FINANCE

Financial statements for TVA for 1982 through 1984 are included in Figures 14–16.

PERSONNEL

TVA has traditionally enjoyed a reputation for excellent labor relations and high employee morale and loyalty, but recently a number of problems have surfaced.

Human Resources

Personnel at TVA are divided into two major groups: (1) salary policy (encompassing professional and related technical, administrative, clerical, custodial, and public safety fields) and (2) trades and labor (operating and maintenance and all construction). Because TVA has always done its own construction, cancellation of nuclear projects has resulted in significant cuts in employment level from a peak of 51,714 in 1980.

Pay and Promotion

Although they are federal government employees, the TVA Board has total authority to fix compensation independently of Civil Service laws. In practice, pay levels are usually similar to Civil Service. Pay levels are based on prevailing rates in a specified labor market vicinity and are negotiated with TVA by the Salary Policy Employee Panel and the Tennessee Valley Trades and Labor Council representing, respectively, the various bargaining units of the salaried and the hourly employee groups. Salary positions are classified into seven schedules, and the basic pay schedule and eligibility period for within-grade increases in each schedule are specified in detail. Eligibility for promotions and salary increases for some schedules and upper level grades are in the merit range (performance beyond satisfactory service).

The TVA directors contend that inadequate salaries have made TVA a training ground for managers for the industry (Engardio, 1985). They claim that their best managers are being lost because of federal pay caps that limit salaries to $72,300, a claim that has been publicly disputed by at least one congressman (*Huntsville Times,* 1985j). Despite the controversy and TVA's current large operating losses, the TVA Board within the past month approved salary raises totalling $4.59 million for almost 4,000 lower and middle-level managers (*Huntsville Times,* 1985k).

Benefits

TVA offers a variety of benefits including voluntary medical and dental expense programs and free protective eyewear. Self-development training is encouraged by permitting altered work schedules. Partly because of TVA's status as a federal agency, some benefits, such as annual and sick leave and holidays, are not negotiable. In short, TVA offers an adequate benefits program.

Motivation

The pay issue is a highly visible symptom of an apparently more serious employee morale problem expressed primarily as distrust of management. Some of the problems undoubtedly are related to the severe cutbacks and layoffs resulting from the badly managed nuclear projects. A more serious issue, however, is that most of the personnel problems are related to employee fears about reporting safety concerns. On September 30 of this year, a 5-year legal battle was settled when TVA was forced to reinstate (with back pay plus damages) an employee 'whistle-blower' who had been transferred for discussing potential safety violations with NRC inspectors (*Huntsville Times,* 1985l).

Fear of retaliation by supervisors caused many employees to take their safety concerns to congressional aides and the NRC; and, as a result, TVA is spending $3.6 million to have a consulting firm interview all employees. Despite these events and TVA policy statements, one TVA safety expert remains concerned "that TVA leaders still have not shown an 'overall commitment' to quality assurance" (Engardio, 1985: 86).

Training

TVA has a documented training policy including a TVA-wide orientation program, selected reading materials, and explanation of safety hazards for new employees. Occupational qualifying and developmental training are offered. The supervisors are responsible for continuous informal on-the-job training including demonstrating in their own work the application of TVA policies and procedures.

Employee attitudes toward safety are often criticized by those inside and outside the agency. Even if TVA policy statements on training are adequate, the implementation probably can be improved. For example, employee failures to pass welding recertification tests resulted recently in further delays and additional inspections at the Watts Bar plant (*Huntsville Times,* 1985m).

As the firm phases from the construction to operating phase in its nuclear program, either considerable retraining or layoffs and new recruitment will be necessary. TVA has recognized this need and is trying to retrain employees for the transition to operation of facilities.

Recruitment and Hiring

TVA has been an attractive organization to work for, particularly for recent college graduates. With shortages of power engineers now an industry problem, however, TVA may face difficulties in recruiting unless it can solve some of its current problems and improve its image both internally and externally.

EPILOGUE: REMARKS BY JOHN B. WATERS, DIRECTOR TENNESSEE VALLEY AUTHORITY BEFORE THE UNITED STATES SENATE SUBCOMMITTEE ON REGIONAL AND COMMUNITY DEVELOPMENT JULY 15, 1985, WASHINGTON, D. C.

Mr. Chairman, you have already heard about TVA's power program and its natural resource development efforts. I'd like to focus for a little while on what TVA accomplishes through its congressionally-funded programs for community and economic development.

But, first I'd like to take the opportunity to let you know that, along with chairman Dean, I'm a native of the Tennessee Valley and have had a chance to see firsthand what TVA has helped this region do. There are plenty of people where I come from that can remember what life was like before TVA brought electricity to rural communities, or controlled flooding along the river, or helped farmers get more out of their land, or helped create new jobs where they were desperately needed. These are the kind of people, Mr. Chairman, that don't come to Washington to testify, they never appear on anybody's list of

FIGURE 14   STATEMENTS OF INCOME AND RETAINED EARNINGS: POWER PROGRAM

For the years ended September 30, 1984, 1983, and 1982	1984		1983		1982	
	kWh	Amount	kWh	Amount	kWh	Amount
			(thousands)			
Operating revenues						
Sales of electric energy						
Municipalities and cooperatives	80,700,297	$3,189,653	76,305,236	$2,936,006	75,681,355	$2,815,440
Federal agencies	11,162,287	648,847	16,352,790	693,909	16,670,674	670,902
Industries	16,455,426	685,249	13,065,280	583,180	15,490,317	626,437
Electric utilities	317,950	14,358	157,764	7,958	353,778	13,828
Interdivisional	390,224	16,997	352,705	15,116	350,764	14,273
Revenue credit due customers	—	150,000*	—	152,000*	—	183,732*
Total sales of electric energy	109,026,184	4,405,104	106,233,775	4,084,169	108,546,888	3,957,148
Rents		27,847		16,525		16,737
Discounts and penalties		3,168		2,244		868
Other miscellaneous revenues		16,951		11,381		7,049
Total operating revenues		4,453,070		4,114,319		3,981,802
Operating expenses						
Production						
Fuel		1,364,903		1,359,587		1,322,235
Other		586,722		469,914		534,903
Transmission		50,091		48,444		45,107
Customer accounts		24,893		19,007		9,059
Power consumer services		20,316		17,684		9,095
Demonstration of power use		19,775		17,364		16,890
Research, development, and demonstrations		41,666		61,462		58,777
General and administrative		83,617		79,358		76,635
Payments in lieu of taxes		170,172		165,193		163,461
Amortization of loss on cancelled nuclear generating units		145,000		—		—
Provision for depreciation		267,388		247,054		225,095
Total operating expenses		2,774,543		2,485,067		2,461,257
Operating income		1,678,527		1,629,252		1,520,545

FIGURE 14   STATEMENTS OF INCOME AND RETAINED EARNINGS: POWER PROGRAM (*Continued*)

For the years ended September 30, 1984, 1983, and 1982	1984		1983		1982	
	kWh	Amount	kWh	Amount	kWh	Amount
			(thousands)			
Other income and deductions						
Interest income		$ 28,946		$ 8,466		$ 1,343
Charge related to loss on cancelled nuclear generating units		800,000*		204,168*		256,647*
Other, net		15,467*		2,725*		3,298*
Total other income and deductions		786,521*		198,427*		258,602*
Income before interest charges		892,006		1,430,825		1,261,943
Interest charges						
Interest on long-term debt		1,508,975		1,437,271		1,260,832
Other interest expense		49,483		52,363		121,481
Allowance for borrowed funds used during construction		532,976*		498,301*		511,745*
Amortization of long-term debt discount and expense		973		988		974
Net interest charges		1,026,455		992,321		871,542
Net income (loss)		(134,449)		438,504		390,401
Return on appropriation investment		93,657		106,567		109,478
Increase (decrease) in retained earnings reinvested		(228,106)		331,937		280,923
Retained earnings reinvested at beginning of period		1,728,690		1,396,753		1,115,830
Retained earnings reinvested at end of period		$1,500,584		$1,728,690		$1,396,753

*Deduct

FIGURE 15 BALANCE SHEETS

September 30, 1984 and 1983	Power program 1984	Power program 1983	All programs 1984	All programs 1983
		(thousands of dollars)		

Assets

Property, plant, and equipment
substantially all at original cost
  Completed plant

Multipurpose dams	$ 541,066	$ 535,162	$ 1,407,133	$ 1,275,846
Single-purpose dams	386,974	361,818	386,974	361,818
Steam production plants	3,771,947	3,504,784	3,771,947	3,504,784
Nuclear production plants	2,715,051	2,594,372	2,715,051	2,594,372
Other electric plant	2,878,304	2,761,134	2,878,304	2,761,134
Other plant	—	—	283,506	286,681
	10,293,342	9,757,270	11,442,915	10,784,635
Less accumulated depreciation and depletion	2,842,136	2,607,937	3,067,431	2,819,415
Completed plant, net	7,451,206	7,149,333	8,375,484	7,965,220
Construction in progress	6,526,589	5,839,895	6,743,958	6,138,787
Deferred nuclear generating projects, net	—	2,667,051	—	2,667,051
	6,526,589	8,506,946	6,743,958	8,805,838
Nuclear fuel	548,210	457,239	548,210	457,239
Less accumulated amortization	527,924	416,479	527,924	416,479
Nuclear fuel, net	20,286	40,760	20,286	40,760
Total	13,998,081	15,697,039	15,139,728	16,811,818

Investment funds

at amortized cost	145,123	103,348	145,123	103,348

Current assets

Cash	131,485	59,981	261,310	270,469
Accounts receivable	606,429	450,542	620,870	466,743
Inventories, principally at average cost	693,797	767,831	709,460	783,780
Total	1,431,711	1,278,354	1,591,640	1,520,992

Deferred charges and other assets

Loans and other long-term receivables	312,197	279,314	349,924	311,989
Recoverable cost of cancelled nuclear generating units	149,000	—	149,000	—
Unamortized cost of cancelled nuclear generating units	2,716,099	1,004,360	2,716,099	1,004,360
Spent nuclear fuel disposal costs	—	102,869	—	102,869
Mine and mill development costs, net	196,294	267,461	196,294	267,461
Energy conservation costs, net	73,661	68,102	73,661	68,102
Unamortized debt issue and reacquisition expense	5,966	6,558	5,966	6,558
Total	3,453,217	1,728,664	3,490,944	1,761,339
Total assets	$19,028,132	$18,807,405	$20,367,435	$20,197,497

FIGURE 15   BALANCE SHEETS (*Continued*)

September 30, 1984 and 1983	Power program 1984	Power program 1983	All programs 1984	All programs 1983
		(thousands of dollars)		

Capitalization and liabilities

Proprietary capital

Appropriation investment

Congressional appropriations	$ 1,419,426	$ 1,414,354	$ 4,166,207	$ 4,080,578
Transfers of property from other Federal agencies, net	23,795	23,905	58,402	58,540
	1,443,221	1,438,259	4,224,609	4,139,118
Less repayments to General Fund of the U.S. Treasury	595,059	575,059	636,785	616,786
Appropriation investment	848,162	863,200	3,587,824	3,522,332
Retained earnings reinvested in the power program	1,500,584	1,728,690	1,500,584	1,728,690
Accumulated net expense of nonpower programs	—	—	1,482,155*	1,341,471*
Total	2,348,746	2,591,890	3,606,253	3,909,511

Long-term debt

Principal	14,525,000	14,275,000	14,525,000	14,275,000
Less unamortized discount	4,172	4,457	4,172	4,547
Total	14,520,828	14,270,453	14,520,828	14,270,453

Other liabilities

Decommissioning of nuclear plant	41,302	31,752	41,302	31,752
Reclamation of coal properties	11,792	—	11,792	—
Disposal costs of spent nuclear fuel	—	157,000	—	157,000
Cancellation costs for nuclear generating units	127,555	127,769	127,555	127,769
Total	180,649	316,521	180,649	316,521

Current liabilities

Short-term debt

U.S. Treasury	150,000	150,000	150,000	150,000
Federal Financing Bank	685,000	565,000	685,000	565,000
Short-term debt	835,000	715,000	835,000	715,000
Accounts payable	602,159	369,951	654,708	417,188
Refund due power customers	150,000	157,718	150,000	157,718
Employees' accrued leave	34,281	30,675	51,812	45,658
Payrolls accrued	23,647	25,883	35,363	36,094
Interest accrued	332,822	329,314	332,822	329,314
Total	1,977,909	1,628,541	2,059,705	1,700,972

Commitments and contingencies

Total capitalization and liabilities	$19,028,132	$18,807,405	$20,367,435	$20,197,497

*Deduct

FIGURE 16 STATEMENTS OF CHANGES IN FINANCIAL POSITION

For the years ended September 30, 1984, 1983, and 1982	Power program			All programs		
(thousands of dollars)	1984	1983	1982	1984	1983	1982
Source of funds						
Program sources						
Net power income or loss*	$ 134,449*	$ 438,504	$ 390,401	$ 134,449*	$ 438,504	$ 390,401
Items not requiring funds	750,546	20,000	20,019	750,546	20,000	20,019
Funds from power operations	616,097	458,504	410,420	616,097	458,504	410,420
Sale of power assets, principally nuclear fuel sales	137,399	183,795	312,055	137,399	183,795	312,055
Funds from power program	753,496	642,299	722,475	753,496	642,299	722,475
Net expense of nonpower programs				140,684*	110,540*	103,871*
Add items not requiring funds				18,592	9,849	9,519
Funds used in nonpower operations				122,092*	100,691*	94,352*
Sale of nonpower facilities				975	1,592	916
Funds used in nonpower programs				121,117*	99,099*	93,436*
Debt sources						
Long-term bonds						
Issues	250,000	850,000	2,100,000	250,000	850,000	2,100,000
Short-term notes						
Issues	8,275,000	2,855,000	3,870,000	8,275,000	2,855,000	3,870,000
Redemptions	8,155,000*	2,875,000*	4,595,000*	8,155,000*	2,875,000*	4,595,000*
Total debt sources	370,000	830,000	1,375,000	370,000	830,000	1,375,000
Other sources						
Recovery of mine and mill development costs through litigation	56,000	—	—	56,000	—	—
Sale of equipment at cancelled and deferred nuclear units	25,955	28,094	6,872	25,955	28,094	6,872
Liability for disposal of spent nuclear fuel	—	95,834	—	—	95,834	—
Liability for cancellation costs for nuclear generating units, net of adjustments	241*	70,416*	212,334	214*	70,416*	212,334
Congressional appropriations	1,285	1,141	1,677	85,629	216,433	129,162
Property transfers	110*	59	10*	137*	400	36*
Total other sources	82,916	54,712	220,873	167,233	270,345	348,332
Total source of funds	$1,206,412	$1,527,011	$2,318,348	$1,169,612	$1,643,545	$2,352,371

FIGURE 16

For the years ended September 30, 1984, 1983, and 1982	Power program			All programs		
	1984	1983	1982	1984	1983	1982
	(thousands of dollars)					
Disposition of funds						
Expended for plant and equipment, excluding allowance for borrowed funds used	$ 863,242	$1,228,271	$1,814,102	$ 919,586	$1,295,626	$1,911,812
Less:						
Depreciation and depletion allowances charged to construction clearing accounts and other asset categories	10,872	10,458	9,301	12,966	12,641	12,424
Cost of removing retired facilities and salvage from retained materials	7,998*	6,816*	3,149*	9,270*	7,118*	9,211
	860,368	1,224,629	1,807,950	915,890	1,290,103	1,890,177
Payments to U.S. Treasury						
Return on appropriation investment	93,657	106,567	109,478	93,657	106,567	109,478
Repayments of appropriation investment	20,000	20,000	20,000	20,000	20,000	20,000
	113,657	126,567	129,478	113,657	126,567	129,478
Investment funds	42,691	43,995	59,066	42,691	43,995	59,066
Changes in other assets and liabilities						
Loans and other long-term receivables	32,888	15,516*	54,322	32,641	17,335*	67,449
Spent nuclear fuel disposal costs	172,616	102,869	—	172,616	102,869	—
Mine and mill development cost	9,117	1,603*	24,310	9,117	1,603*	24,310
Energy conservation cost	29,976	32,524	35,231	29,976	32,524	35,231
Cancellation costs for nuclear generating units net of adjustments	214*	70,416*	212,334	214*	70,416*	212,334
Payment of cancellation costs for nuclear generating units	21,324	14,148	—	21,324	14,148	—
	265,707	62,006	326,197	265,460	60,187	339,324
Changes in working capital (increase or decrease*)						
Cash	71,504	5,449*	40,165*	9,159*	50,800	103,041*
Accounts receivable	155,887	56*	37,148	154,127	4,828	40,651
Inventories	74,034*	20,863*	204,730	74,320*	27,351*	203,900
	153,357	26,368*	201,713	70,648	28,277	141,510
Less other current liabilities (excluding short-term debt)	229,368	96,182*	206,056	238,734	94,416*	207,184
	76,011*	69,814	4,343*	168,086*	122,693	65,674*
Total disposition of funds	$1,206,412	$1,527,011	$2,318,348	$1,169,612	$1,643,545	$2,352,371

*Deduct

"expert" witnesses, but they know in their hearts what TVA has meant to them.

Also, before I get into the specifics of our community and economic development efforts, I want to say a few words about the concept of "regional development" because I think this approach to achieving social and economic progress is very important—especially when the region is a true region and not one just artificially drawn on a map.

The Tennessee Valley watershed is just such a region; it is tied together in nature with a geographical, ecological, and social integrity. That's not to say that there's no diversity in the region—there is—but the area encompassed by the Tennessee River watershed is best viewed as a whole. Unique opportunities and problems exist in this region because of particular characteristics of the natural and human resources that stretch from one end of the valley to the other. These problems and opportunities are best addressed through a cooperative regional approach. And a cooperative regional approach is just what TVA strives to incorporate into its community and economic development programs.

Just as TVA's efforts to help develop the region's natural resources are guided by a central proposition, TVA's economic and community development programs are also guided by a set of principles based on a particular conception of what a federally-supported regional development agency should do.

Our view is that such an agency should build local initiative and help communities stand on their own two feet, that limited federal funds should be leveraged through cooperative projects to attract private and public contributions at the local level, that such cooperative projects should address practical, down-to-earth problems of local communities, and that community and economic development should take into full account the continual interplay between humans and their environment.

We also believe firmly that TVA should *not* be offering programs that duplicate those of other government agencies, programs that don't yield positive results, and most especially, programs that are not truly needed. Common sense would dictate this for any responsible government organization.

As a regional development agency, Mr. Chairman, TVA virtually stands alone. There are few, if any, other federal agencies with an explicit responsibility for regional economic development that also have a direct involvement in the creation and management of a region's basic energy and natural resource infrastructure. TVA is

unique in its ability to guide and apply the benefits of this infrastructure to the region's sustained, balanced growth. TVA's power system and natural resource development efforts are purposefully managed to help the region and its communities prosper. While TVA's congressionally-funded programs specifically aimed at community and economic development are vital links in the chain, TVA's overall effort to bring about progress in the region goes far beyond these specific initiatives. And that is what gives the Tennessee Valley Authority an edge when it comes to making economic development happen.

In viewing TVA's programs that focus specifically on community and economic development, the themes of *self-reliance, cooperation, interdependency,* and *practicality* are useful guides. . . .

Through the operation of our power system, our waterway system, our natural resource development programs, and our community and economic development activities, we are doing what we can to help the Tennessee Valley region and nation, and we don't shy away from saying so, Mr. Chairman.

But we want to make it clear, that we're doing so mainly with our own resources. The federal investment in TVA's regional development programs, although crucial, does not represent an "unfair" investment in the region and that investment by itself certainly does not give the valley region a federally sponsored advantage over any other region.

If the valley does have an advantage, that advantage comes from its own resources and the resources of its people which are its true building blocks for growth and progress.

REFERENCES

Articles of Agreement. 1985. Articles of agreement between the Tennessee Valley Authority and the Salary Policy Employee Panel and supplementary agreements as of January 7, 1985.

Brody, M. 1985. A way to line up cheap electricity. *Fortune,* 111 (6): 134–137.

Business Week. 1985. Utility fortunes dim with demand. March 22: 241.

Callahan, N. 1980. *TVA: Bridge over troubled waters.* South Brunswick, N.J.: A. S. Barnes & Company.

Chandler, W. U. 1984. *The myth of TVA: Conservation and development in the Tennessee Valley, 1933–1983.* Cambridge, Mass.: Ballinger Publishing Company.

Cheuse, A. 1983. Tripping the lights fantastic. *Boston Globe,* Magazine Section, May 29: 8ff. Rpr. in *Social Issues Resources Series: 3,* Article 69.

Citizen's Guide to TVA. 1984. Publication TVA/OGM/10-84/12. Knoxville, Tenn.: Tennessee Valley Authority.

Cook, J. 1985. Nuclear follies. *Forbes,* 135 (3): 82–100.

Dean, C. H. 1985a. *Remarks by C. H. Dean, Jr., Chairman, Tennessee Valley Authority.* Paper presented before the Select Committee on Energy, Legislative Assembly of Ontario, Toronto, Canada, September 26.

Droze, W. H. 1983. The TVA, 1945–80: The power company. In E. Hargrove & P. Conkin (Eds.), *TVA: Fifty years of grassroots bureaucracy:* 66–85. Urbana, Ill.: University of Illinois Press.

Electrical World. 1981a. French reactor gets applause from U.S. group. February, 195: 23–24.

Electrical World. 1981b. Personalities: Charles H. Dean. August, 194: 60.

Electrical World. 1984. TVA realigns nuclear responsibilities. May, 198: 21.

Engardio, P. 1985. Can a chastened TVA reform its nuclear ways? *Business Week,* July 15: 83, 86.

Fenn, S. 1984. *America's electric utilities: Under siege and in transition.* New York: Praeger Publishers.

Fortune. 1985. The recovery will keep its cool. July 22, 112: 34–41.

Freeman, R. M. 1985. Energy conservation: Investing in an energy secure future. (Published chapter furnished by TVA; source unknown.)

Hobday, V. C. 1969. *Sparks at the grassroots: Municipal distribution of TVA electricity in Tennessee.* Knoxville: The University of Tennessee Press.

Holden, C. 1984. New directions for TVA? *Science,* 224 (4651): 852.

Huntsville Times. 1985a. Flippo says TVA records dispute pay contention. September 24: C–1.

Huntsville Times. 1985b. Inspector general proposed for TVA. October 1: A1–A2.

Huntsville Times. 1985c. Bevill says TVA non-power budget will clear Congress. October 2: F–1.

Huntsville Times. 1985d. House members, TVA board exchange barbs. September 19: C–2.

Huntsville Times. 1985e. But where were TVA's friends last week? September 22: B–3.

Huntsville Times. 1985f. No Browns Ferry power until April. September 25: F–1.

Huntsville Times. 1985g. NRC: TVA safest because N-plants are shut down. September 16.

Huntsville Times. 1985h. Denton sponsors bill for TVA post. October 10: A–7.

Huntsville Times. 1985i. TVA in line to obtain $113 million for projects. October 10: A–7.

Huntsville Times. 1985j. Flippo says TVA records dispute pay contention. September 24: C–1.

Huntsville Times. 1985k. TVA oks raises of $4.59 million. September 30: A–1.

Huntsville Times. 1985l. TVA reinstates 'whistleblower' to old job. October 1: C–1.

Huntsville Times. 1985m. 32 Watts Bar welders fail tests. September 27: C–1.

Huntsville Times. 1985n. TVA agrees to hire inspector general. October 18: A–1.

Joskow, P. L., & Schmalensee, R. 1983. *Markets for power: An analysis of electric utility deregulation.* Cambridge, Mass.: The MIT Press.

Leiserson, A. 1983. Administrative management and political accountability. In E. Hargrove & P. Conkin (Eds.), *TVA: Fifty years of grass-roots bureaucracy:* 122–149. Urbana, Ill.: University of Illinois Press.

Lyman, F. 1980. The human factor. *Environmental Action,* 11. Rpr. in *Social Issues Resources Series: 3,* Article 18.

Magnet, M. 1985. It's shape up or shake out in a shook-up world: The service 500. *Fortune,* 111 (12): 166–172.

Myers, R. J. 1985. A dimmer future for cogeneration. *Fortune,* 112 (8): 29.

Neuse, S. M. 1983. TVA at age fifty: Reflections and retrospect. *Public Administration Review,* 43: 491–499.

Owen, M. 1973. *The Tennessee Valley Authority.* New York: Praeger Publishers.

Sheppeard, L. 1985. Private communication. TVA Information Office, September 30, 1985.

Standard & Poor's Industry Surveys. 1984. Utilities—electric: Current analysis. August 9, 152 (32): U1–U37.

Steffy, R. C. 1985. FY 1986 final rate review presentation at TVA Board of Directors Meeting, August 29.

Tennessee Valley Authority. 1981. Seven ratemaking standards to encourage conservation and efficiency approved by TVA board. TVA news release TVA 4516 (10–2–80), April 1, Knoxville, Tenn.

Tennessee Valley Authority. 1982. Allocation of low-cost power benefits and assignment of benefits in rate design. TVA news release TVA 4516 (10–2–81), April 2. Knoxville, Tenn.

Tennessee Valley Authority. 1984a. *Organization bulletin*. I TVA, September 27.

Tennessee Valley Authority. 1984b. *1984 Annual report*. Knoxville, Tenn.: Tennessee Valley Authority.

Tennessee Valley Authority. 1984c. *Power engineering*. 1984 power program summary, Vol. 1. Knoxville, Tenn.: TVA.

Tennessee Valley Authority. 1985a. *Background on fiscal year 1986 budget request for TVA*. Knoxville, Tenn.: TVA.

Tennessee Valley Authority. 1985b. *Load forecast and power supply summary prepared for fiscal year 1986*. Chattanooga, Tenn.: TVA Power and Engineering, Power Planning Staff.

Tennessee Valley Authority Act. May 18, 1933. Public No. 17, 73d Congress, 1st Session [H.R. 5081]. 48 Stat. 58.

U.S. Department of Commerce. 1985. *Statistical abstract of the United States*. Washington, D.C.: U.S. Government Printing Office.

Wall Street Journal. 1985. Competition can power utilities into the black. October 14: 14.

TEXAS INSTRUMENTS, INC.

M. Afzalur Rahim
Western Kentucky University

Texas Instruments (TI) grew from a tiny geophysical services company founded in 1930 to a world leader in electronics. It has stayed on the technological edge of electronics for more than a quarter of a century. TI is engaged in the development, manufacture, and sale of a variety of products in the electrical and electronics industries for industrial, consumer, and government markets. These products consist of semiconductors (such as integrated circuits, and electrical and electronic control devices), government electronics (such as radar, infrared surveillance systems, and missile guidance and control systems), and digital products (such as minicomputers, data terminals, electronic calculators, and learning aids).

Patrick Haggerty headed the company from 1945 to 1976. This was TI's golden era uring which decentralization gave rise to a flood of innovations. Under Haggerty TI grew into the largest manufacturer of integrated circuits, a huge defense contractor, and a major power in minicomputers. During the 1970s, TI was a shining star of American technology. TI was admired by industry analysts as an innovative, aggressive outfit that was up to the challenge of beating the Japanese in consumer electronics. It was during this time Mark Shepherd, Jr., became chairman of the board and CEO and J. Fred Bucy became president of TI. The future goal of TI was to sell $15 billion worth of goods and services by the late 1980s. TI's three primary market thrusts were semiconductors,

distributed computing, and consumer electronics. Technology had been and will continue to be the key to TI's strategy.

One of TI's corporate strategies is to compete in fast-growing markets throughout the world. It has more than 77,800 employees working in more than 50 plants in 18 countries. TI's worldwide operations are linked by a data communications network. This network relays information through a system of 18 satellite channels, 14 earth stations, 1,500 terrestrial circuits, 65 mainframe computers, 500 minicomputers, and 32,000 terminals, including more than 10,000 TI Professional Computers (Dove, 1985).

INDUSTRY ANALYSIS

In 1983 the electronics industry rebounded from two years of limited sales growth. Leading the way in this outstanding recovery was the semiconductor segment of the industry. The economic recovery as well as an insatiable demand for microprocessors was largely responsible for the explosive growth. Sales increased in 1984 to $15.2 billion, a 37% increase over 1983's $11 billion. The Semiconductor Industry Association (SIA) has predicted a 24% increase in 1985 to $18.9 billion and a 19% rise to $22.4 billion in 1986.

Standard & Poor's predicts the profits of its semiconductor-components stock price group (Advanced Micro Devices, Intel, Motorola, National Semiconductors, and TI) to rise dramatically in 1985, possibly reaching 240% over 1984. This is in sharp contrast to the 1983 decline of 24%, which was partially due to the heavy losses reported by TI in its now defunct home computer business. Due to a lack of capital investment in the 1981–82 industry recession, a shortage of capacity had existed during 1983–84, creating a significant backlog of orders. There was some relief in 1985 from projects that were begun in 1983–84.

While most economists are expecting the recovery to remain on course in 1986, a downturn in growth during the latter half of the year is possible. The increase in capital spending in 1983 and 1984 is a reason for some concern since debt was used to finance much of the expansion. This has made the industry highly leveraged and very sensitive to volume savings. One possible downturn in semiconductor volume stems from a potential decline in the personal computer market, especially compatibles. At present IBM compatibles consume approximately 10% of the semiconductor industry's output.

Despite the potential problems in the industry's expansion program, the demand for semiconductors is expected to rise as new applications are developed. In short, many industry experts feel growth in the semiconductor industry is assured.

A second area of the electronics industry where TI is very strong is in government electronics. The total federal electronics market, which was $37.1 billion in 1984, is expected to grow to $42 billion by 1987. Much of this growth will come from increases in defense spending for electronics. Rebuilding the nation's arsenal has been a major priority of the Reagan Administration. Defense projects, such as stealth weaponry, radar, and communication systems, all of which require enormous quantities of electronic gear, will continue to fuel the growth. Also, the recent rejuvenation of the MX missile system by Congress is sure to help continued growth.

The other area of electronics in which TI is involved is digital products. These products include minicomputers, electronic data terminals and peripherals, electronic calculators, and learning aids. As will be discussed later, TI withdrew from the consumer home computer market in October 1983. Growth is expected to stem from new product innovations. Other industries not directly related to the electronics industry in which TI is involved are geophysical services and metallurgical materials. Geophysical services are not expected to show much improvement, since the market has remained weak in the past few years.

PRODUCTS

Semiconductors

TI was destined for greatness from the day in 1954 when a TI vice president stunned an engineers' conference in Dayton, Ohio, by pulling a handful of mass produced silicon transistors from his coat pocket. TI exemplified the new semiconductor industry, which grew rapidly, creating new markets from a stream of dazzling technological breakthroughs. Today TI is stronger than ever in semiconductors. Dollar sales are increasing about 25% vs. worldwide market growth of about 19%. TI is the world's leading chip producer. It is also the leading producer of semiconductors in Europe. In 1984 it led the American entry into the market for the new-generation, 256-kilobit dynamic random access memory chip. Semiconductors should continue to post higher profits, although a weak demand is expected to continue (Esposito, 1985).

Computers

The home computer sprang from TI's desire to find a mass market for its newest microprocessor. In 1980 TI introduced its home computer. TI used more than 1,000 retail outlets to distribute its computers. In 1981 J.C. Penney included TI's computer in its fall catalog. This was the only home computer that the chain was selling. TI tried to outmaneuver the competitors with heavy rebates. While TI pioneered the market for home computers, it greatly ignored the market for microcomputers aimed at professionals and very small businesses, computers that sell in the $1,000 to $10,000 range. TI's 99/4 was aimed at the ordinary American family. Yet it was a flop in the marketplace because the price was higher for most families, while computer buffs considered the product too unsophisticated.

In June 1983 TI announced its withdrawal from home computer business. TI took $660 million in writeoffs and posted a net loss of $145 million even after claiming an unusual tax credit. Two days after this announcement the TI stockholders "collectively took a $1.2 billion pasting as the price on TI dropped by more than $50 a share, to

107'' (Chakravarty, 1984, p. 38). TI's decision to withdraw from home computers also cost it a lot of credibility.

In late 1981 TI introduced its first computer for small businesses. Electronics experts were surprised to learn that the new models were not designed to use a popular computer-operating system called CP/M, which provides the basis for many of the leading software programs. Instead, TI had developed alternative programs. This was a critical mistake. Some industry analysts believe that TI deliberately chose to disregard CP/M simply because the company did not write or sell the programs. In 1983 TI launched its Professional Computer. It was successful in selling the product through its own sales force to commercial markets but efforts to sell it through computer stores failed.

In late 1984 TI introduced a lap-top personal computer called Pro-Lite. Some industry analysts are skeptical about the market potential. But TI believes the lap-top computer market will grow faster than the desktop computer market during the next two to three years.

TI's personal computer business is losing money and market share. Its basic mistake was to challenge the IBM PC rather than accept it as the industry standard (Mason & Ticer, 1985).

Defense Electronics

TI got into the defense business in 1941 when it was called Geophysical Services, Inc. Its strengths in semiconductors allowed it to build its defense electronics business in the 1970s and 1980s. In 1983 the defense electronics division had revenues of $1.2 billion. Besides its pace-setting research in semiconductors, TI has developed a series of state-of-the-art radar and missile-guidance systems for the U.S. military. As the Reagan Administration's planned defense buildup gathers force, these technologies could become huge money-makers. In 1984 it added a major program of full production of the High-Speed Anti-Radiation Missile (HARM), intended to destroy an enemy's ground-based radar systems. This program may be worth some $5 billion over the next 10 years.

Watches

TI entered the watch market with an aggressive pricing strategy that succeeded for awhile. But as the market began demanding more fashion and features, TI failed to adapt. It was unable to match the Japanese marketing blitz and after two years of losses abandoned the field altogether in 1981.

Calculators

Programmable calculators were once TI's exclusive market. But it has lost market share steadily during the past four years. However, TI's share of the U.S. professional calculator market still stands at about 50%. Hewlett-Packard is squeezing TI out of the high-priced end of the calculator market while the Japanese have cornered sales of its other models. In 1981 TI launched a line of price leaders that started at $10 to combat the Japanese.

Learning Aids

TI has been dominant in the educational product market since no company has matched its line of talking-learning aids, a consumer category that the company pioneered in 1978 with Speak and Spell. The invention of this talking computer was brought about by TI's vigorous research and development. It has also introduced Speak and Read, Speak and Math, and Touch and Tell.

MANAGEMENT STYLE

Mark Shepherd, Jr., became the chief executive officer in 1969, taking over from former chairman and CEO Patrick Haggerty. When Haggerty retired in 1976, Shepherd also became the chairman. Shepherd subsequently passed the CEO title to President J. Fred Bucy. Shepherd has an electrical engineering background and was responsible for setting up TI's semiconductor operations in 1954. After working at every major division at TI, Bucy became president when Haggerty retired. Bucy started with TI as a physicist.

The leadership style of the two top executives was characterized as authoritarian. Bucy and Shepherd were reluctant to delegate much authority to other managers, resulting in almost every important decision being made by them. This has caused much frustration among upper and middle managers. TI has lost group vice presidents and executive vice presidents because of the abrasive management style of Bucy and Shepherd. One longtime group manager recalls, ''If Bucy and Shepherd didn't like something, they'd interrupt the presentation by saying, That's bull! If that's all you have to say, we don't want to hear it. Another time they walked out on my presentation because they didn't like what I had to say." "We spent more time saying what Fred and Mark wanted to hear, than saying what we thought," said another middle-level manager who recently left TI. Management meetings were sometimes punctuated by table-pounding, table-kicking, and flying objects." Many former employees describe Shepherd and Bucy as "meddlesome and hot-tempered." These two executives drove off some of TI's best scientists and managers. Such strong personalities have created a corporate culture which can be characterized as Exploitive Authoritative as conceptualized by Likert (1967).

In April 1985 Bucy unexpectedly announced his decision to retire early. The directors announced the promotion of Executive Vice-President Jerry R. Junkins to president and CEO of the company. His "elevation to president and chief executive signaled the end of an abrasive management style that many felt had contributed to a fat catalogue of the company's misfortunes" (O'Reilly, 1985, p. 60). Junkins, an engineer from Iowa, who had spent 28 years at TI, is widely regarded as a likable manager who is willing to listen to the employees.

Shepherd remains a potential obstacle. Although he has lost some of his power, he kept control of TI's strategic planning, communication, legal, and finance departments as its "chief corporate officer."

ORGANIZATION STRUCTURE

TI's problems in the consumer market stem partly from its matrix organization structure. Under this system a product-customer center (PCC) was created whenever there was a clear match between a product and a market. This system, which was created by Haggerty, gave the manager of the PCC complete responsibility for profits and losses, but not enough authority to control the functional departments, such as manufacturing and marketing. In essence the PCC manager didn't have enough authority over the functional departments to get the job done.

These problems were particularly evident in the digital watch and programmable calculator PCCs. The problem resulted from disagreements among managers of PCC and functional departments about the demand for each line of business. This partly resulted in the loss of considerable market share to Hewlett-Packard in the programmable calculator business.

President Bucy had attempted to solve the problem with the PCCs by cutting back a number of them. For example, in semiconductor operations, cutting back on PCCs meant going from about 18 small units to seven large ones that report directly to a vice-president instead of through divisional managers.

STRATEGIC PLANNING SYSTEM

Another of Haggerty's legacies, the planning system known as Objectives, Strategies, and Tactics (OST), is slowly being done away with. Under this system, top management and the board of directors are responsible for setting objectives, such as to be a leader of semiconductors, and other managers and engineers design strategies to achieve those objectives. Blueprints of these strategies are sent down to very low-level managers, requiring them to handle both day-to-day operations as well as the development of strategies. Since most managers are more concerned with their operating results rather than strategies that may not bear directly on their operating responsibilities, strategy development was often pushed aside.

TI is moving away from the heavy paperwork requirements of the old OST system and substituting a computerized data base. The computer can make predictions about the financial requirement of a proposed product development project in 30 seconds, a job that used to take managers a week to complete. The main problem with this computerized planning system is that Bucy and Shepherd used to consistently second-guess its results, rendering it practically worthless.

It is currently following three different corporate strategies. Because it is a dominant firm in its industry it is following a keep-the-offensive strategy. Being in a young emerging industry allows TI to also follow a grow/build strategy. Another strategy of TI is to be a low-cost producer.

MARKETING STRATEGY

When TI dropped its digital watches, outsiders were sure that the company's vaunted management systems had finally gone awry. Competitors proclaimed that past marketing and technological sins had finally caught up with the electronics giant. TI's management was determined to solve what had grown into a fundamental problem for the company—its shortcoming in marketing. The managers freely admitted that they were insensitive to marketing needs of the company.

Nowhere has that insensitivity been so clearly dem-

TABLE 1   CONSOLIDATED FINANCIAL STATEMENTS

(In millions of dollars except for share amounts)	For the year ended December 31		
	1985	1984	1983
Income and retained earnings			
Net sales bilied	$4,924.5	$5,741.6	$4,579.8
Operating costs and expenses			
Cost of goods and services sold	4,071.2	4,189.6	3,908.4
General, administrative and marketing	816.9	858.1	901.0
Employees' retirement and profit sharing plans	64.2	168.1	58.5
Total	4,952.3	5,215.8	4,867.9
Profit (loss) from operations	(27.8)	525.8	(288.1)
Plant-closing and employment-reduction costs	(63.8)	—	—
Other income (expense) net	17.0	9.6	.9
Interest on loans	(40.4)	(48.9)	(36.0)
Income (loss) before provision (credit) for income taxes	(115.0)	486.5	(323.2)
Provision (credit) for income taxes	3.7	170.5	(177.8)
Net income (loss)	(118.7)	316.0	(145.4)
Retained earnings at beginning of year	1,241.3	973.9	1,167.1
Cash dividends declared on common stock ($2.00 per share in 1985, 1984 and 1983)	(50.1)	(48.6)	(47.8)
Retained earnings at end of year	$1,072.5	$1,241.3	$ 973.9
Earnings (loss) per common share (average outstanding during year)	$ (4.76)	$ 13.05	$ (6.09)
Changes in financial position			
Sources of cash			
Net income (loss)	(118.7)	$ 316.0	$ (145.4)
Depreciation	515.9	422.6	351.4
Net (increase) decrease in working capital (excluding cash and short-term investments, loans payable and current portion long-term debt, and dividends payable)	(54.8)	(144.8)	123.9
Provided from operations	342.4	593.8	329.9
Net change in total long-term debt	2.6	156.3	11.0
Deferral of pension contributions	76.9	—	—
Sales and other common stock transactions	56.0	69.3	35.0
Other	(29.3)	36.1	(42.8)
	448.6	855.5	333.1
Uses of cash			
Additions (net) to property, plant and equipment	484.8	704.7	454.1
Dividends paid on common stock	49.8	48.3	47.6
Increase in deferred taxes and other assets	11.5	21.3	54.4
Decrease (increase) in loans payable	18.1	(8.3)	12.1
	564.2	766.0	568.2
Increase (decrease) in cash and short-term investments	$ (115.6)	$ 89.5	$ (235.1)

TABLE 2   BALANCE SHEET

	December 31 1985	December 31 1984
Assets		
Current assets		
Cash and short-term investments	$ 158.8	$ 274.4
Accounts receivable, less allowance for losses of $68.1 in 1985 and $119.1 in 1984	620.1	793.7
Inventories (net of progress billings)	447.7	489.2
Deferred taxes and prepaid expenses	304.1	301.1
Total current assets	1,530.7	1,858.4
Property, plant and equipment at cost	2,775.6	2,577.1
Less accumulated depreciation	(1,325.6)	(1,096.0)
Property, plant and equipment (net)	1,450.0	1,481.1
Deferred taxes and other assets	95.4	83.9
Total assets	$3,076.1	$3,423.4
Liabilities and stockholders' equity		
Current liabilities		
Loans payable and current portion long-term debt	$ 29.6	$ 46.3
Accounts payable and accrued expenses	1,024.7	1,122.6
Income taxes payable	56.7	135.0
Accrued retirement and profit sharing contributions	5.3	96.0
Dividends payable	12.6	12.3
Total current liabilities	1,128.9	1,412.2
Long-term debt	381.9	380.7
Deferred credits and other liabilities	137.6	90.0
Stockholders' equity (common shares outstanding at year-end: 1985 25,167,670 1984 24,616,098)	1,427.7	1,540.5
Total liabilities and stockholders' equity	$3,076.1	13,423.4

onstrated as in the company's consumer products operations. The lack of marketing skills certainly was a major factor in the failure of its watch business. TI simply did not try to understand the consumer, nor would it listen to the marketplace.

In an attempt to raise the company's marketing skills to a par with its highly respected capabilities in manufacturing and technology, TI started to institutionalize marketing throughout the consumer products division. TI appointed Grant A. Dove, as senior vice-president for marketing. He was a longtime TIer who was on its policy and corporate development committees. He replaced 26 different advertising agencies with New York's McCann-Erickson, Inc. to handle TI's worldwide advertising. Dove tripled radio and television advertising expenditures. He pursued an aggressive pricing strategy, espe-

cially in the calculator business and later in the home computer business.

When TI dropped its home computers most of the problems were the same as with the watches. Some industry observers believe that TI's failure in the home computer business was due to both marketing and engineering problems. After the home computer failure, TI hired a top marketing person, Peter Field, from Procter & Gamble to develop and coordinate its marketing strategies. This shows that TI is beginning to get serious about its marketing problems.

FINANCIAL ANALYSIS

The Consolidated Income Statements and Balance Sheets for the financial years 1983–85 and Summary of Selected

TABLE 3 SUMMARY OF SELECTED FINANCIAL DATA (Millions of Dollars)

Year ended December 31	1985	1984	1983	1982	1981	1980	1979	1978	1977	1976
Net sales billed	$4,924.5	$5,741.6	$4,579.8	$4,326.6	$4,206.0	$4,074.7	$3,224.1	$2,549.9	$2,046.5	$1,658.6
Operating costs and expenses	4,952.3	5,215.8	4,867.9	4,090.9	3,953.1	3,656.0	2,904.8	2,296.4	1,835.7	1,496.0
Profit (loss) from operations	(27.8)	525.8	(288.1)	235.7	252.9	418.7	319.3	253.5	210.8	162.6
Other income (expense) net	(46.8)	9.6	.9	10.5	(36.6)	4.6	8.9	12.3	9.3	23.8
Interest on loans	(40.4)	(48.9)	(36.0)	(33.1)	(41.3)	(44.3)	(19.5)	(8.4)	(9.2)	(8.3)
Income (loss) before provision (credit) for income taxes	(115.0)	486.5	(323.2)	213.1	175.0	379.0	308.7	257.4	210.9	178.1
Provision (credit) for income taxes	3.7	170.5	(177.8)	69.1	66.5	166.8	135.8	117.1	94.3	80.7
Net income (loss)	(118.7)	316.0	(145.4)	144.0	108.5	212.2	172.9	140.3	116.6	97.4
Earnings (loss) per common share (average outstanding during year)	$(4.76)	$13.05	$(6.09)	$6.10	$4.62	$9.22	$7.58	$6.15	$5.11	$4.25
Cash dividends declared per common share	2.00	2.00	2.00	2.00	2.00	2.00	2.00	1.76	1.41	1.08
Common shares (average shares outstanding during year in thousands)	24,948	24,210	23,862	23,609	23,483	23,021	22,799	22,794	22,842	22,933

December 31	1985	1984	1983	1982	1981	1980	1979	1978	1977	1976
Working capital	$ 401.8	$ 446.2	$ 221.2	$ 568.2	$ 432.1	$ 327.9	$ 200.7	$ 304.3	$ 365.7	$ 364.8
Property, plant and equipment (net)	1,450.0	1,481.1	1,199.0	1,096.3	1,105.5	1,097.4	812.5	572.7	394.1	302.9
Total assets	3,076.1	3,423.4	2,713.3	2,631.4	2,310.5	2,413.7	1,908.2	1,494.1	1,234.3	1,110.2
Long-term debt	381.9	380.7	225.1	214.0	211.7	211.7	17.6	19.1	29.7	38.2
Stockholders' equity	1,427.7	1,640.5	1,202.7	1,360.8	1,260.1	1,164.5	952.9	821.3	723.9	642.8
Employees	77,872	86,563	80,696	80,007	83,714	89,875	85,779	78,571	68,521	66,162
Stockholders of record	34,456	30,701	32,856	28,994	31,460	28,370	28,405	26,247	24,438	22,425

Financial Data for the financial years 1976–85 are shown in Tables 1, 2, and 3, respectively (Texas Instruments, 1985).

Net sales billed for 1985 were $4,924 million, a decline of 14% compared with $5,742 in 1984 (up 25% over 1983). This was caused primarily by a substantial reduction in semiconductor shipments. Lower semiconductor volume and sharp price declines in these products were the principal reasons for a loss from operations of 27.8 million for the year, compared with a profit from operations of $525.8 million in 1984. The pretax loss for the year was $115 million, including a $63.8 million charge taken in the third quarter to reflect the costs of plant closings and employment reductions. Net loss for the year was $118.7 million, or $4.76 per share, compared with net income of $316 million, or $13.5 per share, in 1984.

The net income for TI in 1984 was $316 million, compared with 1983's net loss of $145.4 million. Earnings per share in 1984 were $13.05. In 1983, TI had a net loss of $6.09 per share.

REFERENCES

Chakravarty, S.N. (1984, April 23). Recovering from the trauma. *Forbes*, pp. 38–39.

Dove, G.A. (1985, May 16). *Texas Instruments and international competition in a high-technology society.* Dallas, TX: The Dallas Council of World Affairs.

Esposito, E.J. (Ed.). (1985, Spring). *Moody's handbook of common stock: Special features.* New York: Moody's Investors Service.

Likert, R. (1967). *Human organization: Its management and value.* New York: McGraw-Hill.

Mason, T., & Ticer, S. (1985, June 10). Troubled Texas Instruments turns to a cooler head. *Business Week*, p. 50.

O'Reilly, B. (1985, July 8). Texas Instruments: New boss, big job. *Fortune*, pp. 60–61, 64.

Texas Instruments. (1985). *Annual report.* Dallas, TX: Texas Instruments.

TURNER BROADCASTING SYSTEM, INC. (A and B)

Neil H. Snyder
University of Virginia

TED TURNER: ENTREPRENEUR

In 1962, at age 24, Ted Turner faced some very difficult decisions—more difficult, in fact, than most people, including businesspeople, ever face. His father committed suicide and left an outdoor (billboard) advertising business that was $6 million in debt and short of cash. Rejecting the advice of the company's bankers who believed Turner was too inexperienced to run the company, he chose not to sell the firm, but instead, to build it. Immediately, he sold some of the company's assets to improve its cash position, refinanced its debt, renegotiated contracts with customers, hired new sales people, and literally turned the company around. By 1969, the company's debt was paid off, and in 1970, having secured the future of Turner Advertising, Ted Turner purchased Channel 17, an Atlanta independent/UHF television station. Although Channel 17 is widely recognized today as a profitable business, in 1970 it was two years old, losing $50,000 per month, and competing in a market dominated by three firmly-rooted network stations in Atlanta.

Recently, due in large measure to his phenomenal financial success, journalists have begun to explore Ted Turner, the man. Below are excerpts from a *Wall Street Journal* article:

Associates of broadcaster Ted Turner like to retell the story of his victory in a 1979 yachting race because they think it says it all about the man.

Mr. Turner's boat, *Tenacious,* battled 40-foot waves whipped by 65-knot winds in the Irish Sea to win the Fastnet race. Of the 306 boats that started the race, only 87 finished, and in one of ocean racing's greatest tragedies, 19 sailors drowned.

After his extraordinary display of skill and courage, Mr. Turner at dockside callously reminded his somber British hosts that in the 16th century the Spanish Armada ran into similar trouble. "You ought to be thankful there are storms like that," he said, "or you'd all be speaking Spanish". . . .

The flamboyant Southerner, called a visionary by some and a buffoon by others, seems a bit of both. Widely referred to as "Terrible Ted" and "The Mouth of the South," he has been charged with hypocrisy for preaching family values and then appearing drunk in public, and for criticizing the networks' TV "garbage" while boasting to Playboy magazine that he has photographed nude women. . . .

Friends and colleagues attribute both Mr. Turner's

successes and his excesses to a personality riddled with contradictions. "Ted is a brilliant person," says Irwin Mazo, a former Turner accountant, "but he also borders on egomania." Although he often talks hard-line conservatism, Mr. Turner seems genuinely concerned about pet liberal issues like overpopulation, world hunger and nuclear proliferation. He presides over a major news organization but says he limits his newspaper reading to glances at *USA Today* and the Atlanta papers' sports section. He professes to admire the courtly values of the Old South yet often treats his senior executives like servants.

The conflicting sides are cemented by an overwhelming tenacity. "He competes in everything he does," says Jim Roddey, a former Turner executive and sailing buddy who has known him for 25 years. "He sails like he conducts business—it's all or nothing." Indeed, when he saw an Atlanta Braves game-night promotion threatened by lack of participants, he jumped into the contest: He rolled a baseball around the infield with his nose and emerged with blood streaming from forehead to chin.

That incident, his friends say, demonstrates both Mr. Turner's love of publicity and his willingness to sacrifice his dignity in his drive to win. . . .

Mr. Turner was thrust into the business world more than 20 years ago, when his father committed suicide immediately after selling most of the family billboard business. Then 24 years old, Mr. Turner challenged the would-be buyers and regained control of the company. "He could have lost it all," recalls Mr. Mazo, the accountant. But then as apparently now, says Mr. Mazo, "Ted is willing to put all his chips on the table and roll the dice."

In 1970, with the billboard business reestablished, Mr. Turner gambled next on buying a floundering Atlanta UHF television station. In 1976, he transformed it into one of the nation's most profitable stations by having its signal bounced off a satellite and into the nation's cable-TV systems. He channeled Turner Broadcasting's profits from the superstation into a round-the-clock news service dubbed Cable News Network. Five years later, as CNN approaches profitability, Mr. Turner is looking for a new challenge.

Throughout, Mr. Turner's revolutionary moves have been scoffed at by the broadcasting establishment, just as brokers now are scoffing at his CBS takeover bid. Even Turner confidants have been skeptical about his moves. "He's made about $500 million and at least $400 million of that was on deals I told him not to do," chuckles Mr.

Roddey, the former Turner executive who admits to advising the company to stick with billboards. . . .

Mr. Turner's management technique isn't any more conventional. "He's not a manager," says Mr. Roddey. "He's not hands-on. He always used to tell me I was getting bogged down in the details, like making the payroll."

But the volatile executive is "a very tough guy to work for," says Reese Schonfeld, the first president of CNN, who left after a dispute with Mr. Turner over hiring and firing. "I've seen him abuse a lot of people. Once you let him humiliate you, he'll walk all over you." Mr. Schonfeld says Mr. Turner has a habit of ordering his senior executives to fetch drinks for him.

Not all Turner employees have such gripes. Lower-level workers at CNN, housed in the basement of Turner Broadcasting's Atlanta headquarters, say their encounters with Mr. Turner are infrequent and non-confrontational. But life in Turner's executive suite looks stressful: In June 1983, for example, when Mr. Bevins was 36, he was struck by a heart attack while in Mr. Turner's office. Mr. Bevins declines to discuss the incident. . . .

In recent years, however, both Mr. Turner and his company have toned down. Aides say the change began when Mr. Turner began to realize that obtaining control of a network might someday be within his grasp. He began to position himself for an eventual combination, they say.

For Mr. Turner, that meant dropping off the interview trail and scaling down his public excesses. He repeatedly declined to be interviewed for this story, for instance. While hardly prim these days, "he's become more discreet," says one longtime Turner employee. And with age, his friends say, has come a dose of maturity. "Lately he talks a lot about world peace, nuclear war, improving the environment," says Gary Jobson, tactician aboard many of Mr. Turner's winning yachts (*Wall Street Journal,* April 19, 1985, pages 1 and 6).

Turner's perspective on business is interesting to say the least. He is quoted as saying,

I don't think winning is everything. It's a big mistake when you say that I think trying to win is what counts. Be kind and fair and make the world a better place to live, that's what's important. . . . I think the saddest people I've ever met were people with a lot of wealth. If you polled 90 percent of the people and asked them what they want most, most would want to be millionaires. I'll tell you, you've got to be one to know how unimportant it is. . . . I'm blessed with some talents. I've made a lot of money, more than I ever thought I would. . . . But if I continue to be successful, I would like to serve my fellow man in some way other than doing flips at third base. . . . People want leadership, somebody to rally around, and I want to be a leader (*Atlanta Constitution,* January 8, 1977).

CREATING A NETWORK: WTBS, THE SUPERSTATION

WTBS is the pioneer of the SuperStation concept. Owned and operated by the Turner Broadcasting System Inc., it is an independent UHF television station, Channel 17 in Atlanta, Georgia, whose signal is beamed via satellite to television households nationwide. Ted Turner, TBS President and Chairman of the Board, purchased Channel 17 in January 1970. By merging the then Turner Communications Corporation with Rice Broadcasting, he gained control of the television outlet, which became WTCG, flagship station of the Turner Communications Group.

Realizing that WTCG's programming could be made available by satellite to millions of television viewers throughout the country, Turner originated the Super-Station concept. In short, the "SuperStation" is a reworking of the traditional television network concept, in which one station acts as original programming supplier for a multiplicity of distant cable markets. On December 16, 1976, WTCG made history, as its signal was beamed to cable systems nationwide via a transponder on RCA's Satcom I satellite. Satcom I was replaced by Satcom III-R in January 1982, and by Galaxy I in January 1985.

In 1979, the Turner Communications Group was renamed Turner Broadcasting System Inc., and, to reflect this change, the WTCG call letters became WTBS. The company estimates that, as of February 29, 1984, WTBS was beamed into approximately 75% of U.S. cable homes and 35% of U.S. television homes.

WTBS broadcasts twenty-four hours per day, acquiring its programming primarily from film companies, syndicators of programs that have run successfully on television networks, and its sports affiliates. WTBS currently has available 4,100 film titles for its programming needs, the majority of which are available for multiple runs. In addition, approximately 500 titles are under contract and will become available for programming purposes in the future. Approximately 23% of the purchased program-

ming has been obtained from Viacom International, Inc. and 17% from MCA. WTBS has not obtained more than 10% of its purchased programming needs from any other single supplier, and approximately 1900 hours of programming broadcast on WTBS during 1983 were produced internally, or under contract. Exhibits 1, 2, 3, 4, 5, and 6 are descriptions of internally produced programs. WTBS plans to produce more programs internally in the future.

WTBS derives revenue from the sale of advertising time, and advertising prices depend on the size of WTBS' viewing audience and the amount of available time sold. Since February 1981, the A.C. Nielsen Company has been measuring the audience level of WTBS for use by the company and its advertisers. The demand for advertising time on cable television is significantly lower than that for advertising time on the three major networks because of the relatively small size of the cable network audiences and the fact that cable has not penetrated significantly in many of the major urban markets. The Board of Directors of TBS anticipates that the continued growth of the cable television (CATV) industry, particularly in the major urban markets, will result in increased demand on the part of advertisers.

The revenues of WTBS also include amounts obtained from "direct response" advertising, which represent fees received by the company for the sale of products it promotes by advertisement. The company broadcasts advertisements for the products during unsold advertising time, and the products are ordered directly by viewers through the company by mail or telephone. WTBS collects a fee for each order. In 1983, these fees amounted to 6.6% of total advertising revenues for WTBS.

Advertising time for WTBS as well as the company's cable news services is marketed and sold by the company's own advertising sales force consisting of approximately 101 persons located in sales offices in New York, Chicago, Detroit, Los Angeles, and Atlanta.

According to the *Wall Street Journal* (April 19, 1985):

It's hard to laugh at Mr. Turner's operations now, or at least the WTBS operation. His superstation, one of the nation's most popular cable services, now beams a steady diet of sports, movies and reruns into almost 34 million U.S. households, or about 84% of all homes equipped for cable.

It has revolutionized the cable-television business, says Ira Tumpowsky, a Young & Rubicam Inc. senior vice president who oversees the agency's cable-TV buying. "He's the

EXHIBIT 1   **Portrait of America.**

PORTRAIT OF AMERICA

PORTRAIT OF AMERICA, an in-depth, 60-part documentary series exploring each of the United States and U.S. territories, highlights the SuperStation program lineup. Filmed on location, this ambitious, five-year series of hour-long specials marks the most comprehensive look ever at the pieces which make up the greatest nation on earth.

Hosted and narrated by award-winning television, film and stage star Hal Holbrook, *PORTRAIT OF AMERICA* reveals unusual characters, depicts interesting places and delves into the ingenuity, beauty and heritage of American life with insatiable curiosity. Each episode focuses on a single state, commonwealth or territory, painting a close-up, modern picture of the land and its people, framed in the flavor of local culture and the strength of American history.

"We're taking an insightful look at the diversity of people and resources of this nation, rather than dwelling on its weaknesses," says WTBS President Robert Wussler.

PORTRAIT OF AMERICA, originated by TBS Board Chairman and President R.E. "Ted" Turner, has been cited by numerous organizations for outstanding television achievement. The series has been honored with a George Foster Peabody Award, one of electronic journalism's most prestigious prizes, and a variety of top film festival awards.

Recommended by the National Education Association for viewing by students, the award-winning *PORTRAIT OF AMERICA* airs four times a month to ensure viewing availability. The SuperStation presents the first telecast during prime time, with replays scheduled for late night, weekend early fringe and weekend daytime. The series successfully debuted in January 1983 with a profile of Virginia, followed in the first 18 months by programs featuring Nevada, Georgia, Puerto Rico, Florida, Texas, Oregon, Iowa, Indiana, New Jersey, New Mexico, Connecticut, Idaho, Wisconsin, Missouri, North Dakota, Louisiana and Maine. A new *PORTRAIT OF AMERICA* episode will be introduced every month, with the entire series continuing for five years.

"This project is yet another example of the impact cable television can have on viewers across the nation," says *PORTRAIT OF AMERICA* Executive Producer Ira Miskin. "TBS intends to make a tangible contribution to a nation long starved for reinforcement of its faith in what makes America great."

EXHIBIT 2   **Jacques Cousteau.**

JACQUES COUSTEAU

In the Turner Broadcasting System tradition of quality family programming, the SuperStation offers exciting first-run Cousteau Society specials and a regularly scheduled series of hour-long documentaries, *THE UNDERSEA WORLD OF JACQUES COUSTEAU.*

Scheduled for 1985 is a seventh and final hour to the successful *COUSTEAU/AMAZON* series. The special explores the cocaine and drug trafficking problem in Amazonia, a major source of cocaine brought into the United States.

Also new from The Cousteau Society in 1985 is a two-hour documentary on the 2,348-mile Mississippi River, offering the most comprehensive look Cousteau has ever made at a water system in the United States.

In 1984, the SuperStation aired *COUSTEAU/ AMAZON*, a six-hour documentary covering the

"Calypso's" 18-month expedition into South America's Amazon River Basin, where teams of environmental scientists explored the uncharted. Narrated by Joseph Campanella, the series gives new insight into the world's second longest river, its abundant lifeforms, its people and its future.

An encore presentation of the entire seven-hour *COUSTEAU/AMAZON* series is scheduled for early 1985.

COUSTEAU/AMAZON has received national acclaim, being called "an extraordinary video venture" by the *Chicago Tribune.* The *Philadelphia Inquirer* has said, "What makes a Cousteau show utterly different from any other is the decency, humanity and worth of the man himself. His character shines through the screen." The series is "as gorgeous as you'd expect it to be," said the *Atlanta Constitution,* while *The Hollywood Reporter* applauded it as "uplifting and entertaining." *Daily Variety* said of the documentary, which took two years to produce, "It's been worth the wait."

During past seasons, the SuperStation debuted two more beautiful Cousteau films: *ST. LAWRENCE: STAIRWAY TO THE SEA,* a fascinating study of the Great Lakes-Inland Waterway System; and *CRIES FROM THE DEEP,* a stirring investigation of the struggle for survival between men and animals in the Canadian North Atlantic.

THE UNDERSEA WORLD OF JACQUES COUSTEAU, which airs Sundays at 5:35-6:35 PM (ET), combines scientific knowledge with beauty and aquatic adventure to create one of television's most highly acclaimed documentary series.

Captain Jacques-Yves Cousteau and son Jean-Michel have devoted their lives to making people aware of nature and its processes. They have set the tone for many of today's environmental action efforts and are symbols of mankind's concern for the health and well-being of future generations.

Jacques Cousteau

Jean-Michel Cousteau

Cable's Most Popular Network

SuperStationWTBS

EXHIBIT 3 **Good News.**

GOOD NEWS

Liz Wickersham

GOOD NEWS

GOOD NEWS, an innovative, uplifting and positively entertaining approach to the news, airs on SuperStation WTBS Sundays at 10:05 AM (ET). The half-hour program recaps the week's most inspiring news from around the world, with host Liz Wickersham reporting the positive, healthy and creative side of human events.

Now in its second year, *GOOD NEWS* has become basic cable's highest rated, originally produced, regularly scheduled, non-sports program. It offers lifestyle features, revealing interviews with some of the entertainment industry's most celebrated stars and unique looks at the hottest box office attractions and music videos.

News items designed to evoke smiles and boost spirits are gathered for *GOOD NEWS* through the worldwide resources of Turner Broadcasting's Cable News Network. *GOOD NEWS* is an original WTBS production, conceived by TBS Board Chairman R.E. "Ted" Turner, and produced by WTBS' award-winning writers/producers, Bonnie and Terry Turner.

Liz Wickersham became known to SuperStation viewers as host of *THE LIGHTER SIDE.* Prior to joining TBS in March 1982, she was a successful model and actress. She has been seen in many popular publications, including *Glamour, Mademoiselle* and *Cosmopolitan,* and has appeared in episodes of television's "One Life to Live," "The Edge of Night," "B.J. and the Bear" and "Magnum, P.I."

GOOD NEWS airs Sundays at 10:05-10:35 AM (ET) on SuperStation WTBS.

Cable's Most Popular Network

SuperStationWTBS

EXHIBIT 4   Down to Earth.

Carol Mansell

Dick Sargent

Ronnie Schell

DOWN TO EARTH

DOWN TO EARTH, SuperStation WTBS' first made-for-cable situation comedy, offers fun for the whole family on Fridays at 6:35-7:05 PM (ET).

Produced in Los Angeles by The Arthur Company in association with Procter & Gamble Productions Inc., *DOWN TO EARTH* follows the mishaps of a zany, endearing angel named Ethel MacDoogan, sent to earth for one final chance to win her wings. Through her daily efforts as their housekeeper, Ethel brings the Preston family, a widower and his three children, closer together and finally has earned her wings.

Ethel, who wants to remain on earth, now is assigned the task of aiding others, in addition to her role with the Prestons. Ethel (born 1887, died 1925) must report her earthly activities to Lester Luster, one of the head angels who can recall Ethel to heaven if she makes too many major blunders.

Modern living, from aerobics to home computers, is a revelation to this angel. Mix a large portion of naivete with a healthy dash of curiosity and a pinch of mischief and that's Ethel, *DOWN TO EARTH* with her late 20th century entourage. The Preston family consists of Richard, 38, an inventor's agent; Duane, 16, who is primarily concerned with his image; Lissy, 14, who begins to date; and Jay Jay, 8, the only one who knows Ethel is an angel.

Carol Mansell, who appeared in the title role of the Kennedy Center production "Really Rosie," stars as Ethel Methel MacDoogan. Ronnie Schell, who portrayed Gomer Pyle's best friend "Duke" on the hit television series "Gomer Pyle, USMC" is Lester Luster. Dick Sargent, who starred as Darrin Stephens on the long-running comedy "Bewitched," plays Richard Preston.

David Kaufman (Duane), Kyle Richards (Lissy) and Randy Josselyn (Jay Jay) round out the cast.

Cable's Most Popular Network

SuperStationWTBS

EXHIBIT 5 The Catlins.

Danny Nelson is
Medgar Quinn

Joseph Rainer is
Dirk Stack

Mary Nell Santacroce is
Catherine Catlin

THE CATLINS

THE CATLINS is a fascinating weekday series aired exclusively on SuperStation WTBS, and brought to you in part by the Brands at Procter & Gamble. Each exciting half-hour episode of *THE CATLINS* airs Monday through Friday at 11:05 AM (ET).

Set in Atlanta, the action centers around the wealthy and powerful Catlin family, whose feuds, romances, intrigues, laughs and triumphs weave a captivating contemporary drama.

Headed by Catherine Catlin, a tough-minded matriarch, the family consists of eight core members. T.J. Catlin is Catherine's son and Chairman of the Board of the family's financial empire. He and his wife Annabelle, an aristocratic Southern Belle, have five children. Matthew, their oldest child, is a handsome and highly respected cardiologist. Maggie is a brilliant and beautiful lawyer. Jonathan is the middle son, a straight-laced man who is desperate to prove himself. Beau is the family's dashingly attractive, devil-may-care black sheep. And Jennifer, the youngest Catlin, is a beautiful but naive young woman.

The Catlins are a rich and politically influential group, but they face major and minor complications in their efforts to stay on top. Most of their foils are generated by the antagonistic Quinn family, consisting of Medgar and his sons Seth and Cullen. The mutual dislike between the Catlins and the Quinns creates an electric and suspenseful atmosphere throughout their lives.

Other continuing characters on *THE CATLINS* include Dirk Stack, a slick-talking entrepreneur; Stacy Manning, a journalist whose first priority is herself; Woody Thorpe, a hardworking "good ol' boy" trying to become a success; and Babe Chalifoux, an undercover F.B.I. agent.

Tune in and keep up with *THE CATLINS* as the adventures unfold, weekdays on the SuperStation.

Cable's
Most
Popular
Network

SuperStationWTBS

EXHIBIT 6   World of Audubon.

WORLD OF AUDUBON

WORLD OF AUDUBON is an exciting new environmental series telecast on SuperStation WTBS. Airing quarterly throughout 1985, *WORLD OF AUDUBON* explores and celebrates the beauty and majesty of nature in fast-paced magazine format programs guaranteed to be soaring experiences.

The National Audubon Society, in its first long-term television effort, joins Turner Broadcasting System and the SuperStation in bringing the bracing and bewildering vitality of the great outdoors into focus as a fragile and beautiful treasure. *WORLD OF AUDUBON* highlights the splendors of the earth as cameras capture the teeming wildlife realm, showing that the world is full of glorious things.

"But," warns the National Audubon Society, "the wonders of wildlife are in danger!"

Hosted by veteran actor and environmentalist Cliff Robertson, each hour-long edition of *WORLD OF AUDUBON* uses remarkable on-location photography and interviews with noted conservationists to cover a variety of issues.

"The preservation of our planet's environment and its wildlife is one of the most important issues facing mankind today," says TBS Board Chairman and President R.E. "Ted" Turner. "We must be deeply concerned about the type of world we leave for future generations." National Audubon Society President Dr. Russell Peterson declares, "Of all the projects Audubon is working on, few compare in importance to this initiative with Ted Turner. It is a great opportunity for the National Audubon Society to reach the public with our very important message."

WORLD OF AUDUBON includes magnificently photographed segments on sea otters in Big Sur, CA; rare pink flamingos in Great Inagua, West Indies; bald eagles in Alaska; and grizzly bears in Yellowstone National Park. There are revealing interviews with actor Richard Chamberlain, who is working to preserve California's scenic Tuolumne River; with actress Pam Dawber ("Mork and Mindy"), who is a solar energy proponent; and with Margaret Owings, who is founder of "Friends of the Sea Otter."

WORLD OF AUDUBON's Academy Award-winning host Cliff Robertson is an active conservationist. His stage, film and television credits are numerous. He was selected personally by President John F. Kennedy to portray the President as a young World War II Navy Lieutenant in "PT-109." Robertson displayed his acting versatility by portraying a mentally-retarded man in the 1968 film, "Charly," for which he won an Academy Award.

WORLD OF AUDUBON is originated by R.E. "Ted" Turner and is a co-production of Turner Broadcasting System and the National Audubon Society.

Cliff Robertson

Cable's Most Popular Network

SuperStationWTBS

person who moved cable from a reception industry to a marketing industry,'' the advertising executive says.

TBS Sports

In January 1976, TBS acquired the Atlanta Braves professional baseball club, and on December 29, 1976, the Atlanta Hawks professional basketball club was acquired. Although both teams have consistently lost money, they have provided TBS with excellent sports programming, and the Atlanta Braves, ''America's Team,'' have a national following. TBS aired 150 Braves games and 41 Hawks games in 1984.

Along with a full schedule of Atlanta Braves baseball and Atlanta Hawks basketball, TBS Sports offers NCAA basketball, NBA basketball, NCAA football, Southeastern Conference football, and a variety of special sports presentations. For example, TBS Sports telecast the NASCAR circuit's Richmond 400, college football's Hall of Fame Bowl, and World Championship Wrestling during 1984.

Recently, baseball Commissioner Peter Ueberroth persuaded Ted Turner to make annual payments to other major-league teams if he continued to broadcast Braves games across the nation over his cable station. Turner has agreed to make these payments, totalling more than $25 million according to the *Wall Street Journal* (April 19, 1985), into a central fund for five years. This agreement is a compromise. Ueberroth had wanted to end nationwide cable broadcasts of baseball games, since they were hurting the profits of teams in other cities. Ueberroth is reported to have said that superstations are the most serious problem facing professional baseball (*Richmond Time Dispatch,* Jan. 28, 1985).

Ted Turner is said to be as creative with his sports franchises as he is with TBS. For example, the *Wall Street Journal* (April 19, 1985) concluded that:

Even in the stodgy game of baseball, Mr. Turner has displayed some business acumen. The Atlanta Braves franchise that he bought in 1976 was mired in mediocrity. Mr. Turner beefed up its farm system, paid top dollar to lure stars from elsewhere, and transmitted across the nation practically every game the team played. Average attendance at Braves' home games last year was 21,834, triple the figure for 1975. The Braves are widely considered pennant contenders this season.

In baseball, as in his other businesses, Mr. Turner has managed to outrage both his employees and his peers. Mr. Turner once tried to demote a slumping star to the minor leagues. At another point, he named himself manager of the team. Such antics led to a collision with the then-commissioner of baseball, Bowie Kuhn, and to Mr. Turner's temporary suspension from the game. According to one biography, Mr. Turner pleaded with Mr. Kuhn: ''I am very contrite. I would bend over and let you paddle my behind, hit me over the head with a Fresca bottle.''

CNN

Through its subsidiary Cable News Network, Inc. (CNN), which began broadcasting on June 1, 1980, TBS provides a twenty-four-hour news programming service which is available to CATV systems throughout the United States and in some foreign countries. The programming includes comprehensive reporting of domestic and international news, sports, business and weather, plus analysis, commentary and reports by its staff of experts and investigative reporters. CNN obtains news reports from its bureaus in various U.S. and foreign cities. Each of these bureaus is equipped to provide live reports to CNN's transmission facility in Atlanta thereby providing the capability for live coverage of news events around the world. In addition, news is obtained through wire services, television news services by agreement with television stations in various locations worldwide, and from free-lance reporters and camera crews.

CNN employs over 160 journalists, executives and technicians. The news channel was initially received by 193 CATV systems serving approximately 1.7 million subscribers. As of December 31, 1983, 4,278 CATV systems serving approximately 25.1 million subscribers received CNN's programming.

According to the *Wall Street Journal* (April 19, 1985):

During its five years of losses, CNN has grown to become the nation's most popular cable service, available in some 32 million homes. And this year, the company indicates, CNN should move into the black. Though still not an equal of the high-powered network news operations, CNN is nipping at their heels, and doing it on a bargain-basement budget.

CNN is weak on features says Jim Snyder, News vice president of Post-Newsweek Stations Inc., the broadcasting division of the Washington Post Co., but it covers breaking news ''as well as anybody.'' A recent Washington Journalism Review assessment of the channel carried the headline ''CNN Takes Its Place Beside the Networks.''

CNN Headline News

CNN offered another 24-hour news service to cable operators effective December 31, 1981. Referred to as

CNN Headline News (CNN HN), this service utilizes a concise, fast-paced format, programming in half-hour cycles throughout the day. CNN HN employs approximately 225 people, and its start-up required the construction and furnishing of a studio facility and additional transmitting facilities. The resources and expertise of CNN is utilized by CNN HN for accumulation of news material. Its revenues are derived from the sale of advertising on CNN HN and from fees charged for the syndication of CNN HN directly to over-the-air television and radio stations.

The number of cable homes receiving the CNN HN signal increased from approximately 5,400,000 in October 1983 to approximately 9,100,000 as a direct result of TBS' agreement to acquire CNN HN's major cable news competitor (The Satellite News Channel). Despite this increase in cable homes, TBS executives do not expect CNN HN to be profitable in 1984.

Cable Music Channel

On October 26, 1984, TBS launched its own brand of video-clip programming to compete with MTV. The Cable Music Channel started with 2.5 million households, about half the expected subscriber count company executives had predicted. However, by November 30, 1984, the Cable Music Channel's title and affiliate list was sold to MTV Networks Inc. for $1.5 million in cash and advertising commitments at a loss of $2.2 million. Cable Music Channel President/TBS Executive Vice President Robert Wussler acknowledges that operator resistance was largely responsible. "We didn't get the homes and we weren't about to get 3 or 5 million homes. We surveyed the field, felt we had a good product, but the industry obviously embraced MTV, the future in terms of acquiring subs was bleak and we felt strongly that this was our best course of action" (*CableVision*, December 10, 1984).

KEY EXECUTIVES & OWNERSHIP

Ted Turner is aided by highly qualified, experienced men. Robert J. Wussler, Executive Vice President, had twenty-one years experience with CBS, including his appointment as president of the CBS Sports Division, before joining TBS in August, 1981.

William C. Bevins, Jr. is Vice President of Finance, Secretary and Treasurer as well as a director of the com-

pany. Previously, he was affiliated with Price Waterhouse for ten years, most recently as Senior Manager.

Henry L. (Hank) Aaron has been Vice President-Director of Player Development for the Atlanta Braves since 1976, and the Vice President of Community Relations and a director of the company since 1980. He was previously a professional baseball player with a total of twenty-eight years of experience in professional sports, and he holds the world's record for the most home runs hit by a professional baseball player.

Burt Reinhardt became President of CNN in 1982 and a director of CNN in 1983. He was employed by the company in 1979 and was instrumental in organizing CNN. Previously, he served as Executive Vice-President of UPI Television News and Executive Vice President of the Non-Theatrical and Educational Division of Paramount Pictures.

Gerald Hogan joined the company in 1971 and served as General Sales Manager of WTBS from 1979 until 1981. He became Senior Vice President of Turner Broadcasting Sales, Inc. in 1982.

Henry Gillespie joined TBS in 1982 as Chairman of the Board of Turner Program Services, Inc. Prior to that, he served as President of Columbia Pictures Television Distribution and President of Viacom Enterprises.

J. Michael Gearon has been a director of the company, President of Hawks Management Company, and general partner of Atlanta Hawks, Ltd., operator of the Atlanta Hawks professional basketball team, since 1979. He previously owned a real estate brokerage and development firm in Atlanta, Georgia.

OWNERSHIP PHILOSOPHY

Currently, Ted Turner owns 86% of the common shares outstanding. Exhibit 7 presents TBS common stock ownership of selected individuals. Most of the stockholders besides Turner and his family are either directors or executive officers of TBS.

FINANCIAL ISSUES

Debt Philosophy

TBS is a highly leveraged company that emphasizes the building of asset values. Presently, the company has a $190 million revolving credit agreement extending until 1987, and $133 million of this credit line has been borrowed. Concerning long term debt, the company has in-

EXHIBIT 7   COMMON STOCK OWNERSHIP

Name of beneficial owner	Amount	Percent of class
R. E. Turner	17,579,922	86.2%
William C. Bevins, Jr.	20,000	0.1%
Peter A. Dames	98,910	0.5%
Karl Eller	1,000	—
Tench C. Coxe	128,285	0.6%
J. Michael Gearon	31,500	0.2%
Martin B. Seretean	20,800	0.1%
William C. Bartholomay	210,700	1.0%
Allison Thornwell, Jr.	215,912	1.1%
All directors and officers as a group (27 persons)	18,421,489	90.4%

*From 1984 Annual 10-K Report

curred debt restructuring fees which it expenses as interest based on the weighted average of the principal balance outstanding throughout the term of the agreement. The company paid restructuring fees of $3,650,000 during 1983, and the balance due at year end is classified as current and long-term in accordance with the payment terms of the agreements.

Under terms of its 1983 debt agreement, the company is limited with regard to additional borrowings, cash dividends, and acquisition of the company's common stock. TBS is also required, among other things, to maintain minimum levels of working capital and to meet specified current ratio requirements. It is important to note that the company was not in compliance with certain restrictive covenants of its loan agreement on December 31, 1983. TBS received waivers of these restrictions from lenders; accordingly, the amounts due have been classified in accordance with the original terms of the agreement.

Owner's Equity

Characteristic of firms in the growth stage of the business life cycle, TBS has experienced mostly negative earnings since its inception (see Exhibit 8). Most of its losses have resulted from the high start-up costs associated with the divisions that have been created in the past ten years. Exhibit 9 shows balance sheet information for the years 1977 to 1983.

Working Capital

During 1983, the company was unable to generate sufficient cash flow from operations to meet its needs. Working capital deficits were primarily funded through short term credit lines and financing agreements with vendors, program suppliers and others during the first three quarters of the year. A large percentage of cash outflow resulted from the debt restructuring fees.

TBS faces several uncertainties that could arise out of normal operations that might require additional cash. However, management feels that the current financing program will be adequate to meet the company's anticipated needs. In the unlikely event that these uncertainties do materialize and require cash in excess of the anticipated amounts, because of limitations in existing loan agreements, there is no assurance that the company can obtain additional borrowings which might be needed to meet these excess needs.

Dividend Policy

TBS has not paid a cash dividend since 1975. In view of the unavailability of funds to the company and restrictions in its loan agreements against any dividend payments, it is not anticipated that dividends will be paid to holders of its common stock in the foreseeable future.

EXHIBIT 8 TURNER BROADCASTING COMPANY
HISTORICAL COMMON SIZE INCOME STATEMENT (Dollars in Thousands)

	1977		1978		1979		1980		1981		1982		1983	
Revenue:														
Broadcasting	19573	51.9%	23434	62.1%	27789	73.7%	35495	65.0%	55329	58.2%	96647	58.3%	136217	60.7%
Cable production	0	0.0%	0	0.0%	0	0.0%	7201	13.2%	27738	29.2%	49708	30.0%	65169	29.0%
Sports	6706	17.8%	8181	21.7%	7395	19.6%	9211	16.9%	8840	9.3%	16263	9.8%	21401	9.5%
Management fees	1782	4.7%	2094	5.6%	2285	6.1%	2473	4.5%	2835	3.0%	2717	1.6%	1462	0.7%
Other	738	2.0%	134	0.4%	252	0.7%	230	0.4%	305	0.3%	306	0.2%	283	0.1%
Total revenue	28799	76.3%	33843	89.7%	37721	100.0%	54610	100.0%	95047	100.0%	165641	100.0%	224532	100.0%
Cost of expenses:														
Cost of operation	12767	33.8%	13219	35.0%	16997	45.1%	35124	64.3%	49036	51.6%	81187	49.0%	105695	47.1%
S, G & admin.	10729	28.4%	12736	33.8%	14460	38.3%	25218	46.2%	37067	39.0%	60343	36.4%	80722	36.0%
Amortization film contracts	1178	3.1%	1571	4.2%	2290	6.1%	2803	5.1%	4010	4.2%	7497	4.5%	8674	3.9%
Amort player/ other contracts	1556	4.1%	1599	4.2%	1508	4.0%	1210	2.2%	0	0.0%		0.0%		0.0%
Depreciation of P, P & E	934	2.5%	1037	2.7%	1222	3.2%	2172	4.0%	3469	3.6%	4182	2.5%	4706	2.1%
Interest expense/ amort debt.	1291	3.4%	1323	3.5%	2098	5.6%	4437	8.1%	9673	10.2%	13084	7.9%	14383	6.4%
Other	1251	3.3%	0	0.0%	0	0.0%	0	0.0%	0	0.0%	0	0.0%	0	0.0%
Total costs & expenses	29706	78.8%	31485	83.5%	38575	102.3%	70964	129.9%	103255	108.6%	166293	100.4%	214170	95.4%
Income (loss) from operation	−907	−2.4%	2358	6.3%	−854	−2.3%	−16354	−29.9%	−8208	−8.6%	−652	−0.4%	10362	4.6%
Equity loss-limited partners	−1053	−2.8%	−1225	−3.2%	−2014	−5.3%	−2905	−5.3%	−5215	−5.5%	−2698	−1.6%	−3350	−1.5%
Income before gains or dispos.	−1960	−5.2%	1133	3.0%	−2868	−7.6%	−19259	−35.3%	−13423	−14.1%	−3350	−2.0%	7012	3.1%
Gain on disposition of prop.	0	0.0%	395	1.0%	312	0.8%	15694	28.7%	0	0.0%	0	0.0%	0	0.0%
Income bef. tax & extra. items	−1960	−5.2%	1528	4.1%	−2556	−6.8%	−3575	−6.5%	−13423	−14.1%	−3350	−2.0%	7012	3.1%
Provision (benefit) for taxes	−728	−1.9%	669	1.8%	−1060	−2.8%	200	0.4%	0	0.0%	0	0.0%	0	0.0%
Income bef. extra. items	−1232	−3.3%	860	2.3%	−1496	−4.0%	−3775	−6.9%	−13423	−14.1%	−3350	−2.0%	7012	3.1%
Gain on prepayment of debt	0	0.0%	343	0.9%	0	0.0%	0	0.0%	0	0.0%	0	0.0%	0	0.0%
Net income (loss)	−1232	−3.3%	1203	3.2%	−1496	−4.0%	−3775	−6.9%	−13432	−14.1%	−3350	−2.0%	7012	3.1%

EXHIBIT 9   TURNER BROADCASTING COMPANY
HISTORICAL COMMON SIZE BALANCE SHEET (Dollars in Thousands)

	1977		1978		1979		1980		1981		1982		1983	
Current assets														
Cash	1351	3.6%	154	0.4%	342	0.9%	489	0.9%	504	0.5%	538	0.3%	594	0.3%
Accounts receivable	3537	9.4%	4951	13.1%	6322	16.8%	10662	19.5%	18868	19.9%	25728	15.5%	34186	15.2%
Less: allow for doubt accts	431	1.1%	547	1.5%	415	1.1%	793	1.5%	1164	1.2%	1997	1.2%	2418	1.1%
Net accounts receivable	3106	8.2%	4404	11.7%	5907	15.7%	9869	18.1%	17704	18.6%	23731	14.3%	31768	14.1%
Prepaid expenses	1250	3.3%	563	1.5%	585	1.6%	552	1.0%	1086	1.1%	1378	0.8%	2177	1.0%
Notes pay-able—S-T	0	0.0%	0	0.0%	0	0.0%	0	0.0%	0	0.0%	0	0.0%	0	0.0%
Curr port def prog prod cost		0.0%		0.0%		0.0%		0.0%		0.0%	2490	1.5%	2660	1.2%
Film contract rights—current	1128	3.0%	2055	5.4%	2570	6.8%	2521	4.6%	3495	3.7%	4516	2.7%	12163	5.4%
Other current assets	1359	3.6%	528	1.4%	644	1.7%	1591	2.9%	1433	1.5%	2585	1.6%	2305	1.0%
Total current assets	8194	21.7%	7704	20.4%	10048	26.6%	15022	27.5%	24222	25.5%	35238	21.3%	51667	23.0%
Film contract rights	3193	8.5%	5632	14.9%	7537	20.0%	5660	10.4%	9464	10.0%	15633	9.4%	26057	11.6%
Inv. in limited partnerships	1000	2.7%	2578	6.8%	2480	6.6%	2027	3.7%	900	0.9%	1900	1.1%	1633	0.7%
Net prop., plant & equipment	6543	17.3%	7784	20.6%	13381	35.5%	26647	48.8%	28698	30.2%	67555	40.8%	71505	31.8%
Notes receivable—L-T	1146	3.0%	404	1.1%	514	1.4%	920	1.7%	0	0.0%	0	0.0%	0	0.0%
Deferred program prod costs	0	0.0%	0	0.0%	0	0.0%	0	0.0%	0	0.0%	4460	2.7%	11432	5.1%
Deferred charges	0	0.0%	0	0.0%	0	0.0%	0	0.0%	9623	10.1%	6585	4.0%	13926	6.2%
Net contract rights	6165	16.3%	4947	13.1%	3628	9.6%	2784	5.1%	2084	2.2%	1583	1.0%	1246	0.6%
Intangible assets	0	0.0%	0	0.0%	0	0.0%	0	0.0%	0	0.0%	0	0.0%	25567	11.4%
Other assets	1624	4.3%	1349	3.6%	1696	4.5%	958	1.8%	1970	2.1%	2232	1.3%	2805	1.2%
Total assets	27865	73.9%	30398	80.6%	39284	104.1%	54018	98.9%	76961	81.0%	135186	81.6%	205838	91.7%

874

	1		2		3		4		5		6		7	
Current liabilities														
Accounts payable	2043	5.4%	2615	6.9%	1351	3.6%	2079	3.8%	3926	4.1%	7548	4.6%	6954	3.1%
Accrued expenses	0	0.0%	0	0.0%	1752	4.6%	7196	13.2%	11152	11.7%	16750	10.1%	22551	10.0%
Deferred income	0	0.0%	0	0.0%	216	0.6%	700	1.3%	2226	2.3%	7220	4.4%	7083	3.2%
Short-term borrowings	0	0.0%	0	0.0%	6642	17.6%	17907	32.8%	42783	45.0%	49924	30.1%	0	0.0%
Long-term debt—current	5411	14.3%	4910	13.0%	2704	7.2%	8430	15.4%	3005	3.2%	4266	2.6%	14473	6.4%
Obligation-film RTS (current)	0	0.0%	0	0.0%	3344	8.9%	2456	4.5%	3465	3.6%	5613	3.4%	11317	5.0%
Debt restructure fees (cur)	0	0.0%	0	0.0%	0	0.0%	0	0.0%	2253	2.4%	3000	1.8%	3650	1.6%
Income taxes payable	0	0.0%	0	0.0%	0	0.0%	163	0.3%	0	0.0%	0	0.0%	0	0.0%
Total current liabilities	7454	19.8%	7525	19.9%	16009	42.4%	38931	71.3%	68810	72.4%	94321	56.9%	66028	29.4%
Long-term debt	15968	42.3%	16329	43.3%	14158	37.5%	9825	18.0%	7165	7.5%	42802	25.8%	122404	54.5%
Unfunded pension cost	283	0.8%	283	0.8%	283	0.8%	283	0.5%	283	0.3%		0.0%		0.0%
Deferred income taxes	1076	2.9%	1980	5.2%	918	2.4%	918	1.7%	2834	3.0%		0.0%		0.0%
Deferred income	0	0.0%	0	0.0%	0	0.0%	0	0.0%	1313	1.4%	646	0.4%	562	0.3%
Debt restructure fees payable	0	0.0%	0	0.0%	0	0.0%	0	0.0%	4207	4.4%	3000	1.8%	650	0.3%
Obligations—emp. contracts	0	0.0%	0	0.0%	1410	3.7%	2221	4.1%	2560	2.7%	3442	1.8%	5201	2.3%
Obligations—film rights	0	0.0%	0	0.0%	3631	9.6%	2662	4.9%	3943	4.1%	7379	4.5%	13959	6.2%
Other liabilities	0	0.0%	0	0.0%	0	0.0%	0	0.0%	0	0.0%	1097	0.7%	7507	3.3%
Total liabilities	24781	65.7%	26117	69.2%	36409	96.5%	54840	100.4%	91115	95.9%	152687	92.2%	216311	96.3%
Common stock, PAR .125	1024	2.7%	1024	2.7%	2663	7.1%	2663	4.9%	2663	2.8%	2663	1.6%	2663	1.2%
Capital in excess	1541	4.1%	1572	4.2%	291	0.8%	602	1.1%	1508	1.6%	1508	0.9%	1508	0.7%
Retained earnings (deficit)	1095	2.9%	2298	6.1%	802	2.1%	-2973	-5.4%	-16396	-17.3%	-19746	-11.9%	-12734	-5.7%
Total stockholders' equity	3660	9.7%	4894	13.0%	3756	10.0%	292	0.5%	-12225	-12.9%	-15575	-9.4%	-8563	-3.8%

EXHIBIT 9 TURNER BROADCASTING COMPANY
HISTORICAL COMMON SIZE BALANCE SHEET (Dollars in Thousands) (*Continued*)

	1977		1978		1979		1980		1981		1982		1983	
Less shares of stock—treasury		0.0%		0.0%		0.0%		0.0%		0.0%	−474	−0.3%	−754	−0.3%
Notes rec—sales of CS—treas		0.0%		0.0%		0.0%		0.0%		0.0%	−1452	−0.9%	−1156	−0.5%
Treasury stock	−576	−1.5%	−613	−1.6%	−881	−2.3%	−1114	−2.0%	−1929	−2.0%	−1926	−1.2%	−1910	−0.9%
Total stockholders' equity	6744	17.9%	9175	24.3%	6631	17.6%	−530	−1.0%	−26379	−27.8%	−17501	−10.6%	−10473	−4.7%
Total liabilities & S.E.	31525	83.6%	35292	93.6%	43040	114.1%	54310	99.5%	64736	68.1%	135186	81.6%	205838	91.7%

Capital Structure

Presently, 97% of TBS' capital structure consists of long term debt. In the fourth quarter of 1984, TBS was considering a public offering to raise $125 million to pay off its bank debt. The company planned to use a combination of ten year notes, stocks and warrants to raise the capital. Based on preliminary plans, the offering would boost the number of shares outstanding from the current 20.3 million to 22.2 million, reducing the percentage of shares held by Turner from 87% to 79%.

INDUSTRY AND COMPETITION

The dramatic increase in the number of alternative sources of television broadcasting has led to a measurable drop in the audience shares of the three major networks. Consequently, there is a great deal of pressure for change in the television industry. Pay and ad-supported cable, independent broadcast stations and videocassettes are all seen as contributing to the decline. In the next decade, it is believed that television entertainment may shift toward a broader range of outlets including ad-hoc and regional networks, pay-per-view networks and more reasonably priced videocassette recorders.

Networks

Although television audience viewing is growing, the big three networks are concerned about the decline in their audience shares and about when the decline will stop. The availability of syndicated programs is becoming scarce as new broadcasters race to buy up existing shows. However, networks have an advantage in this competition because of their programming expertise and facilities. Exhibit 10 shows how precipitous the decline in network television audience share was between 1975–76 and 1981–82.

Independents

Independent television stations have experienced phenomenal growth in the past fifteen years. In 1971, there were 65 independent broadcasters serving 30 markets in the United States with losses of $24 million. In 1980, 179 independent stations served 86 markets with profits of $158 million. This growth can be largely attributed to the FCC's financial interest rule which prohibits the big three networks from syndicating programs that they originally aired and from owning any financial interest in programming produced by others. The independents thus have been able to compete against the networks by airing former network hit shows at key times during the day, including prime time.

Cable

The cable industry is in the midst of a gigantic building boom which can be attributed to two advances. First, there was an increase in the number of channels picked up by cable operators from 12 to 54. Second, in 1975, Home

EXHIBIT 10   Decline in network TV audience.
(Needham Harper Steers, based on data from A. C. Nielsen.)

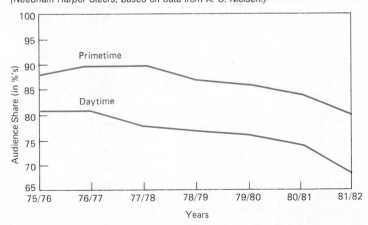

Box Office (HBO) started sending its signal via satellite and other stations, including WTBS, followed and were able to easily attain national distribution for their cable programming.

The Fall 1984 Cable Study Report conducted by Mediamark Research, Inc. found that the median age of pay television subscribers was 35.2 years with an average yearly income of $29,879. *Cablevision,* the trade magazine of the cable industry, projects that the percentage of pay television subscribers will jump from 23% of the population in 1984 to 27% in 1986. Most of the cable industry's profits will be invested in the wiring of additional homes, particularly those in major urban areas. The high costs associated with wiring these areas had kept cable operators out previously. Now, cities represent more than four-fifths of the potential market.

Ad-Supported Cable

With the emergence of cable television as a national delivery system, many media people became excited about a concept called "narrowcasting." Narrowcasting consists of the programming of one particular type of entertainment (i.e., ESPN—a sports channel) that enables a programmer to target his audience and thus attract specific advertisers at higher rates. Although several narrowcasting networks exist, their success has been very limited because of the lack of quality programming. Dave Martin, vice-president for broadcasting at Campbell-Ewall said, "Narrowcasting allows an advertiser to take advantage of a specific opportunity. . . . If it works, though, there is nothing on the mass level that will parallel the opportunity of true narrowcasting to a target audience." Another good example of successful narrowcasting is Music Television (MTV). Narrowcasting is not the only form of ad-supported cable. Stations such as WTBS in Atlanta, WGN in Chicago, and WOR in New York have been successful with their broad-based programming.

Pay Television

Pay television has been the leader in the cable industry, and it is currently experiencing significant change. Most of the change is being introduced by motion picture companies who are trying to become more directly involved in pay television. For example, Columbia Pictures teamed up with Time, Inc., parent of HBO, and CBS in an attempt to grab a large share of the pay T.V. market and to become involved in pay-per-view (PPV) television. PPV requires a subscriber to pay an additional fee to view certain major programs. Thus far, most PPV has not been profitable because of the high prices viewers must pay for the programs.

A major threat to large pay television systems comes from smaller private delivery systems. For example, SMATV is a private system that picks up cable signals using a satellite disk and sends the signal via cable to a group of apartment houses, hotels, or clusters of private homes. SMATV has been extremely effective in urban areas previously ignored by other cable systems. This system does not offer the potential, however, of other systems such as MDS (multipoint distribution system) or DBS (direct broadcast satellite).

FCC Rulings

Television broadcasting is subject to the jurisdiction of the Federal Communications Commission (FCC) under the Communications Act of 1934, as amended. Among other things, FCC regulations govern the issuance, term, renewal, and transfer of licenses which must be obtained by persons to operate any television station. The FCC's recent proposal to repeal its network syndication and financial interest rules is strongly supported by the three major networks. Currently, the networks cannot syndicate their own programs, nor can they have a financial interest in programs produced by others. This rule prevents the networks from making money from their shows in syndication. Independent television stations, on the other hand, have grown substantially under this rule because of their ability to air former hit shows.

Independent broadcasters argue that repeal of the financial interest rule will increase the possibility of the networks' monopolizing and withholding off-network, syndicated, prime time entertainment programming. However, CBS, NBC and ABC contend that this possibility would not materialize, since the networks have neither the incentive nor the opportunity to discriminate against the independents.

To make the television industry more competitive, the FCC is preparing to adopt a plan to expand the 7-7-7 rule to the 12-12-12 rule. Currently, television station owners are allowed to own only seven AM and seven FM radio stations in addition to seven television stations. This limitation was adopted in the 1950's to encourage program diversity in the marketplace. Under the new plan, media companies would be allowed to own as many as twelve television stations only if the audience reach of the stations does not exceed 25% of the national viewing audience. This plan would eventually result in an increase in the number of television station owners capable of competing with the three major broadcast networks.

Another important issue facing the FCC concerns the re-examination of the fairness doctrine, the thirty-five-year-old requirement that broadcasters cover "controversial issues" and air contrasting views. FCC Chairman Mark S. Fowler says that "the government shouldn't be the one to decide what's fair and what isn't" (*Business Week,* May 7, 1984). However, defenders of the fairness doctrine counter that the airwaves are a scarce public resource that must be protected from abuse. Under Fowler's administration, the FCC has continued to expand its deregulatory efforts by abolishing regulations and relaxing rules that restrict regional concentration and multiple ownership of broadcast stations. "These are the areas where the agency must regulate, but in the choice between competition and regulation, competition is far better for the consumer," says Fowler (*Business Week,* May 7, 1984).

The Changing Landscape of Competition

Clearly, competition in the home entertainment industry, in general, and television, in particular, are changing. VCR's are the hottest items going. Exhibit 11 shows how rapidly factory sales of VCR's have risen since 1982. Exhibit 12 shows that firms competing in the cable in-

dustry have made significant progress over the last twenty years "wiring" homes in our nation. Finally, Exhibit 13 shows how rapidly sales of videocassette tapes have increased. There can be no doubt that the landscape of competition is changing.

OUTLOOK FOR THE FUTURE

The future of the cable industry is still bright. According to Robert J. Wussler, Executive Vice President of TBS, "I don't think the momentum is out of the game, although I certainly think the bloom is off the rose. But all you have to do is come to a couple of cable conventions and see that there's still enough money around and there are still enough young people around to execute all the ideas people can dream up. No, there's still a lot of momentum around, even if it's not the gold rush" (*Broadcasting,* December 12, 1983). Wussler believes broadcasting in general has hit a plateau or is shrinking. Due to the rise of independents, cable, direct broadcast satellites, video cassette recorders, and our various life styles, he does not believe broadcasting is becoming more powerful. According to Wussler, broadcasters do not need to worry about getting bigger again, but instead they must worry about getting smaller and about how they are going to manage being smaller. As for cable industry growth, Wussler does not see many limitations. Although it is a tough business to get into today because it requires a lot of capital and there are channel capacity problems, the future is bright.

If the cable industry continues to grow and supersta-

EXHIBIT 11 **Factory sales in billions of dollars.**
(Electronic Industries Association figures for 1985 are projected; appeared in the Richmond Times-Dispatch, *July 5, 1985.)*

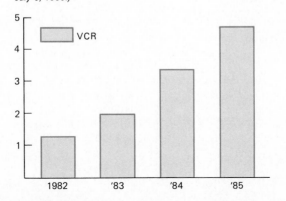

EXHIBIT 12   **Homes with cable TV (in millions, rounded).**
(National Cable Television Association using Arbitron estimates for 1985; appeared in the Richmond Times-Dispatch, *July 4, 1985.)*

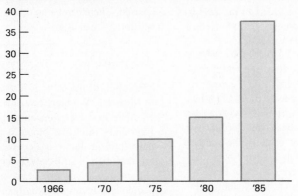

Figures are as of Jan. 1, except for 1985, when May statistics were used.

tions proliferate, TBS will face more competition. According to the *Wall Street Journal* (April 19, 1985), some industry observers have questioned whether Turner Broadcasting could hold up if superstation imitators proliferated beyond the handful now operating. But Bonnie Cook, an analyst for J.C. Bradford & Co. in Nashville, dismisses that notion. She believes that anybody can transform a television station into a superstation, but cable systems can carry only a limited number of channels. Thus, it is unlikely that the number of superstations will increase dramatically.

Television broadcasting is changing. In early 1985, Capital Cities Communications, Inc. purchased ABC, and in April 1985 Ted Turner made a move to acquire CBS for $5.4 billion including no cash. This acquisition attempt attracted praise, criticism, and ridicule. According to the *Wall Street Journal* (April 19, 1985),

> Mr. Turner has long broadcast his drive to run a network. Some associates contend that this desire became almost an obsession after Capital Cities Communications Inc. last month agreed to acquire American Broadcasting Cos. CBS

EXHIBIT 13   **Sales to dealers in millions of units.**
(Electronic Industries Association figures for 1985 are projected; appeared in the Richmond Times-Dispatch, *July 5, 1985.)*

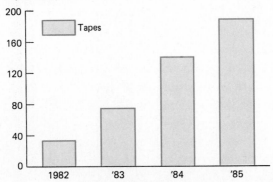

thus was seen as Mr. Turner's last chance, because RCA, the parent of NBC, was probably too big to be taken over.

William C. Bevins Jr., the financial vice president of Turner Broadcasting, denies that the ABC acquisition move forced Mr. Turner's hand. But he concedes that the trans-action 'certainly crystallized where the various regulatory agencies stood and that the timing was propitious.'

The package offered by Turner, which is reputed to be made up primarily of junk bonds, is presented below:

TURNER BROADCASTING SYSTEM INC'S. PACKAGE FOR CBS
For each of CBS's 30 million shares, Turner offers the following package:

Type of security	Face value
$46 of 15% 7-year senior note	$ 46.00
$46 of 15½% 15-year senior debenture	46.00
$10.31 of 5-year Series A Zero coupon note	5.00
$11.91 of 6-year Series B Zero coupon note	5.00
$15.90 of 8-year Series C Zero coupon note	5.00
$18.38 of 9-year Series D Zero coupon note	5.00
$30.00 of 16¼ 20-year senior subordinated debenture	30.00
1 share of $2.80 preferred	16.50
0.75 share of Class B common	16.50
Total	$175.00*

*This is the face value of the offer for each CBS share. Analysts say there isn't any way of currently evaluating the market value of the package because the issues don't yet exist.

Source: Wall Street Journal, April 19, 1985

CBS rejected Turner's offer as inadequate and took steps to prevent a takeover. Andy Rooney, a regular on the television program ''60 Minutes'', had this to say about Turner's offer,

Ted Turner, the Atlanta, Ga., money operator, yachtsman and baseball team owner, has applied to the Federal Communications Commission for its approval of his scheme to take CBS away from its present owners. He has offered CBS stockholders a grabbag of what are known on Wall Street as ''junk bonds'' for their shares in CBS. . . .

I offer my services in trying to locate a new anchorman for the CBS Evening News and someone else to do pieces at the end of ''60 Minutes'' because if Ted Turner takes over CBS, I doubt very much that Dan Rather will want his job and I know darn well I won't (*Richmond Times Dispatch,* April 25, 1985).

On May 7, 1985, TBS announced a first quarter loss of $741,000, compared with a $5.3 million loss a year earlier.

AN ABORTED TAKEOVER ATTEMPT

For many years, Ted Turner's interest in acquiring a major television network was widely known. Finally in late April 1985, Ted Turner made his move and announced his intention to purchase CBS, a goal that seemed unattainable since CBS is 17 times bigger than TBS. In preparation for this action, CNN had been offered for sale to the three major networks in 1981. CBS offered $250 million and NBC $200 million. One of Turner's stipulations about the sale of CNN was that he was to be paid in stock. When the networks realized that this deal would make Turner the largest single stockholder of the company acquiring CNN, they promptly withdrew their offers. As recently as March 1985, Turner was still trying to entice CBS into a deal that would enable Turner to gain control of CBS in a friendly manner, but his attempts failed. Undaunted, Ted Turner, together with the aid of E.F. Hutton & Co., made an offer to the shareholders of CBS to gain control of the network by exchanging debt for stock in a hostile takeover attempt.

Turner's plan was to acquire 73% of CBS's 30 million outstanding shares of stock (5% more than the 67% required by New York State for the merger to take place). To do this, TBS would have had to borrow heavily and offer a variety of high risk debt securities in exchange for the CBS stock. At the time of the offer, CBS's net worth was estimated at $7.6 billion, or $254 a share. The face value of Turner's offer was for $175 a share in securities, but estimates of the market value of the offer ranged from $155 to $130 a share.

Besides TBS stock, the other securities offered to CBS shareholders were low-quality, high risk junk bonds paying 15% interest or higher and zero coupon bonds which require the payment of the principal and interest in a lump sum at maturity. Zeros would have allowed Turner to borrow $600 million and pay nothing until 1990. In addition, each share of TBS offered to CBS shareholders would have had only 1/10 of a vote. Thus, Turner would have maintained control of 73% of the voting rights in TBS stock.

If Turner's offer had been accepted, he would have acquired the broadcast network and 4 of the 5 CBS owned and operated television stations. Turner had planned to sell one station, the CBS records group, the CBS publishing group, ratio stations and various other holdings for $3.1 billion and to apply the proceeds from these sales to the debt. Selling off these pieces of CBS would have reduced the total cost of the deal from $7.6 billion to $4.5 billion. Exhibit 14 presents a financial summary of the offer to CBS.

From the perspective of CBS stockholders, the proposed offer would result in the exchange of a $3 per year CBS dividend for $21.71 in interest and preferred stock

dividends from TBS. Although the offer sounds very appealing, Wall Street analysts expressed concern about the security of the TBS assets.

The CBS Response

To ward off the hostile takeover attempt, CBS had several alternatives. One option was to find a "white knight," a more suitable and friendly merger partner. Another possibility, and the one preferred by CBS directors, was to increase their debt and buy back their own stock. By raising additional debt, CBS would make their acquisition by Turner even riskier, because the combined debt of CBS and TBS after the merger would virtually guarantee failure. Additionally, the stock repurchase would leave fewer shares available for purchase by Turner.

Subsequently, CBS purchased 6.4 million shares of their stock, roughly 21% of the shares outstanding, at a cost of $960 million. The price paid by CBS for the stock was $40 per share in cash, plus $110 per share in senior notes at 10⅞% interest due to mature in 1995. A "poison pill," a maneuver designed to make CBS an unattractive takeover target in the future, was added by the placing of limits on the amount of debt CBS can carry. The plan

---

EXHIBIT 14   A SUMMARY OF THE OFFER MADE BY TED TURNER TO ACQUIRE CBS

		Face value	Estimated market value
1)	Interest bearing "junk bonds"*	$122.00	$105.00
2)	Zero coupon notes**	20.00	19.00
3)	TBS stock***	16.50	15.00
	—1 share preferred		
	—¾ share class B common		
	Total	$175.50	$150.00

Estimated total market value of offer—$4.5 billion

*15% senior notes due 1992
15.5% senior debenture due 2000
16.25% senior subordinated debenture due 2005
**four series with maturity range 1990–1994 with effective interest rate of 15%
***one share preferred $2.64

also included the sale of $123 million in new convertible preferred shares to institutional investors.

To prevent the repurchase plan, Turner filed a suit against CBS accusing its directors of a breach of fiduciary duty. The complaint alleged that the board was motivated by self interest and that it was attempting to insulate the CBS shareholders from Turner's offer. On July 30, both the FCC and a federal judge in Atlanta ruled that the board had acted in a fair and reasonable manner and in the best interest of the company. Lacking sufficient cash to compete with the CBS stock repurchase offer and lacking the ability to wage a proxy battle, these rulings ended any hope Ted Turner had of gaining control of CBS.

Repercussions

TBS reported that it lost $6.7 million on revenues of $99.3 million in the second quarter of 1985. In total, the takeover attempt cost TBS $18.2 million. According to *Newsweek*, it may have been worth it to Turner just to be in the spotlight for a few weeks (*Newsweek*, April 29, 1985).

The cost of the failed merger attempt to CBS was very high. They purchased approximately 21% of their stock at a cost of $960 million. Since the takeover attempt ended, CBS has had serious financial difficulties and several members of its top management group have been dismissed.

UNION CARBIDE OF INDIA, LTD. (1985)

Arthur D. Sharplin
Bentley College

December 2, 1984 began as a typical day in the central Indian city of Bhopal. Shoppers moved about the bustling, open-air market. Here and there a customer haggled with a merchant. Beasts of burden, donkeys and oxen, pulled carts or carried ungainly bundles through the partly paved streets. Children played in the dirt. In the shadow of a Union Carbide pesticide plant, tens of thousands of India's poorest citizens milled about the shanty town they called home. A few miles away, wealthy Indians lived in opulence rivaling that of the first-class districts of London or Paris. Inside the plant, several hundred Indian workers and managers went about their duties, maintaining and operating the systems which produced the mildly toxic pesticide Sevin. Most of the plant was shut down for maintenance and it was operating at far below capacity.

At about 11 o'clock that evening, one of the operators noticed that the pressure in a methyl isocyanate (MIC) storage tank read 10 pounds per square inch—four times normal. The operator was not concerned, thinking that the tank may have been pressurized with nitrogen by the previous shift. Around midnight several of the workers noticed that their eyes had begun to water and sting, a signal experience had taught them indicated an MIC leak. The leak, a small but continuous drip, was soon spotted.

The research assistance of Aseem Shukla is gratefully acknowledged.

The operators were still not alarmed because minor leaks at the plant were quite common. It was time for tea and most of the crew retired to the company canteen, resolving to correct the problem afterwards.

By the time the workers returned it was too late. The MIC tank pressure gauge was pegged. The leak had grown much larger and the entire area of the MIC tanks was enveloped in the choking fumes. The workers tried spraying water on the leak to break down the MIC. They sounded the alarm siren and summoned the fire brigade. As the futility of their efforts became apparent, many of the workers panicked and ran upwind—some scaling the chain-link and barbed-wire fence in their frantic race for survival.

By one o'clock, only a supervisor remained in the area. He stayed upwind, donning his oxygen breathing apparatus every few minutes to check the various gauges and sensors. Pressure in the MIC tank had forced open a relief valve and the untreated MIC vapor could be seen escaping from an atmospheric vent line 120 feet in the air.

The cloud of deadly white gas was carried by a south-easterly wind toward the Jai Prakash Nagar shanties. The cold temperature of the December night caused the MIC to settle towards the ground (in the daytime, or in the summer, convection currents probably would have raised and diluted the MIC).

As the gaseous tentacles reached into the huts there was panic and confusion. Many of the weak and elderly died where they lay. Some who made it into the streets were blinded. "It was like breathing fire," one survivor said. As word of the gas leak spread, many of Bhopal's affluent were able to flee in their cars. But most of the poor were left behind. When the gas reached the railroad station, supervisors who were not immediately disabled sent our word along the tracks and incoming trains were diverted. This cut off a possible means of escape but may have saved hundreds of lives. Because the whole station was quickly enveloped in gas, arriving trains would have been death traps for passengers and crews.

Of Bhopal's total population of about 1,000,000, an estimated 500,000 fled that night, most on foot. The surrounding towns were woefully unprepared to accept the gasping and dying mass of people. Thousands waited outside hospitals for medical care. There was no certainty about how to treat the gas victims and general purpose medical supplies were in hopelessly short supply. Inside the hospitals and out, screams and sobs filled the air. Food supplies were quickly exhausted. People were even afraid to drink the water, not knowing if it was contaminated.

During the second day, relief measures were better organized. Several hundred doctors and nurses from nearby hospitals were summoned to help medical personnel in Bhopal. Just disposing of the dead was a major problem. Mass cremation was necessary. Islamic victims, whose faith allows burial rather than cremation, were piled several deep in hurriedly dug graves. Bloated carcasses of cattle and dogs littered the city. There was fear of a cholera epidemic. Bhopal's mayor said, "I can say that I have seen chemical warfare. Everything so quiet. Goats, cats, whole families—father, mother, children— all lying silent and still. And every structure totally intact. I hope never again to see it."

By the third day, the city had begun to move toward stability, if not normalcy. The Union Carbide plant had been closed and locked. A decision was made to consume the 30 tons of MIC that remained by using it to make pesticide. Most of the 2,000 dead bodies had been disposed of, however inappropriately. The more than 100,000 injured were being treated as rapidly as the limited medical facilities would allow, although many simply sat in silence, blinded and maimed by an enemy they had never known well enough to fear. For them, doctors predict an increased risk of sterility, kidney and liver infections, tuberculosis, vision problems, and brain damage. The potential for birth defects and other long-term effects

is not clear. However, months after the incident newspapers reported a high incidence of stillbirths and congenital deformities among the population which was affected by the gas.

COMPANY BACKGROUND

The Ever-Ready Company, Ltd. (of Great Britain) began manufacturing flashlight batteries in Calcutta in 1926. The division was incorporated as the Ever-Ready Company (India), Ltd. in 1934 and became a subsidiary of Union Carbide Corporation of New York. The name of the Indian company was changed to National Carbide Company (India), Ltd. in 1949 and to Union Carbide (India), Ltd. (UCIL) in 1959. The 1926 capacity of 40 million dry cell batteries per year was expanded to 767 million by the 1960s. In 1959, a factory was set up in India to manufacture the flashlights themselves.

By the 1980s, UCIL was involved in five product areas: batteries, carbon and metals, plastics, marine products, and agricultural chemicals. Table 1 provides production statistics for UCIL products. The company eventually operated fourteen plants at eight locations, including the headquarters operation in Calcutta. Union Carbide's petrochemical complex, established in Bombay in 1966, was India's first.

UCIL began its marine products operation with two shrimping ships in 1971. The business is completely export oriented and employs fifteen deep sea trawlers. Processing facilities are located off the east and west coasts of India. The trawlers now harvest deep sea lobsters in addition to shrimp.

In 1979, UCIL initiated a letter of intent to manufacture dry cell batteries in Nepal. A 77.5 percent owned subsidiary was set up in Nepal in 1982 and construction of a Rs. 18 million plant was begun.

The agricultural products division of UCIL was started in 1966 with only an office in Bombay. Agreement was reached with the Indian government in 1969 to set up a pesticide plant at Bhopal. Land was rented to UCIL for about $40 per acre per year. The initial investment was small, only $1 million, and the process was simple. Concentrated Sevin powder was imported from the USA, diluted with non-toxic powder, packaged, and sold. Under the technology transfer provisions of its agreement with UCIL, Union Carbide Corporation (USA) was obligated to share its more advanced technologies with UCIL. Eventually the investment at Bhopal grew to exceed $25

TABLE 1   PRODUCTION STATISTICS

Class of goods	1983 Capacity	Production levels					
		1983	1982	1981	1980	1979	1978
Batteries (millions of pieces)	792	510.4	512.2	411.3	458.8	460.3	430.3
Flashlight cases (millions of pieces)	7.5	6.7	6.7	7.4	6.9	6.4	5.7
Arc Carbons (millions of pieces)	9.0	7.5	7.0	7.0	6.7	6.2	6.1
Industrial Carbon Electrodes and Shapes (millions of pieces)	2.5	0.5	0.5	0.5	0.3	0.5	0.2
Photo-engravers' Plates/ Strips for Printing (tonnes*)	1,200	412.0	478.0	431.0	339.0	469.0	506.0
Stellite castings, head facings and tube rods (tonnes)	150	17.5	12.7	16.4	14.5	15.8	18.2
Electrolytic Manganese Dioxide (tonnes)	4,500	3,335	3,085	3,000	2,803	2,605	2,700
Chemicals (tonnes)	13,600	7,349	6,331	6,865	7,550	8,511	8,069
Polyethylene (tonnes)	20,000	18,144	17,290	19,928	19,198	16,324	12,059
MIC based pesticides (tonnes)	5,000	1,647	2,308	2,704	1,542	1,496	367
Marine products (tonnes)	5,500	424	649	642	601	648	731

*One tonne = 1,000 kilograms = 2,214 pounds. One British long ton = 2,240 pounds. One U.S. ton = 2,000 pounds.
Source: The Stock Exchange Foundation, Bombay, India, The Stock Exchange Official Directory, Vol. XVII/29, July 18, 1983.

million and the constituents of Sevin were made there. Another Union Carbide insecticide, called Temik, was made in small quantities at Bhopal.

UCIL's assets grew from Rs. 558 million in 1974 to Rs. 1,234 million in 1983 (the conversion rate stayed near 9 rupees to the dollar during this period, moving to about 12.50 as the dollar strengthened worldwide during 1984 and 1985—see Table 3). The *Economic Times* of India ranked UCIL number 21 in terms of sales among Indian companies. Union Carbide Corporation (USA) owned 50.9 percent of UCIL's stock and Indian citizens and companies owned the remainder. When Indira Gandhi was voted out of office in 1977, the Janata (Peoples') Party strengthened the Foreign Exchange Regulation Act (FERA) (see inset). As a result, IBM and Coca-Cola pulled out of India. IBM's business in India was taken over by ICIM (International Computers Indian Manufacturers), a domestic firm. Another similar firm was set up to perform the maintenance services for the existing IBM computers.

Since 1967 the chairman of the board of UCIL has been an Indian, and foreign membership on the eleven-member board of directors has been limited to four. One expert on Indian industry affairs said, ''Though the foreigners on the board are down to four from six in previous years, they continue to hold sway over the affairs of the company.'' Major capital expenditures by UCIL were required to be approved by Union Carbide Corporation. Also, the Bhopal plant submitted monthly reports to U.S. corporate headquarters detailing operations and safety procedures. And inspections of the plant were carried out from time to time by Union Carbide technical specialists.

OPERATIONS AT BHOPAL

On the surface, the UCIL insecticide factory is a typical process plant. A wide diversity of storage tanks, hoppers, and reactors are connected by pipes. There are many pumps and valves and a number of tall vent lines and

THE FOREIGN EXCHANGE REGULATION ACT

The Act was originally enacted as a temporary measure in 1947 and made permanent in 1957. It was revised and redrafted in 1973. It covers various aspects of foreign exchange transactions, including money changing, buying or selling foreign exchange in India or abroad, having an account in a bank outside India, and remitting money abroad.

The purpose of the Act is to restrict outflow of foreign exchange and to conserve hard currency holdings in India. One requirement of the Act is that any company in which the non-resident interest is more than 40 percent "shall not carry on in India or establish in India any branch or office without the special permission of the Reserve Bank of India." But the Reserve Bank of India has authority to exempt a company from the provisions of the Act. The 40 percent requirement was changed to 49 percent by Rajiv Gandhi's government.

High technology companies are frequently exempted from the equity ownership provisions of the Act. Other companies which have operated in India for many years are sometimes exempted if they agree not to expand their Indian operations.

Policies in India regarding nationalization of foreign-owned companies have varied. A number of major oil companies have been nationalized. For example, Indian Oil Corporation, Bharat Petroleum, and Hindustan Petroleum used to be, respectively, Burmah Shell, Mobil, and Stanvae (Standard Vacuum Oil Company, an Esso unit). More typically, a multinational company is asked to reduce its holdings to 49 percent or less by offering shares to the Indian public and Indian financial institutions. Multinationals which have diluted equity to meet the 49 percent requirement include CIBA-GEIGY, Parke-Davis, Bayer (aspirin), Lever Brothers (which operates as Hindustan Lever in India), Lipton, and Brooke-Bond.

---

ducts. Ponds and pits are used for waste treatment and several railway spur lines run through the plant. Figure 1 is a diagram of the factory. Figure 1a is a schematic of just the MIC manufacturing process. The pesticide plant was designed and supplied by Union Carbide Corporation, which sent engineers to India to supervise construction.

Sevin is made through a controlled chemical reaction involving alpha-naphthol and MIC. Alpha-naphthol is a brownish granular material and MIC is a highly reactive liquid which boils and becomes a gas at usual daytime temperatures. When plans were first made to begin production of alpha-naphthol at Bhopal in 1971, a pilot plant was set up to manufacture the product. Because the pilot plant was successful, a full-size alpha-naphthol plant (in fact, the world's largest) was constructed and placed in operation in 1977.

In the meantime, work had begun on the ill-fated MIC plant. But even before the MIC plant was completed in 1979, problems began to crop up with the alpha-naphthol plant, resulting in a shutdown for modifications in 1978. In February 1980, the MIC plant was placed into service. The alpha-naphthol plant continued in various stages of shutdown and partial operation through 1984. Mr. V. P. Gokhale, managing director of UCIL, called the alpha-naphthol plant a "very large mistake." But he said the company was forced to build it to keep its operating license from the Indian government. The Bhopal factory was designed to produce 5,000 tons per year of Sevin but never operated near capacity. UCIL has generally been the third largest producer of pesticides in India, sometimes slipping to number four.

FINANCE

Tables 2, 3, 4, and 5 and Figure 2 provide financial facts and figures for UCIL. As mentioned earlier, Union Carbide Corporation (USA) holds 50.9 percent of UCIL's common shares. The remainder are publicly traded on major Indian stock exchanges. Most of these shares are held by about 24,000 individuals. However, a number of institutional investors own substantial blocks. The Indian government does not directly own any UCIL stock, although the Life Insurance Corporation of India, the country's largest insuror and owner of many UCIL shares, is owned by the Indian Government. During the months before the Bhopal disaster, UCIL's common shares hovered around Rs. 30, but dropped to a low of Rs. 15.8 on December 11, recovering only slightly in succeeding weeks.

In 1975, the United States Export-Import bank in cooperation with First National Citibank of New York agreed to grant loans of $2.5 million to buy equipment for the MIC project. Also, the Industrial Credit and In-

FIGURE 1   **The UCIL pesticide factory at Bhopal.**

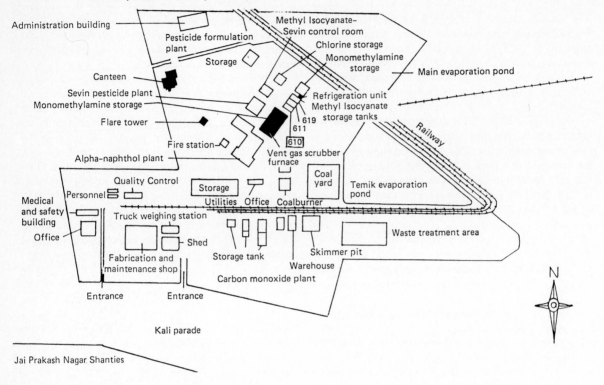

FIGURE 1a   **The methyl isocyanate manufacturing process.**

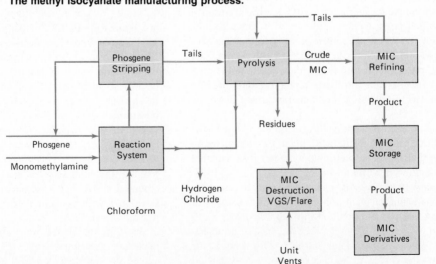

TABLE 2 SUMMARY OF INCOME STATEMENTS

For years ended December 25	1984 rs. lakhs	1983 rs. lakhs	1982 rs. lakhs
Income			
Sales (excluding value of products used internally rs. 57,65.80 lakhs— Previous year rs. 53,92.51 lakhs)	222,89.77	210,19.60	206,38.14
Other sources	1,32.40	1,96.06	2,83.28
	224,22.17	212,15.66	209,21.42
Expenditure			
Materials consumed	99,16.01	91,59.84	95,46.63
Excise duty	34,03.09	28,58.85	28,65.04
Operating expenses	65,97.52	66,68.39	60,98.25
Depreciation	5,01.12	4,75.79	4,16.14
Interest	4,73.15	5,75.29	5,26.61
	208,90.89	197,38.16	194,52.67
Profit before taxation	15,31.28	14,77.50	14,68.75
Provision for taxation	7,10.00	5,45.20	5,02.00
Profit after taxation	8,21.28	9,32.30	9,66.75
Transfer to investment allowance reserve	1,05.00	75.00	1,90.00
	7,16.28	8,57.30	7,76.75
Transfer from development rebate reserve	13.08	9.38	1.22
Balance brought forward from previous year	1,07.92	0.00	26.30
Available for appropriation	8,37.28	8,66.68	8,04.27
Appropriations			
Debenture stock redemption reserve	1,00.00	70.00	90.00
Unclaimed dividends paid	0.01	0.01	0.03
Interim dividend (@ R. 0.50 per share)	1,62.92	0.00	
Proposed dividend (subject to taxation)	0.00	4,88.75	4,88.75
General reserve	0.00	2,00.00	2,25.49
Balance carried forward to balance sheet	5,74.35	1,07.92	0.00

Notes: 1. 1 lakh = 100,000
2. Placement of commas in numbers differs from American practice.

TABLE 3   WHOLESALE PRICE LEVELS IN THE U.S. AND INDIA AND DOLLAR-TO-RUPEE CONVERSION RATES, 1974–1984

Year	U.S. producer price index*	India wholesale price index**	Conversion rate§
1974	161.1	169.2	8.111
1975	175.1	175.8	8.914
1976	183.6	172.4	8.985
1977	195.8	185.4	8.703
1978	197.1	185.0	8.189
1979	215.8	206.5	8.108
1980	244.5	248.1	7.872
1981	269.8	278.4	8.728
1982	280.7	285.3	9.492
1983	285.2	308.5	10.129
1984	291.1	334.0	11.402
1985			11.930§§

*Wholesale Price Index before 1978. Arithmetic average of January–December monthly figures. Base year, 1967 (January–December).
**Arithmetic average of April–March monthly figures. Base year, 1970 (April 1970–March 1971).
§Arithmetic average of monthly figures (rupees per dollar).
§§October 7, 1985, only.

vestment Corporation of India (ICICI) authorized a Rs. 21.5 million loan, part of which was drawn in 1980. Finally, long-term loans were provided by several Indian financial institutions and insurance companies. Some of these loans were guaranteed by the State Bank of India.

Profits of several million dollars from the Bhopal facility were originally predicted for 1984. Several factors kept these expectations from being realized. First, an economic recession made farmers more cost conscious and caused them to search for less expensive alternatives to Sevin. Second, a large number of small-scale producers were able to undersell the company, partly because they were exempt from excise and sales taxes. Seventeen of these firms bought MIC from UCIL and used it to make products virtually identical to Sevin and Temik. Finally, a new generation of low cost pesticides was becoming available. With sales collapsing, the Bhopal plant because a money loser in 1981. By late 1984, the profit estimate for that year had been adjusted downward to a $4 million *loss* based on 1,000 tons of output, one-fifth of capacity.

To forestall what may have seemed inevitable economic failure, extensive cost cutting efforts were carried out. The staff at the MIC plant was cut from twelve operators on a shift to six. The maintenance team was reduced in size. In a number of instances, faulty safety devices remained unrepaired for weeks. Because a refrig-

eration unit, designed to keep the methyl isocyanate cool, continued to malfunction, it was shut down. Though instrumentation technology advanced at Union Carbide's other pesticide plants, the innovations were only partly adopted at Bhopal.

The UCIL directors disclaim fault for the incident. The "Report of the Directors," included in UCIL's 1984 annual report, states,

"At no time had any significant fault been found with the working or safety precautions taken by your Company. Your Company had taken all safety precautions to avoid any accident in the Plant, which had been operated all along with trained and qualified operators."

PERSONNEL

Until 1982, a cadre of American managers and technicians worked at the Bhopal plant. The Americans were licensed by the Indian government only for fixed periods. While in India, they were expected to train Indian replacements. From 1982 onward, no American worked at Bhopal. While major decisions, such as approval of the annual budget, were cleared with Union Carbide, USA, day to day details such as staffing and maintenance were left to the Indian officials.

TABLE 4   SUMMARY OF BALANCE SHEETS

As of December 25	1984 Rs. lakhs		1983 Rs. lakhs		1982 Rs. lakhs	
Funds employed						
Fixed assets						
Goodwill at cost	30.00		30.00		30.00	
Fixed assets	44,18.59		41,07.55		40,51.60	
Capital expenditure in progress	2,23.36	46,71.95	5,50.51	46,88.06	4,43.86	45,25.46
Investments		1,37.48		92.37		96.52
Current assets						
Stores & spares at cost	7,32.53		6,86.16		6,40.67	
Stocks	32,63.68		30,05.56		31,32.50	
Sundry debtors	16,27.25		23,93.25		30,00.83	
Cash & bank balances	5,38.88		4,23.79		5,22.05	
Loans & advances	12,23.91		8,87.32		7,87.21	
Interest accrued on investments	0.03		0.25		0.25	
	73,86.28		73,96.33		80,83.51	
Less: Current liabilities	20,53.60		21,34.92		23,36.49	
Provisions	6,10.68		10,07.14		10,71.12	
	26,64.28		31,42.06		34,07.61	
Net current assets		47,22.00		42,54.27		46,75.90
		95,31.43		90,34.70		92,97.88
Financed by						
Share capital & reserves						
Share capital—issued & subscribed	32,58.30		32,58.30		32,58.30	
Reserves and surplus	35,97.32	68,55.62	29,38.97	61,97.27	24,95.43	57,53.73
Loan capital						
Secured loans	13,53.56		14,33.75		22,32.15	
Unsecured loans	13,22.25	26,75.81	14,03.68	28,37.43	13,12.00	35,44.15
		95,31.43		90,34.70		92,97.88

Notes: 1. 1 lakh = 100,000
2. Placement of commas in numbers differs from American practice.

TABLE 5 SUMMARY OF COMMON STOCK ISSUES

	Paid-up common stock		
Year	# of shares	Total amount rs.	Remarks
1959– 1960	2,800,000	28,000,000	800,000 right shares issued premium Rs. 2.50 per share proportion 2:5.
1964	3,640,000	36,400,000	840,000 right shares issued at a premium of Rs. 4 per share in the proportion 3:10.
1965	4,095,000	40,950,000	455,000 bonus shares issued in the proportion 1:8.
1968	8,190,000	81,900,000	2,047,500 right shares issued at par in proportion 1:2. 2,047,500 bonus shares issued in proportion 1:2.
1970	12,285,000	122,850,000	4,095,000 bonus shares issued in the proportion 1:2.
1974	18,427,500	184,275,000	6,142,500 bonus shares issued in the proportion 1:2.
1978	21,722,000	217,220,000	3,294,500 shares issued at a premium of Rs. 6 per share to resident Indian shareholders, the company's employees, and financial institutions.
1980	32,583,000	325,830,000	10,861,000 bonus shares issued in proportion 1:2.

In general, the engineers at the Bhopal plant were among India's elite. Most new engineers were recruited from the prestigious Indian Institutes of Technology and paid wages comparable with the best offered in Indian industry. Successful applicants for engineering jobs with UCIL were provided two years of training before being certified for unsupervised duty.

Until the late seventies, only first class science graduates or persons with diplomas in engineering were employed as operators at Bhopal. New hires were given six months of theoretical instruction followed by on-the-job training. As cost cutting efforts proceeded in the eighties, standards were lowered significantly. Some operators with only a high school diploma were employed and training was much less rigorous than before. In addition, the number of operators on shift was reduced by about half and many supervisory positions were eliminated.

The Indian managers developed strong ties with the local political establishment. A former police chief became the plant's security contractor and a local political party boss got the job as company lawyer. *Newsweek* reports that a luxurious guest house was maintained and lavish parties thrown there for local dignitaries.

In general, wages at the Bhopal plant were well above those available in domestic firms. A janitor, for example, earned Rs. 1,000 per month compared to less than Rs. 500 elsewhere. Still, as prospects continued downward after 1981, a number of senior managers and the best among the plant's junior executives began to abandon ship. The total work force at the plant dropped from a high of about 1500 to 950. This reduction was accomplished through voluntary departures rather than layoffs. An Indian familiar with operations at Bhopal said, "The really competent and well trained employees, especially managers and supervisors, got sick of the falling standards and indifferent management and many of them quit despite high salaries at UCIL. Replacements were made on an ad hoc basis. Even guys from the consumer products division, who only knew how to make batteries, were drafted to run the pesticide plant."

MARKETING

The population of India is over 700 million persons, while its land area is only about one-third that of the United

FIGURE 2   **UCIL financial charts.**

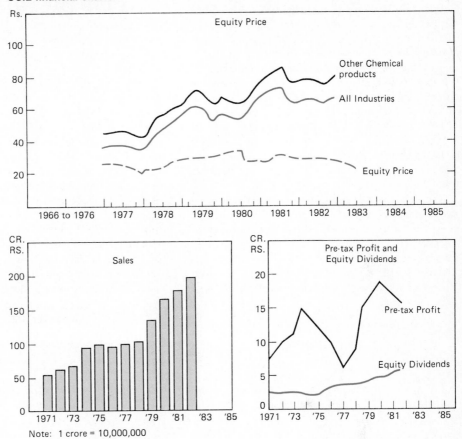

Note: 1 crore = 10,000,000

States. Three-fourths of India's people depend on agriculture for a livelihood. Fewer than one-third are literate. Modern communications and transportation facilities connect the major cities, but the hundreds of villages are largely untouched by twentieth century technology. English tends to be at least a second language for most Indian professionals but not for ordinary Indians. There are 16 officially recognized languages in the country. The national language is Hindi, which is dominant in five of India's 22 states. The working classes speak hundreds of dialects, often unintelligible to citizens just miles away.

India's farmers offer at best a challenging target market. They generally eke out a living from small tracts of land. Most have little more than subsistence incomes and are reluctant to invest what they have in such modern innovations as pesticides. They are generally ignorant of

the right methods of application and, given their linguistic diversity and technological isolation, are quite hard to educate. To advertise its products, UCIL has used billboards and wall posters as well as newspaper and radio.

Radio is the most widely used advertising medium in India. The state-owned radio system includes broadcasts in local languages. Companies can buy advertising time on the stations but it is costly to produce commercials in so many dialects. Much of the state-sponsored programming, especially in rural areas, is devoted to promoting agriculture and instructing farmers about new techniques. Often the narrators mention products such as Sevin and Temik by name.

Movies provide another popular promotional tool. Most small towns have one or more cinema houses and rural people often travel to town to watch the shows.

Advertisements appear before and after main features and are usually produced in regional languages (though not in local dialects).

Until recently, television was available only in the cities. During 1984, a government program spread TV relay stations at the rate of more than one each day, with the result that 80 percent of the population was within the range of a television transmitter by the end of the year. Still, few rural citizens had access to television receivers.

Pesticides sales are highly dependent on agricultural activity from year to year. In years of drought, like 1980 and 1982, UCIL's pesticide sales have suffered severe setbacks. In 1981, abundant rains helped spur pesticide sales.

Figure 3 is a map of India. India has a very extensive network of railways. The total track mileage is second only to the USSR. The road and highway system crisscrosses the areas in between railway lines. The railway system was especially significant to UCIL's pesticide operation because Bhopal lies near the junction of the main east-west and north-south tracks in India. Bhopal is also just south of the vast Indo-Gangetic plain, the richest farming area in India. An Indian familiar with the agricultural economy remarked, "Overall, physical distribution of pesticides is not too monumental a task. Getting farmers to use them and teaching them how are the real problems."

The marketing division for agricultural products was headquartered in Hyderabad. Under the headquarters were eight branch offices scattered all over the country. Sales were through a network of distributors, wholesalers, and retailers. Sales representatives from the branch offices booked orders from the distributors and wholesalers. Retailers got their requirements from wholesalers, who, in turn, were supplied by distributors. The distributors got their stocks from the branch offices. The branch office "godowns" (warehouses) were supplied directly from the Bhopal plant. The retailers' margin was fifteen percent. Wholesalers and distributors each received about five percent. Most of the retailers were family- or individually-owned although some of UCIL's pesticides were sold through government agricultural sales offices.

FIGURE 3   **Map of India.**

EVENTS OF 1985

In early 1985, the government of India cancelled the operating license of the Bhopal plant, clearing the way for the plant's dismantlement. The likelihood that this would happen provoked a Bhopal political leader to remark, "We've lost 2,000 lives, now must we lose 2,000 jobs?"

Manslaughter and other charges were filed against UCIL executives. Union Carbide Corporation chairman Warren Anderson had been briefly detained by Indian officials when he went to India shortly after the incident. Still, both companies continued for months to enjoy good relations with the Indian government. This may have been true in part because many leading Indian citizens and institutions have a financial interest in UCIL. And, except for the Bhopal incident, Union Carbide had an excellent safety record in India.

Warren Anderson said, "The name of the game is not to nail me to the wall but to provide for the victims of the disaster." He said he expected to be mainly concerned with the incident for the rest of his working life. Union Carbide Corporation offered to help provide funding for a hospital to treat the Bhopal victims. The company also contributed $1 million to a victims' relief fund. UCIL offered to build a new plant, one that would use nontoxic inputs, on the Bhopal site. One proposal was for a non-hazardous "Formulation Plant" to be constructed by UCIL and operated by the state government. Alternatively, UCIL suggested a battery factory to be owned and operated by the company. Both ideas were turned down in a letter dated May 15, 1985.

Within months after the incident, Union Carbide (USA) faced lawsuits in amounts far exceeding the company's net worth. That company's stock dropped from its mid-fifties trading range to the low thirties. A dozen or more American attorneys signed up thousands of Bhopal victims and relatives of victims and filed suits in America purporting to represent them. The Attorney General of India was authorized to sue Union Carbide in an American court. He stated that compensation had to be in accordance with American standards. A Minneapolis law firm which specializes in product liability cases was retained to represent India.

By March 1985, the streets of Bhopal were bustling again. There were cars, cattle, and crowds of people. But everywhere there were reminders of the disaster. Many wore dark glasses and covered their faces with shrouds to protect their injured eyes from the sunlight or to keep others from seeing their blindness. At the city's main police station, women and children continued to seek help. Vegetables shriveled by the poison gas were putting forth green shoots here and there. Occasionally, someone still fell sick from eating fish contaminated by MIC.

In the modernistic masonry-and-glass headquarters in Danbury, Connecticut, Union Carbide officials could look out on the beautiful Connecticut countryside and consider how best to manage the company's public affairs and how to grapple with the needs in India. Half a world away, in philosophical as well as physical distance, the poor of Jai Prakash Nagar, then poorer than ever, peered out from their shanties onto dusty streets and undoubtedly pondered quite different questions: From where would tomorrow's food come? How long would the pain inside and the dimming of vision last? And, just as importantly, what source of wealth would replace the pesticide plant? And how long would it be before its effects were felt?

In late June 1985, a lawsuit consolidating about 100 claims was filed in the U.S. by famed attorney F. Lee Bailey and his associates. The Indian government continued to press its lawsuit and to engage in out of court negotiations with Union Carbide. As the lawsuits in America moved forward, the legal issues involved became clearer: (1) Should the cases be tried in U.S. Courts or in Indian Courts? Both legal systems are based on English common law, but punitive damages are almost unheard of in Indian courts and compensatory damage awards are much lower than in America. (2) Should settlements be based on American standards simply because Union Carbide, the 51 percent parent of UCIL, is an American company, or on the much lower standards in India? (3) Who is responsible for the incident—Union Carbide, the Indian managers at Bhopal, the mostly Indian board of directors of UCIL, or the Indian government? (4) Which victims should be represented by the Indian government and which by the U.S. attorneys who went to India after the incident and signed up clients? (5) Did Union Carbide fail to properly warn the Indian managers at UCIL of the dangers posed by MIC? (6) Did Union Carbide fail to insure that appropriate safety equipment was installed at the Bhopal facility?

Negotiations between Union Carbide and Asoke K. Sen, the Indian Law Minister, seemed to have broken down in June 1985. Union Carbide had made a $230 million offer, with payment to be spread over twenty years. Mr. Sen said the offer was worth only $100 million in current terms and continued, "Union Carbide's offer is based on a total lack of appreciation of the magnitude of the problem, so is hardly worth consideration." He said that doctors have treated 200,000 Indians injured by the gas leak and that the government is having to build 15,000 housing units and a 100-bed hospital to care for the most seriously ill.

On the other hand, a Union Carbide spokesperson said that $100 million could "pay the heirs of each dead person 100 years annual income . . . and the seriously injured 20 years annual income," leaving funds left over. The U.S. district judge under whom the Indian court cases were consolidated requested that Union Carbide pay $5 million in emergency aid, but that was rejected by the Indian officials. Mr. Sen said that India had already spent several times more than that on relief and that $5 million would not serve a critical need. A $268 million "five-year master plan" of economic development was announced by Indian officials in August 1985, but funding had not been approved. The plan called for redevelopment near the plant and in the city of Bhopal including building 5,000 houses, 12 hospitals, an electric trolley transportation system, and a number of "work sheds" to employ and train the unskilled and semi-skilled among the gas victims.

As Union Carbide (USA) struggled to recover from the disaster and restore its favorable public image, four events thrust the company back to the forefront of national and international news coverage. In June 1985, hundreds of persons were poisoned by California watermelons grown on soil to which the Union Carbide pesticide Temik had been applied (improperly applied, according to the company). In August, a leak of the chemical intermediate aldecarb oxime at the company's Institute, West Virginia plant, the only U.S. facility to make MIC, sent 135 people to hospitals. A few days later another accidental discharge of chemicals at a Union Carbide plant just miles from the Institute facility caused a public health scare. Finally, GAF Corporation increased its holdings of Union Carbide stock and announced an effort to gain control of the corporation. Union Carbide managers rushed to erect take-over barriers and took actions to make the company less desirable as a merger candidate. Union Carbide Corporation (USA) was reorganized into two separately-incorporated divisions, one for chemicals and plastics and one for other products. As part of the reorganization, the company wrote down various assets by nearly $1 billion (almost none of this was related to UCIL) and made plans to spend $500 million of surplus in the employee retirement fund "for general corporate purposes."

Even though West Virginia governor Arch Moore publicly criticized Union Carbide's handling of the aldecarb oxime leak and CEO Warren Anderson admitted that the company had waited too long to warn residents, Union Carbide stock moved about $50 a share for the first time since the Bhopal incident.

A number of UCIL employees and gas victims interviewed nearly a year after the incident generally agreed that "Union Carbide" (no distinction was made between the U.S. parent and its Indian subsidiary) and the government were to blame, that proper safety measures could have prevented the disaster, that the plant should be dismantled, and that the victims should receive economic and medical help as well as compensation for their injuries. A visitor to the area at about that time wrote,

> I saw the notorious UCIL plant from a distance. There are no plans to reopen it. Most of the workers have found other jobs. Bhopal looks normal on the surface, but a claims court right opposite the railway station with a big crowd of widows and dependents who had come to take their claims was a grim reminder.
>
> Also got some first hand accounts. Most of the railway personnel are coughing and wheezing even now. There are lots of people whose lungs have been permanently damaged (the corrosive nature of the gas has caused fibrosis, i.e., formation of scar tissue, so lung volume has reduced).

As the end of 1985 approached, there were few indications of progress toward settling the lawsuits. None of the victims had been compensated. UCIL was essentially out of the pesticide business, although the company's other divisions, especially those involving batteries and flashlights, remained profitable. UCIL's common stock traded near 30 rupees (Rs. 30) where it had been before the disaster and Union Carbide Corporation common stock was still trading above $50.

WHEELING-PITTSBURGH STEEL COMPANY (B)

Neil H. Snyder
University of Virginia

INTRODUCTION

On December 5, 1968, Wheeling Steel Corporation merged with Pittsburgh Steel Company to form Wheeling-Pittsburgh Steel Company (W-P). W-P is engaged in the manufacturing, processing, and fabricating of steel and steel products. Exhibits 1 through 4 contain pertinent information about W-P's products. The firm is currently the seventh largest integrated steel company in the United States. W-P has eleven operating plants and fourteen subsidiaries. Exhibits 5 and 6 show the location of W-P's plants and its subsidiary companies, respectively.

HEADING FOR A CRISIS

In 1978, Dennis J. Carney became chairman of W-P, and he faced several major problems including the company's

low market share, poor reputation with its customers, erratic earnings, and old equipment. To deal with these problems, Carney embarked on a campaign to upgrade the company's facilities with funds obtained from a multitude of sources (see Exhibit 7). By increasing W-P's debt to modernize, a very heavy burden was placed on an already struggling organization. In 1983, W-P's bank credit lines expired and the company ended 1984 with its tenth loss in eleven quarters. Exhibits 8 through 10 show selected financial data, stock price information, and financial ratios, respectively.

Twice in two years Carney had persuaded the United Steel Workers Union (USW) to help W-P by granting wage concessions in excess of $150 million. However, these concessions were not necessarily a sign of good labor/management relations. In fact, the USW and Chairman Carney were constantly at odds. Carney was viewed by the union as a highly controversial, autocratic, and abrasive leader. In the four years during which Carney was chairman, five top level W-P executives resigned, and he is reported to have alienated a W-P director, and the company's largest stockholder, Allen Paulson, with his management style.

W-P's losses during 1982, 1983, and 1984 totalled more than $172 million. In addition, the company's long-term debt increased to more than $500 million in 1983, and its interest expense approached $60 million per year.

EXHIBIT 1   PERCENTAGE CONTRIBUTIONS TO SALES REVENUES

Products	1984	1983	1982
Hot & cold rolled sheet & strip	41.9%	35.8%	25.5%
Coated sheet	16.6	19.6	16.6
Fabricated	14.9	15.5	15.7
Tin mill	11.1	18.0	17.0
Rail products	8.9	5.3	4.2
Seamless tubular	1.2	0.2	8.4
Welded tubular	0.3	1.5	4.8
Other	5.1	4.3	7.8
	100.0%	100.0%	100.0%

EXHIBIT 2   SHIPMENTS BY PRODUCT CLASS (Net Tons)

Products	1984	1983	1982
Hot & cold rolled sheet & strip	53.6%	47.1%	37.3%
Coated sheet	13.2	16.7	17.1
Fabricated	10.5	10.9	12.1
Rail products	10.4	7.1	6.0
Tin mill	3.7	14.9	16.8
Seamless tubular	0.7	0.1	4.0
Welded tubular	0.4	1.3	4.3
Other	2.5	1.9	2.3
	100.0%	100.0%	100.0%

EXHIBIT 3   SHIPMENTS BY MAJOR MARKET CLASSIFICATION (Net Tons)

Market class	1984	1983	1982
Automotive	11%	15%	15%
Intermediate markets	45	38	27
Construction	13	15	17
Containers	10	13	14
Appliances	5	7	8
Oil & gas	1	1	7
Rail transportation	10	7	5
Other	5	4	7
	100%	100%	100%

EXHIBIT 4   PRINCIPAL MARKETS AND MAJOR MARKET CLASSIFICATIONS TO WHICH
RESPECTIVE CLASSES OF PRODUCTS WERE SOLD, BASED UPON SHIPMENTS
(Net Tons)

Products	Automotive			Construction			Containers		
	1984	1983	1982	1984	1983	1982	1984	1983	1982
Hot & cold rolled sheet & strip	11%	17%	25%	4%	6%	7%	8%	8%	9%
Tin mill	7	6	6	—	—	2	60	62	69
Coated sheet	38	38	28	10	15	16	—	—	—
Fabricated	—	—	—	79	82	88	—	—	—
Seamless tubular	—	—	1	—	1	1	—	—	—
Welded tubular	—	1	—	—	32	21	—	—	—

Products	Appliances			Oil & Gas			Intermediate		
	1984	1983	1982	1984	1983	1982	1984	1983	1982
Hot & cold rolled sheet & strip	7%	11%	14%	—%	—%	—%	65%	53%	36%
Tin mill	10	8	9	—	—	—	21	22	22
Coated sheet	6	5	6	—	—	—	43	38	44
Fabricated	—	—	2	—	—	—	20	18	10
Seamless tubular	—	—	—	96	99	97	4	—	1
Welded tubular	—	—	1	23	31	23	77	33	46

EXHIBIT 5   WHEELING-PITTSBURGH STEEL CORPORATION'S PLANTS

Canfield, Ohio
Martins Ferry, Ohio
Mingo Junction, Ohio
Steubenville, Ohio
Yorkville, Ohio

Allenport, Pennsylvania
Monessen, Pennsylvania

Benwood, West Virginia
Follansbee, West Virginia
Beech Bottom, West Virginia
Wheeling, West Virginia

EXHIBIT 6   WHEELING-PITTSBURGH SUBSIDIARY COMPANIES

Consumers Mining Company*
W-P Coal Company*
Ft. Duquesne Coal Company*
Gateway Coal Company
Harmar Coal Company
Mingo Oxygen Company*
Monessen Southwestern Railway Company*
Pittsburgh-Canfield Corporation*
Three Rivers Coal Company*
Wheeling-Empire Company
Wheeling Gateway Coal Company
Wheeling-Itasca Company
Wheeling-Pittsburgh Trading Company
WMI, Inc.

*These wholly-owned subsidiaries filed petitions for relief under Chapter 11 of the Federal Bankruptcy laws in the U.S. Bankruptcy Court for the Western District of Pennsylvania.

EXHIBIT 7   WHEELING-PITTSBURGH DEBT

Secured long-term debt holders (millions)

Mitsubishi Corporation*	$177.4
Prudential	51.7
Metropolitan Life	51.7
Aetna	20.7
Connecticut General	18.0
New York Life	15.1
Mutual of New York	13.2
Northwestern Mutual	13.2
Teachers	10.3
Pennsylvania IDA	9.0
Equitable	6.7
Massachusetts Mutual	4.2
John Hancock	3.4
Total	$394.6

Revolving working capital loans (millions)

Manufacturers Hanover	$24.8
Royal Bank of Canada	20.7
Security Pacific	16.5
Pittsburgh National Bank	8.3
Manufacturers National—Detroit	8.3
Continental Illinois	8.3
Canadian Imperial Bank	8.3
National Bank of Canada	8.3
Bank of Nova Scotia	8.3
First Pennsylvania Bank	4.1
North Carolina National	4.1
Total	$120.0

*Guaranteed in event of default by eleven bank lenders.

EXHIBIT 8   WHEELING-PITTSBURGH'S FINANCIAL SITUATION (Thousands)

	1981	1982	1983	1984
Net sales	$1,151,112	$755,083	$772,320	$1,049,215
Net income	60,059,000	(58,769,000)	(54,080,000)	(59,376,000)
NI/Sh com stock	14.28	(15.98)	(15.74)	(14.12)
Pref div declared	3,763,000	4,976,000	8,373,000	8,308,000
Depreciation	42,989,000	38,219,000	40,361,000	48,729,000
Plant imprvmnts	110,177,000	160,211,000	91,905,000	26,878,000
Working capital	195,477,000	230,026,000	101,216,000	124,968,000
Long-term debt	358,733,000	495,915,000	513,928,000	527,291,000
Raw steel productn	2,944,000	1,818,000	2,222,000	2,304,000
Shipments (tons)	2,146,000	1,368,000	1,642,000	2,320,000

EXHIBIT 9   WHEELING-PITTSBURGH'S STOCK PRICES

	6% Prior preferred		$5 Cumulative preferred		Common shares	
	High	Low	High	Low	High	Low
1978	58.75	45.00	49.50	40.50	14.00	9.00
1979	48.00	42.75	38.875	34.125	20.00	15.625
1980	42.75	38.25	38.75	31.50	23.375	17.625
1981	40.00	38.00	34.00	30.00	32.50	25.625
1982	38.50	34.00	33.00	28.00	17.00	13.0
1983	42.50	38.25	34.00	31.00	28.00	22.25
1984	38.00	32.00	36.00	25.00	22.50	13.625

EXHIBIT 10   WHEELING-PITTSBURGH'S FINANCIAL RATIOS

	1981	1982	1983	1984
Current	1.86	2.57	1.42	1.61
Debt	.58	.63	.69	.71
Debt-equity	.77	1.15	1.39	1.56
Times interest earned	2.93	(1.93)	(.92)	(.03)
Inventory turnover	6.74	4.73	5.09	6.30
Total assets turnover	1.03	.63	.62	.86
Gross profit margin	.0852	(.0086)	(.0137)	.0779
Profit margin on sales	.0522	(.0778)	(.0700)	(.0566)
Return on total assets	.0713	(.0194)	(.0133)	(.0016)
Return on equity	.1283	(.1363)	(.1468)	(.1761)

To avoid bankruptcy, Carney turned to the USW and W-P's creditors for help in meeting the company's principal and interest payments. Exhibit 11 shows W-P's debt repayment schedule.

The USW stated that it was the creditors' turn to help the company, but the creditors were unwilling to do so unless the USW agreed to help as well. Eventually, the USW relented. However, this time they presented a list of demands that included a complete restructuring of the company's long-term debt, two union seats on the company's board of directors, and a large share of W-P's common stock. W-P's creditors agreed to defer $90 million of debt due in 1985 and in 1986 in exchange for a lien on the company's $300 million in current assets. The USW found the creditors' offer unacceptable, because it provided too little help and because it would have given them a major claim on W-P's assets. The impasse in negotiations continued until April 16, 1985 when Wheeling-Pittsburgh filed for Chapter 11 bankruptcy.

The repercussions of W-P's bankruptcy and the implications for the steel industry, as a whole, are far reaching. Foremost is the issue of wage renegotiation. After declaring bankruptcy, W-P made it clear that it would not continue to honor previous labor agreements, and the company entered into negotiations with the union which culminated in the union's rejection of W-P's proposed 30% wage and benefit cut. Finally, the bankruptcy court was asked to rule on the wage issue. If the court ruled in W-P's favor, the company's lower wage rates coupled with court protection from its creditors would place W-P in an excellent competitive position when it emerged from Chapter 11. Moreover, the ruling might set a downward

EXHIBIT 11   W-P'S DEBT REPAYMENT FOR THE NEXT FIVE YEARS (IN THOUSANDS)*

	1985	1986	1987	1988	1989
First mortgage bonds:					
5.45% Series A due 1985	$12,600	$ —	$ —	$ —	$ —
9.50% Series D due 1994	3,187	3,187	3,187	3,187	3,187
4% Mortgage due 2001	376	391	407	423	447
Senior secured notes:					
11% Series A due 2001	3,493	3,493	3,493	3,493	3,493
11% Series B due 2001	2,007	2,007	2,007	2,007	2,007
11% Series C due 1994	2,590	2,710	3,250	3,250	3,250
Notes payable to banks	—	40,000	40,000	40,000	—
8% Supplier loan due 1985	2,412	—	—	—	—
8.5% Supply contract, 1987	14,000	14,000	14,001	—	—
Loan agreement:					
"A" Tranche 12.875%, 1991	—	7,300	14,600	14,600	14,600
"B" Tranche 13% due 1991	—	—	—	10,000	20,000
Long-term leases:					
Revenue bond lease Obligations at 6.75% to 9.25% due 2005	1,470	505	535	570	610
Other lease obligations due 1991	497	563	349	312	310
11% Notes of W-P Coal Company due 1993	1,864	1,864	1,864	1,864	1,864
14% Notes of Ft. Duquesne Coal Company due 1992	697	798	914	1,046	1,198
Amount reclassified due to filing a petition for reorganization under Chapter 11	(39,495)	—	—	—	—
Total	5,698	76,818	84,607	80,752	50,960

*Represents debt scheduled for payment in the indicated years prior to the Corporation's filing a petition for reorganization under Chapter 11 of the bankruptcy laws except for the amount reclassified for 1985.

trend in steel industry wage rates, thus making the domestic steel industry more competitive with foreign producers. Ultimately, the court ruled in W-P's favor.

After the ruling, W-P proposed to cut labor costs by 18%, or to about $17.50 an hour on the average. Previously, the USW had stated that if the average hourly wage were set lower than $18.50, the union would strike. Additionally, W-P indicated that it would not be able to make a $5 million pension fund payment due at the end of July 1985. For all practical purposes, this would end the health and life insurance benefits of W-P workers and place those pensioned in a precarious position. On July 21, 1985, the steel industry experienced its first major strike in twenty-six years. Eight thousand three hundred W-P employees walked off their jobs (*Wall Street Journal,* February 5, 1985 to July 21, 1985).

THE STEEL INDUSTRY

The steel industry is confronted with a host of problems which have caused several companies in the industry to contemplate bankruptcy. Included in this list are high labor costs, weak prices, and increasing foreign competition. Part of the problem is the product. Demand for steel is derived demand, meaning that its demand is contingent upon the demand for products in which it is used. Manufacturers of cars, bridges, ships, machine tools and appliances are end-use buyers of steel. Since they are durable goods, purchases of these products can be postponed by consumers during economic downturns. Thus, steel

demand is highly sensitive to inventory cycles, business cycle changes, the long-term investment outlook, and the rate of overall economic growth (Bossong, "Industry Perspective: The Steel Industry—Stagnation, Decay, or Recovery" *Business Economics,* July 1985).

Price-Elasticity

The cost of steel usually represents only a small percentage of the cost of the end-use products in which it is used. However, steel producers are faced with extremely price-elastic demand because of the homogeneity of the product and the lack of brand name differences. Thus far, steel producers have not differentiated their products effectively. To maintain market share and compete, steel producers must discount their prices when the demand for steel declines or competition intensifies. This practice has caused a steady decrease in steel prices over the past several years (See Exhibit 12). The problem is worsened by foreign steel producers who engage in "dumping", or selling steel products in the U.S. at prices below production costs.

Imports

Recently, the steel industry has experienced a surge in imports which, in 1984, claimed 26.4% of the U.S. domestic steel market (see Exhibits 13 and 14). Government-imposed restrictions have attempted to help the domestic industry. For example, during 1964–1974 Vol-

EXHIBIT 12   **Composite real prices received by U.S. producers.**

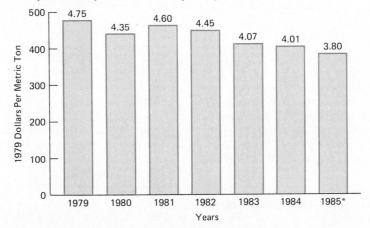

EXHIBIT 13   U.S. STEEL INDUSTRY
IMPORTS

	A Import levels		
	Imports, all steel mill products (thousands of net tons)	Market penetration (percent of total market)	Imports, semi-finished steel* (thousands of net tons)
1984	26,163	26.4%	1,516
1983	17,070	20.5%	822
1982	16,662	21.8%	717
1981	19,898	18.9%	790
1980	15,495	16.3%	155
1979	17,518	15.2%	345
1978	21,135	18.1%	414
1977	19,307	17.8%	298
1976	14,285	14.1%	240
1975	12,012	13.5%	243

	B Percent increase (decrease)	
	Imports, all steel mill products	Imports, semi-finished steel
1983–84	53.3%	84.4%
1982–83	2.4%	14.6%
1981–82	(16.3%)	(9.2%)
1980–81	28.4%	409.7%
1979–80	(11.5%)	(55.1%)
1978–79	(17.1%)	(16.7%)
1977–78	9.5%	38.9%
1976–77	35.2%	24.2%
1975–76	18.9%	(1.2%)

*Examples of semi-finished steel are ingots, billets, and slabs.
Source: American Iron and Steel Institute (AISI) Annual Statistical Report—1984.

untary Restraint Agreements between the U.S. and foreign steel producing nations were in force. It was hoped that U.S. steel companies would use this period of protection to modernize their facilities. Yet, the industry's capital outlays fell below the 1968 level for each of the following six years, while wages and dividend payments rose considerably (Kawahito, "Relative Profitability of the U.S. and Japanese Steel Industries," *Columbia Journal of World Business,* Fall 1984).

In 1983 and 1984, when steel imports were approaching their highest levels of U.S. market share, many U.S.

firms reacted by filing lawsuits charging foreign producers with dumping. President Reagan responded by announcing a new voluntary agreement in October, 1984, which was designed to hold steel imports to a little over 20% of U.S. market share until 1989. As of October, 1985, Voluntary Restraint Agreements had been reached with fourteen nations. The result of President Reagan's actions became visible in July, 1985, when imports declined sharply. From June to July, steel imports fell from 2.3 million tons to 1.5 million tons (*Iron Age,* October 4, 1985).

EXHIBIT 14   U.S. STEEL INDUSTRY
IMPORTS BY COUNTRIES OF ORIGIN

A Import volume (thousands of net tons)					
	1984	1983	1982	1981	1980
Canada	3,167	2,379	1,844	2,899	2,370
Latin America	3,132	2,415	974	782	630
Europe	9,963	5,310	6,775	8,077	4,744
Asia & Africa	9,685	6,761	6,939	8,011	7,620
Australia & Oceania	216	206	130	129	132
Total imports of steel mill products	26,163	17,070	16,662	19,898	15,495

B Percent of total imports					
	1984	1983	1982	1981	1980
Canada	12.1%	13.9%	11.1%	14.6%	15.3%
Latin America	12.0%	14.2%	5.8%	3.9%	4.1%
Europe	38.1%	31.1%	40.7%	40.6%	30.6%
Asia & Africa	37.0%	39.6%	41.6%	40.3%	49.2%
Australia & Oceania	0.8%	1.2%	0.8%	0.6%	0.8%
Total imports of steel mill products	100.0%	100.0%	100.0%	100.0%	100.0%

U.S. market penetration					
	1984	1983	1982	1981	1980
Canada	3.2%	2.9%	2.4%	2.7%	2.5%
Latin America	3.2%	2.9%	1.3%	0.8%	0.7%
Europe	10.1%	6.4%	8.9%	7.7%	5.0%
Asia & Africa	9.8%	8.1%	9.1%	7.6%	8.0%
Australia & Oceania	0.2%	0.2%	0.2%	0.1%	0.1%
Total imports of steel mill products	26.4%	20.5%	21.8%	18.9%	16.3%

Source: AISI Annual Statistical Report—1984.

Capacity

Domestic steel production capacity experienced almost no growth between 1960 and 1980. Furthermore, the capacity of U.S. steel producers has been cut drastically since 1980 in an effort to bring it in line with demand. In 1980, domestic steel production capacity was 154 million tons; it was 134 million tons in 1984; and it is expected to fall to 120 million tons by 1987. Even though U.S. producers have reduced their capacity, they continue to use only a portion of that capacity. Exhibit 15 shows that the capacity utilization problem is one that is becoming more severe.

Cost Control

Cost control is another major concern of domestic steel producers. Labor and energy costs represent a large portion of total costs, and they have become the target of manufacturers' cost reduction efforts. Since a large part of their labor force is unionized, steel producers must

EXHIBIT 15

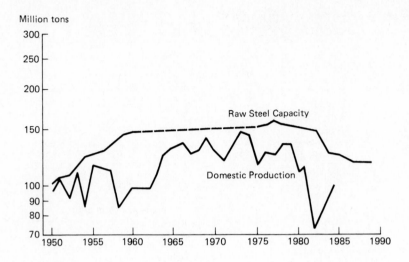

Million tons

bargain with the United Steel Workers Union (USW) to set wage and benefit rates for labor contracts. Labor costs in the steel industry exceeded the manufacturing sector average by more than 90% in 1982. Additionally, although energy consumption per ton of steel produced decreased by 2% between 1973 and 1981 for U.S. firms, Japanese firms cut their energy consumption per ton by 11% during this time (Kawahito, 1984).

In 1982, the aggregate net loss of the six largest domestic steel producers reached over three billion dollars, and only slight improvements have been made since 1982 (Exhibit 16). These firms experienced losses in the first quarter of 1985 which amounted to an average of seventeen dollars per ton. In 1984, their average loss was six

dollars per ton. Exhibits 17 through 20 provide additional information about the global steel industry.

Due to the depressed condition of the steel industry, some companies are selling their most profitable units to improve their financial position. Other firms are seeking mergers with foreign steel producers. In April 1984, an agreement was reached between Nippon KoKan (NKK), Japan's second largest steel producer, and National Steel, the U.S.'s fourth largest producer. NKK bought 50% of National, and it plans to spend one billion dollars to modernize National's facilities. The improvement project is expected to cut National's operating costs by about $44 million per year. Mergers and joint ventures are two of the most attractive alternatives for domestic steel produc-

EXHIBIT 16 **Aggregate net profits of the six largest domestic producers.**

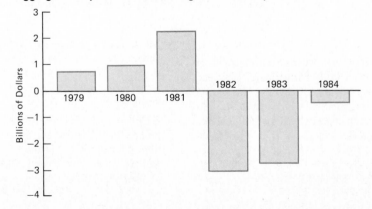

EXHIBIT 17   MARKET SHARE BY FIRM

		1950			1960		
		A	B	C	A	B	C
U.S. Steel		22.6	28.4	28.0	18.7	26.3	25.2
Bethlehem		10.9	13.7	13.5	11.4	16.0	15.3
Republic		6.4	8.0	7.9	5.4	7.6	7.3
J&L	merged	6.8	8.5	8.4	7.0	9.8	9.4
Youngstown	1978						
National	merged	4.0	5.0	5.0	5.3	7.5	7.1
Granite City	1971						
Armco		3.0	3.8	3.7	5.0	7.0	6.7
Inland		3.3	4.1	4.1	5.1	7.2	6.9
Wheeling	merged						
Pittsburgh	1968	3.3	2.9	2.9	2.6	3.7	3.5
Total of above		60.3	74.5	73.5	60.5	85.1	81.4
Other domestic		20.3	25.5	25.2	10.6	14.9	14.3

		1970			1981		
		A	B	C	A	B	C
U.S. Steel		21.0	23.1	20.2	16.6	19.1	15.5
Bethlehem		13.6	15.2	13.2	11.6	13.3	10.9
Republic		6.7	7.4	6.4	6.5	7.5	6.1
J & L	merged	8.4	9.3	8.1	7.6	8.7	7.1
Youngstown	1978						
National	merged	7.3	8.0	7.0	6.6	7.6	6.2
Granite City	1971						
Armco		5.4	5.9	5.2	5.8	6.7	5.4
Inland		4.7	5.2	4.5	5.8	6.7	5.4
Wheeling	merged						
Pittsburgh	1968	2.9	3.2	2.8	2.1	2.4	2.0
Total of above		70.2	77.3	67.4	67.6	72.0	58.6
Other domestic		20.6	22.7	19.8	24.4	28.0	22.8

Note: A = Millions of net tons, B = Percent of domestic shipments, C = Percent of domestic and imported shipments

Source: Steel: Upheaval in a Basic Industry, by Barnett and Schorsch, Cambridge, Mass., Ballinger, 1983.

ers to acquire badly needed capital for improvements, since many of them are highly leveraged. Additionally, mergers and joint ventures give foreign firms easier access to the U.S. market.

A JOINT VENTURE

After two unsuccessful attempts to form joint ventures, in February 1984 W-P and Nisshin Steel Corporation of Japan reached an agreement. W-P registered to offer one million shares of common stock at $35 per share, and Nisshin Steel agreed to purchase 500,000 shares under the pre-emptive rights offering. Allen E. Paulson, Chairman and President of Gulfstream Aerospace Corporation, and a member of W-P's Board, agreed to purchase the remaining 500,000 shares. This transaction increased Paulson's holdings in W-P from 31.7% to 35.3% and gave Nisshin a 10% interest in the company. As part of the joint venture agreement, W-P invested approximately $10 million in the Japanese steelmaker's stock. As a result of this agreement, a $40 million production line will be con-

EXHIBIT 18   U.S. STEEL INDUSTRY
INTERNATIONAL COMPARATIVE COST STRUCTURE: COSTS PER METRIC TON SHIPPED
(At Actual Operating Rates)

	1980				
	U.S.	Japan	W. Germany	U.K.*	France
Revenue	$507.24	$426.66	$506.96	$514.23	$501.61
Labor	$175.11	$93.88	$164.56	$452.81	$172.87
Raw materials	292.12	259.61	289.68	456.63	299.96
Financial costs	39.93	82.85	63.04	159.57	105.53
Total costs/ton	$507.16	$436.33	$517.29	$1,069.02	$578.36
Exogenous cost factor				−342.70	
				$726.32	
Pretax profit/ton	$0.08	$26.32	($10.33)	($212.09)	($76.74)

*Strike year in the UK.

	1981				
	U.S.	Japan	W. Germany	U.K.	France
Revenue	$574.28	$496.52	$440.60	$456.59	$433.64
Labor	$185.19	$108.11	$145.10	$144.76	$143.14
Raw materials	320.58	287.85	284.26	384.86	296.39
Financial costs	39.76	93.32	57.29	77.06	90.60
Total costs/ton	$545.52	$489.28	$486.63	$ 606.68	$530.13
Pretax profit/ton	$28.75	$7.24	($46.03)	($150.10)	($96.49)

	1982				
	U.S.	Japan	W. Germany	U.K.	France
Revenue	$581.17	$453.79	$463.15	$453.11	$447.73
Labor	$214.54	$96.99	$162.08	$134.94	$146.08
Raw materials	359.18	279.30	289.84	342.07	293.42
Financial costs	65.34	84.04	66.03	76.32	94.33
Total costs/ton	$639.06	$460.33	$517.95	$553.32	$533.83
Pretax profit/ton	($57.89)	($6.54)	($54.80)	($100.21)	($86.10)

	1983				
	U.S.	Japan	W. Germany	U.K.	France
Revenue	$533.37	$467.43	$436.64	$413.48	$419.49
Labor	$173.08	$101.27	$152.94	$93.96	$156.80
Raw materials	345.44	274.54	268.17	290.01	257.52
Financial costs	64.62	96.08	60.86	53.40	91.47
Total costs/ton	$583.14	$471.89	$481.97	$437.36	$505.78
Pretax profit/ton	($49.77)	($4.47)	($45.33)	($23.89)	($86.29)

EXHIBIT 18 U.S. STEEL INDUSTRY
INTERNATIONAL COMPARATIVE COST STRUCTURE: COSTS PER METRIC TON SHIPPED
(At Actual Operating Rates) (*Continued*)

	1984				
	U.S.	Japan	W. Germany	U.K.	France
Revenue	$542.56	$450.30	$405.02	$378.95	$387.79
Labor	$149.10	$91.73	$117.18	$81.43	$128.20
Raw materials	347.00	256.84	245.17	262.86	235.42
Financial costs	66.85	88.71	46.63	46.21	72.77
Total costs/ton	$562.95	$437.28	$408.98	$390.51	$436.39
Pretax profit/ton	($20.39)	$13.02	($3.95)	($11.56)	($48.61)

	1985 (Jan.–June average)				
	U.S.	Japan	W. Germany	U.K.	France
Revenue	$523.90	$425.43	$387.11	$359.20	$368.03
Labor	$139.10	$83.05	$95.33	$64.66	$105.44
Raw materials	329.98	242.50	231.57	252.08	224.59
Financial costs	64.85	82.34	39.17	36.33	57.25
Total costs/ton	$533.93	$407.89	$366.07	$333.07	$387.38
Pretax profit/ton	($10.03)	$17.54	$21.04	$6.14	($19.36)

Source: World Steel Dynamics (WSD) Price/Cost Monitor Report #7

EXHIBIT 19 U.S. STEEL INDUSTRY
INTERNATIONAL COMPARATIVE UNIT LABOR COSTS
(At Actual Operating Rates)

	U.S.		
	Manhours per ton shipped	Labor cost per hour	Unit labor cost (labor cost per ton shipped)
1980	9.17	× $19.06 =	$174.78
1981	8.90	× $20.78 =	$184.94
1982	8.65	× $24.67 =	$213.40
1983	7.28	× $23.70 =	$172.54
1984	6.67	× $22.36 =	$149.14
1985 (Jan–Jun)	6.02	× $23.10 =	$139.06

EXHIBIT 19   U.S. STEEL INDUSTRY
INTERNATIONAL COMPARATIVE UNIT LABOR COSTS
(At Actual Operating Rates) (*Continued*)

	Japan				
	Manhours per ton shipped		Labor cost per hour		Unit labor cost (labor cost per ton shipped)
1980	9.15	×	$10.25	=	$93.79
1981	9.36	×	$11.55	=	$108.11
1982	8.90	×	$10.90	=	$97.01
1983	8.47	×	$11.96	=	$101.30
1984	7.71	×	$11.89	=	$91.67
1985 (Jan–Jun)	7.51	×	$11.06	=	$83.06

	U.K.				
	Manhours per ton shipped		Labor cost per hour		Unit labor cost (labor cost per ton shipped)
1980	46.02	×	$9.96	=	$458.36
1981	15.06	×	$9.57	=	$144.12
1982	14.86	×	$9.14	=	$135.82
1983	11.87	×	$7.92	=	$94.01
1984	11.68	×	$6.98	=	$81.53
1985 (Jan–Jun)	10.49	×	$6.18	=	$64.83

	W. Germany				
	Manhours per ton shipped		Labor cost per hour		Unit labor cost (labor cost per ton shipped)
1980	11.04	×	$14.93	=	$164.83
1981	11.00	×	$13.19	=	$145.09
1982	12.26	×	$13.28	=	$162.81
1983	12.05	×	$12.71	=	$153.16
1984	10.21	×	$11.49	=	$117.31
1985 (Jan–Jun)	9.25	×	$10.30	=	$95.28

	France				
	Manhours per ton shipped		Labor cost per hour		Unit labor cost (labor cost per ton shipped)
1980	11.22	×	$15.39	=	$172.68
1981	11.31	×	$12.66	=	$143.19
1982	12.04	×	$12.15	=	$146.29
1983	12.14	×	$12.87	=	$156.24
1984	11.59	×	$11.01	=	$127.61
1985 (Jan–Jun)	10.86	×	$9.71	=	$105.45

Source: WSD Price/Cost Monitor Report #7

EXHIBIT 20   U.S. STEEL INDUSTRY
WORLD PRODUCTION AND CAPACITY UTILIZATION
World Gross Capacity Utilization (Percent of Capacity)

	U.S.	Japan	EEC	Developing world	Communist world
1973	97.0	88.4	85.8	65.7	89.7
1974	94.4	84.9	87.4	68.0	88.0
1975	76.8	73.1	63.5	68.4	88.5
1976	80.7	73.0	68.4	71.8	88.3
1977	79.0	64.9	62.1	70.2	87.2
1978	86.9	65.0	65.6	73.9	90.2
1979	87.9	71.5	69.2	78.1	87.4
1980	72.8	70.1	64.1	79.1	85.5
1981	77.5	63.9	63.7	72.5	81.1
1982	48.5	63.0	56.8	70.1	80.0
1983	55.3	61.6	59.0	67.6	83.1
Forecast					
1984E	70.0	66.3	66.3	67.1	83.9
1985E	80.8	70.8	73.2	68.5	85.3
1986E	91.3	79.7	81.8	68.2	92.2
1987E	71.8	78.7	76.9	64.9	89.2
1990E	78.3	86.0	75.5	70.5	90.0

Source: World Steel Dynamics, *The Steel Strategist #10*, Paine Webber, Inc., December, 1984.

structed at one of W-P's existing plants in the Ohio River Valley. The line is expected to be operating by 1986 and will produce rust-resistant galvanized steel for the auto industry. The production of rust-resistant steel is one of the few markets that is growing in the industry (W-P 1984 10K Report).

MODERNIZATION PROGRAM

Over the last six years, W-P has been heavily involved in a modernization program that will enable the firm to satisfy its customers' demands for better quality and service, while remaining competitive with foreign and domestic steel producers. Between 1979 and 1983, W-P spent approximately $536 million modernizing its facilities. During this time, the company's spending to enhance production facilities grew more than 5 times faster than the domestic industry average and more than 4 times faster than the average for Japanese firms. The construction of a new railroad rail mill utilizing the most advanced technology available in the world at a cost of $105 million consumed the lion's share of the firm's investment capital. Another component of the modernization plan was the

construction of a new two-strand continuous slab caster and a new five-strand continuous bloom caster at a cost of $175 million.

These two casters employ the most advanced technology for quality control available in the world. The technology was obtained from Japan and Germany, and it utilizes automated and computerized equipment that will enable W-P to increase quality, expand production, conserve energy, and decrease operating costs. Mitsubishi financed the project, and the equipment was supplied by Hitachi Corporation of Japan and Mannesmann Demag AG of West Germany. Technical assistance and engineering for the slab caster was provided by the Nippon Steel Corporation. Technical assistance for the bloom caster was provided by August Thyssen-Hutte AG of West Germany (1983 10K Report).

Additionally, as part of their modernization program, W-P spent $15.7 million upgrading its 80 inch hot strip mill at its Steubenville plant. This expenditure was necessary for W-P to comply with Environmental Protection Agency (EPA) requirements. Since 1979, W-P has invested over $100 million to comply with other EPA regulations dealing with air and water quality control measures, and the company anticipates the promulgation of additional environmental regulations that will result in significant increases in its overall capital and operating expenditures.

THE FUTURE

On September 19, 1985, the *Wall Street Journal* reported that Dennis Carney was expected to resign on September 20 to pave the way for a strike settlement. Although it was suggested that Carney might change his mind, they said it "is extremely unlikely, chiefly because of the severance guarantee. The United Steel Workers union, whose protests in part contributed to Mr. Carney's anticipated resignation, have informally agreed to resume bargaining in earnest if Mr. Carney departs" (*Wall Street Journal,* September 19, 1985).

According to Jerry Flint, the Steel Industry could be on the verge of an amazing recovery. Says he,

"It's easy to be negative about steel. Turnarounds that never came. Write-offs of $4.4 billion in assets and $7 billion in losses in four years. The six largest companies lost $325 million in the fourth quarter alone and this is in a strong economy. For the price of a couple TV stations, you could buy the great Bethlehem Steel Co. with its $5 billion in sales and 45,000 employees. . . .

Drop steel imports 3 million tons to 4 million tons. Let the capital goods business improve, not a boom, just a normal upswing, enough to add another couple million tons to steel sales. Let the United Steel Workers union cooperate to cut labor costs in the bargaining this spring. You know what happens? The bloodletting in the steel industry ends, and the profits begin to flow, this year. . . .

First, ask about productivity. This may be the untold miracle of American industry. "We're producing steel at fewer man-hours per ton in America than anybody else in the world now," says Lynn Williams, president of the United Steelworkers of America. "We have 4.6 man-hours in a ton, and by the end of this year it will be 4," says David Roderick, chairman of U.S. Steel. At Bethlehem productivity last year improved 5% from 1984, which was improved 12% from 1983, which was improved 15% from 1982. . . .

Quality is another major plus. It's no secret that U.S. steel wasn't matching up. A few years ago the reject rate on Japanese steel was 1% to 1.5%, while American-made metal was running 5% to 10%, says George Ferris, who once headed Ford Motor Co.'s steel operations and now runs Wheeling-Pittsburgh Steel. In an auto plant example, a bad coil means taking down the press for half an hour to change it, and losing production of 300 to 450 stampings. Today the American Steelmakers say they are as good as anybody. "We're all [U.S. and Japan] around a 2%" reject rate, says Ferris. "Yes, we've seen the quality of steel improve," says Roger Smith, chairman of General Motors. But he asks for even better quality, plus better steels, lighter, rustproof, more dent-resistant. . . .

Right now the biggest "if" in the turnaround is the union question. While U.S. productivity is high, wages and benefits are even higher—$17.18 an hour pay and $24.84 with benefits at Bethlehem. One product study on hot-rolled band, for example, showed 3.6 man-hours per ton in the U.S. to 3.4 in Japan, 6.9 in Brazil, 4.6 in Britain and 5.5 in Korea. But the $20-plus labor cost meant $84 per ton for that hot-rolled against $16 for Korea and $37 for Japan" (*FORBES,* March 10, 1986).

THE WOMEN'S CLUB, LTD.

Joseph W. Leonard
Miami University

The Women's Club, Ltd. (TWCL) is the only women's club in the United States owned and operated by the women as owners. It is designed for women of all ages to develop themselves physically, socially, culturally, and creatively. TWCL began operations on December 15, 1981, and is run through various committees, elected officials, and an elected board of directors.

TWCL is located in Boise, a city with a population of slightly over 100,000. Boise, the state capital, is a predominantly white city with a very vocal and active Mormon minority. While there is no major industry located there, there are three national corporate headquarters: Hewlett-Packard, Albertson's (grocery chain), and Morris-Knudsen (construction company). The downtown area, like many other downtown areas across the country, is struggling to compete with suburban shopping areas, but still provides an adequate number of retail stores, restaurants, and theaters, in a very picturesque setting.

The building and property which house TWCL were purchased from Utah Mortgage for $885,000, and were recently appraised at $1¼ million. To raise enough capital for the down payment, members purchased owner-certif-

This case was prepared by Bradley A. Dicks under the direction of Joseph W. Leonard of Miami University as a basis for class discussion rather than to illustrate either effective or ineffective handling of organizational issues and practices.

icates for $1,000 each. Within the first two months, 120 of these certificates were sold. During 1982, in accordance with the mortgage contract, a series of balloon payments totaling $36,500 were paid to reduce the principal (see Exhibit 1). Due to a renegotiated contract in June of 1982, $30,799 in interest payments would be due on March 15, 1983 as well. This brought the total balance due to $729,299.

To provide working capital, an investor group of three individuals was formed on December 15, 1981. Together, they lent TWCL $17,000 at 12% interest and secured the loan with a second mortgage on the building and property. A fourth investor lent $20,000 at 17% interest and secured the loan with the signatures of the four officers of TWCL. The entire loan plus interest was repaid on March 3, 1982.

Presently there are 210 owner-members that show strong support when financial needs arise. In May of 1982, over $9,000 was raised in one night; and on another occasion, $14,000 was raised within one week to meet the October balloon payment.

FINANCIAL OUTLOOK

Exhibits 2 and 3 show TWCL's balance sheet and income statement.

In 1983, a 15 year commercial real estate loan was

EXHIBIT 1   MORTGAGE INFORMATION

Purchase price	$855,000
Down payment, 12/15/81	(120,000)
Balloon payment, 3/14/82	(10,000)
Balloon payment, 6/14/82	(5,000)
Balloon payment, 7/14/82	(5,000)
Balloon payment, 9/14/82	(1,500)
Balloon payment, 10/14/82	(15,000)
Principal due, 3/15/83	$698,500

requested and secured by TWCL for $850,000. The loan was secured by a first mortgage on the land and building.

The reason for the loan was to refinance and provide working capital for the following:

Utah mortgage	
principal	$698,500
interest at 18%	30,799
Investor group	
principal	$17,000
interest	3,060
Operating capital	100,641
	$850,000

TWCL plans to repay this loan from five income sources: (1) member dues, (2) initiation fees, (3) restaurant sales, (4) bar sales, and (5) physical department fees. Secondary sources of repayment are: (1) the sale of owner certificates, (2) catering and banquet income, and (3) special events.

The request for operating capital of $100,641 is to offset a projected $100,000 negative cash flow for the next two years (i.e., until there is enough growth in the membership to attain positive cash flows).

COMPETITION

The Women's Club, Ltd. is very unique in the programs that it offers its women and in the fact that it is the only

EXHIBIT 2   THE WOMEN'S CLUB, LTD.
BALANCE SHEET (Year Ending December 31, 1982)

Current assets		Current liabilities	
Cash	$4,234	Accounts payable	$10,317
Dues receivable	869	Prepaid dues	7,062
Membership contracts receivable	4,960	Taxes payable	17,869
Inventory	2,054	Deferred revenue, current	5,760
Prepaid expenses	1,841	Interest payable	7,805
Refundable deposits	3,259	Mortgages payable	736,918
	17,217		785,731
Property & equipment		Deferred revenue, net	26,664
Land	226,575	Total liabilities	812,395
Building	628,425		
Office equipment	11,020	Member's equity	
Accumulated depreciation	(24,240)	Memberships	166,694
	841,780	Acc. deficit	(120,092)
		Total equity	46,602
		Total liabilities	
Total assets	$858,997	& equity	$858,997

EXHIBIT 3   THE WOMEN'S CLUB, LTD.
STATEMENT OF LOSS AND ACCUMULATED DEFICIT
(Year Ending December 31, 1982)

Revenue	
Dues	196,911
Restaurant and bar	63,041
Catering and banquets	22,513
Special events	16,961
Other	6,392
Interest	2,846
	308,664
Expenses	
Interest	117,382
Payroll and payroll taxes	110,615
Restaurant and bar	31,455
Special events	14,048
Utilities	34,050
Repairs and maintenance	25,165
Depreciation	24,240
Licenses and taxes	16,962
Insurance	9,690
Office supplies	9,086
Advertising	4,192
Other	19,070
	415,955
Net loss	(107,291)
Accumulated deficit, beginning of year	(12,801)
Accumulated deficit, end of year	(120,092)

club that offers ownership to its members. Most of the competition stresses physical fitness; only the YWCA offers social, cultural, and arts programs; and none of the other clubs have a full dining room.

A summary of the primary competition and their fees structure is as follows:

1 Eastgate Health Club—open to members only and offers one year memberships for $15.00 per month.

2 Court House, Inc.—

  1 Aerobic and dance classes only, $80.00 plus $25.00 per month;

  2 Nautilus weight program only, $80.00 plus $27.00 per month;

  3 Racquetball courts only, $160.00 plus $35.00 per month;

  4 Programs 1 & 2, $80.00 plus $32.96 per month; and

  5 Programs 1, 2, & 3, $160 plus $48.41 per month.

3 Family Fitness Center—lifetime membership of $1,700.00 plus $400 per child.

4 Lady Fitness—(women only), one year membership, $189.00; two year membership, $289.00

5 YWCA—$15.00 annual membership dues entitles member to $10.00 discount on all classes and 30¢ (per hour) discount on child care.

A comparative listing of the facilities, programs, and services offered by TWCL and the five primary competitors is contained in Exhibit 4.

TWCL'S FACILITIES

Dining Room and Kitchen
  Open from 6:00 am to 9:00 pm, Monday thru Friday; seats 44. Available to members and guests; serves sandwiches, salads, soups, omelettes, juices, and fruits;

EXHIBIT 4   OFFERINGS BY TWCL AND COMPETITORS

	TWCL	Court house	Eastgate	Family fitness	Lady fitness	YWCA
Facilities						
Basketball & Volleyball court				X		
Dining room	X					
Dressing room	X	X	X	X	X	X
Jacuzzi/whirlpool	X	X	X	X	X	
Jogging track				X		
Racquetball court		X		X		
Sauna/steamroom	X	X	X	X	X	
Showers	X	X	X	X	X	X
Swimming pool	X	X		X		
Tanning booths			X		X	
Weight equipment	X	X	X	X	X	
Fitness programs						
Floor aerobics	X	X	X	X	X	X
Jazzercise	X					
Slimnastics	X		X		X	X
Swim classes	X					
Private swim lessons	X					
Tai chi	X					X
Weight loss/nutrition	X			X	X	
Yoga	X					
Other services						
Child care		X	X		X	X
Masseuse	X				X	
Towel service	X					
Social/cultural programs						
Arts & crafts	X					X
Speakers/seminars	X					X
Theatres/luncheons	X					X

with a main entree (changes daily); hot and cold beverages, wine, and beer.

Indoor Swimming Pool
Heated 48 foot pool with four swimming lanes, has two enclosed showers. Classes include water exercise, beginning and intermediate swimming, private lessons, and open time for lap swimming.

Indoor Jacuzzi
Seats ten people, heated to 101°F.

Dry Heat Sauna
Accommodates four adults lying down (or 16 seated).

Exercise Equipment Room
5 different pieces of equipment to exercise upper and lower body;
2 exercise bikes;
1 set of barbells weights;
2 jogging trampolines.
Room is carpeted with a mirrored wall.

Masseuse Room

Dressing Room
156 individual lockers with carpeted change areas;
6 private tiled showers with change areas;

2 sinks and vanity areas, equipped with hair dryers and curling irons;

4 restrooms.

Large Meeting Room/Floor Exercise Room
35 × 66 foot hardwood floor auditorium;

Large stage with curtains, drapes, lighting and sound system;

Built-in oak storage cabinets;

Used for theater, lectures, banquets, dances, special events, and physical fitness classes such as aerobics, jazzercise, slimnastics, and others.

Small Meeting Room
18 × 22 foot carpeted room; used for small meetings, classes in management of stress, French, bridge lessons, and others.

Arts & Crafts Room
3 circular work counters with 4 stools each;

1 pottery kiln;

Classes include oil painting, water color, pottery, and stained glass.

Library
Built-in bookshelves; fireplace; 4 sofas; a quiet area for studying or small meetings.

Lobby
Receptionist and cashier counter;

Small waiting/greeting room.

Administrative Areas
Offices for the manager, the bookkeeper, and catering manager.

Public Restrooms

Storage Rooms

(Note: See Exhibit 5 on page 918 for a detailed physical layout of TWCL.)

MEMBERSHIP

Any woman 19 years of age or older may apply for membership. The classes of memberships are as follows:

1 Inactive Owner-Member—$1,100 certificate. This is an investment certificate. The holder owns one share in TWCL for each certificate. The holder has voting rights, but cannot use the facility or participate in any activities which are not open to the public.

2 Active Owner-Member—$1,100 certificate plus $40 monthly dues. This member owns one share in TWCL and has voting rights. The monthly dues entitle the holder to full use of the facilities and its activities. For events which require an additional fee, the Active Owner receives a small discount.

3 Lifetime Owner-Member—$1,100 certificate plus $3,900 lump sum dues. This member has the same rights and privileges as the Active Owner, but pays no monthly dues.

4 Program Member—$150 initiation fee plus $40 monthly dues (with a minimum agreement of six months at a time). This member is entitled to full use of the facilities and participation in the activities.

5 Business Member—A business organization may purchase any one of the above four membership types, but the organization must designate the person who will have use of the facilities.

6 One Month Program Member—$45. This is a use-only membership for one month. This member has no voting rights but does have full use of the facilities and its activities. After one month, the person must decide whether to become an Owner or a Program Member.

7 Weekend Program Member—$20. This is a use-only membership, which allows the person full use of the facilities on Saturday and Sunday only.

8 Weekly Program Member—This is a use-only membership that can be purchased by owners or program members for their guests. The person has full use of the facilities for one week.

Management

The Women's Club, Ltd. is owned by its members and operates through its board of directors, which consists of nine elected women.

The president of TWCL is Mary Johnson; she provides expertise in management, personnel, and budgeting. She is currently the office manager for the Central Engineering Department of the Morris-Knudsen Construction Company, and has 12 years total employment with the company in positions involving budgeting systems, personnel, and resource management. Ms. Johnson previously spent three years with the Intermountain Glass Company, and nine years with the Western Equipment Company.

The vice-president is Joan Cochrane; she provides expertise in business and food service. Her experience includes ten years as current co-owner of Precision Manu-

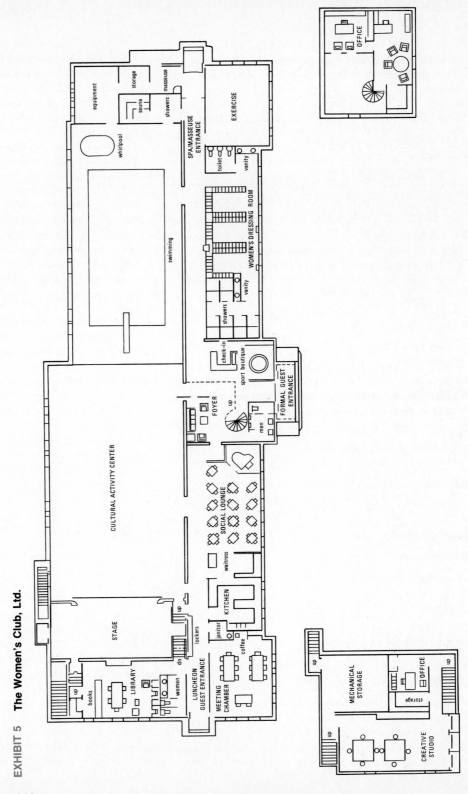

EXHIBIT 5   The Women's Club, Ltd.

918

facturing Company, five years as the past owner of the U-Stick Cannery, and five years as the past owner of Kuna Drive-in.

Joyce Sager, the treasurer, provides expertise in fiscal management, nutrition, public health, state government, personnel, and teaching. She served seven years as the program director of a major nutrition program for the Idaho Department of Health and Welfare. In this capacity, Ms. Sager administered a $5 million statewide program and oversaw nine local health agencies and 56 clinic locations. She previously spent two years as a public health nutritionist with the Southwest District Health Department, dietitian with St. Alphonsus Hospital, and nutrition instructor at Boise State Univesity. Ms. Sager's education includes a masters degree in public health nutrition from University of California-Berkeley, and a B.S. in Food & Nutrition from the University of California-Davis.

The secretary is Jeanette Pauli who for the past 25 years has been the corporate secretary for the Title Insurance Company.

These four officers, along with the other five members of the board, hire the manager who handles the day-to-day operations of TWCL. The primary responsibilities of the manager are: assisting in annual budget preparation, planning promotional and public relations activities, planning long term club/member activities and programs. In addition, the manager must enforce TWCL policies and rules, and submit reports and other information to the board as required. To carry out these responsibilities, the manager must spend her time preparing budgets and working with the treasurer; supervising department heads, who are in turn responsible for hiring, training, and evaluating their respective staffs; and overseeing advertising, fund-raising, and membership campaigns. In carrying out this last duty, a considerable amount of time is spent making public presentations, coordinating public relations activities, and closely monitoring membership recruitment.

The manager of TWCL is Ruth Dicks; she has expertise in bookkeeping, marketing, sales, and office management. She spent four years as owner of Brad Realty, Inc., a real estate business in Ohio, and spent 15 years as co-owner of Insurance Consultants, Inc., a casualty insurance agency with over $2 million in assets. Ms. Dicks was formerly the treasurer for TWCL and is currently on the Boise Chamber of Commerce.

In addition to the board of directors, TWCL has three key financial advisors: Marilyn Clapp, who is currently the manager of the Tax Collection Department of the local IRS branch office; Bonnie Johnson, a CPA; and Margorie Moon, the Idaho State Treasurer.

The unwritten/undrawn organizational chart for TWCL is approximated in Exhibit 6.

EXHIBT 6   **Organizational structure.**

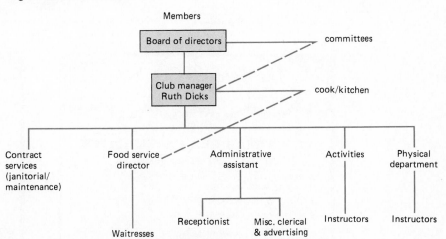

Note: It is unclear where the kitchen/cook should be placed in the organizational structure.

MARKETING & SALES

TWCL's market area consists of women who live or work in Boise or the surrounding area. The primary marketing task since its organization has been to attract members. The most effective sales method for TWCL has been member referrals. Members invite female guests to use the facilities or join in the activities. The manager then meets with potential members on the premises and discusses with them each type of membership available. When the potential members become familiar with TWCL, these guests frequently join. The members are very proud of their club and do an excellent job of selling its benefits to potential members.

EXHIBIT 7　Advertising.

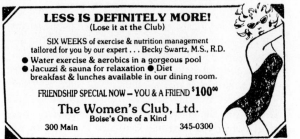

Recruitment of new members continues to be a vital activity for TWCL. Membership drives are held periodically throughout the year and a committee for membership expansion meets weekly to report on its activities. Ms. Dicks would like to spend about half of her time on membership recruitment activities but is not able to do so as a result of other day-to-day requirements.

Another method used by TWCL is newspaper advertising. These advertisements (see page 920) are developed by the Club Manager with the help of an advertising committee. Available funds (cash) are limited and thus the number and size of ads are restricted. TWCL has no formal advertising budget. TWCL also uses flyers placed in local retail stores and businesses announcing new membership drives, holiday specials, and special upcoming events.

TWCL also tries to take advantage of other promotional activities. In 1981, TWCL gathered 6,000 names on a petition to influence a major department store to locate in downtown Boise. That effort generated a considerable amount of publicity, including several TV interviews with Ruth Dicks on the local 6 o'clock news. TWCL attempts to participate in other newsworthy events and with other community-minded groups. An example of this was TWCL's sponsorship of the Boise Special Olympics. This activity gained favorable publicity and supported TWCL's goal of being community service–minded.

TWCL PROGRAMS

The Women's Club, Ltd. has a wide range of events to develop each of its members physically, socially, intel-

EXHIBIT 8   NOVEMBER—PHYSICAL EDUCATION PROGRAM

		A.M.			P.M.	
Mon.	6:00–6:45 A.M.	Body Contouring	(M)	12:00N–1:00P	Yoga	(D)
	6:45–7:45 A.M.	Slimnastics	(J)	4:30P–6:15P	Lap Swimming	
	9:00–10:00 A.M.	Slimnastics	(K)	5:30P–6:30P	Jazzercise	(D)
	9:30–10:30 A.M.	Yoga	(R)			
	10:30–11:00 A.M.	Water Aerobics	(Kr)			
	11:00–11:30 A.M.	Water Exercise	(S)			
Tue.	6:45–7:45 A.M.	Slimnastics	(J)	5:30P–6:30 P	Water Exercise	(M)
	9:00–10:00 A.M.	Slimnastics	(C)	5:30P–6:30P	Aerobics	(K)
	10:30–11:00 A.M.	Water Aerobics	(M)			
	11:00–11:30 A.M.	Water Exercise	(S)			
Wed.	6:00–6:45 A.M.	Body Contouring	(M)	12:00N–1:00P	Yoga	(D)
	6:45–7:45 A.M.	Slimnastics	(J)	4:30P–6:15P	Lap Swimming	
	9:00–10:00 A.M.	Slimnastics	(K)	6:30P–7:00P	Beg. Swim Lsns	(M)
	10:30–11:00 A.M.	Water Aerobics	(Kr)	7:00P–7:30P	Int. Swim Lsns	(M)
	11:00–11:30 A.M.	Water Exercise	(S)	5:30P–6:30P	Jazzercise	(D)
Thur.	6:45–7:45 A.M.	Slimnastics	(S)	4:30P–6:15P	Lap Swimming	
	9:00–10:00 A.M.	Slimnastics	(K)	5:30P–6:30P	Aerobics	(K)
	10:30–11:00 A.M.	Water Aerobics	(M)	5:30P–6:30P	Water Exercise	(M)
	11:00–11:30 A.M.	Water Exercise	(M)	5:30P–6:30P	Yoga	(R)
				6:30P–7:30P	Water Safety	(M)
Fri.	6:45–7:45 A.M.	Slimnastics	(J)			
	9:00–10:00 A.M.	Slimnastics	(K)			
	10:30–11:00 A.M.	Water Aerobics	(Kr)			
	11:00–11:30 A.M.	Water Exercise	(S)			
Sat.	9:30–10:30 A.M.	Jazzercise	(D)			
	10:30–11:30 A.M.	Aerobics	(K)			

Instructor code:	(C)	Chris	(M)	Marilynn	(J)	Justine	(Kr)	Kris
	(K)	Karen	(S)	Shannon	(R)	Reekman	(D)	Debbie

lectually, and culturally. The members' physical needs are met by classes in slimnastics, yoga, jazzercise, water aerobics, water exercises, and a body contouring program. A popular offering is the ''red eye special'', a body contouring and slimnastics session from 6 to 7:45 A.M. which is followed by a diet breakfast in the club restaurant. Social needs are met through many interest groups such as the bridge club. Also, the restaurant features a TGIF social event each Friday. There are many cultural programs available such as classes in painting, stained glass, flower arrangement, pottery, and water color. An especially significant cultural activity is the ''Women in the Arts'' event. Recently, TWCL launched the ''300

Main'' Lecture Series to educate both their members and the general public on topics of wide interest and local significance. (Exhibit 8 on page 921 shows a typical week's physical education program schedule.)

These widely varied social, professional, and cultural reasons that bring women to TWCL have resulted in a diverse membership which includes 210 owner members and 198 program members. While all ages and income levels are represented, the majority of the membership ranges between 30 and 55 years of age and includes business and professional women, as well as young mothers and retired women.

WORLD VIEW TRAVEL AGENCY, INC.

James C. Makens
Wake Forest University

In January of 1983, the president and the general manager of World View Travel were discussing the possible need for new strategies to meet increased competition, deregulation of the industry, and to take advantage of a market they both regarded as unsaturated.

HISTORY OF THE COMPANY

World View Travel was located in a southwestern city of 150,000 population and was owned by Rene Townsend and her husband Bob. Although Bob was a full partner he continued to work full time in his career as a pathologist and did not participate in the active management of the company. Rene served as president and shared management responsibilities with Sylvia Franklin, the general manager.

After ten years of operation, World View had become the largest travel agency in town with five million dollars in gross billings and sixteen employees. Prior to estab-

The case was written by James C. Makens of The Babcock Graduate School of Management of Wake Forest University. It was not designed to present an illustration of either effective or ineffective handling of administrative problems. This case was based on an actual firm whose identification has been disguised as well as the individuals involved. Copyright © 1983: James C. Makens

lishing World View, Rene had worked two years for a competitive travel agency. At that time only two travel agencies existed in town with eight or nine employees each. By 1983, competition had grown to eleven agencies including an in-house firm within a large electronics company which served as the area's largest employer.

The growth of World View had been fairly consistent and some in the industry regarded it as extraordinary. In the first year of operation World View recorded over one million dollars in billings. Growth occurred each subsequent year despite the existence of two recessions in the ten years. However, the percentage of growth in recession years was less than in years when the economy was stronger. The years 1981 and 1982 had proven to be ones in which little growth had occurred. The corresponding U.S. recession had undoubtedly been a major contributing factor to the leveling in sales but Rene and Sylvia were concerned that the plateau might also signal a need for new marketing strategies.

CITY LOCATION

The southwestern city in which World View was located consisted of approximately 150,000 residents with approximately 30% classified as minority. The largest part of the minority population were Mexican Americans.

Blacks represented approximately one fourth of the minority group.

The city was heavily represented by a middle class and although there were lower income areas there were surprisingly few areas that could be regarded as slums. This was due to a combination of a good industrial base, good public administration and a civic pride among the residents. There were four major employers in the area and many smaller ones. The city was corporate headquarters for a company listed on the New York Stock Exchange and one listed on the American Exchange. These were involved in electronics and pharmaceuticals.

The predominant industries in the city were banking-finance, insurance, pharmaceuticals, and electronics. The city also boasted a large medical complex which attracted many patients from outside the area and two universities.

The city was located on a major interstate highway and was served by three major airlines and two commuters. Two national hotel chains operated downtown properties and several chains operated motels along the interstate highway. Three or four of the restaurants in town could be regarded as good but none were known for consistent excellence in service or food. Many fast food establishments existed and represented the normal mix of hamburgers, pizza, and chicken. The city had an attractive shopping mall and a small convention center which was to be markedly improved in size and quality within the next four years. It was felt that the addition of a new convention center would enable the city to attract visitors from a wider area and would also attract new visitor services. A major hotel had expressed interest in entering the city.

The mayor had recently called for the formation of a blue ribbon council to study tourism. This included representatives from several segments of the city with a good mixture of industrial and cultural interests. The city had grown as a commercial crossroads rather than as a result of nearby natural attractions such as seashore or mountains. Nevertheless, there was a strong opinion that the number of travellers to the city could be increased through a combination of attractive facilities and events.

The recession which was currently affecting the nation had created national unemployment of over ten percent. This city had witnessed a 5.5% unemployment. Although the city was not considered to be a boom city it had enjoyed growth during the past ten years and was located in a region of the nation which was generally regarded as a growth area.

COMPETITION

Eleven travel agencies existed in the city. One of these was an in-house agency for the largest employer in town. Consequently, very little direct business was generated by this company for any of the ten independent agencies.

Among the ten independent agencies, one had originally intended to specialize in group travel but had soon become a full service agency and did not specialize in groups to any greater degree than the others. All the agencies offered a mixture of services and were not particularly distinguishable in terms of product offering or market segments served.

The two agencies which had been the only competitors in town when World View began operation, continued to serve as strong competition even though they were now smaller than World View. Both firms had suffered the death of the owners, had undergone considerable turnover in personnel and seemed to be currently lacking in direction.

The largest increase in numbers of travel agencies had occurred three or four years earlier and there currently seemed to be relative stability in the industry. There were no rumors of new firms opening in town or major expansion by competitors but this was subject to change at anytime.

A major effect of increased competition had been a heightened public awareness of the benefits of using a travel agency. One of the major airlines serving the area reported that the volume of tickets which came from travel agencies had risen from 40% in 1975 to nearly 80% in 1982. Despite an increase in awareness on the part of the traveling public there were still many individuals and smaller companies who did not consistently use the services of a travel agent. There were also many clients who were unfamiliar with the multiple service offerings of a travel agency. Rene and Sylvia mentioned that clients sometimes expressed surprise upon learning that World View could make hotel and auto rental reservations.

DESCRIPTION OF WORLD VIEW TRAVEL

After establishing World View Travel, Rene personally called upon companies in the area and asked for their travel business. This approach proved to be so successful that after only three years of operation her agency was as large as any competitor. Most of the calls were made to individuals Rene or her husband knew through prior business or social settings. Rene admitted to having a distaste for "cold calls" to organizations and firms unknown to her and preferred to call persons in which a prior contact of some kind had been established. In several cases, these were referrals by friends or satisfied clients. Time after time she was told by the prospect that this was the first time the owner or manager of a travel agency had ever asked them for their business.

LOCATION

The location of World View was not conducive to walk in traffic nor to provide visual exposure to the public. World View leased space in a new office building located on a side street in a light industrial park. The street was not a thoroughfare and dead ended in a culdesac. A sign in front identified World View Travel but was not larger nor particularly distinct from the signs of neighboring businesses. There was little reason for anyone to visit the building unless they had specifically come to see someone at World View or one of the neighboring tenants.

CLIENT MIX

The mix of billings in 1982 for World View was approximately 56% commercial and 44% group and individual. Of the commercial accounts six clients had billings of $500,000 or more. These were the larger companies in town. World View did most of the travel business for the second largest employer in town. However, Rene said that this business was not evenly distributed among all departments within the company. She was certain there were two or three major departments within the client company that did not deal with World View.

The rest of the commercial business came from a mixture of small and medium sized companies. Rene and Sylvia emphasized that they had purposely tried to have a large mix of commercial clients. Rene stated she felt it was likely that on a time per client basis, the sales productivity and earnings were less for small clients than for large ones. She felt that from a standpoint of the bottom line, her agency would probably be better off with fewer of the smaller commercial clients and more of the larger ones. For instance, "We probably could get every bit of the business of the second largest employer in town. However, that frightens us since we would then have too many of our eggs in one basket. At this point, we feel we're

better off with a larger number of corporate clients even if some are relatively unproductive."

An analysis of revenues for 1982 indicated that 40% resulted from corporate business, 45% came from personal and vacation billings and 15% were listed as group.

When corporate travel was excluded, and group was compared only to personal and vacation revenue it was found that the ratio was 1 to 4 in favor of personal and vacation travel.

Revenue comparisons between international and domestic billings revealed that revenue from all international billings contributed 15% while domestic contributed 85%. This occurred despite the fact that commissions from international averaged 9.8% as opposed to 8.8% from domestic.

Nearly all of the services performed by World View in 1982 could be considered as "outbound." A small percentage consisted of making local reservations for corporate clients and helping with inbound groups such as sales meetings and seminars in which corporate clients brought visitors to the local area.

In reviewing the current customer and product mix, Rene commented that she felt commercial business would be significantly more important in the future. The failure of other agencies to gain reputations as strong corporate service firms meant that World View could strengthen its relationship with the area's major employers resulting in more travel billings. Rene also expressed interest in moving toward the meeting and convention planning business on both an inbound and outbound basis. She believed that corporate clients were receptive to professional outside assistance in this area and that in the future professional fees could be charged for this service. If a decision was made to expand in this area, changes or additions to the number of sales personnel would be needed.

PERSONNEL

The personnel count for World View totaled fifteen full time female employees and one part time who worked half days. Of these, five were involved in non-sales functions including one bookkeeper, Rene, Sylvia, one person to double check fares plus general office work and one errand girl. This left eleven employees with direct sales responsibilities. Of these, four were assigned to corporate sales, one to group sales and six to "front office". The six known as front office sales personnel handled a mix of group and personal-vacation and business travel. The percentage mix between group and personal travel varied by each of the six saleswomen depending upon a variety of factors such as their experiences, interests, and contacts. For example, one of these with twenty years experience in travel demonstrated a strong interest in group sales. She was not afraid to follow up leads and to aggressively seek this business. Rene and Sylvia had been considering asking her to specialize in group sales. Others seemed far more comfortable with personal travel. None of the salesforce spent much time out of the office. None had an expense account and unless they specifically requested to entertain a client for lunch, all business entertainment was conducted by Rene.

The educational backgrounds of the corporate and personal saleswomen were quite different. The four in corporate sales did not hold college degrees. The typical educational background of this group was a high school diploma or one year beyond in a junior college or trade school. All but one of the saleswomen who specialized in personal sales held college degrees. The individual without a degree had attended several years of specialized trade school and had a background as assistant manager of a savings and loan prior to working for World View.

Rene explained the difference in backgrounds as a result of the nature of work demanded by each position. Corporate sales work tended to be routine and repetitive. It demanded someone who enjoyed working with details, doing clerical type tasks and someone who was very thorough so that few errors were made and nothing was left to chance for the client. Although personal travel also required precision it offered a wider variety of challenges to the salesperson and allowed more creativity than corporate.

Different compensation systems existed for those in corporate and personal sales. Those who had responsibility for corporate sales were paid a salary plus end of month bonus. The bonus was determined using a formula which called for a dollar sales productivity four times in excess of gross salary. Once the productivity level had been reached, a salesperson would obtain 20% of the excess revenue above the 4 × salary. The addition of a support-staff person meant that each corporate salesperson was relieved of certain clerical chores which left more time for sales. It was felt that the addition of the support-staff person increased sales productivity and that the formula for a bonus should reflect the change. Prior to the change, those in corporate sales were realizing more from their bonus than from their salary.

A corporate salesperson would begin with an annual salary of $9,000–$10,000 per year. After a period of six months to a year those in corporate sales realized incomes of $14,000–$20,000 including the bonus. The personal (front office) salesperson also started at $9–$10,000 per year and worked on a salary plus bonus basis. The formula used for this group called for sales productivity of three times gross salary rather than four times. This was felt to be equitable since this group received less staff support. Annual income for experienced salespeople in this area ranged from $14,000–$22,000.

In addition to monetary compensation, all members of the salesforce were eligible for "fam" trips throughout the year.[1] Those in corporate sales generally obtained two short fam trips per year and those in personal sales averaged 2–2½ longer ones per year. The typical fam trip for those in corporate sales was domestic in nature. Individuals in personal sales were more likely to obtain international fam trips.

Fam trips were regarded by Rene and Sylvia as more than non monetary motivating tools. They were regarded as professionally desirable and necessary for persons who sold travel. After visting a new destination on a fam trip, the salesperson was expected to make a brief presentation to the rest of the salesforce. This individual was also expected to share expertise concerning destination areas with other members of the salesforce when the need occurred.

ADVERTISING AND PROMOTION

Advertising was not regarded as an activity which deserved a heavy budget appropriation. Rene confined advertising to the Yellow Pages. Advertisements were purchased in high school annuals and theatre programs but these were regarded as contributions in terms of their effect upon sales. A limited number of baggage tags and flight bags were purchased which had the name of World View but these were limited in quantity and given only to selected clients. Rene felt that the best advertising a travel agency could acquire was word-of-mouth referrals based on professional service for clients.

A special corporate relations program existed which

[1]The term "fam trip" refers to familiarization trips. These are provided free or at a greatly reduced cost to travel agents by suppliers such as airlines or destination areas as a means of acquainting travel agents with travel services and destinations.

seemed to have been very successful. This consisted of the following factors:

1 A $100,000 automatic free flight insurance policy for corporate clients who flew on tickets issued by World View.

2 A Corporate Rate Hotel Program. A handbook of nearly 350 pages was given to all corporate clients. This contained names of hotels and the best corporate rates available to them.

3 An emergency 800 number which could be used in case of a travel problem anywhere in the U.S.

4 A special training program for executive secretaries to acquaint them with the basics of business travel. This seminar was conducted at the offices of World View and had been popular with executive secretaries.

5 A regular newsletter which was sent to clients.

6 The addition of a special staff person to recheck all fares to insure the lowest cost to the client.

7 A computer generated statistical capability to assist major clients in analyzing their travel expenditures and trends.

THE FUTURE

The past ten years had been rewarding ones for World View. Rene and Sylvia were confident that their travel agency was as well equipped to meet future opportunities and challenges as any in town. In assessing the agency's present strengths, Rene stated there were five factors which she felt would be invaluable in planning future strategies. First, World View was automated beyond the levels of all other competitors. This had begun five years ago when the agency purchased a stand-alone mini-computer to assist in bookkeeping. Since then, Rene had added the computer system available through United Airlines known as the Apollo system. Rene felt that automation had been the principle factor which allowed World View to efficiently serve commercial accounts and had made this sector of the agency the most profitable part. Rene said the agency was committed to computerized automation and would continue to use new technology as it became available.

Second, the strength of the salesforce. Sylvia emphasized that the salesforce for World View was the most committed of any agency she had seen. Turnover was comparatively low and there was a good esprit de corps among the employees.

Third, the agency had developed a good reputation in the community. This was particularly important in the case of corporate clients who seemed to regard World View as the most professional agency in town.

Fourth, the company was in good financial condition. Rene pointed out that bankers had told her they would be

EXHIBIT I   DECEMBER 1982 SALES RECORDS OF MEMBERS OF SALESFORCE—WORLD VIEW TRAVEL

	Years experience as travel agent	Billings
Corporate sales		
Melanie Lamb	10	$69,000
Virginia Fare	5	$60,000
Carol Gifford	1½	$55,000
*Nancy Senate		
Personal and group sales		
Arlene Felton	20	$61,000
Janice Grant	5	$38,000
Marian Terple	4	$44,000
*Gloria Barrett		
Glenda Riggins		
**Kristine Fraser		
**Amy Clarke		

*These members of the sales force have under 6 months' experience.
**Maternity leave

happy to consider loan requests from World View at any time.

Fifth, the management team of Rene and Sylvia worked well. "If a buyer ever took us over the new owner would probably ask one of us to leave to cut administrative costs. We understand that working as a team we increase administrative costs but there is a terrific symbiotic relationship here that works well and just can't be measured in dollars and cents. We honestly feel we are one of the few agencies in town giving much thought to future strategies. Most seem to think in terms of the short run only."

Despite their optimism, Rene and Sylvia admitted there were outside variables which had to be considered which could dramatically affect the entire travel agency industry. A worsening in the U.S. and world economy would certainly affect the travel market. Only a week previous, *The Wall Street Journal* had carried a front page article describing the fears of many that a world depression was going to occur in 1983 or 84. Although it appeared that the bottom of the recessionary trough had been reached and that recovery was at hand, there were ample economic storm clouds to feed a pessimistic appraisal of the future.

Another consideration was a possible change in travel habits within the corporate and personal travel sectors. Articles had been written which described a future reduction in business travel due to advances in communications technology. Holiday Inns had installed satellite discs in several of their properties and were encouraging corporations to hold meetings on a regional level with satellite communication hookups between several Holiday Inns. This would permit corporations to hold national meetings without the expense of flying large numbers of personnel to a central meeting site. New telephone companies were offering discount rates and improved technology to businesses and individuals. It was impossible to predict what the effect of a breakthrough such as Phonavision might have upon the travel industry.

During the recession year of 1982 many international vacation destinations had reported a poor year. At the same time, many states had reported an excellent tourist year. This seemed to be particularly true for resort areas which could be reached within a few hours. Gasoline prices had actually dropped and employed Americans could seriously plan for summer vacation trips. Airlines and buses were aware of this change and were fighting for market share in a depressed economy. Greyhound offered a transcontinental fare for $99 from coast to coast.

Airlines were also offering discounted fares between major markets such as New York to Los Angeles or New York to Miami. Rates as low as $69 between New York and Miami were being advertised. Virtually all air carriers other than commuters were offering some form of discount fare. It was almost impossible for the average traveler to keep track of these offerings or in many cases to clearly understand them. Manufacturers such as Kodak, Polaroid and Chevrolet had offered travel discounts on certain airlines to the public as incentives for purchasing their products. Airlines were offering travel clubs in which discounts or free flights could be obtained after flying a specified number of miles on a particular carrier.

One of the outside variables which offered the greatest uncertainty to travel agents was the continuing effects of deregulation in air transportation. The movement toward less government regulation of air transportation had begun during President Carter's administration and had continued under President Reagan. The purpose of deregulation had been to encourage greater competition within the travel industry and reduce the importance of the U.S. government in the establishment of air fares, selection of routes, arbitrator of disputes and other areas which affected the structure and conduct of the air transportation industry. One of the eventual aims of deregulation was to disband the Civil Aeronautics Board.

The effects of deregulation had been dramatically seen in 1982 with the bankruptcy of Braniff International Airlines. This was followed by the bankruptcy of Altair, a small east coast airline. At the same time, new airlines had sprung up such as People Express and Muse Air. These and others entered by serving a specific market and offered discount fares.

Deregulation had affected travel agents through increased complexity in numbers of fares available from airlines. The effect had also been quite evident surrounding the bankruptcy of Braniff. Now, a new aspect of deregulation looked as though it could present travel agents with a direct challenge to traditional methods of doing business. The effects of a ruling known as the "Maximum Tariff Rule" issued by the CAB in October, 1981 had still not greatly affected travel agents but it and successive CAB rulings posed the potential for drastic change.

Prior to October, 1981 all domestic airlines were required to file each of their fares with the CAB. After filing, neither the airline nor travel agents were permitted to sell tickets at prices above or below these prices. Under the new rule carriers were required only to file their standard coach fare in any market as the maximum fare to be charged. Airlines were not required to file discount fares or other special prices. This essentially meant that airlines and agents could cut prices. It was felt this would lead to large discounts for large organizations such as corporations.

Despite the ruling, there generally was not a great deal of price cutting or shared commissions by travel agents with large corporate clients. This was partially forestalled by the fact that the major airlines continued to file all their fares with the CAB. The airlines also advised travel agents not to engage in price cutting to preferred customers.

Nevertheless, a few travel agents in the U.S. such as one in Indianapolis did cut prices. TWA and American Airlines responded by removing ticketing validation plates from the travel agency. In spite of the fact that widespread discounting or commission sharing by travel agents had not occurred, the possibility now existed and could not be discounted for the future. The ruling had also opened the door for airlines to bypass travel agents and offer discount prices to large groups such as conventions and corporations.

The Maximum Tariff Rule was not the only legal change emanating from Washington. Changes in two other rules were also under serious consideration by the CAB. These were known as the Exclusivity Rule and the 20% Rule. The Exclusivity Rule stated that only appointed travel agents were eligible to receive commissions from the carriers for the sale of air transportation. In January 1983, the entire U.S. travel agent industry was concerned with the end of the Exclusivity Rule. Various future scenarios were being predicted including supermarket chains and department stores directly selling airline tickets at discount prices.

The 20% Rule stated that a travel agency owned by a larger corporation could not do more than 20% of its total air ticketing volume for the needs of the parent corporation without becoming ineligible for commissions. Otherwise, airlines would consider it as an in-house travel department and not an independent travel agency.

It seemed apparent that changes in the rules governing methods of operation of travel agencies and the competitive environment would be forthcoming. The effect upon travel agencies and World View in particular were not apparent.

In spite of changes that might occur, Rene and Sylvia spoke very encouragingly of the future. Both felt that the most difficult years were behind them and that the future offered excellent opportunities for growth. Rene summarized her feelings by saying, "World View Travel may look quite different ten or even five years from now but we intend to remain the leading travel agency in this area. In fact there is no reason we have to confine our plans to this area. We proved we were capable of success in this market and there is no reason we can't think in far broader terms. We have the organization, the know how and the desire to grow, its just a matter of setting our objectives, deciding upon a strategy and getting on with the task."

Page numbers in *italic* indicate exhibits.